Quantitative Aptitude

R. Gupta's®

Quantitative Aptitude

A Comprehensive Book for Various Recruitment and Entrance Examinations

✦ IBPS-CWE Bank PO & MT ✦ Bank Specialist Officers ✦ SBI PO ✦ RBI ✦ UPSC ✦ LIC/GIC–AAO/ADO ✦ Railway Exam ✦ SSC ✦ IGNOU ✦ NIFT ✦ IB ACIO ✦ SI of Police ✦ SBI Clerk etc.

Shambhu Nath Jha

&

RPH Editorial Board

RAMESH PUBLISHING HOUSE, NEW DELHI

Published by
O.P. Gupta *for* Ramesh Publishing House

Admin. Office
12-H, New Daryaganj Road, Opp. Officers' Mess
New Delhi-110002 ✆ 23275224, 23245124

E-mail: info@rameshpublishinghouse.com
For Online Shopping: www.rameshpublishinghouse.com

Showroom
• Balaji Market, Nai Sarak, Delhi-6 ✆ 23253720, 23282525
• 4457, Nai Sarak, Delhi-6, ✆ 23918938

Book Code: R-1121

17th Edition: November 2024

ISBN: 978-93-86298-39-3

Price: ₹ 680

Printed at: J.P. Enterprises, Delhi

CONTENTS

QUANTITATIVE APTITUDE

1

NUMBER SYSTEM

In our System of numeration, numbers are written by using the symbols 0, 1, 2, 3, 4, 5, 6, 7, 8 and 9 with each symbol getting a value depending on the place it occupies. These symbols are called digits. A number related to the objects in a collection gives an idea of how many objects are there in the collection.

The number 789345126 can be represented as:

Ten crores	Crores	Ten Lacs (Millions)	Lacs	Ten Thousands	Thousands	Hundreds	Tens	Units
10^8	10^7	10^6	10^5	10^4	10^3	10^2	10^1	10^0
7	8	9	3	4	5	1	2	6

This number can be read as : "Seventy-eight crores, ninety-three lacs, forty-five thousands, one hundred twenty six".

1. **Natural Numbers or Positive Integers (N = 1, 2, 3, 4, 5 .....):** These are also called counting numbers. When two natural numbers are added or multiplied together, the result is always a natural number. Therefore, all positive integers, used for counting objects, are always **natural numbers** whereas zero together with negative integers and fractional numbers are not natural numbers.
2. **Whole Numbers: (W = 0, 1, 2, 3, 4, 5, ...):** The number '0' together with the natural numbers gives us the numbers which are called **whole numbers,** e.g., 0, 1, 2, 3, 4 ..... etc. whereas –10, –15, –12 ..... or $\frac{1}{5}, \frac{2}{9}, \frac{4}{5}$..... etc. are not whole numbers.
3. **Integers: (I = ..., –5, –4, –3, –2, –1, 0, 1, 2, 3, 4, 5, ...):** The negative numbers together with the whole numbers are called integers. The numbers –1, –2, –3, –4, –5, ... are called negative integers and 1, 2, 3, 4, 5, ..., *i.e.,* natural numbers are called positive integers. The number 0 is simply an integer, *i.e.,* it is neither positive nor negative.
4. **Rational Numbers:** A rational number is a number that can be put in the form $\frac{p}{q}$ where p and q are both integers and $q \neq 0$, e.g., $8, -\frac{7}{5}, -\frac{3}{4}, \frac{1}{7}, 0$ .... are all rational numbers i.e. a rational number may be positive, zero or negative.
5. **Irrational Numbers:** An irrational number is a number that can not be put in the form $\frac{p}{q}$ where p and q are both integers and $q \neq 0$, e.g., $\sqrt{5}, \sqrt{11}, \sqrt{15}, 3 + \sqrt{5}$ .... etc. are all irrational numbers.

6. Real Numbers: All those numbers which are either rational or irrational, are called real numbers, e.g., $\frac{11}{17}, \frac{19}{21}, -\frac{7}{8}, \sqrt{7}, 8 + \sqrt{3}$ etc. are real numbers.

7. Even Numbers: All those numbers which are exactly divisible by 2, are called 'even numbers', e.g., 2, 8, 14, 28, 52 etc. are even numbers.

8. Odd Numbers: All those numbers which are not exactly divisible by 2, are called 'odd numbers', e.g., 1, 3, 5, 7, 9, 19 etc. are odd numbers.

9. Composite Numbers: The numbers which are divisible not only by 1 or themselves, but by some other numbers also, are called the 'composite numbers'. In other words, the numbers which have more than two factors are called 'composite numbers.', e.g., 4, 9, 15, 18, 27, ... etc. are composite numbers.

10. Prime Numbers: The numbers which have only two factors, 1 and the number itself are called 'prime numbers', e.g., 2, 5, 11, 19, 23, 31, ... etc. are prime numbers.

11. Co-primes: Two numbers which have only 1 as the common factor are called 'co-primes'. 5 and 7 are co-primes. So are 15 and 16.

12. Twin Primes: Two prime numbers which differ by 2, are called 'twin primes', e.g., 3, 5; 5, 7; 11, 13; 71, 73 are some pairs of twin primes.

13. Consecutive Numbers: The numbers which are following or coming after other numbers in regular order, are called consecutive numbers. 4, 6, 8, 10 are consecutive even numbers and 9, 11, 13, 15 are consecutive odd numbers. 3, 4, 5, 6, 7 ..... etc. are consecutive numbers in the natural order of the number series.

PROPERTIES OF CONSECUTIVE NUMBERS

(a) The product of two consecutive numbers is exactly divisible by 2.

e.g., $1 \times 2 = 2$ which is exactly divisible by 2.
$3 \times 4 = 12$ which is exactly divisible by 2.
$4 \times 5 = 20$ which is exactly divisible by 2.

(b) The product of three consecutive numbers is exactly divisible by 6.

e.g., $1 \times 2 \times 3 = 6$; which is exactly divisible by 6.
$2 \times 3 \times 4 = 24$, which is exactly divisible by 6.
$3 \times 4 \times 5 = 60$, which is exactly divisible by 6.

(c) The product of four consecutive numbers is exactly divisible by 24.

e.g., $1 \times 2 \times 3 \times 4 = 24$, which is exactly divisible by 24.
$2 \times 3 \times 4 \times 5 = 120$, which is exactly divisible by 24.
$3 \times 4 \times 5 \times 6 = 360$, which is exactly divisible by 24.

(d) The product of five consecutive numbers is exactly divisible by 120.

e.g., $1 \times 2 \times 3 \times 4 \times 5 = 120$, which is exactly divisible by 120.
$2 \times 3 \times 4 \times 5 \times 6 = 720$, which is exactly divisible by 120.
$3 \times 4 \times 5 \times 6 \times 7 = 6720$, which is exactly divisible by 120.

(e) The difference between the squares of two consecutive odd numbers is always exactly divisible by 8.

e.g., $3^2 - 1^2 = 9 - 1 = 8$, which is exactly divisible by 8.
$5^2 - 3^2 = 25 - 9 = 16$, which is exactly divisible by 8.
$7^2 - 5^2 = 49 - 25 = 24$ which is exactly divisible by 8.

(f) If 1 is added to the product of either two odd consecutive numbers or two even consecutive numbers, the result obtained will be a perfect square number,

e.g., $2 \times 4 + 1 = 8 + 1 = 9 = 3^2$, which is a perfect square number.
$5 \times 7 + 1 = 35 + 1 = 36 = 6^2$, which is a perfect square number.
$9 \times 11 + 1 = 99 + 1 = 100 = 10^2$, which is a perfect square number.

(g) The sum of two consecutive numbers is equal to the difference between their squares.

e.g., $1 + 2 = 3 = 2^2 - 1^2 = 3$
$4 + 5 = 9 = 5^2 - 4^2 = 9$
$5 + 6 = 11 = 6^2 - 5^2 = 11$

(h) The sum of the cubes of three consecutive numbers is exactly divisible by their own sum.

e.g., $1^3 + 2^3 + 3^3 = 1 + 8 + 27 = 36 = (1 + 2 + 3) \times 6$
$4^3 + 5^3 + 6^3 = 64 + 125 + 216 = 405 = (4 + 5 + 6) \times 27$

TESTS FOR DIVISIBILITY OF NUMBERS

1. **Divisibility by 2:** A number is divisible by 2, if its units digit is 0, 2, 4, 6 or 8. For example, each of the numbers 130, 244, 566, 278, ... etc. is divisible by 2.
2. **Divisibility by 3:** A number is divisible by 3, if the sum of its digits is a multiple of 3. For example, each of the numbers 312, 213, 456 is divisible by 3 since sum of digits in each of these numbers is (3 + 1 + 2 = 6), (2 + 1 + 3 = 6) and (4 + 5 + 6 = 15) respectively, each of which is a multiple of 3.
3. **Divisibility by 4:** A number is divisible by 4, if the number formed by its digits in ten's and unit's places is divisible by 4. For example, numbers formed by ten's and unit's digits of 1132, 1312, 1400 and 1348 are 32, 12, 00 and 48 respectively which are divisible by 4. Hence, these numbers also are divisible by 4.
4. **Divisibility by 5:** A number is divisible by 5, if its unit's digit is either 0 or 5. For example, each of the numbers 100, 205, 315, 435 is divisible by 5 since unit's digit in each of these numbers is either 0 or 5.
5. **Divisibility by 6:** A number is divisible by 6, if it is divisible by both 2 and 3.
6. **Divisiblity by 8:** A number is divisible by 8, if the number formed by its digits in hundred's, ten's and unit's places is divisible by 8. For example, numbers formed by hundred's, ten's and unit's digits of 1864, 1024, 2008 and 5000 are 864, 024, 008 and 000 respectively which are divisible by 8. Hence, these numbers also are divisible by 8.
7. **Divisibility by 9:** A number is divisible by 9, if the sum of its digits is a multiple of 9. For example, each of the numbers 23409, 454554, 66636 is divisible by 9 since sum of digits in each of these numbers is (2 + 3 + 4 + 0 + 9 = 18), (4 + 5 + 4 + 5 + 5 + 4 = 27) and (6 + 6 + 6 + 3 + 6 = 27) respectively, each of which is a multiple of 9.
8. **Divisibility by 10:** A number is divisible by 10, if its unit's digit is zero. For example, each of the numbers 50, 80, 1310, 1400 is divisible by 10 since unit's digit in each of these numbers is 0.
9. **Divisibility by 11:** A number is divisible by 11, if the difference of the sum of its digits in even places and the sum of its digits in odd places (starting from unit's place) is either 0 or a multiple of 11. For example, each of the numbers 909183, 540045 and 184712 is divisible by 11 since in each of the numbers difference of the sum of digits in even places and sum of the digits in odd places is [(9 + 9 + 8) – (0 + 1 + 3) = 22], [(5 + 0 + 4) – (4 + 0 + 5) = 0] and [(8 + 7 + 2) – (1 + 4 + 1) = 11] respectively, each of which is either '0' or a multiple of '11'.

10. **Divisibility by 12:** A number is divisible by 12, if it is divisible by 3 and 4 both.
    For example, take a number 769824
    (i) Sum of digits = 7 + 6 + 9 + 8 + 2 + 4 = 36, it is divisible by 3.
    (ii) The number has 24 as its last two digits, which is divisible by 4.
    Hence, 769824 is divisible by 3 and 4 both, so it is divisible by 12.
11. **Divisibility by 14:** A number is divisible by 14, if it is divisible by 2 and 7 both.
12. **Divisibility by 15:** A number is divisible by 15, if it is divisible by 3 and 5 both.
13. **Divisibility by 16:** A number is divisible by 16, if the number formed by its last four digits is divisible by 16.
    For example, take a number 9877856, the number formed by its last four digits is 7856, which is divisible by 16. Hence, the number 9877856 is divisible by 16.
14. **Divisibility by 24:** A number is divisible by 24, if it is divisible by 3 and 8 both.
15. **Divisibility by 40:** A number is divisible by 40, if it is divisible by 5 and 8 both.
16. **Divisibility by 80:** A number is divisible by 80, if it is divisible by 5 and 16 both.

[**Note:** If a number is divisible by two co-primes separately, then the number will be also divisible by the product of co-primes.]

Digit in unit's place in the product of any given numbers: Digit in unit's place in the product of any two or more given numbers is the digit in the unit's place in the product of the digits in unit's place of the given numbers. For example, in the product of 444 × 312 × 864, digit in unit's place is the digit in the unit's place in the product of 4 × 2 × 4.

Since 4 × 2 × 4 = 32 where digit in unit's place is 2.

∴ Digit is unit's place in the product of given numbers will be 2.

Ascending Order: If in a given number series, numbers are written in increasing order, then the number series is said to be written in ascending order. e.g., 25, 30, 41, 50 or –10, –8, –6, –2 etc. are series in ascending order.

Descending Order: If in a given number series, numbers are written in decreasing order, then the number series is said to be written in descending order. e.g., 50, 41, 30, 25, or –2, –6, –8, –10 etc. are series in descending order.

Place Value and Face Value of a digit:

Place Value: Numbers are written by using the symbols 0, 1, 2, 3, 4, 5, 6, 7, 8 and 9 called digits, with each digit getting a value depending on the place it occupies. This value assigned to the digit due to its placement, is called place value. For example, in the number 56, digit 6 is placed in unit's place and 5 in ten's place. Therefore, place value of 6 in 56 is 6 × 1 = 6 and that of 5 is 5 × 10 = 50.

Face Value: In a number face value of a digit is the digit itself. For example, in 42, the face value of digit 2 is 2 and that of digit 4 is 4.

Additive Inverse: If sum of two numbers is zero, then each of the numbers (called addends) is called additive inverse of the other. For example, if $a + b = 0$, then 'b' is additive inverse of 'a' and *vice versa.*

Multiplicative Inverse: If a and b are two rational numbers such that $a \times b = 1$, then each is called the multiplicative inverse of the other.

Note: $\frac{p}{q}$ and $\frac{q}{p}$ are also called multiplicative inverse of each other. The multiplicative inverse of zero does not exist.

An important formula in respect of division of whole numbers

Dividend = Divisor × Quotient + Remainder

or Divisor = $\dfrac{\text{Dividend} - \text{Remainder}}{\text{Quotient}}$

or Quotient = $\dfrac{\text{Dividend} - \text{Remainder}}{\text{Divisor}}$

SOME IMPORTANT FACTS

(i) The smallest natural number or positive integer is (+1).
(ii) The greatest negative integer is –1
(iii) The number '0' is neither positive nor negative integer.
(iv) 1 is only such number which is neither a prime number nor a composite number.
(v) 2 is only such number which is an even number as well as a prime number.
(vi) 2 is the smallest prime number.
(vii) The number of prime numbers between 1 to 100 is 25.
(viii) A square number may have 0, 1, 4, 5, 6 or 9 in its unit's place.
(ix) A cubic number may have any digit from 0 to 9 in its unit's place.

Things to remember while solving problems on whole numbers

(a) Sum of numbers from 1 to n = $\dfrac{n(n+1)}{2}$ (where n is the number of terms)

(b) Number of odd numbers from 1 to n = $\left(\dfrac{\text{Last odd number} + 1}{2}\right)$

(c) Sum of odd numbers from 1 to n = (Number of odd numbers)^2

(d) Number of even numbers from 1 to n = $\left(\dfrac{\text{Last even number}}{2}\right)$

(e) Sum of even numbers from 1 to n = Number of even numbers × (Number of even numbers + 1)

MULTIPLICATION BY SHORT CUT METHODS

1. Multiplication by Distributive law:

(i) a . (b + c) = a × b + a × c *(ii)* a × (b – c) = a × b – a × c

Ex. (i) 735 × 386 + 725 × 614 = 735 . (386 + 614) = 735 × 1000
= 735000

Ex. (ii) 688 × 99 = 688 (100 – 1) = 688 × 100 – 688 × 1
= 68800 – 688 = 68112

2. *(a)* Finding the square of a number having 5 at its unit's place,

Such as, $(65)^2$, $(75)^2$, $(85)^2$ etc.

As, 65^2

Now, 6 × (6 + 1) = 6 × 7 = 42, then put 25 as its last two digits.

Hnce, $(65)^2 = 4225$

$(75)^2 = 5625$ ($\because$ 7 × 8 = 56)

$(35)^2 = 1225$ ($\because$ 3 × 4 = 12)

***(b)* Multiplication of 25 and 35, such numbers having 5 at their unit's places and difference of their ten's places digits is 1.**

25×35

First we multiply $2 \times (3 + 1) = 2 \times 4 = 8$, then put 75 as its last two digits', such as

$25 \times 35 = 875$

$35 \times 45 = 1575$ $[\because 3 \times (4 + 1) = 15]$

$65 \times 75 = 4875$ $[\because 6 \times (7 + 1) = 48]$

***(c)* Multiplication of numbers containing 9 as its ten's place.**

Such as, 91×91

Here, $(100 - 91) \times (100 - 91) = 9 \times 9 = 81$

& also, $9 + 9 = 18$

Now, $(100 - 18) = 82$

Hence, $91 \times 91 = 8281$

Similarly,

$91 \times 93 = 8463$ $[\because 9 + 7 = 16$ & $100 - 16 = 84, 9 \times 7 = 63]$

$95 \times 97 = 9215$ $[\because 5 + 3 = 8$ & $100 - 8 = 92, 5 \times 3 = 15]$

$99 \times 99 = 9801$ $[\because 1 + 1 = 2$ & $100 - 2 = 98, 1 \times 1 = 01]$

3. Multiplication of a number by 5^n :

Such as, $8274 \times 5^3 = \frac{8274000}{2^3} = \frac{8274000}{8} = 1034250$

In this method, we put 3 zeros to the right hand of the multiplicand and divide the number so formed by 2^3.

Algebraic Formulae :

(i) $(a + b)^2 = a^2 + 2ab + b^2$

(ii) $(a - b)^2 = a^2 - 2ab + b^2$

(iii) $a^2 - b^2 = (a + b)(a - b)$

(iv) $(a + b)^2 + (a - b)^2 = 2(a^2 + b^2)$

(v) $(a + b)^2 - (a - b)^2 = 4ab$

(vi) $(a + b)^2 = (a - b)^2 + 4ab$

(vii) $(a - b)^2 = (a + b)^2 - 4ab$

(viii) $(a + b + c)^2 = a^2 + b^2 + c^2 + 2ab + 2bc + 2ca$

(ix) $(a + b)^3 = a^3 + b^3 + 3ab(a + b)$

(x) $(a - b)^3 = a^3 - b^3 - 3ab(a - b)$

(xi) $a^3 + b^3 = (a + b)(a^2 - ab + b^2) = (a + b)^3 - 3ab(a + b)$

(xii) $a^3 - b^3 = (a - b)(a^2 + ab + b^2) = (a - b)^3 + 3ab(a - b)$

(xiii) $a^3 + b^3 + c^3 - 3abc = (a + b + c)(a^2 + b^2 + c^2 - ab - bc - ca)$

(xiv) If, $a + b + c = 0$, then, $a^3 + b^3 + c^3 = 3abc$

Some Basic division Tricks:
(i) $(x^n + a^n)$ is divisible by $(x + a)$ for all odd values of n.
(ii) $(x^n - a^n)$ is divisible by $(x - a)$ for all values of n.
(iii) $(x^n - a^n)$ is divisible by $(x + a)$ for all even values of n.

Example 1 : What is the sum of first four prime numbers?
Solution: Sum of first four prime numbers = 2 + 3 + 5 + 7 = 17.

Example 2 : What is the number of prime factors of $(6)^{10} \times (7)^{17} \times (55)^{27}$?
Solution: $(6)^{10} \times (7)^{17} \times (55)^{27} = 2^{10} \times 3^{10} \times 7^{17} \times 5^{27} \times 11^{27}$
$\therefore$ No. of prime factors = 10 + 10 + 17 + 27 + 27 = 91.

Example 3 : Find the number of prime factors in the product of $(25)^{12} \times (10)^7 \times (14)^7$.
Solution: $(25)^{12} \times (10)^7 \times (14)^7 = 5^{12} \times 5^{12} \times 2^7 \times 5^7 \times 2^7 \times 7^7 = 5^{12+12+7} \times 2^{7+7} \times 7^7 = 5^{31} \times 2^{14} \times 7^7$
$\therefore$ No. of prime factors = 31 + 14 + 7 = 52.

Example 4 : Is 979 a prime number?
Solution: The approximate square root of 979 is 32.
Prime numbers less than 32 are 2, 3, 5, 7, 11, 13, 17, 19, 23, 29, 31. We observe that 979 is divisible by 11, so it is not a prime number.

Example 5 : Prime factors of a number are 2, 2, 3, 7. Find the number.
Solution: The number is equal to the product of prime factors.
$\therefore$ 2 × 2 × 3 × 7 = 84 is the required number.

Example 6 : What is the sum of all primes between 70 and 100?
Solution: Prime numbers between 70 and 100 are 71, 73, 79, 83, 89 and 97.
$\therefore$ Sum of 71 + 73 + 79 + 83 + 89 + 97 = 492.

Example 7 : What is the least prime number of three digits?
Solution: Least number of 3 digits = 100.
But 100 is not a prime number, so the number next to 100 is 101 and it is prime number.

Example 8 : What is the difference in face value and local value of 5 in 7501?
Solution: The local value of 5 in 7501 = 500 and intrinsic value of 5 in 7501 = 5.
$\therefore$ Required difference = 500 – 5 = 495.

Example 9 : Which one of the following is the pair of twin primes?
(i) 5, 11 *(ii)* 7, 11 *(iii)* 11, 17 *(iv)* 1, 3 *(v)* 17, 19
Solution: Twin primes are the pairs of those prime numbers whose difference is 2. In the given alternatives, (17, 19) is such a pair of two prime numbers whose difference is 2.

Example 10: Which of the following is the pair of co-primes?
(i) 6, 9 *(ii)* 9, 12 *(iii)* 10, 21 *(iv)* 12, 22 *(v)* 18, 27
Solution: Co-prime is the pair of such numbers whose common factor is nothing except 1. In the given alternatives (10, 21) is such a pair in which common factor is nothing except 1.

Example 11: What will be the unit's digit in the value of $(4137)^{753}$?
Solution: Here, the unit's digit of 4137 is 7 and the index is 753.
But we know $(7)^1 = 7$, $(7)^2 = 49$, $(7)^3 = 343$, $(7)^4 = 2401$, $(7)^5 = 16807$
Hence, unit's digit is repeated after each 4 index.
The unit's digit in $(7)^{753}$ = `the unit's digit in $(7)^{752+1}$
Here, the required unit's digit is $(7)^1 = 7$

Example 12: What is the unit number in the value of $(729)^{59}$

Solution: Unit digit in $(729)^{59}$ = Unit digit in $(729)^{2 \times 29 + 1} = (9)^1 = 9$

Example 13: What will come in place of unit digit in the value of $(7)^{35} \times (3)^{71} \times (11)^{55}$?

Solution: On dividing (35 – 1) by 4; remainder = 2

Unit number in $(7)^{35}$ = unit no. in $(7)^{2+1}$ = unit no. in 7^3 = unit no. of 343 = 3

On dividing (55 – 1) by 4; remainder = 2

Unit number in $(11)^{55}$ = unit no. in $(1)^{2+1}$ = 1

On dividing (71 – 1) by 4; remainder = 2

Unit number in $(3)^{71}$ = unit no. in $(3)^{2+1}$ = 7

∴ Unit number of $(7)^{35} \times (3)^{71} \times (11)^{55}$ = Unit number of $3 \times 7 \times 1 = 1$ Ans.

Example 14: What is at the unit place of $(742)^{75}$?

Solution: Here, $N^n = (742)^{75}$

Dividing the index 75 by 4 we have remainder 3.

∴ $(742)^{75}$ will have the same number at the unit place of $(742)^3$ and the number at the unit place of $(742)^3$ is 8 because, $2 \times 2 \times 2 = 8$.

Example 15: Which digits cannot be on the place of unit digit when any number is squared?

Solution: If a number is squared, it will end with one of these numbers *i.e.*, 0, 1, 4, 5, 6 or 9. Hence it will never end with 2, 3, 7 or 8.

Example 16: The average of 7 consecutive integers is 7. Find the average of the square of those integers.

Solution: After using formula: Average of square $= \dfrac{1}{\text{No. of integer}} \times \left[\dfrac{n_1(n_1+1)(2n_1+1)}{6} - \dfrac{n_2(n_2+1)(2n_2+1)}{6}\right]$

where $n_1 = \text{Average} + \dfrac{\text{No. of integer} - 1}{2} = 7 + \dfrac{7-1}{2} = 10$

and $n_2 = 7 - \dfrac{7+1}{2} = 3$

∴ $\text{Average} = \dfrac{1}{7}\left[\dfrac{10 \times 11 \times 21}{6} - \dfrac{3 \times 4 \times 7}{6}\right] = \dfrac{1}{7}(385 - 14) = \dfrac{371}{7} = 53$ Ans.

Example 17: What will be the sum of odd numbers between 110 to 320?

Solution: Sum of odd numbers between 1 to 320 = $(160)^2$ = 25600.

No of odd numbers between 1 to 110 = $\dfrac{110}{2} = 55$

∴ Sum of odd numbers between 1 to 110 = $(55)^2$ = 3025

∴ Sum of odd numbers between 110 to 320 = 25600 – 3025 = 22575 **Ans.**

Example 18: What will be the sum of even numbers between 1 to 40?

Solution: Number of even numbers between 1 to 40 = $\dfrac{40}{2} = 20$

∴ Sum of even numbers between 1 to 40 = $20(20 + 1) = 20 \times 21 = 420$

Example 19 : The digit in unit's place in the product of 36* × 39 × 967 × 951 is 1. Which number should replace the asterisk*?

Solution: Unit's digits in numbers 39, 967 and 951 are 9, 7 and 1 respectively.

∴ Product of 9, 7 and 1 = $9 \times 7 \times 1 = 63$ in which unit digit is 3.

But, by the question
$36* \times 39 \times 967 \times 951$, unit digit is 1.
∴ 7 should be replaced the asterisk because $7 \times 3 = 21$ in which digit in unit's place is 1.

Example 20: What will be the sum of odd numbers between 1 to 200?

Solution: Number of odd numbers between 1 to $n = \left(\dfrac{\text{Last odd number} + 1}{2}\right)$

∴ Number of odd numbers between 1 to 200 $= \dfrac{199+1}{2} = 100$

∴ Sum of odd nos. between 1 to 200 = (Number of odd numbers)^2 = $(100)^2 = 10000$.

Example 21: A number when divided by 899 gives a remainder of 63. If the same number is divided by 29, then what will be the remainder?

Solution: Number $= D \times Q + R$
$= 899 \times K + 63$
$= 31 \times 29 \times K + 29 \times 2 + 5$
$= 29\,(31K + 2) + 5$
∴ The remainder when the number is divided by 29 is 5 Ans.

Example 22: If 30 x 0103 is divisible by 11, then, what is the value of x?

Solution: If a number is divisible by 11, the difference between the sum of the digits at the even places and sum of digits at odd places should be zero or a multiple of 11.
∵ The sum of the digits in the even places = 0 and the sum of the digits in the odd places
$= 3 + x + 1 + 3 = 7 + x$

∴ $(7 + x) - 0 = 11$
$x = 11 - 7 = 4$.

Example 23 : What least value must be given to * so that the number 91876 * 2 is divisible by 8?
Solution: By hit and trial method, we find that 632 is divisible by 8. Hence * must be replaced by 3.

Example 24: A number on being divided by 5 and 7 successively leaves the remainders 2 and 4 respectively. Find the remainder when the same number is divided by $5 \times 7 = 35$.

Solution:

5	A	
7	B	2
C	4	

In the above arrangement, A is the number which, when divided by 5, gives B as a quotient and leaves 2 as a remainder. Again, when B is divided by 7, it gives C as a quotient and 4 as a remainder.
For simplicity, we may take C = 1
∴ $B = 7 \times 1 + 4 = 11$
and $A = 5 \times 11 + 2 = 57$
Now, when 57 is divided by 35, we get 22 as the remainder.

Example 25: What least number must be subtracted from 1294, so that the remainder when divided by 9, 11, 13 will leave in each case the same remainder 6?

Solution: The number when divided by 9, 11, 13 leaving remainder 6
= (L.C.M. of 9, 11, 13) + 6 = 1287 + 6 = 1293
∴ Required number = 1294 – 1293 = 1.

Example 26 : $7^{12} - 4^{12}$ is exactly divisible by which numbers?

Solution: Two factors of $7^{12} - 4^{12}$ are necessarily (7 + 4) (7 – 4) because 12 is even numbers.
But (7 + 4) (7 – 4) = 11 × 3 = 33
Hence, $7^{12} - 4^{12}$ is exactly divisible by 3, 11 and 33.

Example 27 : A certain number when successively divided by 8 and 11 leaves remainders 3 and 7 respectively. Find the remainder if the same number is divided by 88.

Solution:

5	A	
7	B	2
	C	4

For simplicity, we take C = 1; then, B = 11 × 1 + 7 = 18 and A = 8 × 18 + 3 = 147
when 147 is divided by 88 it gives a remainder 59.
Hence, the required remainder = 59

Example 28 : In a division sum, the divisor is ten times the quotient and five times the remainder. If the remainder is 46 determine the dividend.

Solution: Let the quotient be Q and the remainder be R.
According to the question,

$$\text{Divisor} = 5 \times 46 = 230$$

$$\text{Quotient} = \frac{230}{10} = 23$$

$$\therefore \quad \text{Dividend} = \text{Divisor} \times \text{Quotient} + \text{Remainder}$$

$$= 230 \times 23 + 46 = 5290 + 46 = 5336$$

Example 29 : A number when divided by the sum of 555 and 445 gives two times their difference as quotient and 30 as the remainder. Find the number.

Solution: According to the question,

$$\text{Divisor} = 555 + 445 = 1000$$

$$\text{Quotient} = (555 - 445) \times 2 = 110 \times 2 = 220$$

$$\text{Remainder} = 30$$

$$\text{Dividend} = ?$$

$$\text{Dividend} = (\text{Divisor} \times \text{Quotient}) + \text{Remainder}$$

$$= (1000 \times 220) + 30 = 220000 + 30$$

$$= 220030.$$

Example 30 : When a certain number is multiplied by 13, the product consists entirely of fives. What is the smallest such number?

Solution: By hit and trial method, we find that the smallest number consisting entirely of fives and exactly divisible by 13 is 555555.
On dividing 555555 by 13, we get 42735 as quotient.

Example 31 : If $\frac{72 \times x}{27 \times 48}$ is a natural number then what will be the least value of x?

Solution: $\frac{72 \times x}{27 \times 48}$ is a natural number or a positive integer.

$\because$ 1 is the smallest positive integer

$$\therefore \frac{72 \times x}{27 \times 48} = 1 \Rightarrow x = \frac{27 \times 48}{72} = 18$$

Hence, the least value of x will be 18.

Example 32: If in a question of division divisor is 9, quotient is 114 and remainder is 5, then what will be the dividend?

Solution:

$$\begin{aligned} \text{Dividend} &= \text{Divisor} \times \text{Quotient} + \text{Remainder} \\ &= 9 \times 114 + 5 \\ &= 1026 + 5 = 1031 \end{aligned}$$

Example 33: If a number 19^{35} is divided by 18, then what will be the remainder?

Solution:

$$\begin{aligned} 19 &= 18 \times 1 + 1, \textit{ i.e.}, 18 \times \text{quotient} + 1 \\ 19^2 &= (18 \times 1 + 1) \times 19 = 18 \times 19 + 19 \\ &= 18 \times 19 + 18 + 1 \\ &= 18 \times 20 + 1, \textit{ i.e.}, 18 \times \text{quotient} + 1 \\ 19^3 &= (18 \times 20 + 1) \times 19 = 18 \times 380 + 19 \\ &= 18 \times 380 + 18 + 1 \\ &= 18 \times 381 + 1, \textit{ i.e.}, 18 \times \text{quotient} + 1 \\ \text{Similarly, } 19^{35} &= 18 \times \text{quotient} + 1 \end{aligned}$$

Hence, it is clear that 1 will be left as remainder if 19^{35} is divided by 18.

Example 34: A smallest numbei multiplied by 9 and then 9 is added to the product. If the sum so obtained is completely divisible by 17 then what is that smallest number?

Solution: Let the smallest number be x.

According to the question,

$x \times 9 + 9 = 9\ (x + 1)$ is a number which is completely divisible by 17.

Hence, it is clear that x should be at least 16, because $9\ (16 + 1) = 9 \times 17$, which is completely divisible by 17.

Required smallest number = 16.

Example 35: Find the largest number which divides 25, 73 and 97 leaving an equal remainder in each case.

Solution:

$$\because \quad \text{Number} = \text{Divisor} \times \text{Quotient} + \text{Remainder}$$

$$25 = 24 \times 1 + 1 \quad \text{... } (i)$$

$$73 = 24 \times 3 + 1 \quad \text{... } (ii)$$

$$97 = 24 \times 4 + 1 \quad \text{... } (iii)$$

It is clear from the above three equations that 24 is the largest number which divides the given three numbers leaving 1 as remainder in each case.

Example 36: If the number 135 * 7 is completely divisible by 9, then which number should replace the asterisk (*) ?

Solution: We know that a number is divisible by 9 only if the sum of its digits is a multiple of 9.

In the given number 135 * 7, sum of all other digits except the digit in place of (*) is (1 + 3 + 5 + 7 = 16).

Hence, digit 2 should replace the asterisk to form the sum of the digits of the number a multiple of 9.

Example 37 : If a three-digit number 4A3 is added to another three digit number 984, their sum is a four-digit number 13 B7 which is completely divisible by 11. What will be the value of (A + B)?

Solution: A number is divisible by 11 if the difference of the sum of its digits in even places and the sum of its digits in odd places (starting from unit's place) is either 0 or a multiple of 11.

According to the condition of the problem,

The number 13 B7 is completely divisible by 11

$\therefore\ (1 + B) - (3 + 7) = 0$

$1 + B - 10 = 0$

$B = 9$

$\therefore$ The four digit number will be 1397

Now, $4\,A3 + 984 = 1397$

$\Rightarrow\ 4\,A3 = 1397 - 984$

$\Rightarrow\ 4\,A3 = 413$

$\therefore\ A = 1$

Hence, it is clear that $(A + B) = 1 + 9 = 10$

Example 38 : If $\left(9\frac{3}{x}\right)\times\left(y\frac{7}{9}\right) = 16\frac{2}{3}$, then what will be the values of x and y?

Solution: Since the product of two numbers is $16\frac{2}{3}$. Therefore it is obvious that the digit 1 will replace y because $9 \times 1 = 9$ which is less than 16.

Now, $9\frac{3}{x} \times 1\frac{7}{9} = 16\frac{2}{3} \Rightarrow 9\frac{3}{x}\times\frac{16}{9} = \frac{50}{3}$

$\Rightarrow 9\frac{3}{x} = \frac{75}{8} \qquad \Rightarrow\ 9\frac{3}{x} = 9\frac{3}{8} \qquad \Rightarrow x = 8$

Therefore, values of x and y will be 8 and 1 respectively.

Example 39 : What will be the digit in unit's place in the product of 302, 244, 538 and 117.

Solution: Since digits in units place in the given numbers are 2, 4, 8 and 7 respectively.

$\therefore 2 \times 4 \times 8 \times 7 = 448$ in which digit in unit's place is 8.

Hence, the digit in unit's place in the product of the given numbers will also be 8.

Example 40 : How many numbers between 1 to 300 are completely divisible by 13?

Solution: $\because\ 300 = 13 \times 23 + 1$

$\therefore$ Between 1 to 300, there are 23 such numbers which are completely divisible by 13.

Example 41 : What is additive inverse of $\frac{3}{7}$?

Solution: We know that if sum of two numbers is 0, then each of the numbers is additive inverse of the other.

Therefore additive inverse of $\frac{3}{7}$ is $-\frac{3}{7}$, because $\frac{3}{7}-\frac{3}{7}=0$

Example 42 : What will be the multiplicative inverse of $-\frac{7}{8}$?

Solution: Multiplicative inverse (reciprocal) of $-\frac{7}{8}$ is $-\frac{8}{7}$ because $\left(-\frac{7}{8}\right)\times\left(-\frac{8}{7}\right) = 1$

Example 43: What is the sum of the numbers between 1 to 500.

Solution: Sum of numbers from 1 to $n = \frac{n(n+1)}{2}$ (where n is the number of terms)

$\therefore$ Sum of numbers from 1 to 500

$$= \frac{500\ (500+1)}{2} = \frac{500 \times 501}{2} = \frac{250500}{2} = 125250$$

Example 44: Find out the sum of the numbers between 100 to 150.

Solution: Sum of the numbers between 1 to 150$= \frac{150(150+1)}{2} = \frac{150 \times 151}{2} = 11325$

Sum of the numbers between 1 to 99$= \frac{99\ (99+1)}{2} = \frac{99 \times 100}{2} = 4950$

$\therefore$ Sum of the numbers between 100 to 150= 11325 – 4950 = 6375

Example 45: What will be the sum of even numbers between 70 to 200?

Solution: Number of even numbers between 1 to 200 $= \frac{200}{2} = 100$

$\therefore$ Sum of even numbers between 1 to 200

$$= 100 \times (100 + 1) = 100 \times 101 = 10100.$$

Now, number of even numbers between 1 to 69 $= \frac{68}{2} = 34$

$\therefore$ Sum of even numbers between 1 to 69

$$= 34 \times (34 + 1) = 34 \times 35 = 1190$$

$\therefore$ Sum of even numbers between 70 to 200 = 10100 – 1190 = 8910.

Example 46: Saurabh was asked to multiply a given number by $\frac{7}{8}$ but instead he multiplied the given number by $\frac{17}{8}$. If his answer was 30 more than the correct answer, what was the number given under the question?

Solution: Let the given number be x.

$\therefore$ Correct answer $= x \times \frac{7}{8} = \frac{7x}{8}$

Incorrect answer $= x \times \frac{17}{8} = \frac{17x}{8}$

According to the question, $\frac{17x}{8} = \frac{7x}{8} + 30$

$\therefore$ $\frac{17x}{8} - \frac{7x}{8} = 30 \Rightarrow \frac{10x}{8} = 30 \Rightarrow x = \frac{30 \times 8}{10} = 24.$

$\therefore$Required number was 24.

EXERCISE

1. 2, 4, 6, 8, 10, ..., are

(*a*) prime numbers (*b*) odd numbers (*c*) even numbers (*d*) natural numbers

2. 2, 3, 5, 7, 11, and 13 are

(*a*) even numbers (*b*) odd numbers (*c*) prime numbers (*d*) natural numbers

3. The prime numbers between 1 to 100 are
(*a*) 20 (*b*) 22 (*c*) 25 (*d*) 30

4. The only even prime number is
(*a*) 2 (*b*) 67 (*c*) 79 (*d*) 98

5. Which of the following is not a prime number?
(*a*) 79 (*b*) 83 (*c*) 87 (*d*) 97

6. Which of the following is a prime number?
(*a*) 117 (*b*) 147 (*c*) 149 (*d*) 159

7. The next number in the sequence 1, 7, 3, 9, 5, 11, ... is—
(*a*) 7 (*b*) 13 (*c*) 15 (*d*) 17

8. In the sequence 4, 9, ..., 25, 36 the missing number is—
(*a*) 14 (*b*) 16 (*c*) 20 (*d*) 21

9. In the sequence 17, ..., 18, 15, 19, 14, 20, 13 the missing number is—
(*a*) 5 (*b*) 10 (*c*) 12 (*d*) 16

(For questions 11 to 14, let means add the first number to twice the second number).*

10. The value of 5*4 is
(*a*) 20 (*b*) 9 (*c*) 11 (*d*) 13

11. The value of 7*0 is
(*a*) 7 (*b*) 9 (*c*) 14 (*d*) 0

12. The value of [1*2] * 3 is
(*a*) 5 (*b*) 7 (*c*) 9 (*d*) 11

13. The value of 3*[0*6] is
(*a*) 18 (*b*) 23 (*c*) 27 (*d*) 29

(For questions 14 to 16, let Δ means square the first number and add the second).

14. The value of 2 Δ 10 is—
(*a*) 12 (*b*) 14 (*c*) 22 (*d*) 102

15. The value of 6 Δ 7 is—
(*a*) 42 (*b*) 43 (*c*) 54 (*d*) 59

16. The value of [3 × 2] Δ 9 is—
(*a*) 42 (*b*) 45 (*c*) 87 (*d*) 91

*(For questions 17 to 19, let ** means increase the first number by 2 and then multiply by the second number).*

17. The value of 5**3 is
(*a*) 15 (*b*) 25 (*c*) 21 (*d*) 17

18. The value of [3**3]**4 is
(*a*) 68 (*b*) 60 (*c*) 54 (*d*) 36

19. The value of [5**0]**3 is
(*a*) 0 (*b*) 6 (*c*) 15 (*d*) 21

20. The smallest whole number which is divisible by 3 and also by the next two greater prime number is—
(*a*) 15 (*b*) 21 (*c*) 60 (*d*) 105

21. A number is called perfect, when it is equal to the sum of all its divisions excluding the number itself, e.g., 6 = 1 + 2 + 3. The other perfect number less than 32 is—
(a) 8 (b) 12 (c) 16 (d) 28

22. The smallest number of four digits is—
(a) 1001 (b) 0001 (c) 0010 (d) 1000

23. The largest number of four digits is—
(a) 1000 (b) 9000 (c) 9009 (d) 9999

24. If 'a' is an odd number, 'b' is an even number and 'c' is odd then, $a + b + c$ is—
(a) odd number (b) even number (c) prime number (d) any number

25. The product of two prime numbers is a—
(a) prime number (b) even number
(c) odd number (d) composite number

26. Prime factors of a number are 2, 2, 3, 7. The number is—
(a) 14 (b) 41 (c) 48 (d) 84

27. The largest number which is a factor of 56 as well as 84 is—
(a) 2 (b) 7 (c) 14 (d) 28

28. L.C.M. of 6, 9, 12, 18 is—
(a) 28 (b) 36 (c) 38 (d) 42

29. If 'x' and 'y' are both odd numbers, which of the following numbers must be an even number?
(a) $x + y$ (b) $x \times y$ (c) $xy + 2$ (d) $2x + y$

30. 'a' is less than 'b' then, which of the following numbers is greater than 'a' and less than 'b'?
(a) $\frac{a+b}{2}$ (b) $\frac{ab}{2}$ (c) $b^2 - a^2$ (d) ab

31. $a + b + c + d$ is a positive number, a minimum of 'x' of the number a, b, c and d must be positive, where 'x' is equal to—
(a) –1 (b) 2 (c) 3 (d) 4

32. There are four numbers A, B, C and D. Average of the first three i.e., A, B and C is 15 and that of B, C and D is 16. If the last number, i.e., D is 19, then the first number is—
(a) 15 (b) 16 (c) 17 (d) 18

33. Think of a number, divide it by 9 and add 9 to it, if the result is 27, the number is—
(a) 18 (b) 21 (c) 100 (d) 162

34. Of the three numbers, the first is twice the second and thrice the third. If the average of three is 22, the three numbers are—
(a) 12, 18, 36 (b) 18, 12, 36 (c) 36, 12, 18 (d) 36, 18, 12

35. The number which when added to itself 10 times gives 264. The number is—
(a) 20 (b) 22 (c) 24 (d) 26

36. If a person is standing on the sixth number in the queue from both the ends, the total persons in the queue are—
(a) 9 (b) 11 (c) 12 (d) 13

37. A number 'x' when multiplied by 5 and added to three times its own gives 64, the number is—
(a) 8 (b) 12 (c) 14 (d) 18

38. If the sum of two numbers 'x' and 'y' is equal to twice the first number, the second number 'y' is—
(a) $> x$ (b) $< x$ (c) $= x$ (d) negative number

39. The excess of thrice a certain number over 11 is 19. The number is—
(*a*) 8 (*b*) 9 (*c*) 10 (*d*) 11

40. The difference between the squares of two consecutive numbers is 25. The numbers are—
(*a*) 11, 12 (*b*) 12, 13 (*c*) 15, 14 (*d*) 14, 13

41. The sum of two digits of a number is 15. If 9 is added to the number, the digits are reversed. The number is—
(*a*) 78 (*b*) 87 (*c*) 69 (*d*) 96

42. A number which when multiplied by 11 is as much above 180 as it was originally below it. The number is—
(*a*) 25 (*b*) 30 (*c*) 40 (*d*) 45

43. Divide Rs. 53 among X, Y, Z so that X may receive Rs. 7 more than Y, and Y may receive Rs. 8 more than Z.
(*a*) 10, 15, 18 (*b*) 18, 10, 25
(*c*) 20, 12, 27 (*d*) 25, 18, 10

44. If $a = 16$ and $b = 15$, then what is the value of $\frac{a^2+b^2+ab}{a^3-b^3} = ?$
(*a*) $\frac{1}{2}$ (*b*) $\frac{1}{3}$ (*c*) 1 (*d*) 2

45. Find the number which when multiplied by 16 is increased by 225.
(*a*) 13 (*b*) 14 (*c*) 15 (*d*) 16

46. What is the largest number of four digits which is exactly divisible by 88?
(*a*) 9999 (*b*) 9988 (*c*) 9944 (*d*) 9998

47. If $\frac{a}{b} = \frac{4}{3}$, then $\frac{3a+2b}{3a-2b} = ?$
(*a*) 2 (*b*) 3 (*c*) 4 (*d*) 5

48. If $\frac{x}{y} = \frac{3}{4}$, then the value of $\frac{6}{7}+\frac{y-x}{y+x} = ?$
(*a*) 1 (*b*) 2 (*c*) 3 (*d*) 4

49. If the number $(10^n - 1)$ is divisible by 11, then n is—
(*a*) odd number (*b*) even number (*c*) any number (*d*) multiple of 11

50. $\left(1-\frac{1}{3}\right)\left(1-\frac{1}{4}\right)\left(1-\frac{1}{5}\right)...\left(1-\frac{1}{n}\right) = ?$
(*a*) $\frac{42}{29}$ (*b*) $\frac{n-1}{n}$ (*c*) $\frac{2}{n}$ (*d*) 0

51. $\left(2-\frac{1}{3}\right)\left(2-\frac{3}{5}\right)\left(2-\frac{5}{7}\right)...\left(2-\frac{997}{999}\right) = ?$
(*a*) $\frac{997}{999}$ (*b*) ∞ (*c*) $\frac{997}{3}$ (*d*) $\frac{1001}{3}$

52. Divide 48 into two parts such that 7 times the first part added to 5 times the second part is 246. Find the first part.
(*a*) 2 (*b*) 3 (*c*) 4 (*d*) 5

53. The sum of a number and its reciprocal is thrice the difference of the number and its reciprocal. Find the number.

(a) $\sqrt{2}$ (b) $\sqrt{3}$ (c) $\sqrt{5}$ (d) $\sqrt{7}$

54. What should be added to the product of four consecutive odd numbers to make it a perfect square?

(a) 13 (b) 14 (c) 15 (d) 16

55. A boy was asked to find $\frac{7}{9}$ of a fraction. He made a mistake of dividing the fraction by $\frac{7}{9}$ and so got an answer which exceeded the correct answer by $\frac{8}{21}$. Find the correct answer.

(a) $\frac{2}{3}$ (b) $\frac{5}{7}$ (c) $\frac{7}{12}$ (d) $\frac{7}{15}$

56. If 40% of a number is 360, what will be 15% of 15% of that number?

(a) 11.5 (b) 20.25 (c) 15.5 (d) 21.75

57. The sum of two numbers is 25 and the difference of their square is 75. Find the difference between the numbers.

(a) 2 (b) 3 (c) 4 (d) 5

58. Ram eats 8 bananas in the morning, 5 in the afternoon and 2 in the evening. How many dozens of bananas does he eat in a day.

(a) $1\frac{1}{4}$ (b) $\frac{1}{4}$ (c) $\frac{3}{13}$ (d) $14\frac{17}{30}$

59. What should come in place of the question mark (?) in the following equation?

$$47^{7.5} \div 47^{\frac{3}{2}} \times 47^{-3} = \left(\sqrt{47}\right)^{?}$$

(a) 5 (b) 6 (c) 7 (d) 8

60. $\sqrt{256\sqrt{16 \div ?}} = 16$

(a) 8 (b) 16 (c) 4 (d) 256

61. Compute the following: $7+\cfrac{2}{5+\cfrac{3}{4+\cfrac{2}{3+\cfrac{1}{4}}}}$

(a) $\frac{831}{113}$ (b) $\frac{47}{12}$ (c) $\frac{900}{113}$ (d) $\frac{14}{17}$

62. There are 408 boys and 312 girls in a school, which are to be divided into equal sections of either boys or girls alone. Find the maximum number of boys or girls that can be placed in a section. Also find the total number of sections thus formed.

(a) 10, 20 (b) 24, 30 (c) 24, 40 (d) 30, 30

63. A wine seller had three types of wine, 403 gallon of 1st type, 434 gallon of 2nd type, 465 gallon of 3rd type. Find the least possible number of casks of equal size in which different type of wine can be filled without mixing.

(a) 41 (b) 42 (c) 0 (d) 43

64. The least value of K when 7K25 is divisible by 5 is—
(a) 0 (b) 1 (c) 2 (d) 3

65. Simplify : $\frac{.0203 \times 2.92}{.0073 \times 14.5 \times .7}$
(a) .8 (b) .2 (c) .7 (d) .07

66. A reception party was held in a five star hotel and the charges per plate were as many rupees as the number of plates used. The total charges came to be Rs. 15129. How many rupees were charged per plate?
(a) 120 (b) 121 (c) 122 (d) 123

67. The difference between place values of 7 and 3 in the number 527435 is—
(a) 5 (b) 4 (c) 6970 (d) 45

68. If the largest three digit number is subtracted from the smallest five-digit number, then the remainder is—
(a) 9000 (b) 9001 (c) 90001 (d) 1

69. 9548 + 7314 = 8362 + ?
(a) 8410 (b) 8230 (c) 8600 (d) 8500

70. 7589 – ? = 3434
(a) 11023 (b) 4155 (c) 3246 (d) 721

71. 9358 – 6014 + 3127 = ?
(a) 6741 (b) 6561 (c) 6471 (d) 6381

72. 39798 + 3798 + 378 = ?
(a) 49532 (b) 43984 (c) 43974 (d) 43576

73. What should be the maximum value of B in the following equation?
5A9 – 7B2 + 9C6 = 823
(a) 9 (b) 7 (c) 6 (d) 5

74. In the given sum, "?" stands for which digit?
? + 1? + 2? + ?3 + ?1 = 21?
(a) 9 (b) 8 (c) 6 (d) 4

75. 360 × 17 = ?
(a) 6130 (b) 6120 (c) 5320 (d) 5120

76. 587 × 999 = ?
(a) 615173 (b) 614823 (c) 587523 (d) 586413

77. 12345679 × 72 = ?
(a) 999999998 (b) 898989898
(c) 888888888 (d) 88888888

78. (217 × 217 + 183 × 183) is equal to
(a) 81268 (b) 80698 (c) 80578 (d) 79698

79. A positive integer, which when added to 1000, gives a sum which is greater than when it is multiplied by 1000. This positive integer is—
(a) 7 (b) 5 (c) 3 (d) 1

80. What number should replace x in this multiplication problem?

$$\begin{array}{r} 3\,x\,4 \\ 4 \\ \hline 1216 \end{array}$$

(a) 5 (b) 4 (c) 2 (d) 0

81. What should come in place of ★ mark in the given equation?

1 ★ 544 ÷ 148 = 78

(a) 6 (b) 4 (c) 2 (d) 1

82. When a certain number is multiplied by 13, the product consists entirely of fives. The smallest such number is—

(a) 42735 (b) 42515 (c) 42135 (d) 41625

83. A boy multiplies 987 by a certain number and obtains 559981 as his answer. If in the answer, both 9's are wrong, but the other digits are correct, then correct answer will be—

(a) 556581 (b) 555681 (c) 555181 (d) 553681

84. The smallest value of n, for which $2n + 1$ is not a prime number, is—

(a) 5 (b) 4 (c) 3 (d) 2

85. The sum of all possible two-digit number formed from three different one-digit natural numbers, when divided by the sum of the original three numbers is equal to—

(a) 11 (b) 18 (c) 22 (d) 36

86. For the integer n, if n^3 is odd, then which of the following statements is/are true?

I. n is odd II. n^2 is odd III. n^2 is even

(a) I only (b) II only (c) I and II only (d) I and III only

87. There are four prime numbers written in ascending order. The product of the first three is 385 and that of the last three is 1001. The last number is—

(a) 19 (b) 17 (c) 13 (d) 11

88. If we write all the whole numbers from 200 to 400, then how many of these contain the digit 7 once and only once?

(a) 36 (b) 35 (c) 34 (d) 32

89. The digit in unit's place of the product 81 × 82 × .... × 89 is—

(a) 8 (b) 6 (c) 2 (d) 0

90. The digit in the unit's place of the number represented by $(7^{95} - 3^{58})$ is—

(a) 7 (b) 6 (c) 4 (d) 0

91. The unit's digit in the product $(7^{71} \times 6^{59} \times 3^{65})$ is:

(a) 6 (b) 4 (c) 2 (d) 1

92. x is an even number then x^{4n}, where n is a positive integer, will always have—

(a) 6 in the units place (b) Zero in the unit's place

(c) Either 0 or 6 in the unit's place (d) None of these

93. If $(64)^2 - (36)^2 = 20x$, then the value of x is—

(a) 180 (b) 140 (c) 120 (d) 70

94. If the number 357 ★ 25 ★ is divisible by both 3 and 5, then the missing digits in the unit's place and thousandth place respectively are—

(a) 0, 4 (b) 5, 4 (c) 5, 6 (d) 0, 6

95. Which of the following numbers is exactly divisible by 24?
(*a*) 3125736 (*b*) 537804 (*c*) 63810 (*d*) 35718

96. How many of the following numbers are divisible by 132?
264, 396, 462, 792, 968, 2178, 5184, 6336
(*a*) 7 (*b*) 6 (*c*) 5 (*d*) 4

97. The difference between the squares of two consecutive odd integers is always divisible by:
(*a*) 8 (*b*) 7 (*c*) 6 (*d*) 3

98. The sum of three consecutive odd numbers is always divisible by:
I. 3 II. 2 III. 6 IV. 5
(*a*) only I (*b*) only II (*c*) only I & III (*d*) only II and IV

99. A 4-digit number is formed by repeating a 2-digit number such as 2525, 3232 etc. Any number of this form is exactly divisible by:
(*a*) 13 (*b*) 11
(*c*) 7 (*d*) smallest 3-digit prime number

100. The number 3 1 1 3 1 1 3 1 1 3 1 1 3 1 1 3 1 1 is:
(*a*) Divisible by 11 but not by 3 (*b*) Divisible by 3 but not by 11
(*c*) Divisible by 3 and 11 both (*d*) Neither divisible by 3 nor by 11

101. 325325 is a six-digit number. It is divisible by:
(*a*) 13 only (*b*) 11 only (*c*) 7 only (*d*) All 7, 11 and 13

102. Which of the following numbers is exactly divisible by all prime numbers between 1 and 17.
(*a*) 515513 (*b*) 510510 (*c*) 440440 (*d*) 345345

103. Find the number which is nearest to 457 and exactly divisible by 11.
(*a*) 462 (*b*) 460 (*c*) 451 (*d*) 450

104. The number of times 99 is subtracted from 1111 so that remainder is less than 99, is
(*a*) 13 (*b*) 12 (*c*) 11 (*d*) 10

105. When the sum of two numbers is multiplied by 5, the product is divisible by 15. Which one of the following pairs of numbers satisfies the above condition?
(*a*) 250, 341 (*b*) 245, 342 (*c*) 240, 335 (*d*) None of these

106. What least number must be subtracted from 427398 so that remaining number is divisible by 15?
(*a*) 11 (*b*) 6 (*c*) 5 (*d*) 3

107. The smallest number that must be added to 803642 in order to obtain a multiple of 11 is—
(*a*) 9 (*b*) 7 (*c*) 4 (*d*) 1

108. The greatest number by which the product of three consecutive multiples of 3 is always divisible is:
(*a*) 243 (*b*) 162 (*c*) 81 (*d*) 54

109. The smallest number of five-digits exactly divisible by 476 is:
(*a*) 47600 (*b*) 10476 (*c*) 10472 (*d*) 10000

110. In a divison of a question with zero remainder, a candidate took 12 as divisor instead of 21. The quotient obtained by him was 35. The correct quotient is:
(*a*) 20 (*b*) 13 (*c*) 12 (*d*) zero

111. The difference between two numbers is 1365. When the larger number is divided by the smaller one, the quotient is 6 and the remainder is 15. The smaller number is:
(*a*) 360 (*b*) 295 (*c*) 270 (*d*) 240

112. When a number is divided by 13, the remainder is 11. When the same number is divided by 17, the remainder is 9. What is the number?
(*a*) 369 (*b*) 349 (*c*) 339 (*d*) Data inadequate

113. When a number is divided by 31, the remainder is 29. When the same number is divided by 16, what will be the remainder?
(*a*) 15 (*b*) 13 (*c*) 11 (*d*) Data inadequate

114. A number when divided by 119 leaves 19 as remainder. If the same number is divided by 17, the remainder obtained is:
(*a*) 10 (*b*) 7 (*c*) 3 (*d*) 2

115. A number when divided by 296 gives a remainder 75. When the same number is divided by 37, then the remainder will be:
(*a*) 11 (*b*) 8 (*c*) 2 (*d*) 1

116. A number when divided by 114 leaves the remainder 21. When the same number is divided by 19, then the remainder will be
(*a*) 21 (*b*) 7 (*c*) 2 (*d*) 1

117. If x is a whole number, then $x^2 (x^2 - 1)$ is always divisible by:
(*a*) x (*b*) $12 - x$ (*c*) 24 (*d*) 12

118. $4^{61} + 4^{62} + 4^{63} + 4^{64}$ is divisible by:
(*a*) 13 (*b*) 11 (*c*) 10 (*d*) 3

119. In dividing a number by 585, a student applied the method of short division. He divided the number successively by 5, 9 and 13 (factor of 585) and got the remainders 4, 8 and 12. If he had divided the number by 585, the remainder would have been:
(*a*) 584 (*b*) 292 (*c*) 144 (*d*) 24

120. A number was divided successively in order by 4, 5 and 6. The remainder were respectively 2, 3 and 4. The number is:
(*a*) 1908 (*b*) 954 (*c*) 476 (*d*) 214

121. A number when divided successively by 4 and 5 leaves remainders 1 and 4 respectively. When it is successively divided by 5 and 4, then the respective remainders will be
(*a*) 4, 1 (*b*) 3, 2 (*c*) 2, 3 (*d*) 1, 2

122. When a number divided by 6 leaves a remainder 3. When the square of the same number is divided by 6, the remainder is:
(*a*) 3 (*b*) 2 (*c*) 1 (*d*) zero

EXPLANATORY ANSWERS

1. The numbers divisible by 2 are called even numbers, since, 4, 6, 8, 10 are divisible by 2, hence these are even numbers.

2. 2, 3, 5, 7, 11 and 13 are prime numbers.

3. The prime numbers between 1 to 100 are : 2, 3, 5, 7, 11, 13, 17, 19, 23, 29, 31, 37, 41, 43, 47, 53, 59, 61, 67, 71, 73, 79, 83, 89 and 97 i.e., 25 numbers.

4. 2 is the only even prime number.

5. 87 is divisible by 3, therefore it is not a prime number.

6. 149 is not divisible by any number, therefore it is a prime number.

7. In the sequence 1, 7, 3, 9, 5, 11 ... the alternate numbers differ by 2, *i.e.*, first and third number differ by 2, similarly the difference of second and fourth number is 2. Thus, next number in the series should be 5 + 2 = 7.

8. The sequence 4, 9, ..., 25, 36 contains the square of natural numbers, *i.e.*, 2^2, 3^2, 4^2, 5^2, 6^2. Thus the missing number is 4^2, *i.e.*, 16.

9. In the sequence 17, ..., 18, 15, 19, 14, 20, 13, the next alternate number is one more than the previous alternate number, *i.e.*, 17 + 1 = 18, 18 + 1 = 19, 19 + 1 = 20. Also the second number and fourth number differ by 1, *i.e.*, 13 + 1 = 14, 14 + 1 = 15, 15 + 1 = 16 is the required missing number).
[* *means add the first number to the twice of the second number*].

10. 5 + [2 × 4] = 5 + 8 = 13

11. 7 + [2 × 0] = 7 + 0 = 7

12. [1 + (2 × 2)] + 2 × 3 = 5 + 6 = 11

13. 3*[0*6] = 3*[0 + 2 × 6] = 3* 12 = 3 + 2 × 12 = 27
[Δ *means square the first number and add the second number.*]

14. 2 Δ 10 = 2 × 2 + 10 = 14

15. 6 Δ 7 = 6 × 6 + 7 = 43

16. [3 × 2] Δ 9 = 6 Δ 9 = 6 × 6 + 9 = 45
[***means increase the first number by 2 and then multiply by the second number*].

17. 5**3 = [5 + 2] × 3 = 21

18. [3**3]**4 = [(3 + 2) × 3] ** 4 = 15** 4 = [15 + 2] × 4 = 68

19. [5**0]**3 = [(5 + 2) × 0] **3 = 0**3 = [0 + 2] × 3 = 6

20. The number should be divisible by 3, 5 and 7. Thus L.C.M. of 3, 5, 7 is equal to 105 which is the required number.

21. 28 is multiple of 1, 2, 4, 7, 14.
Also 1 + 2 + 4 + 7 + 14 = 28

22. The smallest number of four digits is 1000.

23. The largest number of four digits is 9999.

24. Out of *a, b, c*; *a* is odd and *c* is odd while *b* is even. The sum of two odd numbers is even, *i.e.*, $a + c$ = even = d. Also, the sum of two even numbers is even, *i.e.*, $d + b$ = even.
$\therefore a + b + c$ = Even number.

25. Product of two prime numbers is never a prime number but it is either an odd number or an even number.

26. The number is equal to the product of prime factors.
∴ 2 × 2 × 3 × 7 = 84 is the required number.

27. Find H.C.F. of 56, 84 which is equal to 28.

28. L.C.M. of 6, 9, 12, 18, is 36.

29. Since the sum of two odd numbers is always even number, therefore, $x + y$ is even number.

30. Average of two different numbers is always between the two numbers.

31. If all numbers were not positive, then the sum could not be positive. If *a, b, c* were all – 1 and *d* were 5, then $a + b + c + d$ would be positive, so *(b), (c), (d)* are incorrect.

32. $\frac{A+B+C}{3} = 15,$ or, $A + B + C = 15 \times 3 = 45$ ... *(i)*

$\frac{B+C+D}{3} = 16,$ or $B + C + D = 48$ ... *(ii)*

$D = 19$

$\therefore B + C + 19 = 48$ or, $B + C = 48 - 19 = 29$

But, $A + B + C = 45$

Putting the value of $B + C = 29$ in the above equation *(i)*, we get $A + 29 = 45$

$\therefore A = 45 - 29 = 16.$

33. Let the number is x.

$\therefore \frac{x}{9}+9 = 27$ or, $\frac{x}{9} = 27 - 9 = 18$ $\therefore x = 18 \times 9 = 162.$

34. Let the third number $= x$

$\therefore$ First number $= 3x$ Second number $= \frac{3x}{2}$

$\therefore \frac{1}{3}\left[x+3x+\frac{3x}{2}\right] = 22 \Rightarrow \frac{11}{2}x = 66$

$\Rightarrow x = \frac{66 \times 2}{11} = 12 =$ Third number,

$12 \times 3 = 36 =$ First number, $\frac{12 \times 3}{2} = 18 =$ Second number.

35. Let the number is x.

Then, $x + 10x = 264$

$\Rightarrow 11x = 264$ $\therefore x = \frac{264}{11} = 24$

36. If the person is standing at sixth number in the queue from both sides, that means there are five persons ahead and five persons behind him. Hence, total number of persons in the queue is $5 + 1 + 5 = 11$.

37. $5 \times x + 3x = 64$ $\Rightarrow 8x = 64$ $\therefore x = \frac{64}{8} = 8$

38. $x + y = 2x$

$\therefore y = 2x - x = x$

39. Let the number is x.

$\therefore 3x - 11 = 19$ $\Rightarrow 3x = 19 + 11 = 30$ $\therefore x = \frac{30}{3} = 10$

40. Let the numbers are x and $(x + 1)$

$\therefore (x + 1)^2 - x^2 = 25$

$\Rightarrow x^2 + 1 + 2x - x^2 = 25$

$\Rightarrow 2x + 1 = 25$

$\Rightarrow 2x = 25 - 1 = 24$

$\therefore x = \frac{24}{2} = 12$

$\therefore x + 1 = 12 + 1 = 13$

Hence, the numbers are 12, 13.

41. Let x be the digit in units place. Digit in ten's place is then $15 - x$.

$\therefore$ The number $= 10\ (15 - x) + x$

The new number with reverse digits $= 10 \times x + (15 - x)$

$\therefore\ 10(15 - x) + x + 9 = 10x + 15 - x$

$\Rightarrow 150 - 10x + x + 9 = 9x + 15$

$\Rightarrow\ 18x = 144 \qquad x = \dfrac{144}{18} = 8$

The digit of ten's place $= 15 - 8 = 7$

$\therefore$ The required number = 78.

42. Let the number is x

$\therefore\ 180 - x = 11x - 180$

$\Rightarrow\ 180 + 180 = 11x + x \qquad \Rightarrow 360 = 12x,$

$\Rightarrow\ x = \dfrac{360}{12} = 30.$

43. Let Y receives Rs. a. Then X receives Rs. $(a + 7)$ and Z receives Rs. $(a - 8)$

But, $a + 7 + a + a - 8 =$ Rs. 53

$\Rightarrow 3a - 1 = 53, \qquad \Rightarrow 3a = 53 + 1$

$\Rightarrow 3a = 54, \qquad \therefore a = \dfrac{54}{3} =$ Rs. 18. = Y's share

X's share $= a + 7 = 18 + 7 =$ Rs. 25

Z's share $= a - 8 = 18 - 8 =$ Rs. 10.

44. Given $a = 16$ and $b = 15$, then $\dfrac{a^2+b^2+ab}{a^3-b^3} = \dfrac{a^2+b^2+ab}{(a-b)\left(a^2+b^2+ab\right)} = \dfrac{1}{a-b} = \dfrac{1}{16-15} = 1$

45. Let the required no. $= x$

then, $16x - x = 225$

$\Rightarrow\ 15x = 225$

$\therefore\ x = 15$

46. The greatest no. of 4 digit = 9999

Now, after dividing 9999 by 88, we get Remainder = 55

Hence, the largest 4 digit no. = 9999 – 55 = 9944

47. $\dfrac{3a+2b}{3a-2b} = \dfrac{3\frac{a}{b}+2}{3\frac{a}{b}-2} = \dfrac{3\times\frac{4}{3}+2}{3\times\frac{4}{3}-2} = \dfrac{6}{2} = 3$

48. $\dfrac{6}{7}+\dfrac{y-x}{y+x} = \dfrac{6}{7}+\dfrac{1-x/y}{1+x/y} = \dfrac{6}{7}+\dfrac{1-3/4}{1+3/4} = \dfrac{6}{7}+\dfrac{1}{7} = 1$

49. n is even number.

50. $\dfrac{2}{3}\times\dfrac{3}{4}\times\dfrac{4}{5}\times\ldots\times\dfrac{n-1}{n} = \dfrac{2}{n}$

51. $\dfrac{5}{3}\times\dfrac{7}{5}\times\dfrac{9}{7}\times\ldots\times\dfrac{1001}{999} = \dfrac{1001}{3}$

52. Let the first part = x then 2nd part = $(48 - x)$

By question, $7x + 5(48 - x) = 246$

$\Rightarrow \quad 2x = 246 - 240$

$\therefore \quad x = 3$

53. Let the no. $= x$ then its reciprocal $= \frac{1}{x}$

By the question, $\left(x + \frac{1}{x}\right) = 3\left(x - \frac{1}{x}\right)$

$\Rightarrow \quad \frac{x^2 + 1}{x} = \frac{3(x^2 - 1)}{x}$ $\Rightarrow x^2 + 1 = 3x^2 - 3$

$\Rightarrow \quad 3x^2 - x^2 = 3 + 1$

$\therefore \quad x = \sqrt{2}$.

54. Let the four consecutive odd numbers be $(2x - 3)$, $(2x - 1)$, $(2x + 1)$ and $(2x + 3)$

$\therefore$ Their product $= (2x - 1)(2x + 1)(2x - 3)(2x + 3)$

$= (4x^2 - 1)(4x^2 - 9)$

$= 16x^4 - 40x^2 + 9$

$= (4x^2 - 5)^2 - 16$

Hence, on adding 16, the result will be a perfect square.

55. : Let the required fraction = x

then, by the question $x \div \frac{7}{9} - x \times \frac{7}{9} = \frac{8}{21}$

$\Rightarrow \quad x \times \frac{9}{7} - \frac{7x}{9} = \frac{8}{21}$

$\Rightarrow \quad \frac{32x}{63} = \frac{8}{21}$

$\Rightarrow \quad x = \frac{8}{21} \times \frac{63}{32} = \frac{3}{4}$

Hence, the correct answer $= \frac{3}{4} \times \frac{7}{9} = \frac{7}{12}$.

56. Let a number be x

then 40% of $x = 360$

$\Rightarrow \frac{40}{100} \times x = 360$ $\therefore x = 360 \times \frac{100}{40} = 900$

Now by the question, 15% of 15% of 900 $= \frac{15}{100} \times \frac{15}{100} \times 900 = \frac{81}{4} = 20.25$.

57. Let two numbers are a and b

Given, $a + b = 25$

and $a^2 - b^2 = 75$

$\Rightarrow (a + b)(a - b) = 75$ $\Rightarrow (a - b) = \frac{75}{(a+b)} = \frac{75}{25} = 3$.

58. Total dozen of bananas Ram eats in a day $= \frac{8}{12} + \frac{5}{12} + \frac{2}{12} = \frac{15}{12} = 1\frac{1}{4}$

59. $47^{7.5} \div 47^{\frac{3}{2}} \times 47^{-3} = \left(\sqrt{47}\right)^{?}$

Let ? = x

then $(47)^{\frac{15}{2}} \div (47)^{\frac{3}{2}} \times (47)^{-3} = (47)^{\frac{x}{2}}$

$\Rightarrow (47)^{\frac{15}{2}-\frac{3}{2}-3} = (47)^{\frac{x}{2}}$ $\Rightarrow (47)^{\frac{6}{2}} = (47)^{\frac{x}{2}}$ $\therefore x = 6$

60. $\sqrt{256\sqrt{16 \div ?}} = 16$

$\Rightarrow \sqrt{16 \times 16\sqrt{16 \div x}} = 16$ [Let ? = x]

$\Rightarrow 16\sqrt{16 \div x} = 16 \Rightarrow \sqrt{16 \div x} = 1 \Rightarrow 16 \div x = 1$

$\therefore x = 16$

61. $7+\cfrac{2}{5+\cfrac{3}{4+\cfrac{2}{3+\cfrac{1}{4}}}} = 7+\cfrac{2}{5+\cfrac{3}{4+\cfrac{2}{\frac{13}{4}}}}$

$= 7+\cfrac{2}{5+\cfrac{3}{4+\cfrac{8}{13}}} = 7+\cfrac{2}{5+\cfrac{3}{\frac{60}{13}}} = 7+\cfrac{2}{5+\cfrac{13}{20}} = 7+\cfrac{2}{\frac{113}{20}} = 7+\frac{40}{113} = \frac{831}{113}$

62.

```
312) 408( 1
     312
     96 ) 312 ( 3
          288
           24 )96 ( 4
               96
               ×
```

$\therefore$ Maximum number of girls or boys that can be placed in a section = 24 and total number of such section = $\frac{408}{24}+\frac{312}{24}$ = 17 + 13 = 30

63.

```
403 ) 434 ( 1              31 ) 465 ( 15
      403                        31
      31 ) 403 ( 13              155
           31                    155
           93                     ×
           93
           ×
```

For least possible number of casks of equal size, the size of the casks must be the greatest and it is 31 gallon.

$\therefore$ Required number = $\frac{403}{31}+\frac{434}{31}+\frac{465}{31}$ = 13 + 14 + 15 = 42

64. Least value of $k = 0$

65. $\frac{.0203 \times 2.92}{.0073 \times 14.5 \times .7} = \frac{203 \times 292}{73 \times 145 \times 7} = \frac{4}{5} = .8$

66. Let the no. of plates $= x$ then cost of one plate $= x$

$\therefore$ cost of total plate $= x \times x = x^2$

By the question $x^2 = 15129$

$\therefore \quad x = \sqrt{15129} = \sqrt{123 \times 123} = 123.$

67. Place value of 7 in 527435 = 7000

Place value of 3 in 527435 = 30

Hence, their difference = 7000 − 30 = 6970

68. Required remainder = 10000 − 999 = 9001

69. ? = (9548 + 7314) − 8362 = 16862 − 8362 = 8500

70. ? = 7589 − 3434 = 4155

71. ? = 9358 + 3127 − 6014 = 12485 − 6014 = 6471

72. ? = 39798 + 3798 + 378 = 43974

73. Here, 1 + A + C − B = 12

$\Rightarrow$ A + C − B = 11

By putting A = C = 9, we get B = 7

$$\begin{array}{r} 1\ 1 \\ 5\ A\ 9 \\ +\ 9\ 6\ 6 \\ -\ 7\ B\ 2 \\ \hline 8\ 2\ 3 \end{array}$$

74. Here, $x + (10 + x) + (20 + x) + (10x + 3) + (10x + 1) = 200 + 10 + x$

$\Rightarrow 23x + 34 = 210 + x \quad \Rightarrow \quad 22x = 176 \quad \therefore x = 8$

75. 360 × 17= 360 × (20 − 3) = 360 × 20 − 360 × 3

= 7200 − 1080 = 6120

76. 587 × 999 = 587 × (1000 − 1) = 587000 − 587 = 586413

77. 1234679 × 72 = 12345679 (100 − 28)

= 12345679 (100 + 2 − 30)

= 1234567900 + 24691358 − 370370370

= 1259259258 − 370370370 = 888888888

78. (217 × 217 + 183 × 183) $= \frac{1}{2} \times 2\,(217^2 + 183^2)$

$= \frac{1}{2}[(217 + 183)^2 + (217 - 183)^2]$

$= \frac{1}{2}[(400)^2 + (34)^2]$

$= \frac{1}{2}[160000 + 1156]$

$= \frac{1}{2} \times 161156$

$= 80578$

79. Here, $1000 + 1 = 1001$
& $1000 \times 1 = 1000$
Now, $1001 > 1000$
Hence, required positive integer is 1.

80. Here, $(300 + 10x + 4) = 1216$
$\Rightarrow 1216 + 40x = 1216$
$\Rightarrow 40x = 0$
$\therefore\ x = 0$

81. 1 ★ 544 = 148 × 78 = 11544
Hence, ★ = 1

82. It is clear that product will be 555555

Hence, required number $= \dfrac{555555}{13} = 42735$

83. Here, $947 = 3 \times 7 \times 47$
Hence, the required number must be divisible by each of 3, 7 and 47.
Here, (c) and (d) are not divisible by 3 and (a) is also not divisible by 7.
Hence, required answer is (b).

84. Here, $2 \times 2 + 1 = 5$, $2 \times 3 + 1 = 7$, $2 \times 4 + 1 = 9$ (Not a prime no.)
Hence, required value of $n = 4$

85. Let three different one digit natural numbers be x, y and z.
Then, sum of all possible two digits numbers
$= (10x + y) + (10y + x) + (10x + z) + (10z + x) + (10y + z) + (10z + y)$
$= 22x + 22y + 22z = 22\ (x + y + z)$
Hence, required number = 22.

86. If n^3 is odd, then n and n^2 will be also odd.

87. Let four prime numbers be a, b, c and d respectively.

Now, $\dfrac{abc}{bcd} = \dfrac{385}{1001} \quad \Rightarrow \dfrac{c}{d} = \dfrac{5}{13}$

Hence, $a = 5$ and $d = 13$

88. The whole numbers between 200 to 300 containing the digit 7 once and only once are, 207, 217, 227, 237, 247, 257, 267, 270, 271`, 272, 273, 274, 275, 276, 278, 279, 287, 297 = 18
Similarly between 300 to 400 = 18
Hence, total number of such numbers = 18 + 18 = 36

89. Required digit = digit in unit place in $(1 \times 2 \times 3 \times 4 \times 5 \times 6 \times 7 \times 8 \times 9) = 0$

90. Here, $7^{95} = 7^{(23 \times 4 + 3)}$
Hence, digit in unit place in $7^{(23 \times 4 + 3)} = 3$
Now, $3^{58} = 3^{(14 \times 4 + 2)}$
Hence, digit in unit place in $3^{(14 \times 4 + 2)} = 9$
So, required digit = 13 − 9 = 4

91. $(7^{71} \times 6^{59} \times 3^{65}) = [7^{(17 \times 4 + 3)} \times 6^{(14 \times 4 + 3)} \times 3^{(16 \times 4 + 1)}]$
Hence, required digit = Unit digit in $(3 \times 6 \times 3) = 4$

92. Here, $x^{4n} = (2^4)^n$ or, $(4^4)^n$ or, $(6^4)^n$
Hence, they will always have 6 in the unit's place.

93. Here, $x = \frac{(64+36)(64-36)}{20} = \frac{100 \times 28}{20} = 140$

94. 357 ★ 25 ★
For divisible by 5, the last digit must be either 0 or 5.
If last digit is 0, then other required digit will be 2 or 5 or 8
Hence, the numbers are (0, 2) or (0, 5) or (0, 8)
If last digit is 5, then other required digit will be 0 or 3 or 6 or 9
Hence, the numbers are (5, 0) or (5, 3) or (5, 6) or (5, 9)
So, correct option is (c)

95. For divisible by 24, the number must be divisible by 3 and 8 both.
Here only 736 is divisible by 8.
Sum of the digits = 3 + 1 + 2 + 5 + 7 + 3 + 6 = 27, which is divisible by 3.
Hence, 3125736 is divisible by 24.

96. The number divisible by 132, must be divisible by 3, 4 and 11 each.
968 is not divisible by 3
462 and 2178 are not divisible by 4.
5184 is not divisible by 11.
Hence, 264, 396, 792 and 6336 are divisible by 132.

97. Let two consecutive odd numbers are $(2n + 1)$ and $(2n + 3)$
Hence, $(2n + 3)^2 - (2n + 1)^2 = 4n^2 + 12n + 9 - 4n^2 - 4n - 1$
$= 8n + 8 = 8(n + 1)$
which is always divisible by 8.

98. Let three consecutive odd numbers are $(2n + 1)$, $(2n + 3)$ and $(2n + 5)$
Now, $(2n + 1) + (2n + 3) + (2n + 5) = (6n + 9) = 3(2n + 3)$
which is divisible by 3.

99. The smallest 3-digit prime number = 101
Now, 2525 = 25 × 101 and 3232 = 32 × 101
Hence, each such number is divisible by the smallest 3-digit prime number.

100. Sum of digits = 35 (not divisible by 3)
Now, (sum of digits at odd places) – (sum of digits at even place)
= 19 – 16 = 3 (not divisible by 11)
Hence, the number is neither divisible by 3 nor by 11.

101. 325325 is divisible by all 7, 11 and 13.

102. 515513 and 345345 are not divisible by 2.
440440 is not divisible by 3.
Hence, 510510 is exactly divisible by all prime numbers between 1 and 17.

103. The numbers 451 and 462 are divisible by 11, in which 462 is nearest to 457.

104. 1111 = 99 × 11 + 22
Hence, required number = 11

105. Here, $5x$ (sum of numbers) is divisible by 15
Hence, it is clear that sum of numbers is divisible by 3
Now, 250 + 341 = 591 (Divisible by 3)
So, the required pair is 250, 341.

106. $427398 = 15 \times 28493 + 3$
Hence, required number to be subtracted = 3

107. $803642 = 11 \times 73058 + 4$
Hence, required number to be added = 11 – 4 = 7

108. Let the three consecutive multiples of 3 are $3n$, $3(n + 1)$, $3(n + 2)$
Now, $3n \times 3(n + 1) \times 3(n + 2) = 27n\ (n^2 + 3n + 2)$
Putting, $n = 1$ then, $27 \times 1\ (1^2 + 3 \times 1 + 2) = 27 \times 6 = 162$
Hence, required number = 162

109. $10000 = 476 \times 21 + 4$
Hence, the required number $= 10000 + (476 - 4)$
$= 10000 + 472$
$= 10472$

110. The number $= 12 \times 35 = 420$
Hence, correct quotient $= 420 \div 21 = 20$

111. Here, $(x + 1365) = 6x + 15$
$\Rightarrow 5x = 1350$

$$\therefore\ x = \frac{1350}{5} = 270$$

Hence, the smaller number = 270

112. Here, $13x + 11 = 17y + 9$
$\Rightarrow\ 13x - 17y = -2$
By putting $x = 26$ and $y = 20$, we get the above result
Hence, required number $= 13 \times 26 + 11 = 338 + 11 = 349$.

113. The number $= 31x + 29$.
Here, given data is inadequate.

114. The number $= 119x + 19$
$= 17 \times 7x + 17 + 2$
$= 17\ (7x + 1) + 2$
Hence, required remainder = 2

115. The number $= 296x + 75$
$= 37 \times 8x + 37 \times 2 + 1$
$= 37\ (8x + 2) + 1$
Hence, required remainder = 1

116. The number $= 114x + 21$
$= 19 \times 6x + 19 + 2$
$= 19(6x + 1) + 2$
Hence, the required remainder = 2

117. $x^2 (x^2 - 1)$

By putting, $x = 2$, we get

$2^2 (2^2 - 1) = 4 \times 3 = 12$

Hence, $x^2 (x^2 - 1)$ is always divisible by 12.

118. $4^{61} + 4^{62} + 4^{63} + 4^{64} = 4^{61} (1 + 4 + 4^2 + 4^3)$

$= 4^{61} (5 + 16 + 64)$

$= 4^{61} \times 85$

$= 4^{60} \times 340$

Hence, it is divisible by 10.

119.

$$\begin{array}{r|l} 5 & a \\ \hline 9 & b-4 \\ \hline 13 & c-8 \\ \hline & 1-12 \end{array}$$

Now, $c = 13 \times 1 + 12 = 25$

$b = 9c + 8 = 9 \times 25 + 8 = 233$

$a = 5b + 4 = 5 \times 233 + 4 = 1165 + 4 = 1169$

$1169 = 585 \times 1 + 584$

Hence, required remainder = 584

120.

$$\begin{array}{r|l} 4 & a \\ \hline 5 & b-2 \\ \hline 6 & c-3 \\ \hline & 1-4 \end{array}$$

Now, $c = 6 \times 1 + 4 = 10$

$b = 5c + 3 = 5 \times 10 + 3 = 53$

$a = 4b + 2 = 4 \times 53 + 2 = 212 + 2 = 214$

Hence, required remainder = 214

121.

$$\begin{array}{r|l} 4 & a \\ \hline 5 & b-1 \\ \hline & 1-3 \end{array}$$

Now, $b = 5 \times 1 + 4 = 9$; $a = 4b + 1 = 4 \times 9 + 1 = 37$

$$\begin{array}{r|l} 5 & 37 \\ \hline 4 & 7-2 \\ \hline & 1-3 \end{array}$$

Hence, respective remainder are = 2, 3

122. The number = $6x + 3$

Now, $(6x + 3)^2 = 36x^2 + 36x + 9$

$= (36x^2 + 36x + 6) + 3$

$= 6(6x^2 + 6x + 1) + 3$

Hence, required remainder = 3

BASIC MATHEMATICAL OPERATIONS (SIMPLIFICATION)

Simplification is a mathematical operation by which a complex expression of numbers or fractions is converted into a simpler or less difficult form. It is erroneous to solve this type of questions on random basis and a very appropriate method is to apply BODMAS Rule for arriving at the solution of such problems. Each of the letters of the word 'BODMAS' when explained serially, has following implications:

1.	B	→	Bracket	[{ (¯) }]
2.	O	→	of	of
3.	D	→	Division	÷
4.	M	→	Multiplication	×
5.	A	→	Addition	+
6.	S	→	Subtraction	–

Therefore, for simplification, we should remove the brackets first. Thereafter operation for 'of', then for 'division', after that the operation for 'multiplication' and thereafter for 'addition' and at last operation for 'subtraction' should be carried out.

Important Notes

A. In mathematical operations the word 'of' indicates multiplication.

B. While removing brackets, first of all bar bracket '–' and after that small bracket '( )' is removed. Thereafter the curly bracket '{ }' and at last square bracket [ ] is removed.

Example 1.: Simplify the following expression:

$$800 \div 8 \text{ of } 4 \times [40 - \{35 - (\overline{20 - 10} \div 2) + 6\}]$$

Solution: For simplifying the given expression we will first remove bar bracket '–', then the small bracket '( )', thereafter the curly bracket '{ }' and at last the square bracket '[ ]'. 'BODMAS' Rule is applied to solve the expression.

$\therefore\ 800 \div 8 \text{ of } 4 \times [40 - \{35 - (\overline{20 - 10} \div 2) + 6\}]$

$= 800 \div 8 \text{ of } 4 \times [40 - \{35 - (10 \div 2) + 6\}]$

$= 800 \div 8 \text{ of } 4 \times [40 - \{35 - 5 + 6\}] = 800 \div 8 \text{ of } 4 \times [40 - \{41 - 5\}]$

$= 800 \div 8 \text{ of } 4 \times [40 - 36] = 800 \div 8 \text{ of } 4 \times 4 = 800 \div 32 \times 4$

$= \dfrac{800}{32} \times 4 = 100$

Example 2: Simplify the following expressions:

(a) $375 + 150 \div 25$

(b) $288 \div 36 \div 18$

(c) $2280 \times 24 + 24 - 20$

(d) $46 \times (128 - 48) \div 200$

(e) $6 \text{ of } 76 \div 4 \times 24 - 6 + 8$

(f) $\dfrac{(72 \div 24) \text{ of } 48 \times 6 + 18 \div 6}{(2+18) \text{ of } 12 \div 2 \text{ of } 3 \times (100 \div 75)}$

(g) $\dfrac{(86 \times 30) + (192 \div 48)}{(32 \times 22) - (21 \times 12)}$

(h) $4 \times 4 + 4 + (4 \times 4 \div 4 + 40)$

Solution:

(a) $375 + 150 \div 25 = 375 + \dfrac{150}{25} = 375 + 6 = 381$

(b) $288 \div 36 \div 18 = \dfrac{288}{36} \div 18 = 8 \div 18 = \dfrac{8}{18} = \dfrac{4}{9}$

> **Note:** *In case a sign is followed by an identical sign, the mathematical operation is carried out from left to right.*

(c) $2280 \times 24 + 24 - 20 = 54720 + 24 - 20 = 54724$

(d) $46 \times (128 - 48) \div 200 = 46 \times 80 \div 200 = 46 \times \dfrac{80}{200} = 18.4$

(e) $6 \text{ of } 76 \div 4 \times 24 - 6 + 8 = 456 \div 4 \times 24 - 6 + 8 = \dfrac{456}{4} \times 24 - 6 + 8$

$= 114 \times 24 - 6 + 8 = 2736 - 6 + 8 = 2744 - 6 = 2738$

(f) $\dfrac{(72 \div 24) \text{ of } 48 \times 6 + 18 \div 6}{(2+18) \text{ of } 12 \div 2 \text{ of } 3 \times (100 \div 75)} = \dfrac{\left(\dfrac{72}{24}\right) \text{ of } 48 \times 6 + 18 \div 6}{20 \text{ of } 12 \div 2 \text{ of } 3 \times \left(\dfrac{100}{75}\right)}$

$= \dfrac{3 \text{ of } 48 \times 6 + 18 \div 6}{20 \text{ of } 12 \div 2 \text{ of } 3 \times \dfrac{4}{3}} = \dfrac{144 \times 6 + 18 \div 6}{240 \div 6 \times \dfrac{4}{3}} = \dfrac{144 \times 6 + 3}{40 \times \dfrac{4}{3}}$

$= \dfrac{864 + 3}{160/3} = \dfrac{867 \times 3}{160} = \dfrac{2601}{160}$

(g) $\dfrac{(86 \times 30) + (192 \div 48)}{(32 \times 22) - (21 \times 12)} = \dfrac{2580 + 4}{704 - 252} = \dfrac{2584}{452}$

(h) $4 \times 4 + 4 + (4 \times 4 \div 4 + 40) = 4 \times 4 + 4 + \left(4 \times \dfrac{4}{4} + 40\right)$

$= 4 \times 4 + 4 + (4 \times 1 + 40) = 4 \times 4 + 4 + (4 + 40) = 4 \times 4 + 4 + 44$

$= 16 + 4 + 44 = 20 + 44 = 64$

Example 3: Simplyfy:

(a) $\dfrac{2.8\times2.8-1.2\times1.2}{2.8-1.2}$ (b) $(6.8)^2 + 6.8 \times 6.4 + (3.2)^2$

Solution:

(a) $\because \dfrac{2.8\times2.8-1.2\times1.2}{2.8-1.2} = \dfrac{(2.8)^2-(1.2)^2}{2.8-1.2} = \dfrac{(2.8+1.2)\,(2.8-1.2)}{2.8-1.2} = 2.8 + 1.2 = 4$

$[\because a^2 - b^2 = (a+b)(a-b)]$

(b) $\because (6.8)^2 + 6.8 \times 6.4 + (3.2)^2 = (6.8)^2 + 2 \times 3.2 \times 6.8 + (3.2)^2$

$= (6.8 + 3.2)^2 = (10)^2 = 100$ $[\because a^2 + 2ab + b^2 = (a+b)^2]$

Example 4: Find the value of the following:

(a) $\dfrac{\left(\sqrt{5}+\dfrac{1}{\sqrt{5}}\right)^2-2}{\dfrac{2}{5}\text{ of }13}$ (b) $\dfrac{4.669\times4.669-2.331\times2.331}{(4.669)^3+(2.331)^3+21\times(4.669)\times2.331}$

(c) $\left(2^{\frac{3}{2}}+3^2\right)\left(2^{\frac{3}{2}}-3^2\right)$ (d) $\dfrac{7.61\times7.61\times7.61-7.61\times.11\times22.5-(.11)^3}{1.75\times1.75\times1.75+1.75\times.75\times7.5+(.75)^3}$

(e) $\dfrac{2.33\times2.33\times2.33+7.67\times7.67\times7.67}{2.33\times2.33-2.33\times7.67+7.67\times7.67}$ (f) $\left(\dfrac{14.4^2-3.4^2}{14.4+3.4}\right)\times3\text{ of }25\div5$

Solution:

(a) $\dfrac{\left(\sqrt{5}+\dfrac{1}{\sqrt{5}}\right)^2-2}{\dfrac{2}{5}\text{ of }13} = \dfrac{\left(\sqrt{5}\right)^2+2.\sqrt{5}\cdot\dfrac{1}{\sqrt{5}}+\left(\dfrac{1}{\sqrt{5}}\right)^2-2}{\dfrac{2}{5}\text{ of }13} = \dfrac{5+2+\dfrac{1}{5}-2}{\dfrac{26}{5}} = \dfrac{\dfrac{26}{5}}{\dfrac{26}{5}} = 1$

$[\because (a+b)^2 = a^2 + 2ab + b^2]$

(b) $\dfrac{4.669\times4.669-2.331\times2.331}{(4.669)^3+(2.331)^3+21\times4.669\times2.331}$

$= \dfrac{(4.669)^2-(2.331)^2}{(4.669)^3+(2.331)^3+3\times4.669\times2.331(4.669+2.331)}$

$= \dfrac{(4.669-2.331)\,(4.669+2.331)}{(4.669\;+\;2.331)^3}$

$[\because a^2 - b^2 = (a-b)(a+b),\ a^3 + b^3 + 3ab(a+b) = (a+b)^3]$

$= \dfrac{(4.669-2.331)\times7}{7^3} = \dfrac{2.338}{49} = .034$

(c) $\left(2^{\frac{3}{2}}+3^2\right)\left(2^{\frac{3}{2}}-3^2\right) = \left(2^{\frac{3}{2}}\right)^2-\left(3^2\right)^2$ $[\because (a+b)(a-b) = a^2 - b^2]$

$= 2^3 - 3^4 = 8 - 81 = -73$

(*d*) $\dfrac{7.61\times7.61\times7.61-7.61\times.11\times22.5-(.11)^3}{1.75\times1.75\times1.75+1.75\times.75\times7.5+(.75)^3}$

$= \dfrac{(7.61)^3-7.61\times.11\times3(7.61-.11)-(.11)^3}{(1.75)^3+1.75\times.75\times3\,(1.75+.75)+(.75)^3} = \dfrac{(7.61-.11)^3}{(1.75+.75)^3}$ [$\because a^3 - ab \times 3\,(a - b) - b^3 = (a - b)^3$

$a^3 + ab \times 3\,(a + b) + b^3 = (a + b)^3$]

$= \left(\dfrac{7.50}{2.50}\right)^3 = 3^3 = 27$

(*e*) $\dfrac{2.33\times2.33\times2.33+7.67\times7.67\times7.67}{2.33\times2.33-2.33\times7.67+7.67\times7.67} = \dfrac{(2.33)^3+(7.67)^3}{(2.33)^2-2.33\times6.67+(7.67)^2}$

$= (2.33 + 7.67) = 10.00$ $\left[\because \dfrac{a^3+b^3}{a^2-ab+b^2} = a+b\right]$

(*f*) $\left[\dfrac{14.4^2-3.4^2}{14.4+3.4}\right]\times3 \text{ of } 25\div5 = \left[\dfrac{(14.4+3.4)(14.4-3.4)}{(14.4+3.4)}\right]\times3 \text{ of } 25\div5$

[$\because a^2 - b^2 = (a + b)\,(a - b)$]

$= [(14.4 - 3.4)] \times 3 \text{ of } 25 \div 5 = 11 \times 3 \text{ of } 25 \div 5$

Now, according to BODMAS rule operation for 'of' has to be carried out first.

Therefore, $11 \times 3 \text{ of } 25 \div 5 = 11 \times 75 \div 5 = 11 \times 15 = 165$

Example 5: Find the value of 6 of $30 \div 5 \times 2 - 4$

Solution : According to BODMAS rule, mathematical operation for 'of' has to be carried out first, thereafter mathematical operations for 'division', multiplication, addition and subtraction have to carried out in subsequent steps.

$6 \text{ of } 30 \div 5 \times 2 - 4 = 180 \div 5 \times 2 - 4 = 36 \times 2 - 4 = 72 - 4 = 68$

Example 6: Simplify : $7680 \div 256 \div 64 \div 8$

Solution: $7680 \div 256 \div 64 \div 8 = \dfrac{7680}{256} \div 64 \div 8 = 30 \div 64 \div 8$

$= \dfrac{30}{64} \div 8 = \dfrac{15}{32} \div 8 = \dfrac{15}{32\times8} = \dfrac{15}{256}$

Example 7: Simplify: $\dfrac{24+24\times12-8}{160+18\times12-72}$

Solution: $\dfrac{24+24\times12-8}{160+18\times12-72} = \dfrac{24+288-8}{160+216-72} = \dfrac{312-8}{376-72} = \dfrac{304}{304} = 1$

Example 8: Simplify: $\dfrac{12\times12\times12-1\times1\times1}{12\times12+12\times1+1\times1}$

Solution: This problem can be solved quite easily with the help of algebraic expression:

$\dfrac{12\times12\times12-1\times1\times1}{12\times12+12\times1+1\times1} = \dfrac{(12)^3-(1)^3}{(12)^2+12\times1+1^2} = \dfrac{(12-1)\,[(12)^2+12\times1+(1)^2]}{[(12)^2+12\times1+(1)^2]} = 12 - 1 = 11$

[$\because a^3 - b^3 = (a - b)\,(a^2 + ab + b^2)$]

Example 9: Simplify: 3720 ÷ 30 – 2 × (36 + 48 ÷ 24)

Solution: $3720 \div 30 - 2 \times (36 + 48 \div 24) = 3720 \div 30 - 2 \times \left(36+\frac{48}{24}\right) = 3720 \div 30 - 2 \times (36 + 2)$

$$= 3720 \div 30 - 2 \times 38 = \frac{3720}{30} - 2 \times 38$$

$$= 124 - 2 \times 38 = 124 - 76 = 48$$

Example 10: Simplify: $3 \div \left[(8-5) \div \left\{(4-2) \div \left(2+\frac{8}{13}\right)\right\}\right]$

Solution: $3 \div \left[(8-5) \div \left\{(4-2) \div \left(2+\frac{8}{13}\right)\right\}\right] = 3 \div \left[(8-5) \div \left\{2 \div \frac{34}{13}\right\}\right]$

$$= 3 \div \left[3 \div \frac{2\times 13}{34}\right] = 3 \div \left[\frac{3\times 34}{26}\right] = \frac{3\times 26}{3\times 34} = \frac{13}{17}$$

Example 11: Simplify: $40 \times [280 - \{25 - (15 - \overline{8-3}) \div 2\} + 6]$

Solution: Brackets will have to be removed First the bar bracket, then the small bracket, after that the curly bracket, and at last the square bracket will be cleared

$\therefore 40 \times [280 - \{25 - (15 - \overline{8-3}) \div 2) + 6]$

$= 40 \times [280 - \{25 - (15 - 5) \div 2\} + 6$

$= 40 \times [280 - \{25 - 10 \div 2\} + 6]$

$= 40 \times [280 - \{25 - 5\} + 6]$

$= 40 \times [280 - 20 + 6]$

$= 40 \times 266 = 10640$

Example 12: Simplify: $\frac{30^2 - 18^2 \times 2}{30-18}$

Solution: $\frac{30^2 - 18^2 \times 2}{30-18} = \frac{900 - 324\times 2}{12} = \frac{900-648}{12} = \frac{252}{12} = 21$

Example 13: Simplify: $\frac{1.35\times 1.35 - 2.40\times 1.35 + 1.20\times 1.20}{1.35-1.20}$

Solution: $\frac{1.35\times 1.35 - 2.40\times 1.35 + 1.20\times 1.20}{1.35-1.20}$

$$= \frac{1.35\times 1.35 - 2\times 1.20\times 1.35 + 1.20\times 1.20}{(1.35-1.20)}$$

$$= \frac{(1.35)^2 - 2\times 1.20\times 1.35 + (1.20)^2}{(1.35-1.20)} = \frac{(1.35-1.20)^2}{(1.35-1.20)}$$

$[\because a^2 - 2ab + b^2 = (a - b)^2]$

$= 1.35 - 1.20 = .15.$

Example 14: Simplify: $\dfrac{1}{2+\dfrac{1}{3+\dfrac{1}{1+\dfrac{1}{4}}}}$

Solution: This type of fraction is solved from the bottom.

$$\therefore \quad \frac{1}{2+\dfrac{1}{3+\dfrac{1}{1+\dfrac{1}{4}}}}=\frac{1}{2+\dfrac{1}{3+\dfrac{1}{\dfrac{5}{4}}}}=\frac{1}{2+\dfrac{1}{3+\dfrac{4}{5}}}$$

$$=\frac{1}{2+\dfrac{1}{\dfrac{19}{5}}}=\frac{1}{2+\dfrac{5}{19}}=\frac{1}{\dfrac{43}{19}}=\frac{19}{43}.$$

Example 15: Simplify: $b-\left[b-(a+b)-\left\{b-\left(b-\overline{a-b}\right)\right\}+2a\right]$

Solution: $b-\left[b-(a+b)-\left\{b-\left(b-\overline{a-b}\right)\right\}+2a\right]$

$= b-\left[b-(a+b)-\left\{b-(b-a+b)\right\}+2a\right]$

$= b-\left[b-a-b-\{b-b+a-b\}+2a\right]$

$= b-\left[b-a-b-\{a-b\}+2a\right]$

$= b-\left[b-a-b-a+b+2a\right]$

$= b-b$

$= 0$

Example 16: $\frac{4}{15}$ of $\frac{5}{7}$ of a number is greater than $\frac{4}{9}$ of $\frac{2}{5}$ of the same number by 8. What is half of that number?

Solution: Let the number be x.

Now, $\frac{4}{15}\times\frac{5}{7}x-\frac{4}{9}\times\frac{2}{5}\times x=8$

$\Rightarrow \quad \frac{4}{21}x-\frac{8}{45}x=8 \qquad \Rightarrow \quad \frac{60x-56x}{315}=8$

$\Rightarrow \quad \frac{4x}{315}=8 \qquad \therefore \quad x=\frac{8\times 315}{4}=630$

Hence, half of this number $=\frac{1}{2}\times 630=315$

Example 17: Simplify: $108 \div 36$ of $\frac{1}{4}+\frac{2}{5}\times 3\frac{1}{4}$

Solution: $108 \div 36$ of $\frac{1}{4}+\frac{2}{5}\times\frac{13}{4}$

$$= 108 \div 36 \times \frac{1}{4} + \frac{2}{5} \times \frac{13}{4}$$

$$= 108 \div 9 + \frac{2}{5} \times \frac{13}{4}$$

$$= 12 + \frac{13}{10}$$

$$= \frac{120+13}{10} = \frac{133}{10} = 133 = 13\frac{3}{10}$$

Example 18: Simplify: $.6 \times .6 + .6 \div 6$

Solution: $.6 \times .6 + .6 \div 6$

$= .6 \times .6 + .1$

$= .36 + .1 = .46$

Example 19: Simplify: $\dfrac{\frac{7}{2} \div \frac{5}{2} \times \frac{3}{2}}{\frac{7}{2} \div \frac{5}{2} \; of \; \frac{3}{2}} \div 5.25$

Solution: $\dfrac{\frac{7}{2} \times \frac{2}{5} \times \frac{3}{2}}{\frac{7}{2} \div \frac{15}{4}} \div 5.25$

$$= \frac{\frac{21}{10}}{\frac{7}{2} \times \frac{4}{15}} \div 5.25 \quad = \frac{21}{10} \times \frac{15}{14} \times \frac{1}{5.25}$$

$$= \frac{9}{4} \times \frac{100}{525} \quad = \frac{3}{7}$$

Example 20: Find the value of x,

$$8.5 - \left\{5\frac{1}{2} - \left(7\frac{1}{2} + 2.8 \div x\right)\right\} \times 4.25 \div (0.2)^2 = 306$$

Solution: $8.5 - \left\{\frac{11}{2} - \left(\frac{15}{2} + 2.8 \div x\right)\right\} \times 4.25 \div 0.04 = 306$

$$\Rightarrow 8.5 - \left\{\frac{11}{2} - \left(\frac{15}{2} + 2.8 \times \frac{1}{x}\right)\right\} \times 4.25 \div 0.04 = 306$$

$$\Rightarrow 8.5 - \left\{\frac{11}{2} - \frac{15}{2} - \frac{2.8}{x}\right\} \times 4.25 \div 0.04 = 306$$

$$\Rightarrow 8.5 - \left\{-2 - \frac{2.8}{x}\right\} \times \frac{4.25}{0.04} = 306$$

$$\Rightarrow 8.5 - \left\{-\frac{425}{2} - \frac{297.5}{x}\right\} = 306$$

$$\Rightarrow 8.5+\frac{425}{2}+\frac{297.5}{x}=306$$

$$\Rightarrow \frac{17+425}{2}+\frac{297.5}{x}=306$$

$$\Rightarrow \frac{297.5}{x}=306-221$$

$$\Rightarrow \frac{297.5}{x}=85$$

$$\therefore x=\frac{297.5}{85}=3.5$$

Example 21: If $\frac{x}{4}-\frac{x-3}{6}=1$, then find the value of x.

Solution: $\frac{x}{4}-\frac{x-3}{6}=1$

$$\Rightarrow \frac{3x-2x+6}{12}=1$$

$$\Rightarrow x+6=12$$

$$\therefore x=6$$

Example 22: $\frac{a}{b}=\frac{3}{4}$ and $8a+5b=22$, then find the value of a.

Solution: Now, $\frac{a}{b}=\frac{3}{4}$ $\quad\therefore\ b=\frac{4}{3}a$

Again, $8a+5b=22$

$$\Rightarrow 8a+5\times\frac{4}{3}a=22$$

$$\Rightarrow \frac{44a}{3}=22$$

$$\therefore a=\frac{22\times 3}{44}=\frac{3}{2}$$

Example 23: If $\dfrac{2x}{1+\dfrac{1}{1+\dfrac{x}{1-x}}}=1$, then find the value of x.

Solution: $\dfrac{2x}{1+\dfrac{1}{1+\dfrac{x}{1-x}}}=1 \quad \Rightarrow \dfrac{2x}{1+\dfrac{1}{\dfrac{1-x+x}{1-x}}}=1 \quad \Rightarrow \dfrac{2x}{1+1-x}=1 \quad \Rightarrow 2x=2-x$

$$\Rightarrow 3x=2 \qquad \therefore x=\frac{2}{3}$$

Example 24: If $2x + 3y = 34$ and $\frac{x+y}{y} = \frac{13}{8}$, then find the value of $5y + 7x$.

Solution: $2x + 3y = 34$ ....(i)

and also, $8x + 8y = 13y$

$\Rightarrow \quad 8x = 5y$

$\therefore \quad x = \frac{5}{8}y$

Now from equation *(i)*,

We have, $2 \times \frac{5}{8}y + 3y = 34$

$\Rightarrow \frac{5}{4}y + 3y = 34$

$\Rightarrow \frac{5y+12y}{4} = 34$

$\Rightarrow \frac{17y}{4} = 34 \quad \therefore y = \frac{4\times 34}{17} = 8$

Now, $2x + 3y = 34 \quad \Rightarrow 2x + 3 \times 8 = 34$

$\Rightarrow 2x = 10 \quad \therefore x = 5$

Now, $5y + 7x = 5 \times 8 + 7 \times 5 = 40 + 35 = 75$

Example 25: If $2x + 3y + z = 55$, $x + z - y = 4$ and $y - x + z = 12$, then what are the values of x, y and z?

Solution: Here, $2x + 3y + z = 55$ ...(i)

$x + z - y = 4$ ...(ii)

$y - x + z = 12$ ...(iii)

On adding equations (ii) and (iii) we get

$2z = 16$

$\therefore \quad z = 8$

Putting the value of z in equation (ii), we get

$x + 8 - y = 4$

$\therefore \quad x = y - 4$

Now from equation (i),

$2(y - 4) + 3y + 8 = 55$

$\Rightarrow \quad 2y - 8 + 3y + 8 = 55$

$\Rightarrow \quad 5y = 55$

$\therefore \quad y = 11$

$x = y - 4 = 11 - 4 = 7$

Hence, $x = 7$, $y = 11$ and $z = 8$

Example 26: Find the value of $\left(1-\frac{1}{3}\right)\left(1-\frac{1}{4}\right)\left(1-\frac{1}{5}\right)...\left(1-\frac{1}{100}\right)$

Solution: $\left(1-\frac{1}{3}\right)\left(1-\frac{1}{4}\right)\left(1-\frac{1}{5}\right)...\left(1-\frac{1}{100}\right)$

$= \frac{2}{3}\times\frac{3}{4}\times\frac{4}{5}\times...\times\frac{99}{100} \quad = \frac{2}{100} = \frac{1}{50}$

Example 27: Simplify : $99\frac{48}{49}\times 245$

Solution: $99\frac{48}{49}\times 245$

$= \left(100-\frac{1}{49}\right)\times 245$

$= 24500 - 5 = 24495$

Example 28: A tin of oil was $\frac{4}{5}$ full, when 6 bottles of oil were taken out and four bottles of oil were poured into it, it was $\frac{3}{4}$ full. How many bottles of oil can the tin contain?

Solution: Let capacity of the tin = x bottles

Now, $\frac{4}{5}x-6+4=\frac{3}{4}x$

$\Rightarrow \frac{4}{5}x-\frac{3}{4}x=2$

$\Rightarrow \frac{16x-15x}{20}=2$

$\Rightarrow x = 40$

Hence, tin can contain 40 bottles of oil.

Example 29: A board 7 ft. 9 inches long is divided into 3 equal parts. What is length of each part?

Solution: Length of each part = $\frac{\text{7ft 9 inches}}{3}=\frac{(84+9)\text{ inches}}{3}=\frac{93}{3}$ inches

= 31 inches

= 2 ft. 7 inches

Example 30: Two pens and three pencils cost Rs. 86. Four pens and a pencil cost Rs. 112. Find the cost of a pen and that of a pencil.

Solution: Let cost of a pen and a pencil be Rs. x and Rs. y respectively.

Then, $2x + 3y = 86$ ...(i)

$4x + y = 112$ ...(ii)

Multiplying equation (i) by 2 and subtracting (ii), we get

$4x + 6y = 172$

$4x + y = 112$

$- \quad - \quad -$

$5y = 60$

$\therefore \quad y = 12$

Putting the value of y in equation (i)

$2x + 3 \times 12 = 86$

$\Rightarrow \quad 2x = 86 - 36$

$\Rightarrow \quad 2x = 50$

$\therefore \quad x = 25$

Hence, cost of a pen = Rs. 25

cost of a pencil = Rs. 12

Example 31: When an amount was distributed among 14 boys, each of them got Rs. 80 more than the amount received by each boy when the same amount is distributed equally among 18 boys. What was the amount?

Solution: Let the total amount be Rs. x

Now, $\frac{x}{14} - \frac{x}{18} = 80$

$\Rightarrow \quad \frac{9x - 7x}{126} = 80$

$\Rightarrow \quad \frac{x}{63} = 80$

$\therefore \quad x = 80 \times 63 = 5040$

Then, total amount = Rs. 5040

Example 32: Kiran had 85 currency notes in all, some of which were Rs. 100 denomination and remaining of Rs. 50 denomination. The total amount of all these currency notes was Rs. 5000. How much amount did she have in the denomination of Rs. 50?

Solution: Let the number of Rs. 50 denomination be x then number of Rs. 100 will be $(85 - x)$.

Then, $(85 - x) \times 100 + x \times 50 = 5000$

$\Rightarrow 8500 - 100x + 50x = 5000$

$\Rightarrow 50x = 3500$

$\therefore x = 70$

Hence the required amount $= 70 \times 50$ = Rs. 3500

Example 33: A train starts full of passengers. At the first station, it drops one-third of the passengers and takes 280 more. At the second station, it drops one half the new total and takes 12 more. On arriving at the third station, it is found to have 248 passengers. Find the number of passengers in the beginning.

Solution: Let in the beginning total number of passengers be x.

At the first station,

Number of passengers left $= x - \frac{x}{3} + 280 = \frac{2x}{3} + 280$

At the second station,

Number of passengers left $= \frac{1}{2}\left(\frac{2x}{3} + 280\right) + 12$

$= \frac{x}{3} + 140 + 12 = \frac{x}{3} + 152$

Now, $\frac{x}{3} + 152 = 248$

$\Rightarrow \frac{x}{3} = 96$

$\therefore x = 3 \times 96 = 288$

Hence, number of passengers in the beginning was 288.

Example 34: In a certain office, $\frac{1}{3}$ of the workers are women, $\frac{1}{2}$ of the women are married and $\frac{1}{3}$ of the married women have children. If $\frac{3}{4}$ of the men are married and $\frac{2}{3}$ of the married men have children. What part of the workers are without children?

Solution: Let total number of workers be x.

Then number of women workers = $\frac{x}{3}$ and number of men workers = $\frac{2x}{3}$

Now, number of married women = $\frac{1}{2} \times \frac{x}{3} = \frac{x}{6}$

Number of married women having children = $\frac{1}{3} \times \frac{x}{6} = \frac{x}{18}$

Now, number of married men = $\frac{3}{4} \times \frac{2x}{3} = \frac{x}{2}$

Number of married men having children = $\frac{2}{3} \times \frac{x}{2} = \frac{x}{3}$

Hence, number of workers having children = $\frac{x}{18} + \frac{x}{3} = \frac{x + 6x}{18} = \frac{7x}{18}$

Then, number of workers having no children = $1 - \frac{7x}{18} = \frac{11x}{18}$

So, $\frac{11}{18}$ part of the workers are without children.

Example 35: A man spends $\frac{2}{5}$ of his salary on house rent, $\frac{3}{10}$ of his salary on food and $\frac{1}{8}$ of his salary on conveyance. If he has Rs. 1400 left with him, find his expenditure on food and conveyance.

Solution: Let the man's salary be Rs. x.

The amount of salary left = $x - \left(\frac{2}{5}x + \frac{3}{10}x + \frac{1}{8}x\right) = x - \left(\frac{16x + 12x + 5x}{40}\right) = x - \frac{33x}{40}$ = Rs. $\frac{7x}{40}$

Now, $\frac{7x}{40} = 1400$ $\therefore x = \frac{40 \times 1400}{7}$ = Rs. 8000

Then, expenditure on food and conveyance = $\frac{3}{10}x + \frac{1}{8}x = \frac{17x}{40} = \frac{17 \times 8000}{40}$ = Rs. 3400

Example 36: A man divides Rs. 8600 among 5 sons, 4 daughters and 2 nephews. If each daughter receives four times as much as each nephew and each son receives five times as much as each nephew. How much does each daughter receive?

Solution: Let the share of each nephew = Rs. x

Then, share of each son = Rs. $5x$

and also, share of each daughter = Rs. $4x$

Now, $5 \times 5x + 4 \times 4x + 2 \times x = 8600$

$\Rightarrow$ $25x + 16x + 2x = 8600$ $\Rightarrow 43x = 8600$ $\therefore x = 200$

Hence, share of each daughter = Rs. $4x$ = 4×200

= Rs. 800

EXERCISE

1. The value of 51 ÷ 17 ÷ 3 is:
(a) 9 (b) 4 (c) 3 (d) 1

2. What will be the value of 40 × 2 ÷ 10 + 5 – 4?
(a) 5 (b) 8 (c) 11 (d) 9

3. The value of 28 × 104 ÷ (18 + 6) + 3 is:
(a) $124\frac{1}{3}$ (b) $104\frac{1}{3}$ (c) $125\frac{1}{3}$ (d) 128

4. If $75^2 - 65^2 = 2x$, then value of x is:
(a) 715 (b) 700 (c) 688 (d) 711

5. The value of 99 × 14 ÷ 11 ÷ 0.7 is:
(a) 2.9 (b) 1.6 (c) 1.8 (d) 2.8

6. If 45 – [28 – {37 – (15 – ?) }] = 58, then which of the following should replace the sign of interrogation (?)?
(a) 18 (b) 17 (c) 13 (d) 19

7. The value of $8\frac{1}{3}+5\frac{1}{4}\times 13\frac{1}{5} \div 6\frac{3}{5}$ is:
(a) $19\frac{1}{3}$ (b) $18\frac{1}{2}$ (c) $21\frac{1}{3}$ (d) $22\frac{1}{2}$

8. The value of $\frac{14}{3}$ of $\frac{5}{8}$ of 72 is:
(a) 209 (b) 217 (c) 210 (d) 199

9. What will be the value of 10 × 10 × 10 ÷ (20 ÷ 10 × 10 – 10) + 6?
(a) 108 (b) 111 (c) 106 (d) 114

10. What will be the value of $\dfrac{\frac{1}{3}\times 20 \div 4}{\frac{1}{4}\times 25 \div 5}$?
(a) $\frac{7}{3}$ (b) $\frac{4}{3}$ (c) $\frac{5}{3}$ (d) $\frac{10}{3}$

11. Which of the following is the standard form of $\dfrac{(24\times 13)+(28\div 7)}{(24+13)-\left(\frac{14}{3}\text{of}\frac{5}{8}\right)}$?
(a) $\frac{3792}{409}$ (b) $\frac{4792}{309}$ (c) $\frac{3792}{411}$ (d) $\frac{3092}{409}$

12. If $\dfrac{144+32\div ?-8}{35\div\frac{1}{2}\text{of}\frac{1}{2}} = 1$, then which of the following should replace the sign of interrogation?
(a) 7 (b) 6 (c) 10 (d) 8

13. What is the value of $\frac{2.70\times2.70+4.30\times4.30+8.60\times2.70}{2.70+4.30}$?

(a) 6.8 *(b)* 7.0 *(c)* 7.6 *(d)* 8.5

14. What will be the value of $\frac{\left(\sqrt{6}+\frac{1}{\sqrt{6}}\right)^2}{\frac{1}{2}\text{of } 18 + 4}+\frac{2}{3}$?

(a) $\frac{101}{78}$ *(b)* $\frac{104}{71}$ *(c)* $\frac{101}{88}$ *(d)* $\frac{99}{57}$

15. 1150 ÷ 50 ÷ 23 + 15 = ?

(a) 16 *(b)* 20 *(c)* 22 *(d)* 18

16. What is the value of $1+\frac{1}{1+\frac{1}{1+\frac{9}{16}}}$?

(a) $\frac{44}{31}$ *(b)* $\frac{55}{41}$ *(c)* $\frac{66}{41}$ *(d)* $\frac{77}{51}$

17. $\frac{(.08)^3+(.011)^3}{(.08)^2-.08\times.011+(.011)^2}=?$

(a) .087 *(b)* .091 *(c)* .077 *(d)* .067

18. What is the value of $22 \div \left[(28-13)\div\{(32-8)\div\left(5+\frac{1}{3}\right)\}\right]$?

(a) 7.9 *(b)* 6.8 *(c)* 6.6 *(d)* 5.7

19. What is the value of $\frac{(20^2-10^2)\div5\times3+10}{\frac{1}{3}\text{ of } 27+10\div2+1}$?

(a) $10\frac{2}{3}$ *(b)* $14\frac{1}{3}$ *(c)* 15 *(d)* $12\frac{2}{3}$

20. What is the value of $11^2 - 6^2 \div 6 \times \frac{5}{2}$ = 2 of 10?

(a) 126 *(b)* 108 *(c)* 110 *(d)* 125

21. What is the value of $\frac{25}{3}-\frac{4}{7}\text{ of }\frac{7}{5}+\frac{11}{3}\div\frac{2}{3}-4$?

(a) $8\frac{1}{15}$ *(b)* $9\frac{1}{30}$ *(c)* $7\frac{1}{30}$ *(d)* $9\frac{1}{5}$

22. What is the value of 35 × .07 – 21 × .03?

(a) 2.75 *(b)* 1.72 *(c)* 1.82 *(d)* 2.13

23. What is the value of $60 \times [35 - \{25 - (18 - \overline{9-3}) \div 11\}]$?

(a) $566\frac{5}{7}$ (b) $665\frac{5}{11}$ (c) $665\frac{8}{11}$ (d) $765\frac{5}{11}$

24. $\dfrac{140 - 44 \times 9 \div 3}{\frac{1}{2} \text{ of } 18 \div 9 + 2} = ?$

(a) $2\frac{2}{3}$ (b) $3\frac{1}{3}$ (c) $4\frac{2}{3}$ (d) $6\frac{4}{5}$

25. Find the value of: 20% of 8 + 18% of 15 ÷ 5 of 10

(a) 2.546 (b) 1.654 (c) 1.456 (d) 2.654

26. What is the value of $4\frac{1}{3} \times 5\frac{1}{3} \div 6\frac{1}{3} \div \frac{1}{3} + 5\frac{1}{3} - 2\frac{1}{3}$?

(a) $14\frac{14}{19}$ (b) $13\frac{19}{21}$ (c) $13\frac{18}{19}$ (d) $17\frac{8}{11}$

27. What is the value of $\frac{19}{17}$ of $\frac{28}{5}$ of $\left(\frac{17}{3} \div \frac{5}{3} \text{ of } 6\frac{1}{3}\right)$?

(a) $4\frac{9}{25}$ (b) $3\frac{8}{23}$ (c) $3\frac{9}{24}$ (d) $3\frac{9}{25}$

28. What is the value of $\left(17^{\frac{3}{2}} + 11^{3/2}\right)\left(17^{\frac{3}{2}} - 11^{3/2}\right)$?

(a) 3852 (b) 3582 (c) 3782 (d) 3258

29. What is the value of $1 + \dfrac{1}{1 + \dfrac{1}{1 + \dfrac{1}{3}}}$?

(a) $1\frac{4}{7}$ (b) $2\frac{4}{7}$ (c) $3\frac{4}{7}$ (d) $4\frac{4}{7}$

30. What is the value of $3 - [9 + \{14 - (6 - \overline{3-21})\}]$?

(a) 0 (b) 4 (c) 18 (d) 6

31. $\dfrac{\left(2\frac{2}{3} + 3\frac{4}{7}\right)^2 + \left(2\frac{2}{3} - 3\frac{4}{7}\right)^2}{\left(\frac{8}{3}\right)^2 + \left(\frac{25}{7}\right)^2} = ?$

(a) 1 (b) $\frac{1}{2}$ (c) 2 (d) 4

32. $\dfrac{4\frac{1}{7} - 2\frac{1}{4}}{3\frac{1}{2} + 1\frac{1}{7}} \div \dfrac{1}{2 + \dfrac{1}{2 + \dfrac{1}{5 - \frac{1}{5}}}} = ?$

(a) 3 (b) $\frac{1}{8}$ (c) 8 (d) 1

33. Find the value of: $\frac{5.66 \times 5.66 - 4.44 \times 4.44}{2 - .78} + (6.53 \times 8.34 - 6.53 \times 5.17 - 6.53 \times 3.17)$

(a) 10.1 (b) 9.01 (c) 10.8 (d) 11.2

34. $(8 \div 88) \times 8888088 = ?$

(a) 8008008 (b) 808088 (c) 808080 (d) 808008

35. $1260 \div 15 \div 7 = ?$

(a) 588 (b) 122 (c) 58 (d) 12

36. $2 - [2 - \{2 - 2(2 + 2)\}] = ?$

(a) 6 (b) – 6 (c) 4 (d) – 4

37. $100 \times 10 - 100 + 2000 \div 100 = ?$

(a) 979 (b) 920 (c) 780 (d) 29

38. $3640 \div 14 \times 16 + 340 = ?$

(a) 3500 (b) 4500 (c) 3525 (d) 4480

39. $25 - 5\ [2 + 3\ \{2 - 2\ (5 - 3) + 5\} - 10] \div 4 = ?$

(a) 5 (b) 25 (c) 23.25 (d) 23.75

40. $(-5)\ (4)\ (2) \left(-\frac{1}{2}\right)\left(\frac{3}{4}\right) = ?$

(a) 15 (b) –15 (c) 30 (d) –30

41. A boy was asked to write the value of $(2)^5 \times (9)^2$. He wrote 2592. The difference between the obtained and the actual value is:

(a) $2^3 \times 9^4$ (b) $2^2 \times 9^3$ (c) 2×9^2 (d) zero

42. Which of the following will come in place of both the question marks in the following equation?

$$\frac{128 \div 16 \times ? - 7 \times 2}{7^2 - 8 \times 6 + ?^2} = 1$$

(a) 6 (b) 3 (c) 7 (d) 9

43. $\frac{180 \times 15 - 12 \times 20}{140 \times 8 + 2 \times 55} = ?$

(a) 2 (b) 4 (c) $\frac{4}{5}$ (d) 6

44. $\frac{(6+6+6+6) \div 6}{4+4+4+4 \div 4} = ?$

(a) $3\frac{6}{13}$ (b) $\frac{4}{13}$ (c) $\frac{3}{2}$ (d) 1

45. $\dfrac{-\frac{1}{2} - \frac{2}{3} + \frac{4}{5} - \frac{1}{3} + \frac{1}{5} + \frac{3}{4}}{\frac{1}{2} + \frac{2}{3} - \frac{4}{3} + \frac{1}{3} - \frac{1}{5} - \frac{4}{5}} = ?$

(a) 1 (b) –2 (c) $\frac{-10}{3}$ (d) $-\frac{3}{10}$

46. If $\frac{1}{3}+\frac{1}{2}+\frac{1}{x}=4$, then find the value of x.

(a) $\frac{24}{11}$ (b) $\frac{18}{5}$ (c) $\frac{6}{19}$ (d) $\frac{5}{18}$

47. $\frac{1}{\left(2\frac{1}{3}\right)}+\frac{1}{\left(1\frac{3}{4}\right)}=?$

(a) 1 (b) 2 (c) $\frac{1}{2}$ (d) $4\frac{1}{12}$

48. Which of the folloiwng pairs of fractions adds up to a number greater than 5?

(a) $\frac{13}{5}, \frac{11}{6}$ (b) $\frac{11}{4}, \frac{8}{3}$ (c) $\frac{7}{3}, \frac{11}{5}$ (d) $\frac{5}{3}, \frac{3}{4}$

49. $1+\frac{1}{2}+\frac{1}{4}+\frac{1}{7}+\frac{1}{14}+\frac{1}{28}$ is equal to:

(a) 2 (b) 3 (c) 2.5 (d) 3.5

50. $1 \div [1 + 1 \div \{1 + 1 \div (1 + 1 \div 2)\}] = ?$

(a) 1 (b) 2 (c) $\frac{1}{2}$ (d) $\frac{5}{8}$

51. $18 - [5 - \{6 + 2 (7 - 8 - 5)\}] = ?$

(a) 32 (b) 27 (c) 15 (d) 13

52. $\frac{8-|5-(-3+2)|\div 2}{|5-3|-|5-8|\div 3}=?$

(a) 5 (b) 4 (c) 3 (d) 2

53. The difference of $1\frac{3}{16}$ and its reciprocal is equal to:

(A) $\frac{105}{304}$ (b) $\frac{15}{34}$ (c) $\frac{15}{16}$ (d) $\frac{4}{3}$

54. Supply the two missing figures in order indicated by x and y in the given equation, the fraction being in their lowest terms:

$$5\frac{1}{x}\times y\frac{3}{4}=20$$

(a) 5, 3 (b) 4, 1 (c) 3, 3 (d) 3, 1

55. $5\frac{2}{3}\div ?\frac{5}{6}=2$

(a) 5 (b) 4 (c) 3 (d) 2

56. Find the value of ★ in the following: $1\frac{2}{3}\div\frac{2}{7}\times\frac{\bigstar}{7}=1\frac{1}{4}\times\frac{2}{3}\div\frac{1}{6}$

(a) 6 (b) 0.6 (c) $\frac{1}{6}$ (d) 0.006

57. $\frac{3}{8}$ of 168 × 15 ÷ 5 + ? = 549 ÷ 9 + 235

(a) 296 (b) 189 (c) 174 (d) 107

58. $\frac{3}{5}$ of $\frac{4}{7}$ of $\frac{5}{9}$ of $\frac{7}{8}$ of 504 = ?

(a) 63 (b) 84 (c) 69 (d) 96

59. $6\frac{5}{6}\times 5\frac{1}{3}+17\frac{2}{3}\times 4\frac{1}{2}=?$

(a) $112\frac{1}{3}$ (b) $116\frac{17}{18}$ (c) $115\frac{17}{18}$ (d) $112\frac{17}{18}$

60. When $\left(\frac{1}{2}-\frac{1}{4}+\frac{1}{5}-\frac{1}{6}\right)$ is divided by $\left(\frac{2}{5}-\frac{5}{9}+\frac{3}{5}-\frac{7}{18}\right)$, the quotient is:

(a) $5\frac{1}{10}$ (b) $3\frac{3}{10}$ (c) $3\frac{1}{6}$ (d) $2\frac{1}{18}$

61. $\dfrac{\frac{1}{3}+\frac{3}{4}\left(\frac{2}{5}-\frac{1}{3}\right)}{1\frac{2}{3}\ of\ \frac{3}{4}-\frac{1}{4}\ of\ \frac{4}{5}}=?$

(a) $\frac{23}{63}$ (b) $\frac{23}{55}$ (c) $\frac{23}{40}$ (d) $\frac{1}{63}$

62. The value of $\left(\frac{5}{7}\ of\ 1\frac{6}{13}\right)\div\left(2\frac{5}{7}\div 3\frac{1}{4}\right)$ is—

(a) $\frac{4}{5}$ (b) $\frac{3}{4}$ (c) $\frac{5}{4}$ (d) 1

63. A student was asked to solve the fraction $\dfrac{\frac{7}{3}+1\frac{1}{2}\ of\ \frac{5}{3}}{2+1\frac{2}{3}}$ and his answer was $\frac{1}{4}$. By how much was his answer wrong?

(a) $\frac{23}{44}$ (b) $\frac{3}{44}$ (c) $1\frac{3}{44}$ (d) $\frac{23}{40}$

64. $9-1\frac{2}{9}$ of $3\frac{3}{11}\div 5\frac{1}{7}$ of $\frac{7}{9}=?$

(a) 9 (b) 8 (c) $\frac{5}{4}$ (d) $8\frac{32}{81}$

65. $\frac{4335}{4(?)24}\div 1\frac{7}{8}=\frac{289}{528}$; then ? is:

(a) 1 (b) 2 (c) 3 (d) 4

66. $4\frac{1}{2}\times 4\frac{1}{3}-8\frac{1}{3}\div 5\frac{2}{3}=?$

(a) $18\frac{1}{34}$ (b) $11\frac{33}{34}$ (c) $\frac{7}{17}$ (d) 8

67. $2\frac{3}{4} \div 2\frac{2}{3} \div 1\frac{1}{12} = ?$

(a) $\frac{169}{144}$ (b) $\frac{99}{104}$ (c) $1\frac{1}{4}$ (d) $\frac{39}{48}$

68. 7 is added to a certain number, the sum is multiplied by 5 the product is divided by 9 and 3 is subtracted from the quotient. The remainder left is 12. Find the number.

(a) 60 (b) 40 (c) 30 (d) 20

69. If $x \oplus y = x^2 + 2y$, what is the value of p if $4 \oplus (3 \oplus p) = 50$?

(a) 12.5 (b) 8 (c) 7 (d) 4

70. If $a \star b = \frac{ab}{a+b}$, find the value of $3 \star (3 \star -1)$.

(a) $\frac{2}{3}$ (b) -1 (c) -1.5 (d) -3

71. If $x \star y = x^2 + y^2 - xy$, then the value of $9 \star 11$ is:

(a) 121 (b) 113 (c) 103 (d) 93

72. $a \star b = 2a - 3b + ab$, then $3 \star 5 + 5 \star 3$ is equal to:

(a) 28 (b) 26 (c) 24 (d) 22

73. Two-fifth of one-fourth of three-seventh of a number is 15. What is the half of that number?

(a) 175 (b) 196 (c) 75 (d) 275

74. If $\frac{4}{5}$ of an estate be worth Rs. 16,800, then the value of $\frac{3}{7}$ of the estate will be:

(a) Rs. 90,000 (b) Rs. 72,000 (c) Rs. 21,000 (d) Rs. 9,000

75. By how much does $\frac{6}{7/8}$ exceed $\frac{6/7}{8}$?

(a) $7\frac{5}{6}$ (b) $7\frac{3}{4}$ (c) $6\frac{3}{4}$ (d) $6\frac{1}{8}$

76. By how much is three-fifth of 350 greater than four-seventh of 210?

(a) 120 (b) 100 (c) 90 (d) 75

77. The simplified value of $\frac{\frac{1}{3} \div \frac{1}{3} \times \frac{1}{3}}{\frac{1}{3} \div \frac{1}{3} \text{ of } \frac{1}{3}} - \frac{1}{9}$ is:

(a) 1 (b) $\frac{1}{3}$ (c) $\frac{1}{9}$ (d) 0

78. $3034 - (1002 \div 20.04) = ?$

(a) 3029 (b) 2993 (c) 2984 (d) 2543

79. $11.6 + 9.28 \div 0.2828 \div 0.07 = ?$

(a) 27.56 (b) 27.2 (c) 9.56 (d) 9.2

80. $0.008 \times 0.01 \times 0.0072 \div (0.12 \times 0.0004) = ?$

(a) 1.2 (b) 1.02 (c) 0.12 (d) 0.012

81. $5.8 \times 2.5 + 0.6 \times 6.75 + 139.25 = ?$

(a) 160.30 (b) 158.40 (c) 157.80 (d) 157.30

82. $8\frac{2}{7}$ of $1568 + 265.75 = ? + 2455.60$

(a) 11250.15 (b) 10802.15 (c) 10578.15 (d) 10354.15

83. If $x = \frac{a}{a-1}$ and $y = \frac{1}{a-1}$, then

(a) $x > y$ if $a < 1$ (b) $x > y$

(c) $x = y$ if $a < 1$ (d) $x = y$

84. If $\frac{x}{y} = \frac{4}{5}$, then the value of $\left(\frac{4}{7} + \frac{2y - x}{2y + x}\right)$ is:

(a) 2 (b) $1\frac{1}{7}$ (c) 1 (d) $\frac{3}{7}$

85. What is the value of $\frac{x+y}{x-y}$ if $\frac{x}{y} = 7$?

(a) $\frac{7}{8}$ (b) $\frac{4}{3}$ (c) $\frac{2}{3}$ (d) $\frac{1}{3}$

86. $3 - [1.6 - \{3.2 - (3.2 + 2.25 \div x)\}] = 0.65$; then the value of x is:

(a) 7 (b) 3 (c) 0.7 (d) 0.3

87. $2.002 + 7.9\,\{2.8 - 6.3\,(3.6 - 1.5) + 15.6\} = ?$

(a) 42.845 (b) 40.843 (c) 4.2845 (d) 2.002

88. If $(a + b + 2c + 3d)(a - b - 2c + 3d) = (a - b + 2c - 3d)(a + b - 2c - 3d)$; then $2bc$ is equal to:

(a) a^2d^2 (b) $3ad$ (c) $\frac{3a}{2d}$ (d) $\frac{3}{2}$

89. If $\frac{2a+b}{a+4b} = 3$, then the value of $\frac{a+b}{a+2b}$ is:

(a) $\frac{10}{9}$ (b) $\frac{10}{7}$ (c) $\frac{5}{9}$ (d) $\frac{2}{7}$

90. If $3x + 7 = x^2 + p = 7x + 5$, then the value of p is:

(a) $8\frac{1}{2}$ (b) $8\frac{1}{4}$

(c) $\frac{1}{2}$ (d) Cannot be determined

91. $\frac{a}{3} = \frac{b}{4} = \frac{c}{7}$, then what is the value of $\frac{a+b+c}{c}$?

(a) 7 (b) 2 (c) $\sqrt{2}$ (d) $\frac{1}{\sqrt{7}}$

92. If $\frac{a}{x}+\frac{y}{b}=1$ and $\frac{b}{y}+\frac{z}{c}=1$, then $\frac{x}{a}+\frac{c}{z}$ is equal to:

(a) $\frac{y}{b}$ (b) 1 (c) $\frac{b}{y}$ (d) 0

93. If $0 < a < 1$, then the value of $a + \frac{1}{a}$ is:

(a) greater than 4 (b) less than 4
(c) greater than 2 (d) less than 2

94. If $2 = x + \cfrac{1}{1+\cfrac{1}{3+\cfrac{1}{4}}}$, then the value of x is:

(a) $\frac{21}{17}$ (b) $\frac{18}{17}$ (c) $\frac{13}{17}$ (d) $\frac{12}{17}$

95. The value of $\cfrac{1}{2+\cfrac{1}{2+\cfrac{1}{2-\cfrac{1}{2}}}}$ is:

(a) $\frac{8}{19}$ (b) $\frac{8}{3}$ (c) $\frac{19}{8}$ (d) $\frac{3}{8}$

96. The value of $\cfrac{2+\cfrac{1}{3\frac{4}{5}}}{2+\cfrac{1}{3+\cfrac{1}{1+\cfrac{1}{4}}}}$ is:

(a) $\frac{8}{7}$ (b) $\frac{3}{7}$ (c) $\frac{1}{7}$ (d) 1

97. The value of $\cfrac{2}{2+\cfrac{2}{3+\cfrac{2}{3+\cfrac{2}{3}}}\times 0.39}$ is:

(a) $\frac{99}{111}$ (b) $\frac{100}{111}$ (c) $\frac{101}{111}$ (d) $\frac{10}{11}$

98. $8-8\times\dfrac{2\frac{1}{5}-1\frac{2}{7}}{2-\dfrac{1}{6-\frac{1}{6}}}$ is simplified to:

(a) 8 (b) 6 (c) 4 (d) 2

99. $\dfrac{1}{1+\dfrac{\frac{2}{3}}{1+\frac{2}{3}+\dfrac{\frac{8}{9}}{1-\frac{2}{3}}}}$ is equal to:

(a) $\frac{15}{13}$ (b) $\frac{13}{11}$ (c) $\frac{13}{15}$ (d) $\frac{11}{13}$

100. If $\dfrac{37}{13}=2+\dfrac{1}{x+\dfrac{1}{y+\frac{1}{z}}}$; where x, y and z are natural numbers, then x, y, z are:

(a) 11, 2, 5 (b) 5, 2, 11 (c) 1, 5, 2 (d) 1, 2, 5

101. Which of the following values of x and y satisfy the equations I and II:

I. $3x + y = 19$ II. $x - y = 9$

(a) 7, 2 (b) 7, –2 (c) –7, 2 (d) –7, –2

102. If $\frac{x}{5}-\frac{x}{6}=4$ then find the value of x.

(a) 120 (b) 100 (c) –100 (d) –120

103. If $a + b = 5$ and $3a + 2b = 20$, then the value of $(3a + b)$ is:

(a) 25 (b) 20 (c) 15 (d) 10

104. If $4x + 5y = 83$ and $\frac{3x}{2y}=\frac{21}{22}$, then the value of $(y - x)$ is

(a) 11 (b) 7 (c) 4 (d) 3

105. If $2x + 3y = 31$, $y - z = 4$ and $x + 2z = 11$, then the value of $(x + y + z)$ is:

(a) 16 (b) 15 (c) 13 (d) 12

106. If $2x + 3y = 17$, $y + 2z = 15$ and $x + y = 9$, then the value of $(4x + 3y + z)$ is:

(a) 45 (b) 43 (c) 42 (d) 41

107. If $3x - 5y = 5$ and $\frac{x}{x+y}=\frac{5}{7}$ then the value of $(x - y)$ is:

(a) 9 (b) 6 (c) 4 (d) 3

108. $\frac{3}{4}\left(1+\frac{1}{3}\right)\left(1+\frac{2}{3}\right)\left(1-\frac{2}{5}\right)\left(1+\frac{6}{7}\right)\left(1-\frac{12}{13}\right)$ is simplified to:

(a) $\frac{1}{8}$ (b) $\frac{1}{7}$ (c) $\frac{1}{6}$ (d) $\frac{1}{5}$

109. $\left(1+\frac{1}{2}\right)\left(1+\frac{1}{3}\right)\left(1+\frac{1}{4}\right)\ldots\left(1+\frac{1}{120}\right)$ is simplified to:

(a) 121 (b) 60.5 (c) 40.5 (d) 30

110. The value of $\left(1-\frac{1}{2}\right)\left(1-\frac{1}{3}\right)\left(1-\frac{1}{4}\right)\ldots\left(1-\frac{1}{n}\right)$ is:

(a) $\frac{2}{n(n+1)}$ (b) $\frac{2(n-1)}{n}$ (c) $\frac{2}{n}$ (d) $\frac{1}{n}$

111. The value of $\left(999\frac{1}{7}+999\frac{2}{7}+999\frac{3}{7}+999\frac{4}{7}+999\frac{5}{7}+999\frac{6}{7}\right)$ is:

(a) 5997 (b) 5994 (c) 5979 (d) 2997

112. $999\frac{995}{999}\times 999$ is simplified to:

(a) 999824 (b) 998999 (c) 998996 (d) 990809

113. $\frac{3}{1^2.2^2}+\frac{5}{2^2.3^2}+\frac{7}{3^2.4^2}+\frac{9}{4^2.5^2}+\frac{11}{5^2.6^2}+\frac{13}{6^2.7^2}+\frac{15}{7^2.8^2}+\frac{17}{8^2.9^2}+\frac{19}{9^2.10^2}$ is simplified to:

(a) $\frac{101}{100}$ (b) 1 (c) $\frac{99}{100}$ (d) $\frac{1}{100}$

114. $1+\frac{1}{4\times 3}+\frac{1}{4\times 3^2}+\frac{1}{4\times 3^3}$ is simplified to:

(a) $\frac{11}{18}$ (b) $\frac{121}{108}$ (c) $\frac{3}{2}$ (d) $\frac{31}{2}$

115. $\frac{1}{1\cdot 2\cdot 3}+\frac{1}{2\cdot 3\cdot 4}+\frac{1}{3\cdot 4\cdot 5}+\frac{1}{4\cdot 5\cdot 6}$ is simplified to:

(a) $\frac{17}{30}$ (b) $\frac{13}{30}$ (c) $\frac{11}{30}$ (d) $\frac{7}{30}$

116. The total monthly salary of 4 men and 2 women is Rs. 46,000. If a woman earns Rs. 500 more than a man, what is the monthly salary of a woman?

(a) Rs. 9000 (b) Rs. 8000 (c) Rs. 7500 (d) Rs. 6500

117. Along a yard 225 meters long, 26 trees are planted at equal distances, one tree being at each end of the yard. What is the distance between two consecutive trees?

(a) 15 meters (b) 10 meters (c) 9 meters (d) 8 meters

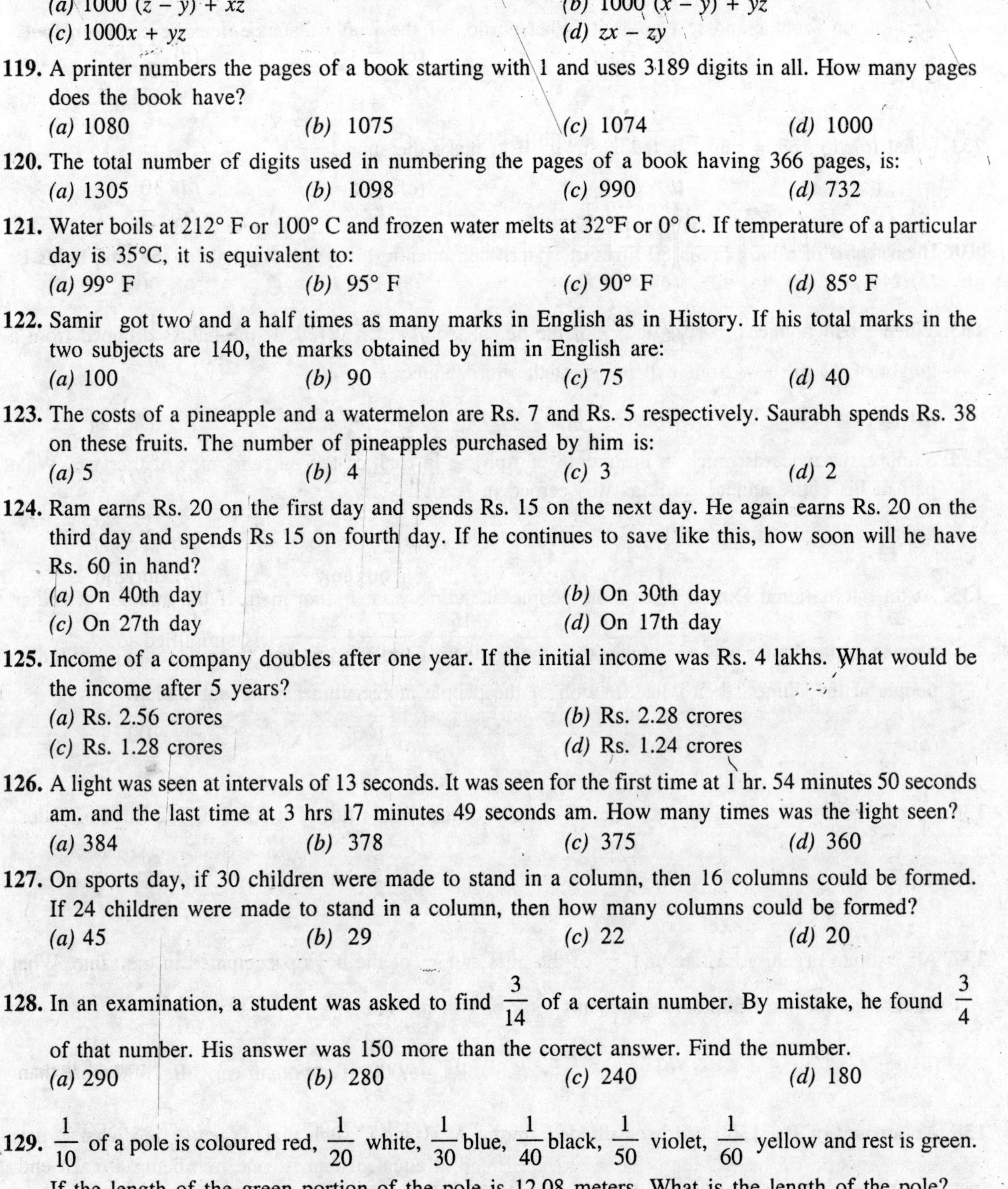

118. It costs Rs. x each to make the first thousand copies of a compact disc and Rs. y to make each subsequent copy. If z is greater than 1000, how much will it cost to z copies of the compact disc?
(*a*) $1000(z - y) + xz$ (*b*) $1000(x - y) + yz$
(*c*) $1000x + yz$ (*d*) $zx - zy$

119. A printer numbers the pages of a book starting with 1 and uses 3189 digits in all. How many pages does the book have?
(*a*) 1080 (*b*) 1075 (*c*) 1074 (*d*) 1000

120. The total number of digits used in numbering the pages of a book having 366 pages, is:
(*a*) 1305 (*b*) 1098 (*c*) 990 (*d*) 732

121. Water boils at 212° F or 100° C and frozen water melts at 32°F or 0° C. If temperature of a particular day is 35°C, it is equivalent to:
(*a*) 99° F (*b*) 95° F (*c*) 90° F (*d*) 85° F

122. Samir got two and a half times as many marks in English as in History. If his total marks in the two subjects are 140, the marks obtained by him in English are:
(*a*) 100 (*b*) 90 (*c*) 75 (*d*) 40

123. The costs of a pineapple and a watermelon are Rs. 7 and Rs. 5 respectively. Saurabh spends Rs. 38 on these fruits. The number of pineapples purchased by him is:
(*a*) 5 (*b*) 4 (*c*) 3 (*d*) 2

124. Ram earns Rs. 20 on the first day and spends Rs. 15 on the next day. He again earns Rs. 20 on the third day and spends Rs 15 on fourth day. If he continues to save like this, how soon will he have Rs. 60 in hand?
(*a*) On 40th day (*b*) On 30th day
(*c*) On 27th day (*d*) On 17th day

125. Income of a company doubles after one year. If the initial income was Rs. 4 lakhs. What would be the income after 5 years?
(*a*) Rs. 2.56 crores (*b*) Rs. 2.28 crores
(*c*) Rs. 1.28 crores (*d*) Rs. 1.24 crores

126. A light was seen at intervals of 13 seconds. It was seen for the first time at 1 hr. 54 minutes 50 seconds am. and the last time at 3 hrs 17 minutes 49 seconds am. How many times was the light seen?
(*a*) 384 (*b*) 378 (*c*) 375 (*d*) 360

127. On sports day, if 30 children were made to stand in a column, then 16 columns could be formed. If 24 children were made to stand in a column, then how many columns could be formed?
(*a*) 45 (*b*) 29 (*c*) 22 (*d*) 20

128. In an examination, a student was asked to find $\frac{3}{14}$ of a certain number. By mistake, he found $\frac{3}{4}$ of that number. His answer was 150 more than the correct answer. Find the number.
(*a*) 290 (*b*) 280 (*c*) 240 (*d*) 180

129. $\frac{1}{10}$ of a pole is coloured red, $\frac{1}{20}$ white, $\frac{1}{30}$ blue, $\frac{1}{40}$ black, $\frac{1}{50}$ violet, $\frac{1}{60}$ yellow and rest is green. If the length of the green portion of the pole is 12.08 meters. What is the length of the pole?
(*a*) 30 m (*b*) 20 m (*c*) 18 m (*d*) 16 m

130. A person travels 3.5 km from place A to place B. Out of this distance, he travels $1\frac{2}{3}$ km on bicycle, $1\frac{1}{6}$ km on scooter and rest on foot. What portion of the whole distance does he cover on foot?

(a) $\frac{5}{6}$ *(b)* $\frac{4}{21}$ *(c)* $\frac{4}{11}$ *(d)* $\frac{3}{19}$

131. What fraction of $\frac{4}{7}$ must be added to itself to make the sum $1\frac{1}{14}$?

(a) $\frac{15}{14}$ *(b)* $\frac{7}{8}$ *(c)* $\frac{4}{7}$ *(d)* $\frac{3}{19}$

132. If one-third of a tank holds 80 litres of water, then quantity of water that half of the tank holds is:

(a) 240 *l* *(b)* 120 *l* *(c)* 100 *l* *(d)* 90 *l*

133. When a ball bounces, it rises to $\frac{3}{4}$ of the height from which it fell. If the ball is dropped from a height of 32 m, how high will it rise at the third bounce?

(a) 13 *m* *(b)* $13\frac{1}{4}$ *m* *(c)* $13\frac{1}{2}$ *m* *(d)* $14\frac{1}{2}$ *m*

134. Samir earns twice as much in the month of April as in each of the other months of the year. What part of his entire annual earnings was earned in April?

(a) $\frac{2}{13}$ *(b)* $\frac{2}{11}$ *(c)* $\frac{1}{6}$ *(d)* $\frac{1}{7}$

135. At an International Dinner, $\frac{1}{5}$ of the people attending were Indian men. If the number of Indian women at the dinner was $\frac{2}{3}$ greater than the number of Indian men, and there were no other Indian people at the dinner, then what fraction of the people at the dinner were not Indian?

(a) $\frac{7}{15}$ *(b)* $\frac{2}{3}$ *(c)* $\frac{2}{5}$ *(d)* $\frac{1}{5}$

136. $\frac{1}{4}$ of a tank holds 135 litres of water. What part of the tank is full of it contains 180 litres of water?

(a) $\frac{2}{5}$ *(b)* $\frac{2}{3}$ *(c)* $\frac{1}{3}$ *(d)* $\frac{1}{6}$

137. An institute organised a fate and $\frac{1}{5}$ of the girls and $\frac{1}{8}$ of the boys participated in the same. What fraction of the total number of students took part in the fate?

(a) $\frac{3}{13}$ *(b)* $\frac{2}{13}$ *(c)* $\frac{1}{13}$ *(d)* None of these

138. An amount of Rs. 1360 has been divided among A, B and C such that A gets $\frac{2}{3}$ of what B gets and B gets $\frac{1}{4}$ of what C gets. What is the share of B?

(a) Rs. 300 *(b)* Rs. 240 *(c)* Rs. 160 *(d)* Rs. 120

139. A man has divided his total money in his will in such a way that half of it goes to his wife, $\frac{2}{3}$*rd* of the remaining among his three sons equally and the rest among his four daughters equally. If each daughter gets Rs. 20,000, then how much money will each son get?

(a) Rs. 54,333.33 *(b)* Rs. 53,333.33
(c) Rs. 50,333.33 *(d)* Rs. 48,533.33

140. A boy read $\frac{3}{8}$*th* of a book on one day and $\frac{4}{5}$*th* of the remainder on another day. If there were 30 pages unread, how many pages did the book contain?

(a) 250 *(b)* 240 *(c)* 260 *(d)* 300

141. One-third of Saurabh's savings in National Savings Certificate is equal to one-half of his savings in Public Provident Fund. If he has Rs. 1,50,000 as total savings how much has he saved in Public Provident Fund?

(a) Rs. 90,000 *(b)* Rs. 60,000 *(c)* Rs. 50,000 *(d)* Rs. 30,000

142. The liquid contained in a bucket can fill four large bottles or seven small bottles. A full large bottles is used to fill an empty small bottle. What fraction of liquid is left over in the large bottle, when the small one is full?

(a) $\frac{5}{7}$ *(b)* $\frac{4}{7}$ *(c)* $\frac{3}{7}$ *(d)* $\frac{2}{7}$

143. Ram gave one-fourth of the amount he had to Shyam. Shyam in turn gave half of what he received from Ram to Mohan. If the difference between the remaining amount with Ram and the amount received by Mohan is Rs. 500, how much money did Shyam receive from Ram?

(a) Rs. 400 *(b)* Rs. 300 *(c)* Rs. 200 *(d)* Rs. 100

144. The marks scored in an examination are connected from 50 to 10 for the purpose of internal assessment. The highest marks were 47 and the lowest were 14. The difference between the maximum and the minimum internal assessment scores is:

(a) 7.4 *(b)* 6.6 *(c)* 4.8 *(d)* 3.3

145. To fill a tank, 25 buckets of water is required. How many buckets of water will be required to fill the same tank if the capacity of the bucket reduced to two-fifth of its present?

(a) $62\frac{1}{2}$ *(b)* $60\frac{1}{2}$ *(c)* 60 *(d)* 62

146. A fires 5 shots to B's 3 but A kills only once in 3 shots, while B kills once in 2 shots. When B missed 27 times, A has killed:

(a) 90 birds *(b)* 72 birds *(c)* 60 birds *(d)* 30 birds

147. One third of the boys and one-half of the girls of a college participated in a social work project. If the number of participating students is 300 out of which 100 are boys, what is the total number of students in the college?

(a) 800 *(b)* 700 *(c)* 600 *(d)* 500

148. $\dfrac{\left(\frac{3}{5}\right)^3 - \left(\frac{2}{5}\right)^3}{\left(\frac{3}{5}\right)^2 - \left(\frac{2}{5}\right)^2}$ is simplified to:

(a) 1 (b) $\frac{21}{25}$ (c) $\frac{19}{25}$ (d) $\frac{1}{5}$

149. $\left(\frac{147\times147+147\times143+143\times143}{147\times147\times147-143\times143\times143}\right)$ is simplified to:

(a) 4 (b) $\frac{1}{290}$ (c) 290 (d) $\frac{1}{4}$

150. $\frac{785\times785\times785+435\times435\times435}{785\times785-785\times435+435\times435}=?$

(a) 1320 (b) 1220 (c) 785 (d) 350

151. $\frac{(13)^3+7^3}{(13)^2+7^2-?}=20$

(a) 91 (b) 81 (c) 100 (d) 64

152. If $\frac{x^2+y^2+z^2-64}{xy-yz-zx}=-2$ and $x+y=32$, then find the value of z.

(a) 5 (b) 4 (c) 3 (d) 2

153. If $a+b+c=13$, $a^2+b^2+c^2=69$, then what is the value of $(ab+bc+ca)$.

(a) 75 (b) 69 (c) 50 (d) 60

154. $\frac{\left(1+\frac{1}{1+\frac{1}{100}}\right)\left(1+\frac{1}{1+\frac{1}{100}}\right)-\left(1-\frac{1}{1+\frac{1}{100}}\right)\left(1-\frac{1}{1+\frac{1}{100}}\right)}{\left(1+\frac{1}{1+\frac{1}{100}}\right)+\left(1-\frac{1}{1+\frac{1}{100}}\right)}$ is simplified to:

(a) $\frac{101}{200}$ (b) 101 (c) 200 (d) $\frac{200}{101}$

155. $\frac{\left(3\frac{2}{3}\right)^2-\left(2\frac{1}{2}\right)^2}{\left(4\frac{3}{4}\right)^2-\left(3\frac{1}{3}\right)^2}\div\frac{3\frac{2}{3}-2\frac{1}{2}}{4\frac{3}{4}-3\frac{1}{3}}$ is simplified to:

(a) $\frac{97}{74}$ (b) $\frac{74}{97}$ (c) $\frac{37}{97}$ (d) $\frac{97}{37}$

156. $\frac{(469+174)^2-(469-174)^2}{469\times174}$ is simplified to:

(a) 2 (b) 3 (c) 4 (d) 5

157. If $\frac{x^2-1}{x+1}$ = 4, then what is the value of x ?

(a) 5 (b) 4 (c) 3 (d) 2

158. If $a - b = 3$ and $a^2 + b^2 = 29$ then ab = ?

(a) 18 (b) 15 (c) 12 (d) 10

159. On Children's Day, sweets were to be equally distributed among 175 children in a school. 35 children were absent on that day and therefore each child got 4 sweets extra. How many sweets are available for distribution in total?

(a) 2800 (b) 2750 (c) 2700 (d) 2850

160. A man has some hens and cows. If the number of heads be 48 and the number of feet equals 140. Then find the number of hens.

(a) 26 (b) 24 (c) 23 (d) 22

161. Eight people are planning to share equally the cost of a rental car. If one person withdraws from the arrangement and the others share equally the entire cost of the car, then the share of each of the remaining persons increased by:

(a) $\frac{7}{8}$ (b) $\frac{1}{9}$ (c) $\frac{1}{8}$ (d) $\frac{1}{7}$

162. Free notebooks were distributed equally among children of a class. The number of notebooks each child got was one-eighth of the number of children. Had the number of the children been half, each child would have got 16 notebooks. How many notebooks were distributed in total?

(a) 512 (b) 500 (c) 450 (d) 412

163. A man has Rs. 480 in the denominations of one-rupee notes, five-rupee notes and ten-rupee notes. The number of notes of each denomination is equal. Find the total number of notes he has:

(a) 90 (b) 75 (c) 60 (d) 45

164. In a group of buffaloes and ducks the number of feet are 24 more than twice the number of heads. Find the number of buffaloes in the group.

(a) 12 (b) 10 (c) 8 (d) 6

165. A total of 324 coins of 20 paise and 25 paise make a sum of Rs. 71. What is the number of 25 paise coins?

(a) 200 (b) 144 (c) 124 (d) 120

166. N number of persons decided to raise Rs. 3 lakhs by equal contributions from each. Had they contributed Rs. 50 each extra, the contribution would have been Rs. 3.25 lakhs. Find the value of N.

(a) 600 (b) 550 (c) 400 (d) 500

167. A cricket team won 3 matches more than they lost. If a win gives them 2 points and loss (–1) point, If their score is 23, then how many matches in all have they played?

(a) 40 (b) 37 (c) 20 (d) 17

168. There are two examination room A and B. If 10 students are sent from A to B, then the number of students in each room is equal. If 20 students are sent from B to A, then the number of students in A is double the number of students in B. Find the number of students in room A.

(a) 200 (b) 100 (c) 80 (d) 90

169. In an examination, a student scores 4 marks for every correct answer and loses 1 mark for every wrong answer. If he attempts in all 60 questions and secures 130 marks. Find the number of questions he attempts correctly.

(a) 42 (b) 40 (c) 38 (d) 35

170. Ram gets on the elevator at the 11th floor of a building and rides up at the rate of 57 floors per minute. At the same time Mohan gets on an elevator at the 51st floor of the same building and rides down at the rate of 63 floors per minute. If they continue travelling at these rates, then at which floor will their paths cross?

(*a*) 40 (*b*) 37 (*c*) 30 (*d*) 28

171. If cost of 2 tables and 3 chairs is Rs. 3500 and cost of 3 tables and 2 chairs is Rs. 4000, then find the cost of a table.

(*a*) Rs. 1500 (*b*) Rs. 1000 (*c*) Rs. 750 (*d*) Rs. 500

172. A sum of Rs. 312 was divided among 100 boys and girls in such a way that each boy get Rs. 3.60 and each girl Rs. 2.40. Find the number of girls.

(*a*) 65 (*b*) 60 (*c*) 40 (*d*) 35

173. The cost of 2 sarees and 4 shirts is Rs. 1600. With the same money one can buy one saree and 6 shirts. Then find the cost of 12 shirts:

(*a*) Rs. 4800 (*b*) Rs. 3600 (*c*) Rs. 2400 (*d*) Rs. 1200

174. The cost of 10 chairs is equal to that of 4 tables. The cost of 15 chairs and 2 tables together is Rs. 4000. Find the cost of 12 chairs and 3 tables.

(*a*) Rs. 3900 (*b*) Rs. 3840 (*c*) Rs. 3750 (*d*) Rs. 3500

175. In a regular week, there are 5 working days and for each day, the working hours are 8. A man gets Rs. 2.40 per hour for regular work and Rs. 3.20 per hour for overtime. If he earns Rs. 432 in 4 weeks. Then how many hours does he work for?

(*a*) 195 (*b*) 180 (*c*) 175 (*d*) 160

176. A certain number of tennis balls were purchased for Rs. 450. Five more balls could have been purchased in the same amount if each ball was cheaper by Rs. 15. Find the number of balls which was purchased.

(*a*) 25 (*b*) 20 (*c*) 15 (*d*) 10

EXPLANATORY ANSWERS

1. $\because 51 \div 17 \div 3 = \frac{51}{17} \div 3 = 3 \div 3 = \frac{3}{3} = 1$

2. $\because 40 \times 2 \div 10 + 5 - 4 = 40 \times \frac{2}{10} + 5 - 4 = 8 + 5 - 4 = 9$

3. $\because 28 \times 104 \div (18 + 6) + 3 = 28 \times 104 \div 24 + 3$

$= 28 \times \frac{104}{24} + 3 = 28 \times \frac{13}{3} + 3 = \frac{364}{3} + 3 = \frac{373}{3} = 124\frac{1}{3}$

4. $\because 75^2 - 65^2 = 2x \Rightarrow (75 + 65)(75 - 65) = 2x$

$[\because a^2 - b^2 = (a + b)(a - b)]$

$\Rightarrow 140 \times 10 = 2x \Rightarrow x = 70 \times 10 = 700$

$\therefore$ Value of x is 700.

5. $\because .99 \times 14 \div 11 \div 0.7$

$= .99 \times \frac{14}{11} \div 0.7 = \frac{.99 \times 14}{11 \times 0.7} = 1.8$

6. $\because$ 45 – [28 – {37 – (15 – ?)}] = 58

$\Rightarrow$ 45 – [28 – {37 – 15 + ?}] = 58

$\Rightarrow$ 45 – [28 – {22 + ?}] = 58

$\Rightarrow$ 45 – [28 – 22 – ?} = 58

$\Rightarrow$ 45 – 28 + 22 + ? = 58

$\Rightarrow$ 39 + ? = 58

$\Rightarrow$? = 58 – 39 = 19

Therefore, the interrogation sign should be replaced by 19.

7. $\because 8\frac{1}{3}+5\frac{1}{4}\times 13\frac{1}{5}\div 6\frac{3}{5}$

$=\frac{25}{3}+\frac{21}{4}\times\frac{66}{5}\div\frac{33}{5}=\frac{25}{3}+\frac{21}{4}\times\frac{66}{5}\times\frac{5}{33}$

$=\frac{25}{3}+\frac{21}{2}=\frac{50+63}{6}=\frac{113}{6}=18\frac{5}{6}$

8. $\because \frac{14}{3}$ of $\frac{5}{8}$ of $72=\frac{14\times 5\times 72}{3\times 8}=210$

9. 10 × 10 × 10 ÷ (20 ÷ 10 × 10 – 10) + 6

$= 10\times 10\times 10\div\left(\frac{20}{10}\times 10-10\right)+6$

= 10 × 10 × 10 ÷ (20 – 10) + 6

$= 10\times 10\times 10\div 10+6=10\times 10\times\frac{10}{10}+6$

= 10 × 10 × 1 + 6 = 100 + 6 = 106

10. $\because \dfrac{\frac{1}{3}\times 20\div 4}{\frac{1}{4}\times 25\div 5}=\dfrac{\frac{1}{3}\times 5}{\frac{1}{4}\times 5}=\dfrac{\frac{5}{3}}{\frac{5}{4}}=\frac{4}{3}$

11. $\because \dfrac{(24\times 13)+(28\div 7)}{(24+13)-\left(\frac{14}{3}\text{ of }\frac{5}{8}\right)}=\dfrac{312+4}{37-\frac{35}{12}}=\dfrac{316}{\frac{409}{12}}=\dfrac{3792}{409}$

12. If $\dfrac{144+32\div ?-8}{35\div\frac{1}{2}\text{ of }\frac{1}{2}}=1\Rightarrow\dfrac{144+\frac{32}{?}-8}{35\div\frac{1}{4}}=1\Rightarrow\dfrac{136+\frac{32}{?}}{\frac{35}{\frac{1}{4}}}=1$

$\Rightarrow 136+\frac{32}{?}=35\times 4=140$

$\Rightarrow \frac{32}{?}=140-136=4 \qquad \Rightarrow ?=\frac{32}{4}=8$

$\therefore$ Sign of interrogation (?) will be replaced by 8.

13. $\dfrac{2.70\times2.70+4.30\times4.30+8.60\times2.70}{2.70+4.30}$

$= \dfrac{(2.70)^2+(4.30)^2+2\times4.30\times2.70}{2.70+4.30} = \dfrac{(2.70+4.30)^2}{2.70+4.30}$ $[\because a^2 + b^2 + 2ab = (a + b)^2]$

$= 2.70 + 4.30 = 7.00$

14. $\therefore \dfrac{\left(\sqrt{6}+\dfrac{1}{\sqrt{6}}\right)^2}{\dfrac{1}{2}\text{ of } 18 + 4}+\dfrac{2}{3} = \dfrac{(\sqrt{6})^2+\left(\dfrac{1}{\sqrt{6}}\right)^2+2.\sqrt{6}\dfrac{1}{\sqrt{6}}}{9+4}+\dfrac{2}{3}$

$= \dfrac{6+\dfrac{1}{6}+2}{13}+\dfrac{2}{3} = \dfrac{\dfrac{49}{6}}{13}+\dfrac{2}{3} = \dfrac{49}{78}+\dfrac{2}{3} = \dfrac{101}{78}$

15. $1150 \div 50 \div 23 + 15 = \dfrac{1150}{50} \div 23 + 15 = 23 \div 23 + 15$

$= \dfrac{23}{23} + 15 = 1 + 15 = 16.$

16. This type of question is solved starting from the bottom.

$\therefore\ 1+\dfrac{1}{1+\dfrac{1}{1+\dfrac{9}{16}}} = 1+\dfrac{1}{1+\dfrac{1}{\dfrac{25}{16}}}$

$= 1+\dfrac{1}{1+\dfrac{16}{25}} = 1+\dfrac{1}{\dfrac{41}{25}} = 1+\dfrac{25}{41} = \dfrac{66}{41}$

17. $\dfrac{(.08)^3+(.011)^3}{(.08)^2-.08\times.011+(.011)^2}$

$\dfrac{(0.08+.011)\left[(.08)^2-.08\times.011+(.011)^2\right]}{(.08)^2-.08\times.011+(.011)^2}$ $[\because a^3 + b^3 = (a + b)(a^2 - ab + b^2)]$

$= .08 + .011 = .091.$

18. $22 \div \left[(28-13)\div\left\{(32-8)\div\left(5+\dfrac{1}{3}\right)\right\}\right] = 22\div\left[15\div\left\{24\div\dfrac{16}{3}\right\}\right]$

$= 22 \div \left[15\div\dfrac{24}{\dfrac{16}{3}}\right] = 22 \div \left[15\div\dfrac{9}{2}\right] = 22 \div \dfrac{15}{\dfrac{9}{2}} = 22 \div \dfrac{10}{3} = \dfrac{22\times3}{10} = 6.6$

19. $\dfrac{(20^2-10^2)\div 5\times 3+10}{\frac{1}{3}\text{ of } 27+10\div 2+1} = \dfrac{(400-100)\div 5\times 3+10}{9+10\div 2+1} = \dfrac{300\div 5\times 3+10}{9+5+1}$

$= \dfrac{60\times 3+10}{15} = \dfrac{190}{15} = \dfrac{38}{3} = 12\dfrac{2}{3}$

20. $11^2 - 6^2 \div 6 \times \dfrac{5}{2} + 2 \text{ of } 10 = 11^2 - 6^2 \div 6 \times \dfrac{5}{2} + 20$

$= 11^2 - 6 \times \dfrac{5}{2} + 20 = 11^2 - 15 + 20 = 121 + 5 = 126$

21. $\dfrac{25}{3} - \dfrac{4}{7} \text{ of } \dfrac{7}{5} + \dfrac{11}{3} \div \dfrac{2}{3} - 4 = \dfrac{25}{3} - \dfrac{4}{5} + \dfrac{11}{3} \div \dfrac{2}{3} - 4$

$= \dfrac{25}{3} - \dfrac{4}{5} + \dfrac{11}{2} - 4 = \dfrac{83}{6} - \dfrac{24}{5} = \dfrac{415-144}{30} = \dfrac{271}{30} = 9\dfrac{1}{30}$

22. $35 \times .07 - 21 \times .03$
$= 2.45 - .63 = 1.82$

23. $60 \times [35 - \{25 - (18 - \overline{9-3}) \div 11\}]$
$= 60 \times [35 - \{25 - (18 - 6) \div 11\}$
$= 60 \times [35 - \{25 - 12 \div 11\}]$

$= 60 \times \left[35 - \left\{25 - \dfrac{12}{11}\right\}\right] = 60 \times \left[35 - \dfrac{263}{11}\right]$

$= 60 \times \dfrac{122}{11} = 665\dfrac{5}{11}$

24. $\dfrac{140-44\times 9\div 3}{\frac{1}{2}\text{ of } 18\div 9+2} = \dfrac{140-44\times 3}{9\div 9+2} = \dfrac{140-132}{1+2} = \dfrac{8}{3} = 2\dfrac{2}{3}$

25. 20% of 8 + 18% of 15 ÷ 5 of 10
$= 1.60 + 2.70 \div 50$

$= 1.60 + \dfrac{2.70}{50} = \dfrac{82.70}{50} = 1.654$

26. $4\dfrac{1}{3} \times 5\dfrac{1}{3} \div 6\dfrac{1}{3} \div \dfrac{1}{3} + 5\dfrac{1}{3} - 2\dfrac{1}{3}$

$= \dfrac{13}{3} \times \dfrac{16}{3} \div \dfrac{19}{3} \div \dfrac{1}{3} + \dfrac{16}{3} - \dfrac{7}{3} = \dfrac{13}{3} \times \dfrac{16}{19} \div \dfrac{1}{3} + \dfrac{16}{3} - \dfrac{7}{3}$

$= \dfrac{13}{3} \times \dfrac{48}{19} + \dfrac{16}{3} - \dfrac{7}{3} = \dfrac{208}{19} + \dfrac{16}{3} - \dfrac{7}{3}$

$= 10\dfrac{18}{19} + 3 = 13\dfrac{18}{19}$

27. $\frac{19}{17}$ of $\frac{28}{5}$ of $\left(\frac{17}{3} \div \frac{5}{3} \text{ of } 6\frac{1}{3}\right)$

$= \frac{19}{17}$ of $\frac{28}{5}$ of $\left(\frac{17}{3} \div \frac{5}{3} \text{of} \frac{19}{3}\right) = \frac{19}{17}$ of $\frac{28}{5}$ of $\left(\frac{17}{3} \div \frac{95}{9}\right)$

$= \frac{19}{17}$ of $\frac{28}{5}$ of $\frac{153}{285} = \frac{19}{17} \times \frac{28}{5} \times \frac{153}{285} = \frac{84}{25} = 3\frac{9}{25}$

28. $\left(17^{\frac{3}{2}} + 11^{\frac{3}{2}}\right)\left(17^{\frac{3}{2}} - 11^{\frac{3}{2}}\right) = \left(17^{\frac{3}{2}}\right)^2 - \left(11^{\frac{3}{2}}\right)^2$ $[\because (a + b)(a - b) = a^2 - b^2]$

$= 17^{\frac{3}{2}\times 2} - 11^{\frac{3}{2}\times 2} = 17^3 - 11^3 = 4913 - 1331 = 3582.$

29. This type of questions is solved starting from the bottom.

$$1+\cfrac{1}{1+\cfrac{1}{1+\cfrac{1}{3}}} = 1+\cfrac{1}{1+\cfrac{1}{\frac{4}{3}}} = 1+\cfrac{1}{1+\frac{3}{4}} = 1+\cfrac{1}{\frac{7}{4}} = 1+\frac{4}{7} = \frac{11}{7} = 1\frac{4}{7}$$

30. $3 - [9 + \{14 - (6 - \overline{3 - 21})\}] = 3 - [9 + \{14 - (6 + 18\}]$

$= 3 - [9 + \{14 - 24\}] = 3 - [9 - 10] = 3 + 1 = 4.$

31. $$\frac{\left(2\frac{2}{3} + 3\frac{4}{7}\right)^2 + \left(2\frac{2}{3} - 3\frac{4}{7}\right)^2}{\left(\frac{8}{3}\right)^2 + \left(\frac{25}{7}\right)^2} = \frac{\left(\frac{8}{3} + \frac{25}{7}\right)^2 + \left(\frac{8}{3} - \frac{25}{7}\right)^2}{\left(\frac{8}{3}\right)^2 + \left(\frac{25}{7}\right)^2}$$

$$= \frac{2\left[\left(\frac{8}{3}\right)^2 + \left(\frac{25}{7}\right)^2\right]}{\left(\frac{8}{3}\right)^2 + \left(\frac{25}{7}\right)^2} = 2$$ $[\because (a + b)^2 + (a - b)^2 = 2(a^2 + b^2)]$

32. $$\frac{4\frac{1}{7} - 2\frac{1}{4}}{3\frac{1}{2} + 1\frac{1}{7}} \div \cfrac{1}{2+\cfrac{1}{2+\cfrac{1}{5-\frac{1}{5}}}}$$

$$= \frac{\frac{29}{7} - \frac{9}{4}}{\frac{7}{2} + \frac{8}{7}} \div \cfrac{1}{2+\cfrac{1}{2+\cfrac{1}{\frac{24}{5}}}} = \frac{\frac{29\times 4 - 9\times 7}{28}}{\frac{7\times 7 - 8\times 2}{14}} \div \cfrac{1}{2+\cfrac{1}{2+\frac{5}{24}}}$$

$$= \frac{\frac{116-63}{28}}{\frac{49-16}{14}} \div \frac{1}{2+\frac{1}{\frac{53}{24}}} = \frac{\frac{53}{28}}{\frac{65}{14}} \div \frac{1}{2+\frac{24}{53}}$$

$$= \frac{53\times14}{28\times65} \div \frac{1}{\frac{130}{53}} = \frac{53}{130} \div \frac{53}{130} = \frac{53}{130} \times \frac{130}{53} = 1$$

33. $\frac{5.66\times5.66-4.44\times4.44}{2-.78}$ + (6.53 × 8.34 – 6.53 × 5.17 – 6.53 × 3.17)

$= \frac{(5.66)^2-(4.44)^2}{2-.78}$ + 6.53 (8.34 – 5.17 – 3.17)

$= \frac{(5.66+4.44)(5.66-4.44)}{1.22}$ + 6.53 × 0

$= \frac{10.10\times1.22}{1.22}$ + 0 = 10.10 = 10.1.

34. (8 ÷ 88) × 888808 = $\frac{8}{88}\times8888088 = 808008$

35. 1260 ÷ 15 ÷ 7 = 1260 × $\frac{1}{15}\times\frac{1}{7}$ = 12

36. 2 – [2 – {2 – 2(2 + 2)}]
= 2 – [2 – {2 – 8}] = 2 – [2 + 6] = 2 – 8 = – 6

37. 100 × 10 – 100 + 2000 ÷ 100
= 100 × 10 – 100 + 20 = 1000 – 100 + 20 = 920

38. 3640 ÷ 14 × 16 + 340

= 3640 × $\frac{1}{14}$ × 16 + 340 = 4160 + 340 = 4500

39. 25 – 5 [2 + 3 {2 – 2 (5 – 3) + 5} –10] ÷ 4
= 25 – 5 [2 + 3 {2 – 4 + 5} – 10] ÷ 4
= 25 – 5 [2 + 9 – 10] ÷ 4

= 25 – 5 × 1 × $\frac{1}{4}$ = 25 – $\frac{5}{4} = \frac{95}{4}$ = 23.75

40. (–5) (4) (2) $\left(-\frac{1}{2}\right)\left(\frac{3}{4}\right)$ = – 5 × 4 × 2 × $-\frac{1}{2}\times\frac{3}{4}$ = 15

41. $2^5 \times 9^2$ = 32 × 81 = 2592
The required difference = 2592 – 2592 = 0

42. $\dfrac{128 \div 16 \times ? - 7 \times 2}{7^2 - 8 \times 6 + ?^2} = 1$

$\Rightarrow \dfrac{8 \times ? - 7 \times 2}{1 + ?^2} = 1 \Rightarrow 8? - ?^2 = 14 + 1$

$\Rightarrow$? (8 – ?) = 15

By putting ? = 3, we get, 3 (8 – 3) = 15

Hence, ? = 3

43. $\dfrac{180 \times 15 - 12 \times 20}{140 \times 8 + 2 \times 55} = \dfrac{2700 - 240}{1120 + 110} = \dfrac{2460}{1230} = 2$

44. $\dfrac{(6+6+6+6) \div 6}{4+4+4+4 \div 4} = \dfrac{24 \times \frac{1}{6}}{4+4+4+1} = \dfrac{4}{13}$

45. $\dfrac{-\frac{1}{2} - \frac{2}{3} + \frac{4}{5} - \frac{1}{3} + \frac{1}{5} + \frac{3}{4}}{\frac{1}{2} + \frac{2}{3} - \frac{4}{3} + \frac{1}{3} - \frac{1}{5} - \frac{4}{5}} = \dfrac{\frac{3}{4} - \frac{1}{2} - \frac{2}{3} - \frac{1}{3} + \frac{4}{5} + \frac{1}{5}}{\frac{1}{2} - \frac{1}{3} - 1} = \dfrac{\frac{1}{4} - 1 + 1}{-5/6} = \dfrac{1}{4} \times -\dfrac{6}{5} = -\dfrac{3}{10}$

46. $\dfrac{1}{3} + \dfrac{1}{2} + \dfrac{1}{x} = 4 \quad \Rightarrow \dfrac{1}{x} = 4 - \dfrac{5}{6} = \dfrac{19}{6} \qquad \therefore x = \dfrac{6}{19}$

47. $\dfrac{1}{\left(2\frac{1}{3}\right)} + \dfrac{1}{1\frac{3}{4}} = \dfrac{1}{7/3} + \dfrac{1}{7/4} = \dfrac{3}{7} + \dfrac{4}{7} = 1$

48. $\dfrac{13}{5} + \dfrac{11}{6} = \dfrac{78 + 55}{30} = \dfrac{133}{30} = 4\dfrac{13}{30} < 5$

$\dfrac{11}{4} + \dfrac{8}{3} = \dfrac{33 + 32}{12} = \dfrac{65}{12} = 5\dfrac{5}{12} > 5$

49. $1 + \dfrac{1}{2} + \dfrac{1}{4} + \dfrac{1}{7} + \dfrac{1}{14} + \dfrac{1}{28} = \dfrac{28 + 14 + 7 + 4 + 2 + 1}{28} = \dfrac{56}{28} = 2$

50. 1 ÷ [1 + 1 ÷ {1 + 1 ÷ (1 + 1 ÷ 2)}]

$= 1 \div [1 + 1 \div \{1 + 1 \div \frac{3}{2}\}]$

$= 1 \div [1 + 1 \div \{1 + \frac{2}{3}\}] = 1 \div [1 + 1 \div \frac{5}{3}]$

$= 1 \div [1 + \frac{3}{5}] = 1 \times \frac{5}{8} = \frac{5}{8}$

51. $18 - [5 - \{6 + 2(7 - \overline{8-5})\}]$

= 18 – [5 – {6 + 2 (7 – 3)}] = 18 – [5 – {6 + 8}]

= 18 – [5 – 14] = 18 + 9 = 27

52. $\dfrac{8-|5-(-3+2)|\div 2}{|5-3|-|5-8|\div 3} = \dfrac{8-|5+1|\div 2}{2-3\times\frac{1}{3}} = \dfrac{8-6\div 2}{2-1} = 8 - 3 = 5$

53. The required difference $= \dfrac{19}{16}-\dfrac{16}{19} = \dfrac{361-256}{304} = \dfrac{105}{304}$

54. $5\dfrac{1}{x}\times y\dfrac{3}{4} = 20 \quad \Rightarrow \dfrac{5x+1}{x}\times\dfrac{4y+3}{4} = 20$

$\Rightarrow (5x + 1)(4y + 3) = 80x$

By putting $x = y = 3$, we get the required result.

Hence, $x = 3$, $y = 3$

55. Let, $5\dfrac{2}{3}\div x\dfrac{5}{6} = 2$

$\Rightarrow \dfrac{17}{3}\div\dfrac{6x+5}{6} = 2$

$\Rightarrow \dfrac{6x+5}{6} = \dfrac{17}{6} \quad \Rightarrow 6x = 12 \quad \therefore x = 2$

56. Let, $\dfrac{5}{3}\div\dfrac{2}{7}\times\dfrac{x}{7} = \dfrac{5}{4}\times\dfrac{2}{3}\div\dfrac{1}{6}$ $\quad \dfrac{19}{16}-\dfrac{16}{19} = \dfrac{361-256}{304} = \dfrac{105}{304}$

$\Rightarrow \dfrac{5}{3}\times\dfrac{7}{2}\times\dfrac{x}{7} = \dfrac{5}{4}\times\dfrac{2}{3}\times 6$

$\Rightarrow \dfrac{5}{6}x = 5$

$\therefore x = 6$

57. Let, $\dfrac{3}{8}$ of $168\times 15\div 5 + x = 549 \div 9 + 235$

$\Rightarrow 63 \times 15 \times \dfrac{1}{5} + x = 61 + 235$

$\therefore x = 296 - 189 = 107$

58. $\dfrac{3}{5}$ of $\dfrac{4}{7}$ of $\dfrac{5}{9}$ of $\dfrac{7}{8}$ of $504 = \dfrac{3}{5}\times\dfrac{4}{7}\times\dfrac{5}{9}\times\dfrac{7}{8}\times 504 = 84$

59. $\dfrac{41}{6}\times\dfrac{16}{3}+\dfrac{53}{3}\times\dfrac{9}{2} = \dfrac{656}{18} + \dfrac{477}{6} = \dfrac{656+1431}{18} = \dfrac{2087}{18} = 115\dfrac{17}{18}$

60. $\dfrac{\left(\frac{1}{2}-\frac{1}{4}+\frac{1}{5}-\frac{1}{6}\right)}{\left(\frac{2}{5}-\frac{5}{9}+\frac{3}{5}-\frac{7}{18}\right)} = \dfrac{\frac{7}{10}-\frac{5}{12}}{1-\frac{17}{18}} = \dfrac{\frac{42-25}{60}}{\frac{1}{18}} = \dfrac{17}{60}\times 18 = \dfrac{51}{10} = 5\dfrac{1}{10}$

61. $\dfrac{\frac{1}{3}+\frac{3}{4}\left(\frac{2}{5}-\frac{1}{3}\right)}{\frac{5}{3}\text{of}\frac{3}{4}-\frac{1}{4}\text{of}\frac{4}{5}} = \dfrac{\frac{1}{3}+\frac{3}{4}\times\frac{1}{15}}{\frac{5}{4}-\frac{1}{5}} = \dfrac{\frac{1}{3}+\frac{1}{20}}{\frac{21}{20}} = \frac{23}{60}\times\frac{20}{21} = \frac{23}{63}$

62. $\left(\frac{5}{7}\text{of}\frac{19}{13}\right)\div\left(\frac{19}{7}\div\frac{13}{4}\right) = \frac{95}{91}\div\frac{76}{91} = \frac{95}{91}\times\frac{91}{76} = \frac{5}{4}$

63. $\dfrac{\frac{7}{3}+\frac{3}{2}\text{of}\frac{5}{3}}{2+\frac{5}{3}} = \dfrac{\frac{7}{3}+\frac{5}{2}}{\frac{11}{3}} = \frac{29}{6}\times\frac{3}{11} = \frac{29}{22}$

Required difference = $\frac{29}{22}-\frac{1}{4} = \frac{58-11}{44} = \frac{47}{44} = 1\frac{3}{44}$

64. $9-\frac{11}{9}\text{of}\frac{36}{11}\div\frac{36}{7}\text{of}\frac{7}{9} = 9-4\div4 = 9-1 = 8$

65. Let, $\frac{4335}{x}\div\frac{15}{8} = \frac{289}{528}$

$\Rightarrow \frac{4335}{x} = \frac{289}{528}\times\frac{15}{8} = \frac{289\times5}{176\times8}$ $\quad\therefore x = \frac{4335\times176\times8}{289\times5} = 4224$

Hence, ? = 2

66. $\frac{9}{2}\times\frac{13}{3}-\frac{25}{3}\div\frac{17}{3} = \frac{9}{2}\times\frac{13}{3}-\frac{25}{3}\times\frac{3}{17} = \frac{39}{2}-\frac{25}{17} = \frac{613}{34} = 18\frac{1}{34}$

67. $\frac{11}{4}\div\frac{8}{3}\div\frac{13}{12} = \frac{11}{4}\times\frac{3}{8}\times\frac{12}{13} = \frac{99}{104}$

68. Let, $\frac{5(x+7)}{9}-3 = 12$ $\quad\Rightarrow \frac{5(x+7)}{9} = 15$

$\Rightarrow x+7 = \frac{9\times15}{5} = 27$ $\quad\therefore x = 20$

69. Here, $x \oplus y = x^2 + 2y$

$\therefore\ 4 \oplus (3 \oplus p) = 4 \oplus (9 + 2p) = 16 + 18 + 4p = 34 + 4p$

Now, $34 + 4p = 50$

$\Rightarrow 4p = 16$

$\therefore\ p = 4$

70. $a \star b = \frac{ab}{a+b}$

$\therefore\ 3 \star (3\star - 1) = 3 \star \frac{-3}{2} = \frac{-9/2}{3/2} = -3$

71. $x \star y = x^2 + y^2 - xy$

$\therefore\ 9 \star 11 = 9^2 + 11^2 - 9 \times 11 = 81 + 121 - 99 = 103$

72. $a \bigstar b = 2a - 3b + ab$

$\therefore\ 3 \bigstar 5 + 5 \bigstar 3 = 6 - 15 + 15 + 10 - 9 + 15 = 22$

73. Let, $\frac{2}{5} \times \frac{1}{4} \times \frac{3}{7} \times x = 15$

$\Rightarrow \frac{3}{70} x = 15$

$\therefore\ x = \frac{15 \times 70}{3} = 350$

Hence, $\frac{x}{2} = \frac{350}{2} = 175$

74. Let, $\frac{4}{5} \times x = 16{,}800$

$\therefore\ \frac{3}{7} \times x = 16800 \times \frac{5}{4} \times \frac{3}{7}$ = Rs. 9000

75. $\frac{6}{7/8} - \frac{6/7}{8} = \frac{48}{7} - \frac{6}{56} = \frac{384 - 6}{56} = \frac{378}{56} = \frac{27}{4} = 6\frac{3}{4}$

76. $\frac{3}{5} \times 350 - \frac{4}{7} \times 210 = 210 - 120 = 90$

77. $\dfrac{\frac{1}{3} \div \frac{1}{3} \times \frac{1}{3}}{\frac{1}{3} \div \frac{1}{3} \text{ of } \frac{1}{3}} - \frac{1}{9} = \dfrac{1 \times \frac{1}{3}}{\frac{1}{3} \div \frac{1}{9}} - \frac{1}{9} = \dfrac{\frac{1}{3}}{\frac{1}{3} \times 9} - \frac{1}{9} = \frac{1}{9} - \frac{1}{9} = 0$

78. $3034 - (1002 \div 20.04) = 3034 - \frac{1002}{2004} \times 100 = 3034 - 50 = 2984$

79. $11.6 + 9.28 \div 0.464 - 0.2828 \div 0.07$

$= 11.6 + \frac{9280}{464} - \frac{2828}{700} = 11.6 + 20 - 4.04 = 27.56$

80. $0.008 \times 0.01 \times 0.0072 \div (0.12 \times 0.0004)$

$= 0.008 \times 0.01 \times 0.0072 \times \frac{1}{0.000048} = \frac{8 \times 72}{48 \times 1000} = 0.012$

81. $5.8 \times 2.5 + 0.6 \times 6.75 + 139.25 = 14.50 + 4.05 + 139.25 = 157.80$

82. Let, $\frac{58}{7}$ of $1568 + 265.75 = x + 2455.60$

$\Rightarrow 12992 + 265.75 - 2455.60 = x$

$\therefore\ x = 10802.15$

83. $x = \frac{a}{a-1}$ and $y = \frac{1}{a-1}$

Now, $1 + y = 1 + \dfrac{1}{a-1} = \dfrac{a}{a-1} = x$

Hence, $x > y$

84. $\dfrac{x}{y} = \dfrac{4}{5}$ $\quad\therefore\ x = \dfrac{4y}{5}$

Now, $\dfrac{4}{7} + \dfrac{2y-x}{2y+x} = \dfrac{4}{7} + \dfrac{2y - \frac{4y}{5}}{2y + \frac{4y}{5}} = \dfrac{4}{7} + \dfrac{\frac{10-4}{5}}{\frac{10+4}{5}} = \dfrac{4}{7} + \dfrac{3}{7} = 1$

85. $\dfrac{x}{y} = 7$

Then, $\dfrac{x+y}{x-y} = \dfrac{\frac{x}{y}+1}{\frac{x}{y}-1} = \dfrac{7+1}{7-1} = \dfrac{8}{6} = \dfrac{4}{3}$

86. $3 - [1.6 - \{3.2 - (3.2 + 2.25 \div x)\}] = 0.65$

$\Rightarrow 3 - [1.6 - \{3.2 - 3.2 - \dfrac{2.25}{x}\}] = 0.65$

$\Rightarrow 1.6 + \dfrac{2.25}{x} = 3 - 0.65$

$\Rightarrow \dfrac{2.25}{x} = 2.35 - 1.6$

$\Rightarrow x = \dfrac{2.25}{0.75} = 3$

87. $2.002 + 7.9\ \{2.8 - 6.3\ \{3.6 - 1.5) + 15.6\}$

$= 2.002 + 7.9\ \{2.8 - 6.3 \times 2.1 + 15.6\}$

$= 2.002 + 7.9\ \{18.4 - 13.23\}$

$= 2.002 + 7.9 \times 5.17$

$= 2.002 + 40.843$

$= 42.845$

88. Here, $\dfrac{a+b+2c+3d}{a+b-2c-3d} = \dfrac{a-b+2c-3d}{a-b-2c+3d}$

$\Rightarrow \dfrac{2(a+b)}{2(2c+3d)} = \dfrac{2(a-b)}{2(2c-3d)}$ (Applying C & D)

$\Rightarrow \dfrac{a+b}{a-b} = \dfrac{2c+3d}{2c-3d}$

$\Rightarrow \dfrac{2a}{2b} = \dfrac{4c}{6d}$ (Again applying C & D)

$\therefore\ 2bc = 3ad$

89. $\frac{2a+b}{a+4b}=3$

$\Rightarrow 2a + b = 3a + 12b$

$\Rightarrow a = -11b$

$\Rightarrow \frac{a+b}{a+2b}=\frac{-11b+b}{-11b+2b} = \frac{-10b}{-9b}=\frac{10}{9}$

90. $3x + 7 = x^2 + p = 7x + 5$

Now, $3x + 7 = 7x + 5$

$\Rightarrow 4x = 2 \qquad \therefore x = \frac{1}{2}$

Again, $3 \times \frac{1}{2} + 7 = \left(\frac{1}{2}\right)^2 + p$

$\therefore p = \frac{17}{2}-\frac{1}{4}=\frac{33}{4}=8\frac{1}{4}$

91. Let, $\frac{a}{3}=\frac{b}{4}=\frac{c}{7}=k$

Then, $a = 3k;\ b = 4k;\ c = 7k$

Now, $\frac{a+b+c}{c}=\frac{3k+4k+7k}{7k}=\frac{14k}{7k} = 2$

92. $\frac{a}{x}+\frac{y}{b}=1$ and $\frac{b}{y}+\frac{z}{c}=1$

$\Rightarrow \frac{a}{x}=1-\frac{y}{b}=\frac{b-y}{b}$

$\therefore \frac{x}{a}=\frac{b}{b-y}$

Similarly, $\frac{c}{z}=\frac{y}{y-b}$

Now, $\frac{x}{a}+\frac{c}{z}=\frac{b}{b-y}+\frac{y}{y-b}=\frac{b-y}{b-y}=1$

93. $0 < a < 1$, then, $\frac{1}{a}> 1 \qquad \therefore \left(a+\frac{1}{a}\right)> 2$

94. $x+\cfrac{1}{1+\cfrac{1}{3+\cfrac{1}{4}}}=2 \qquad \Rightarrow x + \cfrac{1}{1+\cfrac{4}{13}}=2$

$\Rightarrow x + \frac{13}{17} = 2 \qquad \therefore x = 2 - \frac{13}{17} = \frac{21}{17}$

95. $\dfrac{1}{2+\dfrac{1}{2+\dfrac{1}{2-\dfrac{1}{2}}}} = \dfrac{1}{2+\dfrac{1}{2+\dfrac{2}{3}}} = \dfrac{1}{2+\dfrac{3}{8}} = \dfrac{1}{19/8} = \dfrac{8}{19}$

96. $\dfrac{2+\dfrac{1}{19/5}}{2+\dfrac{1}{3+\dfrac{1}{1+\dfrac{1}{4}}}} = \dfrac{2+\dfrac{5}{19}}{2+\dfrac{1}{3+\dfrac{4}{5}}} = \dfrac{\dfrac{43}{19}}{2+\dfrac{5}{19}} = \dfrac{\dfrac{43}{19}}{\dfrac{43}{19}} = 1$

97. $\dfrac{2}{2+\dfrac{2}{3+\dfrac{2}{3+\dfrac{2}{3}}}\times 0.39} = \dfrac{2}{2+\dfrac{2}{3+2\times\dfrac{3}{11}}\times 0.39} = \dfrac{2}{2+\dfrac{2}{\dfrac{33+6}{11}}\times 0.39}$

$= \dfrac{2}{2+2\times\dfrac{11}{39}\times 0.39} = \dfrac{2}{2+\dfrac{22}{100}} = \dfrac{2\times 100}{222} = \dfrac{100}{111}$

98. $8-8\times\dfrac{\dfrac{11}{5}-\dfrac{9}{7}}{2-\dfrac{1}{6-\dfrac{1}{6}}} = 8-8\times\dfrac{\dfrac{77-45}{35}}{2-\dfrac{6}{35}} = 8-8\times\dfrac{\dfrac{32}{35}}{\dfrac{64}{35}} = 8-8\times\dfrac{1}{2} = 4$

99. $\dfrac{1}{1+\dfrac{\dfrac{2}{3}}{1+\dfrac{2}{3}+\dfrac{8/9}{1-2/3}}} = \dfrac{1}{1+\dfrac{\dfrac{2}{3}}{1+\dfrac{2}{3}+\dfrac{8}{9}\times 3}} = \dfrac{1}{1+\dfrac{\dfrac{2}{3}}{1+\dfrac{10}{3}}} = \dfrac{1}{1+\dfrac{2}{3}\times\dfrac{3}{13}} = \dfrac{1}{\dfrac{15}{13}} = \dfrac{13}{15}$

100. $2+\dfrac{1}{x+\dfrac{1}{y+\dfrac{1}{z}}} = \dfrac{37}{13} \Rightarrow \dfrac{1}{x+\dfrac{1}{y+\dfrac{1}{z}}} = \dfrac{37}{13}-2$

$\Rightarrow x+\dfrac{1}{y+\dfrac{1}{z}} = \dfrac{13}{11} \quad \Rightarrow x+\dfrac{1}{y+\dfrac{1}{z}} = 1+\dfrac{2}{11}$

Then, $x = 1$ & $y + \frac{1}{z} = \frac{11}{2}$ $\Rightarrow y + \frac{1}{z} = 5 + \frac{1}{2}$

Hence, $y = 5$, $z = 2$

Therefore, $x = 1$, $y = 5$, $z = 2$

101. $3x + y = 19$ ...*(i)*

$x - y = 9$ ...*(ii)*

Ading equations *(i)* & *(ii)* and solving we get

$x = 7$ & $y = -2$

102. $\frac{x}{5} - \frac{x}{6} = 4$

$\Rightarrow \frac{x}{30} = 4$

$\therefore x = 120$

103. $a + b = 5$ ...*(i)* $3a + 2b = 20$ ...*(ii)*

Multiplying equation *(i)* by 3 and subtracting from *(ii)* we get

$b = -5$, Now, $a + (-5) = 5$ $\therefore a = 10$

Now, $3a + b = 3 \times 10 + (-5) = 25$

104. $\frac{3x}{2y} = \frac{21}{22}$ $\therefore$ $x = \frac{7}{11}y$

Now, $4x + 5y = 83$

$\Rightarrow 4 \times \frac{7}{11}y + 5y = 83 \Rightarrow \frac{28y + 55y}{11} = 83 \Rightarrow \frac{83y}{11} = 83$ $\therefore y = 11$

Then, $x = \frac{7}{11}y = \frac{7}{11} \times 11 = 7$

Now, $(y - x) = 11 - 7 = 4$

105. $2x + 3y = 31$ ...(i)

$y - z = 4$ ...(ii)

$x + 2z = 11$ ...(iii)

Multiplying equation (ii) by 2 and adding with (iii) we get

$x + 2y = 19$ ...(iv)

Multiplying equation (iv) by 2 and subtracting (i) from it, we get, $y = 7$,

From equation (ii) $z = y - 4 = 7 - 4 = 3$

From equation (iii) $x + 2 \times 3 = 11$ $\therefore x = 5$

Now, $x + y + z = 5 + 3 + 7 = 15$

106. $2x + y = 17$ ...(i)

$y + 2z = 15$ ...(ii)

$x + y = 9$ ...(iii)

Subtracting equation *(iii)* from *(i)*, we get $x = 8$

From equation *(iii)*, $8 + y = 9$ $\therefore y = 1$

From equation *(ii)*, $2z = 15 - 1$ $\therefore z = 7$

Now, $4x + 3y + z = 4 \times 8 + 3 \times 1 + 7 = 42$

107. $3x - 5y = 5$ ...(*i*)

And $\frac{x}{x+y} = \frac{5}{7} \Rightarrow 2x - 5y = 0$ ...(*ii*)

Subtracting equation (*ii*) from (*i*) we get $x = 5$

From (*ii*) $5y = 2 \times 5 \quad \therefore y = 2$

Hence, $x - y = 5 - 2 = 3$

108. $\frac{3}{4}\left(1+\frac{1}{3}\right)\left(1+\frac{2}{3}\right)\left(1-\frac{2}{5}\right)\left(1+\frac{6}{7}\right)\left(1-\frac{12}{13}\right)$

$= \frac{3}{4} \times \frac{4}{3} \times \frac{5}{3} \times \frac{3}{5} \times \frac{13}{7} \times \frac{1}{13} = \frac{1}{7}$

109. $\left(1+\frac{1}{2}\right)\left(1+\frac{1}{3}\right)\left(1-\frac{1}{4}\right)...\left(1+\frac{1}{120}\right)$

$= \frac{3}{2} \times \frac{4}{3} \times \frac{5}{4} \times ... \times \frac{121}{120} = \frac{121}{2} = 60.5$

110. $\left(1-\frac{1}{2}\right)\left(1-\frac{1}{3}\right)\left(1-\frac{1}{4}\right)...\left(1-\frac{1}{n}\right)$

$= \frac{1}{2} \times \frac{2}{3} \times \frac{3}{4} \times ... \times \frac{n-1}{n} = \frac{1}{n}$

111. $999\frac{1}{7} + 999\frac{2}{7} + 999\frac{3}{7} + 999\frac{4}{7} + 999\frac{5}{7} + 999\frac{6}{7}$

$= (999 + 999 + 999 + 999 + 999 + 999) + \left(\frac{1}{7}+\frac{2}{7}+\frac{3}{7}+\frac{4}{7}+\frac{5}{7}+\frac{6}{7}\right)$

$= 5994 + 3 = 5997$

112. $999\frac{995}{999} \times 999 = \left(1000 - \frac{4}{999}\right) \times 999 = 999000 - 4 = 998996$

113. $\frac{3}{1^2.2^2} + \frac{5}{2^2.3^2} + \frac{7}{3^2.4^2} + \frac{9}{4^2.5^2} + \frac{11}{5^2.6^2} + \frac{13}{6^2.7^2} + \frac{15}{7^2.8^2} + \frac{17}{8^2.9^2} + \frac{19}{9^2.10^2}$

$= 1 - \frac{1}{4} + \frac{1}{4} - \frac{1}{9} + \frac{1}{9} - \frac{1}{16} + \frac{1}{16} - \frac{1}{25} + \frac{1}{25} - \frac{1}{36} + \frac{1}{36} - \frac{1}{49} + \frac{1}{49} - \frac{1}{64} + \frac{1}{64} - \frac{1}{81} + \frac{1}{81} - \frac{1}{100}$

$= 1 - \frac{1}{100} = \frac{99}{100}$

114. $1 + \frac{1}{4 \times 3} + \frac{1}{4 \times 3^2} + \frac{1}{4 \times 3^3} = \frac{108+9+3+1}{4 \times 3^3} = \frac{121}{108}$

115. $\frac{1}{1 \cdot 2 \cdot 3} + \frac{1}{2 \cdot 3 \cdot 4} + \frac{1}{3 \cdot 4 \cdot 5} + \frac{1}{4 \cdot 5 \cdot 6} = \frac{120+30+12+6}{1 \cdot 2 \cdot 3 \cdot 4 \cdot 5 \cdot 6} = \frac{168}{720} = \frac{7}{30}$

116. Let the monthly salary of a man be Rs. x then monthly salary of a woman will be Rs. $(x + 500)$

Now, $4x + 2(x + 500) = 46000$

$\Rightarrow 6x = 45000 \quad \therefore \quad x = \text{Rs. } 7500$

Hence, monthly salary of a woman = 7500 + 500 = Rs. 8000

117. Required distance $= \frac{225}{25} = 9$ meters.

118. Required cost $= 1000\,x + (z - 1000)\,y = 1000\,(x - y) + yz$

119. Number of digits from page : 1 to 9 = 9

Number of digits from page : 10 to 99 = 2 × 90 = 180

Number of digits from page : 100 to 999 = 3 × 900 = 2700

Then number of digits in 4-digits page numbers = 3189 − (9 + 180 + 2700)
= 3189 − 2889
= 300

Hence, number of pages in 4 digits number $= \frac{300}{4} = 75$

Therefore, total number of pages of the book = 999 + 75 = 1074

120. Total number of digits = 9 + 2 × 90 + 3 (366 − 99)
= 9 + 180 + 3 × 267 = 189 + 801 = 990

121. $\frac{F-32}{212-32} = \frac{C-0}{100}$

$\Rightarrow \frac{F-32}{180} = \frac{C}{100}$

$\therefore \; F = \frac{180}{100}C + 32$

$= \frac{9}{5} \times 35 + 32 = 95$

Hence, 35° C = 95° F

122. Let the marks obtained in History and English be x & $\frac{5}{2}x$

Now, $x + \frac{5}{2}x = 140 \quad \Rightarrow \frac{7x}{2} = 140 \qquad \therefore x = 40$

Hence, marks obtained in English $= \frac{5}{2} \times 40 = 100$

123. Let the number of pineapple and watermelon be x and y.

Now, $7x + 5y = 38$

$\therefore \; y = \frac{38 - 7x}{5}$

It is clear that x and y will be whole numbers.

only $x = 4$ give the y as a whole number

Hence, number of pineapple = 4

124. In two days, Ram saves Rs. 5
Then in 16 days he will save = 8 × Rs. 5 = Rs. 40
On 17th day he had = Rs. 40 + Rs. 20 = Rs. 60

125. Income after 1 year = 4 × 2 = Rs. 8 lakh
Income after 2 years = 4×2^2 = Rs. 16 lakhs
Similarly, Income after 5 years = 4×2^5 = Rs. 128 lakhs = Rs. 1.28 crores

126.

3 hrs.	17 min.	49 sec
− 1 hr.	54 min.	50 sec
1 hr.	22 min.	59 sec

Time interval = 1 hr. 22 min. 59 sec = (3600 + 1320 + 59) sec = 4979 sec

Hence, the number of times light is seen = $\frac{4979}{13} + 1 = 383 + 1 = 384$

127. Total number of children = 30 × 16 = 480

Required number of columns = $\frac{480}{24} = 20$

128. $\frac{3}{4}x - \frac{3}{14}x = 150 \quad \Rightarrow \quad \frac{15x}{28} = 150 \quad \therefore x = 280$

129. The part of green portion $= 1 - \left(\frac{1}{10} + \frac{1}{20} + \frac{1}{30} + \frac{1}{40} + \frac{1}{50} + \frac{1}{60}\right)$

$$= 1 - \left(\frac{60+30+20+15+12+10}{600}\right)$$

$$= 1 - \frac{147}{600} = \frac{453}{600}$$

Now, $\frac{453}{600}x = 12.08 \quad \therefore \quad x = \frac{12.08 \times 600}{453} = \frac{1208 \times 6}{453} = 16$ m

Hence, length of the pole = 16 m

130. The distance travelled on foot $= 3.5 - \left(\frac{5}{3} + \frac{7}{6}\right) = 3.5 - \frac{17}{6} = \frac{2}{3}$ km

Required portion $= \frac{2}{3 \times 3.5} = \frac{2}{10.5} = \frac{4}{21}$

131. $\frac{4}{7} + \frac{4}{7}x = \frac{15}{14} \quad \Rightarrow \quad \frac{4}{7}(1 + x) = \frac{15}{14}$

$\therefore \ x = \frac{15}{14} \times \frac{7}{4} - 1 = \frac{15}{8} - 1 = \frac{7}{8}$

132. $\frac{1}{3} \times x = 80 \Rightarrow x = 240 \quad \therefore \quad \frac{1}{2}x = 120\ l$

133. Required height = $32 \times \frac{3}{4} \times \frac{3}{4} \times \frac{3}{4} = \frac{27}{2} = 13\frac{1}{2}$ m

134. Required part of his earnings = $\frac{2x}{11x + 2x} = \frac{2}{13}$

135. Let total number of people = x

Then number of Indian people = $\left(\frac{1}{5} + \frac{1}{5} + \frac{1}{5} \times \frac{2}{3}\right)x = \left(\frac{2}{5} + \frac{2}{15}\right)x = \frac{8}{15}x$

Now number of Non-Indian people = $x - \frac{8}{15}x = \frac{7}{15}x$

Hence, required fraction = $\frac{7}{15}$

136. 135 l = $\frac{1}{4}$ of a tank

$\therefore$ 180 l = $\frac{1}{4 \times 135} \times 180 = \frac{1}{3}$ of a tank

137. Required fraction of total number = $\frac{1+1}{5+8} = \frac{2}{13}$

138. Let B gets Rs. x then A and C will be get Rs. $\frac{2}{3}x$ and Rs. $4x$

Now, $\frac{2}{3}x + x + 4x = 1360 \Rightarrow \frac{17x}{3} = 1360 \quad \therefore x = \frac{1360 \times 3}{17}$ = Rs 240

139. Let the total money of the man = Rs. x

Share of his wife = Rs. $\frac{x}{2}$

Share of his each son = $\frac{1}{3} \times \frac{2}{3} \times$ Rs. $\frac{x}{2}$ = Rs. $\frac{x}{9}$

Share of his each daughter = $\frac{1}{4}\left(\frac{x}{2} - \frac{x}{3}\right)$ = Rs. $\frac{x}{24}$

Now, $\frac{x}{24} = 20{,}000 \quad \therefore \frac{x}{9} = \frac{20000 \times 24}{9}$ = Rs. 53,333.33

Hence, share of each son = Rs. 53,333.33

140. Let the total number of pages of the book be x.

Then, $x - \left[\frac{3}{8}x + \frac{4}{5}\left(x - \frac{3}{8}x\right)\right] = 30$

$\Rightarrow x - \left[\frac{3}{8}x + \frac{4}{5} \times \frac{5x}{8}\right] = 30$

$\Rightarrow x - \frac{7x}{8} = 30 \quad \Rightarrow \frac{x}{8} = 30 \quad \Rightarrow x = 240$

Hence, total number of pages = 240

141. Let his savings in National Saving Certificate and Public Provident Fund be Rs. x and Rs. y.

Now, $\frac{1}{3}x = \frac{1}{2}y \quad \therefore \quad x = \frac{3}{2}y$

Now, $x + y = 1{,}50{,}000 \quad \Rightarrow \quad \frac{3}{2}y + y = 1{,}50{,}000$

$\Rightarrow \frac{5y}{2} = 1{,}50{,}000 \quad \therefore \quad y = \text{Rs. } 60{,}000$

142. Let the capacity of a large and a small bottle be $x\ l$ and $y\ l$.

Now, $4x = 7y \quad \therefore \quad y = \frac{4}{7}x$

Hence, liquid remained in large bottle = $x - \frac{4}{7}x = \frac{3x}{7}$

Therefore required fraction = $\frac{3}{7}$

143. Let the amount belonging to Ram be Rs. x

Then amount received by Shyam = Rs. $\frac{x}{4}$

and amount received by Mohan = Rs. $\frac{x}{8}$

Now, remaining amount with Ram = $x - \frac{x}{4}$ = Rs. $\frac{3x}{4}$

Again, $\frac{3x}{4} - \frac{x}{8} = 500 \quad \Rightarrow \quad \frac{5x}{8} = 500 \quad \therefore \quad x = \text{Rs. } 800$

Hence, the amount received by Shyam = Rs. $\frac{x}{4}$ = Rs. $\frac{800}{4}$ = Rs. 200

144. Required difference = $\frac{47}{50} \times 10 - \frac{14}{50} \times 10 = \frac{1}{5} \times 33 = 6.6$

145. $n \times \frac{2}{5}x = 25x \quad \therefore \quad n = \frac{125}{2} = 62\frac{1}{2}$ (where x be the capacity of original bucket)

146. Let total number of shots be x

The number of shots fired by A = $\frac{5}{8}x$

The number of shots fired by B = $\frac{3}{8}x$

The number of shots missed by B = $\frac{1}{2} \times \frac{3}{8} x = \frac{3}{16} x$

The number of killing shots by A = $\frac{1}{3} \times \frac{5}{8} x = \frac{5}{24} x$

Now, $\frac{3}{16} x = 27 \qquad \therefore \quad x = 144$

Then, $\frac{5}{24} x = \frac{5}{24} \times 144 = 30$

Hence, A has killed 30 birds.

147. Let the number of boys and girls be x and y respectively.

$\frac{1}{3} x = 100 \qquad \therefore \quad x = 300$

$\frac{1}{2} y = 200 \qquad \therefore \quad y = 400$

Total number of students = $x + y = 300 + 400 = 700$

148. $\frac{x^3 - y^3}{x^2 - y^2} = \frac{(x-y)(x^2+xy+y^2)}{(x-y)(x+y)} = \frac{x^2+xy+y^2}{x+y}$ (where, $x = \frac{3}{5}$; $y = \frac{2}{5}$)

Now, $\frac{\left(\frac{3}{5}\right)^2 + \frac{3}{5} \times \frac{2}{5} + \left(\frac{2}{5}\right)^2}{\frac{3}{5} + \frac{2}{5}} = \frac{\frac{9}{25} + \frac{6}{25} + \frac{4}{25}}{1} = \frac{19}{25}$

149. $\frac{x^2+xy+y^2}{x^3-y^3} = \frac{(x^2+xy+y^2)}{(x-y)(x^2+xy+y^2)} = \frac{1}{x-y}$ (where, $x = 147$; $y = 143$)

Now, $\frac{1}{x-y} = \frac{1}{147-143} = \frac{1}{4}$

150. $\frac{x^3+y^3}{x^2-xy+y^2} = \frac{(x+y)(x^2-xy+y^2)}{(x^2-xy+y^2)} = x+y$ (where $x = 785$; $y = 435$)

Now, $x + y = 785 + 435 = 1220$

151. $\frac{(13)^3 + 7^3}{(13)^2 + 7^2 - ?} = 20$

$\Rightarrow (13)^2 + (7)^2 - ? = \frac{(13)^3 + (7)^3}{(13+7)} = \frac{(13+7)(13^2 + 7^2 - 13 \times 7)}{(13+7)}$ (Putting, $20 = 13 + 7$)

Now, $13^2 + 7^2 - ? = 13^2 + 7^2 - 91$

$\therefore \; ? = 91$

152. $\dfrac{x^2+y^2+z^2-64}{xy-yz-zx}=-2$

$\therefore\ x^2 + y^2 + z^2 - 64 = -2\,(xy - yz - zx)$ ...(i)

Now, $(x + y - z)^2 = x^2 + y^2 + z^2 + 2\,(xy - yz - zx)$

$\Rightarrow (3z - z)^2 = x^2 + y^2 + z^2 + 2\,(xy - yz - zx)$ $(\because\ x + y = 3z)$

$\therefore\ x^2 + y^2 + z^2 - 4z^2 = -2\,(xy - yz - zx)$ ...(ii)

From (i) and (ii), we get,

$4z^2 = 64 \quad\Rightarrow\quad z^2 = 16 \quad\therefore\quad z = 4$

153. $(a + b + c)^2 = a^2 + b^2 + c^2 + 2(ab + bc + ca)$

$\therefore$ ab + bc + ca $=\dfrac{(a+b+c)^2-(a^2+b^2+c^2)}{2}=\dfrac{(13)^2-69}{2}=\dfrac{169-69}{2}=\dfrac{100}{2}=50$

154. Here, $\dfrac{a^2-b^2}{a+b}=\dfrac{(a+b)(a-b)}{(a+b)}=(a+b)$

Now, $a-b=\left(1+\dfrac{1}{1+\dfrac{1}{100}}\right)-\left(1-\dfrac{1}{1+\dfrac{1}{100}}\right)$

$=\dfrac{1}{101/100}+\dfrac{1}{101/100}=\dfrac{100}{101}+\dfrac{100}{101}=\dfrac{200}{101}$

155. $\dfrac{a^2-b^2}{c^2-d^2}\div\dfrac{a-b}{c-d}=\dfrac{(a-b)(a+b)}{(c+d)(c-d)}\times\dfrac{(c-d)}{(a-b)}=\dfrac{a+b}{c+d}$

Now, $\dfrac{a+b}{c+d}=\dfrac{\dfrac{11}{3}+\dfrac{5}{2}}{\dfrac{19}{4}+\dfrac{10}{3}}=\dfrac{\dfrac{22+15}{6}}{\dfrac{57+40}{12}}=\dfrac{37}{6}\times\dfrac{12}{97}=\dfrac{74}{97}$

156. $\dfrac{(a+b)^2-(a-b)^2}{ab}=\dfrac{4ab}{ab}=4$

157. $\dfrac{x^2-1}{x+1}=4 \quad\Rightarrow\quad \dfrac{(x+1)(x-1)}{(x+1)}=4 \quad\Rightarrow x-1=4 \quad\therefore\ x=5$

158. $(a-b)^2=a^2+b^2-2ab$

$\therefore\ ab=\dfrac{(a^2+b^2)-(a-b)^2}{2}=\dfrac{29-3^2}{2}=\dfrac{20}{2}=10$

159. Let the number of sweets to be given to a student = x

Now, $175x = 140\,(x + 4) \quad\Rightarrow\quad 175x - 140x = 560 \quad\therefore\quad x=\dfrac{560}{35}=16$

Total number of sweets available = 175 × 16 = 2800

160. Let the number of hens and cows be x and y respectively.

Then, $x + y = 48$ $\quad\therefore\quad y = (48 - x)$ ...(i)

Again, $2x + 4(48 - x) = 140$ $\quad\Rightarrow\quad 2x - 4x = 140 - 192$

$\Rightarrow 2x = 52$ $\quad\therefore\quad x = 26$

161. Initially share of each person $= \frac{1}{8}$

New share of each person $= \frac{1}{7}$

Increased in each share $= \frac{1}{7} - \frac{1}{8} = \frac{8-7}{56} = \frac{1}{56}$

Then, share of each person increased by $= \dfrac{\frac{1}{56}}{\frac{1}{8}} = \frac{1}{56} \times 8 = \frac{1}{7}$

162. Let the total number of children be x;

then, share of notebooks of each child $= \frac{x}{8}$

New share of notebooks of each children $= \frac{x}{4}$

Now, $\frac{x}{4} = 16$ $\quad\therefore\quad x = 64$

Total number of note books $= x \times \frac{x}{8} = 64 \times \frac{64}{8} = 512$

163. $x \times 1 + x \times 5 + x \times 10 = 480$ $\quad\Rightarrow\quad 16x = 480$ $\quad\therefore\quad x = 30$

Hence, total number of notes $= 3x = 3 \times 30 = 90$

164. Let the number of buffaloes and duck be x and y respectively.

Now, $4x + 2y - 2(x + y) = 24$ $\quad\Rightarrow\quad 2x = 24$ $\quad\therefore\quad x = 12$

165. Let number of 25 paise coins be x.

Now, $x \times \frac{1}{4} + (324 - x) \times \frac{1}{5} = 71$

$\Rightarrow \frac{x}{4} - \frac{x}{5} = 71 - \frac{324}{5}$ $\quad\Rightarrow\quad \frac{x}{20} = \frac{31}{5}$ $\quad\therefore\quad x = 124$

166. $\frac{3,25,000}{N} - \frac{3,00,000}{N} = 50$ $\quad\Rightarrow\quad \frac{25000}{N} = 50$ $\quad\therefore\quad N = 500$

167. Let the number of matches, they lost be x.

Now, $(x + 3) \times 2 - x \times 1 = 23$ $\quad\Rightarrow\quad x = 17$

Total number of matches $= (x + 3) + x = (17 + 3) + 17 = 37$

168. Let, the number of students in rooms A and B be $x + 20$ and x respectively.

Now, $2(x - 20) = x + 20 + 20$ $\quad\Rightarrow\quad 2x - x = 40 + 40$ $\quad\therefore x = 80$

Hence, number of students in room A $= x + 20 = 80 + 20 = 100$

169. Let the number of correct and wrong answers be x and $(60 - x)$ respectively.

Now, $x \times 4 - (60 - x) \times 1 = 130$ $\quad\Rightarrow\quad 4x + x = 130 + 60$

$\Rightarrow 5x = 190$ $\quad\therefore\quad x = 38$

170. Let they meet after x minute,

Then, $11 + 57x = 51 - 63x \Rightarrow 120x = 40 \quad \therefore x = \frac{1}{3}$ min.

In 1/3 min. Ram will ride up $1/3 \times 57 = 19$ floors.

Hence, they will meet in $11 + 19 = 30$th floor.

171. Let cost of a table and a chair be Rs. x and y respectively.

Now, $2x + 3y = 3500$ ...*(i)* $\quad 3x + 2y = 4000$ ...*(ii)*

Multiplying equation *(i)* by 2 and *(ii)* by 3 and subtracting, we get

$5y = 5000 \quad \therefore \quad y = 1000$

Hence, cost of a table = Rs. 1000

172. Let the number of girls and boys be x and $(100 - x)$ respectively.

Now, $x \times 2.40 + (100 - x) \times 3.60 = 312$

$\Rightarrow 1.20x = 48 \quad \therefore \quad x = \frac{480}{12} = 40$

173. Cost of (2 sarees + 4 shirts) = Rs. 1600

Then, cost of (1 saree + 2 shirts) = Rs. 800 ...(i)

Again, cost of (1 saree + 6 shirts) = Rs. 1600 ...(ii)

Solving equation (i) and (ii) we get,

Cost of 4 shirts = Rs. 800

Hence, cost of 12 shirts = 3 × Rs. 800 = Rs. 2400

174. Here, Cost of 1 table = Cost of $\frac{5}{2}$ chairs.

Cost of (15 chairs + 2 tables) = Cost of (15 chairs + $2 \times \frac{5}{2}$ chairs) = cost of 20 chairs.

Now cost of (12 chairs + 3 tables) = cost of (12 chairs + $3 \times \frac{5}{2}$ chairs) = cost of $\frac{39}{2}$ chairs

Since, cost of 20 chairs = Rs. 4000

$\therefore$ cost of $\frac{39}{2}$ chairs = $\frac{4000}{20} \times \frac{39}{2}$ = Rs. 3900

175. Let, he works x hours for overtime.

Then, $4 \times 5 \times 8 \times$ Rs. $2.40 + x \times$ Rs. 3.20 = Rs. 432

$\Rightarrow 3.20x = 432 - 384 \quad \Rightarrow \quad 3.20x = 48 \quad \therefore \quad x = \frac{480}{32} = 15$ hrs.

Hence, total number of working hours = 160 + 15 = 175

176. Let original cost of each tennis ball = Rs. x

Now, $\frac{450}{x-15} - \frac{450}{x} = 5 \quad \Rightarrow \quad \frac{90(x-x+15)}{x(x-15)} = 1$

$\Rightarrow x^2 - 15x - 1350 = 0 \quad \Rightarrow \quad x^2 - 45x + 30x - 1350 = 0$

$\Rightarrow x(x - 45) + 30(x - 45) = 0 \quad \Rightarrow \quad (x - 45)(x + 30) = 0$

Either, $x = 45$ or, $x = -30$ (Impossible)

Hence, number of balls purchased = $\frac{450}{45} = 10$

3 LCM AND HCF

L.C.M.

Multiple : A number is said to be multiple of other when it is exactly divisible by the other.

Common multiple : A common multiple of two or more numbers is a number which is exactly divisible by each of them. For example, for 2 and 3, common multiples are 6, 12, 18, 24 and so on.

Explanation:

Consider the two numbers 2 and 3

Multiple of 2 are 2, 4, 6, 8, 10, 12, ...

Multiple of 3 are 3, 6, 9, 12, 15, ...

∴ Common multiples are 6, 12, 18, ...

Least Common Multiple (L.C.M.) : L.C.M. of two or more given numbers is the least number which is exactly divisible by each of them. For example,

6 is a common multiple of 2 and 3

12 is also common multiple of 2 and 3

18 is also common multiple of 2 and 3

But 6 is the least common multiple (L.C.M.) of 2 and 3.

Methods to find out L.C.M.

L.C.M. of two or more given numbers is determined by following two methods:

1. By prime factorization method
2. By division method

1. By prime factorization method : Resolve the given numbers into their prime factors and then find the product of the highest power of all the factors that occur in the given numbers. This product will be the L.C.M.

Example 1 : Find the L.C.M. of 40, 50, 60 and 80.

Sol :
$$40 = 2 \times 2 \times 2 \times 5 = 2^3 \times 5$$
$$50 = 2 \times 5 \times 5 = 2 \times 5^2$$
$$60 = 2 \times 2 \times 3 \times 5 = 2^2 \times 3 \times 5$$
$$80 = 2 \times 2 \times 2 \times 2 \times 5 = 2^4 \times 5$$

Here, the prime factors that occur in the given numbers are 2, 3 and 5 and their highest powers are respectively 2^4, 5^2 and 3.

Hence, the required L.C.M. = $2^4 \times 3 \times 5^2 = 1200$.

2. By division method : This is the quicker method to find the prime factors and hence L.C.M.

For determining L.C.M. of the numbers 40, 50, 60 and 80, following process of division is adopted:

2	40, 50, 60, 80
2	20, 25, 30, 40
2	10, 25, 15, 20
5	5, 25, 15, 10
	1, 5, 3, 2

Now required L.C.M. = $2 \times 2 \times 2 \times 5 \times 5 \times 3 \times 2 = 1200$

L.C.M. of decimal : First of all, we find out the L.C.M. of numbers without decimal and then, we see the number in which decimal is given in the minimum digit from right to left. We put the decimal in our result which is equal to that number of digits.

Example : Find the L.C.M. of 0.6, 9.6 and 0.36.

Sol : The given numbers are equivalent to 0.60, 9.60 and 0.36.

Now, we find out the L.C.M. of 60, 960 and 36, which is equal to 2880.

Hence, the required L.C.M. = 28.80.

L.C.M. of fraction : The L.C.M. of two or more fractions is the least fraction or integer which is exactly divisible by each of them.

If $\frac{a}{b}, \frac{c}{d}, \frac{e}{f}$ be the proper fractions, then their L.C.M. is given by

$$\frac{\text{L.C.M. of numerators } a, c, e}{\text{H.C.F. of denominators } b, d, f}$$

An example : Find the L.C.M. of $\frac{1}{2}, \frac{3}{5}, \frac{4}{7}$ and $\frac{5}{12}$.

Sol : $\text{L.C.M.} = \frac{\text{L.C.M. of } 1, 3, 4, 5}{\text{H.C.F. of } 2, 5, 7, 12}$

$$= \frac{60}{1} = 60$$

H.C.F.

Factor : One number is said to be a factor of other when it divides the other exactly. Hence, 5 and 7 are factors of 35.

Common factor : A common factor of two or more numbers is a number that divides each of them exactly. Hence, 5 is a common factor of 15, 25, 35 and 55.

Highest Common Factor (H.C.F.) : H.C.F. of two or more numbers is the largest number by which each given number is divisible without leaving any remainder.

An example : It is required to find the H.C.F. of 6 and 8.

Factors of 6 are 1, 2, 3, 6 and

Factors of 8 are 1, 2, 4, 8.

The common factors are 1, 2, but highest of these is 2. Hence, 2 is the H.C.F.

Note : *The terms Highest Common Divisor (H.C.D.) and Greatest Common Measure (G.C.M.) are often used in the sense of Highest Common Factor (H.C.F.)*

We can find H.C.F. by two methods:

1. By prime factorization method :

An example : Find the H.C.F. of 144, 336 and 2016.

Sol :
$$144 = 2 \times 2 \times 2 \times 2 \times 3 \times 3 = 2^4 \times 3^2$$
$$336 = 2 \times 2 \times 2 \times 2 \times 3 \times 7 = 2^4 \times 3 \times 7$$
$$2016 = 2 \times 2 \times 2 \times 2 \times 2 \times 7 \times 3 \times 3 = 2^5 \times 7 \times 3^2$$

$\therefore$ H.C.F. of given numbers $= 2^4 \times 3 = 48$.

2. By division method : Divide the greater number by the smaller number, divide the divisor by the remainder, divide the remainder by the next remainder, and so on until no remainder is left. The last divisor is the required H.C.F.

An example : Find the H.C.F. of 48, 168 and 324.

Sol :

```
48 ) 168 ( 3
     144
     ----
      24 ) 48 ( 2
           48
           ----
           ××
```

Thus, the H.C.F. of 48 and 168 is 24.

Now, we find out the H.C.F. of 24 and 324

```
24 ) 324 (13
     24
     ----
      84
      72
     ----
      12 ) 24 ( 2
           24
           ----
           ××
```

$\therefore$ Required H.C.F. = 12.

H.C.F. of Decimals : First of all find the H.C.F. of the given numbers ignoring decimals and then put decimal at maximum digits from right to left.

An example : Find the H.C.F. of 0.0012, 1.6 and 2.8.

Sol : First we find the H.C.F. of 12, 16 and 28, which comes to 4.

So, H.C.F. of 0.0012, 1.6 and 2.8 will be 0.0004.

H.C.F. of Fractions : If $\frac{a}{b}, \frac{c}{d}, \frac{e}{f}$, ... be the proper fraction, their H.C.F. is equal to $\frac{\text{H.C.F. of numerators}}{\text{L.C.M. of denominators}}$

An example : Find the H.C.F. of $\frac{54}{9}, 3\frac{9}{17}$ and $\frac{36}{51}$

Sol : Here, $\frac{54}{9} = \frac{6}{1}$; $3\frac{9}{17} = \frac{60}{17}$ and $\frac{36}{51} = \frac{12}{17}$

Hence, the fractions are $\frac{6}{1}, \frac{60}{17}$ and $\frac{12}{17}$

$$\therefore \quad \text{H.C.F.} = \frac{\text{H.C.F. of } 6, 60, 12}{\text{L.C.M. of } 1, 17, 17} = \frac{6}{17}.$$

Relationship Between Two Numbers and Their L.C.M. and H.C.F.

Product of the H.C.F. and the L.C.M. of two numbers is equal to the product of the given numbers.

i.e., 1st number × 2nd number = H.C.F. × L.C.M.

Example 1: *(a)* The L.C.M. and H.C.F. of two numbers are 72 and 6 respectively. If one of the numbers is 18, determine the other.

(b) Product of two numbers is 2560. If H.C.F. of two numbers is 16, determine their L.C.M.

(c) Given that the product of two numbers is 2160 and their H.C.F. is 12. If sum of these two numbers is 96, determine the numbers.

(d) The L.C.M. and H.C.F. of two numbers are 84 and 21 respectively. If the numbers are in the ratio of 1 : 4, then find the larger number?

Solution: *(a)* $\because$ 1st number × 2nd number = H.C.F. of the two numbers × L.C.M. of the numbers

$\therefore$ 18 × 2nd number = 72 × 6

$\therefore$ 2nd number = $\frac{72 \times 6}{18} = 24$

(b) $\because$ Product of the two numbers = L.C.M. × H.C.F.

$\therefore$ 2560 = 16 × L.C.M.

$\therefore$ L.C.M. = $\frac{2560}{16} = 160$

$\therefore$ L.C.M. of the two numbers is 160.

(c) Let the two numbers be x and y respectively.

Now, according to the condition of the problem,

$$x + y = 96$$

$$xy = 2160 \quad \text{... (i)}$$

$\therefore$ $(x - y)^2 = (x + y)^2 - 4xy = (96)^2 - 4 \times 2160$

$= 9216 - 8640 = 576$

$\therefore$ $x - y = \sqrt{576} = 24$ ... *(ii)*

Now, from equations *(i)* and *(ii)*,

$$x + y + x - y = 96 + 24$$

or, $2x = 120 \Rightarrow x = 60$

or, Substituting the value of x in equation *(i)*

$$60 + y = 96 \Rightarrow y = 96 - 60 \Rightarrow y = 36.$$

Hence, it is clear that the two numbers are 60 and 36 respectively.

(d) Let the two numbers be x and $4x$

Now, 1st number × 2nd number = L.C.M. × H.C.F.

or, $x \times 4x = 48 \times 21$

or, $x^2 = \frac{84 \times 21}{4} = 21 \times 21$

or, $x = 21$

$\therefore$ Larger number = 4 × 21 = 84

Example 2 : Determine the H.C.F. of 32, 64, 96 and 128.

Solution:

32 = 2 × 2 × 2 × 2 × 2

64 = 2 × 2 × 2 × 2 × 2 × 2

96 = 2 × 2 × 2 × 2 × 2 × 3

128 = 2 × 2 × 2 × 2 × 2 × 2 × 2

$\therefore$ Required H.C.F. = 2 × 2 × 2 × 2 × 2 = 32

Example 3 : Find the H.C.F. of 8, 9 and 16.

Solution:

```
8 ) 9 ( 1
    8
   ---
   1 ) 8 ( 8
       8
      ---
       ×
```

∴ H.C.F. of 8 and 9 is 1.

Now, we will have to find out the H.C.F. of 1 and 16.

```
1 ) 16 ( 16
    16
   ----
     ×
```

∴ H.C.F. of 1 and 16 is 1

Hence, the required H.C.F. of 8, 9 and 16 is 1.

Example 4 : If $m = 2^5 \times 3^7 \times 5^{10}$ and $n = 2^7 \times 3^8 \times 7^{12}$, determine the H.C.F. of m and n.

Solution:

$$m = 2^5 \times 3^7 \times 5^{10}$$
$$n = 2^7 \times 3^8 \times 7^{12}$$

∴ Common factors in 'm' and 'n' are $2^5 \times 3^7$, which is the H.C.F. of the two quantities.

Example 5 : Find the L.C.M. of 11, 33, 77 and 121.

Solution:

```
11 | 11, 33, 77, 121
   |-----------------
   |  1,  3,  7,  11
```

Hence, required L.C.M. = 11 × 3 × 7 × 11 = 2541

Example 6 : Find the smallest number between 300 and 400 which is exactly divisible by 6, 15 and 18.

Solution: That smallest number will be divisible by the L.C.M. of the given numbers.

Hence, L.C.M. of 6, 15 and 18 :

```
2 | 6, 15, 18
  |-----------
3 | 3, 15,  9
  |-----------
  | 1,  5,  3
```

∴ L.C.M. = 2 × 3 × 5 × 3 = 90

According to the condition of the problem, we have to find out such number between 300 and 400

The required number = 90 × 4 = 360

Example 7 : Find the smallest number which when divided by 25, 35, 45 and 60 leaves a remainder of 18 in each case.

Solution: It is obvious from the given problem that the required smallest number will be 18 more than the L.C.M. of the given numbers.

∴ L.C.M. of the given numbers.

```
5 | 25, 35, 45, 60
  |----------------
3 |  5,  7,  9, 12
  |----------------
  |  5,  7,  3,  4
```

∴ L.C.M. = 5 × 3 × 5 × 7 × 3 × 4 = 6300

The required number = 6300 + 18 = 6318

Example 8 : Find the smallest number which when added to 7, the sum is exactly divisible by 18, 24, 48 and 80.

Solution: It is clear from the given problem that the required smallest number is 7 less than the L.C.M. of the given numbers 18, 24, 48 and 80.

∴ L.C.M. of 18, 24, 48 and 80 :

2	18, 24, 48, 80
2	9, 12, 24, 40
2	9, 6, 12, 20
2	9, 3, 6, 10
3	9, 3, 3, 5
	3, 1, 1, 5

$\therefore$ L.C.M. $= 2 \times 2 \times 2 \times 2 \times 3 \times 3 \times 5 = 720$

Hence, the required number $= 720 - 7 = 713$

Example 9 : Find the largest number which divides 34, 90 and 104 leaving the same remainder in each case.

Solution: The candidates should note that in questions where the largest number is to be found out which divides a set of given three numbers leaving an equal unknown remainder in each case, the H.C.F. of the number obtained on subtracting 1st and 2nd numbers and the number obtained on subtracting 2nd and 3rd numbers will be the required number.

$\therefore$ Number obtained on subtracting 1st and 2nd numbers, *i.e.,* the difference between 34 and 90 $= 90 - 34 = 56$.

And number obtained on subtracting 2nd and 3rd numbers, *i.e,* the difference between 90 and 104 $= 104 - 90 = 14$

$\therefore$ H.C.F. of 56 and 14 :

$$56 = 2 \times 2 \times 2 \times 7$$
$$14 = 2 \times 7$$

$\therefore$ H.C.F. of 56 and 14 $= 2 \times 7 = 14$:

Required number is 14.

Example 10 : The H.C.F. and the L.C.M. of two numbers are 18 and 252 respectively. If one of the numbers is 126, determine the other.

Solution: $\because$ 1st number × 2nd number = H.C.F. × L.C.M.

$\therefore$ $126 \times$ 2nd number $= 18 \times 252$

$\therefore$ 2nd number $= \dfrac{18 \times 252}{126} = 36$

Example 11 : The H.C.F. and the L.C.M. of two numbers are 12 and 120 respectively. If the two numbers are in the ratio of 2 : 5, determine the numbers.

Solution: Let the numbers be $2x$ and $5x$,

$\because$ 1st number × 2nd number = H.C.F. × L.C.M.

$\therefore$ $2x \times 5x = 12 \times 120$

or, $10x^2 = 12 \times 120$

or, $x^2 = \dfrac{12 \times 120}{10} = 12 \times 12$ or, $x = 12$

Therefore, the two numbers are $2 \times 12 = 24$ and $5 \times 12 = 60$ respectively.

Example 12 : Two numbers are in the ratio of 15 : 11. If the H.C.F. of these numbers is 13, determine the numbers.

Solution: Let the numbers be $15x$ and $11x$.

Since the H.C.F. of given numbers is 13 which indicates that 13 is the common factor of these two numbers. Hence, it is obvious that value of x is 13. Therefore, these numbers are $15 \times 13 = 195$ and $11 \times 13 = 143$ respectively.

Example 13 : How many numbers between 200 and 600 are completely divisible by 4, 5 and 6?

Solution: L.C.M. of 4, 5 and 6 = 60

∴ Numbers between 200 and 600 which are completely divisible by 60 are $60 \times 4 = 240$, $60 \times 5 = 300$, $60 \times 6 = 360$, $60 \times 7 = 420$, $60 \times 8 = 480$, $60 \times 9 = 540$ and $60 \times 10 = 600$ respectively. Hence, there are total 7 numbers in between 200 and 600 which are completely divisible by 4, 5 and 6.

Example 14 : Determine the H.C.F. of $\frac{54}{9}$, $3\frac{9}{17}$ and $\frac{36}{51}$.

Solution: $\frac{54}{9} = \frac{6}{1}$, $3\frac{9}{17} = \frac{60}{17}$ and $\frac{36}{51} = \frac{12}{17}$

Now, H.C.F. of $\frac{6}{1}, \frac{60}{17}$ and $\frac{12}{17} = \frac{\text{H.C.F. of 6, 60 and 12}}{\text{L.C.M. of 1, 17 and 17}}$

∵ H.C.F. of 6, 60 and 12 = 6
and L.C.M. of 1, 17 and 17 = 17

∴ Required H.C.F. = $\frac{6}{17}$

Example 15 : Find the L.C.M. of $4\frac{1}{2}$, 3 and $10\frac{1}{2}$.

Solution: $4\frac{1}{2} = \frac{9}{2}$, $10\frac{1}{2} = \frac{21}{2}$

∴ L.C.M. of $\frac{9}{2}, \frac{3}{1}$ and $\frac{21}{2} = \frac{\text{L.C.M. of 9, 3 and 21}}{\text{H.C.F. of 2, 1 and 2}}$

∵ L.C.M. of 9, 3 and 21 = 63
and H.C.F. of 2, 1 and 2 = 1

Hence, required number = $\frac{63}{1} = 63$

Example 16 : Four bells ring respectively at an interval of 6 seconds, 8 seconds, 12 seconds and 18 seconds. They ring together at 12.00 O'clock, then at what time will they ring together again? Also state as to how many times will they ring together during 6 minutes.

Solution: In order to find out the time interval after which they will ring together, we will have to find out the L.C.M. of 6, 8, 12 and 18.

∴ L.C.M. of 6, 8, 12 and 18

2	6, 8, 12, 18
2	3, 4, 6, 9
3	3, 2, 3, 9
	1, 2, 1, 3

∴ L.C.M. = $2 \times 2 \times 3 \times 2 \times 3 = 72$ seconds = 1 minute 12 seconds.
Hence, the four bells will ring together again at 12 hrs. 1 minutes 12 seconds.

∵ 6 minutes = $6 \times 60 = 360$ seconds

∴ Number of times the bells will ring together during 6 minutes = $\frac{360}{72}$
= 5 times

Example 17 : How many times the H.C.F. of 27, 51 and 60 is included in the L.C.M. of these three numbers?

Solution:
$$27 = 3 \times 3 \times 3$$
$$51 = 3 \times 17$$
$$60 = 2 \times 2 \times 3 \times 5$$

$\therefore$ H.C.F. of 27, 51, 60 = 3

L.C.M. of 27, 51, 60 = $2 \times 2 \times 3 \times 3 \times 3 \times 5 \times 17 = 9180$

$$\because \quad \frac{9180}{3} = 3060$$

$\therefore$ H.C.F. of 27, 51 and 60, *i.e.*, 3 is included 3060 times in the L.C.M. of these numbers.

EXERCISE

1. The H.C.F. of 72 and 18 is
(a) 9 *(b)* 72 *(c)* 18 *(d)* 36

2. The L.C.M. of 6, 8, 10 and 12 is
(a) 120 *(b)* 60 *(c)* 240 *(d)* 130

3. The H.C.F. of $\frac{5}{6}, \frac{6}{7}, \frac{7}{8}, \frac{8}{9}$ and $\frac{9}{10}$ is
(a) $\frac{1}{2420}$ *(b)* $\frac{1}{2520}$ *(c)* $\frac{1}{2660}$ *(d)* $\frac{1}{2540}$

4. The L.C.M. of two numbers is 85 and their product is 1020. Their H.C.F. will be
(a) 16 *(b)* 27 *(c)* 12 *(d)* 22

5. The L.C.M. and H.C.F. of two numbers are 4284 and 32 respectively. If one of the numbers is 204, the other is
(a) 672 *(b)* 576 *(c)* 676 *(d)* 572

6. The largest four-digit number divisible by 48, 60 and 64 will be
(a) 7200 *(b)* 9600 *(c)* 8400 *(d)* 10,000

7. L.C.M. of 24, 28, 36 and 44 is a multiple of 24 and which of the following numbers?
(a) 441 *(b)* 231 *(c)* 337 *(d)* 197

8. H.C.F. of 420, 315 and 462 is
(a) 24 *(b)* 28 *(c)* 27 *(d)* 21

9. The smallest number exactly divisible by 3, 4, 6 and 8 is
(a) 26 *(b)* 24 *(c)* 25 *(d)* 28

10. The smallest three-digit number completely divisible by 12, 18 and 24 will be
(a) 72 *(b)* 144 *(c)* 180 *(d)* 224

11. The largest three-digit number, when divided by 6, 9 and 12 leaves 1 as remainder in each case, will be
(a) 887 *(b)* 987 *(c)* 973 *(d)* 730

12. Two numbers are in the ratio of 8 : 15. If their H.C.F. is 4, the numbers are
(a) 32 and 60 *(b)* 16 and 30 *(c)* 80 and 150 *(d)* 64 and 120

13. The largest number that will divide 226 and 272 leaving 1 and 2 as remainders respectively, is
(a) 36 *(b)* 45 *(c)* 55 *(d)* 59

14. Which of the following is the greatest common divisor of 1170 and 102?
(a) 8 *(b)* 4 *(c)* 6 *(d)* 3

15. A number, when 3 is added to it, becomes divisible by 36, 45 and 50. The smallest such number is
(a) 987 *(b)* 798 *(c)* 986 *(d)* 897

16. The least perfect square number which is completely divisible by 10, 20, 30 and 40 is
(a) 4800 *(b)* 3600 *(c)* 4400 *(d)* 2500

17. The product of two numbers is 2160 and their H.C.F. is 12. How many such pairs of numbers can be possibly formed?
(a) 3 *(b)* 1 *(c)* 2 *(d)* None

18. The greatest number that will divide 366, 513 and 324 leaving the same remainder in each case is
(a) 21 *(b)* 18 *(c)* 27 *(d)* 42

19. The sum of two numbers is 216 and their H.C.F. is 27. These numbers are
(a) 60 and 90 *(b)* 81 and 135 *(c)* 64 and 128 *(d)* 30 and 84

20. The L.C.M. of two numbers is 45 times their H.C.F. If the sum of the L.C.M. and the H.C.F. of these two numbers is 1150 and one of the numbers is 125, then the other number is
(a) 256 *(b)* 225 *(c)* 250 *(d)* 255

21. The H.C.F. and the L.C.M. of two numbers are 50 and 250 respectively. On dividing one of these numbers by 2, 50 is obtained as quotient. The numbrs are
(a) 100, 125 *(b)* 80, 100 *(c)* 125, 100 *(d)* 200, 250

22. The largest three-digit number, which when successively divided by 6, 9 and 12, leaves 3 as remainder in each case, is
(a) 575 *(b)* 795 *(c)* 957 *(d)* 525

23. The greatest number that will divide 33, 64 and 80 leaving 3, 4 and 5 as remainders respectively, is
(a) 10 *(b)* 20 *(c)* 15 *(d)* 22

24. The H.C.F. of three numbers is 12. If the three numbers are in the ratio of 1 : 2 : 3, then the numbers are
(a) 14, 28, 42 *(b)* 12, 24, 36 *(c)* 15, 30, 45 *(d)* 24, 48, 72

25. The greatest four-digit number completely divisible by 2, 3, 4 and 5 is
(a) 9960 *(b)* 9690 *(c)* 8990 *(d)* 9980

26. Three bells ring respectively at an interval of 15 seconds, 20 seconds and 24 seconds. If they ring continuously for 12 minutes then how many times, during this period, will they ring together?
(a) 2 times *(b)* 6 times *(c)* 5 times *(d)* 3 times

27. The smallest number, on being successively divided by 5, 6, 8, 9 and 12 leaves 1 as remainder in each case and is completely divisible by 13, will be
(a) 4603 *(b)* 6305 *(c)* 4503 *(d)* 3601

28. If in the process of finding H.C.F. of two numbers by continued division method, 49 is the last divisor and quotients obtained (from the beginning) are 17, 3 and 2 respectively, then the numbers are
(a) 432 and 4929 *(b)* 343 and 5929
(c) 388 and 5880 *(d)* 472 and 5930

29. A, B and C start running together in a particular direction from a particular point on a 12 kms long circular path. If the speeds of A, B and C are 3 kms/h, 7 kms/h and 13 kms/h respectively, then after how many hours will they meet together again?

(a) 8 (b) 6 (c) 12 (d) 10

30. Which of the following has most numbers of divisors?

(a) 182 (b) 176 (c) 101 (d) 99

31. Expressed in simplest form : $\frac{1095}{1168}$

(a) $\frac{25}{26}$ (b) $\frac{17}{26}$ (c) $\frac{15}{16}$ (d) $\frac{13}{16}$

32. Expressed in lowest terms : $\frac{128352}{238368}$

(a) $\frac{9}{13}$ (b) $\frac{7}{13}$ (c) $\frac{5}{13}$ (d) $\frac{3}{4}$

33. A number n is said to be perfect, if the sum of all its divisors (excluding n itself) is equal to n. A perfect number is

(a) 21 (b) 15 (c) 9 (d) 6

34. HCF of $4 \times 27 \times 3125$, $8 \times 9 \times 25 \times 7$ and $16 \times 81 \times 5 \times 11 \times 49$ is

(a) 1260 (b) 540 (c) 360 (d) 180

35. Which is of the following is a co-primes?

(a) (23, 92) (b) (21, 35) (c) (18, 25) (d) (16, 62)

36. The LCM of $2^3 \times 3^2 \times 5 \times 11$, $2^4 \times 3^4 \times 5^2 \times 7$ and $2^5 \times 3^3 \times 5^3 \times 7^2 \times 11$ is :

(a) $2^5 \times 3^4 \times 5^3$ (b) $2^3 \times 3^2 \times 5$

(c) $2^5 \times 3^4 \times 5^3 \times 7^2 \times 11$ (d) $2^3 \times 3^2 \times 5 \times 7 \times 11$

37. The G.C.D. of 1.08, 0.36 and 0.9 is

(a) 0.108 (b) 0.18 (c) 0.9 (d) 0.03

38. H.C.F. of 3240, 3600 and a third number is 36 and their L.C.M. is $2^4 \times 3^5 \times 5^2 \times 7^2$. The third number is

(a) $2^3 \times 3^5 \times 7^2$ (b) $2^5 \times 5^2 \times 7^2$ (c) $2^2 \times 5^3 \times 7^2$ (d) $2^2 \times 3^5 \times 7^2$

39. The ratio of two numbers is 3 : 4 and their H.C.F. is 4. Find their L.C.M.

(a) 48 (b) 24 (c) 16 (d) 12

40. Three numbers are in the ratio 1 : 2 : 3 and their HCF is 12. Find the numbers.

(a) 12, 24, 36 (b) 10, 20, 30 (c) 5, 10, 15 (d) 4, 8, 12

41. If the sum of two numbers is 55 and the H.C.F. and L.C.M. of these numbers are 5 and 120 respectively. Find the sum of their reciprocals.

(a) $\frac{120}{11}$ (b) $\frac{11}{120}$ (c) $\frac{601}{55}$ (d) $\frac{55}{601}$

42. The L.C.M. of two numbers is 495 and their HCF is 5. If the sum of the numbers is 100, then find their difference.

(a) 90 (b) 70 (c) 46 (d) 10

43. The LCM and HCF of two numbers are 84 and 21 respectively. If the ratio of the two numbers is 1 : 4. Find the larger of two numbers.
(*a*) 108 (*b*) 84 (*c*) 48 (*d*) 12

44. The HCF of two numbers is 11 and their LCM is 7700. If one of the number is 275, then find the second number.
(*a*) 318 (*b*) 308 (*c*) 283 (*d*) 279

45. Three numbers are in the ratio of 3 : 4 : 5 and their LCM is 2400. Find their HCF.
(*a*) 200 (*b*) 120 (*c*) 80 (*d*) 40

46. The LCM of two numbers is 48. The numbers are in the ratio of 2 : 3. The sum of the numbers is
(*a*) 64 (*b*) 40 (*c*) 32 (*d*) 28

47. Three numbers which are co-prime to each other are such that the product of the first two is 551 and that of the last two is 1073. Find the sum of three numbers.
(*a*) 89 (*b*) 85 (*c*) 81 (*d*) 75

48. The product of two numbers is 2028 and their HCF is 13. The number of such pair is
(*a*) 4 (*b*) 3 (*c*) 2 (*d*) 1

49. The product of two numbers is 4107. If the H.C.F. of these number is 37, then find the greater number.
(*a*) 185 (*b*) 111 (*c*) 107 (*d*) 101

50. The sum of two numbers is 528 and their H.C.F. is 33. The number of pairs of numbers satisfying the above condition is
(*a*) 12 (*b*) 8 (*c*) 6 (*d*) 4

51. Let N be the greatest number that will divide 1305, 4665 and 6905, leaving the same remainder in each case. Then find the sum of the digits in N.
(*a*) 8 (*b*) 6 (*c*) 5 (*d*) 4

52. Find the greatest number that will divide 43, 91 and 183 so as to leave the same remainder in each case.
(*a*) 13 (*b*) 9 (*c*) 7 (*d*) 4

53. A rectangular courtyard 3.78 m long and 5.25 m wide is to paved exactly with square tiles, all of the same size. What is the largest size of the tile which could be used for the purpose?
(*a*) 7 cm (*b*) 14 cm (*c*) 21 cm (*d*) 42 cm

54. The maximum number of students among them 1001 pens and 910 pencils can be distributed in such a way that each student gets the same number of pens and same number of pencil is
(*a*) 1911 (*b*) 1001 (*c*) 910 (*d*) 91

55. The HCF and LCM of two numbers are 11 and 385 respectively. If one number lies between 75 and 125, then that number is:
(*a*) 110 (*b*) 99 (*c*) 88 (*d*) 77

56. LCM of two prime numbers x and y $(x > y)$ is 161. The value of $3y - x$ is
(*a*) –1 (*b*) –2 (*c*) 2 (*d*) 1

57. The greatest possible length which can be used to measure exactly the length 7m, 3m 85cm, 12m 95 cm is
(*a*) 42 cm (*b*) 35 cm (*c*) 25 cm (*d*) 15 cm

58. Two numbers, both greater than 29, have HCF 29 and LCM 4147. The sum of the numbers is
(*a*) 966 (*b*) 696 (*c*) 669 (*d*) 666

59. The HCF of two numbers is 23 and the other two factors of their LCM are 13 and 14. The larger of the two numbers is
(a) 345 (b) 322 (c) 299 (d) 276

60. The HCF of two numbers is 8. Which one of the following can never be their LCM?
(a) 60 (b) 56 (c) 48 (d) 24

61. The LCM of three different numbers is 120. Which of the following cannot be their HCF?
(a) 35 (b) 24 (c) 12 (d) 8

62. Product of two co-prime numbers is 117. Their LCM should be
(a) 117 (b) 1 (c) 13 (d) 9

63. A, B and C start at the same time in the same direction to run around a circular park. A completes a round in 252 seconds, B in 308 seconds and C in 198 seconds, all starting at the same point. After what time will they meet again at the starting point?
(a) 46 minutes 12 seconds (b) 45 minutes
(c) 42 minutes 36 seconds (d) 26 minutes 18 seconds

64. The least number which when divided by 5, 6, 7 and 8 leaves a remainder 3, but divided by 9 leaves no remainder, is
(a) 3363 (b) 2523 (c) 1683 (d) 1677

65. The least number, which when divided by 48, 60, 72, 108 and 140 leaves 38, 50, 62, 98 and 130 as remainders respectively, is
(a) 15210 (b) 15120 (c) 15110 (d) 11115

66. The least multiple of 7, which leaves a remainder of 4, when divided by 6, 9, 15 and 18 is
(a) 364 (b) 184 (c) 94 (d) 74

67. Let the least number of six digits, which when divided by 4, 6, 10 and 15, leaves in each case the same remainder of 2, be N. The sum of the digits in N is
(a) 6 (b) 5 (c) 4 (d) 3

68. The least number, which when divided by 12, 15, 20 and 54 leaves in each case a remainder of 8, is
(a) 548 (b) 544 (c) 536 (d) 504

69. The smallest number which when subtracted by 7, is divisible by 12, 16, 18, 21 and 28 is
(a) 1032 (b) 1022 (c) 1015 (d) 1008

70. The least number which should be added to 2497 so that the sum is exactly divisible by 5, 6, 4 and 3 is
(a) 33 (b) 23 (c) 13 (d) 3

71. The greatest number of four digits which is divsible by 15, 25, 40 and 75 is
(a) 9800 (b) 9600
(c) 9400 (d) 9000

72. The smallest fraction, which each of $\frac{6}{7}$, $\frac{5}{14}$, $\frac{10}{21}$ will divide exactly, is

(a) $\frac{50}{294}$ (b) $\frac{60}{147}$ (c) $\frac{30}{98}$ (d) $\frac{30}{7}$

73. What will be the least number which when doubled will be exactly divisible by 12, 18, 21 and 30?
(*a*) 2520 (*b*) 1260 (*c*) 630 (*d*) 196

74. Which of the following fraction is the largest
(*a*) $\frac{63}{80}$ (*b*) $\frac{31}{40}$ (*c*) $\frac{13}{16}$ (*d*) $\frac{7}{8}$

75. The greatest number which one dividing 1657 and 2037 leaves remainder 6 and 5 respectively, is:
(*a*) 305 (*b*) 235 (*c*) 127 (*d*) 123

EXPLANATORY ANSWERS

1. $72 = 2 \times 2 \times 2 \times 3 \times 3$
$18 = 2 \times 3 \times 3$
∴ Common factors $= 2 \times 3 \times 3 = 18$
∴ H.C.F. = 18

2. $6 = 2 \times 3$; $8 = 2 \times 2 \times 2$
$10 = 2 \times 5$; $12 = 2 \times 2 \times 3$

It is clear that 2 occurs as prime factor maximum three times, 3 one time and 5 one time.
Hence, required L.C.M. $= 2 \times 2 \times 2 \times 3 \times 5 = 120$

3. H.C.F. of $\frac{5}{6}, \frac{6}{7}, \frac{7}{8}, \frac{8}{9}$ and $\frac{9}{10} = \frac{\text{H.C.F. of } 5,6,7,8 \text{ and } 9}{\text{LCM of } 6,7,8,9 \text{ and } 10}$
Now H.C.F. of 5, 6, 7, 8 and 9 = 1
and L.C.M. of 6, 7, 8, 9 and 10 = 2520

∴ Required H.C.F. $= \frac{1}{2520}$

4. L.C.M. of two numbers × H.C.F. of the numbers = Product of the numbers
∴ 85 × H.C.F. = 1020

∴ H.C.F. $= \frac{1020}{85} = 12$

5. 1st number × 2nd number = LCM × HCF
∴ 204 × 2nd number = 4284 × 32

∴ 2nd number $= \frac{4284 \times 32}{204} = 672$ ∴ 2nd number = 672

6. In this question LCM of the given numbers 48, 60, 64 has to be found out.
$48 = 2 \times 2 \times 2 \times 2 \times 3$;
$60 = 2 \times 2 \times 3 \times 5$
$64 = 2 \times 2 \times 2 \times 2 \times 2 \times 2$
∴ LCM $= 2 \times 2 \times 2 \times 2 \times 2 \times 2 \times 3 \times 5 = 960$
∵ Largest 4-digit number = 9999

∴ 960) 9999 (10
9600
399 ∴ Required number = 9999 − 399 = 9600

7. $24 = 2 \times 2 \times 2 \times 3$

$28 = 2 \times 2 \times 7$

$36 = 2 \times 2 \times 3 \times 3$

$44 = 2 \times 2 \times 11$

$\therefore$ Required LCM $= 2 \times 2 \times 2 \times 3 \times 3 \times 7 \times 11 = 24 \times 231$

Therefore, it is obvious that LCM of the given number is a multiple of 24 and 231.

8. 315) 420 (1
315
105) 315 (3
315
×

$\therefore$ H.C.F. of 315 and 420 is 105

Now, H.C.F. of 105 and 462 :

105) 462 (4
420
42) 105 (2
84
21) 42 (2
42
×

$\therefore$ Required H.C.F. = 21.

9. L.C.M. of 3, 4, 6 and 8

2	3,	4,	6,	8
2	3,	2,	3,	4
3	3,	1,	3,	2
	1,	1,	1,	2

$\therefore$ The required number = LCM of the given numbers $= 2 \times 2 \times 3 \times 2 = 24$.

10. L.C.M. of the given numbers 12, 18 and 24

2	12,	18,	24
2	6,	9,	12
3	3,	9,	6
	1,	3,	2

$\therefore$ L.C.M. $= 2 \times 2 \times 3 \times 3 \times 2 = 72$

$\therefore$ The required 3-digit number which is smallest as well as divisible by 12, 18, and 24 will be $72 \times 2 = 144$.

11. L.C.M. of 6, 9 and 12

3	6,	9,	12
2	2,	3,	4
	1,	3,	2

$\therefore$ LCM $= 3 \times 2 \times 3 \times 2 = 36$.

$\because$ Largest 3-digit number = 999

36) 999 (27
72
279
252
× 27

∴ Largest 3-digit number which is exactly divisible by 6, 9 and 12
$= 999 - 27 = 972$

∴ The required number $= 972 + 1 = 973$

12. Let the numbers be $8x$ and $15x$

$$8x = 2 \times 2 \times 2 \times x$$
$$15x = 3 \times 5 \times x$$

∴ LCM of $8x$ and $15x = 2 \times 2 \times 2 \times x \times 3 \times 5 = 120x$

Now, 1st number × 2nd number = HCF × LCM

$\Rightarrow \quad 8x \times 15x = 4 \times 120x$

$\Rightarrow \quad 120x^2 = 4 \times 120x$

$\Rightarrow \quad x = 4$

∴ Numbers are $8 \times 4 = 32$ and $15 \times 4 = 60$

13. $226 - 1 = 225$ and $272 - 2 = 270$

Now, HCF of 225 and 270

```
225 ) 270 ( 1
      225
      ----
       45 )225 ( 5
           225
           ---
            ×
```

∴ The required number is 45.

14. $1170 = 2 \times 5 \times 3 \times 3 \times 13$

$102 = 2 \times 3 \times 17$

∴ Greatest common divisor $= 2 \times 3 = 6$

15. It is clear from the given conditions of the problem that the smallest number will be 3 less than the LCM of 36, 45 and 50.

∴ LCM of 36, 45 and 50

3	36, 45, 50
2	12, 15, 50
3	6, 15, 25
5	2, 5, 25
	2, 1, 5

∴ LCM $= 3 \times 2 \times 3 \times 5 \times 2 \times 5 = 900$

∴ Required number $= 900 - 3 = 897$.

16. LCM of 10, 20, 30 and 40

2	10, 20, 30, 40
5	5, 10, 15, 20
2	1, 2, 3, 4
	1, 1, 3, 2

∴ LCM $= 2 \times 2 \times 5 \times 3 \times 2$

But the number is a perfect square number

∴ Required number $= 2 \times 2 \times 5 \times 5 \times 3 \times 3 \times 2 \times 2 = 3600$.

17. Product of two numbers = their HCF × their LCM

$$2160 = 12 \times LCM$$

$$\therefore \quad LCM = \frac{2160}{12} = 180$$

Therefore such pairs of numbers in which product of numbers is 2160 and HCF is 12 will be only 2. *i.e.,* 12 × 180 and 36 × 60.

18. Difference between 366 and 513 = 513 – 366 = 147

and difference between 513 and 324 = 513 – 324 = 189

∴ HCF of 147 and 189

```
147 ) 189 ( 1
      147
    × 42 ) 147 ( 3
           126
         × 21 ) 42 ( 2
                42
                 ×
```

∴ The required largest number is 21.

19. Let the numbers be x and y.

∴ $x + y = 216 = 27 \times 8$

Since HCF of these two numbers is 27, hence, common factor of these two numbers is 27. Therefore these numbers will be of the form of 27 × 1, 27 × 2, 27 × 3, ... etc.

According to the condition of the problem sum of these numbers is 216.

∴ The numbers will be 27 × 3 = 81

and 27 × 5 = 135

20. LCM of the two numbers = 45 × HCF

and LCM + HCF = 1150

⇒ 45 × HCF + HCF = 1150

⇒ HCF(45 + 1) = 1150

$$\Rightarrow \quad HCF = \frac{1150}{46} = 25$$

∴ LCM = 45 × 25 = 1125

∵ 1st number × 2nd number = LCM × HCF

∴ 125 × 2nd number = 1125 × 25

$$\therefore \quad \text{2nd number} = \frac{1125 \times 25}{125} = 225.$$

21. According to the condition of the problem, 50 is obtained on dividing one of the numbers by 2

∴ One of the numbers = 50 × 2 = 100

Now, 1st number × 2nd number = LCM × HCF

∴ 100 × 2nd number = 250 × 50

$$\therefore \quad \text{2nd number} = \frac{250 \times 50}{100} = 125$$

Hence, numbers are 100 and 125.

22. LCM of 6, 9 and 12 = 36 and largest 3-digit number = 999

∴ HCF of 36 and 999

$$\begin{array}{r} 36\ )\ 999\ (\ 27 \\ \underline{72} \\ 279 \\ \underline{252} \\ 27 \end{array}$$

∴ Largest three-digit number completely divisible by 6, 9 and 12

= 999 − 27 = 972

Since 3 is left as remainder in each case,

∴ Required largest number of 3-digit = 972 + 3 = 975.

23. 33 − 3 = 30, 64 − 4 = 60 and 80 − 5 = 75

Now, HCF of 30, 60 and 75:

$$30 = 2 \times \underline{3 \times 5}$$
$$60 = 2 \times 2 \times \underline{3 \times 5}$$
$$75 = \underline{3 \times 5} \times 5$$

∵ Common factor = 3 × 5 = 15

∴ Required largest number = 15.

24. Let the numbers be x, $2x$ and $3x$ respectively.

Here, HCF of the three numbers is 12, therefore 12 is the largest common factor of these three numbers.

Thus, it is clear that $x = 12$

∴ These numbers are 12, 24 and 36 respectively.

25. LCM of 2, 3, 4 and 5 = 60

Largest 4-digit number = 9999

$$\begin{array}{r} \text{Now, } 60\ )\ 9999\ (\ 166 \\ \underline{60} \\ 399 \\ \underline{360} \\ \times\ 399 \\ \underline{360} \\ 39 \end{array}$$

∴ Largest 4-digit number completely divisible by 2, 3, 4 and 5

= 9999 − 39 = 9960

∴ Required number = 9960

26. LCM of 15, 20 and 24

5	15, 20, 24
4	3, 4, 24
3	3, 1, 6
	1, 1, 2

LCM = 5 × 4 × 3 × 2 = 120

∵ 12 minutes = 12 × 60 = 720 seconds

∴ Number of times the bells will ring together during 12 minutes

$$= \frac{720}{120} = 6 \text{ times.}$$

27. LCM of 5, 6, 8, 9 and 12 = 360. Hence, the smallest number which when divided by 5, 6, 8, 9 and 12 leaves 1 as remainder in each case will be 360 + 1 = 361. But 361 is not completely divisible by 13. Hence, on considering 360 × 2 + 1, 360 × 3 + 1,... , 360 × n + 1, we conclude that 360 × 10 + 1 = 3601 is the required number.

28. This question is based on finding HCF by continued division method. Now according to the condition of the problem,

Last divisor = 49

and Last quotient = 2

∴ dividend = 49 × 2 = 98

Now, divisor = 98 and quotient = 3

and remainder = 49

∴ dividend = 98 × 3 + 49 = 343

Now, divisor = 343

quotient = 17

and remainder = 98

∴ Dividend = 343 × 17 + 98 = 5829

Therefore, these numbers are 33 and 5829.

29. A, B and C will take 4 hours, $\frac{12}{7}$ hours and $\frac{12}{13}$ hours respectively in completing one round on the circular path.

∴ LCM of $\frac{4}{1}, \frac{12}{7}$ and $\frac{12}{13} = \frac{\text{LCM of 4,12 and 12}}{\text{HCF of 1,7 and 13}}$

∵ LCM of 4, 12 and 12= 12 and HCF of 1, 7 and 13 = 1

∴ Required LCM = $\frac{12}{1} = 12$

Hence, they will meet together again after 12 hrs.

30.

Numbers		*Their divisors*
182	→	1, 2, 7, 13, 14, 26, 91 and 182
176	→	1, 2, 4, 8, 16, 22, 44, 88 and 176
101	→	1 and 101
99	→	1, 3, 9, 11, 33 and 99

Therefore, 176 has the most number of divisors.

31.
```
1095) 1168 ( 1
      1095
      ----
        73 ) 1095 ( 15
              73
             ----
              365
              365
             ----
               ×
```

Hence, HCF of 1095 and 1168 is 73.

Then, $\frac{1095}{1168} = \frac{1095 \div 73}{1168 \div 73} = \frac{15}{16}$

32.
```
128352 ) 238368 ( 1
         128352
       110016 ) 128352 ( 1
                110016
                 18336 ) 110016 ( 6
                         110016
                            ×
```

Hence, HCF of 128352 and 238368 is 18336.

Then, $\dfrac{128352 \div 18336}{238368 \div 18336} = \dfrac{7}{13}$.

33.

Number (n)		*Divisors excluding the number (n)*	*Sum of divisors*
21	→	1, 3, 7	11
15	→	1, 3, 5	9
9	→	1, 3, 3	7
6	→	1, 2, 3	6

Therefore, 6 is a perfect number.

34. $4 \times 27 \times 3125 = 2^2 \times 3^3 \times 5^5$
$8 \times 9 \times 25 \times 7 = 2^3 \times 3^2 \times 5^2 \times 7$
$16 \times 81 \times 5 \times 11 \times 49 = 2^4 \times 3^4 \times 5 \times 7^2 \times 11$
$\therefore$ HCF $= 2^2 \times 3^2 \times 5 = 4 \times 9 \times 5 = 180$

35. HCF of 23 and 92 = 23
HCF of 21 and 35 = 7
HCF of 18 and 25 = 1
HCF of 16 and 62 = 2
Hence, 18 and 25 are co-prime numbers.

36. $2^3 \times 3^2 \times 5 \times 11$; $2^4 \times 3^4 \times 5^2 \times 7$ and $2^5 \times 3^3 \times 5^3 \times 7^2 \times 11$
$\therefore$ LCM $= 2^5 \times 3^4 \times 5^3 \times 7^2 \times 11$

37. GCD of 108, 36 and 90 = 18
Hence, GCD of 1.08, 0.36 and 0.9 = 0.18.

38. $3240 = 2^3 \times 3^4 \times 5$
$3600 = 2^4 \times 3^2 \times 5^2$
HCF $= 36 = 2^2 \times 3^2$
LCM $= 2^4 \times 3^5 \times 5^2 \times 7^2$
Hence, third number $= 2^2 \times 3^5 \times 7^2$.

39. Let the numbers be $3x$ and $4x$; HCF = 4; Hence, $x = 4$
Then, numbers will be 12 and 16; $\therefore$ Their LCM = 48.

40. Let the numbers are x, $2x$ and $3x$; Their HCF = 12
Then, $x = 12$, so the numbers will be 12, 24, 36.

41. Let the number be x and y.
Then, $x + y = 55$; xy = HCF × LCM = 5 × 120

$\therefore$ Sum of their reciprocals $= \dfrac{1}{x} + \dfrac{1}{y} = \dfrac{x+y}{xy} = \dfrac{55}{5 \times 120} = \dfrac{11}{120}$

42. Let the number be x and $(100 - x)$
Now, $x\,(100 - x) = 5 \times 495$
$\Rightarrow x^2 - 100x + 2475 = 0$
$\Rightarrow x^2 - 55x - 45x + 2475 = 0$
$\Rightarrow x\,(x - 55) - 45\,(x - 55) = 0$
$\Rightarrow (x - 45)\,(x - 55) = 0$
Either, $x = 45$ or, $x = 55$
Hence, the numbers are 45 and 55
So, their difference = 55 − 45 = 10

43. Let the two numbers be x and $4x$.
Then, $x \times 4x = 21 \times 84 \quad \Rightarrow x^2 = 21 \times 21 \quad \therefore x = 21$
Hence, larger of two numbers = $4x = 4 \times 21 = 84$

44. Second number = $\dfrac{11 \times 7700}{275} = 308$

45. Let the numbers be $3x$, $4x$ and $5x$.
Then, L.C.M. = $60x$

Now, $60x = 2400 \quad \therefore x = \dfrac{2400}{60} = 40$
Since, the numbers are 3×40, 4×40, 5×40.
Hence, their HCF = 40.

46. Let the two numbers be $2x$ and $3x$; their LCM = $6x$
Now, $6x = 48 \quad \therefore x = 8$
Hence, the numbers are 2×8, 3×8 = 16, 24
Their sum = 16 + 24 = 40.

47. Let the three co-prime numbers are a, b and c respectively,
Now, $ab = 551$ and $bc = 1073$

Now, $\dfrac{ab}{bc} = \dfrac{55}{1073} \Rightarrow \dfrac{a \times b}{b \times c} = \dfrac{29 \times 19}{29 \times 37}$
Hence, three numbers are : 19, 29 and 37; Their sum = 19 + 29 + 37 = 85.

48. Let the two numbers be $13x$ and $13y$

Now, $13x \times 13y = 2028 \quad \therefore xy = \dfrac{2028}{13 \times 13} = 12$
Then, co-primes with product 12 are (1, 12) and (3, 4)
Hence, the requried numbers are $(13 \times 1, 13 \times 12)$ and $(13 \times 3, 13 \times 4)$.
So, there are two such pairs.

49. Let the two numbers be $37x$ and $37y$

Now, $37x \times 37y = 4107 \quad \therefore xy = \dfrac{4107}{37 \times 37} = 3$
Then co-primes with product 3 are (1, 3)
Hence, geater number = $37 \times 3 = 111$.

50. Let the two numbers be $33x$ and $33y$.
Then, $33x + 33y = 528 \Rightarrow 33(x + y) = 528 \quad \therefore (x + y) = 16$
Now, the co-primes with sum 16 are (1, 15), (3, 13), (5, 11) and (7, 9)
Hence, the number of such pairs = 4.

51. N = HCF of (4665 – 1305), (6805 – 4665) and (6905 – 1305)
= HCF of 3360, 2240 and 5600.

52.

```
2240) 3360 ( 1                1120) 5600 ( 5
      2240                          5600
      ----                          ----
      1120 ) 2240 ( 2                 ×
             2240
             ----
               ×
```

Hence, N = HCF of 3360, 2240 and 5600 = 1120
Sum of digits in N = 1 + 1 + 2 + 0 = 4.

52. Greatest number = HCF of (91 – 43), (183 – 91) (183 – 43)
= HCF of 48, 92, 140
= 4

$$\left[\begin{array}{l} \because 48 = 2\times2\times2\times2\times3 \\ 92 = 2\times2\times23 \\ 140 = 2\times2\times5\times7 \end{array}\right]$$

53.

```
378) 525( 1
     378
     ---
     147) 378 ( 2
          294
          ---
           84) 147 ( 1
                84
                --
                63 ) 84 ( 1
                     63
                     --
                     21 ) 63 ( 3
                          63
                          --
                           ×
```

Hence, HCF of 378 cm and 525 cm = 21 cm
So, Largest size of tile = 21 cm.

54. Maximum number of students = HCF of 1001 and 910 = 91

$$\left[\begin{array}{l} \because 1001 = 7\times11\times13 \\ 910 = 2\times5\times7\times13 \end{array}\right]$$

55. Product of two numbers = 11 × 385
= 11 × 5 × 7 × 11 = 55 × 77
Hence, number lies between 75 and 125 is 77.

56. LCM of two prime numbers = product of the numbers = 161 = 23 × 7
Here, $x > y$
So, $x = 23$ & $y = 7$
Now, $3y - x = 3 \times 7 - 23 = -2$.

57. 7m = 700 cm;
3m 85cm = 385 cm;
12m 95cm = 1295 cm

```
385) 700 ( 1
     385
     315) 385 ( 1
          315
           70) 315 ( 4
               280
                35 ) 70 ( 2
                     70
                      ×
```

```
35) 1295 ( 37
    105
     245
     245
      ×
```

Hence, required length = HCF of 700 cm, 385 cm, 1295 cm = 35 cm.

58. Product of two numbers = 29 × 4147 = 29 × 11 × 13 × 29 = 319 × 377
Hence, both the numbers greater than 29 are 319 and 377
∴ Sum of the numbers = 319 + 377 = 696

59. Product of two numbers = 23 × 13 × 14 = 322 × 13
Hence, larger of the two numbers is 322.

60. LCM of two numbers is always divisible by their HCF.
Here, 60 is not divisible by 8. Hence, 60 can never be their LCM.

61. 120 is not divisible by 35. Hence 35 can not be their HCF.

62. Product of two prime numbers = LCM of two prime numbers.

63.

2	252,	308,	198
2	126,	154,	99
3	63,	77,	99
3	21,	77,	33
7	7,	77,	11
11	1,	11,	11
	1,	1,	1

Hence, LCM = 2 × 2 × 3 × 3 × 7 × 11 = 2772
Hence, A, B, C will meet again at the starting point after 2772 sec. = 46 min 12 sec.

64. LCM of 5, 6, 7 and 8 = 840
Hence, required number = 840k + 3
Therefore, least value of k for which (840k + 3) is divisible by 9 is 2.
Hence, required number = 840 × 2 + 3 = 1683.

65. 48 – 38 = 10; 60 – 50 = 10; 72 – 62 = 10; 108 – 98 = 10 and also 140 – 130 = 10
Hence, required number = LCM of (48, 60, 72, 108, 140) – 10 = 15120 – 10 = 15110

2	48,	60,	72,	108,	140
2	24,	30,	36,	54,	70
2	12,	15,	18,	27,	35
3	6,	15,	9,	27,	35
3	2,	5,	3,	9,	35
5	2,	5,	1,	3,	35
	2,	1,	1,	3,	7

Hence, LCM = 2 × 2 × 2 × 3 × 3 × 5 × 2 × 3 × 7 = 15120.

66.

2	6, 9, 15, 18
3	3, 9, 15, 9
3	1, 3, 5, 3
	1, 1, 5, 1

$= 2 \times 3 \times 3 \times 5 = 90$

Hence, LCM of 6, 9, 15 and 18 = 90

Let required number be $90k + 4$, which is multiple of 7.

The least value of $k = 4$, then $90k + 4 = 90 \times 4 + 4 = 364$ which is a multiple of 7.

67. The LCM of 4, 6, 10 and 15 is 60.

Let required number be $60k + 2$, which is least number of 6 digits.

The least value of $k = 1667$ then, $60 \times 1667 + 2 = 100020 + 2 = 100022$.

Hence, N = 100022, Then sum of digits in N = 1 + 2 + 2 = 5.

68.

2	12, 15, 20, 54
2	6, 15, 10, 27
3	3, 15, 5, 27
5	1, 5, 5, 9
	1, 1, 1, 9

$= 2 \times 2 \times 3 \times 5 \times 9 = 540$

Hence, LCM of 12, 15, 20 and 54 is 540. Since, required number = 540 + 8 = 548.

69. LCM of 12, 16, 18, 21 and 28 = 1008 Required number = 1008 + 7 = 1015.

70. LCM of 5, 6, 4 and 3 = 60

when we divide 2497 by 60 remainder is 37. Hence, required number = 60 – 37 = 23.

71. The LCM of 12, 25, 40 and 75 is 600

when we divide greatest number of 4 digits, 9999 by 600, remainder is 399.

Hence, required number = 9999 – 399 = 9600.

72. Required number = $\dfrac{\text{LCM of 6, 15 and 10}}{\text{HCF of 7, 14 and 21}} = \dfrac{30}{7}$.

73. LCM of 12, 18, 21 and 30 is 1260

Hence, required number = $\dfrac{1}{2} \times 1260 = 630$.

74. $\dfrac{63}{80}, \dfrac{31}{40}, \dfrac{13}{16}, \dfrac{7}{8}$ LCM of 80, 40, 16 and 8 = 80

Now, $\dfrac{31}{40} = \dfrac{31 \times 2}{40 \times 2} = \dfrac{62}{80}$; $\dfrac{13}{16} = \dfrac{13 \times 5}{16 \times 5} = \dfrac{65}{80}$; $\dfrac{7}{8} = \dfrac{7 \times 10}{8 \times 10} = \dfrac{70}{80}$ Then, $\dfrac{70}{80} > \dfrac{65}{80} > \dfrac{63}{80} > \dfrac{62}{80}$.

Since, $\dfrac{7}{8} > \dfrac{13}{16} > \dfrac{63}{80} > \dfrac{31}{40}$.

75. Required number = HCF of (1657 – 6) and (2037 – 5) = HCF of 1651 and 2032 = 127.

```
1651) 2032 (1
      1651
      ----
       381) 1651 (4
            1524
            ----
             127) 381 (3
                  381
                  ---
                   ×
```

4 VULGAR AND DECIMAL FRACTION

FRACTION

The relation to represent some part of the body to the whole body is known *Fraction*. For example $\frac{2}{5}$ is a fraction where 2 is the numerator and 5 is the denominator.

Important Facts :

(i) A fraction is also called a rational number.
(ii) A fraction is unity when its numerator and denominator are equal.
(iii) When a fraction is reduced in its lowest term, its numerator and denominator are prime to each other, *i.e.*, they have no common factor.
(iv) The value of fraction is not altered by multiplying or dividing the numerator and the denominator by the same number.

Vulgar or Common Fraction : The fraction such as $\frac{2}{9}, \frac{7}{11}, \frac{3}{10}, \frac{9}{100}$ are called vulgar fraction.

Decimal Fraction : Fractions in which denominators are power of 10 are called decimal fractions.

For example : $\frac{1}{10}, \frac{1}{100}, \frac{7}{1000}$ etc.

Here, $\frac{1}{10}$ is 1 tenths, written as .1

$$\frac{1}{100} = .01$$

$$\frac{7}{1000} = .007$$

$$\frac{13}{100} = .13 \text{ and so on.}$$

Converting a Decimal into a Vulgar Fraction

First of all write down the given number as numerator without the decimal point, and for the denominator write 1 followed by as many zeros as many are there figures after the decimal point. Now reduce the fraction to its lowest terms.

Ex : *(i)* 0.63 $= \frac{63}{100}$

(ii) $0.54 = \frac{54}{100} = \frac{27}{50}$

(iii) $3.013 = 3\frac{013}{1000} = 3\frac{13}{1000}$

Addition and Subtraction of Decimal Fractions

First of all write down the numbers under one another. Other than the decimal point lies in one column. After arranging in this way, we add or subtract in usual fashion.

An example : Add 521 + 52.1 + 5.21 + 0.521

Sol : 521.000
52.100
5.210
0.521 After adding we get 578.831

Multiplication of decimal fraction

1. To multiply by 10, 100, 1000, etc

Example : (i) 63.02 × 10 = 630.2
(ii) 63.02 × 100 = 6302
(iii) 63.02 × 1000= 63020

2. To multiply of two or more decimal fractions.

An example :(i) 5.91 × 13 = 76.83
(ii) 6.32 × 0.59 = 3.7288
(iii) 63.2 × 0.01 = 0.632

Conclusion : First of all multiply the given numbers assuming them without the decimal point. Now mark off the decimal point from extreme right in the product as many places of decimal as is the sum of the number of decimal places in the given numbers.

DIVISION OF DECIMALS

1. When the divisor is a counting number

Example : (i) 4.309 ÷ 10 = 0.4309
(ii) 0.0182 ÷ 14 = 0.0013
(iii) 9.586 ÷ 100 = 0.09586
(iv) $0.05 \div 10^3 = 0.00005$
(v) 0.49 ÷ 7 = 0.07

Conclusion : *(i)* When divisor is the power of 10, then shift the decimal point to the left by as many places of decimal as is the power of 10, prefixing zero if necessary.

(ii) When divisor is other than power of 10, then divide as in the case of integers, and in quotient, put the decimal point to give as many places of decimal as are there in the dividend.

2. When the divisor is a decimal

Example : (i) $0.00066 \div 0.11 = \frac{0.00066}{0.11} = \frac{0.066}{11} = 0.006$

(ii) $42 \div 0.07 = \frac{42}{0.07} = \frac{4200}{7} = 600$

(iii) $32.5 \div 0.0064 = \dfrac{32.5}{0.0064} = \dfrac{325000}{64} = 5078.125$

(iv) $0.0323 \div 0.00017 = \dfrac{0.0323}{0.00017} = \dfrac{3230}{17} = 190$

Recurring Decimal : If in a decimal number a digit or a set of digits is repeated again and again, the decimal is known as recurring decimal.

For example : *(i)* $2.666... = 2.\dot{6}$

(ii) $1.363636... = 1.\dot{3}\dot{6}$ or $1.\overline{36}$

(iii) $7.3424242... = 7.3\dot{4}\dot{2}$ or $7.3\overline{42}$

Recurring decimal numbers are of two types :

(i) Pure and *(ii)* Mixed

***(i)* Pure recurring decimals :** A decmial fraction in which all the figures after the decimal point are repeated is called a pure recurring decimal. For example,

$0.\overline{3}$, $0.\overline{37}$, $3.\overline{4579}$ etc

***(ii)* Mixed recurring decimals :** A decimal fraction in which at least one figure after the decimal point is not repeated is called a mixed recurring decimal. For example,

$0.3\overline{59}$, $0.29\overline{54}$, $0.2\dot{7}$ etc.

Conversion of Recurring into Vulgar Fraction

1. Pure recurring decimals

Rule : Put as many 9's in the denominator at the number of digits under recurring and delete the recurring sign.

For example, $0.\overline{5} = \dfrac{5}{9}$

$0.\overline{35} = \dfrac{35}{99}$

$0.\overline{24} = \dfrac{24}{99} = \dfrac{8}{33}$

2. Mixed Recurring Decimals

For example, *(i)* $0.1\overline{8} =$

Here, numerator = 18 − 1 = 17

and denominator = 9 × 10 = 90

$\therefore$ $0.1\dot{8} = \dfrac{18-1}{90} = \dfrac{17}{90}$

(ii) $0.2\dot{7}\dot{9}$

Here, numerator = 279 − 2 = 277

and denominator = 99 × 10 = 990

$\therefore$ $0.2\overline{79} = \dfrac{279-2}{990} = \dfrac{277}{990}$

(iii) $0.3\overline{56} = \dfrac{356-3}{99 \times 10} = \dfrac{353}{990}$

(iv) $$2.53\dot{6} = 2+\frac{536-53}{9\times 100} = 2+\frac{483}{900}$$

$$= 2+\frac{161}{300} = 2\frac{161}{300}$$

(v) $$0.43\overline{213} = \frac{43213-43}{999\times 100} = \frac{43170}{99900} = \frac{4317}{9990}$$

(vi) $$5.00\overline{983} = 5+\frac{983}{999\times 100} = 5+\frac{983}{99900} = 5\frac{983}{99900}$$

Addition and Subtraction of recurring decimals

Example : *(i)* Add $3.\overline{76}$ and $1.4\overline{576}$ and subtract also.

3.7	676767	67	
1.4	576576	57	
(+) 5.2	253344	24	⇒ $5.2\overline{253344}$
(–) 2.3	100191	10	⇒ $2.3\overline{100191}$

(ii) Subtract $3.\overline{75}$ from $25.5\overline{473}$

25.5	473473	47
3.7	575757	57
21.7	897715	90

Hence, the required subtract = $21.7\overline{897715}$

Multiplication and Division of Recurring Decimal

Example 1 : *(i)* $7.\overline{63}\times 11 = 7\frac{63}{99}\times 11 = 7\frac{7}{11}\times 11 = \frac{84}{11}\times 11 = 84$

(ii) $$0.\overline{09}\times 7.\overline{3} = \frac{9}{99}\times 7\frac{3}{9}$$

$$= \frac{1}{11}\times\frac{66}{9} = \frac{6}{9} = 0.\overline{6}$$

(iii) $$0.\overline{6}\times 7.\overline{3} = \frac{6}{9}\times 7\frac{3}{9}$$

$$= \frac{6}{9}\times\frac{66}{9} = \frac{44}{9} = 4.\overline{8}$$

(iv) $$0.\overline{06}\div 100 = 0.060606...\div 100 = 0.00\overline{06}$$

(v) $$0.7\overline{32}\div 0.02\overline{7} = 0.73\dot{2}\dot{3}\div 0.02\dot{7}\dot{7}$$

$$= \frac{7323-73}{99\times 100}\div\frac{277-2}{99\times 100}$$

$$= \frac{7250}{9900}\div\frac{275}{9900} = \frac{7250}{275} = \frac{290}{11} = 26.\overline{36}\cdot$$

Example 2 : Multiply $0.\dot{0}\dot{9}$ by $7.\dot{3}$

Solution : $0.\dot{0}\dot{9} \times 7.\dot{3} = \frac{9}{99} \times \frac{73-7}{9}$

$= \frac{1}{11} \times \frac{22}{3} = \frac{2}{3}$

$= \frac{6}{9} = 0.\dot{6}$

Example 3 : Divide $0.\dot{6}$ by 0.75

Solution : $0.\dot{6} \div 0.75 = \frac{6}{9} \div \frac{75}{100} = \frac{2}{3} \div \frac{3}{4}$

$= \frac{8}{9} = 0.\dot{8}$

EXERCISE

1. Which of the following is equivalent to $\frac{15}{25}$?

(a) $\frac{150}{25}$ *(b)* $\frac{15}{250}$ *(c)* $\frac{3}{5}$ *(d)* $\frac{60}{75}$

2. If $\frac{9*3}{3*7}$ is equivalent to $\frac{9}{7}$, the sign * is replaced by

(a) ÷ *(b)* × *(c)* + *(d)* –

3. $\frac{5}{6}$ of an hour is equal to

(a) half an hour *(b)* 40 minutes
(c) 50 minutes *(d)* 55 minutes

4. An aircraft uses 2/5 of its fuel in flying 1,250 kilometres. The distance travelled on remaining fuel is

(a) 1875 km *(b)* 2125 km *(c)* 250 km *(d)* 475 km

5. If $\frac{4}{3} * \frac{3}{4} = \frac{16}{9}$, then * means

(a) + *(b)* – *(c)* × *(d)* ÷

6. Which of the following is the largest fraction?

$\frac{3}{15}, \frac{5}{20}, \frac{8}{64}, \frac{25}{1000}$

(a) $\frac{3}{15}$ *(b)* $\frac{5}{20}$ *(c)* $\frac{8}{64}$ *(d)* $\frac{25}{1000}$

7. Six times x increased by 12 is equal to

(a) $\frac{x}{2}$ *(b)* $2x$ *(c)* $6x + 12$ *(d)* $12x + 6$

8. Five times y diminished by 20 is equal to

(a) $5y - 20$ *(b)* $5y + 20$ *(c)* $y/4$ *(d)* $4y$

9. The number less than 15 by 7 is
(*a*) $15x - 7$ (*b*) 15/7 (*c*) 15 (*d*) 8

10. If 21 is add to four times a number, the result is 57. The number is
(*a*) 7 (*b*) 8 (*c*) 9 (*d*) 10

11. A number, the sum of whose fourth and fifth parts exceeds their third part by 28, is
(*a*) 120 (*b*) 240 (*c*) 220 (*d*) 160

12. Which fraction should be added to the sum of $5\frac{3}{4}$, $4\frac{4}{5}$ and $7\frac{3}{8}$ to make the result a whole number?
(*a*) $\frac{1}{40}$ (*b*) $\frac{2}{40}$ (*c*) $\frac{3}{40}$ (*d*) $\frac{4}{40}$

13. $\frac{1}{15}+\frac{3}{15}+\frac{5}{15}+\frac{6}{15} = ?$
(*a*) $\frac{10}{15}$ (*b*) $\frac{3}{5}$ (*c*) $\frac{4}{5}$ (*d*) 1

14. A number one-sixth of which exceeds its one-ninth by 100 is
(*a*) 600 (*b*) 900 (*c*) 1500 (*d*) 1800

15. The sum of 1/2, 1/4 and 1/8 of a number is 28. The number is
(*a*) 28 (*b*) 32 (*c*) 36 (*d*) 42

16. The sum of 1/9, 1/3, 1/6 and 7/18 of a number is 150. The number is
(*a*) 120 (*b*) 130 (*c*) 140 (*d*) 150

17. Which is the greatest? .999, .1011, .1995, .9985
(*a*) .999 (*b*) .1011 (*c*) .1995 (*d*) .9985

18. In decimal system, $9\frac{1}{8}$ may be represented as
(*a*) 9.18 (*b*) 9.125 (*c*) 9.025 (*d*) 9.225

19. $2.205 \div 0.15 = ?$
(*a*) 1.47 (*b*) 14.7 (*c*) 147 (*d*) 0.147

20. G.C.M. of .24, 3.2 and 16.0 is
(*a*) 80 (*b*) 8 (*c*) .8 (*d*) .08

21. L.C.M. of .24, 3.2 and 16.0 is
(*a*) .48 (*b*) 4.8 (*c*) 48 (*d*) 480

22. A pole has 0.5 of its length in mud, 0.25 of its length in water and 2 metres above water. The total length of the pole is
(*a*) 8 metres (*b*) 5 metres (*c*) 4 metres (*d*) 2 metres

23. $\sqrt{1/3}$ is equal to
(*a*) 0.57 (*b*) 0.35 (*c*) 0.30 (*d*) 3.00

24. How many times does 2/3 of 1/2 go into half of third?
(*a*) 2 (*b*) 1/2 (*c*) 1/3 (*d*) 2/3

25. The eleventh part of $990\frac{990}{990}$ is
(*a*) 99.0 (*b*) 99.99 (*c*) 90 (*d*) 90.9

26. A train started from Delhi at 6.00 A.M. On the next (second) station 1/3 passengers got down and 96 got in. On the next (third) station, 1/2 of the total passengers, present in the train, got down and 12 came in. Now there were 248 passengers in the train. When the train started from Delhi, total number of passengers was

(*a*) 435 (*b*) 564 (*c*) 654 (*d*) 736

27. 1 ÷ [1 + 1 ÷ {1 + 1 ÷ 1(1 + 1 ÷ 2)}] is equal to

(*a*) 1 (*b*) 2 (*c*) $\frac{5}{8}$ (*d*) zero

28. 1.25 × 1.25 + 2.75 × 2.75 + 2.5 × 2.75 is equal to

(*a*) 4.000 (*b*) 16.000 (*c*) 26.1250 (*d*) 28.2350

29. What fraction of an hour is second?

(*a*) $\frac{1}{24}$ (*b*) $\frac{1}{60}$ (*c*) $\frac{1}{120}$ (*d*) $\frac{1}{3600}$

30. G.C.M. of 1.6 and 0.72 is equal to

(*a*) 8 (*b*) .8 (*c*) .08 (*d*) .008

31. $\frac{4}{5}$ of 0.025 is equal to

(*a*) 0.0002 (*b*) 0.002 (*c*) 0.02 (*d*) 0.2

32. Divide $0.7\dot{3}\dot{2}$ by $0.02\dot{7}$.

(*a*) $26.\dot{3}\dot{6}$ (*b*) $25.\dot{2}\dot{5}$ (*c*) 0 (*d*) $27.\dot{7}$

33. Divide $0.\dot{6}$ by 0.75

(*a*) $0.\dot{8}$ (*b*) 0.75 (*c*) 0 (*d*) $0.\dot{6}7\dot{5}$

34. Which of the following fractions is greater than $\frac{3}{4}$ and less than $\frac{5}{6}$?

(*a*) $\frac{9}{10}$ (*b*) $\frac{4}{5}$ (*c*) $\frac{2}{3}$ (*d*) $\frac{1}{2}$

35. What is the difference between the biggest and the smallest fraction among $\frac{2}{3}$, $\frac{3}{4}$, $\frac{4}{5}$ and $\frac{5}{6}$?

(*a*) $\frac{1}{30}$ (*b*) $\frac{1}{20}$ (*c*) $\frac{1}{12}$ (*d*) $\frac{1}{6}$

36. Which of the following are in ascending order?

(*a*) $\frac{19}{21}, \frac{11}{14}, \frac{16}{19}$ (*b*) $\frac{16}{19}, \frac{19}{21}, \frac{11}{14}$ (*c*) $\frac{16}{19}, \frac{11}{14}, \frac{19}{21}$ (*d*) $\frac{11}{14}, \frac{16}{19}, \frac{19}{21}$

37. Which of the following are in desending order of their value?

(*a*) $\frac{11}{17}, \frac{7}{11}, \frac{5}{9}, \frac{8}{15}$ (*b*) $\frac{11}{17}, \frac{7}{11}, \frac{8}{15}, \frac{5}{9}$ (*c*) $\frac{5}{9}, \frac{8}{15}, \frac{11}{17}, \frac{7}{11}$ (*d*) $\frac{5}{9}, \frac{7}{11}, \frac{8}{15}, \frac{11}{17}$

38. Which part contains the fractions in ascending order?

(*a*) $\frac{2}{5}, \frac{3}{5}, \frac{1}{3}, \frac{4}{7}, \frac{5}{6}, \frac{6}{7}$ (*b*) $\frac{1}{3}, \frac{2}{5}, \frac{3}{5}, \frac{5}{6}, \frac{4}{7}, \frac{6}{7}$ (*c*) $\frac{1}{3}, \frac{2}{5}, \frac{3}{5}, \frac{4}{7}, \frac{5}{6}, \frac{6}{7}$ (*d*) $\frac{1}{3}, \frac{2}{5}, \frac{4}{7}, \frac{3}{5}, \frac{5}{6}, \frac{6}{7}$

39. Which part contains the fractions in ascending order?

(a) $\frac{8}{9}, \frac{9}{11}, \frac{7}{9}, \frac{2}{3}, \frac{3}{5}$ (b) $\frac{3}{5}, \frac{2}{3}, \frac{7}{9}, \frac{9}{11}, \frac{8}{9}$ (c) $\frac{3}{5}, \frac{2}{3}, \frac{9}{11}, \frac{7}{9}, \frac{8}{9}$ (d) $\frac{2}{3}, \frac{3}{5}, \frac{7}{9}, \frac{9}{11}, \frac{8}{9}$

40. If $47.2506 = 4A + \frac{7}{B} + 2C + \frac{5}{D} + 6E$, then the value of $5A + 3B + 6C + D + 3E$ is

(a) 213.0003 (b) 153.6003 (c) 53.603 (d) 53.6003

41. 832.58 – 242.31 = 779.84 – ?

(a) 179.57 (b) 189.57 (c) 199.57 (d) 205.05

42. 138.009 + 341.981 – 146.305 = 123.6 + ?

(a) 220.085 (b) 210.085 (c) 120.85 (d) 120.085

43. 12.1212 + 17.0005 – 9.1102 = ?

(a) 20.1015 (b) 20.0115 (c) 20.0105 (d) 20.0015

44. 617 + 6.017 + 0.617 + 6.0017 = ?

(a) 629.6357 (b) 6296.357 (c) 62.965 (d) 6.2963

45. 1 + 0.1 + 0.01 + 0.001 = ?

(a) 1.111 (b) 1.003 (c) 1.011 (d) 1.001

46. 3 × 0.3 × 0.03 × 0.003 × 30 = ?

(a) 0.0243 (b) 0.00243 (c) 0.000243 (d) 0.0000243

47. 0.04 × 0.0162 = ?

(a) 6.48×10^{-6} (b) 6.48×10^{-5} (c) 6.48×10^{-4} (d) 6.48×10^{-3}

48. 40.83 × 1.02 × 1.2 = ?

(a) 58.7952 (b) 49.97592 (c) 42.479532 (d) 41.64660

49. 0.014 × 0.014 = ?

(a) 196 (b) 19.6 (c) 0.00196 (d) 0.000196

50. 16.02 × 0.001 = ?

(a) 1.6021 (b) 0.1602 (c) 0.01602 (d) 0.001602

51. If $1.125 \times 10^k = 0.001125$, then the value of k is

(a) –1 (b) –2 (c) –3 (d) –4

52. What will come in place of question mark in the following equation?

54.(?) 3 + 543 + 5.43 = 603.26

(a) 8 (b) 7 (c) 6 (d) 5

53. What is the value of $\frac{1}{0.04}$?

(a) 25 (b) 2.5 (c) $\frac{2}{5}$ (d) $\frac{1}{40}$

54. 4.036 ÷ 0.04 = ?

(a) 10.09 (b) 1.009 (c) 1009 (d) 100.9

55. Consider the following quotients:

I. 368.39 ÷ 17 II. 170.50 ÷ 62 III. 875.65 ÷ 83

Their correct sequence in decreasing order is
(a) III, I, II (b) II, III, I (c) II, I, III (d) I, III, II

56. If $\frac{144}{0.144} = \frac{14.4}{x}$, then value of x is
(a) 144 (b) 14.4 (c) 1.44 (d) 0.0144

57. $0.04 \times ? = 0.000016$
(a) 0.0004 (b) 0.004 (c) 0.04 (d) 0.4

58. The price of commodity A increases by 40 paise every year, while the price of commodity B increases by 15 paise every year. If in 2001, the price of commodity A was Rs. 4.20 and that of B was Rs. 6.30, in which year commodity A will cost 40 paise more than the commodity B?
(a) 2013 (b) 2012 (c) 2011 (d) 2010

59. A tailor has 37.5 m of cloth and he has to make 8 pieces out of a meter of cloth. How many pieces can he make out of this cloth?
(a) 400 (b) 360 (c) 320 (d) 300

60. What is the value of $6.\overline{46}$ in the fractional form?
(a) $\frac{640}{99}$ (b) $\frac{640}{100}$ (c) $\frac{64640}{1000}$ (d) $\frac{646}{99}$

61. The fractional form of $2.1\overline{36}$ is
(a) $2\frac{3}{22}$ (b) $2\frac{1}{22}$ (c) $\frac{47}{220}$ (d) $\frac{68}{495}$

62. The least among the following is
(a) $(0.2)^2$ (b) $0.\overline{2}$ (c) $1 \div 0.2$ (d) 0.2

63. The fractional form of $0.\overline{47}$ is
(a) $\frac{46}{99}$ (b) $\frac{46}{90}$ (c) $\frac{47}{99}$ (d) $\frac{47}{90}$

64. The fractional form of 0.125125...... is
(a) $\frac{125}{999}$ (b) $\frac{119}{993}$ (c) $\frac{63}{487}$ (d) $\frac{63}{999}$

65. The fractional form of 0.232323 .... is
(a) $\frac{23}{100}$ (b) $\frac{23}{99}$ (c) $\frac{23}{90}$ (d) $\frac{2}{9}$

66. If $\frac{1}{6.198} = 0.16134$, then the value of $\frac{1}{0.0006198}$ is
(a) 16134 (b) 1613.4 (c) 0.16134 (d) 0.016134

67. If $213 \times 16 = 3408$, then $1.6 \times 21.3 = ?$
(a) 340.8 (b) 34.08 (c) 3.408 (d) 0.3408

68. If $\frac{547.527}{0.0082} = x$, then the value of $\frac{547527}{82}$ is
(a) $\frac{x}{100}$ (b) $\frac{x}{10}$ (c) $100x$ (d) $10x$

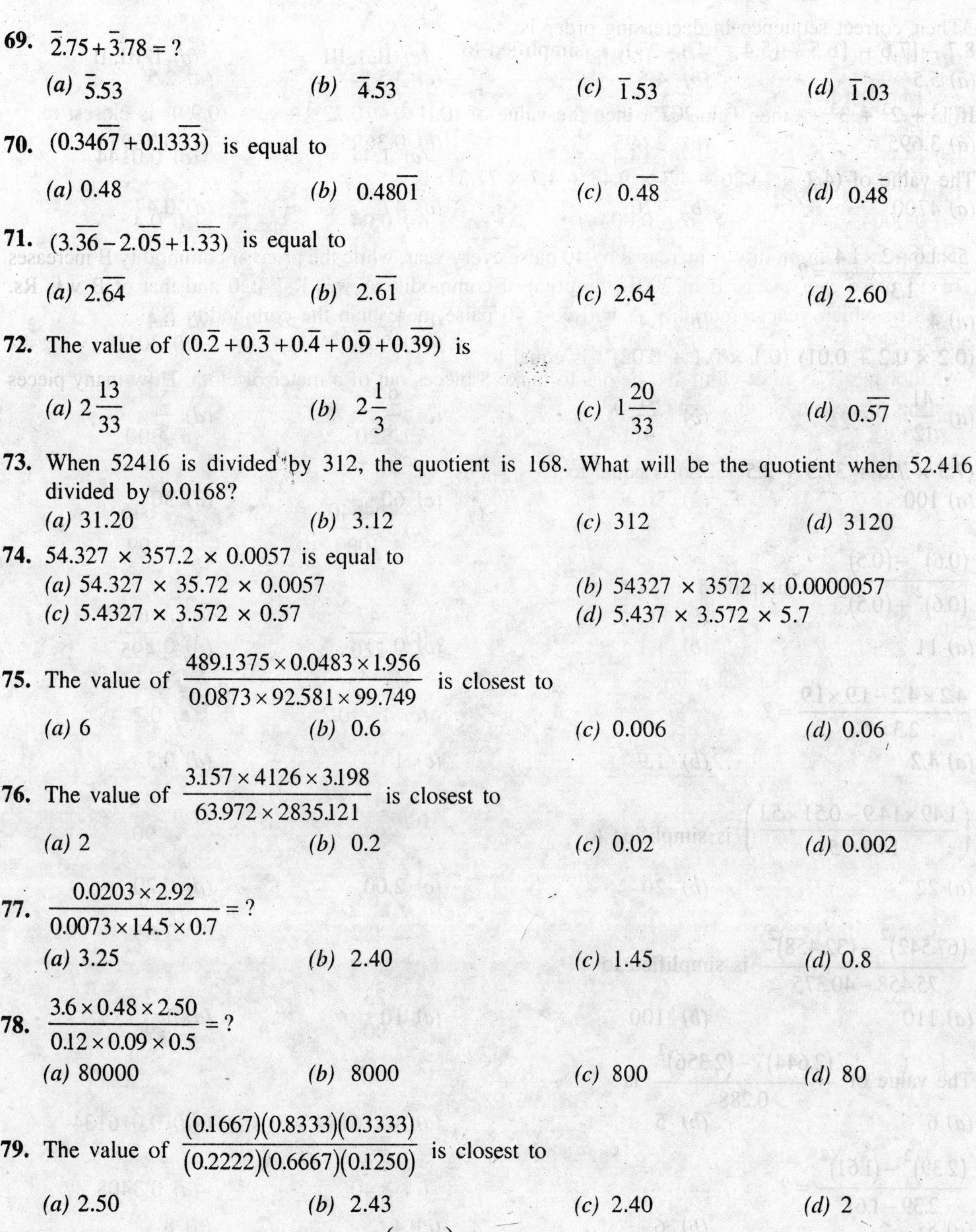

69. $\bar{2}.75+\bar{3}.78=?$

(a) $\bar{5}.53$ (b) $\bar{4}.53$ (c) $\bar{1}.53$ (d) $\bar{1}.03$

70. $(0.34\overline{67}+0.13\overline{33})$ is equal to

(a) 0.48 (b) $0.48\overline{01}$ (c) $0.\overline{48}$ (d) $0.4\bar{8}$

71. $(3.\overline{36}-2.\overline{05}+1.\overline{33})$ is equal to

(a) $2.\overline{64}$ (b) $2.\overline{61}$ (c) 2.64 (d) 2.60

72. The value of $(0.\bar{2}+0.\bar{3}+0.\bar{4}+0.\bar{9}+0.\overline{39})$ is

(a) $2\frac{13}{33}$ (b) $2\frac{1}{3}$ (c) $1\frac{20}{33}$ (d) $0.\overline{57}$

73. When 52416 is divided by 312, the quotient is 168. What will be the quotient when 52.416 is divided by 0.0168?

(a) 31.20 (b) 3.12 (c) 312 (d) 3120

74. 54.327 × 357.2 × 0.0057 is equal to

(a) 54.327 × 35.72 × 0.0057 (b) 54327 × 3572 × 0.0000057
(c) 5.4327 × 3.572 × 0.57 (d) 5.437 × 3.572 × 5.7

75. The value of $\frac{489.1375\times0.0483\times1.956}{0.0873\times92.581\times99.749}$ is closest to

(a) 6 (b) 0.6 (c) 0.006 (d) 0.06

76. The value of $\frac{3.157\times4126\times3.198}{63.972\times2835.121}$ is closest to

(a) 2 (b) 0.2 (c) 0.02 (d) 0.002

77. $\frac{0.0203\times2.92}{0.0073\times14.5\times0.7}=?$

(a) 3.25 (b) 2.40 (c) 1.45 (d) 0.8

78. $\frac{3.6\times0.48\times2.50}{0.12\times0.09\times0.5}=?$

(a) 80000 (b) 8000 (c) 800 (d) 80

79. The value of $\frac{(0.1667)(0.8333)(0.3333)}{(0.2222)(0.6667)(0.1250)}$ is closest to

(a) 2.50 (b) 2.43 (c) 2.40 (d) 2

80. If $1.5x = 0.04y$, then the value of $\left(\frac{y-x}{y+x}\right)$ is

(a) $\frac{0.73}{77}$ (b) $\frac{7.3}{77}$ (c) $\frac{73}{77}$ (d) $\frac{730}{77}$

81. $8.7 - [7.6 - \{6.5 - (5.4 - \overline{4.3 - 2})\}]$ is simplified to
(*a*) 5.5 (*b*) 4.5 (*c*) 3.5 (*d*) 2.5

82. If $1^3 + 2^3 + 3^3 + ... + 9^3 = 2025$, then the value of $(0.11)^3 + (0.22)^3 + ... + (0.99)^3$ is closest to
(*a*) 3.695 (*b*) 2.695 (*c*) 0.3695 (*d*) 0.2695

83. The value of $(4.7 \times 13.26 + 4.7 \times 9.43 + 4.7 \times 77.31)$ is
(*a*) 4700 (*b*) 470 (*c*) 47 (*d*) 0.47

84. $\dfrac{5 \times 1.6 - 2 \times 1.4}{1.3} = ?$
(*a*) 4 (*b*) 1.4 (*c*) 1.2 (*d*) 0.4

85. $(0.2 \times 0.2 + 0.01)\ (0.1 \times 0.1 + 0.02)^{-1}$ is equal to
(*a*) $\dfrac{41}{12}$ (*b*) $\dfrac{41}{4}$ (*c*) $\dfrac{9}{5}$ (*d*) $\dfrac{5}{3}$

86. $(7.5 \times 7.5 + 37.5 + 2.5 \times 2.5)$ is equal to
(*a*) 100 (*b*) 80 (*c*) 60 (*d*) 30

87. $\dfrac{(0.6)^4 - (0.5)^4}{(0.6)^2 + (0.5)^2}$ is simplified to
(*a*) 11 (*b*) 1.1 (*c*) 0.11 (*d*) 0.1

88. $\dfrac{4.2 \times 4.2 - 1.9 \times 1.9}{2.3 \times 6.1} = ?$
(*a*) 4.2 (*b*) 1.9 (*c*) 1 (*d*) 0.5

89. $\left(\dfrac{1.49 \times 14.9 - 0.51 \times 5.1}{14.9 - 5.1}\right)$ is simplified to
(*a*) 22 (*b*) 20 (*c*) 2.00 (*d*) 0.20

90. $\dfrac{(67.542)^2 - (32.458)^2}{75.458 - 40.375}$ is simplified to
(*a*) 110 (*b*) 100 (*c*) 10 (*d*) 1

91. The value of $\dfrac{(2.644)^2 - (2.356)^2}{0.288}$ is
(*a*) 6 (*b*) 5 (*c*) 4 (*d*) 1

92. $\dfrac{(2.39)^2 - (1.61)^2}{2.39 - 1.61} = ?$
(*a*) 8 (*b*) 6 (*c*) 4 (*d*) 8

93. Evaluate : $\dfrac{0.2 \times 0.2 + 0.2 \times 0.02}{0.044}$
(*a*) 2 (*b*) 1 (*c*) 0.4 (*d*) 0.004

94. Simplify : $\dfrac{(2.3)^3 - 0.027}{(2.3)^2 + 0.69 + 0.09}$

(*a*) 3.4 (*b*) 2 (*c*) 1.6 (*d*) 0

95. Evaluate : $\dfrac{(0.96)^3 - (0.1)^3}{(0.96)^2 + 0.096 + (0.1)^2}$

(*a*) 1.06 (*b*) 0.97 (*c*) 0.95 (*d*) 0.86

96. Simplify : $\dfrac{8.94 \times 8.94 \times 8.94 - 3.56 \times 3.56 \times 3.56}{8.94 \times 8.94 + 8.94 \times 3.56 + 3.56 \times 3.56}$

(*a*) 53.8 (*b*) 0.0538 (*c*) 5.38 (*d*) 0.538

97. $\left[\dfrac{8(3.75)^2 + 1}{(7.5)^2 - 6.5}\right]$ is simplified to

(*a*) 8.5 (*b*) 4.75 (*c*) 2.75 (*d*) 9/5

98. The value of $\left[\dfrac{10.3 \times 10.3 \times 10.3 + 1}{10.3 \times 10.3 - 10.3 + 1}\right]$ is

(*a*) 12.3 (*b*) 11.3 (*c*) 10.3 (*d*) 9.3

99. $\left[\dfrac{0.125 + 0.027}{0.5 \times 0.5 + 0.09 - 0.15}\right]$ is simplified to

(*a*) 1 (*b*) 0.8 (*c*) 0.2 (*d*) 0.08

100. Simplify: $\left[\dfrac{(0.051)^3 + (0.041)^3}{(0.051)^2 - 0.051 \times 0.041 + (0.041)^2}\right]$

(*a*) 0.92 (*b*) 0.092 (*c*) 0.0092 (*d*) 0.00092

101. $\dfrac{(0.137 + 0.098)^2 - (0.137 - 0.098)^2}{0.137 \times 0.098}$ is simplified to

(*a*) 4 (*b*) 0.25 (*c*) 0.235 (*d*) 0.039

102. For what value of x, the expression $(11.98 \times 11.98 + 11.98 \times x + 0.02 \times 0.02)$ will be a perfect square?

(*a*) 0.4 (*b*) 0.04 (*c*) 0.2 (*d*) 0.02

EXPLANATORY ANSWERS

1. $\dfrac{15}{25} = \dfrac{3 \times 5}{5 \times 5} = \dfrac{3}{5}$

2. $\dfrac{9 * 3}{3 * 7} = \dfrac{9}{7}$, or, $\dfrac{9 \times 3}{7 \times 3} = \dfrac{9}{7}$, $\therefore$ The sign * is ×.

3. $\frac{5}{6}$ of 1 hr. $= \frac{5}{6} \times 60$ minutes $= 50$ minutes.

4. Remaining fuel $= 1 - \frac{2}{5} = \frac{5-2}{5} = \frac{3}{5}$

Distance flown by $\frac{2}{5}$ of fuel = 1250 km.

Distance flown by full fuel $= \frac{1250}{2/5} = \frac{1250 \times 5}{2}$ km.

Distance flown by $\frac{3}{5}$ of fuel $= \frac{1250 \times 5 \times 3}{2 \times 5} = 1875$ km.

6. $\frac{3}{15} = \frac{1}{5}, \frac{8}{64} = \frac{1}{8}, \frac{5}{20} = \frac{1}{4}, \frac{25}{1000} = \frac{1}{40}$

Now, the fractions are $\frac{1}{5}, \frac{1}{4}, \frac{1}{8}, \frac{1}{40}$

∴ The largest fraction is $\frac{1}{4} = \frac{5}{20}$

7. $x \times 6 + 12 = 6x + 12$

8. $5 \times y - 20 = 5y - 20$

9. $15 - 7 = 8$

10. Let the number be x

∴ $4x + 21 = 57$ or, $4x = 57 - 21 = 36$

Hence, $x = \frac{36}{4} = 9$

11. Let the number be x

∴ $\frac{x}{4} + \frac{x}{5} = \frac{x}{3} + 28$

⇒ $\frac{9x}{20} = \frac{x}{3} + 28$

⇒ $\frac{9x}{20} - \frac{x}{3} = 28$ ⇒ $\frac{27x - 20x}{60} = 28$

∴ $x = \frac{28 \times 60}{7} = 240.$

12. $5\frac{3}{4} + 4\frac{4}{5} + 7\frac{3}{8} = \frac{23}{4} + \frac{24}{5} + \frac{59}{8} = \frac{717}{40}$

717/40 becomes whole number when 3/40 is added to it, *i.e.,*

$\frac{717}{40} + \frac{3}{40} = \frac{720}{40} = 18$ which is a whole number.

13. $\frac{1}{15} + \frac{3}{15} + \frac{5}{15} + \frac{6}{15} = \frac{1+3+5+6}{15} = \frac{15}{15} = 1$

14. Let the number be x

$$\frac{x}{6} = \frac{x}{9} + 100$$

$$\Rightarrow \quad \frac{x}{6} - \frac{x}{9} = 100, \quad \Rightarrow \frac{x}{18} = 100$$

$$\therefore \quad x = 100 \times 18 = 1800.$$

15. Let the number be x

$$\therefore \quad \frac{x}{2} + \frac{x}{4} + \frac{x}{8} = 28, \quad \Rightarrow \frac{7x}{8} = 28$$

$$\therefore \quad x = \frac{28 \times 8}{7} = 32.$$

16. Let the number be x

$$\therefore \quad \frac{x}{9} + \frac{x}{3} + \frac{x}{6} + \frac{7x}{18} = 150$$

$$\Rightarrow \quad \frac{2x + 6x + 3x + 7x}{18} = \frac{18x}{18} = 150$$

$$\therefore \quad x = 150.$$

17. .999 is the greatest.

18. $9\frac{1}{8} = 9 + \frac{1}{8} = 9 + .125 = 9.125$

19. $2.205 \div 0.15 = \frac{2.205}{.15} = \frac{2205}{1000} \times \frac{100}{15}$

$$= \frac{2205}{150} = 14.7.$$

20. G.C.M. of .24, 3.2 and 16.0

$$= \text{G.C.M. of } \frac{24, 320 \text{ and } 1600}{100}$$

$$= \frac{8}{100} = 0.08$$

21. L.C.M. of .24, 3.2 and 16.0 = L.C.M. of $\frac{24, 320 \text{ and } 1600}{100} = \frac{4800}{100} = 48.$

22. Let total length of the pole = x

Pole above water $= x - [0.5x + 0.25x]$

$= 0.25x$; But, $0.25x = 2$ metres

$$\therefore \quad x = \frac{2 \times 100}{25} = 8 \text{ metres}$$

23. $$\sqrt{\frac{1}{3}} = \frac{\sqrt{1}}{\sqrt{3}} = \frac{1}{\sqrt{3}} = \frac{1}{1.732} = \frac{1000}{1732} = 0.57$$

24.
$$\frac{2}{3} \text{ of } \frac{1}{2} = \frac{2}{3} \times \frac{1}{2} = \frac{1}{3}$$
$$\frac{1}{2} \text{ of } \frac{1}{3} = \frac{1}{6}$$
$$\therefore \quad \frac{1}{6} \div \frac{1}{3} = \frac{1}{6} \times \frac{3}{1} = \frac{1}{2}$$

25. Eleventh part of $990\frac{990}{990} = 990\frac{990}{990} \div 11 = \frac{990}{11} = 90$

26. When train started from Delhi, let number of passengers was x. On next station, 1/3 got down and 96 got in.

Now passengers in train $= x - \frac{x}{3} + 96 = \frac{2x}{3} + 96$

On next station 1/2 of it got down and 12 got in, *i.e.*,

$\frac{1}{2}\left[\frac{2x}{3} + 96\right]$ got down and 12 got in

Now passengers in train $= \frac{2x}{3} + 96 - \left[\frac{x}{3} + 48\right] + 12$

$$= \frac{2x}{3} - \frac{x}{3} + 96 - 48 + 12 = 248$$

$\therefore \quad x = [248 - 60] \times 3 = 188 \times 3 = 564.$

27. $1 \div [1 + 1 \div \{1 + 1 \div (1 + 1 \div 2)\}]$

$= 1 \div [1 + 1 \div \{1 + 1 \div \frac{3}{2}\}]$

$= 1 \div [1 + 1 \div \frac{5}{3}]$

$= 1 \div \frac{8}{5} = \frac{5}{8}$

28. Put $1.25 = a$ and $2.75 = b$, then,

$1.25 \times 1.25 + 2.75 \times 2.75 + 2 \times 1.25 \times 2.75$

$= a^2 + b^2 + 2ab = (a + b)^2$

$= (1.25 + 2.75)^2 = (4)^2 = 16$

29. 1 second $= \frac{1}{60 \times 60} = \frac{1}{3600}$ hour

30. G.C.M. of 1.6 and 0.72 is 0.08

31. $\frac{4}{5} \times 0.025 = \frac{4}{5} \times \frac{25}{1000} = \frac{1}{50} = 0.02$

32.
$$0.7\dot{3}\dot{2} \div 0.02\dot{7} = 0.73\dot{2}\dot{3} \div 0.02\dot{7}$$
$$= \frac{7323 - 73}{9900} \div \frac{27 - 2}{900}$$
$$= \frac{290}{11} = 26.\dot{3}\dot{6}$$

33. $0.\dot{6} \div 0.75 = \frac{6}{9} \div \frac{75}{100}$

$= \frac{2}{3} \div \frac{3}{4} = \frac{2}{3} \times \frac{4}{3} = \frac{8}{9} = 0.\dot{8}$

34. $\frac{3}{4} = 0.75$, $\frac{5}{6} = 0.833$, $\frac{9}{10} = 0.9$, $\frac{4}{5} = 0.8$, $\frac{2}{3} = 0.66$, $\frac{1}{2} = 0.5$

Hence, 0.8 is greater than 0.75 and less than 0.833.

Therefore, $\frac{4}{5}$ is greater than $\frac{3}{4}$ and less than $\frac{5}{6}$.

35. Here, $\frac{2}{3} = 0.66$, $\frac{3}{4} = 0.75$, $\frac{4}{5} = 0.8$, $\frac{5}{6} = 0.833$.

Hence, biggest fraction = $\frac{5}{6}$ and smallest fraction = $\frac{2}{3}$

Their difference = $\frac{5}{6} - \frac{2}{3} = \frac{1}{6}$.

36. Here, $\frac{19}{21} = 0.904$; $\frac{11}{14} = 0.785$; $\frac{16}{19} = 0.842$

Hence, $0.785 < 0.842 < 0.904$

$\therefore \frac{11}{14} < \frac{16}{19} < \frac{19}{21}$

37. Here $\frac{11}{17} = 0.647$; $\frac{7}{11} = 0.636$; $\frac{5}{9} = 0.555$; $\frac{8}{15} = 0.533$

Hence, $0.647 > 0.636 > 0.555 > 0.533$

$\therefore \frac{11}{17} > \frac{7}{11} > \frac{5}{9} > \frac{8}{15}$

38. Here, $\frac{2}{5} = 0.4$; $\frac{3}{5} = 0.6$; $\frac{1}{3} = 0.33$; $\frac{4}{7} = 0.57$; $\frac{5}{6} = 0.83$; $\frac{6}{7} = 0.85$

Hence, $0.33 < 0.4 < 0.57 < 0.6 < 0.83 < 0.85$

$\therefore \frac{1}{3} < \frac{2}{5} < \frac{4}{7} < \frac{3}{5} < \frac{5}{6} < \frac{6}{7}$

39. Here, $\frac{8}{9} = 0.88$; $\frac{9}{11} = 0.81$; $\frac{7}{9} = 0.77$; $\frac{2}{3} = 0.66$; $\frac{3}{5} = 0.6$

Hence, $0.6 < 0.66 < 0.77 < 0.81 < 0.88$

$\therefore \frac{3}{5} < \frac{2}{3} < \frac{7}{9} < \frac{9}{11} < \frac{8}{9}$

40. Here, $47.2506 = 4A + \frac{7}{B} + 2C + \frac{5}{D} + 6E$ ...(i)

But, $47.2506 = 40 + 7 + 0.2 + 0.05 + 0.0006$ ...(ii)

By comparing (i) and (ii), we get

$4A = 40 \Rightarrow A = 10; \frac{7}{B} = 7 \Rightarrow B = 1; 2C = 0.2 \Rightarrow C = 0.1$

$\frac{5}{D} = 0.05 \Rightarrow D = 100; 6E = 0.0006 \Rightarrow E = 0.0001$

Now, $5A + 3B + 6C + D + 3E = 5 \times 10 + 3 \times 1 + 6 \times 0.1 + 100 + 3 \times 0.0001$
$= 50 + 3 + 0.6 + 100 + 0.0003 = 153.6003$

41. ? = (779.84 + 242.31) − 832.58 = 1022.15 − 832.58 = 189.57

42. ? = (138.009 + 341.981) − (146.305 + 123.6)
= 479.990 − 269.905 = 210.085

43. ? = 12.1212 + 17.0005 − 9.1102 = 29.1217 − 9.1102 = 20.0115

44. ? = 617 + 6.107 + 0.617 + 6.0017 = 629.6357

45. ? = 1 + 0.1 + 0.01 + 0.001 = 1.111

46. ? = 3 × 0.3 × 0.03 × 0.003 × 30 = 0.00243

47. ? = 0.04 × 0.0162 = 0.000648 = 6.48×10^{-4}

48. ? = 40.83 × 1.02 × 1.2 = 41.6466 × 1.2 = 49.97592

49. ? = 0.014 × 0.014 = 0.000196

50. ? = 16.02 × 0.001 = 0.01602

51. Here, $1.125 \times 10^k = 0.001125 = 1.125 \times 10^{-3}$

$\therefore k = -3$

52. Let, $x + 543 + 5.43 = 603.26$

$\therefore x = 603.26 - 548.43 = 54.83$

Now, 54. (?) 3 = 54.83 ⇒ ? = 8

53. $\frac{1}{0.04} = \frac{100}{4} = 25$

54. $4.036 \div 0.04 = \frac{4036}{40} = \frac{1009}{10} = 100.9$

55. I. $\frac{368.39}{17} = 21.67$ II. $\frac{170.50}{62} = 2.75$ III. $\frac{875.65}{83} = 10.55$

Hence, 21.67 > 10.55 > 2.75

∴ Their sequence in decreasing order will be I, III, II

56. Here, $\frac{144}{0.144} = \frac{14.4}{x} \Rightarrow x = \frac{14.4 \times 0.144}{144} = 0.0144$

57. $? = \frac{0.000016}{0.04} = \frac{0.0016}{4} = 0.0004$

58. Let commodity A will cost 40 paise more than B after t years.

Then, $(4.20 + 0.40t) - (6.30 + 0.15t) = 0.40$

$\Rightarrow -2.10 + 0.25\,t = 0.40$

$\therefore\ t = \dfrac{2.50}{0.25} = \dfrac{250}{25} = 10$

Hence, A will cost 40 paise more than B after 10 years 2001 i.e., 2011.

59. Required number of pieces = 37.5 × 8 = 300

60. $6.\overline{46} = 6\dfrac{46}{99} = \dfrac{640}{99}$

61. $2.1\overline{36} = 2\dfrac{136-1}{990} = 2\dfrac{135}{990} = 2\dfrac{3}{22}$

62. $(0.2)^2 = 0.04;\ \ 0.\overline{2} = \dfrac{2}{9} = 0.22;\ \ \dfrac{1}{0.2} = \dfrac{10}{2} = 5;\ 0.2.$

The least among them is 0.04 i.e., $(0.2)^2$

63. $0.\overline{47} = \dfrac{47}{99}$

64. $0.125125\ ......\ = 0.\overline{125} = \dfrac{125}{999}$

65. $0.232323\ ......\ = 0.\overline{23} = \dfrac{23}{99}$

66. Here, $\dfrac{1}{6.198} = 0.16134$

Then, $\dfrac{1}{0.0006198} = \dfrac{1}{6.198} \times 10000 = 0.16134 \times 10000 = 1613.4$

67. Here, 213 × 16 = 3408

Then, $1.6 \times 21.3 = \dfrac{16}{10} \times \dfrac{213}{10} = \dfrac{3408}{100} = 34.08$

68. $\dfrac{547.527}{0.0082} = x$

Then, $\dfrac{547527}{82} = \dfrac{547.527 \times 1000}{0.0082 \times 10000} = \dfrac{547.527}{0.0082} \times \dfrac{1}{10} = \dfrac{x}{10}$

69. $\overline{2}.75 + \overline{3}.78 = -2 + .75 - 3 + .78 = -5 + 1.53 = \overline{4}.53$

70. $\left(0.34\overline{67} + 0.13\overline{33}\right) = \dfrac{3467-34}{9900} + \dfrac{1333-13}{9900} = \dfrac{3433+1320}{9900}$

$= \dfrac{4753}{9900} = \dfrac{4801-48}{9900} = 0.48\overline{01}$

71. $3.\overline{36} - 2.\overline{05} + 1.\overline{33} = (3 + 0.\overline{36}) + (1 + 0.\overline{33}) - (2 + 0.\overline{05})$

$$= \left[4 + \left(\frac{36}{99} + \frac{33}{99}\right)\right] - \left[2 + \frac{5}{99}\right] = 2 + \left(\frac{69}{99} - \frac{5}{99}\right)$$

$$= 2 + \frac{64}{99} = 2.\overline{64}$$

72. $0.\overline{2} + 0.\overline{3} + 0.\overline{4} + 0.\overline{9} + 0.\overline{39}$

$$= \frac{2}{9} + \frac{3}{9} + \frac{4}{9} + \frac{9}{9} + \frac{39}{99} = \frac{18}{9} + \frac{39}{99} = 2 + \frac{39}{99} = 2 + \frac{13}{33} = 2\frac{13}{33}$$

73. $\frac{52416}{312} = 168 \Rightarrow \frac{52416}{168} = 312$

Then, $\frac{52.416}{0.0168} = \frac{52416 \times 10^{-3}}{168 \times 10^{-4}} = \frac{52416}{168} \times 10 = 312 \times 10 = 3120$

74. Here, 54.327 × 357.2 × 0.0057 = 5.437 × 3.572 × 5.7
Because number of decimal places in both sides are equal *i.e.* 8.

75. $\frac{489.1375 \times 0.0483 \times 1.956}{0.0873 \times 92.581 \times 99.749} \approx \frac{489 \times 0.05 \times 2}{0.09 \times 93 \times 100} = \frac{489 \times 5 \times 2}{9 \times 93 \times 100}$

$$= \frac{163}{279} \times \frac{1}{10} = \frac{0.58}{10} = 0.058 \approx 0.06$$

76. $\frac{3.157 \times 4126 \times 3.198}{63.972 \times 2835.121} \approx \frac{3.2 \times 4126 \times 3.2}{64 \times 2835} = \frac{32 \times 4126 \times 32}{64 \times 2835} \times \frac{1}{100}$

$$= \frac{66016}{2835} \times \frac{1}{100} = \frac{23.2}{100} = 0.232 \approx 0.2$$

77. $\frac{0.0203 \times 2.92}{0.0073 \times 14.5 \times 0.7} = \frac{203 \times 292 \times 10^{-6}}{73 \times 145 \times 7 \times 10^{-6}} = \frac{4}{5} = 0.8$

78. $\frac{3.6 \times 0.48 \times 2.50}{0.12 \times 0.09 \times 0.5} = \frac{36 \times 48 \times 250 \times 10^{-5}}{12 \times 9 \times 5 \times 10^{-5}} = 800$

79. $\frac{(0.1667)(0.8383)(0.3333)}{(0.2222)(0.6667)(0.1250)} = \frac{3333}{2222} \times \frac{0.1667 \times 0.8383}{0.6667 \times \frac{125}{1000}}$

$$= \frac{3}{2} \times \frac{\frac{1}{6} \times \frac{5}{6}}{\frac{2}{3} \times \frac{1}{8}} = \frac{3}{2} \times \frac{1}{6} \times \frac{5}{6} \times \frac{3}{2} \times \frac{8}{1} = \frac{5}{2} = 2.50$$

80. $1.5x = 0.04y \Rightarrow \frac{x}{y} = \frac{0.04}{1.5} = \frac{4}{150} = \frac{2}{75}$

Now, $\frac{y-x}{y+x} = \frac{1-\frac{x}{y}}{1+\frac{x}{y}} = \frac{1-\frac{2}{75}}{1+\frac{2}{75}} = \frac{73/75}{77/75} = \frac{73}{77}$

81. $8.7 - [7.6 - \{6.5 - \{5.4 - \overline{4.3-2}\,)\}]$
$= 8.7 - [7.6 - \{6.5 - (5.4 - 2.3)\}]$
$= 8.7 - [7.6 - \{6.5 - 3.1\}]$
$= 8.7 - [7.6 - 3.4]$
$= 8.7 - 4.2 = 4.5$

82. Here, $1^3 + 2^3 + 3^3 + ... + 9^3 = 2025$
Now, $(0.11)^3 + (0.22)^3 + (0.33)^3 + ... + (0.99)^3$
$= (0.11)^3\ [1^3 + 2^3 + 3^3 + ... + 9^3]$
$= 0.001331 \times 2025 = 2.695275 \approx 2.695$

83. $4.7 \times 13.26 + 4.7 \times 9.43 + 4.7 \times 77.31$
$= 4.7\ (13.26 + 9.43 + 77.31)$
$= 4.7 \times 100.00 = 470$

84. $\frac{5\times1.6-2\times1.4}{1.3} = \frac{8-2.8}{1.3} = \frac{5.2}{1.3} = \frac{52}{13} = 4$

85. $(0.2 \times 0.2 + 0.01)\ (0.1 \times 0.1 + 0.02)^{-1}$
$= \frac{(0.04+0.01)}{(0.01+0.02)} = \frac{0.05}{0.03} = \frac{5}{3}$

86. $7.5 \times 7.5 + 37.5 + 2.5 \times 2.5$
$= 7.5 \times 7.5 + 2 \times 7.5 \times 2.5 + 2.5 \times 2.5$
$= (7.5 + 2.5)^2 = (10)^2 = 100$

87. $\frac{(0.6)^4-(0.5)^4}{(0.6)^2+(0.5)^2} = \frac{\left[(0.6)^2\right]^2-\left[(0.5)^2\right]^2}{(0.6)^2+(0.5)^2} = \frac{\left[(0.6)^2+(0.5)^2\right]\left[(0.6)^2-(0.5)^2\right]}{\left[(0.6)^2+(0.5)^2\right]}$

$= (0.6)^2 - (0.5)^2 = 0.36 - 0.25 = 0.11$

88. $\frac{4.2\times4.2-1.9\times1.9}{2.3\times6.1} = \frac{(4.2)^2-(1.9)^2}{(4.2-1.9)\ (4.2+1.9)} = \frac{(4.2+1.9)(4.2-1.9)}{(4.2+1.9)\ (4.2-1.9)} = 1$

89. $\frac{1.49\times14.9-0.51\times5.1}{14.9-5.1} = \frac{1.49\times1.49\times10-0.51\times0.51\times10}{1.49\times10-0.51\times10}$

$= \frac{10\left[(1.49)^2-(0.51)^2\right]}{10(1.49-0.51)} = \frac{(1.49+0.51)(1.49-0.51)}{(1.49-0.51)} = 1.49 + 0.51 = 2$

90. $$\frac{(67.542)^2-(32.458)^2}{75.458-40.374}=\frac{(67.542+32.458)(67.542-32.458)}{35.084}$$

$$=\frac{100\times 35.084}{35.084}=100$$

91. $$\frac{(2.644)^2-(2.356)^2}{0.288}=\frac{(2.644+2.356)(2.644-2.356)}{0.288}$$

$$=\frac{5\times 0.288}{0.288}=5$$

92. $$\frac{(2.39)^2-(1.61)^2}{2.39-1.61}=\frac{(2.39+1.61)(2.39-1.61)}{(2.39-1.61)}=2.39+1.61=4$$

93. $$\frac{0.2\times 0.2+0.2\times 0.2}{0.044}=\frac{0.04+0.004}{0.044}=\frac{0.044}{0.044}=1$$

94. $$\frac{(2.3)^3-0.027}{(2.3)^2+0.69+0.09}=\frac{(2.3)^3-(0.3)^3}{(2.3)^2+2.3\times 0.3+(0.3)^2}$$

$$=\frac{(2.3-0.3)\left[(2.3)^2+2.3\times 0.3+(0.3)^2\right]}{\left[(2.3)^2+2.3\times 0.3+(0.3)^2\right]}=2.3-0.3=2$$

95. $$\frac{(0.96)^3-(0.1)^3}{(0.96)^2+0.096+(0.1)^2}=\frac{(0.96-0.1)\left[(0.96)^2+0.96\times 0.1+(0.1)^2\right]}{(0.96)^2+0.96\times 0.1+(0.1)^2}$$

$$=0.96-0.1$$
$$=0.86$$

96. $$\frac{8.94\times 8.94\times 8.94-3.56\times 3.56\times 3.56}{8.94\times 8.94+8.94\times 3.56+3.56\times 3.56}=\frac{(8.94)^3-(3.56)^3}{8.94\times 8.94+8.94\times 3.56+3.56\times 356}$$

$$=\frac{(8.94-3.56)\left[(8.94)^2+8.94\times 3.56+(3.56)^2\right]}{\left[(8.94)^2+8.94\times 3.56+(3.56)^2\right]}=8.94-3.56=5.38$$

97. $$\left[\frac{8(3.75)^3+1}{(7.5)^2-65}\right]=\frac{(2\times 3.75)^3+1^3}{(7.5)^2-6.5}$$

$$= \frac{(7.5)^3 + 1^3}{(7.5)^2 - 6.5} = \frac{(7.5+1)\left[(7.5)^2 - 7.5 \times 1 + 1^2\right]}{(7.5)^2 - 6.5}$$

$$= \frac{8.5 \times \left[(7.5)^2 - 7.5 + 1\right]}{(7.5)^2 - 6.5} = \frac{8.5 \times \left[(7.5)^2 - 6.5\right]}{(7.5)^2 - 6.5} = 8.5$$

98. $\dfrac{10.3 \times 10.3 \times 10.3 + 1}{10.3 \times 10.3 - 10.3 + 1} = \dfrac{(10.3)^3 + (1)^3}{(10.3)^2 - 10.3 \times 1 + 1^2} = \dfrac{(10.3+1)\left[(10.3^2) - 10.3 \times 1 + 1^2\right]}{\left[(10.3)^2 - 10.3 \times 1 + 1^2\right]} = 10.3 + 1 = 11.3$

99. $\dfrac{0.125 + 0.027}{0.5 \times 0.5 + 0.09 - 0.15} = \dfrac{(0.5)^3 + (0.3)^3}{(0.5)^2 + (0.3)^2 - 0.5 \times 0.3} = \dfrac{(0.5+0.3)\left[(0.5)^2 + (0.3)^2 - 0.5 \times 0.3\right]}{\left[(0.5)^2 + (0.3)^2 - 0.5 \times 0.3\right]} = 0.5 + 0.3 = 0.8$

100. $\dfrac{(0.051)^3 + (0.041)^3}{(0.051)^3 - 0.051 \times 0.041 + (0.041)^2} = \dfrac{(0.051+0.41)\left[(0.051)^2 - 0.051 \times 0.041 + (0.41)^2\right]}{\left[(0.051)^2 - 0.051 \times 0.41 + (0.041)^2\right]}$

$$= 0.051 + 0.041 = 0.092$$

101. $\dfrac{(0.137 + 0.098)^2 - (0.137 - 0.098)^2}{0.137 \times 0.098}$

$$= \frac{(0.137)^2 + (0.098)^2 + 2 \times 0.137 \times 0.098 - (0.137)^2 - (0.098)^2 + 2 \times 0.137 \times 0.098}{0.137 \times 0.098}$$

$$= \frac{4 \times 0.137 \times 0.098}{0.137 \times 0.098} = 4$$

102. $11.98 \times 11.98 + 11.98x + 0.02 \times 0.02$

$(12)^2 = (11.98 + 0.02)^2 = (11.98)^2 + (0.02)^2 + 2 \times 11.98 \times 0.02$

$= (11.98)^2 + (0.02)^2 + 0.04 \times 11.98$

Hence, required value of $x = 0.04$

NUMBER SERIES

In this type of questions a sequence of numbers is given, which are usually called TERMS of the sequence. All the terms of the sequence are arranged according to a certain rule/pattern. It can be seen that each number of the given sequence changes from the preceding one in a particular order. The candidates are required to study carefully the given sequence to perceive the pattern of change and discern the rule/ pattern which is being followed by the terms of the sequence.

Finding out the wrong term in the Series: In this type of questions a sequence or group of numbers is given in which all others except one are similar in some respect. The one term of the sequence does not follow the same pattern/rule as is followed by the others. This one is the wrong term in the series. Candidates are required to find out the one which does not conform to the rule used in writing the series and is different from the others and therefore does not fit in the sequence.

For example, in the series 7, 28, 63, 124, 215, 342, 511, one term is wrong and this wrong term has to be found out.

A careful scrutiny of the sequence reveals that terms of the sequence are in the following order:

$2^3 - 1, 3^3 - 1, 4^3 - 1, 5^3 - 1, 6^3 - 1, 7^3 - 1, 8^3 - 1.$

Therefore, second term of the sequence, *i.e.*, 28 should be replaced by 26 so that all the terms of the series follow a particular order. Hence, 28 is the wrong term in the series.

Finding out the missing term of the series: In this type of questions, a number series is given in which a blank space or question mark is provided in place of any one term or element of the series. All terms of the series including the missing term at the question mark form a series i.e., the term at the blank space follow the same pattern/rule as is followed by other terms. Candidates are required to study carefully the pattern and find out the term from the given alternatives to fit in the blank space or to replace the question mark.

For Example: In the sequence 6, 24, 60, ?, 210, 336, one term is missing. A scrutiny of the terms will reveal that the terms of the sequence are arranged in the following order:

$2^3 - 2, 3^3 - 3, 4^3 - 4, 5^3 - 5, 6^3 - 6, 7^3 - 7.$

Therefore, fourth term in place of question mark will be $5^3 - 5 = 120$.

Composite (or Compound) series: The composite (or compound) series is one which is obtained by combining two or more different series. Terms or elements of a compound or composite series follow two or more patterns. For example, a number sequence, 1, 1, 4, 3, 9, 5, 16, 7, 25, 9, ? is given in which the question mark has to be replaced by an appropriate term. Here, we can find out that the series constitutes two different sequences. One is 1, 4, 9, 16, 25 and the other is 1, 3, 5, 7, 9. Therefore, 36, should replace the question mark. This is because the numbers in the given series are in the order of $1^2, 2^2, 3^2, 4^2, 5^2, 6^2$. Thus, the term in place of the question mark is the term of the first sequence.

Example (1 to 4): Directions: *Given below are four number series. Each of these number series contains a wrong term. You have to perceive the pattern/rule which is being followed by the terms of the series and find out the wrong term of the series to replace by a correct one from amongst the alternatives given.*

1. 240, 240, 120, 40, 20, 2
(*a*) 15 (*b*) 1 (*c*) 10 (*d*) 50 (*e*) 60

2. 9, 25, 49, 89, 121, 169, 225
(*a*) 64 (*b*) 16 (*c*) 36 (*d*) 81 (*e*) 210

3. 3, 3, 6, 18, 70, 360
(*a*) 3 (*b*) 360 (*c*) 6 (*d*) 18 (*e*) 70

4. 1, 16, 9, 64, 25, 216, 49
(*a*) 25 (*b*) 216 (*c*) 160 (*d*) 144 (*e*) 90

1. (*c*)**:** A careful study of the given number sequence will reveal that if 20 is replaced by 10 then two successive terms of the sequence will form the ratio of 1 : 1, 2 : 1, 3 : 1, 4 : 1 and 5 : 1 respectively. Therefore, the term given in alternative (*c*) is the correct answer.

2. (*d*)**:** If 89 is replaced by 81, then the following number series will be formed
$3^2, 5^2, 7^2, 9^2, 11^2, 13^2, 15^2$.
Therefore, alternative (*d*) is the correct alternative.

3. (*e*)**:** If each term of the given sequence is multiplied by its place number in the sequence, then next term of the sequence could be found out. Therefore 70, *i.e.*, 5th term of the series should be replaced by 72. Hence, alternative (*e*) is the correct answer.

4. (*d*)**:** One can note that each of the terms of the sequence, except 216, is a perfect square. Therefore if 216 is replaced by 144, then all terms will become perfect squares and terms of the sequence could be written in the following manner:
$1^2, 4^2, 3^2, 8^2, 5^2, 12^2, 7^2$
Therefore, alternative (*d*) is the correct answer.

EXERCISE

Directions (Qs. 1 to 25): *In each of the questions from 1 to 25, a number series is given followed by five alternatives. One term/element of the given series is wrong, i.e., it does not conform to the rule used in writing the series. This wrong term is depicted in the following alternatives. Spot out that wrong term/element and mark your answer.*

1. 5, 15, 30, 135, 405, 1215, 3645
(*a*) 3645 (*b*) 5 (*c*) 405 (*d*) 1215 (*e*) 30

2. 2, 3, 6, 10, 18, 27, 54
(*a*) 10 (*b*) 27 (*c*) 3 (*d*) 6 (*e*) 18

3. 3, 4, 8, 17, 33, 49, 94
(*a*) 17 (*b*) 8 (*c*) 4 (*d*) 33 (*e*) 49

4. 36, 49, 100, 144, 196, 256, 324
(*a*) 256 (*b*) 36 (*c*) 49 (*d*) 144 (*e*) 100

5. 508, 250, 124, 60, 28, 12, 4
(a) 28 (b) 124 (c) 60 (d) 12 (e) 250

6. 16, 17, 21, 30, 45, 71, 107
(a) 16 (b) 107 (c) 45 (d) 21 (e) 71

7. 380, 188, 92, 48, 20, 8, 2
(a) 48 (b) 20 (c) 92 (d) 8 (e) 188

8. 325, 259, 202, 160, 127, 105, 94
(a) 94 (b) 105 (c) 202 (d) 259 (e) 127

9. 8, 13, 21, 32, 47, 63, 83
(a) 32 (b) 83 (c) 13 (d) 21 (e) 47

10. 3, 5, 6, 7, 10, 11, 13, 14, 15, 16
(a) 10 (b) 7 (c) 11 (d) 16 (e) 5

11. 2, 3, 5, 8, 15, 21, 34, 55
(a) 5 (b) 8 (c) 3 (d) 21 (e) 15

12. 2, 5, 10, 18, 26, 37, 50
(a) 37 (b) 18 (c) 5 (d) 50 (e) 2

13. 1, 4, 7, 11, 16, 22, 29
(a) 4 (b) 11 (c) 22 (d) 29 (e) 1

14. 4, 6, 9, 18, 34, 59, 95
(a) 34 (b) 6 (c) 18 (d) 95 (e) 9

15. 3, 18, 38, 78, 123, 178, 24
(a) 3 (b) 18 (c) 123 (d) 178 (e) 38

16. 1, 6, 16, 26, 76, 156, 316
(a) 316 (b) 26 (c) 1 (d) 156 (e) 76

17. 12, 18, 27, 90, 270, 945, 3780
(a) 945 (b) 270 (c) 27 (d) 18 (e) 12

18. 5, 11, 23, 47, 96, 191, 383
(a) 191 (b) 23 (c) 96 (d) 47 (e) 11

19. 112, 114, 120, 124, 132, 142, 154
(a) 132 (b) 142 (c) 124 (d) 114 (e) 120

20. 54, 43, 34, 26, 22, 19, 18
(a) 26 (b) 18 (c) 43 (d) 22 (e) 34

21. 15, 45, 90, 360, 1080, 2160, 6480
(a) 6480 (b) 1080 (c) 360 (d) 2160 (e) 90

22. 8, 12, 16, 23, 32, 43, 56
(a) 12 (b) 23 (c) 18 (d) 43 (e) 23

23. 3, 8, 15, 24, 34, 48, 63
(a) 48 (b) 24 (c) 34 (d) 63 (e) 15

24. 11, 12, 14, 17, 20, 26, 32
(a) 14 (b) 17 (c) 26 (d) 32 (e) 20

25. 2, 9, 17, 65, 126, 217, 344
(*a*) 17 (*b*) 126 (*c*) 217 (*d*) 344 (*e*) 9

Directions (Qs. 26 to 50): *In each of the questions below a number series has been given followed by five alternatives. One term/element of the given number series is wrong. Find out that wrong term and spot out a number from the alternatives which will replace the wrong term of the series.*

26. 95, 86, 73, 62, 47, 30, 11
(*a*) 90 (*b*) 75 (*c*) 64 (*d*) 35 (*e*) 15

27. 0, 9, 64, 169, 576, 1225
(*a*) 225 (*b*) 360 (*c*) 444 (*d*) 556 (*e*) 630

28. 5, 10, 17, 26, 39, 50, 65
(*a*) 39 (*b*) 36 (*c*) 37 (*d*) 42 (*e*) 63

29. 1, 4, 10, 22, 46, 95, 190
(*a*) 74 (*b*) 25 (*c*) 94 (*d*) 101 (*e*) 116

30. 2, 9, 28, 65, 126, 216, 344
(*a*) 38 (*b*) 217 (*c*) 356 (*d*) 66 (*e*) 125

31. 3, 4.5, 9, 22.5, 67.5, 270, 945
(*a*) 236.25 (*b*) 175.5 (*c*) 62.5 (*d*) 140 (*e*) 5.5

32. 7, 14, 56, 168, 336, 1344, 2688, 8064
(*a*) 3032 (*b*) 5032 (*c*) 4032 (*d*) 2680 (*e*) 332

33. 299, 178, 97, 48, 24, 14, 13
(*a*) 175 (*b*) 295 (*c*) 23 (*d*) 10 (*e*) 7

34. 11, 15, 17, 19, 23, 25
(*a*) 14 (*b*) 18 (*c*) 21 (*d*) 10 (*e*) 13

35. 58, 57, 54, 50, 42, 33, 22
(*a*) 48 (*b*) 49 (*c*) 52 (*d*) 30 (*e*) 18

36. 3, 10, 19, 31, 43, 58, 75
(*a*) 20 (*b*) 18 (*c*) 30 (*d*) 42 (*e*) 72

37. 7, 9, 17, 42, 91, 172, 293
(*a*) 16 (*b*) 25 (*c*) 36 (*d*) 8 (*e*) 49

38. 105, 85, 60, 30, 0, –45, –90
(*a*) –5 (*b*) 55 (*c*) –10 (*d*) 15 (*e*) –35

39. 2100, 2000, 1600, 1200, 700, 100
(*a*) 1900 (*b*) 1800 (*c*) 2150 (*d*) 750 (*e*) 50

40. 90, 72, 56, 40, 30, 20, 12
(*a*) 32 (*b*) 18 (*c*) 25 (*d*) 42 (*e*) 50

41. 169, 121, 80, 49, 25, 9, 1
(*a*) 100 (*b*) 81 (*c*) 36 (*d*) 16 (*e*) 4

42. 3, 4, 10, 32, 136, 685, 4116
(*a*) 35 (*b*) 135 (*c*) 40 (*d*) 33 (*e*) 4110

43. 8, 14, 26, 48, 98, 194, 386
(*a*) 60 (*b*) 50 (*c*) 72 (*d*) 96 (*e*) 108

44. 7, 28, 63, 124, 215, 342, 511
(a) 26 *(b)* 65 *(c)* 123 *(d)* 216 *(e)* 360

45. 49, 48, 45, 42, 33, 24, 13
(a) 53 *(b)* 34 *(c)* 38 *(d)* 40 *(e)* 12

46. 4, 25, 100, 289, 652, 1369, 2500
(a) 2022 *(b)* 342 *(c)* 676 *(d)* 978 *(e)* 1580

47. 1, 3, 7, 19, 42, 89, 184
(a) 8 *(b)* 9 *(c)* 24 *(d)* 30 *(e)* 182

48. 2, 6, 8, 16, 20, 28, 35, 45
(a) 9 *(b)* 25 *(c)* 36 *(d)* 144 *(e)* 14

49. 1, 3, 7, 15, 31, 65, 127, 255
(a) 63 *(b)* 34 *(c)* 45 *(d)* 250 *(e)* 122

50. 720, 120, 24, 8, 2, 1, 1
(a) 10 *(b)* 6 *(c)* 110 *(d)* 640 *(e)* 3

Directions (Qs. 51to 97): *In each of the questions below a number series is given followed by five alternatives. One term of the given number series is missing. Find that missing term out and mark your answer.*

51. 1, 3, 5, 7, 9, ?
(a) 11 *(b)* 14 *(c)* 17 *(d)* 19 *(e)* 15

52. 2, 1, 3, 2, ?, 3
(a) 8 *(b)* 7 *(c)* 6 *(d)* 5 *(e)* 4

53. 1, 4, 9, ?, 25, 36
(a) 21 *(b)* 36 *(c)* 16 *(d)* 15 *(e)* 14

54. 2, 7, 14, 23, 34, ?
(a) 48 *(b)* 45 *(c)* 42 *(d)* 52 *(e)* 51

55. 1, 8, 27, 64, 125, ?
(a) 225 *(b)* 216 *(c)* 420 *(d)* 320 *(e)* 215

56. 6, 25, ?, 123, 214, 341
(a) 65 *(b)* 70 *(c)* 72 *(d)* 62 *(e)* 45

57. ?, 6, 12, 20, 30, 42
(a) 1 *(b)* 3 *(c)* 2 *(d)* 4 *(e)* 5

58. 5, 8, 10, 13, 15, ?
(a) 17 *(b)* 20 *(c)* 22 *(d)* 15 *(e)* 18

59. 6, ?, 60, 120, 210, 336
(a) 31 *(b)* 27 *(c)* 24 *(d)* 38 *(e)* 31

60. 2, 5, 10, 17, 26, ?
(a) 132 *(b)* 140 *(c)* 142 *(d)* 37 *(e)* 136

61. 2, 12, 30, 56, 90, ?
(a) 133 *(b)* 140 *(c)* 142 *(d)* 132 *(e)* 140

62. 10, 17, 26, ?, 50, 65
(a) 42 *(b)* 37 *(c)* 38 *(d)* 41 *(e)* 29

63. 5, 10, 20, 40, 80, ?

(*a*) 280 (*b*) 166 (*c*) 172 (*d*) 160 (*e*) 180

64. 216, 125, ?, 27, 8, 1

(*a*) 36 (*b*) 64 (*c*) 16 (*d*) 51 (*e*) 53

65. 4, 27, 256, 3125, 46656, ?

(*a*) 5764801 (*b*) 576811 (*c*) 676801 (*d*) 567801 (*e*) 568000

66. ?, 23, 34, 45, 56, 78

(*a*) 15 (*b*) 18 (*c*) 32 (*d*) 31 (*e*) 12

67. ?, 100, 75, 50, 25, 0

(*a*) 1100 (*b*) 1250 (*c*) 1750 (*d*) 125 (*e*) 1235

68. $\frac{1}{2}, \frac{1}{4}, \frac{1}{8}, ?\ \frac{1}{32}, \frac{1}{64}$

(*a*) $\frac{1}{16}$ (*b*) $\frac{1}{10}$ (*c*) $\frac{1}{20}$ (*d*) $\frac{1}{25}$ (*e*) $\frac{1}{36}$

69. $\frac{1}{2}, \frac{3}{2}, \frac{5}{2}, ?, \frac{9}{2}, \frac{11}{2}$

(*a*) $\frac{8}{3}$ (*b*) $\frac{5}{3}$ (*c*) $\frac{14}{3}$ (*d*) $\frac{7}{2}$ (*e*) $\frac{9}{2}$

70. 512, 128, 32, 8, 2, ?

(*a*) $\frac{1}{4}$ (*b*) $\frac{1}{2}$ (*c*) $\frac{1}{8}$ (*d*) $\frac{1}{16}$ (*e*) $\frac{1}{32}$

71. 12, 21, 24, 42, 36, ?

(*a*) 65 (*b*) 64 (*c*) 163 (*d*) 70 (*e*) 63

72. 1432, 4321, 3214, ?

(*a*) 2140 (*b*) 1143 (*c*) 2143 (*d*) 1743 (*e*) 2142

73. 294, 42, 6, ?

(*a*) $\frac{6}{49}$ (*b*) $\frac{3}{7}$ (*c*) $\frac{4}{7}$ (*d*) $\frac{6}{7}$ (*e*) $\frac{2}{7}$

74. 8, 11, 16, 23, ?

(*a*) 35 (*B*) 38 (*c*) 40 (*d*) 36 (*e*) 32

75. 18, 45, 72, 99, ?

(*a*) 125 (*b*) 216 (*c*) 140 (*d*) 128 (*e*) 126

76. 9, 13, 17, 21, ?

(*a*) 36 (*b*) 42 (*c*) 25 (*d*) 16 (*e*) 40

77. 0, 1, 16, 81, 256, ?

(*a*) 525 (*b*) 316 (*c*) 666 (*d*) 625 (*e*) 624

78. 14, 78, 252, ?

(*a*) 420 (*b*) 412 (*c*) 512 (*d*) 620 (*e*) 612

79. 84, 260, 630, ?

(*a*) 1302 (*b*) 1032 (*c*) 1230 (*d*) 1941 (*e*) 1532

80. 1, 12, 123, 1234, ?, 123456
(*a*) 13245 (*b*) 12345 (*c*) 12432 (*d*) 1231 (*e*) 1347

81. $\frac{1}{2}, \frac{9}{2}, \frac{25}{2}, ?, \frac{81}{2}$
(*a*) $\frac{49}{2}$ (*b*) 36 (*c*) $\frac{49}{3}$ (*d*) 32 (*e*) 16

82. 4, 20, 60, ?, 900
(*a*) 250 (*b*) 300 (*c*) 330 (*d*) 160 (*e*) 310

83. 22, 44, 77, 33, 55, ?
(*a*) 120 (*b*) 110 (*c*) 115 (*d*) 119 (*e*) 116

84. $\frac{5}{6}, \frac{9}{7}, \frac{13}{8}, ?, \frac{21}{10}$
(*a*) $\frac{19}{9}$ (*b*) $\frac{17}{9}$ (*c*) $\frac{21}{2}$ (*d*) $\frac{11}{2}$ (*e*) $\frac{45}{2}$

85. 51, 68, 85, ?, 119
(*a*) 101 (*b*) 1.5 (*c*) 108 (*d*) 109 (*e*) 102

86. 1527, 1424, 1321, ?, 1115
(*a*) 1218 (*b*) 1318 (*c*) 1128 (*d*) 1821 (*e*) 1281

87. 18, 27, 36, ?, 54
(*a*) 46 (*b*) 45 (*c*) 55 (*d*) 49 (*e*) 50

88. 2, 7, 14, ?, 34
(*a*) 23 (*b*) 21 (*c*) 18 (*d*) 25 (*e*) 28

89. 21, 32, 43, ?, 65
(*a*) 27 (*b*) 9 (*c*) 46 (*d*) 54 (*e*) 51

90. 69, 73, 81, ?, 121
(*a*) 98 (*b*) 70 (*c*) 97 (*d*) 99 (*e*) 120

91. 13, 31, 15, ?, 17
(*a*) 18 (*b*) 27 (*c*) 25 (*d*) 46 (*e*) 35

92. 42, 39, 44, 46, 43
(*a*) 41 (*b*) 38 (*c*) 45 (*d*) 42 (*e*) 40

93. ?, 3, 4, 6, 7
(*a*) 0 (*b*) 2 (*c*) 1 (*d*) 4 (*e*) 5

94. ?, 15, 24, 35, 48
(*a*) 6 (*b*) 7 (*c*) 8 (*d*) 3 (*e*) 5

95. 1, 1, 1, 2, 4, 8, 3, 9, ?
(*a*) 27 (*b*) 26 (*c*) 25 (*d*) 16 (*e*) 22

96. 9, 14, 21, 30, ?
(*a*) 45 (*b*) 44 (*c*) 49 (*d*) 41 (*e*) 50

97. 1, 1, 1, 4, 2, ?, 9
(*a*) 3 (*b*) 2 (*c*) 1 (*d*) 5 (*e*) 7

EXPLANATORY ANSWERS

1. Each term of the series is obtained by multiplying the previous term by 3. Therefore the particular order is: 5, (5 × 3 = 15), (15 × 3 = 45), (45 × 3 = 135), (135 × 3 = 405), (405 × 3 = 1215), (1215 × 3 = 3645), ... and so on. Hence, alternative *(e)* consists of the wrong term.

2. In the given sequence second term is 1.5 the first, the third term is 2 times the second and so on. Therefore, alternative *(a)* consists of the wrong term.

3. In the given sequence difference between successive terms is in the order of 1^2, 2^2 3^2 ...... Therefore, 58 should replace 49 to form the series. Hence, alternative *(e)* consists of the wrong term.

4. Terms of the series would be 6^2, 8^2, 10^2, 12^2, ... 18^2 if 49 is replaced by 64. Therefore, alternative *(c)* consists of the wrong term.

5. If 250 is replaced by 252, then difference between successive terms of the series will be in the order of 256, 128, 64, 32, 16, 8 respectively which from a particular order. Therefore, alternative *(e)* consists of the wrong term.

6. If 45 is replaced by 46, then difference between successive terms of the series will be in the order of 1^2, 2^2, 3^2, 4^2 ...... Therefore, alternative *(c)* contains the wrong term of the series.

7. If 48 is replaced by 44, then difference between successive terms of the series will be in the order of 192, 96, 48, 24, 12 and 6. Therefore, alternative *(a)* consists of the wrong term.

8. A careful scrutiny of the sequence reveals that the second term of the sequence is obtained on subtracting 55 from the first term. Third term of the series is obtained on subtracting 44 from the second term. Fourth term is obtained on subtracting 33 from the third term. This very pattern is followed by remaining terms of the sequence. Therefore, alternative *(c)* contains the wrong term.

9. 46 should replace 47 in the given series because a quick scrutiny indicates that the difference between successive terms of the series is in the order of 5, 8, 11, 14, 17, 20 ..... . The difference between fifth and fourth elements should obviously be 14 and therefore, 47 should be replaced by 46. Hence, alternative *(e)* contains the wrong term of the given series.

10. 16 is the only term in the series which is a perfect square. Therefore, alternative *(d)* consists of the wrong term.

11. If 15 is replaced by 13 then a particular order of terms in the series will be formed in which sum of two successive terms is equal to the next term. Therefore, alternative *(e)* consists of the wrong term.

12. If 18 is replaced by 17 then terms of the series will be arranged in the order of $1^2 + 1$, $2^2 + 1$, $3^2 + 1$ ..... $7^2 + 1$. Therefore, alternative *(b)* consists of the wrong term.

13. If first term of the series is replaced by 2 then difference between successive terms of the series will be in the order of 2, 3, 4, 5, 6, 7. Therefore, alternative *(e)* consists of the wrong term of the sequence.

14. If 6 is replaced by 5 then difference between successive terms will be in the order of 1, 4, 9, 16, 25, 36. Therefore, alternative *(b)* contains the wrong term.

15. : In the given sequence 3 is the only term which is a prime number. Therefore, alternative *(a)* consists of the wrong term.

16. If 26 is replaced by 36, then an order is obtained in which every next term of the series will be equal to twice the preceding term plus 4.

17. If 27 is replaced by 36, then a particular order is obtained in the series. That particular order is 12, 12 × 1.5 = 18, 18 × 2 = 36, 36 × 2.5 = 90, 90 × 3 = 270 and so on. Therefore, alternative *(c)* consists of the wrong term.

18. The difference between successive elements changes in a well-defined manner. A quick scrutiny of the given series shows that the difference between successive elements of the series is in the order of 6, 12, 24, 48, 96, 192. Therefore, it is obvious that 96 i.e. fifth term of the series should be replaced by 95. Hence, alternative *(c)* is the alternative which contains the wrong term.

19. A careful scrutiny of the number series reveals that if 120 is replaced by 118, then the difference between successive terms of the series will be in the order of 2, 4, 6, 8, 10, 12. Therefore, alternative *(e)* consists the wrong term of the series.

20. If 26 is replaced by 27, then difference between successive terms of the series will be in the order of 11, 9, 7, 5, 3, 1. Therefore, alternative *(a)* consists the wrong term of the series.

21. A quick scrutiny of the series reveals that second term is three times the first, third term is two times the second and fourth term is four times the third. The same pattern is being followed by the remaining terms of the series. Therefore, 6480 should be replaced by $2160 \times 4 = 8640$. Hence, alternative *(a)* contains the wrong term.

22. If 12 is replaced by 11, then difference between successive terms of the series will be in an order of 3, 5, 7, 9, 11, 13. Therefore, alternative *(a)* consists the wrong term.

23. A quick study of the series reveals that if 34 is replaced by 35, then difference between successive terms of the series will be in the order of 5, 7, 9, 11, 13 .... Therefore, alternative *(c)* consists the wrong term.

24. A careful study of the series reveals that if 20 is replaced by 21 then difference between successive terms will be in the order of 1, 2, 3, 4, ... *etc.* which constitute a particular order. Therefore alternative *(e)* contains the wrong term of the series.

25. If 17 is replaced by 28, then terms of the series will be in the order of $1^3 + 1$, $2^3 + 1$, $3^3 + 1$, $4^3 + 1$, $5^3 + 1$, $6^3 + 1$ and $7^3 + 1$. Therefore, alternative *(a)* consists the wrong term.

26. If 73 is replaced by 75, then difference between successive terms of the series will be in the order of 9, 11, 13, 15, 17 and 19. Therefore, alternative *(b)* is the correct alternative.

27. If 169 is replaced by 225, then the terms will get arranged in a particular series, *i.e.*, $(1^2 - 1)^2$, $(2^2 - 1)^2$, $(3^2 - 1)^2$, $(4^2 - 1)^2$, $(5^2 - 1)^2$ and $(6^2 - 1)^2$. Therefore, alternative *(a)* is the correct alternative.

28. If 39 is replaced by 37, then the terms of the series will be in a particular order of $2^2 + 1$, $3^2 + 1$, $4^2 + 1$, ... *etc.* Therefore, alternative *(c)* is the correct alternative.

29. A quick scrutiny of the series reveals that each term of the series is two more than twice the previous term. Therefore, 95 should be replaced by 94. Hence, alternative *(c)* is the correct alternative.

30. If 216 is replaced by 217, then terms of the series will get arranged in the order of $1 \times (1)^2 + 1$, $2\times (2)^2 + 1$, $3 \times (3)^2 + 1$, $4 \times (4)^2 + 1$ ..... *etc.* Therefore, alternative *(b)* is the correct answer.

31. A careful study of the series reveals that ratio of successive terms is in the order of 1.5, 2, 2.5, 3, 3.5 and 4. Therefore, 270 should be replaced by 236.25. Hence, alternative *(a)* is the correct answer.

32. A careful scrutiny of the given series reveals that second term is two times the first, third term is four times the second and fourth term is three times the third The same pattern is being followed by the remaining terms of the series. Therefore, 2688 should be replaced by 4032. Hence alternative *(e)* is the correct alternative.

33. If 24 is replaced by 23, then difference between successive terms will be in the order of 11^2, 9^2, 7^2, 5^2, ... *etc.* Therefore, correct alternative is *(c)*.

34. If 15 is replaced by 13, then difference between successive terms will be in the order of 2, 4, 2, 4 ..... and so on. Therefore, alternative *(e)* is the correct alternative.

35. A careful scrutiny of the series reveals that if 50 is replaced by 49, then difference between successive terms will in the order of 1, 3, 5, 7, 9, 11. Therefore, alternative *(b)* is the correct answer.

36. If 31 is replaced by 30, then difference between successive terms will be in the order of 7, 9, 11, 13, 15 and 17. Therefore, alternative *(c)* is the correct answer.

37. It is obvious from the given series that if 9 is replaced by 8, then difference between successive terms will be in the order of 1^2, 3^2, 5^2, 7^2, 9^2 and 11^2. Therefore, alternative *(d)* is the correct answer.

38. 0 should be replaced by –5. Thus, the difference between successive terms of the series will be in the order of 20, 25, 30, 35, 40, 45. Therefore, alternative *(a)* is the correct alternative.

39. It is obvious from the given series that if 2000 is replaced by 1900, then difference between successive terms will be in the order of 200, 300, 400, 500, 600. Therefore, alternative *(a)* is the correct answer.

40. If 40 is replaced by 42, then difference between successive terms of the series will be in the order of 18, 16, 14, 12, 10 and 8. Therefore, correct alternative is *(d)*.

41. A careful scrutiny of the series reveals that if 80 is replaced by 81, then the series will be arranged in the order of 13^2, 11^2, 9^2, 7^2, 5^2, 3^2, 1^2. Therefore, *(b)* is the correct alternative.

42. If 32 is replaced by 33, then the order of terms in the series will be in the following manner:
Second term = (1st term + 1) × 1 = (3 + 1) × 1 = 4
Third term = (2nd term + 1) × 2 = (4 + 1) × 2 = 10
Fourth term = (3rd term + 1) × 3 = (10 + 1) × 3 = 33.
Therefore, alternative *(d)* is the correct answer.

43. If 48 is replaced by 50, then each term of the series is obtained on subtracting 2 from twice its previous term. Therefore, alternative *(b)* is the correct answer.

44. If 28 is replaced by 26 then terms of the series get arranged in a particular order, *i.e.*, $2^3 - 1$, $3^3 - 1$, $4^3 - 1$, $5^3 - 1$, $6^3 - 1$, $7^3 - 1$ and $8^3 - 1$. Therefore, alternative *(a)* is the correct alternative.

45. If 42 is replaced by 40 then difference between successive terms of the series will be in the order of 1, 3, 5, 7, 9 and 11. Therefore, alternative *(d)* is the correct answer.

46. If 652 is replaced by 676, then terms of the series get arranged in a particular order, *i.e.*, $(1^2 + 1)^2$, $(2^2 + 1)^2$, $(3^2 + 1)^2$, $(4^2 + 1)^2$, $(5^2 + 1)^2$, $(6^2 + 1)^2$ and $(7^2 + 1)^2$. Therefore, alternative *(c)* is the correct answer.

47. *(a)* **48.** *(c)* **49.** *(a)* **50.** *(b)*

51. A quick scrutiny reveals that $(2n - 1)$ rule is being followed by the terms of the series, where n is place number of the terms. Therefore, in place of the sixth term 2 × 6 – 1 = 11 will be kept. Hence, sign of interrogation (?) should be replaced by 11. Alternative *(a)* is the correct alternative.

52. Given series is a composite one. Two different series constitute the given series.
e.g., (1) Series of terms in odd places = 2, 3, 4, ...
(2) Series of terms in even places = 1, 2, 3, ...
Therefore, alternative *(e)* is the correct answer.

53. Terms follow the rule of n^2 in constituting the series where n is place number of the terms. Therefore, the correct series will be 1, 4, 9, 16, 25, 36, ... *etc.* Hence, alternative *(c)* is the correct answer.

54. $(n^2 - 2)$ rule is being followed by the terms of the series in forming the series where n = 2, 3, 4, 5, 6 ..... *etc.* Therefore, it is obvious that alternative *(b)* is the correct answer.

55. Pattern of n^3 is being followed by the terms of the series where n is the place number of the terms. Therefore, alternative *(b)* is the correct answer.

56. $(n^3 - 2)$ rule is being followed by the terms of the series in forming the series where $n = 2, 3, 4, 5, 6$ *etc*. Therefore, alternative *(d)* is the correct answer.

57. $(n^2 - n)$ rule is being followed by the terms of the series forming the series where $n = 2, 3, 4, 5,$ ..... *etc*. Therefore, alternative *(c)* is the correct answer.

58. Second term of the series is obtained by adding 3 in the first term and third term is obtained by adding 2 in the second term and so on. Therefore, alternative *(e)* is the correct answer.

59. Terms of the series follow the rule of $(n^3 - n)$ in forming the series where $n = 2, 3, 4, 5$ ..... *etc*. Therefore, alternative *(c)* is the correct answer.

60. Difference between successive terms changes in a well-defined manner. A quick scrutiny of the series indicates that difference between successive terms is in the order of 3, 5, 7, 9, ... The next difference should obviously be 11 and hence, the missing number should be 37. Therefore, alternative *(d)* is the correct answer.

61. The given terms of the series are in the order of $\underline{1 \times 2}, \underline{3 \times 4}, \underline{5 \times 6}, \underline{7 \times 8}, \underline{9 \times 10}, \underline{11 \times 2}$. Therefore, alternative *(d)* is the correct alternative in place of the question mark.

62. The difference between successive terms is in the order of 7, 9, 11, 13, 15 ..... .Hence, 37 should replace the question mark and therefore, alternative *(b)* is the correct answer.

63. The ratio between successive terms is 1 : 2. Therefore alternative *(d)* is the correct alternative to replace the question mark.

64. In the given series, n^3 rule has been followed by the terms of the series where $n = 6, 5, 4, 3,$ .... Therefore, alternative *(b)* is the correct answer.

65. In this series terms of the series follow n^n rule where $n = 2, 3, 4, 5$ .... *etc*. Therefore, alternative *(a)* is the correct answer.

66. The given series has been formed in the order $1 \times 2 = 12$, $2 \times 3 = 23$, $\underline{3 \times 4 = 34}$ ..... Therefore, alternative *(e)* is the correct answer.

67. Each successive term of the series is obtained by subtracting 25 from the previous term of the given series. Therefore, alternative *(d)* is the correct answer.

68. Terms of the series are obtained by multiplying each previous term by $\frac{1}{2}$. Therefore, alternative *(a)* is the correct answer.

69. Terms of the series are obtained on applying $\left(\frac{2n-1}{2}\right)$ rule where n is the place number of the terms in the series. Therefore, alternative *(d)* should replace the question mark.

70. Terms of the series are obtained on dividing each previous term by 4. Therefore, alternative *(b)* is the correct term to replace the question mark.

71. Digits of the first term interchange places in the second term. Similarly, digits of the third term interchange places in the fourth term. Folloiwng the same pattern the digits of the fifth term will interchange their places in sixth term. Therefore, 36 of the fifth term will become 63 in the sixth term. Hence, alternative *(e)* is the correct alternative to replace the question mark.

72. Order of digits has been depicted in this number series. Hence, alternative *(c)* is the correct alternative to replace the question mark.

73. Terms of the series are obtained on dividing each previous term by 7. Therefore, alternative *(d)* is the correct answer.

74. Terms of the series are obtained on applying $(n^2 + 7)$ rule where n is the place number of the terms in the series. Therefore, alternative *(e)* is the correct answer to replace the question mark in the series.

75. A quick scrutiny of the given series indicates that the difference between successive elements of the series is constant i.e. each element of the series is 27 more than the preceding element. Therefore, 126 should come in place of the question mark.

76. In this series each element of the series is 4 more than the preceding element. Therefore, 25 should replace the question mark. Hence, alternative *(c)* is the correct answer.

77. Terms of the series are obtained on applying (n^4) rule where $n = 0, 1, 2, 3,$ .... *etc* respectively. Therefore, alternative *(d)* is the correct answer.

78. Terms of the series are obtained on applying $(n^4 - n)$ rule where $n = 2, 3, 4,$ ..... *etc* respectively. Therefore, alternative *(d)* is the correct answer.

79. Terms of the series are obtained on applying $(n^4 + n)$ rule where $n = 3, 4, 5,$ ..... *etc* respectively. Therefore, alternative *(a)* is the correct answer.

80. In the given series elements of the series have been arranged in the following manner:
First term = 1
Second term = 1 × 2 = 12
Third term = 1 × 2 × 3 = 123
Fourth term = 1 × 2 × 3 × 4 = 1234
Therefore, fifth term in place of the question mark = 1 × 2 × 3 × 4 × 5 = 12345

81. Terms of the series are obtained on applying $\left(\frac{2n-1}{2}\right)^2$ rule where value of n is in the order of 1, 2, 3, ... *etc.* Therefore, alternative *(a)* is the correct answer.

82. Terms of the series are alternately multiplied by 5 and 3 to obtain the next term. Therefore, alternative *(b)* is the correct answer.

83. Each term of the series is a multiple of 11. Therefore, alternative *(b)* is the correct answer.

84. In the given fractions of the series, each successive numerator is 4 more than the preceding one and successive denominators are in the order of the natural numbers. Therefore, alternative *(b)* is the correct answer.

85. Each successive element of the series is 17 more than the preceding element of the series. Thus, alternative *(e)* is the correct answer.

86. Each successive element of the series is 103 less than the preceding element. Therefore, alternative *(a)* should replace the given question mark.

87. Each successive term of the series is obtained on adding 9 to the preceding term. Therefore, alternative *(b)* is the correct answer.

88. The difference between successive elements of the series are 5, 7, 9, ... The number in place of question mark should, therefore, obviously be 23 and hence, the correct alternative is *(a)*.

89. In the given series, the difference between successive elements of the series is 11. Therefore, alternative *(d)* is the correct answer.

90. *(c)** **91.** *(e)* **92.** *(a)* **93.** *(c)* **94.** *(c)* **95.** *(a)* **96.** *(d)* **97.** *(c)*

6 SQUARE ROOTS AND CUBE ROOTS

The square root of a number is the number which when multiplied by itself produces the number in question. We use the radical sign '$\sqrt{\ }$' for the 'positive square root'.

Square root of a given number may be obtained by following two methods:

1. By Prime Factorization Method
2. By Division Method

1. SQUARE ROOT OF A PERFECT SQUARE NUMBER BY PRIME FACTORIZATION METHOD:

This method is most suitable when the given number is a small perfect square number. In this method we adopt the following steps:

(a) Find the prime factors of the given number.
(b) Make pairs of similar factors.
(c) Take one number from each pair and multiply together.

Given below are a few examples to illustrate the method explained above.

Square root of 9

$= \sqrt{9} = \sqrt{3 \times 3} = 3$

Similarly,

Square root of 25 = $\sqrt{25} = \sqrt{5 \times 5} = 5$

Square root of 36 = $\sqrt{36} = \sqrt{2 \times 2 \times 3 \times 3} = 2 \times 3 = 6$

Square root of 49 = $\sqrt{49} = \sqrt{7 \times 7} = 7$

Square root of 121 = $\sqrt{121} = \sqrt{11 \times 11} = 11$

Example 1. Find the square root of 32 + $\sqrt{5+\sqrt{121}}$.

Solution: Square root of 32 + $\sqrt{5+\sqrt{121}} = \sqrt{32+\sqrt{5+\sqrt{121}}} = \sqrt{32+\sqrt{5+11}}$

$= \sqrt{32+\sqrt{16}} = \sqrt{32+4} = \sqrt{36} = \sqrt{2 \times 2 \times 3 \times 3} = 2 \times 3 = 6$

Example 2. Find the square root of $128 + \sqrt{261-\sqrt{25}}$.

Solution: Square root of $128 + \sqrt{261-\sqrt{25}} = \sqrt{128+\sqrt{261-\sqrt{25}}} = \sqrt{128+\sqrt{261-5}}$

$= \sqrt{128+\sqrt{256}} = \sqrt{128+16} = \sqrt{144} = 12$

Example 3. Find the square root of $\sqrt{121}-\sqrt{16}-\sqrt{9}$.

Solution: Square root of $\left(\sqrt{121}-\sqrt{16}-\sqrt{9}\right) = \sqrt{\left(\sqrt{121}-\sqrt{16}-\sqrt{9}\right)}$

$= \sqrt{\sqrt{11\times11}-\sqrt{4\times4}-\sqrt{3\times3}} = \sqrt{11-4-3} = \sqrt{4}$

$= \sqrt{2\times2} = 2$

Example 4. Find the square root of $\sqrt{256}+\sqrt{81}+\sqrt{576}$.

Solution: Square root of $\sqrt{256}+\sqrt{81}+\sqrt{576} = \sqrt{\sqrt{256}+\sqrt{81}+\sqrt{576}}$

$= \sqrt{\sqrt{16\times16}+\sqrt{9\times9}+\sqrt{24\times24}} = \sqrt{16+9+24} = \sqrt{49}$

$= \sqrt{7\times7} = 7$

2. SQUARE ROOT OF A PERFECT SQUARE NUMBER BY DIVISION METHOD

When numbers are very large or can not easily be factorised we use this method. This method is also applicable when the factors do not form complete pairs or the numbers are given in decimal form. In this method we divide the given square number into pairs of two digits beginning with the unit's digit. For example.

Find the square root of 1681.

We first divide the number into pairs of two digits beginning with the unit's digit and then apply division method for finding the square root of the given number.

Thus,

```
        41
   4 | 16  81
     | 16
     |--------
  81 |     81
     |     81
     |--------
     |     ×
```

Hence, Square root of 1681 is 41.

Example 5. Find the square root of 104976.

Solution :

```
          324
    3 | 10 49 76
      |  9
      |---------
   62 |   149
      |   124
      |---------
  644 |   2576
      |   2576
      |---------
      |     ×
```

∴ Square root of 104976 is 324.

Example 6. Find the Square root of 180625.

Solution :

```
          425
    4 | 18 06 25
      | 16
      |---------
   82 |    206
      |    164
      |---------
  845 |   4225
      |   4225
      |---------
      |     ×
```

∴ Square root of 180625 is 425.

Example 7. Find the Square root of 211600.

Solution :

```
          460
    4 | 21 16 00
      | 16
      |---------
   86 |   516
      |   516
  920 |---------
      |    ×
```

∴ Square root of 211600 is 460.

Example 8. Find the greatest number of four digits which is a perfect square.
Solution : ∵ The greatest four digit number is 9999

```
          99
    9 | 99 99
      | 81
      |------
  189 | 1899
      | 1701
      |------
      |  198
```

∴ The greatest perfect square number of four digits is 9999 – 198 = 9801.

Example 9. Find the least number of six digits which is a perfect square.
Solution : ∵ The least six-digit number = 100000

```
          316
    3 | 10 00 00
      |  9
      |---------
   61 | 100
      |  61
      |---------
  626 | 3900
      | 3756
      |---------
      |  144
```

∴ 100000 = $(316)^2$ + 144 which is not a perfect square number.
∴ The least perfect square number of six digits = $(317)^2$
∴ The required number is 317 × 317 = 100489.

Example. 10 Find the least number which must be added to 3488 so that the sum becomes a perfect square.

Solution:

```
          59
     5 | 34 88
       | 25
       |------
   109 |  988
       |  981
       |------
       |    7
```

∴ $3488 = (59)^2 + 7$, which is not a perfect square number.

∵ $(60)^2 = 3600$

∴ $3600 - 3488 = 112$

Hence, it is clear that 112 should be added to 3488 so that the resulting number a perfect square.

Example 11. Find the least number which must be subtracted from 9985 so that the remainder becomes a perfect square.

Solution :

```
          99
     9 | 99 85
       | 81
       |------
   189 | 18 85
       | 17 01
       |------
       |  184
```

∴ $9985 = (99)^2 + 184$.

Hence, it is clear that 184 should be subtracted from 9985 so that the resulting number a perfect square.

Example 12. In Tarun's birthday party 1521 toffees in total were distributed among children. If the number of toffees given to each child was the same as the number of children in the party, how many children attended the birthday party?

Soluton : The total number of children will be square root of 1521

```
         39
     3 | 15 21
       |  9
       |------
    69 | 621
       | 621
       |------
       |  ×
```

∴ Square root of 1521 = $\sqrt{1521} = 39$.

∴ Number of Children = 39

3. SQUARE ROOT OF DECIMAL FRACTIONS: Division method is quite appropriate for finding the square root of decimal fractions. For example:

Find the square root of .001849.

```
       .043
    4 | 00 18 49
      |    16
      |---------
   83 |   249
      |   249
      |---------
      |    ×
```

∴ Square root of .001849 is .043.

Example 13. Find the value of $\sqrt{2}$ upto three decimal places.

Solution :

	1.414
1	$2.\overline{00}\ \overline{00}\ \overline{00}$
	1
24	100
	96
281	400
	281
2824	11900
	11296
	604

$\therefore\ \sqrt{2} = 1.414$

Example 14. Find the square root of 7 upto three decimal places.

Solution :

	2.6457
2	$7.\overline{00}\ \overline{00}\ \overline{00}\ \overline{00}$
	4
46	300
	276
524	2400
	2096
5285	30400
	26425
52907	397500
	370349
	27151

$\therefore\ \sqrt{7} = 2.6457$

$\therefore$ Required square root of 7 upto three decimal places is 2.646.

Example 15. Find the square root of $\dfrac{4}{\sqrt{3}}$.

Solution: $\because\ \dfrac{4}{\sqrt{3}} = \dfrac{4}{\sqrt{3}} \times \dfrac{\sqrt{3}}{\sqrt{3}} = \dfrac{4 \times \sqrt{3}}{3}$

$= \dfrac{4 \times 1.73205}{3} = 2.30940$ or, 2.309400

	1.519
1	$2.\overline{30}\ \overline{94}\ \overline{00}$
	1
25	130
	125
301	594
	301
3029	29300
	27261
	20391

$\therefore$ Required square root of $\dfrac{4}{\sqrt{3}} = 1.519.$

Example 16. What will be the square root of .000529?

Solution :

```
        .023
    ┌──────────
  2 │ .00 05 29
    │     04
    ├──────────
 43 │    129
    │    129
    ├──────────
    │     ×
```

∴ Required square root of .000529 = .023.

Example 17. Find the square root of 27.4576

Solution :

```
          5.24
      ┌──────────
    5 │ 27.45 76
      │ 25
      ├──────────
  102 │  245
      │  204
      ├──────────
 1044 │  4176
      │  4176
      ├──────────
      │    ×
```

∴ Required square root of 27.4576 = 5.24.

Example 18. Find the square root of .327184.

Solution :

```
          .572
      ┌──────────
    5 │ .3271 84
      │  25
      ├──────────
  107 │  771
      │  749
      ├──────────
 1142 │  2284
      │  2284
      ├──────────
      │    ×
```

∴ Required square root of .327184 = .572.

Example 19. Find the square root of $\frac{2}{5}$.

Solution : $\because \frac{2}{5}$ = .4 or, .400000 ∴ Square root of .400000

```
          .632
      ┌──────────
    6 │ .4000 00
      │  36
      ├──────────
  123 │  400
      │  369
      ├──────────
 1262 │  3100
      │  2524
      ├──────────
      │   576
```

∴ Required square root of .4 or $\frac{2}{5}$ is .632.

CUBE ROOTS

The Cube root of a number is the number, the third power of which gives the number in question. The Symbol used for cube root is '$\sqrt[3]{\ }$'. We can find the cube root of a number by prime factorization method only.

For example, 2 × 2 × 2 = 8. ∴ Cube root of 8 is 2.

Therefore, cube root of 8 = $\sqrt[3]{8} = \sqrt[3]{2\times2\times2} = 2$

Similarly, cube root of 27 = $\sqrt[3]{27} = \sqrt[3]{3\times3\times3} = 3$

cube root of 64 = $\sqrt[3]{64} = \sqrt[3]{4\times4\times4} = 4$

cube root of 216 = $\sqrt[3]{216} = \sqrt[3]{6\times6\times6} = 6$

Example 20. Find the cube root of 512.

Solution: Cube root of 512 = $\sqrt[3]{512}$

$= \sqrt[3]{\underline{2\times2\times2}\times\underline{2\times2\times2}\times\underline{2\times2\times2}}$

$= 2 \times 2 \times 2 = 8.$

Example 21. Find the cube root of 8000.

Solution: Cube root of 8000 = $\sqrt[3]{8000} = \sqrt[3]{20\times20\times20} = 20.$

Example 22. Find the cube root of 3375.

Solution: Cube root of 3375 = $\sqrt[3]{3375}$

$= \sqrt[3]{\underline{3\times3\times3}\times\underline{5\times5\times5}} = 3\times5 = 15.$

Example 23. Find the value of $\sqrt[3]{50+\sqrt{121}+\sqrt{9}}$.

Solution : $\sqrt[3]{50+\sqrt{121}+\sqrt{9}} = \sqrt[3]{50+11+3} = \sqrt[3]{64}$

$= \sqrt[3]{4\times4\times4} = 4$

$\therefore$ Value of $\sqrt[3]{50+\sqrt{121}+\sqrt{9}} = 4.$

Example 24. What will be the value of $\sqrt[3]{.000064}$?

Solution: $\sqrt[3]{.000064} = \sqrt[3]{.04\times.04\times.04} = .04$

$\therefore$ Value of $\sqrt[3]{.000064} = .04.$

Example 25. What will be the value of $\sqrt[3]{\sqrt{.000729}}$?

Solution : $\sqrt[3]{\sqrt{.000729}} = \sqrt[3]{\sqrt{.027\times.027}} = \sqrt[3]{.027}$

$= \sqrt[3]{.3\times.3\times.3} = .3$

$\therefore$ Value of $\sqrt[3]{\sqrt{.000729}} = .3.$

Example 26. What will be the value of $\sqrt[3]{\sqrt{441}+\sqrt{16}+\sqrt{4}}$?

Solution : $\sqrt[3]{\sqrt{441}+\sqrt{16}+\sqrt{4}} = \sqrt[3]{\sqrt{21\times21}+\sqrt{4\times4}+\sqrt{2\times2}}$

$= \sqrt[3]{21+4+2} = \sqrt[3]{27} = \sqrt[3]{3\times3\times3} = 3$

$\therefore$ Value of $\sqrt[3]{\sqrt{441}+\sqrt{16}+\sqrt{4}} = 3.$

Example 27. Find the value of $\sqrt[3]{1325+\sqrt{20+\sqrt{256}}}$.

Solution : $\sqrt[3]{1325+\sqrt{20+\sqrt{256}}} = \sqrt[3]{1325+\sqrt{20+16}}$

$= \sqrt[3]{1325+\sqrt{36}} = \sqrt[3]{1325+6} = \sqrt[3]{1331}$

$= \sqrt[3]{11\times11\times11} = 11.$

Example 28. Find the Square root of 2025.

Solution: Square root of 2025 = $\sqrt{2025} = \sqrt{\underline{3\times3}\times\underline{3\times3}\times\underline{5\times5}} = 3 \times 3 \times 5 = 45$.

Example 29. Find the square root of 3025.

Solution:

$$\begin{array}{r|l} & 55 \\ \hline 5 & \overline{30}\ \overline{25} \\ & 25 \\ \hline 105 & 525 \\ & 525 \\ \hline & \times \end{array}$$

∴ Required square root of 3025 = 55.

Example 30. Find the cube root of 2197.

Solution: Cube root of 2197 = $\sqrt[3]{2197}$

$= \sqrt[3]{13\times13\times13} = 13.$

Example 31. Find the value of $\sqrt{\dfrac{121}{289}}$.

Solution: $\because \sqrt{\dfrac{121}{289}} = \dfrac{\sqrt{121}}{\sqrt{289}} = \dfrac{\sqrt{11\times11}}{\sqrt{17\times17}} = \dfrac{11}{17}$.

Example 32. $\sqrt{\dfrac{3969}{1681}} = \dfrac{\sqrt{3969}}{\sqrt{1681}}$.

∴ We will have to find out the Square roots of 3969 and 1681

$$\begin{array}{r|l} & 63 \\ \hline 6 & \overline{39}\ \overline{69} \\ & 36 \\ \hline 123 & 369 \\ & 369 \\ \hline & \times \end{array}$$

∴ Square root of 3969 is 63, and

$$\begin{array}{r|l} & 41 \\ \hline 4 & \overline{16}\ \overline{81} \\ & 16 \\ \hline 81 & 81 \\ & 81 \\ \hline & \times \end{array}$$

∴ Square root of 1681 is 41

$$\therefore \quad \frac{\sqrt{3969}}{\sqrt{1681}} = \frac{63}{41}.$$

Example 33: Find the square root of $\sqrt{\dfrac{10000}{6561}}$.

Solution: Square root of $\sqrt{\dfrac{10000}{6561}} = \sqrt{\sqrt{\dfrac{10000}{6561}}}$

$$\because \quad \sqrt{\frac{10000}{6561}} = \frac{\sqrt{10000}}{\sqrt{6561}}$$

∴ Square root of 10000 and square root of 6561 will be found out.

∵ $$\text{Square root of } 10000 = \sqrt{10000} = \sqrt{100 \times 100} = 100$$

And

```
         81
    8 | 65 61
      | 64
 161  | 161
      | 161
      |  ×
```

∴ Square root of 6561 = 81

∴ $$\sqrt{\frac{10000}{6561}} = \frac{100}{81}$$

∴ $$\sqrt{\sqrt{\frac{10000}{6561}}} = \sqrt{\frac{100}{81}} = \frac{\sqrt{100}}{\sqrt{81}} = \frac{\sqrt{10 \times 10}}{\sqrt{9 \times 9}} = \frac{10}{9}.$$

Example 34. Find the square root of 530.8416.

Solution:

```
          23.04
    2  | 530.8416
       | 4
   43  | 130
       | 129
 4604  | 18416
       | 18416
       |   ×
```

∴ Square root of 530.8416 = 23.04.

Example 35. Find the square root of $\frac{3}{8}$ upto three decimal places.

Solution: ∵ $$\frac{3}{8} = .375 \text{ or } .375000$$

Hence, to find out the square root of $\frac{3}{8}$ we have to find out the square root of .375000.

```
          .612
     6 | .375 000
       | 36
   121 |  150
       |  121
  1222 |  2900
       |  2444
       |   456
```

∴ Square root of $\frac{3}{8}$ or .375000 = .612.

Example 36. Find the value of: $\sqrt{\sqrt[3]{64} + \sqrt[3]{125} + \sqrt[3]{343}}$

Solution:

$$\sqrt[3]{64} = \sqrt[3]{4 \times 4 \times 4} = 4$$

$$\sqrt[3]{125} = \sqrt[3]{5 \times 5 \times 5} = 5$$

and $$\sqrt[3]{343} = \sqrt[3]{7 \times 7 \times 7} = 7$$

∴ $$\sqrt{\sqrt[3]{64} + \sqrt[3]{125} + \sqrt[3]{343}} = \sqrt{4+5+7} = \sqrt{16} = \sqrt{2 \times 2 \times 2 \times 2} = 2 \times 2 = 4$$

Example 37. If $\sqrt{2+\frac{2}{49}} = \frac{x}{14}$, what will be the value of x?

Solution: $\because$ $\sqrt{2+\frac{2}{49}} = \sqrt{\frac{100}{49}} = \frac{\sqrt{100}}{\sqrt{49}} = \frac{\sqrt{10\times10}}{\sqrt{7\times7}} = \frac{10}{7}$

$\therefore$ $\sqrt{2+\frac{2}{49}} = \frac{x}{14}$,

or $\frac{10}{7} = \frac{x}{14}$

or $x = \frac{10\times14}{7} = 20$

$\therefore$ Value of $x = 20$.

Example 38. Find the value of x if $\frac{x^2}{2304} = \frac{6}{x}$.

Solution: $\frac{x^2}{2304} = \frac{6}{x}$

$\Rightarrow$ $x^2 \times x = 6 \times 2304$

$\Rightarrow$ $x^3 = 2 \times 3 \times 2\times 2 \times 2 \times 2 \times 2 \times 2 \times 2 \times 2 \times 3 \times 3$

$\Rightarrow$ $x^3 = \sqrt[3]{2\times2\times2\times2\times2\times2\times2\times2\times2\times3\times3\times3}$

$\Rightarrow$ $x = 2 \times 2 \times 2 \times 3 = 24$

$\therefore$ Value of $x = 24$.

Example 39. If $\sqrt{(0.4\times.04\times a)} = 0.4 \times .04 \times \sqrt{b}$, then find the value of a/b.

Solution: $\sqrt{(0.4\times.04\times a)} = 0.4 \times .04 \times \sqrt{b}$

$\Rightarrow$ $\sqrt{(0.4\times.04\times a)} = \sqrt{0.16\times.0016\times b}$

$\Rightarrow$ $.4 \times .04 \times a = 0.16 \times .0016 \times b$

$\Rightarrow$ $\frac{a}{b} = \frac{0.16\times.0016}{.4\times.04} = 0.016$

$\therefore$ Value of $\frac{a}{b} = .016$

Example 40. Find the smallest number by which 750 be multiplied or divided so that the product or quotient becomes a perfect square number.

Solution: The prime factors of 750 are:

$750 = 2 \times 3 \times 5 \times 5 \times 5 = 30 \times 25$

$= 30 \times (5)^2$

From the above, we find that in the prime factorization of 750, 30 is not a perfect square number and 25 is a perfect square number.

∴ If we multiply or divide 750 by 30, the resulting number in each case will be a perfect square numbers.

Hence, it is clear that *(i)* on multiplying 750 by 30:

$$750 \times 30 = 30 \times 30 \times 5^2 = 30^2 \times 5^2$$, which is a perfect square number.

and *(ii)* on dividing 750 by 30:

$$750 \div 30 = \frac{30}{30} \times 5^2 = 5^2$$

which is a perfect square number.

∴ The required smallest number is 30.

Example 41. The sum of Rs. 5760 is to be divided among a few children in such a way that each child gets as many 10 paise coins as the total number of children. Find the amount received by each of the children.

Solution: Rs. 5760 = 576000 paise = 57600 coins of ten paise.

Here, number of children = Square root of 57600.

```
       240
   2 | 5 76 00
     | 2
  44 | 176
     | 176
 480 | ×
```

∴ Numbers of children = 240

Amount received by each child = 240 × 10 = 2400 paise = Rs. 24.

EXERCISE

1. The square root of $5\frac{4}{9}$ is:

A. $\frac{8}{3}$ B. $\frac{7}{3}$ C. $\frac{5}{3}$ D. $\frac{1}{2}$

2. What will be value of the square root of 15625?

A. 115 B. 135 C. 125 D. 145

3. Square root of $\sqrt{1296}$ will be:

A. 6 B. 36 C. 16 D. 26

4. Cube root of 10648 is:

A. 12 B. 32 C. 22 D. 18

5. Square root of 176.252176 is:

A. 12.262 B. 13.272 C. 13.372 D. 15.572

6. What will be the square root of 72 upto three decimal places?

A. 8.485 B. 6.465 C. 8.845 D. 8.465

7. Square root of $7+\sqrt{7}$ upto three decimal places will be:

A. 3.105 B. 3.203 C. 3.125 D. 3.015

8. What will be the value of $\sqrt{676} + \sqrt{784} - \sqrt{289}$?

A. 38 B. 42 C. 37 D. 36

9. If $\frac{x}{7} = \frac{28}{x}$, what will be the value of x?

A. 12 B. 21 C. 18 D. 14

10. If $\sqrt{1+\frac{x}{144}} = \frac{13}{12}$, what will be the value of x?

A. 25 B. 24 C. 36 D. 28

11. If $\sqrt{18225} = 135$, what will be the value of $\sqrt{18225} + \sqrt{182.25} + \sqrt{1.8225}$?

A. 129.75 B. 149.85 C. 157.85 D. 149.65

12. The value of $\sqrt{95+\sqrt{13+\sqrt{144}}}$ is:

A. 12 B. 11 C. 10 D. 19

13. If 50% of ? = 20% of 10, which of the following should replace the sign (?)?

A. 16 B. 12 C. 13 D. 16

14. If $\frac{1}{\sqrt{144}} = \frac{x}{7}$ then the value of x will be:

A. $\frac{1}{3}$ B. $\frac{1}{18}$ C. $\frac{1}{9}$ D. $\frac{1}{27}$

15. If $\sqrt{4} + \sqrt{16} + \sqrt{25} = \sqrt{?}$, which of the following will replace the sign of interrogation (?)?

A. 100 B. 81 C. 256 D. 121

16. If $\sqrt{.81} + \sqrt{.0049} =$?, which of the following should replace the sign of interrogation (?)?

A. . 97 B. .83 C. 1.01 D. .99

17. If $(625)^2 = 390625$, then the value of $\sqrt{.00390625}$ will be:

A. .0625 B. 0.625 C. .00625 D. .000625

18. $x \otimes y = \sqrt{(x+1)(y+1)^2}$, then the value of $3 \otimes 7$ will be:

A. 21 B. 16 C. 18 D. 28

19. The cube root of 8^4 is:

A. 16 B. 8 C. 4 D. 64

20. By what smallest number 270 be multiplied so that the resulting number becomes a perfect cube?

A. 121 B. 109 C. 100 D. 99

21. By what smallest number 675 be multiplied so that the product becomes a perfect square number?

A. 2 B. $\frac{3}{5}$ C. 4 D. 3

22. If the approximate square root of 80 is 8.94. What will be the value of $\sqrt{20}$?

A. 3.37 B. 4.47 C. 4.87 D. 4.40

23. What will be the value of $\sqrt[3]{32+\sqrt{1012+\sqrt{144}}}$?

A. 4 B. 6 C. 5 D. 8

24. What will be the square root of $\left(\sqrt[3]{0.00000064}\right) \times \sqrt{2.56}$?

A. .06 B. .08 C. .05 D. .04

25. If $\frac{\sqrt{?}}{4} = \frac{1}{3}$, what will be in place of (?)?

A. $\frac{16}{3}$ B. $\frac{16}{9}$ C. $\frac{21}{16}$ D. $\frac{4}{3}$

26. If 30% of $\sqrt{?}$ + 15% of 40 = 11, what should replace the sign of interrogation (?)?

A. $\frac{2500}{9}$ B. $\frac{2400}{7}$ C. $\frac{2300}{11}$ D. $\frac{2200}{7}$

27. Find the least number of four digits which is a perfect square.

A. 1025 B. 1125 C. 1016 D. 1024

28. What least number should be subtracted from 11125 so that the resulting number becomes a perfect square?

A. 100 B. 99 C. 81 D. 90

29. In an orchard 4624 plants have been arranged in such a way that the number of plants in each row is the same as the number of rows. How many plants have been arranged in a row?

A. 63 B. 68 C. 78 D. 58

30. An Army General arranges his soldiers in such a way that the number of rows is the same as the number of columns. In doing so, he finds that 100 soldiers are left out. If the total number of soldiers is 14500, find the number of soldiers in each row.

A. 110 B. 105 C. 120 D. 115

31. Kanchan had 537 toffees. On her birthday she distributed among her friends the toffees in such a way that her each friend got as many toffees as was the number of her friends. In doing so, 8 toffees were left with her. Total number of her friends is:

A. 22 B. 23 C. 24 D. 27

32. A sum of Rs. 676 was deposited with a co-operative society by its members in a certain month. If each member of the society deposited as much amount (in paise) as was the number of members of the society, what was the number of members of the society?

A. 270 B. 260 C. 272 D. 280

33. $\left(\frac{\sqrt{625}}{11} \times \frac{14}{\sqrt{25}} \times \frac{11}{\sqrt{196}}\right)$ is simplified to

(a) 11 *(b)* 8 *(c)* 6 *(d)* 5

34. Simplify : $\sqrt{41-\sqrt{21+\sqrt{19-\sqrt{9}}}}$

(a) 6.4 *(b)* 6 *(c)* 5 *(d)* 3

35. Evaluate : $\sqrt{10+\sqrt{25+\sqrt{108+\sqrt{154+\sqrt{225}}}}}$

(a) 10 *(b)* 8 *(c)* 6 *(d)* 4

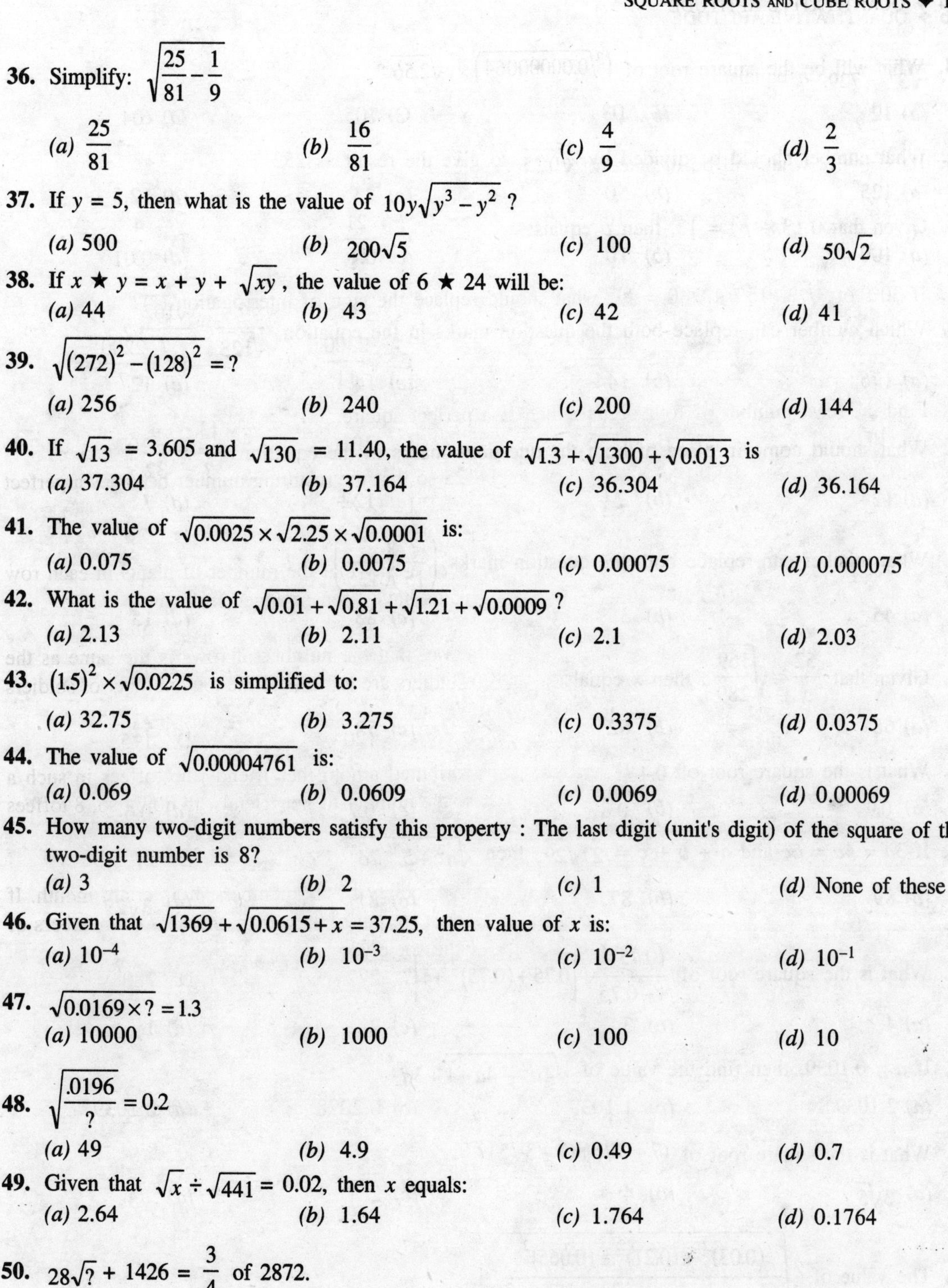

36. Simplify: $\sqrt{\frac{25}{81} - \frac{1}{9}}$

(a) $\frac{25}{81}$ (b) $\frac{16}{81}$ (c) $\frac{4}{9}$ (d) $\frac{2}{3}$

37. If $y = 5$, then what is the value of $10y\sqrt{y^3 - y^2}$?

(a) 500 (b) $200\sqrt{5}$ (c) 100 (d) $50\sqrt{2}$

38. If $x \bigstar y = x + y + \sqrt{xy}$, the value of $6 \bigstar 24$ will be:

(a) 44 (b) 43 (c) 42 (d) 41

39. $\sqrt{(272)^2 - (128)^2} = ?$

(a) 256 (b) 240 (c) 200 (d) 144

40. If $\sqrt{13} = 3.605$ and $\sqrt{130} = 11.40$, the value of $\sqrt{1.3} + \sqrt{1300} + \sqrt{0.013}$ is

(a) 37.304 (b) 37.164 (c) 36.304 (d) 36.164

41. The value of $\sqrt{0.0025} \times \sqrt{2.25} \times \sqrt{0.0001}$ is:

(a) 0.075 (b) 0.0075 (c) 0.00075 (d) 0.000075

42. What is the value of $\sqrt{0.01} + \sqrt{0.81} + \sqrt{1.21} + \sqrt{0.0009}$?

(a) 2.13 (b) 2.11 (c) 2.1 (d) 2.03

43. $(1.5)^2 \times \sqrt{0.0225}$ is simplified to:

(a) 32.75 (b) 3.275 (c) 0.3375 (d) 0.0375

44. The value of $\sqrt{0.00004761}$ is:

(a) 0.069 (b) 0.0609 (c) 0.0069 (d) 0.00069

45. How many two-digit numbers satisfy this property : The last digit (unit's digit) of the square of the two-digit number is 8?

(a) 3 (b) 2 (c) 1 (d) None of these

46. Given that $\sqrt{1369} + \sqrt{0.0615 + x} = 37.25$, then value of x is:

(a) 10^{-4} (b) 10^{-3} (c) 10^{-2} (d) 10^{-1}

47. $\sqrt{0.0169 \times ?} = 1.3$

(a) 10000 (b) 1000 (c) 100 (d) 10

48. $\sqrt{\frac{.0196}{?}} = 0.2$

(a) 49 (b) 4.9 (c) 0.49 (d) 0.7

49. Given that $\sqrt{x} \div \sqrt{441} = 0.02$, then x equals:

(a) 2.64 (b) 1.64 (c) 1.764 (d) 0.1764

50. $28\sqrt{?} + 1426 = \frac{3}{4}$ of 2872.

(a) 1444 (b) 1296 (c) 676 (d) 576

51. $\sqrt{3^n} = 729$, n equals:

(a) 12 (b) 10 (c) 8 (d) 6

52. What number should be divided by $\sqrt{0.25}$ to give the result as 25?

(a) 125 (b) 50 (c) 25 (d) 12.5

53. Given that $0.13 \div p^2 = 13$, then p equals:

(a) 100 (b) 10 (c) 0.1 (d) 0.01

54. Which number can replace both the question marks in the equation $\frac{?}{\sqrt{128}} = \frac{\sqrt{162}}{?}$?

(a) 196 (b) 144 (c) 14 (d) 12

55. What should come in place of both the questions marks in the equation $\frac{4\frac{1}{2}}{?} = \frac{?}{32}$?

(a) 12 (b) $7\frac{1}{2}$ (c) $12\frac{1}{2}$ (d) 7

56. What number can replace both the question marks $\left(\frac{?}{15}\right)\left(\frac{?}{135}\right) = 1$?

(a) 45 (b) 35 (c) 25 (d) 15

57. Given that $\frac{52}{x} = \sqrt{\frac{169}{289}}$, then x equals:

(a) 68 (b) 62 (c) 58 (d) 52

58. What is the square root of $0.\bar{4}$?

(a) $0.\bar{9}$ (b) $0.\bar{8}$ (c) $0.\bar{7}$ (d) $0.\bar{6}$

59. If $3a = 4b = 6c$ and $a + b + c = 27\sqrt{29}$, then $\sqrt{a^2 + b^2 + c^2}$ is:

(a) 89 (b) 87 (c) 81 (d) $3\sqrt{29}$

60. What is the square root of $\frac{(0.75)^3}{1-0.75} + \left[0.75 + (0.75)^2 + 1\right]$?

(a) 4 (b) 3 (c) 2 (d) 1

61. If $a = 0.1039$, then find the value of $\sqrt{4a^2 - 4a + 1} + 3a \cdot$

(a) 2.1039 (b) 1.1039 (c) 0.2078 (d) 0.1039

62. What is the square root of $(7+3\sqrt{5})\,(7-3\sqrt{5})$?

(a) $3\sqrt{5}$ (b) 4 (c) 2 (d) $\sqrt{5}$

63. The value of $\sqrt{\frac{(0.03)^2 + (0.21)^2 + (0.065)^2}{(0.003)^2 + (0.021)^2 + (0.0065)^2}}$ is:

(a) 10^3 (b) 10^2 (c) 10 (d) 0.1

64. The value of $\left(\sqrt{3}-\frac{1}{\sqrt{3}}\right)^2$ is:

(a) $\frac{\sqrt{3}}{4}$ (b) $\frac{4}{3}$ (c) $\frac{4}{\sqrt{3}}$ (d) $\frac{3}{4}$

65. $\sqrt{\frac{0.081\times0.484}{0.0064\times6.25}}$ simplifies to:

(a) 9 (b) 99 (c) 0.99 (d) 0.9

66. The closest value of $\frac{3\sqrt{12}}{2\sqrt{28}}\div\frac{2\sqrt{21}}{\sqrt{98}}$ is:

(a) 1.6026 (b) 1.6007 (c) 1.0727 (d) 1.0605

67. If $\sqrt{2}=1.414$, then the value of $\sqrt{8}+2\sqrt{32}-3\sqrt{128}+4\sqrt{50}$ is:

(a) 8.876 (b) 8.526 (c) 8.484 (d) 8.426

68. Given $3\sqrt{5}+\sqrt{125}=17.88$, then the value of $\sqrt{80}+6\sqrt{5}$ is:

(a) 22.35 (b) 21.66 (c) 20.46 (d) 13.41

69. $\frac{\sqrt{80}-\sqrt{112}}{\sqrt{45}-\sqrt{63}}$ is equal to:

(a) $1\frac{3}{4}$ (b) $1\frac{7}{9}$ (c) $1\frac{1}{3}$ (d) $\frac{3}{4}$

70. By how much does $\sqrt{12}+\sqrt{18}$ exceed $\sqrt{3}+\sqrt{2}$:

(a) $3(\sqrt{3}-\sqrt{2})$ (b) $2(\sqrt{3}-\sqrt{2})$ (c) $\sqrt{3}+2\sqrt{2}$ (d) $\sqrt{2}-4\sqrt{3}$

71. Given $\sqrt{1+\frac{55}{729}}=1+\frac{x}{27}$, then x equals:

(a) 7 (b) 5 (c) 3 (d) 1

72. Three fifth of the square of a certain number is 126.15, then the number is:

(a) 210.25 (b) 145 (c) 75.69 (d) 14.5

73. The greatest four-digit perfect square number is:

(a) 9981 (b) 9900 (c) 9801 (d) 9000

74. The smallest number added to 680621 to make the sum a perfect square is:

(a) 8 (b) 6 (c) 5 (d) 4

75. What is the least number which should be subtracted from 0.000326 to make it a perfect square?

(a) 0.04 (b) 0.02 (c) 0.000004 (d) 0.000002

76. Find the smallest number by which 5808 should be multiplied so that the product becomes a perfect square.

(a) 11 (b) 7 (c) 3 (d) 2

77. The least perfect square, which is divisible by each of 21, 36, and 66 is:

(a) 231444 (b) 214434 (c) 214344 (d) 213444

78. If $\sqrt{5} = 2.236$, then find the value of $\frac{\sqrt{5}}{2} - \frac{10}{\sqrt{5}} + \sqrt{125}$.

(*a*) 10.062 (*b*) 8.944 (*c*) 7.826 (*d*) 5.59

79. The approximate value of $\frac{1+\sqrt{0.01}}{1-\sqrt{0.1}}$ is:

(*a*) 1.7 (*b*) 1.6 (*c*) 1.1 (*d*) 0.6

80. $\sqrt{\frac{0.16}{0.4}}$ is equal to:

(*a*) 0.6 (*b*) 0.63 (*c*) 0.2 (*d*) 0.02

81. If $x = \frac{\sqrt{3}+1}{\sqrt{3}-1}$ and $y = \frac{\sqrt{3}-1}{\sqrt{3}+1}$; then find the value of $\left(x^2 + y^2\right)$.

(*a*) 15 (*b*) 14 (*c*) 13 (*d*) 10

82. If $x = \left(7 - 4\sqrt{3}\right)$, then the value of $\left(x + \frac{1}{x}\right)$ will be:

(*a*) $14 + 8\sqrt{3}$ (*b*) 14 (*c*) $8\sqrt{3}$ (*d*) $3\sqrt{3}$

83. Simplify: $\left(\frac{2+\sqrt{3}}{2-\sqrt{3}} + \frac{2-\sqrt{3}}{2+\sqrt{3}} + \frac{\sqrt{3}-1}{\sqrt{3}+1}\right)$

(*a*) $2 + \sqrt{3}$ (*b*) $2 - \sqrt{3}$ (*c*) $4 - \sqrt{3}$ (*d*) $16 - \sqrt{3}$

84. $\frac{3+\sqrt{6}}{5\sqrt{3} - 2\sqrt{12} - \sqrt{32} + \sqrt{50}}$ simplifies to:

(*a*) $\sqrt{3}$ (*b*) 3 (*c*) $3\sqrt{2}$ (*d*) 6

85. Given $\sqrt{2} = 1.414$, the square root of $\frac{\sqrt{2}-1}{\sqrt{2}+1}$ is closest to:

(*a*) 1.414 (*b*) 0.586 (*c*) 0.414 (*d*) 0.172

86. If $\frac{5+2\sqrt{3}}{7+4\sqrt{3}} = a + b\sqrt{3}$ then:

(*a*) $a = 6,\ b = 11$ (*b*) $a = 11,\ b = -6$ (*c*) $a = -11,\ b = 6$ (*d*) $a = -11,\ b = -6$

87. $\frac{\sqrt{7}+\sqrt{5}}{\sqrt{7}-\sqrt{5}}$ equals:

(*a*) $6 + \sqrt{35}$ (*b*) $6 - \sqrt{35}$ (*c*) 2 (*d*) 1

88. $\left[\frac{3\sqrt{2}}{\sqrt{6}-\sqrt{3}} - \frac{4\sqrt{3}}{\sqrt{6}-\sqrt{2}} - \frac{6}{\sqrt{8}-\sqrt{12}}\right]$ is equal to:

(*a*) 1 (*b*) $5\sqrt{3}$ (*c*) $\sqrt{3} + \sqrt{2}$ (*d*) $\sqrt{3} - \sqrt{2}$

89. $\left[2+\sqrt{2}+\dfrac{1}{2+\sqrt{2}}-\dfrac{1}{2-\sqrt{2}}\right]$ is simplified to:

(a) $2\sqrt{2}$ (b) $2+\sqrt{2}$ (c) 2 (d) $2-\sqrt{2}$

90. $\dfrac{1}{(\sqrt{9}-\sqrt{8})}-\dfrac{1}{(\sqrt{8}-\sqrt{7})}+\dfrac{1}{(\sqrt{7}-\sqrt{6})}-\dfrac{1}{(\sqrt{6}-\sqrt{5})}+\dfrac{1}{(\sqrt{5}-\sqrt{4})}$ equals:

(a) 5 (b) 1 (c) $\dfrac{1}{3}$ (d) 0

91. If $\sqrt{5}=2.2361$, $\sqrt{3}=1.7321$, then $\dfrac{1}{\sqrt{5}-\sqrt{3}}$ equals:

(a) 2 (b) 1.9841 (c) 1.984 (d) 1.98

EXPLANATORY ANSWERS

1. Square root of $5\frac{4}{9}$ = Squre root of $\dfrac{49}{9}=\sqrt{\dfrac{49}{9}}=\dfrac{\sqrt{7\times7}}{\sqrt{3\times3}}=\dfrac{7}{3}$.

2.

$$\begin{array}{r|l} & 125 \\ \hline 1 & \overline{1}\ \overline{56}\ \overline{25} \\ & 1 \\ \hline 22 & 56 \\ & 44 \\ \hline 245 & 1225 \\ & 1225 \\ \hline & \times \end{array}$$

∴ Square root of 15625 = 125.

3. Square root of $\sqrt{1296}=\sqrt{\sqrt{1296}}=\sqrt{\sqrt{6\times6\times6\times6}}=\sqrt{6\times6}=6$

4. Cube root of 10648 = $\sqrt[3]{10648}=\sqrt[3]{2\times2\times2\times11\times11\times11}$ = 2 × 11 = 22.

5.

$$\begin{array}{r|l} & 13{,}272 \\ \hline 1 & \overline{1}\ \overline{76}.\ \overline{25}\ \overline{21}\ \overline{76} \\ & 1 \\ \hline 23 & 76 \\ & 69 \\ \hline 262 & 725 \\ & 524 \\ \hline 2647 & 19121 \\ & 18529 \\ \hline 26542 & 59276 \\ & 53084 \\ \hline & 6192 \end{array}$$

∴ Square root of 176.252176 = 13.272.

6. $\because$ 72 = 72.000000

$$
\begin{array}{r|l}
 & 8.485 \\
\hline
8 & \overline{72}.\overline{00}\,\overline{00}\,\overline{00} \\
 & 64 \\
\hline
164 & 800 \\
 & 656 \\
\hline
1688 & 14400 \\
 & 13504 \\
\hline
16565 & 89600 \\
 & 82825 \\
\hline
 & 6775
\end{array}
$$

Square root of 72.000000 upto three decimal places = 8.485

7. $\because$ $\sqrt{7} = \sqrt{7.000000}$

$$
\begin{array}{r|l}
 & 2.645 \\
\hline
2 & \overline{7}.\overline{00}\,\overline{00}\,\overline{00} \\
 & 4 \\
\hline
46 & 300 \\
 & 276 \\
\hline
524 & 2400 \\
 & 2096 \\
\hline
5285 & 30400 \\
 & 26425 \\
\hline
 & 3975
\end{array}
$$

$\therefore$ Square root of 7 upto three decimal places = $\sqrt{7} = 2.645$.

According to question, $7 + \sqrt{7} = 7 + 2.645 = 9.645$

$\therefore$ $\sqrt{9.645} =$

$$
\begin{array}{r|l}
 & 3.105 \\
\hline
3 & \overline{9}.\overline{64}\,\overline{50}\,\overline{00} \\
 & 9 \\
\hline
61 & 64 \\
 & 61 \\
\hline
6205 & 35000 \\
 & 31025 \\
\hline
 & 3975
\end{array}
$$

$\therefore$ $\sqrt{7+\sqrt{7}} = \sqrt{9.645} = 3.105.$

8. $\sqrt{676} = \sqrt{26 \times 26} = 26,$

$\sqrt{784} = \sqrt{28 \times 28} = 28$

and $\sqrt{289} = \sqrt{17 \times 17} = 17$

$\therefore$ $\sqrt{676} + \sqrt{784} - \sqrt{289} = 26 + 28 - 17 = 37.$

9. $\frac{x}{7} = \frac{28}{x}$

$\Rightarrow x^2 = 7 \times 28$ $\Rightarrow x^2 = 7 \times 7 \times 2 \times 2$

$\Rightarrow x = \sqrt{7 \times 7 \times 2 \times 2}$ $\Rightarrow x = 7 \times 2 = 14.$

10. $\sqrt{1+\frac{x}{144}} = \frac{13}{12}$ $\Rightarrow 1+\frac{x}{144} = \left(\frac{13}{12}\right)^2$

$\Rightarrow \quad \frac{144+x}{144} = \frac{169}{144} \qquad \Rightarrow 144 + x = 169 \quad \Rightarrow \ x = 169 - 144 \quad \Rightarrow x = 25.$

11. $\sqrt{18225} = 135$ (given)

$\therefore \ \sqrt{182.25} = 13.5$ and $\sqrt{1.8225} = 1.35$

$\therefore \ \sqrt{18225} + \sqrt{182.25} + \sqrt{1.8225} = 135 + 13.5 + 1.35 = 149.85.$

12. $\sqrt{95+\sqrt{13+\sqrt{144}}} = \sqrt{95+\sqrt{13+12}} = \sqrt{95+\sqrt{25}}$

$= \sqrt{95+5} = \sqrt{100} = \sqrt{10\times10} = 10.$

13. 50% of $\sqrt{?}$ = 20% of 10

$\therefore \ \frac{1}{2}\times\sqrt{?} = \frac{20}{100}\times10 = 2 \ \therefore \ \sqrt{?} = 2\times2 = 4$

$\Rightarrow \ ? = 4^2 = 16.$

14. $\frac{1}{\sqrt{441}} = \frac{\sqrt{x}}{7} \qquad \Rightarrow \qquad \frac{1}{21} = \frac{\sqrt{x}}{7}$

$\Rightarrow \ \sqrt{x} = \frac{7}{21} = \frac{1}{3} \qquad \Rightarrow \qquad x = \left(\frac{1}{3}\right)^2 = \frac{1}{9}.$

$\therefore$ Value of x is $\frac{1}{9}$

15. $\because \ \sqrt{4} = 2,\ \sqrt{16} = 4$ and $\sqrt{25} = 5$

$\therefore \ \sqrt{4} + \sqrt{16} + \sqrt{25} = \sqrt{?}$ (given)

$\Rightarrow \ 2 + 4 + 5 = \sqrt{?}$ or $\sqrt{?} = 11$

$\Rightarrow \ ? = (11)^2 = 121$

$\therefore$ Sign of interrogation should be replaced by 121.

16. $\sqrt{.81} = \sqrt{.9\times.9} = .9$

and $\sqrt{.0049} = \sqrt{.07\times.07} = .07$

$\therefore \ \sqrt{.81} + \sqrt{.0049} = .9 + .07 = .97$

$\therefore$ Sign of interrogation should be replaced by .97.

17. $\because \ (625)^2 = 390625$

$\therefore \ \sqrt{.00390625} = \sqrt{10^{-8}\times390625}$

$= \ \sqrt{10^{-8}\times(625)^2} = \sqrt{10^{-4}\times625\times10^{-4}\times625}$

$= \ 10^{-4}\times625 = .0625.$

18. $\because \qquad x \otimes y = \sqrt{(x+1)(y+1)^2}$

$\therefore \qquad 3 \otimes 7 = \sqrt{(3+1)(7+1)^2}$

$= \sqrt{4\times8^2} = 2\times8 = 16.$

19. Cube root of $8^4 = \sqrt[3]{8^4}$

$= \sqrt[3]{8 \times 8 \times 8 \times 8}$

$= \sqrt[3]{\underline{8 \times 2} \times \underline{8 \times 2} \times \underline{8 \times 2}}$

$= 8 \times 2 = 16$

20. $270 = 2 \times 5 \times 3 \times 3 \times 3$

$= 10 \times \underline{3 \times 3 \times 3}$

From the above, we find that the number 10 does not make a group of three.

∴ If we multiply 270 by (10 × 10 = 100), the product would be $\underline{10 \times 10 \times 10} \times \underline{3 \times 3 \times 3}$ which is a perfect cube.

21. $675 = 3 \times 3 \times 3 \times 5 \times 5 = 3 \times 3^2 \times 5^2$

From the above, we find that only a factor 3 is left unpaired

∴ If we multiply 675 by 3 the product would be $\underline{3 \times 3} \times 3^2 \times 5^2$ which is a perfect square.

∴ The required smallest number is 3.

22. $\sqrt{80} = 8.94$ (given)

∴ $\sqrt{20} = \sqrt{\frac{20 \times 4}{4}} = \sqrt{\frac{80}{4}} = \frac{8.94}{2} = 4.47$ ∴ Value of $\sqrt{20} = 4.47$

23. ∵ $\sqrt[3]{32 + \sqrt{1012 + \sqrt{144}}} = \sqrt[3]{32 + \sqrt{1012 + 12}}$

$= \sqrt[3]{32 + \sqrt{1024}} = \sqrt[3]{32 + 32} = \sqrt[3]{64} = \sqrt[3]{4 \times 4 \times 4} = 4$

24. $\sqrt[3]{0.000000064} = \sqrt[3]{.004 \times .004 \times .004} = .004$

∴ $\sqrt[3]{0.000000064} \times \sqrt{2.56} = .004 \times 1.6 = .0064$

∴ Square root of $\left(\sqrt[3]{.000000064} \times \sqrt{2.56}\right)$

= Square root of .0064 $= \sqrt{.0064} = \sqrt{.08 \times .08} = .08$

25. $\frac{\sqrt{?}}{4} = \frac{1}{3}$ $\Rightarrow \sqrt{?} = \frac{4}{3}$ $\Rightarrow ? = \frac{4}{3} \times \frac{4}{3} = \frac{16}{9}$

∴ Sign of interrogation (?) should be replaced by $\frac{16}{9}$.

26. 30% of $\sqrt{?}$ + 15% of 40 = 11

∴ $\frac{30}{100} \times \sqrt{?} + \frac{15}{100} \times 40 = 11$

$\Rightarrow \frac{30\sqrt{?}}{100} + \frac{600}{100} = 11$ $\Rightarrow 30\sqrt{?} + 600 = 1100$

$\Rightarrow 30\sqrt{?} = 1100 - 600$ $\Rightarrow 30\sqrt{?} = 500$

$$\Rightarrow \sqrt{?} = \frac{500}{30} = \frac{50}{3}$$

$$\Rightarrow ? = \frac{50}{3} \times \frac{50}{3} = \frac{2500}{9}$$

27. The least number of four digits = 1000

Square root of 1000

$$\begin{array}{r|l} & 31 \\ \hline 3 & \overline{10}\ \overline{00} \\ & 9 \\ \hline 61 & 100 \\ & 61 \\ \hline & 39 \end{array}$$

∴ $1000 = (31)^2 + 39$ which is not a perfect square number

∴ The least number of four digits is $32^2 = 32 \times 32 = 1024$.

28. Square root of 11125

$$\begin{array}{r|l} & 105 \\ \hline 1 & \overline{1}\,\overline{11}\ \overline{25} \\ & 1 \\ \hline 205 & 1125 \\ & 1025 \\ \hline & 100 \end{array}$$

The remainder 100 shows that if we subtract 100 from 11125, the resulting number will be a perfect square.

∴ 100 is to be subtracted from 11125.

29. Number of plants that have been arranged in a row will be square root of 4624.

$$\therefore \sqrt{4624} = \begin{array}{r|l} & 68 \\ \hline 6 & \overline{46}\ \overline{24} \\ & 36 \\ \hline 128 & 1024 \\ & 1024 \\ \hline & \times \end{array}$$

∴ Number of plants arranged in a row will be 68.

30. Number of soldiers in each row will be square root of 14500 – 100 = 14400

∴ Square root of 14400 = $\sqrt{14400} = \sqrt{12 \times 10 \times 12 \times 10} = 12 \times 10 = 120$.

31. Total number of Kanchan's friends = Square root of (537 – 8 = 529)

$$\begin{array}{r|l} & 23 \\ \hline 2 & \overline{5}\ \overline{29} \\ & 4 \\ \hline 43 & 129 \\ & 129 \\ \hline & \times \end{array}$$

∴ Total number of her friends = 23.

32. $\because$ Rs. 676 = 676 × 100 = 67600 Paise

$\therefore$ Number of members of the society = Square root of 67600

$$\begin{array}{r|l} & 260 \\ 2 & \overline{6}\ \overline{76}\ \overline{00} \\ & 4 \\ \hline 46 & 276 \\ & 276 \\ \hline 520 & \times \end{array}$$

$\therefore$ Number of members = 260.

33. $\left(\frac{\sqrt{625}}{11} \times \frac{14}{\sqrt{25}} \times \frac{11}{\sqrt{196}}\right) = \frac{25}{11} \times \frac{14}{5} \times \frac{11}{14} = 5$

34. $\sqrt{41-\sqrt{21+19-\sqrt{9}}} = \sqrt{41-\sqrt{21+\sqrt{19-3}}} = \sqrt{41-\sqrt{21+\sqrt{16}}} = \sqrt{41-\sqrt{21+4}}$

$= \sqrt{41-\sqrt{25}} = \sqrt{41-5} = \sqrt{36} = 6$

35. $\sqrt{10+\sqrt{25+\sqrt{108+\sqrt{154+\sqrt{225}}}}} = \sqrt{10+\sqrt{25+\sqrt{108+\sqrt{154+15}}}}$

$= \sqrt{10+\sqrt{25+\sqrt{108+\sqrt{169}}}} = \sqrt{10+\sqrt{25+\sqrt{108+13}}} = \sqrt{10+\sqrt{25+\sqrt{121}}}$

$= \sqrt{10+\sqrt{25+11}} = \sqrt{10+\sqrt{36}} = \sqrt{10+6} = \sqrt{16} = 4$

36. $\sqrt{\frac{25}{81}-\frac{1}{9}} = \sqrt{\frac{25-9}{81}} = \sqrt{\frac{16}{81}} = \frac{\sqrt{16}}{\sqrt{81}} = \frac{4}{9}$

37. $y = 5$

Then, $10y\sqrt{y^3 - y^2} = 10 \times 5\sqrt{5^3 - 5^2} = 50\sqrt{125-25} = 50 \times \sqrt{100} = 50 \times 10 = 500$

38. Here, $x \star y = x + y + \sqrt{xy}$

$\therefore$ $6 \star 24 = 6 + 24 + \sqrt{6 \times 24} = 30 + \sqrt{144} = 30 + 12 = 42$

39. $\sqrt{(272)^2 - (128)^2} = \sqrt{(272+128)(272-128)} = \sqrt{400 \times 144} = 20 \times 12 = 240$

40. Given, $\sqrt{13} = 3.605$ and $\sqrt{130} = 11.40$

Then, $\sqrt{1.3} + \sqrt{1300} + \sqrt{0.013} = \frac{\sqrt{130}}{10} + 10\sqrt{13} + \frac{\sqrt{130}}{100} = \frac{11.40}{10} + 10 \times 3.605 + \frac{11.40}{10.0}$

$= 1.140 + 36.05 + 0.1140 = 37.304$

41. $\sqrt{0.0025} \times \sqrt{2.25} \times \sqrt{0.0001} = 0.05 \times 1.5 \times 0.01 = 0.00075$

42. $\sqrt{0.01}+\sqrt{0.81}+\sqrt{1.21}+\sqrt{0.0009} = 0.1 + 0.9 + 1.1 + 0.03 = 2.13$

43. $(1.5)^2 \times \sqrt{0.0225} = 2.25 \times 0.15 = 0.3375$

44. $\sqrt{0.00004761} = \dfrac{\sqrt{4761}}{\sqrt{100000000}} = \dfrac{69}{10000} = 0.0069$

45. A two-digit number having 8 at its unit place cannot be a perfect square.

46. $\sqrt{1369}+\sqrt{1.0615+x} = 37.25$

$\Rightarrow 37 + \sqrt{0.0615+x} = 37.25 \Rightarrow \sqrt{0.0615+x} = 0.25$

$\Rightarrow 0.0615 + x = 0.0625 \qquad \therefore x = 0.0625 - 0.0615 = 0.001 = 10^{-3}$

47. $\sqrt{0.0169 \times ?} = 1.3 \qquad \Rightarrow 0.0169 \times ? = 1.69 \qquad \therefore ? = \dfrac{1.69}{0.0169} = \dfrac{16900}{169} = 100$

48. $\sqrt{\dfrac{0.0196}{?}} = 0.2 \Rightarrow \dfrac{0.0196}{?} = 0.04 \therefore ? = \dfrac{0.0196}{0.04} = \dfrac{1.96}{4} = 0.49$

49. Here, $\sqrt{x} \div \sqrt{441} = 0.02 \Rightarrow \sqrt{\dfrac{x}{441}} = 0.02 \Rightarrow \dfrac{x}{441} = 0.0004$

$\therefore x = 441 \times 0.0004 = 0.1764$

50. $28\sqrt{?} + 1426 = \dfrac{3}{4}$ of $2872 \qquad \Rightarrow 28\sqrt{?} = \dfrac{3}{4} \times 2872 - 1426$

$\Rightarrow 28\sqrt{?} = 2154 - 1426 \qquad \Rightarrow 28\sqrt{?} = 728$

$\Rightarrow \sqrt{?} = \dfrac{728}{28} = 26 \qquad \therefore ? = (26)^2 = 676$

51. $\sqrt{3^n} = 729 \qquad \Rightarrow \sqrt{3^n} = 3^6$

$\Rightarrow 3^n = 3^{12} \qquad \therefore n = 12$

52. Required number $= 25 \times \sqrt{0.25} = 25 \times 0.5 = 12.5$

53. $0.13 \div p^2 = 13 \qquad \Rightarrow p^2 = \dfrac{0.13}{13} = 0.01 \qquad \therefore p = \sqrt{0.01} = 0.1$

54. Here, $?^2 = \sqrt{162 \times 128} = 144 \qquad \therefore ? = \sqrt{144} = 12$

55. Here, $?^2 = \dfrac{9}{2} \times 32 = 9 \times 16 \qquad \therefore ? = \sqrt{9 \times 16} = 3 \times 4 = 12$

56. Here, $?^2 = 15 \times 135 \qquad \therefore ? = \sqrt{15 \times 135} = \sqrt{15 \times 15 \times 9} = 15 \times 3 = 45$

57. Here, $x = 52 \times \sqrt{\dfrac{289}{169}} = 52 \times \dfrac{17}{13} = 4 \times 17 = 68$

58. $\sqrt{0.\bar{4}} = \sqrt{\dfrac{4}{9}} = \dfrac{2}{3} = 0.\bar{6}$

59. Here, $3a = 4b = 6c$ $\quad \therefore a = 2c$ and $b = \dfrac{3}{2}c$

Now, $a + b + c = 27\sqrt{29}$ $\quad \Rightarrow 2c + \dfrac{3}{2}c + c = 27\sqrt{29}$ $\quad \Rightarrow \dfrac{9c}{2} = 27\sqrt{29}$

$\therefore$ $c = 6\sqrt{29}$ Again, $a = 2c = 2 \times 6\sqrt{29} = 12\sqrt{29}$ Now, $b = \dfrac{3}{2}c = \dfrac{3}{2} \times 6\sqrt{29} = 9\sqrt{29}$

Then, $\sqrt{a^2 + b^2 + c^2}$ $\sqrt{\left(12\sqrt{29}\right)^2 + \left(9\sqrt{29}\right)^2 + \left(6\sqrt{29}\right)^2}$

$= \sqrt{144 \times 29 + 81 \times 29 + 36 \times 29} = \sqrt{(144 + 81 + 36) \times 29} = \sqrt{261 \times 29}$

$= \sqrt{9 \times 29 \times 29} = 3 \times 29 = 87$

60. $\sqrt{\dfrac{(0.75)^3}{(1-0.75)} + \left[0.75 + (0.75)^2 + 1\right]} = \sqrt{\dfrac{(0.75)^3 + (1-0.75)\left[1 + (0.75)^2 + 0.75 \times 1\right]}{(1-0.75)}}$

$\sqrt{\dfrac{(0.75)^3 + 1^3 - (0.75)^3}{(1-0.75)}} = \sqrt{\dfrac{1}{0.25}} = \dfrac{1}{0.5} = \dfrac{10}{2} = 2$

61. Given, a = 0.1039,

Then, $\sqrt{4a^2 - 4a + 1} + 3a = \sqrt{1^2 - 2 \times 1 \times 2a + (2a)^2} + 3a = \sqrt{(1-2a)^2} + 3a$

$= 1 - 2a + 3a = 1 + a = 1 + 0.1039 = 1.1039$

62. $\sqrt{\left(7 + 3\sqrt{5}\right)\left(7 - 3\sqrt{5}\right)} = \sqrt{(7)^2 - \left(3\sqrt{5}\right)^2} = \sqrt{49 - 45} = \sqrt{4} = 2$

63. $\sqrt{\dfrac{(0.03)^2 + (0.21)^2 + (0.065)^2}{(0.003)^2 + (0.021)^2 + (0.0065)^2}} = \sqrt{\dfrac{10^2\left[(0.003)^2 + (0.021)^2 + (0.0065)^2\right]}{(0.003)^2 + (0.021)^2 + (0.0065)^2}} = \sqrt{10^2} = 10$

64. $\left(\sqrt{3} - \dfrac{1}{\sqrt{3}}\right)^2 = \left(\dfrac{3-1}{\sqrt{3}}\right)^2 = \left(\dfrac{2}{\sqrt{3}}\right)^2 = \dfrac{4}{3}$

65. $\sqrt{\dfrac{0.081\times0.484}{0.0064\times6.25}}=\sqrt{\dfrac{81\times484\times10^{-6}}{64\times625\times10^{-6}}}=\dfrac{9\times22}{8\times25}=\dfrac{99}{100}=0.99$

66. $\dfrac{3\sqrt{12}}{2\sqrt{28}}\div\dfrac{2\sqrt{21}}{\sqrt{98}}=\dfrac{3}{2}\times\dfrac{1}{2}\times\dfrac{\sqrt{12}}{\sqrt{28}}\times\dfrac{\sqrt{98}}{\sqrt{21}}=\dfrac{3}{4}\times\sqrt{2}=\dfrac{3}{4}\times1.414$ $= 3 \times 0.3535 = 1.0605$

67. Given $\sqrt{2}=1.414$

Then, $\sqrt{8}+2\sqrt{32}-3\sqrt{128}+4\sqrt{50}=2\sqrt{2}+8\sqrt{2}-24\sqrt{2}+20\sqrt{2}$

$=6\sqrt{2}=6\times1.414=8.484$

68. Given, $3\sqrt{5}+\sqrt{125}=17.88$ $\Rightarrow 3\sqrt{5}+5\sqrt{5}=17.88$ $\therefore 8\sqrt{5}=17.88$

Then, $\sqrt{80}+6\sqrt{5}=4\sqrt{5}+6\sqrt{5}=10\sqrt{5}=\dfrac{10}{8}\times17.88$ $= 5 \times 4.47 = 22.35$

69. $\dfrac{\sqrt{80}-\sqrt{112}}{\sqrt{45}-\sqrt{63}}=\dfrac{4\sqrt{5}-4\sqrt{7}}{3\sqrt{5}-3\sqrt{7}}=\dfrac{4\left(\sqrt{5}-\sqrt{7}\right)}{3\left(\sqrt{5}-\sqrt{7}\right)}=\dfrac{4}{3}=1\dfrac{1}{3}$

70. Here, $\left(\sqrt{12}+\sqrt{18}\right)-\left(\sqrt{3}+\sqrt{2}\right)=2\sqrt{3}+3\sqrt{2}-\sqrt{3}-\sqrt{2}=\sqrt{3}+2\sqrt{2}$

71. $\sqrt{1+\dfrac{55}{729}}=1+\dfrac{x}{27}\Rightarrow\sqrt{\dfrac{729+55}{729}}=1+\dfrac{x}{27}\Rightarrow\sqrt{\dfrac{784}{729}}=1+\dfrac{x}{27}$

$\Rightarrow \dfrac{28}{27}-1=\dfrac{x}{27}$ $\Rightarrow \dfrac{1}{27}=\dfrac{x}{27}$ $\therefore x=1$

72. Let, the number be x,

Then, $\dfrac{3}{5}\times x^2=126.15 \Rightarrow x^2=\dfrac{5}{3}\times126.15$ $\therefore x^2=210.25$

$\therefore x=\sqrt{210.25}=14.5$

73. The greatest four-digit number = 9999

```
   9 | 99 99 (99
     | 81
 189 | 18 99
     | 17 01
     |  1 98
```

$\therefore$ The required number = 9999 − 198 = 9801.

74.

```
    8 | 68 06 21 (825
      | 64
  162 |  4 06
      |  3 24
 1645 |    82 21
      |    82 25
      |       −4
```

Hence, required smallest number to be added is 4.

75.

$$\begin{array}{r|l} 0 & 0.\ 00\ 03\ 26\ (0.018 \\ & \ \ 00 \\ \hline 1 & \ \ \ \ 03 \\ & \ \ \ \ \ \ 1 \\ \hline 28 & \ \ \ \ 226 \\ & \ \ \ \ 224 \\ \hline & \ \ \ \ \ \ \ \ 2 \end{array}$$

Hence, least number to be subtracted is 0.000002.

76.

$$\begin{array}{r|l} 2 & 5808 \\ \hline 2 & 2904 \\ \hline 2 & 1452 \\ \hline 2 & 726 \\ \hline 3 & 363 \\ \hline 11 & 121 \\ \hline & 11 \end{array}$$

Hence, $5808 = 2^2 \times 2^2 \times 3 \times 11^2$

Hence, required least number to be multiplied is 3.

77. LCM of 21, 36 and 66 is 2772.

Now $2772 = 2^2 \times 3^2 \times 7 \times 11$

Hence, required number $= 2772 \times 77 = 213444$

78. $\sqrt{5} = 2.236$ (Given)

Then, $\dfrac{\sqrt{5}}{2} - \dfrac{10}{\sqrt{5}} + \sqrt{125} = \dfrac{\sqrt{5}}{2} - \dfrac{10}{\sqrt{5}} \times \dfrac{\sqrt{5}}{\sqrt{5}} + 5\sqrt{5} = \dfrac{\sqrt{5}}{2} - 2\sqrt{5} + 5\sqrt{5}$

$= \dfrac{\sqrt{5}}{2} + 3\sqrt{5} = \dfrac{(1+6)\sqrt{5}}{2} = \dfrac{7}{2}\sqrt{5} = \dfrac{7}{2} \times 2.236 = 7 \times 1.118 = 7.826$

79. $\dfrac{1+\sqrt{0.01}}{1-\sqrt{0.1}} = \dfrac{1+0.1}{1-0.316} = \dfrac{1.1}{0.684} = \dfrac{1100}{684}$

$= \dfrac{275}{171} = 1.6$

$$\begin{array}{r|l} 3 & 0\ .\ \overline{10}\ \overline{00}\ \overline{00}\ \ (0.316 \\ & \ \ \ \ 9 \\ \hline 61 & \ \ \ \ 100 \\ & \ \ \ \ \ 61 \\ \hline 626 & \ \ \ \ 3900 \\ & \ \ \ \ 3756 \\ \hline & \ \ \ \ \ 144 \end{array}$$

80. $\sqrt{\dfrac{0.16}{0.4}} = \sqrt{0.4} = 0.63$

$$\begin{array}{r|l} 6 & 0\ .\ \overline{40}\ \overline{00}\ \overline{00}\ \ (0.632 \\ & \ \ \ \ 36 \\ \hline 123 & \ \ \ \ 400 \\ & \ \ \ \ 369 \\ \hline 1262 & \ \ \ \ 3100 \\ & \ \ \ \ 2524 \\ \hline & \ \ \ \ \ 576 \end{array}$$

81. Given, $x = \dfrac{\sqrt{3}+1}{\sqrt{3}-1}, \quad y = \dfrac{\sqrt{3}-1}{\sqrt{3}+1}$

Then, $x^2 + y^2 = (x + y)^2 - 2xy = \left[\frac{\sqrt{3}+1}{\sqrt{3}-1} + \frac{\sqrt{3}-1}{\sqrt{3}+1}\right]^2 - 2 \times \frac{\left(\sqrt{3}+1\right)}{\left(\sqrt{3}-1\right)} \times \frac{\left(\sqrt{3}-1\right)}{\left(\sqrt{3}+1\right)}$

$$= \left[\frac{\left(\sqrt{3}+1\right)^2 + \left(\sqrt{3}-1\right)^2}{\left(\sqrt{3}-1\right)\left(\sqrt{3}+1\right)}\right]^2 - 2 = \left(\frac{3+1+2\sqrt{3}+3+1-2\sqrt{3}}{3-1}\right)^2 - 2$$

$$= \left(\frac{8}{2}\right)^2 - 2 = 16 - 4 = 14$$

82. Given, $x = \left(7 - 4\sqrt{3}\right)$

Then, $\frac{1}{x} = \frac{1}{7-4\sqrt{3}} = \frac{1}{\left(7-4\sqrt{3}\right)} \times \frac{\left(7+4\sqrt{3}\right)}{\left(7+4\sqrt{3}\right)} = \frac{7+4\sqrt{3}}{49-48} = 7 + 4\sqrt{3}$

Now, $x + \frac{1}{x} = 7 - 4\sqrt{3} + 7 + 4\sqrt{3} = 14$

83. $\left(\frac{2+\sqrt{3}}{2-\sqrt{3}} + \frac{2-\sqrt{3}}{2+\sqrt{3}} + \frac{\sqrt{3}-1}{\sqrt{3}+1}\right) = \frac{\left(2+\sqrt{3}\right)^2 + \left(2-\sqrt{3}\right)^2}{\left(2-\sqrt{3}\right)\left(2+\sqrt{3}\right)} + \frac{\sqrt{3}-1}{\sqrt{3}+1} \times \frac{\sqrt{3}-1}{\sqrt{3}-1}$

$$= \frac{4+3+2\sqrt{3}+4+3-2\sqrt{3}}{4-3} + \frac{\left(\sqrt{3}-1\right)^2}{\left(\sqrt{3}+1\right)\left(\sqrt{3}-1\right)} = \frac{14}{1} + \frac{3+1-2\sqrt{3}}{3-1}$$

$$= 14 + \frac{2\left(2-\sqrt{3}\right)}{2} = 14 + 2 - \sqrt{3} = 16 - \sqrt{3}$$

84. $\frac{3\sqrt{6}}{5\sqrt{3} - 2\sqrt{12} - \sqrt{32} + \sqrt{50}} = \frac{3+\sqrt{6}}{5\sqrt{3} - 4\sqrt{3} - 4\sqrt{2} + 5\sqrt{2}} = \frac{3+\sqrt{6}}{\sqrt{3}+\sqrt{2}}$

$$= \frac{3+\sqrt{6}}{\sqrt{3}+\sqrt{2}} \times \frac{\sqrt{3}-\sqrt{2}}{\sqrt{3}-\sqrt{2}} = \frac{3\sqrt{3}+\sqrt{18}-3\sqrt{2}-\sqrt{12}}{3-2}$$

$$= \frac{3\sqrt{3}+3\sqrt{2}-3\sqrt{2}-2\sqrt{3}}{1} = \sqrt{3}$$

85. Given, $\sqrt{2} = 1.414$

Then, $\sqrt{\frac{\sqrt{2}-1}{\sqrt{2}+1}} = \sqrt{\frac{\left(\sqrt{2}-1\right)}{\left(\sqrt{2}+1\right)} \times \frac{\left(\sqrt{2}-1\right)}{\left(\sqrt{2}-1\right)}} = \sqrt{\frac{\left(\sqrt{2}-1\right)^2}{2-1}} = \sqrt{2} - 1 = 1.414 - 1 = 0.414$

86. $\frac{5+2\sqrt{3}}{7+4\sqrt{3}}=a+b\sqrt{3}$

L.H.S. $=\frac{5+2\sqrt{3}}{7+4\sqrt{3}}\times\frac{7-4\sqrt{3}}{7-4\sqrt{3}}=\frac{35+14\sqrt{3}-20\sqrt{3}-24}{49-48}=11-6\sqrt{3}$

Now, $a+b\sqrt{3}=11-6\sqrt{3}$

Hence, $a=11,\ b=-6$

87. $\frac{\sqrt{7}+\sqrt{5}}{\sqrt{7}-\sqrt{5}}=\frac{(\sqrt{7}+\sqrt{5})}{(\sqrt{7}-\sqrt{5})}\times\frac{(\sqrt{7}+\sqrt{5})}{(\sqrt{7}+\sqrt{5})}=\frac{7+5+2\sqrt{35}}{7-5}$

$=\frac{2(6+\sqrt{35})}{2}=6+\sqrt{35}$

88. $\frac{3\sqrt{2}}{\sqrt{6}-\sqrt{3}}-\frac{4\sqrt{3}}{\sqrt{6}-\sqrt{2}}-\frac{6}{\sqrt{8}-\sqrt{12}}$

$=\frac{3\sqrt{2}}{\sqrt{6}-\sqrt{3}}\times\frac{\sqrt{6}+\sqrt{3}}{\sqrt{6}+\sqrt{3}}-\frac{4\sqrt{3}}{\sqrt{6}-\sqrt{2}}\times\frac{\sqrt{6}+\sqrt{2}}{\sqrt{6}+\sqrt{2}}-\frac{6}{2\sqrt{2}-2\sqrt{3}}$

$=\frac{3(\sqrt{12}+\sqrt{6})}{6-3}-\frac{4(\sqrt{18}+\sqrt{16})}{6-2}-\frac{3}{\sqrt{2}-\sqrt{3}}\times\frac{\sqrt{2}+\sqrt{3}}{\sqrt{2}+\sqrt{3}}$

$=\frac{3(2\sqrt{3}+\sqrt{6})}{3}-\frac{4(3\sqrt{2}+\sqrt{6})}{4}-\frac{3(\sqrt{12}+\sqrt{3})}{2-3}$

$=2\sqrt{3}+\sqrt{6}-3\sqrt{2}-\sqrt{6}+3\sqrt{2}+3\sqrt{3}$

$=5\sqrt{3}$

89. $2+\sqrt{2}+\frac{1}{2+\sqrt{2}}-\frac{1}{2-\sqrt{2}}$

$=2+\sqrt{2}+\frac{2-\sqrt{2}-2-\sqrt{2}}{(2+\sqrt{2})(2-\sqrt{2})}=2+\sqrt{2}-\frac{2\sqrt{2}}{4-2}=2+\sqrt{2}-\frac{2\sqrt{2}}{2}=2$

90. $\frac{1}{\sqrt{9}-\sqrt{8}}-\frac{1}{\sqrt{8}-\sqrt{7}}+\frac{1}{\sqrt{7}-\sqrt{6}}-\frac{1}{\sqrt{6}-\sqrt{5}}+\frac{1}{\sqrt{5}-\sqrt{4}}$

$$= \frac{1}{(\sqrt{9}-\sqrt{8})}\times\frac{(\sqrt{9}+\sqrt{8})}{(\sqrt{9}+\sqrt{8})}-\frac{1}{(\sqrt{8}-\sqrt{7})}\times\frac{(\sqrt{8}+\sqrt{7})}{(\sqrt{8}+\sqrt{7})}+\frac{1}{(\sqrt{7}-\sqrt{6})}\times\frac{(\sqrt{7}+\sqrt{6})}{(\sqrt{7}+\sqrt{6})}-\frac{1}{(\sqrt{6}-\sqrt{5})}\times\frac{(\sqrt{6}+\sqrt{5})}{(\sqrt{6}+\sqrt{5})}+\frac{1}{(\sqrt{5}-\sqrt{4})}\times\frac{(\sqrt{5}+\sqrt{4})}{(\sqrt{5}+\sqrt{4})}$$

$$= \frac{\sqrt{9}+\sqrt{8}}{9-8}-\frac{\sqrt{8}+\sqrt{7}}{8-7}+\frac{\sqrt{7}+\sqrt{6}}{7-6}-\frac{\sqrt{6}+\sqrt{5}}{6-5}+\frac{\sqrt{5}+\sqrt{4}}{5-4}$$

$$= \sqrt{9}+\sqrt{8}-\sqrt{8}-\sqrt{7}+\sqrt{7}+\sqrt{6}-\sqrt{6}-\sqrt{5}+\sqrt{5}+\sqrt{4}$$

$$= \sqrt{9}+\sqrt{4} = 3+2 = 5$$

91. $\sqrt{5} = 2.2361$ and $\sqrt{3} = 1.7321$

Then, $\frac{1}{\sqrt{5}-\sqrt{3}} = \frac{1}{\sqrt{5}-\sqrt{3}}\times\frac{\sqrt{5}+\sqrt{3}}{\sqrt{5}+\sqrt{3}} = \frac{\sqrt{5}+\sqrt{3}}{5-3} = \frac{2.2361+1.7321}{2}$

$$= \frac{3.9682}{2} = 1.9841$$

7 RATIO AND PROPORTION

RATIO

In ratio we compare two quantities of the same kind and consider what multiple, part or parts one is of the other. In comparing 8 with 4, observe that it is 2 times 4. This comparison can be represented as $8 \div 4$ or $\frac{8}{4}$.

Hence, *ratio is that relation between two numbers which is expressed by the fraction, the numerator is which is the measure of the first quantity and denominator is the measure of the second quantity.*

If the terms of a ratio be multiplied or divided by the same quantity the value of the ratio remains unaltered.

Thus, 3 : 4 is the same as 9 : 12 and 9 : 12 is the same as 3 : 4.

PROPORTION

The equality of two ratio is called proportion.

Consider the two ratios:

Ist ratio	2nd ratio
5 : 15	7 : 21

Since, 5 is one-third of 15 and 7 is one-third of 21, the two ratios are equal. The equality of two ratios is called proportion and the numbers 5, 15, and 7, 21 are said to be in **proportion.**

The proportion may be written as 5 : 15 : : 7 : 21 (5 is to 15 as 7 is to 21)

$\Rightarrow \quad 5 : 15 = 7 : 21$

$$\Rightarrow \quad \frac{5}{15} = \frac{7}{21}$$

The numbers 5, 15, 7 and 21 are called the terms. 5 is the first term, 15 the second, 7 the third, and 21 the fourth.

The first and fourth terms, *i.e.*, 5 and 21 are called extremes (end terms), and the second and the third terms, *i.e.*, 15 and 7 are called the **means** (middle terms), 21 is called the fourth proportional.

Some Important Facts:

1. If a and b are two quantities, then

(a) Duplicate ratio of $a : b = a^2 : b^2$

(b) Sub-duplicate ratio of $a : b = \sqrt{a} : \sqrt{b}$

(c) Triplicate ratio of $a : b = a^3 : b^3$

(d) Sub-triplicate ratio $a : b = \sqrt[3]{a} : \sqrt[3]{b}$

(e) Inverse or reciprocal ratio of $a : b = \frac{1}{a} : \frac{1}{b}$

(f) Third proportional to 'a' and 'b' $= \frac{b^2}{a}$

2. If A : B = $x : y$ and B : C = $p : q$, then

(a) $A : C = \frac{x \times p}{y \times q}$

(b) $A : B : C = px : py : qy$

3. In what *ratio* the two kinds of tea must be mixed together one at Rs. x per kg and another at Rs. y per kg, so that the mixture may cost Rs. z per kg?

$$\text{Ratio} = \frac{z - y}{x - z}$$

4. A grey hound persues a hare as takes J_1 leaps for every J_2 leaps of the hare. If K_1 leaps of the hound are equal to K_2 leaps of the hare, then the Ratio of speeds of the hound and hare is

$$\frac{J_2 \times K_1}{J_1 \times K_2}$$

5. The incomes of two persons are in the ratio of $a : b$ and their expenditure are in the ratio of $x : y$. If the saving of each person is Rs. s, then income of each is Rs. $\frac{as(y-x)}{ay-bx}$ and Rs. $\frac{bs(y-x)}{ay-bx}$ respectively.

6. In a mixture of z litre, the ratio of milk and water is $x : y$. If another p litres of water is added to the mixture, the ratio of milk and water in the resulting mixture $= \frac{xz}{yz + p(x+y)}$

7. There are four members a, b, c and d, then formula for

(a) What should be added to each of these numbers so that the remaining numbers may be proportional $= \frac{ad - bc}{(b+c)-(a+d)}$

(b) What should be subtracted from each of these numbers so that the remaining numbers may be proportional $= \frac{ad - bc}{(a+d)-(b+c)}$

8. In a mixture the ratio of milk and water is $a : b$. If in this mixture another K litre of water is added, then the ratio of milk and water in the resulting mixture becomes $a : m$. Then the quantity of milk in the original mixture $= \frac{ak}{m-b}$ and quantity of water $= \frac{bk}{m-b}$

Example 1 : A, B and C are three quantities of the same kind. Their ratios are A : B = 3 : 4, B : C = 5 : 6, find the ratio between A and C.

Solution: $\frac{A}{B} = \frac{3}{4}$ and $\frac{B}{C} = \frac{5}{6}$

$\Rightarrow \frac{A}{C} = \frac{A}{B} \times \frac{B}{C} = \frac{3}{4} \times \frac{5}{6} = \frac{5}{8}$

Hence, the ratio between A and C is 5 : 8.

Alter :

A	:	B	:	C
3	:	4		
		↓		
		5	:	6
15	:	20	:	24

Multiply the numbers joined by arrows. The products so obtained will give the required ratio. This can be illustrated as follows:

A	:	B	:	C
3 × 5	:	5 × 4	:	4 × 6
15	:	20	:	24

Hence, the ratio between A and C
=15 : 24 = 5 : 8

Example 2 : Find the third proportional to 5 and 15.

Solution: Suppose the third proportional to 5 and 15 is x.

5 : 15 : : 15 : x

But the product of the extremes is equal to the square of the mean.

$\Rightarrow \quad 5 \times x = 15 \times 15$

$\Rightarrow \quad x = \frac{15 \times 15}{5} = 45$

The required third proportional = 45

Example 3 : Compound the ratios 2 : 3, 4 : 5 and 6 : 7

Solution: Required ratio = (2 × 4 × 6) : (3 × 5 × 7)
= 48 : 105

Example 4 : A stick 1.4 m long casts a shadow 1.3 m long at the same time when a pole casts a shadow 5.2 m long. Find the length of the pole.

Solution: Let the length of the pole be x m.

Then, 1.3 : 5.2 : : 1.4 : x

$\Rightarrow \quad x = \frac{5.2 \times 14}{1.3} = 5.6 \text{ m}$

Example 5 : How many men must be employed to finish a piece of work in 15 days, which 5 men can do in 24 days.

Solution: This problem based on inverse proposition.

The term may now be put as:

Days		Days		Men	
15	:	24	: :	5	: No. of men required

$\Rightarrow$ Number of men required $\frac{24 \times 5}{15} = 8$

Alter : To finish the work in 24 days, the number of men required = 5

To finish the work in 1 day, the number of men required = 5 × 24

To finish the work in 15 days, the number of men required = $\frac{5 \times 24}{15} = 8$

Example 6 : An amount is to be divided among A, B and C in the ratio of 3 : 5 : 6 respectively. If the difference between A and B's share is Rs. 600, what is C's share?

Solution: Trick : $\frac{A}{3} = \frac{B}{5} = \frac{C}{6}$

$\Rightarrow \quad A = \frac{C}{2}, B = \frac{5C}{6}$

$B - A = 600$

$\Rightarrow \quad \frac{5C}{6} - \frac{C}{2} = 600 \Rightarrow C = \text{Rs. } 1800$

Example 7 : The ratio of prices of two cows was 23 : 16. Two years later when the price of the first had risen by Rs. 447 and that of the second by 10%, the ratio of their prices become 20 : 11. What is their original prices?

Solution: Let prices of two cows be Rs. 23*x* and Rs. 16*x*

$\therefore \quad \frac{23x + 447}{16x + 10\% \text{ of } 16x} = \frac{20}{11}$

$\Rightarrow \quad \frac{23x + 477}{16x + 1.6x} = \frac{20}{11}$

$\Rightarrow \quad \frac{23x + 477}{17.6x} = \frac{20}{11}$

$\Rightarrow \quad 253x + 5247 = 352x$

$\Rightarrow \quad 99x = 5247$

$\Rightarrow \quad x = \frac{5247}{99} = 53$

∴ Original price of the first cow = Rs. (23 × 53) = Rs. 1219
and, that for the 2nd cow = Rs. (16 × 53) = Rs. 848

Example 8 : What will be the area of a rectangle if the ratio of length and breadth is 4 : 3 and its perimeter is 140 meter?

Sol : As perimeter = $2(l + b) = 2(4 + 3) = 14$

$\Rightarrow \quad 14x = 140 \Rightarrow x = 10$

∴ Area of rectangle = $lb = 4 \times 3 \times 10^2 = 1200$ sqm.

Example 9 : One third of Rakesh's marks in English equals a half of his marks in Hindi. If he got 150 marks in these two subject together, how many marks did he get in Hindi?

Solution: $\frac{\text{English}}{3} = \frac{\text{Hindi}}{2}$

∴ English : Hindi = 3 : 2

∴ Hindi's marks = $\frac{2}{5} \times 150 = 60$

Example 10 : The students in three classes are in the ratio 2 : 3 : 5. If 20 students are increased in each classes, the ratio changes to 4 : 5 : 7. What is the total number of students in the three classes before the increase?

Solution: $(2x + 20) : (3x + 20) : (5x + 20) = 4 : 5 : 7$

$$\Rightarrow \quad \frac{2x+20}{4} = \frac{3x+20}{5} = \frac{5x+20}{7} \Rightarrow x = 10$$

$\therefore$ Number of students before increase $= 2x + 3x + 5x = 10x = 100$

Example 11 : The first, second and third class fares between two stations were 10 : 8 : 3 and the number of first, second and third class passengers between the two station in a year was 3 : 4 : 10. The sale of tickets to passengers running between two stations in the year was Rs. 8050. How much was realised by the sale of second class tickets?

Solution: Ratio between the first class, second class and third class fares

$= 10 : 8 : 3$

Ratio between the numbers of passengers of first class, second class and third class = 3 : 4 : 10

The ratio between the total amounts collected by the sale of 1st class, 2nd class and 3rd class passengers can be found out by compounding the above two ratios because the total collection is proportional to the fares as well as the numbers of passengers.

The ratio between the money collected from first, second and third class passengers

$= 10 \times 3 : 8 \times 4 : 3 \times 10 = 30 : 32 : 30 = 15 : 16 : 15$

Sum of ratio numbers $= 15 + 16 + 15 = 46$

$\therefore$ Amount realised by the sale of second class tickets $= 8050 \times \frac{16}{46}$

$= \text{Rs. } 2800$

Example 12 : Rakesh has Rs. 5130 in the form of 1, 2 and 5 rupee notes. If these notes be in the ratio 3 : 7 : 8, find the number of 5 rupee note he has.

Solution: Let these note be $3x$, $7x$ and $8x$

Ratio of their values $= 3x \times 1 : 7x \times 2 : 8x \times 5$

$= 3x : 14x : 40x = 3 : 14 : 40$

Value of 5 rupee note $= \text{Rs. } 5130 \times \frac{40}{57} = \text{Rs. } 3600$

$\therefore$ Number of these notes $= \frac{3600}{5} = 720$

Example 13 : The sum of three numbers is 174. The ratio of second number to the third number is 9 : 16 and the ratio of first number to the third one is 1 : 4. Find the second number.

Solution: $b : c = 9 : 16$ and $a : c = 1 : 4$

$$\therefore \quad \frac{a}{b} = \frac{a}{c} \times \frac{c}{b} = \frac{1}{4} \times \frac{16}{9} = \frac{4}{9}$$

$\therefore \quad a : b = 4 : 9$ and $b : c = 9 : 16$

$\Rightarrow \quad a : b : c = 4 : 9 : 16$

$\therefore \quad$ Second number $= \frac{9}{29} \times 174 = 54$

Example 14 : The ratio between the rates of walking of A and B is 2 : 3. If the time taken by B to cover a certain distance is 36 minutes, find the time in minutes taken by A to cover that much distance.

Solution: Ratio of rates of walking = inverse ratio of time taken

$$\therefore \quad \frac{2}{3} = \frac{36}{x}$$

$\Rightarrow \quad 2x = 108 \Rightarrow x = 54$ minutes

Example 15 : A and B have incomes in the ratio 5 : 3. The expenses of A, B and C are in the ratio 8 : 5 : 2. If C spends Rs. 2000 and B saves Rs. 700, find A's saving.

Solution: Let the incomes of A and B be Rs. $5x$ and Rs. $3x$ respectively.

Let their expenses be $8y$, $5y$ and $2y$

Then, $2y = 2000 \Rightarrow y = 1000$

Also, $3x - 5y = 700 \Rightarrow 3x = 5700 \Rightarrow x = 1900$

$\therefore$ A's saving $= (5x - 8y) = (5 \times 1900 - 8 \times 1000) =$ Rs. 1500

Example 16 : Last year the ratio between the salaries of A and B was 3 : 4. But the ratio of their individual salaries between last year and this year were 4 : 5 and 2 : 3 respectively. If the sum of their present salaries is Rs. 4160, then how much is the salary of A now?

Solution: Let their last year's salaries be $3x$ and $4x$

This year's salaries are $\frac{5}{4} \times 3x$ and $\frac{3}{2} \times 4x$

i.e., $\frac{15x}{4}$ and $6x$ $\therefore$ $\frac{15x}{4} + 6x = 4160 \Rightarrow 39x = 16640$

$\Rightarrow 3x = 1280$

$\therefore$ A's salary now $= \frac{5}{4} \times 3x = \frac{5}{4} \times 1280 =$ Rs. 1600

Example 17 : If 35% of A's income is equal to 25% of B's income, then find the ratio of their income.

Solution: $\frac{35}{100}x = \frac{25}{100}y \Rightarrow \frac{x}{y} = \frac{25}{35} = \frac{5}{7}$

$\therefore$ $x : y = 5 : 7$

Example 18 : Sand and cement were mixed in the ratio 3 : 1 to make 100 tonnes. How much sand must be added to make the ratio 6 : 1?

Solution: The quantity of sand $= \frac{3 \times 100}{3+1} = 75$ tonnes

and the quantity of cement $= \frac{1 \times 100}{3+1} = 25$ tonnes

Suppose we add x tonnes of sand to make the ratio 6 : 1,

then $\frac{75 + x}{25} = \frac{6}{1}$

$\Rightarrow$ $75 + x = 150$

$\therefore$ $x = 150 - 75 = 75$ tonnes

Example 19 : In a mixture of 60 litres, the ratio of milk and water is 2 : 1. What amount of water must be added to make the ratio 1 : 2?

Solution: Milk $= \left(60 \times \frac{2}{3}\right) = 40$ litres

Water $= (60 - 40) = 20$ litres

$\therefore$ $\frac{40}{20 + x} = \frac{1}{2}$

$\therefore$ $20 + x = 80 \Rightarrow x = 60$ litres.

Hence, water to be added = 60 litres

Example 20 : 729 ml of a mixture contains milk and water in the ratio 7 : 2. How much more water is to be added to get a new mixture containing milk and water in the ratio of 7 : 3?

Solution: Milk $= \left(729 \times \frac{7}{9}\right) = 567$ ml

Water $= \left(729 \times \frac{2}{9}\right) = 162$ ml

$\therefore \quad \frac{567}{162 + x} = \frac{7}{3} \Rightarrow 7(162 + x) = 3 \times 567$

$\therefore \quad 7x = 1701 - 1134$

$\Rightarrow \quad x = \frac{567}{7} = 81$ ml.

Example 21 : In a mixture of 35 litres, the ratio of milk and water is 4 : 1. Another 7 litres of water is added to the mixture. Find the ratio of milk and water in the resulting mixture.

Solution: Ratio of milk and water = 4 : 1

Milk $= 35 \times \frac{4}{5} = 28$ litres

Water $= 35 \times \frac{1}{5} = 7$ litres

In the new mixture, Milk = 28 litres

and water = 7 + 7 = 14 litres

$\therefore$ Ratio = 28 : 14 = 2 : 1.

Example 22 : The sum of present ages of two brothers is 36 years. After 4 years their age will be 5 : 6. Find the age of the elder brother.

Solution: Let the age of the elder brother be x years.

$\therefore$ Age of the younger brother = $36 - x$ years

$\therefore \quad \frac{36 - x + 4}{x + 4} = \frac{5}{6}$

$\Rightarrow \quad \frac{40 - x}{x + 4} = \frac{5}{6}$

$\Rightarrow \quad 5x + 20 = 240 - 6x$

$\Rightarrow \quad 11x = 220$

$\therefore \quad x = 20$ years

Example 23 : The average age of 3 girls is 20 years and their ages are in the proportion 3 : 5 : 7. Find the age of the youngest girl.

Solution: Their total age = 3 × 20 = 60 years.

Let their ages be $3x$, $5x$ and $7x$ years.

Then, $3x + 5x + 7x = 60$

$\Rightarrow \quad x = 4$

$\therefore$ Age of the youngest girl = $3x$ = 12 years.

Example 24 : A father's age was 5 times his son's age 5 years ago and will be 3 times son's age after 2 years. What is the ratio of their present ages?

Solution: Let son's age 5 years ago = x years
Then, father's age at that time = $5x$ years
After 2 years, son's age = $x + 7$ years
After 2 years, father's age = $5x + 7$ years
$\therefore \quad 3(x + 7) = 5x + 7 \quad \Rightarrow \quad x = 7$
$\therefore$ Father's age now = $(5x + 5) = 40$ years
and son's age now = $(x + 5) = 12$ years
$\therefore$ Ratio of their present ages = 40 : 12 = 10 : 3

Example 25 : The ages of Mahesh and Suresh are in the ratio 2 : 3. After 12 years, their ages will be in the ratio 11 : 15. What is the age of Suresh?

Solution: Let their ages be $2x$ and $3x$ years.

$$\Rightarrow \quad \frac{2x+12}{3x+12} = \frac{11}{15}$$

$$\Rightarrow \quad 15(2x + 12) = 11\,(3x + 12)$$

$$\Rightarrow \quad 3x = 48 \Rightarrow x = 16$$

$\therefore$ Age of Suresh = $3x$ = 48 years.

Example 26 : Men, women and children are employed to do a work in the proportion of 1 : 2 : 3 and their wages are in the proportion of 6 : 3 : 2. When 50 men are employed, total wages of all the hands amount to Rs. 450. Find the weekly wages paid to a man, a woman and a child.

Solution: Men : Women : Children = 1 : 2 : 3
But number of men = 50
$\therefore$ No. of women = 50 × 2 = 100
and No. of children = 50 × 3 = 150
If a man gets Rs. 6 a woman gets Rs. 3 and a child gets Rs. 2
$\therefore$ Total wages received by all = 50 × 6 + 100 × 3 + 150 × 2 = Rs. 900
If total wages are Rs. 900, then a man's wage = Rs. 6

If total wages are Rs. 450, then a man's wage = $\frac{6}{900} \times 450$ = Rs. 3

$\therefore$ Weekly wages of a man = 7 × 3 = Rs. 21
Ratio between the wages of a man and a woman = 6 : 3

$\therefore$ Weekly wages of a woman = $\frac{3}{6} \times 21$ = Rs. 10.50

Ratio between the wages of a man and a child = 6 : 2

$\therefore$ Weekly wages of a child = $\frac{2}{6} \times 21$ = Rs. 7

Example 27 : An employer reduces the number of his employees in the ratio of 9 : 8 and increases the wages in the ratio of 14 : 15. Find in what ratio the wage bill is increased or decreased and find the difference in the amount of bill, if it was previously Rs. 1890.

Solution: Ratio of decrease of employees = 9 : 8
Ratio of increase in wages = 14 : 15
$\therefore$ Ratio of wage bills = 9 × 14 : 8 × 15 = 126 : 120 = 21 : 20
Now, if the previous wage bills is Rs. 21,
then differnce in two bills = 21 − 20 = Re. 1
Now, if the previous wage bill is Rs. 1890,

then, difference in the bills = $\frac{1}{21} \times 1890$ = Rs. 90

Example 28 : A sum of Rs. 3115 is divided among P, Q and R such that if Rs. 25, Rs. 28 and Rs. 52 be diminished from their shares respectively, the remainders shall be in the ratio of 8 : 15 : 20. Find the share of each.

Solution: The total sum after deduction = 3115 – (25 + 28 + 52) = Rs. 3010

Their diminished share is in the ratio 8 : 15 : 20

$\therefore$ P's diminished share $= \frac{3010}{43} \times 8 = \text{Rs. } 560$

Q's diminished share $= \frac{3010}{43} \times 15 = \text{Rs. } 1050$

R's diminished share $= \frac{3010}{43} \times 20 = \text{Rs. } 1400$

$\therefore$ P's share = 560 + 25 = Rs. 585

Q's share = 1050 + 28 = Rs. 1078

R's share = 1400 + 52 = Rs. 1452

Example 29 : How many one-rupee coins, 50 P coins and 25 P coins, of which the numbers are proportional to 4, 5 and 6 are together worth Rs. 32?

Solution: The ratio of values of a rupee, 50 P and 25 P coins

$= 4 \times 100 : 5 \times 50 : 6 \times 25 = 8 : 5 : 3$

Since, 8 + 5 + 3 = 16

$\therefore$ The value of rupee coins $= \frac{32}{16} \times 8 = 16$

The value of 50 P coins $= \frac{32}{16} \times 5 = 10$

And the value of 25 P coins $= \frac{32}{16} \times 3 = 6$

$\therefore$ The number of Rupee coins = 16 × 1 = 16

The number of 50 P coins = 10 × 2 = 20

And the number of 25 P coins = 6 × 4 = 24

Example 30 : The estate of a bankrupt person worth of Rs. 21000 is to be divided among four creditors whose debts are : P's to Q's as 2 : 3, Q's to R's as 4 :5, R's to S's as 6 : 7. What amount must each receive?

Solution: P : Q = 2 : 3

Q : R = 4 : 5

R : S = 6 : 7

P : Q : R = 2 × 4 : 3 × 4 : 3 × 5 = 8 : 12 : 15

R : S = 6 : 7 = 15 : 17.5

P : Q : R : S = 8 : 12 : 15 : 17.5 = 16 : 24 : 30 : 35

Since, 16 + 24 + 30 + 35 = 105

P's share $= \frac{21000}{105} \times 16 = \text{Rs. } 3200$

Q's share $= \frac{21000}{105} \times 24 = \text{Rs. } 4800$

$$\text{R's share} = \frac{21000}{105} \times 30 = \text{Rs. } 6000$$

$$\text{And S's share} = \frac{21000}{105} \times 35 = \text{Rs. } 7000$$

Example 31 : The speed of three cars are in the ratio of 3 : 4 : 5. What is the ratio between times taken by them to travel the same distance?

Solution: Ratio of time taken $= \frac{1}{3}:\frac{1}{4}:\frac{1}{5} = 20 : 15 : 12$

Example 32 : The sides of a triangle are in the ratio $\frac{1}{3}:\frac{1}{4}:\frac{1}{5}$ and its perimeter is 94 cm. What is the length of smallest side?

Solution: Ratio of sides $= \frac{1}{3}:\frac{1}{4}:\frac{1}{5} = 20 : 15 : 12$

$\therefore$ Length of smallest side $= 94 \times \frac{12}{47} = 24$ cm

Example 33 : What must be added to each term of the ratio 7 : 13 so that the ratio becomes 2 : 3?

Solution: $\frac{7+x}{13+x} = \frac{2}{3}$

$\Rightarrow$ $3(7 + x) = 2(13 + x)$

$\Rightarrow$ $21 + 3x = 26 + 2x$

$\Rightarrow$ $3x - 2x = 26 - 21 \Rightarrow x = 5$

Example 34 : What number should be added to each one of 6, 14, 18, 38 to make it equally proportionate?

Solution: $\frac{6+x}{14+x} = \frac{18+x}{38+x}$

$\Rightarrow$ $(6 + x)(38 + x) = (14 + x)(18 + x)$

$\Rightarrow$ $228 + 44x + x^2 = 252 + 32x + x^2$

$\Rightarrow$ $44x + 228 = 32x + 252$

$\Rightarrow$ $12x = 24 \Rightarrow x = 2$

Example 35 : What number should be subtracted from each of the numbers 54, 71, 75 and 99 so that the remainders may be proportional?

Solution: $\frac{54-x}{71-x} = \frac{75-x}{99-x}$

$\Rightarrow$ $(54 - x)(99 - x) = (75 - x)(71 - x)$

$\Rightarrow$ $x^2 - 153x + 5346 = x^2 - 146x + 5325 \Rightarrow x = 3$

EXERCISE

1. If A : B = 6 : 7 and B : C = 8 : 9, then A : B : C is:

   (a) 24 : 28 : 63 *(b)* 48 : 28 : 63 *(c)* 48 : 56 : 63 *(d)* None of these

2. The sum of two numbers is 20 and their difference is $2\frac{1}{2}$. What is the ratio of the numbers?

   (a) 11 : 7 *(b)* 9 : 11 *(c)* 9 : 7 *(d)* None of these

3. If 0.7 of one number is equal to 0.075 of another, what is the ratio of the two numbers?
(a) 6 : 14 (b) 3 : 28 (c) 5 : 7 (d) None of these

4. If 10% of x is the same as 20% of y, then $x : y$ is equal to :
(a) 1 : 2 (b) 2 : 1 (c) 5 : 1 (d) 10 : 1

5. Two numbers are in the ratio 3 : 5. If each number is increased by 10, the ratio becomes 5 : 7. The numbers are:
(a) 3, 5 (b) 7, 9 (c) 13, 22 (d) 15, 25

6. The mean proportional between 0.32 and 0.02 is:
(a) 0.34 (b) 0.3 (c) 0.16 (d) 0.08

7. The sum of three numbers is 98. If the ratio between the first and second be 2 : 3 and that between the second and third be 5 : 8, then what is the second number?
(a) 20 (b) 30 (c) 10 (d) 40

8. One man adds 3 litres of water to 12 litres of milk and another 4 litres of water to 10 litres of milk. What is the ratio of the strenghts of the milk in the two mixtures?
(a) 15 : 25 (b) 25 : 28 (c) 28 : 25 (d) None of these

9. Rs. 425 is divided among 4 men, 5 women and 6 boys such that the share of a man, a woman and a boy may be in the ratio of 9 : 8 : 4. What is the share of a woman?
(a) Rs. 34 (b) Rs. 24 (c) Rs. 44 (d) None

10. A vessel contains liquids P and Q in the ratio 5 : 3. If 6 litres of the mixture are removed and the same quantity of liquid q is added, the ratio becomes 3 : 5. What quantity does the vessel hold?
(a) 40 litres (b) 50 litres (c) 30 litres (d) None of these

11. A bucket contains a mixture of two liquids P and Q in the proportion 7 : 5. If 9 litres of the mixture is replaced by 9 litres of liquid Q, then the ratio of the two liquid becomes 7 : 9. How much of the liquid P was there in the bucket?
(a) 11 litres (b) 21 litres (c) 31 litres (d) None of these

12. Three glasses P, Q and R with their capacities in the ratio 2 : 3 : 4 are filled with a mixture of spirit and water. The ratio of spirit to water in P, Q and R is 1 : 5, 3 : 5 and 5 : 7 respectively. If the contents of these glasses are mixed together, what is the ratio of spirit to water in the mixture?
(a) 14 : 27 (b) 23 : 47 (c) 25 : 47 (d) None of these

13. A and B are two alloys of gold and copper prepared by mixing metals in proportions 7 : 2 and 7 : 11 respectively. If equal quantities of the alloys are melted to form a third alloy C, the proportion of gold and copper in C will be
(a) 5 : 9 (b) 5 : 7 (c) 7 : 5 (d) 9 : 5

14. Gold is 19 times as heavy as water and copper 9 times as heavy as water. The ratio in which these two metals be mixed so that the mixtures is 15 times as heavy as water is:
(a) 1 : 2 (b) 2 : 3 (c) 3 : 2 (d) 19 : 135

15. The contents of two vessels containing water and milk are in the ratio 1 : 2 and 2 : 5 are mixed in the ratio 1 : 4. The resulting mixture will have water and milk in the ratio:
(a) 21 : 54 (b) 31 : 74 (c) 27 : 74 (d) None of these

16. One year ago, the ratio between Mahesh and Suresh's salaries was 3 : 5. The ratio of their individual salaries of last year and present year are 2 : 3 and 4 : 5 respectively. If their total salaries for the present year are Rs. 4300, what is the present salary of Mahesh?
(a) Rs. 1800 (b) Rs. 1900 (c) Rs. 1600 (d) None of these

17. The ratio of P's and Q's income last year was 3 : 4. The ratio of their own incomes of last year and this year is 4 : 5 and 2 : 3 respectively. If the total sum of their present income is Rs. 4160. What is the present income of P?
(a) Rs. 1500 *(b)* Rs. 1400 *(c)* Rs. 1600 *(d)* None of these

18. The monthly salary of A, B, C is in the proportion of 2 : 3 ; 5. If C's monthly salary is Rs. 1200 more than that of A, then B's annual salary is:
(a) Rs. 14400 *(b)* Rs. 24000 *(c)* Rs. 1200 *(d)* Rs. 2000

19. Rs. 1050 is divided among P, Q and R. The share of P is $\frac{2}{5}$ of the combined share of Q and R. Thus P gets:
(a) Rs. 200 *(b)* Rs. 300 *(c)* Rs. 400 *(d)* Rs. 420

20. The ratio between Sumit's and Prakash's age at present is 2 : 3. Sumit is 6 years younger than Prakash. The ratio of Sumit's age to Prakash's age after 6 years will be:
(a) 1 : 2 *(b)* 2 : 3 *(c)* 3 : 4 *(d)* 3 : 8

21. The ratio between the ages of Kamla and Savitri is 6 : 5 and the sum of their ages is 44 years. The ratio of their ages after 8 years will be:
(a) 5 : 6 *(b)* 7 : 8 *(c)* 8 : 7 *(d)* 14 : 13

22. Vinay got thrice as many marks in Maths as in English. The proportion of his marks in Maths and History is 4 : 3. If his total marks in Maths, English and History is 250 then, what is his marks in English?
(a) 120 *(b)* 90 *(c)* 40 *(d)* 80

23. The areas of two spheres are in the ratio 1 : 4. the ratio of their volumes is:
(a) 1 : 2 *(b)* 1 : 4 *(c)* 1 : 8 *(d)* 1 : 6

24. A certain amount was divided between Kavita and Reena in the ratio 4 : 3. If Reena's share was Rs. 2400, the amount is:
(a) Rs. 5600 *(b)* Rs. 3200 *(c)* Rs. 9600 *(d)* None of these

25. The prices of scooter and television set are in the ratio 3 : 2. If a scooter costs Rs. 6000 more than the television set, the price of the television set is:
(a) Rs. 6000 *(b)* Rs. 10000 *(c)* Rs. 12000 *(d)* Rs. 18000

26. In a class, the number of boys is more than the number of girls by 12% of the total strength. The ratio of the boys to girls is:
(a) 11 : 14 *(b)* 14 : 11 *(c)* 25 : 28 *(d)* 28 : 25

27. A right circular cylinder and a right circular cone have the same radius and the same volume. The ratio of the height of the cylinder to that of the cone is:
(a) 3 : 5 *(b)* 2 : 5 *(c)* 3 : 1 *(d)* 1 : 3

28. A circle and a square have same area. Therefore, the ratio of the side of the square and the radius of the circle is :
(a) $\sqrt{\pi}:1$ *(b)* $1:\sqrt{\pi}$ *(c)* $1 : \pi$ *(d)* $\pi : 1$

29. A, B and C can do a work in 20, 25 and 30 days respectively. They undertook to finish the work together for Rs. 2220, then the share of A exceeds that of B by:
(a) Rs. 120 *(b)* Rs. 180 *(c)* Rs. 300 *(d)* Rs. 600

30. A bag contains 25 paise, 10 paise and 5 paise coins in the ratio 1 : 2 : 3. If their total value is Rs. 30, the number of 5 paise coin is:
(a) 50 *(b)* 100 *(c)* 150 *(d)* 200

31. If Rs. 782 be divided into three parts, proportional to $\frac{1}{2}:\frac{2}{3}:\frac{3}{4}$; then the first part is:
(a) Rs. 204 (b) Rs. 196 (c) Rs. 190 (d) Rs. 182

32. Salary of Samir and Saurabh are in the ratio 2 : 3. If the salary of each is increased by Rs. 4000, the new ratio becomes 40 : 57. What is Saurabh's present salary?
(a) Rs. 38,000 (b) Rs. 35,000 (c) Rs. 30,000 (d) Rs. 25,000

33. In a bag, there are coins of 25p, 10p and 5p in the ratio of 1 : 2 : 3. If there are Rs. 30 in all, how many 5p coins are there?
(a) 200 (b) 150 (c) 100 (d) 50

34. Two numbers are in the ratio 1 : 2. If 7 is added to both, their ratio changes to 3 : 5. The greater number is:
(a) 32 (b) 28 (c) 26 (d) 24

35. Two numbers are in the ratio 3 : 5. If 9 is subtracted from each, the new numbers are in the ratio 12 : 23. The smaller number is:
(a) 55 (b) 49 (c) 33 (d) 27

36. The salaries of A, B, C are in the ratio 2 : 3 : 5. If the increments 15%, 10% and 20% are allowed respectively in their salaries, then what will be the new ratio of their salaries?
(a) 20 : 23 : 33 (b) 23 : 33 : 60 (c) 10 : 11 : 20 (d) 2 : 3 : 10

37. If 40% of a number is equal to two-third of another number, what is the ratio of first number to the second number?
(a) 7 : 3 (b) 5 : 3 (c) 3 : 7 (d) 2 : 5

38. A sum of money is to be distributed among A, B, C, D in the proportion of 5 : 2 : 4 : 3. If C gets Rs. 1000 more than D, what is B's share?
(a) Rs. 2500 (b) Rs. 2000 (c) Rs. 1500 (d) Rs. 1000

39. The ratio of the number of boys and girls in a college is 7 : 8. If the percentage increase in the number of boys and girls be 20% and 10% respectively, what will be the new ratio?
(a) 19 : 20 (b) 21 : 22 (c) 17 : 18 (d) 8 : 9

40. Seats for Mathematics, Physics and Chemistry in a school are in the ratio 5 : 7 : 8. There is a proposal to increase these seats by 40%, 50% and 75% respectively. Find the ratio of increased seats?
(a) 3 : 4 : 5 (b) 6 : 8 : 9 (c) 6 : 7 : 8 (d) 2 : 3 : 4

41. Two numbers are respectively 20% and 50% more than a third number. The ratio of two numbers is:
(a) 6 : 7 (b) 4 : 5 (c) 3 : 5 (d) 2 : 5

42. A and B together have Rs. 1210. If $\frac{4}{15}$ of A's amount is equal to $\frac{2}{5}$ of B's amount, how much amount does B have?
(a) Rs. 664 (b) Rs. 550 (c) Rs. 484 (d) Rs. 460

43. A sum of Rs. 1300 is divided among P, Q, R and S such that $\frac{\text{P's share}}{\text{Q's share}} = \frac{\text{Q's share}}{\text{R's share}} = \frac{\text{R's share}}{\text{S's share}} = \frac{2}{3}$. Then P's share is:
(a) Rs. 320 (b) Rs. 240 (c) Rs. 160 (d) Rs. 140

44. A fraction which bears the same ratio to $\frac{1}{27}$ that $\frac{3}{11}$ does to $\frac{5}{9}$, is equal to:
(a) 55 (b) $\frac{3}{11}$ (c) $\frac{2}{11}$ (d) $\frac{1}{55}$

45. The sum of three numbers is 98. If the ratio of the first to the second is 2 : 3 and that of the second to the third is 5 : 8, then the second number is:

(*a*) 58 (*b*) 48 (*c*) 30 (*d*) 20

46. If Rs. 510 be divided among A, B, C is such a way that A gets $\frac{2}{3}$ of what B gets and B gets $\frac{1}{4}$ of what C gets, then their shares are respectively:

(*a*) Rs. 150, Rs. 300, Rs. 60 (*b*) Rs. 120, Rs. 240, Rs. 150
(*c*) Rs. 60, Rs. 90, Rs. 360 (*d*) None of these

47. Gold is 19 times as heavy as water and copper is 9 times as heavy as water. In what ratio should these be mixed to get an alloy 15 times as heavy as water?

(*a*) 3 : 2 (*b*) 1 : 2 (*c*) 2 : 3 (*d*) 1 : 1

48. An amount of Rs. 2430 is divided among A, B and C such that if their shares be reduced by Rs. 5, Rs. 10 and Rs. 15 respectively, the remainder shall be in the ratio of 3 : 4 : 5. Then B's share was:

(*a*) Rs. 810 (*b*) Rs. 800 (*c*) Rs. 790 (*d*) Rs. 605

49. An amount of Rs. 735 was divided between A, B and C. If each of them had received Rs. 25 less, their share would have been in the ratio of 1 : 3 : 2. The money received by C was:

(*a*) Rs. 245 (*b*) Rs. 225 (*c*) Rs. 200 (*d*) Rs. 195

50. In a mixture of 60 litres, the ratio of milk and water is 2 : 1. If the ratio is to be 1 : 2, then the quantity of water to be further added is:

(*a*) 60 litres (*b*) 40 litres (*c*) 30 litres (*d*) 20 litres

51. Ratio of the earnings of A and B is 4 : 7. If the earnings of A increases by 50% and those of B decreases by 25%, the new ratio of their earnings becomes 8 : 7. What are the A's earnings?

(*a*) Rs. 28000 (*b*) Rs. 21000 (*c*) Rs. 26000 (*d*) Data inadequate

52. If 10% of x = 20% of y, then $x : y$ is equal to:

(*a*) 10 : 1 (*b*) 5 : 1 (*c*) 2 : 1 (*d*) 1 : 2

53. x varies inversely as square of y. Given that $y = 2$ for $x = 1$. The value of x for $y = 6$ will be equal to:

(*a*) $\frac{1}{9}$ (*b*) $\frac{1}{3}$ (*c*) 9 (*d*) 3

54. One-fourth of sixty per cent of a number is equal to two-fifth of twenty per cent of another number. What is the respective ratio of the first number to the second number?

(*a*) 8 : 15 (*b*) 5 : 9 (*c*) 8 : 13 (*d*) 4 : 7

55. If $ab = 36$, which of the following proportions is correct?

(*a*) $a : 9 = 4 : b$ (*b*) $a : 6 = b : 6$ (*c*) $a : 18 = b : 3$ (*d*) $9 : a = 4 : b$

56. 20% of a number is equal to 50% of second number. What is the ratio of the first number to the second?

(*a*) 2 : 5 (*b*) 5 : 2 (*c*) 2 : 3 (*d*) 3 : 2

57. In a school ratio of boys to girls is 4 : 5. When 100 girls leave the school ratio becomes 6 : 7. How many boys are there in the school?

(*a*) 1200 (*b*) 1300 (*c*) 1500 (*d*) 1600

58. Ratio of earnings of A and B is 4 : 5 respectively. If the earnings of A increases by 20% and the earnings of B decreases by 20%, the new ratio of their earnings became 6 : 5 respectively. What is A's earnings?

(*a*) Rs. 26,400 (*b*) Rs. 27,500 (*c*) Rs. 22,000 (*d*) Data inadequate

59. A sum of money is divided among A, B, C and D in the ratio of 3 : 7 : 9 : 13 respectively. If the share of A and C together is Rs. 11,172, then what is the difference between the amounts of B and D?

(a) Rs. 6086 *(b)* Rs. 5586
(c) Rs. 6834 *(d)* Rs. 7672

60. A sum of money is to be divided equally amongst A, B and C in the respective ratio of 3 : 4 : 5 and another sum of money is to be divided between E and F equally. If F got Rs. 1050 less than A, how much amount did B receive?

(a) Rs. 1500 *(b)* Rs. 2000 *(c)* Rs. 750 *(d)* Data inadequate

61. The total number of boys in a school are 24% more than the total number of girls in the school. What is the respective ratio of the total number of boys to the total number of girls in the school?

(a) 21 : 19 *(b)* 19 : 21 *(c)* 31 : 25 *(d)* 25 : 31

62. A sum of Rs. 817 is divided among A, B and C such that 'A' receives 25% more than 'B' and 'B' receives 25% less than 'C'. What is A's share in the amount?

(a) Rs. 304 *(b)* Rs. 285 *(c)* Rs. 247 *(d)* Rs. 228

63. The ratio of the number of boys and girls in a school is 3 : 2. If 20% of the boys and 25% of the girls are scholarship holders, what percentage of the students does not get the scholarship?

(a) 80% *(b)* 78% *(c)* 70% *(d)* 56%

64. The speeds of three cars are in the ratio 5 : 4 : 6. The ratio between the time taken by them to travel the same distances is:

(a) 12 : 15 : 10 *(b)* 10 : 12 : 15 *(c)* 6 : 4 : 5 *(d)* 5 : 4 : 6

65. 20 litres of a mixture contains milk and water in the ratio 5 : 3. If 4 litres of this mixture be replaced by 4 litres of milk, the ratio of milk to water in the new mixture would be:

(a) 4 : 3 *(b)* 8 : 3 *(c)* 7 : 3 *(d)* 2 : 3

66. 15 litres of mixture contains 20% alcohol and rest water. If 3 litres of water be mixed with it, the percentage of alcohol in the new mixture would be:

(a) $18\frac{1}{2}\%$ *(b)* 17% *(c)* $16\frac{2}{3}\%$ *(d)* 15%

67. A sum of Rs. 53 is divided among A, B, C in such a way that A gets Rs. 7 more than what B gets and B gets Rs. 8 more than what C gets. The ratio of their shares is:

(a) 15 : 8 : 30 *(b)* 18 : 25 : 10
(c) 25 : 18 : 10 *(d)* 16 : 9 : 18

68. A and B are two alloys of gold and copper prepared by mixing metals in the ratio 7 : 2 and 7 : 11 respectively. If equal quantities of the alloys are melted to form a third alloy C. Then what is the ratio of gold and copper in C?

(a) 9 : 5 *(b)* 7 : 5 *(c)* 5 : 9 *(d)* 5 : 7

69. The least whole number which when subtracted from both the terms of the ratio 6 : 7 gives a ratio less than 16 : 21 is:

(a) 6 *(b)* 4 *(c)* 3 *(d)* 2

70. The ratio of incomes of A and B is 5 : 4 and the ratio of their expenditures is 3 : 2. If at the end of the year each saves Rs. 1600, then income of A is:

(a) Rs. 4400 *(b)* Rs. 4000 *(c)* Rs. 3600 *(d)* Rs. 3400

EXPLANATORY ANSWERS

1. $A : B = 6 : 7$
$B : C = 8 : 9$
$\therefore \quad A : B : C = 6 \times 8 : 7 \times 8 : 7 \times 9$
$= 48 : 56 : 63$

2. $$\text{Ratio} = \frac{20 + \frac{5}{2}}{20 - \frac{5}{2}} = \frac{22.5}{17.5} = \frac{225}{175} = \frac{9}{7} = 9 : 7$$

3. We have, $0.7x = 0.075\, y$

$$\frac{x}{y} = \frac{0.075}{0.7} = \frac{75}{700}$$
$$= \frac{3}{28} = 3:28$$

4. 10% of $x = 20\%$ of y

$$\Rightarrow \quad \frac{10}{100}x = \frac{20}{100}y$$

$$\therefore \quad \frac{x}{10} = \frac{y}{5} \quad \Rightarrow \frac{x}{y} = \frac{10}{5} = \frac{2}{1} \Rightarrow x:y = 2 : 1$$

5. Let the number be $3x$ and $5x$.

Then, $$\frac{3x+10}{5x+10} = \frac{5}{7}$$
$\Rightarrow \quad 7(3x + 10) = 5(5x + 10)$
$\Rightarrow \quad 21x + 70 = 25x + 50$
$\Rightarrow \quad 4x = 20 \Rightarrow x = 5$

So, the numbers are 15, 25.

6. Mean proportional $= \sqrt{0.32 \times 0.02} = \sqrt{0.0064} = 0.08$

7. The ratio among the three numbers is

$2 : 3$
$5 : 8$
and $10 : 15 : 24$

$$\therefore \text{ The second number} = \frac{98}{10+15+24} \times 15 = 30$$

8. Strength of milk in the first mixture $= \dfrac{12}{12+3} = \dfrac{12}{15}$

Strength of milk in the second mixture $= \dfrac{10}{10+4} = \dfrac{10}{14}$

$\therefore$ The ratio of their strengths $= \dfrac{12}{15} : \dfrac{10}{14} = 12 \times 14 : 15 \times 10 = 28 : 25$

9. The ratio of shares of group of men, women and boys

$$= 9 \times 4 : 8 \times 5 : 4 \times 6 = 9 : 10 : 6$$

$\therefore$ Share of 5 women $= \dfrac{425}{9+10+6} \times 10 = \text{Rs. } 170$

$\therefore$ Share of 1 woman $= \dfrac{170}{5} = \text{Rs. } 34$

10. Let the vessel contains $5x$ litres and $3x$ litres of liquid P and Q respectively. The removed quantity contains

$$\frac{16}{5+3} \times 5 = 10 \text{ litres of P}$$

and $16 - 10 = 6$ litres of Q.

Now, $(5x - 10) : (3x - 6 + 16) = 3 : 5$

$\Rightarrow \quad \dfrac{5x-10}{3x+10} = \dfrac{3}{5}$

$\Rightarrow \quad 25x - 50 = 9x + 30$

$\Rightarrow \quad 16x = 80 \Rightarrow x = 5$

$\therefore$ Vessel contains $8x = 8 \times 5 = 40$ litres.

11. Let the two liquids P and Q are $7x$ litres and $5x$ litres repectively.

Now, when 9 litres of mixture are taken out,

P remains $7x - 9\left(\dfrac{7}{7+5}\right) = 7x - \dfrac{9 \times 7}{12} = \left(7x - \dfrac{21}{4}\right)$ litres

and Q remains $5x - 9\left(\dfrac{5}{7+5}\right) = 5x - \dfrac{9 \times 5}{12} = \left(5x - \dfrac{15}{4}\right)$ litres

Now, when 9 litres of liquid Q are added,

$$\left(7x - \frac{21}{4}\right) : \left(5x - \frac{15}{4} + 9\right) = 7 : 9$$

$\Rightarrow \quad \dfrac{7x - \dfrac{21}{4}}{5x - \dfrac{15}{4} + 9} = \dfrac{7}{9}$

$\Rightarrow \quad 63x - \dfrac{189}{4} = 35x + \dfrac{147}{4}$

$\Rightarrow \quad 28x = \dfrac{189}{4} + \dfrac{147}{4} = \dfrac{336}{4} = 84$

$\Rightarrow \quad x = \dfrac{84}{28} = 3 \Rightarrow 7x = 7 \times 3 = 21$ litres.

12. P : Q : R

2 : 3 : 4

Spirit : Water = 1 : 5, 3 : 5 and 5 : 7

When they are mixed, the ratio of spirit to water

$$= \left(2\times\frac{1}{1+5}+3\times\frac{3}{3+5}+4\times\frac{5}{5+7}\right):\left(2\times\frac{5}{1+5}+3\times\frac{5}{3+5}+4\times\frac{7}{5+7}\right)$$

$$= \left(\frac{1}{3}+\frac{9}{8}+\frac{5}{3}\right):\left(\frac{5}{3}+\frac{15}{8}+\frac{7}{3}\right) = \frac{25}{8}:\frac{47}{8} = 25 : 47$$

13. Gold in C $= \left(\frac{7}{9}+\frac{7}{18}\right) = \frac{21}{18} = \frac{7}{6}$

Copper in C $= \left(\frac{2}{9}+\frac{11}{18}\right) = \frac{15}{18} = \frac{5}{6}$

$\therefore$ Gold : Copper $= \frac{7}{6}:\frac{5}{6} = 7 : 5$

14. Let 1 gm of gold be mixed with x gm of copper to give $(1 + x)$ gm of mixture.

Now, $1G = 19w$

and $1C = 9w$

and mixture $= 15w$

Now, 1 gm gold + x gm copper

$= (1 + x)$ gm mixture

$\therefore \quad 19w + 9w \times x = (1 + x) \times 15w$

Thus, $4w = 6wx$

$\Rightarrow \quad x = \frac{4w}{6w} = \frac{4}{6} = \frac{2}{3}$

So, the required ratio is $1:\frac{2}{3}$, *i.e.*, 3 : 2.

15.

	Water	*Milk*
Vessel I	$\frac{1}{3}$	$\frac{2}{3}$
Vessel II	$\frac{2}{7}$	$\frac{5}{7}$

From vessel I, $\frac{1}{5}$ is taken and from vessel II, $\frac{4}{5}$ is taken. Therefore, the ratio of water to milk in the new vessel

$$= \left(\frac{1}{3}\times\frac{1}{5}+\frac{2}{7}\times\frac{4}{5}\right):\left(\frac{2}{3}\times\frac{1}{5}+\frac{5}{7}\times\frac{4}{5}\right)$$

$$= \left(\frac{1}{15}+\frac{8}{35}\right):\left(\frac{2}{15}+\frac{20}{35}\right) = \frac{31}{105}:\frac{74}{105} = 31 : 74$$

16. The ratio of Mahesh's salary for the two years = 2 : 3

The ratio of Suresh's salary for the two years = 4 : 5

We have also given that the ratio of their salary during the last year = 3 : 5

Now, we change the antecedents (2 and 4) of the first two ratios so that the antecedents in the first becomes 3 (antecedent of the third ratio) and the antecedent in the second becomes 5 (consequent of the third ratio).

Thus, $2:3 = 3:\frac{9}{2}$ and $4:5 = 4\left(\frac{5}{4}\right):5\left(\frac{5}{4}\right) = 5:\frac{25}{4}$

Now, it is clear that the ratio of their salaries for the present year is $\frac{9}{2}:\frac{25}{4} = 18:25$

$\therefore$ The present salary of Mahesh $= \frac{4300}{18+25}\times 18 =$ Rs. 1800

17. The ratio of present incomes $= 3\times\frac{5}{4}:4\times\frac{3}{2} = \frac{15}{4}:\frac{12}{2} = 30:48 = 5:8$

$\therefore$ P's present income $= \frac{4160}{5+8}\times 5 =$ Rs. 1600

18. Let the monthly salary of A, B, C be $2x$, $3x$ and $5x$

Then, $5x - 2x = 1200$

or, $3x = 1200 \quad \therefore x = 400$

B's monthly salary $= 3x = 3 \times 400 =$ Rs. 1200

19. P : (Q + R) = 2 : 5

$\therefore$ P's share = Rs. $\left(1050\times\frac{2}{7}\right)$ = Rs. 300

20. Let their ages be $2x$ and $3x$ years.

$\Rightarrow \quad 3x - 2x = 6 \;\Rightarrow x = 6$

Sumit's age = 12 years

Prakash's age = 18 years

After 6 years, Sumit's age = 18 years and Prakash's age = 24 years

$\therefore$ Ratio of their ages = 18 : 24 = 3 : 4

21. Let their ages be $6x$ and $5x$ years.

$\therefore 6x + 5x = 44 \quad \Rightarrow 11x = 44 \Rightarrow x = 4$

So, their present ages are 24 years and 20 years

$\therefore$ Ratio of their ages after 8 years = 32 : 28 = 8 : 7

22. M = 3E and $\frac{M}{H} = \frac{4}{3}$

$\therefore H = \frac{3}{4}M = \frac{3}{4}\times 3E = \frac{9}{4}E$

Now, M + E + H = 250 $\Rightarrow 3E + E + \frac{9}{4}E = 250$

$\therefore$ 25E = 1000 or, E = 40

23. $\frac{4\pi r^2}{4\pi R^2} = \frac{1}{4}$

$\therefore \quad \frac{r^2}{R^2} = \frac{1}{4}$ and so $\frac{r}{R} = \frac{1}{2}$

$\therefore \quad \dfrac{r^3}{R^3} = \dfrac{1}{8}$

Hence, $\quad \dfrac{\frac{4}{3}\pi r^3}{\frac{4}{3}\pi R^2} = \dfrac{1}{8}$

Thus, their volumes are in the ratio 1 : 8.

24. Let their shares be Rs. $4x$ and Rs. $3x$

Then, $3x = 2400 \quad \Rightarrow x =$ Rs. 800

$\therefore$ Total amount $= 7x = 7 \times 800 =$ Rs. 5600

25. Let the price of a scooter be Rs. $3x$ and that of a television set be Rs. $2x$

Then, $3x - 2x = 6000 \quad \Rightarrow x = 6000$

$\therefore$ Cost of a television set $= 2x = 2 \times 6000 =$ Rs. 12000

26. Let the number of boys and girls be x and y respectively.

Then, $(x - y) = 12\%$ of $(x + y)$.

$$\Rightarrow \quad x - y = \frac{3}{25}(x + y)$$

$$\Rightarrow \quad 25x - 25y = 3x + 3y$$

$$\Rightarrow \quad 22x = 28y$$

$$\Rightarrow \quad \frac{x}{y} = \frac{28}{22} = \frac{14}{11}$$

$\Rightarrow$ Ratio = 14 : 11

27. Let the heights of the cylinder and cone be h and H respectively.

Then, $\pi r^2 h = \dfrac{1}{3}\pi r^2 H \quad \Rightarrow \dfrac{h}{H} = \dfrac{1}{3}$

So, their heights in the ratio = 1 : 3

28. Let the side of the square be x and the radius of the circle be y. Then,

$$x^2 = \pi y^2$$

$$\Rightarrow \quad \frac{x^2}{y^2} = \pi \quad \Rightarrow \frac{x}{y} = \sqrt{\pi}$$

$$\therefore \quad x : y = \sqrt{\pi} : 1$$

29. Ratio of shares of A, B, and C $= \dfrac{1}{20} : \dfrac{1}{25} : \dfrac{1}{30} = 15 : 12 : 10$

$\therefore$ A's share = Rs. $\left(2220 \times \dfrac{15}{37}\right)$ = Rs. 900

B's share = $\left(2220 \times \dfrac{12}{37}\right)$ = Rs. 720

Thus, the share of A exceeds that of B by Rs. (900 – 720) = Rs. 180.

30. Ratio of their values $= \frac{1}{4} : \frac{2}{10} : \frac{3}{20} = 5 : 4 : 3$

$\therefore$ Value of 5 paise coins $= \text{Rs.}\left(30 \times \frac{3}{12}\right) = \text{Rs. } 7.50$

$\therefore$ Number of 5 paise coins $= \frac{750}{5} = 150$

31. Here ratio $= \frac{1}{2} : \frac{2}{3} : \frac{3}{4} = 6 : 8 : 9$

Hence, Ist part $= \frac{6}{6+8+9} \times \text{Rs. } 782 = \frac{6}{23} \times \text{Rs.} 782 = \text{Rs. } 204$

32. Let their original salaries be Rs. $2x$ and Rs. $3x$

Then, $\frac{2x+4000}{3x+4000} = \frac{40}{57} \Rightarrow 120x + 1{,}60{,}000 = 114x + 2{,}28{,}000$

$\Rightarrow 6x = 68000 \qquad \therefore x = \frac{68000}{6} = \frac{34000}{3}$

Hence, Saurabh's present salary = Rs. $(3x + 4000)$ = Rs. $(34000 + 4000)$ = Rs. 38000

33. Let the number of coins of 25p, 10p and 5p be x, $2x$ and $3x$ respectively.

Then, $x \times \frac{1}{4} + 2x \times \frac{1}{10} + 3x \times \frac{1}{20} = 30 \Rightarrow \frac{5x+4x+3x}{20} = 30$

$\Rightarrow \frac{3x}{5} = 30 \qquad \therefore x = \frac{5 \times 30}{3} = 50$

Hence, number of 5p coins $= 3x = 3 \times 50 = 150$

34. Let the two number be x and $2x$

Then, $\frac{x+7}{2x+7} = \frac{3}{5} \Rightarrow 6x + 21 = 5x + 35 \qquad \therefore x = 14$

The greater number $= 2x = 2 \times 14 = 28$

35. Let the two numbers be $3x$ and $5x$

Then, $\frac{3x-9}{5x-9} = \frac{12}{23} \Rightarrow 69x - 207 = 60x - 108$

$\Rightarrow 9x = 99 \qquad \therefore x = 11$

Hence, the smaller number $= 3x = 3 \times 11 = 33$

36. Let the salaries of A, B and C be Rs. $2x$, Rs. $3x$ and Rs. $5x$ respectively.

Then, new salary of A $= \frac{115}{100} \times \text{Rs. } 2x = \text{Rs. } \frac{23x}{10}$

New salary of B $= \frac{110}{100} \times \text{Rs. } 3x = \text{Rs.} \frac{33x}{10}$

New salary of C $= \frac{120}{100} \times \text{Rs. } 5x = \text{Rs. } 6x$

The ratio of their new salaries $= \frac{23x}{10} : \frac{33x}{10} : 6x = 23 : 33 : 60$

37. Let 40% of $x = \frac{2}{3}$ of $y \Rightarrow \frac{40}{100} \times x = \frac{2}{3} y$

$\Rightarrow \frac{x}{y} = \frac{2}{3} \times \frac{5}{2} = \frac{5}{3}$

Hence, required ratio = 5 : 3

38. Let the share of A, B, C and D be Rs. $5x$, Rs. $2x$, Rs. $4x$ and Rs. $3x$ respectively.
Then, $4x - 3x = 1000$ $\therefore x = 1000$
Hence, B's share = Rs. $2x$ = Rs. 2×1000 = Rs. 2000

39. Let the number of boys and girls be $7x$ and $8x$ initially.

Now, number of boys $= \frac{120}{100} \times 7x = \frac{42x}{5}$

And number of girls $= \frac{110}{100} \times 8x = \frac{44x}{5}$

Hence, their new ratio $= \frac{42x}{5} : \frac{44x}{5} = 21 : 22$

40. Let the number of seats for Mathematics, Physics and Chemistry be $5x$, $7x$ and $8x$, originally.
Now,

Number of seats for Mathematics $= \frac{140}{100} \times 5x = 7x$

Number of seats for Physics $= \frac{150}{100} \times 7x = \frac{21x}{2}$

Number of seats for Chemistry $= \frac{175}{100} \times 8x = 14x$

Hence, ratio of increased seats $= 7x : \frac{21x}{2} : 14x = 2 : 3 : 4$

41. Let the two numbers be $\frac{120x}{100} = \frac{6x}{5}$ and $\frac{150x}{100} = \frac{3x}{2}$

Their ratio $= \frac{6x}{5} : \frac{3x}{2} = 12x : 15x = 4 : 5$

42. Let amount of A and B be Rs. x and Rs. y respectively.

Then, $\frac{4}{15} x = \frac{2}{5} y$ $\therefore x = \frac{3}{2} y$

Now, $x + y = 1210 \Rightarrow \frac{3}{2} y + y = 1210 \Rightarrow \frac{5y}{2} = 1210 \therefore y = \frac{1210 \times 2}{5}$ = Rs. 484

Hence, amount of B = Rs. 484

43. Let the share of P, Q, R and S be Rs. p, Rs. q, Rs. r and Rs. s respectively.

Now, $\frac{p}{q} = \frac{q}{r} = \frac{r}{s} = \frac{2}{3}$

Then, $p = \frac{2}{3}q$; $q = \frac{2}{3}r$; $r = \frac{2}{3}s$

$= \frac{2}{3} \times \frac{2}{3} \times \frac{2}{3}s$; $= \frac{2}{3} \times \frac{2}{3}s$

$= \frac{8}{27}s$; $= \frac{4}{9}s$

Now, $\frac{8}{27}s + \frac{4}{9}s + \frac{2}{3}s + s = 1300 \Rightarrow \frac{65s}{27} = 1300$

$\therefore s = \frac{27 \times 1300}{65} = \text{Rs. } 540$

Hence, P's share = Rs. p = Rs. $\frac{8}{27}s$ = Rs. $\frac{8}{27} \times 540$ = Rs. 160

44. Let the fraction be x

Then, $x : \frac{1}{27} = \frac{3}{11} : \frac{5}{9} \Rightarrow x \times 27 = \frac{3}{11} \times \frac{9}{5}$

$\therefore x = \frac{3}{11} \times \frac{9}{5} \times \frac{1}{27} = \frac{1}{55}$

45. Let the three numbers be a, b and c

Then, $a : b = 2 : 3$ and $b : c = 5 : 8$

Hence, $a : b : c = 10 : 15 : 24$

Now, Second number $= \frac{15}{10+15+24} \times 98 = \frac{15}{49} \times 98 = 30$

46. Let the share of A, B and C be Rs. a, Rs. b and Rs. c

$a = \frac{2}{3} \times b$ and also, $b = \frac{1}{4}c$;

$= \frac{2}{3} \times \frac{1}{4}c = \frac{1}{6}c$

Now, $a : b : c = \frac{1}{6}c : \frac{1}{4}c : c = 2 : 3 : 12$

Share of A $= \frac{2}{2+3+12} \times 510 = \frac{2}{17} \times 510 =$ Rs. 60

Share of B $= \frac{3}{17} \times 510$ = Rs. 90

Share of C $= \frac{12}{17} \times 510$ = Rs. 360

47. Let the ratio of gold to copper in the mixture be $x : y$.

Now, $\frac{19x+9y}{x+y} = 15 \Rightarrow 4x = 6y \quad \therefore x : y = 3 : 2$

48. Let the share of A, B and C be Rs. $(3x + 5)$, Rs. $(4x + 10)$ and Rs. $(5x + 15)$ respectively.
Now, $3x + 5 + 4x + 10 + 5x + 15 = 2430 \Rightarrow 12x = 2400 \quad \therefore x = 200$
Hence, B's share $= 4x + 10 = 4 \times 200 + 10 =$ Rs. 810

49. Let the share of A, B, C be Rs. $(x + 25)$, Rs $(3x + 25)$ and Rs. $(2x + 25)$ respectively.
Then, $x + 25 + 3x + 25 + 2x + 25 = 735 \quad \Rightarrow 6x = 660 \quad \therefore x = 110$
Hence, money received by C = Rs. $(2 \times 110 + 25)$ = Rs. 245

50. The amount of milk $= \frac{2}{3} \times 60 = 40\ l$

The amount of water $= \frac{1}{3} \times 60 = 20\ l$

Let the $x\ l$ water required for ratio 1 : 2.

Then, $\frac{40}{20+x} = \frac{1}{2} \quad \Rightarrow 20 + x = 80 \quad \therefore x = 60\ l$

51. Let the initial earnings of A and B be Rs. $4x$ and Rs. $7x$.

New earnings of A $= \frac{150}{100} \times 4x =$ Rs. $6x$

New earnings of B $= \frac{75}{100} \times 7x =$ Rs. $\frac{21x}{4}$

Now, $6x : \frac{21x}{4} = 8 : 7$

$\Rightarrow \frac{6x \times 4}{21x} = \frac{8}{7}$

This expression does not give the value of x. Hence, data is inadequate.

52. Here, $\frac{10}{100} \times x = \frac{20}{100} \times y \quad \Rightarrow \frac{x}{y} = \frac{2}{1} \quad \therefore x : y = 2 : 1$

53. Here, $x \propto \frac{1}{y^2} \Rightarrow xy^2 = k \quad \therefore k = 1.2^2 = 4$

Now, $xy^2 = k \Rightarrow x \,.\, 6^2 = 4 \therefore x = \frac{4}{36} = \frac{1}{9}$

54. Let two number be x and y, then,

$\frac{1}{4} \times \frac{60}{100} \times x = \frac{2}{5} \times \frac{20}{100} \times y \quad \Rightarrow \frac{3}{20} x = \frac{2}{25} y \quad \therefore \frac{x}{y} = \frac{8}{15}$

Hence, required ratio = 8 : 15

55. Here $ab = 36$

From option a, $\quad \frac{a}{9} = \frac{4}{b} \quad \therefore ab = 36$ (correct).

From option b, $\quad \frac{a}{6} = \frac{b}{6} \quad \therefore a = b$ (incorrect).

From option *c*, $\frac{a}{18}=\frac{b}{3}$ $\therefore a = 6b$ (incorrect).

From option *d*, $\frac{9}{a}=\frac{4}{b}$ $\therefore \frac{a}{b}=\frac{9}{4}$ (incorrect).

56. Let the number be x and y, then

$\frac{20}{100}\times x=\frac{50}{100}\times y \Rightarrow \frac{x}{y}=\frac{5}{2}$

Hence, required ratio = 5 : 2

57. Let initially number of boys and girls be $4x$ and $5x$.

Now, $\frac{4x}{5x-100}=\frac{6}{7} \Rightarrow 15x - 300 = 14x \quad \therefore x = 300$

Hence, number of boys = $4x = 4 \times 300 = 1200$

58. Let the earnings of A and B be Rs. $4x$ and Rs. $5x$ initially.

New earnings of A = $\frac{120}{100}\times 4x$ = Rs. $\frac{24x}{5}$

and earnings of B = $\frac{80}{100}\times 5x$ = Rs. $4x$

Then, $\frac{24x}{5} : 4x = 6 : 5 \Rightarrow \frac{24x}{5\times 4x}=\frac{6}{5}$

It does not give the value of x, hence, data is inadequate.

59. Let the share of A, B, C and D be Rs. $3x$, Rs. $7x$, Rs. $9x$ and Rs. $13x$ respectively.

Now, $3x + 9x = 11172 \Rightarrow 12x = 11172 \quad \therefore x = 931$

Hence, difference of amounts of B and D is

$13x - 7x = 6x = 6 \times 931$ = Rs. 5586

60. Here absolute value is not given, hence, data is inadequate.

61. Let total number of girls be x then total number of boys will be $\frac{124x}{100}=\frac{31x}{25}$

Hence, required ratio = $\frac{31x}{25} : x = 31 : 25$

62. Here, A : B = 125 : 100 = 5 : 4

B : C = 75 : 100 = 3 : 4

Hence, A : B : C = 15 : 12 : 16

Now, Share of A = $\frac{15}{15+12+16}\times$ Rs. 817 = $\frac{15}{43}\times$ Rs. 817 = Rs. 285

63. Let number of boys and girls be $3x$ and $2x$ respectively. Then total number of students = $3x + 2x = 5x$

Number of studetns who do not getting scholarships = $\frac{80}{100}\times 3x+\frac{75}{100}\times 2x=\frac{12x}{5}+\frac{3x}{2}=\frac{39x}{10}$

Hence, required percentage = $\frac{39x}{10\times 5x}\times 100 = 78\%$

64. Ratio of speeds = 5 : 4 : 6 (when they travel same distance)

Then, ratio of time taken = $\frac{1}{5}:\frac{1}{4}:\frac{1}{6}=\frac{1}{5}\times 60:\ \frac{1}{4}\times 60;\ \frac{1}{6}\times 60$

= 12 : 15 : 10

65. In 16 litres mixture, the amount of milk = $\frac{5}{8}\times 16 = 10l$

and the amount of water = $\frac{3}{8}\times 16 = 6l$

In new 20 litres mixture, the amount of milk = 10 + 4 = $14l$

and the amount of water = $6l$

Hence, the required ratio = 14 : 6 = 7 : 3

66. In original mixture, the amount of alcohol = $\frac{20}{100}\times 15 = 3l$

In new mixture, the percentage of alcohol = $\frac{3}{18}\times 100 = 16\frac{2}{3}\%$

67. Let the share of A, B, C be Rs. $(x + 15)$, Rs. $(x + 8)$ and Rs. x respectively.

Now, $x + 15 + x + 8 + x = 53 \Rightarrow 3x + 23 = 53 \quad \therefore x = \frac{30}{3} = 10$

Hence, the share of A, B, C will be Rs. 25, Rs. 18 and Rs. 10.

∴ Requried ratio = 25 : 18 : 10

68. The gold in mixture C = $\frac{7}{9}+\frac{7}{18}=\frac{21}{18}=\frac{7}{6}$

The copper in mixture C = $\frac{2}{9}+\frac{11}{18}=\frac{15}{18}=\frac{5}{6}$

Hence, their required ratio = $\frac{7}{6}:\frac{5}{6}$ = 7 : 5

69. Let the least whole number be x.

Then, $\frac{6-x}{7-x}<\frac{16}{21} \Rightarrow 126 - 21x < 112 - 16x$

$\Rightarrow 126 - 112 < 21x - 16x \quad \Rightarrow 5x > 14 \quad \Rightarrow x > 2.8$

Hence, least such whole number = 3

70. Let the incomes of A and B be Rs. $5x$ and Rs. $4x$ and their expenditures be Rs. $3y$ and Rs. $2y$ respectively.

Hence,
$5x - 3y = 1600$ ...(i)
$4x - 2y = 1600$ ...(ii)

Multiplying equation (i) by 2 and (ii) by 3 and subtracting

$10x - 6y = 3200$
$12x - 6y = 4800$
$-\quad +\quad -$

$-2x = -1600 \Rightarrow x = 800$

Hence, income of A = Rs. $5x$ = Rs. 5 × 800 = Rs. 4000

8

AVERAGE

AVERAGE

The average of any number of quantities of the same kind can be found by dividing their sum by their number. Thus,

$$\text{Average} = \frac{\text{Sum of quantities}}{\text{No. of quantities}}$$

$$\text{Sum of quantities} = \text{Their average} \times \text{Their number}$$

$$\text{Number of quantities} = \frac{\text{Sum of quantities}}{\text{Their average}}$$

When a body coveres the same distance at two different speeds p km/hr and q km/hr, then its average speed for the whole journey is $\frac{2pq}{p+q}$ km/hr.

Example 1 : The weight of 5 boys in a class are 49.6 kg, 39.8 kg, 40.8 kg, 45.2 kg and 24.6 kg. Find their average weight.

Solution: Total weight of 5 boys = 49.6 + 39.8 + 40.8 + 45.2 + 24.6 = 200 kg

$\therefore$ Average weight = $\frac{200}{5}$ = 40 kg

Example 2 : A man's average daily expenditutre is Rs. 10 during May, Rs. 14 during June and Rs. 15 during July. Find the average daily expenditure for the three months.

Solution: Total expenditure = 10 × 31 + 14 × 30 + 15 × 31
= 310 + 420 + 465 = Rs, 1195

The number of days = 31 + 30 + 31 = 92

$\therefore$ The average daily expenditure = Rs. $\frac{1195}{92}$ = Rs. 13 approximately.

Example 3 : The average score of a cricketer for 10 matches is 38.9 runs. If the average for the first six matches is 42, find the average for the last 4 matches.

Solution: Total runs of the last four matches = 10 × 38.9 – 6 × 42 = 137

$\therefore$ Average = $\frac{137}{4}$ = 34.25 run

Example 4 : A man bought 2 toys for Rs. $5\frac{1}{2}$ each, 3 toys for Rs. $3\frac{2}{3}$ each and 6 toys for Rs. $1\frac{5}{6}$ each. Find the average price of per toy.

Sol : Total value of the toys = $2\times\frac{11}{2}+3\times\frac{11}{3}+6\times\frac{11}{6}$ = Rs. 33 and the total number of toys $= 2 + 3 + 6 = 11$

$\therefore$ Average = $\frac{33}{11}$ = Rs. 3

Example 5 : The average age of 8 men is increased by 2 years, when two of them, whose ages are 20 and 24 years, are replaced by 2 women. What is the average age of women?

Solution: Two women replace two men aged 20 and 24 years and on account of replacement, ages of 8 men is increased by 2 years

$\therefore$ Total ages of two women = $20 + 24 + 2 \times 8 = 60$ years

$\therefore$ Average age of women = $\frac{60}{2}$ = 30 years.

Example 6 : The average of 13 numbers is 52. The average of first seven of these numers is 48 and the average of the last seven numbers is 58. What is the seventh number?

Solution: Seventh number = $(7 \times 48 + 7 \times 58) - 13 \times 52 = 742 - 676 = 66$

Example 7 : The average age of 25 girls in a class is 10 years. If the teacher's age is included, the average increases by one year. What is the teacher's age?

Solution: Teacher's age = $26 \times 11 - 25 \times 10 = 286 - 250 = 36$ years.

Example 8 : A committee of eight men agrees to collect a sum of money among themselves. The first seven are to pay Rs. 10 and the eight is to pay Rs. 7 more than the average of the eight. Find the total sum to be collected.

Solution: Let average amount = Rs. x

Then, $8x = (7 \times 10) + (x + 7)$

$\therefore$ $7x = 77 \Rightarrow x = 11$

$\therefore$ Total sum = 11×8 = Rs. 88

Example 9 : The average age of 40 soldiers in a troop is 31 years. If the captain's age is included, the average age of all of them still remains the same. What is the captain's age in years?

Solution: Since the average remains the same, the age of the captain and the average age of soldiers should be the same, *i.e.*, 31 years

Example 10 : The average age of 8 persons increases by 2 years when a person comes in place of another person who is 24 years old. What is the age of the new person?

Solution: Age of new person = $8 \times 2 + 24 = 16 + 24 = 40$ years

Example 11 : The average weight of 10 men in a boat is increased by 1.6 kg when a man, whose weight is 79 kg, is replaced by a new man. Find the weight of the new man.

Solution: Weight of the new man = $79 + 1.6 \times 10 = 79 + 16 = 95$ kg

Example 12 : The average age of 33 students and their teacher is 18 years. If the class teacher is 51 years old, what would be the average age of the students?

Solution: Average age of the students = $\frac{18\times 34-51}{33} = \frac{612-51}{33}$ = 17 years

Example 13 : The average runs scored by each player of a team in a one-day match is 22. The average score of the first five players is 35 runs and the average score of the last five players is 8. What is the score of the sixth player?

Solution: Runs scored by the sixth player = $22 \times 11 - (35 \times 5 + 8 \times 5)$

$= 242 - 215 = 27$ runs

Example 14 : The batting average for 50 innings of a cricket player is 60 runs. His highest score exceeds his lowest score by 182 runs. If these two innings are excluded, the average of remaining 48 innings is 58 runs. Find the highest score of the player.

Solution: His scores in the two excluded innings = 50 × 60 – 48 × 58 = 3000 – 2784 = 216 runs

Let the highest score is x

Now, $x + (x - 182) = 216 \Rightarrow x = 199$

Hence, the highest score of the player = 199 runs

Example 15 : The average of 7 consecutive integers is 7. Find the average of the squares of these integers.

Solution: $$\text{Sum of Squares} = \frac{1}{\text{No. of integers}} \times \left[\frac{n_1(n_1+1)(2n_1+1)}{6} - \frac{n_2(n_2+1)(2n_2+1)}{6}\right]$$

Where, $$n_1 = \text{Average} + \frac{\text{No. of integers} - 1}{2}$$

and $$n_2 = \text{Average} - \frac{\text{No. of integers} + 1}{2}$$

In the above case;

$$n_1 = 7 + \frac{7-1}{2} = 10$$

$$n_2 = 7 - \frac{7+1}{2} = 3$$

$$\therefore \quad \text{Sum of Squares} = \frac{1}{7}\left[\frac{10 \times 11 \times 21}{6} - \frac{3 \times 4 \times 7}{6}\right] = \frac{1}{7}[385 - 14]$$

$$= \frac{371}{7} = 53$$

Example 16 : The average daily temperature from 9th January to 16th January (both days inclusive) was 38.6° and that from 10th to 17th (both days inclusive) was 39.2°. The temperature of 9th was 34.6°. What was the temperature of 17th January?

Solution: Total sum of temperature for 9th to 16th January = 8 × 38.6° = 308.8°

Total sum of temperature for 10th to 17th January = 8 × 39.2° = 313.6°

Temperature on 9th January = 34.6°

Temperature from 10th to 16th January = 308.8° – 34.6° = 274.2°

∴ Temperature on 17th January = 313.6° – 274.2° = 39.4°

Example 17 : The average temperature of the town in the first four days of a month was 58°. The average for the second, third, fourth and fifth day was 60°. If the temperature of the first and fifth day were 7 : 8. What is the temperature on the fifth day?

Solution: Total sum of the temperature for first four days = 4 × 58° = 232°

Total sum of 2nd to 5th day = 4 × 60° = 240°

∴ Difference of the temperature of 5th and 1st day of the month

= 240° – 232° = 8°

Also, ratio of temperatures of 5th and 1st day = 8 : 7

In this case, the difference is 1°, then temperature of 5th day is 8°

But actual difference = 8°

$$\therefore \text{ Temperature on 5th day} = \frac{8}{1} \times 8° = 64°$$

Example 18 : The average temperature for Monday, Tuesday and Wednesday was 36°C. The average temperature for Tuesday, Wednesday and Thursday was 38°C and that for Thursday was 37°C. What was the temperature on Monday?

Solution: Average temperature for Monday, Tuesday and Wednesday = 36°C

∴ Total temperature for Monday, Tuesday and Wednesday = 3 × 36 = 108 °C

Since average temp. for Tuesday, Wednesday and Thursday = 38 °C

∴ Total temperature for Tuesday, Wednesday and Thursday = 3 × 38 = 114°C

But temperature for Thursday = 37°C

∴ Total temperature for Tuesday and Wednesday = 114 – 37 = 77°C

∴ Temperature on Monday = 108 – 77 = 31°C

Example 19 : The average salary of Prakash, Jayesh and Kailash is Rs.1100. The average salary of Prakash and Kailash is Rs. 900. What is Jayesh's salary?

Solution: Total salary of Prakash, Jayesh and Kailash = Rs. (1100 × 3) = Rs. 3300

Total salary of Prakash and Kailash = Rs (900 × 2) = Rs. 1800

∴ Salary of Jayesh = Rs. (3300 – 1800) = Rs. 1500

Example 20 : The average salary of 20 workers in a factory is Rs. 1900 per month. If the manager's salary is added, the average salary becomes Rs.2000 per month. What is the manager's annual salary?

Solution: Total salary of 20 workers = 20 × 1900 = Rs. 38000

Total salary of 20 workers and manager = 21 × 2000 = Rs. 42000

∴ Manager's monthly salary = Rs. (42000 – 38000) = Rs. 4000

∴ Manager's annual salary = 12 × 4000 = Rs. 48000

Example 21 : The average weight of 45 passengers on board of an aircraft is 50 kg. If the weight of 5 members of the crew is added, the average is reduced by half kilogram. What is the average weight of the crew members?

Solution: Total weight of 45 passengers = 45 × 50 = 2250 kg

and the total weight of 45 passengers and the 5 crew = 50 × 49.5 = 2475 kg

∴ Total weight of 5 crews = 2475 – 2250 = 225 kg

∴ Average weight of 5 crews = $\frac{225}{5}$ = 45 kg

Example 22 : The average of runs scored by the eleven players of a cricket team is 60. If the runs scored by the captain are neglected, the average of runs scored by the remaining players increases by 5. How many runs were scored by the captain?

Solution: The total runs scored by the captain = 11 × 60 – 10 × 65 = 660 – 650 = 10 runs

Example 23 : The average sales of gas lighters of 24 salesman excluding Mukesh is 46 pieces per day whereas Mukesh alone sells 96 pieces per day. What will be the average sells of gas lighters if Mukesh's sells is also included in it?

Solution: The average sells of gas lighters including Mukesh's sell = $\frac{24 \times 46 + 96}{25} = \frac{1104 + 96}{25}$ = 48 pieces.

Example 24 : The average of Mukesh's marks in 7 subjects is 75. His average in 6 subjects excluding Science is 72. How many marks did he get in Science?

Solution: Marks in Science = 7 × 75 – 6 × 72 = 525 – 432 = 93 marks

Example 25 : A motorist complete the journey between A and B at a constant speed of 20 kmph and covers the returns journey from B to A at a constant speed of 30 kmph. What was the average speed?

Solution: Time taken by motorist to go from A to B = $\frac{60}{20}$ = 3 hours and Time taken by motorist to go from B to A = $\frac{60}{30}$ = 2 hours

∴ Total time taken = 3 + 2 = 5 hours, and total distance covered = 60 + 60 = 120 km

∴ Average speed = $\frac{120}{5}$ = 24 kmph

Example 26 : The average salary of Raju, Mahesh and Mukesh is Rs. 800 and the average salary of Mahesh, Mukesh and Sohan is Rs. 900 and if Sohan's salary is Rs. 900, what is Raju's salary?

Solution: Average salary of Raju, Mahesh and Mukesh = Rs. 800

∴ Total salary of Raju, Mahesh and Mukesh = 800 × 3 = Rs. 2400

Since the average salary of Mahesh, Mukesh and Sohan = Rs. 900

∴ Total salary of Mahesh, Mukesh and Sohan = 900 × 3 = Rs. 2700

∴ Total salary of Mahesh and Mukesh = 2700 – 900 = Rs. 1800

∴ Salary of Raju = 2400 – 1800 = Rs. 600

Example 27 : The average of three numbers of which greatest is 16, is 12. Smallest is half of the greatest, then find the remaining number.

Solution: Average of three numbers = 12

∴ Total of three numbers = 12 × 3 = 36

But the greatest number = 16

∴ The smallest number = 8

∴ The remaining number = 36 – 16 – 8 = 12

Example 28 : The average of marks obtained by Sohan in seven subjects is 68. His average in six subjects excluding Mathematics is 70. How many marks did he get in Mathematics?

Solution: Marks in Mathematics = (68 × 7 – 70 × 6) = (476 – 420) = 56 marks

Example 29 : The average of marks obtained by Sunil in History and Mathematics is 60%. If he got 90 marks out of 150 in Mathematics, how much did he get in History, out of 100?

Solution: Total marks obtained by Sunil = 60% of (150 + 100) = 150 marks

∴ Marks obtained in History = 150 – 90 = 60 marks

Example 30 : There are 20 students with an average height of 125 cm in a class. 5 students with an average height of 116 cm leave the class. What is the average height of the class now?

Solution: Average = $\left(\frac{20 \times 125 - 5 \times 116}{15}\right)$cm = $\left(\frac{2500 - 580}{15}\right)$cm = 128 cm

Example 31: The average weight of three person A, B and C is 84 kg. Another man D joins the group and the average now becomes 80 kg. If another man E, whose weight is 3 kg more than that of D, replaces A, then the average weight of B, C, D and E becomes 79 kg. What is the weight of A?

Solution: Total weight of A, B and C = 3 × 84 = 252 kg

and total weight of A, B, C and D = 4 × 80 = 320 kg

∴ Weight of D = (320 – 252) kg = 68 kg

and weight of E = (68 + 3) = 71 kg

Now, weight of B, C and D = (316 – 71) kg = 245 kg

⇒ weight of A = (320 – 245) kg = 75 kg

Example 32 : The averge weight of 8 men is increased by 2 kg when one of the men, whose weight is 50 kg is replaced by a new man. Find the weight of the new man.

Solution: Weight increased = (8 × 2) = 16 kg

∴ Weight of new man = (50 + 16) = 66 kg

Example 33 : The average of 10 numbers is calculated as 15. It is discovered later on that while calculating the average one number, namely 36 was wrongly read is 26. Find the correct average.

Solution: Sum of numbers = (10 × 15 – 26 + 36) = 160

$$\therefore \text{ Correct average} = \frac{160}{10} = 16$$

Example 34. The average of 25 results is 18; that of first twelve is 14 and of last twelve is 17. Find the thirteenth result.

Solution: Thirteenth result = (25 × 18 – 12 × 14 + 12 × 17) = 78

Example 35 : There were 35 students in a hostel. If the number of students increased by 7, the expenses of the mess were increased by Rs. 42 per day while the average expenditure per head diminished by Re. 1. What was the original expenditure of the mess?

Solution: Let the original expenditure = Rs. x

$$\text{Then, } \frac{x}{35} - \frac{x+42}{42} = 1$$

$$\Rightarrow 42x - 35(x + 42) = 35 \times 42$$

$$\Rightarrow 7x = 35 \times 42 + 35 \times 42$$

$$\Rightarrow x = \frac{2 \times 35 \times 42}{7} = 420$$

Example 36 : A person purchased 40 pieces of fruits, *i.e.*, apples and mangoes and paid Rs. 24. Had he purchased as many apples as mangoes and as many mangoes as apples, he would have paid Rs. 16. The cost of an apple is Re. 0.70. Find the cost of 7 apples and 9 mangoes.

Solution: Total no. of fruits = 40

In the first case,

Let the no. of apples = x

Then, the no. of mangoes = 40 – x

∴ Cost of x apples + cost of (40 – x) mangoes = Rs. 24 ...*(i)*

In the second case,

Cost of (40 – x) apple + cost of x mangoes = Rs. 16 ...*(ii)*

From *(i)* and *(ii)*

Cost of 40 apples + cost of 40 mangoes = 24 + 16 = Rs. 40

$$\therefore \text{ Cost of 1 apple + cost of 1 mango} = \frac{40}{40} = \text{Re. } 1$$

Since, cost of 1 apple = Re. 0.70

∴ Cost of 1 mango = 1 – 0.70 = Re. 0.30

Hence, cost of 7 apples and 9 mangoes = 0.70 × 7 + 0.30 × 9 = Rs. 7.60

Example 37 : Average cost of 5 cows and 4 horses is Rs. 450. The average cost of 4 cows and 5 horses is Rs. 540. What is the cost of 7 cows and 7 horses?

Solution: Total cost of 5 cows and 4 horses = 450 × 9 = Rs. 4050 ...*(i)*

and the total cost of 4 cows and 5 horses = 540 × 9 = Rs. 4860 ...*(ii)*

From *(i)* and *(ii)*, we get
Cost of 9 cows and 9 horses = 4050 + 4860 = Rs. 8910

$\therefore$ Cost of 1 cow and 1 horse = $\frac{8910}{9}$ = Rs. 990

$\Rightarrow$ Cost of 7 cows and 7 horses = 990 × 7 = Rs. 6930

Example 38 : The average temperature of Sunday, Monday, Tuesday and Wednesday was 38° and that of Monday, Tuesday, Wednesday and Thursday was 40°. If the temperature on Sunday was 30°, what was the temperature of Thursday?

Solution: Total temperature of Sunday, Monday, Tuesday and Wednesday = (4 × 38) = 152°C
$\therefore$ Total temperature of Monday, Tuesday and Wednesday = (152 – 30) = 122°C
Total temperature of Monday, Tuesday, Wednesday and Thursday = (4 × 40) = 160°C
$\therefore$ Temperature of Thursday = (160 – 122) = 38°C

Example 39 : The mean temperature of Sunday to Tuesday was 37°C and of Monday to Wednesday was 34°C. If the temperature on Wednesday was $\frac{4}{5}$ th that of Sunday. What was the temperature on Wednesday?

Solution: Total temperature of Sunday, Monday and Tuesday = (3 × 37) = 111°C ...*(i)*
and total temperature of Monday, Tuesday and Wednesday = (3 × 34) = 102°C
Let the temperature on Sunday = x

Then, the temperature on Wednesday = $\frac{4}{5}x$

Subtracting *(ii)* from *(i)*, we get

$$x - \frac{4}{5}x = 9$$

$$\Rightarrow \quad x = 45°C$$

$\therefore$ Temperature on Wednesday = $\left(\frac{4}{5} \times 45\right)$ = 36°C

Example 40 : Average temperature of first 4 days of a week is 38.6°C and that of the last 4 days is 40.3°C. If the average temperature of the week be 39.1°C, find the temperature on 4th day.

Solution: Let the temperature on 4th day = x
Then, 4 × 38.6 + 4 × 40.3 – x = 7 × 39.1 $\Rightarrow$ x = 41.9°C

Example 41 : The average earning of an engineer for the first four days of a week is Rs. 18 and for the last four days is Rs. 22. If he earns Rs. 20 on the fourth day, then what is his average earning in whole week?

Solution: Total earning in whole week = Rs. (4 × 18 + 4 × 22 – 20) = Rs. 140

$\therefore$ Average earning = Rs. $\left(\frac{140}{7}\right)$ = Rs. 20

Example 42 : A shopkeeper earned Rs. 504 in 12 days. His average income for the first four days was Rs. 40 a day. What is his average income for the remaining day?

Solution: Let the average income for remaining 8 days be Rs. x a day.
Then, 4 × 40 + 8 × x = 504

$$\Rightarrow \quad 8x = 344$$

$$\therefore \quad x = 43$$

$\therefore$ Required average = Rs. 43

Example 43 : The average age of the husband and wife at the time of their marriage 6 years ago was 28 years 6 months. Now, the average age of the husband, wife and a child is 24 years. How old is the child?

Solution: The total age of husband and wife 6 years ago = $\left(28\frac{1}{2} \times 2\right)$ = 57 years

The total age of husband and wife now = (57 + 12) years = 69 years

The total age of husband, wife and the child now

= (24 × 3) years = 72 years

∴ The age of the child = (72 – 69) years = 3 years.

Example 44 : Ten years ago, the average age of a family of 4 members was 24 years. Two children having been born, the average age of the family is same today. What is the present age of the youngest child if they differ in age by 2 years?

Solution: Ten years ago, total age of family = 24 × 4 = 96 years

∴ Total present age of the family (excluding child) = 96 + 40 = 136 years

Total present age of the family (including 2 children) = 24 × 6 = 144 years

∴ Total age of two children = 144 – 136 = 8 years

Let the age of one child be x, then the age of other child = $x + 2$

∴ $x + (x + 2) = 8$

⇒ $2x = 6$

∴ $x = 3$ years Ans.

Trick

$x + x + 2 = (24 \times 6 - 24 \times 4 + 4 \times 10)$

⇒ $2x + 2 = 8$

∴ $x = 3$ years

Example 45 : The average score of a cricketer for 10 matches is 38.9 runs. If the average for the first 6 matches is 42, what is the average for last 4 matches?

Solution: Let the required average be x.

Then, $(6 \times 42) + 4 \times x = (38.9 \times 10)$

⇒ $x = 34.25$

Hence, the average score for last 4 matches = 34.25 runs.

EXERCISE

1. The average of the fractions $1\frac{1}{2}$, $2\frac{1}{3}$, $3\frac{1}{3}$ and $4\frac{5}{6}$ is

(*a*) 2 (*b*) $2\frac{1}{2}$ (*c*) 3 (*d*) 4

2. The average of first nine multiples of 3 is

(*a*) 12.0 (*b*) 12.5 (*c*) 15.0 (*d*) 18.5

3. The average of 13 numbers is 68, the average of first 7 numbers is 63 and the average of last 7 numbers is 70. What is the 7th number?

(*a*) 43 (*b*) 45 (*c*) 47 (*d*) 49

4. One third of a certain journey was covered at the rate of 25 km per hour, one-fourth at the rate of 30 km per hour and the rest at the 50 km per hour. What is the average speed per hour for whole journey?

(a) $33\frac{1}{3}$ kmph (b) $44\frac{1}{4}$ kmph (c) $22\frac{1}{2}$ kmph (d) 33 kmph

5. Nine men went to a hotel. Eight of them spent Rs. 3 for each over their meals and the ninth spent Rs. 2 more than the average expenditure of all the nine. What is the total money spent by them?
(a) Rs. 29.25 (b) Rs. 29.50 (c) Rs. 29 (d) Rs. 30

6. An establishment is permitted an average monthly contingency expenditure of Rs. 500 per month during the financial year. When a trial check was made at the end of the first nine months of the year it was found that the average monthly contingency expenditure worked out to be Rs. 511. What average monthly expenditure for the next three months should be aimed at in order to attain the permissible average of Rs. 500 per month for the whole year?
(a) Rs. 567 (b) Rs. 467 (c) 367 (d) Rs. 667

7. Average age of 8 persons increased by 2 years, when two men whose ages are 20 and 24 years are replaced by two women. What is the average age of women?
(a) 30 years (b) 31 years (c) 28 years (d) 33 years

8. A man had seven children. When their average age was 12 years, the child who was 6 years of age died. What was the average of the surviving children 5 years after the death of the child?
(a) 15 years (b) 16 years (c) 17 years (d) 18 years

9. The weight of a body, calculated as the average of seven different experiments is 53.735 grams. The average of the first three is 54.005 grams, the fourth was greater than the fifth by 0.004 gram, while the average of the sixth and seventh was 0.010 gram less than the average of the first three. What is the weight of the body as obtained by the fourth experiment?
(a) 53.068 gm (b) 53.078 gm (c) 53.086 gm (d) 53.072 gm

10. A batsman has a certain average of runs for 16 innings. In the 17th innings, he makes a score of 85 runs thereby increasing his average by 3. What is the average after the 17th inning?
(a) 33 runs (b) 34 runs (c) 37 runs (d) 36 runs

11. The average of 50 numbers is 38. If two numbers namely 45 and 55 are discarded, the average of the remaining numbers is
(a) 36.5 (b) 37 (c) 37.5 (d) 37.52

12. The average of 6 observations is 12. A new seventh observation is included and the new average is decreased by 1. The seventh observation is
(a) 1 (b) 3 (c) 5 (d) 6

13. A man whose bowling average is 12.4 takes 5 wickets for 26 runs and thereby decreases his average by 0.4. The number of wickets, taken by him, before his last match, is
(a) 85 (b) 78 (c) 72 (d) 64

14. The average of marks obtained by 120 candidates was 35. If the average of marks of passed candidates was 39 and that of failed candidates was 15, the number of candidates who passed the examination is
(a) 100 (b) 110 (c) 120 (d) 150

15. The average of three numbers is 42. The first is twice the second and the second is twice the third. The difference between the largest and the smallest number is
(a) 18 (b) 36 (c) 54 (d) 72

16. Out of three numbers, the first is twice the second and is half of the third. If the average of the three numbers is 56, the three numbers in order are

(a) 48, 96, 24 (b) 48, 24, 96 (c) 96, 24, 48 (d) 96, 48, 24

17. The average age of 30 students in a class is 12 years. The average age of a group of 5 of the students is 10 years and that of another group of 5 of them is 14 years. The average age of the remaining students is

(a) 8 years (b) 10 years (c) 12 years (d) 14 years

18. Out of four numbers, the average of first three is 15 and that of the last three is 16. If the last number is 19, the first is

(a) 15 (b) 16 (c) 18 (d) 19

19. The average age of an adult class is 40 years. 12 new students with an average age of 32 years join the class, thereby decreasing the average by 4 years. The original strength of the class was

(a) 10 (b) 11 (c) 12 (d) 15

20. The average age of 24 students in a class is 10. If the teacher's age is included, the average increases by one. The age of the teacher is

(a) 25 (b) 30 (c) 35 (d) 40

21. The average age of A, B, C and D five years ago was 45 years. By including X, the present age of all the five is 49 years. The present age of X is

(a) 64 years (b) 48 years (c) 45 years (d) 40 years

22. The average expenditure of a man for the first five months is Rs. 120 and for the next seven months it is Rs. 130. If he saves Rs. 290 in that year, his monthly average income is

(a) Rs. 1000 (b) Rs. 1800 (c) Rs. 2000 (d) Rs. 2500

23. The average weight of a class of 40 students is 40 kg. If the weight of the teacher be included, the average weight increases by 500 gms. The weight of the teacher is

(a) 40.5 kg (b) 60 kg (c) 60.5 kg (d) 62 kg

24. The average weight of 8 persons is increased by 2.5 kg when one of them whose weight is 56 kg is replaced by a new man. The weight of the new man is

(a) 66 kg (b) 75 kg (c) 76 kg (d) 86 kg

25. If a, b, c, d, e are five consecutive odd numbers, their average is

(a) $5(a + 4)$ (b) $\frac{abcde}{5}$

(c) $5(a + b + c + d + e)$ (d) None of these

26. The average of four positive integers is 72.5. The highest integer is 117 and the lowest integer is 15. The difference between the remaining two integers is 12. Which integer is higher of these two remaining integers?

(a) 85 (b) 84 (c) 73 (d) 70

27. Out of the three given numbers, the first number is twice the second and thrice the third. If the average of three numbers is 121, what is the difference between the first and third number?

(a) 144 (b) 77 (c) 99 (d) 132

28. The average of 5 consecutive odd numbers A, B, C, D and E is 41. What is the product of A and E?

(a) 1591 (b) 1665 (c) 1517 (d) 1677

29. The average of 5 consecutive even numbers A, B, C, D and E is 34. What is the product of B and D?

(a) 1152 (b) 1368 (c) 1224 (d) 1088

30. The average of four consecutive odd numbers is 12. What is the lowest odd number?
(a) 3 *(b)* 5 *(c)* 7 *(d)* 9

31. The average of four consecutive even numbers is one-fourth of the sum of these numbers. What is the difference between first and the last number?
(a) 2 *(b)* 4 *(c)* 6 *(d)* 8

32. A student was asked to find the average of the numbers 3, 11, 7, 9, 15, 13, 8, 19, 17, 21, 14 and x. He found the average to be 12. What should be the number in place of x?
(a) 31 *(b)* 17 *(c)* 7 *(d)* 3

33. The average of 20 numbers is zero. Of them, at the most how many may be greater than zero?
(a) 19 *(b)* 10 *(c)* 1 *(d)* 0

34. In Samir's opinion, his weight is greater than 65 kg but less than 72 kg. His brother does not agree with Samir and he thinks that Samir's weight is greater than 60 kg but less than 70 kg. His mother's view is that his weight cannot be greater than 68 kg. If all of them are correct in their estimation, What is the average of different probable weights of Samir?
(a) 66.5 kg *(b)* 66 kg *(c)* 67 kg *(d)* 68 kg

35. A family consists of grand parents, parents and three grand children. The average age of the grand parents is 67 years, that of the parents is 35 years and that of the grand children is 6 years. What is the average age of the family?
(a) $32\frac{1}{7}$ years *(b)* $31\frac{5}{7}$ years *(c)* $30\frac{5}{7}$ years *(d)* $29\frac{1}{7}$ years

36. The average annual income (in Rs.) of certain agricultural workers is S and that of other workers is T. The number of agricultural workers is 11 times that of the other workers. Then the average monthly income (in Rs.) of all the workers is:
(a) $\frac{11S+T}{12}$ *(b)* $\frac{1}{11S}+T$ *(c)* $\frac{S+11T}{12}$ *(d)* $\frac{S+T}{2}$

37. The average age of the boys in a class is 16 years and that of the girls is 15 years. The average age for the whole class is:
(a) 16 years *(b)* 15.5 years *(c)* 15 years *(d)* Data inadequate

38. The sum of three consecutive odd numbers is 38 more than the average of these numbers. What is the first of these numbers?
(a) 19 *(b)* 17 *(c)* 13 *(d)* Data inadequate

39. The average of a non-zero number and its square is 5 times the number. What is the number?
(a) 295 *(b)* 29 *(c)* 17 *(d)* 9

40. If a, b, c, d, e are five consecutive numbers, their average is:
(a) $(a + 2)$ *(b)* $5(a + b + c + d + e)$ *(c)* $\frac{abcde}{5}$ *(d)* $5\ (a + 2)$

41. The average of a, b, c is M and $ab + bc + ca = 0$, then the mean of a^2, b^2, c^2 is:
(a) $9M^2$ *(b)* $6M^2$ *(c)* $3M^2$ *(d)* M^2

42. The average of six numbers is 3.95. The average of two of them is 3.4, while the average of other two is 3.85. What is the average of remaining two numbers?
(a) 4.8 *(b)* 4.7 *(c)* 4.6 *(d)* 4.5

43. 16 children are to be divided into two groups A and B of 10 and 6 children. The average per cent marks obtained by the children of group A is 75 and the average per cent marks of all the 16 children is 76. What is the average per cent marks of children of group B?

(*a*) $78\frac{2}{3}$ (*b*) $78\frac{1}{3}$ (*c*) $77\frac{2}{3}$ (*d*) $77\frac{1}{3}$

44. The average of five numbers is 27. If one number is excluded, the average becomes 25. The excluded number is

(*a*) 35 (*b*) 30 (*c*) 27 (*d*) 25

45. The average score of a cricketer for ten matches is 38.9 runs. If the average for the first six matches is 42, then find the average for the last four matches?

(*a*) 35 (*b*) 34.25 (*c*) 33.5 (*d*) 33.25

46. The average age of 35 students in a class is 16 years. The average age of 21 students is 14. What is the average age of remaining 14 students?

(*a*) 19 years (*b*) 18 years (*c*) 17 years (*d*) 15 years

47. The average of 50 numbers is 30. If two numbers, 35 and 40 are discarded, then the average of the remaining numbers is nearly:

(*a*) 29.68 (*b*) 29.27 (*c*) 28.78 (*d*) 28.32

48. The average of six numbers is x and average of three of these is y. If the average of remaining three is z, then:

(*a*) $2x = y + z$ (*b*) $x = 2y + 22$ (*c*) $x = y + z$ (*d*) None of these

49. The average weight of 16 boys in a class is 50.25 kgs and that of the remaining 8 boys 45.15 kgs. Find the average weight of all the boys in the class.

(*a*) 49.25 kgs (*b*) 48.55 kgs (*c*) 48 kgs (*d*) 47.55 kgs

50. A library has an average of 510 visitors on Sundays and 240 on other days. The average number of visitors per day in a month of 30 days beginning with a Sunday is:

(*a*) 285 (*b*) 280 (*c*) 276 (*d*) 250

51. Out of 9 persons, 8 persons spent Rs. 30 each for their meals. The ninth one spent Rs. 20 more than the average expenditure of all the nine. The total money spent by all of them was:

(*a*) Rs. 400.50 (*b*) Rs. 292.50 (*c*) Rs. 290 (*d*) Rs. 260

52. A car owner buys diesel at Rs. 7.50, Rs. 8 and Rs. 8.50 per litre for three successive years. What approximately is the average cost per litre of diesel if he spends Rs 4000 each year?

(*a*) Rs. 9 (*b*) Rs. 8.50 (*c*) Rs. 8 (*d*) Rs. 7.98

53. If the average marks of three batches of 55, 60 and 45 students is 50, 55 and 60, then average marks of all the students is:

(*a*) 55 (*b*) 54 (*c*) 54.68 (*d*) 55.68

54. If the arithmetic mean of seventy-five numbers is calculated, it is 35. If each number is increased by 5, then mean of new number is:

(*a*) 90 (*b*) 70 (*c*) 40 (*d*) 30

55. Of the three numbers, the average of first and second is greater than the average of the second and third by 15. What is the difference between the first and the third of the three numbers?

(*a*) 60 (*b*) 45 (*c*) 30 (*d*) 15

56. Of the four numbers, whose average is 60, the first is one-fourth of the sum of the last three. The first number is:

(*a*) 60.25 (*b*) 48 (*c*) 45 (*d*) 15

57. In first 10 overs of a cricket game, the run rate was only 3.2. What should be the run rate in the remaining 40 overs to reach the target of 282 runs?
(a) 7 *(b)* 6.75 *(c)* 6.5 *(d)* 6.25

58. A grocer has a sale of Rs. 6435, Rs. 6927, Rs. 6855, Rs. 7230 and Rs. 6562 for five consecutive months. How much sale must he has in the sixth month so that he gets an average sale of Rs. 6500?
(a) Rs. 6991 *(b)* Rs. 6001 *(c)* Rs. 5991 *(d)* Rs. 4991

59. The average price of 10 books is Rs. 12, while the average price of 8 of these books is Rs. 11.75. Of the remaining two books, if the price of one book is 60% more than the price of the other, what is the price of these two books?
(a) Rs. 12, Rs. 14 *(b)* Rs. 10, Rs. 16 *(c)* Rs. 8, Rs. 12 *(d)* Rs. 5, Rs. 7.50

60. The average of 8 numbers is 20. The average of first two numbers is $15\frac{1}{2}$ and that of the next three is $21\frac{1}{3}$. If the sixth number be less than the seventh and eighth numbers by 4 and 7 respectively, then the eighth number is:
(a) 27 *(b)* 25 *(c)* 22 *(d)* 18

61. Of the three numbers, first is twice the second and second is twice the third. The average of the reciprocal of the numbers is $\frac{7}{72}$. The numbers are:
(a) 36, 18, 9 *(b)* 24, 12, 6 *(c)* 20, 10, 5 *(d)* 16, 8, 4

62. Of the four numbers, the first is twice the second, the second is one-third of the third and third is 5 times of the fourth. The average of the number is 24.75. Which is the largest of these number?
(a) 45 *(b)* 30 *(c)* 25 *(d)* 9

63. A company produces on an average 4000 items per month for the first three months. How many items it must produce on an average per month over the next 9 months, to average 4375 items per month over the whole year?
(a) 4710 *(b)* 4680 *(c)* 4600 *(d)* 4500

64. The average of runs of a cricket player of 10 innings was 32. How many runs must he make in his next inning so as to increase this average of runs by 4?
(a) 76 *(b)* 70 *(c)* 86 *(d)* 80

65. The average monthly salary of 20 employees of an organisation is Rs. 1500. If the manager's salary is added, then the average salary increases by Rs. 100. Find the manager's monthly salary?
(a) Rs. 4800 *(b)* Rs. 3600 *(c)* Rs. 2400 *(d)* Rs. 2000

66. The average monthly income of A and B is Rs. 5050. The average monthly income of B and C is Rs. 6250 and the average monthly income of A and C is Rs. 5200. What is monthly income of A?
(a) Rs. 5000 *(b)* Rs. 4050 *(c)* Rs. 4000 *(d)* Rs. 3500

67. The average temperature of the town in the first four days of a month was 58 degrees.The average for the second, third, fourth and fifth days was 60 degrees. If the temperatures of the first and fifth days were in the ratio 7 : 8, then what is the temperature on the fifth day?
(a) 66 degrees *(b)* 64 degrees *(c)* 62 degrees *(d)* 60 degrees

68. The average age of 15 students of a class is 15 years. Out of these the average age of 5 students is 14 years and that of the other 9 students is 16 years. The age of the 15th student is:

(a) $15\frac{2}{7}$ years (b) 15 years (c) 14 years (d) 11 years

69. The mean of 50 observations was 36. It was found latter that an observation 48 was wrongly taken as 23. The corrected new mean is:
(a) 39.1 (b) 36.5 (c) 36.1 (d) 35.2

70. The average age of 36 students in a group is 14 years. When teacher's age is included to it, the average increases by 1. The teacher's age in years is:
(a) 55 (b) 51 (c) 45 (d) 40

71. The average weight of A, B and C is 45 kg. If the average weight of A and B be 40 kg and that of B and C be 43 kg, then weigth of B is:
(a) 31 kg (b) 26 kg (c) 20 kg (d) 17 kg

72. The average weight of three boys A, B and C is $54\frac{1}{3}$ kg, while the average weight of three boys B, D and E is 53 kg. The average weight of A, B, C, D and E is:
(a) 53.2 kg (b) 53.8 kg (c) 52.4 kg (d) Data inadequate

73. A pupil's marks were wrongly entered as 83 instead of 63. Dut to that the average marks for the class got increased by half. What is the number of pupils in the class?
(a) 73 (b) 40 (c) 40 (d) 10

74. Average of ten positive numbers is $\overline{x}$. If each number is increased by 10%, then $\overline{x}$:
(a) is increased by 10% (b) may increase
(c) may decrease (d) remains unchanged

75. The average weight of 3 men A, B and C is 84 kg. Another man joins in the group and the average now becomes 80 kg. If another man E, whose weight is 3 kg more than that of D, replaces A, then the average weight of B, C, D and E becomes 79 kg. What is the weight of A?
(a) 80 kg (b) 75 kg (c) 72 kg (d) 70 kg

76. A cricketer whose bowling average is 12.4 runs per wicket takes 5 wickets for 26 runs and thereby decreases his average by 0.4. The number of wickets taken by him till the last match was:
(a) 85 (b) 80 (c) 72 (d) 64

77. The average weight of 45 students in a class is 52 kg. Five of them whose average weight is 48 kg leave the class and other 5 students whose average weight is 54 kg join the class. What is the new average weight (in kg) of the class?
(a) $53\frac{2}{3}$ kg (b) $52\frac{2}{3}$ kg (c) $53\frac{1}{2}$ kg (d) $52\frac{1}{2}$ kg

78. A cricketer has a certain average for 10 innings. In the eleventh inning, he scored 108 runs, thereby increasing his average by 6 runs. His new average is:
(a) 60 runs (b) 55 runs (c) 52 runs (d) 48 runs

79. The average age of 8 men is increased by 2 years when two of them whose ages are 21 years and 23 years are replaced by two new men. The average age of the two new men is:
(a) 30 years (b) 28 years (c) 24 years (d) 22 years

80. The average weight of 8 persons increases by 2.5 kg when a new person comes in place of one of them weighing 65 kg. What might be the weight of the new person?
(a) 90 kg (b) 85 kg (c) 80 kg (d) 75 kg

81. The captain of a cricket team of 11 members is 26 years old and the wicket keeper is 3 years older. If the ages of these two are excluded, the average age of the remaining players is one year less than the average age of the whole team. What is the average age of the team?
(*a*) 22 years (*b*) 25 years (*c*) 24 years (*d*) 23 years

82. The average weight of a class of 24 students is 35 kg. If the weight of the teacher be included, the average rises by 400 g. What is the weight of the teacher?
(*a*) 55 kg (*b*) 53 kg (*c*) 50 kg (*d*) 45 kg

83. The average salary of all the workers in a workshop is Rs. 8000. The average salary of 7 technicians is Rs. 12000 and the average salary of the rest is Rs. 6000. The total number of workers in the workshop is:
(*a*) 23 (*b*) 22 (*c*) 21 (*d*) 20

84. The arithmetic mean of the scores of a group of students in a test was 52. The brightest 20% of them secured a mean score of 80 and the dullest 25% a mean score of 31. The mean score of remaining 55% is:
(*a*) 54.6 approx. (*b*) 51.4 approx. (*c*) 50 (*d*) 45

85. 3 years ago, the average age of family of 5 members was 17 years. A baby having been born, the average age of the family is the same today. What is the present age of the baby?
(*a*) 3 years (*b*) 2 years (*c*) $1\frac{1}{2}$ years (*d*) 1 year

86. The average age of a husband and his wife was 23 years at the time of their marriage. After five years they have a one-year old child. The average age of the family now, is:
(*a*) 29.3 years (*b*) 28.5 years (*c*) 23 years (*d*) 19 years

87. The average age of students of a class is 15.8 years. The average age of boys in the class is 16.4 years and that of the girls is 15.4 years. The ratio of the number of boys to the number of girls in the class is:
(*a*) 3 : 5 (*b*) 3 : 4 (*c*) 2 : 3 (*d*) 1 : 2

88. In an examination, a student's average marks were 63 per paper. If he had obtained 20 more marks for his Geography paper and two more marks for his History paper, his average per paper would have been 65. What were the number of papers in the examination?
(*a*) 12 (*b*) 11 (*c*) 10 (*d*) 9

EXPLANATORY ANSWERS

1. Average $= \frac{1}{4}\left(\frac{3}{2}+\frac{7}{3}+\frac{10}{3}+\frac{29}{6}\right) = \left(\frac{9+14+20+29}{24}\right) = \frac{72}{24} = 3$

2. Average $= \frac{3(1+2+3+4+5+6+7+8+9)}{9} = \frac{135}{9} = 15$

3. Average of 13 numbers = 68
$\therefore$ Total of 13 numbers = 13 × 68 = 884
Average of last 7 numbers = 70
$\therefore$ Total of last 7 numbers = 7 × 70 = 490
$\therefore$ Average of first 6 numbers = 884 – 490 = 394

∴ Average of first 7 numbers = 63
∴ Total of first 7 numbers = 63 × 7 = 441
∴ 7th number = 441 − 394 = 47

4. Let the total distance covered during journey = 60 km

$\frac{1}{3}$ of the distance covered during journey = $60 \times \frac{1}{3} = 20$ km

$\frac{1}{4}$ of the distance covered during journey = $\frac{1}{4} \times 60 = 15$ km

∴ The distance covered during the rest of journey = 60 − (20 + 15) = 25 km

Time taken to cover 20 km at 25 km/h = $\frac{20}{25}$ hours = $\frac{4}{5}$ hour

Time taken to cover 15 km at 30 km/h = $\frac{15}{30}$ hours = $\frac{1}{2}$ hour

Time taken to cover 25 km at 50 km/h = $\frac{25}{50}$ hours = $\frac{1}{2}$ hour

Total time taken $= \frac{4}{5} + \frac{1}{2} + \frac{1}{2} = \frac{9}{5}$ hours

Hence average speed per hour $= 60 \div \frac{9}{5} = \frac{60 \times 5}{9} = \frac{100}{3}$ km / h $= 33\frac{1}{3}$ km / h

5. Let the average expenditure of all the nine = Rs. x
Now amount spent by eight = Rs. 3 × 8 = Rs. 24
and total spent by the ninth = Rs. $x + 2$

$$\Rightarrow \quad \frac{26 + x}{9} = x$$

∴ Average amount spent by nine = $\frac{26 + x}{9}$

Total amount spent by nine = $24 + x + 2 = 26 + x$

$$\Rightarrow \quad 9x = 26 + x$$

or, $\quad 8x = 26$

$$\Rightarrow \quad x = \frac{26}{8} = \text{Rs. } 3.25$$

Hence total money spent = Rs. (3.25 × 9) = Rs. 29.25

6. Average monthly expenditure permitted = Rs. 500
Total expenditure permitted for 12 months = Rs. 500 × 12 = Rs. 6000
Expenditure incurred during the first nine months =Rs. 511 × 9 = Rs. 4,599
Expenditure for the last three month = Rs. (6000 − 4599) = Rs. 1,401

∴ Average monthly expenditure for the three months = Rs. $\frac{1401}{3}$ = Rs. 467

7. Total increase in the age of 8 persons = 2 × 8 = 16 years
Total age of two men being replaced = 20 + 24 = 44 years

Total of the age of two women = 44 + 16 = 60 years

$\Rightarrow$ The average age of women = $\frac{60}{2}$ = 30 years.

8. Average age of 7 children = 12 years
Total ages of 7 children = 12 × 7 = 84 years
Age of 1 child who died = 6 years
Total ages of remaining 6 children = 84 – 6 = 78 years

$\therefore$ Average age of 6 children = $\frac{78}{6}$ = 13 years

$\therefore$ Average age of 6 children after 5 years = 13 + 5 = 18 years

9. Total weight of 7 experiments = 53.735 × 7 = 376.145 gm
Total weight of first three = 54.005 × 3 = 162.015 gm
The average of the 6th and 7th was 0.010 gm less than that of the first three.
$\therefore$ Average of the 6th and 7th = 54.005 – 0.010 = 53.995 gm
$\therefore$ Total of the 6th and 7th = 53.995 × 2 = 107.990 gm
Thus, total of 4th and 5th = 376.145 – (162.015 + 107.990) = 106.140 gm
The fourth was greater than the fifth by 0.004 gm

$$\therefore \quad \text{The fifth} = (106.140 - 0.004) \times \frac{1}{2} = \frac{106.136}{2} = 53.068 \text{ gm}$$

Hence, the fourth = 53.068 + 0.004 = 53.072 gm

10. Average increase in the score of 17 innings = 3 runs
Total increase in the score of 17 innings = 3 × 17 = 51 runs
$\therefore$ His average of 16 innings = 85 – 51 = 34 runs
Hence, average after the 17th innings = 34 + 3 = 37 runs

11. Total of 50 numbers = 50 × 38 = 1900
Total of 48 numbers = 1900 – (45 + 55) = 1800

$$\therefore \quad \text{Average} = \frac{1800}{48} = 37.5$$

12. Seventh observation = (7 × 11 – 6 × 12) = 5

13. Suppose the number of wickets taken before the last match = x

$$\Rightarrow \quad \frac{12.4x + 26}{x + 5} = 12$$

$$\Rightarrow \quad 12.4x + 26 = 12x + 60$$

$$\Rightarrow \quad x = 85$$

14. Let the number of candidates who passed = x

$\Rightarrow$ 39 × x + 15 × (120 – x) = 120 × 35

$$\Rightarrow \quad 24x = 4200 - 1800$$

$$\therefore \quad x = \frac{2400}{24} = 100$$

15. Let the third number = x
Then, second number = $2x$ and first number = $4x$

$\therefore \quad \frac{x+2x+4x}{3} = 42$

$\Rightarrow \quad \frac{7x}{3} = 42 \Rightarrow x = \frac{42 \times 3}{7}$

$\Rightarrow \quad x = 18$

So, (largest) – (smallest) = $(4x - x) = 3x = 54$

16. Let second number $= x$

Then, first number $= 2x$

and third number $= 4x$

$\therefore \quad \frac{x+2x+4x}{3} = 56$

$\Rightarrow \quad \frac{7x}{3} = 56$

$\Rightarrow \quad 7x = 56 \times 3$

$\Rightarrow \quad x = 24$

So, the numbers are 48, 24 , 96

17. Let, the required average age be x

Then, $5 \times 10 + 5 \times 14 + 20 \times x = 30 \times 12$

$\Rightarrow \quad 20x = 360 - 120$

$\Rightarrow \quad 20x = 240$

$\Rightarrow \quad x = 12$

18. Sum of four numbers = $(15 \times 3 + 19) = 64$

Sum of last three numbers = $(16 \times 3) = 48$

$\therefore$ First number $= (64 - 48) = 16$

19. Let the original strength $= x$

Then, $40x + 12 \times 32 = (x + 12) \times 36$

$\Rightarrow \quad 40x + 384 = 36x + 432$

$\Rightarrow \quad 4x = 48$

$\Rightarrow \quad x = 12$

20. Age of the teacher $= (25 \times 11 - 24 \times 10)$ years = 35 years

21. Present age of $x = [(49 \times 5) - (4 \times 45 + 4 \times 5)]$ years = 45 years

22. Total income $= (120 \times 5 + 130 \times 7 + 290)$ = Rs. 1800

23. Weight of the teacher $= (41 \times 40.5 - 40 \times 40)$ kg = 60.5 kg

24. Total increase $= (8 \times 2.5)$ kg = 20 kg

Weight of new man = $(56 + 20)$kg = 76 kg

25. Average $= \frac{a+(a+2)+(a+4)+(a+6)+(a+8)}{5} = (a + 4)$

26. Let the remaining two positve integers be x and $x + 12$

Now, $117 + x + 12 + x + 15 = 4 \times 72.5 \Rightarrow 2x + 144 = 290$

$\Rightarrow 2x = 146 \qquad \therefore \; x = 73$

Hence, required number $= x + 12 = 73 + 12 = 85$

27. Let the three numbers be x, $\frac{x}{2}$ and $\frac{x}{3}$ respectively,

Now, $\frac{1}{3}\left(x+\frac{x}{2}+\frac{x}{3}\right)=121 \Rightarrow \frac{11x}{6} = 121 \times 3$

$\therefore\ x = \frac{121\times3\times6}{11} = 198$

Hence, required difference $= x-\frac{x}{3}=\frac{2x}{3}=\frac{2}{3}\times198=132$

28. Let 5 consecutive odd numbers be $(x + 1)$, $(x + 3)$, $(x + 5)$, $(x + 7)$ and $(x + 9)$ respectively.

Now, $\frac{x+1+x+3+x+5+x+7+x+9}{5}=41 \Rightarrow 5x + 25 = 205$

$\Rightarrow 5x = 180 \qquad \therefore\ x = 36$

Then, $A = x + 1 = 36 + 1 = 37$; $\qquad E = x + 9 = 36 + 9 = 45$

Hence, their product $= 37 \times 45 = 1665$

29. Let 5 consecutive even numbers A, B, C, D and E be x, $x + 2$, $x + 4$, $x + 6$ and $x + 8$ respectively.

Now, $\frac{x+x+2+x+4+x+6+x+8}{5} = 34 \Rightarrow 5x + 20 = 170$

$\Rightarrow 5x = 150 \qquad \therefore\ x = 30$

Then, $B = x + 2 = 30 + 2 = 32$; $\qquad D = x + 6 = 30 + 6 = 36$

Hence, their product $= 32 \times 36 = 1152$

30. Let 4 consecutive odd numbers be $(x + 1)$, $(x + 3)$, $(x + 5)$ and $(x + 7)$.

Now, $\frac{x+1+x+3+x+5+x+7}{4}=12 \Rightarrow 4x + 16 = 48$

$\Rightarrow 4x = 32 \quad \therefore\ x = 8$

Hence, lowest odd number $= x + 1 = 8 + 1 = 9$

31. Let 4 consecutive even numbers be x, $(x + 2)$, $(x + 4)$ and $(x + 6)$.

Hence, required difference $= x + 6 - x = 6$

32. Here, $\frac{3+11+7+9+15+13+8+19+17+21+14+x}{12}=12$

$\Rightarrow 137 + x = 144 \qquad \therefore\ x = 7$

33. Average of 20 numbers is zero.

Hence, sum of 20 numbers will be zero. In which there may be sum of 19 numbers is positive if their sum is $+x$ when 20th term $= -x$.

34. In Ist case : $65 < x < 72$

In IInd case : $60 < x < 70$

In IIIrd case : $x < 68$

From the above three cases, we get, $65 < x < 68$

Hence, x may be either 66 or 67 kg.

Then, required average $=\frac{66+67}{2}=\frac{133}{2} = 66.5$ kg

35. Average age of family = $\dfrac{2\times 67+2\times 35+3\times 6}{6}=31\dfrac{5}{7}$ years.

36. The required average monthly income = $\dfrac{11\,S+T}{11+1}=\dfrac{11\,S+T}{12}$

37. The average age of the boys = 16 years
The average age of the girls = 15 years
Hence, number of boys and girls are not given so it is quite impossible to find out the average age for the whole class. Therefore, data is inadequate.

38. Let three consecutive odd numbers be $(x + 1)$, $(x + 3)$ & $(x + 5)$

Then, average = $\dfrac{x+1+x+3+x+5}{3}=\dfrac{3x+9}{3}=x+3$

Now, $x + 1 + x + 3 + x + 5 = x + 3 + 38$
$\Rightarrow 2x + 6 = 38$ $\Rightarrow 2x = 32$ $\therefore\ x = 16$
Hence, Ist number = $x + 1 = 16 + 1 = 17$

39. Let the number be x

Then, $\dfrac{x+x^2}{2}=5x$ $\Rightarrow x^2 - 9x = 0;$ $\Rightarrow x(x - 9) = 0$

Either $x = 0$ (Impossible) or, $x = 9$
Hence, number = 9

40. Here, a, b, c, d and e are five consecutive numbers.
then, $b = a + 1$; $c = a + 2$; $d = a + 3$ and $e = a + 4$

Now, Their average $=\dfrac{a+b+c+d+e}{5}=\dfrac{a+a+1+a+2+a+3+a+4}{5}$

$=\dfrac{5a+10}{5}=\dfrac{5(a+2)}{5}=a+2$

41. Here, $\dfrac{a+b+c}{3}=M$ $\therefore\ a + b + c = 3M$
Now, $(a + b + c)^2 = a^2 + b^2 + c^2 + 2(ab + bc + ca)$
$\Rightarrow (3M)^2 = a^2 + b^2 + c^2 + 2 \times 0$ $(\because ab + bc + ca = 0)$

$\Rightarrow a^2 + b^2 + c^2 = 9M^2$ $\therefore$ $\dfrac{a^2+b^2+c^2}{3}=\dfrac{9M^2}{3}=3M^2$

42. Required average of remaining two numbers = $\dfrac{6\times(3.95)-(2\times 3.4+2\times 3.85)}{2}$

$=\dfrac{23.70-14.50}{2}=\dfrac{9.20}{2}=4.6$

43. The average per cent marks of children of group B = $\dfrac{16\times 76-10\times 75}{6}=\dfrac{1216-750}{6}=\dfrac{466}{6}=77\dfrac{2}{3}$

44. The excluded number = $5 \times 27 - 4 \times 25 = 135 - 100 = 35$

45. Average of last 4 matches = $\dfrac{10\times 38.9-6\times 42}{4}=\dfrac{389-252}{4}=\dfrac{137}{4}=34.25$

46. The average age of remaining 14 students $= \dfrac{35\times16-21\times14}{14} = \dfrac{560-294}{14} = \dfrac{266}{14} = 19$

47. The average of remaining 48 numbers $= \dfrac{50\times30-(35+40)}{48} = \dfrac{1500-75}{48} = \dfrac{1425}{48} = 29.68$

48. Here, $x = \dfrac{3y+3z}{6} \Rightarrow x = \dfrac{y+z}{2} \quad \therefore 2x = y + z$

49. The average weight of all the boys in the class $= \dfrac{16\times50.25+8\times45.15}{16+8} = \dfrac{804+361.20}{24} = \dfrac{1165.20}{24}$

$= 48.55$ kgs

50. For the given condition, there are 5 Sundays in that month.
Now, average number of visitors per day in a month of 30 days.

$\dfrac{5\times510+25\times240}{30} = \dfrac{2550+6000}{30} = \dfrac{8550}{30} = 285$

51. Let Rs. x be the average of their expenditure, then,

$\dfrac{8\times\text{Rs. }30+x+\text{Rs. }20}{9} = x \Rightarrow 240 + 20 + x = 9x$

$\Rightarrow 8x = 260 \qquad \therefore x = \text{Rs. } 32.50$

Hence, total expenditure = 9 × Rs. 32.50 = Rs. 292.50

52. Total consumption of diesel in three years $= \dfrac{4000}{7.5} + \dfrac{4000}{8} + \dfrac{4000}{8.5}$

$= \dfrac{1600}{3} + 500 + \dfrac{8000}{17}$

$= \dfrac{27200+25500+24000}{51}$

$= \dfrac{76700}{51} l$

Total expenditure on diesel in three years = 3 × Rs. 4000 = Rs. 12000

Hence, average cost per litre of diesel $= \dfrac{12000\times51}{76700} = \dfrac{6120}{767} = \text{Rs. } 7.98$

53. Required average Marks $= \dfrac{55\times50+60\times55+45\times60}{55+60+45} = \dfrac{8750}{160} = 54.68$

54. Here, Mean of new number $= \dfrac{75\times35+75\times5}{75} = \dfrac{75(35+5)}{75} = 40$

55. Let the three numbers be x_1, x_2 and x_3

Now, $\dfrac{x_1+x_2}{2} = \dfrac{x_2+x_3}{2} + 15$

$\Rightarrow \dfrac{x_1-x_3}{2} = 15 \qquad \therefore x_1 - x_3 = 30$

56. Let the four numbers be x_1, x_2, x_3 and x_4.

Now, $\frac{1}{4}(x_2 + x_3 + x_4) = x_1 \quad \therefore x_2 + x_3 + x_4 = 4x_1$

Again, $\frac{x_1 + x_2 + x_3 + x_4}{4} = 60$

$\Rightarrow x_1 + 4x_1 = 240 \quad \Rightarrow 5x_1 = 240 \quad \therefore x_1 = 48$

57. Total runs in first 10 overs = 10 × 3.2 = 32

Remaining runs required in 40 overs = 282 – 32 = 250

Required run rate = $\frac{250}{40} = 6.25$

58. Let the sale in sixth month = Rs. x, then

$$\frac{6435 + 6927 + 6855 + 7230 + 6562 + x}{6} = 6500$$

$\Rightarrow 34009 + x = 39000 \quad \therefore x = \text{Rs. } 4991$

59. Let the price of remaining two books be Rs. x and Rs. $\frac{8x}{5}$

Now, $x + \frac{8x}{5} = 10 \times 12 - 8 \times 11.75 = 120 - 94$

$\Rightarrow \frac{13x}{5} = 26 \quad \therefore \quad x = \frac{5 \times 26}{13} = \text{Rs. } 10$ and $\frac{8x}{5} = \frac{8 \times 10}{5} = \text{Rs. } 16$

Hence, price of remaining two books are Rs. 10 and Rs. 16

60. Let the sixth, seventh and eighth numbers are x, $x + 4$ and $x + 7$.

Sum of last three numbers = $8 \times 20 - (2 \times \frac{31}{2} + 3 \times \frac{64}{3})$

$\Rightarrow x + x + 4 + x + 7 = 160 - 95 \Rightarrow 3x + 11 = 65$

$\Rightarrow 3x = 54 \quad \therefore x = 18$

New eighth number = $x + 7 = 18 + 7 = 25$

61. Let the three numbers be x, $\frac{x}{2}$, $\frac{x}{4}$ then,

$\frac{1}{3}\left(\frac{1}{x} + \frac{2}{x} + \frac{4}{x}\right) = \frac{7}{72} \quad \Rightarrow \frac{7}{x} = \frac{7}{24} \quad \therefore x = 24$

Hence, three numbers will be 24, 12, 6.

62. Let four numbers be x, $\frac{x}{2}$, $\frac{3x}{2}$ and $\frac{3x}{10}$ respectively.

Now, $\frac{1}{4}\left(x + \frac{x}{2} + \frac{3x}{2} + \frac{3x}{10}\right) = 24.75 \quad \Rightarrow \left(3x + \frac{3x}{10}\right) = 99$

$\Rightarrow \quad \frac{33x}{10} = 99 \qquad \therefore\ x = \frac{99 \times 10}{33} = 30$

Hence, the largest number = $\frac{3x}{2} = \frac{3}{2} \times 30 = 45$

63. Let x be the number of average items per month for next 9 months.

Now, $\frac{3 \times 4000 + 9 \times x}{12} = 4375 \quad \Rightarrow 12000 + 9x = 52500$

$\Rightarrow\ 9x = 52500 - 12000 \qquad \therefore\ x = \frac{40500}{9} = 4500$

64. Let he makes x runs in 11th inning.

Now, $\frac{10 \times 32 + x}{11} = 36 \quad \Rightarrow 320 + x = 396 \quad \therefore\ x = 76$

65. Let manager's salary be Rs. x, then

$\frac{20 \times 1500 + x}{21} = 1600 \quad \Rightarrow 30{,}000 + x = 33600 \quad \therefore\ x =$ Rs. 3600

66. Here, monthly income of 2(A + B + C) = 2 (5050 + 6250 + 5200)

∴ Monthly income of (A + B + C) = Rs. 16500

Hence, Monthly income of A = Monthly income of (A + B + C) – Monthly income of (B + C)

= 16500 – 2 × 6250 = 16500 – 12500

= Rs. 4000

67. Let temperature of the town in five days are $7x$, x_1, x_2, x_3 and $8x$ degrees respecitvely; Then,

$7x + x_1 + x_2 + x_3 = 4 \times 58 = 232$ ...(i)

And $x_1 + x_2 + x_3 + 8x = 4 \times 60 = 240$ ...(ii)

Now, Subtracting *(i)* and *(ii)*, we get,

$8x - 7x = 240 - 232 \qquad \therefore\ x = 8$

Hence, temperature of the town on fifth day = $8x = 8 \times 8 = 64$ degrees.

68. The age of the 15th student = 15 × 15 – (5 × 14 + 9 × 16) = 225 – 214 = 11 years

69. The corrected new mean = $\frac{50 \times 36 + (48 - 23)}{50} = \frac{1825}{50} = 36.5$

70. Let the teacher's age be x years, then $\frac{36 \times 14 + x}{37} = 15$

$\Rightarrow 504 + x = 555 \qquad \therefore\ x = 51$

Hence, age of teacher = 51 years

71. The weight of B = weigth of A and B + weight of B and C – weight of A, B and C

= 2 × 40 + 2 × 43 – 3 × 45 = 80 + 86 – 135 = 31 kg

72. The weight of three boys (A + B + C) = $3 \times \frac{163}{3} = 163$ kg

The weight of three boys (B + D + E) = 3 × 53 = 159 kg

Now, it is quite clear that without the absolute value of B the average weight of A, B, C, D and E can not be determined. Hence, data is inadequate.

73. Let the total number of pupils in the class be x; then,

$$\frac{83-63}{x}=\frac{1}{2} \quad \Rightarrow \frac{20}{x}=\frac{1}{2} \quad \therefore x = 40$$

74. Here, new average = $\dfrac{10\times\overline{x}+10\times\frac{1}{10}\overline{x}}{10}=\dfrac{10\left(\overline{x}+\frac{1}{10}\overline{x}\right)}{10}=\dfrac{11}{10}\overline{x}$

Hence, new mean is increased by 10%.

75. Here, weight of D = 4 × 80 – 3 × 84 = 68 kgs

Then, weight of E = 68 + 3 = 71 kgs

The weight of B + C = 4 × 79 – (68 + 71) = 177 kgs

Now, weight of A = 3 × 84 – 177 = 252 – 177 = 75 kgs.

76. Let the number of wickets taken by him be x till the last match.

Then, $\dfrac{x\times 12.4+26}{x+5}=12 \Rightarrow 12.4x + 26 = 12x + 60$

$\Rightarrow 0.4x = 34 \qquad \therefore \; x = \dfrac{340}{4}=85$

77. New average weight = $\dfrac{45\times 52-5\times 48+5\times 54}{45}=\dfrac{2340-240+270}{45}=\dfrac{2370}{45}=\dfrac{158}{3}$ kgs = $52\dfrac{2}{3}$ kgs

78. Let the average of runs for 10 innings be x, then

$\dfrac{10\times x+108}{11}=x+6 \quad \Rightarrow 10x + 108 = 11x + 66 \qquad \therefore x = 42$

Hence, new average = 42 + 6 = 48 runs

79. Let the age of two new men be x_1 and x_2 years and initially average age of 8 men be x years, then

$\dfrac{8x-(21+23)+x_1+x_2}{8} = x + 2$

$\Rightarrow 8x - 44 + x_1 + x_2 = 8x + 16 \qquad \Rightarrow x_1 + x_2 = 60$

Hence, the average age of two new men = $\dfrac{x_1+x_2}{2}=\dfrac{60}{2}$ = 30 years

80. Let the originally average weight of 8 persons be x kgs. and the weight of new person be x_1 kg then,

$\dfrac{8x-65+x_1}{8} = x + 2.5 \quad \Rightarrow 8x - 65 + x_1 = 8x + 20$

$\therefore \; x_1 = 20 + 65 = 85$ kgs

81. Let the average age of the team is x years, then,

$\dfrac{11x-(26+29)}{9}=(x-1)$

$\Rightarrow 11x - 55 = 9x - 9 \quad \Rightarrow 2x = 46 \qquad \therefore x = 23$ years

82. Let the weight of the teacher be x kgs, then

$\frac{24 \times 35 + x}{25} = 35.4$ $\Rightarrow$ $840 + x = 885$ $\therefore$ $x = 45$ kgs

83. Let the total number of workers be x, then,

$\frac{7 \times 12000 + (x-7) \times 6000}{x} = 8000$

$\Rightarrow 84000 + 6000x - 42000 = 8000x$ $\Rightarrow 2000x = 42000$ $\therefore x = 21$

Hence, total number of workers = 21

84. Let the total number of studetns be 100 and mean score of remaining 55% be x, then,

$\frac{20 \times 80 + 25 \times 31 + 55 \times x}{100} = 52$

$\Rightarrow 55x = 5200 - 2375$ $\therefore x = \frac{2825}{55} = 51.36 \approx 51.4$

85. Let the present age of the baby be x years, then

$\frac{5 \times 20 + x}{6} = 17$

$\Rightarrow 100 + x = 102$ $\therefore x = 2$ years

86. Required average age = $\frac{2 \times 28 + 1}{3} = \frac{57}{3} = 19$ years

87. Let the number of boys and girls be x and y, then,

$\frac{x \times 16.4 + y \times 15.4}{x + y} = 15.8$ $\Rightarrow 16.4x + 15.4y = 15.8x + 15.8y$

$\Rightarrow 0.6x = 0.4y$ $\therefore \frac{x}{y} = \frac{2}{3}$

Hence, required ratio = 2 : 3

88. Let the total number of papers be x; then,

$\frac{63x + 20 + 2}{x} = 65$ $\Rightarrow 63x + 22 = 65x$

$\Rightarrow 2x = 22$ $\therefore x = 11$

Hence, number of papers = 11.

9 SURDS AND INDICES

SURDS

If x is a rational number and n is a positive integer, such that $x^{1/n} = \sqrt[n]{x}$ is irrational, since $\sqrt[n]{x}$ is called a surd of order n.

Laws of Surds:

(i) $\sqrt[n]{x} = x^{1/n}$ (ii) $\left(\sqrt[n]{x}\right)^m = \sqrt[n]{x^m}$ (iii) $\sqrt[m]{\sqrt[n]{x}} = \sqrt[mn]{x}$

(iv) $\left(\sqrt[n]{x}\right)^n = x$ (v) $\sqrt[n]{xy} = \sqrt[n]{x} \times \sqrt[n]{y}$ (vi) $\sqrt[n]{\frac{a}{b}} = \frac{\sqrt[n]{a}}{\sqrt[n]{b}}$

We know that $x \times x = x^2$, $x \times x \times x = x^3$,
$x \times x \times x \times x = x^4$ ....., $x \times x \times x \times x \times x$ .... n times $= x^n$.
In the given quantity x^n, x is called **base** and n is called **exponent** or **index** or **power**. We read x^n as x raised to the power n or, nth power of x.

Laws of Indices:

Law 1: *When m and n are natural numbers or positive integers and x is a non-zero real number, then* $x^m \times x^n = x^{m+n}$.

Example 1: Evaluate the following using law of exponents:

(a) $a^3 \times a^4 \times a^7$
(b) $b \times b^3 \times b^5 \times b^{10}$
(c) $5 \times 5^3 \times 5^8$
(d) $x^{3x-4} + 2x^{x-1} + (2x-1)^{x+1}$, (where $x = 3$)
(e) $a^3\, bc^2 \times ab^4\, c^3 \times 5bc$
(f) $10^{2/5} \times 10^{4/5} \times 10^{\frac{1}{5}} \times 10^{3/5}$

Solution: (a) $a^3 \times a^4 \times a^7 = a^{3+4+7} = a^{14}$
(b) $b \times b^3 \times b^5 \times b^{10} = b^1 \times b^3 \times b^5 \times b^{10} = b^{1+3+5+10} = b^{19}$
(c) $5 \times 5^3 \times 5^8 = 5^1 \times 5^3 \times 5^8 = 5^{1+3+8} = 5^{12}$
(d) $x^{3x-4} + 2x^{x-1} + (2x-1)^{x+1}$
$= 3^{3\times3-4} + 2 \times 3^{3-1} + (2\times3-1)^{3+1}$
$= 3^{9-4} + 2 \times 3^2 + (6-1)^4 = 3^5 + 2 \times 9 + 5^4$
$= 243 + 18 + 625 = 886$

(e) $a^3 bc^2 \times ab^4 c^3 \times 5bc$

$= a^3 \times a \times b \times b^4 \times b \times c^2 \times c^3 \times c \times 5$

$= 5a^{(3+1)}\, b^{(1+4+1)}\, c^{(2+3+1)} = 5a^4 b^6 c^6$

(f) $10^{2/5} \times 10^{\frac{4}{5}} \times 10^{\frac{1}{5}} \times 10^{\frac{3}{5}}$

$= 10^{\frac{2}{5}+\frac{4}{5}+\frac{1}{5}+\frac{3}{5}} = 10^{\frac{2+4+1+3}{5}} = 10^{\frac{10}{5}} = 10^2 = 100$

Law 2: *When m and n are natural numbers or positive integers and x is a non-zero real number,*

$$\text{then } x^m \div x^n = \frac{x^m}{x^n} = x^{m-n}, \text{ if } m > n \text{ and } \frac{x^m}{x^n} = \frac{1}{x^{n-m}}, \text{ if } n > m.$$

Example 2: Simplify the following using laws of exponents.

(a) $a^9 \div a^7$ *(b)* $24\, a^7 b^5 c^2 \div 3a^5 b^3 c^4$ *(c)* $4^3 \times 2^4 \div 2^{10}$

(d) $\dfrac{x^{-3}y^2z^{-2}}{xy^{-1}z}$ *(e)* $\left(\dfrac{a^3b^2}{ab}\right) \div \left(\dfrac{ab}{a^2b^3}\right)$ *(f)* $\dfrac{x^{-2}y^{-4}}{x^{-3}y^{-1}} \div \dfrac{y^{-2}}{x^{-1}}$

Solution:

(a) $a^9 \div a^7 = \dfrac{a^9}{a^7} = a^{9-7} = a^2$

(b) $24\, a^7 b^5 c^2 \div 3a^5 b^3 c^4$

$$= \frac{24a^7b^5c^2}{3a^5b^3c^4} = 8\left(\frac{a^7}{a^5}\right)\left(\frac{b^5}{b^3}\right)\left(\frac{c^2}{c^4}\right) = 8\, a^{(7-5)}\, b^{(5-3)} \left(\frac{1}{c^{4-2}}\right) = \frac{8a^2b^2}{c^2}$$

(c) $4^3 \times 2^4 \div 2^{10}$

On applying BODMAS rule,

$$4^3 \times 2^4 \div 2^{10} = 4^3 \times \frac{2^4}{2^{10}} = 4^3 \times \frac{1}{2^{10-4}} = 4^3 \times \frac{1}{2^6} = \frac{4\times4\times4}{2\times2\times2\times2\times2\times2} = 1$$

(d) $$\frac{x^{-3}y^2z^{-2}}{xy^{-1}z} = \left(\frac{x^{-3}}{x^1}\right)\left(\frac{y^2}{y^{-1}}\right)\left(\frac{z^{-2}}{z}\right) = \left(\frac{1}{x^{1+3}}\right)\left(y^{2+1}\right)\left(\frac{1}{z^{1+2}}\right) = \frac{1}{x^4}.y^3.\frac{1}{z^3} = \frac{y^3}{x^4z^3}$$

(e) $$\frac{a^3b^2}{ab} \div \frac{ab}{a^2b^3} = \frac{\frac{a^3b^2}{ab}}{\frac{ab}{a^2b^3}} = \frac{a^3b^2 \times a^2b^3}{ab \times ab} = \frac{a^5b^5}{a^2b^2} = a^3b^3$$

(f) $$\because \frac{x^{-2}y^{-4}}{x^{-3}y^{-1}} \div \frac{y^{-2}}{x^{-1}} = \frac{\frac{x^{-2}y^{-4}}{x^{-3}y^{-1}}}{\frac{y^{-2}}{x^{-1}}} = \frac{x^{-2}.y^{-4} \times x^{-1}}{x^{-3}.y^{-1} \times y^{-2}} = \frac{x^{-3}y^{-4}}{x^{-3}.y^{-3}} = y^{-4+3} = y^{-1} = \frac{1}{y}$$

Law 3: *When m and n are natural numbers or positive integers and x is a non-zero real number, then* $(x^m)^n = x^{mn}$.

Example 3: Evaluate the following:

(a) $(a^4)^3 \times (b^3)^2$ (b) $(x^2)^3 . (y^3)^2$ (c) $(3^3)^4 \times 9^5 \div 27^2$

(d) $[(x^2)^4]^3 \div [(x)^2]^3$ (e) $(6^2)^3 \times 12^4 \div [4^5 \times 9^4]$ (f) $\left[\left(\frac{2^{-1}}{3^{-4}}\right)^7 \div \left(\frac{3^{-5}}{2^{-2}}\right)^{-5}\right] 2^{-4}\, 3^{-2}$

Solution : (a) $(a^4)^3 . (b^3)^2 = a^{4\times 3} . b^{3\times 2} = a^{12} b^6$

(b) $(x^2)^3 . (y^3)^2 = x^{2\times 3} . y^{3\times 2} = x^6 y^6$

(c) $(3^3)^4 \times 9^5 \div 27^2 = (3^3)^4 \times \frac{9^5}{27^2} = \frac{27^4 \times 9^5}{27^2}$

$= 27^{4-2} . 9^5 = 27^2 . 9^5 = (3^3)^2 . (3^2)^5 = 3^{3\times 2} . 3^{2\times 5} = 3^6 . 3^{10} = 3^{16}$

(d) $\left[\left(x^2\right)^4\right]^3 = \left[x^{2\times 4}\right]^3 = x^{2\times 4\times 3} = x^{24}$ and $[(x)^2]^3 = (x^2)^3 = x^{2\times 3} = x^6$

$\therefore \{(x^2)^4\}^3 \div \{(x)^2\}^3 = \frac{x^{24}}{x^6} = (x)^{24-6} = (x)^{18}$

(e) $(6^2)^3 \times 12^4 \div (4^5 \times 9^4)$

$= 6^{2\times 3} \times (4 \times 3)^4 \div (4^5 \times (3^2)^4) = 6^6 \times 4^4 \times 3^4 \div (4^5 \times 3^{2\times 4})$

$= \frac{6^6 \times 4^4 \times 3^4}{4^5 \times 3^8} = \frac{6^6}{4^{5-4} . 3^{8-4}} = \frac{6^6}{4.3^4} = \frac{6\times 6\times 6\times 6\times 6\times 6}{4\times 3\times 3\times 3\times 3} = 144$

(f) $\because \left(\frac{2^{-1}}{3^{-4}}\right)^7 = \frac{2^{-1\times 7}}{3^{-4\times 7}} = \frac{2^{-7}}{3^{-28}} = \frac{3^{28}}{2^7}$ and $\left(\frac{3^{-5}}{2^{-2}}\right)^{-5} = \frac{3^{-5\times -5}}{2^{-2\times -5}} = \frac{3^{25}}{2^{10}}$

$\therefore \left[\left(\frac{2^{-1}}{3^{-4}}\right)^7 \div \left(\frac{3^{-5}}{2^{-2}}\right)^{-5}\right] 2^{-4} . 3^{-2}$

$= \left(\frac{3^{28}}{2^7} \div \frac{3^{25}}{2^{10}}\right) 2^{-4} . 3^{-2} = \frac{3^{28} \times 2^{10} \times 2^{-4}}{2^7 \times 3^{25}} = 3^{28-25-2} \times 2^{10-4-7} = 3^1 \times 2^{-1} = \frac{3}{2}$

Law 4: *When m and n are natural numbers or positive integers and x and y are non-zero real numbers, then* $(xy)^m = x^m \times y^m$.

Example 4: Evaluate the following:

(a) $(5x^4)^2 . (3y^3)^4$ (b) $(a^p\, b^{-2q})^3 . (a^2\, b^3)^{2P}$

(c) $\left[\left(2^{-2/3}\right)^{-5/3}\right]^{9/10} + \left[\left(3^{-6/7}\right)^{-3/2}\right]^{7/9}$ (d) $(a^{-x}\, b^{3y})^6 \div (a^3\, b^{-1})^{-4x}$

(e) $[(2.5x)^2 + [3.(4x-1)]^{-2}$ (where, $x = 2$) (f) $\frac{(2\times 3)^4}{27}+\frac{(5\times 4)^3}{16}-\frac{6^5}{(3^2)^2}$

Solution: (a) $(5x^4)^2.(3y^3)^4 = 5^2.(x^4)^2\,3^4.(y^3)^4 = 25x^{4\times 2}.81y^{3\times 4} = 2025x^8y^{12}$

(b) $(a^p.b^{-2q})^3.(a^2.b^3)^{2p} = a^{(p\times 3)}.b^{(-2q\times 3)}.a^{(2\times 2p)}.b^{(3\times 2p)}$

$= a^{3p}.b^{-6q}.a^{4p}.b^{6p} = a^{(3p+4p)}.b^{(6p-6q)} = a^{7p}.b^{-6(q-p)}$ or $a^{7p}b^{6(p-q)}$

(c) $\left[\left(2^{-2/3}\right)^{-5/3}\right]^{9/10} = \left[2^{-\frac{2}{3}\times\frac{-5}{3}}\right]^{\frac{9}{10}} = (2^{10/9})^{9/10} = 2^{10/9\times 9/10} = 2^1 = 2$

and $\left[\left(3^{-6/7}\right)^{-3/2}\right]^{7/9} = \left(3^{-6/7\times -3/2}\right)^{7/9} = (3^{9/7})^{7/9} = 2^{9/7\times 7/9} = 3^1 = 3$

$\therefore \left[\left(2^{-2/3}\right)^{-5/3}\right]^{9/10} + \left[\left(3^{6/7}\right)^{-3/2}\right]^{7/9} = 2 + 3 = 5$

(d) $(a^{-x}b^{3y})^6 \div (a^3b^{-1})^{-4x} = (a^{-x\times 6}.b^{3y\times 6}) \div (a^{3\times -4x}.b^{-1\times -4x})$

$= (a^{-6x}.b^{18y}) \div (a^{-12x}.b^{4x}) = \frac{a^{-6x}.b^{18y}}{a^{-12x}.b^{4x}} = a^{-6x+12x}.b^{18y-4x} = a^{6x}.b^{18y-4x}$

(e) $(2.5x)^2 + [3.(4x-1)]^{-2}$

$= [2.(5\times 2)]^2 + [3.(4\times 2-1)]^{-2}$ ($\because x = 2$)

$= (2\times 10)^2 + (3\times 7)^{-2} = (20)^2 + (21)^{-2} = 400 + \frac{1}{(21)^2} = 400 + \frac{1}{441} = \frac{176401}{441}$

(f) $\frac{(2\times 3)^4}{27}+\frac{(5\times 4)^3}{16}-\frac{6^5}{(3^2)^2} = \frac{2^4\times 3^4}{3^3}+\frac{5^3\times 4^3}{4^2}-\frac{(2\times 3)^5}{3^4}$

$= 2^4\times 3^{4-3} + 5^3\times 4^{3-2} - 2^5\times 3^{5-4} = 2^4\times 3^1 + 5^3\times 4^1 - 2^5\times 3^1$

$= 16\times 3 + 125\times 4 - 32\times 3 = 48 + 500 - 96 = 452$

ROOT:

If 'x' is a positive real number, 'n' an integer and 'a' is a natural number such that $x^n = a$, then it means nth root of a is x. It is generally denoted as:

$$x^n = a \text{ or } x = \sqrt[n]{a} = a^{\frac{1}{n}}$$

Similarly, if x is a positive real number, 'p' an integer and 'q' is a natural number such that $x^{p/q} = a$ (where a is a non-zero real number) then it means that qth root of x is equal to pth root of 'a'.

$$\text{i.e., } x^{\frac{p}{q}} = a \Rightarrow \left(x^{\frac{1}{q}}\right)^p = a \Rightarrow x^{\frac{1}{q}} = a^{\frac{1}{p}} \Rightarrow \sqrt[q]{x} = \sqrt[p]{a}$$

2nd root of a number is called square root and 3rd root is called cube root.

Example 5: Calculate:

(a) $8^{2/3}$ (b) $\left(2\frac{1}{4}\right)^{-\frac{1}{2}}$ (c) $(27)^{-\frac{2}{3}}$

(d) $\left[\sqrt[3]{x^2y^5}\right]^6$ *(e)* $\left[\left(\sqrt[3]{a^{-5}}\right)^{\frac{3}{4}}\right]^{-\frac{4}{5}}$ *(f)* $\left[\left(\sqrt[3]{5}\right)^{5/6}\right]^{-12}\left[\left(\sqrt{5}\right)^{-\frac{3}{4}}\right]^{10} \div \left[\left(\sqrt[3]{5}\right)^{\frac{15}{2}}\right]^{-\frac{14}{5}}$

Solution: *(a)* $8^{\frac{2}{3}} = \left(8^{\frac{1}{3}}\right)^2 = \left(\sqrt[3]{8}\right)^2 = \left(\sqrt[3]{2\times2\times2}\right)^2 = 2^2 = 4$

(b) $\left(2\frac{1}{4}\right)^{-\frac{1}{2}} = \left(\frac{9}{4}\right)^{-\frac{1}{2}} = \left(\sqrt{\frac{9}{4}}\right)^{-1} = \left(\sqrt{\frac{3}{2}\times\frac{3}{2}}\right)^{-1} = \left(\frac{3}{2}\right)^{-1} = \frac{2}{3}$

(c) $(27)^{-\frac{2}{3}} = \left[(27)^{\frac{1}{3}}\right]^{-2} = \left(\sqrt[3]{27}\right)^{-2} = \left(\sqrt[3]{3\times3\times3}\right)^{-2} = (3)^{-2} = \frac{1}{3^2} = \frac{1}{9}$

(d) $\left[\left(\sqrt[3]{x^2y^5}\right)\right]^6 = \left[\left(x^2.y^5\right)^{\frac{1}{3}}\right]^6 = \left[x^{\frac{2}{3}}.y^{\frac{5}{3}}\right]^6 = x^{\frac{2}{3}\times6}.y^{\frac{5}{3}\times6} = x^4.y^{10}$

(e) $\left[\left(\sqrt[3]{a^{-5}}\right)^{\frac{3}{4}}\right]^{-\frac{4}{5}} = \left[\left(\left(a^{-5}\right)^{\frac{1}{3}}\right)^{\frac{3}{4}}\right]^{-\frac{4}{5}} = \left[\left(a^{-5\times\frac{1}{3}}\right)^{\frac{3}{4}}\right]^{-\frac{4}{5}} = \left(a^{-5\times\frac{1}{3}\times\frac{3}{4}}\right)^{-\frac{4}{5}} = \left(a^{-5\times\frac{1}{3}\times\frac{3}{4}\times-\frac{4}{5}}\right) = a^1 = a$

(f) $\left[\left(\sqrt[3]{5}\right)^{\frac{5}{6}}\right]^{-12} = \left[\left((5)^{\frac{1}{3}}\right)^{\frac{5}{6}}\right]^{-12} = 5^{\frac{1}{3}\times\frac{5}{6}\times-12} = 5^{-\frac{10}{3}}$

$\left[\left(\sqrt{5}\right)^{-\frac{3}{4}}\right]^{10} = \left[\left((5)^{\frac{1}{2}}\right)^{-\frac{3}{4}}\right]^{10} = 5^{\frac{1}{2}\times\frac{-3}{4}\times10} = 5^{\frac{-15}{4}}$

And $\left[\left(\sqrt[3]{5}\right)^{\frac{15}{2}}\right]^{-\frac{14}{5}} = \left[\left((5)^{\frac{1}{3}}\right)^{\frac{15}{2}}\right]^{-\frac{14}{5}} = 5^{\frac{1}{3}\times\frac{15}{2}\times\frac{-14}{5}} = 5^{-7}$

$\therefore \left[\left(\sqrt[3]{5}\right)^{\frac{5}{6}}\right]^{-12}.\left[\left(\sqrt{5}\right)^{\frac{-3}{4}}\right]^{10} \div \left[\left(\sqrt[3]{5}\right)^{\frac{15}{2}}\right]^{-\frac{14}{5}} = 5^{-\frac{10}{3}}.5^{-\frac{15}{4}} \div 5^{-7}$

$= \frac{5^{-\frac{10}{3}}.5^{-\frac{15}{4}}}{5^{-7}} = 5^{-\frac{10}{3}}.5^{-\frac{15}{4}}.5^{+7} = 5^{-\frac{10}{3}-\frac{15}{4}+7} = 5^{-\frac{1}{12}}$

Important Note: *If x is any rational number other than zero, then* $x^0 = 1$

When the base is a non-zero real number and exponent is negative integer: Here, we shall find out the value of x^{-n} (where $x \neq 0$ and a positive integer).

From the first law of exponent,

$x^{-n} \times x^n = x^{-n+n} = x^0$

$\Rightarrow x^{-n} \times x^n = 1$ ($\because x^0 = 1$)

Dividing both sides by x^n,

$x^{-n} = \dfrac{1}{x^n}$, Similarly, $x^n = \dfrac{1}{x^{-n}}$

Hence, x^{-n} means the reciprocal of x^n.

Example 6: Find the value of $\sqrt[6]{7^{12}}$

Solution: $\sqrt[6]{7^{12}} = \left(7^{12}\right)^{\frac{1}{6}} = 7^{12\times\frac{1}{6}} = 7^2 = 7 \times 7 = 49$

Example 7: What will be the value of $\left(3\frac{1}{2}\right)^{-3}$?

Solution: $\left(-3\frac{1}{2}\right)^{-3} = \left(-\frac{7}{2}\right)^{-3} = \dfrac{1}{\left(-\frac{7}{2}\right)^3} = \left(-\frac{2}{7}\right)^3 = \dfrac{-2}{7} \times \dfrac{-2}{7} \times \dfrac{-2}{7} = \dfrac{-8}{343}$

Example 8: Find the value of $p^2 \times p^5 \times p^8 \times p^6 \times p^{14}$

Solution: $\because$ $p^2 \times p^5 \times p^8 \times p^6 \times p^{14}$

$p^{2+5+8+6+14} = p^{35}$

Example 9: Find the value of $(3^4)^4 \times 9^6 \div (27^7 \times 3^9)$.

Solution: $(3^4)^4 \times 9^6 = 3^{4\times 4} \times (3^2)^6 = 3^{16} \times 3^{2\times 6} = 3^{16} \times 3^{12} = 3^{16+12} = 3^{28}$

And, $(27^7 \times 3^9) = (3^3)^7 \times 3^9 = 3^{3\times 7} \times 3^9 = 3^{21} \times 3^9 = 3^{21+9} = 3^{30}$

$\therefore$ $(3^4)^4 \times 9^6 \div (27^7 \times 3^9) = 3^{28} \div 3^{30} = \dfrac{3^{28}}{3^{30}} = \dfrac{1}{3^{30-28}} = \dfrac{1}{3^2} = \dfrac{1}{9}$

Example 10: Find the value of $(3^4)^4 \times 9^6 \div 27^7 \times 3^9$.

Solution: Here, according to BODMAS rule we should first do the operation of 'division' and then the operation of 'multiplication'.

$$(3^4)^4 \times 9^6 \div 27^7 \times 3^9 = (3^4)^4 \times \frac{9^6}{27^7} \times 3^9 = \frac{3^{4\times4}(3^2)^6 \times 3^9}{\left(3^3\right)^7}$$

$$= \frac{3^{16} \times 3^{12} \times 3^9}{3^{21}} = 3^{16+12+9-21} = 3^{16}$$

Example 11: If $5\sqrt{5} \times 5^3 \div 5^{-3/2} = 5^{a+2}$, what is the value of a?

Solution: $5\sqrt{5} \times 5^3 \div 5^{-3/2} = 5^{a+2}$

$$\Rightarrow \frac{5 \times 5^{\frac{1}{2}} \times 5^3}{5^{-3/2}} = 5^{a+2} \qquad \Rightarrow 5^{1+\frac{1}{2}+3+3/2} = 5^{a+2}$$

$$\Rightarrow 5^6 = 5^{a+2} \qquad \Rightarrow 6 = a + 2 \qquad \Rightarrow \qquad a = 6 - 2 = 4$$

Example 12: Find the value of $\frac{2^{n+4} - 2(2^n)}{2(2^{n+3})} + 2^{-3}$

Solution: $$\frac{2^{n+4} - 2(2^n)}{2(2^{n+3})} + 2^{-3} = \frac{2^n.2^4 - 2.2^n}{2.2^n.2^3} + \frac{1}{2^3} = \frac{2^n(2^4 - 2)}{2^n(2^4)} + \frac{1}{2^3}$$

$$= \frac{2^4 - 2}{2^4} + \frac{1}{2^3} = \frac{16-2}{16} + \frac{1}{8} = \frac{14}{16} + \frac{1}{8} = \frac{7}{8} + \frac{1}{8} = 1$$

Example 13: Find the value of $\left[\left(\frac{a^{-1}b^2}{a^2b^{-4}}\right)^7 \div \left(\frac{a^3b^{-5}}{a^{-2}b^3}\right)^{-5}\right].(a^{-4}.b^{-2})$

Solution: $$\left(\frac{a^{-1}b^2}{a^2b^{-4}}\right)^7 = \left(\frac{b^{2+4}}{a^{2+1}}\right)^7 = \left(\frac{b^6}{a^3}\right)^7 = \frac{b^{42}}{a^{21}}$$

And $$\left(\frac{a^3b^{-5}}{a^{-2}b^3}\right)^{-5} = \left(\frac{a^{3+2}}{b^{3+5}}\right)^{-5} = \left(\frac{a^5}{b^8}\right)^{-5} = \frac{a^{-25}}{b^{-40}} = \frac{b^{40}}{a^{25}}$$

$$\therefore \left[\left(\frac{a^{-1}b^2}{a^2b^{-4}}\right)^7 \div \left(\frac{a^3b^{-5}}{a^{-2}b^3}\right)^{-5}\right].(a^{-4}.b^{-2}) = \left(\frac{b^{42}}{a^{21}} \div \frac{b^{40}}{a^{25}}\right)(a^{-4}.b^{-2})$$

$$= \left(\frac{b^{42} \times a^{25}}{a^{21} \times b^{40}}\right)(a^{-4}.b^{-2}) \quad = (b^{42-40} \times a^{25-21})\,(a^{-4}.b^{-2}) \quad = (b^2 \times a^4)\,(a^{-4}.b^{-2})$$

$$= a^{4-4}.\ b^{2-2} = a^0.b^0 = 1 \qquad [\because b^0 = 1, a^0 = 1]$$

Example 14: Find the value of $\left(\frac{x^a}{x^b}\right)^{a+b}.\left(\frac{x^b}{x^c}\right)^{b+c}.\left(\frac{x^c}{x^a}\right)^{c+a}$

Solution: $$\left(\frac{x^a}{x^b}\right)^{a+b} = (x^{a-b})^{a+b} = x^{(a-b)(a+b)} = x^{a^2-b^2}$$

Similarly, $\left(\frac{x^b}{x^c}\right)^{b+c} = x^{b^2-c^2}$ And $\left(\frac{x^c}{x^a}\right)^{c+a} = x^{c^2-a^2}$

$$\therefore \quad \left(\frac{x^a}{x^b}\right)^{a+b}\cdot\left(\frac{x^b}{x^c}\right)^{b+c}\cdot\left(\frac{x^c}{x^a}\right)^{c+a} = x^{a^2-b^2}.x^{b^2-c^2}.x^{c^2-a^2}$$

$$= x^{a^2-b^2+b^2-c^2+c^2-a^2} = x^0 = 1.$$

Example 15: Find the value of $\left(3+\frac{1}{\sqrt{3}}+\frac{1}{3+\sqrt{3}}+\frac{1}{\sqrt{3}-3}\right)$

Solution: $3+\frac{1}{\sqrt{3}}+\frac{1}{3+\sqrt{3}}+\frac{1}{\sqrt{3}-3} = 3+\frac{\sqrt{3}}{3}+\frac{1}{3+\sqrt{3}}-\frac{1}{3-\sqrt{3}}$

$$= \frac{9+\sqrt{3}}{3}+\frac{3-\sqrt{3}-3-\sqrt{3}}{\left(3+\sqrt{3}\right)\left(3-\sqrt{3}\right)} = \frac{9+\sqrt{3}}{3}-\frac{2\sqrt{3}}{6} = \frac{9+\sqrt{3}-\sqrt{3}}{3} = \frac{9}{3} = 3$$

Example 16: Find the greatest among the numbers:

$\sqrt[3]{9}, \sqrt{3}, \sqrt[4]{16}, \sqrt[6]{80}$

Solution: Here, LCM of 3, 2, 4, 6 = 12, then

$\sqrt[3]{9} = \sqrt[12]{9^4} = \sqrt[12]{6561};\qquad \sqrt{3} = \sqrt[12]{3^6} = \sqrt[12]{729}$

$\sqrt[4]{16} = \sqrt[12]{16^3} = \sqrt[12]{4096};\qquad \sqrt[6]{80} = \sqrt[12]{80^2} = \sqrt[12]{6400}$

Hence, $\sqrt[12]{6561} > \sqrt[12]{6400} > \sqrt[12]{4096} > \sqrt[12]{729}$

$\Rightarrow \sqrt[3]{9} > \sqrt[6]{80} > \sqrt[4]{16} > \sqrt{3}$, **so, $\sqrt[3]{9}$ is the greatest among the numbers.**

Example 17: If $x = \sqrt{3}+\sqrt{2}$, then find the value of $\left(x^3+\frac{1}{x^3}\right)$

Solution: Here, $x = \sqrt{3}+\sqrt{2}$

Then, $\frac{1}{x} = \frac{1}{\sqrt{3}+\sqrt{2}} = \frac{1}{\sqrt{3}+\sqrt{2}}\times\frac{\sqrt{3}-\sqrt{2}}{\sqrt{3}-\sqrt{2}} = \frac{\sqrt{3}-\sqrt{2}}{3-2} = \sqrt{3}-\sqrt{2}$

Hence, $x^3+\frac{1}{x^3} = \left(\sqrt{3}+\sqrt{2}\right)^3+\left(\sqrt{3}-\sqrt{2}\right)^3$

$$= \left(\sqrt{3}\right)^3+\left(\sqrt{2}\right)^3+9\sqrt{2}+6\sqrt{3}+\left(\sqrt{3}\right)^3-\left(\sqrt{2}\right)^3-9\sqrt{2}+6\sqrt{3}$$

$$= 3\sqrt{3}+6\sqrt{3}+3\sqrt{3}+6\sqrt{3} = 18\sqrt{3}$$

Example 18: Find the value of $\frac{3\sqrt{2}}{\sqrt{6}+\sqrt{3}}-\frac{2\sqrt{6}}{\sqrt{3}+1}+\frac{2\sqrt{3}}{\sqrt{6}+2}$

Solution: $\frac{3\sqrt{2}}{\sqrt{6}+\sqrt{3}}-\frac{2\sqrt{6}}{\sqrt{3}+1}+\frac{2\sqrt{3}}{\sqrt{6}+2}$

$$= \frac{3\sqrt{2}(\sqrt{6}-\sqrt{3})}{(\sqrt{6}+\sqrt{3})(\sqrt{6}-\sqrt{3})} - \frac{2\sqrt{6}(\sqrt{3}-1)}{(\sqrt{3}+1)(\sqrt{3}-1)} + \frac{2\sqrt{3}(\sqrt{6}-2)}{(\sqrt{6}+2)(\sqrt{6}-2)}$$

$$= \frac{3\sqrt{2}(\sqrt{6}-\sqrt{3})}{6-3} - \frac{2\sqrt{6}(\sqrt{3}-1)}{3-1} + \frac{2\sqrt{3}(\sqrt{6}-2)}{6-4}$$

$$= \sqrt{12}-\sqrt{6}-\sqrt{18}+\sqrt{6}+\sqrt{18}-2\sqrt{3} = 2\sqrt{3}-2\sqrt{3} = 0$$

Example 19: If $x = 2 + 2^{2/3} + 2^{1/3}$, then find the value of $x^3 - 6x^2 + 6x$.

Solution: Here, $x = 2 + 2^{2/3} + 2^{1/3}$

$\Rightarrow (x - 2) = (2^{2/3} + 2^{1/3})$

$\Rightarrow (x - 2)^3 = (2^{2/3} + 2^{1/3})^3$

$\Rightarrow x^3 - 6x^2 + 12x - 8 = (2^{2/3})^3 + (2^{1/3})^3 + 3.2^{2/3}.\ 2^{1/3}\ (2^{2/3} + 2^{1/3})$

$\Rightarrow x^3 - 6x^2 + 12x - 8 = 4 + 2 + 6(x - 2)$ $\quad [\because (2^{2/3} + 2^{1/3}) = (x - 2)]$

$\Rightarrow x^3 - 6x^2 + 12x - 6x = 6 + 8 - 12$

$\therefore x^3 - 6x^2 + 6x = 2$

Example 20: If $a^x = b$; $b^y = c$; $c^z = a$, then find the value of xyz.

Solution: $a = c^z = (b^y)^z = [(a^x)^y]^z$

$\Rightarrow \quad a = a^{xyz}$

Hence, $xyz = 1$

Example 21: What will come in place of the question mark (?) in the following equation?

$$18^{3.5} \div 27^{3.5} \times 6^{3.5} = 2^?$$

Solution: $18^{3.5} \times \frac{1}{27^{3.5}} \times 6^{3.5} = (3^2 \times 2)^{3.5} \times \frac{1}{(3^3)^{3.5}} \times (2 \times 3)^{3.5}$

$= 3^7 \times 2^{3.5} \times \frac{1}{3^{10.5}} \times 2^{3.5} \times 3^{3.5} = 2^7 \times 3^{10.5} \times \frac{1}{3^{10.5}} = 2^7$

Now, $2^? = 2^7$

$\therefore ? = 7$

Example 22: Find the value of $(2^{1/4}-1)(2^{3/4}+2^{1/2}+2^{1/4}+1)$

Solution: Let $2^{1/4} = x$, then given expression will be

$= (x - 1)(x^3 + x^2 + x + 1) = (x - 1)[x^2(x + 1) + (x + 1)]$

$= (x - 1)(x + 1)(x^2 + 1) = (x^4 - 1) = [(2^{1/4})^4 - 1] = 2 - 1 = 1$

EXERCISE

1. What is the value of $a^5 \times a^7$?

(a) a^{35} (b) a^2 (c) a^{12} (d) $a^{5/7}$

2. $(x^{2/3})^{-3/4}$ is equivalent to:

(a) $\frac{1}{x}$ (b) $\frac{1}{\sqrt{x}}$ (c) $\frac{1}{x^2}$ (d) $\frac{1}{x^{-2}}$

3. Third power of 4 is equivalent to:
(*a*) 64 (*b*) 81 (*c*) 12 (*d*) 49

4. What is the difference between the third power of 2 and the second power of 3?
(*a*) 2 (*b*) 5 (*c*) 3 (*d*) 1

5. The value of $\left(-\frac{1}{125}\right)^{-\frac{2}{3}}$ is:
(*a*) $\frac{1}{25}$ (*b*) 25 (*c*) 5 (*d*) $\frac{1}{5}$

6. The value of $(8)^{-(2^{-2})}$ is:
(*a*) $2^{-1/4}$ (*b*) $2^{-3/4}$ (*c*) $2^{3/4}$ (*d*) $2^{-\frac{1}{2}}$

7. If $\sqrt{2^n} = 64$, what will be the value of *n*?
(*a*) 8 (*b*) 4 (*c*) 12 (*d*) 16

8. $(100)^0$ is equivalent to:
(*a*) 0 (*b*) 10 (*c*) 1 (*d*) 100

9. If $10^{2/5} \times 10^{8/5} = 10^n$, the value of *n* is:
(*a*) 2 (*b*) 3 (*c*) 6 (*d*) 4

10. The value of $27^3 \times 3^4 \div 3^{10}$ is equal to:
(*a*) 9 (*b*) 27 (*c*) 81 (*d*) $\frac{1}{27}$

11. The expression $\frac{(-1)^{132}}{5^{-1}+3^{-1}}$ is equivalent to:
(*a*) $\frac{16}{9}$ (*b*) $-\frac{15}{8}$ (*c*) $\frac{15}{8}$ (*d*) $\frac{17}{8}$

12. The value of $6a^3 b^3 c^2 \div 2ab^2 c$ is:
(*a*) $3a^2 bc$ (*b*) $3a b^2 c$ (*c*) $3a^2 b^2 c^2$ (*d*) $3a^3 b^3 c^3$

13. $\sqrt{\frac{1}{\left(\frac{3}{4}\right)^{-2}}}+\sqrt[3]{\frac{27}{64}}$ is equivalent to:
(*a*) $\frac{2}{3}$ (*b*) $\frac{4}{5}$ (*c*) $\frac{13}{12}$ (*d*) $\frac{3}{2}$

14. The positive exponential function of $\frac{a^{-3} \cdot a^{-4}}{a^{-5}}$ is:
(*a*) a^2 (*b*) $\frac{1}{a^3}$ (*c*) $\frac{1}{a^4}$ (*d*) $\frac{1}{a^2}$

15. $\sqrt[3]{x^6} \div \sqrt[3]{x^{12}} \times x^{-3} \times \sqrt[3]{x^9}$ is equivalent to:
(*a*) $2x$ (*b*) 1 (*c*) $\frac{1}{3x^2}$ (*d*) $\frac{1}{x}$

16. The value of $\left(\frac{2^3}{3^2}\right)^{2/3} \times \left(\frac{3^3}{2^2}\right)^{2/3}$ is:

(a) $6^{4/3}$ (b) $8^{2/3}$ (c) $6^{2/3}$ (d) $9^{\frac{1}{3}}$

17. $(16)^{-3/4} + 2^{-3} + (8)^{-2/3}$ is equivalent to:

(a) $\frac{1}{2}$ (b) $\frac{3}{2}$ (c) $\frac{9}{2}$ (d) $\frac{5}{4}$

18. The value of $12x^2y^4z^3 \div (2xy^2 \times 3yz^2)$ will be:

(a) $2xyz$ (b) xyz (c) $\frac{1}{xyz}$ (d) $\frac{2}{xyz}$

19. $\left[\left(2a^2\right)^3\right]^3 \left[\left(3a^3\right)^2\right]^2 \div \left[\left(6a^6\right)^2\right]^2$ is equivalent to:

(a) $36a^6$ (b) $32\ a^6$ (c) $32\ a^4$ (d) $34\ a^5$

20. The value of $\frac{x^{-2}.y^{-4}}{x^{-3}.y^{-1}} \div \frac{y^{-2}}{x^{-1}}$ is:

(a) y (b) $\frac{1}{y}$ (c) xy (d) $\frac{1}{xy}$

21. $\frac{\left[\left(3^{-2}\right)^{-5}\right]^{1/5} + \left[\left(4^{-3}\right)^{-6}\right]^{1/6} - 1}{\left[\left(2^{-3}\right)^{-4}\right]^{1/4}}$ is equivalent to:

(a) 9 (b) 8 (c) 27 (d) $\frac{1}{3}$

22. If $\sqrt{4^3} \times (4)^{3/2} \div 4^{-3} = 2^x$, the value of x will be:

(a) 16 (b) 8 (c) 12 (d) 4

23. $\left(\frac{x}{y}\right)^{a-b} \left(\frac{x}{y}\right)^{b-c} \left(\frac{x}{y}\right)^{c-a}$ is equivalent to:

(a) 1 (b) 0 (c) xyz (d) $x^2\ y^2\ z^2$

24. $\frac{3^{n+3} - 3^{n+1} + 3^n}{2\left(3^{n-1}\right)} + 2^{-1}$ is equivalent to:

(a) 32 (b) 39 (c) 35 (d) 38

25. $\left(\frac{x^a}{x^{-b}}\right)^{a^2 - ab + b^2} \left(\frac{x^b}{x^{-c}}\right)^{b^2 - bc + c^2} \left(\frac{x^c}{x^{-a}}\right)^{c^2 - ca + a^2}$ is equivalent to:

(a) $x^{(a^2 + b^2 + c^2)}$ (b) $x^{2\,(a^3 + b^3 + c^3)}$

(c) $x^{2\,(a^3 - b^3 - c^3)}$ (d) $\frac{1}{x^{2\,(a^3 + b^3 + c^3)}}$

26. $\left(\frac{x^b}{x^c}\right)^{\frac{1}{bc}} \times \left(\frac{x^c}{x^a}\right)^{\frac{1}{ac}} \times \left(\frac{x^a}{x^b}\right)^{\frac{1}{ab}}$ is equivalent to:

(a) x^{b^2-ac} (b) $\frac{1}{x^{(ab+b^2-c^2)}}$ (c) $x^{(a^3+b^3+c^3-abc)}$ (d) 1

27. The value of $\left(\frac{x^b}{x^c}\right)^a \cdot \left(\frac{x^c}{x^a}\right)^b \cdot \left(\frac{x^a}{x^b}\right)^c$ is:

(a) 1 (b) $x^{2(a+b+c)}$

(c) $\frac{1}{x^{(a^2+b^2+c^2)}}$ (d) $x^{(a^2+b^2+c^2-ab-bc-ca)}$

28. What should come in place of the question mark in the following question?

$2^{0.2} \times 64 \times 8^{1.3} \times 4^{0.2} = 8^?$

(a) 2.5 (b) 3.7 (c) 3.2 (d) None of these

29. The value of $[(10)^{150} \div (10)^{146}]$ is:

(a) 10^6 (b) 100000 (c) 10000 (d) 1000

30. Find the value of $\frac{1}{(216)^{-2/3}} + \frac{1}{(256)^{-3/4}} + \frac{1}{(32)^{-1/5}}$

(a) 109 (b) 107 (c) 105 (d) 102

31. If $\left(\frac{a}{b}\right)^{x-1} = \left(\frac{b}{a}\right)^{x-3}$, then the value of x is:

(a) $\frac{7}{2}$ (b) 2 (c) 1 (d) 1/2

32. The value of $\frac{(243)^{0.13} \times (243)^{0.07}}{(7)^{0.25} \times (49)^{0.075} \times (343)^{0.2}}$ is:

(a) $2\frac{2}{7}$ (b) $1\frac{3}{7}$ (c) $\frac{7}{3}$ (d) 3/7

33. $(25)^{7.5} \times (5)^{2.5} \div (125)^{1.5} = 5^?$

(a) 17.5 (b) 16 (c) 13 (d) 8.5

34. $(64)^{-1/2} - (-32)^{-4/5} = ?$

(a) $\frac{3}{16}$ (b) $\frac{1}{16}$ (c) $\frac{3}{8}$ (d) $\frac{1}{8}$

35. $(17)^{3.5} \times (17)^? = 17^8$

(a) 4.5 (b) 4.25 (c) 2.75 (d) 2.5

36. $(1000)^7 \div 10^{18} = ?$

(a) 10000 (b) 1000 (c) 100 (d) 10

37. $(0.04)^{-1.5} = ?$

(a) 625 (b) 250 (c) 125 (d) 25

38. $(256)^{0.16} \times (256)^{0.09} = ?$

(a) 256.25 (b) 64 (c) 16 (d) 4

39. If $2^{2n-1} = \frac{1}{8^{n-3}}$, then find the value of n.

(a) 3 (b) 2 (c) 0 (d) –2

40. If $5\sqrt{5} \times 5^3 \div 5^{-3/2} = 5^{a+2}$, then find the value of a.

(a) 8 (b) 6 (c) 5 (d) 4

41. If $5^a = 3125$, then find the value of $5^{(a-3)}$:

(a) 1625 (b) 625 (c) 125 (d) 25

42. $\left(\frac{x^b}{x^c}\right)^{(b+c-a)} \cdot \left(\frac{x^c}{x^a}\right)^{(c+a-b)} \cdot \left(\frac{x^a}{x^b}\right)^{(a+b-c)} = ?$

(a) x^{a+b+c} (b) $x^{ab+bc+ca}$ (c) 1 (d) x^{abc}

43. $\frac{1}{1+x^{(b-a)}+x^{(c-a)}} + \frac{1}{1+x^{(a-b)}+x^{(c-b)}} + \frac{1}{1+x^{(b-c)}+x^{(a-c)}} = ?$

(a) x^{a+b+c} (b) x^{a-b-c} (c) 1 (d) 0

44. $\frac{1}{1+a^{(n-m)}} + \frac{1}{1+a^{(m-n)}} = ?$

(a) a^{m+n} (b) 1 (c) $\frac{1}{2}$ (d) 0

45. $\frac{(243)^{n/5} \times 3^{2n+1}}{9^n \times 3^{n-1}} = ?$

(a) 3^n (b) 9 (c) 3 (d) 1

46. If $x = 3+2\sqrt{2}$, then find the value of $\left(\sqrt{x} - \frac{1}{\sqrt{x}}\right)$.

(a) $3\sqrt{3}$ (b) $2\sqrt{2}$ (c) 2 (d) 1

47. If m and n are whole numbers such that $m^n = 121$, then find the value of $(m-1)^{n+1}$.

(a) 1000 (b) 121 (c) 10 (d) 1

48. If $10^{0.48} = x$, $10^{0.70} = y$ and $x^z = y^2$, then what is the approximate value of z?

(a) 3.7 (b) 2.9 (c) 1.88 (d) 1.45

49. $\frac{2^{n+4} - 2 \times 2^n}{2 \times 2^{(n+3)}} + 2^{-3}$ is simplified to:

(a) 1 (b) $\left(-2^{n+1} + \frac{1}{8}\right)$ (c) $\left(\frac{9}{8} - 2^n\right)$ (d) 2^{n+1}

50. Given that $3^x - 3^{x-1} = 18$, then find the value of x^x.

(a) 216 (b) 27 (c) 8 (d) 3

51. Given that $2^x = 4^y = 8^z$ and $\left(\frac{1}{2x}+\frac{1}{4y}+\frac{1}{6z}\right)=\frac{24}{7}$, then find the value of z.

(a) $\frac{7}{64}$ (b) $\frac{7}{48}$ (c) $\frac{7}{32}$ (d) $\frac{7}{16}$

52. Given that $2^x = 3^y = 6^{-z}$, then find the value of $\left(\frac{1}{x}+\frac{1}{y}+\frac{1}{z}\right)$.

(a) $-\frac{1}{2}$ (b) $\frac{3}{2}$ (c) 1 (d) 0

53. Given that $a^x = b^y = c^z$ and $b^2 = ac$, then find the value of y.

(a) $\frac{2xz}{(x+z)}$ (b) $\frac{xz}{2(z-x)}$ (c) $\frac{xz}{2(x-z)}$ (d) $\frac{xz}{x+2}$

54. Given that $3^{(x-y)} = 27$ and $3^{(x+y)} = 243$, then x is equal to:

(a) 6 (b) 4 (c) 2 (d) 0

55. If $x = 5+2\sqrt{6}$, then find the value of $\frac{x-1}{\sqrt{x}}$.

(a) $2\sqrt{3}$ (b) $\sqrt{3}$ (c) $2\sqrt{2}$ (d) $\sqrt{2}$

56. Given that $abc = 1$, then find the value of $\left(\frac{1}{1+a+b^{-1}}+\frac{1}{1+b+c^{-1}}+\frac{1}{1+c+a^{-1}}\right)$.

(a) ab (b) $\frac{1}{ab}$ (c) 1 (d) 0

57. If a, b, c are real numbers, then the value of $\sqrt{a^{-1}b}\cdot\sqrt{b^{-1}c}\cdot\sqrt{c^{-1}a}$ is:

(a) 1 (b) $\frac{1}{abc}$ (c) $\sqrt{abc}$ (d) abc

EXPLANATORY ANSWERS

1. $a^5 \times a^7 = a^{5+7} = a^{12}$ $[\because x^m \times x^n = x^{m+n}]$

2. $\left[x^{2/3}\right]^{-\frac{3}{4}} = x^{\frac{2}{3}\times\frac{-3}{4}} = x^{-\frac{1}{2}} = \frac{1}{x^{\frac{1}{2}}} = \frac{1}{\sqrt{x}}$ $\left[\because \left(x^m\right)^n = x^{mn}\right]$

3. Third power of 4 = $4^3 = 4 \times 4 \times 4 = 64$

4. Third power of 2 = $2^3 = 2 \times 2 \times 2 = 8$
And second power of 3 = $3^2 = 3 \times 3 = 9$
$\therefore$ Difference = $9 - 8 = 1$

5. $$\left(-\frac{1}{125}\right)^{-\frac{2}{3}} = \frac{1}{\left(-\frac{1}{125}\right)^{\frac{2}{3}}} = (-125)^{\frac{2}{3}} = [(-125)^{1/3}]^2 = [(-5 \times -5 \times -5)^{1/3}]^2$$
$$= (-5)^2 = -5 \times -5 = 25$$

6. $$8^{-\left(2^{-2}\right)} = 8^{-\left(\frac{1}{2^2}\right)} = 8^{-\frac{1}{4}} = \frac{1}{8^{\frac{1}{4}}} = \frac{1}{(2\times2\times2)^{\frac{1}{4}}} = \frac{1}{(2)^{\frac{3}{4}}} = 2^{-\frac{3}{4}}$$

7. $\sqrt{2^n} = 64 \Rightarrow 2^n = (64)^2 \Rightarrow 2^n = (2 \times 2 \times 2 \times 2 \times 2 \times 2)^2$
$\Rightarrow 2^n = (2^6)^2 \Rightarrow 2^n = 2^{6 \times 2} = 2^{12} \Rightarrow n = 12.$

8. If any given number (suppose x) is a rational number other than zero, then $x^0 = 1$.

9. $\because 10^{2/5} \times 10^{8/5} = 10^n \Rightarrow 10^{2/5 + 8/5} = 10^n \Rightarrow 10^{10/5} = 10^n \Rightarrow 10^2 = 10^n \Rightarrow n = 2$
Hence, the value of n is 2.

10. $$27^3 \times 3^4 \div 3^{10} = 27^3 \times \frac{3^4}{3^{10}} = \frac{(3\times3\times3)^3 \times 3^4}{3^{10}} = \frac{\left(3^3\right)^3 \times 3^4}{3^{10}} = \frac{3^9 \times 3^4}{3^{10}} = \frac{3^{9+4}}{3^{10}} = \frac{3^{13}}{3^{10}}$$
$$= 3^{13-10} = 3^3 = 3 \times 3 \times 3 = 27$$

11. $$\frac{(-1)^{132}}{5^{-1}+3^{-1}} = \frac{\left((-1)^2\right)^{66}}{5^{-1}+3^{-1}} = \frac{(1)^{66}}{5^{-1}+3^{-1}} = \frac{1}{\frac{1}{5}+\frac{1}{3}} = \frac{1}{\frac{3+5}{15}} = \frac{1}{\frac{8}{15}} = \frac{15}{8}$$

12. $$6a^3b^3c^2 \div 2ab^2c = \frac{6a^3b^3c^2}{2ab^2c} = 3a^{3-1}b^{3-2}c^{2-1} = 3a^2bc$$

13. $$\sqrt{\frac{1}{\left(\frac{3}{4}\right)^{-2}}} + \sqrt[3]{\frac{27}{64}} = \sqrt{\left(\frac{3}{4}\right)^2} + \sqrt[3]{\frac{3\times3\times3}{4\times4\times4}} = \sqrt{\left(\frac{3}{4}\right)^2} + \sqrt[3]{\left(\frac{3}{4}\right)^3} = \frac{3}{4}+\frac{3}{4} = \frac{6}{4} = \frac{3}{2}$$

14. $$\frac{a^{-3}.a^{-4}}{a^{-5}} = \frac{a^5}{a^3.a^4} = \frac{a^5}{a^7} = \frac{1}{a^{7-5}} = \frac{1}{a^2}$$

Therefore, positive exponential function of $\frac{a^{-3}.a^{-4}}{a^{-5}}$ will be $\frac{1}{a^2}$.

15. $\sqrt[3]{x^6} \div \sqrt[6]{x^{12}} \times x^{-3} \times \sqrt[3]{x^9} = \dfrac{\left(x^6\right)^{\frac{1}{3}}}{\left(x^{12}\right)^{\frac{1}{6}}} \times x^{-3} \times \left(x^9\right)^{\frac{1}{3}}$ [According to BODMAS rule]

$$= \frac{x^{6\times\frac{1}{3}} \times x^{-3} \times x^{9\times\frac{1}{3}}}{x^{12\times\frac{1}{6}}} = \frac{x^2 \times x^{-3} \times x^3}{x^2} = x^0 = 1$$

16. $\left(\dfrac{2^3}{3^2}\right)^{\frac{2}{3}} \times \left(\dfrac{3^3}{2^2}\right)^{\frac{2}{3}} = \left(\dfrac{2^3}{3^2} \times \dfrac{3^3}{2^2}\right)^{\frac{2}{3}} = (2\times 3)^{\frac{2}{3}} = 6^{\frac{2}{3}}$ $[\because (xy)^m = x^m . y^m]$

17. $16^{-\frac{3}{4}} + 2^{-3} + 8^{-\frac{2}{3}} = \dfrac{1}{(16)^{3/4}} + \dfrac{1}{2^3} + \dfrac{1}{(8)^{2/3}} = \dfrac{1}{\left(2^4\right)^{3/4}} + \dfrac{1}{2^3} + \dfrac{1}{\left(2^3\right)^{2/3}}$

$$= \frac{1}{2^3} + \frac{1}{2^3} + \frac{1}{2^2} = \frac{1}{8} + \frac{1}{8} + \frac{1}{4} = \frac{1}{2}$$

18. $12x^2y^4z^3 \div (2xy^2 \times 3yz^2) = \dfrac{12x^2y^4z^3}{2xy^2 \times 3yz^2} = 2xyz$

19. $[(2a^2)^3]^3\ [(3a^3)^2]^2 \div [(6a^6)^2]^2 = (8a^6)^3 .\ (9a^6)^2 \div (36a^{12})^2 = \dfrac{(8)^3 . a^{18} . (9)^2 . a^{12}}{(36)^2 . a^{24}} = 32a^6$

20. $\dfrac{x^{-2}y^{-4}}{x^{-3}.y^{-1}} \div \dfrac{y^{-2}}{x^{-1}} = \dfrac{x^{-2}y^{-4}.x^{-1}}{x^{-3}.y^{-1}.y^{-2}} = x^0y^{-1} = \dfrac{1}{y}$

21. $\dfrac{\left[\left(3^{-2}\right)^{-5}\right]^{1/5} + \left[\left(4^{-3}\right)^{-6}\right]^{1/6} - 1}{\left[\left(2^{-3}\right)^{-4}\right]^{1/4}} = \dfrac{3^{-2\times -5\times 1/5} + 4^{-3\times -6\times 1/6} - 1}{2^{-3\times -4\times 1/4}}$

$$= \frac{3^2 + 4^3 - 1}{2^3} = \frac{9 + 64 - 1}{8} = \frac{72}{8} = 9$$

22. $\sqrt{4^3} \times 4^{3/2} \div 4^{-3} = 2^x \Rightarrow \dfrac{4^{3/2} \times 4^{3/2}}{4^{-3}} = 2^x \Rightarrow \dfrac{4^3}{4^{-3}} = 2^x \Rightarrow 4^6 = 2^x$

$\Rightarrow (2^2)^6 = 2^x \Rightarrow 2^{12} = 2^x \Rightarrow x = 12$

$\therefore$ Value of x is 12.

23. $\left(\dfrac{x}{y}\right)^{a-b} \left(\dfrac{x}{y}\right)^{b-c} \left(\dfrac{x}{y}\right)^{c-a} = \left(\dfrac{x}{y}\right)^{a-b+b-c+c-a} = \left(\dfrac{x}{y}\right)^0 = 1$

24. $\frac{3^{n+3}-3^{n+1}+3^n}{2\left(3^{n-1}\right)}+2^{-1}=\frac{3^n \cdot 3^3-3^n \cdot 3+3^n}{2.3^n .3^{-1}}+2^{-1}$

$$=\frac{3^3-3+1}{2.3^{-1}}+2^{-1}=\frac{3^4-3^2+3}{2}+\frac{1}{2}=\frac{81-9+3}{2}+\frac{1}{2}=\frac{76}{2}=38$$

25. $\left(\frac{x^a}{x^{-b}}\right)^{a^2-ab+b^2}=\left(x^{a+b}\right)^{a^2-ab+b^2}$

$= x^{(a+b)(a^2-ab+b^2)} = x^{a^3+b^3}$ $[\because a^3+b^3=(a+b)(a^2-ab+b^2)]$

Similarly, $\left(\frac{x^b}{x^{-c}}\right)^{b^2-bc+c^2}=x^{b^3+c^3}$ and $\left(\frac{x^c}{x^{-a}}\right)^{c^2-ca+a^2}=x^{c^3+a^3}$

$\therefore \left(\frac{x^a}{x^{-b}}\right)^{a^2-ab+b^2}\left(\frac{x^b}{x^{-c}}\right)^{b^2-bc+c^2}\left(\frac{x^c}{x^{-a}}\right)^{c^2-ca+a^2}$

$= x^{a^3+b^3}.x^{b^3+c^3}.x^{c^3+a^3} = x^{a^3+b^3+b^3+c^3+c^3+a^3} = x^{2(a^3+b^3+c^3)}$

26. $\left(\frac{x^b}{x^c}\right)^{\frac{1}{bc}}=\left(x^{b-c}\right)^{\frac{1}{bc}}=x^{\frac{b-c}{bc}}=x^{\frac{1}{c}-\frac{1}{b}}$

Similarly, $\left(\frac{x^c}{x^a}\right)^{\frac{1}{ac}}=x^{\frac{1}{a}-\frac{1}{c}}$ and $\left(\frac{x^a}{x^b}\right)^{\frac{1}{ab}}=x^{\frac{1}{b}-\frac{1}{a}}$

$\therefore \left(\frac{x^b}{x^c}\right)^{\frac{1}{bc}}.\left(\frac{x^c}{x^a}\right)^{\frac{1}{ac}}.\left(\frac{x^a}{x^b}\right)^{\frac{1}{ab}}=x^{\frac{1}{c}-\frac{1}{b}}\times x^{\frac{1}{a}-\frac{1}{c}}\times x^{\frac{1}{b}-\frac{1}{a}}=x^{\frac{1}{c}-\frac{1}{b}+\frac{1}{a}-\frac{1}{c}+\frac{1}{b}-\frac{1}{a}}=x^0=1$

27. $\left(\frac{x^b}{x^c}\right)^a=\frac{\left(x^b\right)^a}{\left(x^c\right)^a}=\frac{x^{ab}}{x^{ac}}$ Similarly, $\left(\frac{x^c}{x^a}\right)^b=\frac{x^{bc}}{x^{ab}}$ and $\left(\frac{x^a}{x^b}\right)^c=\frac{x^{ac}}{x^{bc}}$

$\therefore \left(\frac{x^b}{x^c}\right)^a.\left(\frac{x^c}{x^a}\right)^b.\left(\frac{x^a}{x^b}\right)^c=\frac{x^{ab}}{x^{ac}}.\frac{x^{bc}}{x^{ab}}.\frac{x^{ac}}{x^{bc}}=1$

28. $2^{0.2}\times 64\times 8^{1.3}\times 4^{0.2}=2^{0.2}\times 2^6\times (2^3)^{1.3}\times (2^2)^{0.2}=2^{0.2}\times 2^6\times 2^{3.9}\times 2^{0.4}$

$$=2^{10.5}=\left(2^3\right)^{\frac{10.5}{3}}=8^{3.5}$$

Now, $8^? = 8^{3.5}$ Hence, $? = 3.5$

29. $(10)^{150} \div (10)^{146} = 10^{(150-146)} = 10^4 = 10000$

30. $\dfrac{1}{(216)^{-2/3}} + \dfrac{1}{(256)^{-3/4}} + \dfrac{1}{(32)^{-1/5}} = (6^3)^{2/3} + (4^4)^{3/4} + (2^5)^{1/5}$

$= 6^2 + 4^3 + 2 = 36 + 64 + 2 = 102$

31. Here, $\left(\dfrac{a}{b}\right)^{x-1} = \left(\dfrac{b}{a}\right)^{x-3} \Rightarrow x - 1 = 3 - x \qquad \Rightarrow 2x = 4 \quad \therefore x = 2$

32. $\dfrac{(243)^{0.13} \times (243)^{0.07}}{(7)^{0.25} \times (49)^{0.075} \times (343)^{0.2}} = \dfrac{(3^5)^{0.13} \times (3^5)^{0.07}}{(7)^{0.25} \times (7^2)^{0.075} \times (7^3)^{0.2}}$

$= \dfrac{(3)^{0.65} \times (3)^{0.35}}{(7)^{0.25} \times (7)^{0.15} \times (7)^{0.6}} = \dfrac{(3)^{(0.65+0.35)}}{(7)^{(0.25+0.15+0.6)}} = \dfrac{3^1}{7^1} = \dfrac{3}{7}$

33. $(25)^{7.5} \times (5)^{2.5} \div (125)^{1.5} = (5^2)^{7.5} \times (5)^{2.5} \div (5^3)^{1.5}$

$= \quad 5^{15} \times 5^{2.5} \div 5^{4.5} = 5^{(15+2.5-4.5)} = 5^{13}$

Now, $5^? = 5^{13}$

$\therefore \quad ? = 13$

34. $(64)^{-1/2} - (-32)^{-4/5} = (2^6)^{-1/2} - (-2^5)^{-4/5} = 2^{-3} - (-2)^{-4} = \dfrac{1}{8} - \dfrac{1}{(-2)^4} = \dfrac{1}{8} - \dfrac{1}{16} = \dfrac{1}{16}$

35. $(17)^{3.5} \times (17)^? = 17^8 \Rightarrow (17)^? = 17^{8-3.5} = 17^{4.5} \qquad \therefore \quad ? = 4.5$

36. $(1000)^7 \div 10^{18} = (10^3)^7 \div 10^{18} = 10^{21-18} = 10^3 = 1000$

37. $(0.04)^{-1.5} = [(0.2)^2]^{-1.5} = (0.2)^{-3} = \dfrac{1}{0.008} = \dfrac{1000}{8} = 125$

38. $(256)^{0.16} \times (256)^{0.09} = (256)^{(0.16+0.09)} = (2^8)^{0.25} = 2^2 = 4$

39. Here, $2^{2n-1} = \dfrac{1}{8^{n-3}} \qquad \Rightarrow 2^{2n-1} = (2^3)^{3-n} \qquad \Rightarrow 2^{2n-1} = 2^{9-3n}$

$\Rightarrow 2n - 1 = 9 - 3n \qquad \Rightarrow 5n = 10 \qquad \Rightarrow n = 2$

40. $5\sqrt{5} \times 5^3 \div 5^{-3/2} = 5^{a+2} \qquad \Rightarrow 5^{3/2} \times 5^3 \div 5^{-3/2} = 5^{a+2}$

$\Rightarrow \quad 5^{(3/2+3+3/2)} = 5^{a+2} \qquad \Rightarrow \quad 5^6 = 5^{a+2} \qquad \Rightarrow \quad a + 2 = 6 \qquad \therefore \quad a = 4$

41. $5^a = 3125 \quad \Rightarrow \quad 5^a = 5^5 \quad \therefore \quad a = 5$

Now, $5^{(a-3)} = 5^{(5-3)} = 5^2 = 125$

42. $\left(\dfrac{x^b}{x^c}\right)^{(b+c-a)} \cdot \left(\dfrac{x^c}{x^a}\right)^{(c+a-b)} \cdot \left(\dfrac{x^a}{x^b}\right)^{(a+b-c)}$

$= \left[x^{(b-c)}\right]^{(b+c-a)} \cdot \left[x^{(c-a)}\right]^{(c+a-b)} \cdot \left[x^{(a-b)}\right]^{(a+b-c)}$

$$= x^{\left(b^2+bc-ab-bc-c^2+ac\right)} \cdot x^{\left(c^2+ac-bc-ac-a^2+ab\right)} \cdot x^{\left(a^2+ab-ac-ab-b^2+bc\right)}$$

$$= x^{\left(b^2-ab-c^2+ac+c^2-bc-a^2+ab+a^2-ac-b^2+bc\right)} = x^0 = 1$$

43. $\dfrac{1}{1+x^{(b-a)}+x^{(c-a)}}+\dfrac{1}{1+x^{(a-b)}+x^{(c-b)}}+\dfrac{1}{1+x^{(b-c)}+x^{(a-c)}}$

$$= \frac{1}{1+\frac{x^b}{x^a}+\frac{x^c}{x^a}}+\frac{1}{1+\frac{x^a}{x^b}+\frac{x^c}{x^b}}+\frac{1}{1+\frac{x^b}{x^c}+\frac{x^a}{x^c}}$$

$$= \frac{1}{\frac{x^a+x^b+x^c}{x^a}}+\frac{1}{\frac{x^a+x^b+x^c}{x^b}}+\frac{1}{\frac{x^a+x^b+x^c}{x^c}} = \frac{x^a+x^b+x^c}{x^a+x^b+x^c} = 1$$

44. $\dfrac{1}{1+a^{(n-m)}}+\dfrac{1}{1+a^{(m-n)}} = \dfrac{1}{1+\frac{a^n}{a^m}}+\dfrac{1}{1+\frac{a^m}{a^n}} = \dfrac{1}{\frac{a^m+a^n}{a^m}}+\dfrac{1}{\frac{a^m+a^n}{a^n}} = \dfrac{a^m+a^n}{a^m+a^n} = 1$

45. $\dfrac{(243)^{n/5}\times 3^{2n+1}}{9^n\times 3^{n-1}} = \dfrac{\left(3^5\right)^{n/5}\times 3^{2n+1}}{\left(3^2\right)^n\times 3^{n-1}} = \dfrac{3^n\times 3^{2n+1}}{3^{2n}\times 3^{n-1}} = 3^2 = 9$

46. $x = 3+2\sqrt{2} = 2+1+2\sqrt{2} = \left(\sqrt{2}+1\right)^2$

$\therefore\quad \sqrt{x} = \left(\sqrt{2}+1\right) \quad\Rightarrow\quad \dfrac{1}{\sqrt{x}} = \dfrac{1}{\sqrt{2}+1}\times\dfrac{\sqrt{2}-1}{\sqrt{2}-1} = \dfrac{\sqrt{2}-1}{2-1} = \sqrt{2}-1$

Hence, $\sqrt{x}-\dfrac{1}{\sqrt{x}} = \sqrt{2}+1-\sqrt{2}+1 = 2$

47. $m^n = 121$, Hence, value of $m = 11$ and $n = 2$

Then, $(m-1)^{n+1} = (11-1)^{2+1} = (10)^3 = 1000$

48. $x = 10^{0.48}$, $y = 10^{0.70}$

$x^z = y^2 \Rightarrow (10^{0.48})^z = (10^{0.70})^2 \Rightarrow 10^{0.48z} = 10^{1.40} \Rightarrow 0.48z = 1.40$

$\therefore\quad z = \dfrac{1.40}{0.48} = \dfrac{140}{48} \simeq 2.9$

49. $\dfrac{2^{n+4}-2\times 2^n}{2\times 2^{(n+3)}}+2^{-3} = \dfrac{2^{n+4}-2^{n+1}}{2^{n+4}}+2^{-3} = \dfrac{2^{n+1}\left(2^3-1\right)}{2^{n+1}.2^3}+\dfrac{1}{8} = \dfrac{7}{8}+\dfrac{1}{8} = 1$

50. $3^x - 3^{x-1} = 18 \Rightarrow 3^{x-1}(3-1) = 18 \Rightarrow 3^{x-1} = 9 \Rightarrow 3^{x-1} = 3^2$

$\Rightarrow x - 1 = 2 \quad \therefore x = 3$

Now, $x^x = 3^3 = 27$

51. $2^x = 4^y = 8^z \Rightarrow 2^x = 2^{2y} = 2^{3z}$ Hence, $x = 2y = 3z$

Now, $\frac{1}{2x}+\frac{1}{4y}+\frac{1}{6z}=\frac{24}{7} \Rightarrow \frac{1}{6z}+\frac{1}{6z}+\frac{1}{6z}=\frac{24}{7} \Rightarrow \frac{3}{6z}=\frac{24}{7}$ $(\because\ 2x = 4y = 6z)$

$\Rightarrow z = \frac{7\times 3}{24\times 6}=\frac{7}{48}$

52. Let $2^x = 3^y = 6^{-z} = k$, then,

$k^{1/x} = 2;\ k^{1/y} = 3;\ k^{-1/z} = 6$

Now, $2 \times 3 = 6 \Rightarrow k^{1/x} \times k^{1/y} = k^{-1/z} \Rightarrow k^{\left(\frac{1}{x}+\frac{1}{y}\right)} = k^{-1/z}$

$\Rightarrow \frac{1}{x}+\frac{1}{y}=-\frac{1}{z}$ $\therefore \frac{1}{x}+\frac{1}{y}+\frac{1}{z}=0$

53. Let, $a^x = b^y = c^z = k$, then,

$a = k^{1/x};\ b = k^{1/y};\ c = k^{1/z}$

Now, $b^2 = ac \Rightarrow (k^{1/y})^2 = k^{1/x} \times k^{1/z} \Rightarrow k^{2/y} = k^{1/x + 1/z}$

$\Rightarrow \frac{2}{y}=\frac{1}{x}+\frac{1}{z} \Rightarrow \frac{2}{y}=\frac{x+z}{xz}$ $\therefore y=\frac{2xz}{x+z}$

54. $3^{(x-y)} = 27 \Rightarrow 3^{(x-y)} = 3^3$ $\therefore x - y = 3$ ...(i)

Again, $3^{(x+y)} = 243 \Rightarrow 3^{(x+y)} = 3^5$ $\therefore x + y = 5$ ...(ii)

Solving equations (i) & (ii) we get, $x = 4$

55. $x = 5+2\sqrt{6} = 3+2+2\sqrt{3}\times\sqrt{2} = \left(\sqrt{3}+\sqrt{2}\right)^2$

$\therefore \sqrt{x} = \sqrt{3}+\sqrt{2}$

Now, $\frac{x-1}{\sqrt{x}}=\frac{5+2\sqrt{6}-1}{\sqrt{3}+\sqrt{2}}=\frac{4+2\sqrt{6}}{\sqrt{3}+\sqrt{2}}\times\frac{\sqrt{3}-\sqrt{2}}{\sqrt{3}-\sqrt{2}}=\frac{\left(4+2\sqrt{6}\right)\left(\sqrt{3}-\sqrt{2}\right)}{3-2}$

$=\frac{4\sqrt{3}+2\sqrt{18}-4\sqrt{2}-2\sqrt{12}}{1}$ $= 4\sqrt{3}+6\sqrt{2}-4\sqrt{2}-4\sqrt{3} = 2\sqrt{2}$

56. $\frac{1}{1+a+b^{-1}}+\frac{1}{1+b+c^{-1}}+\frac{1}{1+c+a^{-1}}=\frac{1}{1+a+b^{-1}}+\frac{b^{-1}}{b^{-1}+1+b^{-1}c^{-1}}+\frac{a}{a+ac+1}$

$=\frac{1}{1+a+b^{-1}}+\frac{b^{-1}}{b^{-1}+1+a}+\frac{a}{a+b^{-1}+1}$ $\left(\because\ abc=1 \Rightarrow b^{-1}c^{-1}=a\ \&\ b^{-1}=ac\right)$

$=\frac{1+a+b^{-1}}{1+a+b^{-1}}=1$

57. $\sqrt{a^{-1}b}\cdot\sqrt{b^{-1}c}\cdot\sqrt{c^{-1}a} = a^{-1/2}\cdot b^{1/2}\cdot b^{-1/2}\cdot c^{1/2}\cdot c^{-1/2}\cdot a^{1/2}$

$= a^{\left(\frac{1}{2}-\frac{1}{2}\right)}\cdot b^{\left(\frac{1}{2}-\frac{1}{2}\right)}\cdot c^{\left(\frac{1}{2}-\frac{1}{2}\right)}$ $= a^0 . b^0 . c^0 = 1\cdot 1\cdot 1 = 1$

10 PROBLEMS BASED ON NUMBERS

In this chapter, for solving problems based on numbers, we frame algebraic expressions for finding the values of the unknown quantities from the known ones which leads us to the formation of an equation or a system of equations. Equations are solved to find the solution of the given problem.

Example 1: $\frac{1}{4}$th of $\frac{2}{5}$th of a number is 82. What is the number?

Solution: Let the number be x, then,

$$\frac{1}{4}\times\frac{2}{5}\times x = 82 \Rightarrow \frac{1}{10}x = 82 \qquad \therefore x = 820$$

Example 2: The sum of three consecutive numbers is 39. Find the largest number.

Solution: Let the three consecutive numbers are x, $x + 1$ and $x + 2$

then, $x + x + 1 + x + 2 = 39 \quad \Rightarrow 3x + 3 = 39 \quad \Rightarrow 3x = 36 \quad \therefore x = 12$

Hence, the largest number $= x + 2 = 12 + 2 = 14$

Example 3: The product of two positive successive numbers is 3192. What is the smallest number?

Solution: Let the two successive numbers are x and $(x + 1)$, then

$x(x + 1) = 3192 \quad \Rightarrow x^2 + x - 3192 = 0$

$\Rightarrow x^2 + 57x - 56x - 3192 = 0 \quad \Rightarrow x(x + 57) - 56(x + 57) = 0$

$\Rightarrow (x - 56)(x + 57) = 0$

Then either, $x = 56$ or, $x = -57$ (Impossible).

Hence, numbers = 56, 57

The smallest number = 56.

Example 4: If the difference between a number and one-fifth of it is 84, what is the number?

Solution: Let the number be x, then,

$$x - \frac{1}{5}x = 84 \quad \Rightarrow \frac{4x}{5} = 84; \quad \therefore x = \frac{84\times 5}{4} = 105$$

Example 5: The difference between a two-digit number and the number obtained by interchanging the two digits of the number is 9. The sum of the two digits of the number is 15. What is the product of two digits of the two digit number?

Solution: Let the two-digit number be $10x + y$, then,

$10x + y - (10y + x) = 9 \quad \Rightarrow 9x - 9y = 9 \quad \therefore x - y = 1 \quad ...(i)$

And also, $x + y = 15 \quad ...(ii)$

Solving equations *(i)* and *(ii)* we get $x = 8$, $y = 7$

Hence, required product $= 8 \times 7 = 56$

Example 6: The product of two consecutive even numbers is 16128. Find the larger number?

Solution: Let the two consecutive even numbers are x and $(x + 2)$, then

$x(x + 2) = 16128$ $\Rightarrow x^2 + 2x - 16128 = 0$

$\Rightarrow x^2 + 128x - 126x - 16128 = 0$ $\Rightarrow x(x + 128) - 126(x + 128) = 0$

$\Rightarrow (x - 126)(x + 128) = 0$ $\therefore x = 126$ (Taking +ve value only).

Hence, the larger number = 126 + 2 = 128

Example 7: If the digits of a two-digit number are interchanged, the number so obtained is greater than the original number by 27. If the sum of the digits of the number is 11, what is the original number?

Solution: Let the two-digit number be $10x + y$, then

$10y + x - (10x + y) = 27$ $\Rightarrow 9(y - x) = 27$ $\therefore y - x = 3$ ...(*i*)

And also, $x + y = 11$ ...(*ii*)

After solving (*i*) and (*ii*), we get, $x = 4, y = 7$

Hence, required number = $10x + y = 47$

Example 8: What is the greater of two numbers whose product is 1092 and the sum of the two numbers exceeds their difference by 42?

Solution: Let the two numbers be x and y, then

$xy = 1092$ ...(*i*)

And also, $x + y - (x - y) = 42$ $\Rightarrow 2y = 42$ $\therefore y = 21$

Now, $x = \frac{1092}{21} = 52$

Hence, the greater number = 52

Example 9: The sum of five consecutive numbers A, B, C, D and E is 190. What is the product of B and C?

Solution: Let 5 consecutive numbers be $x, (x + 1), (x + 2), (x + 3)$ and $(x + 4)$,

Then, $x + x + 1 + x + 2 + x + 3 + x + 4 = 190$

$\Rightarrow 5x + 10 = 190$ $\Rightarrow 5x = 180$ $\therefore x = 36$

Hence, B = 36 + 1 = 37, C = 36 + 2 = 38

Required product = 37 × 38 = 1406.

Example 10: Two numbers are such that their difference, their sum and their product are in the ratio of 1 : 7 : 24. What is the product of numbers?

Solution: Let the numbers be x and y, then,

$(x - y) : (x + y) : xy = 1 : 7 : 24$

Now, $\frac{(x-y)}{x+y} = \frac{1}{7}$ $\Rightarrow 7x - 7y = x + y$ $\Rightarrow 6x = 8y$ $\Rightarrow x = \frac{4}{3}y,$

Then, $x + y = \frac{4}{3}y + y = \frac{7}{3}y$ & $x.y = \frac{4}{3}y.y = \frac{4}{3}y^2$

Again, $\frac{7/3y}{4/3y^2} = \frac{7}{24}$ $\Rightarrow \frac{7}{4y} = \frac{7}{24}$ $\Rightarrow 4y = 24$ $\therefore y = 6$

Then, $x = \frac{4}{3}y = \frac{4}{3} \times 6 = 8$

Hence, the product of the numbers = 8 × 6 = 48

Example 11: When 7,807 is divided into three parts in such a way that first part is greater than second by 193 and third is 207 less than the second part. What is the second number?

Solution: Let the second part be x, then first and third will be $x + 193$ and $x - 207$ respectively, then

$x + 193 + x + x - 207 = 7,807$ $\Rightarrow 3x - 14 = 7807$

$\Rightarrow 3x = 7821$ $\therefore x = 2607$

Hence, second number = 2607

Example 12: Of the three numbers, the sum of first two is 45; the sum of second and the third is 55 and sum of third and thrice the first is 90. Find the third number?

Solution: Let the three numbers are a, b and c then,

$a + b = 45;$ $b + c = 55;$ $3a + c = 90;$

Now, $b = 45 - a$ and also, $c = 55 - b = 55 - (45 - a) = 10 + a$

Again, $3a + c = 90 \Rightarrow 3a + 10 + a = 90 \Rightarrow 4a = 80 \therefore a = 20$

Hence, third number = 20 + 10 = 30

Example 13: If $(73)^2$ is subtracted from the square of a number, the answer so obtained is 5075. What is the number?

Solution: Let the number be x, then

$x^2 - (73)^2 = 5075$ $\Rightarrow x^2 = 5075 + 5329 = 10404$

$\therefore x = \sqrt{10404} = 102$

Example 14: If $(57)^2$ is added to the square of a number, the answer so obtained is 8010. What is the number?

Solution: Let the number be x; then

$x^2 - 57^2 = 8010$ $\Rightarrow x^2 = 8010 - 3249 = 4761$

$\therefore x = \sqrt{4761} = 69$

Example 15: The sum of squares of two numbers is 1700 and difference of their squares is 348. Find the numbers.

Solution: Let the two numbers be x and y, then

$x^2 + y^2 = 1700$ ...*(i)*

$x^2 - y^2 = 348$ ...*(ii)*

Solving these two equations, we get $x^2 = 1024$ $\therefore x = 32$

$y^2 = 676$ $\therefore y = 26$

Hence, two numbers are 32 and 26.

Example 16: If the difference between a number and one-fifth of it is 84, what is the number?

Solution: Let the number be x, then

$$x - \frac{x}{5} = 84 \Rightarrow \frac{4x}{5} = 84 \quad \therefore x = \frac{5 \times 84}{4} = 105$$

Example 17: If 10% of a number is subtracted from it, the result is 1800. What is the number?

Solution: Let the number be x, then

$$x - \frac{10}{100}x = 1800$$

$$\Rightarrow \frac{9x}{10} = 1800 \quad \therefore x = \frac{10 \times 1800}{9} = 2000$$

Example 18: Three-fourth of two-third of one-fifth of a number is 15. What is the 50 percent of that number?

Solution: Let the number be x, then

$$\frac{3}{4}\times\frac{2}{3}\times\frac{1}{5}\times x = 15 \quad \Rightarrow \frac{1}{10}x = 15 \quad \therefore x = 10 \times 15 = 150$$

Hence, 50% of the number $= \frac{50}{100}\times 150 = 75$

Example 19: The product of two numbers is 36 times the difference between these two. What is absolute value of sum of these two numbers?

Solution: Let the two numbers be x and y, then

$$xy = 36\,(x - y)$$

Now, $(x + y)^2 = (x - y)^2 + 4xy$

$= (x - y)^2 + 4 \times 36\,(x - y) = (x - y)^2 + 144\,(x - y)$

Hence, the absolute value of $(x - y)$ is not known, so $(x + y)$ can not be determined.

Example 20: The product of a number and its square root is 8. What is the number?

Solution: Let the number be x, then

$x.\sqrt{x} = 8$

$\Rightarrow x^{3/2} = (2^2)^{3/2} \quad \therefore x = 2^2 = 4$

Example 21: If x and y are two such digits in 65 xy such that the number formed is exactly divisible by 80. Then find the value of $x + y$.

Solution: If the number formed by last three digits is divisible by 8 then the number is divisible by 8. If we put $x = 6$, $y = 0$ then the number 6560 is exactly divisible by 80 as 656 is divisible by 8. Hence, sum of the required number $= x + y = 6 + 0 = 6$.

Example 22: The sum of A, B and C is 3800. If A is one-third of B and B is one-fifth of C, then what is the value of C?

Solution: Let C be the x, then B and A will be $\frac{x}{5}$ and $\frac{x}{15}$, then $\frac{x}{15}+\frac{x}{5}+x = 3800$

$$\Rightarrow \frac{19x}{15} = 3800 \quad \therefore x = \frac{15\times 3800}{19} = 3000$$

Hence, C = 3000

Example 23: Of six consecutive numbers the sum of first three is 27. What is the sum of next three?

Solution: Let first three consecutive numbers be x, $(x + 1)$ and $(x + 2)$, then

$x + (x + 1) + (x + 2) = 27 \quad \Rightarrow 3x + 3 = 27 \quad \Rightarrow 3x = 24 \quad \Rightarrow x = 8$

Then, next three consecutive numbers will be $(x + 3)$, $(x + 4)$ & $(x + 5)$

Now, their sum $= x + 3 + x + 4 + x + 5 = 3x + 12 = 3 \times 8 + 12 = 36$

Example 24: Sum of two numbers is equal to sum of their reciprocals. What will be the product of the numbers?

Solution: Let two numbers be x and y, then,

$$x + y = \frac{1}{x}+\frac{1}{y} = \frac{x+y}{xy} \quad \therefore xy = \frac{x+y}{x+y} = 1$$

Hence, product of the numbers = 1

Example 25: The product of two positive numbers is 24. The greater is $1\frac{1}{2}$ times the smaller. What are the numbers?

Solution: Let two numbers be x and $\frac{3}{2}x$; then

$x \times \frac{3}{2}x = 24 \quad \Rightarrow x^2 = \frac{24 \times 2}{3} = 16 \quad \therefore x = 4$

Other number $= \frac{3}{2} \times 4 = 6$

Hence, two numbers = 4, 6

Example 26: The sum of a rational number and its reciprocal is $\frac{13}{6}$. Find the number.

Solution: Let the number be x, then

$x + \frac{1}{x} = \frac{13}{6} \quad \Rightarrow \frac{x^2+1}{x} = \frac{13}{6} \quad \Rightarrow 6x^2 - 13x + 6 = 0$

$\Rightarrow 6x^2 - 9x - 4x + 6 = 0 \quad \Rightarrow 3x(2x - 3) - 2(2x - 3) = 0$

$\Rightarrow (3x - 2)(2x - 3) = 0$

Hence, either $x = \frac{2}{3}$ or, $x = \frac{3}{2}$

Example 27: Find a number such that when 15 is subtracted from 7 times the number, the result is 10 more than twice the number.

Solution: Let the number be x, then

$7x - 15 = 2x + 10 \quad \Rightarrow 5x = 25 \quad \therefore x = 5$

Example 28: If the sum of two numbers is 42 and their product is 437, then find the absolute difference between the numbers?

Solution: Let the two numbers be x and y, then

$x + y = 42, \quad xy = 437$

$(x - y)^2 = (x + 2)^2 - 4xy = (42)^2 - 4 \times 437 = 1764 - 1748 = 16$

$\therefore x - y = \sqrt{16} = 4$

Hence, required difference = 4

Example 29: A fraction becomes $\frac{2}{3}$, when 1 is added to numerator and denominator both. But when 1 is subtracted from numerator and denominator both it becomes $\frac{1}{2}$. Find the fraction?

Solution: Let fraction be $\frac{x}{y}$; then

$\frac{x+1}{y+1} = \frac{2}{3} \quad \Rightarrow 3x + 3 = 2y + 2 \quad \Rightarrow 3x - 2y = -1 \quad ...(i)$

Again, $\frac{x-1}{y-1} = \frac{1}{2} \quad \Rightarrow 2x - 2 = y - 1 \quad \Rightarrow 2x - y = 1 \quad ...(ii)$

Solving equation (i) & (ii) we get $x = 3$ and $y = 5$

Hence, fraction $= \frac{3}{5}$

Example 30: If three numbers are added in pairs, the sums equal to 10, 19 and 21. What are the numbers?

Solution: Let the three numbers are a, b and c, then

$a + b = 10$ ...(i) $b + c = 19$ ...(ii) $a + c = 21$ ...(iii)

Adding all the three equations, we get, $2(a + b + c) = 10 + 19 + 21$

$\Rightarrow a + b + c = 25$ ...(iv)

Subtracting equations *(i)*, *(ii)*, *(iii)* from *(iv)*, we get

$c = 25 - 10 = 15$, $a = 25 - 19 = 6$, $b = 25 - 21 = 4$

Thus, the numbers are 6, 4 and 15.

EXERCISE

1. The difference between the squares of two consecutive numbers is 35. Find the numbers.
   (a) 17, 18 *(b)* 16, 17 *(c)* 18, 19 *(d)* 19 , 20
2. A positive number when decreased by 4, is equal to 21 times the reciprocal of the number. Find the number.
   (a) 6 *(b)* 7 *(c)* 8 *(d)* 5
3. The sum of two numbers is thrice their difference. If smaller number is 10, find the greater number.
   (a) 20 *(b)* 25 *(c)* 30 *(d)* 35
4. If one-fourth of one-third of one-half of a number is 15, find the number.
   (a) 300 *(b)* 360 *(c)* 350 *(d)* 400
5. The sum of the digits of a two-digit number is 8. If the digits are reversed, the number is decreased by 54. Find the number.
   (a) 71 *(b)* 62 *(c)* 53 *(d)* None of these
6. A number whose fifth part increased by 5 is equal to its fourth part diminished by 5. Find the number.
   (a) 150 *(b)* 200 *(c)* 250 *(d)* 300
7. Three numbers are in the ratio of 3 : 4 : 5. The sum of the largest and smallest equals the sum of the third and 52. Find the smallest number.
   (a) 40 *(b)* 45 *(c)* 38 *(d)* 39
8. If 16% of 40% of a number is 8, find the number.
   (a) 200 *(b)* 150 *(c)* 125 *(d)* 100
9. The sum of three numbers is 68. If the ratio between first and second be 2 : 3 and that between second and third be 5 : 3, then find the second number.
   (a) 30 *(b)* 25 *(c)* 35 *(d)* 40
10. The sum of seven numbers is 235. The average of the first three is 23 and that of the last three is 42. Find the fourth number.
    (a) 25 *(b)* 30 *(c)* 35 *(d)* 40
11. The sum of two numbers is 80. If the larger number is 5 more than 4 times the smaller number. Find the numbers.
    (a) 50, 30 *(b)* 45, 35 *(c)* 65, 15 *(d)* 15, 55
12. A two-digit number is 6 times the sum of digits. If 2 is subtracted from unit digit and 1 is subtracted from ten's digit, the number obtained is seven times the sum of digits. Find the number.
    (a) 54 *(b)* 64 *(c)* 78 *(d)* 70

13. If each of the numerator and denominator of a fraction is increased by 1, the fraction obtained is 7/8 and if each of them is decreased by 1, the fraction obtained is 6/7. Find the fraction.
(a) $\frac{13}{14}$ *(b)* $\frac{12}{13}$ *(c)* $\frac{15}{13}$ *(d)* $\frac{13}{15}$

14. The sum of digits of a three-digit number is 10 and the digit in the middle of this three digit number is equal to the sum of the remaining two digits. If the first and the third digits are interchanged, the value of this number increases by 99. Find the number.
(a) 385 *(b)* 253 *(c)* 154 *(d)* 374

15. The difference between a two-digit number and the number obtained by interchanging the position of digits of the number is 27. What is the difference between the digits of that number?
(a) 2 *(b)* 3 *(c)* 4 *(d)* 5

16. The sum of two-digit number is 12 and the difference between the two digits of the two-digit number is 6. What is the two-digit number?
(a) 39 *(b)* 84
(c) 93 *(d)* Cannot be determined

17. A number consists of two-digit, whose sum is 8. If 18 is subtracted from the number the digits interchange their places. The number is:
(a) 44 *(b)* 35 *(c)* 62 *(d)* 53

18. The difference between two-digit number and the number obtained by interchanging the two digits of the number is 9. The sum of the digits of the number is 15. What is the product of the two digits of the two-digit number?
(a) 54 *(b)* 72 *(c)* 56 *(d)* None of these

19. The difference between a two digit number and the number obtained by interchanging the two digits of the same number is 9. The sum of the digits of two-digit number is 17. What is the product of the two digits of the two-digit number?
(a) 64 *(b)* 63 *(c)* 72 *(d)* None of these

20. The product of two consecutive even number is 5328. What is the smaller number?
(a) 70 *(b)* 68 *(c)* 74 *(d)* 72

21. The product of two successive numbers is 6162. Find the larger number.
(a) 78 *(b)* 77 *(c)* 81 *(d)* 79

22. The product of two successive numbers is 3192, what is the smaller number?
(a) 59 *(b)* 58 *(c)* 57 *(d)* 56

23. The multiplication of two consecutive numbers is 8556. What is the smaller number?
(a) 94 *(b)* 92 *(c)* 93 *(d)* 91

24. A number is doubled and 9 is added. If the resultant is trebled it becomes 75. What is such number?
(a) 6 *(b)* 8 *(c)* 3.5 *(d)* None of these

25. A number is decreased by 4 and divided by 6, the result is 8. What would be the result if 2 is subtracted from the number and then it is divided by 5?
(a) 12 *(b)* 11 *(c)* 10 *(d)* 9

26. If the sum of two numbers is 22 and the sum of their squares is 404, then the product of the numbers is:
(a) 88 *(b)* 80 *(c)* 44 *(d)* 40

27. Find a positive number which when increased by 17 is equal to 60 times the reciprocal of the number.
(*a*) 20 (*b*) 17 (*c*) 10 (*d*) 3

28. The sum of a whole number and its reciprocal is one-eighth of 34. What is the product of the number and its square root?
(*a*) 27 (*b*) 32 (*c*) 8 (*d*) None of these

29. Twenty times a positive integer is less than its square by 96. What is the integer?
(*a*) 30 (*b*) 25 (*c*) 24 (*d*) 20

30. If 50 is subtracted from two-third of a number, the result is equal to the sum of 40 and one-fourth of that number? What is the number?
(*a*) 336 (*b*) 246 (*c*) 216 (*d*) 174

31. The sum of one-half and one-fifth of a number exceeds one-third of that number by $7\frac{1}{3}$. What is that number?
(*a*) 30 (*b*) 20 (*c*) 18 (*d*) 15

32. Find the number which when multiplied by 15 is increased by 196.
(*a*) 28 (*b*) 26 (*c*) 20 (*d*) 14

33. Two-third of a positive number and $\frac{25}{216}$ of its reciprocal are equal. What is such number?
(*a*) $\frac{144}{25}$ (*b*) $\frac{25}{144}$ (*c*) $\frac{12}{5}$ (*d*) $\frac{5}{12}$

34. Thrice the square of a natural number is decreased by 4 times the number is equal to 50 more than the number. What is that number?
(*a*) 10 (*b*) 6 (*c*) 5 (*d*) 4

35. If sum of a number and its square is 182. The number is:
(*a*) 28 (*b*) 26 (*c*) 15 (*d*) 13

36. If doubling a number and adding 20 to the result gives the same result as multiplying the number by 8 and taking away 4 from the product. What is the number?
(*a*) 6 (*b*) 4 (*c*) 3 (*d*) 2

37. The sum of two numbers is 40 and their difference is 4. Find the ratio of the numbers.
(*a*) 22 : 9 (*b*) 21 : 19 (*c*) 11 : 18 (*d*) 11 : 9

38. The sum of two numbers is 25 and their difference is 13. What is their product?
(*a*) 325 (*b*) 315 (*c*) 114 (*d*) 104

39. The sum of two numbers is 22. Five times of one number is equal to 6 times the other. Find the greater of the two number.
(*a*) 16 (*b*) 15 (*c*) 12 (*d*) 10

40. The product of two natural numbers is 17. Then find the sum of the reciprocals of their squares.
(*a*) 289 (*b*) $\frac{1}{289}$ (*c*) $\frac{289}{290}$ (*d*) $\frac{290}{289}$

41. If the sum of two numbers is 33 and their difference is 15; what is the smaller number?
(*a*) 18 (*b*) 15 (*c*) 12 (*d*) 9

42. One-fifth of a number is equal to $\frac{5}{8}$ of another number. If 35 is added to the first number, it becomes four times of the second number. Find the second number.
(a) 125 (b) 70 (c) 40 (d) 25

43. The sum of three numbers is 264. If the first number be twice the second and third number be one-third of the first, find the second number.
(a) 84 (b) 72 (c) 54 (d) 48

44. If $2\frac{1}{2}$ is added to a number and the sum multiplied by $4\frac{1}{2}$ and 3 is added to the product and dividing the sum by $1\frac{1}{5}$, the quotient becomes 25. The number is:
(a) $5\frac{1}{2}$ (b) $4\frac{1}{2}$ (c) $3\frac{1}{2}$ (d) $2\frac{1}{2}$

45. The difference between two positive integers is 3. If the sum of their squares is 369. What is the sum of the numbers?
(a) 81 (b) 33 (c) 27 (d) 25

46. The product of two numbers is 120 and the sum of their squares is 289. What is the sum of the numbers?
(a) 23 (b) 69 (c) 20 (d) None of these

47. The sum of two numbers is 40 and their product is 375. The sum of their reciprocals is:
(a) $\frac{75}{8}$ (b) $\frac{75}{4}$ (c) $\frac{8}{75}$ (d) $\frac{1}{40}$

48. If the two numbers are differ by 5 and their product is 336. What is the sum of two numbers?
(a) 51 (b) 37 (c) 28 (d) 21

49. The product of two numbers is 192 and the sum of these two numbers is 28, then the smaller number is:
(a) 18 (b) 16 (c) 14 (d) 12

50. The product of two numbers is 45 and the sum of their squares is 106. What are the numbers?
(a) 45, 1 (b) 5, 19 (c) 5, 9 (d) 3, 5

51. If the sum and difference of two numbers are 20 and 8 respectively. What is the difference of their squares?
(a) 180 (b) 160 (c) 28 (d) 12

52. The product of two numbers is 9375 and the quotient, when the larger one is divided by the smaller, is 15. What is the sum of the numbers?
(a) 425 (b) 400 (c) 395 (d) 380

53. The difference between two integers is 5. Their product is 500. What are the numbers?
(a) 21, 26 (b) 30, 25 (c) 20, 25 (d) 15, 20

54. In a two-digit number, unit's digit exceeds its ten's digit by 2 and that the product of the given number and sum of its digits is equal to 144. What is the number?
(a) 46 (b) 42 (c) 26 (d) 24

55. A two-digit number exceeds the sum of the digits of that number by 18. If the digit at the unit's place is double the digit at the ten's place, then the number is:
(a) 84 (b) 48 (c) 42 (d) 24

56. In a two-digit number, the digit at the unit's place is four times the digit at the ten's place and sum of the digits is equal to 10. The number is:
(a) 28 (b) 82 (c) 14 (d) 41

57. The sum of the squares of three consecutive natural numbers is 2030, the second number is:
(a) 28 (b) 27 (c) 26 (d) 25

58. The sum of three consecutive multiples of 3 is 72. The largest number is:
(a) 36 (b) 27 (c) 24 (d) 21

59. The sum of three consecutive odd numbers is 20 more than the first of these numbers. The second number is:
(a) 13 (b) 11 (c) 9 (d) 7

60. Three times the first of three consecutive odd integers is 3 more than twice the third. What is the third integer?
(a) 15 (b) 13 (c) 11 (d) 9

61. A number of two digits has 3 for its unit's digit, and the sum of digits is $\frac{1}{7}$ of the number itself. What is the number?
(a) 73 (b) 63 (c) 53 (d) 43

62. What is the sum of two consecutive even numbers, the difference of whose squares is 84?
(a) 46 (b) 42 (c) 38 (d) 34

63. The product of three consecutive even numbers when divided by 8 is 720. What is the product of their square roots?
(a) 120 (b) $42\sqrt{10}$ (c) $24\sqrt{10}$ (d) $12\sqrt{10}$

64. The sum of four consecutive even integers is 1284. What is the greatest number?
(a) 326 (b) 324 (c) 322 (d) 320

65. The sum of three consecutive numbers is 87. What is the greatest number?
(a) 30 (b) 29 (c) 28 (d) 26

66. The difference between a two-digit number and the number obtained by interchanging the digits is 36. What is the difference between the sum and the difference of the digits of the number if the ratio between the digits of the number is 1 : 2?
(a) 16 (b) 8 (c) 6 (d) 4

67. The sum of the digits of a two-digit number is $\frac{1}{5}$ of the difference between the number and the number obtained by interchanging the positions of the digits. Then the difference between the digits of that number is:
(a) 7 (b) 9 (c) 5 (d) Data inadequate

68. The difference between a two-digit number and the number obtained by interchanging the positions of its digits is 36. The difference of the two digits of the number is:
(a) 9 (b) 5 (c) 4 (d) 3

69. A number consists of two digits. If the digits interchange places and the new number is added to the original number, then the resulting number will be divisible by:
(a) 11 (b) 9 (c) 5 (d) 3

70. The difference between the numerator and the denominator of a fraction is 5. If 5 is added to its denominator, the fraction is decreased by $1\frac{1}{4}$. The fraction is:

(a) $\frac{1}{4}$ (b) $3\frac{1}{4}$ (c) $2\frac{1}{4}$ (d) $1\frac{1}{4}$

71. In a pair of fractions, fraction A is twice the fraction B and the product of two fractions is $\frac{2}{25}$. The fraction A is:

(a) $\frac{3}{5}$ (b) $\frac{2}{5}$ (c) $\frac{1}{5}$ (d) $\frac{1}{25}$

72. In a two-digit number the product of the digits is 8. When 18 is added to the number, then the digits are reversed. What is the number?

(a) 81 (b) 42 (c) 24 (d) 18

73. In a two-digit number, the digit at the unit's place is more than twice the digit at the ten's place by 1. If the digits at the unit's place and ten's place are interchanged, the difference between the newly formed number and the original number is less than the original number by 1. The original number is:

(a) 73 (b) 49 (c) 37 (d) 25

74. A number consists of two digits such that the digit at the ten's place is less by 2 than the digit in the unit's place. Three times the number added to 6/7 times the number obtained by reversing the digits equals 108, what is the sum of the digits of the number?

(a) 9 (b) 8 (c) 7 (d) 6

75. The denominator of a fraction is 3 more than the numerator. If the numerator as well as the denominator is increased by 4, the fraction becomes $\frac{4}{5}$. The original fraction is:

(a) $\frac{7}{10}$ (b) $\frac{10}{13}$ (c) $\frac{5}{8}$ (d) $\frac{8}{11}$

76. The product of two fractions is $\frac{14}{15}$ and their quotient is $\frac{35}{24}$. What is the greater fraction?

(a) $\frac{7}{3}$ (b) $\frac{7}{4}$ (c) $\frac{7}{6}$ (d) $\frac{4}{5}$

77. A two-digit number is three times the sum of its digits and if 45 is added to it, the digits are reversed. What is the number?

(a) 72 (b) 32 (c) 27 (d) 23

78. The digit at the unit's place of a number is equal to the digit at the ten's place of half of that number and the digit at the ten's place of that number is less than the digit at unit's place of half of the number by 1. The sum of the digits of the number is 7. Then number is:

(a) 43 (b) 52 (c) 34 (d) 25

79. The sum of squares of three numbers is 138, while the sum of their products taken to at a time is 131. What is their sum?

(a) 35 (b) 30 (c) 25 (d) 20

80. If the numerator of a fraction is increased by 2 and the denominator is increased by 3, the fraction becomes $\frac{7}{9}$ and if both the numerator as well as the denominator are decreased by 1, the fraction becomes $\frac{4}{5}$. The original fraction is:

(a) $\frac{17}{21}$ (b) $\frac{13}{16}$ (c) $\frac{9}{11}$ (d) $\frac{5}{6}$

81. The numerator and denominator of a fraction are in the ratio of 2 : 3. If 6 is subtracted from the numerator, the result is a fraction that has value $\frac{2}{3}$ of the original fraction. What is the numerator of the original fraction?

(a) 36 (b) 27 (c) 18 (d) 6

82. The sum of four numbers is 64. If you add 3 to the first number, 3 is subtracted from the second number, the third is multiplied by 3 and the fourth is divided by 3, then all the results are equal. The difference between the largest and the smallest of the original number is:

(a) 32 (b) 30 (c) 27 (d) 21

83. If 1 is added to the denominator of a fraction, the fraction becomes $\frac{1}{2}$. If 1 is added to the numerator of the fraction, the fraction becomes 1. What is the fraction?

(a) $\frac{3}{2}$ (b) $\frac{3}{4}$ (c) $\frac{2}{3}$ (d) $\frac{1}{3}$

84. What is the greater of the two numbers whose product is 640, if the sum of the two numbers exceeds their difference by 32?

(a) 45 (b) 50 (c) 55 (d) 40

85. The product of two consecutive odd numbers is 1763. What is the larger number?

(a) 43 (b) 39 (c) 41 (d) 37

86. The sum of the squares of 2 numbers is 146 and the square root of one of them is $\sqrt{5}$. The cube of the other number is:

(a) 1111 (b) 1221 (c) 1331 (d) 1441

87. If $(12)^3$ is subtracted from the square of a number, the result so obtained is 976. What is the number?

(a) 58 (b) 56 (c) 54 (d) 52

88. If $(26)^2$ is subtracted from square of a number, the result so obtained is 549. What is the number?

(a) 35 (b) 33 (c) 29 (d) 41

89. When the digits of the two-digits number are interchanged, the number so obtained is less than the original number by 54. If in the original number the digit at the unit's place is one-fourth of the digit at the ten's place. Find the original number?

(a) 62 (b) 41 (c) 28 (d) 82

90. Two numbers are such that their sum is 16 and their product is 55. What is the sum of their reciprocals?

(a) $\frac{27}{55}$ (b) $\frac{16}{55}$ (c) $\frac{37}{45}$ (d) $\frac{38}{85}$

91. The sum of squares of two numbers is 80 and square of difference between the two numbers is 36. What is the product of two numbers?

(a) 11 (b) 22 (c) 33 (d) 26

92. The double of a positive whole number is 50 times the value of its reciprocal. What is the number?
(a) 20 (b) 10 (c) 5 (d) 2

93. Two numbers are such that their product, their sum and their difference are in the ratio of 6 : 2 : 1 respectively. Their sum is:
(a) 16 (b) 20 (c) 24 (d) 30

EXPLANATORY ANSWERS

1. Let the two consecutive numbers be x and $(x + 1)$.
Then $(x + 1)^2 - x^2 = 35 \Rightarrow x^2 + 2x + 1 - x^2 = 35$
$\Rightarrow 2x = 34 \quad \therefore \quad x = 17$
Hence, numbers are 17, 18

2. Let the positive number be x, then

$$(x - 4) = 21 \times \frac{1}{x} \Rightarrow x^2 - 4x - 21 = 0$$
$$\Rightarrow x^2 - 7x + 3x - 21 = 0 \Rightarrow x(x - 7) + 3(x - 7) = 0$$
$$\Rightarrow (x + 3)(x - 7) = 0$$

Either, $x = -3$ (Impossible) or, $x = 7$
Hence, number = 7

3. Let the greater number be x, then
$$x + 10 = 3(x - 10) \Rightarrow 2x = 40 \therefore x = 20$$

4. Let the number be x, then,
$$\frac{1}{4} \times \frac{1}{3} \times \frac{1}{2} x = 15 \Rightarrow x = 15 \times 24 = 360$$

5. Let the two-digit number be $10x + y$, then
$$x + y = 8 \quad ...(i)$$
And also, $10x + y - (10y + x) = 54 \Rightarrow 9x - 9y = 54 \quad \therefore \quad x - y = 6 \quad ...(ii)$
Solving equations (i) & (ii), we get $x = 7$, $y = 1$
Then number = $10 \times 7 + 1 = 71$

6. Let the number be x, then
$$\frac{x}{5} + 5 = \frac{x}{4} - 5 \Rightarrow \frac{x}{4} - \frac{x}{5} = 10 \Rightarrow \frac{x}{20} = 10 \quad \therefore \quad x = 200$$

7. Let the three numbers be $3x$, $4x$ and $5x$ respectively;
Then, $3x + 5x = 4x + 52 \Rightarrow 4x = 52 \quad \therefore \quad x = 13$
Hence, the smallest number = $3 \times 13 = 39$

8. Let the number be x, then
$$\frac{16}{100} \times \frac{40}{100} \times x = 8 \Rightarrow \frac{8}{125} \times x = 8 \quad \therefore \quad x = 125$$

9. Let three numbers be a, b, c then,
$$a : b = 2 : 3 \text{ and } b : c = 5 : 3$$
Hence, $a : b : c = 10 : 15 : 9$
$$\text{The second number} = \frac{15}{34} \times 68 = 30$$

10. Fourth number $= 235 - (3 \times 23 + 3 \times 42) = 235 - 195 = 40$

11. Let the smaller number be x, then larger will be $4x + 5$, then
$x + 4x + 5 = 80 \quad \Rightarrow 5x = 75 \quad \therefore \quad x = 15 \ \& \ 4x + 5 = 65$

12. Let the two-digit number be $10x + y$, then
$10x + y = 6(x + y) \quad \Rightarrow \quad 4x - 5y = 0$ ...(i)
And also, $10(x - 1) + (y - 2) = 7(x - 1 + y - 2)$
$\Rightarrow \quad 10x + y - 12 = 7x + 7y - 21$
$\Rightarrow \quad 3x - 6y = -9$
$\Rightarrow \quad x - 2y = -3$ ...(ii)
Solving equations (i) & (ii) we get $x = 5$ and $y = 4$
Hence, number $= 10 \times 5 + 4 = 54$

13. Let the fraction be $\frac{x}{y}$, then

$\frac{x+1}{y+1} = \frac{7}{8} \quad \Rightarrow 8x + 8 = 7y + 7 \quad \Rightarrow 8x - 7y = -1$ ...(i)

Again, $\frac{x-1}{y-1} = \frac{6}{7} \quad \Rightarrow 7x - 7 = 6y - 6 \quad \Rightarrow 7x - 6y = 1$ ...(ii)

Solving equations (i) and (ii) we get $x = 13$ and $y = 15$

$\therefore$ Fraction $= \frac{13}{15}$

14. Let the three-digit number be $100x + 10y + z$, then
$x + y + z = 10$ ...(i) $\quad x + z = y$ ...(ii)
From equations (i) & (ii) we get, $y = 5$ and $x + z = 5$ ...(iii)
Again, $100z + 10y + x - (100x + 10y + z) = 99$
$\Rightarrow \quad 99z - 99x = 99 \quad \therefore \quad z - x = 1$ ...(iv)
Solving (iii) and (iv), we get $x = 2$, $z = 3$.
Hence, number $= 100 \times 2 + 10 \times 5 + 3 = 253$

15. Let the two-digit number be $10x + y$, then
$10x + y - (10y + x) = 27 \quad \Rightarrow 9x - 9y = 27 \quad \Rightarrow x - y = 3$

16. Let the two number be $10x + y$, then
$x + y = 12$ ...(i) & also $x - y = 6$ or, $y - x = 6$ ...(ii)
Solving these equations, we get the numbers 93 or 39
Hence, single value of the number cannot be determined.

17. Let the two-digit number be $10x + y$, then, $x + y = 8$ ...(i)
And also, $10x + y - 18 = 10y + x \quad \Rightarrow 9x - 9y = 18 \quad \therefore x - y = 2$ ...(ii)
Solving these two equations, we get $x = 5$ and $y = 3$
Hence, number $= 10 \times 5 + 3 = 53$

18. Let the two-digit number be $10x + y$; then $x + y = 15$ ...(i)
And, $10x + y - 9 = 10y + x \quad \Rightarrow \quad 9x - 9y = 9 \quad \therefore \quad x - y = 1$ ...(ii)
Solving (i) and (ii) we get $x = 8$ and $y = 7$
Hence, their product $= 8 \times 7 = 56$

19. Let the two digit number be $10x + y$; then

$x + y = 17$ ...(i)

And $10x + y - 10y - x = 9 \Rightarrow 9x - 9y = 9 \quad \therefore x - y = 1$ ...(ii)

Solving these two equations, we get $x = 9$ and $y = 8$

Hence, their product $= 9 \times 8 = 72$

20. Let the two consecutive even numbers are x and $(x + 2)$

Then, $x(x + 2) = 5328 \Rightarrow x^2 + 2x - 5328 = 0$

$\Rightarrow x^2 + 74x - 72x - 5328 \Rightarrow x(x + 74) - 72(x + 74) = 0$

$\Rightarrow (x - 72)(x + 74) = 0$

$\therefore x = 72$ (Taking positive value only)

Hence, smaller number = 72

21. Let the two successive numbers be x and $(x + 1)$; then

$x(x + 1) = 6162 \Rightarrow x^2 + x - 6162 = 0 \Rightarrow (x + 79)(x - 78) = 0$

$\therefore x = 78$ (Taking positive value only)

Hence, larger number = 78 + 1 = 79

22. Let the two successive numbers be x and $(x + 1)$; then

$x(x + 1) = 3192 \Rightarrow x^2 + x - 3192 = 0 \Rightarrow (x + 57)(x - 56) = 0$

$\therefore x = 56$ (Taking positive value only)

Hence, smaller number = 56

23. Let the two successive numbers be x and $(x + 1)$; then

$x(x + 1) = 8556 \Rightarrow x^2 + x - 8556 = 0 \Rightarrow (x + 93)(x - 92) = 0$

$\therefore x = 92$ (Taking positive value only)

Hence, smaller number = 92

24. Let the number be x; then

$3(2x + 9) = 75 \Rightarrow 2x + 9 = 25 \Rightarrow 2x = 16 \quad \therefore x = 8$

25. Let the number be x; then

$$\frac{x-4}{6} = 8 \Rightarrow x - 4 = 48 \quad \therefore x = 52$$

Hence, required number $= \dfrac{52-2}{5} = 10$

26. Let the two numbers be x and y; then

$x + y = 22$ ...(i) $\quad x^2 + y^2 = 404$ ...(ii)

Now, $(x + y)^2 = x^2 + y^2 + 2xy$

$$\Rightarrow (22)^2 = 404 + 2xy \Rightarrow 2xy = 484 - 404 \quad \therefore xy = \frac{80}{2} = 40$$

Hence, product of the number = 40

27. Let the positive number be x; then

$$(x + 17) = 60 \times \frac{1}{x} \Rightarrow x^2 + 17x - 60 = 0$$

$(x + 20)(x - 3) = 0 \quad \therefore x = 3$ (only positive value)

Hence, number = 3

28. Let the whole number be x; then

$$x + \frac{1}{x} = \frac{1}{8} \times 34 \Rightarrow \frac{x^2+1}{x} = \frac{17}{4} \Rightarrow 4x^2 - 17x + 4 = 0$$

$\Rightarrow (4x - 1)(x - 4) = 0$ $\quad \therefore x = 4$ (whole number)

Hence, required product = $4 \times \sqrt{4} = 4 \times 2 = 8$

29. Let the positive integer be x; then

$x^2 - 20x = 96 \Rightarrow x^2 - 20x - 96 = 0 \Rightarrow (x + 4)(x - 24) = 0$

$\therefore$ $x = 24$ (A positive value)

30. Let the number be x; then

$$\frac{2}{3}x - 50 = \frac{x}{4} + 40 \Rightarrow \frac{2}{3}x - \frac{x}{4} = 90 \Rightarrow \frac{5x}{12} = 90 \quad \therefore x = \frac{90 \times 12}{5} = 216$$

31. Let the number be x; then

$$\left(\frac{x}{2} + \frac{x}{5}\right) = \frac{x}{3} + \frac{22}{3} \Rightarrow \frac{7x}{10} - \frac{x}{3} = \frac{22}{3} \Rightarrow \frac{11x}{30} = \frac{22}{3} \quad \therefore x = \frac{30 \times 22}{3 \times 11} = 20$$

32. Let the number be x; then

$15x = x + 196 \Rightarrow 14x = 196 \quad \therefore x = 14$

33. Let the positive number be x; then

$$\frac{2}{3}x = \frac{25}{216} \times \frac{1}{x} \Rightarrow x^2 = \frac{25 \times 3}{2 \times 216} = \frac{25}{144} \quad \therefore x = \frac{5}{12}$$

34. Let the natural number be x; then

$3x^2 - 4x = x + 50 \Rightarrow 3x^2 - 5x - 50 = 0 \Rightarrow (3x + 10)(x - 5)$

$\therefore$ $x = 5$ (A natural number)

35. Let the number be x; then

$x^2 + x = 182 \Rightarrow x^2 + x - 182 = 0 \Rightarrow (x + 14)(x - 13) = 0$

$\Rightarrow x = 13$ (A positive value)

36. Let the number be x; then

$2x + 20 = 8x - 4 \Rightarrow 6x = 24 \quad \therefore x = 4$

37. Let the two numbers be x and y; then

$x + y = 40$ ...(i) $\quad x - y = 4$ ...(ii)

Solving these two equations, we get, $x = 22$ and $y = 18$

Hence, required ratio = 22 : 18 = 11 : 9

38. Let the two numbers be x and y; then

$x + y = 25$ ...(i) $\quad x - y = 13$ ...(ii)

Solving these two equations, we get, $x = 19$, $y = 6$

Hence, their product = $19 \times 6 = 114$

39. Let the two numbers be x and y; then

$x + y = 22$ ...(i) $\quad 5x = 6y \Rightarrow x = \frac{6}{5}y$ ...(ii)

Now from equations (i) and (ii)

$\frac{6}{5}y + y = 22 \Rightarrow \frac{11y}{5} = 22 \quad \therefore \; y = 10$ and $x = \frac{6}{5} \times 10 = 12$

Hence, greater number = 12

40. Let the two numbers are x and y;
then $xy = 17$ then only possible value of x and y are 17 and 1.

Then, $\frac{1}{x^2} + \frac{1}{y^2} = \frac{1}{289} + 1 = \frac{290}{289}$

41. Let the two numbers be x and y; then

$x + y = 33$ ...(i) $\qquad x - y = 15$ ...(ii)

Solving these two equations, we get $x = 24$ & $y = 9$.
Hence, smaller number = 9

42. Let the two numbers be x and y; then

$\frac{1}{5}x = \frac{5}{8}y \quad \therefore \; x = \frac{25}{8}y$ ...(i)

And $x + 35 = 4y \Rightarrow 4y - \frac{25}{8}y = 35 \Rightarrow \frac{7y}{8} = 35 \quad \therefore \; y = \frac{8 \times 35}{7} = 40$

Hence, second number = 40

43. Let the second number be x, then first and third will be $2x$ and $\frac{2}{3}x$

Then, $2x + x + \frac{2}{3}x = 264 \Rightarrow \frac{11x}{3} = 264 \quad \therefore \; x = \frac{3 \times 264}{11} = 72$

44. Let the number be x; then

$$\frac{\frac{9}{2}\left(x + \frac{5}{2}\right) + 3}{6/5} = 25 \Rightarrow \frac{9}{2}\left(\frac{2x+5}{2}\right) + 3 = 30$$

$$\Rightarrow \frac{9}{2}\left(\frac{2x+5}{2}\right) = 27 \Rightarrow 2x + 5 = \frac{27 \times 4}{9}$$

$$\Rightarrow 2x = 12 - 5 \quad \therefore \quad x = \frac{7}{2} = 3\frac{1}{2}$$

45. Let the two positive integers be x and y; then

$x - y = 3$ ...*(i)* $\qquad x^2 + y^2 = 369$ ...*(ii)*

Now, $(x - y)^2 = x^2 + y^2 - 2xy$

$\Rightarrow \; (3)^2 = 369 - 2xy \Rightarrow 2xy = 360 \quad \therefore \; xy = 180$

Again, $(x + y)^2 = (x - y)^2 + 4xy = (3)^2 + 4 \times 180 = 729$

$\therefore \; x + y = \sqrt{729} = 27$

46. Let two numbers be x and y; then

$xy = 120$ ...*(i)* $\qquad x^2 + y^2 = 289$ ...*(ii)*

Now, $(x + y)^2 = x^2 + y^2 + 2xy = 289 + 2 \times 120 = 529$

$\therefore \; x + y = \sqrt{529} = 23$

47. Let the two numbers be x and y; then

$x + y = 40$ ...(i) $xy = 375$ ...(ii)

From equations (i) & (ii)

$$\frac{x+y}{xy} = \frac{40}{375} \Rightarrow \frac{1}{x} + \frac{1}{y} = \frac{8}{75}$$

48. Let the two numbers be x and y; then

$x - y = 5$ ...(i) $xy = 336$ ...(ii)

Now, $(x + y)^2 = (x - y)^2 + 4xy = (5)^2 + 4 \times 336 = 1369$

$\therefore$ $(x + y) = \sqrt{1369} = 37$

49. Let the two numbers be x and y; then

$xy = 192$ ...*(i)* $x + y = 28$ ...(ii)

$(x - y)^2 = (x + y)^2 - 4xy = (28)^2 - 4 \times 192 = 784 - 768 = 16$

$\therefore$ $x - y = 4$ ...(iii)

Solving equations *(ii)* and *(iii)* we get $x = 16$, $y = 12$.

Hence, smaller number = 12

50. Let the two numbers be x and y; then

$xy = 45$ ...(i) $x^2 + y^2 = 106$ ...(ii)

$(x + y)^2 = x^2 + y^2 + 2xy = 106 + 2 \times 45 = 196$

$\therefore$ $x + y = 14$ ...(iii)

Now, $(x - y)^2 = x^2 + y^2 - 2xy = 106 - 2 \times 45 = 16$

$\therefore$ $(x - y) = 4$ ...(iv)

Solving equations (iii) and (iv), we get $x = 9$ and $y = 5$

Hence, numbers are 9, 5.

51. Let two numbers be x and y; then

$x + y = 20$ ...(i) $x - y = 8$ ...(ii)

$x^2 - y^2 = (x + y)(x - y) = 20 \times 8 = 160$

52. Let the two numbers are x and y; then

$xy = 9375$ ...(i) $\frac{x}{y} = 15$ $\therefore x = 15y$ ...(ii)

Now from equations (i) and (ii), we get

$$15y \times y = 9375 \Rightarrow y^2 = \frac{9375}{15} \quad \therefore \; y = \sqrt{625} = 25$$

Then, $x = 15 \times 25 = 375$

Hence, $x + y = 375 + 25 = 400$

53. Let the two numbers be x and y; then

$x - y = 5$ ...(i) $xy = 500$ ...(ii)

$(x + y)^2 = (x - y)^2 + 4xy = (5)^2 + 4 \times 500 = 2025$

$\therefore$ $(x + y) = \sqrt{2025} = 45$ ...(iii)

Solving equations (i) and (iii), we get $x = 25$ and $y = 20$

Hence, numbers are 20 and 25

54. Let the ten's place digit and unit's place digit be x and $x + 2$.
Then, number $= 10x + x + 2 = 11x + 2$;
Sum of the digits $= x + x + 2 = 2x + 2$
Now, $(11x + 2)(2x + 2) = 144$ $\Rightarrow 22x^2 + 26x + 4 = 144$
$\Rightarrow 11x^2 + 13x - 70 = 0$ $\Rightarrow (x - 2)(11x + 35) = 0$
Hence, $x = 2$
$\therefore$ Number $= 10 \times 2 + 2 + 2 = 24$

55. Let the digits at unit's and ten's places be $2x$ and x; then
$(10 \times x + 2x) - (x + 2x) = 18$ $\Rightarrow 12x - 3x = 18$
$\Rightarrow 9x = 18$ $\therefore x = 2$
Hence, number $= 10 \times 2 + 4 = 24$

56. Let the digits at ten's and unit's places be x and $4x$;
then, $x + 4x = 10 \Rightarrow x = 2$
Hence, number $= 10 \times 2 + 8 = 28$

57. Let three consecutive natural numbers be x, $(x + 1)$ and $(x + 2)$;
then, $x^2 + (x + 1)^2 + (x + 2)^2 = 2030$
$\Rightarrow x^2 + x^2 + 2x + 1 + x^2 + 4x + 4 = 2030$ $\Rightarrow 3x^2 + 6x - 2025 = 0$
$\Rightarrow x^2 + 2x - 675 = 0$ $\Rightarrow (x + 27)(x - 25) = 0$
Hence, $x = 25$
$\therefore$ Second number $= 25 + 1 = 26$

58. Let the three consecutive multiples of 3 are $3x$, $3(x + 1)$ and $3(x + 2)$
then, $3x + 3(x + 1) + 3(x + 2) = 72$
$\Rightarrow 9x + 9 = 72$ $\Rightarrow 9x = 63$
$\therefore x = 7$
Hence, largest number $= 3(7 + 2) = 3 \times 9 = 27$

59. Let the three consecutive odd numbers be $(x + 1)$, $(x + 2)$ and $(x + 5)$
then, $x + 1 + x + 3 + x + 5 = x + 1 + 20$
$\Rightarrow 2x + 8 = 20$ $\therefore x = 6$
Hence, the second number $= 6 + 3 = 9$

60. Let the three consecutive odd numbers be $(x + 1)$, $(x + 3)$, $(x + 5)$;
then, $3(x + 1) = 2(x + 5) + 3 \Rightarrow x = 10$
Hence, third number $= 10 + 5 = 15$

61. Let the digit at the ten's place be x;
then, number $= 10x + 3$
Now, $x + 3 = \frac{1}{7}(10x + 3)$ $\Rightarrow 7x + 21 = 10x + 3$ $\Rightarrow 3x = 18$
$\therefore x = 6$
Hence, number $= 10 \times 6 + 3 = 63$

62. Let the two consecutive even numbers be x and $(x + 2)$;
then, $(x + 2)^2 - x^2 = 84$ $\Rightarrow x^2 + 4x + 4 - x^2 = 84$ $\Rightarrow 4x = 80$ $\therefore x = 20$
Hence, $x + x + 2 = 2x + 2 = 2 \times 20 + 2 = 42$

63. Product of their square root $= \sqrt{8 \times 720} = 4 \times 6\sqrt{10} = 24\sqrt{10}$

64. Let the four consecutive even numbers are x, $x + 2$, $x + 4$, $x + 6$; then

$x + x + 2 + x + 4 + x + 6 = 1284 \quad \Rightarrow 4x = 1272 \quad \therefore \Rightarrow x = 318$

Hence, the greatest number = 318 + 6 = 324

65. Let the three consecutive numbers be x, $x + 1$ and $x + 2$; then

$x + x + 1 + x + 2 = 87 \quad \Rightarrow 3x = 84 \quad \Rightarrow x = 28$

Hence, the greatest number = 28 + 2 = 30

66. Let the digits at the ten's place and unit's place be $2x$ and x;

then, $10 \times 2x + x - 10 \times x + 2x = 36 \quad \Rightarrow 9x = 36 \quad \therefore x = 4$

Hence, the required difference = $(2x + x) - (2x - x) = 2x = 2 \times 4 = 8$

67. Let the number be $10x + y$; then

$x + y = \frac{1}{5}(10x + y - 10y - x) \quad \Rightarrow 5x + 5y = 9x - 9y \quad \therefore (x - y) = \frac{5}{9}(x + y)$

Hence, value of $(x + y)$ is not known so $(x - y)$ cannot be determined.

68. Let the number be $10x + y$;

then, $10x + y - 10y - x = 36 \quad \Rightarrow 9(x - y) = 36 \quad \therefore (x - y) = 4$

69. Let the number be $10x + y$; then

$10x + y + 10y + x = 11(x + y)$

Hence, resulting number will be divisible by 11.

70. Let the numerator and denominater be $x + 5$ and x; then

$\frac{x+5}{x+5} = \frac{x+5}{x} - \frac{5}{4} \quad \Rightarrow \frac{x+5}{x} = 1 + \frac{5}{4} \quad \Rightarrow \frac{x+5}{x} = \frac{9}{4}$

$\Rightarrow 4x + 20 = 9x \quad \Rightarrow 5x + 20 \quad \therefore x = 4$

Hence, fraction = $\frac{x+5}{x} = \frac{9}{4} = 2\frac{1}{4}$

71. Let the fraction B and A be x and $2x$; then

$x \times 2x = \frac{2}{25} \quad \Rightarrow x^2 = \frac{1}{25} \quad \therefore x = \frac{1}{5}$

Hence, fraction A = $2x = \frac{2}{5}$

72. Let the number be $10x + y$; then

$xy = 8$ ...(i)

Also, $10x + y + 18 = 10y + x \quad \Rightarrow 9(x - y) = -18 \quad \therefore x - y = -2$ ...(ii)

Now, $(x + y)^2 = (x - y)^2 + 4xy = (-2)^2 + 4 \times 8 = 36$

$\therefore \quad x + y = 6$ ...(iii)

Solving the equations (ii) and (iii) we gét, $x = 2$ and $y = 4$

Hence, number = $10 \times 2 + 4 = 24$

73. Let digits at the ten's place and unit's place be x and $(2x + 1)$;

then, $10(2x + 1) + x - 10x - 2x - 1 = 10x + 2x + 1 - 1$

$\Rightarrow \quad 9x + 9 = 12x \quad \Rightarrow 3x = 9 \quad \therefore x = 3 \ \&\ 2x + 1 = 7$

Hence, number = $10 \times 3 + 7 = 37$

74. Let digits at unit's place and ten's place be x and $x - 2$, then

$$3[10\,(x-2) + x] + \frac{6}{7}[10x + x - 2] = 108$$

$$\Rightarrow \quad 33x - 60 + \frac{6}{7}(11x - 2) = 108 \Rightarrow \frac{231x + 66x - 12}{7} = 168$$

$$\Rightarrow \quad 297x = 1176 + 12 \qquad \Rightarrow x = \frac{1188}{297} = 4$$

Hence, sum of the digits = $x + x - 2 = 2x - 2 = 2 \times 4 - 2 = 6$

75. Let the numerator and denominator be x and $x + 3$; then

$$\frac{x+4}{x+3+4} = \frac{4}{5} \quad \Rightarrow \frac{x+4}{x+7} = \frac{4}{5}$$

$\Rightarrow 5x + 20 = 4x + 28 \qquad \therefore x = 8$

Hence, fraction = $\dfrac{x}{x+3} = \dfrac{8}{11}$

76. Let the two fraction be x and y; then

$$xy = \frac{14}{15} \quad ...(i) \qquad \frac{x}{y} = \frac{35}{24} \quad ...(ii)$$

Now from equations (i) and (ii)

$$xy \times \frac{x}{y} = \frac{14}{15} \times \frac{35}{24} \qquad \Rightarrow \quad x^2 = \frac{49}{36} \qquad \therefore \; x = \frac{7}{6}$$

Hence, greater fraction = $\dfrac{7}{6}$

77. Let the number be $10x + y$ then

$10x + y = 3\,(x + y) \qquad \Rightarrow 7x - 2y = 0 \qquad ...(i)$

Also, $10x + y + 45 = 10y + x \qquad \Rightarrow 9x - 9y = -45 \qquad \therefore x - y = -5 \quad ...(ii)$

Solving equations (i) and (ii) we get, $x = 2$ and $y = 7$

Hence, number = $10 \times 2 + 7 = 27$

78. Let the number be $10x + y$; then

$$\frac{10x+y}{2} = 10y + (x + 1) \qquad \Rightarrow 10x + y = 20y + 2x + 2 \qquad \Rightarrow 8x - 19y = 2 \; ...(i)$$

Also, $x + y = 7$ ..(ii)

Solving equations (i) and (ii) we get $x = 5$ and $y = 2$

Hence, number = $10 \times 5 + 2 = 52$

79. Let the three numbers be x, y and z; then,

$x^2 + y^2 + z^2 = 138 \quad ...(i) \qquad xy + yz + zx = 131 \quad ...(ii)$

Then, $(x + y + z)^2 = x^2 + y^2 + z^2 + 2(xy + yz + zx) = 138 + 2 \times 131 = 400$

$$\therefore \quad x + y + z = \sqrt{400} = 20$$

80. Let the original fraction = $\frac{x}{y}$; then

$\frac{x+2}{y+3}=\frac{7}{9} \Rightarrow 9x + 18 = 7y + 21 \Rightarrow 9x - 7y = 3$ ...(i)

Again, $\frac{x-1}{y-1}=\frac{4}{5} \Rightarrow 5x - 5 = 4y - 4 \Rightarrow 5x - 4y = 1$ ...(ii)

Solving equations (i) and (ii) we get, $x = 5$ and $y = 6$

Hence, fraction = $\frac{x}{y}=\frac{5}{6}$

81. Let the original numerator and denominator be $2x$ and $3x$;

then, $\frac{2x-6}{3x}=\frac{2}{3}\times\frac{2}{3} \Rightarrow \frac{x-3}{x}=\frac{2}{3} \Rightarrow 3x - 9 = 2x \therefore x = 9$

Hence, required numerator = $2 \times 9 = 18$

82. Let the four numbers be a, b, c and d; then

$a + 3 = b - 3 = 3c = \frac{d}{3}$

Hence, $b = a + 6$; $c = \frac{a+3}{3}$; $d = 3(a + 3) = 3a + 9$

Again, $a + b + c + d = 64 \Rightarrow a + a + 6 + \frac{a+3}{3} + 3a + 9 = 64$

$\Rightarrow 5a + \frac{a+3}{3} = 49 \Rightarrow \frac{16a+3}{3} = 49 \Rightarrow 16a = 147 - 3$

$\therefore a = \frac{144}{16} = 9$

Hence, $d - c = 3a + 9 - \frac{a+3}{3} = \frac{8a+24}{3} = \frac{8\times9+24}{3} = \frac{96}{3} = 32$

83. Let fraction be $\frac{x}{y}$; then

$\frac{x}{y+1}=\frac{1}{2} \Rightarrow 2x = y + 1 \Rightarrow 2x - y = 1$ ...(i)

Again, $\frac{x+1}{y}=1 \Rightarrow x - y = -1$ ...(ii)

Solving equations (i) and (ii) we get $x = 2$ and $y = 3$

Hence, fraction = $\frac{2}{3}$

84. Let the two numbers be x and y; then

$xy = 640$ ...(i)

Also, $(x+y)-(x-y)=32 \Rightarrow 2y = 32 \Rightarrow y = 16$

From equation *(i)*, $x = \frac{640}{y} = \frac{640}{16} = 40$

85. Let the two consecutive odd numbers be $(x + 1)$ and $(x + 3)$;
Then, $(x + 1)(x + 3) = 1763$ $\Rightarrow x^2 + 4x + 3 = 1763$
$\Rightarrow x^2 + 4x - 1760 = 0$ $\Rightarrow (x + 44)(x - 40) = 0$
Hence, $x = 40$
$\therefore$ Larger number $= 40 + 3 = 43$

86. One number $= \left(\sqrt{5}\right)^2 = 5$
Let other number be x; then
$x^2 + 5^2 = 146 \Rightarrow x^2 = 121 \therefore x = 11$
Hence, $x^3 = (11)^3 = 1331$

87. Let the number be x; then,
$x^2 - 12^3 = 976 \Rightarrow x^2 = 1728 + 976$
$\therefore x = \sqrt{2704} = 52$

88. Let the number be x; then
$x^2 - (26)^2 = 549 \Rightarrow x^2 = 549 + 676 \therefore x = \sqrt{1225} = 35$

89. Let the digits at unit's and ten's place be x and $4x$; then
$10 \times 4x + x - 10x - 4x = 54 \Rightarrow 27x = 54 \quad \therefore x = 2$
Hence, required number $= 10 \times 4x + x = 41x = 41 \times 2 = 82$

90. Let the two numbers be x and y; then
$x + y = 16$ ...(i) $xy = 55$ ...(ii)
Hence, $\frac{x+y}{xy} = \frac{16}{55} \quad \therefore \frac{1}{x} + \frac{1}{y} = \frac{16}{55}$

91. Let the two numbers be x and y; then
$x^2 + y^2 = 80$ ...(i)
$(x - y)^2 = 36$ ...(ii)
Now, $(x - y)^2 = x^2 + y^2 - 2xy$
$\Rightarrow 36 = 80 - 2xy \Rightarrow 2xy = 44 \therefore xy = 22$

92. Let the positive whole number be x; then
$2x = 50 \times \frac{1}{x} \Rightarrow x^2 = 25 \Rightarrow x = 5$

93. Let the two numbers be x and y; then
$xy : (x + y) : (x - y) = 6 : 2 : 1$
Now, $\frac{x-y}{x+y} = \frac{1}{2} \Rightarrow 2x - 2y = x + y \Rightarrow x = 3y,$
$x + y = 3y + y = 4y$ & $xy = 3y.y = 3y^2$
Now, $\frac{x+y}{xy} = \frac{2}{6} \Rightarrow \frac{4y}{3y^2} = \frac{2}{6} \therefore y = 3 \times \frac{4}{3} = 4$
Then, $x = 3 \times 4 = 12$
Hence, $x + y = 12 + 4 = 16$

11 PROBLEMS BASED ON AGES

IMPORTANT FACTS:

1. The present age of the father is x times the age of his son. T years hence, the father's age become y times the age of his son. Then the present ages of the father and his son are:

   Present age of the son = $\frac{(y-1)T}{x-y}$ years and age of the father = $\frac{(y-1)\,T \times y}{x-y}$ years

2. T years ago, the father's age was x times that of his son and at present the father's age is y times the age of his son. Then their present ages are:

   Son's age = $\frac{T(x-1)}{x-y}$ years; Father's age = $\frac{T(x-1)}{x-y} \times y$ years.

Example 1: The ratio of the present ages of Samir and Saurabh is 7 : 8. If 4 years ago, the ratio of their ages be 5 : 6, then find the present age of Saurabh?

Solution: Let the present ages of Samir and Saurabh be $7x$ and $8x$ years respectively; then

$$\frac{7x-4}{8x-4} = \frac{5}{6} \quad \Rightarrow 42x - 24 = 40x - 20 \quad \Rightarrow 2x = 4 \quad \therefore x = 2$$

Hence, present age of Saurabh = $8x = 8 \times 2 = 16$ years.

Example 2: The sum of the ages of a son and father is 56 years. After 4 years, the age of the father will be three times that of the son. What is the age of the son?

Solution: Let ages of the son and father be x and $(56 - x)$ years respectively.

Then, $$\frac{x+4}{56-x+4} = \frac{1}{3} \quad \Rightarrow 3x + 12 = 60 - x \quad \Rightarrow 4x = 48 \quad \therefore x = 12$$

Hence, age of the son = 12 years.

Example 3: Six year back Rani was half of that of Nilam in age. Four years hence, the respective ratio of their ages would be 3 : 5. How is Nilam at present?

Solution: Let six years back the age of Rani and Nilam were x and $2x$ years respectively. Hence, their present ages are $(x + 6)$ and $(2x + 6)$ years; then

$$\frac{x+6+4}{2x+6+4} = \frac{3}{5} \quad \Rightarrow 5x + 50 = 6x + 30 \quad \therefore x = 20$$

Hence, present age of Nilam = $2x + 6 = 2 \times 20 + 6 = 46$ years.

Example 4: The age of Ram is 4 times the age of Shyam. If 5 years hence, Ram's age would be $1\frac{1}{2}$ times that of Shyam. What are their present ages?

Solution: Let the present age of Ram and Shyam be $4x$ and x years; then

$\frac{4x+5}{x+5}=\frac{3}{2}$ $\Rightarrow 8x+10 = 3x + 15$ $\Rightarrow 5x = 5$ $\therefore\ x = 1$

Hence, $4x = 4 \times 1 = 4$ years and $x = 1$ year

Example 5: The sum of present ages of Ashok, Anil and Ajay is 75 years. If 5 years ago the ratio of their ages was 3 : 4 : 5, what is the present age of Anil?

Solution: Let 5 years ago, the age of Ashok, Anil and Ajay were $3x$, $4x$ and $5x$ years. Then, their present ages are $(3x + 5)$, $(4x + 5)$ and $(5x + 5)$ years.

Now, $3x + 5 + 4x + 5 + 5x + 5 = 75$ $\Rightarrow 12x = 60$ $\therefore x = 5$

Hence, present age of Anil $= 4x + 5 = 4 \times 5 + 5 = 25$ years

Example 6: The ratio of ages of the father and his son at present is 12 : 5. The difference of their age is 28 years. What will be the ratio of their ages after 8 years?

Solution: Let the present ages of father and his son be $12x$ and $5x$ years respectively; then

$12x - 5x = 28$ $\Rightarrow 7x = 28$ $\therefore x = 4$

Now, $12x = 12 \times 4 = 48$ years and $5x = 5 \times 4 = 20$ years

After 8 years their age will be $48 + 8 = 56$ years and $20 + 8 = 28$ years

Hence, their ratio = 56 : 28 = 2 : 1

Example 7: The ratio of ages of Ajay and Vijay at present is 3 : 2. 8 years earlier, the ratio was 5 : 3. What are their present ages?

Solution: Let the present ages of Ajay and Vijay are $3x$ years and $2x$ years respectively; then

$\frac{3x-8}{2x-8}=\frac{5}{3}$ $\Rightarrow 9x - 24 = 10x - 40$ $\therefore x = 16$

Hence, $3x = 3 \times 16 = 48$ years and $2x = 2 \times 16 = 32$ years

So, their present ages are 48 years and 32 years.

Example 8: One year ago the ratio between Samir and Saurabh's age was 4 : 3. One year hence, the ratio of their ages will be 5 : 4. What is the sum of their present ages in years?

Solution: Let one year ago ages of Samir and Saurabh was $4x$ and $3x$ years respectively; then

$\frac{4x+2}{3x+2}=\frac{5}{4}$ $\Rightarrow 16x + 8 = 15x + 10$ $\therefore x = 2$

Hence, sum of their present ages $= 4x + 1 + 3x + 1 = 7x + 2 = 7 \times 2 + 2 = 16$ years.

Example 9: Ratio of present ages of Ramesh and Suresh is 4 : 3. Ramesh will be 26 years old after 6 years. How old is Suresh now?

Solution: Let the present ages of Ramesh and Suresh be $4x$ and $3x$ years respectively; then

$4x + 6 = 26$ $\Rightarrow 4x = 20$ $\therefore\ x = 5$

Hence, present age of Suresh $= 3x = 3 \times 5 = 15$ years.

Example 10: At the time of marriage a man was 6 years elder to his wife but 12 years after the marriage, his age was $\frac{6}{5}$ times the age of his wife. What were their ages at the time of marriage?

Solution: Let at the time of marriage the age of man and his wife be $x + 6$ and x years respectively;

then, $\frac{x+6+12}{x+12}=\frac{6}{5}$ $\Rightarrow 5x + 90 = 6x + 72$ $\Rightarrow x = 18$

Hence, at the time of marriage, the age of the man $= x + 6 = 18 + 6 = 24$ years and the age of his wife $= x$ years $= 18$ years.

Example 11: The product of the age of Mahesh and Dinesh is 240. If the twice the age of Dinesh is more than Mahesh's age by 4 years, find the age of Dinesh?

Solution: Let the age of Mahesh and Dinesh be $2x - 4$ and x years respectively; then

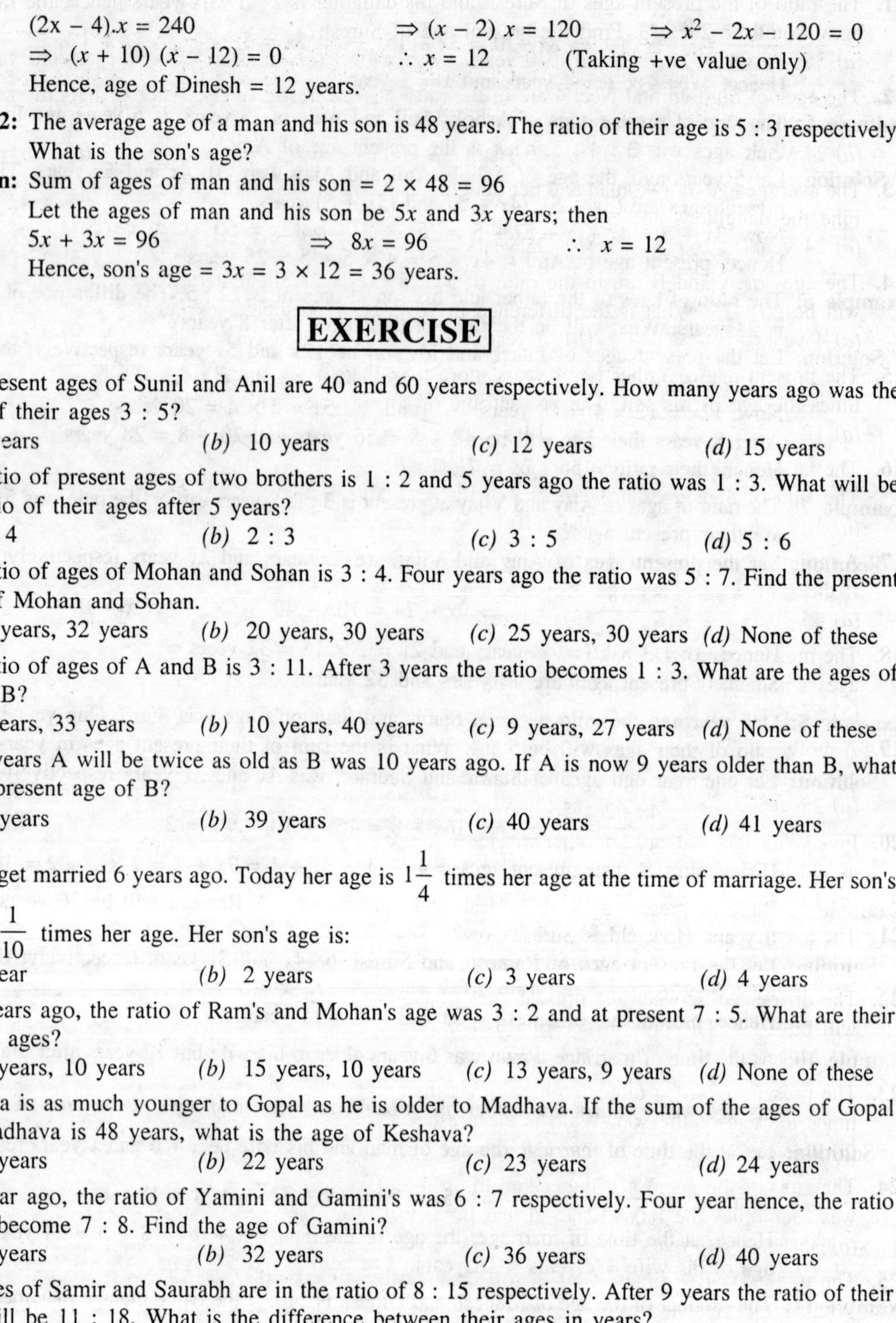

$(2x - 4).x = 240$ $\Rightarrow (x - 2)\, x = 120$ $\Rightarrow x^2 - 2x - 120 = 0$

$\Rightarrow (x + 10)(x - 12) = 0$ $\therefore x = 12$ (Taking +ve value only)

Hence, age of Dinesh = 12 years.

Example 12: The average age of a man and his son is 48 years. The ratio of their age is 5 : 3 respectively. What is the son's age?

Solution: Sum of ages of man and his son = $2 \times 48 = 96$

Let the ages of man and his son be $5x$ and $3x$ years; then

$5x + 3x = 96$ $\Rightarrow 8x = 96$ $\therefore x = 12$

Hence, son's age = $3x = 3 \times 12 = 36$ years.

EXERCISE

1. The present ages of Sunil and Anil are 40 and 60 years respectively. How many years ago was the ratio of their ages 3 : 5?

(a) 5 years (b) 10 years (c) 12 years (d) 15 years

2. The ratio of present ages of two brothers is 1 : 2 and 5 years ago the ratio was 1 : 3. What will be the ratio of their ages after 5 years?

(a) 1 : 4 (b) 2 : 3 (c) 3 : 5 (d) 5 : 6

3. The ratio of ages of Mohan and Sohan is 3 : 4. Four years ago the ratio was 5 : 7. Find the present ages of Mohan and Sohan.

(a) 24 years, 32 years (b) 20 years, 30 years (c) 25 years, 30 years (d) None of these

4. The ratio of ages of A and B is 3 : 11. After 3 years the ratio becomes 1 : 3. What are the ages of A and B?

(a) 9 years, 33 years (b) 10 years, 40 years (c) 9 years, 27 years (d) None of these

5. In 10 years A will be twice as old as B was 10 years ago. If A is now 9 years older than B, what is the present age of B?

(a) 38 years (b) 39 years (c) 40 years (d) 41 years

6. Radha get married 6 years ago. Today her age is $1\frac{1}{4}$ times her age at the time of marriage. Her son's age is $\frac{1}{10}$ times her age. Her son's age is:

(a) 1 year (b) 2 years (c) 3 years (d) 4 years

7. Two years ago, the ratio of Ram's and Mohan's age was 3 : 2 and at present 7 : 5. What are their present ages?

(a) 14 years, 10 years (b) 15 years, 10 years (c) 13 years, 9 years (d) None of these

8. Keshava is as much younger to Gopal as he is older to Madhava. If the sum of the ages of Gopal and Madhava is 48 years, what is the age of Keshava?

(a) 21 years (b) 22 years (c) 23 years (d) 24 years

9. One year ago, the ratio of Yamini and Gamini's was 6 : 7 respectively. Four year hence, the ratio would become 7 : 8. Find the age of Gamini?

(a) 30 years (b) 32 years (c) 36 years (d) 40 years

10. The ages of Samir and Saurabh are in the ratio of 8 : 15 respectively. After 9 years the ratio of their ages will be 11 : 18. What is the difference between their ages in years?

(a) 20 years (b) 21 years (c) 22 years (d) 24 years

11. The ratio of the present ages of Suresh and his daughter is 2 : 1. Six years hence, the ratio of their ages would be 23 : 13. Find the present age of Suresh?
(*a*) 35 years (*b*) 40 years (*c*) 45 years (*d*) 50 years

12. The ages of Surabhi and Neerja are in the ratio of 6 : 7 respectively. After 6 years the ratio of their ages will be 15 : 17. Find the age of Neerja.
(*a*) 24 years (*b*) 26 years (*c*) 28 years (*d*) 32 years

13. The average age of a woman and her daughter is 42 years. The ratio of their ages is 2 : 1 respectively. Find the daughter's age.
(*a*) 24 years (*b*) 28 years (*c*) 30 years (*d*) 32 years

14. The ages of A and B are in the ratio of 11 : 13 respectively. After 7 years the ratio of their ages will be 20 : 23. What is the difference in years between their ages?
(*a*) 4 years (*b*) 5 years (*c*) 6 years (*d*) 7 years

15. The present age of father is 34 years more than that of his son. 12 years ago, father's age was 18 times the age of his son. The present age of son in years is:
(*a*) 12 (*b*) 14 (*c*) 16 (*d*) 18

16. The ratio of the ages of two persons is 4 : 7 and age of one of them is more than other by 30 years. The sum of their ages in years is:
(*a*) 100 (*b*) 110 (*c*) 120 (*d*) 130

17. A father is older than his first son by 30 years, the first son is older than the second son by 10 years. If the sum of their ages be 95 years, find the age of father.
(*a*) 45 years (*b*) 50 years (*c*) 55 years (*d*) 65 years

18. The present age of Deepak is 3 times the present age of his son. Five years hence, the ratio of their ages will be 34 : 13 respectively. The present age of Deepak is:
(*a*) 58 years (*b*) 60 years (*c*) 63 years (*d*) 68 years

19. A mother is 25 years older than her daughter. Five years ago, the age of the mother was 6 times the age of the daughter. What is the present age of mother?
(*a*) 25 years (*b*) 29 years (*c*) 32 years (*d*) 35 years

20. Five years ago, Mayank's mother was three times as old as Mayank. After five years she will be twice as old as Mayank. The present age of Mayank is:
(*a*) 13 years (*b*) 15 years (*c*) 20 years (*d*) 30 years

21. The average age of A, B and C is 25 years. The ratio of their age is 3 : 5 : 7. What is the age of A?
(*a*) 12 years (*b*) 15 years (*c*) 18 years (*d*) 21 years

22. The difference between the present ages of P and Q is 4 years. The ratio of their ages after 5 years will be 9 : 8. The present age of P is:
(*a*) 24 years (*b*) 30 years (*c*) 32 years (*d*) None of these

23. The present age of a father is three times the age of his son. Five years ago, father's age was four times the age of the son. What is the presetn age of son?
(*a*) 20 years (*b*) 18 years (*c*) 15 years (*d*) 12 years

24. The sum of the ages of a father and his son is 45 years. Five years ago, the product of their ages was four times the father's age at that time. What are their present ages?
(*a*) 35 years, 10 years (*b*) 36 years, 9 years (*c*) 37 years, 8 years (*d*) 39 years, 6 years

25. The mother is five times older than her son. After 4 years, the sum of their ages will be 44 years. What is the present age of the son?
(*a*) 5 years (*b*) 6 years (*c*) 7 years (*d*) 8 years

26. The difference between the present ages of Arun and Barun is 14 years. Seven years ago the ratio of their ages was 5 : 7 respetively. The present age of Barun is :
(a) 35 years *(b)* 42 years *(c)* 49 years *(d)* 56 years

27. The respective ratio of the ages of Shami, Nammi and Pammi is 3 : 4 : 5. The sum of their ages is 48 years. What will be the respective ratio of their ages 8 years hence?
(a) 4 : 5 : 6 *(b)* 5 : 6 : 7 *(c)* 5 : 7 : 8 *(d)* 6 : 7 : 8

28. The ratio between the ages of Ram and Mohan is 4 : 5 and that between Mohan and Anil is 5 : 6. If sum of the ages of three be 90 years, what is the age of Mohan?
(a) 20 years *(b)* 24 years *(c)* 25 years *(d)* 30 years

29. Three years ago, the average age of a family of five members was 17 years. A baby having been born, the average age of the family is the same as what was three years ago. The present age of the baby is:
(a) 6 months *(b)* 9 months *(c)* 1 year *(d)* 2 years

30. 5 years ago, the average age of Ram and Shyam was 20 years. Now, the average age of Ram, Shyam and Mohan is 30 years. What will be Mohan's age 10 years hence?
(a) 50 years *(b)* 45 years *(c)* 40 years *(d)* 35 years

31. Present age of Rahul is 5 years less than Ritu's present age. If 3 years ago Ritu's age was x years, which of the following represents Rahul's present age in years?
(a) $x - 2$ *(b)* $x + 3$ *(c)* $x + 5$ *(d)* $x + 11$

32. The present age of Sanyal is 3 times the present age of his son. Six years hence, the ratio of their ages will be 5 : 2 respectively. The present age of Sanyal is:
(a) 48 years *(b)* 50 years *(c)* 54 years *(d)* 60 years

33. The ratio of the present ages of Rahul and Reshmi is 2 : 1. The ratio of their ages after 30 years will be 7 : 6. The present age of Rahul is:
(a) 20 years *(b)* 12 years *(c)* 10 years *(d)* 6 years

34. The difference between the ages of a boss and his subordinate is 16 years. Four years ago, the respective ratio of the ages of the boss and subordinate was 11 : 7. The present age of the subordinate is:
(a) 28 years *(b)* 32 years *(c)* 36 years *(d)* 40 years

35. The ratio of ages of Namrata and Divya is 4 : 3. The sum of their ages is 28 years. The ratio of their ages after 4 years will be:
(a) 3 : 4 *(b)* 5 : 4 *(c)* 5 : 6 *(d)* 6 : 5

36. Ten years ago, the age of Divya was half of the age of Namrata. If the ratio of present ages of both is 3 : 4, the sum of their present ages is:
(a) 35 years *(b)* 30 years *(c)* 25 years *(d)* 18 years

37. At present, the ratio between the ages of Gopal and Madhawa is 4 : 3. After 6 years, Gopal's age will be 26 years. The present age of Madhawa is:
(a) 21 years *(b)* $19\frac{1}{2}$ years *(c)* 15 years *(d)* 12 years

38. The sum of the ages of Ram, Shyam and Mohan is 93 years. Ten years ago, the ratio of their ages was 2 : 3 : 4. The present age of Mohan is:
(a) 38 years *(b)* 34 years *(c)* 32 years *(d)* 24 years

39. The present ages of three persons are in the ratio of 4 : 7 : 9. Eight years ago, the sum of their ages was 56. What are their present ages in years?
(a) 30, 40, 50 *(b)* 20, 35, 45 *(c)* 16, 28, 36 *(d)* 8, 20, 28

40. The ratio between the present ages of A and B is 5 : 3 respectively. The ratio between A's age 4 years ago and B's age 4 years hence is 1 : 1. The ratio between A's age 4 years hence and B's age 4 years ago is:

(a) 4 : 1 (b) 3 : 1 (c) 2 : 1 (d) 1 : 3

41. The ratio of ages of a man and his wife is 4 : 3. After 4 years, this ratio will be 9 : 7. If at the time of marriage, the ratio was 5 : 3, then how many years ago were they married?

(a) 15 years (b) 12 years (c) 10 years (d) 8 years

42. A is two years older than B, who is twice as old as C. If the sum of the ages of A, B and C be 27, then the age of B in years is:

(a) 10 (b) 9 (c) 8 (d) 7

43. Sudha's grandfather was 8 times older to her 16 years ago. He would be 3 times of her age 8 years from now. Eight years ago, what was the ratio of Sudha's age to that of her grandfather?

(a) 11 : 53 (b) 3 : 8 (c) 1 : 5 (d) 1 : 2

44. The sum of ages of A and B is 12 years more than the sum of ages of B and C. Then C is how many years younger than A?

(a) 10 (b) 12 (c) 24 (d) Data inadequate

45. Ram got married 8 years ago. His present age is $\frac{6}{5}$ times his age at the time of marriage. Ram's sister was 10 years younger to him at the time of his marriage. What is the present age of Ram's sister?

(a) 40 years (b) 38 years (c) 36 years (d) 32 years

46. Q is as much younger than R as he is older than T. If sum of the ages of R and T is 50 years, what is the difference between R and Q's age?

(a) 2.5 years (b) 2 years (c) 1 year (d) Data inadequate

47. The sum of the ages of 5 children born at the interval of 3 years each is 50 years. The age of youngest child is:

(a) 10 years (b) 8 years (c) 4 years (d) None of these

48. A father said to his son, "I was as old as you are at present at the time of your birth." If the father's age is 38 years now. Five years ago the age of son was:

(a) 38 years (b) 33 years (c) 19 years (d) 14 years

49. A person said "Take my age three years hence, multiply it by 3 and then subtract 3 times my age three years ago and hence everybody will know how old I am". The age of person in years is:

(a) 32 (b) 24 (c) 20 (d) 18

50. Nisha's father was 38 years of age when she was born while her mother was 36 years old when her brother four years younger to her was born. The difference of ages of her parents is:

(a) 8 years (b) 6 years (c) 4 years (d) 2 years

EXPLANATORY ANSWERS

1. Let x years ago, the ratio of their ages was 3 : 5, then

$$\frac{40-x}{60-x} = \frac{3}{5} \quad \Rightarrow 200 - 5x = 180 - 3x \qquad \Rightarrow 2x = 20 \qquad \therefore\ x = 10 \text{ years}$$

2. Let their present ages be x and $2x$ years; then

$\frac{x-5}{2x-5} = \frac{1}{3}$ $\Rightarrow 3x - 15 = 2x - 5$ $\therefore\ x = 10$

Hence, their present ages 10 years and 20 years

Required ratio = $\frac{10+5}{20+5} = \frac{3}{5} = 3 : 5$

3. Let the ages of Mohan and Sohan be $3x$ years and $4x$ years;

then, $\frac{3x-4}{4x-4} = \frac{5}{7}$ $\Rightarrow 21x - 28 = 20x - 20$ $\therefore\ x = 8$

Hence, their present ages, $3x = 3 \times 8 = 24$ years; $4x = 4 \times 8 = 32$ years.

So, their ages 24 and 32 years.

4. Let the ages of A and B be $3x$ and $11x$ years; then

$\frac{3x+3}{11x+3} = \frac{1}{3}$ $\Rightarrow 9x + 9 = 11x + 3$ $\Rightarrow 2x = 6$ $\therefore\ x = 3$

Hence, their present age, $3x = 3 \times 3 = 9$ years; $11x = 11 \times 3 = 33$ years

5. Let the present age of B and A be x and $(x + 9)$ years; then,

$2(x - 10) = x + 19$ $\Rightarrow$ $2x - x = 19 + 20$ $\therefore$ $x = 39$ years

6. Let the present age of Radha be x years; then

$\frac{5}{4}(x - 6) = x$ $\Rightarrow$ $5x - 30 = 4x$ $\therefore$ $x = 30$ years

Hence, her son's age = $\frac{1}{10} \times 30 = 3$ years

7. Let the present ages of Ram and Mohan are $7x$ and $5x$ years; then

$\frac{7x-2}{5x-2} = \frac{3}{2}$ $\Rightarrow 14x - 4 = 15x - 6$ $\therefore x = 2$

Hence, their present ages : $7 \times 2 = 14$ years and $5 \times 2 = 10$ years

8. Let the present ages of Madhava, Keshava and Gopal are a, b and c years respectively, then

$b - a = c - b$ $\Rightarrow 2b = a + c$ $\therefore$ $b = \frac{a+c}{2}$

Hence, the age of Keshava = $\frac{48}{2} = 24$ years

9. Let one year ago the ages of Yamini and Gamini were $6x$ and $7x$ years respectively; then

$\frac{6x+5}{7x+5} = \frac{7}{8}$ $\Rightarrow 48x + 40 = 49x + 35$ $\therefore x = 5$

Hence, present ago of Gamini = $7x + 1 = 7 \times 5 + 1 = 36$ years

10. Let the present ages of Samir and Saurabh are $8x$ and $15x$ years respectively; then

$\frac{8x+9}{15x+9} = \frac{11}{18}$ $\Rightarrow 144x + 162 = 165x + 99$ $\Rightarrow$ $21x = 63$ $\therefore\ x = 3$

Hence, difference of their ages = $15x - 8x = 7x = 7 \times 3 = 21$ years

11. Let the present ages of Suresh and his daughter be $2x$ and x years respectively; then

$\frac{2x+6}{x+6} = \frac{23}{13}$ $\Rightarrow 26x + 78 = 23x + 138$ $\Rightarrow 3x = 60$ $\therefore\ x = 20$

Hence, present age of Suresh = $2 \times 10 = 40$ years

12. Let the present ages of Surabhi and Neerja are $6x$ and $7x$ years respectively; then,

$\frac{6x+6}{7x+6} = \frac{15}{17}$ $\Rightarrow 102x + 102 = 105x + 90$ $\Rightarrow 3x = 12$ $\therefore x = 4$

Hence, present ages of Neerja = $7 \times 4 = 28$ years

13. Let the present ages of woman and her daugher be $2x$ and x years respectively; then

$2x + x = 2 \times 42$ $\Rightarrow 3x = 84$ $\therefore$ $x = 28$

Hence, present age of her daughter = 28 years

14. Let the present ages of A and B are $11x$ and $13x$ years respectively; then

$\frac{11x+7}{13x+7} = \frac{20}{23}$ $\Rightarrow 253x + 161 = 260x + 140$ $\Rightarrow 7x = 21$ $\therefore x = 3$

Hence, difference of their ages = $13x - 11x = 2x = 2 \times 3 = 6$ years

15. Let the present ages of father and his son be $x + 34$ and x years respectively; then

$18(x - 12) = x + 34 - 12$ $\Rightarrow 18x - 216 = x + 22$ $\Rightarrow 17x = 238$ $\therefore x = 14$

Hence, present age of his son = 14 years

16. Let the present ages of two persons be $4x$ and $7x$ years respectively; then

$7x - 4x = 30$ $\Rightarrow 3x = 30$ $\therefore x = 10$

Hence, sum of their ages = $4x + 7x = 11x = 11 \times 10 = 110$ years

17. Let ages of father and his two sons are x, $(x - 30)$ and $(x - 40)$ years respectively; then

$(x + x - 30) + x - 40 = 95 \Rightarrow 3x = 165$ $\therefore x = 55$

Hence, age of the father = 55 years.

18. The present age of Deepak and his son be $3x$ and x years respectively; then

$\frac{3x+5}{x+5} = \frac{34}{13}$ $\Rightarrow 39x + 65 = 34x + 170$ $\Rightarrow 5x = 105$ $\therefore\ x = 21$

Hence, present age of Deepak = $3x = 3 \times 21 = 63$

19. Let the present ages of mother and her daughter are $(x + 25)$ and x years respectively; then

$6(x - 5) = x + 25 - 5$ $\Rightarrow$ $6x - 30 = x + 20$ $\Rightarrow 5x = 50$ $\therefore x = 10$

Hence, the age of the mother = $10 + 25 = 35$ years

20. Let 5 years ago Mayank's age = x years and Mother's age = $3x$ years

After 5 years $2(x + 10) = 3x + 10$ $\Rightarrow 2x + 20 = 3x + 10$ $\Rightarrow$ $x = 10$

Present age of Mayank = $x + 5 = 10 + 5 = 15$ years

21. Let the present ages of A, B and C are $3x$, $5x$ and $7x$ years respectively; then

$3x + 5x + 7x = 3 \times 25$ $\Rightarrow 15x = 75$ $\therefore$ $x = 5$

Hence, age of A = $3x = 3 \times 5 = 15$ years

22. Let the present ages of P and Q be $(x + 4)$ and x years;

then, $\frac{x+4+5}{x+5} = \frac{9}{8}$ $\Rightarrow$ $8x + 72 = 9x + 45$ $\therefore x = 27$

Hence, present age of P = $27 + 4$ = 31 years

23. Let the present age of father and his son are $3x$ and x years respectively; then
$4(x - 5) = 3x - 5 \Rightarrow 4x - 20 = 3x - 5 \quad \therefore x = 15$ years

24. Let the present ages of father and his son be x and $(45 - x)$ years respectively; then
$(x - 5)(45 - x - 5) = 4(45 - x - 5) \quad \Rightarrow x - 5 = 4 \quad \therefore x = 9$
Now, son's age $= 45 - x = 45 - 9 = 36$ years

25. Let the present ages of mother and her son be $5x$ and x years respectively; then
$5x + 4 + x + 4 = 44 \quad \Rightarrow 6x = 36 \quad \therefore x = 6$ years

26. Let the present ages of Arun and Barun are x and $x + 14$ years respectively; then

$$\frac{x-7}{x+14-7} = \frac{5}{7} \Rightarrow 7x - 49 = 5x + 35 \Rightarrow 2x = 84 \quad \therefore x = 42$$

Hence, age of Barun $= 42 + 14 = 56$ years

27. Let the present ages of Shami, Nammi and Pammi are $3x$, $4x$ and $5x$ years respectively;
then, $3x + 4x + 5x = 48 \quad \Rightarrow 12x = 48 \quad \therefore x = 4$
Hence, their present ages are 12, 16 and 20 years respectively.
So, required ratio $= (12 + 8) : (16 + 8) : (20 + 8) = 20 : 24 : 28 = 5 : 6 : 7$

28. Here, ratio of ages of Ram, Mohan and Anil $= 4 : 5 : 6$
Let their present ags be $4x$, $5x$ and $6x$ years respectively;
then $4x + 5x + 6x = 90 \quad \Rightarrow 15x = 90 \quad \therefore x = 6$
Hence, age of Mohan $= 5 \times 6 = 30$ years

29. The present age of baby $= 17 \times 6 - 20 \times 5 = 2$ years

30. The present age of Mohan $= 3 \times 30 - 2 \times 25 = 90 - 50 = 40$ years
10 years hence, the age of Mohan $= 40 + 10 = 50$ years

31. Ritu's present age $= x + 3$ years
Hence, present age of Rahul $= x + 3 - 5 = x - 2$ years

32. Let the present age of Sanyal and his son be $3x$ and x years respectively; then

$$\frac{3x+6}{x+6} = \frac{5}{2} \Rightarrow 6x + 12 = 5x + 30 \quad \therefore x = 18$$

Hence, age of Sanyal $= 3 \times 18 = 54$ years

33. Let the present age of Rahul and Reshmi be $2x$ and x years respectively; then

$$\frac{2x+30}{x+30} = \frac{7}{6} \Rightarrow 12x + 180 = 7x + 210 \Rightarrow 5x = 30 \quad \therefore x = 6$$

Hence, present age of Rahul $= 2 \times 6 = 12$ years

34. Let the present age of the boss and his subordinate be $(x + 16)$ and x years respectively; then

$$\frac{x+16-4}{x-4} = \frac{11}{7} \Rightarrow 7x + 84 = 11x - 44 \Rightarrow 4x = 128 \quad \therefore x = 32 \text{ years}$$

35. Let the present ages of Namrata and Divya are $4x$ and $3x$ years respectively; then
$4x + 3x = 28 \quad \therefore x = 4$
Hence, their present ages are 16 and 12 years.
So, required ratio $= (16 + 4) : (12 + 4) = 20 : 16 = 5 : 4$

36. Let the present ages of Divya and Namrata are $3x$ and $4x$ years respectively; then

$\frac{3x-10}{4x-10}=\frac{1}{2}$ $\Rightarrow 6x - 20 = 4x - 10$ $\Rightarrow 2x = 10$ $\therefore x = 5$

Hence, sum of their ages = $3x + 4x = 7x = 7 \times 5 = 35$ years

37. Let the present ages of Gopal and Madhawa are $4x$ and $3x$ years respectively; then

$4x + 6 = 26$ $\Rightarrow 4x = 20$ $\therefore x = 5$

Hence, present age of Madhawa = $3x = 3 \times 5 = 15$ years

38. Let 10 years ago, ages of Ram, Shyam and Mohan were $2x$, $3x$ and $4x$ years respectively; then

$2x + 10 + 3x + 10 + 4x + 10 = 93$ $\Rightarrow 9x = 63$ $\therefore x = 7$

Hence, present age of Mohan = $4x + 10 = 4 \times 7 + 10 = 38$ years

39. Let the present ages of three persons are $4x$, $7x$ and $9x$ years respectively; then

$4x - 8 + 7x - 8 + 9x - 8 = 56$ $\Rightarrow 20x = 80$ $\therefore x = 4$

Hence, their present ages are $4 \times 4 = 16$ years, $7 \times 4 = 28$ years and $9 \times 4 = 36$ years respectively.

40. Let the present ages of A and B are $5x$ and $3x$ years respectively; then,

$\frac{5x-4}{3x+4}=1$ $\Rightarrow 5x - 4 = 3x + 4$ $\Rightarrow 2x = 8$ $\therefore x = 4$

Hence, their present ages are 20 years and 12 years.

So, required ratio = (20 + 4) : (12 – 4) = 24 : 8 = 3 : 1

41. Let the present ages of the man and his wife are $4x$ and $3x$ years respectively; then

$\frac{4x+4}{3x+4}=\frac{9}{7}$ $\Rightarrow 28x + 28 = 27x + 36$ $\therefore x = 8$

Hence, their present ages are $4 \times 8 = 32$ years and $3 \times 8 = 24$ years

If t years ago they were married, then

$\frac{32-t}{24-t}=\frac{5}{3}$ $\Rightarrow 96 - 3t = 120 - 5t$ $\Rightarrow 2t = 24$ $\therefore t = 12$ years

42. Let the ages of A, B and C are $(x + 2)$, x and $\frac{x}{2}$ years respectively, then

$x + 2 + x + \frac{x}{2} = 27$ $\Rightarrow \frac{5x}{2}=25$ $\therefore x = \frac{2\times 25}{5} = 10$ years

43. Let 16 years ago, the age of Sudha and her grandfather were x and $8x$ years respectively; then

$3(x + 16 + 8) = 8x + 16 + 8$ $\Rightarrow 3x + 72 = 8x + 24$ $\Rightarrow 5x = 48$ $\therefore x = \frac{48}{5}$

Hence, required ratio $= (x + 8) : (8x + 8) = \left(\frac{48}{5}+8\right):\left(8\times\frac{48}{5}+8\right)$

$= \left(\frac{88}{5}\right):\left(\frac{424}{5}\right) = 11 : 53$

44. Here, (A + B) – (B + C) = 12 $\therefore$ A – C = 12

Hence, C is 12 years younger than A.

45. Let the present age of Ram be x years; then

$$\frac{x}{x-8}=\frac{6}{5} \Rightarrow 5x = 6x - 48 \quad \therefore \quad x = 48$$

Hence, present age of Ram's sister = 48 – 10 = 38 years.

46. Here, $Q - T = R - Q \quad \therefore \quad Q=\frac{R+T}{2}$

Hence, age of $Q = \frac{50}{2} = 25$ years

Here, absolute value of age of R is not known.

So, the difference between R and Q's age cannot be determined. Hence, data is inadequate.

47. Let age of youngest child be x years; then

$$x + (x + 3) + (x + 6) + (x + 9) + (x + 12) = 50 \quad \Rightarrow 5x = 20 \quad \therefore x = 4 \text{ years}$$

48. Let the age of father was x years at the time of his son's birth, then present age of father and his son will be $2x$ and x years,

Now, $2x = 38 \quad \therefore \quad x = 19$ years

Hence, 5 years ago the age of son was 19 – 5 = 14 years

49. Let the present age of the person be x years; then

$$3(x + 3) - 3(x - 3) = 3x + 9 - 3x + 9 = 18 \text{ years}$$

Hence, age of the person = 18 years

50. The difference of ages of her parents = (38 + 4) – 36 = 42 – 36 = 6 years.

12

CHAIN RULE

IMPORTANT FACTS

Rule of Three : The method of finding the 4th term of a proportion, when the other three are given, is called the rule of three or simple proportion.

Compound proportion : If three or more quantities are such that the value of one quantity depends on other remaining quantities, then these quantities are said to be in compound proportion. To understand it, we take an example: If 8 men can plough 80 acres of field in 24 days, in how many days can 36 men plough 450 acres?

Solution: First of all we write the given quantities or variables namely men, acres and days in a row. We write the unknown quantity to the extreme right which supposed to be x. Then we put a downward arrow mark (↓) to the right as shown below :

Men	Acres	Days
8	80	24 ↓
36	450	x ↓

Now, we compare the relationship of various variables with the last quantity to be determined. If the relationship is of direct proportion we mark the arrow in the same direction. If the relationship is of inverse proportion, we mark the arrow in the opposite direction. We go on comparing to the last quantity and putting arrow marks accordingly.

The above relation can be expressed as follows:

Men	Acres	Days
8 ↑	80 ↓	24 ↓
36 ↑	450 ↓	x ↓

Now, we change the arrows in ratio. We do it in the direction of arrows. Thus, we have

$$\frac{24}{x} = \frac{80}{450} \times \frac{36}{8}$$

$$\Rightarrow \quad x \times 80 \times 36 = 24 \times 450 \times 8$$

$$\Rightarrow \quad x = \frac{24 \times 450 \times 8}{80 \times 36} = 30 \text{ days}$$

Note : *We write the digit at the tail of arrow first and then the digit at head of arrow.*

Example 1: If 72 men can do a certain piece of work in 50 days, in how many days will 30 men do it?

Solution: Clearly less no. of men, more no. of days, so inverse ratio of men is equal to ratio of time taken.

Now, Let the required no. of days be x.

then, 30 : 72 : : 50 : x

$$\Rightarrow \quad \frac{30}{72} = \frac{50}{x}$$

$$\Rightarrow \quad x = \frac{72 \times 50}{30} = 120 \text{ days.}$$

Example 2: If 30 dolls cost Rs. 90, what do 40 dolls cost?

Solution: Clearly more dolls, more cost

So, ratio of dolls is the same as ratio of costs

Now, Let the required cost be Rs. x

then, 30 : 40 : : 90 : x

$$\Rightarrow \quad \frac{30}{40} = \frac{90}{x} \Rightarrow x = \frac{90 \times 40}{30} = 120$$

Example 3: 20 men complete one-third of a piece of work in 20 days. How many more men should be employed to finish the remaining of the work in 25 more days?

Solution: Here, work done = $\frac{1}{3}$

Work to be done = $1 - \frac{1}{3} = \frac{2}{3}$

Now, Let the required no. of men = x

work	days	men
$\frac{1}{3}$ ↓	20 ↑	20 ↓
$\frac{2}{3}$	25	x

$$\text{Now,} \quad \frac{20}{x} = \frac{25}{20} \times \frac{\frac{1}{3}}{\frac{2}{3}}$$

$$\Rightarrow \quad \frac{20}{x} = \frac{25}{20} \times \frac{1}{3} \times \frac{3}{2}$$

$$\Rightarrow \quad x = \frac{20 \times 20 \times 2}{25} = 32$$

But 20 men has been employed, so 12 more men should be employed.

Example 4: If 18 pumps can raise 2170 tonnes of water in 10 days, working 7 hours a day, in how many days will 16 pumps raise 1736 tonnes working 9 hours a day?

Solution: Let the required days be x

Pumps	Water	Working hours	Days
18 ↑	2170 ↓	7 ↑	10 ↓
16	1736	9	x

$$\text{Since,} \quad \frac{10}{x} = \frac{9}{7} \times \frac{2170}{1736} \times \frac{16}{18}$$

$$\therefore \quad x = \frac{10 \times 7 \times 1736 \times 18}{9 \times 2170 \times 16} = 7 \text{ days}$$

Example 5: If 17 labourers can dig a ditch 26 metres long in 18 days, working 8 hours a day, how many more labourers should be engaged to dig a similar ditch 39 metres long in 6 days, each labourer working 9 hours a day?

Solution:

length	working hours	days	labourers
26 ↓	8 ↑	18 ↑	17 ↓
39	9	6	x

$$\text{Since, } \frac{17}{x} = \frac{26}{39} \times \frac{9}{8} \times \frac{6}{18}$$

$$\therefore x = \frac{17 \times 39 \times 8 \times 18}{26 \times 9 \times 6} = 68$$

So, more labourers to be engaged = (68 – 17) = 51

Example 6: If 4 examiners can examine a certain number of answer books in 8 days by working 5 hours a day; for how many hours a day would 2 examiners have to work in order to examine twice the number of answer books in 20 days?

Solution:

books	Days	Examiners	Working hours
1 ↓	8 ↑	4 ↑	5 ↓
2	20	2	x

$$\text{Since, } \frac{5}{x} = \frac{1}{2} \times \frac{20}{8} \times \frac{2}{4}$$

$$\therefore x = \frac{5 \times 2 \times 8 \times 4}{20 \times 2} = 8 \text{ hours per day}$$

Example 7: 3 men and 4 boys earn Rs. 264 in 8 days. 2 men and 3 boys earn Rs. 184 in the same specified time. In how many days 6 men and 7 boys will earn Rs. 315?

Solution: 3 men and 4 boys earn Rs. 264

2 men and 3 boys earn Rs. 184

Hence, the time of their earning is the same.

∴ The ratio of both these terms will be equal

$$i.e., \frac{3 \text{ men} + 4 \text{ boys}}{2 \text{ men} + 3 \text{ boys}} = \frac{264}{184} = \frac{33}{23}$$

⇒ 69 men + 92 boys = 66 men + 99 boys

⇒ 3 men = 7 boys

∴3 men + 4 boys = 7 boys + 4 boys = 11 boys

6 men + 7 boys = 14 boys + 7 boys = 21 boys.

Now, Let the number of required days = x

Boys	Earning	Days
11 ↑	264 ↓	8 ↓
21	315	x

$$\text{Therefore, } \frac{8}{x} = \frac{21}{11} \times \frac{264}{315}$$

$$\therefore \quad x = \frac{8 \times 11 \times 315}{21 \times 264} = 5 \text{ days.}$$

Hence, the required no. of days = 5

Example 8: If 80 persons can finish a work within 16 days by working 6 hours a day, then how many hours per day should 64 persons work to complete that very job within 15 days?

Solution:

Persons	Days	Hours	
80 ↑	16 ↑	6 ↓	More hours, Less Days (Indirect Variation)
64	15	x	More hours, Less persons (Indirect Variation)

Hence, $\frac{x}{6} = \frac{16}{15} \times \frac{80}{64}$ $\qquad \therefore x = \frac{16}{15} \times \frac{80}{64} \times 6 = 8$ hours

Example 9: 60 men consume 280 kgs of rice in 14 days. In how many days will 30 men consume 120 kgs of rice?

Solution:

Men	Kgs	Days
60 ↑	280 ↓	14 ↓
30	120	x

Hence, $\frac{x}{14} = \frac{120}{280} \times \frac{60}{30}$ $\qquad \therefore x = \frac{120}{280} \times \frac{60}{30} \times 14 = 12$ days

Example 10: A contractor undertakes to do a piece of work in 40 days. He engages 100 men at the beginning and 100 more after 35 days and completes the work in stipulated time. If he has not engaged the additional men how many days behind the schedule the work would have been finished?

Solution:

Men	Days
200 ↑	5 ↓
100	x

Hence, $\frac{x}{5} = \frac{200}{100}$ $\qquad \therefore x = 2 \times 5 = 10$ days

Required number of days = 10 – 5 = 5 days

EXERCISE

1. If 15 men can do a certain amount of work in 20 days working 8 hours a day, in how many days will 10 men do three times the work working 6 hours a day?
   (*a*) 120 days (*b*) 70 days (*c*) 100 days (*d*) None of these

2. 400 persons working 9 hours a day complete $\frac{1}{4}$th of the work in 10 days. Find the number of additional persons, working 8 hours per day required to complete the remaining work in 20 days.
   (*a*) 275 (*b*) 200 (*c*) 225 (*d*) 250

3. The shadow of a tower which is 80 metres high is 16 metres at particular time on a day. Find the height of a tree which casts a shadow of 9 metres, under the similar condition on the same time and day.
   (*a*) 40 metres (*b*) 45 metres (*c*) 50 metres (*d*) 60 metres

4. 15 persons complete a job in 3 days. How many days will 10 persons take to complete the same job?
   (*a*) 2 (*b*) $2\frac{2}{3}$ (*c*) $3\frac{1}{4}$ (*d*) $4\frac{1}{2}$

5. 16 men can complete a piece of work in 8 days. In how many days can 12 men complete the same piece of work?

(a) $10\frac{2}{3}$ *(b)* $9\frac{1}{3}$ *(c)* 9 *(d)* 10

6. In a canteen 238 kgs of rice is required for a week. How much rice required for 49 days?

(a) 1566 kg *(b)* 1666 kg *(c)* 1764 kg *(d)* 1650 kg

7. 17 men can complete a piece of work in 12 days. In how many days can 6 men complete the same piece of work?

(a) 26 days *(b)* 28 days *(c)* 32 days *(d)* 34 days

8. A fort has provision for 50 days. After 15 days a reinforcement of 150 men arrives and the provision now lasts 25 days. How many men were there in the fort?

(a) 300 *(b)* 225 *(c)* 275 *(d)* 200

9. A fort has supply of foodstuff for 150 soldiers for 45 days. After 10 days, 25 soldiers leave. How long the food will last for the remaining soldiers at the same rate?

(a) 35 days *(b)* 40 days *(c)* 41 days *(d)* 42 days

10. 40 men consume 60 kgs of rice in 15 days, then in how many days will 30 men consume 12 kgs of rice?

(a) 9 days *(b)* $6\frac{1}{4}$ days *(c)* 4 days *(d)* $3\frac{1}{4}$ days

11. If 30 men working 7 hours a day can do a piece of work in 18 days, in how many days will 21 men working 8 hours a day do the same piece of work?

(a) 20 *(b)* $22\frac{1}{2}$ *(c)* 25 *(d)* 30

12. In a fort there is provisions for 40 days for 275 persons. If after 16 days 125 persons leave the fort for how many more days the provisions will last?

(a) 35 days *(b)* 44 days *(c)* 45 days *(d)* 53 days

13. A canteen requires 105 kgs of wheat for a week. How many kgs of wheat will it require for 58 days?

(a) 406 *(b)* 536 *(c)* 708 *(d)* 870

14. 18 men complete a piece of work in 5 days. In how many days can 21 men complete the same piece of work?

(a) $3\frac{2}{7}$ *(b)* $4\frac{2}{7}$ *(c)* 4 *(d)* $5\frac{2}{7}$

15. 60 men could complete a work in 250 days. They worked together for 200 days. After that the work had to be stopped for 10 days due to bad weather. How many more men should be engaged to complete the work in time?

(a) 20 *(b)* 18 *(c)* 15 *(d)* 10

16. 12 pumps working 6 hours a day can empty a completely filled reservoir in 15 days. How many such pumps working 9 hours a day will empty the same reservoir in 12 days?

(a) 9 *(b)* 10 *(c)* 12 *(d)* 15

17. A contractor undertook to complete a project in 90 days and employed 60 men on it. After 60 days, he found that $\frac{3}{4}$ of the work has already been completed. How many men can he discharge so that the project may completed exactly on time?

(a) 15 *(b)* 20 *(c)* 30 *(d)* 40

18. 50 people consume 350 kgs of rice in 30 days. In how many days will 35 people consume 50 kgs of rice?
(*a*) 3 (*b*) 4 (*c*) 6 (*d*) 7

19. A canteen requires 525 kgs of wheat for a week. How many kgs of wheat will it require for 30 days?
(*a*) 1950 (*b*) 2100 (*c*) 2250 (*d*) 2400

20. 56 men can complete a piece of work in 24 days. In how many days can 42 men complete the same piece of work?
(*a*) 48 (*b*) 32 (*c*) 20 (*d*) 16

21. Two carpenters can complete 2 table in 2 days. In 5 days, 6 carpenters can complete x tables, where x is:
(*a*) 18 (*b*) 15 (*c*) 12 (*d*) 10

22. If a quarter kg of potato costs 60 paise, how many paise will 200 gm cost?
(*a*) 72 paise (*b*) 56 paise (*c*) 54 paise (*d*) 48 paise

23. The price of 6 toys is Rs. 264.37, What will be the approximate price of 5 toys?
(*a*) Rs. 240 (*b*) Rs. 220 (*c*) Rs. 200 (*d*) Rs. 180

24. If the cost of x meters of wire is d rupees, then what is the cost of y meters of wire at the same rate?
(*a*) Rs. $\frac{yd}{x}$ (*b*) Rs. yd (*c*) Rs. xd (*d*) Rs. $\frac{xy}{d}$

25. A man completes $\frac{5}{8}$ of a job in 10 days. At this rate, how many more days will he take to finish the job?
(*a*) 4 (*b*) 5 (*c*) 6 (*d*) 7

26. A flagstaff 17.5 m high casts a shadow of length 40.25 m. The height of the building, which casts a shadow of length 28.75m under similar condition will be:
(*a*) 21.25 m (*b*) 17.5 m (*c*) 12.5 m (*d*) 10 m

27. An industrial loom weaves 0.128 metre of cloth every second. Approximately, how many seconds will it take for the loom to weave 25 meters of cloth?
(*a*) 488 (*b*) 204 (*c*) 195 (*d*) 178

28. In a camp, there is a meal for 120 men or 200 children. If 150 children have taken the meal, how many men will be catered to with the remaining meal?
(*a*) 50 (*b*) 40 (*c*) 30 (*d*) 20

29. A wheel that has 6 cogs is meshed with a larger wheel of 14 cogs. When the smaller wheel has made 21 revolutions, then the number of revolutions made by the larger wheel is:
(*a*) 16 (*b*) 12 (*c*) 9 (*d*) 5

30. Running at the same constant rate, 6 identical machines can produce a total of 270 bottles per minute. At this rate, how many bottles could 10 such machines produce in 4 minutes?
(*a*) 1400 (*b*) 1600 (*c*) 1800 (*d*) 2000

31. 4 mat-weavers can weave 4 mats in 4 days. At the same rate, how many mats would be woven by 8 mat-weavers in 8 days?
(*a*) 16 (*b*) 14 (*c*) 12 (*d*) 8

32. If 12 carpenters, working 6 hours a day, can make 460 chairs in 24 days, how many chairs will 18 carpenters make in 36 days, each working 8 hours a day?
(*a*) 1380 (*b*) 1320 (*c*) 1260 (*d*) 920

33. If 7 spiders makes 7 webs in 7 days, then in how many days 1 spider will make 1 web?

(a) 7 (b) $\frac{7}{6}$ (c) 3 (d) 1

34. If 5 men or 9 women can do a piece of work in 19 days, then 3 men and 6 women will do the same work in how many days?

(a) 21 (b) 18 (c) 15 (d) 12

35. 8 men can reap 80 hectares in 24 days, then how many hectares can 36 men reap in 30 days?

(a) 450 (b) 425 (c) 400 (d) 350

36. 39 persons can repair a road in 12 days, working 5 hours a day. In how many days will 30 persons, working 6 hours a day, complete the work?

(a) 15 (b) 14 (c) 13 (d) 10

37. In a dairy farm, 40 cows eat 40 bags of husk in 40 days. In how many days one cow will eat one bag of husk?

(a) 80 (b) 40 (c) $\frac{1}{40}$ (d) 1

38. 3 pumps, working 8 hours a day, can empty a tank in 2 days. How many hours a day must 4 pumps work to empty the tank in 1 day?

(a) 12 (b) 11 (c) 10 (d) 9

39. 10 men, working 6 hours a day can complete a work in 18 days. How many hours a day must 15 men work to complete the same work in 12 days?

(a) 15 (b) 12 (c) 10 (d) 6

40. 400 persons, working 9 hours a day complete $\frac{1}{4}$*th* of the work in 10 days. The number of additional persons, working 8 hours a day, required to complete the remaining work in 20 days, is:

(a) 275 (b) 250 (c) 675 (d) 200

41. 20 men complete $\frac{1}{3}$*rd* of a piece of work in 20 days. How many more men should be employed to finish the rest of the work in 25 more days?

(a) 20 (b) 15 (c) 12 (d) 10

42. If 9 examiners can examine a certain number of answer books in 12 days, working 5 hours a day; for how many hours a day would 4 examiners have to work in order to examine twice the number of answer books in 30 days?

(a) 10 (b) 9 (c) 8 (d) 6

43. If x men, working x hours a day, can do x units of work in x days, then y men, working y hours a day would be able to complete how many units of work in y days?

(a) $\frac{y^3}{x^2}$ (b) $\frac{y^2}{x^3}$ (c) $\frac{x^3}{y^2}$ (d) $\frac{x^2}{y^3}$

44. A certain number of men can finish a piece of work in 100 days. If there were 10 men less, it will take 10 days more for the work to be finished. How many men were there originally?

(a) 110 (b) 100 (c) 82 (d) 75

45. Some persons can do a piece of work in 12 days. Two times the number of such persons will do half of that work in:

(a) 12 days (b) 3 days (c) 6 days (d) 4 days

46. 2 men and 7 boys can do a piece of work in 14 days; 3 men and 8 boys can do the same in 11 days. Then 8 men and 6 boys can do three times of this work in

(a) 30 days (b) 4 days (c) 21 days (d) 18 days

47. 12 men and 18 boys, working $7\frac{1}{2}$ hours a day, can do a piece of work in 60 days. If a man works equal to 2 boys, then how many boys will be required to help 21 men to do twice the work in 50 days, working 9 hours a day?

(a) 90 (b) 48 (c) 42 (d) 30

48. If 3 men or 6 boys, working 7 hours a day can do a piece of work in 10 days; how many days will it take to complete a piece of work twice as large with 6 men and 2 boys working together for 8 hours a day?

(a) 9 (b) $8\frac{1}{2}$ (c) $7\frac{1}{2}$ (d) $6\frac{1}{2}$

EXPLANATORY ANSWERS

1. We have to find the number of days, so we compare each of the other items with the number of days, as given below:

Less men, more days required (Indirect Proportion)

Less hours per day, more days required (Indirect Proportion)

More work, more days required (Direct Proportion)

Therefore,

Men	Work	hours/day	Days
15 ↑	1 ↓	8 ↑	20 ↓
10	3	6	x

Since, $\frac{x}{20} = \frac{15}{10} \times \frac{3}{1} \times \frac{8}{6}$

$\therefore \quad x = \frac{15 \times 3 \times 8 \times 20}{10 \times 1 \times 6} = 120$ days

2. Here, work done = $\frac{1}{4}$ part

$\therefore$ Remaining work $= \left(1 - \frac{1}{4}\right) = \frac{3}{4}$

We have to find the number of additional men required, hence we shall compare each other item with the number of men.

Less hours per day, more men required (Indirect proportion)

More work, more men required (Direct proportion)

More days, less men required (Indirect proportion).

Work	Days	Hours/day	Men
$\frac{1}{4}$ ↓	10 ↑	9 ↑	400 ↓
$\frac{3}{4}$	20	8	x

Since, $\frac{x}{400} = \frac{3/4}{1/4} \times \frac{10}{20} \times \frac{9}{8}$

$\Rightarrow \quad x = \frac{3 \times 10 \times 9 \times 400 \times 4}{4 \times 20 \times 8} = 675$

$\therefore$ Additional men $= (675 - 400) = 275$

3. Let the required height of the tree be x metres.

Then $80 : 16 :: x : 9$

$\Rightarrow \quad \frac{80}{16} = \frac{x}{9}$

$\Rightarrow \quad 16x = 9 \times 80$

$x = \frac{9 \times 80}{16} = 45$ metres

Hence, the height of the tree = 45 metres.

4.

Persons	Days	
15 ↑	3 ↓	More days, less persons (Indirect Variations)
10	x	

Now, $\frac{x}{3} = \frac{15}{10} \qquad \therefore \quad x = \frac{15}{10} \times 3 = \frac{9}{2} = 4\frac{1}{2}$ days

5.

Men	Days	
16 ↑	8 ↓	More days, less persons (Indirect Variations)
12	x	

$\Rightarrow \frac{x}{8} = \frac{16}{12} \qquad \therefore \quad x = \frac{16}{12} \times 8 = \frac{32}{3} = 10\frac{2}{3}$ days

6.

Days	Rice (kg)	
7 ↑	238 ↓	More rice, more days (Direct Variations)
49	x	

$\Rightarrow \frac{x}{238} = \frac{49}{7} \qquad \therefore \quad x = \frac{49}{7} \times 238 = 1666$ days

7.

Men	Days	
17 ↑	12 ↓	More days, less men (Indirect Variations)
6	x	

$\Rightarrow \frac{x}{12} = \frac{17}{6} \qquad \therefore \quad x = \frac{17}{6} \times 12 = 34$ days

8. Days ↑ 35, 25   Men ↓ x, $x + 150$

$\Rightarrow \dfrac{x+150}{x} = \dfrac{35}{25} \quad \Rightarrow 1 + \dfrac{150}{x} = \dfrac{35}{25} \quad \Rightarrow \dfrac{150}{x} = \dfrac{10}{25}$

$\therefore\ x = \dfrac{25}{10} \times 150 = 375$

Required number of men = 375 – 150 = 225

9. Soldiers ↑ 150, 125   Days ↓ 35, x

$\Rightarrow \dfrac{x}{35} = \dfrac{150}{125} \qquad \therefore\ x = \dfrac{150}{125} \times 35 = 42$ days

10. Men ↑ 40, 30   Rice (kgs) ↓ 60, 12   Days ↓ 15, x

$\Rightarrow \dfrac{x}{15} = \dfrac{12}{60} \times \dfrac{40}{30} \qquad \therefore\ x = \dfrac{12}{60} \times \dfrac{40}{30} \times 15 = 4$ days

11. Men ↑ 30, 21   Hours ↑ 7, 8   Days ↓ 18, x

$\Rightarrow \dfrac{x}{18} = \dfrac{7}{8} \times \dfrac{30}{21} \qquad \therefore\ x = \dfrac{7}{8} \times \dfrac{30}{21} \times 18 = \dfrac{45}{2} = 22\dfrac{1}{2}$ days

12. Persons ↑ 275, 150   Days ↓ 24, x

$\Rightarrow \dfrac{x}{24} = \dfrac{275}{150} \qquad \therefore\ x = \dfrac{275}{150} \times 24 = 44$ days

13. Days ↑ 7, 58   Rice (kgs) ↓ 105, x More rice, more men (Direct Variations)

$\Rightarrow \dfrac{x}{105} = \dfrac{58}{7} \qquad \therefore\ x = \dfrac{58 \times 105}{7} = 870$ kgs

14. Men ↑ 18, 21   Days ↓ 5, x

$\Rightarrow \dfrac{x}{5} = \dfrac{18}{21} \qquad \therefore\ x = \dfrac{18}{21} \times 5 = \dfrac{30}{7} = 4\dfrac{2}{7}$ days

15. Days — 50, 40 ↑ Men — 60, x ↓

$\Rightarrow \dfrac{x}{60}=\dfrac{50}{40}$ $\therefore\ x=\dfrac{50}{40}\times 60=75$ men

Hence, number of additional men = 75 – 60 = 15

16. Hours — 6, 9 ↑ Days — 15, 12 ↑ Pumps — 12, x ↓

$\Rightarrow \dfrac{x}{12}=\dfrac{15}{12}\times\dfrac{6}{9}$ $\therefore\ x=\dfrac{15}{12}\times\dfrac{6}{9}\times 12=10$ days

17. Work — $\dfrac{3}{4}$, $\dfrac{1}{4}$ ↓ Days — 60, 30 ↑ Men — 60, x ↓

$\Rightarrow \dfrac{x}{60}=\dfrac{60}{30}\times\dfrac{1/4}{3/4}$ $\therefore\ x=\dfrac{60}{30}\times\dfrac{1}{3}\times 60=40$ days

Hence, number of men to be discharged = 60 – 40 = 20

18. People — 50, 35 ↑ Rice (kgs) — 350, 50 ↓ Days — 30, x ↓

$\Rightarrow \dfrac{x}{30}=\dfrac{50}{350}\times\dfrac{50}{35}$ $\therefore\ x=\dfrac{50}{350}\times\dfrac{50}{35}\times 30=\dfrac{300}{49}\simeq 6$ days

19. Days — 7, 30 ↓ Wheat (kgs) — 525, x ↓

$\Rightarrow \dfrac{x}{525}=\dfrac{30}{7}$ $\therefore\ x=\dfrac{30\times 525}{7}=2250$ kgs

20. Men — 56, 42 ↑ Days — 24, x ↓

$\Rightarrow \dfrac{x}{24}=\dfrac{56}{42}$ $\therefore\ x=\dfrac{56}{42}\times 24=32$ days

21. Carpenters — 2, 6 ↓ Days — 2, 5 ↓ Tables — 2, x ↓

$\Rightarrow \dfrac{x}{2}=\dfrac{5}{2}\times\dfrac{6}{2}$ $\therefore\ x=\dfrac{5}{2}\times\dfrac{6}{2}\times 2=15$ days

22. Potato (gm) — Costs (Paise)

250 ↓ 60

200 ↓ x

$$\Rightarrow \frac{x}{60} = \frac{200}{250} \qquad \therefore \quad x = \frac{200}{250} \times 60 = 48 \text{ paise}$$

23. Toys — Cost (Rs.)

6 ↓ 264.37

5 ↓ x

$$\Rightarrow \frac{x}{264.37} = \frac{5}{6} \qquad \therefore \quad x = \frac{5}{6} \times 264.37 \simeq \text{Rs. } 220$$

24. Wire (m) — Cost (Rs)

x ↓ d

y ↓ a

$$\Rightarrow \frac{a}{d} = \frac{y}{x} \qquad \therefore \quad a = \text{Rs. } \frac{yd}{x}$$

25. Job — Days

$\frac{5}{8}$ ↓ 10

$\frac{3}{8}$ ↓ x

$$\Rightarrow \frac{x}{10} = \frac{3/8}{5/8} \qquad \therefore \quad x = \frac{3}{5} \times 10 = 6 \text{ days}$$

26. Shadow (m) — Object (m)

40.25 ↓ 17.5

28.75 ↓ x

$$\Rightarrow \frac{x}{17.5} = \frac{28.75}{40.25} \qquad \therefore \quad x = \frac{28.75 \times 17.5}{40.25} = 12.5 \text{ m}$$

27. Cloth (m) — Time (s)

0.128 ↓ 1

25 ↓ x

$$\Rightarrow \frac{x}{1} = \frac{25}{0.128} \qquad \therefore \quad x = \frac{25}{0.128} \simeq 195 \text{ sec.}$$

28. Children — Men

200 ↓ 120

50 ↓ x

$$\Rightarrow \frac{x}{120} = \frac{50}{200} \qquad \therefore \quad x = \frac{50}{200} \times 120 = 30 \text{ men}$$

29.

Cogs	Revolutions
6 ↑	21 ↓
14	x

$\Rightarrow \dfrac{x}{21} = \dfrac{6}{14}$ $\quad\therefore\quad x = \dfrac{6}{14} \times 21 = 9$ revolutions

30.

Machines	Time (minutes)	Bottles
6 ↓	1 ↓	270 ↓
10	4	x

$\Rightarrow \dfrac{x}{270} = \dfrac{4}{1} \times \dfrac{10}{6}$ $\quad\therefore\quad x = \dfrac{4 \times 10}{6} \times 270 = 1800$ bottles

31.

Mat-weavers	Days	Mats
4 ↓	4 ↓	4 ↓
8	8	x

$\Rightarrow \dfrac{x}{4} = \dfrac{8}{4} \times \dfrac{8}{4}$ $\quad\therefore\quad x = \dfrac{8}{4} \times \dfrac{8}{4} \times 4 = 16$ days

32.

Carpenters	Hours	Days	Chairs
12 ↓	6 ↓	24 ↓	460 ↓
18	8	36	x

$\Rightarrow \dfrac{x}{460} = \dfrac{36}{24} \times \dfrac{8}{6} \times \dfrac{18}{12}$ $\quad\therefore\quad x = \dfrac{3}{2} \times \dfrac{4}{3} \times \dfrac{3}{2} \times 460 = 1380$ chairs

33.

Spiders	Webs	Days
7 ↑	7 ↓	7 ↓
1	1	x

$\Rightarrow \dfrac{x}{7} = \dfrac{1}{7} \times \dfrac{7}{1}$ $\quad\therefore\quad x = \dfrac{1}{7} \times \dfrac{7}{1} \times 7 = 7$ days

34. 5 men $\equiv$ 9 women

$\therefore$ 3 men $= \dfrac{9}{5} \times 3 = \dfrac{27}{5}$ women

Hence, 3 men and 6 women $= \dfrac{27}{5} + 6 = \dfrac{57}{5}$ women

Women	Days
9 ↑	19 ↓
$\dfrac{57}{5}$	x

$\Rightarrow \dfrac{x}{19} = \dfrac{9 \times 5}{57}$ $\quad\therefore\quad x = \dfrac{9 \times 5}{57} \times 19 = 15$ days

35.

Men	Days	Area (hectares)
8 ↓	24 ↓	80 ↓
36	30	x

$\Rightarrow \dfrac{x}{80} = \dfrac{30}{24} \times \dfrac{36}{8}$ $\quad\therefore\quad x = \dfrac{30}{24} \times \dfrac{36}{8} \times 80 = 450$ hectares

36.

Persons	Hours	Days
39 ↑	5 ↑	12 ↓
30	6	x

$\Rightarrow \frac{x}{12} = \frac{5}{6} \times \frac{39}{30}$ $\therefore$ $x = \frac{5}{6} \times \frac{39}{30} \times 12 = 13$ days

37.

Cows	Bags	Days
40 ↑	40 ↓	40 ↓
1	1	x

$\Rightarrow \frac{x}{40} = \frac{40}{1} \times \frac{1}{40}$ $\therefore$ $x = 40$ days

38.

Pumps	Days	Hours
3 ↑	2 ↑	8 ↓
4	1	x

$\Rightarrow \frac{x}{8} = \frac{2}{1} \times \frac{3}{4}$ $\therefore$ $x = \frac{2 \times 3}{4} \times 8 = 12$ days

39.

Men	Days	Hours
10 ↑	18 ↑	6 ↓
15	12	x

$\Rightarrow \frac{x}{6} = \frac{18}{12} \times \frac{10}{15}$ $\therefore$ $x = \frac{3}{2} \times \frac{2}{3} \times 6 = 6$ days

40.

Work	Hours	Days	Persons
$\frac{1}{4}$ ↓	9 ↑	10 ↑	400 ↓
$\frac{3}{4}$	8	20	x

$\Rightarrow \frac{x}{400} = \frac{10}{20} \times \frac{9}{8} \times \frac{3/4}{1/4}$ $\therefore$ $x = \frac{1}{2} \times \frac{9}{8} \times 3 \times 400 = 675$

Hence, number of additional persons = 675 – 400 = 275

41.

Work	Days	Men
$\frac{1}{3}$ ↓	20 ↑	20 ↓
$\frac{2}{3}$	25	x

$\Rightarrow \frac{x}{20} = \frac{20}{25} \times \frac{2/3}{1/3}$ $\therefore$ $x = \frac{4}{5} \times 2 \times 20 = 32$

Hence, number of additional men = 32 – 20 = 12

42.

Examiners	Work	Days	Hours
9 ↑	1 ↓	12 ↑	5 ↓
4	2	30	x

$\Rightarrow \frac{x}{5} = \frac{12}{30} \times \frac{2}{1} \times \frac{9}{4}$ $\therefore$ $x = \frac{12}{30} \times 2 \times \frac{9}{4} \times 5 = 9$ hours

43.

Men	Days	Hours	Work
x ↓	x ↓	x ↓	x ↓
y	y	y	a

$\Rightarrow \quad \frac{a}{x} = \frac{y}{x} \times \frac{y}{x} \times \frac{y}{x} \qquad \therefore \quad a = \frac{y^3}{x^2}$ units

44.

Days	Men
100 ↑	x ↓
110	$x - 10$

$\Rightarrow \quad \frac{x-10}{x} = \frac{100}{110} \qquad \Rightarrow \quad 110x - 1100 = 100x \qquad \Rightarrow 10x = 1100 \quad \therefore \; x = 110$

Hence, initially the number of men = 110

45.

Work	Persons	Days
1 ↓	x ↑	12 ↓
$\frac{1}{2}$	$2x$	a

$\Rightarrow \quad \frac{a}{12} = \frac{x}{2x} \times \frac{1}{2} \qquad \therefore \quad a = \frac{1}{4} \times 12 = 3$ days

46. Here, 14×2 men + 14×7 boys ≡ 11×3 men + 11×8 boys

⇒ 28 men + 98 boys ≡ 33 men + 88 boys ⇒ 5 men = 10 boys ∴ 1 man = 2 boys

Then, 2 men and 7 boys ≡ 4 boys + 7 boys = 11 boys

& also, 8 men and 6 boys ≡ 16 boys + 6 boys = 22 boys

Work	Boys	Days
1 ↓	11 ↑	14 ↓
3	22	x

$\Rightarrow \quad \frac{x}{14} = \frac{11}{22} \times \frac{3}{1} \qquad \therefore \quad x = \frac{1}{2} \times 3 \times 14 = 21$ days

47. Here, 1 man ≡ 2 boys

Now 12 men + 18 boys ≡ 12 men + 9 men = 21 men

Work	Days	Hours	Men
1 ↓	60 ↑	$\frac{15}{2}$ ↑	21 ↓
2	50	9	x

$\Rightarrow \quad \frac{x}{21} = \frac{15}{2 \times 9} \times \frac{60}{50} \times \frac{2}{1} \qquad \therefore \quad x = \frac{15}{2 \times 9} \times \frac{60}{50} \times 2 \times 21 = 42$ men

Hence, number of additional men = 42 – 21 = 21 men

Then, 21 men ≡ 42 boys.

48. Here, 1 man ≡ 2 boys

Then, 6 men and 2 boys ≡ 12 boys + 2 boys ≡ 14 boys

Work	Boys	Hours	Days
1 ↓	6 ↑	7 ↑	10 ↓
2	14	8	x

$\Rightarrow \quad \frac{x}{10} = \frac{7}{8} \times \frac{6}{14} \times \frac{2}{1} \qquad \therefore \quad x = \frac{7}{8} \times \frac{6}{14} \times 2 \times 10 = \frac{15}{2} = 7\frac{1}{2}$ days

13

TIME AND DISTANCE

Important Formulae:

1. Speed = Distance ÷ Time
2. Distance = Time × Speed
3. Time = Distance ÷ Speed
4. x km/hr = $\left(x \times \frac{5}{18}\right)$ m/sec
5. x metres/sec = $\left(x \times \frac{18}{5}\right)$ km/hr.
6. If the speed of a body is changed in the ratio $m : n$, then the ratio of the time taken changes in the ratio $n : m$.
7. When a man covers a certain distance with a speed of x km/h and another equal distance at the rate of y km/h, then for the whole journey, the average speed is given by

$$\text{Average speed} = \frac{2xy}{x+y} \text{ km/h.}$$

Example 1: A man covers a certain distance between his house and office on scooter. Having an average speed of 30 km/h, he is late by 10 min. However, with a speed of 40 km/h, he reaches his office 5 min. earlier. Find the distance between his house and office.

Solution: Let the distance between the house and the office be x km.

$$\text{Difference of time} = 5 - (-10) = 15 \text{ min} = \frac{1}{4} \text{ hr.}$$

$$\text{Here, } \frac{x}{30} - \frac{x}{40} = \frac{1}{4} \quad \Rightarrow \quad \frac{x}{120} = \frac{1}{4} \qquad \therefore\ x = \frac{120}{4} = 30 \text{ km.}$$

Example 2: A boy goes to school at a speed of 4 km/h and returns to the house at a speed of 3 km/h. If he takes 5 hrs. in all, what is the distance between the house and the school?

Solution: Let the distance between house and the school be x km.

$$\frac{x}{4} + \frac{x}{3} = 5 \qquad \Rightarrow \qquad \frac{7x}{12} = 5 \quad \therefore \quad x = \frac{60}{7} \text{ km}$$

Example 3: A motor car does a journey in 12 hours, the first half at 22 km/h and the second half at 23 km/h. Find the total distance.

Solution: Let the total distance = $2x$ km

$$\frac{x}{22}+\frac{x}{23}=12 \Rightarrow \frac{45x}{506}=12.$$

$$\therefore\ x=\frac{12\times 506}{45}=\frac{2024}{15}=134\frac{14}{15}\text{ km.}$$

Example 4: Two man A and B walk from P to Q, a distance of 21 km, at 3 and 4 km an hour respectively. B reaches Q, returns immediately and meet A at R. Find the distance from P to R.

Solution: Let the distance between Q and R be x km; then

$$\frac{21+x}{4}=\frac{21-x}{3} \Rightarrow 63+3x=84-4x \quad \Rightarrow 7x=21 \quad \therefore\ x=3\text{ km}$$

Hence, distance from P to R = 21 – 3 = 18 km

Example 5: A person covers a distance in 40 minutes if he runs at a speed of 45 km per hour on an average. Find the speed at which he must run to reduce the time of journey to 30 minutes.

Solution: Let the required speed = x km/hr; then

$$45\times\frac{40}{60}=x\times\frac{30}{60} \qquad \therefore\ x=45\times\frac{2}{3}\times\frac{2}{1}=60\text{ km/hr}$$

Example 6: A monkey ascends a greased pole 30 metres high. He ascend 3 metres in first minute and slips down 1 metre in the next minute if he keeps on doing so, in what time will it reach the top?

Solution: Given,

Ascending 3 metres in a minute and slipping down in next minute i.e., ascending a total distance of 2 metre in 2 minutes and this way the monkey can ascend a distance of 28 metres in 28 minutes.

Now in the next minute, he has to ascend the rest of the length i.e., 2 metres which he will do in $\frac{2}{3}$ minute and while on reaching at the top of the pole, he will never slip down.

$\therefore$ Total time $= 28\frac{2}{3}$ minutes Ans.

Example 7: A car can complete a journey in 6 hours if it travels at 45 km/hr. At what speed (in km/hr) must it travel in order to complete the journey in 5 hours?

Solution: Distance covered by the car in 6 hours at 45 km/hr = 45 × 6 = 270 kms.

$\therefore$ In the second case speed of the car should be $\frac{270}{5}=54$ km/hr.

Example 8: If wheels of a car with circumference $4\frac{2}{7}$ m revolve 7 times in 4 seconds, find the speed of the car in km/hr.

Solution: Circumference of the wheel $=4\frac{2}{7}=\frac{30}{7}$ m

$\therefore$ Path covered by wheels in 7 revolutions $=\frac{30}{7}\times 7=30$ m

Time taken = 4 seconds

$\therefore$ Speed of the car $=\frac{30}{4}$ m/s $=\frac{30}{4}\times\frac{18}{5}=27$ km/hr.

Example 9: While going to school from her home Monika finds that if she walks at the rate of 5 km/hr, she reaches her school late by 6 minutes. However, if she walks at the rate of 6 km/hr, she reaches the school 6 minutes before. Find the path distance between her home and the school.

Solution: Suppose distance between her home to school = x km

Difference of time = 6 – (–6) = 12 min = $\frac{1}{5}$ hr.

$$\frac{x}{5} - \frac{x}{6} = \frac{1}{5} \Rightarrow \frac{x}{30} = \frac{1}{5} \quad \therefore x = 6 \text{ km}$$

Example 10 : The distance between two towns A and B is 110 kms. A motorist starts from town A towards town B at a speed of 20 km/hr at 7.00 O'clock in the morning and another motorist starts from town B towards town A at a speed of 25 km/hr at 8.00 O'clock in the morning. At what time will they cross each other?

Solution: Let after t hr. starting of B, they cross each other; then

$20(t + 1) + 25t = 110 \quad \Rightarrow 45t = 90 \quad \therefore t = 2$ hr.

Hence, required time = 8 O'clock + 2 hr = 10 O'clock

Example 11 : A car travels a distance of 45 kms at the speed of 15 kms/hr. It covers next 50 kms of its journey at the speed of 25 kms/hr and last 25 kms of its journey at the speed of 10 kms/hr. What is the average speed of the car?

Solution: Average speed = $\frac{45+50+25}{\frac{45}{15}+\frac{50}{25}+\frac{25}{10}} = \frac{120}{7.5}$ = 16 km/hr.

Example 12: Running $\frac{2}{3}$ of its usual speed, a train is 3 hours late. Find the usual time (in hours) to cover the journey.

Solution: Let x km be the distance and v km/hr be the usual speed; then usual time taken = $\frac{x}{v}$ hours.

Now, $\frac{x}{\frac{2}{3}v} - \frac{x}{v} = 3 \quad \Rightarrow \frac{x}{2v} = 3 \quad \therefore \frac{x}{v} = 6$ hrs.

Example 13: Samir drove at the speed of 45 kms/hr from home to resort; Returning over the same route, he got stuck in traffic and took an hour longer, also he could drive only at the speed of 40 kms/hr. How many kilometers did he drive each way.

Solution: Let the distance of each way be x km; then

$$\frac{x}{40} - \frac{x}{45} = 1 \quad \Rightarrow \frac{x}{360} = 1 \quad \therefore x = 360 \text{ km}$$

Example 14: A train travels at a speed of 30 km/hr for 12 minutes and then for the next 8 minutes at a speed of 45 km/hr. What is the average speed for the journey?

Solution: Average speed = $\frac{30 \times \frac{12}{60} + 45 \times \frac{8}{60}}{(12+8) \times \frac{1}{60}} = \frac{360+360}{20} = \frac{720}{20}$ = 36 km/hr

Example 15: The ratio of speeds of two trains is 7 : 8. If the second train runs 400 km in 5 hrs., find the speed of the first train?

Solution: Speed of second train $= \frac{400}{5} = 80$ km/hr

Hence, speed of first train $= \frac{7}{8} \times 80 = 70$ km/hr.

Example 16 : A train travels from Dehradun to Delhi at a speed of 40 km/hr and returns at 60 km/hr. Find the average speed for the entire journey.

Solution: Required average speed $= \frac{2xy}{x+y} = \frac{2 \times 40 \times 60}{40+60} = \frac{4800}{100} = 48$ km/hr.

Example 17: A train travels 200 km at a uniform speed. If the speed had been 10 km/hr less, the journey would have taken forty minutes more. Find the speed of the train?

Solution: Let the usual uniform speed = x km/hr; then

$$\frac{200}{x-10} - \frac{200}{x} = \frac{40}{60} \Rightarrow \frac{200(x-x+10)}{x(x-10)} = \frac{2}{3}$$

$\Rightarrow x^2 - 10x - 3000 = 0$ $\Rightarrow (x - 60)(x + 50) = 0$

$\therefore x = 60$ (Taking +ve value)

Hence, speed of the train = 60 km/hr

EXERCISE

1. A car moving at 48 km/hr completes a journey in 10 hours. By how much the speed of this car should be increased so as to do this journey in 8 hours?

(a) 8 km/hr. (b) 12 km/hr (c) 10 km/hr (d) 15 km/hr

2. Starting from a point at a speed of 4 km/hr a man reaches at a cerain place and returns back to the point from where he had started journey on bicycle at the speed of 16 km/hr. His average speed during the entire journey will be :

(a) 6.4 km/h (b) 8.4 km/h (c) 5.4 km/h (d) 10 km/h

3. A motorist covers a certain distance at a average speed of 48 km/h in 45 minutes. What speed in km/h he must maintain to cover the same distance in 30 minutes?

(a) 66 km/h (b) 79 km/h (c) 80 km/h (d) 72 km/h

4. Two points A and B are 150 km apart. A man completes his onward journey from A to B in 3 hours 20 minutes and return journey from B to A in 4 hours 10 minutes. His average speed during the entire journey will be less than his average speed during the journey from A to B by :

(a) 5 km/h (b) 7.5 km/h (c) 9 km/h (d) 3 km/h

5. A policeman saw a thief at a distance of 200 m. The policeman and the thief started running at the same time. If the policeman runs at a speed of $4\frac{1}{6}$ m per second and the thief at a speed of $3\frac{1}{3}$ m per second, after what time the policeman will catch the thief?

(a) 12 min (b) 10 min (c) 9 min (d) 4 min

6. Kanchan walks from her home at 4 kms per hour and reaches her school 5 minutes late. If she walks at 5 kms per hour, she reaches the school 2½ minutes earlier. How far is the school from her home?
(*a*) 3.5 kms (*b*) 2.5 kms (*c*) 2.75 kms (*d*) 3.2 kms

7. A monkey wants to climb up a glazed pole. He climbs 12 metres in 1 minute and then he slips back 3 metres in the next minute. If the pole is 63 metre high, how long does he take to climb at the top of the pole?
(*a*) $11\frac{1}{4}$ min (*b*) $12\frac{1}{2}$ min (*c*) $12\frac{3}{4}$ min (*d*) $14\frac{3}{4}$ min

8. A and B start walking at the same time on a circular path with circumference 35 metre. If they walk in the same direction at 4 km/hr and 5 km/hr respectively, after what time will they meet together?
(*a*) 35 hours (*b*) 27 hours (*c*) 24 hours (*d*) 40 hours

9. While walking at $\frac{3}{5}$ of his usual speed Kamalkant reaches at his destination late by 30 minutes. His usual time consumed in reaching to his destination is:
(*a*) 32 min (*b*) 40 min (*c*) 45 min (*d*) 42 min

10. The distance between two stations A and B is 300 km. A train leaves the station A with a speed of 40 km/hr. At the same time another train departs from the station B with a speed of 50 km/hr. How much time will these two trains take to cross each other?
(*a*) 3 hrs 40 min (*b*) 3 hrs 20 min (*c*) 2 hrs 20 min (*d*) 3 hrs 45 min

11. Gulshan starts from a place P at 2 p.m. and walks to Q at 5 km per hour. Tarun starts from P at 3 p.m. and follows Gulshan on bicycle at 10 km per hour. By when Tarun will catch Gulshan?
(*a*) At 5.30 p.m. (*b*) At 4.00 p.m. (*c*) At 4.30 p.m. (*d*) At 6.00 p.m.

12. Nilesh goes to school from his village at the speed of 4 km/hr and returns from school to village at the speed of 2 km/hr. If he takes 6 hours in all, then what is the distance between the village and the school?
(*a*) 8 km (*b*) 6 km (*c*) 5 km (*d*) 4 km

13. A school bus covers a distance from a village to school at the speed of 12 km/hr and reaches the school 8 minute late. The next day the bus covers the same distance at the speed of 20 km/hr and reaches the school 10 minutes early. What is the distance between village and the school?
(*a*) 6 km (*b*) 9 km (*c*) 12 km (*d*) 15 km

14. By increasing the speed of the bus by 10 km/hr the time of journey for 72 km is reduced by 36 minutes. What was the original speed of the bus?
(*a*) 30 km/hr (*b*) 35 km/hr (*c*) 40 km/hr (*d*) 45 km/hr

15. A car completes a fixed journey in 8 hours. It covers half distance at the speed of 40 km/hr and rest at the 60 km/hr, the distance of the journey is:
(*a*) 400 km (*b*) 420 km (*c*) 384 km (*d*) 350 km

16. A car covers four consecutive extensions of 3 km each at the speeds of 10 km/hr, 20 km/hr, 30 km/hr and 60 km/hr. Its average speed of journey is:
(*a*) 30 km/hr (*b*) 25 km/hr (*c*) 20 km/hr (*d*) 10 km/hr

17. A girl rides her bicycle 10 km at an average speed of 12 km/hr and another 12 km at an average speed of 10 km/hr. Her average speed for the entire journey is approximately:
(*a*) 12.2 km/hr (*b*) 11.2 km/hr (*c*) 10.8 km/hr (*d*) 10.4 km/hr

18. Raman drove from home to a neighbouring town at the speed of 50 km/hr and on his returning journey, he drove at the speed of 45 km/hr and also took an hour longer to reach home. What distance did he cover each way?

(*a*) 900 km (*b*) 500 km (*c*) 450 km (*d*) 225 km

19. A man takes 6 hours 35 minutes in walking to a certain place and riding back. He would have taken 2 hours less by riding both ways. What would be the time he would take to walk both ways?

(*a*) 10 hours (*b*) 8 hours 35 minutes (*c*) 8 hours 25 minutes (*d*) 8 hrs

20. A man covers a distance of 6 km at the rate of 4 km/hr and other 4 km at 3 km/hr this average speed is

(*a*) $3\frac{5}{9}$ km/hr (*b*) $3\frac{9}{17}$ km/hr (*c*) $5\frac{9}{17}$ km/hr (*d*) $9\frac{3}{17}$ km/hr

21. A person travels three equal distances at a speed of x km/hr, y km/hr and z km/hr respectively. What is the average speed for whole journey?

(*a*) $\frac{xyz}{3(xy+yz+zx)}$ km/h (*b*) $\frac{3xyz}{xy+yz+zx}$ km/h (*c*) $\frac{xy+yz+zx}{xyz}$ km/h (*d*) $\frac{xyz}{xy+yz+zx}$ km/h

22. A train is scheduled to cover the distance between two stations 70 km apart in an hour. If it travels the first 30 km at 60 km/hr can it complete the journey in time without exceeding a speed restriction of 80 km/hr?

(*a*) yes (*b*) no

(*c*) can't be determined (*d*) None of these

23. Manoj walked from Mumbai to Thane on foot. Had he walked one mile/hr faster he would have reached $2\frac{1}{2}$ hrs earlier, but he had walked slower by one mile/hr, he would have taken 5 hrs. more. The distance between Mumbai and Thane is:

(*a*) 20 miles (*b*) 30 miles (*c*) 40 miles (*d*) 60 miles

24. A train covers a distance in 50 minutes, if it runs at a speed of 48 km/hr on an average. The speed at which the train must run to reduce the time of journey to 40 minutes will be:

(*a*) 70 km/hr (*b*) 60 km/hr (*c*) 55 km/hr (*d*) 50 km/hr

25. A car covers its journey at the speed of 80 km/hr in 10 hours. If the same distance is to be covered in 4 hours, by how much the speed of car will have to increase?

(*a*) 12 km/hr (*b*) 10 km/hr (*c*) 8 km/hr (*d*) None of these

26. A person started his journey in the morning. At 11 a.m. he covered $\frac{3}{8}$ of the journey and on the same day at 4.30 p.m. he covered $\frac{5}{6}$ of the journey. He started his journey at:

(*a*) 7.00 a.m. (*b*) 6.30 a.m. (*c*) 6.00 a.m. (*d*) 5.30 a.m.

27. A certain distance is covered by a vehicle at a certain speed. If half of this distance is covered by another vehicle in double the time, the ratio of the speeds of the two vehicles is:

(*a*) 4 : 1 (*b*) 1 : 4 (*c*) 2 : 1 (*d*) 1 : 2

28. A train starts at 7 a.m. from A towards B with a speed of 50 km/hr. Another train from B starts at 8 a.m. with a speed of 60 km/hr towards A. Both of them meet at 10 a.m. at C. The ratio of the distances AC to BC is:

(*a*) 4 : 5 (*b*) 5 : 4 (*c*) 5 : 6 (*d*) 6 : 5

29. Ram arrives at a Bank 15 minutes earlier than scheduled time if he drives his car at 42 km/hr. If he drives car at 35 km/hr he arrives 5 minutes late. The distance of the Bank from his starting point is:
(*a*) 210 km (*b*) 72 km (*c*) 70 km (*d*) 60 km

30. Pratibha covers a distance of 24 km at the speed of 8 km/hr and a distance of 18 km at the speed of 9 km/hr. Further she covers a distance of 12 km at the speed of 3 km/hr. What is her average speed in covering the whole distance?
(*a*) 8 km/hr (*b*) 6 km/hr (*c*) 5.5 km/hr (*d*) 3 km/hr

31. A cyclist rides 24 km at 16 km/h and further 36 km at 15 km/hr. Find his average speed for the journey.
(*a*) 15.38 km/hr (*b*) 15.5 km/hr (*c*) 16 km/hr (*d*) 16.5 km/hr

32. A car is running at a speed of 108 km/hr. Find the distance covered by it in 15 seconds.
(*a*) 450 m (*b*) 475 m (*c*) 500 m (*d*) 550 m

33. How long will a boy take to run round a square field of side 35 meters, If he runs at the rate of 9 km/hr?
(*a*) 56 sec. (*b*) 54 sec. (*c*) 52 sec. (*d*) 50 sec.

34. A person crosses a 600 m long street in 5 minutes. Find his speed in km/hr.
(*a*) 10 (*b*) 8.4 (*c*) 7.2 (*d*) 3.6

35. A man walking at the rate of 5 km/hr crosses a bridge in 15 minutes. What is the length of the bridge in meters?
(*a*) 1250 (*b*) 1000 (*c*) 750 (*d*) 600

36. A truck covers a distance of 550 m in 1 minute whereas a bus covers a distance of 33 km in 45 minutes. The ratio of their speeds is:
(*a*) 50 : 3 (*b*) 3 : 5 (*c*) 4 : 3 (*d*) 3 : 4

37. A train travels at an average of 50 miles/hr for $2\frac{1}{2}$ hrs and then travels at a speed of 70 miles/hr for $1\frac{1}{2}$ hrs. Find the distance travelled by the train in entire 4 hrs.
(*a*) 230 miles (*b*) 200 miles (*c*) 150 miles (*d*) 120 miles

38. Sound is said to travel in air at about 1100 feet/sec. A man hears the axe striking the tree $\frac{11}{5}$ seconds after he sees it strike the tree. Find the distance between the man and the wood chopper.
(*a*) 2629 ft. (*b*) 2500 ft. (*c*) 2420 ft. (*d*) 2197 ft.

39. A motor car starts with the speed of 70 km/hr with its speed increasing every two hours by 10 km/hr. What is the time taken (in hours) in covering 345 km by it?
(*a*) 5 hrs. (*b*) $4\frac{1}{2}$ hrs. (*c*) 4 hrs 5 min. (*d*) 4 hrs

40. A person has to cover a distance of 6 km in 45 minutes. If he covers one-half of the distance in two-thirds of the total time. Find his speed (in km/hr) to cover the remaining distance in remaining time.
(*a*) 15 (*b*) 12 (*c*) 8 (*d*) 6

41. An aeroplane covers a certain distance at a speed of 240 km/hr in 5 hours. What is his speed in covering the same distance in $1\frac{2}{3}$ hrs?
(*a*) 720 km/hr (*b*) 600 hm/hr (*c*) 360 km/hr (*d*) 300 km/hr

42. A train covers a distance of 10 km in 12 minutes. If its speed is decreased by 5 km/hr, find the time taken by it to cover the same distance.
(a) 13 min. 20 sec. *(b)* 13 min. *(c)* 11 min. 20 sec. *(d)* 10 min.

43. The speed of a car increases by 2 km after every one hour. If the distance travelled in first one hour was 35 km. The total distance travelled in 12 hrs. is:
(a) 556 km *(b)* 552 km *(c)* 482 km *(d)* 456 km

44. A salesman travels a distance of 50 km in 2 hours and 30 minutes. How much faster, in kilometer/hour, on an average, must he travel to make such a trip in 5/6 hour less time?
(a) 30 *(b)* 20 *(c)* 15 *(d)* 10

45. A person travels from P to Q at a speed of 40 km/hr and returns by increasing his speed by 50%. Find his average speed for both the trips.
(a) 50 km/hr. *(b)* 48 km/hr. *(c)* 45 km/hr. *(d)* 36 km/hr.

46. A person travels equal distances with speeds of 3 km/hr, 4 km/hr, and 5 km/hr and takes a total time of 47 minutes. What is the total distance in km?
(a) 5 *(b)* 4 *(c)* 3 *(d)* 2

47. A can complete a journey in 10 hrs. He travels first half of the journey at the rate of 21 km/hr and second half at the rate of 24 km/hr. The total journey in km is:
(a) 234 *(b)* 230 *(c)* 224 *(d)* 220

48. A is faster than B. A and B each walk 24 km. The sum of their speeds is 7 km/hr and sum of times taken by them is 14 hours. What is the speed of A?
(a) 7 km/hr *(b)* 5 km/hr *(c)* 4 km/hr *(d)* 3 km/hr

49. A farmer travelled a distance of 61 km in 9 hours. He travelled partly on foot at the rate of 4 km/hr and partly on bicycle at the rate of 9 km/hr. What is the distance travelled on foot?
(a) 17 km *(b)* 16 km *(c)* 15 km *(d)* 14 km

50. The average speed of a train in the onward journey 25% more than that in the return journey. The train halts for one hour on reacting the destination. The total time taken for the complete to and fro journey is 17 hours, covering a distance of 800 km. What is the speed of the train in the onward journey?
(a) 56.25 km/hr *(b)* 52 km/hr *(c)* 47.5 km/hr *(d)* 45 km/hr

51. A man travels 600 km by train at 80 km/hr, 800 km by ship at 40 km/hr, 500 km by aeroplane at 400 km/hr and 100 km by car at 50 km/hr. The average speed for the entire distance is:
(a) $65\frac{5}{123}$ km/hr *(b)* 62 km/hr *(c)* $60\frac{5}{123}$ km/hr *(d)* 60 km/hr

52. A man on tour travels first 160 km at 64 km/hr and next 160 km at 80 km/hr. The average speed for the first 320 km of the tour is:
(a) 71 km/hr *(b)* 71.11 km/hr *(c)* 36 km/hr *(d)* 35.55 km/hr

53. A car travels first one-third of a certain distance with a speed of 10 km/hr, the next one-third distance with a speed of 20 km/hr and last one-third distance with a speed of 60 km/hr. What is the average speed of the car for the whole journey?
(a) 36 km/hr *(b)* 30 km/hr *(c)* 24 km/hr *(d)* 18 km/hr

54. A man covered a certain distance at some speed. If he had moved 3 km/hr faster, he would have taken 40 minutes less. If he had moved 2 km/hr slower, he would have taken 40 minutes more. What is the distance in km?
(a) 40 *(b)* $37\frac{1}{2}$ *(c)* $36\frac{2}{3}$ *(d)* 25

55. A train when moves at an average speed of 40 km/hr, reaches its destination on time. When its average speed becomes 35 km/hr, then it reaches its destination 15 minutes late. What is the distance of the journey?

(*a*) 80 km (*b*) 70 km (*c*) 40 km (*d*) 30 km

56. Walking $\frac{6}{7}$th of his usual speed, a man is 12 minutes too late. The usual time taken by him to cover that distance is:

(*a*) 1 hr 20 min (*b*) 1 hr. 15 min (*c*) 1 hr 12 min (*d*) 1 hr.

57. A car travelling with $\frac{5}{7}$ of its actual speed covers 42 km in 1 hr 40 min 48 sec. What is the actual speed of the car?

(*a*) 35 km/hr (*b*) 30 km/hr (*c*) 25 km/hr (*d*) $17\frac{6}{7}$ km/hr

58. Samir is travelling on his cycle and has calculated to reach point A at 2 P.M., if he trvels at 10 km/hr.; he will reach there at 12 noon if he travels at 15 km/h. At what speed must he travel to reach A at 1 P.M.?

(*a*) 14 km/hr (*b*) 12 km/hr (*c*) 11 km/hr (*d*) 8 km/hr

59. Start from his house one day Saurabh walks at a speed of $2\frac{1}{2}$ km/hr and reaches his school 6 minutes late. Next day he increases his speed by 1 km/hr and reaches the school 6 minutes early. What is the distance of the school from his house?

(*a*) 2 km (*b*) $1\frac{3}{4}$ km (*c*) $1\frac{1}{2}$ km (*d*) 1 km

60. A man can reach a certain place in 30 hours. If he reduces his speed by $\frac{1}{15}$th, he goes 10 km less in that time. What is his speed?

(*a*) 6 km/hr (*b*) $5\frac{1}{2}$ km/hr (*c*) 5 km/hr (*d*) 4 km/hr

61. It takes eight hours for a 600 km journey, if 120 km is done by train and rest by car. It takes 20 minutes more, if 200 km is done by train and rest by car. The ratio of the speed of the train to that of the car is:

(*a*) 4 : 3 (*b*) 3 : 4 (*c*) 3 : 2 (*d*) 2 : 3

62. In covering a distance of 30 km, Abhay takes 2 hours more than Samir. If Abhay doubles his speed then he would take 1 hour less than Samir. Find the speed of Abhay?

(*a*) 7.5 km/hr (*b*) 6.25 km/hr (*c*) 6 km/hr (*d*) 5 km/hr

63. If a person walks at 14 km/hr instead of 10 km/hr, he would have walked 20 km more. What is the actual distance travelled by him?

(*a*) 80 km (*b*) 70 km (*c*) 56 km (*d*) 50 km

64. Excluding stoppages, the speed of a bus is 54 km/hr and including stoppages, it is 45 km/hr. For how many minutes does the bus stop per hour?

(*a*) 20 (*b*) 12 (*c*) 10 (*d*) 9

65. In a flight of 600 km, an aircraft was slowed down due to bad weather. Its average speed for the trip was reduced by 200 km/hr and time of flight increased by 30 minutes. What is the duration of flight?

(*a*) 4 hours (*b*) 3 hours (*c*) 2 hours (*d*) 1 hour

66. With a uniform speed a car covers the distance in 8 hours. Had the speed been increased by 4 km/hr, the same distance could have been covered in $7\frac{1}{2}$ hours. The distance covered is:

(a) 640 km (b) 480 km (c) 450 km (d) 420 km

67. In covering a certain distance, the speeds of A and B is the ratio of 3 : 4. A takes 30 minutes more than B to reach the destination. What is the time taken by A to reach the destination?

(a) $2\frac{1}{2}$ hours (b) 2 hours (c) $1\frac{1}{2}$ hours (d) 1 hour

68. A train can travel 50% faster than a car. Both start from point A at the same time and reach point B 75 kms away from A at the same time. On the way, however, the train lost about 12.5 minutes while stopping at the stations. What is the speed of car?

(a) 130 km/hr (b) 120 km/hr (c) 110 km/hr (d) 100 km/hr

69. Two trains start from P and Q respectively and travel towards each other at a speed of 50 km/hr and 40 km/hr respectively. By the time they meet the first train has travelled 100 km more than the second. What is the distance between P and Q?

(a) 900 km (b) 660 km (c) 630 km (d) 500 km

70. Two cars P and Q start at the same time from A and B which are 120 km apart. If the two cars travel in opposite directions, they meet after one hour and if they travel in same direction (from A towards B), then P meets Q after 6 hours. The speed of the car P is:

(a) 80 km/hr (b) 75 km/hr (c) 70 km/hr (d) 60 km/hr

71. The jogging track in a sports complex is 76 metres in circumference. Sanjay and his wife start from the same point and walk in opposite directions at 4.5 km/hr and 3.75 km/hr respectively. They will meet for the first time in:

(a) 6 min. (b) 5.5 min. (c) 5.28 min. (d) 4.9 min.

72. A thief steals a car at 2.30 p.m. and drives it at 60 km/hr. The theft is discovered at 3 p.m. and the owner sets off in another car at 75 km/h. When will he overtake the thief?

(a) 5.15 p.m. (b) 5 p.m. (c) 4.45 p.m. (d) 4.30 p.m.

73. A walks around a circular field at the rate of one round per hour while B runs around it at the rate of six round per hour. They start in the same direction from the same point at 7.30 a.m. They will first cross each other at:

(a) 8.30 a.m. (b) 8.10 a.m. (c) 7.48 a.m. (d) 7.42 a.m.

74. A and B walk around a circular track. They start at 8 a.m. from the same point in the opposite directions. A and B walk at a speed of 2 rounds per hour and 3 rounds per hour respectively. How many times shall they cross each other before 9.30 a.m.?

(a) 8 (b) 7 (c) 6 (d) 5

75. The distance between two cities A and B is 330 km. A train starts from A at 8 a.m. and travels towards B at 60 km/hr. Another train starts from B at 9 a.m. and travels towards A at 75 km/hr. At what time do they meet?

(a) 11.30 a.m. (b) 11 a.m. (c) 10.30 a.m. (d) 10 a.m.

76. A thief is noticed by a policeman from a distance of 200 m. The thief starts running and the policeman chases him. The thief and the policeman run at the rate of 10 km/hr and 11 km/hr respectively. What is the distance between them after 6 minutes?

(a) 200 m (b) 190 m (c) 150 m (d) 100 m

EXPLANATORY ANSWERS

1. Let he has to increase his speed by x km/hr for given condition; then,
$(48 + x) \times 8 = 48 \times 10 \quad \Rightarrow 48 + x = 60 \quad \therefore x = 12$ km/hr

2. Average speed during the entire journey = $\frac{2xy}{x+y} = \frac{2\times4\times16}{4+16} = \frac{8\times16}{20}$ = 6.4 km/hr.

3. Let required speed be x km/hr; then

$x \times \frac{1}{2} = 48 \times \frac{3}{4} \quad \therefore \; x = 48 \times \frac{3}{4} \times 2 = 72$ km/hr

4. During onward journey from A to B:

Average speed = $\frac{150}{10/3} = \frac{150\times3}{10}$ = 45 km/hr.

During entire jouney :

Average speed = $\frac{300}{\frac{10}{3}+\frac{25}{6}} = \frac{300\times6}{45}$ = 40 km/hr.

Hence, difference of average speed = 45 – 40 = 5 km/hr

5. Suppose the policeman will catch the thief after t seconds

then, $\left(\frac{25}{6}-\frac{10}{3}\right)t = 200 \quad \Rightarrow \frac{5}{6}t = 200 \quad \therefore t = \frac{200\times6}{5}$ = 240 sec = 4 min.

6. Suppose the distance between her house to the school = x km

Difference of time = $\frac{5}{2} - (-5) = \frac{15}{2}$ min = $\frac{1}{8}$ hr.

$\frac{x}{4} - \frac{x}{5} = \frac{1}{8} \quad \Rightarrow \frac{x}{20} = \frac{1}{8} \quad \therefore x = \frac{20}{8}$ = 2.5 km

7. The monkey climbs 12 metres in 1 minute and then he slips back 3 metres in the next minute

$\therefore$ The monkey climbs in the first 2 minutes = 12 – 3 = 9 metres

$\therefore$ In the first 12 minutes the monkey climbs = 9 × 6 = 54 metres

Remaining height of the pole to be covered by the monkey = 63 – 54 = 9 metre

$\therefore$ The monkey will climb the height of 9 metres in the 13th minute

$\because$ The monkey climbs 12 metres in 1 minute

$\therefore$ The monkey will climb 9 metres in $\frac{1}{12}\times9 = \frac{3}{4}$ minute

$\therefore$ Time spent in climbing at the top of the pole = $\left(12+\frac{3}{4}\right)$ minutes = $12\frac{3}{4}$ minutes

8. The two persons walk in the same direction

$\therefore$ Their relative speed = 5 – 4 = 1 km/hr

Distance covered in 1 round on the circular path = 35 km

$\therefore$ They will meet after $\frac{35}{1}$ = 35 hours.

9. Suppose usual speed of Kamalkant is v km/hr and his destination is at a distance of x kms; then usual time taken = $\frac{x}{v}$ hours.

$$\frac{x}{3v/5} - \frac{x}{v} = \frac{1}{2} \quad \Rightarrow \frac{2x}{3v} = \frac{1}{2} \quad \therefore \frac{x}{v} = \frac{3}{4} \text{ hour} = 45 \text{ min.}$$

10. The two trains are moving in the opposite directions

$\therefore$ Relative speed = 40 + 50 = 90 km/hr.

$\therefore$ Time taken to cross each other = $\frac{300}{90} = 3\frac{1}{3}$ hours or, 3 hours 20 minutes.

11. Let Tarun will catch Gulshan after t hours the starting of Tarun; then, $10t = 5(t + 1)$

$\Rightarrow 5t = 5 \therefore t = 1$ hr

Hence, required time = 3 p.m. + 1 hr. = 4 p.m.

12. Let x km be the distance between village and the school; then

$$\frac{x}{4} + \frac{x}{2} = 6 \quad \Rightarrow \frac{3x}{4} = 6 \quad \therefore x = \frac{6 \times 4}{3} = 8 \text{ km}$$

13. Let x km be the distance from village to school, then

$$\frac{x}{12} - \frac{x}{20} = [8 - (-10)] \times \frac{1}{60} \Rightarrow \frac{x}{30} = \frac{18}{60} \quad \therefore x = \frac{18}{60} \times 30 = 9 \text{ km}$$

14. Let original speed of the bus be x km/hr; then

$$\frac{72}{x} - \frac{72}{x+10} = \frac{36}{60} \Rightarrow \frac{72(x+10-x)}{x^2+10x} = \frac{3}{5} \quad \Rightarrow 1200 = x^2 + 10x$$

$$\Rightarrow x^2 + 10x - 1200 = 0 \quad \Rightarrow (x + 40)(x - 30) = 0 \quad \therefore x = 30 \text{ or } x = -40$$

Taking positive value only, so speed of the bus = 30 km/hr.

15. Let the distance of the journey be x km, then,

$$\frac{x}{2 \times 40} + \frac{x}{2 \times 60} = 8 \quad \Rightarrow \frac{5x}{240} = 8 \quad \therefore x = 8 \times 48 = 384 \text{ km}$$

16. Total distance of the journey = 4 × 3 km = 12 km

Total time taken = $\frac{3}{10} + \frac{3}{20} + \frac{3}{30} + \frac{3}{60} = \frac{36}{60} = \frac{3}{5}$ hr.

Hence, average speed = $\frac{12}{3/5} = \frac{12 \times 5}{3} = 20$ km/hr.

17. Average speed = $\frac{10+12}{\frac{10}{12}+\frac{12}{10}} = \frac{22}{61/30} = \frac{22 \times 30}{61} = \frac{660}{61} = 10.8$ km/hr

18. Let his distance of journey of each way be x km; then

$$\frac{x}{45} - \frac{x}{50} - 1 \quad \Rightarrow \frac{x}{450} = 1 \quad \therefore x = 450 \text{ km}$$

19. Here,

Walking to a certain place + riding back = 6 hrs 35 min. ...*(i)*

2 × riding the same distance = 4 hrs 35 min. ...*(ii)*

Multiplying equation *(i)* × 2 and subtracting *(ii)* we get

Time taken in walking both ways = 13 hrs 70 min – 4 hrs. 35 min = 8 hrs. 35 min.

20. His average speed $= \dfrac{6+4}{\dfrac{6}{4}+\dfrac{4}{3}} = \dfrac{10}{17/6} = \dfrac{60}{17} = 3\dfrac{9}{17}$ km/hr

21. Let the equal distances be d km; then,

Average speed $= \dfrac{3d}{\dfrac{d}{x}+\dfrac{d}{y}+\dfrac{d}{z}} = \dfrac{3}{\dfrac{xy+yz+zx}{xyz}} = \dfrac{3xyz}{xy+yz+zx}$ km/hr

22. Time taken in covering 30 km $= \dfrac{30}{60} = \dfrac{1}{2}$ hr

Remaining distance = 70 – 30 = 40 km

Hence, the train has to cover 40 km in $\dfrac{1}{2}$ hr

Hence, speed of the train = 40 × 2 = 80 km/hr

So, the train can complete the journey in time without exceeding a speed restriction of 80 km/hr.

23. Let usual speed be x miles/hr and distance of the destination be d miles

Now, $\dfrac{d}{x} - \dfrac{d}{x+1} = \dfrac{5}{2} \quad \Rightarrow d = \dfrac{5}{2}x(x+1)$ ...(i)

Again, $\dfrac{d}{x-1} - \dfrac{d}{x} = 5 \quad \Rightarrow \quad d = 5x(x-1)$ ...(ii)

From equations (i) and (ii)

$\dfrac{5}{2}x\,(x+1) = 5x\,(x-1) \qquad \Rightarrow x + 1 = 2x - 2 \qquad \therefore \; x = 3$ mile/hr

Now, From *(ii)*, $d = 5 \times 3\,(3 - 1) = 30$ miles

24. Let x km/hr be the required speed of the train; then

$$x \times \frac{40}{60} = 48 \times \frac{50}{60} \quad \therefore \; x = \frac{48 \times 50}{40} = 60 \text{ km/hr}$$

25. Let required speed of the car be x km/hr, then

$4x = 80 \times 10 \qquad \therefore \; x = 200$ km/hr

Hence, increase in speed = 200 – 80 = 120 km/hr

26. Time interval between 11 a.m. to 4.30 p.m. = 5.30 hrs $= \dfrac{11}{2}$ hrs.

Part of journey $= \dfrac{5}{6} - \dfrac{3}{8} = \dfrac{11}{24}$

Now, $\dfrac{11}{24}$ part of journey covered in $\dfrac{11}{2}$ hrs.

Hence, $\frac{3}{8}$ part of journey covered in $\frac{11\times 24}{2\times 11}\times\frac{3}{8}=\frac{9}{2}$ hrs = 4 hrs 30 min.

So, required time = 11 a.m. – 4.30 = 6.30 a.m.

27. Let x km/hr and t hr be the certain speed and certain time.

Then, ratio of their speeds = $\frac{x}{t}:\frac{x}{2\times 2t}=1:\frac{1}{4}$ = 4 : 1

28. AC = 50 × 3 = 150 km; BC = 60 × 2 = 120 km
Hence, AC : BC = 150 : 120 = 5 : 4

29. Let x km be the distance of the bank from his starting point.

Then, $\frac{x}{35}-\frac{x}{42}=[5-(-15)]\times\frac{1}{60}\Rightarrow\frac{x}{210}=\frac{1}{3}\quad\therefore x=70$ km

30. Required average speed = $\frac{24+18+12}{\frac{24}{8}+\frac{18}{9}+\frac{12}{3}}=\frac{54}{9}$ = 6 km/hr

31. Required average speed = $\frac{24+36}{\frac{24}{16}+\frac{36}{15}}=\frac{60}{\frac{3}{2}+\frac{12}{5}}=\frac{60\times 10}{39}$ = 15.38 km/hr

32. Required distance = $108\times\frac{15}{60\times 60}$ km = $\frac{9}{20}$ km = $\frac{9}{20}\times 1000$ = 450 m

33. 9 km/hr = $9\times\frac{5}{18}=\frac{5}{2}$ m/s

Time taken = $\frac{4\times 35}{5/2}$ = 4 × 7 × 2 = 56 sec.

34. Speed = $\frac{600\text{m}}{5\times 60\text{ s}}=2\text{m}/s=2\times\frac{18}{5}$ km/hr = $\frac{36}{5}$ = 7.2 km/hr.

35. 5 km/hr = $5\times\frac{5}{18}$ m/s = $\frac{25}{18}$ m/s

Hence, length of a bridge = $\frac{25}{18}\times 15\times 60$ = 1250 m

36. Speed of the truck = $\frac{550\text{ m}}{1\times 60\text{ s}}=\frac{55}{6}\times\frac{18}{5}$ = 33 km/hr

Speed of the bus = $\frac{33\times 60}{45}$ = 44 km/hr

Hence, ratio of their speeds = 33 : 44 = 3 : 4

37. Total distance travelled = $50 \times \frac{5}{2} + 70 \times \frac{3}{2} = 125 + 105 = 230$ miles

38. Required distance = $1100 \times \frac{11}{5} = 220 \times 11 = 2420$ ft.

39. Distance travelled in 4 hrs = $70 \times 2 + 80 \times 2 = 300$ km

Now, time taken to travel rest of 45 km = $\frac{45}{90} = \frac{1}{2}$ hr

Hence, total time taken = $4\frac{1}{2}$ hrs.

40. One half of the distance = $\frac{1}{2} \times 6$ km = 3 km

Two-thirds of the total time = $\frac{2}{3} \times 45 = 30$ min.

Remaining distance = 6 – 3 = 3 km; Remaining time = 45 – 30 = 15 min

Hence, required speed = $\frac{3}{15/60} = 3 \times 4 = 12$ km/hr

41. Let required speed = x km/hr; then

$x \times \frac{5}{3} = 240 \times 5 \quad \therefore\ x = \frac{240 \times 5 \times 3}{5} = 720$ km/hr.

42. Original speed of the train = $\frac{10}{12/60} = 10 \times 5 = 50$ km/hr

Now, $\quad 45 \times t = 50 \times \frac{12}{60} \Rightarrow t = \frac{10}{45}$ hr

$= \frac{2}{9} hr = \frac{2}{9} \times 60$ min $= 13\frac{1}{3}$ min = 13 min 20 sec.

43. Distance travelled in 12 hrs = 35 + 37 + 39 + ... upto 12 kms.
This is in A.P. having $a = 35$, $d = 2$ & $n = 12$

Hence, their sum = $\frac{12}{2}[2 \times 35 + (12-1) \times 2] = 6\ (70 + 22)$

$= 6 \times 92 = 552$ km

44. Original speed of the salesman = $\frac{50}{5/2} = 20$ km/hr.

Now, $x\left(\frac{5}{2} - \frac{5}{6}\right) = 50 \Rightarrow x \times \frac{5}{3} = 50 \quad \therefore\ x = 30$ km/hr

Hence, increase in speed = 30 – 20 = 10 km/hr

45. Let distance between P to Q = x km

$$\text{Average speed} = \frac{x+x}{\frac{x}{40}+\frac{x}{40\times\frac{150}{100}}} = \frac{2x}{\frac{x}{40}+\frac{x}{60}} = \frac{2\times120}{5} = 48 \text{ km/hr}$$

46. Let the equal distances be x km, then

$$\frac{x}{3}+\frac{x}{4}+\frac{x}{5}=\frac{47}{60} \Rightarrow \frac{47x}{60}=\frac{47}{60} \quad \therefore x = 1 \text{ km}$$

Hence, total distance = $3x = 3 \times 1 = 3$ km

47. Let the total journey be x km, then

$$\frac{x}{2\times21}+\frac{x}{2\times24}=10 \Rightarrow \frac{15x}{336} = 10 \quad \therefore x = \frac{336\times10}{15} = 224 \text{ km}$$

48. Let speeds of A and B are x_1 and x_2 km/hr and times taken by them are t_1 and t_2 hrs, then

$x_1 + x_2 = 7$ km/hr ...(i) $\quad t_1 + t_2 = 14$ hrs ...(ii)

$$\text{Now, } \frac{24}{x_1}+\frac{24}{x_2} = 14 \Rightarrow \frac{24(x_1+x_2)}{x_1x_2} = 14 \quad \therefore x_1x_2 = \frac{24\times7}{14}=12$$

$$\text{Then, } x_1 - x_2 = \sqrt{(x_1+x_2)^2-4x_1x_2} = \sqrt{(7)^2-4\times12} = 1 \quad \text{...(iii)}$$

Solving *(i)* and *(iii)* we get $x_1 = 4$ km/hr

49. Let distance travelled on foot be x km, then,

$$\frac{x}{4}+\frac{61-x}{9}=9 \Rightarrow \frac{9x+244-4x}{36} = 9 \Rightarrow 5x = 36\times9-244$$

$\Rightarrow 5x = 80 \quad \therefore x = 16$ km

50. Let the speeds of return journey and onward journey be x and

$\frac{x\times125}{100}=\frac{5x}{4}$ km/hr, then

$$\frac{4\times400}{5x}+\frac{400}{x}= 17-1 \Rightarrow \frac{320+400}{x} = 16 \quad \therefore x = \frac{720}{16} = 45 \text{ km/hr}$$

$$\text{Hence, speed of onward journey} = \frac{5\times45}{4}=\frac{225}{4} = 56.25 \text{ km/hr}$$

51. $$\text{Required average speed} = \frac{600+800+500+100}{\frac{600}{80}+\frac{800}{40}+\frac{500}{400}+\frac{100}{50}}=\frac{2000}{\frac{15}{2}+20+\frac{5}{4}+2}$$

$$= \frac{2000}{123/4}=\frac{8000}{123}=65\frac{5}{123} \text{ km/hr}$$

52. $$\text{Average speed} = \frac{160+160}{\frac{160}{64}+\frac{160}{80}}=\frac{320}{\frac{5}{2}+2}=\frac{320\times2}{9} = \frac{640}{9}=71.11 \text{ km/hr}$$

53. Let distance of whole journey be x km; then

$$\text{Required average speed} = \frac{x}{\frac{x}{3\times10}+\frac{x}{3\times20}+\frac{x}{3\times60}} = \frac{3\times10\times3}{5} = 18 \text{ km/hr}$$

54. Let x km/hr be the usual speed and d km be the distance of destination, then

$$\frac{d}{x}-\frac{d}{x+3}=\frac{40}{60} \quad \Rightarrow 3d = \frac{2}{3}x(x+3) \quad \therefore d = \frac{2}{9}x(x+3) \text{ ...(i)}$$

Again, $\frac{d}{x-2}-\frac{d}{x}=\frac{40}{60} \quad \Rightarrow 2d = \frac{2}{3}x(x-2) \quad \therefore d = \frac{1}{3}x(x-2)$ ...(ii)

From (i) & (ii), we get,

$$\frac{2}{9}x(x+3) = \frac{1}{3}x(x-2) \quad \Rightarrow 2x + 6 = 3x - 6 \quad \therefore x = 12 \text{ km/hr}$$

Now, from (ii), $d = \frac{1}{3}\times12(12-2) = 4 \times 10 = 40$ km

55. Let x km be the distance of journey; then

$$\frac{x}{35}-\frac{x}{40}=\frac{15}{60} \quad \Rightarrow \frac{x}{7}-\frac{x}{8}=\frac{15}{12} \quad \Rightarrow \frac{x}{56}=\frac{5}{4} \quad \therefore x = 70 \text{ km}$$

56. Let x km/hr be the usual speed and t hr be usual time,

Then, $xt = \frac{6}{7}x\left(t+\frac{12}{60}\right) \quad \Rightarrow 7t = \frac{6(5t+1)}{5} \quad \Rightarrow 5t = 6$

$\therefore t = \frac{6}{5}$ hr. = 1 hr $\frac{1}{5} \times 60$ min = 1 hr 12 min

57. t = 1 hr 40 min. 48 sec. = $\left(1+\frac{40}{60}+\frac{48}{60\times60}\right)$ hr = $\left(1+\frac{2}{3}+\frac{1}{75}\right)$ hr = $\frac{126}{75}=\frac{42}{25}$ hr

Let actual speed be x km/hr., then

$\Rightarrow \frac{5}{7}x\times\frac{42}{25}=42 \quad \therefore x = 35$ km/hr

58. Let x km be the distance of destination, then

$$\frac{x}{10}-\frac{x}{15}=2 \quad \Rightarrow \frac{x}{30}=2 \quad \therefore x = 60 \text{ km}$$

When speed is 10 km/hr, then time = $\frac{60}{10}$ = 6 hr

Required speed = $\frac{60}{5}$ = 12 km/hr

59. Let x km be distance of school from his house; then

$$\frac{2x}{5}-\frac{2x}{7}=\frac{12}{60} \quad \Rightarrow \frac{4x}{35}=\frac{1}{5} \quad \therefore x = \frac{7}{4} = 1\frac{3}{4} \text{ km}$$

60. Let his usual speed be x km/hr; then

Reduced speed = $x - \frac{x}{15} = \frac{14x}{15}$ km/hr

Now, $x \times 30 - \frac{14x}{15} \times 30 = 10 \Rightarrow 2x = 10 \quad \therefore x = 5$ km/hr

61. Let x and y km/hr be the speeds of the train and the car, then

$\frac{120}{x} + \frac{480}{y} = 8 \qquad \Rightarrow \quad \frac{1}{x} + \frac{4}{y} = \frac{1}{15}$ ...(i)

Again, $\frac{200}{x} + \frac{400}{y} = 8.20 \qquad \Rightarrow \quad \frac{1}{x} + \frac{2}{y} = \frac{1}{24}$ ...(ii)

After solving (i) and (ii), we get $x = 60$ km/hr; $y = 80$ km/hr

Hence, $x : y = 60 : 80 = 3 : 4$

62. Let x and y km/hr be the speeds of Abhay and Samir, then

$\frac{30}{x} - \frac{30}{y} = 2 \quad \Rightarrow \quad \frac{1}{x} - \frac{1}{y} = \frac{1}{15}$ ...(i)

and also, $\frac{30}{y} - \frac{30}{2x} = 1 \quad \Rightarrow \quad -\frac{1}{2x} + \frac{1}{y} = \frac{1}{30}$ ...(ii)

Solving (i) and (ii) we get $x = 5$ km/hr

63. Let actual time be t hr, then

$\Rightarrow 14t - 10t = 20 \quad \Rightarrow 4t = 20 \quad \Rightarrow t = 5$ hr.

Hence, actual distance = $10 \times 5 = 50$ km

64. Stoppages of time per hour = $\frac{54-45}{54}$ hr. = $\frac{9}{54} \times 60$ min = 10 min

65. Let actual speed of the aircraft be x km/hr; then

$\frac{600}{x-200} - \frac{600}{x} = \frac{1}{2} \Rightarrow x^2 - 200x - 24000 = 0$

$\Rightarrow (x - 600)(x + 400) = 0 \quad \therefore \; x = 600$ (Taking positive value only)

Hence, duration of flight = $\frac{600}{600} = 1$ hr.

66. Let x km/hr be the actual speed of the car; then

$x \times 8 = (x + 4)\frac{15}{2} \quad \Rightarrow 16x - 15x = 60 \quad \therefore \; x = 60$

Hence, distance covered = $60 \times 8 = 480$ km

67. Ratio of speeds = 3 : 4 $\Rightarrow$ Ratio of time taken = $\frac{1}{3} : \frac{1}{4} = 4 : 3$

Now, $4t - 3t = \frac{1}{2} \qquad \therefore \; t = \frac{1}{2}$; Hence, time taken by A $= 4 \times \frac{1}{2} = 2$ hrs.

68. Let x and $\frac{3x}{2}$ km/hr be the speeds of the car and train;

then, $\frac{75}{x} - \frac{75 \times 2}{3x} = \frac{12.5}{60} \Rightarrow \frac{75}{x} - \frac{50}{x} = \frac{5}{24} \quad \therefore \frac{25}{x} = \frac{5}{24}$

$\therefore\ x = \frac{24}{5} \times 25 = 120$ km/hr

69. Let after t hr they meet; then
$50t - 40t = 100 \Rightarrow 10t = 100 \quad \therefore\ t = 10$ hr
Hence, distance between P and Q = $50t + 40t = 90t = 90 \times 10 = 900$ km

70. Let the speeds of car P and Q be x and y km/hr; then
$x + y = 120$ ...(i) and also, $6(x - y) = 120 \quad \therefore\ x - y = 20$ ...(ii)
Solving equations (i) and (ii), we get, $x = 70$ km/hr
Hence, speed of the car P = 70 km/hr

71. Their relative velocity = 4.5 + 3.75 = 8.25 km/hr
It is clear that they will meet, when they are 726 m apart

Hence, they will meet after = $\frac{726}{1000} \times \frac{1}{8.25}$ hr = $\frac{726}{8250} \times 60$ min = 5.28 min

72. Let the thief will be overtaken after t hrs., then

$60t = \left(t - \frac{1}{2}\right)75 \Rightarrow 15t = \frac{75}{2} \quad \therefore\ t = 2.30$ hr

Hence, required time = 2.30 p.m. + 2.30 hr. = 5 p.m.

73. Relative speed of A and B = 6 – 1 = 5 round per hour
As they are walking around a circular field and also in the same direction, hence they will first meet each other when there is a difference of one round between two.

So, they will first meet after $\frac{1}{5}$ hr = $\frac{1}{5} \times 60$ min = 12 min
Hence, required time = 7.30 a.m. + 12 min = 7.42 a.m.

74. As they are moving in a circular track in opposite direction, hence their relative speed = (2 + 3) = 5 rounds per hours.
So, they will meet 5 times in a hr. and 2 times in half an hour.
Since, they will meet 7 times in 1.30 hr.

75. Let they will meet t hr after starting of A; then
$60t + 75(t - 1) = 330 \Rightarrow 135t = 405 \quad \therefore\ t = 3$ hr.
Hence, required time = 8 a.m. + 3 hr = 11 a.m.

76. Their relative speed = 11 – 10 = 1 km/hr = $\frac{5}{18}$ m/s.

Hence, distance between them after 6 minutes = $\frac{5}{18} \times 6 \times 60 = 100$ m

14

TIME AND WORK

IMPORTANT FACTS:

1. If A can do a piece of work in n days, then work done by A in 1 day = $\frac{1}{n}$.

2. If work done by A in 1 day = $\frac{1}{n}$; then A can finish the whole work in n days.

3. If A is twice as good a workman as B then; Ratio of work done by A and B = 2 : 1
Ratio of times taken by A and B to finish a work = 1 : 2.

Example 1: A can do a piece of work in 6 days. B can do the same work in 3 days. How long would both of them take to do the same work?

Solution: Here, A's 1 day's work = $\frac{1}{6}$ and also B's 1 day's work = $\frac{1}{3}$

Hence, (A + B)'s 1 day's work = $\frac{1}{6}+\frac{1}{3}=\frac{1}{2}$

So, (A + B) could do the same work in 2 days.

Example 2: A and B can do a piece of work in 7 and 8 days respectively. If with the help of C they finish the work in 2 days, then how long would C alone take to finish this work?

Solution: Here, A's 1 day's work = $\frac{1}{7}$ and also B's 1 day's work = $\frac{1}{8}$

Now, (A + B + C)'s 1 day's work = $\frac{1}{2}$

Then, C's 1 day's work = $\frac{1}{2}-\left(\frac{1}{7}+\frac{1}{8}\right)=\frac{1}{2}-\frac{15}{56}=\frac{13}{56}$

Hence, C alone could do the same work = $\frac{56}{13}$ = $4\frac{4}{13}$ days

Example 3: A and B can complete a piece of work in 10 and 15 days respectively. If after working alone for 4 days, A leaves the work and goes home, then how long would B take to finish the remaining work?

Solution: A's 1 days' work = $\frac{1}{10}$; B's 1 day's work = $\frac{1}{4}$

Since, A's 4 day's work = $4 \times \frac{1}{10} = \frac{2}{5}$

Then, remaining work = $1 - \frac{2}{5} = \frac{3}{5}$

Required time = $\frac{3/5}{1/15} = \frac{3}{5} \times 15 = 9$ days

Hence, B could finish the remaining work in 9 days.

Example 4: A, B and C working together can complete a piece of work in 24 days. C alone can complete this work in 48 days. A works twice as fast as B. How long would A take to finish the work working alone?

Solution: Here, (A + B + C)'s 1 day's work = $\frac{1}{24}$; C's 1 day's work = $\frac{1}{48}$

Ratio of work done of A and B = 2 : 1

Hence, ratio of their time taken = 1 : 2

Let A and B can finish the work x and $2x$ days respectively.

Now, $\frac{1}{x} + \frac{1}{2x} + \frac{1}{48} = \frac{1}{24}$ $\Rightarrow$ $\frac{3}{2x} = \frac{1}{48}$ $\therefore x = 72$ days

Example 5: A and B can do a piece of work in 45 and 40 days respectively. They started the work together but after working a few days together A dropped out. If after that B finished the remaining work in 23 days, how long did A work together on this job?

Solution: A's 1 day's work = $\frac{1}{45}$; B's 1 day's work = $\frac{1}{40}$

Hence, (A + B)'s 1 day's work = $\frac{1}{45} + \frac{1}{40} = \frac{17}{360}$

B's 23 day's work = $23 \times \frac{1}{40} = \frac{23}{40}$

Remaining work = $1 - \frac{23}{40} = \frac{17}{40}$

Required time = $\frac{17/40}{17/360} = \frac{360}{40} = 9$ days

Hence, A did work together on this job for 9 days.

Example 6: Samir, Saurabh and Abhay can do a piece of work in 14, 18 and 20 days respectively. They worked together for 4 days and then Samir and Saurabh left Abhay to finish the work alone. If total payment was Rs. 2520, what should each receive?

Solution: Samir's 1 day's work = $\frac{1}{14}$, Saurabh's 1 day's work = $\frac{1}{18}$

Abhay's 1 day's work = $\frac{1}{20}$

Hence, (Samir +Saurabh)'s 4 day's work = $\frac{4}{14}+\frac{4}{18}=\frac{2}{7}+\frac{2}{9}=\frac{32}{63}$

Remaining work = $1-\frac{32}{63}=\frac{31}{63}$, which was completed by abhay.

Now, Share of Samir = $\frac{2}{7}\times$ Rs. 2520 = Rs. 720

Share of Saurabh = $\frac{2}{9}\times$ Rs. 2520 = Rs. 560

Share of Abhay = $\frac{31}{63}\times$ Rs. 2520 = Rs. 1240

Example 7: A and B can do a piece of work in 12 days. B and C can do the same work in 15 days, while C and A can do it in 20 days. In how many days can each of them do the same work?

Solution: (A + B)'s 1 day's work = $\frac{1}{12}$; (B + C)'s 1 day's work = $\frac{1}{15}$; (C + A)'s 1 day's work = $\frac{1}{20}$

Hence, 2 (A + B + C)'s 1 day's work = $\frac{1}{12}+\frac{1}{15}+\frac{1}{20}=\frac{1}{5}$

$\therefore$ (A + B + C)'s 1 day's work = $\frac{1}{10}$

Then, A's 1 day's work = $\frac{1}{10}-\frac{1}{15}=\frac{1}{30}$

B's 1 day's work = $\frac{1}{12}-\frac{1}{30}=\frac{1}{20}$

C's 1 day's work = $\frac{1}{20}-\frac{1}{30}=\frac{1}{60}$

Hence, A, B and C will do the work in 30, 20 and 60 days respectively.

Example 8: A contractor undertakes to complete a work in 20 days. He employs 18 labourers on this job but after 12 days he finds that only half of the work has been done. How many more labourer should he employ to complete the work within the scheduled period?

Solution: Here, remaining part of the work = $\frac{1}{2}$ and remaing number of days = 20 – 12 = 8 days

Hence, $8 \times x = 12 \times 18$ $\quad\therefore\quad x=\frac{12\times 18}{8}=27$

So, number of more labourers = 27 – 18 = 9

Example 9: Two taps A and B can fill a water reservoir in 12 and 15 hours respectively. How long would the two taps take to fill this reservoir if both of them are opened together?

Solution: Taps (A + B) together fill in 1 hour = $\frac{1}{12}+\frac{1}{15}=\frac{3}{20}$ parts

Hence, taps (A + B) would fill the tank in $\frac{20}{3}=6\frac{2}{3}$ hours.

Example 10: A, B and C can complete a piece of work in 12, 18 and 24 days respectively. They begin it together, but C continues till it is finished, A leaves 3 days after they started working and B $1\frac{1}{2}$ days before its completion. In what time is the work finished?

Solution: Here, (A + B + C)'s 3 day's work = $\frac{3}{12}+\frac{3}{18}+\frac{3}{24}=\frac{1}{4}+\frac{1}{6}+\frac{1}{8}=\frac{13}{24}$

Hence, remaining work = $1-\frac{13}{24}=\frac{11}{24}$

Let the work has to be finished now in x days, then,

$$\left(x-\frac{3}{2}\right)\times\frac{1}{18}+x\times\frac{1}{24}=\frac{11}{24} \quad \Rightarrow \quad \frac{x}{3}-\frac{1}{2}+\frac{x}{4}=\frac{11}{24}\times 6$$

$$\Rightarrow \frac{7x}{12}=\frac{11}{4}+\frac{1}{2} \qquad \therefore x=\frac{13}{14}\times\frac{12}{7}=\frac{39}{7}=5\frac{4}{7} \text{ days}$$

Hence, required time = $3+5\frac{4}{7}=8\frac{4}{7}$ days

Example 11: A truck tire has two punctures. The first puncture by itself would make the tire flat in 9 minutes. The second puncture by itself would make the tire flat in 6 minutes. In what time will both the punctures together make the tire flat?

Solution: In 1 minute both the punctures $\frac{1}{9}+\frac{1}{6}=\frac{5}{18}$ leaved the air.

Hence, in $\frac{18}{5}=3.6$ minutes, both the punctures will make the tire flat.

Example 12: If a person makes x toys per hour and another person makes y toys per hour then how many toys made by both persons in 8 hours?

Solution: In 1 hour, both the persons can made $x + y/2$ toys.

So, in 8 hour, both the persons could make $8(x + y/2) = (8x + 4y)$ toys

Example 13: A tank contains 20 gallons of water. If a pump takes $12 - x/10$ minutes to pump one gallon of water out of the tank, how many minutes will it take for the pump to empty the tank?

Solution: 1 gallon of water is pumped out in $\left(12-\frac{x}{10}\right)$ minutes.

Hence, 20 gallon of water is pumped out in $20\left(12-\frac{x}{10}\right)$ minutes = $(240 - 2x)$ minutes

Example 14: A can do a piece of work in 7 days working 9 hours daily and B can do it in 6 days working 7 hours daily. How long will they take to do it, working together $8\frac{2}{5}$ hours a day?

Solution: A can complete the work in 7 × 9 = 63 hours

B can complete the work in 6 × 7 = 42 hours

Hence, (A + B)'s 1 hour's work = $\frac{1}{63}+\frac{1}{42}=\frac{5}{126}$

Then, (A + B)'s $\frac{42}{5}$ hours' work = $\frac{5}{126} \times \frac{42}{5} = \frac{1}{3}$

So, they will complete the work in 3 days.

Example 15: A can do a piece of work in 80 days. He works at it for 10 days then B alone finishes the remaining work in 42 days. In how much time will A and B, working together finish the work?

Solution: A's 10 day's work = $10 \times \frac{1}{80} = \frac{1}{8}$

Remaining work = $1 - \frac{1}{8} = \frac{7}{8}$

Since, $\frac{7}{8}$ work is done by B in 42 days.

∴ Whole work will be done by B in $42 \times \frac{8}{7} = 48$ days

Hence (A + B)'s 1 day's work = $\frac{1}{80} + \frac{1}{48} = \frac{8}{240} = \frac{1}{30}$

So, Both will finish the work in 30 days.

Example 16: A and B working separately can do a piece of work in 9 and 12 days respectively. If they work for a day alternately, A beginning first, then in how many days the work will be completed?

Solution: (A + B)'s 2 days' work = $\frac{1}{9} + \frac{1}{12} = \frac{7}{36}$

Then (A + B)'s 5 pairs (10) days' work = $5 \times \frac{7}{36} = \frac{35}{36}$

Remaining work = $1 - \frac{35}{36} = \frac{1}{36}$, which is done by A in 11th day

$\frac{1}{36}$ work is done by A in $\frac{1}{36} \Big/ \frac{1}{9} = \frac{1}{36} \times 9 = \frac{1}{4}$ day.

Hence, total time taken = $10 + \frac{1}{4} = 10\frac{1}{4}$ days.

EXERCISE

1. 12 boys can do a piece of work in 16 days. In how many days can 6 boys do the same work?

(a) 16 days *(b)* 32 days *(c)* 23 days *(d)* 24 days

2. A can do a piece of work in 8 days while B can do the same work in 16 days. If they start working together, how long would they take to complete half portion of this work?

(a) $2\frac{2}{3}$ days *(b)* $3\frac{5}{7}$ days *(c)* $4\frac{1}{2}$ days *(d)* $3\frac{1}{2}$ days

3. A can do a piece of work in 4 days. B is 50% more efficient than A. How long would B alone take to finish this work?

(a) $3\frac{1}{3}$ days *(b)* $5\frac{1}{4}$ days *(c)* $2\frac{2}{3}$ days *(d)* $1\frac{2}{3}$ days

4. A and B working together complete a work in 35 days. If A takes 60 days to complete it, how long would B alone take to complete it?
(*a*) 64 days (*b*) 72 days (*c*) 81 days (*d*) 84 days

5. A few children working together can do a piece of work in 18 days. If the number of children employed on the work is made double, how long would they take to complete half of the work?
(*a*) $4\frac{1}{2}$ days (*b*) $2\frac{1}{3}$ days (*c*) $8\frac{3}{4}$ days (*d*) $6\frac{1}{2}$ days

6. 10 men or 18 boys can do a piece of work in 15 days. In how many days would 25 men and 15 boys complete the same work working together?
(*a*) $5\frac{1}{2}$ days (*b*) $4\frac{1}{2}$ days (*c*) $6\frac{2}{3}$ days (*d*) $2\frac{1}{3}$ days

7. A can do a piece of work in 40 days. He starts working, but having some other engagements he drops out after 5 days. Thereafter B completes this work in 21 days. How many days would A and B take to complete this work working together?
(*a*) 15 days (*b*) 16 days (*c*) 17 days (*d*) 11 days

8. Two persons A and B can complete a piece of work in 8 hours and 16 hours respectively. If they work at it alternately for an hour, A starting first, in how many hours will the work be finished?
(*a*) $9\frac{1}{3}$ hours (*b*) $10\frac{1}{2}$ hours (*c*) $11\frac{1}{2}$ hours (*d*) $8\frac{1}{2}$ hours

9. 15 men can complete a work in 210 days. They started the work but at the end of 10 days 15 additional men, with double efficiency, were inducted. How many days, in whole, did they take to finish the work?
(*a*) $76\frac{2}{3}$ days (*b*) $84\frac{3}{4}$ days (*c*) $72\frac{1}{2}$ days (*d*) 70 days

10. A and B working together can complete a piece of work in 12 days and B and C working together can complete the same work in 16 days. A worked at it for 5 days and B worked at it for 7 days. C finished the remaining work in 13 days. How many days would C alone take to complete it?
(*a*) 10 days (*b*) 24 days (*c*) 32 days (*d*) 40 days

11. A cistern is filled by a tap in $3\frac{1}{2}$ hours. Due to a leak in the bottom of the cistern, it takes half an hour longer to fill the cistern. If the cistern is full, how long will it take the leak to empty it?
(*a*) 28 hours (*b*) 29 hours (*c*) $31\frac{1}{3}$ hours (*d*) 38 hours

12. A is twice as good a workman as B and thrice as good a workman as C. If C alone can do a piece of work in 24 days, how long would the three persons take to finish the work working together?
(*a*) $3\frac{3}{11}$ days (*b*) $4\frac{4}{7}$ days (*c*) $4\frac{4}{11}$ days (*d*) $3\frac{4}{11}$ days

13. Two pipes can fill a tank in 8 hours and 12 hours respectively whereas an escape pipe can empty it in 6 hours. If the three pipes are opened at 1 p.m., 2 p.m. and 3 p.m. respectively, at what time will the tank be filled?
(*a*) 7.00 a.m. (*b*) 8.00 a.m. (*c*) 5.00 a.m. (*d*) 7.30 a.m.

14. Working 7 hours daily 24 men can complete a piece of work in 27 days. In how many days would 14 men complete the same piece of work working 9 hours daily?
(*a*) 32 days (*b*) 31 days (*c*) 36 days (*d*) 39 days

15. A, B and C undertake to do a piece of work for Rs. 529. If A and B working together do $\frac{19}{23}$ work and B and C working together do $\frac{8}{23}$ work, how should the money be divided among them?
(*a*) Rs. 345, Rs. 102, Rs. 82 (*b*) Rs. 345, Rs. 92, Rs. 92
(*c*) Rs. 330, Rs. 107, Rs. 92 (*d*) Rs. 330, Rs. 92, Rs. 107

16. Two men undertake to do a piece of work for Rs. 1400. First man alone can do this work in 7 days while the second man alone can do this work in 8 days. If they working together complete this work in 3 days with the help of a boy, how should money be divided?
(*a*) Rs. 600, Rs. 500, Rs. 300 (*b*) Rs. 600, Rs. 525, Rs. 275
(*c*) Rs. 600, Rs. 550, Rs. 250 (*d*) Rs. 500, Rs. 525, Rs. 375

17. If 3 men and 5 women can do a piece of work in 8 days and 2 men and 7 boys can do the same work in 12 days. Find the number of boys, the work done by whom can equate the work done by 10 women.
(*a*) 19 boys (*b*) 21 boys (*c*) 23 boys (*d*) 15 boys

18. A, B and C complete a piece of work in 20, 12 and 18 days respectively. They start the work together but A drops out after 4 days and B drops out 2 days before the completion of the work. The work is finished in :
(*a*) $2\frac{22}{25}$ days (*b*) $6\frac{24}{29}$ days (*c*) $5\frac{24}{25}$ days (*d*) $4\frac{24}{25}$ days

19. 'A' can complete a piece of work in 12 days. 'A' and 'B' together can complete the same piece of work in 4 days. In how many days can 'B' alone complete the same piece of work?
(*a*) 18 days (*b*) 15 days (*c*) 8 days (*d*) 6 days

20. 8 men alone can complete a piece of work in 12 days. 4 women alone can complete the same piece of work in 48 days and 10 children alone can complete the piece of work in 24 days. In how many days can 10 men, 4 women and 10 children together complete the piece of work?
(*a*) 6 (*b*) 8 (*c*) 10 (*d*) 15

21. 12 men can complete a piece of work in 36 days. 18 women can complete the same piece of work in 60 days. 8 men and 20 women work together for 20 days. If only women were to complete the remaining piece of work in 4 days, how many women would be required?
(*a*) 40 (*b*) 66 (*c*) 28 (*d*) 70

22. Amit takes twice as much time as Aryan and thrice as much as Ram to finish a piece of work. Together they finish the work in 1 day. What is the time taken by Amit to finish the work?
(*a*) 6 days (*b*) 5 days (*c*) 3 days (*d*) 4 days

23. If A and B work together, they complete a work in 3 days. B and C together complete the same work in 6 days, while A and C complete that work in 8 days. If three of them work together, then in how many days will they complete the work?
(*a*) More than 4 days (*b*) More than 3 days (*c*) Less than 3 days (*d*) Less than 2 days

24. A works twice as fast as B. If B can complete a piece of work independently in 12 days. Find in how many days A and B together can complete the work?
(*a*) 8 days (*b*) 6 days (*c*) 4 days (*d*) 18 days

25. The daily wages of a worker is Rs. 100. Five workers can do a work in 10 days. If you pay Rs. 20 more daily they agree to do 25% more work daily. If the proposal is accepted the total amount could be saved is:
(*a*) RS. 500 (*b*) Rs. 300 (*c*) Rs. 250 (*d*) Rs. 200

26. 12 men take 36 days to do a work while 12 women complete $\frac{3}{4}$th of the same work in 36 days. In how many days 10 men and 8 women together will complete the same work?
(a) 27 days (b) 12 days (c) 6 days (d) Data inadequate

27. Gopal can type 30 words in 1 minute and Madhava 25 words in 1 minute. Ist Gopal typed for 1 minute, then Madhava typed for 1 minute and so on. In this way typing alternately they typed 600 words. The time taken by them in typing these 600 words was:
(a) 22 minutes (b) 21 min. 48 seconds (c) 21 min. 25 seconds (d) 21 minutes

28. A contractor undertook to complete a project in 90 days and employed 60 men on it. After 60 days, he found that $\frac{3}{4}$ of the work has already been completed. How many men can he discharge so that the project may be completed exactly on time?
(a) 15 (b) 20 (c) 30 (d) 40

29. 25 men with 10 boys can do in 6 days as much work as 21 men with 30 boys can do in 5 days. How many boys must help 40 men to do the same work in 4 days?
(a) 5 boys (b) 10 boys (c) 20 boys (d) 40 boys

30. If 12 men and 16 boys can do a piece of work in 5 days and 13 men and 24 boys can do it in 4 days, how long will 7 men and 10 boys take to do it?
(a) $12\frac{1}{3}$ days (b) $10\frac{1}{3}$ days (c) $9\frac{2}{3}$ days (d) $8\frac{1}{3}$ days

31. X and Y can do a work in 12 days, Y and Z in 15 days and Z and X can do the same work in 20 days. How long will they take to complete the work if all the three working together?
(a) 10 days (b) 9 days (c) 8 days (d) $7\frac{1}{2}$ days

32. X and Y can do a work in 12 days and 16 days respectively. Both worked for 3 days and then X left the work. In how many days Y alone can complete the remaining work?
(a) 15 days (b) 12 days (c) 10 days (d) 9 days

33. A can do a work in 30 days, B in 15 days and C in 10 days. If all three work together, how long will they take to do the same work?
(a) 5 days (b) 4 days (c) 3 days (d) 2 days

34. A can do a piece of work in 25 days and B can do it in 20 days. They work together for 5 days and then A goes away. In how many days will B finish the remaining work?
(a) 33 days (b) 20 days (c) 11 days (d) 10 days

35. 12 men and 18 women can complete a work in 6 days whereas 12 women can complete the work in 18 days, 4 days after they (12 men + 18 women) started the work 4 men left, how many days will they take to complete the remaining work?
(a) $2\frac{2}{5}$ days (b) 4 days (c) 3 days (d) 2 days

36. Carpenter A can make a chair in 6 hours, carpenter B in 7 hours and carpenter C in 8 hours. If each carpenter works for 8 hours per day, how many chairs will be made in 21 days?
(a) 79 (b) 73 (c) 67 (d) 61

37. A can do a piece of work in 14 days which B can do in 21 days. They begin together but 3 days before the completion of the work, A leaves off. The total number of days to complete the work is—

(*a*) $13\frac{1}{2}$ days (*b*) $10\frac{1}{5}$ days (*c*) $8\frac{1}{2}$ days (*d*) $6\frac{3}{5}$ days

38. A man can do a piece of work in 5 days, but with the help of his son, he can do it in 3 days. The time taken by the son to do it alone is:

(*a*) 8 days (*b*) $7\frac{1}{2}$ days (*c*) 7 days (*d*) $6\frac{1}{2}$ days

39. A, B and C can complete a piece of work in 24, 6 and 12 days respectively. In how many days will they together complete the same work?

(*a*) 4 days (*b*) $3\frac{3}{7}$ days (*c*) $\frac{7}{24}$ day (*d*) $\frac{1}{24}$ day

40. A can finish a work in 18 days and B can do the same work in half the time taken by A. Then working together the part of the same work they can finish in a day is:

(*a*) $\frac{2}{7}$ (*b*) $\frac{2}{5}$ (*c*) $\frac{1}{9}$ (*d*) $\frac{1}{6}$

41. A man can do a job in 15 days. His father and his son can complete the same work in 20 and 25 days respectively. How long will they take to complete the job if they all work together?

(*a*) More than 10 days (*b*) 6.4 days (*c*) 6 days (*d*) Less than 6 days

42. A and B can do a work in 8 days, B and C can do the same work in 12 days. A, B and C together can finish it in 6 days. A and C together will do it in

(*a*) 12 days (*b*) 8 days (*c*) 6 days (*d*) 4 days

43. Samir can complete a work in 12 days working 8 hours a day. Saurabh can complete the same work in 8 days working 10 hours a day. If both work together, working 8 hours a day, in how many days can they complete the work?

(*a*) $6\frac{6}{11}$ days (*b*) $6\frac{5}{11}$ days (*c*) $5\frac{6}{11}$ days (*d*) $5\frac{5}{11}$ days

44. Gopal and Madhava are working on an assignment. Gopal takes 6 hours to type 32 pages on a computer. While Madhava takes 5 hours to type 40 pages. How much time will take they, working together on two different computers to type an assignment of 110 pages?

(*a*) 8 hrs. 25 min. (*b*) 8 hrs. 15 min. (*c*) 8 hrs. (*d*) 7 hrs. 30 min.

45. A can lay railway track between two given stations in 16 days and B can do the same job in 12 days, with the help of C they did the job in 4 days only. Then C alone can do the job in:

(*a*) 10 days (*b*) $9\frac{3}{5}$ days (*c*) $9\frac{2}{3}$ days (*d*) $9\frac{1}{5}$ days

46. A can do a work in 15 days and B in 20 days. If they work on it together for 4 days, then the fraction of the work that is left is:

(*a*) $\frac{8}{15}$ (*b*) $\frac{7}{15}$ (*c*) $\frac{1}{10}$ (*d*) $\frac{1}{4}$

47. A is 30% more efficient than B. How much time will they, working together, take to complete a job which A alone could have done in 23 days?

(*a*) 20 days (*b*) 15 days (*c*) 13 days (*d*) 11 days

48. P and Q can do a job together in 7 days. P is $1\frac{3}{4}$ times as efficient as Q. The same job can be done by P alone in:

(*a*) $16\frac{1}{3}$ days (*b*) $12\frac{1}{4}$ days (*c*) 11 days (*d*) $9\frac{1}{3}$ days

49. A works twice as fast as B. If B can complete a work in 12 days independently, the number of days in which A and B can together finish the work is:

(*a*) 18 days (*b*) 8 days (*c*) 6 days (*d*) 4 days

50. A can do a piece of work in 4 hours; B and C together can do it in 3 hours, while A and C together can do it in 2 hours. How long will B alone take to do it?

(*a*) 24 hours (*b*) 12 hours (*c*) 10 hours (*d*) 8 hours

51. Nilam can do a piece of work in 20 days. Rani is 25% more efficient than Nilam. The number of days taken by Rani to do the same piece of work is:

(*a*) 25 days (*b*) 18 days (*c*) 16 days (*d*) 15 days

52. A is thrice as good a workman as B and therefore is able to finish a job in 60 days less than B, working together, they can do it in:

(*a*) 30 days (*b*) 25 days (*c*) $22\frac{1}{2}$ days (*d*) 20 days

53. A can do a certain work in the same time in which B and C together can do it. If A and B together could do it in 10 days and C alone in 50 days, then B alone could do it in:

(*a*) 30 days (*b*) 25 days (*c*) 20 days (*d*) 15 days

54. A and B together can do a piece of work in 30 days. A having worked for 16 days, B finishes the remaining work alone in 44 days. In how many days will B finish the whole work alone?

(*a*) 70 days (*b*) 60 days (*c*) 40 days (*d*) 30 days

55. X can do a peice of work in 40 days. He works at it for 8 days and then y finished it in 16 days. How long will they together take to complete the work?

(*a*) 56 days (*b*) 20 days (*c*) 15 days (*d*) $13\frac{1}{3}$ days

56. X and Y do a piece of work in 20 days and 12 days respectively. X started the work alone and then after 4 days Y joined him till the completion of the work. How long did the work last?

(*a*) 20 days (*b*) 15 days (*c*) 10 days (*d*) 6 days

57. A machine P can print one lakh books in 8 hours, machine Q can print the same number of books in 10 hours while machine R can print them in 12 hours. All the machines are started at 9 a.m., while machine P is closed at 11 a.m. and the remaining two machine complete the work. Approximately at what time will the work be finished?

(*a*) 1 p.m. (*b*) 12.30 p.m. (*c*) 12 noon (*d*) 11.30 a.m.

58. A and B can complete a work in 15 days and 10 days respectively. They started doing the work together but after 2 days B had to leave and A alone completed the remaining work. The whole work was completed in:

(*a*) 15 days (*b*) 12 days (*c*) 10 days (*d*) 8 days

59. A does $\frac{4}{5}$ of a work in 20 days. He then calls in B and they together finishing the remaining work in 3 days. How long B alone would take to do the whole work?

(*a*) 40 days (*b*) $37\frac{1}{2}$ days (*c*) 37 days (*d*) 23 days

60. A and B can together finish a work in 30 days. They worked together for 20 days and then B left. After another 20 days, A finished the remaining work. In how many days A alone can finish the job?

(*a*) 60 days (*b*) 54 days (*c*) 50 days (*d*) 40 days

61. A and B can do a piece of work in 30 days, while B and C can do the same work in 24 days and C and A in 20 days. They all work together for 10 days when B and C leave. How many days more will A take to finish the work?

(*a*) 36 days (*b*) 30 days (*c*) 24 days (*d*) 18 days

62. A can finish a work in 24 days, B in 9 days and C in 12 days. B and C started the work but are forced to leave after 3 days. The remaining work was done by A in

(*a*) $10\frac{1}{2}$ days (*b*) 10 days (*c*) 6 days (*d*) 5 days

63. A can finish a work in 18 days and B can do the same work in 15 days. B worked for 10 days and left the job. In how many days, A alone can finish the remaining work?

(*a*) 8 days (*b*) 6 days (*c*) $5\frac{1}{2}$ days (*d*) 5 days

64. A and B together can complete a work in 12 days, A alone can complete it in 20 days. If B does the work only for half a day daily, then in how many days A and B together will complete the work?

(*a*) 20 days (*b*) 15 days (*c*) 11 days (*d*) 10 days

65. A alone can do a piece of work in 6 days and B alone in 8 days. A and B undertook to do it for Rs. 3200. With the help of C, they completed the work in 3 days. How much to be paid to C?

(*a*) Rs. 800 (*b*) Rs. 600 (*c*) Rs. 400 (*d*) Rs. 375

66. A and B can do a piece of work in 45 days and 40 days respectively. They began to do the work together but A leaves after some days and then B completed the remaining work in 23 days. The number of days after which A left the work was:

(*a*) 12 days (*b*) 9 days (*c*) 8 days (*d*) 6 days

67. Ram can do a work in 3 days while M[illegible] can do the same work in 2 days. Both of them finish the work together and get Rs. 150. W[illegible] is the share of Ram?

(*a*) Rs, 75 (*b*) Rs. 70 (*c*) Rs. 60 (*d*) Rs. 30

68. 10 men and 15 women together can complete a work in 6 days. It takes 100 days for one man alone to complete the same work. How many days will be required for one woman alone to complete the same work?

(*a*) 225 days (*b*) 200 days (*c*) 150 days (*d*) 125 days

69. 3 men, 4 women and 6 children can complete a work in 7 days. A woman does double the work a man does and a child does half the work a man does. How many women alone can complete the work in 7 days?

(*a*) 12 (*b*) 10 (*c*) 8 (*d*) 7

70. 10 men can complete a piece of work in 15 days and 15 women can complete the same work in 12 days. If all the 10 men and 15 women work together, in how many days will the work get completed?

(a) $7\frac{2}{3}$ days (b) $6\frac{2}{3}$ days (c) $6\frac{1}{3}$ days (d) 6 days

71. A, B and C can do a piece of work in 20, 30 and 60 days respectively. In how many days can A do the work if he is assisted by B and C on every third day?

(a) 18 days (b) 16 days (c) 15 days (d) 12 days

72. A alone can complete a work in 16 days and B alone in 12 days. Starting with A, they work on alternate days. The total work will be completed in

(a) $13\frac{3}{4}$ days (b) $13\frac{5}{7}$ days (c) 13 days (d) 12 days

73. A man, a woman and a boy can complete a job in 3, 4 and 12 days respectively. How many boys must assist one man and one woman to complete the job in $\frac{1}{4}$ of a day?

(a) 41 (b) 49 (c) 4 (d) 1

74. 12 men complete a work in 9 days. After they have worked for 6 days, 6 more men join them. How many days will they take to complete the remaining work?

(a) 5 days (b) 4 days (c) 3 days (d) 2 days

75. Women can do a work in 16 days. 16 men can complete the same work in 15 days. What is the ratio between the capacity of a man and a woman?

(a) 3 : 5 (b) 5 : 3 (c) 4 : 3 (d) 3 : 4

76. If 6 men and 8 boys can do a piece of work in 10 days while 26 men and 48 boys can do the same in 2 days, the time taken by 15 men and 20 boys in doing the same type of work will be

(a) 7 days (b) 6 days (c) 5 days (d) 4 days

77. If 12 men and 16 boys can do a piece of work in 5 days; 13 men and 24 boys can do it in 4 days, then the ratio of the daily work done by a man to that of a boy is:

(a) 5 : 4 (b) 3 : 2 (c) 3 : 1 (d) 2 : 1

78. 10 women can complete a work in 7 days and 10 children take 14 days to complete the work. How many days will 5 women and 10 children take to complete the work?

(a) 7 days (b) 6 days (c) 5 days (d) 4 days

79. 12 men can complete a piece of work in 4 days, while 15 women can complete the same work in 4 days. 6 men started working on the job and after working for 2 days, all of them stopped working. How many women should be put on the job to complete the remaining work, if it is to be completed in 3 days?

(a) 22 (b) 18 (c) 15 (d) 12

80. 4 men and 6 women can complete a work in 8 days, while 3 men and 7 women can complete it in 10 days. In how many days will 10 women complete it?

(a) 50 (b) 45 (c) 40 (d) 35

81. 24 men can complete a work in 16 days. 32 women can complete the same work in 24 days. 16 men and 16 women started working and worked for 12 days. How many more men are to be added to complete the remaining work in 2 days?

(a) 48 (b) 36 (c) 24 (d) 16

SOLUTIONS

1. $\because$ 12 boys can do a piece of work in 16 days.

$\therefore$ 1 boy will do the same piece of work in 16×12 days.

$\therefore$ 6 boys will do the same piece of work in $\frac{16 \times 12}{6}$ days $= 32$ days.

2. (A + B)'s 1 day's work $= \frac{1}{8} + \frac{1}{16} = \frac{3}{16}$

Hence, (A + B) will do the whole work in $\frac{16}{3}$ days

So, they will do the half portion of the work in $\frac{16}{3 \times 2}$ days $= \frac{8}{3} = 2\frac{2}{3}$ days.

3. A's 1 day's work $= \frac{1}{4}$; Hence, B's 1 day's work $= \frac{150}{100} \times \frac{1}{4} = \frac{3}{8}$

So, B will do the whole work in $\frac{8}{3} = 2\frac{2}{3}$ days.

4. (A + B)'s 1 day's work $= \frac{1}{35}$

and also, A's 1 day's work $= \frac{1}{60}$

Hence, B's 1 day's work $= \frac{1}{35} - \frac{1}{60} = \frac{5}{420} = \frac{1}{84}$

So, B will do the whole work in 84 days.

5. Let number of children be x;

Now x children can do the work in 18 days.

Hence, $2x$ children will do $\frac{1}{2}$ of the work in $\frac{18 \times x}{2x \times 2} = \frac{9}{2}$ days $= 4\frac{1}{2}$ days.

6. 10 men $\equiv$ 18 boys

25 men $\equiv \frac{18}{10} \times 25 = 45$ boys

Hence, 25 men + 15 boys = 45 + 15 = 60 boys

Now, 18 boys can do a piece of work in 15 days.

Hence, 60 boys will do a piece of work in $\frac{15 \times 18}{60} = \frac{9}{2}$ days $= 4\frac{1}{2}$ days.

7. A's 5 days' work $= 5 \times \frac{1}{40} = \frac{1}{8}$

Remaining work $= 1 - \frac{1}{8} = \frac{7}{8}$, which is done by B in 21 days.

Hence, B's 1 day's work $= \frac{7}{8 \times 21} = \frac{1}{24}$

Now, (A + B)'s 1 day's work = $\frac{1}{40}+\frac{1}{24}=\frac{8}{120}=\frac{1}{15}$

Hence, (A + B) will complete the work in 15 days.

8. In 2 hours the part of work = $\frac{1}{8}+\frac{1}{16}=\frac{3}{16}$ will be completed.

Hence, in 5 pairs of hours the part of work = $5\times\frac{3}{16}=\frac{15}{16}$ will be completed

Remaining work = $1-\frac{15}{16}=\frac{1}{16}$ which will be done by A.

Time taken by A to complete the $\frac{1}{16}$ work = $\frac{1/16}{1/8}=\frac{1}{2}$ hour.

Hence, required number of hours = $10+\frac{1}{2}=10\frac{1}{2}$ hours.

9. 15 men's 10 days' work = $10\times\frac{1}{210}=\frac{1}{21}$

Remaining work = $1-\frac{1}{21}=\frac{20}{21}$

Now, (15 men + 15 men having double efficiency)'s 1 day's work = $\frac{1}{210}+\frac{2}{210}=\frac{3}{210}=\frac{1}{70}$

Hence, number of days = $\frac{20/21}{1/70}=\frac{20}{21}\times70=\frac{200}{3}=66\frac{2}{3}$ days

So, required number of total days = $10+66\frac{2}{3}=76\frac{2}{3}$ days.

10. Here, A worked for 5 days, B for 7 days and C for 13 days ≡ (A + B) worked for 5 days, (B + C) for 2 days and C for 11 days.

Let C will complete the work in x days,

Now, (A + B)'s 5 days' work + (B + C)'s 2 days' work + C's 11 days' work = $\frac{5}{12}+\frac{2}{16}+\frac{11}{x}=\frac{13}{24}+\frac{11}{x}$

Again, $\frac{13}{24}+\frac{11}{x}=1 \quad\Rightarrow\quad \frac{11}{x}=\frac{11}{24} \quad \therefore x=24$

Hence, C would alone complete the work in 24 days.

11. In 1 hour $\frac{2}{7}$ cistern is filled by the tap.

Hence, in $\frac{1}{2}$ hour $\frac{2}{14}=\frac{1}{7}$ cistern is filled by the tap.

So, $\frac{1}{7}$ cistern is emptied by the leakage in 4 hours.

So, 1 cistern will be emptied by the leakage in 28 hours.

12. Here, ratio of efficiency of A, B and C = $1 : \frac{1}{2} : \frac{1}{3}$

So, ratio of their time taken to complete the work = 1 : 2 : 3

Now C completes the work in 24 days, so A and B will complete the work in 8 and 16 days respectively.

Hence, (A + B + C)'s 1 day's work = $\frac{1}{8}+\frac{1}{16}+\frac{1}{24}=\frac{11}{48}$

Therefore, (A + B + C) will complete the work in $\frac{48}{11}=4\frac{4}{11}$ days.

13. Let tank will be filled up after t hours of starting of pipe A;

Then, $t\times\frac{1}{8}+(t-1)\times\frac{1}{12}-(t-2)\times\frac{1}{6}=1$

$\Rightarrow t\left(\frac{1}{8}+\frac{1}{12}-\frac{1}{6}\right)-\frac{1}{12}+\frac{1}{3}=1$

$\Rightarrow t\times\frac{1}{24}=1-\frac{1}{4}$ $\qquad \therefore t=\frac{3}{4}\times 24=18$ hours

Hence, required time = 1 p.m. + 18 hours = 7 a.m.

14. Working 7 hours a day 24 men can do the work is 27 days.

Hence, working 9 hours a day 14 men will do the work in $\frac{27\times 24\times 7}{9\times 14}$ = 36 days.

15. The part of work is done by B = $\frac{19}{23}+\frac{8}{23}-1=\frac{4}{23}$

The part of work is done by A = $\frac{19}{23}-\frac{4}{23}=\frac{15}{23}$

The part of work is done by C = $\frac{8}{23}-\frac{4}{23}=\frac{4}{23}$

Hence, share of A = $\frac{15}{23}$ × Rs. 529 = Rs. 345

share of B = $\frac{4}{23}$ × Rs. 529 = Rs. 92

share of C = $\frac{4}{23}$ × Rs. 529 = Rs. 92

So, Their shares are Rs. 345, Rs. 92 and Rs. 92.

16. Both men's 3 day's work = $3\left(\frac{1}{7}+\frac{1}{8}\right)=3\times\frac{15}{56}=\frac{45}{56}$

Remaining work = $1-\frac{45}{56}=\frac{11}{56}$

Ratio of their work done = $\frac{3}{7}:\frac{3}{8}:\frac{11}{56}$ = 24 : 21 : 11

Share of money of first man = $\frac{24}{24+21+11} \times \text{Rs. } 1400 = \frac{24}{56} \times \text{Rs. } 1400 = \text{Rs. } 600$

Share of moeny of second man = $\frac{21}{56} \times \text{Rs. } 1400 = \text{Rs. } 525$

Share of money of the boy = $\frac{11}{56} \times \text{Rs. } 1400 = \text{Rs. } 275$

Hence, their share will be Rs. 600, Rs. 525, Rs. 275.

17. Here, (3 men + 5 women) × 8 ≡ (2 men + 7 boys) × 12

$\Rightarrow$ 40 women ≡ 84 boys $\quad \therefore \quad$ 10 women $\equiv \frac{84}{40} \times 10 = 21$ boys

Hence, work done by 10 women = work done of 21 boys.

18. Let the work has been finished in t days, then

$$4 \times \frac{1}{20} + (t-2) \times \frac{1}{12} + t \times \frac{1}{18} = 1$$

$$\Rightarrow \left(\frac{1}{12} + \frac{1}{18}\right)t - \frac{1}{6} = 1 - \frac{1}{5} \quad \Rightarrow \frac{5}{36}t = \frac{4}{5} + \frac{1}{6} \quad \therefore \quad t = \frac{29}{30} \times \frac{36}{5} = \frac{174}{25} = 6\frac{24}{25} \text{ days.}$$

19. B's 1 day's work = $\frac{1}{4} - \frac{1}{12} = \frac{2}{12} = \frac{1}{6}$

Hence, B alone will complete the work in 6 days.

20. (10 men + 4 women + 10 children)'s 1 day's work = $10 \times \frac{1}{96} + \frac{1}{48} + \frac{1}{24} = \frac{5}{48} + \frac{1}{48} + \frac{1}{24} = \frac{8}{48} = \frac{1}{6}$

Hence, (10 men + 4 women + 10 children) will complete the work in 6 days.

21. (8 men + 20 women)'s 20 day's work = $\frac{8 \times 20}{12 \times 36} + \frac{20 \times 20}{18 \times 60} = \frac{10}{27} + \frac{10}{27} = \frac{20}{27}$

Remaining part of work = $1 - \frac{20}{27} = \frac{7}{27}$

1 woman's 4 days' work = $\frac{4}{18 \times 60} = \frac{1}{270}$

Required number of women = $\frac{7/27}{1/270} = \frac{7}{27} \times 270 = 70$

22. Let Amit, Aryan and Ram can finish the work in x, $\frac{x}{2}$ and $\frac{x}{3}$ days respectively, then

(Amit + Aryan + Ram)'s 1 day's work = $\frac{1}{x} + \frac{2}{x} + \frac{3}{x} = \frac{6}{x}$

Now, $\frac{6}{x} = 1 \quad \therefore \quad x = 6$

Hence, Amit will finish the work in 6 days.

23. 2(A + B + C)'s 1 day's work = $\frac{1}{3}+\frac{1}{6}+\frac{1}{8}=\frac{5}{8}$

Hence, (A + B + C)'s 1 day's work = $\frac{5}{16}$

So, (A + B + C) will complete the work in $\frac{16}{5} = 3\frac{1}{5}$ days, i.e., more than 3 days.

24. Ratio of efficiency of A and B = 2 : 1
Then, ratio of their time taking = 1 : 2
Hence, if B can complete the work in 12 days, then A in 6 days.

Now, (A + B)'s 1 day's work = $\frac{1}{6}+\frac{1}{12}=\frac{3}{12}=\frac{1}{4}$
So, A and B together can complete the work in 4 days.

25. 25% more work daily means
10 days' work ≡ 8 days' work
Hence, saved amount = Rs. 10 × 100 × 5 – Rs. 8 × 120 × 5
= Rs. 5000 – Rs. 4800 = Rs. 200

26. Ratio of work of a man and a woman = $1 : \frac{3}{4} = 4 : 3$

Ratio of their time taking = 3 : 4
Hence, 4 women ≡ 3 men ∴ 8 women ≡ 6 men
Now, 10 men + 8 women ≡ 10 men + 6 men = 16 men
Again, 12 men can complete the work in 36 days

Hence, 16 men will complete the work in $\frac{12 \times 36}{16}$ = 27 days.

27. In 2 minutes the number of words typed by Gopal & Madhava = 30 + 25 = 55
Hence, in 10 pair of minutes the number of words typed by both = 55 × 10 = 550
Then, in 21th minute Gopal will type 30 words.
The number of words typed in 21 minutes = 550 + 30 = 580
Remaining number of words = 600 – 580 = 20 words
Which can be typed by Madhava in 22th minutes
Now, 25 words typed in 1 minute

Hence, 20 words will be typed in $\frac{1}{25}\times 20$ min = $\frac{4}{5}\times 60$ sec = 48 sec.
Therefore, total time taken = 21 min 48 sec.

28. After 60 days remaining work = $1-\frac{3}{4}=\frac{1}{4}$

In 60 days $\frac{3}{4}$ work has been done by 60 men

In 30 days $\frac{1}{4}$ work will be done by $60\times\frac{4}{3}\times\frac{1}{4}\times\frac{60}{30}$ = 40 men.

Hence, required number of men = 60 – 40 = 20 (which are to be discharged).

29. Here, (25 men + 10 boys) × 6 $\equiv$ (21 men + 30 boys) × 5
$\Rightarrow$ 150 men + 60 boys $\equiv$ 105 men + 150 boys
$\Rightarrow$ 45 men $\equiv$ 90 boys   Hence, 1 man $\equiv$ 2 boys
25 men + 10 boys $\equiv$ 50 boys + 10 boys = 60 boys
40 men $\equiv$ 80 boys
In 6 days, the whole work has been done by 60 boys.

Hence, in 4 days, the whole work will be done by $\frac{60 \times 6}{4}$ = 90 boys.
Therefore, required number of boys = 90 – 80 = 10 boys.

30. Here, (12 men + 16 boys) × 5 $\equiv$ (13 men + 24 boys) × 4
$\Rightarrow$ 60 men + 80 boys $\equiv$ 52 men + 96 boys
$\Rightarrow$ 8 men $\equiv$ 16 boys $\therefore$ 1 man $\equiv$ 2 boys
13 men + 24 boys $\equiv$ 26 boys + 24 boys = 50 boys
7 men + 10 boys $\equiv$ 14 boys + 10 boys = 24 boys
Now, 50 boys can do the whole work in 4 days

Hence, 24 boys will do whole work in $\frac{50 \times 4}{24}$ days $= \frac{25}{3} = 8\frac{1}{3}$ days.

31. 2(X + Y + Z)'s 1 day's work $= \frac{1}{12} + \frac{1}{15} + \frac{1}{20} = \frac{12}{60} = \frac{1}{5}$

Hence, (X + Y + Z)'s 1 day's work $= \frac{1}{10}$

Hence, they all together will complete the work in 10 days.

32. (X + Y)'s 3 days' work $= 3\left(\frac{1}{12} + \frac{1}{16}\right) = 3 \times \frac{7}{48} = \frac{7}{16}$

Remaining work $= 1 - \frac{7}{16} = \frac{9}{16}$, which will be done by Y alone.

Hence, number of days $= \frac{9/16}{1/16} = 9$ days

Therefore, remaining work will be completed by Y alone in 9 days.

33. (A + B + C)'s 1 day's work $= \frac{1}{30} + \frac{1}{15} + \frac{1}{10} = \frac{12}{60} = \frac{1}{5}$

Hence, (A + B + C) will do the work in 5 days.

34. (A + B)'s 5 days' work $= \frac{5}{25} + \frac{5}{20} = \frac{1}{5} + \frac{1}{4} = \frac{9}{20}$

Remaining part of work $= 1 - \frac{9}{20} = \frac{11}{20}$; which will be done by 'B';

Hence, number of days taken by B $= \frac{11/20}{1/20} = 11$ days

Therefore, B will finish the remaining work in 11 days.

35. (12 men + 18 women) × 6 ≡ 12 women × 18

⇒ 72 men + 108 women ≡ 216 women

⇒ 72 men ≡ 108 women

Hence, 2 men ≡ 3 women

12 men + 18 women ≡ 18 women + 18 women = 36 women

(12 men + 18 women)'s 4 days' work = $\frac{4}{6} = \frac{2}{3}$

Remaining part of work = $1 - \frac{2}{3} = \frac{1}{3}$; which will be done by 8 men and 18 women ≡ 30 women.

36 women can do the whole work in 6 days

Hence, 30 women will do the $\frac{1}{3}$ work in $\frac{6 \times 36}{30} \times \frac{1}{3} = \frac{12}{5} = 2\frac{2}{5}$ days.

36. Carpenter (A + B + C)'s 8 hours' work = $\frac{8}{6} + \frac{8}{7} + \frac{8}{8} = \frac{4}{3} + \frac{8}{7} + 1 = \frac{73}{21}$ chairs.

Hence, in 21 days when they work 8 hours per day, the number of chairs will be made

$$= \frac{73}{21} \times 21 = 73 \text{ chairs}$$

37. Let total number of days taken to complete the work be *t*.

Hence, $(t - 3) \times \frac{1}{14} + t \times \frac{1}{21} = 1$ $\Rightarrow t\left(\frac{1}{14} + \frac{1}{21}\right) = 1 + \frac{3}{14}$ $\Rightarrow t \times \frac{5}{42} = \frac{17}{14}$

$\Rightarrow t = \frac{17}{14} \times \frac{42}{5} = \frac{51}{5} = 10\frac{1}{5}$ days.

38. His son's 1 day's work = $\frac{1}{3} - \frac{1}{5} = \frac{2}{15}$

Hence, the time taken by his son to do it alone is $\frac{15}{2} = 7\frac{1}{2}$ days.

39. (A + B + C)'s 1 day's work = $\frac{1}{24} + \frac{1}{6} + \frac{1}{12} = \frac{7}{24}$

Hence, they will complete the work in $\frac{24}{7} = 3\frac{3}{4}$ days.

40. (A + B)'s 1 day's work = $\frac{1}{18} + \frac{1}{9} = \frac{3}{18} = \frac{1}{6}$

41. (Man + his father + his son)'s 1 day's work = $\frac{1}{15} + \frac{1}{20} + \frac{1}{25} = \frac{47}{300}$

Hence, they altogether complete the work in $\frac{300}{47} \simeq 6.4$ days

42. (A + 2B + C)'s 1 day's work = $\frac{1}{8} + \frac{1}{12} = \frac{5}{24}$

(A + B + C)'s 1 day's work = $\frac{1}{6}$

Hence, B's 1 day's work = $\frac{5}{24}-\frac{1}{6}=\frac{1}{24}$;

Now, (A + C)'s 1 day's work = $\frac{1}{6}-\frac{1}{24}=\frac{3}{24}=\frac{1}{8}$

Therefore, (A + C) together will do the work in 8 days.

43. (Samir + Saurabha)'s 1 day's work, when both working 8 hours a day = $\frac{1}{12}+\frac{1}{8}\times\frac{8}{10}=\frac{1}{12}+\frac{1}{10}=\frac{11}{60}$

Hence, when they working 8 hours a day they will complete the work in $\frac{60}{11}=5\frac{5}{11}$ days.

44. (Gopal + Madhava)'s 1 hour's work = $\frac{32}{6}+\frac{40}{5}=\frac{16}{3}+8=\frac{40}{3}$ pages

Hence, time taken by them to type 110 pages = $\frac{110}{40/3}=\frac{33}{4}$ hrs.

$= 8 \text{ hrs. } \frac{1}{4}\times 60 \text{ min}$

$= 8$ hrs. 15 min.

45. C's 1 day's job = $\frac{1}{4}-\left(\frac{1}{16}+\frac{1}{12}\right)=\frac{1}{4}-\frac{7}{48}=\frac{5}{48}$

Hence, C alone can do the job in $\frac{48}{5}=9\frac{3}{5}$ days.

46. (A + B)'s 4 days' work = $4\left(\frac{1}{15}+\frac{1}{20}\right)=4\times\frac{7}{60}=\frac{7}{15}$

Hence, the fraction of work that is left = $1-\frac{7}{15}=\frac{8}{15}$

47. Ratio of efficiency of A and B = 130 : 100 = 13 : 10

Hence, ratio of their time taken = 10 : 13

Then time taken by B to complete the work = $13\times\frac{23}{10}=\frac{299}{10}$

So, (A + B)'s 1 day's work = $\frac{1}{23}+\frac{10}{299}=\frac{23}{299}=\frac{1}{13}$

Hence, working together they will complete the job in 13 days.

48. Ratio of efficiency of P and Q = $\frac{7}{4}$: 1 = 7 : 4

Hence, ratio of their time taken = 4 : 7

Let P and Q can finish the job in $4x$ and $7x$ days respectively,

then, $\frac{1}{4x}+\frac{1}{7x}=\frac{1}{7} \quad\Rightarrow\quad \frac{11}{28x}=\frac{1}{7} \quad\Rightarrow\quad \frac{1}{x}=\frac{1}{7}\times\frac{28}{11}=\frac{4}{11};\ x=\frac{11}{4}$

The job can be done by P alone in $4\times\frac{11}{4}$ = 11 days.

49. Ratio of efficiency of A and B = 2 : 1
Hence, ratio of their time taken = 1 : 2
So, A can finish the job in 6 days.

(A + B)'s 1 day's work = $\frac{1}{6}+\frac{1}{12}=\frac{3}{12}=\frac{1}{4}$

Hence, they together will finish the job in 4 days.

50. (A + B + C)'s 1 hour's work = $\frac{1}{4}+\frac{1}{3}=\frac{7}{12}$

B's 1 hour's work = $\frac{7}{12}-\frac{1}{2}=\frac{1}{12}$

Hence, B alone will do the work in 12 hours.

51. Ratio of efficiency of Nilam and Rani = 100 : 125 = 4 : 5
Hence, ratio of their time taking = 5 : 4

Therefore, number of days taken by Rani to complete the work = $\frac{20}{5}\times 4$ = 16 days.

52. Ratio of efficiency of A and B = 3 : 1
Hence, ratio of their time taking = 1 : 3
Let A and B can finish the job in x and $3x$ days respectively.
Now, $3x - x = 60$ $\Rightarrow 2x = 60$ $\therefore\ x = 30$ days
& also, $3x = 3 \times 30 = 90$ days

(A + B)'s 1 day's work = $\frac{1}{30}+\frac{1}{90}=\frac{4}{90}=\frac{2}{45}$

Hence, working together they will finish the job in $\frac{45}{2}=22\frac{1}{2}$ days.

53. (A + B + C)'s 1 day's work = $\frac{1}{10}+\frac{1}{50}=\frac{6}{50}=\frac{3}{25}$

2 A's 1 day's work = $\frac{3}{25}$ ($\because$ A $\equiv$ B + C)

$\therefore$ A's 1 day's work = $\frac{3}{50}$

B's 1 day's work = $\frac{1}{10}-\frac{3}{50}=\frac{2}{50}=\frac{1}{25}$

Hence, B alone could do the work in 25 days.

54. Let 1 day's work of A and B be x and y respectively,

then, $x + y = \frac{1}{30}$

and also, $16x + 44y = 1$ $\Rightarrow 4x + 11y = \frac{1}{4}$ ...(*ii*)

Solving (*i*) & (*ii*), we get $y = \frac{1}{60}$

Hence, B will finish the work in 60 days.

55. X's 8 days' work = $\frac{8}{40} = \frac{1}{5}$

Remaining part of work = $1 - \frac{1}{5} = \frac{4}{5}$, which will be done by Y in 16 days.

Hence, Y's 1 day's work = $\frac{4}{5 \times 16} = \frac{1}{20}$

Therefore (X + Y)'s 1 day's work = $\frac{1}{40} + \frac{1}{20} = \frac{3}{40}$

Hence, (X + Y) will complete the work in $\frac{40}{3} = 13\frac{1}{3}$ days.

56. X's 4 days' work = $\frac{4}{20} = \frac{1}{5}$

Remaining part of work = $1 - \frac{1}{5} = \frac{4}{5}$

(X + Y)'s 1 day's work = $\frac{1}{20} + \frac{1}{12} = \frac{8}{60} = \frac{2}{15}$

Hence, time taken to complete the remaining work = $\frac{4/5}{2/15} = \frac{4}{5} \times \frac{15}{2} = 6$ days

Therefore, total time taken = 4 + 6 = 10 days.

57. In 2 hours machine P will print 1 lakh × $\frac{2}{8}$ = 20,000 books

Remaining number of books = 1,00,000 – 20,000 = 80,000 books which will be printed by machines Q and R

Machines (Q + R)'s 1 hour's work = $\left(\frac{1}{10} + \frac{1}{12}\right) \times 100000 = \frac{11}{60} \times 1,00,000 = \frac{55000}{3}$ books

Hence, time taken by both the machines to print the remaining books $= \frac{80000}{55000/3} = \frac{80000 \times 3}{55000}$

$= 4.36$ hrs. ≈ 4 hrs.

Therefore, required time = 9 a.m. + 4 hrs. = 1 p.m.

58. (A + B)'s 2 days' work = $2\left(\frac{1}{15} + \frac{1}{10}\right) = 2 \times \frac{5}{30} = \frac{1}{3}$

Remaining part of work = $1 - \frac{1}{3} = \frac{2}{3}$, which will be done by A alone.

Hence, time taken by A to complete the remaining work = $\frac{2/3}{1/15} = \frac{2}{3} \times 15 = 10$ days.

Therefore, total time taken to complete the whole work = 2 + 10 = 12 days.

59. A's 1 day's work = $\frac{4}{5 \times 20} = \frac{1}{25}$

After 20 days, remaining part of work = $1 - \frac{4}{5} = \frac{1}{5}$, which will be done by both in 3 days.

Let, B can finish the work in x days, then,

$$3\left(\frac{1}{25}+\frac{1}{x}\right)=\frac{1}{5} \Rightarrow \frac{1}{x}=\frac{1}{15}-\frac{1}{25}=\frac{2}{75}$$

$$\therefore\ x=\frac{75}{2}=37\frac{1}{2} \text{ days.}$$

60. (A + B)'s 20 days' work = $\frac{20}{30}=\frac{2}{3}$

Remaining part of work = $1-\frac{2}{3}=\frac{1}{3}$, which will be done by A alone in 20 days.

Hence, whole work will be done by A alone in 20 × 3 = 60 days.

61. 2 (A + B + C)'s 1 day's work = $\frac{1}{30}+\frac{1}{24}+\frac{1}{20}=\frac{15}{120}=\frac{1}{8}$

Hence, (A + B + C)'s 1 day's work = $\frac{1}{16}$

Now, A's 1 day's work = $\frac{1}{16}-\frac{1}{24}=\frac{1}{48}$

Again, (A + B + C)'s 10 days' work = $10\times\frac{1}{16}=\frac{5}{8}$

Remaining part of work = $1-\frac{5}{8}=\frac{3}{8}$, which will be done by A alone.

Hence, time taken by A to complete the remaining work = $\frac{3/8}{1/48}=\frac{3}{8}\times 48$ = 18 days.

62. (B + C)'s 3 days' work = $3\left(\frac{1}{19}+\frac{1}{12}\right)=3\times\frac{7}{36}=\frac{7}{12}$

Remaining part of work = $1-\frac{7}{12}=\frac{5}{12}$, which will be done by A.

A's 1 day's work = $\frac{1}{24}$

Time taken by A to complete the remaining work = $\frac{5/12}{1/24}=\frac{5}{12}\times 24$ = 10 days.

63. B's 10 days' work = $\frac{10}{15}=\frac{2}{3}$

Remaining part of work = $1-\frac{2}{3}=\frac{1}{3}$; which will be done by A alone.

A's 1 day's work = $\frac{1}{18}$

Hence, time taken by A to complete the remaining work = $\frac{1/3}{1/18}=\frac{1}{3}\times 18-6$ days.

64. B's 1 day's work = $\frac{1}{12}-\frac{1}{20}=\frac{2}{60}=\frac{1}{30}$

Hence, B's $\frac{1}{2}$ day's work = $\frac{1}{60}$

Now, work done by A and B in 1 day = $\frac{1}{20}+\frac{1}{60}=\frac{4}{60}=\frac{1}{15}$

Therefore, the work will be completed by A and B in 15 days.

65. C's 1 day's work = $\frac{1}{3}-\left(\frac{1}{6}+\frac{1}{8}\right)=\frac{1}{3}-\frac{7}{24}=\frac{1}{24}$

Hence, C's 3 days' work = $3 \times \frac{1}{24}=\frac{1}{8}$

Share of money of C = $\frac{1}{8}\times$ Rs. 3200 = Rs. 400

66. B's 23 days' work = $\frac{23}{40}$

Remaining part of work = $1-\frac{23}{40}=\frac{17}{40}$ which has been already done by A and B.

(A + B)'s 1 days' work = $\frac{1}{45}+\frac{1}{40}=\frac{17}{360}$

Hence, time taken by (A + B) to do the same work = $\frac{17/40}{17/360}=\frac{17}{40}\times\frac{360}{17}=9$ days.

67. The ratio of time taken by Ram and Mohan = 3 : 2

Hence, ratio of their efficiency = 2 : 3

Therefore, share of money of Ram = $\frac{2}{2+3}\times$ Rs. 150 = $\frac{2}{5}\times$ Rs. 150 = Rs. 60

68. 10 men's 6 days' work = $10 \times 6 \times \frac{1}{100}=\frac{3}{5}$

Hence, 15 women's 6 days' work = $1-\frac{3}{5}=\frac{2}{5}$

Then, 1 woman's 1 day's work = $\frac{2}{5}\times\frac{1}{15\times 6}=\frac{1}{225}$

Therefore, one woman alone will complete the work in 225 days.

69. Here, 1 woman $\equiv$ 2 men & also, 1 woman = 4 children

Hence, 3 men + 4 women + 6 children $\equiv \frac{3}{2}$ women + 4 women + $\frac{3}{2}$ women $\equiv$ 7 women

Therefore, 7 women alone can complete the work in 7 days.

70. (10 men + 15 women)'s 1 day's work = $\frac{1}{15}+\frac{1}{12}=\frac{9}{60}=\frac{3}{20}$

Hence, 10 men and 15 women will complete the work in $\frac{20}{3}=6\frac{2}{3}$ days.

71. In 3 days the work done by A, B and C = $\frac{3}{20}+\frac{1}{30}+\frac{1}{60}=\frac{12}{60}=\frac{1}{5}$

Hence, whole work done by A, B and C in 5 × 3 = 15 days.

72. In 2 days work done by A and B = $\frac{1}{16}+\frac{1}{12}=\frac{7}{48}$

In 6 pair of days work done by A and B = $6\times\frac{7}{48}=\frac{7}{8}$

Remaining part of work = $1-\frac{7}{8}=\frac{1}{8}$

On 13th day work done by A = $\frac{1}{16}$

Remaining part of work = $\frac{1}{8}-\frac{1}{16}=\frac{1}{16}$

Time taken by B in 14th day = $\frac{1/16}{1/12}=\frac{12}{16}=\frac{3}{4}$ day

Hence, total time taken = $13\frac{3}{4}$ days.

73. (one man + one woman)'s $\frac{1}{4}$ day's work = $\frac{1}{3\times4}+\frac{1}{4\times4}=\frac{1}{12}+\frac{1}{16}=\frac{7}{48}$

Remaining part of work = $1-\frac{7}{48}=\frac{41}{48}$, which will be done by boys alone in $\frac{1}{4}$ day.

One boy's $\frac{1}{4}$ day's work = $\frac{1}{4\times12}=\frac{1}{48}$

Hence, required number of boys = $\frac{41}{48}\Big/\frac{1}{48}=41$

74. 12 men's 6 days' work = $\frac{6}{9}=\frac{2}{3}$

Remaining part of work = $1-\frac{2}{3}=\frac{1}{3}$, which will be done by 18 men.

18 men's 1 day's work = $\frac{18}{9\times12}=\frac{1}{6}$

Hence, required number of days = $\frac{1/3}{1/6}=2$ days.

75. 1 woman's 1 day's work = $\frac{1}{20 \times 16} = \frac{1}{320}$

1 man's 1 day's work = $\frac{1}{15 \times 16} = \frac{1}{240}$

Hence, ratio of capacity of a man and a woman = $\frac{1}{240} : \frac{1}{320} = \frac{1}{3} : \frac{1}{4} = 4 : 3$

76. Here, (6 men + 8 boys) × 10 ≡ (26 men + 48 boys) × 2
⇒ 60 men + 80 boys ≡ 52 men + 96 boys
⇒ 8 men ≡ 16 boys.
Hence, 1 man = 2 boys.
Then, 6 men + 8 boys ≡ 12 boys + 8 boys = 20 boys
and 15 men + 20 boys ≡ 30 boys + 20 boys = 50 boys

Now, 50 boys' 1 day's work = $50 \times \frac{1}{20 \times 10} = \frac{1}{4}$

Hence, 15 men and 20 boys will do the same work in 4 days.

77. Here,
(12 men + 16 boys) × 5 ≡ (13 men + 24 boys) × 4
⇒ 60 men + 80 boys ≡ 52 men + 96 boys
⇒ 8 men ≡ 16 boys
∴ 1 man ≡ 2 boys
Hence, ratio of their daily work done = 2 : 1

78. 5 women's 1 day's work = $5 \times \frac{1}{10 \times 7} = \frac{1}{14}$

10 children's 1 day's work = $\frac{1}{14}$

Hence (5 women + 10 children)'s 1 day's work = $\frac{1}{14} + \frac{1}{14} = \frac{1}{7}$

Therefore, 5 women and 10 children will complete the work in 7 days.

79. 6 men's 2 days' work = $6 \times 2 \times \frac{1}{12 \times 4} = \frac{1}{4}$

Remaining part of work = $1 - \frac{1}{4} = \frac{3}{4}$, which will be done by women alone in 3 days.

1 woman's 1 day's work = $\frac{1}{15 \times 4} = \frac{1}{60}$

Hence, required number of women = $\frac{3/4}{1/60} = \frac{3}{4} \times 60 = 45$

80. Here, (4 men + 6 women) × 8 ≡ (3 men + 7 women) × 10
⇒ 32 men + 48 women ≡ 30 men + 70 women
⇒ 2 men ≡ 22 women

Hence, 1 man $\equiv$ 11 women

4 men + 6 women $\equiv$ 44 women + 6 women = 50 women

10 women's 1 day's work = $10 \times \dfrac{1}{8 \times 50} = \dfrac{1}{40}$

Hence, 10 women will complete the work in 40 days.

81. (16 men + 16 women)'s 1 day's work $= 16 \times \dfrac{1}{24 \times 16} + 16 \times \dfrac{1}{32 \times 24}$

$= \dfrac{1}{24} + \dfrac{1}{48} = \dfrac{1}{16}$

Hence, (16 men + 16 women)'s 14 days' work = $14 \times \dfrac{1}{16} = \dfrac{7}{8}$

Remaining part of work = $1 - \dfrac{7}{8} = \dfrac{1}{8}$, which will be done in 2 days by extra men.

1 man's 2 day's work = $\dfrac{2}{16 \times 24} = \dfrac{1}{192}$

Hence, extra number of men required = $\dfrac{1}{8} \Big/ \dfrac{1}{192} = \dfrac{1}{8} \times 192 = 24$

15

PROBLEMS BASED ON TRAINS

Important Facts :

1. The time taken by a train in passing a signal post or a telegraph pole or a man standing near a railway line = $\frac{\text{Length of the train}}{\text{Speed of the train}}$
2. The time taken by a train of length x passing a railway bridge or a platform or a tunnel or a train of length y at rest = $\frac{x+y}{\text{Speed}}$
3. *(a)* Time taken by faster train of length x and speed u to pass the slower train of length y and speed v in the same direction = $\frac{x+y}{u-v}$

   (b) Time taken by the trains in passing each other while moving in opposite direction = $\frac{x+y}{u+v}$
4. *(a)* Time taken by the train of length x and speed u to cross a man moving with speed v in same direction = $\frac{x}{u-v}$

   (b) Time taken by the train to cross a man moving in the opposite direction = $\frac{x}{u+v}$
5. If two trains start at the same time from two points A and B towards each other and after crossing, they take a and b hours in reaching B and A respectively. Then,

   A's speed : B's speed = $\left(\sqrt{b}:\sqrt{a}\right)$
6. u km/hr = $u \times \frac{5}{18}$ m/s and also, u m/s = $u \times \frac{18}{5}$ km/hr

Example 1: A train 160 m long is running at 40 m/s. In how much time will it pass a platform 40 m long?

Solution: Required time taken = $\frac{(160+40)}{40} = \frac{200}{40}$ = 5 sec.

Example 2: A train 100 m long takes 9 seconds to cross a man walking at 5 km/h in the direction opposite to that of the train. Find the speed of the train.

Sol: Let the speed of the train be x km/h.

Relative speed = $(x + 5)$ km/h = $\frac{5(x+5)}{18}$ m/sec

Now, $\frac{100}{\frac{5(x+5)}{18}} = 9 \quad \Rightarrow x + 5 = \frac{20 \times 18}{9} \quad \therefore x = 35$

Hence, speed of the train = 35 km/h.

Example 3: A train 125 m long is running at 50 km/h. In what time will it pass a man, running at 5 km/hr in the same direction in which the train is running?

Solution: Here, speed of train relative to man

$= (50 - 5)$ km/h $= \left(45 \times \frac{5}{18}\right)$ m/s. $= \frac{25}{2}$ m/sec

$\therefore$ Time taken by the train in passing the man

$= \left(125 \times \frac{2}{25}\right)$ sec $= 10$ sec.

Example 4: A platform is 131 metre long. If the speed of the train of 67 m long is 45 km/h, how long will it take to pass the platform?

Solution: Total distance = 131 + 67 = 198 m

and speed of the train = 45 km/h = $45 \times \frac{5}{18} = \frac{25}{2}$ m/s.

$\therefore$ Time taken to pass the platform = $198 \times \frac{2}{25} = 15.84$ sec.

Example 5: Two trains start from the station A and B towards each other at the rates of 50 km/h and 60 km/h. When they meet, it is found that the second train has travelled 120 km more than the first. Find the distance between the stations.

Solution: Let they will meet after t hours; then

$60t - 50t = 120 \quad \Rightarrow 10t = 120 \quad \therefore t = 12$ hrs.

Hence, required distance = $(60 + 50) \times 12 = 1320$ km

Example 6: If a train moves at the rate of 36 km per hour, what is its speed in metres per second?

Solution: 36 km per hour = $\frac{5}{18} \times 36$ m/s = 10 m/s

Example 7: A train passes a pole in 40 seconds moving at the rate of 36 km per hour. Find the length of the train.

Solution: Required length $= 40 \times 36 \times \frac{5}{18} = 400$ metres.

Example 9: A train of length 150 metres takes 40.5 seconds to cross a tunnel of length 300 metres. What is the speed of the train in km/hr?

Solution: Total distance = 150 m + 300 m = 450 m

Required speed = $\frac{450}{40.5}$ m/s = $\frac{100}{9} \times \frac{18}{5}$ km/hr = 40 km/hr

Example 10: A train 110 m in length runs through a station at the rate of 36 km/hr. How long will it take to pass a given point?

Solution: Time taken $= \dfrac{110}{\left(36 \times \dfrac{5}{18}\right)} = \dfrac{110}{10} = 11$ seconds

Example 11: Two trains are moving in opposite directions at the speed of 50 and 70 km per hour. Their lengths are 150 m and 100 m. The time required for their crossing each other is :

Solution: Required time $= \dfrac{(150+100)\text{ m}}{(50+70)\times\dfrac{5}{18}\text{ m/s}} = \dfrac{250\times 3}{100} = \dfrac{15}{2} = 7\dfrac{1}{2}$ seconds

Example 12: A train 150 metres long running at a speed of 60 km per hour takes 30 seconds to cross a bridge. What is the length of the bridge?

Solution: Distance covered by the train in 30 seconds $= 60 \times \dfrac{5}{18} \times 30 = 500$ m

Length of the bridge = 500 – 150 = 350 m

Example 13: A train starts from station '*x*' @ 60 km per hour and reaches station '*y*' in 45 minutes. If the speed is reduced by 6 kmph, how much more time will the train take to return from station '*y*' to station '*x*'?

Solution: Let *t* hr. taken by the train in returning journey, then,

$54 \times t = 60 \times \dfrac{45}{60} \quad \therefore \; t = \dfrac{45}{54}\text{ hr.} = \dfrac{5}{6} \times 60\text{ min} = 50\text{ min.}$

Required extra (more) time = 50 – 45 = 5 min.

Example 14: A train running at a certain speed takes 20 seconds to cross a signal post and 50 seconds to cross a bridge. If the length of bridge is 300 m, find the length of the train.

Solution: Let length of the train = *x* metres, then

$\dfrac{x}{20} = \dfrac{x+300}{50} \Rightarrow 5x = 2x + 600 \quad \Rightarrow 3x = 600 \quad \therefore \; x = 200\text{ m}$

Example 15: A railway train 140 meters long, travelling at 90 km/hr will overtake another train of length 160 metres and moving in the same direction at 72 km/hr in :

Solution: Difference in speed of two trains = 90 – 72 = 18 km/hr

Total distance= 140 + 160 = 300 m

$\therefore$Time taken $= \dfrac{300}{1000\times 18} = \dfrac{1}{60}$ hr. = 1 minute.

Example 16: Train A starts from a place at 7 a.m. with a speed of 10 km/hr. Another train B starts from the same place at 9 a.m. with a speed of 15 km/hr. When will train B meet train A?

Solution: Let both train will meet in *t* hrs. after starting of train A; then,

$t \times 10 = (t - 2) \times 15$

$\Rightarrow 15t - 10t = 30 \qquad \therefore \; t = 6$ hrs.

Required time = 7 a.m. + 6 hrs = 1 p.m.

EXERCISE

1. A train runs at 45 km per hour. How far does it go in 6 seconds?
(a) 72 m (b) 60 m (c) 75 m (d) 70 m

2. A motorist covers a distance of 39 km in 45 minutes, by moving at a speed of x km/hr for the first 15 minutes, then moving at double the speed for the next 20 minutes and then again moving at his original speed for the rest of journey. Then x is equal to :
(a) 31.2 (b) 36 (c) 40 (d) 52

3. A train travels 82.6 km/hr. How many metres will it travel in 15 minutes?
(a) 206.50 m (b) 2065 m (c) 20650 m (d) 20.65 m

4. If a train running at 72 km/hr crosses a coconut tree standing by the side of the track in 7 seconds, the length of the train is :
(a) 104 m (b) 140 m (c) 504 m (d) 540 m

5. Two trains are moving in the same direction at 45 km/hr and 25 km/hr. The faster train crosses a passenger travelling in the slower one in 18 seconds. The length of the faster train is :
(a) 100 m (b) 120 m (c) 150 m (d) 180 m

6. Two trains are moving at 50 km/hr and 70 km/hr in an opposite direction. Their lengths are 150 m and 100 m respectively. The time they will take to pass each other completely is :
(a) 3 seconds (b) $4\frac{1}{2}$ seconds (c) 5 seconds (d) $7\frac{1}{2}$ seconds

7. A train leaves Delhi at 9 A.M. at a speed of 30 km/hr. Another train leaves at 2 P.M. at a speed of 40 km/hr on the same day and in the same direction. How far from Delhi, will the two trains meet?
(a) 300 km (b) 400 km (c) 600 km (d) 650 km

8. Mumbai Express left Delhi for Mumbai at 14.30 hours travelling at a speed of 60 km/hr, Rajdhani Express left Delhi for Mumbai on the same day at 16.30 hours travelling at a speed of 80 km/hr. How far away from Delhi will the two trains meet?
(a) 120 km (b) 360 km (c) 480 km (d) 500 km

9. A train covers a distance in 50 minutes if it runs at a speed of 48 km/hour on an average. The speed at which the train must run to reduce the time of journey to 40 minutes will be :
(a) 50 km/hr (b) 55 km/hr (c) 60 km/hr (d) 70 km/hr

10. Two trains are running in opposite direction with the speed of 62 km/hr and 40 km/hr respectively. If the length of one train is 250 metres and they cross each other in 18 seconds, what will be the length of the other train?
(a) 125 m (b) 250 m (c) 260 m (d) None of these

11. A train with stoppages travelled a distance at 60 km an hour and without stoppages 90 km an hour. How many minutes per hour the train stops?
(a) 10 minutes (b) 20 minutes (c) 25 minutes (d) 30 minutes

12. The distance of earth from sun is 141,000,000 km and light travels from latter to former in 7 minutes and fifty seconds. Find the velocity of light per second.
(a) 30000 km (b) 3000 km (c) 300000 km (d) 300 km

13. A train passes the platform 60 metres long in 20 seconds and a man standing on the platform in 16 seconds. The speed of the train is :
(a) 38 km/hr (b) 40 km/hr (c) 50 km/hr (d) 54 km/hr

14. A train running at the speed of 20 m/s crosses a pole in 24 seconds less than it requires to cross a platform thrice its length at the same speed. What is the length of the train?
(*a*) 160 m (*b*) 180 m (*c*) 270 m (*d*) 340 m

15. A 180 metres long train crosses a pole in 20 seconds. What is the speed of the train?
(*a*) 9 m/s (*b*) 12 m/s (*c*) 15 m/s (*d*) 18 m/s

16. A train running at 60 km/hr takes 9 seconds to pass a platform. Next it takes 7 seconds to pass a man walking at the rate of 6 km/hr in the same direction. Find the length of the platform?
(*a*) 45 m (*b*) 50 m (*c*) 100 m (*d*) 105 m

17. Two trains travel in the same direction at the speed of 56 km/hr and 29 km/hr respectively. The faster train passes a man in the slower train in 10 seconds. The length of the faster train (in metres) is:
(*a*) 75 (*b*) 80 (*c*) 100 (*d*) 120

18. A train starts from A at 7 a.m. towards B with speed 50 km/hr. Another train from B starts at 8 a.m. with speed 60 km/hr towards A. Both of them meet at 10 a.m. at C. The ratio of the distance AC to BC is:
(*a*) 4 : 5 (*b*) 5 : 4 (*c*) 5 : 6 (*d*) 6 : 5

19. A train running at speed of 90 km/hr crosses a platform double its length in 36 seconds. What is the length of the platform in metres?
(*a*) 200 (*b*) 300 (*c*) 450 (*d*) 600

20. A train 130 metres long crosses a bridge in 21 seconds moving at the speed of 90 km/hr. Find the length of the bridge.
(*a*) 415 m (*b*) 395 m (*c*) 295 m (*d*) 285 m

21. In what time will a 270 m long train cross 180 m long bridge at the speed of 108 km/hr.?
(*a*) 15 sec. (*b*) 9 sec. (*c*) 6 sec. (*d*) 3 sec.

22. A train crosses a 162 m long platform in 18 seconds and other 120 m long platform in 15 seconds. The length of the train is:
(*a*) 100 m (*b*) 90 m (*c*) 80 m (*d*) 70 m

23. A train running at a speed of 90 km/hr crosses a 100 m long platform in 6 seconds. What is the length of the train?
(*a*) 25 m (*b*) 50 m (*c*) 75 m (*d*) 100 m

24. Train A crosses another rest train B in 30 seconds. The length of train B is 140% of the length of train A. The speed of train A is 72 km/hr. What is the difference between the lengths of the two trains?
(*a*) 70 m (*b*) 80 m (*c*) 100 m (*d*) 140 m

25. A train running at a speed of 36 km/hr takes 8 seconds to pass a pole. Find the length of the train.
(*a*) 90 m (*b*) 85 m (*c*) 80 m (*d*) 70 m

26. Two stations A and B are 110 km apart. One train starts from station A at 7 a.m. and travels towards B at 20 km/hr. Another train starts from B at 8 a.m. and travels towards A at a speed of 25 km/hr. At what time will they meet?
(*a*) 1.00 p.m. (*b*) 11.30 a.m. (*c*) 11 a.m. (*d*) 10 a.m.

27. A train 700 m long is running at 72 km/hr. If it crosses a tunnel in 1 minute, the length of the tunnel is:
(*a*) 500 m (*b*) 550 m (*c*) 600 m (*d*) 700 m

28. A train 110 m long passes a telegraph pole in 3 sec. For how long will it take to cross a railway platform 165 m long?
(*a*) $7\frac{1}{2}$ sec. (*b*) 5 sec. (*c*) $4\frac{1}{2}$ sec. (*d*) $3\frac{1}{2}$ sec.

29. A train travels 200 km at a uniform speed. If the speed had been 10 km/hr less, the journey would have taken 40 minutes more. Find the speed of the train?
(a) 40 km/hr (b) 45 km/hr (c) 50 km/hr (d) 60 km/hr

30. A train running at 72 km/hr crosses a 200 m long platform in 22 seconds. The length of the train is:
(a) 220 m (b) 200 m (c) 180 m (d) 240 m

31. A 200 m long train running at 90 km/hr crosses another train 300 m long running at 60 km/hr from opposite direction. The time taken to cross each other is:
(a) 75 sec. (b) 60 sec. (c) 50 sec. (d) 12 sec.

32. Two trains 132 m and 108 m in length respectively are running in opposite directions, one at the rate of 32 km/hr and other at the rate of 40 km/hr. In what time will they be completely clear of each other from the moment they meet?
(a) 13 sec. (b) 12 sec. (c) 11 sec. (d) 10 sec.

33. A train travelling at the speed of 60 km/hr crosses a platform in 20 seconds. What is the length of the train?
(a) 336 m (b) 333 m
(c) 300 m (d) Cannot be determined

34. A train passes a platform 90 metre long in 30 seconds and a man standing on the platform in 15 seconds. The speed of the train is:
(a) 21.6 km/hr (b) 18.4 km/hr (c) 14.6 km/hr (d) 12.4 km/hr

35. A train travelling 25 km/hr leaves Mumbai at 10 a.m. and another train travelling 35 km/hr starts at 3 p.m. in the same direction. How many km from Mumbai will they be together?
(a) $570\frac{1}{2}$ km (b) $550\frac{1}{2}$ km (c) $437\frac{1}{2}$ km (d) $337\frac{1}{2}$ km

36. A train running at a speed of 45 km/hr clears a platform 180 metres long in 24 seconds. The length of the train is:
(a) 130 m (b) 125 m (c) 120 m (d) 110 m

37. A train passes a station platform in 36 seconds and a man standing on the platform in 20 seconds. If the speed of the train is 54 km/hr. What is the length of the platform?
(a) 300 m (b) 240 m (c) 200 m (d) 120 m

38. Two trains are running in opposite directions with the same speed. If the length of each train is 120 m and they cross each other in 12 seconds. Find the speed of each train (in km/hr).
(a) 72 (b) 36 (c) 18 (d) 10

39. Two trains of equal length are running on parallel lines in the same direction at a speed of 46 km/hr and 36 km/hr respectively. The faster train passes the slower train in 36 seconds. What is the length of each train?
(a) 82 m (b) 80 m (c) 72 m (d) 50 m

40. A train 125 m long passes a man, running at 5 km/hr in the same directon in which the train is going, in 10 seconds. What is the speed of train?
(a) 55 km/hr (b) 54 km/hr (c) 50 km/hr (d) 45 km/hr

41. Two trains 140 m and 160 m long run at the speed of 60 km/hr and 40 km/hr respectively in opposite directions on parallel tracks. Find the time (in seconds) which they take to cross each other.
(a) 10.8 (b) 10 (c) 9.6 (d) 9

42. A jogger running at 9 km/hr alongside a railway track is 240 m ahead of the engine of a 120 m long train running at 45 km/hr in the same direction. In how much time will the train pass the jogger?
(*a*) 72 sec (*b*) 36 sec (*c*) 18 sec (*d*) 3.6 sec

43. A train moves past a telegraph post and a bridge 264 m long in 8 seconds and 20 seconds respectively. Find the speed of the train.
(*a*) 79.2 km/hr (*b*) 79 km/hr
(*c*) 70 km/hr (*d*) 69.5 km/hr

44. A 270 m long train running at the speed of 120 km/hr crosses another train running in opposite direction at the speed of 80 km/hr in 9 seconds. Find the length of the other train.
(*a*) 320 m (*b*) 260 m (*c*) 240 m (*d*) 230 m

45. Two goods train each 500 m long are running in opposite directions on parallel tracks. Their speeds are 45 km/hr and 30 km/hr respectively. What is the time taken by the slower train to pass the driver of the faster one?
(*a*) 60 sec. (*b*) 48 sec. (*c*) 24 sec. (*d*) 12 sec.

46. Two trains are moving in opposite directions at the speed of 60 km/hr and 90 km/hr respectively. Their lengths are 1.10 km and 0.9 km respectively. What is the time taken by the slower train to cross the faster train in seconds?
(*a*) 49 (*b*) 48 (*c*) 45 (*d*) 36

47. A train 110 m long is running with a speed of 60 km/hr. In what time will it pass a man who is running at 6 km/hr in the direction opposite to that in which the train is going?
(*a*) 10 sec. (*b*) 7 sec. (*c*) 6 sec. (*d*) 5 sec.

48. How many seconds will a 500 m long train to cross a man walking with a speed of 3 km/hr in the direction of the moving train if the speed of the train is 63 km/hr?
(*a*) 45 (*b*) 40 (*c*) 30 (*d*) 25

49. Two trains one from Howrah to Patna and other from Patna to Howrah, start simultaneously. After they meet, the train reach their destinations after 9 hours and 16 hours respectively. What is the ratio of their speeds?
(*a*) 9 : 16 (*b*) 6 : 7 (*c*) 4 : 3 (*d*) 2 : 3

50. Two trains running in opposite directions cross a man standing on the platform in 27 seconds and 17 seconds respectively and they cross each other in 23 seconds. What is the ratio of their speeds?
(*a*) 3 : 4 (*b*) 3 : 2 (*c*) 2 : 3 (*d*) 1 : 3

51. Two trains, each 100 m long, moving in opposite directions, cross each other in 8 seconds. If one is moving twice as fast the other. What is the speed of the faster train?
(*a*) 75 km/hr (*b*) 60 km/hr (*c*) 45 km/hr (*d*) 30 km/hr

52. Two trains are running at 40 km/hr and 20 km/hr respectively in the same direction. Fast train completely passes a man sitting in the slower train in 5 seconds. Find the length of the fast train.
(*a*) $27\frac{7}{9}$ m (*b*) 27 m (*c*) $23\frac{2}{9}$ m (*d*) 23 m

53. Two trains of equal lengths take 10 seconds and 15 seconds respectively to cross a telegraph post. If the length of the each train be 120 m, in what time (in seconds) will they cross each other travelling in opposite direction?
(*a*) 20 (*b*) 15 (*c*) 12 (*d*) 10

SOLUTIONS

1. Speed = 45 km/hr = $45 \times \frac{5}{18} = \frac{25}{2}$ m/s

Hence, distance covered = $\frac{25}{2} \times 6 = 75$ m

2. Here, $x \times \frac{15}{60} + 2x \times \frac{20}{60} + x \times \frac{10}{60} = 39$

$\Rightarrow 3x + 8x + 2x = 39 \times \frac{60}{5} \quad \Rightarrow 13x = 39 \times 12 \quad \therefore x = \frac{39 \times 12}{13} = 36$

3. Travelled distance = $82.6 \times \frac{15}{60}$ km = 20.65 km = 20650 m

4. Length of the train = $72 \times \frac{5}{18} \times 7 = 140$ m

5. The length of the faster train = $(45 - 25) \times \frac{5}{18} \times 18 = 20 \times 5 = 100$ m

6. Required time = $\frac{(150+100)}{(50+70) \times \frac{5}{18}} = \frac{250 \times 18}{120 \times 5} = \frac{15}{2} = 7\frac{1}{2}$ sec.

7. Let they will meet after t hours from starting the first train.

Then, $t \times 30 = (t - 5)40 \quad \Rightarrow 40t - 30t = 200 \quad \Rightarrow 10t = 200 \quad \therefore t = 20$

Hence, required distance from Delhi = 30 × 20 = 600 km

8. Let they will meet after t hours from starting the Mumbai Express; then

$60t = 80\ (t - 2) \quad \Rightarrow 20t = 160 \quad \therefore t = 8$ hrs.

Hence, required distance from Delhi = 60 × 8 = 480 km

9. Here, $x \times \frac{40}{60} = 48 \times \frac{50}{60} \quad \therefore x = 48 \times \frac{5}{4} = 60$ km/hr

Hence, required speed = 60 km/hr

10. Distance travelled in 18 seconds = $(62 + 40) \times \frac{5}{18} \times 18 = 510$ m

Hence, length of the other train = 510 − 250 = 260 m

11. The train stops per hour = $\frac{90-60}{90}$ hr. = $\frac{1}{3} \times 60$ min = 20 min

12. Time = 7 min 50 sec. = 470 sec.

Velocity of light per second = $\frac{141{,}000{,}000}{470} = 300000$ km

13. Let speed of the train be x m/sec then,

$x \times 20 - x \times 16 = 60 \quad \Rightarrow 4x = 60 \quad \therefore x = 15$m/sec

Hence, speed of the train = $15 \times \frac{18}{5}$ km/hr = 54 km/hr

14. Let length of the train be x m; then

$$\frac{x+3x}{20}-\frac{x}{20}=24 \quad \Rightarrow \frac{3x}{20}=24 \quad \therefore x = 160 \text{ m}$$

15. Speed of the train = $\frac{180}{20}$ = 9m/sec

16. Length of the train = $(60-6)\times\frac{5}{18}\times 7 = 105$ m

Distance covered in 9 sec. = $60\times\frac{5}{18}\times 9 = 150$ m

Hence, length of the platform = 150 − 105 = 45 m

17. Length of the faster train = $(56-29)\times\frac{5}{18}\times 10 = 27\times\frac{5}{18}\times 10 = 75$ m

18. Here, AC = 50 × 3 = 150 km, BC = 60 × 2 = 120 km

Hence, AC : BC = 150 : 120 = 5 : 4

19. Let lengths of train and platform be x and $2x$ m; then,

$$x+2x = 90\times\frac{5}{18}\times 36 \quad \Rightarrow 3x = 900 \quad \therefore x = 300 \text{ m}$$

Hence, length of the platform = $2x$ m = 2 × 300 = 600 m

20. Distance covered in 21 seconds = $90\times\frac{5}{18}\times 21 = 525$ m

Length of the bridge = 525 − 130 = 395 m

21. Speed = 108 km/hr = $108\times\frac{5}{18}$ = 30 m /sec

Required time = $\frac{270+180}{30}=\frac{450}{30}$ = 15 sec

22. Let length of the train be x m; then

$$\frac{162+x}{18}=\frac{120+x}{15} \quad \Rightarrow 5\,(162+x) = 6\,(120+x) \quad \Rightarrow 6x-5x = 810-720 \quad \therefore x = 90 \text{ m}$$

23. Distance covered in 6 seconds = $90\times\frac{5}{18}\times 6 = 150$ m

Length of the train = 150 − 100 = 50 m

24. Let length of the two trains be x m and $\frac{140x}{100}=\frac{7x}{5}$ m, then $x+\frac{7x}{5}=72\times\frac{5}{18}\times 30$

$$\Rightarrow \frac{12x}{5}=600 \quad \therefore x = \frac{5\times 600}{12} = 250 \text{ m}$$

Length of another train = $\frac{7x}{5}=\frac{7}{5}\times 250 = 350$ m

Hence, difference between the lengths = 350 − 250 = 100 m

25. Length of the train = $36 \times \frac{5}{18} \times 8 = 80$ m

26. Let they will meet after t hours from starting the first train; then
$20 \times t + 25\,(t - 1) = 110 \quad \Rightarrow 45t = 135 \quad \therefore\ t = 3$ hrs
Hence, required time = 7 a.m. + 3 hr = 10 a.m.

27. Distance covered in 1 min (60 sec) = $72 \times \frac{5}{18} \times 60 = 1200$ m

Hence, length of the tunnel = 1200 – 700 = 500 m

28. Here, $\frac{165+110}{t} = \frac{110}{3} \quad \Rightarrow \frac{275}{t} = \frac{110}{3} \quad \therefore\ t = \frac{275 \times 3}{110} = \frac{15}{2} = 7\frac{1}{2}$ sec

29. Let usual speed of the train be x km/hr, then,

$\frac{200}{x-10} - \frac{200}{x} = \frac{40}{60} \quad \Rightarrow \frac{200 \times 10}{x^2 - 10x} = \frac{2}{3} \quad \Rightarrow x^2 - 10x = \frac{200 \times 10 \times 3}{2}$
$\Rightarrow x^2 - 10x - 3000 = 0 \quad \Rightarrow (x - 60)\,(x + 50) = 0$
$\therefore\ x = 60$ (Taking positive value)
Hence, speed of the train = 60 km/hr

30. Distance covered in 22 seconds = $72 \times \frac{5}{18} \times 22 = 440$ m

Hence, length of the train = 440 – 200 = 240 m

31. Their relative speed = 90 + 60 = 150 km/hr = $150 \times \frac{5}{18} = \frac{125}{3}$ m/sec

Required time = $\frac{200+300}{125/3} = \frac{500 \times 3}{125} = 12$ sec.

32. Their relative speed = (32 + 40) = 72 km/hr = $72 \times \frac{5}{18} = 20$ m/s

Required time = $\frac{132+108}{20} = \frac{240}{20} = 12$ sec.

33. Distance travelled in 20 sec. = $60 \times \frac{5}{18} \times 20 = \frac{1000}{3}$ m

Here, Length of platform + Length of train = $\frac{1000}{3}$ m

But, length of platform is not given, so length of train cannot be determined.

34. Let speed of the train be x m/s; then
$30x - 15x = 90 \quad \Rightarrow 15x = 90 \quad \therefore\ x = 6$ m/s

Hence, speed of the train = $6 \times \frac{18}{5} = 21.6$ km/hr

35. Let they will meet together after t hours from starting the first train; then

$25t = 35\ (t - 5) \Rightarrow 10t = 175 \quad \therefore\ t = 17.5$ hr.

Required distance from the Mumbai = 25 × 17.5 = 437.5 m

36. Distance covered in 24 seconds $= 45 \times \frac{5}{18} \times 24 = 300$ m

Hence, length of the train = 300 – 180 = 120 m

37. Length of the platform $= 54 \times \frac{5}{18}(36 - 20) = 15 \times 16 = 240$ m

38. Speed of the train $= \frac{1}{2}\left(\frac{120+120}{12}\right) = \frac{1}{2} \times \frac{240}{12} = 10 \text{ m/s} = 10 \times \frac{18}{5} \text{ km/hr} = 36 \text{ km/hr}$

39. Their relative speed $= (46 - 36) \text{ km/hr} = 10 \times \frac{5}{18} = \frac{25}{9}$ m/s

Length of each train $= \frac{1}{2} \times \left(\frac{25}{9} \times 36\right) = 50$ m

40. Their relative speed $= \frac{125}{10} \text{ m/s} = \frac{125}{10} \times \frac{18}{5} = 45$ km/hr

Hence, speed of the train = 45 + 5 = 50 km/hr

41. Their relative speed $= (60 + 40) = 100 \text{ km/hr} = 100 \times \frac{5}{18} \text{ m/s} = \frac{250}{9}$ m/s

Required time $= \frac{140+160}{250/9} = \frac{300 \times 9}{250} = 10.8$ sec.

42. Their relative speed $= (45 - 9) \text{ km/hr} = 36 \times \frac{5}{18} \text{ m/s} = 10$ m/s

Required time $= \frac{240+120}{10} = \frac{360}{10} = 36$ sec.

43. Let speed of the train be x m/s; then,

$x \times 20 - x \times 8 = 264 \Rightarrow 12x = 264 \quad \therefore\ x = 22$ m/s

Hence, speed of the train $= 22 \times \frac{18}{5} \text{ km/hr} = \frac{396}{5} = 79.2$ km/hr

44. Their relative speed $= (120 + 80) \text{ km/hr} = 200 \times \frac{5}{18} \text{ m/sec} = \frac{500}{9}$ m/s

Distance travelled in 9 seconds $= \frac{500}{9} \times 9 = 500$ m

Hence, length of the other train = 500 – 270 = 230 m

45. Their relative speed $= (45 + 30) \text{ km/hr} = 75 \times \frac{5}{18} \text{ m/s} = \frac{125}{6}$ m/s

Required time $= \frac{500+500}{125/6} = \frac{1000 \times 6}{125} = 48$ sec.

46. Required time $= \dfrac{1.10+0.9}{60+90} = \dfrac{2}{150}$ hr $= \dfrac{2\times 60\times 60}{150}$ sec. = 48 sec.

47. Their relative speed = (60 + 6) km/hr $= 66 \times \dfrac{5}{18}$ m/s $= \dfrac{55}{3}$ m/s

Required time $= \dfrac{110}{55/3} = \dfrac{110\times 3}{55} = 6$ sec.

48. Their relative speed = (63 − 3) km/hr $= 60 \times \dfrac{5}{18}$ m/s $= \dfrac{50}{3}$ m/s

Required time $= \dfrac{500}{50/3} = \dfrac{500\times 3}{50} = 30$ sec.

49. Ratio of their speeds $= x_1 : x_2 = \sqrt{t_2} : \sqrt{t_1}$

$= \sqrt{16} : \sqrt{9} = 4 : 3$

50. Let x_1 and x_2 m/s be the speed of two trains and their lengths are l_1 and l_2 m, then,

$l_1 = x_1 \times 27 = 27x_1$; $l_2 = 17x_2$

And also, $\dfrac{l_1+l_2}{x_1+x_2} = 23 \Rightarrow \dfrac{27x_1+17x_2}{x_1+x_2} = 23 \Rightarrow 4x_1 = 6x_2 \Rightarrow \dfrac{x_1}{x_2} = \dfrac{3}{2}$ $\therefore x_1 : x_2 = 3 : 2$

51. Let speeds of two trains be x and $2x$ m/s; then

$\dfrac{100+100}{8} = x + 2x \Rightarrow 3x = 25 \quad \therefore x = \dfrac{25}{3}$ m/s

Speed of faster train $= 2 \times \dfrac{25}{3}$ m/s $= \dfrac{50}{3} \times \dfrac{18}{5}$ km/hr = 60 km/hr

52. Their relative speed = (40 − 20) km/hr $= 20 \times \dfrac{5}{18} = \dfrac{50}{9}$ m/s

Length of the fast train $= \dfrac{50}{9} \times 5 = \dfrac{250}{9}$ m $= 27\dfrac{7}{9}$ m

53. Speed of the Ist train $= \dfrac{120}{10} = 12$ m/s; Speed of IInd train $= \dfrac{120}{15} = 8$ m/s

Their relative speed = (12 + 8) m/s = 20 m/s

Hence, required time $= \dfrac{120+120}{20} = \dfrac{240}{20} = 12$ sec.

16

PIPES & CISTERNS

The fundamental concepts for solving problems on pipes and cisterns are similar to those for Time and Work. Here the work may be positive or negative, *i.e.*, filling or emptying of the tank respectively. Work is done by pipes instead of persons. An inlet pipe (*i.e.*, a pipe connected with a tank and fills it) fills the tank and hence its work is taken as positive. An exit or outlet pipe (*i.e.*, a pipe connected with a tank and empties it) empties the tank and hence its work is taken as negative. A leakage is equivalent to an exit pipe. Since the work here can be positive as well as negative, care must be taken in using proper sign convention.

Important Facts:

1. If a pipe can fill a tank in x hours, then the part filled in 1 hour = $\frac{1}{x}$.
2. If a pipe can empty a tank in y hour, then the part of the tank emptied in 1 hour = $\frac{1}{y}$
3. If two pipes can fill a tank in x and y hours respectively and both the pipes are opened simultaneously then, the part filled in 1 hour = $\frac{1}{x}+\frac{1}{y}$.
4. (*a*) A tap fills a cistern in x hours and the other can empty the cistern in y hours. If both the taps are opened simultaneously, then the net part of the tank filled in 1 hour = $\frac{1}{x}-\frac{1}{y}$; when $y > x$.
   (*b*) A tap can fill a tank in x hours and other can empty in y hours. If both the taps are opened simultaneously, then the net part of tank emptied in 1 hour = $\frac{1}{y}-\frac{1}{x}$; when $x > y$.

Example 1: Two pipes can fill a cistern in 6 min. and 7 min. respectively. If these taps are opened alternately for a minute, in what time will the cistern be filled?

Solution: In 2 minutes the part filled by both pipes = $\frac{1}{6}+\frac{1}{7}=\frac{13}{42}$

In 3 pair of minutes the part filled by both pipes = $3 \times \frac{13}{42} = \frac{13}{14}$

Remaining part = $1 - \frac{13}{14} = \frac{1}{14}$

which is filled by Ist pipe in 7th minute.

Time taken by first pipe to fill up the remaining part = $\frac{1/14}{1/6} = \frac{3}{7}$ minute.

Hence, total time taken = $6\frac{3}{7}$ minutes.

Example 2: Two pipes A and B can fill a cistern in 24 min. and 36 min. respectively. Third pipe C can empty it in 36 min. If all the three pipes are opened, find the time taken to fill the cistern.

Solution: Since, Time taken to fill the cistern by B = time taken to empty the cistern by C

So, the cistern will be filled by A in 24 min.

Example 3: Taps A, B and C, when opened together, fill the tank in 15 hours. Tap A alone can fill it in 10 hours while B alone in 20 hours. How does tap C work?

Solution: In 1 minute part of job done by C = $\frac{1}{15} - \left(\frac{1}{10} + \frac{1}{20}\right) = \frac{1}{15} - \frac{3}{20}$

$$= -\frac{5}{60} = -\frac{1}{12}$$

Hence, tap C can empty the full tank in 12 hours.

Example 4: Two pipes A and B can fill a tank in 24 minutes and 32 minutes respectively. If both the pipes are opened simultaneously, after how much time should B be closed so that the tank is full in 18 minutes?

Solution: In 18 minutes the part filled by A = $18 \times \frac{1}{24} = \frac{3}{4}$

Remaining part = $1 - \frac{3}{4} = \frac{1}{4}$

Time taken by B to fill the remaining part = $\frac{1/4}{1/32}$ = 8 min.

Hence, B should be closed after 8 minutes.

Example 5: A tank has a leak which would empty it in 8 hours. A tap is turned on which admit 6 litres a minute into the tank and it now emptied in 12 hrs. How many litres does the tank holds?

Soluiton: In 1 hour the part filled by the tap = $\frac{1}{8} - \frac{1}{12} = \frac{1}{24}$

Hence, the tap can fill the tank in 24 hours.

Therefore, capacity of the tank = 24 × 60 × 6 = 8640 litres

Example 6: A, B and C are three pipes connected to a tank. A and B together fill the tank in 6 hours. B and C together fill the tank in 10 hours. A and C together fill the tank in $7\frac{1}{2}$ hours. In how much time will A, B and C fill the tank separately?

Solution: In 1 hour the part filled by 2 (A + B + C) = $\frac{1}{6} + \frac{1}{10} + \frac{2}{15} = \frac{12}{30} = \frac{2}{5}$

Hence, in 1 hour the part filled by (A + B + C) = $\frac{1}{2} \times \frac{2}{5} = \frac{1}{5}$

In 1 hour the part filled by A $= \frac{1}{5} - \frac{1}{10} = \frac{1}{10}$

In 1 hour the part filled by B $= \frac{1}{5} - \frac{2}{15} = \frac{1}{15}$

In 1 hour the part filled by C $= \frac{1}{5} - \frac{1}{6} = \frac{1}{30}$

Hence, pipes A, B and C can fill the tank in 10 hours, 15 hours and 30 hours respectively.

Example 7: There are two taps to fill a tank while a third to empty it. When the third tap is closed they can fill the tank in 10 minutes and 12 minutes respectively. If all the three taps be opened, the tank is filled in 15 min. If the first two taps are closed, in what time can the third tap empty the tank when it is full?

Solution: Part of the tank emptied by the third in 1 min $= \left(\frac{1}{10} + \frac{1}{12}\right) - \frac{1}{15} = \frac{7}{60}$

Hence, the full tank will be emptied by third pipe in $\left(\frac{60}{7}\right)$ min $= 8\frac{4}{7}$ minutes

Example 8: Two pipes can fill a reservoir in 10 min and 12 min respectively. A waste pipe in the bottom can drain off 5 litres of water per minute. If the reservoir is empty and all the pipes are opened, it is filled in 7½ minutes, what is the capacity of the reservoir?

Solution: In 1 min the part emptied by waste pipe $= \left(\frac{1}{10} + \frac{1}{12}\right) - \frac{2}{15} = \frac{11}{60} - \frac{2}{15} = \frac{3}{60} = \frac{1}{20}$

Hence, waste pipe can empty the full reservoir in 20 minutes.
Hence, capacity of reservoir = 20 × 5 = 100 litres.

EXERCISE

1. A cistern which could be filled in 9 hours takes one hour more to be filled owing to a leak in its bottom. If the cistern is full, in what time will the leak empty it?
(*a*) 70 hours (*b*) 80 hours (*c*) 90 hours (*d*) 100 hours

2. Two pipes P and Q can fill a cistern in 12 and 15 minutes respectively. Both are opened together, but at the end of 3 minutes the first is turned off. How much longer will the cistern take to fill?
(*a*) $8\frac{1}{4}$ minutes (*b*) $11\frac{1}{4}$ minutes (*c*) $7\frac{1}{4}$ minutes (*d*) $15\frac{1}{4}$ minutes

3. Two pipes A and B would fill a cistern in 20 and 34 minutes respectively. Both pipes being opened, find when the first pipe must be turned off so that the cistern may be just filled in 17 minutes?
(*a*) 10 min. (*b*) 30 min. (*c*) 17 min. (*d*) 34 min.

4. Pipe A and B can fill a tank in 10 hours and 15 hours respectively. Both together can fill it in:
(*a*) 6 hours (*b*) 7 hours (*c*) 8 hours (*d*) 9 hours

5. A cistern is normally filled in 8 hours but takes two hours longer to fill because of a leak in its bottom. If the cistern is full, the leak will empty it in:
(*a*) 20 hours (*b*) 30 hours (*c*) 40 hours (*d*) 50 hours

6. A tap can fill a tank in 12 hours, whereas another can empty it in 18 hours. If both the taps are opened simultaneously, how much time will the tank take to fill?
(a) 36 hours (b) 72 hours (c) 18 hours (d) 12 hours

7. Two taps can fill a tank in 2 hours and 3 hours respectively. If both of them are opened at the same time, the tank will be filled up in:
(a) 2 hours 12 min. (b) 1 hour 12 min. (c) 5 hours (d) None of these

8. A tank can be filled separately by two taps A and B in 45 minutes and 36 minutes respectively. A tap C at the bottom can empty the full cistern in 30 minutes. If the tap C is opened 7 minutes after the two taps A and B are opened, find when the cistern will be full?
(a) 46 minutes (b) 25 minutes (c) 14 minutes (d) None of these

9. There is a leak in the bottom of a cistern. When the cistern had no leak, it was filled in 2½ hours. If now takes half an hour longer, if the cistern is full of water, how long would it take in leaking itself empty, in case the water leaks out at double the rate after half the cistern becomes empty?
(a) 10 hours 10 min. (b) 11 hours 15 min. (c) 9 hours (d) 15 hours 10 min.

10. When the waste pipe is closed, two taps can separately fill a cistern in 10 and 12 minutes respectively. When the waste pipe is opened they together fill it in 15 minutes. How long does it take waste pipe to empty the cistern, when the taps are closed?
(a) 8 min. 34 sec. (b) 7 min. 10 sec. (c) 12 min. (d) 10 min.

11. Two pipes A and B can fill a water tank in 20 and 24 minutes respectively and third pipe C can empty at the rate of 3 gallons per minute. If A, B and C opened together filled the tank in 15 minutes, the capacity (in gallons) of the tank is:
(a) 60 (b) 120 (c) 150 (d) 180

12. Two taps A and B can fill a cistern in 30 minutes and 60 minutes respectively. There is a third exhaust tap C at the bottom of the tank. If all the taps are opened at the same time the cistern will be full in 45 minutes. In what time can exhaust tap C empty the cistern when full?
(a) 40 minutes (b) 36 minutes (c) 35 minutes (d) 30 minutes

13. Two pipes can fill a tank in 10 minutes and 30 minutes respectively and a third pipe can empty the full tank in 20 minutes. If all the three pipes are opened simultaneously, the tank will be filled in:
(a) 12 minutes (b) 10 minutes (c) 8 minutes (d) 6 minutes

14. A certain tank can be filled by pipes A and B separately in 4 and 5 minutes respectively. Whereas pipe C can empty it in 3 minutes. How long will it take to fill or empty the 4/5th full tank, if all the three pipes start together?
(a) $6\frac{2}{7}$ minutes to fill (b) $2\frac{5}{7}$ minutes to fill
(c) $6\frac{6}{7}$ minutes to fill (d) $1\frac{5}{7}$ minutes to fill

15. Two pipes can fill a cistern in 14 hours and 16 hours respectively. The pipes are opened simultaneously and it is found that due to leakage in the bottom, 32 minutes extra are taken for the cistern to be filled up. When the cistern is full, in what time will the leak empty it?
(a) 108 hours (b) 112 hours (c) 116 hours (d) 120 hours

16. 12 pumps working 6 hours a day empty a completely filled reservoir in 15 days. How many such pumps working 9 hours a day will empty the same reservoir in 12 days?
(a) 9 (b) 10 (c) 12 (d) 15

17. A tap takes 36 hours extra to fill a tank due to a leakage equivalent to half its inflow. The inflow can fill the tank in how many hours?
(a) 18 (b) 24 (c) 30 (d) 36

18. A tank can be filled by pipes A and B in 12 minutes and 16 minutes respectively. When full the tank can be emptied by a third pipe in 8 minutes only. If the tank is empty and all the taps are tuned on simultaneously the tank will be full in:
(a) 48 min. (b) 36 min. (c) 24 min. (d) 20 min.

19. A tank is connected to two pipes. One of these pipes can fill the tank in 15 minutes while the other can empty it in 10 minutes. If the tank is initially 3/5th full and both pipes are simultaneously opened, how much time it will take to fill or empty the tank?
(a) 18 minutes (b) 15 minutes (c) 12 minutes (d) 10 minutes

20. A cistern can be filled by pipes A and B in 12 minutes and 10 minutes respectively. The full tank can be emptied by a third pipe C in 8 minutes only. If all the pipes be turned on at the same time, the cistern will be full in:
(a) 17 min. (b) $17\frac{1}{7}$ min. (c) $17\frac{2}{7}$ min. (d) 18 min.

21. Pipes A and B can fill a tank in 10 and 15 hours. How much time will they take together to fill the tank?
(a) 5 hours (b) 6 hours (c) 7 hours (d) 8 hours

22. A cistern can be filled by two taps A and B in 4 hours and 6 hours respectively. When full, the tank can be emptied by a third tap C in 8 hours. If all the taps be turned on at the same time, the cistern will be full in:
(a) 3 hr. 48 min. (b) 3 hr. 42 min (c) 3 hr. 26 min. (d) 3 hr. 18 min.

23. If two pipes function simultaneously, the reservoir will be filled in 12 hours. One pipe fills the reservoir 10 hours faster than the other. How many hours does it take the second pipe to fill the reservoir?
(a) 20 hrs. (b) 25 hrs. (c) 30 hrs. (d) 40 hrs.

24. Two pipes A and B can fill a tank in 24 min. and 32 min. respectively. If both the pipes are opened simultaneously, after how much time B should be close so that the tank is full in 18 minutes?
(a) 6 min. (b) 8 min. (c) 10 min. (d) 12 min.

25. A water tank is two-fifth full. Pipe A can fill a tank in 10 minutes and pipe B can empty it in 6 minutes. If both the pipes are opened, how long will it take to empty or fill the tank completely?
(a) 6 min. to fill (b) 6 min. to empty (c) 9 min. to fill (d) 9 min. to empty

26. A cistern can be filled by a tap in 4 hours while it can be emptied by another tap in 9 hours. If both the taps are opened simultaneously, then after how much time will the cistern get filled?
(a) 7.2 hrs (b) 6.5 hrs. (c) 5 hrs. (d) 4.5 hrs.

27. Two pipes A and B can fill a tank in 12 minutes and 15 minutes respectively. If both the pipes are opened simultaneously, and the pipe A is closed after 3 minues, then how much more time will it take to fill the tank by pipe B?
(a) 8 min 15 sec. (b) 8 min. 5 sec. (c) 7 min. 45 sec. (d) 7 min. 15 sec.

28. A tank is filled by three pipes with uniform flow. The first two pipes operating simultaneously fill the tank in the same time during which the tank is filled by the third pipe alone. The second pipe fills the tank 5 hours faster than the first pipe and 4 hours slower than the third pipe. The time required by the first pipe is:
(a) 30 hrs. (b) 15 hrs. (c) 10 hrs. (d) 6 hrs.

29. One pipe can fill a tank three times as fast as another pipe. If together the two pipes can fill the tank in 36 minutes, then the slower pipe alone will be able to fill the tank in:
(a) 192 min. *(b)* 144 min. *(c)* 108 min. *(d)* 81 min.

30. Three pipes A, B and C can fill a tank from empty to full in 30 minutes, 20 minutes and 10 minutes respectively. When the tank is empty, all the three pipes are opened. A, B and C are filled with the chemical solutions P, Q, R respectively. What is the proportion of solution R in the solutions in the tank after 3 minutes?
(a) $\frac{8}{11}$ *(b)* $\frac{7}{11}$ *(c)* $\frac{6}{11}$ *(d)* $\frac{5}{11}$

31. A tank is filled in 5 hours by three pipes A, B and C. The pipe C is twice as fast as B and B is twice as fast as A. How much time will pipe A alone take to fill the tank?
(a) 40 hrs. *(b)* 35 hrs. *(c)* 30 hrs. *(d)* 25 hrs.

32. Two pipes A and B together can fill a cistern in 4 hours. Had they been opened separately, then B would have taken 6 hours more than A to fill the cistern. How much time will be taken by A to fill the cistern separately?
(a) 8 hrs. *(b)* 6 hrs. *(c)* 2 hrs. *(d)* 1 hr.

33. Three pipes A, B and C can fill a tank in 6 hours. After working it at together for 2 hours, C is closed and A and B can fill the remaining part in 7 hours. How much time will C take alone to fill the tank?
(a) 16 hrs. *(b)* 14 hrs. *(c)* 12 hrs. *(d)* 10 hrs.

34. Three taps A, B and C can fill a tank in 12, 15 and 20 hours respectively. If A is opened all the time and B and C are opened for one hour each alternately, the tank will be full in
(a) 5 hrs. *(b)* 6 hrs. *(c)* $6\frac{2}{3}$ hrs. *(d)* 7 hrs.

35. A large tanker can be filled by two pipes A and B in 60 minutes and 40 minutes respectively. How many minutes will it take to fill the tanker from empty state if B is used for half the time and A and B fill it together for the other half?
(a) 30 min *(b)* 27.5 min *(c)* 20 min *(d)* 15 min

36. Two pipes A and B can fill a tank in 15 minutes and 20 minutes respectively. Both the pipes are opened together but after 4 minutes, pipe A is turned off. The time required to fill the tank is:
(a) 14 min. 40 sec. *(b)* 12 min. 30 sec. *(c)* 11 min. 45 sec. *(d)* 10 min. 20 sec.

37. Two pipes A and B can fill a cistern in $37\frac{1}{2}$ minutes and 45 minutes respectively. Both pipes are opened. The cistern will be filled in just half an hour, if pipe B is turned off after:
(a) 15 min. *(b)* 10 min. *(c)* 9 min. *(d)* 5 min.

SOLUTIONS

1. In 1 hour the part emptied by the leak $= \frac{1}{9} - \frac{1}{10} = \frac{1}{90}$

Hence, the leak can empty the cistern in 90 hours.

2. In 3 minutes the part filled by both pipes P and Q $= 3\times\left(\frac{1}{12}+\frac{1}{15}\right) = 3\times\frac{9}{60} = \frac{9}{20}$

Remaining part = $1 - \frac{9}{20} = \frac{11}{20}$

Time taken by pipe Q to fill the remaining part = $\frac{11/20}{1/15} = \frac{33}{4} = 8\frac{1}{4}$ min.

3. The part of the cistern filled by B in 17 min = $\frac{1}{34} \times 17 = \frac{1}{2}$

Remaining part = $1 - \frac{1}{2} = \frac{1}{2}$

Time taken by A to fill the remaining part = $\frac{1/2}{1/20}$ = 10 min.

Hence, pipe A must be turned off after 10 minutes.

4. In 1 hour the part filled by both pipes = $\frac{1}{10} + \frac{1}{15} = \frac{5}{30} = \frac{1}{6}$

Hence, both pipes can fill the tank in 6 hours.

5. In 1 hour the part emptied by the leak = $\frac{1}{8} - \frac{1}{10} = \frac{1}{40}$

Hence, the leak can empty the full cistern in 40 hours.

6. In 1 hour the part filled by both the taps = $\frac{1}{12} - \frac{1}{18} = \frac{1}{36}$

Hence, both the taps can fill the tank in 36 hours.

7. In 1 hour the part filled by both the taps = $\frac{1}{2} + \frac{1}{3} = \frac{5}{6}$

Hence, both the taps can fill the tank in $\frac{6}{5}$ hours = 1 hr. 12 min.

8. In 7 minutes (A + B) together will fill = $7 \times \left(\frac{1}{45} + \frac{1}{36}\right) = 7 \times \frac{1}{20} = \frac{7}{20}$ tank

Unfilled portion of tank after 7 minutes = $1 - \frac{7}{20} = \frac{13}{20}$ tank

Now, tank filled in 1 minute when A, B and C are opened = $\frac{1}{45} + \frac{1}{36} - \frac{1}{30} = \frac{1}{60}$

$\therefore$ Time required to fill $\frac{13}{20}$ tank = $60 \times \frac{13}{20}$ = 39 minutes

Hence, total time required to fill the tank = 7 + 39 = 46 minutes.

9. The cistern emptied in 1 hour = $\frac{2}{5} - \frac{1}{3} = \frac{1}{15}$ of the cistern *i.e.*, 1 cistern is emptied in 15 hours.

Now, $\frac{1}{2}$ cistern is emptied in $\frac{15}{2}$ hours.

But, remaining half cistern is emptied in $\frac{15}{2} \times \frac{1}{2} = \frac{15}{4}$ hours

∴ Total time taken to empty the cistern = $\frac{15}{2}+\frac{15}{4}=\frac{45}{4}$ hours = 11 hours 15 min.

10. The waste pipe can empty in 1 min. = $\frac{1}{10}+\frac{1}{12}-\frac{1}{15}=\frac{11}{60}-\frac{1}{15}=\frac{7}{60}$ of the cistern.

Hence, the waste pipe can empty the cistern in $\frac{60}{7}$ minutes, *i.e.*, 8 minutes 34 sec. (approx)

11. In 1 minute the part emptied by pipe C = $\left(\frac{1}{20}+\frac{1}{24}\right)-\frac{1}{15}=\frac{11}{120}-\frac{1}{15}=\frac{3}{120}=\frac{1}{40}$

Hence, pipe C can empty the tank in 40 minutes.
Therefore, capacity of the tank = 40 × 3 = 120 gallons.

12. In 1 minute the part emptied by exhaust tap C = $\frac{1}{30}+\frac{1}{60}-\frac{1}{45}=\frac{1}{36}$

Hence, exhaust pipe C can empty the cistern in 36 minutes.

13. In 1 minute the part filled by all the three pipes = $\frac{1}{10}+\frac{1}{30}-\frac{1}{20}=\frac{1}{12}$

Hence, all the three pipes will fill the tank in 12 minutes.

14. In 1 minute the part filled by all the three pipes = $\frac{1}{4}+\frac{1}{5}-\frac{1}{3}=\frac{7}{60}$

Hence, all the three pipes will fill the tank in $\frac{60}{7}$ minutes.

Since, 4/5 th the full tank can be filled by all the three pipes in $\frac{4}{5}\times\frac{60}{7}=\frac{48}{7}=6\frac{6}{7}$ minutes.

15. In 1 hour the part filled by both the pipes = $\frac{1}{14}+\frac{1}{16}=\frac{15}{112}$

Hence, both the pipes will fill the cistern in $\frac{112}{15}$ min.

But due to leakage, the tank will be filled in $\frac{112}{15}+\frac{32}{60}=\frac{120}{15}$ = 8 hrs.

Since, in 1 hr. the part emptied by the leakage = $\frac{15}{112}-\frac{1}{8}=\frac{1}{112}$
Therefore, leakage will empty the tank in 112 hrs.

16. In 1 day working 1 hour a day the filled reservoir can be emptied by 12 × 6 × 15 pumps.

Hence, in 12 days working 9 hours a day the filled reservoir can be emptied by $\frac{12\times6\times15}{12\times9}$

= 10 pumps.

17. Let x hours be the time taken by tap to fill the tank, then $2x$ hours will be the time taken by leakage to empty the tank.

In 1 hour the part filled when both are opened $= \frac{1}{x} - \frac{1}{2x} = \frac{1}{2x}$

Hence, the tank will be filled in $2x$ hours when both are opened.
Now, $2x - x = 36$ $\therefore$ $x = 36$ hrs.
Hence, tap alone will fill the tank in 36 hours.

18. In 1 minute the part filled by all the three taps $= \frac{1}{12} + \frac{1}{16} - \frac{1}{8} = \frac{1}{48}$

Hence, all the three pipes will fill the tank in 48 minutes.

19. In 1 minute the part emptied when both the pipes are opened $= \frac{1}{10} - \frac{1}{15} = \frac{1}{30}$

Hence, in 30 minutes the whole tank will be emptied.

Their $\frac{3}{5}$ part will be emptied in $\frac{3}{5} \times 30 = 18$ minutes.

20. In 1 minute the part filled by the three pipes $= \frac{1}{12} + \frac{1}{10} - \frac{1}{8} = \frac{7}{120}$

Hence, all the three pipes will fill the cistern in $\frac{120}{7} = 17\frac{1}{7}$ minutes.

21. In 1 hour the part filled by both the pipes $= \frac{1}{10} + \frac{1}{15} = \frac{1}{6}$

Hence, both pipes will fill the tank in 6 hours.

22. In 1 hour the part filled by all the three pipes $= \frac{1}{4} + \frac{1}{6} - \frac{1}{8} = \frac{7}{24}$

Hence, all the three pipes will fill the cistern in $\frac{24}{7}$ hr. = 3 hrs. 26 min.

23. Let $(x - 10)$ and x hrs be the time taken by two pipes to fill the reservoir, then,

$\frac{1}{x-10} + \frac{1}{x} = \frac{1}{12}$ $\Rightarrow$ $\frac{2x-10}{x^2-10x} = \frac{1}{12}$ $\Rightarrow$ $x^2 - 34x + 120 = 0$

$\Rightarrow (x - 30)(x - 4) = 0$ $\therefore$ $x = 30$ (Taking 30 only).
Hence, second pipe will fill the reservoir in 30 hours.

24. In 18 minutes the part filled by pipe A $= 18 \times \frac{1}{24} = \frac{3}{4}$

Remaining part $= 1 - \frac{3}{4} = \frac{1}{4}$

Time taken by B to fill the remaining part $= \frac{1/4}{1/32} = 8$ minutes.

25. In 1 minute the part emptied by both the pipes = $\frac{1}{6}-\frac{1}{10}=\frac{1}{15}$

Time taken by both the pipes to empty $\frac{2}{5}$ tank = $\frac{2/5}{1/15}$ = 6 minutes.

26. In 1 hour the part filled by both the taps = $\frac{1}{4}-\frac{1}{9}=\frac{5}{36}$

Hence, Both taps will fill the tank in $\frac{36}{5}$ hrs. = 7.2 hrs.

27. In 3 minutes the part filled by both the pipes = $3\left(\frac{1}{12}+\frac{1}{15}\right) = \frac{9}{20}$

Remaining part = $1 - \frac{9}{20}=\frac{11}{20}$

Time taken by B to fill the remaining part = $\frac{11}{20}\Big/\frac{1}{15}=\frac{33}{4}$ minutes = 8 minutes 15 seconds

28. Let x, $(x - 5)$ and $(x - 9)$ hours be the time taken by three pipes respectively to fill the tank, then

$\frac{1}{x}+\frac{1}{x-5}=\frac{1}{x-9}$ $\Rightarrow$ $\frac{2x-5}{x^2-5x}=\frac{1}{x-9}$

$\Rightarrow x^2 - 18x + 45 = 0$ $\Rightarrow$ $(x - 15)(x - 3) = 0$ $\therefore x = 15$ (Taking 15 only)

Hence, first pipe will fill the tank in 15 hours.

29. Let x and $3x$ minutes taken by the two pipes respectively to fill the tank, then

$\frac{1}{x}+\frac{1}{3x}=\frac{1}{36}$ $\Rightarrow$ $\frac{4}{3x}=\frac{1}{36}$ $\therefore$ $x=\frac{36\times 4}{3}$ = 48 minutes

Hence, time taken by slower pipe = 3 × 48 = 144 minutes to fill the tank.

30. In 3 minutes the part filled by three pipes = $3\left(\frac{1}{30}+\frac{1}{20}+\frac{1}{10}\right)=\frac{11}{20}$

In 3 minutes the part filled by C alone = $3 \times \frac{1}{10}=\frac{3}{10}$

Required proportion = $\frac{3/10}{11/20}=\frac{3}{10}\times\frac{20}{11}=\frac{6}{11}$

31. Let x, $\frac{x}{2}$ and $\frac{x}{4}$ hours be the time taken by pipes A, B and C respectively to fill the tank, then

$\frac{1}{x}+\frac{2}{x}+\frac{4}{x}=\frac{1}{5}$ $\Rightarrow$ $\frac{7}{x}=\frac{1}{5}$ $\therefore$ x = 35 hours.

Hence, time taken by A is 35 hours to fill the tank.

32. Let x and $(x + 6)$ hours be the time taken by pipes A and B respectively to fill the cistern, then

$\frac{1}{x}+\frac{1}{x+6}=\frac{1}{4}$ $\Rightarrow$ $\frac{2x+6}{x^2+6x}=\frac{1}{4}$ $\Rightarrow (x - 6)(x + 4) = 0$ $\therefore x = 6$

(Taking positive value)

Hence, time taken by A alone to fill the cistern is 6 hours.

33. In 2 hours the part filled by all the three pipes $= 2 \times \frac{1}{6} = \frac{1}{3}$

Remaining part $= 1 - \frac{1}{3} = \frac{2}{3}$, which is filled by (A + B) in 7 hours.

Hence, in 1 hour the part filled by (A + B) $= \frac{2}{3 \times 7} = \frac{2}{21}$

Since, in 1 hour the part filled by C alone $= \frac{1}{6} - \frac{2}{21} = \frac{1}{14}$

Threfore, C alone will fill the tank in 14 hours.

34. In 1 hour the part filled by (A + B) $= \frac{1}{12} + \frac{1}{15} = \frac{3}{20}$

In 1 hour the part filled by (A + C) $= \frac{1}{12} + \frac{1}{20} = \frac{2}{15}$

Hence, in 2 hours the part filled by (A + B + C) $= \frac{3}{20} + \frac{2}{15} = \frac{17}{60}$

Then, in 6 hours the part filled by (A + B + C) $= 3 \times \frac{17}{60} = \frac{17}{20}$

Remaining part $= 1 - \frac{17}{20} = \frac{3}{20}$, which is filled by (A + B) in 1 hour.

Hence, total time taken = 6 + 1 = 7 hours.

35. Let the tanker can be filled in x minutes, then

$\frac{x}{2}\left(\frac{1}{60} + \frac{1}{40}\right) + \frac{x}{2} \times \frac{1}{40} = 1 \quad \Rightarrow \frac{x}{2}\left(\frac{1}{60} + \frac{2}{40}\right) = 1 \quad \Rightarrow \frac{x}{2} \times \frac{1}{15} = 1 \quad \therefore x = 30$ min

36. In 4 minutes the part filled by pipes (A + B) $= 4\left(\frac{1}{15} + \frac{1}{20}\right) = \frac{7}{15}$

Remaining part $= 1 - \frac{7}{15} = \frac{8}{15}$

Time taken by B to fill the remaining part $= \frac{8/15}{1/20} = \frac{32}{3}$ min = 10 min. 40 sec.

Hence, total time taken = 4 min. + 10 min. 40 sec. = 14 min. 40 sec.

37. In 30 minutes the part filled by pipe A $= 30 \times \frac{2}{75} = \frac{4}{5}$

The remaining part $= 1 - \frac{4}{5} = \frac{1}{5}$

The time taken by pipe B to fill the remaining part $= \frac{1/5}{1/45} = 9$ minutes.

17

BOATS & STREAMS

When we simply say speed of a boat and swimmer, it usually means speed in still water. If the boat or the swimmer moves against the stream, then it is called *Upstream* and if it moves with the stream, it is called *Downstream.*

Hence, if x km per hour be the man's rate in still water, and y km per hour the rate of the current then

(i) $x + y$ = man's rate with the current (called the downstream)

(ii) $x - y$ = man's rate against the current (called the upstream)

(iii) $x = \frac{1}{2}$ (downstream + upstream)

(iv) $y = \frac{1}{2}$ (downstream – upstream)

Example 1: A boat can travel 35 km downstream in 5 hours. If it covers the same distance upstream in 7 hours, find the speed of the boat in still water.

Solution: Speed of the boat downstream $= \frac{35}{5} = 7$ km/hr.

and speed of the boat upstream $= \frac{35}{7} = 5$ km/hr.

Speed of the boat in still water $= \frac{1}{2}$ (downstream + upstream)

$= \frac{1}{2}(7 + 5) = 6$ km/h

Example 2: A person can row downstream 1 km in 10 minutes and upstream the same distance in 30 minutes. Find the rate of flow of stream.

Solution: Given speed of the person downstream $= \frac{1}{10/60}$ km/h = 6 km/hr

and speed upstream $= \frac{1}{30/60}$ km/h = 2 km/hr

$\therefore$ The rate of flow of stream $= \frac{1}{2}$ (downstream – upstream)

$= \frac{1}{2}(6-2) = \frac{1}{2} \times 4 = 2$ km/h

Example 3: The speed of a boat in still water is 12 km/hr and rate of flow of stream is 4 km/hr. If it, travels upstream for 3 hours 15 minutes find the distance in kms travelled by the boat during this journey.

Solution: Upstream speed = 12 – 4 = 8 km/hr

Hence, distance travelled = $8 \times 3\frac{1}{4} = 8 \times \frac{13}{4} = 26$ km

Example 4: A swimmer covers a distance of 20 km against the current and 30 km in the direction of current. If in each case he takes 5 hours, what is the speed of the current?

Solution: Speed of the swimmer downstream = $\frac{30}{5} = 6$ km/hr.

and speed of the swimmer upstream = $\frac{20}{5} = 4$ km/hr.

Hence, speed of the current = $\frac{1}{2}(6-4) = 1$ km/hr.

Example 5: A man can row 8 km/hr in still water. When the river is running at 4 km/hr, it takes him 1 hour to row a place and back. How far is the place?

Solution: Downstream speed = 8 + 4 = 12 km/hr.
Upstream speed = 8 – 4 = 4 km/hr.
Let required distance be x km, then;

$$\frac{x}{12} + \frac{x}{4} = 1 \Rightarrow \frac{x}{3} = 1 \qquad \therefore x = 3 \text{ km}$$

Example 6: The speed of the current is 5 km/hr. A motorboat goes 10 km upstream and back again to the starting point in 50 minutes. What is the speed of the motorboat in still water?

Solution: Let the speed of the boat = x km/hr.
∴Downstream speed of boat = $x + 5$ km/hr
and upstream speed of boat = $x - 5$ km/hr

$$\therefore \quad \frac{10}{x+5} + \frac{10}{x-5} = \frac{50}{60} \qquad \Rightarrow \quad \frac{20x}{x^2-25} = \frac{5}{6}$$

$\Rightarrow x^2 - 24x - 25 = 0$
$\Rightarrow (x - 25)(x + 1) = 0$
Hence, $x = 25$ km/hr.

Example 7: In 4 hours Ramesh can go 24 km along the current and 12 km against the current in the same time. What is the speed of the current?

Solution: Speed of Ramesh downstream = $\frac{24}{4} = 6$ km/hr.

and speed of Ramesh upstream = $\frac{12}{4} = 3$ km/hr.

Hence, the speed of stream = $\frac{1}{2}(6-3) = \frac{1}{2} \times 3 = \frac{3}{2} = 1\frac{1}{2}$ km/hr.

Example 8: A boat travels upstream from P to Q and downstream from Q to P in 4 hours. If the speed of the boat in still water is 12 km/hr and the speed of the current is 4 km/hr, then what is the distance from P to Q?

Solution: Let distance from P to Q be x km

Downstream speed = 12 + 4 = 16 km/hr

Upstream speed = 12 – 4 = 8 km/hr

Now, $\frac{x}{16}+\frac{x}{8}=4 \quad \Rightarrow \quad \frac{3x}{16}=4 \quad \therefore \ x=\frac{64}{3}=21\frac{1}{3}$ km.

Example 9: A motorboat covers 12 km upstream and 18 km downstream in 3 hours while it covers 36 km upstream and 24 km downstream in 6 ½ hours, what is the speed of the current?

Solution: Let speed of the boat be x km/hr in still water and y km/hr be the speed of current; then

Downstream speed = $(x + y)$ km/hr

Upstream speed = $(x - y)$ km/hr

Now, $\frac{12}{x-y}+\frac{18}{x+y}=3$ ...(i)

$\frac{36}{x-y}+\frac{24}{x+y}=\frac{13}{2}$ ...(ii)

On solving these two equations, we get, $x + y = 12$ & $x - y = 8$

Hence, $y = 1/2\ (12 - 8) = 2$ km/hr

Example 10 : A man can row $9\frac{1}{3}$ km/hr in still water and he finds that it takes him thrice as much time to row up than as to row down the same distance in the river. What is the speed of the current?

Sol: Let speed of the upstream and downstream be x and $3x$ km/hr, then speed of rowing in still water $=\frac{1}{2}(3x+x)=\frac{28}{3}$

$\Rightarrow 2x=\frac{28}{3} \quad \therefore \ x=\frac{14}{3}$ km/hr

Now, speed of the current $=\frac{1}{2}(3x-x)=x=\frac{14}{3}=4\frac{2}{3}$ km/hr

EXERCISE

1. If the speed of a boat in still water is 5 km/hr and its speed against the current is 2.5 km/hr, then what is its speed in the direction of the current?

(a) 7.5 km/hr *(b)* 12 km/hr *(c)* 10 km/hr *(d)* None of these

2. The speed of a motorboat in still water is 9 km/hr and the speed of the stream is 2.5 km/hr. Find the time taken by the motorboat to go 9.1 km against the stream.

(a) 1 hour 24 minutes *(b)* 2 hours 24 minutes

(c) 3 hours 24 minutes *(d)* 4 hours 24 minutes

3. The boat goes 40 km upstream in 8 hours and 36 km downstream in 6 hours. Find the speed of the boat in still water.

(a) 5.5 km/hr *(b)* 6 km/hr *(c)* 6.5 km/hr *(d)* 7 km/hr

4. A boat goes 6 km upstream and back to the starting point in 2 hours. If the current of the stream runs at the rate of 4 km/hr, find the speed of the boat in still water.
(*a*) 6 km/hr (*b*) 8 km/hr (*c*) 10 km/hr (*d*) 12 km/hr

5. A man can swim 3 km/hr in still water. If the velocity of the stream be 2 km/hr, find the time taken by him to swim to a point 10 km upstream and back.
(*a*) 12 hours (*b*) 10 hours (*c*) 8 hours (*d*) 6 hours

6. A boat covers 24 km upstream and 36 km downstream in 6 hours, while it covers 36 km upstream and 24 km downstream in 6½ horus. Find the speed of the current.
(*a*) 2 km/hr (*b*) 4 km/hr (*c*) 6 km/hr (*d*) 8 km/hr

7. A swimmer can swim a certain distance in the direction of current in 5 hours and return the same distance in 7 hours. If the stream flows at the rate of 1 km/hr, find the speed of the swimmer in still water.
(*a*) 3 km/hr (*b*) 4 km/hr (*c*) 5 km/hr (*d*) 6 km/hr

8. A man can row 5 km/hr in still water and the speed of the stream is 1.5 km/hr. He takes an hour when he travels upstream to a place and back again to the starting point. How far is the place from the starting point?
(*a*) 2.275 km (*b*) 3.5 km (*c*) 1.5 km (*d*) None of these

9. A man can row three quarters of a kilometer against the stream in 11¼ minutes and return in 7½ minutes. Find the speed of the man in still water.
(*a*) 3 km/hr. (*b*) 4 km/hr. (*c*) 5 km/hr (*d*) 6 km/hr.

10. The speed of a boat in still water is 6 km/hr and the speed of the stream is 1.5 km/hr. A man rows to a place at a distance of 22.5 km and comes back to the starting point. Find the total time taken by him.
(*a*) 8 hours (*b*) 10 hours (*c*) 12 hours (*d*) 4 hours

11. There is a road beside a river. Two friends started from a place A, moved to a temple situated at another place B and then returned to A again. One of them moves on a cycle at a speed of 12 km/hr, while other sails on a boat at the speed of 10km/hr. If the river flows at the speed of 4 km/hr, then which of the two friends will return to place A first?
(*a*) Cyclist (*b*) Boat sailor (*c*) Both in same time (*d*) None of these

12. A boat running downstream covers a distance of 30 kms in 2 hours. While coming back the boat takes 6 hours to cover the same distance. If speed of the current is half that of the boat. Find the speed of that boat in km/hr.
(*a*) 5 (*b*) 10 (*c*) 15 (*d*) 20

13. A motorboat in still water travels at a speed of 36 km/hr. It goes 56 km upstream in 1 hour 45 minutes. The time taken by it to cover the same distance down the stream will be:
(*a*) 1 hr. 24 minutes (*b*) 2 hr. 21 minutes (*c*) 2 hrs. 25 minutes (*d*) 3 hours

14. A boat covers 20 km downstream and 6 km upstream in 3 hours, while it covers 30 km downstream and 12 km upstream in 5 hours. What is the speed of boat in still water?
(*a*) 6 km/hr (*b*) 8 km/hr (*c*) 10 km/hr (*d*) 12 km/hr.

15. A man can row 40 km upstream and 55 km downstream in 13 hours and 30 km upstream and 44 km downstream in 10 hours. Find the speed of the man in still water and the speed of the current.
(*a*) 8 km/hr; 3 km/hr (*b*) 8 km/hr; 4 km/hr
(*c*) 9 km/hr; 4 km/hr (*d*) 10 km/hr; 5 km/hr.

16. A boat takes 6 hours to travel from place M to N downstream and back from N to M upstream. If the speed of the boat in still water is 4 km/hr; what is the distance between two places?
(*a*) 6 kms (*b*) 8 kms (*c*) 12 kms (*d*) Data inadequate

17. A man can row at a speed of 4½ km/hr in still water. if he takes 2 times as long to row a distance upstream as to row the same distance downstream, then the speed of the stream (in km/hr) is:
(*a*) 1 (*b*) 1.5 (*c*) 2 (*d*) 2.5

18. The current of a river runs at 1 km/hr. A motorboat goes 35 km upstream and back again to the starting point in 12 hours. The speed of the motorboat in the still water is:
(*a*) 9 km/hr (*b*) 8 km/hr (*c*) 7 km/hr (*d*) 6 km/hr

19. A man can row upstream at 8 km/hr and downstream at 13 km/hr. The speed of the stream is:
(*a*) 2.5 km/hr (*b*) 4.2 km/hr (*c*) 5 km/hr (*d*) 10.5 km/hr

20. A man can row the boat with the stream at the speed of 11 km/hr and against the stream at the speed of 8 km//hr, then speed of the stream is:
(*a*) 1.5 km/hr (*b*) 3 km/hr (*c*) 6 km/hr (*d*) 9.5 km/hr

21. A boat can travel with a speed of 13 km/hr in still water. If the speed of the stream is 4 km/hr then the time taken by the boat to go 68 km downstream is:
(*a*) 5 hours (*b*) 4 hours (*c*) 3 hours (*d*) 2 hours

22. A boat running upstream takes 8 hours 48 minutes to cover a certain distance, while it takes 4 hours to cover the same distance running downstream. Find the ratio between the speed of the boat and the speed of the water current respectively.
(*a*) 8 : 3 (*b*) 8 : 5 (*c*) 3 : 2 (*d*) 1 : 2

23. A man takes twice as long to row a distance against the stream as to row the same distance in favour of the stream. What is the ratio of the speed of the boat (in still water) and the stream?
(*a*) 4 : 3 (*b*) 3 : 2 (*c*) 3 : 1 (*d*) 2 : 1

24. A boatman goes 2 km against the current of the stream in 1 hour and goes 1 km along the current in 10 minutes. How long will it take to go 5 km in stationary water?
(*a*) 1 hr. 30 min. (*b*) 1 hr. 15 min. (*c*) 1 hour (*d*) 40 minutes

25. A man's speed with the current is 15 km/hr and the speed of the current is 2.5 km/hr. The man's speed against the current is:
(*a*) 12.5 km/hr (*b*) 10 km/hr (*c*) 9 km/hr (*d*) 8.5 km/hr

26. A boat running downstream covers a distance of 16 km in 2 hours while for covering the same distance upstream, it takes 4 hours. Find the speed of the boat in still water.
(*a*) 10 km/hr (*b*) 8 km/hr (*c*) 6 km/hr (*d*) 4 km/hr

27. Samir can travel 12 miles dowstream in a certain river in 6 hours less than it takes him to travel the same distance upstream. But when he could double his rowing rate for his 24-mile round trip, the downstream 12 miles would then take only one hour less than the upstream 12 miles. Find the speed of the current in miles/hour.
(*a*) $2\frac{2}{3}$ (*b*) $2\frac{1}{3}$ (*c*) $1\frac{2}{3}$ (*d*) $1\frac{1}{3}$

28. A boat takes 90 minutes less to travel 36 miles downstream than to travel the same distance upstream. If the speed of the boat in still water is 10 miles/hr, find the speed of the stream.
(*a*) 4 miles/hr (*b*) 3 miles/hr (*c*) 2.5 miles/hr (*d*) 2 miles/hr

29. A boat covers a certain distance downstream in 1 hour, while it comes back in 1½ hours. If the speed of the stream is 3 km/hr, find the speed of the boat in still water.
(a) 15 km/hr *(b)* 14 km/hr *(c)* 13 km/hr *(d)* 12 km/hr

30. A man can row at 5 km/hr in still water. If the velocity of the current is 1 km and it takes him 1 hour to row to a place and come back, how far is the place?
(a) 3.6 km *(b)* 3 km *(c)* 2.5 km *(d)* 2.4 km

31. A motorboat, whose speed is 15 km/hr in still water goes 30 km downstream and comes back in a total of 4 hours 30 minutes. What is the speed of the stream (in km/hr)?
(a) 10 *(b)* 6 *(c)* 5 *(d)* 4

SOLUTIONS

1. Let the speed of the boat downstream = x km/h.

Now, $5 = \frac{1}{2}(x+2.5)$

$\Rightarrow \quad x = 10 - 2.5 = 7.5$ km/hr.

2. The speed of a boat upstream = (9 – 2.5) km/h = 6.5 km/h

$\therefore$ Required time $= \frac{9.1}{6.5} = \frac{7}{5}$ = 1 hour 24 min.

3. Upstream speed $= \frac{40}{8}$ = 5 km/hr; Downstream speed $= \frac{36}{6}$ = 6 km/hr

Hence, speed of the boat in still water $= \frac{1}{2}(6+5) = \frac{11}{2}$ = 5.5 km/hr

4. Let the speed of a boat in still water = x km/hr; then

$$\frac{6}{x-4} + \frac{6}{x+4} = 2$$

$$\Rightarrow \frac{2x}{x^2-16} = \frac{1}{3}$$

$\Rightarrow x^2 - 6x - 16 = 0$

$\Rightarrow (x - 8)(x + 2) = 0$

Hence, the speed of the boat = 8 km/hr

5. Downstream speed = (3 + 2) = 5 km/hr

Upstream speed = (3 – 2) = 1 km/hr

Required time $= \frac{10}{1} + \frac{10}{5}$ = 12 hrs.

6. Let x km/hr and y km/hr be the speeds of the boat in still water and the speed of the current respectively, then

$$\frac{24}{x-y} + \frac{36}{x+y} = 6 \quad \Rightarrow \quad \frac{4}{x-y} + \frac{6}{x+y} = 1 \qquad \text{...(i)}$$

And, $\dfrac{36}{x-y}+\dfrac{24}{x+y}=\dfrac{13}{2}$ ...(ii)

Solving these two equations, we get

$x + y = 12;\ x - y = 8$

Hence, $y = \dfrac{1}{2}(12-8) = 2$ km/hr

7. Let speed of the swimmer in still water = x km/hr; then
Distance covered = $(x + 1)\,5 = (x - 1)\,7$
$\Rightarrow 2x = 12$ $\quad\therefore\ x = 6$ km/hr.

8. Let required distance be x km, then

$\dfrac{x}{5-1.5}+\dfrac{x}{5+1.5}=1 \quad\Rightarrow\quad \dfrac{x\times 2}{7}+\dfrac{x\times 2}{13}=1$

$\Rightarrow 40x = 91$ $\quad\therefore\ x = 91/40 = 2.275$ km

9. Upstream speed = $\dfrac{3/4}{45/_{4\times60}} = 4$ km/hr

Downstream speed = $\dfrac{3/4}{15/_{2\times60}} = 6$ km/hr

$\therefore$ Speed of the man in still water = $\dfrac{1}{2}(6 + 4) = 5$ km/hr.

10. Required time period = $\dfrac{22.5}{6+1.5}+\dfrac{22.5}{6-1.5}=\dfrac{45}{15}+\dfrac{45}{9} = 8$ hours.

11. Downstream speed = 10 + 4 = 14 km/hr.
Upstream speed = 10 – 4 = 6 km/hr.

Hence, their average speed = $\dfrac{x+x}{\dfrac{x}{14}+\dfrac{x}{6}}=\dfrac{2x}{5x/21}=\dfrac{42}{5} = 8.4$ km/hr.

Since, average speed of cyclist (12 km/hr) > average speed of boat sailor (8.4 km/hr).
Therefore, the cyclist will return to A first.

12. Downstream speed = $\dfrac{30}{2} = 15$ km/hr; Upstream speed = $\dfrac{30}{6} = 5$ km/hr.

Let speed of the boat and speed of the stream be x km/hr and $x/2$ km/hr respectively, then,

$x+\dfrac{x}{2}=15 \quad\Rightarrow\quad \dfrac{3x}{2}=15 \quad\therefore\ x = 10$ km/hr

13. Upstream speed = $\dfrac{56}{1\frac{3}{4}} = 56 \times \dfrac{4}{7} = 32$ km/hr

Hence, speed of the current = 36 – 32 = 4 km/hr
Downstream speed = 36 + 4 = 40 km/hr

Hence, time taken = $\frac{56}{40} = \frac{7}{5}$ hr = 1 hr. 24 min

14. Let x km/hr and y km/hr be the speed of boat in still water and speed of current respectively; then

$$\frac{20}{x+y} + \frac{6}{x-y} = 3 \quad \text{...(i)}$$

and also, $\frac{30}{x+y} + \frac{12}{x-y} = 5 \Rightarrow \frac{15}{x+y} + \frac{6}{x-y} = \frac{5}{2}$ ...(ii)

Solving equations *(i)* & *(ii)* we get, x + y = 10 and $x - y = 6$

Since, $x = \frac{1}{2}(10 + 6) = 8$ km/hr.

15. Let x km/hr and y km/hr be the speed of boat in still water and speed of current respectively; then

$\frac{40}{x-y} + \frac{55}{x+y} = 13$ and also, $\frac{30}{x-y} + \frac{44}{x+y} = 10$ ...(i)

$\Rightarrow \frac{8}{x-y} + \frac{11}{x+y} = \frac{13}{5}$ ...(i) $\Rightarrow \frac{15}{x-y} + \frac{22}{x+y} = 5$ ...(ii)

Solving these two equations, we get $x + y = 11$ and $x - y = 5$

Since, $x = \frac{1}{2}(11 + 5) = 8$ km/hr. and $y = 11 - 8 = 3$ km/hr.

16. Let d km be the distance and x km/hr be the speed of the stream, then

$$\frac{d}{4+x} + \frac{d}{4-x} = 6$$

Here x is not known, so d cannot be determined, hence, data is inadequate.

17. Let x km/hr be speed of the stream, then,
Downstream speed = $(4.5 + x)$ km/hr
Upstream speed = $(4.5 - x)$ km/hr
Now, $(4.5 + x) = 2(4.5 - x)$
$\Rightarrow 3x = 4.5 \therefore x = 1.5$ km/hr.

18. Let x km/hr be the speed of the motorboat in still water, then,

$\frac{35}{x-1} + \frac{35}{x+1} = 12 \Rightarrow \frac{35x}{x^2-1} = 6 \Rightarrow 6x^2 - 35x - 6 = 0$

$\Rightarrow (6x + 1)(x - 6) = 0$ Hence, $x = 6$ km/hr.

19. The speed of the stream = $\frac{1}{2}(13 - 8) = \frac{5}{2} = 2.5$ km/hr.

20. The speed of the stream = $\frac{1}{2}$ (11 – 8) = $\frac{3}{2}$ = 1.5 km/hr.

21. Downstream speed = 13 + 4 = 17 km/hr

The time taken = $\frac{68}{17}$ = 4 hours

22. Let x km/hr and y km/hr be the speed of the boat and speed of the stream respectively,

Now, $8\frac{48}{60}(x-y) = 4(x + y)$

$\Rightarrow 11(x - y) = 5(x + y) \quad \Rightarrow 6x = 16y$

$\therefore x : y = 8 : 3$

23. Let x km/hr and y km/hr be the speed of the boat and speed of the stream respectively, then

$x + y = 2(x - y)$

$\Rightarrow x = 3y$ Hence, $x : y = 3 : 1$

24. Upstream speed = $\frac{2}{1}$ = 2 km/hr

Downstream speed = $\frac{1}{10/60}$ = 6 km/hr

Speed of boatman in still water = $\frac{1}{2}$ (6 + 2) = 4 km/hr

Hence, time taken = $\frac{5}{4}$ hr = 1 hr. 15 min.

25. The man's speed in still water = 15 – 2.5 = 12.5 km/hr
Hence, the men's speed against the current = 12.5 – 2.5 = 10 km/hr

26. Downstream speed = $\frac{16}{2}$ = 8 km/hr.

Upstream speed = $\frac{16}{4}$ = 4 km/hr.

Hence, speed of boat in still water = $\frac{1}{2}$ 8 + 4) = 6 km/hr.

27. Let x km/hr and y km/hr be the speed of rowing in still water and speed of the current respectively; then

$$\frac{12}{x-y} - \frac{12}{x+y} = 6 \quad \Rightarrow \quad \frac{24y}{x^2 - y^2} = 6 \quad \Rightarrow x^2 = y^2 + 4y \qquad ...(i)$$

Again,

$$\frac{12}{2x-y} - \frac{12}{2x+y} = 1 \Rightarrow \frac{24y}{4x^2 - y^2} = 1 \quad \Rightarrow x^2 = \frac{y^2 + 24y}{4} \qquad ...(ii)$$

From equations (i) and (ii), we get,

$$y^2 + 4y = \frac{y^2+24y}{4} \Rightarrow 3y^2 = 8y \quad \therefore \quad y = \frac{8}{3} = 2\frac{1}{3} \text{ miles/hr.}$$

28. Let speed of the stream be x miles/hr, then

$$\frac{36}{10-x} - \frac{36}{10+x} = \frac{90}{60} \quad \Rightarrow \quad \frac{48x}{100-x^2} = 1 \quad \Rightarrow x^2 + 48x - 100 = 0$$

$\Rightarrow (x - 2)(x + 50) = 0 \quad \therefore x = 2$ miles/hr.

29. Let speed of the boat in still water be x km/hr, then,
$(x + 3) \times 1 = (x - 3)\, 3/2$
$\Rightarrow \; 2x + 6 = 3x - 9 \quad \therefore \; x = 15$ km/hr

30. Let the distance of the place be x km, then

$$\frac{x}{5+1} + \frac{x}{5-1} = 1 \quad \Rightarrow \frac{x}{6} + \frac{x}{4} = 1 \quad \therefore \frac{5x}{12} = 1 \quad \therefore x = \frac{12}{5} = 2.4 \text{ km}$$

31. Let speed of the stream be x km/hr, then

$$\frac{30}{15+x} + \frac{30}{15-x} = 4\frac{1}{2} \quad \Rightarrow \quad \frac{30\times 30}{225-x^2} = \frac{9}{2} \quad \Rightarrow \quad \frac{200}{225-x^2} = 1 \quad \Rightarrow x^2 = 225 - 200$$

$\Rightarrow x^2 = 25 \qquad \therefore \; x = 5$ km/hr.

18 ALLIGATION OR MIXTURE

Alligation deals with calculation of values or properties of a mixture. Alligation is the rule that enables us—

(1) to find the proportion in which the two or more ingredients at the given prices must be mixed to yield a mixture at the given price. This is termed as "Alligation Alternate".

(2) to calculate the average or mean value of a mixture when the prices of two or more ingredients which are to be mixed together and proportion in which they are to be mixed are given. This is termed as "Alligation Medial".

1. Rule of Alligation:

$$\frac{\text{Amount of Cheaper ingredient}}{\text{Amount of Dearer ingredient}} = \frac{\text{Cost price of Dearer} - \text{Mean Price}}{\text{Mean Price} - \text{Cost Price of Cheaper}}$$

Here cost price of unit quantity of the mixture is called the *Mean Price*.
The above rule may be represented schematically as under:

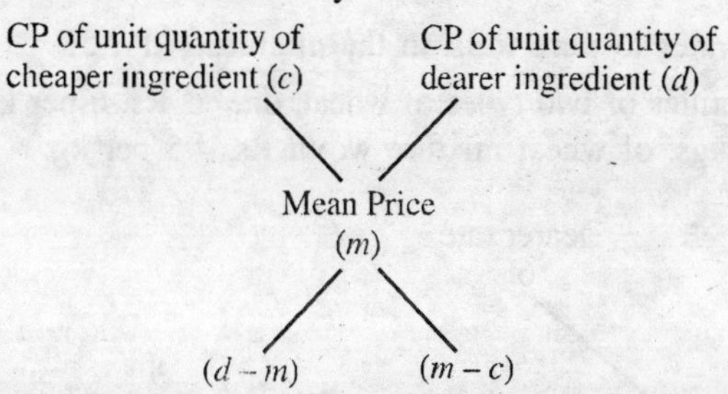

(Cheaper quantity) : (Dearer quantity) = $(d - m) : (m - c)$

This relationship is very helpful in solving problems on mixture involving percentage values, rates, prices, speeds etc.

2. m gm of sugar solution has x % sugar in it. To increase the sugar content in the solution to y %, quantity of sugar need to be added $= \dfrac{m(y-x)}{100-y}$

3. A vessel contains x litres of liquid A. y litres are withdrawn and replaced by liquid B. Next y litres of the mixture is withdrawn and again replaced by liquid B.
This operation is repeated n times.

$$\frac{\text{Quantity of liquid A left after } n\text{th operation}}{\text{Whole quantity of liquid A initially present}} = \left(\frac{x-y}{x}\right)^n \text{ or } \left(1-\frac{y}{x}\right)^n$$

Example 1: In what proportion water be mixed with pure milk in order to make a profit of 20% by selling it at cost price?

Solution: Let cost price of pure milk be Re. 1 per litre.

The SP of mixture = Re. 1 per litre

Profit = 20%

So, CP of 1 litre of mixture = Rs. $\left(1 \times \frac{100}{120}\right)$ = Re. $\frac{5}{6}$

We assume that CP of 1 litre of water is zero.

Using the rule of alligation on 1 litre,

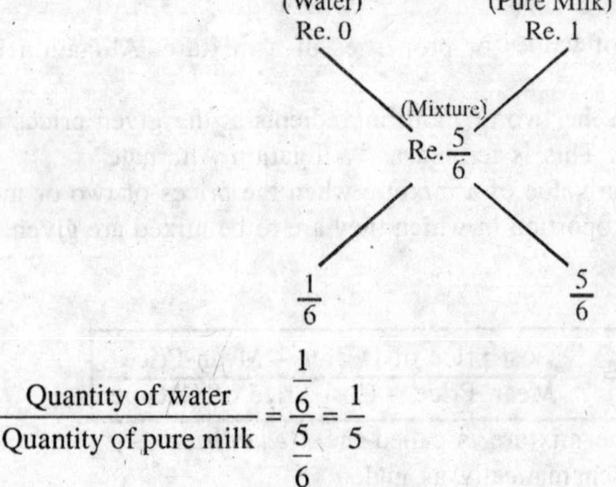

$$\frac{\text{Quantity of water}}{\text{Quantity of pure milk}} = \frac{\frac{1}{6}}{\frac{5}{6}} = \frac{1}{5}$$

or, Ratio of water to pure milk in the mixture = 1 : 5.

Example 2: Find the quantities of two types of wheat, one @ Rs. 6 per kg and the other @ Rs. 4 per kg. to get 20 kgs. of wheat mixture worth Rs. 4.5 per kg.

Solution: Cheaper rate Dearer rate

4 6

4.5

1.5 0.5

$$\frac{\text{Quantity of cheaper wheat}}{\text{Quantity of dearer wheat}} = \frac{1.5}{0.5} = \frac{3}{1}$$

$$\text{Quantity of cheaper wheat} = \frac{3}{3+1} \times 20 = 15 \text{ kgs}$$

$$\text{Quantity of dearer wheat} = \frac{1}{3+1} \times 20 = 5 \text{ kgs.}$$

Example 3: Three glasses of capacity 2 litres, 5 litres and 9 litres contain mixture of milk and water with milk concentrations 90%, 80% and 70% respectively. The contents of three glasses are emptied into a large vessel. Find the milk concentration and ratio of milk to water in the resultant mixture.

Solution: Total quantity of milk = $(2 \times 0.9 + 5 \times 0.8 + 9 \times 0.7) = 12.1$ litres.

Milk concentration in the resultant mixture = $\frac{12.1}{2+5+9} \times 100 = 75.625\%$

Water concentration in the resultant mixture = $100 - 75.625 = 24.375\%$

$$\text{Milk : Water} = \frac{75625}{24375} = \frac{121}{39} = 121 : 39.$$

Example 4: 12 litres of a mixture has wine and water in the ratio 2 : 3. How much water must be added to get wine to water ratio of 3 : 7 in the resultant mixture?

Solution: Fraction of water in the given mixture = $\frac{3}{5}$

For water to be added, fraction = 1

Fraction of water in the resultant mixture = $\frac{7}{10}$

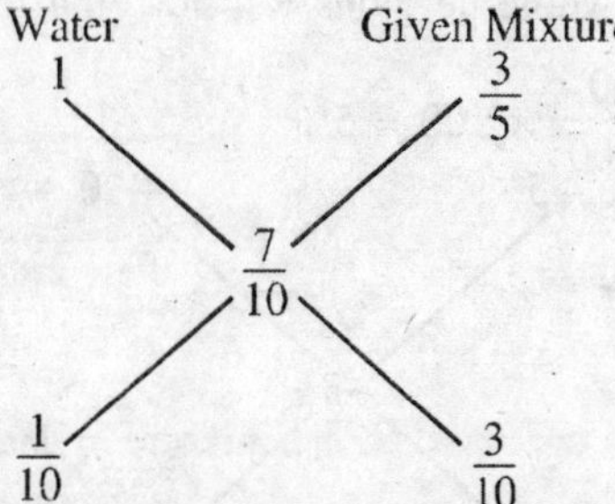

So, water must be added to the mixture in the ratio 1 : 3

Quantity of water to be added = $\frac{1}{3} \times 12 = 4$ litres.

Example 5: 49 litres of milk has 80% milk concentration. How much water be added to make its concentration 70%?

Solution: The given milk has 80% concentration of milk.
Water which is to be added has 0% milk concentration.
Final concentration of solution is 70%.
By alligation rule,

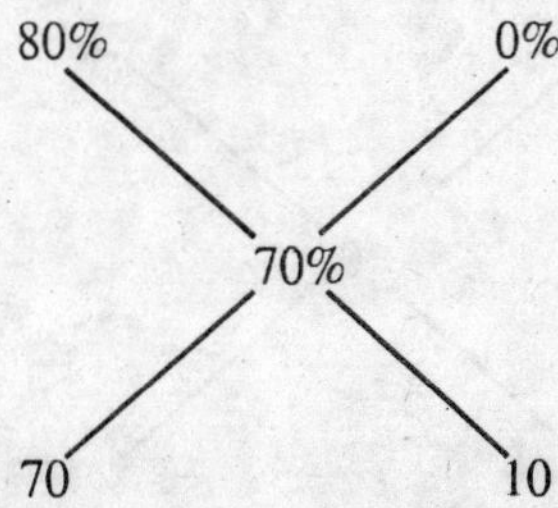

So, water should be added to the given milk in the ratio 10 : 70 or 1 : 7.

$\therefore$ Quantity of water to be added = $\frac{1}{7} \times 49 = 7$ litres.

Example 6: A vessel contains wine with 30% spirit. A part of it is stolen and replaced by same quantity of wine with 10% spirit. The resultant mixture has only 25% spirit. How much of wine was stolen?

Solution:

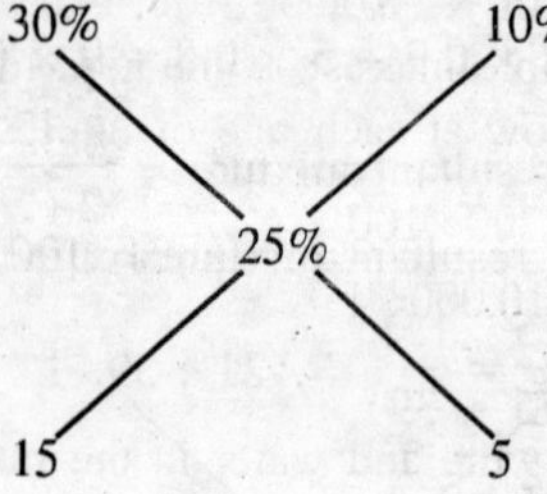

or 3 : 1

Quantity of wine stole = Quantity of 10% wine added.

$$= \frac{1}{3+1} = \frac{1}{4}\text{th the total.}$$

Example 7: A person buys two watches for Rs. 1000. He sells one at a loss of 5% and the other at 20% gain and on the whole he gains Rs. 50. Find the cost price of each watch.

Solution: Overall % profit = $\frac{50}{1000} \times 100 = 5\%$

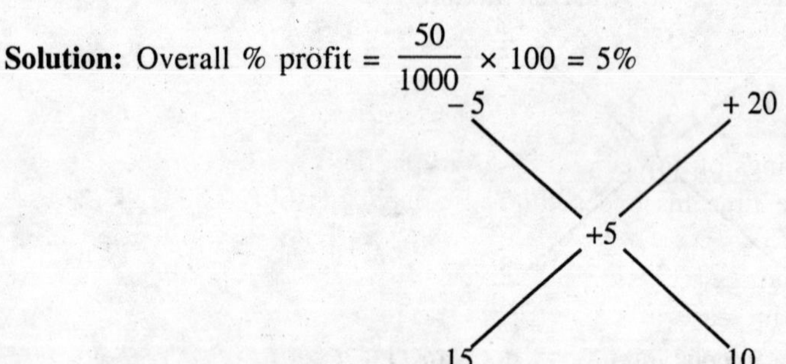

or 3 : 2

CP of watch sold at 5% loss

$$= \frac{3}{3+2} \times 1000 = \text{Rs. } 600$$

CP of watch sold at 20% gain = 1000 – 600 = Rs. 400.

Example 8: A person bought two tables for Rs. 2200. He sells one at 5% loss and the other at 6% profit and thus on the whole he neither gains nor loses. Find the cost price of each.

Solution:

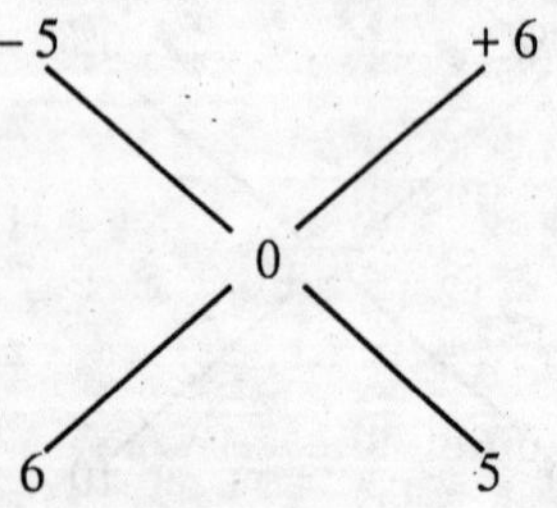

CP of the table sold at 5% loss = $\frac{6}{6+5} \times 2200$ = Rs. 1200

CP of the table sold at 6% profit = $\frac{5}{6+5}$ × 2200 = Rs. 1000

Example 9: A man borrows a total sum of Rs. 10,000 from two sources. To one he pays 10% and to the other 5% per annum simple interest. If the total interest paid by him every year is Rs. 700, how much did he borrow at each rate of interest?

Solution: Average rate of interest = $\frac{700 \times 100}{10{,}000 \times 1} = 7\%$ per annum

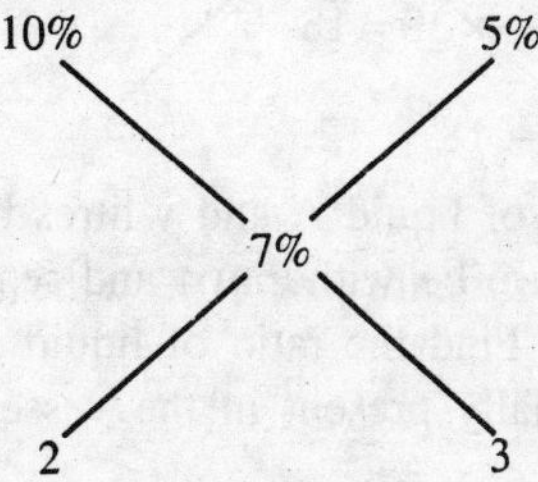

Amount borrowed at 10% = $\frac{2}{2+3}$ × 10,000 = Rs. 4000

Amount borrowed at 5% = $\frac{3}{2+3}$ × 10,000 = Rs. 6000.

Example 10: The expenditure and savings of any employee are in the ratio 3 : 1. His income increases by 16% but at the same time his expenditure also increases by 20%. Find increase or decrease in his savings.

Solution: Here expenditure and savings are two ingredients of income. Therefore, we can write as under, assuming $x\%$ as increase in savings,

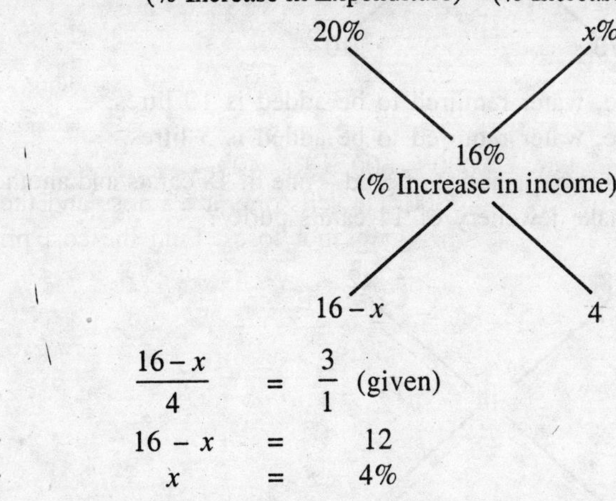

$$\frac{16-x}{4} = \frac{3}{1} \text{ (given)}$$

or $16 - x = 12$

or $x = 4\%$

Example 11: A sum of Rs. 12 is made up of 30 coins which consist of either 50 paise or 25 paise. How many are there of each kind?

Solution: Average value of 30 coins = $\frac{12 \times 100}{30}$ = 40 paise

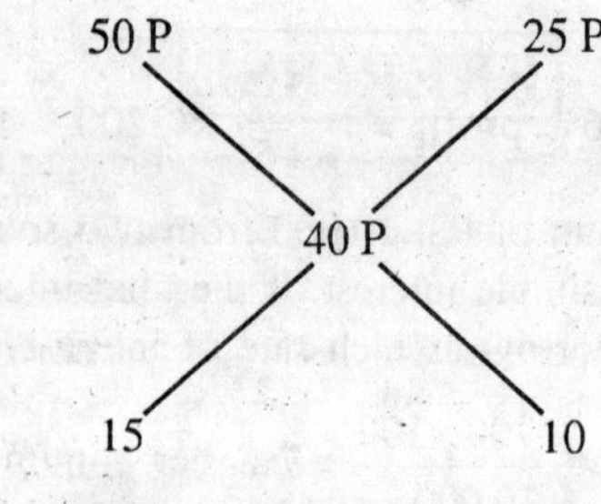

or 3 : 2

No. of 50 P coins = $\frac{3}{3+2} \times 30 = 18$

No. of 25 P coins = 30 – 18 = 12.

Example 12: A vessel contains x litres of liquid A and y litres be withdrawn and replaced by liquid B, then y litres of the mixture be withdrawn and replaced by liquid B, and the opeation is repeated 'n' times in all. Find the ratio of liquid A left after nth operation to the whole quantity of liquid A initially present in the vessel.

Solution: Required Ratio = $\frac{\text{Quantity of liquid A left after nth operation}}{\text{Whole quantity of liquid A initially present}} = \left(1-\frac{y}{x}\right)^n$ or $\left(\frac{x-y}{x}\right)^n$

Example 13: A mixture of 35 litres of spirit and water contains 20% water. How much water must be added to make 30% water in the resultant mixture?

Solution:

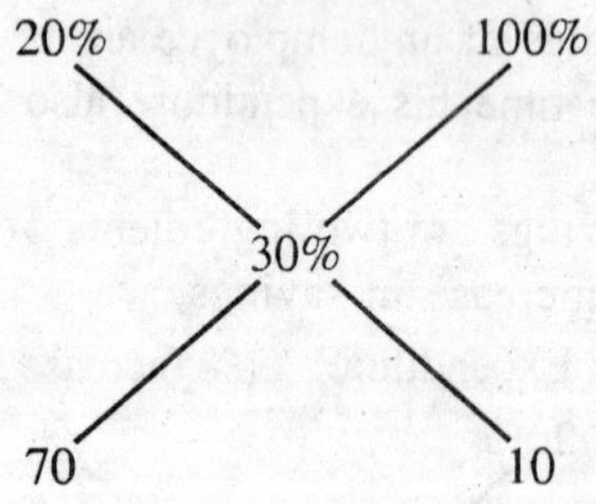

For 70 litres of mixture, water required to be added is 10 litres.

∴ For 35 litres of mixture, water required to be added is 5 litres.

Example 14: In what proportion should two quantities of gold – one of 18 carats and another of 12 carats purity – be mixed to make jewellery of 14 carats purity?

Solution:

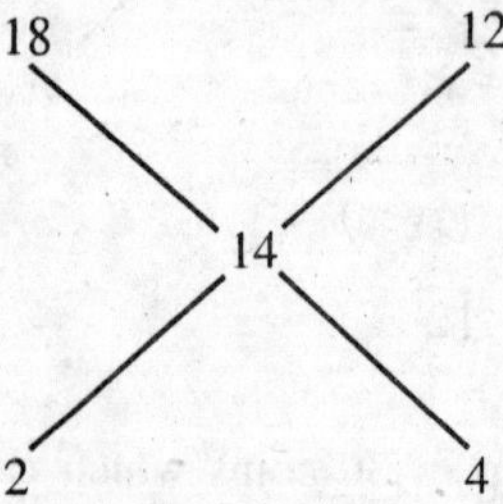

So, $\frac{\text{18 carats}}{\text{12 carats}} = \frac{2}{4} = \frac{1}{2}$ or 1 : 2.

EXERCISE

1. In what proportion must tea at Rs. 62 per kg be mixed with tea at Rs. 72 per kg in order to obtain the mixture worth Rs. 65 per kg?
   A. 4 : 6 B. 7 : 3 C. 2 : 3 D. 4 : 7
2. Find the quantity of rice @ Rs. 10 per kg. which should be mixed with 25 kgs of rice @ Rs. 8 per kg, so that on selling the mixture @ 15 per kg there is 80% profit.
   A. 6 kgs B. 7 kgs C. 3 kgs D. 5 kgs
3. A shopkeeper buys 26 kgs of milk @ Rs. 16 per kg. He also buys from another source an inferior quality of milk @ Rs. 10 per kg. How much quantity of the latter should he buy to mix it with the former so that he can sell the mixture @ Rs. 14 per kg without making any loss?
   A. 13 kgs B. 12 kgs C. 14 kgs D. 16 kgs
4. Two vessels A and B contain milk and water in the ratio 7 : 5 and 17 : 7 respectively. In what ratio mixtures from two vessels should be mixed to get a new mixture containing milk and water in the ratio 5 : 3?
   A. 1 : 2 B. 2 : 1 C. 2 : 3 D. 3 : 2
5. Two vessels A and B contain mixture of milk and water in the ratio 4 : 1 and 9 : 11 respectively. They are mixed in the ratio of 3 : 2. Find the ratio of milk : water in the resulting mixture.
   A. 34 : 16 B. 33 : 17 C. 16 : 34 D. 17 : 33
6. A person has two solutions of sugar with 30% and 50% concentration respectively. In what proportion should he mix two solutions to get 45% concentration in the resulting mixture?
   A. 1 : 3 B. 3 : 1 C. 2 : 3 D. 3 : 2
7. 6 litres of milk and water mixture has 75% milk in it. How much milk should be added to the mixture to make it 90% pure?
   A. 8 litres B. 9 litres C. 10 litres D. 12 litres
8. In what ratio must water be added to spirit to gain 25% by selling it at cost price?
   A. 1 : 4 B. 4 : 1 C. 3 : 4 D. 4 : 3
9. A shopkeeper has 50 kgs of rice. He sells a part of it at 20% profit and the rest at 40% profit. If he gains 25% on the whole, find the quantity of each part.
   A. 12.5 kgs and 37.5 kgs B. 37.5 kgs and 12.5 kgs
   C. 23.5 kgs and 21.5 kgs D. 21.5 kgs and 23.5 kgs
10. A shopkeeper has 100 kgs of tea. He sells a part of it at 20% profit and the rest at 5% loss. If his overall profit is 10%, find the quantity for each part.
    A. 20 kgs B. 25 kgs C. 30 kgs D. 40 kgs
11. A merchant has 160 kgs of wheat. He sells a part of it at 10% profit and the rest of 6% loss. If he incurs 4% loss on the whole, find the quantity for each part.
    A. 120 kgs B. 140 kgs C. 150 kgs D. 160 kgs
12. A man bought a certain quantity of sugar for Rs. 8000. He sells one-fourth of it at 20% loss. At what per cent profit should he sell the remainder stock so as to make an overall profit of 20%?
    A. 20% B. 30% C. 35% D. 40%
13. A person has Rs. 5000. He invests a part of it at 3% per annum and the remainder at 8% per annum simple interest. His total income in 3 years is Rs. 750. Find the sum invested at different rates of interest.
    A. Rs. 2000 and Rs. 3000 B. Rs. 2500 and Rs. 2500
    C. Rs. 3000 and Rs. 2000 D. Rs. 2750 and Rs. 2250

14. A person covers a distance of 100 kms in 10 hours, partly by walking at 7 km/hr and rest by running at 12 km/hr. Find the distance covered in each part.
A. 48 kms B. 72 kms C. 108 kms D. 124 kms

15. The average monthly salary of employees, consisting of officers and workers, of an organisation is Rs. 3000. The average salary of an officer is Rs. 10,000 while that of a worker is Rs. 2000 per month. If there are total 400 employees in the organisation, find the number of officers and workers separately.
A. 300, 100 B. 50, 350 C. 250, 150 D. 310, 90

16. The average daily wages of staff, consisting of supervisors and labourers, of a company is Rs. 50. The average wages of supervisors is Rs. 150 while that of labourers is Rs. 40 per day. If the number of supervisors is 15, find the number of labourers in the company.
A. 150 B. 175 C. 180 D. 200

17. Rs. 675 was divided among 75 boys and girls. Each boy gets Rs. 20 whereas a girl gets Rs. 5. Find the number of boys and girls.
A. 20, 55 B. 15, 60 C. 25, 50 D. 30, 45

18. A sum of Rs. 70 is divided among 10 children. Each boy gets Rs. 10 whereas a girl gets Rs. 5. If the number of boys is 4, find the number of girls.
A. 6 B. 7 C. 8 D. 9

19. From a cask of wine containing 25 litres, 5 litres are withdrawn and the cask is refilled with water. The process is repeated a second and then a third time. Find the quantity of wine left in the cask and also the ratio of wine to water in the resulting mixture.
A 61 : 64 B. 16 : 46 C. 46 : 16 D. 64 : 61

20. A vessel contains 80 litres of milk. 16 litres of milk was taken out of the vessel and replaced by water. Then 16 litres of mixture was withdrawn and again replaced by water. The operation was repeated for third time. How much milk is now left in the vessel?
A. 96.40 litres B. 50.36 litres C. 40.96 litres D. 32.76 litres

21. A vessel contains mixture of liquids A and B in the ratio 3 : 2. When 20 litres of the mixture is taken out and replaced by 20 litres of liquid B, the ratio changes to 1 : 4. How many litres of liquid A was there initially present in the vessel?
A. 12 litres B. 18 litres C. 24 litres D. 22 litres

22. A piece of an alloy of two metals (A and B) weighs 15 gms and costs Rs. 150. If the weights of the two metals be interchanged, the new alloy would be worth Rs. 120. If the price of metal A is Rs. 6 per gm, find the weight of the other metal in the original piece of alloy.
A. 5 gms B. 8 gms C. 10 gms D. 12 gms

23. A container of 90 litres with two liquids A and B, 60% of liquid A and 30% of liquid B are taken out of the vessel. This leaves the container 40% empty. Find the initial quantity of both liquids.
A. 50 litres B. 54 litres C. 57 litres D. 60 litres

24. If 4 kg of an alloy made of 1/4th iron and rest is mixed with 6 kg of another alloy made of 2/3rd iron and rest tin, find the ratio of iron to tin in the resultant mixture.
A. 1 : 1 B. 2 : 1 C. 1 : 2 D. 3 : 2

25. In a courtyard there are many chickens and goats. If heads are counted, it comes to 100 but when legs are counted, it comes to 320. Find the number of chickens and goats in the courtyard.
A. 20, 50 B. 30, 70 C. 40, 60 D. 50, 50

26. A container is full of milk. One-third of milk is taken out of it and replaced by same quantity of water. Then again one-third of the mixture is taken out of it and replaced by the same quantity of water. The process is repeated 4 times. If 16 litres of milk is left in the container at the end of 4th operation, find the capacity of the container.

(a) 76 litres *(b)* 81 litres *(c)* 82 litres *(d)* 85 litres

27. The cost of type-I rice is Rs. 15 per kg and type-II is Rs. 20 per kg. If both type I and type II are mixed in the ratio of 2 : 3, then find the price per kg of the mixed variety.

(a) Rs. 19.50 *(b)* Rs. 19 *(c)* Rs. 18.50 *(d)* Rs. 18

28. A cask full of wine from which 8 litres are drawn and is then filled with water. This operation is performed three more times. The ratio of quantity of wine left in the cask to that of the water is 16 : 81. How much wine did the cask hold originally?

(a) 42 litres *(b)* 32 litres *(c)* 24 litres *(d)* 18 litres

29. Tea worth Rs. 126 per kg and Rs. 135 per kg are mixed with a third variety in the ratio 1 : 1 : 2. If mixture is worth Rs. 153 per kg, the price of the third variety per kg will be:

(a) Rs. 180 *(b)* Rs. 17.50 *(c)* Rs. 170 *(d)* Rs. 169.50

30. In what ratio of water be mixed with milk to gain $16\frac{2}{3}\%$ on selling the mixture at cost price?

(a) 4 : 3 *(b)* 2 : 3 *(c)* 6 : 1 *(d)* 1 : 6

31. In what ratio must a grocer mix two varieties of tea worth Rs. 60 a kg and Rs. 65 a kg so that by selling the mixture at Rs. 68.20 a kg he may gain 10%?

(a) 4 : 5 *(b)* 3 : 5 *(c)* 3 : 4 *(d)* 3 : 2

SOLUTIONS

1. CP of 1 kg. Cheaper tea CP of 1 kg. Dearer tea

Rs. 62 Rs. 72

Mean Price per kg
Rs. 65

$d - m = 7$ $m - c = 3$

Using Alligation rule,

$$\frac{\text{Quantity of cheaper tea}}{\text{Quantity of dearer tea}} = \frac{d-m}{m-c} = \frac{7}{3}$$

Therefore, they must be mixed in the ratio of 7 : 3.

2. Cost price of the mixture = $15 \times \frac{100}{180} = \text{Rs. } \frac{25}{3}$ per kg

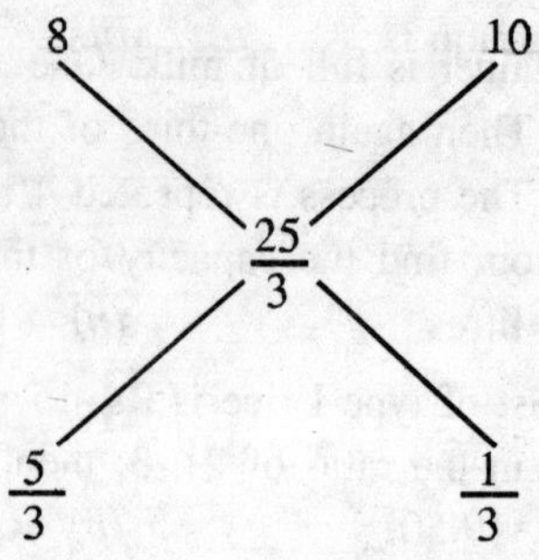

$$\frac{\text{Quantity of rice @ Rs. 8 per kg}}{\text{Quantity of rice @ Rs.10 per kg}} = \frac{5/3}{1/3} = \frac{5}{1}$$

Quantity of rice @ Rs. 10 per kg = $25 \times \frac{1}{5} = 5$ kgs.

3.

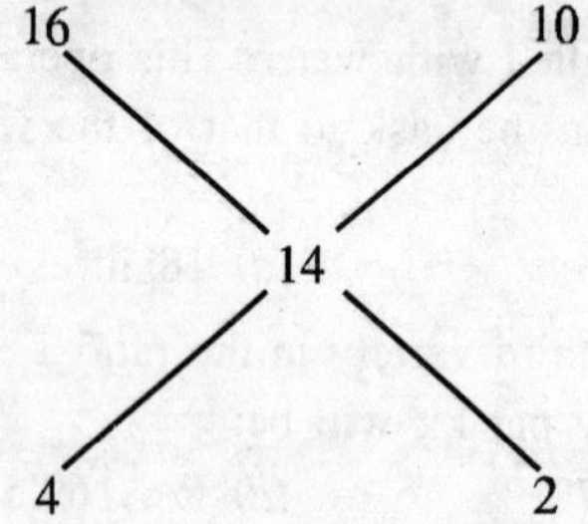

or 2 : 1 $\frac{\text{Quantity of milk @ Rs.10 per kg}}{\text{Quantity of milk @ Rs. 16 per kg}} = \frac{1}{2}$

So, quantity of milk @ Rs. 10 per kg. = $\frac{26}{2} = 13$ kgs.

4. First of all we write the fraction of milk present in three mixtures.

In A : $\frac{7}{12}$

In B : $\frac{17}{24}$

In combination of A and B : $\frac{5}{8}$

We now apply alligation rule on these fractions.

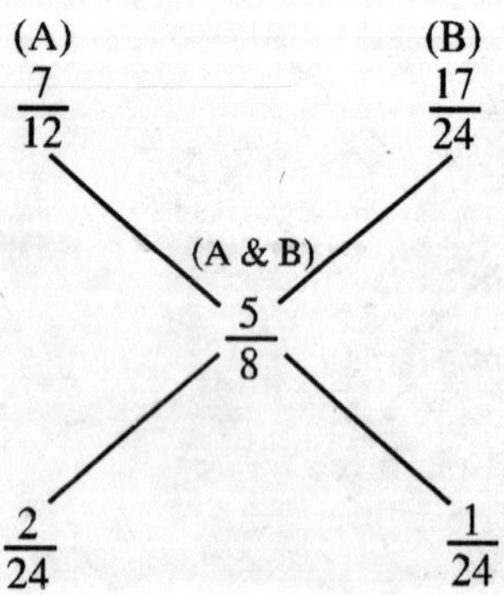

or, 2 : 1

So, Ratio of A : B = 2 : 1.

5. Fraction is *Milk* *Water*

A: $\frac{4}{5}$ $\frac{1}{5}$

B: $\frac{9}{20}$ $\frac{11}{20}$

$(3A + 2B) = A \text{ and } B : \left(\frac{12}{5}+\frac{9}{10}\right) \left(\frac{3}{5}+\frac{11}{10}\right)$

$\frac{33}{10}$ $\frac{17}{10}$

So, Ratio of milk : water in the resulting mixture = 33 : 17.

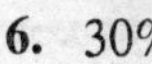

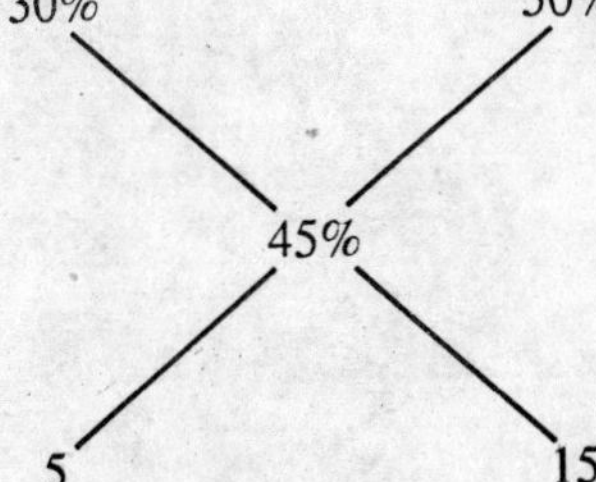

He should mix 30% and 50% in the ratio 5 : 15 or 1 : 3.

$\frac{30\% \text{ Solution}}{50\% \text{ Solution}} = \frac{1}{3}$

or 1 : 3

7. The given solution has 75% milk.
Milk to be added has 100% milk.

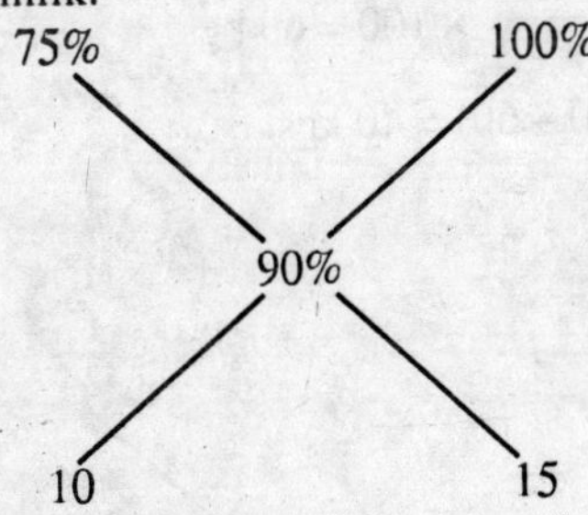

Milk should be added to the given mixture in the ratio 15 : 10 or 3 : 2.

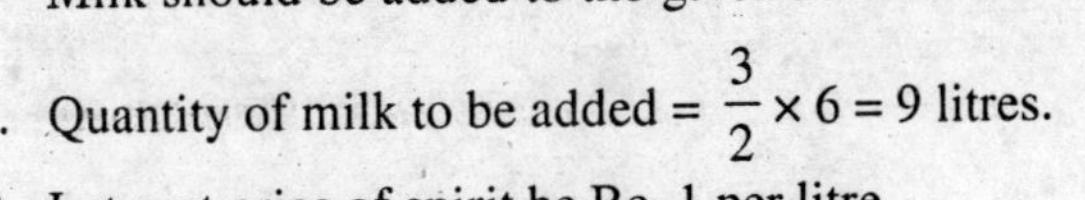

$\therefore$ Quantity of milk to be added = $\frac{3}{2} \times 6 = 9$ litres.

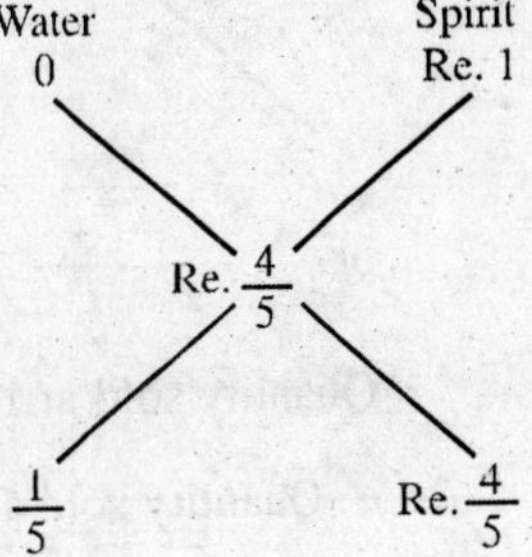

8. Let cost price of spirit be Re. 1 per litre.

Then SP of mixture = Re. 1 per litre

Gain = 25%

So, CP of mixture $= 1 \times \frac{100}{125} = \text{Re. } \frac{4}{5}$

We assume that CP of water is zero.
Using alligation rule on cost price,

Water should be mixed to spirit in the ratio $\frac{1}{5} : \frac{4}{5}$ or 1 : 4.

9.

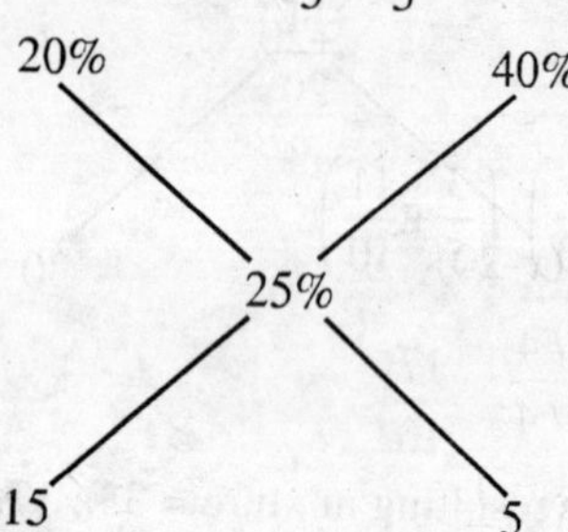

or 3 : 1

Quantity sold at 20% profit $= \frac{3}{3+1} \times 50 = 37.5$ kgs.

Quantity sold at 40% profit $= (50 - 37.5) = 12.5$ kgs.

10.

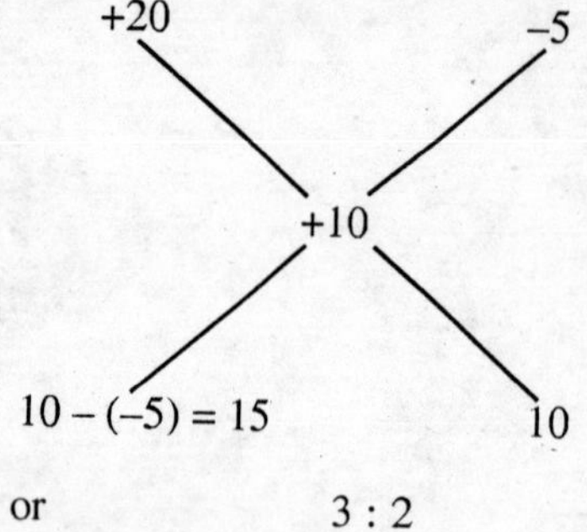

or 3 : 2

Quantity sold at 20% profit $= \frac{3}{3+2} \times 100 = 60$ kgs.

Quantity sold at 5% loss $= (100 - 60) = 40$ kgs.

11.

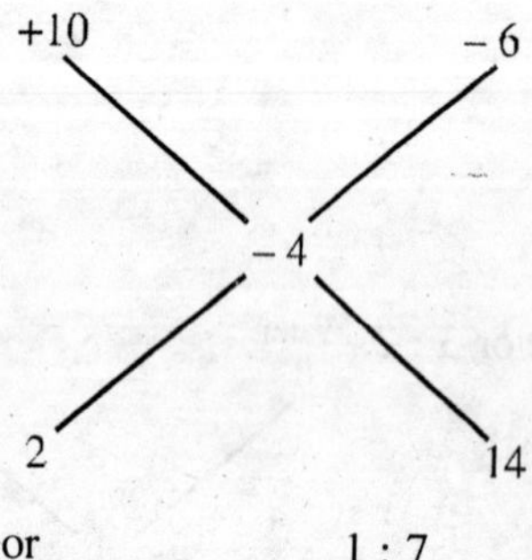

or 1 : 7

Quantity sold at 10% profit $= \frac{1}{1+7} \times 160 = 20$ kgs.

Quantity sold at 6% loss $= 160 - 20 = 140$ kgs.

12. Let the remainder stock be sold at $x\%$ profit.

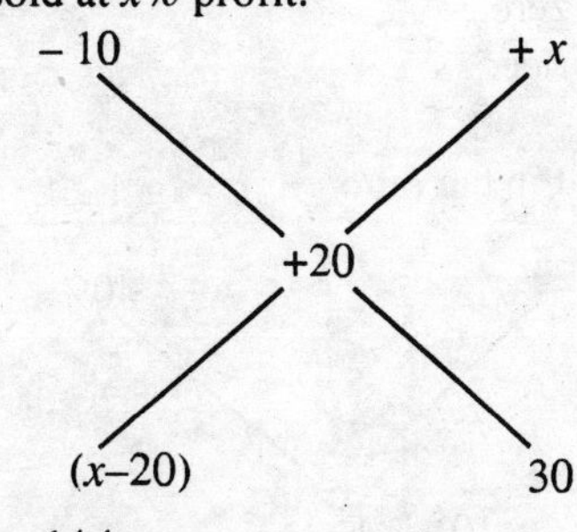

$$\frac{x-20}{30} = \frac{1/4}{3/4}$$

or $\quad x - 20 = 30 \times \frac{1}{3}$

or $\quad x = 20 + 10$

$\quad x = 30\%$ profit.

13. Average rate of interest $= \frac{100 \times 750}{5000 \times 3} = 5\%$ per annum

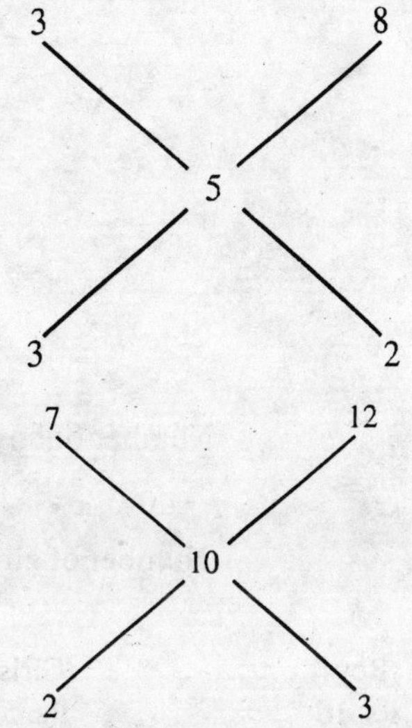

Investment at 3% per annum $= \frac{3}{3+2} \times 5000 =$ Rs. 3000

Investment at 8% per annum $= \frac{2}{3+2} \times 5000 =$ Rs. 2000.

14. Average speed $= \frac{100}{10} = 10$ km/hr.

Ratio of time taken at 7 km/hr to 12 km/hr = 2 : 3

Time taken at 7 km/hr $= \frac{2}{2+3} \times 10 = 4$ hrs.

Distance covered at 7 km/hr = 7 × 4 = 28 km.

Distance covered at 12 km/hr = 100 – 28 = 72 km.

15. Rs. 10,000 Rs. 2000

Rs. 3000

1000 7000

$$\frac{\text{Number of officers}}{\text{Number of workers}} = \frac{1000}{7000} = \frac{1}{7}$$

No. of officers $= \frac{1}{1+7} \times 400 = 50$

No. of workers $= 400 - 50 = 350$

16. 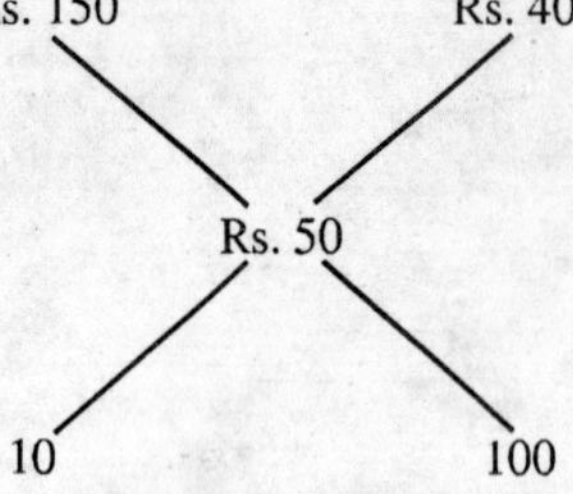

$$\frac{\text{Number of supervisors}}{\text{Number of labourers}} = \frac{10}{100} = \frac{1}{10}$$

Total number of labourers = Total no. of supervisors × 10

= 15 × 10 = 150.

17. Average money per head (boy or girl) = Rs. $\frac{675}{75}$ = Rs. 9

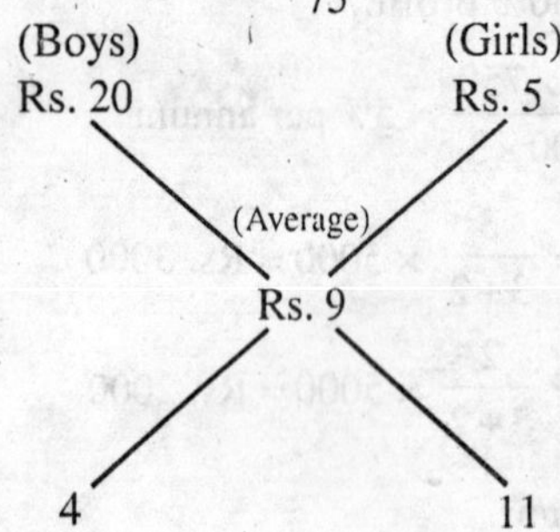

$$\text{Number of boys} = \frac{4}{4+11} \times 75 = 20$$

$$\text{Number of girls} = \frac{11}{4+11} \times 75 = 55.$$

18. 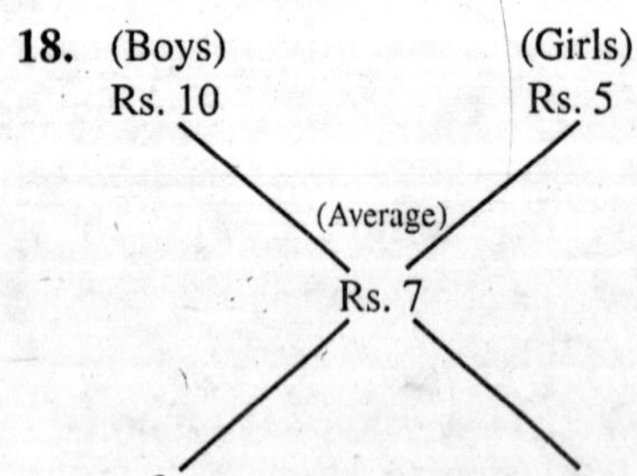

$$\frac{\text{Number of girls}}{\text{Number of boys}} = \frac{3}{2}$$

$$\text{Number of girls} = \frac{3}{2} \times 4 = 6$$

19. Here, quantity of wine left after third operation

$$= \left(1-\frac{5}{25}\right)^3 \times 25 = \left(\frac{4}{5}\right)^3 \times 25 = \frac{64}{125}\times 25 = \frac{64}{5} = 12\frac{4}{5} \text{ litres.}$$

$$\text{Final ratio of wine to water} = \frac{(64/125)}{(1-64/125)}$$

$$= \frac{64/125}{61/125}$$

$$\text{Wine : Water} = \frac{64}{61}.$$

20. $$\text{Amount of milk left} = 80\left(1-\frac{16}{80}\right)^3 = 80\left(\frac{4}{5}\right)^3$$

$$80 \times \frac{64}{125} = 40.96 \text{ litres.}$$

21. % of liquid B initially present in the vessel = $\frac{2}{3+2} \times 100 = 40\%$

% of liquid B finally present in the vessel = $\frac{4}{1+4} \times 100 = 80\%$.

The second solution is liquid B which is being mixed and it has 100% liquid B.
80% of liquid B present in the resultant mixture may be taken as average percentage. So, using rule of alligation on liquid B per cent, we can write,

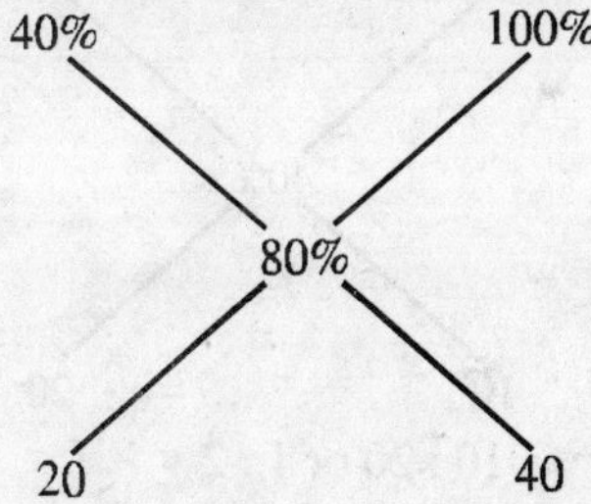

or 1 : 2

The ratio of liquid left in the vessel to liquid B being mixed = 1 : 2

Since the quantity of liquid B being mixed is 20 litres, the quantity of liquid left in the vessel is 10 litres.

Therefore, the total quantity of liquid initially present in the vessel

$$= 10 + 20 = 30 \text{ litres}$$

$$\text{Quantity of liquid A} = \frac{3}{2+3} \times 30 = 18 \text{ litres.}$$

22. If the two alloys are mixed, the mixture would contain 15 gms of each metal and it would cost Rs. (150 + 120) = Rs. 270.

Cost of (15 gms of metal A + 15 gms of metal B) = Rs. 270

Cost of (1 gm of metal A + 1 gm of metal B) = Rs. $\frac{270}{15}$ = Rs. 18

Cost of 1 gm of metal B = Rs. (18 – 6) = Rs. 12

Average cost of original piece of alloy = $\frac{150}{15}$ = Rs. 10 per gm.

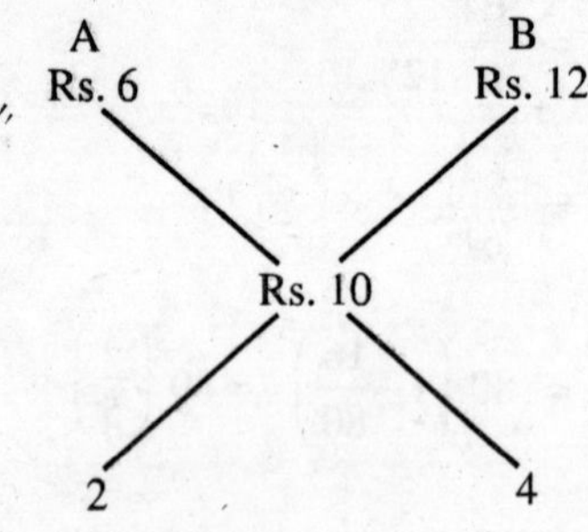

$$\frac{\text{Quantity of metal A}}{\text{Quantity of metal B}} = \frac{2}{4} = \frac{1}{2}$$

$$\text{Quantity of metal B} = \frac{2}{1+2} \times 15 = 10 \text{ gms.}$$

23. Here withdrawal of liquid A and B result into making the container empty. Hence percentage of two liquids withdrawn are two components of the percentage by which the container becomes empty.

Applying the rule of alligation, we get

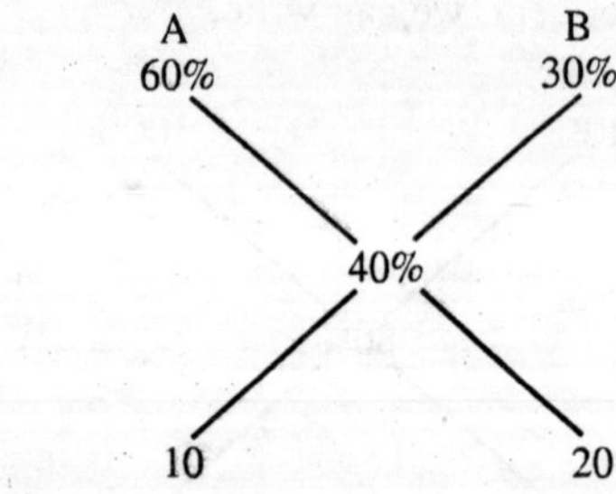

A : B = 10 : 20 or 1 : 2

$$\text{Quantity of liquid} = \frac{1}{1+2} \times 90 = 30 \text{ litres}$$

Quantity of liquid B = 90 – 30 = 60 litres.

24. $$\text{Total quantity of iron} = 4\left(\frac{1}{4}\right) + 6\left(\frac{2}{3}\right) = 1 + 4 = 5 \text{ kg.}$$

Total quantity of tin = (4 + 6) – 5
= 5 kg.

In the resultant mixture, iron : tin = 5 : 5 or 1 : 1.

25. Average no. of legs per head $= \frac{320}{100} = \frac{16}{5}$

or, $3 : 2$

$$\text{No. of goats} = \frac{3}{3+2} \times 100 = 60$$

$$\text{No. of chickens} = 100 - 60 = 40.$$

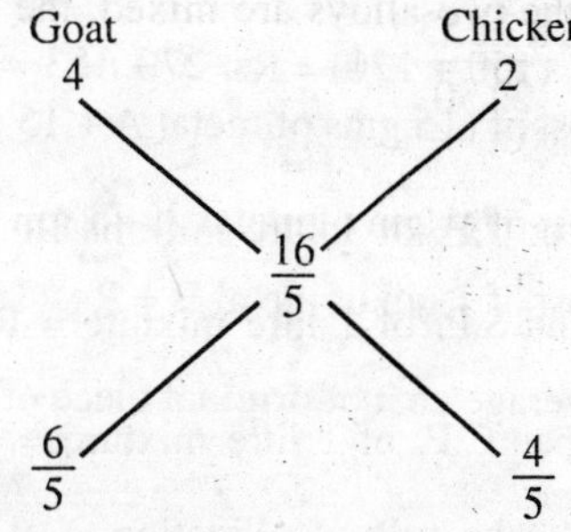

26. Let capacity of the container be x litre; then

$x(1 - 1/3)^4 = 16 \Rightarrow x\left(\frac{2}{3}\right)^4 = 16 \Rightarrow x \times \frac{16}{81} = 16 \quad \therefore x = 81$ litres

27. Let the price per kg of mixed variety be Rs. x; then

By the rule of alligation,

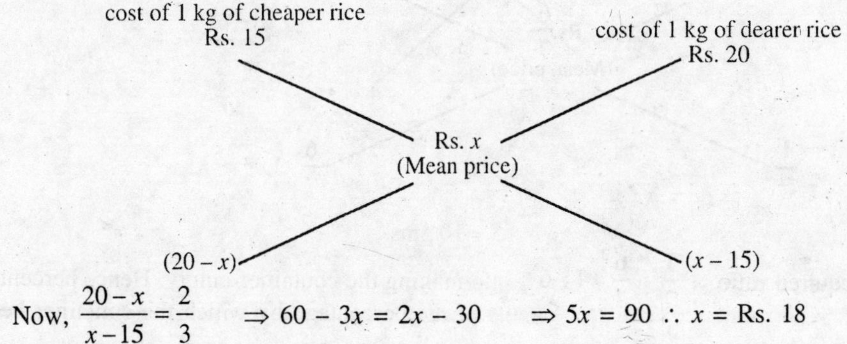

Now, $\frac{20-x}{x-15} = \frac{2}{3} \Rightarrow 60 - 3x = 2x - 30 \Rightarrow 5x = 90 \therefore x = \text{Rs. } 18$

28. Let x litres wine cask hold originally, then

$$\frac{x\left(1-\frac{8}{x}\right)^4}{x} = \frac{16}{81} \Rightarrow \left(1-\frac{8}{x}\right)^4 = \left(\frac{2}{3}\right)^4 \Rightarrow \left(1-\frac{8}{x}\right) = \frac{2}{3}$$

$$\Rightarrow \frac{8}{x} = 1 - \frac{2}{3} \Rightarrow \frac{8}{x} = \frac{1}{3} \quad \therefore x = 24 \text{ litres}$$

29. Here first two varieties of tea are mixed in equal ratio;

So their average price $= \frac{126+135}{2} = \text{Rs. } 130.50$

Let price of the third variety per kg be Rs. x; then now mixture is formed by two varieties one at Rs. 130.50 per kg and other at Rs. x per kg in the same ratio 2 : 2 i.e, 1 : 1

By the rule of alligation,

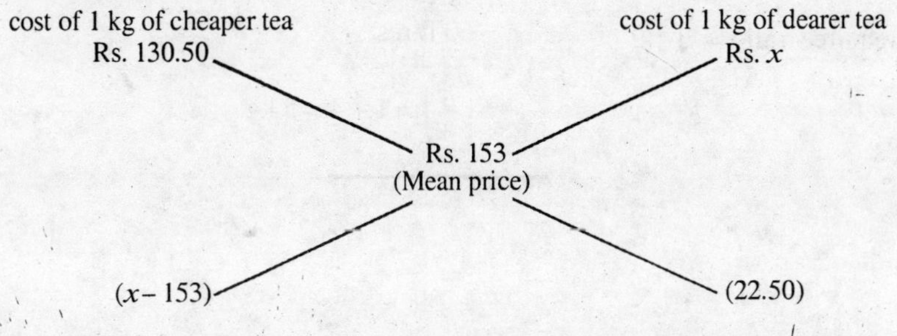

Now, $\frac{x-153}{22.50}=1 \quad \Rightarrow x - 153 = 22.50 \quad \therefore \quad x = \text{Rs. } 175.50$

30. Let C.P. of 1 litre milk be Re. 1, Gain = $16\frac{2}{3}=\frac{50}{3}\%$

and S.P. of 1 litre mixture = Re. 1

then C.P. of 1 litre mixture = $1\times\frac{100\times 3}{350}$ = Re. $\frac{6}{7}$

By the rule of alligation,

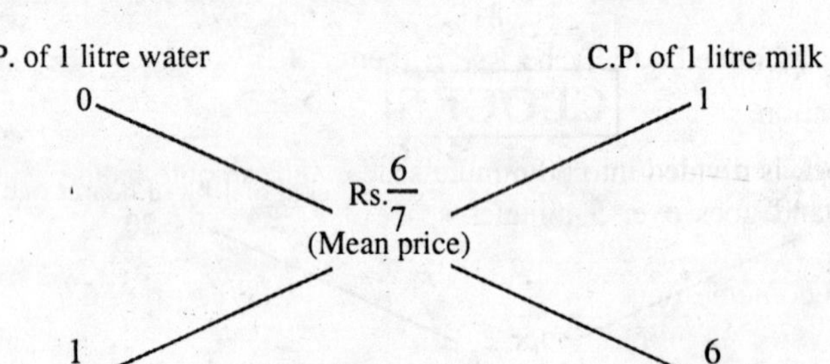

Hence, required ratio = $\frac{1}{7}:\frac{6}{7}=1:6$

31. S.P. of 1 kg mixture = Rs. 68.20, Gain % = 10%

Hence, C.P. of 1 kg mixture = $\frac{100}{110}\times$ Rs. 68.20 = Rs. 62

By the rule of alligation

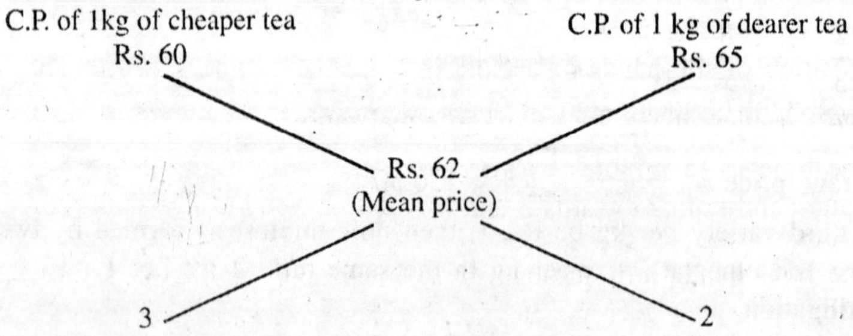

Hence, required ratio = 3 : 2

19

CLOCKS AND CALENDER

CLOCKS

(a) The circular face of a clock is divided into 60 minute spaces. The minute hand passes over 60 minute spaces whilst the hour hand goes over 5 minutes space.

(b) *In every hour*

(i) The hands of a clock coincide once.

(ii) The hands are straight once pointing in opposite direction. The hands are 30 minutes apart in this position.

(iii) The hands are twice at right angles. The hands are 15 minutes apart in this position.

(iv) The minute hand moves through 6° in each minute whereas an hour hand moves through $\frac{1°}{2}$ in each minute: .

(c) *In a day*

(i) The hands coincide 11 times in every 12 hours (because between 11 and 1 o'clock, there is a common position, 12 o'clock when the hands coincide. Hence 22 times in 24 hours.

(ii) The hands point towards each other 11 times in 12 hours (between 5 and 7 there is a common position 6 o'clock when the hands are straight), Hence 22 times in 24 hours.

(iii) The hands of a clock are at right angles twice in every hour, but in 12 hours, they are at right angles 22 times and thus 44 times in a day. There are two positions common in every 12 hours, one at 3 o'clock and second at 9 o'clock.

(iv) Any relative position of the hands of a clock is replaced 11 times in every 12 hours.

(v) The hands are straight (coincide and in opposite direction) 44 times in 24 hours.

Example 1: When the time is 15 minutes past 3, the angle between the two hands of the clock is :

Solution: The minute hand points towards 3 and hour hand shifts from 3rd mark onwards, the angle which the hour hand shifts through in 15 minutes = $15 \times \frac{1°}{2} = 7\frac{1°}{2}$

Hence the angle is $7\frac{1°}{2}$.

Example 2: If a clock takes 22 seconds to strike 12, how much time will it take to strike 6 ?

Solution: In order to hear 12 strikes, there are 11 intervals (12 – 1) and time of each interval is uniform. Hence time to hear each strike is 22 ÷ 11 = 2 seconds. Now to hear 6 strikes, there are (6 – 1) *i.e.* 5 intervals for which the time taken is 5 × 2 = 10 seconds.

Hence it will take 10 seconds for a clock to strike 6.

Example 3: A clock strikes once at 1 o'clock, twice at 2 o'clock, thrice at 3 o'clock, and so on. What is the total number of strikings in a day?

Solution: After every 12 hours, the system is repeated. In 12 hours, the total number of strikes = 1 + 2 + 3 + 4 + 5 + 6 + ... + 12

$$= \frac{12(1+12)}{2} = 78 \qquad \left[\because S_n = \frac{n}{2}(\text{Ist} + \text{Last})\right]$$

$\therefore$ Total number of strikes = 2 × 78 = 156

Example 4: The minute hand of a clock overtakes the hour hand at interval of 65 minutes of correct time. How much a day does the clock gain or lose?

Solution: The minute hand gains 55 minutes spaces over hour hand in 60 minutes in correct clock. But in this case minute hand gains 60 minutes over the hour hand.

Now,55 minutes gained in 60 minutes

60 minutes gained in $\frac{60}{55} \times 60 = 65\frac{5}{11}$ minutes

But minute hand overtakes after 65 minutes.

Hence, gain in 65 minutes = $65\frac{5}{11} - 65 = \frac{5}{11}$ minute

Therefore, gain in 24 hours = $\frac{24 \times 60}{65} \times \frac{5}{11} = \frac{1440}{143} = 10\frac{10}{143}$ min.

Example 5: At what time between 3 and 4 o'clock are the hands of a clock together?

Solution: At 3 o'clock, the minute hand will be 15 minute spaces behind the hour hand. When the two hands are together then minute hands will travel to 15 minutes spaces.

Hence, 55 minutes spaces is gained in 60 minutes.

Then, 15 minutes spaces will be gained in $\frac{60}{55} \times 15$ minutes

$$= \frac{180}{11} = 16\frac{4}{11} \text{ minutes}$$

Hence, they are together at $16\frac{4}{11}$ minute past 3.

Example 6: At what time between 2 and 3 o'clock will the hands of a clock be in same straight line but not together?

Solution: At 2 o'clock hour hand is at 2 and the minute hand at 12. Hence, the two hands are 10 minutes spaced apart.

Hence, the two hands are in same straight line but not together then they will be 30 minute spaces apart.

So, the minute hand will have to gain [30 –(–10)] = 40 minutes spaces over the hour hand.

Now, 55 minute spaces are gained in 60 minutes.

Hence, 40 minute spaces are gained in $\frac{60}{55} \times 40 = \frac{480}{11} = 43\frac{7}{11}$ min.

Example 7: At what time between 5 and 6 o'clock are the hands of a clock be at right angle?

Solution: At 5 o'clock the minute hand in 25 minute spaced behind the hour hand. When the two hands are at right angle, they are 15 minute spaces apart. Between 5 and 6 o'clock both hands are at right angle in two different conditions:

(i) When minute hand is 15 minute spaced behind the hour hand. In this case, minute hand will have to gain (25 – 15) = 10 minute spaces.
Now, 55 minute spaces are gained in 60 minutes

10 minute spaces will be gained in $\frac{60}{55} \times 10 = 10\frac{10}{11}$ minutes.

Hence, they are at right angle at $10\frac{10}{11}$ minutes past 5.

(ii) When minute hand is 15 minute spaced ahead of the hour hand.
In this case, minute hand will have to gain (25 + 15) = 40 min.
Now, 55 minute spaces are gained in 60 minute

Hence, 40 minute spaces will be gained in $\frac{60}{55} \times 40 = 43\frac{7}{11}$ min.

Therefore, they are at right angle at $43\frac{7}{11}$ muinute past 5.

CALENDER

Points to remember

(i) 1 year = 365 days = 52 weeks + 1 day
(∴ An ordinary year contains 1 odd day) .

(ii) 1 leap year = 366 days = 52 weeks + 2 days
(∴ A leap year contains 2 odd days)

(iii) 100 years = 76 ordinary years + 24 leap years
= 76 odd days + 24 × 2 odd days = 124 odd days
= 17 weeks + 5 days
∴ 100 years contain 5 odd days.

(iv) 200 years contain 3 odd days.

(v) 300 years contain 1 odd day.

(vi) 400 years contain no odd day because since there are 5 odd days in 100 years, there will be 20 days in 400 years. But every 4th century is a leap year.

(vii) First January 1 AD was Monday. Therefore we must count days from Sunday.
i.e. Sunday for 0 odd day, Monday for 1 odd day, Tuesday for 2 odd days and so on.

(viii) The first day of a century must either be Monday, Tuesday, Thursday or Saturday.

(ix) Last day of a century cannot be either Tuesday, Thursday or Saturday.

Example 8: What was the day on August 15, 1947.

Solution: August 15, 1947 = 1946 + 1947th year upto August 15
= 1600 + 300 + 46 + Days up to August 15 in lhe year 1947.

No. of odd days in 1600 years = 0
No. of odd days in 300 years = 1
No. of odd days in 35 ordinary years = 35
No. of odd days in 11 leap years = 22
No. of odd days in January = 3
No. of odd days in February = 0
No. of odd days in March = 3
No. of odd days in April = 2
No. of odd days in May = 3
No. of odd days in June = 2
No. of odd days in July = 3
No. of odd days in August = 15
Total No. of odd days = 89

= 89 days = 12 weeks 5 days

∴ It was 5th day *i.e.* 'Friday' on August 15, 1947.

Example 9: Gandhiji was born on Oct. 2,1869, it was Saturday on that day. What was the day on Oct 2, 1870.

Solution: The difference between Oct 2, 1869 and Oct. 2, 1870 is of one year. No. of days in February is 28. After completion of one year 1 odd day increases. Therefore, it was Sunday on Oct., 2, 1870.

Example 10: What was the day on December 31, 1917 ?

Solution: It is not necessary to repeat the whole process. It will be slightly easier to find the day on Jan. 1, 1918. Then Dec. 31, 1917 will be the previous day.

Jan. 1, 1918 = 1900 years + 17 years + 1 day of 1918th year
No. of odd days in 1900 years = 1
No. of odd days in 13 years = 13
No. of odd days in 4 leap years = 8
No. of odd days in January = 1
Total No. of odd days = 23

23 days = 3 weeks + 2 days

∴ Tuesday was on January 1,1918 and Monday was on December 31,1917.

Example 11: Why last day of a century can not be either Tuesday, Thursday or Saturday.

Solution: *Reasoning:* No. of odd days in 1st century = 5
∴ Last day of 1st century will be Friday
No. of odd days in 2 centuries = 3
∴ Last day of IInd century will be Wednesday
No. of odd days in 3 centuries = 1
∴ Last day of IIIrd century will be Monday
No. of Odd days in 4 centuries = 0
∴ 'Last day of IVth century will be Sunday
The same process will be repeated again after it. Therefore last day of any century cannot be either Tuesday, Thursday or Saturday.

Example 12: How calendar of the year 1981 can be used in the year 1987.

Solution: The difference between Jan. 1, 1981 and Jan. 1, 1987 is 6 years in which 1984 is a leap year.
∴ No. of odd days in these 6 years = 6 + 1 = 7 = 1 week + 0 days.
So, in these 6 years no. of odd days are 0. There will be same day on Jan 1, 1981 and Jan 1, 1987. Thus, calendar of 1981 can be used in the year 1987.

EXERCISE

1. What will be the angle between the two hands of clock when it is 3 o'clock?
(a) 30° (b) 60° (c) 90° (d) 100°

2. Through how many degrees a minute hand moves in 1 hour 20 minutes?
(a) 80° (b) 360° (c) 420° (d) 480°

3. When the two hands of a clock are straight in opposite direction. The angle between the two hands is:
(a) 90° (b) 120° (c) 180° (d) 360°

4. When the time is 15 minutes past 5, the angle between the two hands of a clock is:
(a) 60° (b) $67\frac{1°}{2}$ (c) 90° (d) $97\frac{1°}{2}$

5. How many times in twelve hours, the hands of a clock are at right angles?
(a) 4 times (b) 8 times (c) 12 times (d) 22 times

6. At what time between 5 and 6 o'clock, the hands of clock shall be straight (in opposite direction)?
(a) 6 o'clock (b) 55 min. past 5 (c) 5 min. past 6 (d) None of these

7. Any relative position of the hands of a clock is repeated how many times in every 12 hours?
(a) 12 times (b) 11 times (c) 4 times (d) 2 times

8. The hands of a correct clock coincide every:
(a) 60 min (b) $65\frac{5}{11}$ min (c) 65 min (d) None of these

9. A clock rings at 1 o'clock, 2'o clock, 3 o'clock and so on. The number of times it will ring in a week is:
(a) 256 times (b) 168 times (c) 156 times (d) 152 times

10. How many times in a day, the hands of the clock are straight?
(a) 12 times (b) 5 times (c) 44 times (d) 22 times

11. The angle between 4 and 5 o'clock will the hands of a clock coincide?
(a) 21 min. past 4 (b) $21\frac{9}{11}$ min. past 4 (c) 30 min. past 4 (d) None of these

12. The number of relative position of the hands of clock in each of which it is possible for them to change their places, in the course of their revolutions is:
(a) 5 (b) 13 (c) 11 (d) 12

13. Two clocks begin to strike 12 together. One strikes its strokes in 33 seconds and the other in 22 seconds. What is the interval between the 6th stroke of the first and 8th stroke of the second?
(a) 3 seconds (b) 1 second
(c) 11 seconds (d) strikes at the same time

14. What was the day on 1st January, 1 AD?
(a) Sunday (b) Monday (c) Thursday (d) Saturday

15. What was the day on 1st January, 2000 AD?
(a) Wednesday (b) Monday (c) Saturday (d) Tuesday

16. One of the following is a day which cannot be the last day of the century, that day is:
(*a*) Sunday (*b*) Monday (*c*) Tuesday (*d*) Friday

17. One of the following is a day which cannot be the last day of the century, that day is:
(*a*) Sunday (*b*) Monday (*c*) Tuesday (*d*) Friday

18. What was the day on 31st December 1, AD?
(*a*) Monday (*b*) Friday (*c*) Tuesday (*d*) Sunday

19. Which of the following is not a leap year?
(*a*) 1860 AD (*b*) 1900 AD (*c*) 2000 AD (*d*) All are leap years

20. What was the day on 31st December, 1800 AD.?
(*a*) Friday (*b*) Tuesday (*c*) Wednesday (*d*) Sunday

21. How many times does the 29th days of the month occur in 400 consecutive years?
(*a*) 97 times (*b*) 4400 times (*c*) 4497 times (*d*) None of these

22. What was the day on 28th June 2000 if 31st May 2000 was Wednesday?
(*a*) Sunday (*b*) Wednesday (*c*) Saturday (*d*) Sunday

23. If the first day of year 1980 was Tuesday, what was the day on first day of year 1981?
(*a*) Sunday (*b*) Saturday (*c*) Tuesday (*d*) Thursday

24. In which one of the following countries the Gregorian Calendar is not used?
(*a*) England (*b*) China (*c*) Russia (*d*) Brazil

25. Any day in April is always on the same day of the week the corresponding day in:
(*a*) August (*b*) June (*c*) July (*d*) December

26. Given that 5th July 1981 was Sunday, what was the day on 5th April of the same year?
(*a*) Friday (*b*) Monday (*c*) Saturday (*d*) Sunday

27. In a leap year the Ist February and Ist of which of the following month fall on the same day of week?
(*a*) July (*b*) August (*c*) April (*d*) September

SOLUTIONS

1. At 3 o'clock, the hour hand at 3 and minute hand at 12.
So, the two hands are 15 minute spaced apart.
Hence, required angle = $\frac{15}{60} \times 360° = 90°$

2. 1 hour 20 minutes = 80 minutes
Required angle = $\frac{360°}{60} \times 80 = 480°$

3. When two hands of a clock are straight in opposite direction. The angle between two hands is 180°.

4. At 15 minutes past 5,

The angle made by hour hand = $\frac{360°}{12} \times \frac{21}{4} = 157\frac{1°}{2}$

The angle made by minute hand = $\frac{360°}{60°} \times 15 = 90°$

Hence, required angle = $157\frac{1°}{2} - 90° = 67\frac{1°}{2}$

5. 22 times in 12 hours, the hands of a clock are at right angle.

6. At 5 o'clock the hour hand at 5 and minute hand at 12.
Hence, the two hands are 25 minute spaced apart. When the two hands are straight in opposite direction then, minute hand will have to move through (25 + 30) = 55 minute spaces
Now, 55 minute spaces are gained in 60 minutes.
Hence, required time = 5 o'clock + 60 min. = 6 o'clock.

7. Any relative position of the hands of a clock is repeated 11 times in every 12 hours.

8. 55 minute spaces are gained in 60 minute

Hence, 60 minute spaces will be gained in $\frac{60}{55} \times 60 = 65\frac{5}{11}$ minutes

Therefore, the hands of a correct clock coindcide every $65\frac{5}{11}$ minutes.

9. After every 12 hours, the system is repeated. In 12 hours the total number of rings
$= 1 + 1 + 1 + \ldots$ up 12 terms $= 12$
Hence, total number of rings in a week = $7 \times 2 \times 12 = 168$

10. The hands of the clock are straight 44 times in a day.

11. A 4 o'clock the hour hand at 4 hand minute hand at 12, hence both the hands are 20 minute spaced apart. For the coinciding position the minute hand will have to move through 20 minute spaces, then

Time taken = $\frac{60}{55} \times 20 = 21\frac{9}{11}$ minutes

Hence, required time = $21\frac{9}{11}$ minute past 4.

12. The number of relative position of the hands of clock in each of which it is possible for them to change their places, in course of their revolutions is 13.

13. Total time taken in 6th stroke of first = $33 \times 5 = 165$ seconds
Total time taken in 8th stroke of second = $22 \times 7 = 154$ seconds.
Hence, required interval = $165 - 154 = 11$ seconds

14. The day on 1st January, 1 AD was Monday.

15. 1st January 2000 AD = 1600 + 300 + 99 + 1 day
Number of odd days in 1600 years = 0
Number of odd days in 300 years = 1
Number of odd days in 75 ordinary years = 75
Number of odd days in 24 leap years = 48
Number of odd days in January, 2000 = 1
Total number of odd days = 125 days = 17 weeks and 6 days
Hence, 1 January 2000 AD was Saturday.

16. 100 years has 5 odd days, hence their last day will be Friday.
200 years has 3 odd days, hence their last day will be Wednesday.
300 years has 1 odd day, hence their last day will be Monday.
400 years has zero odd day, hence their last day will be Sunday.
Here this order will be continued in successive cycles, so the last day of a century cannot be Tuesday, Thursday or Saturday.

17. The first day of century must either be Monday, Tuesday, Thursday or Saturday.

18. We know that 1st January, 1 AD was Monday.
Now, number of days between 1st January, 1 AD to 31 December, 1 AD are 364 = 52 weeks.
So, 31 December 1, AD was Monday.

19. All are leap years.

20. 31 December, 1800 AD = 1600 years + 200 years
Now, 1600 years has zero odd days
and 200 years has 3 odd days
Hence, total odd days = 3
Hence, 31 December, 1800 AD was Wednesday.

21. First three 100 years has 76 ordinary years each but last 100 years of 400 years has only 75 ordinary years.
Hence, number of months of February in 400 consecutive years in which have only 28 days
$= 3 \times 76 + 75 = 303$
Hence, required number of months $= 12 \times 400 - 303 = 4497$

22. Number of days between 31st May, 2000 and 28 June, 2000 = 28 days = 4 weeks + zero odd day
Hence, 31 May, 2000 was Wednesday, so, 28 June, 2000 was also Wednesday.

23. Since year 1980 was leap year, so, it has 2 odd days.
Here, first day 1980 was Tuesday, so, first day of year 1981 was 2 days after Tuesday i.e., Thursday.

24. In Russia Gregorian Calender is not used.

25. Number of days from April to June = 30 + 31 + 30 = 91 days = 13 week + zero odd day
Hence, any day in April is always on the same day of the corresponding day in July.

26. Number of days between 5th April, 1981 and 5th July, 1981 = 25 + 31 + 30 + 5 = 91 days
Hence, if 5th July, 1981 was Sunday, then 5th April, 1981 was also Sunday.

27. Number of days between February (leap year) and July
= 29 + 31 + 30 + 31 + 30 + 31 = 182 days = 16 weeks + zero odd day
Hence, in a leap year the 1st February and 1st August fall on the same day of week.

20

ALGEBRA AND H.C.F AND L.C.M. OF ALGEBRAIC EXPRESSIONS

It is the branch of mathematics that uses letters and symbols to represent variable quantities and numbers, and to express generalizations about them.

Some Important Formulae

A. $a^2 - b^2 = (a + b)(a - b)$
B. $(a + b)^2 = a^2 + 2ab + b^2$
C. $(a - b)^2 = a^2 - 2ab + b^2$
D. $a^3 + b^3 = (a + b)(a^2 - ab + b^2)$
E. $a^3 + b^3 = (a + b)^3 - 3ab(a + b)$
F. $a^3 - b^3 = (a - b)(a^2 + ab + b^2)$
G. $a^3 - b^3 = (a - b)^3 + 3ab(a - b)$
H. $(a + b)^2 = (a - b)^2 + 4ab$
I. $(a - b)^2 = (a + b)^2 - 4ab$
J. $a^3 + b^3 + c^3 - 3abc = (a + b + c)(a^2 + b^2 + c^2 - ab - bc - ca)$
K. If $a + b + c = 0$, then $a^3 + b^3 + c^3 = 3abc$

Example 1: If $x + \frac{1}{x} = 4$, what will be the value of $x - \frac{1}{x}$?

Solution: $\because$ $\left(x - \frac{1}{x}\right)^2 = \left(x + \frac{1}{x}\right)^2 - 4\left(x \cdot \frac{1}{x}\right)$

$$= 4^2 - 4 \times 1 = 16 - 4 = 12$$

$\therefore$ $x - \frac{1}{x} = \sqrt{12} = \pm 2\sqrt{3}$

Example 2: If $\left(x - \frac{1}{x}\right) = a$, find the value of $x^3 - \frac{1}{x^3}$

Solution: According to formula 'G',

$$x^3 - \frac{1}{x^3} = \left(x - \frac{1}{x}\right)^3 + 3.x.\frac{1}{x}\left(x - \frac{1}{x}\right)$$

$$= a^3 + 3 \times 1 \times a = a^3 + 3a = a(a^2 + 3)$$

Example 3: If $x + \frac{1}{x} = 2$, find the value of $x^4 + \frac{1}{x^4}$

Solution: $x + \frac{1}{x} = 2 \Rightarrow \left(x + \frac{1}{x}\right)^2 = (2)^2$

$\therefore\ x^2 + \frac{1}{x^2} + 2 . x . \frac{1}{x} = 4 \Rightarrow x^2 + \frac{1}{x^2} + 2 = 4$

$\Rightarrow x^2 + \frac{1}{x^2} = 4 - 2 = 2 \quad \therefore \left(x^2 + \frac{1}{x^2}\right)^2 = (2)^2$

$\Rightarrow x^4 + \frac{1}{x^4} + 2.x^2.\frac{1}{x^2} = 4 \quad \therefore x^4 + \frac{1}{x^4} + 2 = 4$

$\Rightarrow x^4 + \frac{1}{x^4} = 4 - 2 \quad \therefore x^4 + \frac{1}{x^4} = 2$

EXERCISE

Directions: *Each of the questions given below is followed by four alternatives of which one is correct. The candidates are required to go through the question and the following alternatives carefully and select the correct answer.*

1. *If* $x + \frac{1}{x} = 15$, then the value of $x^2 + \frac{1}{x^2}$ will be:

A. 228 B. 230 C. 323 D. 223

2. If $x = 12$ and $y = 4$, the value of $(x + y)^{x/y}$ will be:

A. 4096 B. 3896 C. 4196 D. 5086

3. If $x = 9$, $y = \sqrt{17}$, then the value of $\left(x^2 - y^2\right)^{-1/2}$ will be:

A. 2^{-4} B. 2^2 C. 3^{-3} D. 2^{-3}

4. What should be added to $\frac{x}{y}$ to get $\frac{y}{x}$?

A. $\frac{x^2 - y^2}{xy}$ B. $\frac{y^2 - x^2}{xy}$ C. $\frac{2xy}{x^2 - y^2}$ D. $\frac{y^2 - x^2}{2xy}$

5. If $x + y = 2z$, then the value of $\left(\frac{x}{x - z} + \frac{z}{y - z}\right)$ will be:

A. 1 B. 4 C. 3/2 D. 2

6. If $x + y + z = 0$, then the value of $\frac{(x + y)(y + z)(z + x)}{xyz}$ will be:

A. –3 B. –2 C. 0 D. –1

7. If $x + \frac{1}{x} = 3$, the value of $x^4 + \frac{1}{x^4}$ will be:

A. 49 B. 47 C. 37 D. 42

8. If $\left(x + \frac{1}{x}\right)^2 = 0$, then the value of $\left(x^2 + \frac{1}{x^2}\right)$ will be:

A. 1 B. –1 C. 2 D. –2

9. If $\left(a+\frac{2}{a}\right) = 3$, then the value of $\left(a-\frac{2}{a}\right)$ will be:

A. ± 4 B. ± 5 C. ± 2 D. ± 1

10. If $\sqrt{a}+\frac{1}{\sqrt{a}} = 4$, then the value of $a^2 + \frac{1}{a^2}$ will be:

A. 194 B. 199 C. 178 D. 192

11. If $x^2 + y^2 + z^2 = 115$ and $xy + yz + zx = 27$, then the value of $x + y + z$ will be:

A. ± 15 B. ± 13 C. ± 17 D. ± 19

12. If $x = 17$, $y = 15$ and $z = 13$, then the value of $x^2 + y^2 + z^2 - 2xy - 2xz - 2yz$ will be:

A. 111 B. 109 C. 121 D. 120

13. If $x + y = 1$, then the value of $x^3 + y^3 + 3xy$ will be:

A. 1 B. 4 C. 3 D. 7

14. What will be the value of $x^3 + y^3 + z^3 - 3xyz$ if $x + y + z = 16$ and $xy + yz + zx = 78$?

A. 352 B. 452 C. 342 D. 360

15. Which of the following is equivalent to $(x^4 + y^4)(x^2 + y^2)(x + y)(x - y)$?

A. $x^8 - y^8$ B. $x^{10} - y^{10}$ C. $x^6 - y^6$ D. $x^{12} - y^{12}$

SOLUTIONS

1. ∵ $x+\frac{1}{x} = 15$

⇒ $\left(x+\frac{1}{x}\right)^2 = (15)^2 \Rightarrow x^2 + \frac{1}{x^2} + 2.x\frac{1}{x} = 225$

∴ $x^2 + \frac{1}{x^2} = 225 - 2 = 223.$

2. $(x+y)^{x/y} = (12+4)^{12/4} = (16)^3 = 4096.$ [∵ $x = 12, y = 4$]

3. $\left(x^2-y^2\right)^{-1/2} = (81-17)^{-1/2} = (64)^{-1/2} = \frac{1}{\sqrt{64}} = \frac{1}{8} = 2^{-3}.$

4. Suppose A is added to $\frac{x}{y}$, then $\frac{x}{y} + A = \frac{y}{x} \Rightarrow A = \frac{y}{x} - \frac{x}{y} = \frac{y^2-x^2}{xy}$

∴ when $\frac{y^2-x^2}{xy}$ is added to $\frac{x}{y}$, the sum so obtained will be $\frac{y}{x}$.

5. ∵ $x + y = 2z \Rightarrow x - z = z - y = -(y - z)$

∴ $\frac{x}{x-z} + \frac{z}{y-z} = \frac{x}{-(y-z)} + \frac{z}{y-z} = \frac{z-x}{y-z} = 1.$ [∵ $x - z = z - y$]

6. ∵ $x + y + z = 0 \Rightarrow x + y = -z$

$x + y + z = 0 \Rightarrow y + z = -x$

and $x + y + z = 0 \Rightarrow z + x = -y$

∴ $\frac{(x+y)(y+z)(z+x)}{xyz} = \frac{-z.-x.-y}{xyz} = -1.$

7. $\because \quad x+\frac{1}{x}=3 \quad \Rightarrow \quad \left(x+\frac{1}{x}\right)^2=(3)^2$

$\Rightarrow \quad x^2+\frac{1}{x^2}+2.x.\frac{1}{x}=9 \quad \Rightarrow x^2+\frac{1}{x^2}=9-2=7$

$\because \quad x^2+\frac{1}{x^2}=7 \quad \Rightarrow \left(x^2+\frac{1}{x^2}\right)^2=(7)^2$

$\Rightarrow x^4+\frac{1}{x^4}+2.x^2.\frac{1}{x^2}=49 \quad \therefore \quad x^4+\frac{1}{x^4}=49-2=47.$

8. $\left(x+\frac{1}{x}\right)^2=0 \quad \Rightarrow x^2+\frac{1}{x^2}+2x.\frac{1}{x}=0$

$\Rightarrow \quad x^2+\frac{1}{x^2}=-2.$

9. $\because \quad \left(a-\frac{2}{a}\right)^2=\left(a+\frac{2}{a}\right)^2-4.a.\frac{2}{a}=(3)^2-8=9-8=1$

$\therefore \quad \left(a-\frac{2}{a}\right)=\pm\sqrt{1}=\pm 1.$

10. $\because \sqrt{a}+\frac{1}{\sqrt{a}}=4 \Rightarrow \left(\sqrt{a}+\frac{1}{\sqrt{a}}\right)^2=(4)^2=a+\frac{1}{a}+2.\sqrt{a}.\frac{1}{\sqrt{a}}=16$

$\because \quad \left(a+\frac{1}{a}\right)=14 \Rightarrow \left(a+\frac{1}{a}\right)^2=(14)^2$

$\Rightarrow a^2+\frac{1}{a^2}+2.a.\frac{1}{a}=196 \therefore a^2+\frac{1}{a^2}=196-2=194.$

11. $\because \quad (x+y+z)^2=x^2+y^2+z^2+2(xy+yz+zx)$

$\therefore \quad (x+y+z)^2=115+2\times 27=115+54=169$

$\therefore \quad (x+y+z)=\sqrt{169}=\pm 13.$

12. The given expression is equivalent to $(x-y-z)^2$

$\therefore \quad (x-y-z)^2=(17-15-13)^2=(-11)^2=121.$

13. $\because \quad (x+y)^3=x^3+y^3+3xy(x+y)$

$\therefore \quad (1)^3=x^3+y^3+3xy\times 1$

$\therefore \quad 1=x^3+y^3+3xy.$

14. $\because \quad (x+y+z)=16 \Rightarrow (x+y+z)^2=(16)^2$

$=x^2+y^2+z^2+2(xy+yz+zx)=256$

$\therefore \quad x^2+y^2+z^2+2\times 78=256 \Rightarrow x^2+y^2+z^2=256-156=100$

$\therefore \quad x^3+y^3+z^3-3xyz=(x+y+z)[(x^2+y^2+z^2)-(xy+yz+zx)]$

$=16[100-78]=16\times 22=352.$

15. $\because \quad (x^4+y^4)(x^2+y^2)(x+y)(x-y)=(x^4+y^4)(x^2+y^2)(x^2-y^2)$

$=(x^4+y^4)(x^4-y^4)$

$=x^8-y^8.$

H.C.F. AND L.C.M. OF ALGEBRAIC EXPRESSIONS

Highest Common Factor (H.C.F.): The H.C.F. of two or more algebraic expressions (Polynomials) is the largest or the highest common divisor, *i.e.*, the greatest expression (polynomial) that exactly divides each of the given polynomials.

Thus we can conclude that H.C.F. of given polynomials is the greatest or the largest among common factors of the given polynomials.

Lowest Common Multiple (L.C.M.): The L.C.M. of two or more given algebraic expressions (polynomials) is the smallest expression that is exactly divisible by each of the given expressions.

Thus we find that LCM of two or more given algebraic expressions is the smallest expression which is a multiple of each of the given expressions.

Relation between Two Algebraic Expressions and their HCF and LCM: "The product of the HCF and the LCM of two algebraic expressions is equal to the product of the given expressions".

i.e., 1st expression × 2nd expression = HCF × LCM.

Example 1: What will be the HCF of $15x^4y^2$, $20x^3y^3$ and $25x^2y^4$

Solution:

$$15x^4y^2 = 3 \times 5 \times x^4 \times y^2$$
$$20x^3y^3 = 2^2 \times 5 \times x^3 \times y^3$$
$$25x^2y^4 = 5^2 \times x^2 \times y^2$$

$\therefore$ HCF $= 5 \times x^2 \times y^2 = 5x^2y^2$.

Example 2: Find HCF of $x^3 + 3x$, $x^2 + 4x + 3$ and $x^2 + 3x + 2$

Solution:

$$x^3 + 3x = x(x^2 + 3)$$
$$x^2 + 4x + 3 = x^2 + 3x + x + 3$$
$$= x(x + 3) + 1(x + 3) = (x + 3)(x + 1)$$

and
$$x^2 + 3x + 2 = x^2 + x + 2x + 2$$
$$= x(x+1) + 2(x+1) = (x + 1)(x + 2)$$

No factor is common to the three given expressions.

In such a case 1 will always be a common factor and HCF of the given expressions.

$\therefore$ Required HCF = 1.

Example 3: Find the LCM of $2xy$, $7xy^2$ and $4x^2y$.

Solution:

$$2xy = 2 \times x \times y$$
$$7xy^2 = 7x \times y^2$$
$$4x^2y = 2^2 \times x^2 \times y$$

$\therefore$ Required LCM $= 2^2 \times x^2 \times y^2 \times 7 = 28x^2y^2$.

Example 4: What will be the LCM of $a^2 - 1$, $a^3 + 1$, $a^3 - 1$ and $a^6 - 1$?

Solution:

$$a^2 - 1 = (a + 1)(a - 1)$$
$$a^3 + 1 = (a + 1)(a^2 - a + 1)$$
$$a^3 - 1 = (a - 1)(a^2 + a + 1)$$
$$a^6 - 1 = (a^3)^2 - 1^2 = (a^3 + 1)(a^3 - 1)$$
$$= (a + 1)(a^2 - a + 1)(a - 1)(a^2 + a + 1)$$

$\therefore$ Required LCM $= (a + 1)(a - 1)(a^2 - a + 1)(a^2 + a + 1)$

$= (a^3 + 1)(a^3 - 1) = a^6 - 1$.

Example 5: The HCF and the LCM of two algebraic expressions are $(x + 3)$ and $(x^3 - 7x + 6)$ respectively. If one of the expressions is $(x^2 + 2x - 3)$, determine the other.

Solution: Required expression $= \dfrac{\text{H.C.F.}\times\text{L.C.M.}}{\text{Known expression}}$

$$= \frac{(x+3)(x^3 - 7x + 6)}{x^2 + 2x - 3}$$

$\because$ $x^3 - 7x + 6 = (x + 3)(x^2 - 3x + 2) = (x + 3)(x - 2)(x - 1)$

and $x^2 + 2x - 3 = (x + 3)(x + 1)$

$\therefore$ Required expression $= \dfrac{(x+3)(x+3)(x-2)(x-1)}{(x+3)(x-1)} = (x + 3)(x - 2) = x^2 + x - 6.$

EXERCISE

Directions: *Each of the questions given below is followed by four alternatives of which one is correct. The candidates are required to go through the question and the following alternatives carefully and select the correct answer.*

1. Find the HCF of x^3y^2, x^2y^3 and x^4y^4.
A. x^3y^4 B. xy C. x^2y^2 D. x^4y^4

2. The LCM of $12x^3b$, $6a^2b^3$ and $4ab^4$ will be:
A. $6a^3b^4$ B. $12a^4b^3$ C. $8a^2b^2$ D. $12a^3b^4$

3. The LCM of $a^2 - b^2$ and $(a - b)$ is:
A. $a^2 - b^2$ B. $(a - b)$ C. $(b - a)$ D. $b^2 - a^2$

4. The LCM of $4xy^4$ and $6x^2y^2$ is:
A. $6xy^2$ B. $12x^2y^4$ C. $6x^2y^2$ D. $2xy$

5. Product of two algebraic expressions is $x^3(a + b + c)$. If their HCF is x^2, find their LCM
A. $x^2(a + b + c)$ B. $x(a + b + c)$ C. $x^3(a + b + c)$ D. x^2

6. What will be the HCF of $(x^2 + x)$, $(x + 1)^3$ and $(x^3 + 1)$?
A. $(x^3 + 1)$ B. $x(x + 1)^3$ C. $(x + 1)$ D. $(1 + x)^3$

7. What is the LCM of $x^2 - 4$ and $x^2 - 5x + 6$?
A. $(x - 2)(x + 2)(x - 3)$ B. $(x - 2)(x + 2)(x + 3)$
C. $(x + 3)(x - 3)(x + 2)$ D. $(x - 2)^2(x - 3)(x + 4)$

8. The HCF of two polynomials is M and their LCM is L. If one of the polynomials is A, determine the other.
A. MA/L B. LA/M C. ML/A D. MLA

9. Find the HCF of $2x^2 - 5x + 3$ and $6x^2 - 5x + 4$
A. $(2x - 3)$ B. 1 C. $(3x + 4)$ D. $(x + 1)(x + 2)$

10. The LCM of $x^3 - y^3$, $x - y$ and $x^2 + xy + y^2$ will be:
A. $(x^2 - y^2)$ B. $(x - y)$ C. $x^3 - y^3$ D. $x(x + y)$

11. The HCF and the LCM of two algebraic expression are $(a - 5)$ and $2a^3 + 3a^2 - 44a - 105$ respectively. If one of the expressions is $2a^2 - 3a - 35$, the other will be:
A. $a^2 - 2a - 15$ B. $a^2 - 3a - 10$ C. $a^2 - 4a + 15$ D. $2a^2 - 5a + 10$

12. Determine the LCM of $x^2 - x - 12$, $2x^2 - 11x + 15$ and $x^2 - 7x + 12$.
A. $(x - 4)(x + 3)(x - 3)(2x - 5)$ B. $(x + 2)(x - 2)(x - 4)(2x - 5)$
C. $(x + 3)(x + 4)(x - 5)$ D. $(x + 3)(x - 4)(x + 5)$

13. The H.C.F. of $x^2 - 9$, $x^3 - 27$ and $x^2 - 7x + 12$ will be:
A. $(x^2 - 9)$ B. $(x - 3)^2$ C. $(x + 3)$ D. $(x - 3)$

14. The H.C.F. of $x^3 - y^3$, $x^4 + x^2y^2 + y^4$ and $x^3y^2 + x^2y^3 + xy^4$ will be:
A. $x^4 + x^2y^2 + y^4$ B. $x^2 + xy + y^2$ C. $x^2 - xy + y^2$ D. $x(x + y)$

15. Determine the H.C.F. of 50 $a^2b^2c^3$, 80 ab^3c^2 and $120a^2b^3c$.
A. $20a^2b^2c^3$ B. $10ab^2c$ C. $80ab^2c$ D. $10ab^2c^2$

SOLUTIONS

1. $x^3y^2 = x^3 \times y^2$
$x^2y^3 = x^2 \times y^3$
and $x^4y^4 = x^4 \times y^4$
$\therefore$ Required HCF $= x^2 \times y^2 = x^2y^2$.

2. $12a^3b = 2^2 \times 3 \times a^3 \times b$
$6a^2b^3 = 2 \times 3 \times a^2 \times b^3$
$4ab^4 = 2^2 \times a \times b^4$
$\therefore$ Required LCM $= 2^2 \times 3 \times a^3 \times b^4 = 12a^3b^4$.

3. $\because$ $a^2 - b^2 = (a + b)(a - b)$
$a - b = (a - b)$
$\therefore$ Required LCM $= (a + b)(a - b) = a^2 - b^2$.

4. $4xy^4 = 2^2 \times x \times y^4$
$6x^2y^2 = 2 \times 3 \times x^2 \times y^2$
$\therefore$ Required LCM $= 2^2 \times 3 \times x^2 \times y^4 = 12x^2y^4$.

5. Required LCM $= \dfrac{\text{Product of the two expressions}}{\text{Their H.C.F.}}$

$$= \frac{x^3(a+b+c)}{x^2} = x(a + b + c).$$

6. $x^2 + x = x(x + 1)$.
$(x + 1)^3 = (x + 1) \times (x + 1) \times (x + 1)$
and $x^3 + 1 = (x)^3 + (1)^3 = (x + 1)(x^2 - x + 1)$
Required H.C.F. $= (x + 1)$.

7. $x^2 - 4 = (x)^2 - (2)^2 = (x + 2)(x - 2)$
$x^2 - 5x + 6 = x^2 - 3x - 2x + 6 = x(x - 3) - 2(x - 3)$
$= (x - 3)(x - 2)$
$\therefore$ Required LCM $= (x - 2)(x + 2)(x - 3)$.

8. Required expression $= \dfrac{\text{H.C.F.} \times \text{L.C.M.}}{\text{Known expression}} = \dfrac{\text{M} \times \text{L}}{\text{A}} = \dfrac{\text{ML}}{\text{A}}$

9. $2x^2 - 5x + 3 = 2x^2 - 2x - 3x + 3$
$= 2x(x - 1) - 3(x - 1) = (x - 1)(2x - 3)$

and $6x^2 - 5x - 4 = 6x^2 - 8x + 3x - 4$
$= 2x(3x - 4) + 1(3x - 4) = (3x - 4)(2x + 1)$

Since no factor is common to two given expressions, 1 will always be a common factor.
∴ HCF of the given expressions = 1.

10. $x^3 - y^3 = (x - y)(x^2 + xy + y^2)$
$x - y = (x - y)$
$x^2 + xy + y^2 = (x^2 + xy + y^2)$
∴ Required LCM $= (x - y)(x^2 + xy + y^2) = x^3 - y^3$

11. Required expression $= \dfrac{\text{H.C.F.} \times \text{L.C.M.}}{\text{Known expression}}$

$$= \frac{(a-5)(2a^3 + 3a^2 - 44a - 105)}{2a^2 - 3a - 35}$$

$$= \frac{(a-5)(a+3)(2a^2 - 3a - 35)}{2a^2 - 3a - 35}$$

$= (a - 5)(a + 3) = a^2 - 2a - 15.$

12. $x^2 - x - 12 = x^2 - 4x + 3x - 12$
$= x(x - 4) + 3(x - 4) = (x - 4)(x + 3)$
$2x^2 - 11x + 15 = 2x^2 - 6x - 5x + 15$
$= 2x(x - 3) - 5(x - 3)$
$= (x - 3)(2x - 5)$
and $x^2 - 7x + 12 = x^2 - 4x - 3x + 12$
$= x(x - 4) - 3(x - 4)$
$= (x - 4)(x - 3)$
∴ Required LCM $= (x - 4)(x + 3)(x - 3)(2x - 5).$

13. $x^2 - 9 = x^2 - 3^2 = (x + 3)(x - 3)$
$x^3 - 27 = x^3 - 3^3 = (x - 3)(x^2 + 3x + 9)$
and $x^2 - 7x + 12 = x^2 - 4x - 3x + 12$
$= x(x - 4) - 3(x - 4) = (x - 4)(x - 3)$
∴ Required HCF $= (x - 3).$

14. $x^3 - y^3 = (x - y)(x^2 + xy + y^2)$
$x^4 + x^2y^2 + y^4 = x^4 + 2x^2y^2 + y^4 - x^2y^2$
$= (x^2 + y^2)^2 - (xy)^2 = (x^2 + xy + y^2)(x^2 - xy + y^2)$
and $x^3y^2 + x^2y^3 + xy^4 = xy^2(x^2 + xy + y^2)$
∴ Required HCF $= (x^2 + xy + y^2).$

15. $50a^2b^2c^3 = 5^2 \times 2 \times a^2 \times b^2 \times c^3$
$80ab^3c^2 = 5 \times 2^4 \times a \times b^3 \times c^2$
$120a^2b^3c = 3 \times 5 \times 2^3 \times a^2 \times b^3 \times c$
∴ Required HCF $= 5 \times 2 \times a \times b^2 \times c = 10ab^2c.$

21 PERCENTAGE

The word 'per cent' or 'percentage' means 'for every one hundred'. In other words, it gives an indication of rate per hundred. It is denoted by the symbol %.

For example, 5% means 5 out of one hundred or $\frac{5}{100}$.

Remember :

(i) For converting a per cent into a fraction, divide it by 100.

(ii) For converting a fraction into a per cent, multiply it by 100.

(iii) For converting a per cent into a decimal, shift the decimal point two places to the left.

(iv) For converting one given quantity (*x*) as a percentage of another given quantity (*y*), find $\frac{x}{y} \times 100$.

(v) There is no unit of percentage.

Important Facts:

For quickly solving the problems related to percentage, remember following rules:

Rule 1:

(a) Of the given two numbers if the first is *x*% more than the second, then the second will be $\left(\frac{100 \times x}{100 + x}\right)\%$ less than the first.

(b) Of the given two numbers if the first is *x*% less than the second, then the second will be $\left(\frac{100 \times x}{100 - x}\right)\%$ more than the first.

(c) If two numbers are respectively *x*% and *y*% more than a third number, then the first number will be $\left(\frac{100 + x}{100 + y} \times 100\right)\%$ of the second.

(d) If two numbers are respectively *x*% and *y*% less than a third number, then the first number will be $\left(\frac{100 - x}{100 - y} \times 100\right)\%$ of the second.

Example 1 :

(i) A's income is 150% more than B's income. By how much per cent is B's income less than A's income?

(ii) Tarun's income is 40% less than Gulshan's income. By how much per cent is Gulshan's income more than Tarun's?

(iii) Two numbers are respectively 20% and 10% more than a third number. What per cent is the first of the second and by how much per cent is the first number more than the second?

(iv) If the given two numbers are respectively 40% and 50% less than a third number, then what per cent is the first of the second?

Solution : *(i)* Here, A's income is 150% more than B's income, *i.e.*, $x = 150$

$\therefore$ B's income will be $\left(\dfrac{100\times150}{100+150}\right)\%$ less than A's income, $\left(\dfrac{100\times150}{100+150}\right)\% = \dfrac{100\times150}{250}\% = 60\%$

(ii) Since Tarun's income is 40% less than Gulshan's income, *i.e.*, $x = 40$

$\therefore$ Gulshan's income more than Tarun's income $= \dfrac{100\times40}{100-40}\%$

$$= \frac{100\times40}{60}\% = 66\frac{2}{3}\%$$

(iii) The two numbers exceed the third number by 20% and 10% respectively.

$\therefore \quad x = 20,\ y = 10$

$\therefore$ First number will be $\left[\dfrac{(100+20)}{(100+10)}\times100\right]\% = \left[\dfrac{120}{110}\times100\right]\%$

$$= 109\frac{1}{11}\% \text{ of the second number.}$$

$\therefore$ First number will be $109\dfrac{1}{11}\% - 100\% = 9\dfrac{1}{11}\%$ more than the second number.

(iv) Here the 1st number is 40% less and the 2nd number is 50% less than the third number

$\therefore \quad x = 40$ and $y = 50$

Therefore, the first number will be $\left[\dfrac{(100-40)}{(100-50)}\times100\right]\% = \dfrac{60}{50}\times100\%$

$$= 120\% \text{ of the second number.}$$

> **Rule 2 :**
>
> *(a)* If a number or quantity is increased by x% then in order to restore its original value it must be decreased by $\left[\dfrac{100\times x}{100+x}\right]\%$.
>
> *(b)* If a number or quantity is decreased by x% then in order to restore its original value it must be increased by $\left[\dfrac{100\times x}{100-x}\right]\%$.

Example 2 :

(i) The price of a book was increased by 20%. By how much per cent the new price of this book must be decreased to restore its original price?

(ii) If the price of sugar be raised by 25%, find by how much per cent consumption of sugar should be reduced by a housewife so that the expenditure on it may not increase.

(iii) If the price of mangoes goes down by 10%, find the percentage of increase that a family should effect in its consumption so as not to alter expenditure on this account.

(iv) A reduction of 20% in the price of sugar enables a purchaser to buy 2 kg more for Rs 80. Find the price of sugar before reduction.

Solution: *(i)* Percentage increase = 20%

∴ To restore the original price, the new price of the book should be decreased by

$$= \left(\frac{100 \times 20}{100 + 20}\right)\% = \frac{100 \times 20}{120}\% = 16\frac{2}{3}\%$$

(ii) Percentage increase = 25%

To retain the previous expenditure level, consumption of sugar should be reduced by $= \left(\frac{100 \times 25}{100 + 25}\right)\%$

$$= \frac{100 \times 25}{125}\% = 20\%$$

(iii) Percentage decrease in price of mangoes = 10%

To retain the previous expenditure level, consumption of mangoes should be increased by

$$= \left(\frac{100 \times 10}{100 - 10}\right)\% = \frac{100 \times 10}{90}\% = 11\frac{1}{9}\%$$

(iv) Due to reduction in price, Rs. 16 is saved on purchasing the same amount of sugar.

∴ After reduction in price, for Rs. 16 the purchaser buys 2 kg of sugar.

∴ Reduced price of sugar = Rs. 8 per kg

$$\text{Original price} = \frac{100}{(100 - 20)} \times 8 = \frac{100}{80} \times 8 = \text{Rs. 10 per kg}$$

Rule 3 :

(a) If a number is successively increased by $x\%$ and $y\%$ then a single equivalent increase in that number will be $\left(x + y + \frac{xy}{100}\right)\%$

(b) If two successive discounts of $x\%$ and $y\%$ are allowed on a particular amount, then a single discount that is equivalent to the two successive discounts will be $\left(x + y - \frac{xy}{100}\right)\%$

(c) If a number is successively increased by $x\%$, $y\%$ and $z\%$, then a single equivalent increase in that number will be

$$\left[(x + y + z) + \left(\frac{xy + yz + zx}{100}\right) + \frac{(xyz)}{10000}\right]\%$$

(d) If three successive discounts of $x\%$, $y\%$ and $z\%$ are allowed on an amount, then a single discount that is equivalent to the three successive discounts will be

$$\left[x + y + z - \frac{(xy + yz + zx)}{100} + \frac{xyz}{10000}\right]\%$$

Example 3 :

(i) A shopkeeper allows two successive discounts of 30% and 20%. Find a single discount equivalent to these two discounts.

(ii) Find a single equivalent increase in a number that is equivalent to two successive increments of 20% and 10% respectively.

(iii) Two shopkeepers sell a radio of similar brand and type at the same list price Rs. 800. The first allows two successive discounts of 20% and 10% and the second allows the successive discounts of 15% and 15%. Find the difference in discounts offered by the two shopkeepers.

(iv) Find a single discount equivalent to a discount series of 20%, 10% and 5%.

(v) The list price of an article is Rs. 1200. If the dealer allows three successive discounts of 10%, 8% and 5%, find its net selling price.

Solution : (i) ∵ Two successive discounts are 30% and 20%

$$\therefore \text{ Equivalent discount} = \left(30+20-\frac{30\times 20}{100}\right)\% = (50-6)\% = 44\%$$

(ii) ∵ Successive increments = 20% and 10%

$$\therefore \text{ Equivalent increase} = \left(20+10+\frac{20\times 10}{100}\right)\% = (30+2)\% = 32\%$$

$$\text{(iii) Equivalent discount on the radio} = \left(20+10-\frac{20\times 10}{100}\right)\% = (30-2)\% = 28\%$$

$$\therefore \text{ Discount on the list price of radio} = 28\% \text{ of Rs. } 800 = \frac{28\times 800}{100} = \text{Rs. } 224$$

For the Second Shopkeeper :

$$\text{Discount equivalent to the two discounts} = \left(15+15-\frac{15\times 15}{100}\right)\% = (30-2.25)\% = 27.75\%$$

∴ Discount on the list price of radio = 27.75% of Rs. 800

$$= \frac{27.75}{100}\times 800 = \text{Rs. } 222$$

∴ Difference between discounts offered by the two shopkeepers

= Rs. 224 – Rs. 222 = Rs. 2

(iv) The discount series is 20%, 10% and 5%

∴ Equivalent discount

$$= \left(20+10+5-\frac{(20\times 10+10\times 5+5\times 20)}{100}+\frac{20\times 10\times 5}{10000}\right)\%$$

$$= \left(35-\frac{200+50+100}{100}+\frac{1000}{10000}\right)\%$$

$$= \left(35-\frac{350}{100}+\frac{1}{10}\right)\% = (35-3.5+.1)\% = 31.6\%$$

Rule 4 :

(a) If a number is increased by $x\%$ and thereafter reduced by $x\%$, then the number will be reduced by $\left(\frac{x^2}{100}\right)$ per cent.

(b) If a number is reduced by $x\%$ and thereafter increased by $x\%$ then the number will be reduced by $\left(\frac{x^2}{100}\right)$ per cent.

(c) If due to an increase of $x\%$ in the selling price of certain commodity the sell/consumption of the commodity decreases by $y\%$, then gross receipts on account of sale of that commodity will be increased or decreased by $\left(x-y-\frac{xy}{100}\right)\%$, where $x > y$ and will be decreased by $\left(y-x+\frac{xy}{100}\right)\%$, where $y > x$.

Example 4 :

(i) If a number is increased by 10% and thereafter decreased by 10%, then by how much per cent the number has been increased or decreased?

(ii) After 20% in the tax of a commodity, its consumption gets reduced by 30%. Find out the percentage increase or decrease in the income from tax.

(iii) Due to reduction of 20% in the price of sugar a housewife increases her amount of sugar consumption by 20%. What will be the percentage change in her expenditure on this account?

(iv) When the price of radio set was increased by 15%, the number of sets sold reduced by 20%. What was the effect on gross receipts of the shop?

(v) Owing to a reduction of 25% in the selling price of a commodity, its sale was increased by 30%. What was the effect on gross receipts?

Solution : *(i)* ∵ The number is first increased by 10% and later the new number is decreased by 10%

∴ Percentage decrease in the number $= \left(\frac{(10)^2}{100}\right)\% = 1\%$

(ii) Here, $x = 20\%$ and $y = 30\%$

∵ $y > x$

∴ Percentage decrease in the income from tax $= \left(y-x+\frac{xy}{100}\right)\%$

$$= \left(30-20+\frac{20\times 30}{100}\right)\%$$

$$= \left(10+\frac{600}{100}\right) = (10+6)\% = 16\%.$$

(iii) If percentage decrease or percentage increase in price of a commodity is equal to percentage increase or percentage decrease in consumption of the commodity, then the cash receipt from the sale of that commodity or expenditure on consumption of that commodity always goes down.

∴ Percentage decrease in expenditure of that housewife = $\left(\frac{20\times20}{100}\right)\%$ = 4%

(∵ in both cases x = 20)

(iv) ∵ Percentage decrease is more than the percentage increase

∴ Cash receipt will decrease.

percentage decrease = 20% and percentage increase = 15%

∴ Percentage decrease in cash receipt = $\left(y-x+\frac{xy}{100}\right)\%$

$= \left(20-15+\frac{20\times15}{100}\right)\% = (5 + 3)\% = 8\%$

(v) ∵ Percentage increase is more than the percentage decrease

∴ Cash receipt from sale will increase

∵ Percentage increase = 30% and percentage decrease = 25%

∴ Percentage increase or decrease in cash reciept from sale = $\left(y-x-\frac{xy}{100}\right)\%$

$= \left(30-25-\frac{30\times25}{100}\right)\% = (5 - 7.5)\% = -2.5\%$

Minus sign (–) indicates percentage decrease in cash receipt.

∴ Percentage decrease in cash receipt from sale will be 2.5%.

Example 5: Find $6\frac{1}{4}\%$ of Rs. 1600

Solution: $6\frac{1}{4}\%$ of Rs. 1600 = $\frac{25}{4\times100}\times1600$ = Rs. 100.

Example 6: What fraction is equivalent to $8\frac{1}{3}\%$?

Solution: $8\frac{1}{3}\% = \frac{25}{3}\times\frac{1}{100} = \frac{1}{12}$

Example 7: What percentage is equivalent to $\frac{2}{25}$?

Solution: $\frac{2}{25}\times100 = 8\%$

Example 8: Find how much per cent is 40 of 100.

Solution: $\frac{40}{100}\times100 = 40\%$

Example 9: The population of a town has increased from 20000 to 24000. Find the increase per cent.

Solution: Increase in population = 24000 – 20000 = 4000

∴Percentage increase = $\frac{4000}{20000}\times100 = 20\%$

Example 10: The population of a town is 45000. $\frac{11}{18}$th of them are males and the rest females, 40% of the females are married. Find the number of married males.

Solution: Number of males = $\frac{11}{18} \times 45000 = 27500$

$\therefore$No. of females = 45000 – 27500 = 17500

Thus, No. of married females = 40% of 17500 = 7000

$\Rightarrow$ The number of married males = 7000

Example 11: The population of a town is 40,000. If the population increases 20% every year, find the population after 3 years.

Solution: Population after 3 years = $40000\left(1+\frac{20}{100}\right)^3 = 40000 \times \frac{6}{5} \times \frac{6}{5} \times \frac{6}{5} = 69120$

Example 12: The population of a town is 40000. During first year the population increased by 25%. During second year the population increased by 20%. During the third year the population increased by 10%. Find the population after 3 years.

Solution: The population after 3 years = $40000\left(1+\frac{25}{100}\right)\left(1+\frac{20}{100}\right)\left(1+\frac{10}{100}\right) = 40000 \times \frac{5}{4} \times \frac{6}{5} \times \frac{11}{10} = 66000$

Example 13: The population of a town increased by 5% every year. If the present population is 18522. Find the population 3 years ago.

Solution: Population 3 years ago = $\frac{18522}{\left(1+\frac{5}{100}\right)^3} = 18522 \times \frac{20}{21} \times \frac{20}{21} \times \frac{20}{21} = 16000$

Example 14 : The population of a town during the year 2006 was 80000. During the year 2007 the population was 25% more than the previous year and 20% less than the following year. Find the population of the town during the year 2008.

Solution: Population during 2006 = 80000

Population during 2007 is 25% more than the population during 2006.

$\therefore$ Population during 2007 = $80000 \times \frac{125}{100} = 100000$

The population during 2008 = $\frac{100}{80} \times 100000 = 125000$

Example 15: The population of a town increases 4% annually but is decreased by emigration annually to the extent of $\frac{1}{2}$%, what will be the increase per cent in three years?

Solution: Increase in 3 year over 100 = $100 \times \left(1+\frac{7}{2 \times 100}\right)^3 = 100 \times \frac{207}{200} \times \frac{207}{200} \times \frac{207}{200} = \frac{(200+7)^3}{80000}$

$= \frac{(200)^3 + (7)^3 + 4200(200+7)}{80000} = \frac{8869743}{80000} = 110.8718$ $\therefore$ Increase%= 10.8%

Example 16 : In an examination 60% of the candidates passed in English, 55% in Mathematics and 25% failed in both subjects. Find the pass percentage.

Solution: Those failing in mathematics = 100 – 55 = 45%

Those failing in English = 100 – 60 = 40%

Failing in both = 25%

Failing in one or both the subjects = (45 + 40 – 25) = 60%

$\therefore$ Pass % = 100 – 60 = 40%

Example 17: A candidate must get 33% marks to pass. He gets 220 marks and fails by 11 marks. What is the maximum number of marks?

Solution: Let the maximum number of marks be x.

Then, 33% of x = 220 + 11 = 231

$$\Rightarrow \quad x = 231 \times \frac{100}{33} = 700$$

Example 18: Out of a class of 40 girls, 5 were absent and 20% of the remaining failed to do the homework. How many girls who did the homework?

Solution: No. of girls present = 40 – 5 = 35

No. of girls who did not do home work = 20% of 35 = 7

$\therefore$No. of girls who did their home work = 35 – 7 = 28

Example 19: In an examination a candidate who secured 25% marks failed by 60 marks and another candidate who secured 42% marks got 8 marks more than were necessary to pass. What is the total number of marks and the percentage of marks required to pass?

Solution: Let total number of marks = x, then

$$\frac{25}{100} \times x + 60 = \frac{42}{100} - 8 \;\Rightarrow\; \frac{17x}{100} = 68 \quad \therefore \; x = \frac{68 \times 100}{17} = 400$$

$$\text{Now, marks required to pass} = \frac{25}{100} \times 400 + 60 = 160$$

$$\text{Hence, percentage of marks required to pass} = \frac{160}{400} \times 100 = 40\%$$

Example 20: What is the total number of candidates at an examination if 31% fail and the number of those who pass exceeds the numbers of those fail by 247?

Solution: By question, 69% of x – 31% of x = 247

$$\Rightarrow 38\% \text{ of } x = 247 \Rightarrow x = \frac{247 \times 100}{38} = 650$$

Example 21: In an examination 40% students failed in Mathematics, 35% failed in Sanskrit and 15% failed in both the subjects. The number of students passing in both the subjects is 170. Find the total number of students appearing in the examination.

Solution: Failing in one or both the subjects = 40 + 35 – 15 = 60%

$\therefore$ Pass% = 100 – 60 = 40%

Now, 40% = 170

$$\therefore \; 100\% = \frac{170}{40} \times 100 = 425$$

Hence, total numbers of students = 425

Example 22: In an examination, 40% marks are required to pass. A obtains 10% less than the number of marks required to pass. B obtains $11\frac{1}{9}\%$ less than A and C $41\frac{3}{17}\%$ less than the number of marks obtained by A and B together. Does C pass or fail?

Solution: Let the maximum marks = 100

Marks required to pass = 40

Marks secured by A = $40 \times \frac{90}{100} = 36$

Marks secured by B $= 36 \times \frac{\left(100 - 11\frac{1}{9}\right)}{100} = \frac{36 \times 800}{9 \times 100} = 32$ marks

$\therefore$ Total marks obtained by A and B = 36 + 32 = 68

$\therefore$ C's marks $= 68 \times \frac{100 - 41\frac{3}{17}}{100} = \frac{68 \times 1000}{17 \times 100} = 40$ marks,

Hence, C gets required marks to pass.

Example 23: Atul's marks in Science are 20 less than 60% of the total marks obtained by him in Science and Maths together. If his total marks are 250, what are his marks in Maths?

Solution: Marks obtained in Science = 60% of 250 – 20 = $\frac{60}{100} \times 250 - 20 = 130$

$\therefore$ Marks obtained in Maths = 250 – 130 = 120

Example 24: If the numerator of a fraction be increased by 15% and its denominator be diminished by 8%, the value of the fraction is $\frac{15}{16}$. Find the original fraction.

Solution: Let numerator be x and denominator be y.

Then, by question, $\frac{115\% x}{92\% y} = \frac{15}{16}$

$\Rightarrow \frac{x}{y} = \frac{15}{16} \times \frac{92}{115} = \frac{3}{4}$

Example 25: If the duty on an article be reduced by 40% of its price, by how much per cent the consumption of that article increase so that the revenue may be increased by 10%.

Solution: Consumption after the tax is reduced $= \frac{\text{Revenue}}{\text{tax}} = \frac{110}{60\%} = \frac{110 \times 100}{60} = 183\frac{1}{3}$

Hence, percentage increase of consumption = $83\frac{1}{3}\%$

Example 26: If the price of tea be increased by 20%, find by how much per cent a house-holder must reduce his consumption of tea so as not to increase his expenditure?

Solution: Reduction in consumption $= \frac{20}{120} \times 100 = 16\frac{2}{3}\%$

Example 27: If petrol price is reduced by 10%, find by how much a user must increase the consumption of petrol so as not to decrease his expenditure on petrol.

Solution: Increase in petrol = $\frac{10}{100-10}\times 100 = 11\frac{1}{9}\%$

Example 28: The price of milk increases by 25%. If a housewife wants to spend on milk the same amount of money as before, how much per cent less milk she must get?

Solution: Required less per cent of milk = $\frac{25}{(100+25)}\times 100 = 20\%$

Example 29: A reduction of 20% in the price of oranges enables a man to buy 5 oranges more for Rs. 10, what is the price of an orange before reduction?

Solution: Owing to reduction in price of oranges, there is a saving of 20% on Rs. 10 *i.e.,* $\frac{20}{100}\times 10$ = Rs. 2

Reduced price of 1 orange = $\frac{200}{5} = 40$ paise

The original price = $\frac{100}{80}\times 40 = 50$ paise per orange.

Example 30: A's income is $37\frac{1}{2}\%$ less than B's. How much per cent B's income is more than A's.

Solution: Required percentage = $\dfrac{100\times\frac{75}{2}}{100-75/2} = \frac{100\times 75}{125} = 60\%$

Example 31: A man lost $12\frac{1}{2}\%$ of his salary and spent $66\frac{2}{3}\%$ of the remaining and still had Rs. 700. Find his original salary.

Solution: Let his original salary be Rs. x, then

$$\frac{100-25/2}{100}x-\frac{200}{3\times 100}\times\frac{100-25/2}{100}x = 700$$

$$\Rightarrow \frac{175}{2\times 200}x-\frac{2}{3}\times\frac{175}{2\times 100}x = 700 \Rightarrow \frac{7}{8}x-\frac{7}{12}x = 700$$

$$\Rightarrow \frac{7x}{24} = 700 \qquad \therefore x = \frac{24\times 700}{7} = \text{Rs. } 2400$$

Example 32: There are two equal numbers, one increased by $66\frac{2}{3}\%$ and second is decreased by $66\frac{2}{3}\%$. What per cent is the second number less than that of first?

Solution: Let the number be 100

Required percentage = $\dfrac{\frac{200}{3}+\frac{200}{3}}{100+\frac{200}{3}}\times 100 = \frac{400}{500}\times 100 = 80\%$

Example 33: A reduction of 20% in the price of oranges enables a purchaser to obtain 8 oranges more for Rs. 4. Find the reduced price as well as the original price per dozen.

Solution: Saving of 20% on Rs. 4 = $\frac{20}{100} \times 4$ = Re. 0.80 with Re 0.80 he buys 8 oranges.

Thus, the reduced price of oranges per dozen = $0.80 \times \frac{12}{8}$ = Rs. 1.20

The original price per dozen = $\frac{1.20 \times 100}{80}$ = Rs. 1.50

Example 34: Mohan spends 40% of his salary on food items, 50% of the remaining on transport, 30% of the remaining, after spending on food and transport, he spends on clothes and saves the balance. If he saves Rs. 630 every month, what is his monthly salary?

Sol: Let monthly salary be Rs. x

Expenditure on food items = 40% of $x = \frac{2}{5}x$

$\therefore$ Remaining amount = $x - \frac{2}{5}x = \frac{3}{5}x$

Expenditure on transport = 50% of $\frac{3}{5}x = \frac{3}{10}x$

$\therefore$Remaining amount = $\frac{3}{5}x - \frac{3}{10}x = \frac{3x}{10}$

$\therefore$ Expenditure on clothes = 30% of $\frac{3x}{10} = \frac{9x}{100}$

$\therefore$ Remaining amount = $\frac{3x}{10} - \frac{9x}{100} = \frac{21x}{100}$

$\therefore \frac{21x}{100} = 630 \Rightarrow x = \frac{630 \times 100}{21}$ = Rs. 3000

Example 35: 60% of the length of a pole is painted red, 40% of the rest is painted green and 50% of the balance is painted blue. The remaining unpainted length of the pole is 30 cm. Find the length of pole.

Solution: Suppose the total length = 100 m
Since painted red = 60 m
$\therefore$ Balance = 100 – 60 = 40 m

Painted green = $\frac{40}{100} \times 40$ = 16 m

$\therefore$ Balance = 40 – 16 = 24 m

Painted blue= $\frac{50}{100} \times 24$ = 12 m

$\therefore$ Balance = 24 – 12 = 12 m

If balance is 12 m, total length = 100 m

If balance is $\frac{30}{100}$m, total length = $\left(\frac{100}{12} \times \frac{30}{100}\right)$m = 2.5 m

Example 36: A jar full of whisky contains 40% of alcohol. A part of this whisky is replaced by another containing 19% alcohol and now the percentage of alcohol was found to be 26. Find the part of whisky replaced.

Solution: Since Alcohol in first mix = 40 litres and water in it = 60 litres

Let x litres be replaced.

Alcohol in $(100 - x)$ litres $= \dfrac{40}{100}(100-x)$ litres

Alcohol in new x litres $= \left(\dfrac{19}{100}x\right)$

$$\therefore \quad \frac{40}{100}(100-x)+\frac{19x}{100} = 26$$

$$\Rightarrow 4000 - 40x + 19x = 2600$$

$$\Rightarrow x = \frac{1400}{21} = \frac{200}{3}$$

$$\therefore \text{ Part replaced} = \frac{x}{100} = \frac{200}{3\times 100} = \frac{2}{3}$$

Example 37: Two numbers are 20% and 50% more than a third number respectively. What percentage is the first of the second?

Solution: Let third number be x

Then,first number $= \dfrac{120}{100}x = \dfrac{6x}{5}$

andsecond number $= \dfrac{150}{100}x = \dfrac{3x}{2}$

$$\therefore \text{ Required percentage} = \left(\frac{\frac{6x}{5}}{\frac{3x}{2}}\times 100\right)\% = \left(\frac{6x}{5}\times\frac{2}{3x}\times 100\right)\% = 80\%$$

EXERCISE

1. If x is 90% of y, then what per cent of x is y?

(a) 90 (b) 190 (c) 101.1 (d) 111.1

2. A number exceeds 20% of itself by 40. The number is :

(a) 50 (b) 60 (c) 80 (d) 320

3. The price of an article is cut by 10%. To restore it to the former value, the new price must be increased by :

(a) 10% (b) $9\frac{1}{11}\%$ (c) $11\frac{1}{9}\%$ (d) 11%

4. The income of a broker remains unchanged though the rate of commission is increased from 4% to 5%. The percentage of slump business is :

(a) 8% (b) 1% (c) 20% (d) 80%

5. 5% income of A is equal to 15% income of B and 10% income of B is equal to 20% income of C. If income of C is Rs. 2000, then total income of A, B and C is :

(a) Rs. 6000 (b) Rs. 18000 (c) Rs. 20000 (d) Rs. 14000

6. A student who secures 20% marks in an examination fails by 30 marks. Another student who secures 32% gets 42 marks more than those required to pass. The percentage of marks required to pass is:
(a) 20 (b) 25 (c) 28 (d) 30

7. In a college election, a candidate secured 62% of the votes and is elected by a majority of 144 votes. The total number of votes polled is :
(a) 600 (b) 800 (c) 925 (d) 1200

8. What will be 80% of a number whose 200% is 90?
(a) 144 (b) 72 (c) 36 (d) None of these

9. p is six times as large as q. The per cent that q is less than p, is :
(a) $83\frac{1}{3}$ (b) $16\frac{2}{3}$ (c) 90 (d) 60

10. The price of an article has been reduced by 25%. In order to restore the original price, the new price must be increased by :
(a) $33\frac{1}{3}\%$ (b) $11\frac{1}{9}\%$ (c) $9\frac{1}{11}\%$ (d) $66\frac{2}{3}\%$

11. The price of cooking oil has increased by 25%. The percentage of reduction that a family should effect in the use of cooking oil so as not to increase the expenditure on this account is :
(a) 25% (b) 30% (c) 20% (d) 15%

12. In an organisation, 40% of the employees are matriculates, 50% of the remaining are graduates and the remaining 180 are postgraduates. How many employees are graduates?
(a) 360 (b) 240 (c) 300 (d) 180

13. In 40% of the people read newspaper X, 50% read newspaper Y, and 10% read both the papers. What percentage of the people read neither newspaper?
(a) 10% (b) 15% (c) 20% (d) 25%

14. The population of a town increases by 5% annually. If its population in 2008 was 138915, what it was in 2005?
(a) 110000 (b) 100000 (c) 120000 (d) 90000

15. The population of a village is 4500. $\frac{5}{9}$th of them are males and rest females. If 40% of the males are married, then the percentage of married female is :
(a) 35 (b) 40 (c) 50 (d) 60

16. A's income is 10% more than B's. How much per cent is B's income is less than A's?
(a) 10% (b) 7% (c) $9\frac{1}{11}\%$ (d) $6\frac{1}{2}\%$

17. A mixture of 40 litres of milk and water contains 10% water. How much water must be added to make water 20% in the new mixture?
(a) 10 litres (b) 7 litres (c) 5 litres (d) 3 litres

18. If $z = \frac{x^2}{y}$ and x, y both are increased in value by 10%, then the value of z is :
(a) unchanged (b) increased by 10% (c) increased by 11% (d) increased by 20%

19. In an examination, 35% of the examinees failed in G.K. and 25% in English. If 10% of the examinees failed in both, then the percentage of examinees passed will be:
(a) 40% (b) 45% (c) 48% (d) 50%

20. If the price of a television set is increased by 25%, then by what percentage should the new price be reduced to bring the price back to original level?
(*a*) 15% (*b*) 20% (*c*) 25% (*d*) 30%

21. The number of grams of water needed to reduce 9 grams of shaving lotion containing 50% alcohol to a lotion containing 30% alcohol, is :
(*a*) 4 (*b*) 5 (*c*) 6 (*d*) 7

22. A candidate needs 35% marks to pass. If he gets 96 marks and fails by 16 marks, then the maximum marks are :
(*a*) 250 (*b*) 320 (*c*) 300 (*d*) 425

23. In an election one of the two candidates gets 40% votes and loses by 100 votes. Total number of votes is :
(*a*) 500 (*b*) 400 (*c*) 600 (*d*) 1000

24. If the income tax is decreased by 26%, a man's net income increases by $\frac{2}{3}$%. The rate of income tax is:
(*a*) $3\frac{1}{2}$% (*b*) $2\frac{1}{2}$% (*c*) $1\frac{1}{2}$% (*d*) 3%

25. The gross income of a person is Rs. 20000. 10% of his income is exempted from income tax and his net income is Rs. 19100. The rate of income tax is :
(*a*) 3% (*b*) 2% (*c*) 4% (*d*) 5%

26. If the rate of income tax is 5%, the net income of a person is Rs. 17100. If the rate of income tax is 6%, how much will be the net income?
(*a*) 15820 (*b*) 16920 (*c*) 17820 (*d*) 18920

27. The gross income of a person is Rs. 15000, 20% of his income is exempted from income tax and the rate of income tax is Rs. 4%. The net income is :
(*a*) 14520 (*b*) 14620 (*c*) 15520 (*d*) 15620

28. The gross income of a person is Rs. 16000. A part of his income is exempted from income tax and his net income is Rs. 14480. If the rate of income tax is 8%, the income exempted from income tax is :
(*a*) 1600 (*b*) 1700 (*c*) 1800 (*d*) 1500

29. One-eight of a number is 17.25. What will 73% of number be?
(*a*) 82.66 (*b*) 96.42 (*c*) 100.74 (*d*) 138.00

30. If 58% of 960 – x% of 635 = 277.4, find the value of x.
(*a*) 24 (*b*) 36 (*c*) 44 (*d*) 58

31. There are 1225 employees in an organisation, out of which 40% got transferred to different places. How many such employees got transferred?
(*a*) 490 (*b*) 540 (*c*) 630 (*d*) 710

32. In an examination it is required to get 270 of the aggregate marks to pass. A student gets 216 marks and is declared failed by 8% marks. What are the maximum aggregate marks a student can get?
(*a*) 650 (*b*) 675 (*c*) 750 (*d*) 825

33. 56% of a number is 1064. What is 38% of the number?
(*a*) 666 (*b*) 722 (*c*) 856 (*d*) 912

34. The owner of a cell phone shop charges his customer 32% more than the cost price. If a customer paid Rs. 6600 for the cell phone, then what was the cost price of the cell phone?
(*a*) Rs. 5000 (*b*) Rs. 5500 (*c*) Rs. 5800 (*d*) Rs. 6100

35. The difference between 89% of a number and 73% of the same number is 448. What is 49% of that number?
(*a*) 1124 (*b*) 1218 (*c*) 1372 (*d*) 1426

36. Nupur invests Rs. 89856, what is 26% of her annual income in mutual funds. What is her monthly income?
(*a*) Rs. 23980.50 (*b*) Rs. 28800 (*c*) Rs. 28990 (*d*) Rs. 33606.25

37. A fan is listed at Rs. 1400 and discount offered is 10%. What additional discount must be given to bring the net selling price to Rs. 1200?
(*a*) $4\frac{16}{21}\%$ (*b*) 5% (*c*) 6% (*d*) $16\frac{2}{3}\%$

38. If the cost of pins reduced by Rs. 4 per dozen, 12 more pins can be purchased for Rs. 48. The cost of pins per dozen after reduction is:
(*a*) Rs. 8 (*b*) Rs. 12 (*c*) Rs. 16 (*d*) Rs. 20

39. If the price of a commodity is decreased by 20% and its consumption is increased by 20%, what will be the increase or decrease in the expenditure on the commodity?
(*a*) 4% increase (*b*) 4% decrease (*c*) 8% increase (*d*) 8% decrease

40. 72% of the students of a certain class took Biology and 44% took Mathematics. If each student took at least one subject from Biology or Mathematics and 40 took both, then total number of students in the class is:
(*a*) 200 (*b*) 240 (*c*) 250 (*d*) 320

41. In the expression xy^2, the values of both variables x and y are decreased by 20%. By this, the value of the expression is decreased by
(*a*) 40% (*b*) 48.8% (*c*) 51.2% (*d*) 80%

42. 15 litres of mixture contains 20% alcohol and rest water. If 3 litres of water be mixed in it, the percentage of alcohol in the new mixture will be:
(*a*) 15 (*b*) $16\frac{2}{3}$ (*c*) 17 (*d*) $18\frac{1}{2}$

43. The difference between 70% and 55% of a number is 72. The number is:
(*a*) 370 (*b*) 460 (*c*) 480 (*d*) 520

44. 20% of a number is 10% of :
(*a*) half the number (*b*) double the number
(*c*) ten times the number (*d*) twenty times the number

45. 75% of what area is 15 sq. metres?
(*a*) 10 sq. metres (*b*) 15 sq. metres (*c*) 20 sq. metres (*d*) 25 sq. metres

46. In an examination 80% of the students passed in Mathematics and 70% passed in English, while 10% students failed in both the subjects. If 360 students passed in both the subjects, find the total number of students who appeared in the examination.
(*a*) 400 (*b*) 600 (*c*) 630 (*d*) 640

47. In an election, there are two candidates. A candidate secured 57% of the total votes polled and elected by a margin of 2100 votes. Find the total number of votes polled.
(*a*) 15000 (*b*) 17500 (*c*) 18000 (*d*) 21000

48. Electric tax is increased by 20% and its consumption is decreased by 20%. The change in the expenditure is:
(*a*) 4% decrease (*b*) 4% increase (*c*) 5% decrease (*d*) 5% increase

49. A man loses 10% of his money, after spending 20% of the remainder he is left with Rs. 2160. Initially the man had:
(*a*) Rs. 1800 (*b*) Rs. 2500 (*c*) Rs. 3000 (*d*) Rs. 3200

50. In a school 55% of the students are below 9 years of age and the remaining 153 above 9 years of age. The total number of students in the school is:
(*a*) 296 (*b*) 300 (*c*) 340 (*d*) 1000

51. The selling price of certain commodity was reduced by 25%. As a result of it, the sales increased by 30%. What was the effect of it on cash collected by daily sales?
(*a*) 2.5% decrease (*b*) 2.5% increase (*c*) 5% decrease (*d*) 5% increase

52. A cooler marked at Rs. 1500 is offered at Rs. 1350 due to off-season discount. Find the rate of off-season discount offered.
(*a*) 9.5% (*b*) 10% (*c*) 10.5% (*d*) 12%

53. The number of Gypsy-cars sold in 2008 was 16,500 and that sold in 2007 was 16580. How much was the percentage decrease in sales of the Gypsy-cars from 2007 to 2008?
(*a*) less than 1 per cent (*b*) more than 1 per cent
(*c*) zero per cent (*d*) cannot be determined

54. A company decided to sell Rs. 50,000 T.V. set for Rs. 48,000 as a world cup offer. What is the percentage discount offered by the company?
(*a*) 6.5 (*b*) 7 (*c*) 7.5 (*d*) 4

55. 9% of a number is $\frac{81}{200}$, what is $\frac{2}{7}$ of that number?
(*a*) $1\frac{1}{5}$ (*b*) $1\frac{2}{7}$ (*c*) $2\frac{1}{7}$ (*d*) $2\frac{1}{5}$

56. If the numerator of a fraction is increased by 200% and the denominator of the fraction is increased by 120%, the resultant fraction is $\frac{4}{11}$. What is the original fraction?
(*a*) $\frac{4}{15}$ (*b*) $\frac{3}{11}$ (*c*) $\frac{5}{12}$ (*d*) $\frac{6}{11}$

57. What is 170% of 1140?
(*a*) 1824 (*b*) 1881 (*c*) 1938 (*d*) 1995

58. The wheat sold by a grocer contained 10% low quality wheat. What quantity of good quality wheat should be added to 150 kgs of wheat so that the percentage of low quality wheat becomes 5%?
(*a*) 50 kgs (*b*) 85 kgs (*c*) 135 kgs (*d*) 150 kgs

59. If 12% of 350 = x% of 125, then find the value of x.
(*a*) 26.4 (*b*) 28 (*c*) 32.2 (*d*) 33.6

60. 14% of 280 + 18% of 350 = ?
(*a*) 102.2 (*b*) 103.4 (*c*) 105 (*d*) 108.4

61. If 180% of x = 810; Find the value of x.
(*a*) 450 (*b*) 405 (*c*) 350 (*d*) 480

62. Nilam spends 15% of her monthly income on household expenses. She spends 17% of the monthly income in travelling and 6% on medical expenses and saves the rest Rs. 15,500. What is her monthly income?
(*a*) Rs. 20,000 (*b*) Rs. 25,000 (*c*) Rs. 30,000 (*d*) Rs. 35,000

63. The difference between 65% of a number and 25% of the same number is 784. What is 85% of that number?

(a) 1470 (b) 1636 (c) 1666 (d) 1862

64. Samir scored 55% marks in an examination of 680 marks. What are the total marks obtained by Samir?

(a) 306 (b) 340 (c) 374 (d) 408

65. If the numerator of a fraction is increased by 200% and the denominator of the fraction is increased by 150%, then the resultant fraction is $\frac{7}{10}$. What is the original fraction?

(a) $\frac{3}{4}$ (b) $\frac{7}{12}$ (c) $\frac{7}{11}$ (d) $\frac{9}{11}$

66. In an election between two candidates, one got 52% of total valid votes, 25% of the total votes were invalid. The total number of votes were 8400. How many valid votes did the other person get?

(a) 3024 (b) 3054 (c) 3196 (d) 3276

67. When 60% of a number A is added to another number B, B becomes 175% of its previous value. Which one of the following is correct?

(a) A > B (b) B > A (c) A = B (d) Data inadequate

68. The present population of a village is 5500. If the number of males increases by 11% and the number of females increases by 20%, then population will become 6330. What is the present population of females in the village?

(a) 3500 (b) 3000 (c) 2500 (d) 2000

69. Two numbers X and Y are respectively 20% and 28% less than a third number Z. By what percentage is the number Y less than the number X?

(a) 8% (b) 9% (c) 10% (d) 12%

70. The population of a town decreases every year due to death and migration by 5%. The population was 1,20,000 last year. What will be expected population at the end of next year?

(a) 1,02,885 (b) 1,05,300 (c) 1,08,300 (d) 1,09,000

71. A's income is 25% more than B's income. B's income in terms of A's income is:

(a) 75% (b) 80% (c) 90% (d) 96%

72. Two numbers are less than a 3rd number by 30% and 37% respectively. How much per cent is the 2nd number less than the first?

(a) 3% (b) 4% (c) 7% (d) 10%

73. In a school, 75% of the students pass and 20 fail. The number of students appearing from another school is 20 more and 10 more students pass than the former school. The pass percentage of the latter school is:

(a) 60 (b) 70 (c) 75 (d) 85

74. A reduction of 20% in the price of sugar enables a person to get 5.2 kg more sugar for Rs. 130. The original price of sugar per kg is:

(a) Rs. 5 (b) Rs. 5.75 (c) Rs. 6.25 (d) Rs. 7.50

75. Sugar is now being sold at Rs. 15 per kg. During last month its rate was Rs. 13 per kg. Find by how much per cent must a family reduce its consumption to keep the expenditure fixed?

(a) $13\frac{1}{3}\%$ (b) 14% (c) 15% (d) $15\frac{1}{5}\%$

76. Mr. Sanjay spends 80% of his monthly salary on consumable items and 50% of the remaining on clothes and transport. He saves the remaining amount. If his savings at the end of the year are Rs. 5730, how much amount per month he would have spent on clothes and transport?
(a) Rs. 477.50 (b) Rs. 577.50 (c) Rs. 600 (d) Rs. 677.50

77. In an examination, 65% of the students passed in Mathematics, 48% passed in Physics and 30% passed in both. How much per cent of students failed in both the subjects?
(a) 13% (b) 17% (c) 43% (d) 47%

78. The difference of two numbers is 15% of their sum. The ratio of the larger number to the smaller number is
(a) 23 : 11 (b) 23 : 17 (c) 11 : 9 (d) 17 : 11

79. In a village, each of the 60% of families has a cow; each of the 30% has a buffalow and each of the 15% of families has both a cow and buffalo. In all there are 96 families in the village. How many families do not have a cow or a buffalo?
(a) 28 (b) 26 (c) 24 (d) 20

80. p is six times as large as q. The per cent that q is less than p, is
(a) 50 (b) $63\frac{1}{3}$ (c) 70 (d) $83\frac{1}{3}$

81. The population of a village was 9800. In a year, with the increase in population of males by 8% and that of females by 5%, the population of the village became 10458. What was the number of males in the village before increase?
(a) 6048 (b) 5600 (c) 4410 (d) 4200

82. The difference between 58 of a number and 39% of the same number is 247. What is 62% of that number?
(a) 754 (b) 806 (c) 1170 (d) 1300

83. What is 30% of 25% of 3/5th of 9800?
(a) 391 (b) 433 (c) 441 (d) 453

84. Ram's salary is 80% of Shyam's salary and 120% of Mohan's salary. What is Ram's salary if Shyam's salary is Rs. 15000?
(a) Rs. 10000 (b) Rs. 12000 (c) Rs. 12500 (d) Rs. 18000

85. The price of sugar is increased by 10%. By what percentage one must cut down his consumption of sugar, so that no extra amount has to be spent on it?
(a) $9\frac{1}{11}\%$ (b) 10% (c) $11\frac{1}{9}\%$ (d) 12%

86. The air consists of 79.2% of Nitrogen, 20.7% of oxygen, 0.08% of other light gases and remaining gas is Argon. Find out the volume of the air consisting one cubic metre of Argon?
(a) 5 m^3 (b) 50 m^3 (c) 500 m^3 (d) 5000 m^3

87. A man's working hours a day were increased 20% and his wages per hour were increased by 15%. By how much per cent were his daily earning increased?
(a) 35% (b) 38% (c) 40% (d) 42%

88. The price of sugar has been reduced by 10%. How many quintals of sugar can be purchased on reduced rate at the same price of 18 quintals of sugar on the original price?
(a) 20 (b) 21 (c) 22 (d) 25

89. There are 850 students in a class. Out of these 44% are Muslims, 28% Hindus, 10% Sikhs and remaining students belong to the other communities. How many students are there of other communities?

(a) 143 (b) 153 (c) 163 (d) 173

90. A student got 60% average marks in five compulsory subjects. He got equal marks in each of the two optional subjects and if the marks of these two subjects are added to the marks of the compulsory subjects, the average of marks is reduced by 4%. What percentage of marks did he get in each of the optional subjects?

(a) 46% (b) 50% (c) 52% (d) 56%

91. In a committee, 50 people speak French, 20 speak Spanish and 10 speak both Spanish and French. The number of person speaking at least one of these two languages is

(a) 38 (b) 40 (c) 45 (d) 60

92. In an examination it is required to get 36% of the aggregate marks to pass. A student gets 198 marks and is declared failed by 36 marks. What is maximum aggregate marks a student can get?

(a) 450 (b) 480 (c) 550 (d) 650

93. The difference between 40% of a number and 28% of the same number is 198. What is 64% of the number?

(a) 1023 (b) 1056 (c) 1065 (d) 1122

94. The population of a town is 189000. It decreases by 8% in the first year and increases by 5% in the 2nd year. What is the population in the town at the end of 2 years?

(a) 182574 (b) 185472 (c) 191394 (d) 193914

95. The difference between 42% of a number and 35% of the same number is 110.6. What is 60% of that number?

(a) 790 (b) 936 (c) 948 (d) 1106

96. If the numerator of a fraction is increased by 250% and the denominator is increased by 300%, the resultant fraction is 7/9. What is the original fraction?

(a) $\frac{7}{8}$ (b) $\frac{7}{11}$ (c) $\frac{8}{9}$ (d) $\frac{8}{11}$

97. Out of a class of 38 girls, 3 were absent, 20% of the remaining failed to do homework. How many girls did their homework?

(a) 25 (b) 28 (c) 30 (d) 35

98. There is 20% increase in the price of petrol every year. If the price in 2005 was Rs. 20 per litre. What would be the price per litre in 2008?

(a) Rs. 30 (b) Rs. 32 (c) Rs. 33.48 (d) Rs. 34.56

99. Mr. Gopal spends 24% of his monthly income on food and 15% on the education of his children. He spends 25% of the remaining salary on entertainment and 20% on conveyance. He is now left with Rs. 10,736. What is the salary of Mr. Gopal?

(a) Rs. 27,600 (b) Rs. 28,000 (c) Rs. 31,200 (d) Rs. 32,000

100. Exchange rate of dollar vs rupee increases at the rate of 5% per month. If the current rate is Rs. 40 per dollar, What will be the rate at the end of 2 months?

(a) Rs. 44 (b) Rs. 44.1 (c) Rs. 45 (d) Rs. 45.4

101. Saurabh scores 64% marks in 6 papers of 150 marks each. He scores 25% of his total obtained marks in Hindi and English together. How much is his total score for both these papers?

(a) 120 (b) 124 (c) 140 (d) 144

102. When the original price of a toy was increased by 25%, the price of one dozen toys was Rs. 300. What was the original price of one toy?
(a) Rs. 15 (b) Rs. 20 (c) Rs. 24 (d) Rs. 30

103. Samir obtained a total of 1012 marks out of 1150 in an examination. What is his percentage in the examination?
(a) 84 (b) 86 (c) 88 (d) 90

104. 10% of a number is subtracted from it, the result is 1800. The number is
(a) 1900 (b) 2000 (c) 2100 (d) 2140

105. In a village, the number of people increases by 10% every two years. If the total number of people in 2008 was 9680, What was the number of people in 2004?
(a) 6000 (b) 8000 (c) 7500 (d) 9000

106. Anil spent 30% of his monthly salary on food, 20% on transport and saves half of the remaining. If he spends Rs. 800 on transport. What is his annual savings?
(a) Rs. 6000 (b) Rs. 12000 (c) Rs. 18000 (d) Rs. 20000

107. A man spends 75% of his income. His income is increased by 20% and he increased his expenditure by 10%. His savings are increased by
(a) 20% (b) 25% (c) 40% (d) 50%

108. The population of a town is 198000. It increases by 7% in the 1st year and decreases by 5% in the 2nd year. What is the population of the town at the end of two years?
(a) 198900 (b) 201267 (c) 211860 (d) 222453

109. The difference between 38% of a number and 24% of the same number is 135.10. What is 40% of the number?
(a) 370 (b) 378 (c) 386 (d) 394

110. If the numerator of a fraction is increased by 200% and the denominator is increased by 160%, the resultant fraction is $\frac{7}{13}$. What is the original fraction?
(a) $\frac{2}{5}$ (b) $\frac{5}{7}$ (c) $\frac{7}{15}$ (d) $\frac{8}{15}$

111. The difference between 58% of a number and 37% of the same number is 399. What is 72% of that number?
(a) 1330 (b) 1368 (c) 1425 (d) 1913

112. In an examination it is required to get 296 of the total maximum aggregate marks to pass. A student gets 259 marks and is declared failed. The difference of marks obtained by the student and required to pass is 5%. What are the maximum aggregate marks a student can get?
(a) 690 (b) 740 (c) 780 (d) 800

113. In a class of 90 students, amongst 50% of the students each student got number of sweets that are 20% of the total number of students and the amongst remaining 50% of the students each student got number of sweets that are 10% of the total number of students. How many sweets were distributed among 90 students?
(a) 960 (b) 1015 (c) 1215 (d) 1620

114. Mrs. Sharma invests 15% of her monthly salary, i.e., Rs. 4428 in Mutual Funds. Later she invests 18% of her monthly salary on pension policies; also she invests another 9% of her salary on Insurance policies. What is the total montly amount invested by Mrs. Sharma?
(a) Rs. 12.398.4 (b) Rs. 13000 (c) Rs. 13398 (d) Rs. 14000

115. A 78 litre mixture of milk and water contains 20% of water. What quantity of additional water be mixed so that water content in the mixture becomes 30%?

(*a*) 5 litre (*b*) 7 litre (*c*) 8 litre (*d*) 11.1 litre

116. 15 litres of a mixture contains 20% alcohol and rest water. If 3 litres of water be mixed in it, the percentage of alcohol in new mixture will be:

(*a*) 16 (*b*) $16\frac{2}{3}$ (*c*) 17 (*d*) $18\frac{1}{2}$

117. Mr. Samir invests 7% *i.e.*, Rs. 2170, of his monthly salary in mutual funds. Later he invests 18% of his monthly salary in recurring deposits. Also, he invests 6% of his salary on NSC's. What is the total annual amount invested by Mr. Samir?

(*a*) Rs. 1,13,520 (*b*) Rs. 1,15,320 (*c*) Rs. 1,25,320 (*d*) Rs. 1,35,120

118. If 56% of 958 + 67% of 1008 = x% of 2000, then find the value of x.

(*a*) 42.86 (*b*) 47.622 (*c*) 60.592 (*d*) 91.455

119. Find the value of 37% of 150 – 0.05% of 1000.

(*a*) 50 (*b*) 55 (*c*) 55.5 (*d*) 55.55

120. If 14% of 80 + x% of 90 = 31.9, then find the value of x.

(*a*) 16 (*b*) 18 (*c*) 23 (*d*) 26

121. On a test consisting 150 questions carrying 1 mark each, Saurabh answered 80% of the first 75 questions correctly. What per cent of other 75 questions does he need to answer correctly to score 60% on the entire exam?

(*a*) 20 (*b*) 40 (*c*) 50 (*d*) 60

122. If 23% of 8040 + 42% of 545 = x% of 3000, then find the value of x.

(*a*) 56.17 (*b*) 63.54 (*c*) 69.27 (*d*) 71.04

123. If x% of 280 + 18% of 550 = 143.8, then find the value of x.

(*a*) 11 (*b*) 16 (*c*) 18 (*d*) 21

124. A sells his goods at 20% lower price than B and 20% higher price than 'C'. If a customer of B buys goods worth Rs. 200 from C. Find the amount that he can save by doing so.

(*a*) Rs. 50 (*b*) Rs. 100 (*c*) Rs. 150 (*d*) Rs. 200

125. If 32% of x is equal to 40% of y then 32% of y will be equal to what percentage of x?

(*a*) 25 (*b*) 25.6 (*c*) 26 (*d*) 26.6

126. A school has only three classes which contain 40, 50 and 60 students respectively. The pass percentage of these classes are 10%, 20% and 10% respectively. Find the pass percentage of the school.

(*a*) 10 (*b*) $12\frac{1}{3}$ (*c*) $13\frac{1}{3}$ (*d*) 15

127. In an examination, 20% passed in Ist division, 25% in IInd division and 45% passed in IIIrd division. If 124 students failed in the examination, what is the total number of students who appeared in the examination?

(*a*) 800 (*b*) 1216 (*c*) 1240 (*d*) 1364

128. The price of tea increases from Rs. 8 per kg to Rs. 950 per kg. How much consumption of tea should be reduced by a house wife so that the expenditure on it may not increased?

(*a*) $14\frac{4}{5}$% (*b*) 15% (*c*) $15\frac{15}{19}$% (*d*) 16%

129. Maximum marks in three subjects are 50, 50 and 100 respectively. A student secured 50%, 40% and 80% marks in Ist, IInd and IIIrd subject respectively. His aggregate per cent will be:
(a) 62.5% *(b)* 63.5% *(c)* 64% *(d)* 65%

130. A test paper consists of 5 questions. 5% of the students who took the test solved all questions and 5% did not solve any of the questions. Of the remaining students, 25% solved only 1 question and 20% solved 4 questions while $24\frac{1}{2}$% of the total students solved 2 quesions. If the number of students who solved 3 questions is 200, find the total number of students who took the test.
(a) 600 *(b)* 700 *(c)* 800 *(d)* 900

131. A trader spends 50% of his capital as salary to the staff and $33\frac{1}{3}$% of the capital for purchase of commodities. If the cash in hand is Rs. 6000, the capital is
(a) Rs. 32000 *(b)* Rs. 36000 *(c)* Rs. 40000 *(d)* Rs. 45000

132. What percentage of 1 hour is one minute 12 seconds?
(a) 2% *(b)* 3% *(c)* 4% *(d)* 5%

133. In an examination *x* obtained 58% marks and y obtained 43% marks. If difference is of 105 marks, then maximum marks were:
(a) 450 *(b)* 500 *(c)* 600 *(d)* 700

134. If the sales tax be reduced from $3\frac{1}{2}$% to $3\frac{1}{3}$%, then what difference does it make to a person who purchases an article with marked price of Rs. 8400?
(a) Rs. 12 *(b)* Rs. 14 *(c)* Rs. 16 *(d)* Rs. 20

135. Difference of two numbers is 1660. If 75% of one number is 12.5% of the other number, find the two numbers.
(a) 2400, 4100 *(b)* 2450, 4150 *(c)* 2490, 4150 *(d)* 2450, 4190

136. An inspector rejects 0.08% of the meter as defective. How many will he examine to reject 2?
(a) 2000 *(b)* 2200 *(c)* 2500 *(d)* 3000

137. In expressing a length 81.472 km as nearly as possible with three significant digits, find the percentage error.
(a) 0.043% *(b)* 0.034% *(c)* 0.040% *(d)* 0.045%

138. Nilam's Mathematics Test had 75 problems *i.e.*, 10 arithmetic, 30 algebra and 35 geometry problems. Although she answered 70% of the arithmetic, 40% of the algebra and 60% of the geometry problems correctly, she did not pass the test because she got less than 60% of the problems right. How many more questions she would have needed to answer correctly to earn 60% passing grade?
(a) 3 *(b)* 5 *(c)* 7 *(d)* 10

139. A salesman's commission is 5% on all sales upto Rs. 10,000 and 4% on all sales exceeding than. He remits Rs. 31,000 to his parent company after deducting his commission. Find the total sales.
(a) Rs. 32000 *(b)* Rs. 32500 *(c)* Rs. 33000 *(d)* Rs. 33500

140. If 50% of $(x - y)$ = 30% of $(x + y)$, then what percent of x is y?
(a) 20% *(b)* 25% *(c)* 30% *(d)* 35%

141. Sanjay's salary was decreased by 50% and subsequently increased by 50%. How much per cent does he lose?
(a) 15% *(b)* 20% *(c)* 25% *(d)* 30%

142. During one year, the population of a town increased by 5% and during the next year, the population decreased by 5%. If the total population is 9975 at the end of the second year, then what was the population size in the beginning of the first year?

(a) 9000 *(b)* 9500 *(c)* 10,000 *(d)* 10,500

143. The price of a car is Rs. 3,25,000. It was insured to 85% of its price. The car was damaged completely in an accident and the insurance company paid 90% of the insurance. What was the difference between the price of the car and the amount received?

(a) Rs. 81,250 *(b)* Rs. 76,375 *(c)* Rs. 48,750 *(d)* Rs. 32,500

144. A batsman scored 110 runs which included 3 boundaries and 8 sixes. What per cent of his total score did he make by running between the wickets?

(a) $55\frac{5}{11}$ *(b)* $54\frac{6}{11}$ *(c)* $45\frac{5}{11}$ *(d)* 45

145. Nilam went to the shop and bought things worth Rs. 25, out of which 30 paise went on sales tax on taxable purchases. If the tax was 6%, then what was the tax free items?

(a) Rs. 15.70 *(b)* Rs. 19.70 *(c)* Rs. 20 *(d)* Rs. 20.70

146. A fruit seller had some apples. He sells 40% apples and still has 420 apples. Originally, he had:

(a) 700 apples *(b)* 672 apples *(c)* 600 apples *(d)* 588 apples

147. 10% of the voters did not cast their vote in an election between two candidates. 10% of the votes polled were found invalid. The successful candidate got 54% of the valid votes and won by a majority of 1620 votes. The number of voters enrolled on the voters' list was:

(a) 40000 *(b)* 35000 *(c)* 33000 *(d)* 25000

148. In an examination, 5% of the applicants were found ineligible and 85% of the eligible candidates belonged to the general category. If 4275 eligible candidates belonged to other categories, then how many candidates applied for the examination?

(a) 40000 *(b)* 37000 *(c)* 35000 *(d)* 30000

149. If x% of y is 100 and y% of z is 200, then find a relation between x and z.

(a) $z = 4x$ *(b)* $z = \frac{x}{4}$ *(c)* $z = 2x$ *(d)* $z = \frac{x}{2}$

150. If 20% of $a = b$, then b% of 20 is the same as:

(a) 10% of a *(b)* 7% of a *(c)* 6% of a *(d)* 4% of a

151. If x is 90% of y, then what per cent of x is y?

(a) $111\frac{1}{9}$% *(b)* $110\frac{1}{9}$% *(c)* $101\frac{1}{9}$% *(d)* 90%

152. If x is 80% of y, then what per cent of $2x$ is y?

(a) $66\frac{2}{3}$% *(b)* $62\frac{1}{2}$% *(c)* 62% *(d)* $62\frac{2}{3}$%

153. If p% of p is 36, then p is equal to:

(a) 600 *(b)* 60 *(c)* 30 *(d)* 15

154. A spider climbed $62\frac{1}{2}$% of the height of the pole in one hour and in the next hour it covered $12\frac{1}{2}$% of the remaining height. If the height of the pole is 192m, then distance climbed in second hour is:

(a) 9m *(b)* 7m *(c)* 5m *(d)* 3m

155. The sum of number of boys and girls in a school is 150. If the number of boys is x, then the number of girls will become $x\%$ of the total number of students. The number of boys is:
(a) 90 (b) 60 (c) 50 (d) 40

156. Of the 1000 inhabitants of a town, 60% are males of whom 20% are literate. If, of all the inhabitants, 25% are literate, then what per cent of the females of the town are literate?
(a) 37.5 (b) 32.5 (c) 27.5 (d) 22.5

157. In a recent survey, 40% houses contained two or more people. Of those houses containing only one person, 25% were having only a male. What is the percentage of all houses, which contain exactly one female and no males?
(a) 15 (b) 40 (c) 45 (d) 50

158. In a Mathematics examination, the average for the entire class was 80 marks. If 10% of the students scored 95% marks and 20% scored 90 marks, what was the average marks of the remaining students of the class?
(a) 85 (b) 75 (c) 72.5 (d) 65.5

159. A salesman allowed $5\frac{1}{2}\%$ discount on the total sales made by him plus a bonus of $\frac{1}{2}\%$ on the sales over Rs. 10,000. If his total earnings were Rs. 1990, then his total sales (in Rs.) were
(a) 35000 (b) 34000 (c) 32000 (d) 30000

160. Saurabh could save 10% of his income. But two years later when his income is increased by 20%, he could save the same amount only as before. By how much per cent has his expenditure increased?
(a) 24% (b) $23\frac{1}{3}\%$ (c) $22\frac{2}{9}\%$ (d) 22%

161. The price of an article was increased by r %. Later the new price was decreased by r %. If the latest price was Re 1, then the original price was:
(a) $Rs\left(\frac{10000}{10000-r^2}\right)$ (b) $Rs.\frac{\sqrt{1-r^2}}{100}$ (c) $Rs\left(\frac{1-r^2}{100}\right)$ (d) Re. 1

162. Depreciation applicable to an equipment is 20%. The value of the equipment 3 years from now will be less by
(a) 60% (b) 51.2% (c) 48.8% (d) 45%

163. Peter earned 40% more money than Albert. Albert earned 20% less than Michael. Peter earned more than Michael by:
(a) 25% (b) 20% (c) 12% (d) 10%

164. The weight of the container alone is 25% of the container filled wih a certain fluid. When some of the fluid is removed the weight of the container and remaining fluid is 50% of the original total weight. What fractional part of the fluid has been removed?
(a) $\frac{3}{4}$ (b) $\frac{2}{3}$ (c) $\frac{1}{2}$ (d) $\frac{1}{3}$

165. Milk contains 5% water. What quantity of pure milk should be added to 10 litres of milk to reduce this to 2%?
(a) 5 litres (b) 7 litres (c) 10 litres (d) 15 litres

166. In some quantity of ghee, 60% is pure ghee and 40% is vanaspati. If 10 kg of pure ghee is added, then the strength of Vanaspati ghee becomes 20%. The original quantity was
(a) 25 kg (b) 20 kg (c) 15 kg (d) 10 kg

167. Fresh fruit contains 68% water and dry fruit contains 20% water. How much dry fruit can be obtained from 100 kg of fresh fruits?
(*a*) 80 kg (*b*) 52 kg (*c*) 40 kg (*d*) 32 kg

168. Samir's monthly income is 30% more than that of Saurabh. Saurabh's monthly income is 20% less than that of Gopal. If the difference between the monthly incomes of Samir and Gopal is Rs. 800, what is the monthly income of Saurabh?
(*a*) Rs. 12,000 (*b*) Rs. 16,000 (*c*) Rs. 18000 (*d*) Rs. 20000

169. In a certain office, 72% of the workers prefer tea and 44% prefer coffee. If each of them prefer tea or coffee and 40 like both, the total number of workers in the office is
(*a*) 320 (*b*) 250 (*c*) 240 (*d*) 200

170. Out of 450 students of a school, 325 play football, 175 play cricket and 50 neither play football nor cricket. How many students play both football and cricket?
(*a*) 125 (*b*) 100 (*c*) 75 (*d*) 50

171. Due to an increase of 30% in the price of eggs, 3 eggs less are available for Rs. 7.80. The present rate of eggs per dozen is:
(*a*) Rs. 10.40 (*b*) Rs. 9.36 (*c*) Rs. 8.88 (*d*) Rs. 8.64

172. The price of rice is reduced by 2%. How many kilograms of rice can now be bought for the money which was sufficient to buy 49 kg of rice earlier?
(*a*) 51 kg (*b*) 50 kg (*c*) 49 kg (*d*) 48 kg

173. An empty fuel tank of a car was filled with A type petrol. When the tank was half-empty it was filled with B type petrol. Again when the tank was half empty, it was filled with A type petrol. When the tank was half empty again, it was filled with B type petrol. What is the percentage of A type petrol at present in the tank?
(*a*) 50% (*b*) 40% (*c*) 37.5% (*d*) 33.5%

SOLUTIONS

1. $x = 90\%$ of $y \quad \Rightarrow x = \frac{90}{100}y$

Required percentage $= \frac{y}{9y/10} = \frac{10}{9} \times 100 = 111.1\%$

2. $x - 20\%$ of $x = 40 \quad \Rightarrow x - \frac{x}{5} = 40 \Rightarrow \frac{4x}{5} = 40 \quad \Rightarrow x = \frac{40 \times 5}{4} = 50$

3. Required percentage $= \frac{10}{100-10} \times 100 = \frac{10}{90} \times 100 = 11\frac{1}{9}\%$

4. Let the business value changes from x to y

Then 4% of x = 5% of y

$$\Rightarrow \frac{4}{100} \times x = \frac{5}{100} \times y \Rightarrow y = \frac{4}{5}x$$

$\therefore$ Changes in business $= \left(x - \frac{4}{5}x\right) = \frac{1}{5}x$

$\therefore$ Percentage slump in business $= \left(\frac{1}{5}x \times \frac{1}{x} \times 100\right)\% = 20\%$

5. 5% A = 15% B, and 10% B = 20% C

Then, A = 3B and B = 2C

$\therefore$ B = 2C = 2 × 2000 = Rs. 4000

And A = 3B = 3 × 4000 = Rs. 12000

$\therefore$ A + B + C = 12000 + 4000 + 2000 = Rs. 18000

6. $20\% \text{ of } x + 30 = 32\% \text{ of } x - 42$

$\Rightarrow 12\% \text{ of } x = 72$

$\Rightarrow x = \dfrac{72 \times 100}{12} = 600$

Pass Mark = 20% of 600 + 30 = 150

Pass percentage = $\left(\dfrac{150}{600} \times 100\right)\% = 25\%$

7. $(62\% \text{ of } x - 38\% \text{ of } x) = 144 \quad \Rightarrow 24\% \text{ of } x = 144 \quad \Rightarrow x = \dfrac{144 \times 100}{24} = 600$

8. $200\% \text{ of } x = 90$

$\Rightarrow x = \dfrac{90 \times 100}{200} = 45$

$\therefore 80\% \text{ of } x = \left(\dfrac{80}{100} \times 45\right) = 36$

9. $p = 6q$

Required percentage = $\dfrac{6q - q}{6q} \times 100 = \dfrac{5}{6} \times 100 = 83\dfrac{1}{3}\%$

10. Required percentage = $\dfrac{25}{100 - 25} \times 100 = \dfrac{25}{75} \times 100 = 33\dfrac{1}{3}\%$

11. Required reduction = $\left[\dfrac{r}{(100 + r)} \times 100\right] = \left(\dfrac{25}{125} \times 100\right)\% = 20\%$

12. Matriculates = $\dfrac{40}{100} x = \dfrac{2x}{5}$

Remaining = $\left(x - \dfrac{2x}{5}\right) = \dfrac{3x}{5}$

Graduates = $\dfrac{50}{100} \times \dfrac{3x}{5} = \dfrac{3x}{10}$

Remaining = $\dfrac{3x}{5} - \dfrac{3x}{10} = \dfrac{3x}{10}$

Now, $\dfrac{3x}{10} = 180$

$\therefore\ x = \dfrac{10 \times 180}{3} = 600$

$\therefore$ Graduates $= \dfrac{3 \times 600}{10} = 180$

13. Number of people read either one or both = 40 + 50 – 10 = 80%
Hence, number of people read neither newspaper = 100 – 80 = 20%

14. $x \times \left(1 + \dfrac{5}{100}\right)^3 = 138915$

$\Rightarrow x \times \dfrac{21}{20} \times \dfrac{21}{20} \times \dfrac{21}{20} = 138915$

$\Rightarrow \quad x = \dfrac{138915 \times 20 \times 20 \times 20}{21 \times 21 \times 21} = 120000$

15. Males $= \left(\dfrac{5}{9} \times 4500\right) = 2500$

Females = 2000

$\therefore$ Married males $= \dfrac{40}{100} \times 2500 = 1000$

and married females = 1000

$\therefore$ Percentage of married females $= \left(\dfrac{1000}{2000} \times 100\right)\% = 50\%$

16. Required percentage $= \left[\dfrac{10}{(100+10)} \times 100\right]\% = 9\dfrac{1}{11}\%$

17. Water = 10/100 × 40 = 4 litres
Let x litres of water be added,

Then, $x + 4 = \dfrac{20}{100}(40 + x)$ $\Rightarrow 5x + 20 = 40 + x \Rightarrow 4x = 20$ $\therefore\ x = 5$ litres

18. $z = \dfrac{x^2}{y}$

$\therefore$ New value of $z = \dfrac{\left(\dfrac{110}{100}x\right)^2}{\left(\dfrac{110}{100}y\right)} = \dfrac{11}{100}\dfrac{x^2}{y} = \dfrac{11}{10}z$

$\therefore$ Increase percentage $= \dfrac{\left(\dfrac{11}{10}z - z\right)}{z} \times 100 = 10\%$

19. Failed in either one or both subjects = 35 + 25 – 10 = 50%
$\therefore$ Number of examinees passed = (100 – 50) = 50%

20. Required reduction $= \frac{25}{100+25} \times 100 = 20\%$

21. Alcohol in 9 gms $= \left(\frac{50}{100} \times 9\right) = 4.5$ gms.

Let x gm of water be added.

Then, $\frac{4.5}{9+x} \times 100 = 30$

$\Rightarrow 270 + 30x = 450 \quad \Rightarrow 30x = 180 \quad \Rightarrow x = 6$ gms

22. 35% of $x = 96 + 16 = 112$

$\Rightarrow \frac{35}{100} \times x = 112 \Rightarrow x = \frac{112 \times 100}{35} = 320$

23. Out of 100, difference in votes = (60 – 40) = 20

20% of $x = 100$

$\therefore x = \frac{100 \times 100}{20} = 500$

24. 26% of income tax $= \frac{2}{3}\%$ of the net income

$\therefore$ Income tax $= \left[\frac{2}{3} \times \frac{100}{26}\right]\%$ of the net income $= \frac{100}{39}\%$ of the net income

Let net income = Rs. 3900

$\therefore$ Income tax $= 3900 \times \frac{100}{39 \times 100} =$ Rs. 100

$\Rightarrow$ Gross income = Rs. 3900 + Rs. 100 = Rs. 4000

$\therefore$ Rate % of income tax $= \left(\frac{100}{4000} \times 100\right)\% = 2\frac{1}{2}\%$

25. Gross income = Rs. 20000

Income exempted from income tax = 10% of gross income

$\therefore$ Income on which income tax is chargeable = (100 – 10%) = 90% of gross income

$= 20000 \times \frac{90}{100} =$ Rs. 18000

$\therefore$ Total income tax paid on = Rs. 20000 – Rs. 19100 = Rs. 900

$\therefore$ Rate per cent of income tax $= \frac{900}{18000} \times 100 = 5\%$

26. Gross income $= \frac{100}{95} \times 17100 =$ Rs. 18000

New net income $= \frac{94}{100} \times 18000 =$ Rs. 16920

27. Gross income = Rs. 15000

Income on which income tax is chargeable

$= (100 - 20)\% = 80\%$ of gross income

$$= 15000 \times \frac{80}{100} = \text{Rs. } 12000$$

$\therefore$ Income tax paid @ 4% $= 12000 \times \frac{4}{100} = \text{Rs. } 480$

$\therefore$ Net income = 15000 – 480 = Rs. 14520

28. Gross income = Rs. 16000

Net income = Rs. 14840

$\therefore$ Income tax paid = Rs. 16000 – Rs. 14840 = Rs. 1160

$\therefore$ Chargeable income is $= 1160 \times \frac{100}{8} = \text{Rs. } 14500$

Hence, income exempted from income tax = 16000 – 14500 = Rs. 1500

29. The number = 8 × 17.25 = 138.00

73% of the number $= \frac{73}{100} \times 138 = \frac{10074}{100} = 100.75$

30. 58% of 60 – x% of 635 = 277.4

$$\Rightarrow \frac{58}{100} \times 960 - \frac{x}{100} \times 635 = 277.4$$

$$\Rightarrow \frac{127x}{20} = 556.8 - 277.4 \quad \therefore x = \frac{20 \times 279.4}{127} = 44$$

31. The number of employess got transferred $= \frac{40}{100} \times 1225 = 490$

32. Let maximum aggregate marks = x, then

$$\frac{8}{100} \times x = 270 - 216 \quad \therefore x = \frac{54 \times 100}{8} = 675$$

33. Let the number be x; then

$$\frac{56}{100} \times x = 1064 \qquad \therefore x = \frac{1064 \times 100}{56} = 1900$$

Now, 38% of 1900 $= \frac{38}{100} \times 1900 = 722$

34. Let cost price of the cell phone be Rs. x; then

$$x + \frac{32}{100} \times x = 6600 \Rightarrow \frac{132x}{100} = 6600 \quad \therefore x = \frac{100 \times 6600}{132} = \text{Rs. } 5000$$

35. Let the number be x; then

$$(89 - 73) \times \frac{x}{100} = 448 \quad \therefore x = \frac{448 \times 100}{16} = 2800$$

49% of 2800 $= \frac{49}{100} \times 2800 = 1372$

36. Let the Nupur's monthly income = Rs. x, then

$$\frac{26}{100} \times x = \frac{89856}{12} \quad \therefore x = \frac{7488 \times 100}{26} = \text{Rs. } 28800$$

37. Price after 1st discount $= 1400 - \frac{10}{100} \times 1400 =$ Rs. 1260

Hence, additional discount $= \frac{1260-1200}{1260} \times 100 = \frac{60}{1260} \times 100 = 4\frac{16}{21}\%$

38. Let reduced price by Rs. x per dozen, then

$\frac{48}{x} - \frac{48}{x+4} = 1 \Rightarrow \frac{48 \times 4}{x^2 + 4x} = 1 \Rightarrow x^2 + 4x - 192 = 0$

$\Rightarrow (x+16)(x-12) = 0 \qquad \therefore x =$ Rs. 12

39. Let price of a commodity be Rs. 100 and its consumption be 100, then
Now, decrease in commodity $= 100 \times 100 - 80 \times 120 =$ Rs. 400

Hence, decrease percentage $= \frac{400 \times 100}{100 \times 100} = 4\%$

40. Percentage of students who took both the subjects $= (72 + 44) - 100 = 16\%$

Now, $16\% = 40 \qquad \therefore 100\% = \frac{40}{16} \times 100 = 250$

41. Decrease in expression $= xy^2 - \frac{80}{100} \times x\left(\frac{80}{100}y\right)^2$

$= xy^2 - \frac{64}{125}xy^2 = \frac{61xy^2}{125}$

Hence, decrease per cent $= \frac{61xy^2}{125 \times xy^2} \times 100 = 48.8\%$

42. Amount of alcohol $= \frac{20}{100} \times 15 = 3$ litre

Hence, required percentage $= \frac{3}{18} \times 100 = 16\frac{2}{3}\%$

43. Let the number be x; then

$(70-55) \times \frac{1}{100} \times x = 72 \quad \therefore x = \frac{100 \times 72}{15} = 480$

44. Let number be 100, then 20% and 10% of the number be 20 and 10 respectively.
Hence, 20% of a number is 10% of double the number.

45. Let required area be x sq. metre; then

$\frac{75}{100} \times x = 15 \qquad \therefore x = \frac{15 \times 100}{75} = 20$ sq metre

46. Here, percentage of students failed in Mathematics and English be 30% and 20% respectively.
Percentage of students failed either one or both subjects $= 30 + 20 - 10 = 40\%$
Hence, percentage of pass students $= 100 - 40 = 60\%$

Now, $60\% = 360$ $\quad\therefore\ 100\% = \frac{360}{60} \times 100 = 600$

47. Let total number of votes be x; then

$$(57-43) \times \frac{1}{10} x = 2100 \quad \therefore\ x = \frac{100 \times 2100}{14} = 15000$$

48. Let initially electric tax is Rs. 100 and consumption = 100 units
Decrease in consumption = 100 × 100 – 120 × 80 = Rs. 400

$$\text{Hence, decrease percentage} = \frac{400 \times 100}{100 \times 100} = 4\%$$

49. Let initally the man had Rs. x, then

$$\text{amount of money loses} = \frac{10}{100} \times x = \text{Rs.} \frac{x}{10}$$

$$\text{Remaining amount of money} = x - \frac{x}{10} = \text{Rs.} \frac{9x}{10}$$

$$\text{Money spent} = \frac{20}{100} \times \frac{9x}{10} = \text{Rs.} \frac{9x}{50}$$

$$\text{Now, } \frac{9x}{10} - \frac{9x}{50} = 2160 \Rightarrow \frac{36x}{50} = 2160 \qquad \therefore\ x = \frac{2160 \times 50}{36} = \text{Rs. } 3000$$

50. Let total number of students be x, then

$$\frac{45}{100} \times x = 153 \qquad \therefore\ x = \frac{100 \times 153}{45} = 340$$

51. Let the selling price of a commodity be Rs. 100 and number of sales = 100 units
Decrease in daily cash = 100 × 100 – 75 × 130 = Rs. 250

$$\text{Hence, decrease percentage} = \frac{250 \times 100}{100 \times 100} = 2.5\ \%$$

52. Discount per cent $= \frac{1500 - 1350}{1500} \times 100 = \frac{150}{1500} \times 100 = 10\%$

53. Required decrease percentage $= \frac{16580 - 16500}{16580} \times 100 = \frac{80}{16580} \times 100 = 0.48\%$

54. Discount per cent $= \frac{2000}{50,000} \times 100 = 4\%$

55. Let the number be x; then

$$\frac{9}{100} \times x = \frac{81}{200} \qquad \therefore\ x = \frac{100 \times 81}{9 \times 200} = \frac{9}{2}$$

$$\text{Hence, } \frac{2}{7} x = \frac{2}{7} \times \frac{9}{2} = \frac{9}{7} = 1\frac{2}{7}$$

56. Let the fraction be $\frac{x}{y}$; then

$$\frac{x+\frac{200}{100}x}{y+\frac{120}{100}y}=\frac{4}{11} \Rightarrow \frac{3x\times 5}{11y}=\frac{4}{11} \quad \therefore \frac{x}{y}=\frac{4}{11}\times\frac{11}{15}=\frac{4}{15}$$

57. $\frac{170}{100}\times 1140 = 1938$

58. Let x kg of good wheat be added; then

$$\frac{10}{100}\times 150=\frac{5}{100}(150+x) \Rightarrow 150+x=300 \quad \therefore x=150\text{ kg}$$

59. $\frac{12}{100}\times 350=\frac{x}{100}\times 125 \quad \Rightarrow x=\frac{12\times 350}{125}=33.6$

60. $\frac{14}{100}\times 280+\frac{18}{100}\times 350=39.2+63=102.2$

61. $\frac{180}{100}\times x=810 \quad \therefore x=\frac{810\times 5}{9}=450$

62. Let her monthly income be Rs. x; then

$$x-\left(\frac{15}{100}\times x+\frac{17}{100}\times x+\frac{6}{100}\times x\right)=15{,}500$$

$$\Rightarrow x-\frac{38x}{100}=15500 \quad \Rightarrow \frac{62x}{100}=15500$$

$$\therefore x=\frac{15500\times 100}{62}=\text{Rs. }25000$$

63. Let number be x; then

$$x\times(65-25)\times\frac{1}{100}=784 \quad \therefore x=\frac{784\times 100}{40}=1960$$

Hence, $\frac{85}{100}\times 1960=1666$

64. His total marks $=\frac{55}{100}\times 680=374$

65. Let the fraction be x/y; then

$$\frac{x+\frac{200}{100}\times x}{y+\frac{150}{100}\times y}=\frac{7}{10} \Rightarrow \frac{3x\times 2}{5y}=\frac{7}{10} \quad \therefore \frac{x}{y}=\frac{7}{10}\times\frac{5}{6}=\frac{7}{12}$$

66. Total number of valid votes $= 8400 - \frac{25}{100} \times 8400 = 6300$

The number of valid votes which other person got $= \frac{48}{100} \times 6300 = 3024$

67. Here, $\frac{60}{100}\,\text{A} + \text{B} = \frac{175}{100} \times \text{B} \Rightarrow \frac{3}{5}\,\text{A} + \text{B} = \frac{7}{4}\,\text{B} \Rightarrow \frac{3}{5}\,\text{A} = \frac{3}{4}\,\text{B}$

$\therefore \frac{A}{B} = \frac{5}{4}$ Hence, A > B.

68. Let the present population of females and males be x and $(5500 - x)$ respectively; then

$x \times \frac{120}{100} + (5500 - x) \times \frac{111}{100} = 6330$

$\Rightarrow 120x + 610500 - 111x = 633000$

$\Rightarrow 9x = 22500 \qquad \therefore x = \frac{22500}{9} = 2500$

69. Here, $X = \frac{80}{100} Z = \frac{4}{5} Z,\ Y = \frac{72Z}{100} = \frac{18Z}{25}$

Their difference $= \frac{4}{5} Z - \frac{18Z}{25} = \frac{2Z}{25}$

Required percentage $= \frac{2Z/25}{4Z/5} \times 100 = \frac{2Z}{25} \times \frac{5}{4Z} \times 100 = 10\%$

70. Required population $= 1{,}20{,}000 \left(1 - \frac{5}{100}\right)^2 = 1{,}20{,}000 \times \frac{19}{20} \times \frac{19}{20} = 1{,}08{,}300$

71. Let incomes of B and A be Rs. 100 and Rs. 125 respectively.

Required income $= \frac{100}{125} \times 100 = 80\%$

72. Let third number be 100, then two numbers be 70 and 63 respectively.

Required percentage $= \frac{70 - 63}{70} \times 100 = \frac{7}{70} \times 100 = 10\%$

73. $25\% = 20 \qquad \therefore \quad 100\% = \frac{20}{25} \times 100 = 80$

For latter school; number of appearing students = 80 + 20 = 100

number of passed students = 60 + 10 = 70

Hence, pass percentage of latter school is 70%

74. 20% of $130 = \frac{20}{100} \times 130 = 26$

Reduced price per kg $= \frac{26}{5.2} =$ Rs. 5

$\therefore$ Original price per kg = Rs. $5 \times \frac{100}{80}$ = Rs. 6.25

75. Increase percentage = $\frac{15-13}{13} \times 100 = \frac{200}{13}\%$

Required percentage of reduction = $\frac{\frac{200}{13}}{100+\frac{200}{13}} \times 100 = \frac{200}{1500} \times 100 = 13\frac{1}{3}\%$

76. Let monthly salary of Mr. Sanjay = Rs. x, then

Expenditure on consumable items = $\frac{80}{100} \times x$ = Rs. $\frac{4x}{5}$

Remaining amount = $x - \frac{4x}{5}$ = Rs. $\frac{x}{5}$, Then

$\frac{x}{5} - \frac{50}{100} \times \frac{x}{5} = \frac{5730}{12} \Rightarrow \frac{x}{10} = 477.5 \quad \therefore x = 10 \times 477.5 = \text{Rs. } 4775$

Hence, expenditure on clothes and transport = $\frac{4775}{10}$ = Rs. 477.50

77. Percentage of students passed in one or both the subjects = 65 + 48 – 30 = 83%
Hence, percentage of students failed in both subjects = 100 – 83 = 17%

78. Let the two numbers be x and y, where $x > y$,

Then, $x - y = \frac{15}{100}(x+y) \Rightarrow 20x - 3x = 3y + 20y \Rightarrow 17x = 23y$

$\therefore x : y = 23 : 17$

79. Percentage of families having either cow or buffalow or both = 60 + 30 – 15 = 75%
Hence, percentage of families do not have a cow or buffalow = 100 – 75 = 25%

Required number = $\frac{25}{100} \times 96 = 24$

80. Here, $p = 6q$

Reqired percentage = $\frac{6q-q}{6q} \times 100 = \frac{5q}{6q} \times 100 = 83\frac{1}{3}\%$

81. Let the number of males and females be x and $(9800 - x)$ before increase, then

$\frac{108}{100}x + \frac{105}{100}(9800 - x) = 10458$

$\Rightarrow 108x + 1029000 - 105x = 1045800$

$\Rightarrow 3x = 16800 \qquad \therefore x = \frac{16800}{3} = 5600$

82. Let number be x; then

$x \times (58 - 39) \times \frac{1}{100} = 247 \quad \therefore x = \frac{247 \times 100}{19} = 1300$

Hence, required number = $\frac{62}{100} \times 1300 = 806$

83. Required number = $\frac{30}{100}\times\frac{25}{100}\times\frac{3}{5}\times 9800 = 441$

84. Ram's salary = $\frac{80}{100}\times 15000$ = Rs. 12000

85. Required percentge = $\frac{10}{100+10}\times 100 = 9\frac{1}{11}\ \%$

86. Percentage of Argon = 100 – (79.2 + 20.7 + 0.08) = 0.02%
Let required vomume of air = x m^3

Now, $x\times\frac{0.02}{100}=1 \quad \therefore x=\frac{10000}{2}=5000$ m^3

87. Let man's working hours be 100 and wages per hour be Rs. 100 originally;
Hence, increase in earning = 120 × 115 – 100 × 100 = Rs. 3800

Required percentage = $\frac{3800}{100\times 100}\times 100 = 38\%$

88. Let initially rate of sugar per quintal be Rs. 100
and reduced rate per quintal be Rs. 90;
then, $x \times 90 = 18 \times 100 \quad \therefore\ x = 20$ quintal

89. Percentage of other communities = 100 – (44 + 28 + 10) = 18%

Hence, number of other communites = $\frac{18}{100}\times 850 = 153$

90. Let percentage of marks in each optional subject be x%,

then, $\frac{5\times 60+2\times x}{7}=56 \quad \Rightarrow 2x = 392-300 \qquad \therefore x=46$

Hence, required percentage = 46%

91. Required number of person = 50 + 20 – 10 = 60

92. Let the maximum aggregate marks be x, then

$\frac{36}{100}\times x = 198+36 \quad \therefore\ x=\frac{234\times 100}{36}=650$

93. Let the number be x; then

$x\times(40-28)\times\frac{1}{100}=198 \quad \therefore\ x=\frac{198\times 100}{12}=1650$

Hence, $\frac{64}{100}\times 1650 = 1056$

94. Required population = $1{,}89{,}000\left(1-\frac{8}{100}\right)\left(1+\frac{5}{100}\right)$

$= 1{,}89{,}000 \times \frac{23}{25}\times\frac{21}{20}$

= 182574

95. Let the number be x; then

$$x \times (42 - 35) \times \frac{1}{100} = 110.6 \qquad \therefore\ x = \frac{110.6 \times 100}{7} = 1580$$

Hence, $\frac{60}{100} \times 1580 = 948$

96. Let the fraction be $\frac{x}{y}$; then

$$\frac{x + \frac{250}{100}x}{y + \frac{300}{100}y} = \frac{7}{9} \Rightarrow \frac{7x}{2 \times 4y} = \frac{7}{9} \qquad \therefore\ \frac{x}{y} = \frac{7}{9} \times \frac{8}{7} = \frac{8}{9}$$

97. Number of girls, who did their homework $= \frac{80}{100} \times 35 = 28$

98. In 2008 price of petrol per litre $= 20\left(1 + \frac{20}{100}\right)^3 = 20 \times \frac{6}{5} \times \frac{6}{5} \times \frac{6}{5} =$ Rs. 34.56

99. Let the salary of Mr. Gopal be Rs. x; then

Expenditure on food and education $= \frac{24 + 15}{100} \times x =$ Rs. $\frac{39x}{100}$

Remaining salary $= x - \frac{39x}{100} =$ Rs. $\frac{61x}{100}$

Expenditure on entertainment and conveyance $= \frac{25 + 20}{100} \times \frac{61x}{100} =$ Rs. $\frac{549x}{2000}$

$$\text{Now, } \frac{61x}{100} - \frac{549x}{2000} = 10{,}736 \qquad \Rightarrow \frac{671x}{2000} = 10736 \qquad \therefore\ x = \frac{10736 \times 2000}{671} = \text{Rs. } 32000$$

100. Exchange rate of dollar after 2 months $= 40\left(1 + \frac{5}{100}\right)^2 = 40 \times \frac{21}{20} \times \frac{21}{20} =$ Rs. 44.1

101. Saurabh's total score in 6 papers $= 6 \times \frac{64}{100} \times 150 = 576$

Hence, his total score in Hindi and English $= \frac{25}{100} \times 576 = 144$

102. Original price of one dozen toys $= \frac{100}{125} \times 300 =$ Rs. 240

Hence, original price of one toy $= \frac{240}{12} =$ Rs. 20

103. Samir's percentage in examination = $\frac{1012}{1150} \times 100 = 88\%$

104. Let the number be x; then

$$x - \frac{10}{100} \times x = 1800 \Rightarrow \frac{9x}{10} = 1800 \quad \therefore x = \frac{10 \times 1800}{9} = 2000$$

105. The population in 2004 = $\frac{9680}{\left(1 + \frac{10}{100}\right)^2} = 9680 \times \frac{10}{11} \times \frac{10}{11} = 8000$

106. $20\% = 800 \quad \therefore \quad 100\% = \frac{800}{20} \times 100 = \text{Rs. } 4000$

Anil's expenditure on food and transport = $\frac{50}{100} \times 4000 = \text{Rs. } 2000$

Remaining amount = 4000 – 2000 = Rs. 2000

Hence, his monthly savings = $\frac{1}{2} \times 2000 = \text{Rs. } 1000$

Then, his annual savings = 12 × Rs. 1000 = Rs. 12000

107. Let his initial income = Rs. 100, then,
Expenditure = Rs. 75 and Savings = Rs. 25
Now his increased income = Rs. 120, then

Expenditure = $75 \times \frac{110}{100}$ = Rs. 82.5; Savings = 120 – 82.5 = Rs. 37.5

Then, increased percentage of savings = $\frac{37.5 - 25}{25} \times 100 = 50\%$

108. Required population = $198000 \left(1 + \frac{7}{100}\right)\left(1 - \frac{5}{100}\right) = 198000 \times \frac{107}{100} \times \frac{19}{20} = 201267$

109. Let the number be x; then

$$x \times (38 - 24) \times \frac{1}{100} = 135.10 \Rightarrow x \times \frac{14}{100} = 135.10 \quad \therefore x = \frac{13510}{14} = 965$$

Hence, $\frac{40}{100} \times 965 = 386$

110. Let fraction be $\frac{x}{y}$; then

$$\frac{x + \frac{200}{100}x}{y + \frac{160}{100}y} = \frac{7}{13} \quad \Rightarrow \frac{3x \times 5}{13y} = \frac{7}{13} \quad \therefore \frac{x}{y} = \frac{7}{13} \times \frac{13}{15} = \frac{7}{15}$$

111. Let the number be x; then

$$x\times(58-37)\times\frac{1}{100}=399 \Rightarrow x=\frac{399\times 100}{21}=1900$$

Hence, $\frac{72}{100}\times 1900=1368$

112. Here, $5\% = 296-259 \quad \therefore\ 100\%=\frac{37}{5}\times 100=740$

113. Total number of sweets $=\frac{50}{100}\times 90\times\frac{20}{100}\times 90+\frac{50}{100}\times 90\times\frac{10}{100}\times 90$

$$=45\times 18+45\times 9=810+405=1215$$

114. Here, $15\% = \text{Rs. } 4428 \quad \therefore\ 100\%=\frac{4428}{15}\times 100=\text{Rs. } 29520$

Total percentage of investment = 15 + 18 + 9 = 42%

Hence, her total monthly amount invested $=\frac{42}{100}\times 29520=\text{Rs. } 12398.4$

115. Let x litre water will be added; then

$$\frac{20}{100}\times 78+x=\frac{30}{100}(78+x)$$

$$\Rightarrow 2(78+5x)=3(78+x) \Rightarrow 7x=78 \quad \therefore\ x=\frac{78}{7}=11.1 \text{ litre}$$

116. Let percentage of alcohol in new mixture be x%, then

$$\frac{20}{100}\times 15=\frac{x}{100}\times 18 \quad \therefore\ x=\frac{20\times 15}{18}=16\frac{2}{3}\%$$

117. Here, $7\% = 2170 \quad \therefore\ 100\%=\frac{2170}{7}\times 100=\text{Rs. } 31{,}000$

Total percentage of investment = 7 + 18 + 6 = 31%

Hence, total monthly amount invested $=\frac{31}{100}\times 31000=\text{Rs. } 9610$

Since, total annual amount invested = 12 × Rs. 9610 = Rs. 1,15,320

118. $\frac{56}{100}\times 958+\frac{67}{100}\times 1008=\frac{x}{100}\times 2000$

$$\Rightarrow 53648+67536=2000x \qquad \therefore\ x=\frac{121184}{200}=60.592$$

119. $\frac{37}{100}\times 150-\frac{0.05}{100}\times 1000=55.5-0.5=55$

120. $\frac{14}{100}\times 80+\frac{x}{100}\times 90=31.9 \qquad \Rightarrow 0.9x=31.9-11.2 \qquad \therefore\ x=\frac{207}{9}=23$

121. To score 60% on entire examination, number of question needed = $\frac{60}{100} \times 150 = 90$

Number of correct answer in Ist 75 questions = $\frac{80}{100} \times 75 = 60$

Hence, number of correct answer needed in 2nd 75 questions = 90 – 60 = 30

Hence, percentage of questions needed in 2nd 75 questions = $\frac{30}{75} \times 100 = 40\%$

122. $\frac{23}{100} \times 8040 + \frac{42}{100} \times 545 = \frac{x}{100} \times 3000$

$\Rightarrow$ 184920 + 22890 = 3000x

$\therefore x = \frac{207810}{3000} = 69.27$

123. $\frac{x}{100} \times 280 + \frac{18}{100} \times 550 = 143.8$

$\Rightarrow \frac{14x}{5} + 99 = 143.8 \quad \Rightarrow \frac{14x}{5} = 44.8 \quad \therefore x = \frac{44.8 \times 5}{14} = 16$

124. Let A sells in Rs. 100, then B and C sell them in Rs. 120 and Rs. 80 respectively;

Now C sell in Rs. 200, then B sells it $\frac{120}{80} \times 200$ = Rs. 300

Hence, saving amount = 300 –200 = Rs. 100

125. Here, 40% of y = 32% of x

$\therefore$ 32% of $y = \frac{32 \times 32}{40}\%$ of x = 25.6% of x.

126. Total number of students = 40 + 50 + 60 = 150

Total number of students passed = $\frac{10}{100} \times 40 + \frac{20}{100} \times 50 + \frac{10}{100} \times 60 = 4 + 10 + 6 = 20$

Hence, required percentage = $\frac{20}{150} \times 100 = 13\frac{1}{3}\%$

127. Percentage of failed students = 100 – (20 + 25 + 45) = 10%

Hence, 10% = 124 $\quad \therefore 100\% = \frac{124}{10} \times 100 = 1240$

128. Increase% = $\frac{9.50 - 8}{8} \times 100 = \frac{1.50}{8} \times 100 = \frac{75}{4}\%$

Required percentage of reduction = $\frac{\frac{75}{4}}{100 + \frac{75}{4}} \times 100 = \frac{75}{475} \times 100 = 15\frac{15}{19}\%$

129. Total maximum marks of 3 subjects = 50 + 50 + 100 = 200

Total secured marks in 3 subjects = $\frac{50}{100}\times 50+\frac{40}{100}\times 50+\frac{80}{100}\times 100 = 25 + 20 + 80 = 125$

Required percentage = $\frac{125}{200}\times 100 = 62.5\%$

130. Let total number of students = x, then
Number of students solving no any questions, all questions and 2 questions

$$= x\times\left(5+5+\frac{49}{2}\right)\times\frac{1}{100}=\frac{69x}{200}$$

Number of students solving 1 question and 4 questions = $\frac{9x}{10}\times\frac{(25+20)}{100}=\frac{81x}{200}$

Now, number of students solving 3 questions = $x-\left(\frac{69x}{200}+\frac{81x}{200}\right)=\frac{x}{4}$

Hence, $\frac{x}{4}=200 \quad \therefore x = 800$

131. Remaining percentage = $100-\left(50+\frac{100}{3}\right)=\frac{50}{3}\%$

Now, $\frac{50}{3}\%$ = Rs. 6000 $\therefore$ 100% = $\frac{6000\times 3}{50}\times 100$ = Rs. 36000

132. Required percentage = $\frac{60+12}{60\times 60}\times 100 = \frac{72}{60\times 60}\times 100 = 2\%$

133. Let maximum marks be a, then

$a\times(58-43)\times\frac{1}{100}=105 \quad \therefore a=\frac{105\times 100}{15}=700$

134. Required difference = $\left(\frac{7}{2}-\frac{10}{3}\right)\times\frac{1}{100}\times 8400=\frac{1}{6}\times 84$ = Rs. 14

135. Let the two numbers be x and $(x + 1660)$ respectively; then

$\frac{7.5}{100}(x+1660)=\frac{12.5}{100}\times x \quad \Rightarrow 3(x+1660)=5x$

$\Rightarrow 2x = 3\times 1660 \quad \therefore x=\frac{3\times 1660}{2}=2490$

Other number = x + 1660 = 2490 + 1660 = 4150
Hence, two numbers are 2490 and 4150

136. Let the number of meter examined be x; then

$\frac{0.08}{100}\times x=2 \quad \Rightarrow x=\frac{2\times 100\times 100}{8}=2500$

137. Change in length = 81.5 – 81.472 = 0.028 km

Hence, required percentage = $\frac{0.028}{81.472}\times 100 = 0.034\%$

138. The number of questions answered correctly by Nilam = $\frac{70}{100}\times 10+\frac{40}{100}\times 30+\frac{60}{100}\times 35$

$= 7 + 12 + 21 = 40$

Required number of questions for pass = $\frac{60}{100}\times 75 = 45$

Hence, she needed to answer (45 – 40) = 5 questions more.

139. Let his total sales be Rs. x; then

$$\frac{95}{100}\times 10000+\frac{96}{100}\times(x-10000) = 31100$$

$$\Rightarrow 9500+\frac{24}{25}x-9600 = 31100 \quad \Rightarrow \frac{24}{25}x = 31200 \quad \therefore x=\frac{25\times 31200}{24} = \text{Rs. } 32500$$

140. $\frac{50}{100}(x-y)=\frac{30}{100}(x+y) \Rightarrow 2x = 8y \;\; \therefore x = 4y$

Required percentage = $\frac{y}{x}\times 100 = \frac{y}{4y}\times 100 = 25\%$

141. Let present salary of Sanjay = Rs. 100

Hence his decreased salary = Rs. 50

Again, his increased salary = $50+\frac{50}{100}\times 50 = \text{Rs. } 75$

Hence, he loses in his salary = 100 – 75 = Rs. 25

Since, loss percentage = 25%

142. Required Population = $\frac{9975}{\left(1+\frac{5}{100}\right)\left(1-\frac{5}{100}\right)} = 9975\times\frac{20}{21}\times\frac{20}{19} = 10000$

143. The price of a car = Rs. 3,25,000

The amount he received = $\frac{90}{100}\times\frac{85}{100}\times 3{,}25{,}000 = \text{Rs. } 2{,}48{,}625$

Hence, required difference = 3,25,000 – 2,48,625 = Rs. 76,375

144. The number of runs made by running between wickets = 110 – (3 × 4 + 8 × 6) = 50

Required percentage = $\frac{50}{110}\times 100 = 45\frac{5}{11}\%$

145. Let taxable items of worth be Rs. x; then

$$\frac{6}{100}\times x=\frac{30}{100} \qquad \Rightarrow x=\frac{30}{6}=\text{Rs. } 5$$

Hence, amount spent on taxable items = 5 + 0.30 = Rs. 5.30

Since, worth of tax free items = 25 – 5.30 = Rs. 19.70

146. Here, 60% = 420 $\therefore$ 100% = $\frac{420}{60}\times 100 = 700$ apples.

147. Here, $(54-46)\% = 1620 \therefore 100\% = \frac{1620}{8} \times 100 = 20{,}250$

Hence, total valid votes = 20,250

Then, number of votes polled = $\frac{100}{90} \times 20{,}250 = 22500$

Since, the number of voters enrolled on the voter's list = $\frac{100}{90} \times 22500 = 25000$

148. Here, $15\% = 4275 \quad \therefore 100\% = \frac{4275}{15} \times 100 = 28500$

Hence, total number of eligible candidates = 28500

Since, number of candidates applied for examination = $\frac{100}{95} \times 28500 = 30000$

149. Here, $\frac{x}{100} \times y = 100 \quad \therefore \; y = \frac{10000}{x}$ ...(i)

Again, $\frac{y}{100} \times z = 200 \quad \therefore \; y = \frac{20000}{z}$ ...(ii)

From (i) and (ii), we get

$$\frac{1}{x} = \frac{2}{z} \quad \therefore z = 2x$$

150. Here, $b = \frac{20}{100} \times a \quad \Rightarrow b\% \text{ of } 20 = \left(\frac{1}{5} \times 20\right)\% \text{ of } a = 4\% \text{ of } a.$

151. Required percentage $\frac{100}{90} \times 100 = 111\frac{1}{9}\%$

152. Required percentage = $\frac{100}{2 \times 80} \times 100 = 62\frac{1}{2}\%$

153. Here, $\frac{p}{100} \times p = 36 \quad \Rightarrow p^2 = 36 \times 100 \therefore p = 60$

154. The distance climbed in second hour = $\left(100 - \frac{125}{2}\right) \times \frac{25}{2 \times 100} \times 192 = \frac{75}{2 \times 100} \times \frac{1}{8} \times 192 = 9\text{m}$

155. Here, $x + \frac{x}{100} \times 150 = 150 \Rightarrow \frac{5x}{2} = 150 \therefore x = \frac{2 \times 150}{5} = 60$

156. The number of literate males = $\frac{20}{100} \times \frac{60}{100} \times 1000 = 120$

The number of literate females = $\frac{25}{100} \times 1000 - 120 = 250 - 120 = 130$

Total number of females = $\frac{40}{100} \times 1000 = 400$

Required percentage = $\frac{130}{400} \times 100 = 32.5\%$

157. Let total number of houses be 100; then number of houses containing only one person = 60

Hence, required number = $\frac{75}{100} \times 60 = 45$

Since, required percentage = 45%

158. Let the average marks of the remaining students be x; then

$\frac{10 \times 95 + 20 \times 90 + 70 \times x}{100} = 80 \Rightarrow 70x = 8000 - (950 + 1800)$

$\Rightarrow 70x = 5250 \qquad \therefore x = \frac{5250}{70} = 75$

159. Let his total sales = Rs. x; then

$\frac{11}{2 \times 100} \times x + \frac{1}{2 \times 100}(x - 10000) = 1990 \Rightarrow \frac{3x}{50} = 2040$

$\therefore x = \frac{2040 \times 50}{3} =$ Rs. 34000

160. Let originally Saurabh's income be Rs. 100 and his expenditure be Rs. 90.
Again his increased income = Rs. 120 and Expenditure = Rs. 110

Hence, required percentage = $\frac{110 - 90}{90} \times 100 = \frac{20}{90} \times 100 = 22\frac{2}{9}\%$

161. Let the original price be Rs. x; then

$\frac{100 + r}{100} \times \frac{100 - r}{100} \times x = 1 \quad \therefore x = \text{Rs.} \left(\frac{10000}{10000 - r^2}\right)$

162. Let the initial value = Rs. 100, then

Required value = $100\left(1 - \frac{20}{100}\right)^3 = 100 \times \frac{4}{5} \times \frac{4}{5} \times \frac{4}{5} =$ Rs. 51.20

Since, required depreciation % = 100 – 51.20 = 48.8%

163. Let earning of Albert and Peter be Rs. 100 and Rs. 140 respectively, then

Earning of Michael = $\frac{100}{80} \times$ Rs. 100 = Rs. 125

Difference of earnings of Peter and Michael = 140 – 125 = Rs. 15

Hence, required percentage = $\frac{15}{125} \times 100 = 12\%$

164. Let the total weight = x gm, then weight of the container = $\frac{x}{4}$ gm

Now weight of the total filled fluid = $x - \frac{x}{4}$ gm = $\frac{3x}{4}$ gm

Latter weight of the remaining fluid with container = $\frac{50}{100} \times x = \frac{x}{2}$ gm

Now weight of the remaining fluid = $\frac{x}{2} - \frac{x}{4} = \frac{x}{4}$ gm

Hence, required fractional part = $\frac{\frac{3x}{4} - \frac{x}{4}}{\frac{3x}{4}} = \frac{x}{2} \times \frac{4}{3x} = \frac{2}{3}$

165. Let x litre of the milk be added, then

$\frac{95}{100} \times 10 + x = \frac{98}{100}(10 + x) \Rightarrow 9.5 + x = 9.8 + 0.98x$

$\Rightarrow 0.02x = 0.3 \quad \therefore\ x = 30/2 = 15$ litres

166. Let original quantity was x kg, then

$\frac{60}{100} \times x + 10 = \frac{80}{100}(x + 10) \Rightarrow 0.6x + 10 = 0.8x + 8 \quad \Rightarrow 0.2x = 2 \quad \therefore\ x = 20/2 = 10$ kg

167. Fresh fruit contains 68% water and 32% fruit
Dry fruit contains 20% water and 80% fruit
Let required amount of dry fruit be x kg; then

$\frac{32}{100} \times 100 = \frac{80}{100} \times x \quad \therefore\ x = \frac{32 \times 5}{4} = 40$ kg

168. Let monthly income of Saurabh and Samir be Rs. 100 and Rs. 130 respectively, then monthly income of Gopal = $\frac{100}{80} \times 100$ = Rs. 125

Difference between monthly income of Samir and Gopal = 130 – 125 = Rs. 5
Now, if difference is Rs. 5, then monthly income of Saurabh is Rs. 100

Hence, if difference is Rs. 800, then monthly income of Saurabh will be = $\frac{100}{5} \times 800$ = Rs. 16000

169. Percentage of workers prefer tea and coffee both = 72 + 44 – 100 = 16%

Now, 16% = 40 $\quad \therefore\ 100\% = \frac{40}{16} \times 100 = 500$

170. Total number of students who play either cricket or football or both = 450 – 50 = 400
Hence, required number of students = 325 + 175 – 400 = 100

171. Difference of price in Rs. 7.80 = $\frac{30}{100} \times 7.80$ = Rs. 2.34

Present rate of one egg = $\frac{2.34}{3}$ = Re. 0.78

Hence, present rate of one dozen eggs = 12 × Re 0.78 = Rs. 9.36

172. Let original price of the rice = Rs. 100 per kg

Hence, reduced price of the rice = Rs. 98 per kg.

Let x kg of rice is now available for the same price, then

$$x \times 98 = 100 \times 49 \quad \therefore\ x = \frac{100 \times 49}{98} = 50 \text{ kg}$$

173. Let the capacity of the fuel tank = 100 litres

When Ist time B type petrol was filled then A and B types petrol were 50 litre each.

Again when A type petrol was filled in half empty tank then A type and B type were 75 litres and 25 litres respectively.

Hence, their ratio were 3 : 1

Again, when tank was half empty, then

$$\text{Amount of A type petrol} = \frac{3}{3+1} \times 50 = 37.5 \text{ litres}$$

$$\text{\& Amount of B type petrol} = \frac{1}{4} \times 50 = 12.5 \text{ litres}$$

Then tank was filled with B type petrol in half empty tank.

Since, Amount of B type petrol = 12.5 + 50 = 62.5 litres

Hence, percentage of A type petrol at present in the tank is 37.5%.

22 PROFIT & LOSS

A consumer who goes to the market and buys certain goods. The buyer is called a customer and the shopkeeper who sells the goods to him is called a retailer. The retailer purchases goods in turn in bulk from a wholesaler who keeps a large stock of good and in this case, the retailer becomes the customer.

1. Cost price (C.P.) : Cost price is that price at which a particular article is bought. Profit and loss both are marked at cost price.

2. Selling Price (S.P.) : Selling price is that price at which a particular article is sold.

3. Overheads : The expenses incurred on transportation, maintenance, packaging, advertisements and the like are included as *Overhead.* These overheads and the profit when added to the cost price determine the selling price.

4. Profit or Gain : Whenever a person sells an article at price greater than the cost price he is said to have made a profit or gain.

$$\text{Profit or Gain} = \text{S.P.} - \text{C.P.}$$

5. Loss : If S.P. is less than the C.P. there is loss.

$$\text{Loss} = \text{C.P} - \text{S.P}$$

Some Basic Formulae :

(i) Gain = S.P. – C.P.

(ii) Loss = C.P. – S.P.

(iii) $\text{Gain \%} = \dfrac{\text{Gain} \times 100}{\text{C.P.}}$

(iv) $\text{Loss \%} = \dfrac{\text{Loss} \times 100}{\text{C.P.}}$

From these we can write direct expressions for S.P. and C.P.

(v) $\text{S.P.} = \left(\dfrac{100 + \text{Gain\%}}{100}\right) \times \text{C.P.}$ in case of gain or profit

(vi) $\text{S.P.} = \left(\dfrac{100 - \text{Loss\%}}{100}\right) \times \text{C.P.}$ in case of loss

These can be rewritten as

$$\text{C.P.} = \frac{100}{100 + \text{Gain\%}} \times \text{S.P.} \text{ in case of profit}$$

$$\text{C.P.} = \frac{100}{100 - \text{Loss\%}} \times \text{S.P. in case of loss}$$

(vii) If the C.P. of x goods = S.P. of y goods, then

(a) Gain % = $\frac{x-y}{y} \times 100$ [In case of $x > y$]

(b) Loss % = $\frac{y-x}{y} \times 100$ [In case of $y > x$]

(viii) When a man sells two things at the same price each and in this process his loss on first things is $x\%$ and gain on second things is $x\%$, then in such a type question, there is always a loss.

$$\text{Loss \%} = x\% \text{ of } x = \frac{x^2}{100} = \left(\frac{x}{10}\right)^2.$$

$$\text{and Loss} = \frac{2 \times \text{S.P.}}{\left(\frac{100}{x}\right)^2 - 1}$$

(ix) An article is sold at a profit of $x\%$. Had it been sold for Rs. a some more, $y\%$ would have gained. Then,

$$\text{C.P. of an article} = \frac{\text{More gain} \times 100}{\text{Difference in percentage profit}}$$

(x) A dishonest shopkeeper prefers to sell goods at his cost price but uses a false weight of x grams for each kilogram. Then his gain per cent,

$$\text{gain \%} = \frac{\text{Error}}{\text{True value} - \text{Error}} \times 100 = \frac{1000 - x}{x} \times 100$$

or, $$\text{gain \%} = \frac{\text{True weight} - \text{False weight}}{\text{False weight}} \times 100.$$

Example 1: A dishonest dealer professes to sell his goods at cost price, but he uses a weight of 950 gm for the kg. weight. Find his gain per cent.

Solution: Gain % = $\frac{\text{Error}}{\text{True value} - \text{Error}} \times 100 = \frac{50}{950} \times 100 = 5.26\%$

Example 2: A dishonest dealer sells goods at $6\frac{1}{4}\%$ loss on cost price but uses 14 gms instead of 16 gms. What is his percentage profit or loss?

Solution: Suppose the cost price is Rs. p per kg.

Then, he sells the goods for $\text{Rs.}\, p\left(\frac{100 - \frac{25}{4}}{100}\right) = \text{Rs.}\,\frac{15p}{16}$ per kg.

Now, suppose he bought q kg of goods

Then, his total investment = Rs. pq

and his total return = Rs. $\frac{15p}{16}\times q\left(\frac{16}{14}\right)$ = Rs. $\frac{15}{14}pq$

$$\therefore \quad \% \text{ profit} = \frac{\frac{15}{14}pq - pq}{pq}\times 100 = \frac{50}{7} = 7\frac{1}{7}\%$$

Example 3: I sold a book at a profit of 12%. Had I sold it for Rs. 18 more, 18% would have been gained. Find the cost price.

Solution: Cost price $= \frac{\text{More gain} \times 100}{\text{Difference in percentage}} = \frac{18\times 100}{18-12}$ = Rs. 300.

Example 4: A man buys 5 apples for Rs. 3 and sold each for Rs. 2. What did he gain or loss?

Solution: C.P. of apples = Rs. 3 and S.P. of apples = Rs. 2 × 5 = Rs. 10

∴ Gain = Rs. 10 – Rs. 3 = Rs. 7

∴ Gain % $= \frac{7}{3}\times 100 = 233\frac{1}{3}\%$

Example 5: A man bought 7 oranges for a rupee and sold them at a profit of 40%. How many oranges for a rupee he sold?

Solution: C.P. of 1 orange = Re. $\frac{1}{7}$

S.P. of 1 orange = 140% of C.P. = $\frac{140}{100}\times\frac{1}{7}$ = Re. $\frac{1}{5}$

∴ He must sell 5 oranges for a rupee.

Example 6: By selling 11 oranges for a rupee, a man loses 10%. How many for a rupee should he sell to gain 10%?

Solution: S.P. of 1 orange = Re. $\frac{1}{11}$

⇒ New S.P. of 1 orange = $\frac{1}{11}\times\frac{100}{90}\times\frac{110}{100}$ = Re. $\frac{1}{9}$

∴ He must sell 9 oranges for a rupee.

Example 7: If the cost price of 8 articles is equal to the selling price of 10 articles. Find the gain or loss%.

Solution: Loss% $=\frac{2}{10}\times 100 = 20\%$

Example 8: I lose 20% by selling a watch for Rs. 64. What per cent shall I gain or loss by selling it for Rs. 100?

Solution: Rs. 64 =80% of C.P.

∴ Rs. 100 = $\frac{80}{64}\times 100\%$ of C.P. = 125% C.P.

Hence, Gain = 25%

Example 9: What profit per cent is made by selling an article at a certain price, by selling at $\frac{2}{3}$ of that price, there would be a loss of 10%?

Solution: If the C.P. is Rs. 100, then $\frac{2}{3}$ of S.P. = Rs. 100 – Rs. 10 = Rs. 90

$\therefore$ S.P. of the articles = $\text{Rs.}90 \times \frac{3}{2}$ = Rs. 135 $\quad \therefore$ Gain = 35%

Example 10: A man bought two packets of toffees, the same number in each case the first, he bought at $5p$ each but the second at 3 for $13p$. He then mixed them all together and sold them at $70p$ a dozen. Find his gain%.

Solution: Let he purchases a dozen toffee in each case

Hence, cost of 2 dozen = $12 \times 5p + 12 \times \frac{13p}{3} = 112p$

Selling price of 2 dozen = $70 \times 2 = 140p$

Gain = $140p - 112p = 28p \quad \therefore$ Gain% = $\left(\frac{28}{112} \times 100\right)\% = 25\%$

Example 11: A wine merchant buys 10 casks of wine. If he sells his wine at Rs. 5 a litre, he loses Rs. 200; while selling it at Rs. 6 a litre, he would gain Rs. 150 on the whole. Find the number of litre in a cask.

Solution: Let he had x litres of wine contained in 10 casks, selling price of x litres at the rate of 5 rupees a litre, he loses Rs. 200.

$\therefore$Cost price of x litres = $5x + 200$

Cost price of x litres = $6x - 150$, in case of gain of Rs. 150

$\Rightarrow 6x - 150 = 5x + 200$

$\therefore \quad x = 350$

Example 12: A radio dealer marks a radio with a price which is 20% more than the cost price and allows a discount of 10% on it. Find the gain per cent.

Solution: Let C.P. = Rs. 100 and Marked price = Rs. 120

Since, S.P. = 90% of Rs. 120 = Rs. 108 ($\because$ Discount = 10%)

$\therefore$ Gain% = (108 – 100)% = 8%

Example 13: A tradesman marks his goods at such a price that after allowing a discount of 15%, he earns a profit of 20%. Find the marked price of an article which costs him Rs. 850.

Solution: $\therefore$ S.P. = $\text{Rs.}\left(\frac{120}{100} \times 850\right)$ = Rs. 1020

Now, 85% = 1020 $\quad \therefore$ 100% = $\frac{1020}{85} \times 100$ = Rs. 1200

Hence, the marked price = Rs. 1200

Example 14: By selling an article for Rs. 247.50 we get a profit of $12\frac{1}{2}\%$. Find the cost of the article.

Solution: $\therefore$C.P. = $\text{Rs.}\left[\frac{100}{100 + \frac{25}{2}} \times 247.50\right] = \text{Rs.}\left(\frac{100 \times 2}{225} \times 247.50\right)$ = Rs. 220

Example 15: There would be 10% loss if a toy is sold at Rs. 10.80 per piece. At what price should it be sold to earn a profit of 20%?

Solution: Here, 90 : 10.80 : : 120 : x

$$\Rightarrow x = \frac{10.80 \times 120}{90} = 14.40$$

Hence, the toy must be sold for Rs. 14.40.

Example 16: If books bought at prices ranging from Rs. 200 to Rs. 350 are sold at prices ranging from Rs. 300 to Rs. 425, what is the greatest possible profit that might be made in selling 8 books?

Solution: Profit is maximum when C.P. is minimum and S.P. is maximum

$\Rightarrow$ C.P. = Rs. (200 × 8) = Rs. 1600 $\quad\therefore$ S.P. = Rs. (425 × 8) = Rs. 3400

$\therefore$ Gain = Rs. 3400 – Rs. 1600 = Rs. 1800

Example 17 : Mohan bought 25 kg of rice at the rate of Rs. 6 per kg and 35 kg of rice at the rate of Rs. 7 per kg. He mixed the two and sold the mixture at the rate of Rs. 6.75 per kg. What was his gain or loss in the transaction?

Solution: C.P. of 60 kg mix. = Rs. (25 × 6 + 35 × 7) = Rs. 395

and S.P. of 60 kg mix. = Rs. (60 × 6.75) = Rs. 405

$\therefore$ Gain = Rs. (405 – 395) = Rs. 10.

Example 18: A man sold 20 articles for Rs. 60 and gained 20%. How many articles did he buy for Rs. 60?

Solution: $\therefore$ C.P. of 20 articles = Rs.$\left(\frac{100}{120} \times 60\right)$ = Rs. 50

If for Rs. 50 he bought = 20 articles

Since, for Rs. 60 he bought = $\left(\frac{20}{50} \times 60\right)$ = 24 article

Example 19 : Mukesh bought paper sheets for Rs. 7200 and spent Rs. 200 on transport. Paying Rs. 600 he had 330 boxes made which he sold at Rs. 28 each. What is his profit percentage?

Solution: C.P. of 330 boxes = Rs. (7200 + 200 + 600) = Rs. 8000

andS.P. of 330 boxes = Rs. (330 × 28) = Rs. 9240

Now, Gain = Rs. 9240 – Rs. 8000 = Rs. 1240

$\therefore$ Gain% = $\left(\frac{1240}{8000} \times 100\right)\%$ = 15.5%

Example 20: A man sold two houses for Rs. 7.81 lakhs each. On one he gained 5% and on the other, he lost 5%. What per cent is the effect of the sale on the whole?

Solution: Loss% = $\left(\frac{5}{10}\right)^2 = \frac{1}{4}\% = 0.25\%$

Example 21: Sohan bought 4 dozen apples at Rs. 12 per dozen and 2 dozen apples at Rs. 16 per dozen. He sold all of them to earn 20%. At what price per dozen he sells the apples?

Solution: C.P. of 6 dozen apples = Rs. (12 × 4 + 16 × 2) = Rs. 80

$\therefore$ S.P. = Rs.$\left(\frac{120}{100} \times 80\right)$ = Rs. 96

Hence, S.P. per dozen = Rs.$\left(\frac{96}{6}\right)$ = Rs. 16

Example 22: By selling an umbrella for Rs. 30, a shopkeeper gain 20%. During a clearance sale, the shopkeeper allows a discount of 10% of the marked price. Find his gain% during the sale season.

Solution: C.P. = $\left(\frac{100}{120}\times 30\right)$ = Rs. 25

and S.P. = 90% of 30 = Rs. 27

$\therefore$ Gain% = $\left(\frac{2}{25}\times 100\right)\%$ = 8%

Example 23: A shopkeeper allows a discount of 10% on the marked price of an item but changes a sales tax of 8% on the discounted price. If the customer pays Rs. 680.40 as the price including the sales tax, what is the marked price of the item?

Solution: Let marked price = Rs. x

Then, $\frac{90}{100}x+\frac{8}{100}\times\frac{90x}{100}=680.40 \Rightarrow \frac{243x}{250}=680.40 \Rightarrow x=\frac{680.40\times 250}{243}$ $\therefore x$ = Rs. 700

Example 24: The difference between the cost price and sale price of an article is Rs. 240. If the profit per cent is 20, at what price was the article sold?

Solution: Let S.P. = Rs. x, Then, C.P. = $(x - 240)$

$\therefore \frac{240}{(x-240)}\times 100 = 20$

$\Rightarrow x - 240 = 1200$ $\therefore$ x = Rs. 1440

Example 25: By selling motor cycle for Rs. 22600 a person gains 13%, what was his gain?

Solution: C.P. = $\left(\frac{100}{113}\times 22600\right)$ = Rs. 20000

$\therefore$ Gain= Rs. (22600 – 20000) = Rs. 2600

Example 26: A shopkeeper bought locks at the rate of 8 locks for Rs. 34 and sold them at 12 locks for Rs. 57. How many number of locks he should sell to have a profit of Rs. 900?

Solution: Let he purchased 24 locks

$\therefore$ C.P. = $\left(\frac{34}{8}\times 24\right)$ = Rs. 102 and S.P. = $\left(\frac{57}{12}\times 24\right)$ = Rs. 114

To gain Rs. 12, locks purchased = 24

To gain Rs. 900, locks purchased = $\left(\frac{24}{12}\times 900\right)$ = 1800 locks

Example 27: A shopkeeper earns 15% profit on a shirt even after allowing 31% discount on the list price. If the list price is Rs. 125, then find the cost price of the shirt.

Solution: Let C.P. = Rs. x

Then $\frac{115}{100}x=\frac{69}{100}\times 125$ $\therefore x=\frac{69\times 125}{115}$ = Rs. 75

Example 28: Loss incurred by selling a bicycle for Rs. 895 is equal to the profit earned by selling it for Rs. 995. What is the loss/profit in this case?

Solution: Let C.P. = Rs. x

$$(x - 895) = (995 - x) \therefore x = \frac{1890}{2} = \text{Rs. } 945$$

Hence, Loss/Gain = 945 – 895 = Rs. 50

Example 29: A manufacturer sells a pair of glasses to a wholesale dealer at a profit of 18%. The wholesaler sells the same to a retailer at a profit of 20%. The retailer in turn sells them to a customer for Rs. 30.09, thereby earning a profit of 25%. What is the cost price of the manufacturer?

Solution: $\frac{125}{100}$ of $\frac{120}{100}$ of $\frac{118}{100}x = 30.09 \quad \therefore x = \frac{30.09 \times 4 \times 5 \times 50}{5 \times 6 \times 59} = \text{Rs. } 17$

Example 30: If the difference between selling a shirt at a profit of 10% and 15% is Rs. 10, then, find the cost price of the shirt.

Solution: Let C.P. = Rs. x

Then, $\frac{115}{100}x - \frac{110}{100}x = 10 \quad \Rightarrow 5x = 100 \times 10 \quad \therefore x = \text{Rs. } 200$

Example 31: The cost of a shirt after 15% discount is Rs. 102. What was the cost of the shirt before the discount?

Solution: Let the marked price = Rs. x

Then, $\frac{85}{100}x = 102$

$$\therefore x = \text{Rs.}\left(\frac{102 \times 100}{85}\right) = \text{Rs. } 120$$

Example 32 : If a man reduce a selling price of a fan from Rs. 400 to Rs. 380, his loss increases by 20%. What is the cost price of the fan?

Solution: Let C.P. = Rs. x

Increase in loss = $(x - 380) - (x - 400) = 20$

Hence, $\frac{20}{x-400} \times 100 = 20$

$\Rightarrow x - 400 = 100 \quad \therefore x = \text{Rs. } 500$

Example 33: A trader allows a trade discount of 20% and a cash discount of $6\frac{1}{4}\%$ on the marked price of the goods and gets a net gain of 20% on the cost. By how much above the cost should the goods be marked for sale?

Solution: Let the C.P. = Rs. 100 and the marked price = Rs. $(100 + x)$

Hence, $$\text{S.P.} = \frac{\left(100 - \frac{25}{4}\right)}{100} \times \frac{80}{100} \times (100 + x) = \frac{3}{4}(100 + x)$$

Now, $\frac{3}{4}(100 + x) = 120 \quad \Rightarrow x = \text{Rs. } 60;$

Hence, M.P. will be 60% above the C.P.

Example 34: A merchant has 120 kg of rice. He sells a part of it at a profit of 10% and the rest at a profit of 25%. He gains 15% on the whole. Find the quantity of rice he sold at 25% gain.

Solution: Let C.P. of each kg be Re. 1, Then total C.P. = Rs. 120

Let he sells x kg at 25% gain. Then,

$$\frac{125}{100}x+\frac{110}{100}(120-x)=\frac{115}{100}\times 120 \Rightarrow 125x + 13200 - 110x = 13800$$

$$\Rightarrow 15x = 600 \qquad \therefore x = 40 \text{ kg.}$$

Example 35: A wholesaler gains 25% by selling a commodity and a retailer gains 30% by selling it. If the retail value of that commodity is Rs. 325, then find, the wholesale value.

Solution: Wholesaler's value = $\frac{100}{130}\times\frac{100}{125}\times 325 =$ Rs. 200

Example 36: A sells a bicycle to B at a profit of 20% and B sells it to C at a profit of 25%. If C pays Rs. 225 for it, what did A pay for it?

Solution: C.P. for A = $\frac{100}{120}\times\frac{100}{125}\times$ Rs. 225 = Rs. 150

Example 37: A man had a radio to sell. I offered him a sum of money for the radio which he refused as being 13% below the value of the radio. I then offered Rs. 450 more and the second offer was 5% more than the estimated value. What is the value of the radio?

Solution: Here, (105% – 87%) = Rs. 450

$\Rightarrow$ 18% =Rs. 450

Hence, Value of the radio = Rs. $450\times\frac{100}{18}$ = Rs. 2500

Example 38: A man sells out an article at a profit of 25%. Had he bought it at 25% less and sold for Rs. 25 less, he would have still gained 25%. Find the cost of the article.

Solution: Let C.P. be Rs. x; then S.P. = $\frac{125x}{100}$ = Rs. $\frac{5x}{4}$

In 2nd case, C.P. = Rs. $\frac{75x}{100}$ = Rs. $\frac{3x}{4}$; then S.P. = Rs. $\frac{125}{100}\times\frac{3x}{4}$ = Rs. $\frac{15x}{16}$

Now, $\frac{5x}{4}-\frac{15x}{16}=25 \Rightarrow \frac{5x}{16}=25 \qquad \therefore x=\frac{16\times 25}{5}$ = Rs. 80

Example 39 : If goods be purchased for Rs. 450 and one third be sold at a loss of 10%. At what gain per cent should the remainder be sold so as to gain 20% on the whole transaction?

Solution: Cost of one third of the goods = $\frac{1}{3}\times$ Rs. 450 = Rs. 150

S.P. of one third goods = 90% of Rs. 150 = Rs. 135

S.P. of whole goods = 120% of Rs. 450 = Rs. 540

Hence, S.P. of the remaining $\frac{2}{3}$ of the goods = Rs. 540 – Rs. 135 = Rs. 405

But cost of this two-third = Rs. 300

$\therefore$ Gain =Rs. 405 – Rs. 300 = Rs. 105

Hence,Gain% = $\left(\frac{105}{300}\times 100\right)\%$ = 35%

Example 40: A publisher sells books to a retailer at Rs. 5 a copy but allows 25 copies to count as 24. If the retailer sells each of the 25 copies at Rs. 6, what profit per cent, does he make?

Solution: C.P. of 25 copies = 24 × 5 = Rs. 120; S.P. of 25 copies = 25 × 6 = Rs. 150;
Profit= 150 – 120 = Rs. 30

$$\text{Hence, Profit per cent} = \left(\frac{30}{120}\times 100\right)\% = 25\%$$

Example 41: Geeta purchased a suitcase with an additional 10% discount on the reduced price after deducting 20% on the labelled price. If the labelled price of the suitcase was Rs. 1400, at what price did she purchase the suitcase?

Solution: $\text{C.P. for Geeta} = \frac{80}{100}\times\frac{90}{100}\times \text{Rs. } 1400 = \text{Rs. } 1008$

Example 42: The profit earned by selling a watch for Rs. 820 is as much as the loss incurred when it is sold for Rs. 650. What is the cost price of the watch?

Solution: Let C.P. = Rs. x
Now, $820 - x = x - 650 \Rightarrow 2x = 1470 \quad \therefore x = \text{Rs. } 735$

Example 43: Profit earned by selling an article for Rs. 1060 is 20% more than the loss incurred by selling the article for Rs 950. At what price should the article be sold to earn 20% profit?

Solution: Let C.P. = Rs. x

$$\text{Now, } (1060 - x) - (x - 950) = \frac{20}{100}(x - 950)$$

$$\Rightarrow 11x = 11000 \qquad \therefore x = \text{Rs. } 1000$$

$$\text{Hence, S.P.} = \frac{120}{100}\times \text{Rs. } 1000 = \text{Rs. } 1200$$

Example 44: An article is sold at a profit of 20%. If both the cost price and selling price are Rs. 100 less, the profit would be 4% more. Find the cost price.

Solution: Let C.P = Rs. x; then $\text{S.P.} = \text{Rs. } \frac{120x}{100} = \text{Rs. } \frac{6x}{5}$

Again, when C.P. = Rs. $(x - 100)$; then $\text{S.P.} = \text{Rs. } \frac{124}{100}(100 - x) = \text{Rs. } \frac{31}{25}(100 - x)$

$$\text{Now, } \frac{6x}{5} - \frac{31}{25}(100 - x) = 100 \qquad \Rightarrow \frac{3100 - x}{25} = 100 \qquad \therefore x = \text{Rs. } 600$$

Example 45: $\frac{1}{3}$ of a commodity is sold at 15% profit, $\frac{1}{4}$ is sold at 20% profit and the rest at 24% profit. If a total profit of Rs. 62 is earned, then find the value of the commodity.

Solution: Let the value of the commodity was Rs. x

Here, remaining value of commodity $= x - \left(\frac{x}{3} + \frac{x}{4}\right) = \text{Rs. } \frac{5x}{12}$ was sold at 24% profit.

$$\text{Now, profit} = \frac{x}{3}\left(\frac{15}{100}\right) + \frac{x}{4}\left(\frac{20}{100}\right) + \frac{5x}{12}\left(\frac{24}{100}\right) = 62$$

$$\Rightarrow \frac{x}{20} + \frac{x}{20} + \frac{x}{10} = 62 \qquad \Rightarrow \frac{x}{5} = 62 \qquad \therefore x = 62 \times 5 = \text{Rs. } 310$$

Example 46: A man purchases 5 horses and 10 cows for Rs. 10,000. He sells the horses at 15% profit and the cows at 10% loss. Thus he gets Rs. 375 as profit. Find the cost of 1 horse and 1 cow separately.

Solution: Let the cost of 1 hourse be Rs. x; then Net Profit = $\frac{15}{100}\times 5x - \frac{10}{100}(10{,}000 - x) = 375$

$$\Rightarrow \frac{5x}{4} = 1375 \quad \therefore\ x = \frac{4\times 1375}{5} = \text{Rs. } 1100$$

Hence, cost of one horse = Rs. 1100; Cost of one cow = $\frac{10{,}000-(5\times 1100)}{10}$ = Rs. 450

Example 47: Mukesh purchased 20 dozen notebooks at Rs. 48 per dozen. He sold 8 dozen at 10% profit and the remaining 12 dozen at 20% profit. What is his profit percentage in this transaction?

Solution: Cost price of 20 dozen notebooks = 20 × 48 = Rs. 960

S.P. of 20 dozen notebooks = $\frac{110}{100}\times 8\times 48 + \frac{120}{100}\times 12\times 48 = \frac{2112}{5} + \frac{3456}{5}$ = Rs. $\frac{5568}{5}$

Profit = $\frac{5568}{5} - 960 = \text{Rs.}\frac{768}{5}$;

Hence, Profit % = $\frac{768\times 100}{5\times 960} = 16\%$

Example 48: A person sold two watches for Rs. 1000 each. On one he lost 5% but on the other he gained $5\frac{1}{2}\%$. Find his loss or gain. Also find his percentage of gain or loss.

Solution: Here, S.P. of both watches = 2 × Rs. 1000 = Rs. 2000

C.P. of both watches = $\frac{100}{95}\times 1000 + \frac{200}{211}\times 1000$ = 1052.63 + 947.87 = Rs. 2000.50

Loss = 2000.50 – 2000 = Rs. 0.50

Loss % = $\frac{0.50\times 100}{2000.50} \approx 0.025\%$

Example 49: A shopkeeper professes to sell his goods on cost price but uses false weight and gains $11\frac{1}{9}\%$. What weight does he use for a kg?

Solution: False weight = $\frac{100\times \text{True weight}}{\%\text{ gain}+100} = \frac{100\times 1000}{11\frac{1}{9}+100} = \frac{100\times 1000}{\frac{100+900}{9}}$ = 900 gm

Example 50: An article when sold at a gain of 5% yields Rs. 15 more than when sold at a loss of 5%. What is its cost price?

Solution: Let cost price = Rs. x

Now, $\frac{105x}{100} - \frac{95x}{100} = 15 \quad \Rightarrow \frac{x}{10} = 15 \quad \therefore x = \text{Rs. } 150$

EXERCISE

1. Ashok bought 25 kg of rice at the rate of Rs. 6 per kg and 35 kg of rice at the rate of Rs. 7 per kg. He mixed the two and sold the mixture at the rate of Rs. 6.75 per kg. What was his gain or loss in the transaction?
(*a*) Rs. 16 gain (*b*) Rs. 16 loss (*c*) Rs. 10 gain (*d*) None of these
2. A horse and a cow were sold for Rs. 12000 each. The horse was sold at a loss of 20% and the cow at a gain of 20%. The entire transaction resulted in
(*a*) no loss no gain (*b*) loss of Rs. 1000
(*c*) gain of Rs. 1000 (*d*) loss of Rs. 2000
3. Profit after selling a commodity for Rs. 425 is same as loss after selling it for Rs. 355. The cost of the commodity is :
(*a*) Rs. 285 (*b*) Rs. 390 (*c*) Rs. 295 (*d*) Rs. 400
4. Bhajan Singh purchased 120 reams of paper at Rs. 80 per ream. He spent Rs. 280 on transportation, paid octroi at the rate of 40 paise per ream and paid Rs. 72 to the coolie. If he wants to have a gain of 8%, what must be the selling price per ream?
(*a*) Rs. 86 (*b*) Rs. 86.48 (*c*) Rs. 79 (*d*) Rs. 90
5. Ram bought 4 dozen apples at Rs. 12 per dozen and 2 dozen at Rs. 16 per dozen. He sold all of them to earn 20%. At what price per dozen did he sell the apples?
(*a*) Rs. 14.40 (*b*) Rs. 16.00 (*c*) Rs. 16.80 (*d*) Rs. 16.20
6. Jimmy bought paper sheets for Rs. 7200 and spent Rs. 200 in transport. Paying Rs. 600 he had 330 boxes made, which he sold at Rs. 28 each. What is his profit percentage?
(*a*) 15.5 (*b*) 40 (*c*) 50 (*d*) None of these
7. A owns a house worth Rs. 10000. He sells it to B at a profit of 10% based on the worth of the house. B sells the house back to A at a loss of 10%. In this transaction A gets:
(*a*) no profit no loss (*b*) profit of Rs. 1000 (*c*) profit of Rs. 1100 (*d*) profit of Rs. 1200
8. At what price must Kantilal sell a mixture of 80 kg sugar at Rs. 6.75 per kg with 120 kg at Rs. 8 per kg to gain 20%?
(*a*) Rs. 7.50 per kg (*b*) Rs. 8.20 per kg (*c*) Rs. 8.35 per kg (*d*) Rs. 9 per kg
9. Subhash purchased a taperecorder at $\frac{9}{10}$ of its selling price and sold it at 8% more than its S.P. His gain is :
(*a*) 8% (*b*) 10% (*c*) 18% (*d*) 20%
10. A dealer marks his goods 20% above cost price. He then allows some discount on it and makes a profit of 8%. The rate of discount is :
(*a*) 12% (*b*) 10% (*c*) 6% (*d*) 4%
11. A trader lists his articles 20% above C.P. and allows a discount of 10% on cash payment. His gain per cent is :
(*a*) 10% (*b*) 8% (*c*) 6% (*d*) 4%
12. Tarun bought a T.V. with 20% discount on the labelled price. Had he bought it with 25% discount, he would have saved Rs. 500. At what price did he buy the T.V.?
(*a*) Rs. 5000 (*b*) Rs. 8000 (*c*) Rs. 10000 (*d*) Rs. 12000

13. While selling a watch, a shopkeeper gives a discount of 5%. If he gives a discount of 7%, he earns Rs. 15 less as profit. The marked price of the watch is :

(a) Rs. 697.50 *(b)* Rs. 712.50 *(c)* Rs. 787.50 *(d)* None of these

14. Kabir buys an article with 25% discount on its marked price. He makes a profit of 10% by selling it at Rs. 660. The marked price is :

(a) Rs. 600 *(b)* Rs. 700 *(c)* Rs. 800 *(d)* Rs. 885

15. A person bought an article and sold it at a loss of 10%. If he had bought it for 20% less and sold it for Rs. 55 more, he would have had a profit of 40%. The C.P. of the article is :

(a) Rs. 200 *(b)* Rs. 225 *(c)* Rs. 250 *(d)* None of these

16. The purchase tax on an article is levied at the rate of $66\frac{2}{3}\%$ of its wholesale price, while the retailer's profit amounts to 20% of the retail price of the article. What is the wholesale price of an article which is retailed at Rs. 12.50?

(a) Rs. 4 *(b)* Rs. 6 *(c)* Rs. 8 *(d)* Rs. 2

17. The catalogue price of a radio is Rs. 720. If it is sold at a discount of $16\frac{2}{3}\%$ of the catalogue price, the gain is 25%. Find the gain or loss per cent, if it is sold for Rs. 160 below the catalogue price.

(a) $16\frac{2}{3}\%$ *(b)* 16% *(c)* 18% *(d)* 20%

18. A tradesman sells one kind of sugar at Rs. 3 per kg and loses 20 per cent and another kind of sugar at Rs. 5 per kg and gains 25 per cent. He mixes them together in equal proportion and sells the mixture at Rs. 6 per kg. What is his gain %?

(a) $53\frac{26}{31}\%$ *(b)* $51\frac{31}{26}\%$ *(c)* $54\frac{26}{31}\%$ *(d)* $55\frac{26}{31}\%$

19. A dealer sold a machine to a shopkeeper at 20% profit. The shopkeeper sold the machine to a customer so as to get 25% profit for himself. The difference between the selling price of the dealer and that of the shopkeeper was found to be Rs. 129. What is the initial price of the machine?

(a) Rs. 410 *(b)* Rs. 420 *(c)* Rs. 430 *(d)* Rs. 440

20. At a cricket match the contractor provided dinner for 24 persons, and fixed the price so as to gain $12\frac{1}{2}\%$ upon his total outlay. Three of the cricketers being absent, the remaining 21 paid the fixed price for their dinner, and as such the contractor lost 1 rupee. What was the charge of the dinner?

(a) Rs. 2 *(b)* Rs. 3 *(c)* Rs. 4 *(d)* Rs. 5

21. A man bought a horse and cart. If he sold the horse at 10% loss and the cart at 20% gain he would not loss anything. If he sold the horse at 5% loss and the cart at 5% gain he would lose Rs. 10 in the bargain. What did he pay for each?

(a) Rs. 400, Rs. 200 *(b)* Rs. 300, Rs. 300 *(c)* Rs. 250, Rs. 350 *(d)* Rs. 350, Rs. 250

22. A merchant buys 200 kilograms of rice at Rs. 1.25 per kilogram, 400 kilograms of rice at 75 paise per kilogram. He mixes them and sells one third of the mixture at one rupee per kilogram. At what rate should he sell the remaining mixture so that he may earn a profit of 25% on the whole outlay?

(a) Rs. 1.20 *(b)* Rs. 1.22

(c) Rs. 1.30 *(d)* Rs. 1.32

23. A man buys goods and finds that the cost of carriage is 4% on the cost of goods. He is compelled to sell at a loss of 5% of his total outlay. If, however, he had recieved Rs. 32.50 more than he did, he would have gained $2\frac{1}{2}$%. What was the original cost of the goods?

(a) Rs. 416.67 *(b)* Rs. 416 *(c)* Rs. 461.67 *(d)* Rs. 461

24. A businessman sells an old machine for Rs. 1150 after taking some profit. Had he sold it for Rs. 910 his loss would have been $\frac{7}{5}$ of the profit. What was the cost price of that machine?

(a) Rs. 1000 *(b)* Rs. 1050 *(c)* Rs. 1100 *(d)* Rs. 1150

25. The marked price of a radio is 20% more than its cost price. If a discount of 10% is given on the marked price, the gain percentage is:

(a) 8 *(b)* 10 *(c)* 12 *(d)* 15

26. A fan is listed at Rs. 1400 and the discount offered is 10%. What additional discount must be given to bring the net selling price to Rs. 1200?

(a) $4\frac{16}{21}$% *(b)* 5% *(c)* 6% *(d)* $16\frac{2}{3}$%

27. A person blends two varieties of tea-one costing Rs. 160 per kg and other costing Rs. 200 per kg in the ratio 5 : 4. He sells the blended variety at Rs. 192 per kg. What is his profit per cent?

(a) 8 *(b)* 9 *(c)* 10 *(d)* 12

28. Sanjay buys a field of agricultural land for Rs. 3,60,000. He sells one-third at a loss of 20% and two-fifths at a gain of 25%. At what price must he sell the remaining field so as to make an overall profit of 10%?

(a) Rs. 1,00,000 *(b)* Rs. 1,15,000 *(c)* Rs. 1,20,000 *(d)* Rs. 1,25,000

29. The marked price of an electric iron is Rs. 300. The shopkeeper allows a discount of 12% and still gains 10%. If no discount is allowed, his gain per cent would have been:

(a) 20 *(b)* 25 *(c)* 27 *(d)* 30

30. An increase of Rs. 3 in the selling price of an article turns a loss of $7\frac{1}{2}$% into gain of $7\frac{1}{2}$%. What is the cost price (in Rs.) of the article?

(a) 10 *(b)* 15 *(c)* 20 *(d)* 25

31. A car worth Rs. 1,50,000 was sold by X to Y at 5% profit. Y sold back to X at 2% loss. In the entire transaction:

(a) X gained Rs. 3150 *(b)* X gained Rs. 4350 *(c)* Y lost Rs. 3150 *(d)* Y lost Rs. 4350

32. Saurabh bought a radio for Rs. 800 and spent Rs. 400 on it. He sold it for Rs. 1500. What is his gain per cent?

(a) 25% *(b)* 35% *(c)* 52% *(d)* 55%

33. Samir purchased 150 quintals of wheat. One-fourth of the total quantity, he sold at a loss of 10%. At what gain per cent should he sell the remaining wheat to gain 10% on the whole transaction?

(a) $14\frac{1}{2}$% *(b)* $15\frac{2}{3}$% *(c)* $16\frac{2}{3}$% *(d)* $18\frac{2}{3}$%

34. A shopkeeper buys two varieties of rice. One variety costs him Rs. 27 per kg and other Rs. 30 per kg. He mixed them in the ratio of 5 : 3 and sells the blended variety at the rate of Rs. 30 per kg. What is his gain per cent?

(a) 5% *(b)* $6\frac{2}{3}$% *(c)* 7% *(d)* 8%

35. A dishonest dealer sells his goods at the cost price and still earns a profit of 60% by underweight. What weight does he use for a kg?
(*a*) 625 gms (*b*) 750 gms (*c*) 800 gms (*d*) 850 gms

36. A man sells two horses for Rs. 990 each. On one he gains 10% and the other he loses 10%. What is his total percentage of gain or loss in the transaction?
(*a*) 1% gain (*b*) 1% loss (*c*) 2% gain (*d*) 2% loss

37. If a shirt coasting Rs. 385 is sold at a loss of 5% of the cost price, what is the selling price of the shirt?
(*a*) Rs. 364 (*b*) Rs. 364.74 (*c*) Rs. 365 (*d*) Rs. 365.75

38. If the cost price of 24 articles is equal to selling price of 21 articles, find the percentage gain or loss.
(*a*) 12.5 gain (*b*) 12.5% loss (*c*) $14\frac{2}{7}\%$ gain (*d*) $14\frac{2}{7}\%$ loss

39. The profit after selling a pair of trousers for Rs. 863 is the same as the loss incurred after selling the same pair of trousers for Rs. 631. Find the cost price of the pair of trousers.
(*a*) Rs. 747 (*b*) Rs. 750 (*c*) Rs. 763 (*d*) Rs. 800

40. A trader sells 145 metres of cloth for Rs. 12,325 at the profit of Rs. 10 per meter of cloth. Find the cost price of one meter of cloth?
(*a*) Rs. 65 (*b*) Rs. 75 (*c*) Rs. 85 (*d*) Rs. 95

41. The profit obtained after selling an article for Rs. 1,186 is the same as loss incurred after selling the same article for Rs. 1,098. Find the cost price of the article.
(*a*) Rs. 1100 (*b*) Rs. 1135 (*c*) Rs. 1142 (*d*) Rs. 1146

42. On selling an article for Rs. 270 there is a gain of 12.5%. What is its cost price?
(*a*) Rs. 210 (*b*) Rs. 220 (*c*) Rs. 240 (*d*) Rs. 250

43. The cost price of an article is Rs. 7840. To gain 7%, the article should be sold at:
(*a*) Rs. 8000 (*b*) Rs. 8383.80 (*c*) Rs. 8388.80 (*d*) Rs. 8833.80

44. A table clock is sold at a profit of 10%. Had it been sold for Rs. 40 less, there would have been a loss of 10%. What is the cost price?
(*a*) Rs. 150 (*b*) Rs. 175 (*c*) Rs. 200 (*d*) Rs. 324

45. Ram sells a table to Shyam at a profit of 20% and Shyam sells it to Sohan at a profit of 30%. If it costs, Rs. 3120 to Sohan, the cost price of table for Ram is:
(*a*) Rs. 1800 (*b*) Rs. 2000 (*c*) Rs. 2100 (*d*) Rs. 2500

46. A merchant professes to sell tea at the cost price but uses a false weight of 900 gm for a kilogram. His profit per cent in the transaction is:
(*a*) $9\frac{1}{11}\%$ (*b*) 10% (*c*) $11\frac{1}{9}\%$ (*d*) 20%

47. The difference in selling a coat at profits of 4% and 6% is Rs. 12. The cost price of the coat is:
(*a*) Rs. 150 (*b*) Rs. 300 (*c*) Rs. 450 (*d*) Rs.600

48. A shopkeeper marks his goods at a price that would give him 20% profit and allows a discount of 10% in the sale on the marked price. What is his profit or loss per cent in the transaction?
(*a*) 8% profit (*b*) 12% profit (*c*) 30% profit (*d*) 10% loss

49. A manufacturer sells a cooler to a distributor at a profit of 18%. The distributor sells the same to a retailer at a profit of 20%. The retailer, in turns sells it to a customer for Rs. 2124 thereby earning a profit of 25%. What is the cost price for the manufacturer?
(*a*) Rs. 1200 (*b*) Rs. 1300 (*c*) Rs. 1400 (*d*) Rs. 1450

50. A manufactuerer's list price of a table is Rs. 4750. He sells it to a retailer with successive discounts of 15% and 10% with terms : cash 4, 2/20. If the retailer pays the bill on 10th day, what is his cost price?
(*a*) Rs. 1356.08 (*b*) Rs. 3361.08 (*c*) Rs. 3561.08 (*d*) Rs. 4616.10

51. If on selling 12 notebooks any seller makes a profit equal to the selling price of 4 notebooks, what is his profit per cent?
(*a*) $16\frac{2}{3}\%$ (*b*) 20% (*c*) 25% (*d*) 50%

52. A grocer purchased 2 kg of rice at the rate of Rs. 15 per kg and 3 kg of rice at the rate of Rs. 13 per kg. At what price per kg should he sell the mixture to earn $33\frac{1}{3}\%$ profit on the cost price?
(*a*) Rs. 28.00 (*b*) Rs. 20.00 (*c*) Rs. 18.40 (*d*) Rs. 17.40

53. Samir bought a watch with 25% discount on the selling price. If the watch cost her Rs. 1,545. What is the original selling price of the watch?
(*a*) Rs. 2000 (*b*) Rs. 2040 (*c*) Rs. 2050 (*d*) Rs. 2060

54. By selling a watch for Rs. 144 a man loses 10%. At what price should he sell it in order to gain 15%.
(*a*) Rs. 170 (*b*) Rs. 180 (*c*) Rs. 184 (*d*) Rs. 195

55. A shopkeeper sells a television set for Rs. 27600 and earns 15% profit. What was the cost price of the television set?
(*a*) Rs. 24000 (*b*) Rs. 25000 (*c*) Rs. 25500 (*d*) Rs. 27000

56. A man buys two horses for Rs. 1,350.00. He sells one at 6% loss and the other at 7.5% gain. If on the whole transaction he neither gains nor loses then find out the cost price of each horse.
(*a*) Rs. 750, Rs. 600 (*b*) Rs. 650, Rs. 700 (*c*) Rs. 550, Rs. 800 (*d*) Rs. 500, Rs. 850

57. Avinash purchases five cycles at the rate of Rs. 450 per cycle. He spends Rs. 150 on each cycle for repairs. At what price he should sell them to gain a profit of 35%?
(*a*) Rs. 600 (*b*) Rs. 608 (*c*) Rs. 750 (*d*) Rs. 810

58. The marked prices of articles in a shop are 20% more than their cost prices. The shopkeeper gives a discount of Rs. 40 on a purchase of Rs. 960. What is net per cent profit?
(*a*) 10% (*b*) 12% (*c*) 15% (*d*) 18%

59. By selling an article for Rs. 40, there is a loss of 40%. By selling it for Rs. 80 there is:
(*a*) Gain of 20% (*b*) Gain of 10% (*c*) Loss of 10% (*d*) Loss of 20%

60. A wholesaler charges the price of 27 pens for 30 pens from a retailer. The retailer sells them at marked price. What is his gain per cent?
(*a*) $11\frac{1}{9}\%$ (*b*) 12% (*c*) 18% (*d*) 18½%

61. Nilam bought a watch with 24% discount on the selling price. If the watch cost her Rs. 779, what is the original selling price of the watch?
(*a*) Rs. 925 (*b*) Rs. 950 (*c*) Rs. 1000 (*d*) Rs. 1025

62. The profit earned after selling an article for Rs. 536 is the same as loss incurred after selling the article for Rs. 426. What is the cost price of the article?
(*a*) Rs. 448 (*b*) Rs. 470 (*c*) Rs. 481 (*d*) Rs. 500

63. If the cost price of 12 tables is equal to the selling price of 16 tables, find the loss per cent.
(a) 15% (b) 20% (c) 25% (d) 30%

64. How much per cent more than the cost price should a shopkeeper mark his goods so that after giving a discount of 12.5% he makes a profit of 5%?
(a) 15% (b) 17.5% (c) 20% (d) 25%

65. Gopal bought 12 tables for Rs. 12000 and sold them at a profit equal to the cost price of 4 tables. Then find the selling price of 1 table.
(a) Rs. 1100 (b) Rs. 1200 (c) Rs. 1333.33 (d) Rs. 1600

66. A shopkeeper marks his goods at $1\frac{2}{3}$ of his cost price and allows a discount of 10%. What per cent does he gain or lose?
(a) $33\frac{1}{3}$% gain (b) 40% gain (c) 50% gain (d) 50% loss

67. By selling a chair for Rs. 770, a carpenter gained 10% on it. Had he sold it for Rs. 707, what would have been his gain or loss per cent?
(a) 1% gain (b) 7% gain (c) 1% loss (d) 10% loss

68. A merchant sold two cows for Rs. 8400 and Rs. 8800 respectively. If he earns a profit of 20% on the first and 10% on the second, his total profit is:
(a) Rs. 2100 (b) Rs. 2200 (c) Rs. 2400 (d) Rs. 4200

69. A man sells two horses for the same price. On one he makes a profit of 10% on the other a loss of 15%. In the whole transaction, he makes:
(a) $4\frac{4}{39}$% profit (b) $4\frac{4}{39}$% loss (c) $4\frac{5}{39}$% loss (d) $5\frac{4}{39}$% loss

70. A man sold 33 bananas and had a gain equal to selling price of 11 bananas. His profit per cent is:
(a) 28% (b) 30% (c) $33\frac{1}{3}$% (d) 50%

71. A dishonest dealer professes to sell his goods at cost price, but still he gains 25% on his outlay. What weight does he substitute for a kilogram?
(a) 750 gm (b) 800 gm (c) 850 gm (d) 900 gm

72. If S.P. of an article is $\frac{4}{3}$ of C.P., the profit is:
(a) $\frac{1}{3}$% (b) 33% (c) $33\frac{1}{3}$% (d) $33\frac{1}{8}$%

73. The C.P. of 12 articles is equal to selling price of 16 articles. The gain or loss % is:
(a) 25% gain (b) 25% loss (c) $33\frac{1}{3}$% gain (d) $33\frac{1}{3}$% loss

74. A tradesman sold an article at a loss of 20%. If the selling price had been increased by Rs. 100, there would have been a gain of 5%. What was the cost price of the article?
(a) Rs. 350 (b) Rs. 400 (c) Rs. 450 (d) Rs. 500

75. When a producer allows 36% commission on the retail price of his product, he earns a profit of 8.8%. What would be his profit per cent, if the commission is reduced by 24%?
(a) 40% (b) 45.6% (c) 49.6% (d) 50%

76. A retailer buys 40 pens at the marked price of 36 pens from a wholesaler. If he sells these pens giving a discount of 1%, what is the profit per cent?
(a) 5% *(b)* 10% *(c)* 15% *(d)* 20%

77. An uneducated retailer marks his goods at 50% above the cost price and thinking that he will still make 25% profit, offers a discount of 25% on the marked price. What is his actual profit on the sales?
(a) 5% *(b)* 10.5% *(c)* 12.5% *(d)* 15%

78. At what percentage above the C.P. must an article be marked so as to gain 33% after allowing a customer a discount of 5%?
(a) 25% *(b)* 30% *(c)* 35% *(d)* 40%

79. Samir purchased a machine for Rs. 80,000 and spent Rs. 5000 on repair and Rs. 1000 on transport and sold it with 25% profit. At what price did he sell the machine?
(a) Rs. 1,17,500 *(b)* Rs. 1,07,500 *(c)* Rs. 1,06,250 *(d)* Rs. 1,05,100

80. Madhawa bought a scooter for a certain sum of money. He spent 10% of the cost on repairs and sold the scooter for a profit of Rs. 1100. How much did he spend on repairs if he made a profit of 20%.
(a) Rs. 550 *(b)* Rs. 500 *(c)* Rs. 440 *(d)* Rs. 400

81. A shopkeeper sells one transistor for Rs. 840 at a gain of 20% and another for Rs. 960 at a loss of 4%. His total gain or loss per cent is:
(a) $5\frac{15}{17}$% gain *(b)* $6\frac{2}{3}$% gain *(c)* $5\frac{15}{17}$% loss *(d)* $6\frac{2}{3}$% loss

82. The ratio of the cost price and selling price is 4 : 5. The profit per cent is:
(a) 30% *(b)* 25% *(c)* 20% *(d)* $16\frac{2}{3}$%

83. What is the ratio between profit and cost price of an article if ratio between their selling price and cost price is 7 : 5?
(a) 2 : 5 *(b)* 2 : 7 *(c)* 5 : 2 *(d)* 7 : 2

84. If selling price is doubled, the profit triples. What is the profit per cent?
(a) 75% *(b)* 80% *(c)* 100% *(d)* 120%

85. A man gains 20% by selling an article for a certain price. If he sells it at double the price, the percentage of profit will be:
(a) 140% *(b)* 120% *(c)* 100% *(d)* 40%

86. The percentage profit earned by selling an article for Rs. 1920 is equal to the percentage loss incurred by selling the same article for Rs. 1280. At what price should the article be sold to make 25% profit?
(a) Rs. 1800 *(b)* Rs. 2000 *(c)* Rs. 2200 *(d)* Rs. 2400

87. In a certain store, the profit is 320% of the cost price. If the cost increases by 25% but the selling price remains constant, approximately what percentage of the selling price is the profit?
(a) 40% *(b)* 70% *(c)* 90% *(d)* 120%

88. A man buys 2 dozen bananas at Rs. 16 per dozen. After selling 18 bananas at the rate of Rs. 12 per dozen, the shopkeeper reduced the rate to Rs. 4 per dozen. What is the loss percentage?
(a) 37.5% *(b)* 36.5% *(c)* 32.4% *(d)* 25.2%

89. A man sold 18 cots for Rs. 16,800, gaining thereby the cost price of 3 cots. What is the cost price of a cot?
(a) Rs. 800 *(b)* Rs. 750 *(c)* Rs. 700 *(d)* Rs. 650

90. The cost price of 20 articles is the same as the selling price of x articles. If the profit is 25%, then what is the value of x?

(a) 25 *(b)* 18 *(c)* 16 *(d)* 15

91. If the selling price of 50 articles is equal to the cost price of 40 articles, then what is the loss or gain per cent?

(a) 20% gain *(b)* 20% loss *(c)* 25% gain *(d)* 25% loss

92. On an order of 5 dozen boxes of a consumer product, a retailer receives an extra dozen free. This is equivalent to allowing him a discount of:

(a) 20% *(b)* $16\frac{2}{3}\%$ *(c)* $16\frac{1}{3}\%$ *(d)* 15%

93. A shopkeeper mixes three varieties of groundnuts consisting Rs. 50, Rs. 20 and Rs. 30 per kg in the ratio 2 : 4 : 3 in terms of weight and sells the mixture at Rs. 33 per kg. Find his profit per cent.

(a) 12% *(b)* 10% *(c)* 9% *(d)* 8%

94. By mixing two brands of tea and selling the mixture at the rate of Rs. 177 per kg, a shopkeeper makes a profit of 18%. If every 2 kg of one brand costing Rs. 200 per kg, 3 kg of the other brand is added, then how much per kg does the other brand cost?

(a) Rs. 140 *(b)* Rs. 120 *(c)* Rs. 116.66 *(d)* Rs. 115

95. A dairyman pays Rs. 6.40 per litre of milk. He adds water and sells the mixture at Rs. 8 per litre, there by making 37.5% profit. What is the proportion of water to milk received by the customers?

(a) 1 : 15 *(b)* 1 : 10 *(c)* 1 : 7 *(d)* 1 : 5

96. By selling 12 toffees for a rupee, a man loses 20%. How many for a rupee should he sell to get a gain of 20%?

(a) 15 *(b)* 10 *(c)* 8 *(d)* 5

97. Gopal purchased a box full of pencils at the rate of 7 for Rs. 9 and sold all of them at the rate of 8 for Rs. 11 . In the transaction, he gained Rs. 10. How many pencils did the box contain?

(a) 115 *(b)* 114 *(c)* 112 *(d)* 100

98. A man bought toffees at 6 for a rupee. How many for a rupee must he sell to gain 20%.

(a) 6 *(b)* 5 *(c)* 4 *(d)* 3

99. A sells a bicycle to B at a profit of 20%. B sells to C at a profit of 25%. if C pays Rs. 225 for it, the cost price of the bicycle for A is:

(a) Rs. 150 *(b)* Rs. 125 *(c)* Rs. 120 *(d)* Rs. 110

100. A shopkeeper cheat to the extent of 10%, while buying as well as selling by using false weights. What is his total gain?

(a) 21% *(b)* 20% *(c)* 15% *(d)* 12%

101. A fair price shopkeeper takes 10% profit on his goods. He lost 20% goods during theft. What is his loss per cent?

(a) 12% *(b)* 11% *(c)* 10% *(d)* 8%

102. A dishonest dealer professes to sell his goods at cost price. But he uses a false weight and thus gains $6\frac{18}{47}\%$. Find the weight which he uses for a kg.

(a) 960 gm *(b)* 953 gm

(c) 947 gm *(d)* 940 gm

103. A shopkeeper sells two watches for Rs. 308 each. On one he gets 12% profit and on the other 12% loss. His profit or loss per cent in the entire transaction was:

(a) $3\frac{2}{25}\%$ loss (b) $1\frac{11}{25}\%$ profit

(c) $1\frac{11}{25}\%$ loss (d) Neither profit nor loss

104. The difference between the cost price and selling price of an article is Rs. 240. If the profit is 20%, then what is the selling price?

(a) Rs. 1600 (b) Rs. 1400 (c) Rs. 1440 (d) Rs. 1000

105. The cash difference between the selling prices of an article at a profit of 4% and 6% is Rs. 3. What is the ratio of two selling prices?

(a) 52 : 55 (b) 51 : 53 (c) 52 : 53 (d) 51 : 52

106. If a person reduces the selling price of a fan from Rs. 400 to Rs. 380, his loss increases by 2%. What will be his cost price?

(a) Rs. 1000 (b) Rs. 800 (c) Rs. 600 (d) Rs. 500

107. Saurabh bought a microwave oven and paid 10% less than the marked price. He sold it with 30% profit on the price he had paid. Find the profit which Saurabh earns on the marked price.

(a) 30% (b) 25% (c) 20% (d) 17%

108. Ram buys an article for 10% less than its value and sells it for 10% more than its value. What is his gain or loss per cent?

(a) 20% (b) $20\frac{2}{9}\%$ (c) $22\frac{2}{9}\%$ (d) 24%

109. If 5% more is gained by selling price of an article for Rs. 350 than by selling it for Rs. 340, what is the cost price of the article?

(a) Rs. 225 (b) Rs. 200 (c) Rs. 160 (d) Rs. 150

110. A shopkeeper gives 12% additional discount on the discounted price, after giving an initial discount of 20% on the marked price of a radio. If the final selling price of the radio is Rs. 704, then find the marked price?

(a) Rs. 1044.80 (b) Rs. 1000 (c) Rs. 999.28 (d) Rs. 844.80

111. If a company sells a car with labelled price of Rs. 2,72,000 and gives a discount of 4% on Rs. 2,00,000 and 2.5% on the remaining amount of Rs. 72,000, then what is the actual price charged by the company for the car?

(a) Rs. 2,62,000 (b) Rs. 2,60,100

(c) Rs. 2,55,000 (d) Rs. 2,50,000

112. A man purchases 90 clocks and sells 40 clocks at a gain of 10% and 50 clocks at a gain of 20%. If he sold all of them at a uniform profit of 15% then he would have got Rs. 40 less. What is the cost price of each clock?

(a) Rs. 90 (b) Rs. 80 (c) Rs. 60 (d) Rs. 50

113. The difference between a discount of 35% and successive discounts of 20% on a certain bill was Rs. 22. What is the amount of the bill?

(a) Rs. 2400 (b) Rs. 2200 (c) Rs. 2000 (d) Rs. 1100

114. The price of a television is labelled at Rs. 12,000. If successive discounts of 15%, 10% and 5% be allowed, then find the cost price for a customer.
(a) Rs. 8856 (b) Rs. 8756 (c) Rs. 8721 (d) Rs. 8700

115. Applied to a bill for Rs. 1,00,000, the difference between a discount of 40% and two successive discounts of 36% and 4% is:
(a) Rs. 1960 (b) Rs. 1440 (c) Rs. 1400 (d) Nil

116. A fan is listed at Rs. 1500 and a discount of 20% is offered on the marked price. What additional discount must be offered to the customer to bring the net price to Rs. 1104?
(a) 15% (b) 12% (c) 10% (d) 8%

117. Successive discounts of 10%, 12% and 15% amount to a single discount of:
(a) 36.68% (b) 35.28% (c) 32.68% (d) 30.28%

118. Find the selling price of an article if a shopkeeper allows two successive discounts of 5% each on the list price of Rs. 80.
(a) Rs. 72.20 (b) Rs. 72 (c) Rs. 70.20 (d) Rs. 70.10

119. Marked price of an article is Rs. 2000 and it is being sold at successive discounts of 20% and 10%. Its net selling price will be:
(a) Rs. 1700 (b) Rs. 1520 (c) Rs. 1440 (d) Rs. 1400

120. At what price should a shopkeeper mark a radio that costs him Rs. 1200 in order that he may offer a discount of 20% on the marked price and still make a profit of 25%?
(a) Rs. 2025 (b) Rs. 1900 (c) Rs. 1875 (d) Rs. 1675

121. The cost price of an article is 64% of the list price. Calculate the gain per cent after allowing a discount of 12%.
(a) 52% (b) 50.5% (c) 48% (d) 37.5%

122. The list price of a watch is Rs. 720. A man buys it for Rs. 550.80 after getting two successive discounts, the first being 10%, find the second discount per cent.
(a) 18% (b) 15% (c) 14% (d) 12%

123. The price of an article is raised by 30% and then two successive discounts of 10% each are allowed. Ultimately what is the price of the article?
(a) Increased by 5.3% (b) Decreased by 5.3% (c) Increased by 10% (d) Increased by 3%

124. A businessman marked his price of his commodity so as to include a profit of 25%. He allowed discount of 16% on the marked price. What was his actual profit?
(a) 25% (b) 16% (c) 9% (d) 5%

125. Gopal bought an item at 20% discount on its marked price. He sold it with 40% increase on the price he bought it. The new selling price is by what per cent more than the marked price?
(a) 12% (b) 10% (c) 8% (d) 7.5%

126. A trader sold an article offering a discount of 5% and earned a profit of 23.5%. What would have been the percentage of profit earned if no discount was offered?
(a) 30% (b) 25% (c) 20% (d) 10%

127. A trader sells 25 articles at Rs. 45 per article after giving 10% discount and earns 50% profit. If discount is not given, the profit gained is:
(a) $66\frac{2}{3}\%$ (b) 66% (c) $60\frac{2}{3}\%$ (d) 60%

128. A trader sells a badminton racket, whose labelled price is Rs. 30, at a discount of 15% and gives a shuttle cock costing Rs. 1.50 free with each racket. Even then he makes a profit of 20%. What is cost price of a racket?

(*a*) Rs. 21.25 (*b*) Rs. 21 (*c*) Rs. 20 (*d*) Rs. 19.75

129. A tradesman marked his goods at 20% above the cost price. He sold half the stock at the marked price, one quarter at a discount of 20% on the marked price and the rest at a discount of 40% on the marked price. Ultimately what is his total gain?

(*a*) 15% (*b*) 13.5% (*c*) 4.5% (*d*) 2%

130. A shopkeeper marked the selling price of an article at 10% above the cost price. At the time of selling, he allows certain discount and suffers a loss of 1%. What is his allowed discount?

(*a*) 11% (*b*) 10.5% (*c*) 10% (*d*) 9%

131. Kaushal bought a suitcase with 15% discount on the marked price. He sold the suitcase for Rs. 2880 with 20% profit on the marked price. At what price did he buy the suitcase?

(*a*) Rs. 2640 (*b*) Rs. 2604 (*c*) Rs. 2400 (*d*) Rs. 2040

132. A trader fixes the marked price of an item 35% above its cost price. The percentage of discount allowed to gain 8% is:

(*a*) 43% (*b*) 31% (*c*) 27% (*d*) 20%

133. The marked price of cupboard is Rs. 6500. The trader sold it by giving 5% discount on the marked price and earned a profit of 15%. What approximately is the cost price of the cupboard?

(*a*) Rs. 5800 (*b*) Rs. 5600 (*c*) Rs. 5350 (*d*) Rs. 5000

134. A dishonest dealer uses a scale of 90 cm instead of meter scale and claims to sell at cost price. What is his profit per cent?

(*a*) 12% (*b*) $11\frac{1}{9}\%$ (*c*) 10% (*d*) 9%

SOLUTIONS

1. C.P. of 60 kg mixture $=$ Rs. $(25 \times 6 + 35 \times 7) =$ Rs. 395

S.P. of 60 kg mixtire $=$ Rs. $(60 \times 6.75) =$ Rs. 405

$\therefore$ Gain $=$ Rs. $(405 - 395) =$ Rs. 10

2. Loss % $= \left(\frac{20}{10}\right)^2 = (2)^2 = 4\%$

Total S.P. $=$ Rs. 24000

and Total C.P. $=$ Rs. $\left(\frac{100}{96} \times 24000\right) =$ Rs. 25000

$\therefore$ Loss $=$ Rs. $(25000 - 24000) =$ Rs. 1000

3. Let C.P. $=$ Rs. x

Then, $425 - x = x - 355 \Rightarrow 2x = 780 \quad \therefore x =$ Rs. 390

4. C.P. of 1 ream $= 80 + \frac{280}{120} + \frac{72}{120} + 0.40 = 80 + \frac{7}{3} + \frac{3}{5} + \frac{2}{5} =$ Rs. $\frac{250}{3}$

$\therefore$ S.P. of 1 ream $=$ Rs. $\left(\frac{108}{100} \times \frac{250}{3}\right) =$ Rs. 90

5. C.P. of 6 dozen apples = Rs. $(12 \times 4 + 16 \times 2)$ = Rs. 80

$$\therefore \quad \text{S.P.} = \text{Rs.}\left(\frac{120}{100} \times 80\right) = \text{Rs. } 96$$

$$\therefore \quad \text{S.P. per dozen} = \text{Rs.}\left(\frac{96}{6}\right) = \text{Rs. } 16$$

6. $$\text{C.P. of 1 box} = \frac{7200 + 200 + 600}{330} = \text{Rs. } \frac{800}{33}$$

$$\text{Hence, Gain\%} = \frac{28 - \frac{800}{33}}{800/33} \times 100 = \frac{124}{800} \times 100 = 15.5\%$$

7. $$\text{Final C.P. for A} = \frac{110}{100} \times \frac{90}{100} \times \text{Rs. } 10000 = \text{Rs. } 9900$$

$$\text{Hence, profit for A} = \frac{10}{100} \times \text{Rs. } 10{,}000 + \text{Rs. } (10{,}000 - 9900) = \text{Rs. } 1100$$

8. $$\text{C.P. of 1 kg sugar} = \frac{80 \times 6.75 + 120 \times 8}{200} = \text{Rs. } 7.50$$

$$\therefore \quad \text{S.P. of 1 kg} = \text{Rs.}\left(\frac{120}{100} \times 7.50\right) = \text{Rs. 9 per kg}$$

9. Let S.P. = Rs. 100; C.P. for Subhash = $\frac{9}{10} \times 100$ = Rs. 90 and S.P. = Rs. 108

Hence, gain % for Subhash = $\frac{108 - 90}{90} \times 100 = 20\%$

10. Let C.P. be Rs. 100; then Marked price = Rs. 120 and S.P. = Rs. 108

$$\therefore \quad \text{Discount} = \left(\frac{12}{120} \times 100\right)\% = 10\%$$

11. Let C.P. be Rs. 100
Then, marked price = Rs. 120

S.P. = Rs. $\left(\frac{90}{100} \times 120\right)$ = Rs. 108 $\quad \therefore$ Gain % = $\left(\frac{8}{100} \times 100\right)\% = 8\%$

12. Here, 5% = 500 $\quad \therefore \quad$ 100% = $\frac{500}{5} \times 100$ = Rs. 10,000

Hence, labelled price = Rs. 10,000

$\therefore$ S.P. = $\frac{80}{100}$ × Rs. 10,000 = Rs. 8000

13. Let the marked price = Rs. x

Then, $\frac{7x}{100}-\frac{5x}{100}=15 \quad \Rightarrow \frac{x}{50}=15 \quad \therefore x=\text{Rs. } 750$

14. $\text{C.P.} = \frac{100}{110}\times 660 = \text{Rs. } 600$

Hence, $\text{M.P.} = \frac{100}{75}\times 600 = \text{Rs. } 800$

15. Let C.P. = Rs. x, then $\text{S.P.} = \frac{90}{100}\times x = \text{Rs. } \frac{9x}{10}$

Now, when $\text{C.P.} = \text{Rs. } \frac{80x}{100} = \text{Rs. } \frac{4x}{5}$; then $\text{S.P.} = \frac{140}{100}\times\frac{4x}{5} = \text{Rs. } \frac{28x}{25}$

But, $\frac{28x}{25}-\frac{9x}{10}=55 \Rightarrow \frac{11x}{50}=55 \quad \therefore x=\text{Rs. } 250$

16. The retail price of the article = Rs. 12.50 = Rs. $\frac{25}{2}$

Profit of the retailer = 20% of Rs. $\frac{25}{2}$ = Rs. $\frac{5}{2}$

$\therefore$ Retailer's C.P. $= \frac{25}{2}-\frac{5}{2} = \text{Rs. } 10$

Wholesale price $= \frac{100}{100+\frac{200}{3}}\times 10 = \frac{3\times 100}{500}\times 10 = \text{Rs. } 6$

17. $\text{S.P.} = \frac{250}{3\times 100}\times 720 = \text{Rs. } 600$

$\therefore$ $\text{C.P.} = \text{Rs.}\left(600\times\frac{100}{125}\right) = \text{Rs. } 480$

Again, when S.P. = 720 – 160 = Rs. 560, then, gain = 560 – 480 = Rs. 80

$\therefore$ $\text{Gain } \% = \left(80\times\frac{100}{480}\right) = 16\frac{2}{3}\%$

18. C.P. of both kinds of sugar of 1 kg each $= \frac{100}{80}\times 3+\frac{125}{100}\times 5 = \frac{15}{4}+4 = \text{Rs. } \frac{31}{4}$

Hence, C.P. of 1 kg mixture = Rs. $\frac{31}{8}$; then, Gain $= 6-\frac{31}{8} = \text{Rs. } \frac{17}{8}$

$\therefore \text{Gain\%} = \frac{17/8}{31/8}\times 100 = \frac{1700}{31} = 54\frac{26}{31}\%$

19. Let the initial price = Rs. x; then C.P. for dealer = $\frac{120}{100} \times x$ = Rs. $\frac{6x}{5}$

Again, C.P. for shopkeeper = $\frac{125}{100} \times \frac{6x}{5}$ = Rs. $\frac{3x}{2}$

Now, $\frac{3x}{2} - \frac{6x}{5} = 129 \Rightarrow \frac{3x}{10} = 129 \therefore x = \frac{10 \times 129}{3}$ = Rs. 430

20. Let. S.P. of dinner of 1 person = Rs. x; then S.P. of dinner of 21 persons = Rs. $21x$

Now, C.P. of dinner of 24 persons = $24 \times \frac{200}{225} \times x$ = Rs. $\frac{64x}{3}$

$\therefore \frac{64x}{3} - 21x = 1 \Rightarrow \frac{x}{3} = 1 \quad \therefore x$ = Rs. 3

21. Here, 10% C.P. of horse = 20% C.P. of cart; Hence, C.P. of horse = 2 × C.P. of cart;
Let C.P. of cart and horse be Rs. x and Rs. $2x$ respectively; then,

$\frac{5}{100} \times 2x - \frac{5}{100} \times x = 10 \Rightarrow \frac{1}{20}x = 10 \quad \therefore x = 200$

Hence, C.P. of a cart = Rs. 200 and C.P. of a horse = 2 × 200 = Rs. 400

22. C.P. of 600 kg rice = 200 × 1.25 + 400 × 0.75 = Rs. 550

S.P. of 600 kg of rice = $\frac{125}{100} \times 550$ = Rs. 687.50; S.P. of one-third mixture = 200 × 1 = Rs. 200

S.P. of remaining (400 kg) mixture = 687.50 – 200 = Rs. 487.50

Hence, S.P. of remaining 1 kg mixture = $\frac{487.50}{400} \approx$ Rs. 1.22

23. Let his original C.P. = Rs. x; then his total outlay = $x + \frac{4}{100}x$ = Rs. $\frac{26x}{25}$

Since, his S.P. = $\frac{95}{100} \times \frac{26x}{25}$ = Rs. $\frac{247x}{250}$

Now, $\frac{247x}{250} + 32.50 = \frac{205}{200} \times \frac{26x}{25} \Rightarrow \frac{39x}{500} = 32.50 \quad \therefore x = \frac{32.50 \times 500}{39}$ = Rs. 416.67

24. Let his C.P. = Rs. x; then

$\frac{7}{5}(1150 - x) = x - 910 \Rightarrow 8050 - 7x = 5x - 4550 \Rightarrow 12x = 12600 \quad \therefore x$ = Rs. 1050

25. Let C.P. be Rs. 100; then marked price = Rs. 120

Since, S.P. = $\frac{90}{100} \times 120$ = Rs. 108

$\therefore$ Profit = 108 – 100 = Rs. 8, Hence, gain = 8%

26. Let second discount = x%; then

$\frac{90}{100} \times \frac{(100-x)}{100} \times 1400 = 1200 \quad \Rightarrow (100 - x) = \frac{2000}{21} \quad \therefore x = 100 - \frac{2000}{21} = \frac{100}{21} = 4\frac{16}{21}\%$

27. C.P. of 1 kg blended variety of tea = $\frac{5\times160+4\times200}{9}$ = Rs. $\frac{1600}{9}$

Profit = $192-\frac{1600}{9}$ = Rs. $\frac{128}{9}$

Hence, profit % = $\frac{128/9}{1600/9}\times100=\frac{128}{1600}\times100=8\%$

28. S.P. of whole field = $\frac{110}{100}\times3{,}60{,}000$ = Rs. 3,96,000

S.P. of one-third and two-fifths land = $\frac{80}{100}\times\frac{1}{3}\times3{,}60{,}000+\frac{125}{100}\times\frac{2}{5}\times3{,}60{,}000$ = Rs. 2,76,000

Hence, S.P. of remaining land = 3,96,000 – 2,76,000 = Rs. 1,20,000

29. S.P. = $\frac{88}{100}\times300$ = Rs. 264; then C.P. = $\frac{100}{110}\times264$ = Rs. 240

Again, S.P. = Rs. 300; C.P. = Rs. 240; then, Gain = 300 – 240 = Rs. 60

$\therefore$ Gain % = $\frac{60}{240}\times100=25\%$

30. Here, $\left(\frac{15}{2}+\frac{15}{2}\right)\%=3\Rightarrow100\%=\frac{3}{15}\times100$ = Rs. 20

Hence, C.P. of the article = Rs. 20

31. In first case, S.P. for X = $\frac{105}{100}\times1{,}50{,}000$ = Rs. 1,57,500

In IInd case, C.P. for X = $\frac{98}{100}\times1{,}57{,}500$ = Rs. 1,54,350

Hence, X gained = 1,57,500 – 1,54,350 = Rs. 3150

32. Net C.P. = 800 + 400 = Rs. 1200

Gain = 1500 – 1200 = Rs. 300

Hence, Gain% = $\frac{300}{1200}\times100=25\%$

33. Let C.P. of 150 quintal wheat = Rs 100; then

S.P. of 150 quintal wheat = Rs. 110;

Again, S.P. of one-fourth = $\frac{90}{100}\times25$ = Rs. 22.50

Then S.P. of three-fourth = 110 – 22.50 = Rs. 87.50

C.P. of three-fourth = Rs. 75

Hence, required gain% = $\frac{87.50-75}{75}\times100=\frac{50}{3}=16\frac{2}{3}\%$

34. C.P. of 1 kg blended variety $= \dfrac{5\times 27+3\times 30}{8} = \text{Rs. } \dfrac{225}{8}$

Gain $= 30-\dfrac{225}{8} = \text{Rs. } \dfrac{15}{8}$ Hence, gain % $= \dfrac{15/8}{225/8}\times 100 = \dfrac{20}{3} = 6\dfrac{2}{3}\%$

35. Required weight $= \dfrac{100}{160}\times 1000 = 625$ gms.

36. Here, loss % $= \left(\dfrac{10}{10}\right)^2 = 1\%$

37. S.P. $= \dfrac{95}{100}\times 385 = \dfrac{1463}{4} = \text{Rs. } 365.75$

38. Gain% $= \dfrac{24-21}{21}\times 100 = \dfrac{100}{7} = 14\dfrac{2}{7}\%$

39. Let C.P. of 1 pair of trousers = Rs. x; then
$863 - x = x - 631 \quad \Rightarrow 2x = 1494 \quad \therefore x = \text{Rs. } 747$

40. S.P. of 1 metre cloth $= \dfrac{12{,}325}{145} = \text{Rs. } 85$

Hence, C.P. of 1 meter cloth = 85 – 10 = Rs. 75

41. Let cost price of the article = Rs. x; then,
$1186 - x = x - 1098 \Rightarrow 2x = 2284 \quad \therefore x = \text{Rs. } 1142$

42. C.P. $= \dfrac{100}{112.5}\times 270 = \text{Rs. } 240$

43. S.P. $= \dfrac{107}{100}\times 7840 = \text{Rs. } 8388.80$

44. Here, 20% = 40 $\therefore$ 100% $= \dfrac{40}{20}\times 100 = 200$

Hence, C.P. = Rs. 200

45. C.P. for Ram $= \dfrac{100}{120}\times\dfrac{100}{130}\times 3120 = \text{Rs. } 2000$

46. Required pofit per cent $= \dfrac{1000-900}{900}\times 100 = 11\dfrac{1}{9}\%$

47. Here 2% = 12 $\therefore$ 100% $= \dfrac{12}{2}\times 100 = \text{Rs. } 600$

Hence, cost price of coat = Rs. 600

48. Let C.P. = Rs. 100; then marked price = Rs. 120

Since, S.P. = $\frac{90}{100} \times 120$ = Rs. 108

∴ profit = 108 – 100 = Rs. 8; Hence, profit% = 8%

49. Required C.P. = $\frac{100}{118} \times \frac{100}{120} \times \frac{100}{125} \times 2124$ = Rs. 1200

50. Here, retailer pays the bill on 10th day, so discount will be 2%.

Hence, required cost price = $\frac{85}{100} \times \frac{90}{100} \times \frac{98}{100} \times 4750 = \frac{142443}{40}$ = Rs. 3561.08

51. Here, C.P. of 12 books + S.P. of 4 books = S.P. of 12 books
Hence, C.P. of 12 books = S.P. of 8 books

Since, profit% = $\frac{12-8}{8} \times 100$ = 50%

52. C.P. of 1 kg mixture of rice = $\frac{2 \times 15 + 3 \times 13}{5}$ = Rs. 13.80

Hence, S.P. of 1 kg mixture of rice = $\frac{400}{3 \times 100} \times 13.80$ = Rs. 18.40

53. Original S.P. of the watch = $\frac{100}{75} \times 1545$ = Rs. 2060

54. Here, 90% = Rs. 144 ∴ 115% = $\frac{144}{90} \times 115$ = Rs. 184
[∵ When 10% loss, then S.P. = 90% of C.P. and when 15% gain, then S.P. = 115% of C.P.]

55. C.P. of television set = $\frac{100}{115} \times 27600$ = Rs. 24000

56. Let C.P. of two horses be Rs. x and Rs. $(1350 - x)$ respectively.

Then S.P. of two horses = $\frac{94}{100} \times x + \frac{107.5}{100}(1350 - x) = \frac{47x}{50} + \frac{43}{40}(1350 - x)$

Now, $\frac{47x}{50} + \frac{43}{40}(1350 - x)$ ⇒ $\frac{290250 - 27x}{200} = 1350$

⇒ $27x = 290250 - 270000$ ∴ $x = \frac{20250}{27}$ = Rs. 750

Hence, $1350 - x = 1350 - 750$ = Rs. 600
∴ C.P. of two horses are Rs. 750 and Rs. 600 respectively.

57. Net C.P. of 1 cycle = 450 + 150 = Rs. 600

Hence, S.P. of 1 cycle = $\frac{135}{100} \times 600$ = Rs. 810

58. Let C.P. = Rs. x, then marked price = $\frac{120x}{100}$ = Rs. $\frac{6x}{5}$

Now, $\frac{6x}{5} = 960$ $\quad \therefore x = \frac{5 \times 960}{6}$ = Rs. 800

S.P. = 960 – 40 = Rs. 920; profit = 920 – 800 = Rs. 120

Hence, profit % = $\frac{120}{800} \times 100 = 15\%$

59. Here, Rs. 40 = 60% $\therefore$ Rs. 80 = $\frac{60}{40} \times 80 = 120\%$

Hence, gain% = (120 – 100) = 20%

60. Required gain% = $\frac{30-27}{27} \times 100 = 11\frac{1}{9}\%$

61. Original S.P. of the watch = $\frac{100}{76}$ × Rs. 779 = Rs. 1025

62. Let C.P. = x; then
$536 - x = x - 426$ $\quad \Rightarrow 2x = 962 \ \therefore x$ = Rs. 481

63. Loss% = $\frac{16-12}{16} \times 100 = 25\%$

64. Let C.P. = Rs. 100; then S.P. = Rs. 105

Hence, marked price = $\frac{100}{87.5} \times 105$ = Rs. 120

Since, required percentage = 120 – 100 = 20%

65. Cost price of 1 table = $\frac{12000}{12}$ = Rs. 1000

Hence, S.P. of 1 table = $\frac{16 \times 1000}{12}$ = Rs. 1333.33

66. Let C.P. = Rs. 100; then marked price = $\frac{5}{3} \times 100$ = Rs. $\frac{500}{3}$

Since, S.P. = $\frac{90}{100} \times \frac{500}{3}$ = Rs. 150
Hence, Gain % = 150 – 100 = 50%

67. Here, Rs. 770 = 110% $\therefore$ Rs. 707 = $\frac{110}{770} \times 707 = 101\%$

Hence, gain% = 101 – 100 = 1%

68. S.P. of 2 cows = 8400 + 8800 = Rs. 17200

Hence, C.P. of 2 cows = $\frac{100}{120} \times 8400 + \frac{100}{110} \times 8800$ = Rs. 15000

$\therefore$ Total profit = Rs. 17200 – Rs. 15000 = Rs. 2200

69. Let S.P. of each horse = Rs. x; then

C.P. of both horses $= \frac{100}{110} \times x + \frac{100}{85} \times x = \frac{390x}{187}$

Since, loss $= \frac{390x}{187} - 2x = \frac{16x}{187}$

Hence, loss% $= \frac{16x/187}{390x/187} \times 100 = \frac{16}{390} \times 100 = 4\frac{4}{39}\%$

70. Here, C.P. of 33 bananas + S.P. of 11 bananas = S.P. of 33 bananas.
Hence C.P. of 33 bananas = S.P. of 22 bananas

Since, profit % $= \frac{33-22}{22} \times 100 = 50\%$

71. Let he substitutes x gm. for 1 kg; then

$\frac{1000-x}{x} \times 100 = 25 \Rightarrow \frac{1000-x}{x} = \frac{1}{4} \Rightarrow 5x = 4000 \quad \therefore x = 800$ gm

72. Let C.P. = Rs. 100; then S.P. $= \frac{4}{3} \times 100 =$ Rs. $\frac{400}{3}$

Hence, profit % $= \frac{400}{3} - 100 = \frac{100}{3} = 33\frac{1}{3}\%$

73. Loss% $= \frac{16-12}{16} \times 100 = 25\%$

74. The difference of percentage between loss of 20% and gain of 5% = 20 + 5 = 25%

Hence, 25% = Rs. 100 $\therefore$ 100% $= \frac{100}{25} \times 100 =$ Rs. 400

$\therefore$ C.P. = Rs. 400

75. Let retail price be Rs. x; then S.P. $= \frac{64}{100} \times x =$ Rs. $\frac{16x}{25}$

Since, CP $= \frac{100}{108.8} \times \frac{16x}{25} =$ Rs. $\frac{10x}{17}$;

Again, another S.P. $= \frac{88}{100} \times x =$ Rs. $\frac{22x}{25}$

Gain $= \frac{22x}{25} - \frac{10x}{17} =$ Rs. $\frac{124x}{425}$

Hence, gain% $= \frac{124x/425}{10x/17} \times 100 = \frac{124}{10 \times 25} \times 100 = \frac{248}{5} = 49.6\%$

76. Let C.P. of each pen = Re. 1; then

C.P. of 40 pen = Rs. 36 and S.P. of 40 pens $= \frac{99}{100} \times$ Rs. 40 = Rs. 39.60

$\therefore$ Gain% $= \frac{39.60-36}{36} \times 100 = 10\%$

77. Let C.P. = Rs. 100; then marked price = Rs. 150

$\text{S.P.} = \frac{75}{100} \times 150 = \text{Rs. } 112.5$

Hence, actual profit% = 112.5 – 100 = 12.5%

78. Let C.P. = Rs. 100; then S.P. = Rs. 133

Since, marked price $= \frac{100}{95} \times 133 = \text{Rs. } 140$

Required percentage = 140 – 100 = 40%

79. Net, C.P. = 80000 + 5000 + 1000 = Rs. 86000

$\text{S.P.} = \frac{125}{100} \times \text{Rs. } 86000 = \text{Rs. } 1{,}07{,}500$

80. Here, 20% = Rs. 1100 $\therefore$ $100\% = \frac{1100}{20} \times 50 = \text{Rs. } 5500$

Hence, net C.P. = Rs. 5500

Cost of scooter $= \frac{10}{11} \times 5500 = \text{Rs. } 5000$

Hence, cost of repairs = 5500 – 5000 = Rs. 500

81. S.P. of both transistor = 840 + 960 = Rs. 1800

C.P. of both transistor $= \frac{100}{120} \times 840 + \frac{100}{96} \times 960 = \text{Rs. } 1700$

Gain = 1800 – 1700 = Rs. 100

Hence, gain% $= \frac{100}{1700} \times 100 = 5\frac{15}{17}\%$

82. Let C.P. and S.P. be Rs. $4x$ and Rs. $5x$ respectively; then profit% $= \frac{5x - 4x}{4x} \times 100 = 25\%$

83. Let C,P. and S.P. be Rs. $5x$ and Rs. $7x$; then profit $= 7x - 5x =$ Rs. $2x$

Required ratio $= 2x : 5x = 2 : 5$

84. Let S.P. and C.P. are Rs. x and Rs. y; then,

$3(x - y) = 2x - y \qquad \therefore x = 2y;$

Gain $= x - y = 2y - y =$ Rs. y

Gain% $= \frac{y}{y} \times 100 = 100\%$

85. Let C.P. = Rs. 100; then S.P. = Rs. 120

Again, when S.P. = 2 × Rs. 120 = Rs. 240

Then, profit% = 240 – 100 = 140%

86. Let C.P. = Rs. x; then

$\frac{1920 - x}{x} \times 100 = \frac{x - 1280}{x} \times 100 \quad \Rightarrow 2x = 3200 \qquad \therefore x = \text{Rs. } 1600$

Now, required S.P. $= \frac{125}{100} \times \text{Rs. } 1600 = \text{Rs. } 2000$

87. Let C.P. = Rs. 100, then profit = Rs. 320,
Since, S.P. = 100 + 320 = Rs. 420
Now, when C.P. = Rs. 125, then S.P. = Rs. 420
Since, profit = 420 – 125 = Rs. 295

Hence, required percentage = $\frac{295}{420} \times 100 = \frac{1475}{21} \approx 70\%$

88. C.P. of 2 dozen bananas = 2 × Rs. 16 = Rs. 32

S.P. of 2 dozen bananas = $\frac{18}{12} \times$ Rs. 12 + $\frac{6}{12} \times 4$ = Rs. 20

Hence, loss% = $\frac{32-20}{32} \times 100 = \frac{12}{32} \times 100 = 37.5\%$

89. C.P. of a cot = $\frac{16800}{21}$ = Rs. 800

90. Here, $\frac{20-x}{x} \times 100 = 25 \Rightarrow \frac{20-x}{x} = \frac{1}{4} \Rightarrow 5x = 80 \quad \therefore x = 16$

91. Loss % = $\frac{50-40}{50} \times 100 = 20\%$

92. Required discount% = $\frac{1}{6} \times 100 = 16\frac{2}{3}\%$

93. C.P. of mixture of 1 kg = $\frac{2 \times 50 + 4 \times 20 + 3 \times 30}{9} = \frac{270}{9}$ = Rs. 30

Profit % = $\frac{33-30}{30} \times 100 = 10\%$

94. C.P. of 1 kg mixture = $\frac{100}{118} \times 177$ = Rs. 150
Let, the rate of other brand of tea = Rs. x per kg

Since, $\frac{2 \times 200 + 3 \times x}{5} = 150 \Rightarrow 3x = 350 \quad \therefore x =$ Rs. 166.66

95. C.P. of 1 kg mixture = $\frac{100}{137.5} \times 8$ = Rs. $\frac{64}{11}$

Now applying rule of alligation,

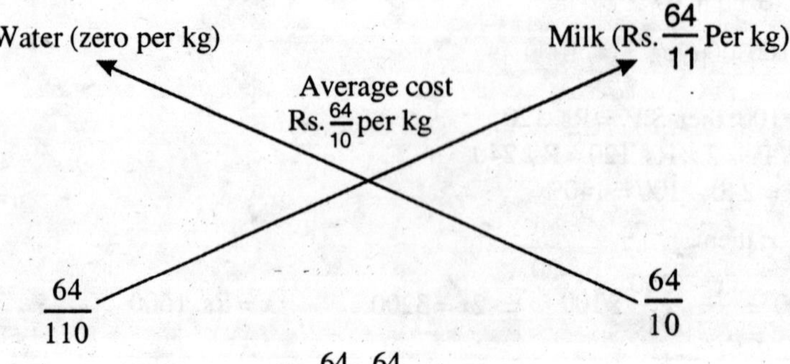

Hence, ratio of water to milk = $\frac{64}{110} : \frac{64}{10} = 1 : 10$

96. C.P. of 1 toffee = $\frac{100}{80} \times \frac{1}{12}$ = Re. $\frac{5}{48}$

For 20% gain, S.P. = $\frac{120}{100} \times \frac{5}{48}$ = Re $\frac{1}{8}$

Hence, S.P. = 8 toffees for a rupee.

97. For 1 pencil, C.P. = Rs. $\frac{9}{7}$; S.P. = Rs. $\frac{11}{8}$

Gain = $\frac{11}{8} - \frac{9}{7}$ = Re $\frac{5}{56}$

Since, gain of Re. $\frac{5}{56}$ for 1 pencil

Hence, gain of Rs. 10 for $\frac{56}{5} \times 10 = 112$ pencils

98. C.P. of one toffee = Re. $\frac{1}{6}$

S.P. of one toffee = $\frac{120}{100} \times \frac{1}{6}$ = Re. $\frac{1}{5}$

Hence, he has to sell 5 toffees for a rupee.

99. Required C.P. = $\frac{100}{120} \times \frac{100}{125} \times 225$ = Rs 150

100. Required gain% = $\left(\frac{100+10}{100}\right)^2 \times 100 - 100 = 121 - 100 = 21\%$

101. Let C.P. = Rs. 100, then S.P. = Rs. 110

The S.P. of remaining goods = $\frac{80}{100}$ × Rs. 110 = Rs. 88

Since, loss% = 100 – 88 = 12%

102. Let he uses x gm weight for a kg; then

$\frac{1000-x}{x} \times 100 = \frac{300}{47} \Rightarrow \frac{1000-x}{x} = \frac{3}{47} \Rightarrow 50x = 47000 \quad \therefore x = 940$ gm

103. Here, loss% = $\left(\frac{12}{10}\right)^2 = \left(\frac{6}{5}\right)^2 = \frac{36}{25} = 1\frac{11}{25}\%$

104. Here, 20% = Rs. 240 ∴ 100% = $\frac{240}{20} \times 100$ = Rs. 1200

Hence, cost price = Rs. 1200; Since, S.P. = $\frac{120}{10} \times 100$= Rs. 1440

105. Let, C.P. = Rs. 100; the two selling prices will be Rs 104 and Rs. 106.
Hence, required ratio = 104 : 106 = 52 : 53

106. Here, 2% = 20 $\quad \therefore\ 100\% = \frac{20}{2} \times 100 = \text{Rs. } 1000$

Hence, C.P. = Rs. 1000

107. Let marked price = Rs. 100; then C.P. for Saurabh = Rs. 90

Since, S.P. for Saurabh $= \frac{130}{100} \times 90 = \text{Rs. } 117$

Required profit percentage = 117 – 100 = 17%

108. Let original value = Rs. 100; then C.P. for Ram = Rs. 90 and also his S.P. = Rs. 110

$$\text{Gain\%} = \frac{110-90}{90} \times 100 = \frac{20}{90} \times 100 = 22\frac{2}{9}\%$$

109. Here, 5% = Rs. 10 $\quad \Rightarrow 100\% = \frac{10}{5} \times 100 = \text{Rs. } 200$

Hence, C.P. = Rs. 200

110. Marked price $= \frac{100}{80} \times \frac{100}{88} \times 704 = \text{Rs. } 1000$

111. Actual price $= \frac{96}{100} \times 2,00,000 + \frac{97.5}{100} \times 72,000 = 1,92,000 + 70,200 = \text{Rs, } 2,62,200$

112. Let C.P. of each clock = Rs. x; then C.P. of 90 clocks = Rs. $90x$
In Ist condition,

$$\text{S.P. of 90 clocks} = 40 \times \frac{110}{100} x + 50 \times \frac{120}{100} \times x = \text{Rs. } 104x$$

In IInd case,

$$\text{S.P. of 90 clocks} = \frac{115}{100} \times 90x = \text{Rs. } \frac{207x}{2}$$

Since, $104x - \frac{207x}{2} = \text{Rs. } 40 \Rightarrow \frac{x}{2} = 40 \quad \therefore x = \text{Rs. } 80$

113. Let the amount of the bill = Rs. x; then,

$$\frac{65}{100}x - \frac{80}{100} \times \frac{80}{100}x = 22 \Rightarrow \frac{x}{100} = 22 \quad \therefore x = \text{Rs. } 2200$$

114. Required cost price $= \frac{85}{100} \times \frac{90}{100} \times \frac{95}{100} \times 12000 = \text{Rs. } 8721$

115. Required difference $= \frac{64}{100} \times \frac{96}{100} \times 1,00,000 - \frac{60}{100} \times 1,00,000 = 61,140 - 60,000 = \text{Rs. } 1140$

116. Let additional discount be $x\%$ then,

$$\frac{80}{100} \times \frac{100-x}{100} \times 1500 = 1104 \quad \Rightarrow 100 - x = 92 \quad \therefore x\% = 8\%$$

117. Let original value = Rs. 100; then

$$\text{S.P.} = \frac{90}{100} \times \frac{88}{100} \times \frac{85}{100} \times 100 = \text{Rs. } 67.32$$

Hence, amount of single discount = 100 – 67.32 = 32.68%

118. Required S.P. = $\frac{95}{100} \times \frac{95}{100} \times 80 = \frac{361}{5} = \text{Rs. } 72.20$

119. Net S.P. = $\frac{80}{100} \times \frac{90}{100} \times 2000 = \text{Rs. } 1440$

120. Required marked price = $\frac{100}{80} \times \frac{125}{100} \times 1200 = \text{Rs. } 1875$

121. Let list price be Rs. 100; then cost price will be Rs. 64 and S.P. = Rs. 88

$$\text{Gain\%} = \frac{88 - 64}{64} \times 100 = \frac{75}{2} = 37.5\%$$

122. Let 2nd discount per cent = $x\%$; then,

$$\frac{90}{100} \times \frac{100 - x}{100} \times 720 = 550.80$$

$$\Rightarrow 100 - x = \frac{55080}{9 \times 72} \qquad \therefore x = 100 - 85 = 15\%$$

123. Let price of the article be Rs. 100; then its raised price = Rs. 130

$$\text{Hence, S.P.} = \frac{90}{100} \times \frac{90}{100} \times 130 = \frac{1053}{10} = \text{Rs. } 105.3$$

Since, price of the article increased by (105.3 – 100) = 5.3%

124. Let C.P. = Rs. 100; then marked price = Rs. 125

$$\text{Hence, S.P.} = \frac{84}{100} \times 125 = \text{Rs. } 105$$

Since, actual profit = 105 – 100 = 5%

125. Let marked price = Rs. 100; then C.P. for Gopal = Rs. 80

$$\text{Since, S.P. for Gopal} = \frac{140}{100} \times 80 = \text{Rs. } 112$$

Hence, required percentage = 112 – 100 = 12%

126. Let marked price = Rs. 100; then S.P. = Rs. 95

$$\text{Since, C.P.} = \frac{100}{123.5} \times 95 = \text{Rs. } \frac{1000}{13}$$

Again, when S.P. = Rs. 100; C.P. = Rs. $\frac{1000}{13}$

$$\text{Gain} = 100 - \frac{1000}{13} = \text{Rs. } \frac{300}{13}$$

$$\text{Gain\%} = \frac{300/13}{1000/13} \times 100 = 30\%$$

127. For one article;

$$\text{Marked price} = \frac{100}{90} \times 45 = \text{Rs. } 50; \text{ C.P.} = \frac{100}{150} \times 45 = \text{Rs. } 30$$

Again, when S.P. = Rs. 50; C.P. = Rs. 30

$$\text{Gain\%} = \frac{50-30}{30} \times 100 = 66\frac{2}{3}\%$$

128. $\text{S.P.} = \frac{85}{100} \times 30 - 1.50 = 25.50 - 1.50 = \text{Rs. } 24$

$$\text{Required C.P.} = \frac{100}{120} \times 24 = \text{Rs. } 20$$

129. Let C.P. = Rs. 100; then marked price = Rs. 120

$$\text{Since, S.P.} = 60 + \frac{1}{4} \times \frac{80}{100} \times 120 + \frac{1}{4} \times \frac{60}{100} \times 120$$

$$= 60 + 24 + 18 = \text{Rs. } 102$$

Hence, gain% = 102 – 100 = 2%

130. Let C.P = Rs. 100; then,

Marked price = Rs. 110 and S.P. = Rs. 99

$$\text{Hence, required discount\%} = \frac{11}{110} \times 100 = 10\%$$

131. $\text{Marked price} = \frac{100}{120} \times 2880 = \text{Rs. } 2400$

$$\text{C.P. for Kaushal} = \frac{85}{100} \times 2400 = \text{Rs. } 2040$$

132. Let C.P. = Rs. 100; then marked price = Rs. 135

If percentage of discount is x%, then

$$\frac{100-x}{100} \times 135 = 108 \quad \Rightarrow 100 - x = 80 \quad \therefore x\% = 20\%$$

133. $\text{Required C.P.} = \frac{95}{100} \times \frac{100}{115} \times 6500 = \text{Rs. } 5369.56 \approx \text{Rs. } 5350$

134. $\text{Required profit \%} = \frac{100-90}{90} \times 100 = \frac{10}{90} \times 100 = 11\frac{1}{9}\%$

23 SIMPLE INTEREST

INTEREST

Interest is the money paid for the use of money borrowed, *i.e.*, extra money paid for using other's money is called *interest.*

The sum borrowed is called the principal. The sum of interest and principal is called the *Amount.*

If the interest on a certain sum borrowed for a certain period is reckoned uniformly, then it is called simple interest, denoted by S.I.

Thus, if A = Amount, P = Principal,
I = Interest, T = Time (in year),
R = Rate per cent per annum, then

(a) $I = \dfrac{P \times R \times T}{100}$ *(b)* $P = \dfrac{100 \times I}{R \times T}$

(c) $T = \dfrac{100 \times I}{P \times R}$ *(d)* $R = \dfrac{100 \times I}{P \times T}$

(e) $P = \dfrac{100\,A}{100 + RT}$ *(f)* A = P + I.

Example 1: If a certain sum of money at simple interest amounts to Rs. 2642 in 3 years and to Rs. 3235 in 4 years, what is the sum and rate of interest?

Solution: Here, P + 3I = 2642; P + 4I = 3235

Then, I = 3235 – 2642 = Rs. 593

Since, P = 2642 – 3 × 593 = Rs. 863

$$\text{Hence,} R = \frac{593 \times 100}{863 \times 1} = 68.71\%$$

Example 2: What annual payment will discharge a debt of Rs. 848 in 4 years at 4% per annum.

Solution: Let annual payment = Rs. *x*; then,

$$x + \frac{x \times 3 \times 4}{100} + x + \frac{x \times 2 \times 4}{100} + x + \frac{x \times 1 \times 4}{100} + x = 848 + \frac{848 \times 4 \times 4}{100}$$

$$\Rightarrow 4x + \frac{6x}{25} = 848\left(1 + \frac{4}{25}\right)$$

$$\Rightarrow \frac{106x}{25} = 848 \times \frac{29}{25} \qquad \therefore x = \frac{848 \times 29}{106} = \text{Rs. } 232$$

Example 3: In what time does a sum of money become four times at the simple interest rate of 5% per annum?

Solution: Let principal = Rs. x; then amount = $4x$

Since, $I = 4x - x =$ Rs. $3x$

Hence, $T = \dfrac{3x \times 100}{x \times 5} = 60$ years

Example 4: A sum of money put out on simple interest double itself in $12\frac{1}{2}$ years. In how many years would it triple itself?

Solution: Let principal = Rs. x; then amount = $2x$; $I = 2x - x =$ Rs. x

$$\text{Rate} = \frac{x \times 100 \times 2}{x \times 25} = 8\%$$

When, principal = Rs. x; Amount = $3x$; then $I = 3x - x =$ Rs. $2x$

$$\therefore \quad T = \frac{2x \times 100}{x \times 8} = 25 \text{ years}$$

Example 5: Simple interest on a sum of money is $\frac{1}{9}$ of the principal, and the number of years is equal to the rate per cent per annum. Find the rate per cent.

Solution: Let T = R = x; then,

$$\frac{P}{9} = \frac{P \times x \times x}{100}$$

$$\Rightarrow \quad x^2 = \frac{100}{9} \quad \therefore x = \frac{10}{3}, \quad \text{Hence, R} = 3\frac{1}{3}\%$$

Example 6: A sum was put at SI at a certain rate for 2 years. Had it been put at 3% higher rate, it would have fetched Rs. 300 more. Find the sum.

Solution: If R = 3%, T = 2 years; then I = Rs. 300

Hence, $P = \dfrac{300 \times 100}{3 \times 2} =$ Rs. 5000

Example 7: *(a)* The rate of interest for the first 2 years is 3% p.a., for the next 3 years is 6% and beyond this, it is 9%. If the simple interest for 10 years is Rs. 2760, then find out the principal.

Solution: Here, $\dfrac{P \times 2 \times 3}{100} + \dfrac{P \times 3 \times 6}{100} + \dfrac{P \times 5 \times 9}{100} = 2760 \Rightarrow 69P = 2760 \times 100 \; \therefore P = \dfrac{2760 \times 100}{69} =$ Rs. 4000

Example 7: *(b)* A man deposits a certain sum in a bank. He gets 4% per annum interest for first 3 years, 5% for next 2 years and 6% beyond that. If he gets Rs. 2000 as simple interest for 8 years, how much money did he deposit in the bank?

Solution: Here, $\dfrac{P \times 4 \times 3}{100} + \dfrac{P \times 5 \times 2}{100} + \dfrac{P \times 6 \times 3}{100} = 2000 \Rightarrow 40P = 2000 \times 100 \; \therefore P = \dfrac{2000 \times 100}{40} =$ Rs.5000

Example 8: The simple interest on a certain sum of money at 4% per annum for 3 years is Rs. 80 more than the interest on the sum for 2 years at 5% per annum. Find the sum.

Solution: Here, $\dfrac{P \times 4 \times 3}{100} - \dfrac{P \times 5 \times 2}{100} = 80 \Rightarrow 2P = 80 \times 100 \quad \therefore P = \dfrac{80 \times 100}{2} =$ Rs. 4000

Example 9: What would be the simple interest on a sum of Rs. 7000 for 4 years at the rate of 5% p.a.?

Solution: $I = \dfrac{7000 \times 5 \times 4}{100} = \text{Rs. } 1400$

Example 10: A sum of money doubles itself in 6 years. In how many years will the amount become four times the principal at the same rate of simple interest?

Solution: Let principal = Rs. x; then amount = Rs. $2x$, Since, I = $2x - x$ = Rs. x

Hence, $R = \dfrac{x \times 100}{x \times 6} = \dfrac{50}{3}\%$

Again, when principal = Rs. x; amount = Rs. $4x$; Since, I = $4x - x$ = Rs. $3x$

Hence, $R = \dfrac{3x \times 100 \times 3}{x \times 50} = 18$ years

Example 11: A sum of money becomes Rs. 815 in 3 years and Rs. 854 in 4 years. Find the principal and rate of interest.

Solution: Here, Interest for 1 year = Rs. 854 – Rs. 815 = Rs. 39

Hence, Simple interest for 3 years = 3 × 39 = Rs. 117

∴ Principal = Rs. 815 – Rs. 117 = Rs. 698

Since, Rate % $= \dfrac{117 \times 100}{698 \times 3} \approx 5.6\%$

Example 12: Simple interest on a sum of Rs. 1600 for 2 years 3 months is Rs. 252. Find the rate of interest per annum.

Solution: Rate per cent $= \dfrac{252 \times 100 \times 4}{1600 \times 9} = 7\%$

Example 13: Simple interest on a sum of Rs. 1500 for 2 years is Rs. 67.50 and for 3 years is Rs. 101.25. Find the rate of interest p.a.

Solution: ∵ Simple interest for one year = Rs. 101.25 – Rs. 67.50 = Rs. 33.75

Hence, Rate per cent $= \dfrac{33.75 \times 100}{1500 \times 1} = \dfrac{9}{4} = 2\tfrac{1}{4}\%$

Example 14: A sum of Rs. 600 amounts to Rs. 720 in 5 years at simple interest. If the rate per annum is further increased by 3%, the amount accrued will be :

Solution: Simple interest = Rs. 720 – Rs. 600 = Rs. 120

Rate $= \dfrac{120 \times 100}{600 \times 5} = 4\%$

when, Rate = (4 + 3)% = 7%

Then, Interest $= \dfrac{600 \times 7 \times 5}{100} = \text{Rs. } 210$

∴ A = Rs. 600 + Rs. 210 = Rs. 810

Example 15: What annual instalment at the rate of 5% per annum must a borrower pay in order to settle a loan of Rs. 6450 in 4 years time.

Solution: Let each annual instalment = Rs. x; then

$$x + \frac{x \times 5 \times 3}{100} + x + \frac{x \times 5 \times 2}{100} + x + \frac{x \times 5 \times 1}{100} + x = 6450 + \frac{6450 \times 5 \times 4}{100}$$

$\Rightarrow \dfrac{43x}{10} = 7740 \qquad \therefore x = \dfrac{7740 \times 10}{43} = \text{Rs. } 1800$

Example 16: Divide Rs. 3200 into two parts in such a manner that the simple interest on the first part for 2½ years at 4% per annum remains equal to two times the simple interest on the second part for 5 years at 3% per annum.

Solution: Let such two parts of Rs. 3200 are Rs. x and Rs. $(3200 - x)$

$$\frac{x \times 4 \times 5}{100 \times 2} = 2 \times \frac{(3200 - x) \times 3 \times 5}{100} \Rightarrow x = 9600 - 3x \Rightarrow 4x = 9600$$

$$\therefore x = \frac{9600}{4} = \text{Rs. } 2400, \text{ since, } 3200 - x = 3200 - 2400 = \text{Rs. } 800$$

Hence, required two parts are Rs. 2400 and Rs. 800

Example 17: If the difference between the simple interest on a certain sum for 4 years at 2½% per annum and the simple interest on the same sum for the same period at 3% per annum is Rs. 75, find the sum.

Solution: Here, $\dfrac{\text{P} \times 3 \times 4}{100} - \dfrac{\text{P} \times 5 \times 4}{100 \times 2} = 75 \Rightarrow \dfrac{\text{P}}{50} = 75 \quad \therefore \text{P} = 50 \times 75 = \text{Rs. } 3750$

Example 18: A man borrowed Rs. 500 at some rate of simple interest and Rs. 700 at 1% higher rate of interest. If after 3 years he had to pay Rs. 165 as total interest on the sum of money borrowed by him in both cases, find the former rate of interest.

Solution: Here, $\dfrac{500 \times \text{R} \times 3}{100} + \dfrac{700 \times (\text{R} + 1) \times 3}{100} = 165 \Rightarrow 36\text{R} + 21 = 165$

$$\therefore \text{R} = \frac{144}{36} = 4\%$$

Example 19: A sum of Rs. 4750 amounts to Rs. 6650 in 4 years at a certain rate of simple interest. In how many years at the same rate of simple interest the sum of Rs. 85000 will amount to Rs. 106250?

Solution: Here,

P = Rs. 4750, T = 4 years, A = Rs. 6650

I = Rs. 6650 – Rs. 4750 = Rs. 1900

$$\text{R} = \frac{1900 \times 100}{4750 \times 4} = 10\%$$

Again, P = Rs. 85000, A = Rs. 106250 and R = 10%

I = Rs. 106250 – Rs. 85000 = Rs. 21250

$$\therefore \quad \text{T} = \frac{21250 \times 100}{85000 \times 10} = 2½ \text{ years.}$$

Example 20: Tarun borrowed Rs. 1000 at 5% per annum simple interest. If each year he pays Rs. 200 for interest and part of debt, find the amount that will be left to be paid back at the end of 3 years.

Solution: Amount to be paid $= 1000 + \dfrac{1000 \times 5 \times 3}{100} = \text{Rs. } 1150$

Amount paid by Tarun = $200 + \frac{200\times5\times2}{100} + 200 + \frac{200\times5\times1}{100} + 200$ = Rs. 630

amount left = 1150 – 630 = Rs. 520

Example 21: A sum of money amounts to Rs. 944 in 3 years at a certain rate of simple interest. If the rate of interest is increased by 25%, then the same sum of money will amount to Rs. 980 during the same time period. Find the sum of money and the former rate of interest.

Solution: Here, if rate = R/4, T = 3 years; then I = 980 – 944 = Rs. 36

Since, $P = \frac{36\times100\times4}{3\times R} = \frac{4800}{R}$

Again, $P + \frac{P\times R\times3}{100} = 944 \Rightarrow P\left(1+\frac{3R}{100}\right) = 944 \quad \Rightarrow \frac{4800}{R}\left(1+\frac{3R}{100}\right) = 944$

$\Rightarrow \frac{4800}{R} + 144 = 944 \qquad \therefore R = \frac{4800}{800} = 6\%$

Since, $P = \frac{4800}{R} = \frac{4800}{6}$ = Rs. 800

Example 22 : Gulshan borrowed a sum of money at the rate of 4% p.a. simple interest. If after 8 years the interest is Rs. 340 less than the sum of money borrowed, find the money borrowed by Gulshan.

Solution: $P - 340 = \frac{P\times4\times8}{100} \Rightarrow P - \frac{8P}{25} = 340 \Rightarrow \frac{17P}{25} = 340 \therefore P = \frac{340\times25}{17}$ = Rs. 500

Example 23: The simple interest of a certain sum of money for 6 years at 4% p.a. is equal to that of Rs. 600 for 2½ year at 8% p.a. Find the sum of money.

Solution: Here, $\frac{P\times6\times4}{100} = \frac{600\times8\times5}{100\times2} \Rightarrow 6P = 600\times5 \therefore P =$ Rs. 500

Example 24: A man lent some money out of Rs. 3600 at 8% p.a. simple interest and remaining sum at 10% p.a. If after 2 years he gets Rs. 636 as total interest, find the sum of money lent out in each case.

Solution : Let the two sums are Rs. x and Rs. $(3600 - x)$ respectively; then

$\frac{x\times8\times2}{100} + \frac{(3600-x)\times10\times2}{100} = 636 \Rightarrow 16x + 72000 - 20x = 63600$

$\Rightarrow 4x = 8400 \therefore x =$ Rs. 2100 and $3600 - x = 3600 - 2100 =$ Rs. 1500

Example 25: A sum of Rs. 9900 is to be divided among A, B and C in such a way that simple interest on each part at 6% p.a. after 1, 2 and 3 years respectively remains equal. The share of A will be how much more than that of C?

Solution: Let shares of A, B and C are Rs. a, Rs b and Rs. c respectively.

Then, $\frac{a\times6\times1}{100} = \frac{b\times6\times2}{100} = \frac{c\times6\times3}{100} \Rightarrow a = 2b = 3c \quad \therefore a : b : c = 6 : 3 : 2$

∴ Sum of proportionals = 6 + 3 + 2 = 11

$\therefore$ A's share = $\frac{6}{11} \times 9900$ = Rs. 5400;

B's share = $\frac{3}{11} \times 9900$ = Rs. 2700;

C's share = $\frac{2}{11} \times 9900$ = Rs. 1800

Hence, it is clear that A's share is 5400 – 1800 = Rs. 3600 more than C's share.

Example 26: Amount of Rs. 12000 at 3% p.a. simple interest in 6 years will be same as that of the sum of Rs. 7500 at a certain rate per cent p.a. in 6 years. Find this rate of interest?

Solution: Here, $12000 + \frac{12000 \times 3 \times 6}{100} = 7500 + \frac{7500 \times R \times 6}{100} \Rightarrow 450\ R = 14160 - 7500$

$\therefore R = \frac{6660}{450} = 14.8\%$

EXERCISE

1. If the simple interest on a certain sum of money at 6% per annum for 3 years is Rs. 90, the sum will be:
(a) Rs. 500 *(b)* Rs. 450 *(c)* Rs. 525 *(d)* Rs. 560

2. If the simple interest on Re. 1 for 1 month is 1 paise, the rate per cent p.a. will be :
(a) 10% *(b)* 8% *(c)* 12% *(d)* 6%

3. A sum of money doubles itself in 20 years. In how many years will it triple itself at the same rate of simple interest?
(a) 30 years *(b)* 50 years *(c)* 40 years *(d)* 45 years

4. If the simple interest on Rs. 500 for 4 years is Rs. 40, find the rate per cent p.a.
(a) 3½% *(b)* 2% *(c)* 2½% *(d)* 3%

5. After what time will the sum of Rs. 2000 become Rs. 2240 at 4% per annum simple interest?
(a) 3 years *(b)* 2 years *(c)* 5 years *(d)* 4 years

6. The simple interest on a certain sum of money is $\frac{25}{64}$ of the sum and the number of years equals the rate per cent p.a. The rate per cent p.a. will be :
(a) $7\frac{1}{2}\%$ *(b)* $5\frac{1}{4}\%$ *(c)* $6\frac{3}{4}\%$ *(d)* $6\frac{1}{4}\%$

7. A sum of money amounts to Rs. 1150 in 3 years and to Rs. 1250 in 5 years at a certain rate per cent p.a. simple interest. The rate per cent p.a. will be :
(a) 5% *(b)* 8% *(c)* 7% *(d)* 6%

8. The simple interest on a sum of Rs. 892 lent out at 6% p.a. for 8 months will be :
(a) Rs. 36.68 *(b)* Rs. 35.68 *(c)* Rs. 48.58 *(d)* Rs. 33.38

9. If the simple interest on a certain sum of money at 6% p.a. for 4½ years is Rs. 81, the sum will be:
(a) Rs. 325 *(b)* Rs. 225 *(c)* Rs. 300 *(d)* Rs. 340

10. A sum of Rs. 1850 lent out for 5 years at 3% p.a. simple interest will amount to:
(a) Rs. 2227.75 *(b)* Rs. 2127.50 *(c)* Rs. 2137.50 *(d)* Rs. 2086.50

11. A lent a sum of Rs. 1250 to B at a certain rate of interest for 3 years and a sum of Rs. 1500 to C at the same rate of interest for 2 years. If he was paid total Rs. 258.75 as interest in both cases, find the rate of interest at which money was lent by him.

(a) $4\frac{1}{6}\%$ *(b)* $6\frac{1}{4}\%$ *(c)* $2\frac{1}{7}\%$ *(d)* $3\frac{5}{6}\%$

12. A invested Rs. 5000 at a certain rate of simple interest and Rs. 4000 for the same period at 1% higher rate of interest. If the interest in both cases is same, the former rate of interest is :

(a) 3% *(b)* 4% *(c)* 6% *(d)* 5%

13. A man lends Rs. 500 for 4 years and Rs. 600 for 3 years at a certain rate of simple interest. If he gets total Rs. 190 as interest in both cases, the rate per cent per annum is :

(a) 8% *(b)* 5% *(c)* 10% *(d)* 4%

14. What annual instalment should be paid to clear the debt of Rs. 645 in 4 years at the rate of 5% p.a. simple interest?

(a) Rs. 160 *(b)* Rs. 185 *(c)* Rs. 180 *(d)* Rs. 190

15. If a certain sum of money at simple interest amounts to Rs. 1900 in 3 years and to Rs. 2050 in 5 years, the rate per cent per annum is :

(a) 4½% *(b)* 3½% *(c)* 2½% *(d)* 5¼%

16. If the simple interest on a sum of money for 5 years is ¼ of the sum, the rate per cent per annum is :

(a) 4% *(b)* 5% *(c)* 8% *(d)* 10%

17. Which of the following sum of money will amount to Rs. 1050 in 5 years at 8% per annum simple interest?

(a) Rs. 750 *(b)* Rs. 825 *(c)* Rs. 775 *(d)* Rs. 730

18. A borrowed Rs. 2500 at a certain rate of simple interest and Rs. 1500 at 3% higher rate of interest. If after 4 years the interest paid by him in both cases is Rs. 1140, the former rate of interest was :

(a) 5% *(b)* 6% *(c)* 8½% *(d)* 5½%

19. A certain sum of money lent out on simple interest amounts to Rs. 1760 in 2 years and to Rs. 2000 in 5 years. Find the sum.

(a) Rs. 1650 *(b)* Rs. 1500 *(c)* Rs. 1580 *(d)* Rs. 1600

20. Out of the sum of Rs. 1550, a part was lent out at 5% p.a. simple interest and the remaining at 8% p.a. simple interest. If the total interest in both cases after 3 years is Rs. 300, the sum of money lent out at 8% p.a. simple interest was:

(a) Rs. 760 *(b)* Rs. 775 *(c)* Rs. 750 *(d)* Rs. 780

21. The simple interest of Rs. 800 is Rs. 216. If the rate per cent of the interest per annum is $\frac{1}{3}$ of the number of years, the rate per cent per annum is :

(a) 2% *(b)* 4% *(c)* 6% *(d)* 3%

22. A and B borrowed an equal sum of money from a money lender at the rate of 8% and 5½% p.a. respectively. If to clear the debt after 4 years, A paid Rs. 550 more than B, the total sum of money taken by them was :

(a) Rs. 12500 *(b)* Rs. 11000 *(c)* Rs. 11500 *(d)* Rs. 10500

23. If a certain sum of money lent out at simple interest amounts to Rs. 368 in 3 years and thereafter to Rs. 400 in another 2 years, the sum lent is :

(a) Rs. 300 *(b)* Rs. 320 *(c)* Rs. 290 *(d)* Rs. 325

24. Girish lent some money to Rajesh at 5% p.a. simple interest. Rajesh lent the entire amount to Omdutt on the same day at 8½% per annum. In this transaction after a year Rajesh earned a profit of Rs. 350. Find the sum of money lent by Girish to Rajesh.
(*a*) Rs. 10,000 (*b*) Rs. 8000 (*c*) Rs. 9500 (*d*) Rs. 10500

25. If simple interest on a certain sum of money for 4 years at 5% p.a. is same as the simple interest on Rs. 840 for 10 years at the rate of 4% p.a., the sum of money is:
(*a*) Rs. 1780 (*b*) Rs. 1660 (*c*) Rs. 1680 (*d*) Rs. 1620

26. A sum of Rs. 2444 is divided among three parts in such a manner that simple interest on the three divided parts at 6% p.a. after 3, 4 and 5 years respectively remains equal. Such three parts will be:
(*a*) Rs. 780, Rs. 1040, Rs. 624 (*b*) Rs. 1040, Rs. 780, Rs. 624
(*c*) Rs. 624, Rs. 780, Rs. 1040 (*d*) Rs. 940, Rs. 880, Rs. 624

27. Amount received by a money lender on lending out a certain sum of money at 3% per annum simple interest for 4 years is same as the amount received by him on lending out the sum of Rs. 6384 at 4% p.a. for 6 years. The sum will be :
(*a*) Rs. 7168 (*b*) Rs. 7278 (*c*) Rs. 7078 (*d*) Rs. 7068

28. If the sum of 8097 is divided among A, B and C in such a manner that amount received from these parts at 4% p.a. simple interest after 4, 5 and 6 years respectively remains equal, then A's part will exceed the B's part by :
(*a*) Rs. 85 (*b*) Rs. 93 (*c*) Rs. 75 (*d*) Rs. 63

29. Sanjay borrowed a total amount of Rs. 30,000 part of it on simple interest, rate of 12 p.c.p.a. and remaining on simple interest rate of 10 p.c.p.a. If at the end of 2 years he paid in all Rs. 36,480 to settle the loan amount, what was the amount borrowed at 12 p.c.p.a.?
(*a*) Rs. 12000 (*b*) Rs. 16000 (*c*) Rs. 17500 (*d*) Rs. 18000

30. Mr. Jha deposits an amount of Rs. 56500 to obtain a simple interest at the rate of 12 p.c.p.a. for 3 years. What total amount will Mr. Jha get at the end of 3 years?
(*a*) Rs. 73420 (*b*) Rs. 75680 (*c*) Rs. 76840 (*d*) Rs. 77540

31. What equal instalment of annual payment will discharge a debt which is due as Rs. 848 at the end of 4 years at 4% per annum simple interest?
(*a*) Rs. 200 (*b*) Rs. 212 (*c*) Rs. 225 (*d*) Rs. 250

32. What interest will be had on Rs. 450 in 2 years if an interest of Re. 0.40 is charged on Re 1 for 4 years?
(*a*) Rs. 30 (*b*) Rs. 60 (*c*) Rs. 90 (*d*) Rs. 120

33. In how many years will Rs. 3000 become Rs. 3840, if the rate of interest is 7% per annum?
(*a*) 3 years (*b*) 3.5 years (*c*) 4 years (*d*) 4.5 years

34. If the rate of interest is 2 paise per rupee per month, then the interest on Rs. 200 in one year will be:
(*a*) Rs. 4 (*b*) Rs. 24 (*c*) Rs. 48 (*d*) Rs. 50

35. In how many years a sum will become double of itself at 20% per annum?
(*a*) 4 years (*b*) 4½ years (*c*) 5 years (*d*) 5½ years

36. The amount of Re. 1 in 5 years at a certain rate of simple interest is Rs. 1.25. What should be the amount of Rs. 600 in two years?
(*a*) Rs. 600 (*b*) Rs. 660 (*c*) Rs. 750 (*d*) Rs. 800

37. Mrs. Nilam obtained an amount of Rs. 8,376 as simple interest on a certain amount at p.c.p.a. after 6 years. Find the amount invested by Mrs. Nilam.
(*a*) Rs. 16,660 (*b*) Rs. 17,180 (*c*) Rs. 17,450 (*d*) Rs. 18,110

38. Madhavi lent Rs. 5000 to Kamla for 5 years and Rs. 3000 to Vimla for 4 years. Find the rate of interest, if Madhavi gets an interest of Rs. 600 in the end.
(a) 1.62% *(b)* 2.5% *(c)* 3% *(d)* 4%

39. Rs. 800 becomes Rs. 956 in 3 years at certain rate of interest. If the rate of interest is increased by 4%, what amounts will Rs. 800 become in 3 years?
(a) Rs. 1020.8 *(b)* Rs. 1025 *(c)* Rs. 1052 *(d)* Data inadequate

40. Mr. Jha invests an amount of Rs.18000 to obtain a simple interest at the rate of 15 per cent per annum for 6 years. What total amount will Mr. Jha get at the end of 6 years?
(a) Rs. 33500 *(b)* Rs. 34000 *(c)* Rs. 34200 *(d)* Rs. 35000

41. Gopal invests an amount of Rs. 10,250 at 4 p.c.p.a. to obtain a total amount of Rs. 12,710 on simple interest after a certain period. For how many years did he invest the amount to obtain the total sum?
(a) 4 years *(b)* 5 years *(c)* 6 years *(d)* 8 years

42. A sum of money doubles itself in 7 years at simple interest. In how many years it will become four fold?
(a) 10 years *(b)* 14 years *(c)* 21 years *(d)* 35 years

43. A sum of money amount to Rs. 767 in 3 years and Rs. 806 in the 4 years at the simple rate of interest of 6%. What is the sum?
(a) Rs. 600 *(b)* Rs. 650 *(c)* Rs. 675 *(d)* Rs. 700

44. A farmer took a loan at 12 per cent per annum at simple interest. After 4 years he settled the loan by paying Rs. 2442. What was the principal amount?
(a) Rs. 1542 *(b)* 1550 *(c)* Rs. 1600 *(d)* Rs. 1650

45. A person invests Rs. 5000 at 5% p.a. simple interest for a certain period and earns Rs. 750. If he earns Rs. 720 on Rs. 6000 in the same time period, what is the rate of interest?
(a) 3% *(b)* 4% *(c)* 5% *(d)* 6%

46. An amount doubles itself at the end of 8 years with a certain rate of simple interest. What will be the total simple interest on Rs. 8000 at that rate at the end of 4 years?
(a) Rs. 2000 *(b)* Rs. 4000 *(c)* Rs. 6000 *(d)* None of these

47. Nisha invests an amount of Rs. 9535 at the rate of 4 per cent per annum to obtain a total amount of Rs. 11442 on simple interest after a certain period. For how many years did she invest the amount to obtain the total sum?
(a) 2 years *(b)* 4 years *(c)* 5 years *(d)* 10 years

48. Ms. Nilam deposits an amount of Rs. 16420 and obtained Rs. 25451 at the end of 5 years. What was the rate of interest per year?
(a) 10.5% *(b)* 11% *(c)* 12% *(d)* 13%

49. What would be the simple interest obtained on an amount of Rs. 3460 at the rate of 8.5% per annum after 6 years?
(a) Rs. 1746 *(b)* Rs. 1756.4 *(c)* Rs. 1764.6 *(d)* Rs. 1766

50. A person borrowed some money at the rate of 6% p.a. for the first two years, at the rate of 9% p.a. for the next 3 years, and at the rate of 14% p.a. for the period beyond 5 years. If he pays a total interest of Rs. 11,400 at the end of 9 years, how much money did he borrow?
(a) Rs. 8000 *(b)* Rs. 10,000 *(c)* Rs. 12,000 *(d)* Rs. 16,000

51. A sum of Rs. 1550 is lent out into two parts, one at 8% and another one at 6%. If the total annual income is Rs. 106, find the money lent at each rate.
(a) Rs. 500, Rs. 1000 *(b)* Rs. 600, Rs. 950 *(c)* Rs. 650, Rs.900 *(d)* Rs. 700, Rs. 950

52. Ram borrows Rs. 5000 for 2 years at 4% p.a. simple interest. He immediately lends it to another person at $6\frac{1}{4}$% p.a. for two years. What is his gain in this transaction per year?
(a) Rs. 167.50 *(b)* Rs. 150 *(c)* Rs. 125 *(d)* Rs. 112.50

53. In how many years, Rs. 150 will produce the same interest at 8% p.a. as Rs. 800 produce in 3 years at 4½ p.a.?
(a) 12 *(b)* 9 *(c)* 8 *(d)* 6

54. A sum invested at 5% simple interest p.a. grows to Rs. 504 in 4 years. The same amount at 10% simple interest p.a. in 2½ years will grow to:
(a) Rs. 550 *(b)* Rs. 525 *(c)* Rs. 450 *(d)* Rs. 420

55. A financer claims to be lending money at simple interest, but he includes the interest every six months for calculating the principal. If he charging an interest of 10%, the effective rate of interest becomes:
(a) 11% *(b)* 10.5% *(c)* 10.25% *(d)* 10%

56. What will be the ratio of simple interest earned by certain amount at the same rate of interest for 6 years and that for 9 years?
(a) 3 : 4 *(b)* 2 : 3 *(c)* 1 : 2 *(d)* 1 : 3

57. At what rate per cent per annum will the simple interest on a sum of money be 2/5 of the amount in 10 years?
(a) $6\frac{2}{3}$% *(b)* 6% *(c)* $5\frac{2}{3}$% *(d)* 4%

58. A sum of money becomes 7/6 of itself in 3 years at a certain rate of simple interest. What is the rate p.a.?
(a) 25% *(b)* 18% *(c)* $6\frac{5}{9}$% *(d)* $5\frac{5}{9}$%

59. A lends Rs. 2500 to B and certain sum to C at the same time at 7% p.a. simple interest. If after four years, A altogether receives Rs. 1120 as interest from B and C, then the sum lent to C is:
(a) Rs. 6500 *(b)* Rs. 4000 *(c)* Rs. 1500 *(d)* Rs. 700

60. Simple interest on a certain amount is 9/16 of the principal. If the numbers representing the rate of interest in per cent and time in years be equal, then time for which the principal is lent out, is:
(a) 7½ years *(b)* 7 years *(c)* 6½ years *(d)* 5½ years

61. A lent Rs. 5000 to B for 2 years and Rs. 3000 to C for 4 years on simple interest at the same rate of interest and received Rs. 2200 in all from both of them as interest. What is the rate of interest per annum?
(a) 10% *(b)* $7\frac{1}{8}$% *(c)* 7% *(d)* 5%

62. If the annual rate of simple interest increases from 10% to 12½%, a person's yearly income increases by Rs. 1250. What is his principal?
(a) Rs. 65000 *(b)* Rs. 60,000 *(c)* Rs. 50,000 *(d)* Rs. 45,000

63. The difference between the simple interest received from two different sources on Rs. 1500 for 3 years is Rs. 13.50. What is the difference between their rates of interest?
(a) 0.4% *(b)* 0.3% *(c)* 0.2% *(d)* 0.1%

64. A sum of Rs. 725 is lent in the beginning of a year at a certain rate of interest. After 8 months, a sum of Rs. 36250 more is lent but at the rate twice the former. At the end of year, Rs. 33.50 is earned as interest from both the loans. Find the original rate of interest.
(a) 6% *(b)* 5% *(c)* 4.5% *(d)* 3.46%

65. Samir invested an amount of Rs. 12,000 at the rate of 10% p.a. simple interest and another amount at the rate of 20% p.a. simple interest. The total interest earned at the end of one year on the total amount invested became 14% p.a. What is the total amount invested?
(*a*) Rs. 25000 (*b*) Rs. 22000 (*c*) Rs. 20000 (*d*) Rs. 18000

66. A money lender finds that due to a fall in the annual rate of interest from 8% to $7\frac{3}{4}\%$, his yearly income diminishes by Rs. 61.50. What is his capital?
(*a*) Rs. 26000 (*b*) Rs. 24,600 (*c*) 23,800 (*d*) Rs. 22,400

67. Divide Rs. 2379 into three parts so that their amounts after 2, 3 and 4 years respectively may be equal, the rate of interest being 5% p.a. at simple interest. What is the first part?
(*a*) Rs. 850 (*b*) Rs. 828 (*c*) Rs. 825 (*d*) Rs. 800

68. Saurabh invested in all Rs. 2600 at 4%, 6% and 8% p.a. simple interest. At the end of the year, he got the same interest in all the three cases. What is the money invested at 4%?
(*a*) Rs. 1200 (*b*) Rs. 800 (*c*) Rs. 600 (*d*) Rs. 200

69. Mr. Sanjay invested an amount of Rs. 13,900 divided in two different schemes P and Q at the simple interest rate of 14% p.a. and 11% p.a. respectively. If the total amount of simple interest earned in 2 years be Rs. 3508 then find the amount invested in scheme Q.
(*a*) Rs. 7500 (*b*) Rs. 7000 (*c*) Rs. 6400 (*d*) Rs. 6000

70. Madhava invested certain amount in three different schemes P, Q and R with the rate of interest 10% p.a., 12% p.a. and 15% p.a. respectively. If the total interest accrued in one year was Rs. 3200 and the amount invested in scheme R was 150% of the amount invested in scheme P and 240% of the amount invested in scheme Q. Find the amount invested in scheme Q.
(*a*) Rs. 6500 (*b*) Rs. 6000 (*c*) Rs. 5500 (*d*) Rs. 5000

71. An amount of Rs. 100000 is invested in two types of shares. The first yield an interest of 9% p.a. and the second 11% p.a. If the total interest at the end of one year is $9\frac{3}{4}\%$, then the total interest at 9% was:
(*a*) Rs. 82,500 (*b*) Rs. 72,500 (*c*) Rs. 62,500 (*d*) Rs. 52,500

SOLUTIONS

1. $P = \dfrac{90 \times 100}{6 \times 3} = \text{Rs. } 500$

2. $\text{Rate} = \dfrac{1 \times 100}{100 \times \frac{1}{12}} = 12\%.$

3. Let principal = Rs. x; Amount = Rs. $2x$; then I = $2x - x$ = Rs. x

$\therefore R = \dfrac{x \times 100}{x \times 20} = 5\%$

Again, if principal = Rs. x; Amount = Rs. $3x$; then I = $3x - x$ = Rs. $2x$

Hence, $T = \dfrac{2x \times 100}{x \times 5} = 40$ years

4. $\text{Rate} = \dfrac{40 \times 100}{500 \times 4} = 2\%$

5. Here, I = 2240 – 2000 = Rs. 240

$\therefore \quad T = \frac{240 \times 100}{2000 \times 4} = 3$ years

6. Let, R = T = x; then

$\frac{25}{64}P = \frac{P \times x \times x}{100} \Rightarrow x^2 = \frac{25 \times 100}{64} \quad \therefore x = \frac{5 \times 10}{8} = \frac{25}{4}; \quad R = 6\frac{1}{4}\%$

7. Here, Simple interest for 2 years = Rs. 1250 – Rs. 1150 = Rs. 100

$\therefore$ Simple interest for 3 years = $\frac{100 \times 3}{2}$ = Rs. 150

Hence, P = Rs. 1150 – Rs. 150 = Rs. 1000

$\therefore \quad \text{Rate} = \frac{50 \times 100}{1000 \times 1} = 5\%$

8. Here, $I = \frac{892 \times 6 \times \frac{2}{3}}{100}$ = Rs. 35.68

9. $P = \frac{81 \times 100 \times 2}{6 \times 9}$ = Rs. 300

10. $I = \frac{1850 \times 3 \times 5}{100}$ = Rs. 277.50

$\therefore$ Amount = Rs. 1850 + Rs. 277.50 = Rs. 2127.50

11. $\frac{1250 \times R \times 3}{100} + \frac{1500 \times R \times 2}{100} = 258.75 \quad \Rightarrow 6750\,R = 25875$

$\therefore \quad R = \frac{25875}{6750} = \frac{23}{6} = 3\frac{5}{6}\%$

12. Here, $\frac{5000 \times R \times T}{100} = \frac{4000 \times (R+1) \times T}{100} \quad \Rightarrow 5R = 4R + 4 \therefore \; R = 4\%$

13. Here, $\frac{500 \times R \times 4}{100} + \frac{600 \times R \times 3}{100} = 190 \quad \Rightarrow 38R = 190 \qquad \therefore R = \frac{190}{38} = 5\%$

14. Let annual instalment be Rs. x; then

$x + \frac{x \times 3 \times 5}{100} + x + \frac{x \times 2 \times 5}{100} + x + \frac{x \times 1 \times 5}{100} + x = 645 + \frac{645 \times 4 \times 5}{100}$

$\Rightarrow \quad 4x + \frac{3x}{10} = 774 \quad \Rightarrow \quad \frac{43x}{10} = 774 \qquad \therefore x = \frac{774 \times 10}{43}$ = Rs. 180

15. Simple interest for 2 years = Rs. 2050 – Rs. 1900 = Rs. 150

$\therefore$ Simple interest for 1 year = Rs. $\frac{150}{2}$ = Rs. 75

Since simple interest for 3 years = Rs. 75 × 3 = Rs. 225

∴ Principal = Rs. 1900 – Rs. 225 = Rs. 1675

Hence, Rate $= \dfrac{75 \times 100}{1675 \times 1} = 4½\%$

16. Rate $= \dfrac{P/4 \times 100}{P \times 5} = 5\%$

17. Here, $P + \dfrac{P \times 8 \times 5}{100} = 1050 \Rightarrow \dfrac{7P}{5} = 1050 \quad \therefore P = \dfrac{1050 \times 5}{7}$ = Rs. 750

18. Here, $\dfrac{2500 \times R \times 4}{100} + \dfrac{1500 \times (R+3) \times 4}{100} = 1140 \Rightarrow 160R = 960 \quad \therefore R = \dfrac{960}{160} = 6\%$

19. Interest for 3 years= Rs. 2000 – Rs. 1760 = Rs. 240

∴ Interest for 1 year = Rs. $\dfrac{240}{3}$ = Rs. 80

And interest for 2 years = Rs. 80 × 2 = Rs. 160

∴ Principal = Rs. 1760 – Rs. 160 = Rs. 1600

20. Let Rs. x and Rs $(1550 - x)$ were lent out at 8% and 5% respectively; then

$\dfrac{x \times 8 \times 3}{100} + \dfrac{(1550 - x) \times 5 \times 3}{100} = 300 \Rightarrow 24x + 23250 - 15x = 30000$

$\Rightarrow 9x = 6750 \quad \therefore x = \dfrac{6750}{9}$ = Rs. 750

21. Let Rate = R then time in years = 3R;

Now, $\dfrac{800 \times R \times 3R}{100} = 216 \Rightarrow 24R^2 = 216 \Rightarrow R^2 = 9 \Rightarrow R = 3\%$

22. Here, $\dfrac{P \times 8 \times 4}{100} - \dfrac{P \times 11 \times 4}{100 \times 2} = 550 \Rightarrow \dfrac{8P}{25} - \dfrac{11P}{50} = 550 \Rightarrow \dfrac{P}{10} = 550 \quad \therefore P = 5500$

Hence, total sum of money = 2P = 2 × 5500 = Rs. 11000

23. S.I. for 2 years = Rs. 400 – Rs. 368 = Rs. 32

∴ S.I. for 1 year = $\dfrac{32}{2}$ = Rs. 16

And S.I. for 3 years = 16 × 3 = Rs. 48

∴ Sum = Rs. 368 – Rs. 48 = Rs. 320

24. $\dfrac{P \times 17 \times 1}{100 \times 2} - \dfrac{P \times 5 \times 1}{100} = 350 \Rightarrow \dfrac{7P}{200} = 350 \quad \therefore P = \dfrac{200 \times 350}{7}$ = Rs. 10,000

25. Here, $\dfrac{P \times 5 \times 4}{100} = \dfrac{840 \times 4 \times 10}{100} \Rightarrow 5P = 8400 \quad \therefore P = \dfrac{8400}{5}$ = Rs. 1680

26. Let three parts be Rs. a, Rs. b and Rs. c respectively; then,

$$\frac{a\times6\times3}{100}=\frac{b\times6\times4}{100}=\frac{c\times6\times5}{100} \Rightarrow 3a = 4b = 5c \quad \therefore a : b : c = 20 : 15 : 12$$

Sum of proportionals = 20 + 15 + 12 = 47

$$a = \frac{20}{47}\times2444 = \text{Rs. } 1040$$

$$b = \frac{15}{47}\times2444 = \text{Rs. } 780$$

and, $$c = \frac{12}{47}\times2444 = \text{Rs. } 624$$

27. Here, $P + \frac{P\times3\times4}{100} = 6384+\frac{6384\times4\times6}{100} \Rightarrow \frac{28P}{25}=\frac{638400+153216}{100}$

$$\therefore P = \frac{791616}{100}\times\frac{25}{28} = \text{Rs. } 7068$$

28. Let parts of A, B and C are Rs. a, Rs. b and Rs. c respectively; then,

$$a + \frac{a\times4\times4}{100}=b+\frac{b\times4\times5}{100}=c+\frac{c\times4\times6}{100} \Rightarrow \frac{29a}{25}=\frac{30b}{25}=\frac{31c}{25}$$

Hence, $a : b : c = 930 : 899 : 870$

Sum of prportionals = 930 + 899 + 870 = 2699

$\therefore$ Out of 8097, A's part $= \frac{930}{2699}\times8097 = \text{Rs. } 2790;$

B's part $= \frac{899}{2699}\times8097 = \text{Rs. } 2697$

Hence, it is clear that A's part exceeds B's part by Rs. 2790 – Rs. 2697 = Rs. 93

29. Let Sanjay borrowed Rs. x and Rs. $(30,000 - x)$ at 12% and 10% p.a. respectively,

Then, $x+\frac{x\times12\times2}{100}+(30000-x)+\frac{(30,000-x)\times10\times2}{100} = 36480$

$\Rightarrow \frac{124x}{100}+\frac{120(30,000-x)}{100} = 36480 \Rightarrow 124x + 3600000 - 120x = 36480 \times 100$

$\Rightarrow 4x = 48000 \quad \therefore x = \text{Rs. } 12000$

30. $I = \frac{56500\times12\times3}{100} = \text{Rs. } 20340$

Hence, Amount = 56500 + 20340 = Rs. 76840

31. Let equal instalment be Rs. x; then

$$x+\frac{x\times4\times3}{100}+x+\frac{x\times4\times2}{100}+x+\frac{x\times4\times1}{100}+x=848$$

$\Rightarrow\ 4x + \dfrac{24x}{100} = 848 \quad \Rightarrow \dfrac{106x}{25} = 848 \quad \therefore\ x = \dfrac{848 \times 25}{106} = \text{Rs. } 200$

32. On Re 1 for 4 years interest of Re 0.40 is charged
Hence, on Rs. 100 for 1 year interest of Rs. 10 is charged

Now, $I = \dfrac{450 \times 10 \times 2}{100} = \text{Rs. } 90$

33. $T = \dfrac{840 \times 100}{3000 \times 7} = 4$ years $\quad (\because\ I = 3840 - 3000 = \text{Rs. } 840)$

34. Rate = 2 paise per rupee per month = 24% p.a.

Then, $I = \dfrac{200 \times 24 \times 1}{100} = \text{Rs. } 48$

35. Let principal be Rs. x, then amount = Rs. $2x$, Hence $I = 2x - x = \text{Rs. } x$

Now, $T = \dfrac{x \times 100}{x \times 120} = 5$ years

36. $I = 1.25 - 1 = 0.25$

Then, $R = \dfrac{0.25 \times 100}{1 \times 5} = 5\%$

Again, $I = \dfrac{600 \times 5 \times 2}{100} = \text{Rs. } 60$

Hence, amount = 600 + 60 = Rs. 660

37. $P = \dfrac{8376 \times 100}{8 \times 6} = \text{Rs. } 17450$

38. $\dfrac{5000 \times R \times 5}{100} + \dfrac{3000 \times R \times 4}{100} = 600 \quad \Rightarrow 250\text{ R} + 120\text{ R} = 600$

$\Rightarrow\ 370R = 600 \quad \therefore\ R = \dfrac{600}{370} = 1.62\%$

39. $I = 956 - 800 = \text{Rs. } 156$

$R = \dfrac{156 \times 100}{800 \times 3} = \dfrac{13}{2}\%$ p.a.

New Rate $= \dfrac{13}{2} + 4 = \dfrac{21}{2}\%$; then

$I = \dfrac{800 \times 21 \times 3}{100 \times 2} = \text{Rs. } 252$

Hence, amount = 800 + 252 = Rs. 1052

40. $I = \dfrac{18000 \times 15 \times 6}{100} = \text{Rs. } 16{,}200$

Hence, amount = 18000 + 16200 = Rs. 34200

41. I = 12710 − 10250 = Rs. 2460 $\quad T = \dfrac{2460 \times 100}{10250 \times 4} = 6$ years

42. Let principal be Rs. x; then amount = Rs. $2x$, Hence, I = $2x - x$ = Rs. x.

$R = \dfrac{x \times 100}{x \times 7} = \dfrac{100}{7}\%$ p.a.

Now, amount = Rs. $4x$; then I = $4x - x$ = Rs. $3x$

Hence, $T = \dfrac{3x \times 100}{x \times \dfrac{100}{7}} = \dfrac{3 \times 100 \times 7}{100} = 21$ years

43. Here, interest, I for 1 year = 806 − 767 = Rs. 39

Hence, 3I = 3 × 39 = Rs. 117 $\quad$ Since, P = 767 − 117 = Rs. 650

44. Let principal = Rs. x, then

$x + \dfrac{x \times 12 \times 4}{100} = 2442 \quad \Rightarrow \dfrac{37x}{25} = 2442 \quad \therefore x = \dfrac{2442 \times 25}{37} = \text{Rs. } 1650$

45. $T = \dfrac{750 \times 100}{5000 \times 5} = 3$ years

Again, $R = \dfrac{720 \times 100}{6000 \times 3} = 4\%$

46. Let principal = Rs. x; then amount = Rs. $2x$; I = $2x - x$ = Rs. x

$R = \dfrac{x \times 100}{x \times 8} = \dfrac{25}{2}\%$ $\quad$ Again, $I = \dfrac{8000 \times 25 \times 4}{100 \times 2} = \text{Rs. } 4000$

47. Here, I = 11442 − 9535 = Rs. 1907, $\quad T = \dfrac{1907 \times 100}{9535 \times 4} = 5$ years

48. I = 25451 − 16420 = Rs. 9031, $\quad R = \dfrac{9031 \times 100}{16420 \times 5} = 11\%$

49. $I = \dfrac{3460 \times 8.5 \times 6}{100} = \text{Rs. } 1764.6$

50. Let he borrowed Rs. x; then

$\dfrac{x \times 6 \times 2}{100} + \dfrac{x \times 9 \times 3}{100} + \dfrac{x \times 14 \times 4}{100} = 11400 \Rightarrow \dfrac{19x}{20} = 11400$

$\therefore x = \dfrac{11400 \times 20}{19} = \text{Rs. } 12000$

51. Let Rs. x and Rs (1550 – x) are lent out at 8% and 6% respectively.

Then, $\frac{x\times8\times1}{100}+\frac{(1550-x)\times6\times1}{100}=106 \Rightarrow 8x + 9300 - 6x = 10600$

$\Rightarrow 2x = 1300 \quad \therefore \; x$ = Rs. 650 and $1550 - x = 1550 - 650$ = Rs. 900

Hence, required two parts are, Rs. 650 and Rs. 900

52. Reqired gain = $\frac{5000\times25\times1}{100\times4}-\frac{5000\times4\times1}{100}=312.50-200$ = Rs. 112.50

53. $I=\frac{800\times9\times3}{100\times2}$ = Rs. 108

Hence, $T=\frac{108\times100}{150\times8}$ = 9 years

54. Here, $P+\frac{P\times5\times4}{100}=504 \Rightarrow \frac{6P}{5}=504 \quad \therefore P=\frac{5\times504}{6}$ = Rs. 420

Now, $I=\frac{420\times10\times5}{100\times2}$ = Rs. 105

Hence, amount = 420 + 105 = Rs. 525

55. Let principal = Rs. 100; then

Interest for 6 months = $\frac{100\times10\times1}{100\times2}$ = Rs. 5

Now, amount = 100 + 5 = Rs. 105

Again, interest for another 6 months = $\frac{105\times10\times1}{100\times2}$ = Rs. 5.25

Hence, amount after 1 year = 105 + 5.25 = Rs. 110.25

Since, effective rate of interest = 110.25 – 100 = 10.25% p.a.

56. Let principal = Rs. 100, then

Required ratio = $\frac{100\times R\times6}{100}:\frac{100\times R\times9}{100}=2:3$

57. Let prinipal = Rs. x, then interest = Rs. $\frac{2}{5}x$

$R=\frac{\frac{2}{5}x\times100}{x\times10}=\frac{2x\times100}{5\times x\times10}=4\%$

58. Let principal = Rs. x; then amount = Rs. $\frac{7x}{6}$; Since, $I=\frac{7x}{6}-x$ = Rs. $\frac{x}{6}$

$R=\frac{x\times100}{6\times x\times3}=\frac{50}{9}=5\frac{5}{9}\%$

59. Let A lends to C Rs. x; then

$\frac{2500\times7\times4}{100}+\frac{x\times7\times4}{100}=1120 \Rightarrow \frac{7x}{25}=1120-700$

$\Rightarrow \dfrac{7x}{25} = 420 \quad \therefore\ x = \dfrac{420 \times 25}{7} = \text{Rs. } 1500$

60. Let principal = Rs. x; then Interest = Rs. $\dfrac{9x}{16}$; and also, Rate = Time = T

Since, $\dfrac{9x}{16} = \dfrac{x \times T \times T}{100} \quad \Rightarrow T^2 = \dfrac{100 \times 9}{16} \therefore\ T = \dfrac{30}{4} = 7\dfrac{1}{2}$ years

61. Here, $\dfrac{5000 \times R \times 2}{100} + \dfrac{3000 \times R \times 4}{100} = 2200$

$\Rightarrow 100R + 120R = 2200 \qquad \Rightarrow 220R = 2200 \qquad \therefore\ R = \dfrac{2200}{220} = 10\%$

62. Let principal = Rs. x; then,

$\dfrac{x \times 25 \times 1}{100 \times 2} - \dfrac{x \times 10 \times 1}{100} = 1250 \quad \Rightarrow \dfrac{x}{8} - \dfrac{x}{10} = 1250$

$\Rightarrow \dfrac{x}{40} = 1250 \qquad \therefore\ x = 1250 \times 40 = \text{Rs. } 50{,}000$

63. Here, $\dfrac{1500 \times R_1 \times 3}{100} + \dfrac{1500 \times R_2 \times 3}{100} = 13.50$

$\Rightarrow 45\ (R_1 - R_2) = 13.50 \qquad \therefore\ R_1 - R_2 = \dfrac{13.50}{45} = 0.3\%$

64. Here, $\dfrac{725 \times R \times 1}{100} + \dfrac{362.50 \times 2R \times 4}{100 \times 12} = 33.50$

$\Rightarrow \dfrac{2175R + 725R}{300} = 33.50 \qquad \Rightarrow 2900\ R = 3 \times 3350 \qquad \therefore\ R = \dfrac{3 \times 3350}{2900} = 3.46\%$

65. Let Samir invested Rs. x at 20% p.a. then,

$\dfrac{12000 \times 10 \times 1}{100} + \dfrac{x \times 20 \times 1}{100} = \dfrac{(12000 + x) \times 14 \times 1}{100}$

$\Rightarrow 168000 + 14x - 20x = 120000 \qquad \Rightarrow 6x = 48000 \qquad \therefore\ x = \text{Rs. } 8000$

Hence, total amount invested = 12000 + 8000 = Rs. 20,000

66. Let his capital = Rs. x; then

$\dfrac{x \times 8 \times 1}{100} - \dfrac{x \times 31 \times 1}{100 \times 4} = 61.50 \quad \Rightarrow \dfrac{x}{400} = 61.50$

$\therefore\ x = 400 \times 61.50 = \text{Rs. } 24600$

67. Let three parts be Rs. x, Rs. y and Rs. z respectively, then

$x + \dfrac{x \times 5 \times 2}{100} = y + \dfrac{y \times 5 \times 3}{100} = z + \dfrac{z \times 5 \times 4}{100}$

$\Rightarrow \dfrac{22x}{20} = \dfrac{23y}{20} = \dfrac{24z}{20}$; then, $y = \dfrac{22}{23}x$ & $z = \dfrac{11x}{12}$

Since, $x + \frac{22x}{20} + \frac{11x}{12} = 2379 \quad \Rightarrow \frac{793x}{276} = 2379$

$\therefore \quad x = \frac{2379 \times 276}{793} = \text{Rs. } 828$

68. Let Saurabh invested Rs. x, Rs. y and Rs. z at 4%, 6% and 8% respectively; then

$\frac{x \times 4 \times 1}{100} = \frac{y \times 6 \times 1}{100} = \frac{z \times 8 \times 1}{100} \Rightarrow 2x = 3y = 4z$

Hence, $y = \frac{2}{3}x$ and $z = \frac{1}{2}x$

Now, $x + \frac{2}{3}x + \frac{1}{2}x = 2600 \quad \Rightarrow \frac{13x}{6} = 2600 \quad \therefore x = \frac{2600 \times 6}{13} = \text{Rs. } 1200$

69. Let Mr. Sanjay invested Rs. x and Rs $(13900 - x)$ in schemes Q and P respectively, then

$\frac{x \times 11 \times 2}{100} + \frac{(13900 - x) \times 14 \times 2}{100} = 3508$

$\Rightarrow 22x + 389200 - 28x = 350800 \quad \Rightarrow 6x = 38400 \quad \therefore \; x = \frac{38400}{6} = \text{Rs. } 6400$

70. Let amount invested in scheme P = Rs. x then amount invested in scheme R = $\frac{150}{100} \times x$

$= \text{Rs. } \frac{3}{2}x$ and also, if amount invested in Scheme Q = Rs. y; then amount invested in Scheme

$R = \frac{240}{100} \times y = \text{Rs. } \frac{12}{5}y$

Since, $\frac{3}{2}x = \frac{12}{5}y \quad \therefore \; x = \frac{8}{5}y$

Hence, $\frac{8y \times 10 \times 1}{5 \times 100} + \frac{y \times 12 \times 1}{100} + \frac{12y \times 15 \times 1}{5 \times 100} = 3200$

$\Rightarrow \frac{4y}{25} + \frac{3y}{25} + \frac{9y}{25} = 3200 \quad \Rightarrow \frac{16y}{25} = 3200 \quad \therefore y = \frac{3200 \times 25}{16} = \text{Rs. } 5000$

71. The amount Rs. x and Rs $(100000 - x)$ are invested at 9% and 11% respectively; then,

$\frac{x \times 9 \times 1}{100} + \frac{(100000 - x) \times 11 \times 1}{100} = \frac{100000 \times 39 \times 1}{100 \times 4}$

$\Rightarrow 9x + 1100000 - 11x = 9{,}75000 \quad \Rightarrow 2x = 1{,}25{,}000$

$\therefore \; x = \frac{1{,}25{,}000}{2} = \text{Rs. } 62{,}500$

24 COMPOUND INTEREST

COMPOUND INTEREST

In business transaction if interest as it becomes due is not paid to the lender but is added on to the principal, the money is said to be lent at *compound interest* and the total sum owed after a given time is called the amount at compound interest for that time.

After a certain period, the difference between the amount and the original principal is called the compound Interest (C.I.).

Some Important Formulae :

Let Principal = P

Time = n years

Rate = r% p.a.

then, the amount,

(*a*) when interest is compounded annually:

$$\text{then,} \quad \text{Amount} = P\left(1+\frac{r}{100}\right)^n$$

(*b*) when interest is compounded half yearly:

$$\text{then,} \quad \text{Amount} = P\left(1+\frac{r/2}{100}\right)^{2n}$$

(*c*) when interest is compounded quarterly :

$$\text{then,} \quad \text{Amount} = P\left(1+\frac{r/4}{100}\right)^{4n}$$

(*d*) when time is fraction of a year, say $4\frac{1}{3}$ years,

$$\text{then,} \quad \text{Amount} = P\left(1+\frac{r}{100}\right)^4 \times \left(1+\frac{\frac{1}{3}r}{100}\right)$$

(*e*) when rates are r_1%, r_2% and r_3% for Ist, IInd and IIIrd year respectively;

$$\text{then,} \quad \text{Amount} = P\left(1+\frac{r_1}{100}\right)\left(1+\frac{r_2}{100}\right)\left(1+\frac{r_3}{100}\right)$$

Example 1: Find the difference between the compound interest and the simple interest for the sum Rs. 2000 at 5% p.a. for 2 years.

Solution: Required difference = $2000\left[\left(1+\frac{5}{100}\right)^2-1\right] - \frac{2000\times5\times2}{100}$

$= 2000\times\frac{41}{400}-200 = 205 - 200 = \text{Rs. } 5$

Example 2: Ram invests Rs. 5000 in a bond which gives interest at 4% per annum during the first year, 5% during the second year and 10% during the third year. How much does he get at the end of third year?

Solution: $A = 5000\left(1+\frac{4}{100}\right)\left(1+\frac{5}{100}\right)\left(1+\frac{10}{100}\right)$

$= 5000\times\frac{26}{25}\times\frac{21}{20}\times\frac{11}{10} = \text{Rs. } 6006.$

Example 3: A certain sum of money doubles itself in 5 years. In how many years will it become 8 times at the same rate of compound interest.

Solution: $2P = P\left(1+\frac{r}{100}\right)^5 \Rightarrow \left(1+\frac{r}{100}\right)^5 = 2$ ...(*i*)

Again, $8P = P\left(1+\frac{r}{100}\right)^n \Rightarrow \left(1+\frac{r}{100}\right)^n = 8 = 2^3$ ...(*i*)

Since, $\left(1+\frac{r}{100}\right)^n = \left(1+\frac{r}{100}\right)^{15}$ [From equation (*i*)]

Hence, n = 15 years

Example 4: A certain amount of money at compound interest grows upto Rs. 51168 in 15 years and upto Rs. 51701 in 16 years. Find the rate per cent per annum.

Solution: Simple interest of Rs. 51168 for 1 year = 51701 – 51168 = Rs. 533

Hence, $r = \frac{533\times100}{51168\times1} = \frac{25}{24} = 1\frac{1}{24}\%$

Example 5: If a sum of Rs. 13040 is to be paid back in two equal annual instalments at $3\frac{3}{4}\%$ per annum, what is the amount of each instalment?

Solution: Let each instalment be Rs. x; then,

$$\frac{x}{\left(1+\frac{15}{4\times100}\right)} + \frac{x}{\left(1+\frac{15}{4\times100}\right)} = 13040 \Rightarrow x.\frac{80}{83} + x.\left(\frac{80}{83}\right)^2 = 13040$$

$$\Rightarrow x.\frac{80}{83}\left(1+\frac{80}{83}\right)=13040 \quad \Rightarrow x.\frac{80}{83}.\frac{163}{83}=13040 \quad \therefore x=\frac{13040\times 83\times 83}{80\times 163}=\text{Rs. } 6889$$

Example 6: If the compound interest of a sum for 3 years at 5% per annum be Rs. 126.10, then what will be the simple interest of the same sum for the same period and at the same rate?

Solution: Here, $126.10=P\left[\left(1+\frac{5}{100}\right)^3-1\right] \Rightarrow 126.10=P\times\frac{1261}{8000} \;\therefore\; P=\frac{1261.10\times 8000}{1261}=\text{Rs. } 800$

Hence, $\text{S.I.}=\frac{800\times 5\times 3}{100}=\text{Rs. } 120$

Example 7: Find the compound interest on Rs. 1000 for 3 years at 5% p.a.

Solution: $\text{C.I.}=1000\left[\left(1+\frac{5}{100}\right)^3-1\right]=1000\left[\left(\frac{21}{20}\right)^3-1\right]$

$$=1000\left[\frac{9261-8000}{8000}\right]=1000\times\frac{1261}{8000}=\text{Rs. } 157.63$$

Example 8: Find the amount of Rs. 4000 for 2 years at 2½% per annum compound interest.

Solution: $A=4000\left(1+\frac{5}{100\times 2}\right)^2=4000\left(\frac{41}{40}\right)^2=\frac{4000\times 41\times 41}{40\times 40}=\text{Rs. } 4202.50.$

Example 9: What sum will amount to Rs. 1352 in 2 years at 4% per annum compound interest?

Solution: Here, $1352=P\left(1+\frac{4}{100}\right)^2$

$$\Rightarrow 1352=P\left(\frac{26}{25}\right)^2$$

$$\therefore \quad P=\frac{1352\times 25\times 25}{26\times 26}=\text{Rs. } 1250$$

Example 10: The population of a village increases by 5% every year. If present population of the village is 4410, what was the population of this village 2 years ago?

Solution: Population of the village 2 years ago $=\frac{4410}{\left(1+\frac{5}{100}\right)^2}=\frac{4410}{\frac{21}{20}\times\frac{21}{20}}=\frac{4410\times 20\times 20}{21\times 21}=4000$

Example 11: Find the amount of Rs. 6400 for 1½ years at 5% per annum, if the interest is compounded semi-annually.

Solution: $A=6400\left(1+\frac{5}{2\times 100}\right)^3$

$$=6400\times\frac{41}{40}\times\frac{41}{40}\times\frac{41}{40}=\text{Rs. } 6892.10$$

Example 12: At what rate per cent compound interest will the sum of Rs. 1250 yield an interest of Rs. 102 in 2 years?

Solution: Here $102 = 1250\left[\left(1+\frac{r}{100}\right)^2 - 1\right] \Rightarrow \left(1+\frac{r}{100}\right)^2 = \frac{51}{625}+1 \Rightarrow \left(1+\frac{r}{100}\right)^2 = \frac{676}{625}$

$\Rightarrow \left(1+\frac{r}{100}\right) = \frac{26}{25} \Rightarrow \frac{r}{100} = \frac{1}{25} \quad \therefore r = 4\%$

Example 13: In what time Rs. 1200 invested at 5% per annum will yield Rs. 123 as compound interest?

Solution: Here, $123 = 1200\left[\left(1+\frac{5}{100}\right)^n - 1\right] \Rightarrow \frac{123}{1200}+1 = \left(\frac{21}{20}\right)^n \Rightarrow \left(\frac{21}{20}\right)^n = \frac{441}{400}$

$\Rightarrow \left(\frac{21}{20}\right)^n = \left(\frac{21}{20}\right)^2 \quad \therefore n = 2$ years

Example 14: A sum of money placed at compound interest amounts to Rs. 5200 in 4 years and to Rs. 5330 in 5 years. Find the rate per cent per annum.

Solution: Simple interest of Rs. 5200 for 1 year = 5330 – 5200 = Rs. 130

Hence, $r = \frac{130\times100}{5200\times1} = 2\frac{1}{2}\%$

Example 15: If the compound interest on a sum of money for 2 years at 4% per annum is Rs. 10 more than the simple interest on the same sum for the same period and at the same rate, find the sum.

Solution: $P\left[\left(1+\frac{4}{100}\right)^2 - 1\right] - \frac{P\times4\times2}{100} = 10 \Rightarrow P\left[\left(\frac{26}{25}\right)^2 - 1\right] - \frac{2P}{25} = 10 \Rightarrow P\left[\frac{51}{625} - \frac{2}{25}\right] = 10$

$\Rightarrow P\times\frac{1}{625} = 10 \quad \therefore$ P = 10 × 625 = Rs. 6250

Example 16: The difference between compound and simple interest on a certain sum of money for 3 years at 10% per annum is Rs. 15.50. Find the sum.

Solution: Here, $P\left[\left(1+\frac{10}{100}\right)^3 - 1\right] - \frac{P\times10\times3}{100} = 15.50 \Rightarrow P\left[\left(\frac{11}{10}\right)^3 - 1\right] - \frac{3P}{10} = 15.50$

$\Rightarrow P\left[\frac{331}{1000} - \frac{3}{10}\right] = 15.50 \Rightarrow P\times\frac{31}{1000} = 15.50 \quad \therefore P = \frac{15.50\times1000}{31}$ = Rs. 500

Example 17: A sum of money placed at compound interest amounts to Rs. 900 in 3 years and to Rs. 990 in 4 years. Find the amount that the sum will yield in 5 years.

Solution: Here, simple interest of 900 for 1 year = 990 – 900 = Rs. 90

Hence, $r = \frac{90\times100}{900\times1} = 10\%$

Since, required amount = $990\left(1+\frac{10}{100}\right) = 990 \times \frac{11}{10}$ = Rs. 1089

Example 18: A and B borrowed a total sum of Rs. 8280 from a money lender at 7% per annum compound interest in such a proportion that to settle his loan after 3 years A paid as much amount as was paid by B after 4 years from the date of borrowing. Find the part of money borrowed by B.

Solution: Let the sums borowed by B and A are Rs. x and Rs $(8280 - x)$ respectively

Now, $(8280 - x)\left(1+\frac{7}{100}\right)^3 = x\left(1+\frac{7}{100}\right)^4 \Rightarrow 8280 - x = x \times \frac{107}{100}$

$\Rightarrow \frac{207x}{100} = 8280 \quad \therefore x = \frac{8280 \times 100}{207} = \text{Rs. } 4000$

Example 19: By how much would the compound interest exceed the simple interest if the sum of Rs. 4800 were invested at 5% per annum for 2 years?

Solution: Required difference $= 4800\left[\left(1+\frac{5}{100}\right)^2 - 1\right] - \frac{4800 \times 5 \times 2}{100}$

$= 4800\left[\left(\frac{21}{20}\right)^2 - 1\right] - 480 = 4800 \times \frac{41}{400} - 480$

$= 492 - 480 = \text{Rs. } 12$

Example 20: A certain sum of money has been placed at compound interest. If the compound interest for the two successive years be Rs. 225 and Rs. 238.50, find the rate per cent per annum.

Solution: Here, simple interest of Rs. 225 for 1 year = 238.50 – 225 = Rs. 13.50

$\therefore \quad r = \frac{13.50 \times 100}{225 \times 1} = 6\%$

Example 21: Two partners Lavkush and Gulshan jointly lent out a sum of Rs. 1682 at 5% per annum compound interest, interest being compounded annually. If after 3 years Lavkush obtained as much amount as was obtained by Gulshan after 5 years, find the parts of money invested by each of them.

Solution: Let parts of Gulshan and Lavkush be Rs. x and Rs. $(1682 - x)$ respectively; then,

$x\left(1+\frac{5}{100}\right)^5 = (1682 - x)\left(1+\frac{5}{100}\right)^3 \Rightarrow x \times \frac{441}{400} = 1682 - x \Rightarrow x \times \frac{841}{400} = 1682$

$\therefore \quad x = \frac{1682 \times 400}{841} = \text{Rs. } 800 \text{ and } 1682 - 800 = \text{Rs. } 882$

Hence, parts of Lavkush and Gulshan are Rs. 882 and Rs. 800 respectively.

Example 22: Ramesh borrowed some money from Vasudev at 4% per annum compound interest. If within two years he cleared his debt by paying two equal annual instalments of Rs. 676, what sum did he borrow?

Solution: Required sum $= \frac{676}{\left(1+\frac{4}{100}\right)} + \frac{676}{\left(1+\frac{4}{100}\right)^2} = 676 \times \frac{25}{26} + 676 \times \frac{625}{676} = 650 + 625 = \text{Rs. } 1275$

Example 23: A sum of Rs. 12610 is divided among three such parts that when put at 5% per annum compound interest, amount received from each part respectively after 2, 3 and 4 years remains equal. Find such three parts of the sum.

Solution: Let three parts be Rs. x, Rs y and Rs z respectively, then

$$\therefore x\left(1+\frac{5}{100}\right)^2 = y\left(1+\frac{5}{100}\right)^3 = z\left(1+\frac{5}{100}\right)^4$$

$$\Rightarrow x = \frac{21}{20}y = \frac{441}{400}z; \text{ Hence, } y = \frac{20}{21}x \text{ and } z = \frac{400x}{441}$$

$$\text{Since, } x + \frac{20x}{21} + \frac{400x}{441} = 12610 \Rightarrow \frac{1261x}{441} = 12610 \quad \therefore x = \frac{12610 \times 441}{1261} = \text{Rs. } 4410$$

EXERCISE

1. What will be the compound interest on Rs. 8000 for 3 years at 5% p.a.?
(a) Rs. 1361 *(b)* Rs. 1261 *(c)* Rs. 1260 *(d)* Rs. 1250

2. What will be the amount if a sum of Rs. 2500 is invested for 1 year at 4% per annum compound interest, interest being compounded half-yearly?
(a) Rs. 2625 *(b)* Rs. 2601 *(c)* Rs. 2830 *(d)* Rs. 2901

3. Find the compound interest on Rs. 2560 for ½ year at 12½% per annum, interest payable quarterly.
(a) Rs. 3720.50 *(b)* Rs. 2722.50 *(c)* Rs. 2752.50 *(d)* Rs. 2250.50

4. After how many years will Rs. 3375 become Rs. 4096 at $6\frac{2}{3}$% per annum compound interest?
(a) 4 years *(b)* 2 years *(c)* 2½ years *(d)* 3 years

5. A certain sum of money placed at compound interest amounts to Rs. 110 in 1 year and to Rs. 121 in 2 years. The rate of interest per annum is :
(a) 5% *(b)* 10% *(c)* 8% *(d)* 4%

6. The present population of a city is 80,000. If the rate of growth is 5% per year, find its population after 3 years.
(a) 88,100 *(b)* 95,600 *(c)* 92,610 *(d)* 84,600

7. First year's interest on a sum of money placed at compound interest at the rate of 8% per annum is Rs. 72. What will be interest for the second year?
(a) Rs. 77.76 *(b)* Rs. 78.66 *(c)* Rs. 85.66 *(d)* Rs. 78.76

8. The difference between compound and simple interest on a certain sum of money for 2 years at 5% per annum is Rs. 21. Find the sum.
(a) Rs. 7200 *(b)* Rs. 8400 *(c)* Rs. 9200 *(d)* Rs. 8500

9. In how many years will a sum of Rs. 19200 placed at 10% per annum compound interest yield an interest of Rs. 4032?
(a) 1½ years *(b)* 2½ years *(c)* 2 years *(d)* 3 years

10. The compound interest on a certain sum of money invested for 3 years at 5% per annum is Rs. 1891.50. What will be the simple interest on the same sum at the same rate for 2 years?
(a) Rs. 1700 *(b)* Rs. 1200 *(c)* Rs. 1500 *(d)* Rs. 2100

11. The simple interest on a sum of Rs. 4800 for 2 years is Rs. 768. What will be the compound interest on the same sum at the same rate and for the same period?
(a) Rs. 798.72 (b) Rs. 870.75 (c) Rs. 920.69 (d) Rs. 884.20

12. A sum of money lent out at a certain rate of simple interest amounts to Rs. 6600 in 2 years and to Rs. 6900 in 3 years. What will be the compound interest on the same sum of money if lent out at the same rate for 2 years?
(a) Rs. 605 (b) Rs. 715 (c) Rs. 615 (d) Rs. 595

13. If the first year's interest on a certain sum of money placed at 5% p.a. compound interest is Rs. 1200, what will be the interest for the third year?
(a) Rs. 1220 (b) Rs. 1323 (c) Rs. 1423 (d) Rs. 1330

14. If a certain sum of money placed at compound interest amounts to Rs. 960 in 3 years and to Rs. 1000 in 4 years, find the rate of compound interest.
(a) $4\frac{1}{6}\%$ (b) $5\frac{1}{6}\%$ (c) $2\frac{1}{3}\%$ (d) 3%

15. What would be the compound interest on Rs. 3200 at 25% per annum for 3 years?
(a) Rs. 2050 (b) Rs. 2775 (c) Rs. 3050 (d) Rs. 3180

16. A sum of money placed at compound interest becomes four times itself in 2 years. In how many years will it amount to eight times itself?
(a) 2 years (b) 3 years (c) 4 years (d) 8 years

17. What sum will amount to Rs. 169 in 2 years at 4% per annum compound interest?
(a) Rs. 156.25 (b) Rs. 150.25 (c) Rs. 165.75 (d) Rs. 170.25

18. Sonu and Monu lent out an equal sum of money for 2 years at $6\frac{1}{4}\%$ per annum on simple interest and compound interest respectively. If Monu gets Rs. $3\frac{1}{8}$ more interest than Sonu, find the sum of money lent out by each of them.
(a) Rs. 820 (b) Rs. 980 (c) Rs. 750 (d) Rs. 800

19. For obtaining the difference between compound and simple interest on a certain sum of money invested for 3 years at 5% p.a., we must multiply the sum of money by :
(a) 0.007625 (b) 0.007645 (c) 0.008625 (d) 0.007525

20. A sum of money placed at compound interest doubles itself in 10 years. In how many years will it amount to four times itself?
(a) 16 years (b) 20 years (c) 15 years (d) 30 years

21. A man deposits Rs. 1200 in a bank on the 1st day of each year. If the bank pays 5% per annum compound interest on deposited sum of money, what will be the amount to his credit on the 10th day of the second year?
(a) Rs. 2560 (b) Rs. 2460 (c) Rs. 2370 (d) Rs. 2860

22. The difference between simple and compound interest on a sum of Rs. P for 2 years at $r\%$ per annum will be :
(a) $P\left(\frac{100}{r}\right)^2$ (b) $\frac{\left(\frac{100}{r}\right)^2}{P}$ (c) $\frac{P}{\left(\frac{100}{r}\right)^2}$ (d) $\frac{\left(\frac{r}{100}\right)^2}{P}$

23. If a certain sum of money placed at compound interest amounts to Rs. 518.48 in 2 years and to Rs. 614.55 in 3 years, the rate of compound interest per annum will be :
(*a*) 17.5% (*b*) 18.52% (*c*) $19\frac{1}{3}\%$ (*d*) 18.36%

24. What will be the amount of Rs. 1500 after 3 years if the rate of compound interest per annum is 3%, 4% and 5% for the first, second and third year respectively?
(*a*) Rs. 1780.14 (*b*) Rs. 1880.40 (*c*) Rs. 1687.14 (*d*) Rs. 1785.60

25. If the difference between compound and simple interest on a certain sum of money for 3 years at 5% per annum is Rs. 244, the sum is :
(*a*) Rs. 40000 (*b*) Rs. 25000 (*c*) Rs. 30000 (*d*) Rs. 32000

26. The simple interest on a sum of Rs. 1800 for 2 years is Rs. 108. What would be the compound interest on the same sum of money for the same period if the rate of interest were further increased by 4%?
(*a*) Rs. 260.82 (*b*) Rs. 245.80 (*c*) Rs. 270.72 (*d*) Rs. 250.82

27. The simple interest on a sum of money for 2 years is Rs. 400 and the compound interest on the same sum for the same period and at the same rate is Rs. 410. Find the rate per cent per annum.
(*a*) 8% (*b*) 5% (*c*) 3% (*d*) 4%

28. The difference between simple and compound interest on a sum of Rs. 2000 for 3 years at 20% per annum will be:
(*a*) Rs. 248 (*b*) Rs. 236 (*c*) Rs. 256 (*d*) Rs. 266

29. A sum of money placed at compound interest amounts to Rs. 800 in 4 years and to Rs. 840 in 5 years. In 6 years this will amount to :
(*a*) Rs. 841 (*b*) Rs. 877 (*c*) Rs. 876 (*d*) Rs. 882

30. A borrowed from a bank Rs. 8000 for 2 years at 5% per annum compound interest and B borrowed from a money lender a certain sum of money for 3 years at 4% per annum compound interest. If after expiry of their respective loan period, each of them pay an equal amount to clear off their debts, find the sum of money borrowed by B from the money lender.
(*a*) Rs. 7840.25 (*b*) Rs. 7820.75 (*c*) Rs. 8840.25 (*d*) Rs. 8200

31. A man purchased a sewing machine for Rs. 5000. If due to sustained use value of this sewing machine depreciates by 6% annually, find its value after 3 years.
(*a*) Rs. 3775.67 (*b*) Rs. 4152.92 (*c*) Rs. 4250.25 (*d*) Rs. 4356.25

32. What will be the difference between compound and simple interest on Rs. 11,000 for 2 years at 6% per annum?
(*a*) Rs. 39.60 (*b*) Rs. 41.40 (*c*) Rs. 38.70 (*d*) Rs. 35.50

33. Find the sum on which the difference between compound and simple interest for 3 years at 10% per annum will be Rs. 868.
(*a*) Rs. 29500 (*b*) Rs. 27625 (*c*) Rs. 28500 (*d*) Rs. 28000

34. Two friends A and B jointly lent out Rs. 81,600 at 4% per annum compound interest, payable annually. 2 years after A gets the same amount as B gets after 3 years. The investment made by B was :
(*a*) Rs. 30,000 (*b*) Rs. 40,000 (*c*) Rs. 45,000 (*d*) Rs. 38,000

35. The amount obtained from an investment of Rs. 3025 at 10% per annum compound interest for 3 years is equal to the amount obtained from the investment of a certain sum of money at 10% per annum compound interest for 5 years. Find the sum of investment in the second case.
(*a*) Rs. 2500 (*b*) Rs. 2415 (*c*) Rs. 2480 (*d*) Rs. 2550

36. Present ages of Tarun and Gulshan are 12 years and 10 years respectively. They want to deposit in Post Office a total sum of Rs. 5204 in such a proportion that at the age of 15, each of them may get an equal amount. If the Post Office pays 4% p.a. compound interest on the total sum of deposit, find the part of money deposited by each of them.
(*a*) Rs. 2500, Rs. 2704 (*b*) Rs. 2704, Rs. 2500
(*c*) Rs. 2804, Rs. 2400 (*d*) Rs. 2204, Rs. 3000

37. What would be the compound interest obtained on an amount of Rs. 7800 at the rate of 5% p.a. after 3 years?
(*a*) Rs. 1229.475 (*b*) Rs. 1235.685 (*c*) Rs. 1248.750 (*d*) Rs. 1287.68

38. A sum of money amounts to Rs. 4840 in 2 years and to Rs. 5324 in 3 years at compound interest compounded annually. What is the rate of interest per annum?
(*a*) 8% (*b*) 9% (*c*) 10% (*d*) 11%

39. The difference between compound interest (compounded annually) and simple interest on a certain sum of money at 10% per annum for 2 years is Rs. 40. Find the sum.
(*a*) Rs. 3200 (*b*) Rs. 3600 (*c*) Rs. 4000 (*d*) Rs. 4200

40. At what rate per cent per annum will a sum of Rs. 8000 amounts to Rs. 9261 at compound interest in $1\frac{1}{2}$ years, interest being compounded half yearly?
(*a*) 5% (*b*) 8% (*c*) 10% (*d*) 12%

41. The compound interest for two years on a certain amount at 8% p.a. is Rs. 416. What would be the compound interest for 3 years for the same amount in the same rate?
(*a*) Rs. 449.28 (*b*) Rs. 624 (*c*) Rs. 649.28 (*d*) Rs. 1261.28

42. Samir invested Rs. 15000 at the rate of interest 10% p.a. for 1 year. If the interest compound six months. What amount will Samir get at the end of the year?
(*a*) Rs. 16,500 (*b*) Rs. 16525.50 (*c*) Rs. 16537.50 (*d*) Rs. 18,150

43. Mr. Jha invests a certain amount for a 2 years at 6% p.a. to obtain a total amount of Rs. 33,384 at the end of 2 years. What was the amount invested by Mr. Jha?
(*a*) Rs. 24560 (*b*) Rs. 29,712 (*c*) Rs. 30000 (*d*) None of these

44. The compound interest on Rs. 2500 at the rate of 6% p.a. after 2 years will be:
(*a*) Rs. 309 (*b*) Rs. 318 (*c*) Rs. 320 (*d*) None of these

45. What will be difference in the interests obtained by investing Rs. 500 for 2 years at the rate of 10% p.a. compounded yearly and Rs. 800 at the rate of 10% compounded half-yearly for 1 year?
(*a*) Rs. 20 (*b*) Rs. 23 (*c*) Rs. 27 (*d*) Rs. 30

46. The difference between simple and compound interest on a sum of money at 5% p.a. for 2 years is Rs. 25. Find the sum.
(*a*) Rs. 1000 (*b*) Rs. 5000 (*c*) Rs. 10,000 (*d*) Rs. 11000

47. The value of machinery depreciates every year by 20%. Calculate the value of the machinery bought for Rs. 6,250, at the end of third year.
(*a*) Rs. 3200 (*b*) Rs. 3500 (*c*) Rs. 4500 (*d*) Rs. 5000

48. The population of a town is 198000. It increases by 7% in the Ist year and decreases by 5% in the IInd year. What is the population of the town at the end of 2 years?
(*a*) 198900 (*b*) 201267 (*c*) 211860 (*d*) 222453

49. What will be the difference in simple and compound interests at the rate of 12% p.a. on the sum Rs. 960 after 2 years?
(*a*) Rs. 13.824 (*b*) Rs. 20.224 (*c*) Rs. 24.04 (*d*) Rs. 31

50. Under a scheme of investment, the rate of interest is 4% and the interest is compounded three monthly. What will be the amount if a man invests Rs. 2000 for 1 year under this scheme?
(*a*) Rs. 2060 (*b*) Rs. 2081.21 (*c*) Rs. 2100.25 (*d*) Rs. 2125.54

51. A bank offers 5% compound interest calculated on half-yearly basis. A customer deposits Rs. 1600 each on 1st January and 1st July of a year. At the end of the year, the amount he would have gained by the way of interest is:
(*a*) Rs. 123 (*b*) Rs. 122 (*c*) Rs. 121 (*d*) Rs. 120

52. The compound interest on a certain sum for 2 years at 10% per annum is Rs. 525. The simple interest on the same sum for double the time at half the rate per cent per annum is:
(*a*) Rs. 800 (*b*) Rs. 600 (*c*) Rs. 500 (*d*) Rs. 400

53. What is the difference between the compound interests on Rs. 5000 for 1½ years at 4% p.a. compounded yearly and half yearly?
(*a*) Rs. 8.30 (*b*) Rs. 4.80 (*c*) Rs. 3.06 (*d*) Rs. 2.04

54. There is 60% increase in an amount in 6 years at simple interest. What will be the compound interest of Rs. 12000 after 3 years at the same rate?
(*a*) Rs. 6240 (*b*) Rs. 3972 (*c*) Rs. 3120 (*d*) Rs. 2160

55. The simple interest on a certain sum of money for 3 years at 8% p.a. is half the compound interest on Rs. 4000 for 2 years at 10% p.a. The sum invested on simple interest is:
(*a*) Rs. 2000 (*b*) Rs. 1750 (*c*) Rs. 1650 (*d*) Rs. 1550

56. A sum of money is borrowed and paid back in two annual instalments of Rs. 882 each allowing 5% compound interest. What was the sum borrowed?
(*a*) Rs. 1700 (*b*) Rs. 1680 (*c*) Rs. 1640 (*d*) Rs. 1620

57. What annual payment will discharge a debt of Rs. 1025 due in 2 years at the rate of 5% compound interest?
(*a*) Rs. 560.75 (*b*) Rs. 560 (*c*) Rs. 551.25 (*d*) Rs. 550

58. The least number of complete years in which a sum of money put at 20% compound interest will be more than doubled is:
(*a*) 6 (*b*) 5 (*c*) 4 (*d*) 3

59. The effective annual rate of interest corresponding to a nominal rate of 6% per annum payable half-yearly is:
(*a*) Rs. 6.09% (*b*) 6.08% (*c*) 6.07% (*d*) 6.06%

60. On a sum of money, the simple interest for 2 years is Rs. 660, while the compound interest is Rs. 696.30, the rate of interest being the same in both cases. Find the rate of interest.
(*a*) Rs. 12% (*b*) 11% (*c*) 10% (*d*) 9%

SOLUTIONS

1. $\therefore$ C.I.= $8000\left[\left(1+\frac{5}{100}\right)^3-1\right] = 8000\left[\left(\frac{21}{20}\right)^3-1\right] = \frac{8000\times1261}{8000}$ = Rs. 1261

2. A = $2500\left(1+\frac{2}{100}\right)^2 = 2500\left(\frac{51}{50}\right)^2 = \frac{2500\times51\times51}{50\times50}$ = Rs. 2601

3. Amount = $2560\left(1+\frac{25}{8\times100}\right)^2 = \frac{2560\times33\times33}{32\times32}$ = Rs. 2722.50

4. Here, $4096 = 3375\left(1+\frac{20}{3\times100}\right)^n \Rightarrow \frac{4096}{3375} = \left(1+\frac{1}{15}\right)^n \Rightarrow \left(\frac{16}{15}\right)^3 = \left(\frac{16}{15}\right)^n \quad \therefore n = 3$ years

5. Here, simple interest of Rs. 110 for 1 year = 121 – 110 = Rs. 11

Hence, rate $= \frac{11\times100}{110\times1} = 10\%$

6. Population of the city after 3 years $= 80{,}000\left(1+\frac{5}{100}\right)^3$

$= 80{,}000\times\frac{21}{20}\times\frac{21}{20}\times\frac{21}{20} = 92610$

7. Second year's interest = 72 + 8% of 72 $= 72+\frac{72\times8}{100} = 72 + 5.76 =$ Rs. 77.76

8. Here, $P\left[\left(1+\frac{5}{100}\right)^2-1\right]-\frac{P\times5\times2}{100} = 21 \Rightarrow P\left[\frac{441}{400}-1\right]-\frac{P}{10} = 21$

$\Rightarrow P\left[\frac{41}{400}-\frac{1}{10}\right] = 21 \Rightarrow P\times\frac{1}{400} = 21 \quad \therefore P = 21\times400 =$ Rs. 8400

9. Amount = Rs. 19200 + Rs. 4032 = Rs. 23232

Now, $23232 = 19200\left(1+\frac{10}{100}\right)^n \Rightarrow \frac{23232}{19200} = \left(\frac{11}{10}\right)^n \Rightarrow \frac{121}{100} = \left(\frac{11}{10}\right)^n \Rightarrow \left(\frac{11}{10}\right)^2 = \left(\frac{11}{10}\right)^n$

$\therefore$ $n = 2$ years

10. Here, $1891.50 = \text{P}\left[\left(1+\frac{5}{100}\right)^3-1\right] \Rightarrow 1891.50 = \text{P}\left[\left(\frac{21}{20}\right)^3-1\right]$

$\Rightarrow 1891.50 = \text{P}\left(\frac{1261}{8000}\right) \quad \therefore \text{P} = \frac{1891.50\times8000}{1261} =$ Rs. 12000

Now, S.I. $= \frac{12000\times5\times2}{100} =$ Rs. 1200

11. Rate $= \frac{768\times100}{4800\times2} = 8\%$

$\therefore$ C.I. $= 4800\left[\left(1+\frac{8}{100}\right)^2-1\right] = 4800\left[\left(\frac{27}{25}\right)^2-1\right] = \frac{4800\times104}{625} =$ Rs. 798.72

12. Here, 1 year's S.I. = Rs. 6900 – Rs. 6600 = Rs. 300

$\therefore$ 2 year's S.I. = 300 × 2 = Rs. 600

$\therefore$ Principal = Rs. 6600 – Rs. 600 = Rs. 6000

Hence, Rate $= \frac{600\times100}{6000\times2} = 5\%$

$\therefore$ $$\text{C.I.} = 6000\left[\left(1+\frac{5}{100}\right)^2 - 1\right] = 6000\left[\left(\frac{21}{20}\right)^2 - 1\right] = \frac{6000\times 41}{400} = \text{Rs. } 615$$

13. Required interest = $1200\left(1+\frac{5}{100}\right)^2 = 1200\times\frac{21}{20}\times\frac{21}{20}$ = Rs. 1323

14. Here, simple interest of Rs. 960 for 1 year = 1000 – 960 = Rs. 40

Hence, Rate = $\frac{40\times 100}{960\times 1} = \frac{25}{6} = 4\frac{1}{6}\%$

15. Compound interest = $3200\left[\left(1+\frac{25}{100}\right)^3 - 1\right] = 3200\left[\left(\frac{5}{4}\right)^3 - 1\right] = \frac{3200\times 61}{64}$ = Rs. 3050

16. Here, $4P = P\left(1+\frac{r}{100}\right)^2$ $\therefore$ $\left(1+\frac{r}{100}\right) = 2$ ...(*i*)

Now, $8P = P\left(1+\frac{r}{100}\right)^n \Rightarrow \left(1+\frac{r}{100}\right)^n = 2^3 = \left(1+\frac{r}{100}\right)^3$ [from equation (*i*)]

Hence, n = 3 years

17. Here, $169 = P\left(1+\frac{4}{100}\right)^n$ $\therefore$ $P = \frac{169\times 25\times 25}{26\times 26}$ = Rs. 156.25

18. Here, $P\left[\left(1+\frac{25}{4\times 100}\right)^2 - 1\right] - \frac{P\times 25\times 2}{100\times 4} = \frac{25}{8} \Rightarrow P\times\frac{33}{256} - \frac{P}{8} = \frac{25}{8}$

$\Rightarrow P\times\frac{1}{256} = \frac{25}{8}$ $\therefore$ $P = \frac{25}{8}\times 256$ = Rs. 800

19. Let difference between compound and simple interest be Rs. x; then,

$$P\left[\left(1+\frac{5}{100}\right)^3 - 1\right] - \frac{P\times 5\times 3}{100} = x \Rightarrow P\times\frac{1261}{8000} - \frac{3P}{20} = x \Rightarrow P\times\frac{61}{8000} = x \;\therefore\; x = 0.007625P$$

20. Here, $2P = P\left(1+\frac{r}{100}\right)^{10}$ $\therefore$ $\left(1+\frac{r}{100}\right)^{10} = 2$ ...(*i*)

Now, $4P = P\left(1+\frac{r}{100}\right)^n \Rightarrow \left(1+\frac{r}{100}\right)^n = 2^2 = \left(1+\frac{r}{100}\right)^{20}$ [From equation (*i*)]

$\therefore$ n = 20 years

21. Required amount = $1200\left(1+\frac{5}{100}\right) + 1200 = 1200\times\frac{21}{20} + 1200$ = 1260 + 1200 = Rs. 2460

22. Required difference = $P\left[\left(1+\frac{r}{100}\right)^2 - 1\right] - \frac{P\times r\times 2}{100} = P\left(\frac{2r}{100} + \left(\frac{r}{100}\right)^2 - \frac{2r}{100}\right) = P\Big/\left(\frac{100}{r}\right)^2$

23. Simple interest of Rs. 518.48 for 1 year = 614.55 – 518.48 = Rs. 96.07

Hence, Rate = $\frac{96.07 \times 100}{518.48 \times 1}$ = 18.52%

24. Amount = $1500\left[\left(1+\frac{3}{100}\right)\left(1+\frac{4}{100}\right)\left(1+\frac{5}{100}\right)\right] = 1500 \times \frac{103}{100} \times \frac{104}{100} \times \frac{105}{100}$ = Rs. 1687.14

25. Here, $P\left[\left(1+\frac{5}{100}\right)^3 - 1\right] - \frac{P \times 5 \times 3}{100} = 244 \Rightarrow P \times \frac{1261}{8000} - \frac{3P}{20} = 244$

$\Rightarrow P \times \frac{61}{8000} = 244 \qquad \therefore P = \frac{244 \times 8000}{61}$ = Rs. 32000

26. $\because$ Rate = $\frac{108 \times 100}{1800 \times 2}$ = 3%

New rate = (3 + 4)% = 7%

$\therefore$ C.I. = $1800\left[\left(1+\frac{7}{100}\right)^2 - 1\right] = 1800\left[\left(\frac{107}{100}\right)^2 - 1\right] = 1800\left[\frac{11449 - 10000}{10000}\right] = \frac{1800 \times 1449}{10000}$

= Rs. 260.82

27. Simple interest for 2 years = Rs. 400

Hence, simple interest or compound interest for 1 year = Rs. 200

Now, $200\left(1+\frac{r}{100}\right) = 210$

$\Rightarrow \frac{r}{100} = \frac{21}{20} - 1 \qquad \therefore r = \frac{1}{20} \times 100$ = 5%

28. Required difference = $2000\left[\left(1+\frac{20}{100}\right)^3 - 1\right] - \frac{2000 \times 20 \times 3}{100} = 2000 \times \frac{91}{125} - 1200$

= 1456 – 1200 = Rs. 256

29. Here, simple interest of Rs. 800 for 1 year = 840 – 800 = Rs. 40

Hence, rate = $\frac{40 \times 100}{800 \times 1}$ = 5%

Since, required amount = $840\left(1+\frac{5}{100}\right) = 840 \times \frac{21}{20}$ = Rs. 882

30. Here, $8000\left(1+\frac{5}{100}\right)^2 = P\left(1+\frac{4}{100}\right)^3 \Rightarrow 8000 \times \frac{21}{20} \times \frac{21}{20} = P \times \left(\frac{26}{25}\right)^3$

$\therefore$ P = $20 \times 441 \times \frac{25}{26} \times \frac{25}{26} \times \frac{25}{26}$ = Rs. 7840.25

31. Here, value of the machine after 3 years = $5000\left(1-\frac{6}{100}\right)^3 = 5000 \times \frac{47}{50} \times \frac{47}{50} \times \frac{47}{50}$ = Rs. 4152.92.

32. Required difference = $11000\left[\left(1+\frac{6}{100}\right)^2-1\right]-\frac{11000\times6\times2}{100}=11000\times\frac{309}{2500}-1320$

$= 1359.60 - 1320 =$ Rs. 39.60

33. Here, $P\left[\left(1+\frac{10}{100}\right)^3-1\right]-\frac{P\times10\times3}{100}=868 \Rightarrow P\times\frac{331}{1000}-\frac{3P}{10}=868$

$\Rightarrow P\times\frac{31}{1000}=868 \quad \therefore\ P=\frac{868\times1000}{31}=$ Rs. 28000

34. Let investment of B and A be Rs. x and Rs. $(81600 - x)$ respectively, then

$(81600-x)\left(1+\frac{4}{100}\right)^2 = x\left(1+\frac{4}{100}\right)^3 \Rightarrow \frac{26x}{25}=81600-x$

$\Rightarrow \frac{51x}{25}=81600 \quad \therefore\ x=\frac{81600\times25}{51}=$ Rs. 40,000

35. Here, $P\left(1+\frac{10}{100}\right)^5=3025\left(1+\frac{10}{100}\right)^3 \Rightarrow P\times\left(\frac{11}{10}\right)^2=3025 \quad \therefore\ P=\frac{3025\times100}{121}=$ Rs. 2500

36. Let shares of Tarun and Gulshan be Rs. x and Rs. $(5204 - x)$ respectively; then

$x\left(1+\frac{4}{100}\right)^3=(5204-x)\left(1+\frac{4}{100}\right)^5 \Rightarrow x=(5204-x)\times\frac{676}{625}$

$\Rightarrow \frac{625x}{676}+x=5204 \Rightarrow \frac{1301x}{676}=5204 \quad \therefore\ x=\frac{5204\times676}{1301}=$ Rs. 2704

Now, $5204 - x = 5204 - 2704 =$ Rs. 2500

Hence, shares of Tarun and Gulshan are Rs. 2704 and Rs. 2500.

37. C.I. $= 7800\left[\left(1+\frac{5}{100}\right)^3-1\right]=7800\left[\frac{9261}{8000}-1\right]$

$= 7800\times\frac{1261}{8000}=$ Rs. 1229.475

38. Here, simple interest of Rs. 4840 for 1 year $= 5324 - 4840 =$ Rs. 484

Since, rate $=\frac{484\times100}{4840\times1}=10\%$

39. Here, $P\left[\left(1+\frac{10}{100}\right)^2-1\right]-\frac{P\times10\times2}{100}=40$

$\Rightarrow P\left[\frac{121}{100}-1\right]-\frac{20P}{100}=40 \Rightarrow P\left[\frac{21}{100}-\frac{20}{100}\right]=40 \quad \therefore\ P = 40\times100 =$ Rs. 4000

40. Here, $9261 = 8000\left(1+\frac{r}{100}\right)^3 \Rightarrow \left(1+\frac{r}{100}\right)^3 = \left(\frac{21}{20}\right)^3$

$\Rightarrow 1+\frac{r}{100}=\frac{21}{20} \Rightarrow \frac{r}{100}=\frac{1}{20} \quad \therefore r = \frac{1}{20}\times 100$ = 5% per half-yearly

Hence, rate of interest = 10% p.a.

41. Required C.I. $= 416\left(1+\frac{8}{100}\right) = 416\times\frac{27}{25}$ = Rs. 449.28

42. $A = 15000\left(1+\frac{5}{100}\right)^2 = 15000\times\frac{441}{400}$ = Rs. 16537.50

43. Here, $P\left(1+\frac{6}{100}\right)^2 = 33{,}384 \quad \therefore P = 33384 \times \frac{50}{53}\times\frac{50}{53} \approx$ Rs. 29712

44. C.I. $= 2500\left[\left(1+\frac{6}{100}\right)^2 - 1\right] = 2500\left[\frac{2809}{2500}-1\right] = 2500 \times \frac{309}{2500}$ = Rs. 309

45. Ist C.I. $= 500\left[\left(1+\frac{10}{100}\right)^2 - 1\right] = 500\left[\frac{121}{100}-1\right] = 500 \times \frac{21}{100}$ = Rs. 105

IInd C.I. $= 800\left[\left(1+\frac{5}{100}\right)^2 - 1\right] = 800\left[\frac{441}{400}-1\right] = 800 \times \frac{41}{400}$ = Rs. 82

Hence, required difference = 105 − 82 = Rs. 23

46. Here, $P\left[\left(1+\frac{5}{100}\right)^2 - 1\right] - \frac{P\times 5\times 2}{100} = 25 \Rightarrow P\left[\frac{441}{400}-1\right] - \frac{10P}{100} = 25$

$\Rightarrow P\left[\frac{41}{400}-\frac{10}{100}\right] = 25 \Rightarrow P \times \frac{1}{400} = 25 \quad \therefore P = 25 \times 400 =$ Rs. 10,000

47. Required value $= 6250\left(1-\frac{20}{100}\right)^3 = 6250\times\frac{64}{125} =$ Rs. 3200

48. Required population $= 19800\left(1+\frac{7}{100}\right)\left(1-\frac{5}{100}\right)$

$= 19800 \times \frac{107}{100}\times\frac{19}{20} = 201267$

49. Required difference $= 960\left[\left(1+\frac{12}{100}\right)^2-1\right]-\frac{960\times12\times2}{100}$

$= 960\left[\frac{784}{625}-1\right]-230.4 = 960\times\frac{159}{625}-230.4$

$= 244.224 - 230.4 =$ Rs. 13.824

50. Required amount $= 2000\left[1+\frac{1}{100}\right]^4 = 2000\times1.04060401 \approx$ Rs. 2081.21

51. Total amount $= 1600\left(1+\frac{5}{2\times100}\right)^2+1600\left(1+\frac{5}{2\times100}\right)$

$= 1600\times\frac{1681}{1600}+1600\times\frac{41}{40} = 1681 + 1640 =$ Rs. 3321

Hence, required interest = 3321 – 3200 = Rs. 121

52. Here, $P\left[\left(1+\frac{10}{100}\right)^2-1\right]=525 \Rightarrow P\left[\frac{121}{100}-1\right]=525$

$\Rightarrow P\times\frac{21}{100} = 525 \quad \therefore\ P = \frac{525\times100}{21} =$ Rs. 2500

Hence, required S.I. $= \frac{2500\times5\times4}{100} =$ Rs. 500

53. Ist C.I. $= 5000\left(1+\frac{4}{100}\right)\left(1+\frac{4}{2\times100}\right) = 5000\times\frac{26}{25}\times\frac{51}{50} =$ Rs. 5304

IInd C.I. $= 5000\left(1+\frac{2}{100}\right)^3 = 5000\times\left(\frac{51}{50}\right)^3 =$ Rs. 5306.04

Hence, required difference = 5306.04 – 5304 = Rs. 2.04

54. Let, P = Rs. 100; then S.I. = Rs. 60

Since, rate $= \frac{60\times100}{100\times6} = 10\%$ p.a.

Hence, C.I. $= 12000\left[\left(1+\frac{10}{100}\right)^3-1\right] = 12000\left[\frac{1331}{1000}-1\right]$

$= 12000\times\frac{331}{1000}$

= Rs. 3972

55. Here, C.I. $= 4000\left[\left(1+\frac{10}{100}\right)^2-1\right] = 4000\left[\frac{121}{100}-1\right] = 4000\times\frac{21}{100} =$ Rs. 840

Then S.I. = Rs. 420

Since, required sum $= \frac{420\times100}{8\times3} =$ Rs. 1750

56. Required sum $= \frac{882}{\left(1+\frac{5}{100}\right)} + \frac{882}{\left(1+\frac{5}{100}\right)^2} = 882\left[\frac{20}{21}+\left(\frac{20}{21}\right)^2\right]$

$= 882\times\frac{20}{21}\left(1+\frac{20}{21}\right) = 882\times\frac{20}{21}\times\frac{41}{21} =$ Rs. 1640

57. Let annual payment be Rs. x; then

$$\frac{x}{\left(1+\frac{5}{100}\right)}+\frac{x}{\left(1+\frac{5}{100}\right)^2} = 1025 \Rightarrow x.\frac{20}{21}+x.\left(\frac{20}{21}\right)^2 = 1025$$

$\Rightarrow x.\frac{20}{21}\times\frac{41}{21} = 1025$ $\quad\therefore x = \frac{1025\times21\times21}{20\times41} =$ Rs. 551.25

58. Here, $P\left(1+\frac{20}{100}\right)^n > 2P \Rightarrow \left(\frac{6}{5}\right)^n > 2$

Hence, if $n = 4$ then, $\left(\frac{6}{5}\right)^4 = \frac{1296}{625} > 2$

So, $n = 4$ years

59. Let, P = Rs. 100; then

$A = 100\left(1+\frac{3}{100}\right)^2 = 100\times1.0609 =$ Rs. 106.09

Hence, C.I. = 106.09 – 100 = Rs. 6.09

So, required effective rate = 6.09% p.a.

60. Here, S.I. for 1 year = Rs. 330

Since, simple interest of Rs. 330 for 1 year = 696.30 – 660 = Rs. 36.30

Hence, required rate $= \frac{36.30\times100}{330\times1} = \frac{3630}{330} = 11\%$

25 PARTNERSHIP

When two or more than two persons agree to invest money to run a business jointly, this association or deal is called *partnership* and those who invest money are called *pertners.* The total investment is called the *capital.*

Kind of partners : There are two kinds of partners.

1. Working or active partner : When a partner devotes his time for the business in addition to invest his money, he is called a working partner. With mutual agreement, the active partners get some fixed percentage of profit as *working allowance.*

2. Sleeping or non-active partner : A partner who simply invests money, but does not attend to the business is called a sleeping partner.

Kind of partnership :

(i) **Simple partnership :** If the capitals of several partners are invested for the same period, it is called a simple partnership.

(ii) **Compound or complex partnership :** If the capitals of the partners are invested for diffrent intervals of time, the partnership is called compound or complex.

Example 1: If A and B enter into a partnership, A contributes Rs. 7000 and B contributes Rs. 10000. If the profit at the end of the year amounts to Rs. 7310, what would be the share of B in the profit?

Solution: Ratio of their capitals = 7000 : 10000 = 7 : 10

Hence, share of B = $\frac{10}{17} \times 7310 =$ Rs. 4300

Example 2: A and B started a business with the investment of Rs. 4000 and Rs. 6000 respectively. In what ratio the profit earned at the end of the year will be distributed between them?

Solution: $\because$ Ratio of the capitals of A and B = 4000 : 6000 = 2 : 3

$\therefore$ profit of A and B will be in the ratio of 2 : 3

Example 3: Gulshan and Tarun invested Rs. 3900 and Rs. 4200 respectively in a business. If at the end of the year there was a profit of Rs. 2025 in the business, what will be the gain of Gulshan?

Solution: Ratio of the capitals of Gulshan and Tarun = 3900 : 4200 = 13 : 14

Hence, Share of Gulshan in the profit = $\frac{13}{27} \times 2025$ = Rs. 975.

Example 4: Ram and Shyam invested Rs. 400 and Rs. 600 respectively in a business. If at the end of the year Shyam gets Rs. 120 as profit, what will be the share of Ram in the profit.

Solution: Ratio of their capitals = 400 : 600 = 2 : 3

Ram's Share in the profit = $\frac{2}{3} \times 120$ = Rs. 80.

Example 5 : A, B and C started a business with the investment of Rs. 5000, Rs. 7000 and Rs. 8000 respectively. If at the end of the year total profit is Rs. 8000, what will be the gain of each?

Solution: Ratio of their capitals = 5000 : 7000 : 8000 = 5: 7 : 8

Sum of proportionals = 5 + 7 + 8 = 20

∴ A's share in the profit $= \frac{5}{20} \times 8000$ = Rs. 2000

B's share in the profit $= \frac{7}{20} \times 8000$ = Rs. 2800

C's share in the profit $= \frac{8}{20} \times 8000$ = Rs. 3200

Example 6: Sumeet, Sanju and Deepak started a business with respective investment of Rs. 5000, Rs. 6000 and Rs. 7000. Sumeet is an active partner and hence he gets 10% of the profit separately. If at the end of the year total profit is Rs. 8000, what will be the total gain of Sumeet?

Solution: Total profit incurred = Rs. 8000

Separate 10% profit for Sumeet = 10% of 8000 = $\frac{8000 \times 10}{100}$ = Rs. 800

∴ Remaining sum of profit = Rs. 8000 – Rs. 800 = Rs. 7200

Ratio of capitals invested by Sumeet, Sanju and Deepak = 5000 : 6000 : 7000 = 5 : 6 : 7

Sum of proportionals = 5 + 6 + 7 = 18

∴ Share of Sumeet in the remaining sum of profit = $\frac{5}{18} \times 7200$ = Rs. 2000

Hence, total profit earned by Sumeet = Rs. 2000 + Rs. 800 = Rs. 2800

Example 7: Ajay, Sanjay and Girish invested Rs. 5000, Rs. 7000 and Rs. 8000 respectively in a business. If at the end of the year total profit was Rs. 16000, by how much the profit of Girish will exceed the profit of Ajay?

Solution: Ratio of capital of Ajay, Sanjay and Girish = 5000 : 7000 : 8000 = 5 : 7 : 8

Difference between the proportionals of Girish and Ajay = 8 – 5 = 3

Total profit = Rs. 16000

∴ Profit of Girish exceeds the profit of Ajay by = $\frac{3}{20} \times 16000$ = Rs. 2400.

Example 8: A, B and C started a business with respective investment of Rs. 5000, Rs. 4000 and Rs. 2000. A took back his amount after 4 months and B took back his amount after 6 months. If at the end of the year, there was a total profit of Rs. 5100, what will be the share of each of them in the profit?

Solution: This question is related to compound Partnership. Therefore, total profit will be divided in the ratio of the product of their capitals and time

Ratio of Capitals of A, B and C = (5000 × 4) : (4000 × 6) : (2000 × 12) = 5 : 6 : 6

Sum of the proportionals = 5 + 6 + 6 = 17

Share of A in the profit = $\frac{5}{17} \times 5100$ = Rs. 1500

Share of B in the profit = $\frac{6}{17} \times 5100$ = Rs. 1800

Share of C in the profit = $\frac{6}{17} \times 5100$ = Rs. 1800.

Example 9: A started a business with an investment of Rs. 80000. After 3 months, B also joined him with an investent of Rs. 50000. If at the end of the year total profit is Rs. 23,500, what profit will each of them get?

Solution: Ratio of Capitals of A and B = (80000 × 12) : (50000 × 9) = 32 : 15

∴ A's profit = $\frac{32}{47} \times 23500$ = Rs. 16000

B's profit = $\frac{15}{47} \times 23500$ = Rs. 7500

Example 10: A, B and C together took under lease a pasture ground for Rs. 415. If A put his 25 cows out to graze for 6 months, B put his 40 cows out to graze for 8 months and C put his 30 cows out to graze for whole the year in this pasture ground, find the lease amount paid by each of them.

Solution: Ratio of shares of A, B and C = (25 × 6) : (40 × 8) : (30 × 12) = 150 : 320 : 360 = 15 : 32 : 36

Sum of proportionals = 15 + 32 + 36 = 83

Total lease amount paid = Rs. 415

Amount paid by A = $\frac{15}{83} \times 415$ = Rs. 75

Amount paid by B = $\frac{32}{83} \times 415$ = Rs. 160

Amount paid by C = $\frac{36}{83} \times 415$ = Rs. 180

Example 11: Rajesh and Suresh invested Rs. 8000 and Rs. 1000 respectively in a business. After 6 months Naresh also joined them with an investment of Rs. 6000. If at the end of 3 years total profit is Rs. 9660, what profit will each of them get?

Solution: Ratio of their capitals = (8000 × 36) : (1000 × 36) : (6000 × 30) = 8 : 1 : 5

Share of Rajesh in the profit = $\frac{8}{14} \times 9660$ = Rs. 5520

Share of Suresh in the profit = $\frac{1}{14} \times 9660$ = Rs. 690

Share of Naresh in the profit = $\frac{5}{14} \times 9660$ = Rs. 3450

Example 12: Radheyshyam, Mukesh and Sheesh Ram together started a business. Radheyshyam invested Rs. 500 for 2 years. Mukesh invested Rs. 400 for 15 months and Sheesh Ram invested Rs. 300 for 10 months. If at the end total profit is Rs. 577.50 what will be the gain of Radheyshyam?

Solution: Ratio of their capitals = (500 × 24) : (400 × 15) : (300 × 10) = 4 : 2 : 1

Hence, Share of Radheyshyam in the profit = $\frac{4}{7} \times 577.50$ = Rs. 330

Example 13: A, B and C together took under lease a pasture ground for some amount. A put his 40 cows out to graze in this ground for 10 months, B put his 50 cows out to graze in this ground for 5 months and C put his 75 cows out to graze in this ground for 4 months. If A pays Rs. 80 as lease amount, for how much the pasture ground was taken under lease?

Solution: Ratio of shares of A, B and C = $(40 \times 10) : (50 \times 5) : (75 \times 4) = 8 : 5 : 6$

$\because$ Lease amount paid by A = Rs. 80

$\therefore$ Total lease amount = $\frac{80}{8} \times 19$ = Rs. 190

Example 14: A and B invested Rs. 2600 and Rs. 2800 respectively in a business. If at the end of 6 months, there was a profit of Rs. 1350 in the business, what will be the gain of A?

Solution: Ratio of their capitals = 2600 : 2800 = 13 : 14

Share of A in the profit = $\frac{13}{27} \times 1350$ = Rs. 650.

Example 15: A and B start a business with the investment of Rs. 7500 and Rs. 6000 respectively. B is an active partner and therefore he gets 12½% of the profit separately for supervision of the trade. If total profit of the business is Rs. 2160, what will be the profit of B?

Solution: Separate profit of B for supervision of the trade = $\frac{25}{200} \times 2160$ = Rs. 270

Remaining profit = Rs. 2160 – Rs. 270 = Rs. 1890

Ratio of capitals of A and B = 7500 : 6000 = 5 : 4

B's share in the profit = $\frac{4}{9} \times 1890$ = Rs. 840

Hence, total profit of B = Rs. 840 + Rs. 270 = Rs. 1110

Example 16: Sanju started a business with an investment of Rs. 75000. After 3 months, Lavakush also joined him with an investment of Rs. 60000. If at the end of the year total profit is Rs. 16000, what will be the gain of Lavakush?

Solution: Ratio of their capitals = $(75000 \times 12) : (60000 \times 9) = 5 : 3$

$\therefore$ Profit of Lavakush = $\frac{3}{8} \times 16000$ = Rs. 6000

Example 17: A, B and C started a business in partnership. A invested $\frac{1}{3}$rd part of the total capital and B invested equal to the investment of A and C. If annual profit of the business is Rs. 840, what will be the gain of each of them?

Solution: Let total capital = Rs. x; then capital of A = Rs. $\frac{x}{3}$

and also capital of (B + C) = Rs. $\frac{2x}{3}$. If capital of B = Rs. y; then

$y = \frac{x}{3} + \frac{2x}{3} - y \Rightarrow 2y = x \quad y = \text{Rs. } \frac{x}{2}$ and also share of C = $\frac{2x}{3} - \frac{x}{2}$ = Rs. $\frac{x}{6}$

Now, Ratio of their capitals = $\frac{x}{3} : \frac{x}{2} : \frac{x}{6} = 2 : 3 : 1$

Hence, share of A = $\frac{2}{6} \times 840$ = Rs. 280; share of B = $\frac{3}{6} \times 840$ = Rs. 420;

Share of C = $\frac{1}{6} \times 840$ = Rs. 140

Example 18: A, B and C started a business with a total investment of Rs. 14000. If at the end of the year, A, B and C gets profit of Rs. 337.50, Rs. 1125 and Rs. 637.50 respectively, how much did each of them invest in the business?

Solution: Ratio of the investment of A, B and C = 337.50 : 1125 : 637.50 = 9 : 30 : 17

Sum of proportionals = 9 + 30 + 17 = 56

$$\text{A's capital} = \frac{9}{56} \times 14000 = \text{Rs. } 2250$$

$$\text{B's capital} = \frac{30}{56} \times 14000 = \text{Rs. } 7500$$

$$\text{C's capital} = \frac{17}{56} \times 14000 = \text{Rs. } 4250$$

Example 19: A, B and C started a business with the investment of Rs. 15000, Rs. 18000 and Rs. 17000 respectively. After 4 months, A invested Rs. 5000 more and 2 months after that C took away Rs. 4000. If at the end of 15 months there was a profit of Rs. 15380 in the business, what will be the gain of each of them?

Solution: A's capital for 1 month = 15000 × 4 + 20000 × 11 = Rs. 2,80,000

B's capital for 1 month = 18000 × 15 = Rs. 2,70,000

C's capital for 1 month = 17000 × 6 + 13000 × 9 = Rs. 2,19,000

∴ Ratio of their capitals = 280000 : 270000 : 219000 = 280 : 270 : 219

Sum of proportionals = 280 + 270 + 219 = 769

Total profit= Rs. 15380

$$\therefore \text{A's share in profit} = \frac{280}{769} \times 15380 = \text{Rs. } 5600$$

$$\text{B's share in profit} = \frac{270}{769} \times 15380 = \text{Rs. } 5400$$

$$\text{C's share in profit} = \frac{219}{769} \times 15380 = \text{Rs. } 4380$$

Example 20: A, B and C together make a profit of Rs. 7200 in a business. If A invested Rs. 8000 in the business and A and C make profit of Rs. 1920 and Rs. 2880 respectively. What did B invest in the business?

Solution: Total profit in the business = Rs. 7200

B's profit = 7200 – (1920 + 2880) = Rs. 2400

A's capital = Rs. 8000, A's profit = Rs. 1920

$$\therefore \text{Capital invested by B} = \frac{8000}{1920} \times 2400 = \text{Rs. } 10000$$

Example 21: Gulshan, Tarun and Kamalkant invested Rs. 400, Rs. 700 and Rs. 300 respectively in a business. If at the end of the year Gulshan makes a profit of Rs. 160 in the business, find the total profit in the business.

Solution: Ratio of their capitals = 400 : 700 : 300 = 4 : 7 : 3

Profit of Gulshan = Rs. 160

$$\therefore \text{Total profit in the business} = \frac{160}{4} \times 14 = \text{Rs. } 560$$

Example 22: A and B started a business with capitals in the ratio of 5 : 8. After 5 months, B took back his amount. If they got profit in the ratio 2 : 3, for how many months A's capital continued in the business?

Sol: Let A's capital continued in the business for x months; then

Ratio of their capitals = $(5 \times x) : (8 \times 5) = x : 8$

Now, $x : 8 = 2 : 3 \qquad \therefore \ x = \frac{2}{3} \times 8 = 5\frac{1}{3}$ months

Example 23 : A, B and C together rented a house for 2 years at Rs. 1080 per year. They live in the house jointly for 5 months. After that C leaves off 8 months after B also leaves the house and thereafter A alone lives in this house. Find the amount of rent paid by each of them.

Solution: Amount of rent for 1 year = Rs. 1080

1 month's rent when A, B and C live together = $\frac{1080}{12}$ = Rs. 90

Rent to be paid by each of them = Rs. $\frac{90}{3}$ = Rs. 30

When A and B live together

Amount of rent to be paid by each of them = $\frac{90}{2}$ = Rs. 45

when A alone lives in the house

Amount of rent to be paid by A = Rs. 90

∴Rent paid by C = Rs. 30 × 5 = Rs. 150

Rent paid by B = 30 × 5 + 45 × 8 = 150 + 360 = Rs. 510

Rent paid by A = 30 × 5 + 45 × 8 + 90 × 11

= 150 + 360 + 990 = Rs. 1500

EXERCISE

1. A and B started a business with the investment of Rs. 80000 and Rs. 60000 respectively. At the end of the year total profit in the business will be divided between them in the ratio of :
(a) 2 : 3 *(b)* 3 : 4 *(c)* 2 : 1 *(d)* 4 : 3

2. A and B started a business in partnership with the investment of Rs. 4000 and Rs. 6000 respectively. If at the end of the year total profit is Rs. 2250, what will each of them get?
(a) Rs. 900, Rs. 1350 *(b)* Rs. 800, Rs. 1450
(c) Rs. 1000, Rs. 1250 *(d)* Rs. 1200, Rs. 1050

3. Sonu, Monu and Mohit together start a business with the investment of Rs.1800, Rs. 1500 and Rs. 1600 respectively. If at the end of the year, Monu gains a profit of Rs. 900 the total profit in the business is :
(a) Rs. 2880 *(b)* Rs. 2940 *(c)* Rs. 3200 *(d)* Rs. 3240

4. Omdutt started a business with a capital of Rs. 8000. After six months, Sanjay joined him with investment of some capital. If at the end of the year each of them gets equal amount as profit, how much did Sanjay invest in the business?
(a) Rs. 18000 *(b)* Rs. 17500 *(c)* Rs. 16000 *(d)* Rs. 16500

5. A, B and C buy a farm for Rs. 100000. A contributes Rs. 40000 in it. They sell it, and from the profit B gets Rs. 2750 and C gets Rs. 1750. What would be the profit of A?
(a) Rs. 2780 *(b)* Rs. 3000 *(c)* Rs. 3280 *(d)* Rs. 2785

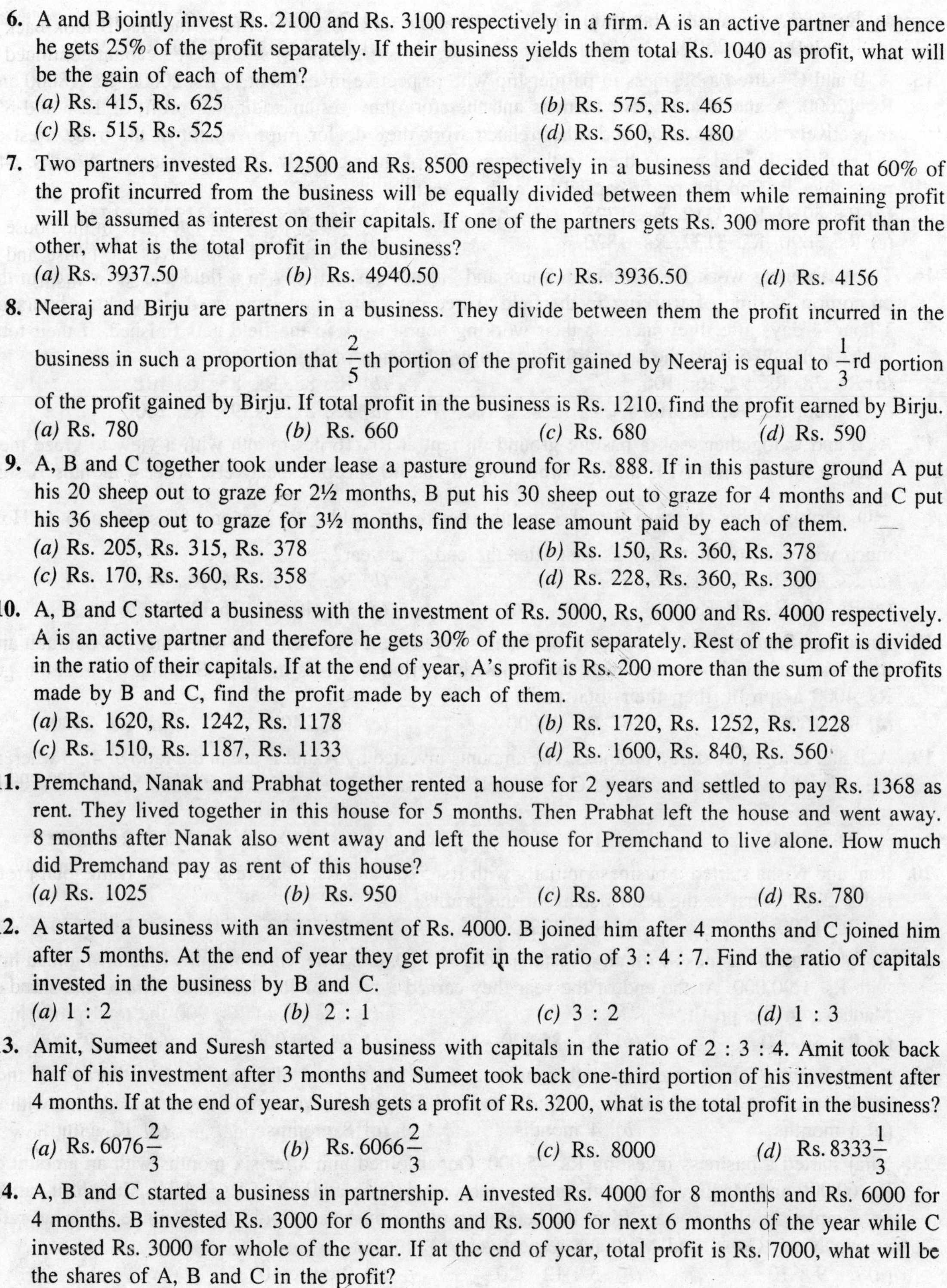

6. A and B jointly invest Rs. 2100 and Rs. 3100 respectively in a firm. A is an active partner and hence he gets 25% of the profit separately. If their business yields them total Rs. 1040 as profit, what will be the gain of each of them?
(a) Rs. 415, Rs. 625 *(b)* Rs. 575, Rs. 465
(c) Rs. 515, Rs. 525 *(d)* Rs. 560, Rs. 480

7. Two partners invested Rs. 12500 and Rs. 8500 respectively in a business and decided that 60% of the profit incurred from the business will be equally divided between them while remaining profit will be assumed as interest on their capitals. If one of the partners gets Rs. 300 more profit than the other, what is the total profit in the business?
(a) Rs. 3937.50 *(b)* Rs. 4940.50 *(c)* Rs. 3936.50 *(d)* Rs. 4156

8. Neeraj and Birju are partners in a business. They divide between them the profit incurred in the business in such a proportion that $\frac{2}{5}$th portion of the profit gained by Neeraj is equal to $\frac{1}{3}$rd portion of the profit gained by Birju. If total profit in the business is Rs. 1210, find the profit earned by Birju.
(a) Rs. 780 *(b)* Rs. 660 *(c)* Rs. 680 *(d)* Rs. 590

9. A, B and C together took under lease a pasture ground for Rs. 888. If in this pasture ground A put his 20 sheep out to graze for 2½ months, B put his 30 sheep out to graze for 4 months and C put his 36 sheep out to graze for 3½ months, find the lease amount paid by each of them.
(a) Rs. 205, Rs. 315, Rs. 378 *(b)* Rs. 150, Rs. 360, Rs. 378
(c) Rs. 170, Rs. 360, Rs. 358 *(d)* Rs. 228, Rs. 360, Rs. 300

10. A, B and C started a business with the investment of Rs. 5000, Rs, 6000 and Rs. 4000 respectively. A is an active partner and therefore he gets 30% of the profit separately. Rest of the profit is divided in the ratio of their capitals. If at the end of year, A's profit is Rs. 200 more than the sum of the profits made by B and C, find the profit made by each of them.
(a) Rs. 1620, Rs. 1242, Rs. 1178 *(b)* Rs. 1720, Rs. 1252, Rs. 1228
(c) Rs. 1510, Rs. 1187, Rs. 1133 *(d)* Rs. 1600, Rs. 840, Rs. 560

11. Premchand, Nanak and Prabhat together rented a house for 2 years and settled to pay Rs. 1368 as rent. They lived together in this house for 5 months. Then Prabhat left the house and went away. 8 months after Nanak also went away and left the house for Premchand to live alone. How much did Premchand pay as rent of this house?
(a) Rs. 1025 *(b)* Rs. 950 *(c)* Rs. 880 *(d)* Rs. 780

12. A started a business with an investment of Rs. 4000. B joined him after 4 months and C joined him after 5 months. At the end of year they get profit in the ratio of 3 : 4 : 7. Find the ratio of capitals invested in the business by B and C.
(a) 1 : 2 *(b)* 2 : 1 *(c)* 3 : 2 *(d)* 1 : 3

13. Amit, Sumeet and Suresh started a business with capitals in the ratio of 2 : 3 : 4. Amit took back half of his investment after 3 months and Sumeet took back one-third portion of his investment after 4 months. If at the end of year, Suresh gets a profit of Rs. 3200, what is the total profit in the business?
(a) Rs. $6076\frac{2}{3}$ *(b)* Rs. $6066\frac{2}{3}$ *(c)* Rs. 8000 *(d)* Rs. $8333\frac{1}{3}$

14. A, B and C started a business in partnership. A invested Rs. 4000 for 8 months and Rs. 6000 for 4 months. B invested Rs. 3000 for 6 months and Rs. 5000 for next 6 months of the year while C invested Rs. 3000 for whole of the year. If at the end of year, total profit is Rs. 7000, what will be the shares of A, B and C in the profit?

(a) Rs. 2800, Rs. 2400, Rs. 1800 (b) Rs. 2500, Rs. 2600, Rs. 1900
(c) Rs. 2600, Rs. 2500, Rs. 1900 (d) Rs. 2000, Rs. 2700, Rs. 2300

15. A, B and C started a business in partnership with respective investment of Rs. 20000, Rs. 18000 and Rs. 12000. A and B are active partners and therefore they get an additional profit of 12% and 8% respectively for supervision and other related work they do for improvement of the trade. Rest of the profit is divided among them in the proportion of their capitals. If profit made by A is Rs. 648 more than B, find the profit earned by each of them.
(a) Rs. 3960, Rs. 3312, Rs. 1728 (b) Rs. 4960, Rs. 3312, Rs. 1728
(c) Rs. 3690, Rs. 3132, Rs. 1820 (d) Rs. 5960, Rs. 3600, Rs. 1750

16. Three labourers work for 5 hours, 6 hours and 7 hours respectively in a field and get wages in the proportion of time of working in the field. Three days after they increase their working hours by 1 hour. 4 days after they increase their working hours, work in the field gets finished. If their total wages is Rs. 276, find the share of wages earned by each of them.
(a) Rs. 78, Rs, 92, Rs. 106 (b) Rs. 88, Rs. 87, Rs. 101
(c) Rs. 80, Rs. 90, Rs. 106 (d) Rs. 81, Rs. 95, Rs. 100

17. A, B and C together took a pasture ground on rent at Rs. 16 per month with a view to graze their sheep in this ground. A, B and C owned 70, 50 and 40 sheep respectively. After 4 months A sold $\frac{2}{7}$th portion of his sheep to B and 3 month after that C sold $\frac{2}{5}$th portion of his sheep to A. How much will each of them pay as rent after the end of a year?
(a) Rs. 70, Rs. 70, Rs. 52 (b) Rs. 76, Rs. 76, Rs. 40
(c) Rs. 80, Rs. 76, Rs. 36 (d) Rs. 40, Rs. 76.30, Rs. 76

18. Samir and Saurabh started a joint firm. Samir's investment was thrice the investment of Saurabh and the period of his investment was two times the period of investment of Saurabh. If Saurabh got Rs. 4000 as profit, then their total profit is:
(a) Rs. 16000 (b) Rs. 20000 (c) Rs. 24000 (d) Rs. 28000

19. A, B and C together start a business. The amounts invested by A and B are in the ratio of 4 : 3 whereas the ratio of investments of B and C is 2 : 3. If the total profit earned is Rs. 46000, what is C's share in the profit?
(a) Rs. 14000 (b) Rs. 15000 (c) Rs. 16000 (d) Rs. 18000

20. Rani and Nisha started a business initially with Rs. 5100 and Rs. 6600 respectively. If the total profit is Rs. 2730, what is the Rani's share in the profit?
(a) Rs. 1190 (b) Rs. 1200 (c) Rs. 1530 (d) Rs. 1540

21. Gopal started a business with an investment of Rs. 1,20,000. After three months Madhava joined him with Rs. 1,90,000. At the end of the year they earned a profit of Rs. 1,75,000. What is the share of Madhava in the profit?
(a) Rs. 80,000 (b) Rs. 85,000 (c) Rs. 90,000 (d) Rs, 95,000

22. A and B enter into partnership with capitals as 5 : 6. At the end of 8 months A withdraws. If they receive profit in the ratio of 5 : 9, find how long B's capital was used?
(a) 3 months (b) 4 months (c) 8 months (d) 12 months

23. Niraj started a business investing Rs. 45,000, Gopal joined him after six months with an amount of Rs. 60,000 and Madhava joined them after one year with an amount of Rs. 1 lakh. The profit earned on completion of two years from the beginning of the business should be distributed in what ratio among Niraj, Gopal and Madhava respectively?
(a) 5 : 9 : 10 (b) 5 : 12 : 20 (c) 9 : 9 : 10 (d) 9 : 12 : 20

24. Three partners invested Rs. 2000, Rs. 2500 and Rs. 1000 respectively in a business. What will be the share of the third partner in a profit of Rs. 880?

(*a*) Rs. 160 (*b*) Rs. 180 (*c*) Rs. 350 (*d*) Rs. 400

25. Kaushal and Kamlesh are partners in a business, Kaushal contributes one-thirds of the capital for 9 months and Kamlesh received two-fifths of the profits. For how long Kamlesh's money was used in the business?

(*a*) 2 months (*b*) 3 months (*c*) 4 months (*d*) 5 months

26. Amar, Shubham and Shivam enter into a business. Amar invests some amount at the beginning. Shubham invests double the amount after six months and Shivam invests thrice the amount after 8 months. They earn a profit of Rs. 45,000 at the end of the year. What is Shivam's share in the profit?

(*a*) Rs. 9000 (*b*) Rs. 12,000 (*c*) Rs. 15,000 (*d*) Rs. 25,000

27. Rani, Samir and Saurabh rented a set of DVD's at a rent of Rs. 578. If they used it for 8 hours, 12 hours and 14 hours respectively, what is Saurabh's share of rent to be paid?

(*a*) Rs. 192 (*b*) Rs. 204 (*c*) Rs. 215 (*d*) Rs. 238

28. Rita and Nilam started a workshop jointly by investing Rs. 9000 and Rs. 10500 respectively. After 4 months Nisha joined them by investing Rs. 12500, while Nilam withdrew Rs. 2000. At the end of the year there was a profit of Rs. 4770. Find the share of each.

(*a*) Rs. 1620, Rs. 1500, Rs. 1400 (*b*) Rs. 1620, Rs. 1650, Rs. 1500

(*c*) Rs. 2000, Rs. 1800, Rs, 1500 (*d*) Rs. 2400, Rs. 1650, Rs. 1500

29. The ratio of investments of Kaushal and Guddu is 11 : 12 and the ratio of their profits is 2 : 3. If Kaushal invested the money for 8 months, find for how much time Guddu invested his money.

(*a*) 3 months (*b*) 6 months (*c*) 8 months (*d*) 11 months

30. Ram started a business with an investment of Rs. 50,000. After 4 months Shyam joined with an investment of Rs. 80,000. If in one year the profit is Rs. 62,000, what amount Shyam would get as profit?

(*a*) Rs. 11000 (*b*) Rs. 14000 (*c*) Rs. 16000 (*d*) Rs. 32000

31. Ashok started a business investing Rs. 50,000. After one year he invested another Rs. 30,000 and Anil also joined him with a capital of Rs. 70,000. If the profit earned in three years from the starting business was Rs. 87,500, then find the share of Anil in the profit.

(*a*) 35,000 (*b*) Rs. 32,500 (*c*) Rs. 37,500 (*d*) Rs. 38,281

32. A, B and C entered into a partnership investing Rs. 12000, Rs. 15000 and Rs. 18000 respectively. B is also a working partner and gets 20% of the profit for his work. After 3 months A withdraws Rs. 3000, while C deposited Rs. 3000 after 6 months of the starting of business. Find the share of B in an annual profit of Rs. 36875.

(*a*) Rs. 12000 (*b*) Rs. 15000 (*c*) Rs. 17375 (*d*) Rs. 18000

33. A, B and C enter into a partnership with capitals Rs. 40,000, Rs. 80,000 and Rs. 1,20,000 respectively. At the end of the first year, B withdraws Rs. 40,000 while at the second year, C withdraws Rs. 80,000. In what ratio will the profit be shared at the end of 3 years?

(*a*) 2 : 3 : 6 (*b*) 3 : 4 : 7 (*c*) 4 : 5 : 7 (*d*) 4 : 5 : 9

34. A and B started a partnership business investing the amount in the ratio of 3 : 5. C joined them after six months with an amount equal to that of B. In what proportion should the profit at the end of one year be distributed among A, B and C?

(*a*) 3 : 5 : 2 (*b*) 3 : 10 : 5 (*c*) 4 : 5 : 10 (*d*) 6 : 10 : 5

35. A, B and C enter into a partnership in the ratio of $\frac{7}{2}:\frac{4}{3}:\frac{6}{5}$. After 4 months, A increase his share by 50%. If the total profit at the end of one year is Rs. 21,600, then B's share in the profit is:
(a) Rs. 4000 *(b)* Rs. 3600 *(c)* Rs. 2400 *(d)* Rs. 2100

36. A and B entered into partnership with capitals in the ratio 4 : 5. After 3 months, A withdrew 1/4 of his capital and B withdrew 1/5 fo his capital. The gain at the end of 10 months was Rs. 760. What is the A's share in this profit?
(a) Rs. 430 *(b)* Rs. 380 *(c)* Rs. 360 *(d)* Rs. 330

37. A, B and C enter into a partnership with their share in the ratio $\frac{1}{2}:\frac{1}{3}:\frac{1}{4}$. After 2 months, A withdraws half of his capital and after 10 months, a profit of Rs. 378 is divided among them. B's share in this profit is:
(a) Rs. 168 *(b)* Rs. 156 *(c)* Rs. 144 *(d)* Rs. 129

38. A, B and C enter into business partnership. It was agreed that A would invest Rs. 6500 for 6 months, B Rs. 8400 for 5 months and C Rs. 10,000 for 3 months. A wants to be the working member for which he was to receive 5% of the profit. The profit earned was Rs. 7400. What is the share of B in this profit?
(a) Rs. 2840 *(b)* Rs. 2800 *(c)* Rs. 2660 *(d)* Rs. 1900

39. A and C invested amounts in the ratio 2 : 1 in a business, whereas the ratio between amount invested by A and B was 3 : 2. If Rs. 1,57,300 was their profit, B's share in that profit was:
(a) Rs. 72,600 *(b)* Rs. 48,400 *(c)* Rs. 36,300 *(d)* Rs. 24,200

40. In a business A and B are partners. A contributes 1/4 of the capital for 15 months and B received 2/3 of the profit. For how long B's money was used?
(a) 1 year *(b)* 10 months *(c)* 9 months *(d)* 6 months

41. A began a business with Rs. 85000. He was joined afterwards by B with Rs. 42,500. For how much period does B join, if the profit at the end of year are divided in the ratio 3 : 1?
(a) 8 months *(b)* 6 months *(c)* 5 months *(d)* 4 months

42. Three partners shared the profit in a business in the ratio 5 : 7 : 8. They had partnered for 14 months, 8 months and 7 months respectively. Their ratio of investment is:
(a) 10 : 15 : 17 *(b)* 20 : 49 : 64 *(c)* 21 : 35 : 65 *(d)* 35 : 47 : 64

43. A starts business with Rs. 3500 and after 5 months, B joins as a partner. After a year the profit is divided in the ratio 2 : 3. The capital of B is:
(a) Rs. 9000 *(b)* Rs. 8500 *(c)* Rs. 8000 *(d)* Rs. 7500

44. Two friends X and Y started a business investing in the ratio of 5 : 6. Z joined them after six months investing amount equal to that of Y's. At the end of the year, 20% profit was earned which was equal to Rs. 98,000. The amount invested by Z was:
(a) Rs. 2,15,000 *(b)* Rs. 2,10,000 *(c)* Rs. 2,00,000 *(d)* Rs. 1,80,000

SOLUTIONS

1. Ratio between their profits = 80000 : 60000 = 4 : 3

2. Ratio of capitals of A and B = 4000 : 6000 = 2 : 3

A's share in the profit = $\frac{2}{5} \times 2250$ = Rs. 900

B's share in the profit = $\frac{3}{5} \times 2250$ = Rs. 1350

3. Ratio of their capitals = 1800 : 1500 : 1600 = 18 : 15 : 16
Sum of proportionals = 18 + 15 + 16 = 49
Monu's profit = Rs. 900

$\therefore$ Total profit in the business = $\frac{900}{15} \times 49$ = Rs. 2940

4. Investment by Omdutt for 1 month = Rs. 8000 × 12 = Rs. 96000
Let Sanjay invested Rs. x for 6 months
$\therefore$ Capital of Sanjay for 1 month = Rs. $x \times 6$ = Rs. $6x$
Now, $6x = 96000$ $\therefore$ x = Rs. 16000

5. Here, ratio of capitals of A and (B + C) = 40000 : 60000 = 2 : 3
Profit of (B + C) = 2750 + 1750 = Rs. 4500

Hence, A's profit = $\frac{4500}{3} \times 2$ = Rs. 3000

6. Separate profit for A = $\frac{1040 \times 25}{100}$ = Rs. 260
Remaining profit = Rs. (1040 − 260) = Rs. 780
Ratio of capitals of A and B = 2100 : 3100 = 21 : 31

A's profit = $\frac{21}{52} \times 780$ = Rs. 315

B's profit = $\frac{31}{52} \times 780$ = Rs. 465

Total profit of A = Rs. (315 + 260) = Rs. 575
Therefore A and B will make profit of Rs. 575 and Rs. 465 respectively.

7. Ratio of their capitals = 12500 : 8500 = 25 : 17
Hence, sum of their ratios = 25 + 17 = 42 and difference of ratios = 25 − 17 = 8

Now total profit taken as interest = $\frac{300}{8} \times 42$ = Rs. 1575

Hence, total profit in the business = $\frac{100}{40} \times 1575$ = Rs. 3937.50

8. Let shares of Neeraj and Birju in profit are Rs. x and Rs. y respectively; then,

$\frac{2}{5}x = \frac{1}{3}y$ $\therefore$ $x : y = 5 : 6$

Hence, share of Birju = $\frac{6}{11} \times 1210$ = Rs. 660

9. Ratio of their shares = (20 × 5/2) : (30 × 4) : (36 × 7/2) = 25 : 60 : 63
Sum of proportionals = 25 + 60 + 63 = 148
Total lease amount = Rs. 888

$\therefore$ Amount paid by A = $\frac{25}{148} \times 888$ = Rs. 150

Amount paid by B = $\frac{60}{148} \times 888$ = Rs. 360

Amount paid by C = $\frac{63}{148} \times 888$ = Rs. 378

10. Ratio of capitals of A, B and C = 5000 : 6000 : 4000 = 5 : 6 : 4
Let total profit in the business = Rs. x; then

$$\frac{30x}{100} + \frac{5}{15} \times \frac{70x}{100} - \frac{(6+4)}{15} \times \frac{70x}{100} = 200 \Rightarrow \frac{8x}{15} - \frac{7x}{15} = 200 \quad \therefore x = \text{Rs. } 3000$$

Hence, A's profit = $\frac{8 \times 3000}{15}$ = Rs. 1600; B's profit = $\frac{6}{15} \times \frac{7 \times 3000}{10}$ = Rs. 840;

C's profit = $\frac{4}{15} \times \frac{7 \times 3000}{10}$ = Rs. 560

11. Rent for 1 month = $\frac{1368}{24}$ = Rs. 57

Total rent paid by Premchand = $5 \times \frac{57}{3} + 8 \times \frac{57}{2} + 11 \times 57$ = 95 + 228 + 627 = Rs. 950

12. Let, B and C invest Rs. x and Rs. y respectively
∴ Ratio of their capitals = 48000 : $8x$: $7y$
But given ratio of the profits = 3 : 4 : 7

$$8x : 7y = 4 : 7 \Rightarrow \frac{x}{y} = \frac{1}{2} \quad \text{Hence, } x : y = 1 : 2$$

13. Ratio of capitals of Amit, Sumeet and Suresh
= (2 × 3 + 1 × 9) : (3 × 4 + 2 × 8) : (4 × 12) = 15 : 28 : 48
Sum of the ratios = 15 + 28 + 48 = 91

∴ Total profit in the business = $\frac{91}{48} \times 3200 = \text{Rs. } 6066\frac{2}{3}$

14. Ratio of their capitals
= (4000 × 8 + 6000 × 4) : (3000 × 6 + 5000 × 6) : (3000 × 12)
= 56000 : 48000 : 36000 = 14 : 12 : 9
Sum of proportionals = 14 + 12 + 9 = 35

Share of A in the profit = $\frac{14}{35} \times 7000$ = Rs 2800

Share of B in the profit = $\frac{12}{35} \times 7000$ = Rs. 2400

Share of C in the profit = $\frac{9}{35} \times 7000$ = Rs. 1800

15. Ratio of their capitals = 20000 : 18000 : 12000 = 10 : 9 : 6
Let total profit in the business = Rs. x; then

$$\left(\frac{12x}{100} + \frac{10}{25} \times \frac{80x}{100}\right) - \left(\frac{8x}{100} + \frac{9}{25} \times \frac{80x}{100}\right) = 648 \Rightarrow \frac{11x}{25} - \frac{46x}{125} = 648$$

$\Rightarrow \frac{9x}{125} = 648 \qquad \therefore x = \frac{648 \times 125}{9} = \text{Rs. } 9000$

Hence, share of A = $\frac{11x}{25} = \frac{11 \times 9000}{25} = \text{Rs. } 3960;$

Share of B = $\frac{46x}{125} = \frac{46 \times 9000}{125} = \text{Rs. } 3312$

Share of C = $\frac{6}{25} \times \frac{80x}{100} = \frac{6}{25} \times \frac{4}{5} \times 9000 = \text{Rs. } 1728$

16. Ratio of their working hours = $(5 \times 3 + 6 \times 4) : (6 \times 3 + 7 \times 4) : (7 \times 3 + 8 \times 4) = 39 : 46 : 53$
Sum of proportionals = 39 + 46 + 53 = 138

$\therefore$ Wages for the 1st labourer = $\frac{39}{138} \times 276 = \text{Rs. } 78$

Wages for the 2nd labourer = $\frac{46}{138} \times 276 = \text{Rs. } 92$

Wages for the 3rd labourer = $\frac{53}{138} \times 276 = \text{Rs. } 106$

17. Number of sheep of A for 1 month = $[70 \times 4 + (70 - \frac{2}{7} \times 70) \times 3 + (70 - \frac{2}{7} \times 70 + \frac{2}{5} \times 40) \times 5]$
= 280 + 150 + 330 = 760

Number of sheep of B for 1 month = $[50 \times 4 + (50 + \frac{2}{7} \times 70) \times 8] = 200 + 560 = 760$

Number of sheep of C for 1 month = $[40 \times 7 + (40 - \frac{2}{5} \times 40) \times 5] = 280 + 120 = 400$

Hence, ratio of their sheep = 760 : 760 : 400 = 19 : 19 : 10
Sum of proportionals = 19 + 19 +10 = 48
1 year's rent of the pasture ground = 16 × 12 = Rs. 192

$\therefore$ Rent to be paid by A = $\frac{19}{48} \times 192 = \text{Rs. } 76$

Rent to be paid by B = $\frac{19}{48} \times 192 = \text{Rs. } 76$

Rent to be paid by C = $\frac{10}{48} \times 192 = \text{Rs. } 40$

18. Ratio of Capitals of Samir and Saurabh = (3 × 2) : (1 × 1) = 6 : 1
Saurabh's profit = Rs. 4000
Hence, total profit in the business = 7 × Rs. 4000 = Rs. 28000

19. A : B = 4 : 3 and B : C = 2 : 3, Therefore, A : B : C = 8 : 6 : 9

Hence, C's profit = $\frac{9}{23} \times 46000 = \text{Rs. } 18000$

20. Ratio of their Capitals = 5100 : 6600 = 17 : 22

Hence, Rani's profit = $\frac{17}{39} \times 2730 = \text{Rs. } 1190$

21. Ratio of the capitals of Gopal and Madhava = (1,20,000 × 12) : (1,90,000 × 9) = 16 : 19

Hence, Madhava's profit = $\frac{19}{35} \times 1{,}75{,}000$ = Rs. 95,000

22. Let the B's capital was used for x months; then
Ratio of their capitals = (5 × 8) : (6 × x) = 20 : 3x

Now, $\frac{20}{3x} = \frac{5}{9}$ $\quad \therefore x = \frac{20 \times 9}{5 \times 3}$ = 12 months

23. Ratio of capitals of Niraj, Gopal and Madhava
= (45000 × 24) : (60000 × 18) : (1,00,000 × 12) = 9 : 9 : 10
Hence, ratio of their profits = 9 : 9 : 10

24. Ratio of their capitals = 2000 : 2500 : 1000 = 4 : 5 : 2

Hence, profit of third partner = $\frac{2}{11} \times 880$ = Rs. 160

25. Let money of Kamlesh was used for x months;

Then, ratio of their capitals = $\left(\frac{1}{3} \times 9\right) : \left(\frac{2}{3} \times x\right)$ = 9 : 2x

The ratio of their profit = $\frac{3}{5} : \frac{2}{5}$ = 3 : 2

Hence, $\frac{9}{2x} = \frac{3}{2}$ $\quad \therefore x = \frac{9 \times 2}{2 \times 3}$ = 3 months

26. Ratio of capitals of Amar, Shubham and Shivam = (1 × 12) : (2 × 6) : (3 × 4) = 1 : 1 : 1

Hence, Shivam's profit = $\frac{1}{3} \times 45000$ = Rs. 15000

27. Ratio of shares of Rani, Samir and Saurabh = 8 : 12 : 14 = 4 : 6 : 7

Hence, Saurabh's share in rent = $\frac{7}{17} \times 578$ = Rs. 238

28. Ratio of capitals of Rita, Nilam and Nisha
= (9000 × 12) : (10500 × 4 + 8500 × 8) : (12500 × 8)
= 54 : 55 : 50

Rita's profit = $\frac{54}{159} \times 4770$ = Rs. 1620;

Nilam's profit = $\frac{55}{159} \times 4770$ = Rs. 1650;

Nisha's profit = $\frac{50}{159} \times 4770$ = Rs. 1500

29. Let Guddu invested his money for x months; then
Ratio of their capitals = (11 × 8) : (12 × x) = 22 : 3x

Now, $\frac{22}{3x} = \frac{2}{3}$ $\quad \therefore x = \frac{22 \times 3}{2 \times 3}$ = 11 months

30. Ratio of their capitals = (50,000 × 12) : (80,000 × 8) = 15 : 16

Hence, Shyam's profit = $\frac{16}{31} \times 62{,}000$ = Rs. 32000

31. Ratio of their capitals = (50000 × 12 + 80000 × 24) : (70000 × 24) = 3 : 2

Hence, Anil's profit = $\frac{2}{5} \times 87500$ = Rs. 35000

32. Ratio of their capitals = (12000 × 3 + 9000 × 9) : (15000 × 12) : (18000 × 6 + 21000 × 6)

= 13 : 20 : 26

B's share for extra work = $\frac{20}{100} \times 36875$ = Rs. 7375

Rest of profit = 36875 – 7375 = Rs. 29500

B's profit = $\frac{20}{59} \times 29500$ = Rs. 10000

Hence, total share of B = 7375 + 10000 = Rs. 17375

33. Ratio of their capitals
= (40000 × 36) : (80000 × 12 + 40000 × 24) : (1,20,000 × 24 + 40000 × 12)
= 3 : 4 : 7
Hence, ratio of their profits = 3 : 4 : 7

34. Ratio of their capitals = (3 × 12) : (5 × 12) : (5 × 6) = 6 : 10 : 5
Hence, ratio of their profits = 6 : 10 : 5

35. Ratio of their initial capitals = $\frac{7}{2} : \frac{4}{3} : \frac{6}{5}$ = 105 : 40 : 36
Ratio of their capitals on which profit will be divided

$= (105 \times 4 + \frac{150}{100} \times 105 \times 8) : (40 \times 12) : (36 \times 12)$

= 35 : 10 : 9

Hence, B's profit = $\frac{10}{54}$ × 21600 = Rs. 4000

36. Ratio of their capitals = $[4 \times 3 + (4 - \frac{1}{4} \times 4) \times 7] : [5 \times 3 + (5 - \frac{1}{5} \times 5) \times 7]$

= 33 : 43

Hence, A's profit = $\frac{33}{76}$ × 760 = Rs. 330

37. Ratio of their capitals = $\frac{1}{2} : \frac{1}{3} : \frac{1}{4}$ = 6 : 4 : 3
Ratio of their capital on which profit will be divided
= [6 × 2 + 3 × 10] : (4 × 12) : (3 × 12) = 7 : 8 : 6

Hence, B's profit = $\frac{8}{21} \times 378$ = Rs. 144

38. Share of A for extra work = $\frac{5}{100} \times 7400$ = Rs. 370

Rest of profit = 7400 − 370 = Rs. 7030

Ratio of their capitals = (6500 × 6) : (8400 × 5) : (10000 × 3) = 13 : 14 : 10

Hence, B's profit = $\frac{14}{37} \times 7030$ = Rs. 2660

39. Here, A : C = 2 : 1 ⇒ C : A = 1 : 2 and A : B = 3 : 2

Hence, C : A : B = 3 : 6 : 4, then, A : B : C = 6 : 4 : 3

∴ B's profit = $\frac{4}{13} \times 157300$ = Rs. 48400

40. Let B's money was used for x months; then

Ratio of their capitals = $\left(\frac{1}{4} \times 15\right) : \left(\frac{3}{4} \times x\right) = 5 : x$

Ratio of their profits = $\frac{1}{3} : \frac{2}{3} = 1 : 2$

Hence, $\frac{5}{x} = \frac{1}{2}$ ∴ x = 10 months

41. Let B was joined for x months; then

$\frac{85000 \times 12}{42500 \times x} = \frac{3}{1}$ ∴ $x = \frac{85000 \times 12}{42500 \times 3}$ = 8 months

42. Let they invest Rs. x, Rs. y and Rs. z for 14 months, 8 months and 7 months respectively; then

$14x : 8y : 7z = 5 : 6 : 8$ ⇒ $\frac{14x}{8y} = \frac{5}{7}$ ∴ $y = \frac{49x}{20}$

Again, $\frac{14x}{7z} = \frac{5}{8}$ ∴ $z = \frac{16x}{5}$

Since, $x : y : z = x : \frac{49x}{20} : \frac{16x}{5} = 20 : 49 : 64$

43. Let the capital of B = Rs. x; then

$\frac{3500 \times 12}{x \times 7} = \frac{2}{3}$ ∴ $x = \frac{3500 \times 12 \times 13}{7 \times 2}$ = Rs. 9000

44. Let total capial = Rs. a; then

$\frac{20}{100} \times a = 98000$ ∴ a = 98000 × 5 = Rs. 4,90,000

If their individual capitals are Rs. $5x$, Rs. $6x$ and Rs. $6x$ respectively,

Then, $(5x \times 12) + (6x \times 12) + (6x \times 6) = 490000 \times 12$

⇒ $168x = 490000 \times 12$ ∴ $x = \frac{490000 \times 12}{168}$ = 35000

Hence, amount invested by $Z = 6x = 6 \times 35000$ = Rs. 2,10,000

26

FACTORISATION

The process of expressing a polynomial as a product of two or more polynomials of smaller degrees is called *factorising polynomials.* Thus when an expression is the product of two or more expressions, each of these expressions is called a *factor* of the product. Following methods are used:

A. *Common Factor:*

For example,

1st term = $42a^2b = 7ab \times 6a$; 2nd term = $7ab^2 = 7ab \times b$

Therefore, here $7ab$ is the common factor. On dividing $42a^2b + 7ab^2$ by $7ab$, the quotient obtained is $(6a + b)$

$\therefore$ Required factor = $7ab(6a + b)$.

B. *Factorising polynomials by properly grouping terms of the expression.*

For example,

$$ab^2 - 1 - b^2 + a$$

Expression $ab^2 - 1 - b^2 + a = ab^2 - b^2 + a - 1$

$= b^2(a - 1) + 1(a - 1)$

$= (a - 1)(b^2 + 1)$.

C. *Finding factors when the polynomial is the difference of two squares.*

For example, if we have to find the factors of $25x^4 - 16y^4$,

$$25x^4 = (5x^2)^2 \text{ and } 16y^4 = (4y^2)^2$$

$\therefore$ $25x^4 - 16y^4 = (5x^2)^2 - (4y^2)^2$, which is of the form $a^2 - b^2$

$\therefore$ Required factors = $(5x^2 + 4y^2)(5x^2 - 4y^2)$.

D. *Finding factors when the polynomial of the form of a perfect square:*

For example, if we have to find the factors of $x^4 + x^2y + y^4$, we add twice the product of the square roots of x^4 and y^4 *i.e.,* $2x^2y^2$ to the given expression so as to make it a perfect square.

$\therefore$ $x^4 + x^2y^2 + y^4 = (x^2)^2 + 2x^2y^2 + (y^2)^2 - x^2y^2$

$= (x^2 + y^2)^2 - (xy)^2$ [This is of the form $a^2 - b^2$]

$\therefore$ Required factors = $(x^2 + y^2 - xy)(x^2 + y^2 - xy)$.

E. *Finding factors when the polynomial is a second degree trinomial:*

The type is of the form $ax^2 + bx + c$, where a is a positive integer and b and c are either positive or negative integers.

There are following two cases in factorisation of such polynomials:

I. When $a = 1$, *i.e.,* the given polynomial is of the form $x^2 + bx + c$

II. When a = a positive integer other than 1, *i.e.,* the given polynomial is of the form $ax^2 + bx + c$.

F. *Finding factors when the polynomial is the sum and difference of two cubes:* The given polynomials in this case are of the forms $x^3 + y^3$ and $x^3 - y^3$.

G. *Finding factors by Remainder Theorem:* If a polynomial is divided by one of its factors then the remainder obtained is zero
i.e., if $(x - a)$ is a factor of $p(x)$, then $p(a) = 0$.

Example 1: Factorise $8(x + y) - 4a(x + y) + 12ab(x + y)$

Solution: $8(x + y) - 4a(x + y) + 12ab(x + y) = 4(x + y)\quad[2 - a + 3ab]$

Example 2: Find the factors of $Ax^2 + Ay^2 + 10x^2 + 10y^2 + Axy + 10xy$

Solution: $Ax^2 + Ay^2 + 10x^2 + 10y^2 + Axy + 10xy$

$= (Ax^2 + Ay^2 + Axy) + (10x^2 + 10y^2 + 10xy)$

$= A(x^2 + y^2 + xy) + 10(x^2 + y^2 + xy)$

$= (x^2 + y^2 + xy)(A + 10)$

Example 3: Factorise $x^2 - 26x + 25$

Solution: $x^2 - 26x + 25 = x^2 - 25x - x + 25$

$= x(x - 25) - 1(x - 25) = (x - 25)(x - 1)$

Example 4: Factorise $36x^3 - 625x$

Solution: $36x^3 - 625x = x(36x^2 - 625)$

$= x[(6x)^2 - (25)^2] = x(6x - 25)(6x + 25)$

Example 5: Factorise $1 - 81p^4$

Solution: $1 - 81p^4 = (1)^2 - (9p^2)^2$

$= (1 + 9p^2)(1 - 9p^2)$

$= (1 + 9p^2)[(1)^2 - (3p)^2]$

$= (1 + 9p^2)(1 + 3p)(1 - 3p)$

Example 6: Factorise $8x^2 + 2x - 15$

Solution: Here we have to find two numbers whose product is 8×-15, *i.e.*, -120 and sum is $+2$.

By trial we find these to be $+12$ and -10.

$\therefore\quad 8x^2 + 2x - 15 = 8x^2 + 12x - 10x - 15 = 4x(2x + 3) - 5(2x + 3)$

$= (2x + 3)(4x - 5)$

Example 7: Factorise $1 + 10x + 25x^2$

Solution: $1 + 10x + 25x^2 = 1^2 + 2.5x + (5x)^2$, which is of the form $a^2 + 2ab + b^2$

$= (1 + 5x)^2$

Example 8: Factorise $49x^4 - 15x^2y^2 + 121y^4$

Solution: $49x^4 - 15x^2y^2 + 121y^4 = (7x^2)^2 + 154x^2y^2 + (11y^2) - 154x^2y^2 - 15x^2y^2$

$= (7x^2 + 11y^2)^2 - 169x^2y^2$

$= (7x^2 + 11y^2)^2 - (13xy)^2$

$= (7x^2 + 11y^2 + 13xy)(7x^2 + 11y^2 - 13xy)$

Example 9: Factorise $x(x - 1) - y(y - 1)$

Solution: $x(x - 1) - y(y - 1) = x^2 - x - y^2 + y = (x^2 - y^2) - (x - y)$

$= (x + y)(x - y) - (x - y) = (x - y)(x + y - 1)$

Example 10: Factorise $x^2 + y^2 - z^2 - 2xy$

Solution: $x^2 + y^2 - z^2 - 2xy = (x^2 + y^2 - 2xy) - z^2$

$= (x - y)^2 - z^2 = (x - y + z)(x - y - z)$

Example 11: Factorise $a^2 + \frac{1}{a^2} + 3 - 2a - \frac{2}{a}$

Solution: $a^2 + \frac{1}{a^2} + 3 - 2a - \frac{2}{a} = \left(a^2 + \frac{1}{a^2} + 2\right) - 2a - \frac{2}{a} + 1$

$$= \left(a + \frac{1}{a}\right)^2 - 2\left(a + \frac{1}{a}\right) + 1$$

$$= x^2 - 2x + 1 \qquad \left[\text{suppose } a + \frac{1}{a} = x\right]$$

$$= (x - 1)^2$$

$$= \left(a + \frac{1}{a} - 1\right)^2 \qquad \text{[on substituting the value of } x\text{]}$$

Example 12: Find the factors of $(a - b)^3 + (b - c)^3 + (c - a)^3$

Solution: Suppose $(a - b) = x, (b - c) = y$ and $(c - a) = z$

$\therefore \quad (a - b) + (b - c) + (c - a) = x + y + z$

$\Rightarrow \quad 0 = x + y + z$

$\therefore \quad x + y = -z \qquad$ ..... *(i)*

$\therefore \quad (x + y)^3 = (-z)^3$

or $\quad x^3 + y^3 + 3xy(x + y) = -z^3$

or $\quad x^3 + y^3 + 3xy(-z) = -z^3 \qquad$ [on substituting $x + y = -z$ from eqn. *(i)*]

or $\quad x^3 + y^3 - 3xyz = -z^3$

or $\quad x^3 + y^3 + z^3 = 3xyz$

$\therefore \quad (a - b)^3 + (b - c)^3 + (c - a)^3 = 3(a - b)(b - c)(c - a)$

Example 13: If the expression $(x^3 + ax^2 - bx + 4)$ is completely divisible by $(x^2 + 3x + 4)$, find the values of a and b.

Solution: $x^2 + 3x - 4 = x^2 + 4x - x - 4$

$$= x(x + 4) - 1(x + 4) = (x + 4)(x - 1)$$

Since the expression $(x^3 + ax^2 - bx + 4)$ is completely divisible by $x^3 + 3x + 4$

$\therefore$ $(x - 1)$ and $(x + 4)$ will be factors of $x^3 + ax^2 - bx + 4$, *i.e.*, on substituting $x = 1$ and $x = -4$ in the expression, the remainder will be zero.

On substituting $x = 1$:

$1^3 + a(1)^2 - b(1) + 4 = 0$

or $\quad 1 + a - b + 4 = 0$

$\Rightarrow \quad a - b = -5 \qquad$ ..... *(i)*

On substituting $x = -4$:

$(-4)^3 + a(-4)^2 - b(-4) + 4 = 0$

or $\quad -64 + 16a + 4b + 4 = 0$

$\Rightarrow \quad 4a + b = 15 \qquad$ ..... *(ii)*

From equations *(i)* & *(ii)*

$$5a = 10 \Rightarrow a = \frac{10}{5} = 2$$

On substituting the value of a in equation *(i)*, $2 - b = -5 \Rightarrow b = 7$

Therefore value of a and b will be 2 and 7 respectively.

EXERCISE

Directions: *Each of the questions given below is following by four alternatives of which one is correct. The candidates are required to go through the questions and the following alternatives carefully and select the correct answer.*

1. Factors of $x^2 - 25$ are:
A. $(x-1)(x-25)$ B. $(x+25)(x-1)$ C. $(x+5)(x-5)$ D. $(x-5)(x-5)$

2. Square of $\left(x-\frac{1}{x}\right)$ will be
A. $x^2-2-\frac{1}{x^2}$ B. $x^2-2+\frac{1}{x^2}$ C. $x^2-4-\frac{1}{x^2}$ D. $x^2-2+\frac{1}{x}$

3. Factors of $36-9x^2$ will be:
A. $(6+3x)(6-3x)$ B. $(3x-6)(6-3x)$ C. $(3x+6)(3x-6)$ D. $(12x-3x)(3+3x)$

4. Factors of $8x^3+y^3$ are:
A. $(2x+y)(4x^2-2xy+y^2)$ B. $(2x+y)(4x^2+2xy+y^2)$
C. $(2x-y)(4x^2-2xy+y^2)$ D. $(2x+y)(4x^2-2xy-y^2)$

5. If the expression x^3+5x^2-2+k is completely divisible by $(x-1)$, the value of k will be:
A. –3 B. –8 C. –3 D. –4

6. Find the factors of $x^2+3x-10$
A. $(x-1)(x-10)$ B. $(x-2)(x+5)$ C. $(x+2)(x-5)$ D. $(x+2)(x+5)$

7. Factors of $(x+y)^3-x-y$ are:
A. $(x-y)[(x-y)^2-1]$ B. $(x-y)[(x+y)^2-1]$
C. $(x+y)[(x+y)^2+1]$ D. $(x-y)[(x+y)^2+1]$

8. Factors of $x^3y^3z^3-27$ are:
A. $(xyz-3)(x^2y^2z^2+3xyz+9)$ B. $(xyz+3)(x^2y^2z^2+3xyz+9)$
C. $(3-xyz)(x^2y^2z^2-3xyz+9)$ D. $(xyz-3)(x^2y^2+y^2z^2+z^2x^2)$

9. If $2x-3=a$, find the value of $8x^3-18ax$
A. a^4+16 B. a^3+27 C. a^3+64 D. a^3+125

10. Factors of $1000+c^3$ are:
A. $(10-c)(100-10c+c^2)$ B. $(10+c)(100+10c+c^2)$
C. $(10+c)(100-10c+c^2)$ D. $(10+c)(100-10c+c^2)$

11. If $x=\sqrt{3}$, the value of $x^4+2+\frac{1}{x^4}$ will be:
A. $\frac{9}{100}$ B. $\frac{81}{100}$ C. $\frac{101}{9}$ D. $\frac{100}{9}$

12. Factors of $4x^2+8x-5$ will be:
A. $(2x-1)(2x+5)$ B. $(2x+1)(2x+5)$ C. $(2x-5)(2x-1)$ D. $(2x+5)(1-2x)$

13. Factors of $a^2+\frac{1}{4}+a$ will be:
A. $\left(a+\frac{1}{2}\right)\left(a-\frac{1}{2}\right)$ B. $\left(a+\frac{1}{2}\right)^2$ C. $\left(a+\frac{1}{2}\right)^3$ D. $\left(a+\frac{1}{2}\right).a$

14. What should be added to $(1 + 8x)$ so that the expression obtained may be a perfect square?

A. $8x^2$ B. $9x^2$ C. $16x^2$ D. $25x^2$

15. If $(x - 2)$ is a factor of $x^2 + 2x - a$, the value of a will be:

A. 8 B. 6 C. 11 D. 3

16. Factors of $x^8 + x^4 - 30$ will be:

A. $(x^4 - 5)(x^4 + 6)$ B. $(x^4 + 5)(x^4 - 6)$ C. $(x^4 + 5)(x^4 + 6)$ D. $(x^4 - 10)(x^4 + 3)$

17. Factors of $xy(z^2 + 1) + z(x^2 + y^2)$ will be:

A. $(zx - y)(yz - x)$ B. $(zx + y)(yz + x)$ C. $(xy + z)(yz + x)$ D. $xyz \times (x + y + z)$

18. The value of $\dfrac{789 \times 789 - 211 \times 211}{789 - 211}$ will be:

A. 981 B. 1100 C. 1000 D. 999

SOLUTIONS

1. $x^2 - 25 = (x)^2 - (5)^2$, [which is of the form $a^2 - b^2$]

$= (x + 5)(x - 5)$.

2. According to question:

Square of $\left(x - \frac{1}{x}\right) = \left(x - \frac{1}{x}\right)^2$

$= x^2 - 2.x.\frac{1}{x} + \left(\frac{1}{x}\right)^2 = x^2 - 2 + \frac{1}{x^2}$.

3. $36 - 9x^2 = (6)^2 - (3x)^2$ [which is of the form $a^2 - b^2$]

$= (6 + 3x)(6 - 3x)$.

4. $8x^3 + y^3 = (2x)^3 + (y)^3$ [which is of the form $a^3 + b^3$]

$= (2x + y)[(2x)^2 - 2x.y + (y)^2]$

$= (2x + y)(4x^2 - 2xy + y^2)$.

5. Since the expression $x^3 + 5x^2 - 2 + k$ is completely divisible by $(x - 1)$

$\therefore$ on substituting $x = 1$ in the given expression, its value will be zero

i.e., $(1)^3 + 5(1)^2 - 2 + k = 0 \Rightarrow 1 + 5 - 2 + k = 0$

$\Rightarrow \quad 4 + k = 0 \Rightarrow k = -4$

Hence value of k is -4.

6. $\because \quad x^2 + 3x - 10 = x^2 + 5x - 2x - 10$

$= x(x + 5) - 2(x + 5) = (x - 2)(x + 5)$

7. $\because \; (x + y)^3 - x - y = (x + y)^3 - (x + y) = (x + y)[(x + y)^2 - 1]$.

8. $\because \quad x^3y^3z^3 - 27 = (xyz)^3 - (3)^3$ [which is of the form $a^3 - b^3$]

$= (xyz - 3)[(xyz)^2 + xyz.3 + (3)^2]$

$= (xyz - 3)(x^2y^2z^2 + 3xyz + 9)$.

9. $\because \quad 2x - 3 = a$

$\Rightarrow \quad 2x = a + 3 \Rightarrow x = \dfrac{a + 3}{2}$

$\because \quad 8x^3 - 18ax = 8.\left(\frac{a+3}{2}\right)^3 - 18a.\left(\frac{a+3}{2}\right) = (a+3)^3 - 9a.(a+3)$

$= a^3 + 3.a.3(a+3) + 3^3 - 9a(a+3)$

$= a^3 + 9a(a+3) + 27 - 9a(a+3) = (a^3 + 27).$

10. $\because \quad 1000 + c^3 = (10)^3 + (c)^3$ [which is of the form $a^3 + b^3$]

$= (10 + c)\,[(10)^2 - 10c + (c)^2]$

$= (10 + c)\,(100 - 10c + c^2).$

11. $\because \quad x^4 + 2 + \frac{1}{x^4} = (x^2)^2 + 2.x^2.\frac{1}{x^2} + \left(\frac{1}{x^2}\right)^2 = \left(x^2 + \frac{1}{x^2}\right)^2$

$\therefore$ On substituting $x = \sqrt{3}$

$= \left((\sqrt{3})^2 + \frac{1}{(\sqrt{3})^2}\right)^2 = \left(3 + \frac{1}{3}\right)^2$

$= \left(\frac{10}{3}\right)^2 = \frac{100}{9}.$

12. $\because \quad 4x^2 + 8x - 5 = 4x^2 + 10x - 2x - 5$

$= 2x(2x + 5) - 1(2x + 5) = (2x - 1)\,(2x + 5).$

13. $\because \quad a^2 + \frac{1}{4} + a = (a)^2 + 2.\frac{1}{2}.a + \left(\frac{1}{2}\right)^2 = \left(a + \frac{1}{2}\right)^2.$

14. A trinomial is a perfect square if two of its terms are perfect squares and the third term is equal to twice the product of the square roots of the other two terms. Hence it is clear that when $16x^2$ is added to $1 + 8x$, the expression obtained is $16x^2 + 8x + 1$, *i.e.*, $(4x)^2 + 2.4x.1 + (1)^2$ which is a perfect square.

15. Since $(x - 2)$ is a factor of $x^2 + 2x - a$

$\therefore$ On substituting $x = 2$ in the expression, the result obtained will be zero

$\therefore \quad (2)^2 + 2.2 - a = 0$

or $\quad 4 + 4 - a = 0$

or $\quad a = 8$

16. $\because \quad x^8 - x^4 - 30 = x^8 - 6x^4 + 5x^4 - 30$

$= x^4(x^4 - 6) + 5\,(x^4 - 6)$

$= (x^4 + 5)\,(x^4 - 6).$

17. $\because \quad xy(z^2 + 1) + z(x^2 + y^2) = xyz^2 + xy + zx^2 + y^2z = (xyz^2 + zx^2) + y^2z + xy$

$= zx(yz + x) + y(yz + x) = (zx + y)\,(yz + x).$

18. Suppose $\quad 789 = a,\ 211 = b$

$\therefore \quad \frac{789 \times 789 - 211 \times 211}{789 - 211} = \frac{a^2 - b^2}{a - b} = \frac{(a+b)(a-b)}{a-b} = a + b$

On substituting the value of a and b

$\therefore \quad a + b = 789 + 211 = 1000.$

27

QUADRATIC EQUATION

Definition: A polynomial equation in which the highest power of the unknown variable is two. The general form of a quadratic equation in the variable x is

$ax^2 + bx + c = 0$

where, a, b and c are constant.

Solution of a Quadratic Equation

Consider the quadratic equation

$ax^2 + bx + c = 0; a \neq 0$

Dividing by a both sides, we get

$$x^2 + \frac{b}{a}x + \frac{c}{a} = 0$$

$$x^2 + 2\frac{b}{2a}x + \left(\frac{b}{2a}\right)^2 - \left(\frac{b}{2a}\right)^2 + \frac{c}{a} = 0$$

or, $$\left(x + \frac{b}{2a}\right)^2 = \frac{b^2}{4a^2} - \frac{c}{a}$$ or, $$\left(x + \frac{b}{2a}\right) = \pm\sqrt{\frac{b^2 - 4ac}{4a^2}}$$

or, $$x = \frac{-b}{2a} \pm \frac{\sqrt{b^2 - 4ac}}{2a}$$ or, $$x = \frac{-b \pm \sqrt{b^2 - 4ac}}{2a}$$

$b^2 - 4ac = \text{D}$ is called discriminant.

(*a*) If D > 0 then there are real and distinct roots given by

$$\alpha = \frac{-b + \sqrt{b^2 - 4ac}}{2a}, \ \beta = \frac{-b - \sqrt{b^2 - 4ac}}{2a}$$

(*b*) If D = 0, there are real and equal roots

$$\alpha = \beta = \frac{-b}{2a}$$

(*c*) If D < 0, there are no real roots.

Sum of the roots, $\alpha + \beta = \frac{-b}{a}$

Product of the roots, $\alpha\beta = \frac{c}{a}$

Expressions of the type $\alpha^2 + \beta^2$, $\alpha^3 + \beta^3$ etc. are called symmetric functions.

$$\alpha^2 + \beta^2 = (\alpha + \beta)^2 - 2\alpha\beta$$

and $$\alpha^3 + \beta^3 = (\alpha + \beta)^3 - 3\alpha\beta(\alpha + \beta).$$

Example 1: The roots of the equation $6x^2 - 5x - 21 = 0$ are

(*a*) $-\frac{7}{3}$ and $-\frac{3}{2}$ (*b*) $\frac{7}{3}$ and $\frac{3}{2}$ (*c*) $\frac{7}{3}$ and $-\frac{3}{2}$ (*d*) $-\frac{7}{3}$ and $\frac{3}{2}$

Solution: $6x^2 - 14x + 9x - 21 = 0$

$\Rightarrow 2x(3x - 7) + 3(3x - 7) = 0 \Rightarrow (3x - 7)(2x + 3) = 0$

$\Rightarrow x = \frac{7}{3},\ x = -\frac{3}{2}$

Example 2: The roots of the quadratic equation $abx^2 + (b^2 - ac)x - bc = 0$ are

(*a*) $\frac{c}{b}, \frac{b}{a}$ (*b*) $\frac{c}{b}, -\frac{b}{a}$ (*c*) $-\frac{c}{b}, \frac{b}{a}$ (*d*) $-\frac{c}{b}, -\frac{b}{a}$

Solution: $abx^2 + b^2x - acx - bc = 0$

$\Rightarrow bx(ax + b) - c(ax + b) = 0$

$\Rightarrow (bx - c)(ax + b) = 0$

$\Rightarrow x = \frac{c}{b}, -\frac{b}{a}$

Example 3: If α and β are the roots of the quadratic equation $3x^2 + 3x + 2 = 0$ then $\alpha^3 + \beta^3 =$ ......

(*a*) $-\frac{1}{3}$ (*b*) -1 (*c*) 1 (*d*) None of the above

Solution: $a = 3,\ b = 3,\ c = 2$

$\Rightarrow \alpha + \beta = -1,\ \alpha\beta = \frac{2}{3}$

$$\alpha^3 + \beta^3 = (-1)^3 - 3 \times \frac{2}{3} \times (-1)$$

$$= -1 + 2 = 1$$

Example 4: If α and β are the roots of the quadratic equation $x^2 - 7x + 3 = 0$ then the equation whose roots are 2α and 2β is

(*a*) $x^2 + 14x + 12 = 0$ (*b*) $x^2 + 14x - 12 = 0$ (*c*) $x^2 - 14x - 12 = 0$ (*d*) $x^2 - 14x + 12 = 0$

Solution: $\alpha + \beta = 7,\ \alpha\beta = 3$

$\alpha' = 2\alpha,\ \beta' = 2\beta$

$s' = \alpha' + \beta' = 2(\alpha + \beta) = 14$

$p' = \alpha'\beta' = 4\alpha\beta = 12$

Required equation : $x^2 - 14x + 12 = 0$

Example 5: The value of p for which the quadratic equation $3x^2 - px + 5 = 0$ has no real roots

(*a*) $p \geq 2\sqrt{15}$ (*b*) $\frac{7}{3}$ $p = \pm 2\sqrt{15}$ (*c*) $p \leq -2\sqrt{15}$ (*d*) None of these

Solution: $a = 3$, $b = -p$, $c = 5$

Equation has no real roots $\Rightarrow D < 0$

$\Rightarrow (-p)^2 - 4 \times 3 \times 5 < 0 \qquad \Rightarrow p^2 < 60$

$\Rightarrow \qquad p^2 < \left(2\sqrt{15}\right)^2 \qquad \Rightarrow \qquad -2\sqrt{15} < p < 2\sqrt{15}$

Example 6: The values of x satisfying the equation $4^x - 5(2^x) + 4 = 0$ are

(*a*) 0 and 2 (*b*) 0 and –2 (*c*) 2 and –2 (*d*) None of these

Solution: $\left(2^x\right)^2 - 5\left(2^x\right) + 4 = 0$

Let $2^x = y$

$\Rightarrow \quad y^2 - 5y + 4 = 0 \qquad \Rightarrow (y - 1)(y - 4) = 0$

$\Rightarrow \quad y = 1, 4 \qquad \Rightarrow \quad 2^x = 1;\ 2^x = 4$

$\Rightarrow \quad 2^x = 2^0;\ 2^x = 2^2 \qquad \Rightarrow \quad x = 0, x = 2$

Example 7: The values of x satisfying the equation $\left(\frac{x}{x+1}\right)^2 - 5\left(\frac{x}{x+1}\right) + 6 = 0$; are

(*a*) $2, \frac{3}{2}$ (*b*) $2, -\frac{3}{2}$ (*c*) $-2, \frac{3}{2}$ (*d*) $-2, -\frac{3}{2}$

Solution: Let, $\frac{x}{x+1} = y$

$\Rightarrow \quad y^2 - 5y + 6 = 0 \qquad \Rightarrow (y - 2)(y - 3) = 0$

$\Rightarrow \quad y = 2, y = 3 \qquad \Rightarrow \quad \frac{x}{x+1} = 2;\ \frac{x}{x+1} = 3$

$\Rightarrow \quad x = 2x + 2;\ x = 3x + 3 \quad \Rightarrow x = -2, x = -\frac{3}{2}$

Example 8: A motor boat whose speed is 15 km/hr in still water goes 40 km downstream and comes back in a total of 6 hours. The speed of the stream is

(*a*) 9 km/hr (*b*) 7 km/hr (*c*) 5 km/hr (*d*) 3 km/hr

Solution: Let speed of the stream be x km/hr.

Speed downstream = $(15 + x)$ km/hr

and speed upstream = $(15 - x)$ km/hr

$$\frac{40}{15+x} + \frac{40}{15-x} = 6$$

$\Rightarrow \quad \frac{40(15-x+15+x)}{(15+x)(15-x)} = 6 \qquad \Rightarrow \qquad 225 - x^2 = 200$

$\Rightarrow \quad x^2 = 25 \qquad \therefore \qquad x = 5$

The speed of the stream = 5 km/hr

Example 9: The length of a rectangle exceeds its breadth by 8 cm and the area of the rectangle is 240 cm^2.

The dimension of the rectangle are

(*a*) 28 cm × 20 cm (*b*) 20 cm × 12 cm (*c*) 16 cm × 24 cm (*d*) None of these

Solution: Let breadth be x cm

$\Rightarrow$ length = $(x + 8)$ cm $\Rightarrow$ $(x + 8)x = 240$

$\Rightarrow$ $x^2 + 8x - 240 = 0$ $\Rightarrow$ $(x + 20)(x - 12) = 0$

$\Rightarrow$ $x = -20, x = 12$

$x = -20$ is impossible

Then, breadth = 12 cm

and length = 20 cm

$\therefore$ dimensions = 20 cm × 12 cm

EXERCISE

1. The equation whose roots are 5, 9 is :
A. $x^2 - 5x + 14 = 0$ B. $x^2 - 14x + 14 = 0$ C. $x^2 - 45x + 14 = 0$ D. $x^2 - 14x + 45 = 0$

2. If α, β be the values of x satisfying the equation $x^2 - px + q = 0$, the value of $\frac{1}{\alpha}+\frac{1}{\beta}$ is :
A. $\frac{q}{p}$ B. $-\frac{p}{q}$ C. $\frac{p}{q}$ D. $\frac{1}{q}$

3. Find the values of 'p' for which the quadratic equation $px^2 + 4x + 1 = 0$ has real roots.
A. $p \le 4$ B. $p \ge 6$ C. $p \ge 4$ D. None of these

4. Determine 'k' such that the quadratic equation $x^2 + 7(3 + 2k) - 2x(1 + 3k) = 0$ has equal roots.
A. 2, –10/9 B. 3, –10/9 C. 2, 10/9 D. None of these

5. For what value of 'k' the equation
$(k + 3)x^2 - (5 - k)x + 1 = 0$ has coincident roots?
A. 1, 13 B. 1, 12 C. 3, 13 D. None of these

6. Find the value of 'k' so that the sum of the roots of equation $3x^2 + (2x + 1)x - k + 5 = 0$ is equal to the product of roots.
A. 4 B. 2 C. 3 D. –6

7. Find the value of 'p' so that equation $4x^2 - 8px + 9 = 0$ has roots whose difference is 4.
A. ±3 B. ±2/5 C. ±5/2 D. None of these

8. Find the value of 'm' so that the equation $9x^2 - 8mx - 9 = 0$ has one root as the negative of the other.
A. 0 B. 1 C. 2 D. None of these

9. If α and β are the roots of $x^2 - 2x - 1 = 0$, find the value of $\alpha^2\beta + \beta^2\alpha$.
A. –3 B. –2 C. 2 D. None of these

10. If a and b are the roots of the equation $x^2 - 5x + 6 = 0$, find the value of $(a^2 - b^2)$.
A. ±3 B. ±5 C. ±4 D. None of these

11. For what values of 'p' for which the quadratic equation $px^2 - 4x + p$ has real linear factors?
A. $-2 \le p < 3$ B. $-2 \le p \le 2$ C. $-2 \ge p \le 2$ D. None of these

12. For what values of 'p' the equation
$(1 + p) x^2 + 2(1 + 2p)x + (1 + p) = 0$ has coincident roots?
A. 2/3, 0 B. –2/3, 0 C. –3/2, 0 D. None of these

13. If a and b are the roots of the quadratic equation $3x^2 + 8x + 2 = 0$, find the value of $a^3 + b^3$.
A. 368/27 B. –368/27 C. –368/24 D. None of these

14. If a and b are the roots of the quadratic equation $6x^2 - x - 2 = 0$, from an equation whose roots are a^2 and b^2?
A. $36x^2 - 25x + 4 = 0$ B. $36x^2 + 25x + 4 = 0$ C. $6x^2 - 25x + 4 = 0$ D. None of these

15. If a and b are the roots of the quadratic equation $2x^2 - 6x + 3 = 0$, find the value of $a^3 + b^3 - 3ab(a^2 + b^2) - 3ab(a + b)$.
A. –27 B. –25 C. 27 D. None of these

16. $z^4 + 3z - 4 = 0$
A. 1 B. ±1 C. –1 D. None of these

17. $x - \sqrt{25 - x^2} = 1$
A. 3 B. 4 C. –4 D. None of these

18. $\sqrt{3x - 5} + \sqrt{x + 2} = 3$
A. 2 B. 1 C. 3 D. None of these

19. If α, β are the roots of a quadratic equation such that $\alpha + \beta = 24$ and $\alpha - \beta = 8$, the quadratic equation is
A. $x^2 - 24x + 128 = 0$ B. $x^2 - 8x + 16 = 0$ C. $x^2 - 24x + 12 = 0$ D. $x^2 - 16x + 20 = 0$

20. If α, β are the roots of a quadratic equation : $x^2 - 3kx + k^2 = 0$, find the values of k if $\alpha^2 + \beta^2 = \frac{7}{4}$.
A. $\pm\frac{1}{3}$ B. $\pm\frac{1}{2}$ C. $\pm\frac{1}{4}$ D. $\pm\frac{1}{5}$

21. Find the value of k so that the sum of the roots of the quadratic equation $kx^2 + 2x + 3k = 0$ is equal to their product.
A. $\frac{2}{3}$ B. $\frac{-2}{3}$ C. $\frac{3}{2}$ D. $\frac{-3}{2}$

22. If α, β are the roots of the quadratic equation $x^2 - 8x + p = 0$, find the value of p if $\alpha^2 + \beta^2 = 40$.
A. 8 B. 10 C. 12 D. 6

23. Find the value of k such that the quadratic equation $x^2 - (k + 6)x + 2(2k - 1) = 0$ has sum of the roots as half of their product.
A. 1 B. 2 C. 3 D. 7

24. If the sum and product of roots of the quadratic equation $ax^2 - 5x + c$ are both equal to 10, find the value of a and c.
A. 2, 3 B. $\frac{1}{3}, 5$ C. $\frac{1}{2}, 5$ D. 3, 5

25. If α and β are the roots of $x^2 + x - 2 = 0$, find the value of $\alpha^{-1} + \beta^{-1}$.
A. 1 B. $\frac{1}{2}$ C. $\frac{1}{3}$ D. 3

SOLUTIONS

1. Roots are 5 and 9

Sum of the roots = 5 + 9 = 14

Product of roots = 5 × 9 = 45

$\therefore$ x^2 – Sum of roots (x) + Product of roots = 0 $\Rightarrow x^2 - 14x + 45 = 0$

2. $\alpha+\beta=p,\ \alpha\beta=q$ $\qquad \therefore \dfrac{1}{\alpha}+\dfrac{1}{\beta}=\dfrac{\alpha+\beta}{\alpha\beta}=\dfrac{p}{q}$

3. For real roots $D \geq 0$

$\Rightarrow (4)^2-4.p.1\geq 0 \Rightarrow 16\geq 4p \Rightarrow 4p\leq 16 \Rightarrow p\leq 4$

4. For equal roots $D=0$

$\Rightarrow [2(1+3k)]^2-4.7(3+2k)=0 \Rightarrow 4(1+6k+9k^2)-28(3+2k)=0 \Rightarrow 1+6k+9k^2-21-14k=0$

$\Rightarrow 9k^2-8k-20=0 \Rightarrow (k-2)(9k+10)=0$

Hence, $k=2, -\dfrac{10}{9}$

5. For coincident roots, $D=0$

Now, $[-(5-k)]^2-4\times(k+3)\times 1=0$

$\Rightarrow 25+k^2-10k-4k-12=0 \Rightarrow k^2-14k+13=0 \Rightarrow (k-13)(k-1)=0$

$\therefore\ k=13, 1$

6. $\alpha+\beta=\alpha\beta$

$$\frac{-(2k+1)}{3}=\frac{-k+5}{3}$$

$$-2k-1=-k+5$$

$$k=-6$$

7. $\alpha+\beta=\dfrac{8p}{4}=2p;\ \ \alpha\beta=\dfrac{9}{4}$

$\alpha+\beta=2p \qquad \alpha-\beta=4$(Given)

Now, $(\alpha-\beta)^2=(\alpha+\beta)^2-4\alpha\beta$

$\Rightarrow (4)^2=(2p)^2-4\times\dfrac{9}{4} \Rightarrow 16=4p^2-9 \Rightarrow 25=4p^2 \Rightarrow p^2=\dfrac{25}{4} \Rightarrow p=\pm\dfrac{5}{2}$

8. Let α, β are roots

$\alpha+\beta=\dfrac{8m}{9}$

But, $\alpha=-\beta$

Thus, $\alpha+\beta=0 \Rightarrow 8m=0 \Rightarrow m=0$

9. Here, $\quad \alpha+\beta=2, \alpha\beta=-1$

Now, $\alpha^2\beta+\alpha\beta^2=\alpha\beta(\alpha+\beta)=-1(2)=-2$

10. Here, $a + b = 5; ab = 6$

$$a^2 - b^2 = (a+b)(a-b) = (a+b)\sqrt{(a+b)^2 - 4ab} = 5.\sqrt{5^2 - 4\times 6} = 5.(\pm 1) = \pm 5$$

11. For real linear factors,

$D \geq 0 \Rightarrow 16 - 4p^2 \geq 0 \Rightarrow p^2 \leq 4$

Thus, $-2 \leq p \leq 2$

12. For coincident roots,

$$D = 0 \Rightarrow \left[2(1+2p)\right]^2 - 4(1+p)^2 = 0 \Rightarrow 1 + 4p^2 + 4p - 1 - p^2 - 2p = 0 \Rightarrow 3p^2 + 2p = 0$$

$$\Rightarrow p(3p+2) = 0 \Rightarrow p = 0, -\frac{2}{3}$$

13. Here, $a + b = \frac{8}{3}$ and $ab = \frac{2}{3}$

$$a^3 + b^3 = (a+b)^3 - 3ab(a+b) = \left(\frac{8}{3}\right)^3 - 3 \times \frac{2}{3} \times \frac{8}{3} = \frac{512}{27} - \frac{16}{3} = \frac{368}{27}$$

14. $a + b = \frac{1}{6}$

$$ab = -\frac{2}{6} = -\frac{1}{3} \Rightarrow a^2b^2 = \frac{1}{9}$$

$$a^2 + b^2 = (a+b)^2 - 2ab = \left(\frac{1}{6}\right)^2 - 2\times -\frac{1}{3} = \frac{1}{36} + \frac{2}{3} = \frac{25}{36}$$

Thus, required equation

$$= x^2 - \frac{25}{36}x + \frac{1}{9} = 0 \Rightarrow 36x^2 - 25x + 4 = 0$$

15. Here, $a + b = 3; ab = \frac{3}{2}$

Now, $a^3 + b^3 - 3ab(a^2 + b^2) - 3ab(a + b) = (a+b)^3 - 3ab(a+b) - 3ab\left[(a+b)^2 - 2ab\right] - 3ab(a+b)$

$$= (3)^3 - 3\times\frac{3}{2}\times 3 - 3\times\frac{3}{2}\left[3^2 - 2\times\frac{3}{2}\right] - 3\times\frac{3}{2}\times 3 = 27 - \frac{27}{2} - \frac{9}{2}\times 6 - \frac{27}{2} = -27$$

16. $z^4 + 3z^2 - 4 = 0$

Let $x = z^2$ or $x^2 + 3x - 4 = 0$ or $(x+4)(x-1) = 0$

$x = -4 \quad x = 1$

Thus, $z^2 = -4$ (Impossible)

So, $z^2 = 1 \Rightarrow z = \pm 1$

17. $x - \sqrt{25 - x^2} = 1 \Rightarrow x - 1 = \sqrt{25 - x^2}$

Squaring both sides,

$$\Rightarrow (x-1)^2 = 25 - x^2 \Rightarrow x^2 + 1 - 2x = 25 - x^2 \Rightarrow 2x^2 - 2x - 24 = 0 \Rightarrow x^2 - x - 12 = 0$$

$$\Rightarrow (x-4)(x+3) = 0 \Rightarrow x = 4, -3$$

18. $\sqrt{3x-5}+\sqrt{x+2}=3$

$\Rightarrow \sqrt{3x-5}=3-\sqrt{x+2} \Rightarrow 3x-5=9+x+2-6\sqrt{x+2} \Rightarrow 2x-16=-6\sqrt{x+2} \Rightarrow x-8=-3\sqrt{x+2}$

$\Rightarrow x^2-16x+64=9(x+2) \Rightarrow x^2-25x+46=0 \Rightarrow (x-23)(x-2)=0 \Rightarrow x=23, 2$

19. $\because$ $\alpha+\beta=24$ ...(*i*)

and $\alpha-\beta=8$ ...(*ii*)

Adding equation (*i*) and (*ii*), we get

$$2\alpha=32 \Rightarrow \alpha=16$$

Subtracting equation (*ii*) from (*i*), we get

$$2\beta=16 \Rightarrow \beta=8$$

$\therefore$ Product of the roots i.e.

$$\alpha.\beta=16\times 8=128$$

We know that the quadratic equation whose roots are α and β is

$$x^2-(\alpha+\beta)x+\alpha.\beta=0 \Rightarrow x^2-24x+128=0$$

which is the required quadratic equation.

20. The given quadratic equation is $x^2-3kx+k^2=0$.

Hence $a=1$, $b=-3k$, $c=k^3$.

$\because$ α, β are the roots of the given quadratic equation:

$\therefore$ $$\alpha+\beta=-\frac{b}{a}=-\frac{-3k}{1}=3k \qquad \alpha.\beta=\frac{c}{a}=\frac{k^2}{1}=k^2$$

$\therefore$ $$(\alpha+\beta)^2=\alpha^2+\beta^2+2\alpha\beta \Rightarrow (3k)^2=\frac{7}{4}+2k^2 \qquad \left[\because \alpha^2+\beta^2=\frac{7}{4}\right]$$

$\Rightarrow$ $$9k^2-2k^2=\frac{7}{4} \Rightarrow 7k^2=\frac{7}{4} \Rightarrow k^2=\frac{1}{4}$$

$\therefore$ $$k=\pm\sqrt{\frac{1}{4}}=\pm\frac{1}{2}.$$

21. $\left.\begin{aligned} kx^2+2x+3k=0 \\ ax^2+bx+c=0 \end{aligned}\right\} \Rightarrow a=k,\ b=2,\ c=3k.$

Sum of roots $=\dfrac{-b}{a}=\dfrac{-2}{k}$

Product of the roots $=\dfrac{c}{a}=\dfrac{3k}{k}$.

Since sum of roots = Product of roots

$\Rightarrow$ $$\frac{-2}{k}=\frac{3k}{k}$$

$$\frac{-2}{k}=\frac{3}{1}$$

$\Rightarrow$ $$3k=-2 \Rightarrow k=\frac{-2}{3}.$$

22. $\because$ α, β are the roots of the quadratic equation

$$x^2 - 8x + p = 0$$

Here $\quad a = 1,\ b = -8,\ c = p$

$$\therefore \quad \alpha + \beta = -\frac{b}{a} = \frac{8}{1} = 8$$

and $\quad \alpha \, . \, \beta = \frac{c}{a} = \frac{p}{1} = p$

Now, $\quad (\alpha + \beta)^2 = \alpha^2 + \beta^2 + 2\alpha.\beta$

$\Rightarrow \quad (8)^2 = 40 + 2p \Rightarrow 64 = 40 + 2p \Rightarrow 2p = 64 - 40 = 24$

$$\therefore \quad p = \frac{24}{2} = 12.$$

23. The given quadratic equation is:

$x^2 - (k + 6)x + 2(2k - 1) = 0$

Here, $a = 1$, $b = -(k + 6)$, $c = 2(2k - 1)$

Sum of the roots $= \dfrac{-b}{a} = k + 6$

Product of the roots $= \dfrac{c}{a} = 2(2k - 1)$

According to the given condition:

Sum of the roots $= \dfrac{1}{2} \times$ Product of the roots

$\Rightarrow \quad k + 6 = \dfrac{1}{2} \times 2(2k - 1) \Rightarrow k + 6 = 2k - 1 \Rightarrow 6 + 1 = 2k - k$

$$k = 7.$$

24. $ax^2 - 5x + c = 0$

Here, $\quad b = -5$

Sum of the roots $= \dfrac{-b}{a} = \dfrac{-(-5)}{a} = \dfrac{5}{a}$

and product of the roots $= \dfrac{c}{a}$

According to the given, we have

$$\frac{5}{a} = 10 \Rightarrow a = \frac{5}{10} = \frac{1}{2} \text{ and } \frac{c}{a} = 10 \Rightarrow c = 10.a = 10 \times \frac{1}{2} = 5$$

Hence, $\quad a = \dfrac{1}{2}$ and $c = 5$.

25. $\quad x^2 + x - 2 = 0$

$\therefore \quad \alpha + \beta = -1,\ \alpha\beta = -2$

$$\alpha^{-1} + \beta^{-1} = \frac{1}{\alpha} + \frac{1}{\beta} = \frac{\beta + \alpha}{\alpha\beta} = \frac{-1}{-2} = \frac{1}{2}.$$

28

LOGARITHMS

Logarithms is a very important tool used for simplification of mathematical calculations and problems involving long multiplications, divisions and powers. It is an equivalent form of expressing an exponential identity.

Definition: The logarithm of any number to a given base is the index of the power to which the base must be raised in order to equal the given number.

If b be any number and p and N two other numbers such that $b^p = N$, then p is called the logarithm of N to the base b and is written as $\log_b N$. Thus the exponential identity $b^p = N$ is equivalent to logarithmic identity $\log_b N = p$.

Exponential	*Logarithmic*
$b^p = n$	$\log_b N = p$
$3^2 = 9$	$\log_3 9 = 2$
$4^{-2} = \frac{1}{16}$	$\log_4\left(\frac{1}{16}\right) = -2$
$4^{-2} = 0.0625$	$\log_4 (0.0625) = -2$
$64^{1/3} = 4$	$\log_{64}(4) = \frac{1}{3}$

Properties of Logarithms:

(i) $a^{\log_a^x} = x;\ a \neq 0, \pm 1, x > 0.$

(ii) $a^{\log_b^x} = x^{\log_b^a}\ ;\ a > 0, b > 0, \neq 1, x > 0.$

(iii) $\log_a a = 1, \log_a 1 = 0;\ a > 0, \neq 1.$

(iv) $\log_a x = \dfrac{1}{\log_x a};\ x, a > 0, \neq 1.$

(v) $\log_a x = \log_b x.\log_a b = \dfrac{\log_b x}{\log_b a};\ a, b > 0, \neq 1, x > 0.$

(vi) For $x, y > 0, a > 0, \neq 1$

(a) $\log_a (x.y) = \log_a x + \log_a y$

(b) $\log_a (x/y) = \log_a x - \log_a y$

(c) $\log_a (x^n) = n \log_a x.$

(vii) For $x > 0, a > 0, \neq 1$

(a) $\log_a n\ (x) = \left(\dfrac{1}{n}\right) \log_a x$ *(b)* $\log_a n\ (x^m) = \left(\dfrac{m}{n}\right) \log_a x$

Example1: Rewrite the following equations in the logarithm form:

(i) $4^{3/2} = 8$, (ii) $5^0 = 1$, (iii) $\left(2\sqrt{2}\right)^{-2/3} = \frac{1}{2}$

Solution: (i) $\log_4 8 = \frac{3}{2}$ (ii) $\log_5 1 = 0$ (iii) $\log_{2\sqrt{2}} \frac{1}{2} = -\frac{2}{3}$

Example 2: Rewrite the following equalities in the exponential form:

(i) $\log_2 32 = 5$, (ii) $\log_{5\sqrt{5}} 5 = \frac{2}{3}$ and (iii) $\log_{100} 0.1 = -\frac{1}{2}$

Solution: (i) $32 = 2^5$, (ii) $5 = \left(5\sqrt{5}\right)^{2/3}$ and (iii) $0.1 = 100^{-1/2}$

Example 3: Using the identity $a \log_a{}^n = n$, find

(i) $3^{-1/2} \log_3{}^9$ (ii) $2^2 . 2^{-\log_2{}^5}$ (iii) $10^{\log 10^m} + \log 10^n$

Solution: (i) $3^{-½} \log_3{}^9 = 3^{\log 3^{9^{-1/2}}} = 9^{-½} = \frac{1}{3}$

(ii) $2^2 . 2^{-\log_2{}^5} = 4.2 \log_2{}^{5^{-1}} = 4.5^{-1} = 4/5$

(iii) $10^{\log 10^m} + \log 10^n = 10^{\log 10^{mn}} = mn$

Example 4: Compute without using tables:

(i) $\log_\pi \tan (0.25\pi)$ (ii) Evaluate $\log (216\sqrt{6})$ to the base 6.

Solution: (i) $\log_\pi \tan (0.25\pi) = \log_\pi \tan\left(\frac{1}{4}\pi\right) = \log_\pi .1 = 0$

(ii) $\log_6 216\sqrt{6} = \log_6 6^{7/2} = 7/2$.

Example 5: Compute $\log_{30} 8$ if $\log_{30} 3 = a$ and $\log_{30} 5 = b$.

Solution: $\log_{30} 8 = 3 \log_{30} 2 = 3\log_{30} \frac{30}{15} = 3[1 - \log_{30} 3 - \log_{30} 5] = 3(1 - a - b)$

Example 6: Simplify $7 \log \frac{16}{15} + 5 \log \frac{25}{24} + 3 \log \frac{81}{80}$

Solution: Given expression= $7\log\left(\frac{2^4}{3\times 5}\right) + 5\log\left(\frac{5^2}{3\times 2^3}\right) + 3\log\left(\frac{3^4}{5\times 2^4}\right)$

$= 7 [4 \log 2 - \log 3 - \log 5] + 5 [2 \log 5 - \log 3 - 3 \log 2] + 3 [4 \log 3 - \log 5 - 4 \log 2] = \log 2$

Example 7: Find the least integer n such that $7^n > 10^5$, given that $\log_{10} 343 = 2.5353$.

Solution: $\log_{10} 343 = \log 7^3 = 3 \log 7 = 2.5353$. $\therefore \log 7 = \frac{1}{3}(2.5353) = 0.8451$. Now $7^n > 10^5$

If $n \log 7 > 5 \log_{10} 10 \Rightarrow n. 0.8451 > 5 \Rightarrow n > \frac{5}{0.8451}$ Hence, $n > 6$

Clearly, there can be infinite values of n satisfying the above inequality but there is only one least value of n which is clearly 6.

Example 8: Determine b satisfying $\log_{\sqrt{8}} b = 3\frac{1}{3}$.

Solution: Here, $b = (\sqrt{8})^{10/3} = (2^{3/2})^{10/3} = 2^5 = 32$.

Example 9: Prove that $|\log_b a + \log_a b| \geq 2$ where a and b are positive numbers not unity.

Solution: Since, $a \neq 1$, $b \neq 1$, $a > 0$, $b > 0$, $\log_b a$ and $\log_a b$ are both positive or both negative.
Hence,
$|\log_b a + \log_a b| = |\log_b a| + |\log_a b|$ ...(1)
Since A.M. of two positive quantities is greater than their G.M.,

we get, $\dfrac{|\log_b a| + |\log_a b|}{2} > \sqrt{\log_b a \log_a b} = 1,$ ...(2)

Hence, from (1) and (2) we obtain $|\log_b a + \log_a b| > 2$.

Example 10: Prove that $\log_{10} 2$ lies between $\frac{1}{4}$ and $\frac{1}{3}$.

Solution: $\log_{10} 2 > \frac{1}{4}$ if $2 > 10^{1/4}$.

that is, $\log_{10} 2 > \frac{1}{4}$ if $2^4 > 10$, which is true.

Again, $\log_{10} 2 < \frac{1}{3}$ if $2 < 10^{1/3}$, *i.e.* if $2^3 < 10$, which is again true. Hence, $\frac{1}{4} < \log_{10} 2 < \frac{1}{3}$.

Example 11: Prove that $\log_2 3$ is an irrational number.

Solution: Suppose, if possible, that $\log_2 3$ is rational.

So we assume, $\log_2 3 = \dfrac{p}{q}$

where p and q are positive integers having no factor in common.
Then $3 = 2^{p/q} \Rightarrow 3^q = 2^p$.
which is impossible since 3^q is odd and 2^p is even. Hence, $\log_2 3$ cannot be rational, that is, it is irrational.

Example 12: Given that $\log_l x$, $\log_m x$ and $\log_n x$ are in arithmetic progression, Note that $x \neq 1$. Then prove that $n^2 = (ln)^{\log_l m}$

Solution: Taking reciprocals, we get $\log_x l$, $\log_x m$, $\log_x n$ are in H.P.

$\therefore \log_x m = \dfrac{2\log_x l \log_x n}{\log_x l + \log_x n} \Rightarrow \log_x m/\log_x l = \log_x n^2/\log_x ln$

Writing the above in exponential form, we get $n^2 = (ln) \log_l^m$

Example 13: If $n = 1983!$, complete the sum $\dfrac{1}{\log_2 n} + \dfrac{1}{\log_3 n} + \dfrac{1}{\log_4 n} + ... + \dfrac{1}{\log_{1983} n}$

Solution: Since, $\log_b a = \dfrac{1}{\log_a b}$, the expression

$= \log_n 2 + \log_n 3 + \log_n 4 + ... + \log_n 1983$

$= \log_n (2.3.4 ..... 1983) = \log_n 1983!$

$= \log_n n = 1.$ [$\because$ 1983! = n]

Example 14: If $\dfrac{\log a}{b-c} = \dfrac{\log b}{c-a} = \dfrac{\log c}{a-b}$, prove that $a^a.b^b.c^c = 1$.

Solution: Let $\dfrac{\log a}{b-c} = \dfrac{\log b}{c-a} = \dfrac{\log c}{a-b} = k$.

Then $\log a = k(b-c)$,

$\log b = k(c-a)$ and $\log c = k(a-b)$.

Now $a \log a + b \log b + c \log c = a.k(b-c) + b.k(c-a) + c.\,k(a-b) = 0$

$\therefore \log a^a b^b c^c = 0 \Rightarrow a^a b^b c^c = 1$.

Note that here it is understood that $a > 0, b > 0, c > 0$ and $a \neq 1, b \neq 1, c \neq 1$.

Example 15: If n is a natural number such that $n = p_1^{a_1}, p_2^{a_2}, p_3^{a_3}, \ldots\ldots p_k^{a_k}$ and $p_1, p_2, \ldots\ldots p_k$ are distinct primes, then show that $\log_n \geq k \log 2$.

Solution: Since, n is a natural number and p_i's are primes, it follows that a_i's are also natural numbers.

Taking logarithms of both sides of given relation, we get $\log n = \sum_{i=1}^{k} a_i \log p_i \geq \sum_{i=1}^{k} a_i \log 2 \geq$ $k \log 2$, since each $a \geq 1$.

Example 16: If $a^2 + b^2 = 7ab$, prove that $\log \frac{1}{3}(a+b) = \frac{1}{2}[\log a + \log b]$.

Solution: From $a^2 + b^2 = 7ab$, we have $(a+b)^2 = 9ab$. $\Rightarrow \left(\dfrac{a+b}{3}\right)^2 = ab$.

Taking logarithms of both sides, we get, $\log \frac{1}{3}(a+b) = \frac{1}{2}[\log a + \log b]$

Example 17: Prove that identity $\log_a n \log_b n + \log_b n \log_c n + \log_c n \log_a n = \log_a n \log_b n \log_c n / \log_{abc} n$.

Solution: L.H.S. $= \dfrac{1}{\log_n a \log_n b} + \dfrac{1}{\log_n b \log_n c} + \dfrac{1}{\log_n c \log_n a} = \dfrac{\log_n c + \log_n a + \log_n b}{\log_n a \log_n b \log_n c}$

$= \dfrac{\log_n abc}{\log_n a \log_n b \log_n c} = \dfrac{\log_a n \log_b n \log_c n}{\log_{abc} n} =$ R.H.S.

Example 18: If $a > 0, c > 0, b = \sqrt{ac}, a \neq 1, c \neq 1, ac \neq 1$ and $n > 0$, Prove that $\dfrac{\log_a n}{\log_c n} = \dfrac{\log_a n - \log_b n}{\log_b n - \log_c n}$

Solution: R.H.S. $= \dfrac{(1/\log_n a) - (1/\log_n b)}{(1/\log_n b) - (1/\log_n c)} = \dfrac{\log_n b - \log_n a}{\log_n c - \log_n b} \cdot \dfrac{\log_n c}{\log_n a} = \dfrac{\log_n (b/a)}{\log_n (c/b)} \cdot \dfrac{\log_n c}{\log_n a} = \dfrac{\log_n c}{\log_n a} = \dfrac{\log_a n}{\log_c n}$

$[\because b = \sqrt{ac} \Rightarrow b^2 = ac \Rightarrow b/a = c/b]$

Example 19: Solve the following equations for real roots:

(a) $\dfrac{2^{x^2}}{2^{2x}} - 8 = 0$

(b) $3^{2x} - 3^{x+1} - 3^{x-1} + 1 = 0$.

Solution: *(a)* The given equation can be written as $\dfrac{2^{x^2}}{2^{2x}} = 8$ $\Rightarrow 2^{x^2 - 2x} = 2^3$

Hence, $x^2 - 2x = 3 \quad \Rightarrow x^2 - 2x - 3 = 0 \quad \Rightarrow (x-3)(x+1) = 0; \quad \therefore x = 3, -1$.

(b) $3^{2x} - 3^{x+1} - 3^{x-1} + 1 = 0$ $\Rightarrow 3^{2x} - 3.3^x - \frac{3^x}{3} + 1 = 0 \Rightarrow 3.3^{2x} - 10.3^x + 3 = 0$

Let $3^x = a$; then

$3a^2 - 10a + 3 = 0$; On solving we get $a = 3$ or, $\frac{1}{3}$ Since, $3^x = 3$ $\therefore x = 1$; If $3^x = \frac{1}{3}$ $\therefore$

$x = -1$

Hence, $x = \pm 1$

Example 20: Solve $\log_x (3x^2 + 10x) = 3$.

Solution: The domain of x is $x > 0$, $x \neq 1$. The given equation is equivalent to $\Rightarrow 3x^2 + 10x = x^3$

$\Rightarrow x^3 - 3x^2 - 10x = 0$ $\Rightarrow x(x - 5)(x + 2) = 0$

Since, $x = 0$ and $x = -2$ do not lie in the domain of x, the only solution of the given equation is $x = 5$.

Example 21: Prove that $\log_{10}\left[98 + \sqrt{x^3 - x^2 - 12x + 36}\right] = 2$.

Solution: The equation can be written as $\left[98 + \sqrt{x^3 - x^2 - 12x + 36}\right] = 10^2 = 100$

$\Rightarrow \sqrt{x^3 - x^2 - 12x + 36} = 2 \Rightarrow x^3 - x^2 - 12x + 36 = 4$

$\Rightarrow x^3 - x^2 - 12x + 32 = 0 \Rightarrow x^2(x + 4) - 5x(x + 4) + 8(x + 4) = 0$

$\Rightarrow (x + 4)(x^2 - 5x + 8) = 0$ $\therefore x = -4$.

$$\Rightarrow x = \frac{5 \pm \sqrt{25 - 32}}{2} = \frac{5 \pm \sqrt{-7}}{2}$$

If we consider only real roots, then the only solution is $x = -4$.

Example 22: For $a > 0$, solve for x the equations $2\log_x a + \log_{ax} a + 3\log_{a^2 x} a = 0$.

Solution: The given equation can be written as $\frac{2}{\log_a x} + \frac{1}{\log_a a + \log_a x} + \frac{3}{2\log_a a + \log_a x} = 0$.

Now put $\log_a x = y$. Then $\frac{2}{y} + \frac{1}{1+y} + \frac{3}{2+y} = 0$

$\Rightarrow 2(1 + y)(2 + y) + y(2 + y) + 3y(1 + y) = 0$ $\Rightarrow 6y^2 + 11y + 4 = 0$

$\Rightarrow 6y^2 + 8y + 3y + 4 = 0$ $\Rightarrow (3y + 4)(2y + 1) = 0$, $\therefore y = -\frac{4}{3}$ or, $-\frac{1}{2}$.

Hence, $\log_a x = -\frac{4}{3}$ or $-\frac{1}{2}$ $\therefore x = a^{-4/3}$ or $a^{-1/2}$.

Example 23: Prove that $4^{\log_9 3} + 9^{\log_2 4} = 10^{\log_x 83}$

Solution: Since, $\log_9 3 = \log_{3^2} 3 = \frac{1}{2}$,

$\log_2 4 = \log_2 2^2 = 2$ and $\log_x 83 = \log_{10} 83 \log_x 10$.

The equation can be written as $4^{1/2} + 9^2 = 10^{\log_{10} 83 \log_x 10}$

$\Rightarrow 83 = \left(10^{\log_{10} 83}\right)^{\log_x 10}$ $\Rightarrow 83 = 83^{\log_x 10}$

Hence, $\log_x 10 = 1$ when $x = 10$.

Example 24: Prove that $\log_{10}(x^2 - x - 6) - x = \log_{10}(x + 2) - 4$.

Solution. The equation can be written as $\log_{10}\left(\frac{x^2 - x - 6}{x+2}\right) = x - 4$

$\Rightarrow \log_{10}\frac{(x-3)(x+2)}{(x+2)} = x - 4 \Rightarrow \log_{10}(x - 3) = x - 4 \qquad \Rightarrow x - 3 = 10^{(x-4)}$ ...(1)

By trial, $x = 4$ is the solution of (1) which is therefore the solution of the given equation. Observe that $x > 4$ or $x < 4$ does not satisfy (1). Hence, $x = 4$ is the only solution of the original equation.

Example 25: Solve $\log_{16} x + \log_4 x + \log_2 x = 7$.

Sol. The given equation can be re-written as $\log_{2^4} x + \log_{2^2} x + \log_2 x = 7$

$\Rightarrow \frac{1}{4}\log_2 x + \frac{1}{2}\log_2 x + \log_2 x = 7 \Rightarrow \frac{7}{4}\log_2 x = 7 \qquad \Rightarrow \log_2 x = 4.$

Hence, $x = 2^4 = 16$.

Example 26: Solve $4^x - 3^{x-1/2} = 3^{x+1/2} - 2^{2x-1}$.

Solution The given equation can be re-written as $2^{2x} + 2^{2x-1} = 3^{x-1/2} + 3^{x+1/2}$

$\Rightarrow \quad 2^{2x}\left(1+\frac{1}{2}\right) = 3^x\left(\frac{1}{\sqrt{(3)}}+\sqrt{3}\right)$

$\Rightarrow 3.2^{2x-1} = 4.3^{x-1/2} \qquad \Rightarrow 2^{2x-3} = 3^{x-3/2}$

Now by trial, $x = 3/2$ is one solution.

Now taking logarithm to the base 10, we get $(2x - 3)\log_{10}2 = \left(x-\frac{3}{2}\right)\log_{10}3$

$\Rightarrow \quad (2\log 2 - \log 3)\,.\,x = \frac{3}{2}(2\log 2 - \log 3).$ This also gives $x = 3/2$.

Hence, $x = 3/2$ is the only solution.

Example 27: If $\log 2 = 0.30103$, $\log 3 = 0.4771213$, $\log 7 = 0.8450980$, then solve $21^x = 2^{2x+1}.\,5^x$

Solution: We write the given equation as $(7 \times 3)^x = 2^{2x+1}.\,(10/2)^x$

Taking logarithm of both sides, we have

$x(\log 7 + \log 3) = (2x + 1)\log 2 + x(\log 10 - \log 2)$

$\Rightarrow x[\log 7 + \log 3 - 2\log 2 - \log 10 + \log 2] = \log 2$

$\Rightarrow x[\log 7 + \log 3 - \log 2 - 1] = \log 2$

$\Rightarrow x[0.8450980 + 0.4771213 - 0.3010300 - 1] = 0.30103$

$\Rightarrow x(0.0211893) = 0.30103 \therefore x = 14.207$ (approx.)

Example 28: Solve $3^x 5^y = 75$, $3^y 5^x = 45$.

Solution: Dividing the given equations, we get $3^{x-y}.\,5^{y-x} = \frac{75}{45} \Rightarrow \left(\frac{3}{5}\right)^{x-y} = \left(\frac{3}{5}\right)^{-1}$.

Hence, $x - y = -1$ ...(1)

Again multiplying the equations, we get $(3^x \times 5^x)(3^y \times 5^y) = 75 \times 45 \Rightarrow 15^{x+y} = 15^3$

Hence, $x + y = 3$ ...(2)

Solving (1) and (2), we get $x = 1, y = 2$

By trial method $x = 1, y = 2$ satisfy both the equations.

Example 29: Solve $\log_y x + \log_x y = 2$, $x^2 + y = 12$.

Solution: The first equation can be written as $\log_y x + \dfrac{1}{\log_y x} = 2$

$\Rightarrow (\log_y x)^2 - 2\log_y x + 1 = 0 \Rightarrow (\log_y x - 1)^2 = 0$ *i.e.* $\log_y x = 1$

This gives $x = y$ $(x > 0, y > 0, x \neq 1)$.

Then second given equation gives $x^2 + x - 12 = 0$ $\Rightarrow (x + 4)(x - 3) = 0$.

Since, $x = -4$ is not in the domain of x, the only solution is $x = y = 3$.

Example 30: Solve $2^{x+y} = 6^y$, $3^x = 3.2^{y+1}$

Solution: Taking log, we have $(x + y)\log 2 = y(\log 2 + \log 3)$,

$\therefore x \log 2 = y \log 3$ ...(1)

$x \log 3 = \log 3 + (y + 1)\log 2$ ...(2)

Now solve for x and y.

$$x = \frac{\log_{10} 3}{\log_{10} 3 - \log_{10} 2},\ y = \frac{\log_{10} 2}{\log_{10} 3 - \log_{10} 2}.$$

EXERCISE

1. $\log_5 5 \log_4 9 \log_3 2$ simplifies to:
   (a) 2 (b) 1 (c) 5 (d) None of these
2. $\log_3 11.\log_{11} 13.\log_{13} 15.\log_{15} 27 = ?$
   (a) 1 (b) 2 (c) 3 (d) None of these
3. $\log_{2\sqrt{2}} 512 = ?$
   (a) 4 (b) 5 (c) 6 (d) 7
4. If $A = \log_2 \log_2 \log_4 256 + 2\log_{\sqrt{2}} 2$, then A equals:
   (a) 2 (b) 3 (c) 5 (d) 7
5. $25^{(1/2 + \log_{1/5} 27 + \log_{125} 81)} = ?$
   (a) 0 (b) 1 (c) 10/81 (d) $5\sqrt[3]{9}/81$
6. The domain of the function $\sqrt{(\log_{0.5} x)}$ is:
   (a) $(1, \infty)$ (b) $(0, \infty)$ (c) $(0, 1)$ (d) $(0.5, 1)$
7. If $\log_{10} 3 = 0.477$, the no. of digits in 3^{40} is:
   (a) 18 (b) 19 (c) 20 (d) 21
8. If $a^x = b$, $b^y = c$, $c^z = a$, then value of xyz is:
   (a) 0 (b) 1 (c) 2 (d) 3
9. $7\log(16/15) + 5\log(25/24) + 3\log(81/80) = ?$
   (a) 0 (b) 1 (c) log 2 (d) log 3
10. If $\log_{16} x + \log_4 x + \log_2 x = 14$, then $x = ?$
    (a) 16 (b) 32 (c) 64 (d) None of these
11. If $N = m!$ (m is a fixed positive integer > 2), then $\dfrac{1}{\log_2 N} + \dfrac{1}{\log_3 N} + \ldots\ldots\ldots + \dfrac{1}{\log_m N}$ is equal to:
    (a) –1 (b) 0 (c) 1 (d) 2

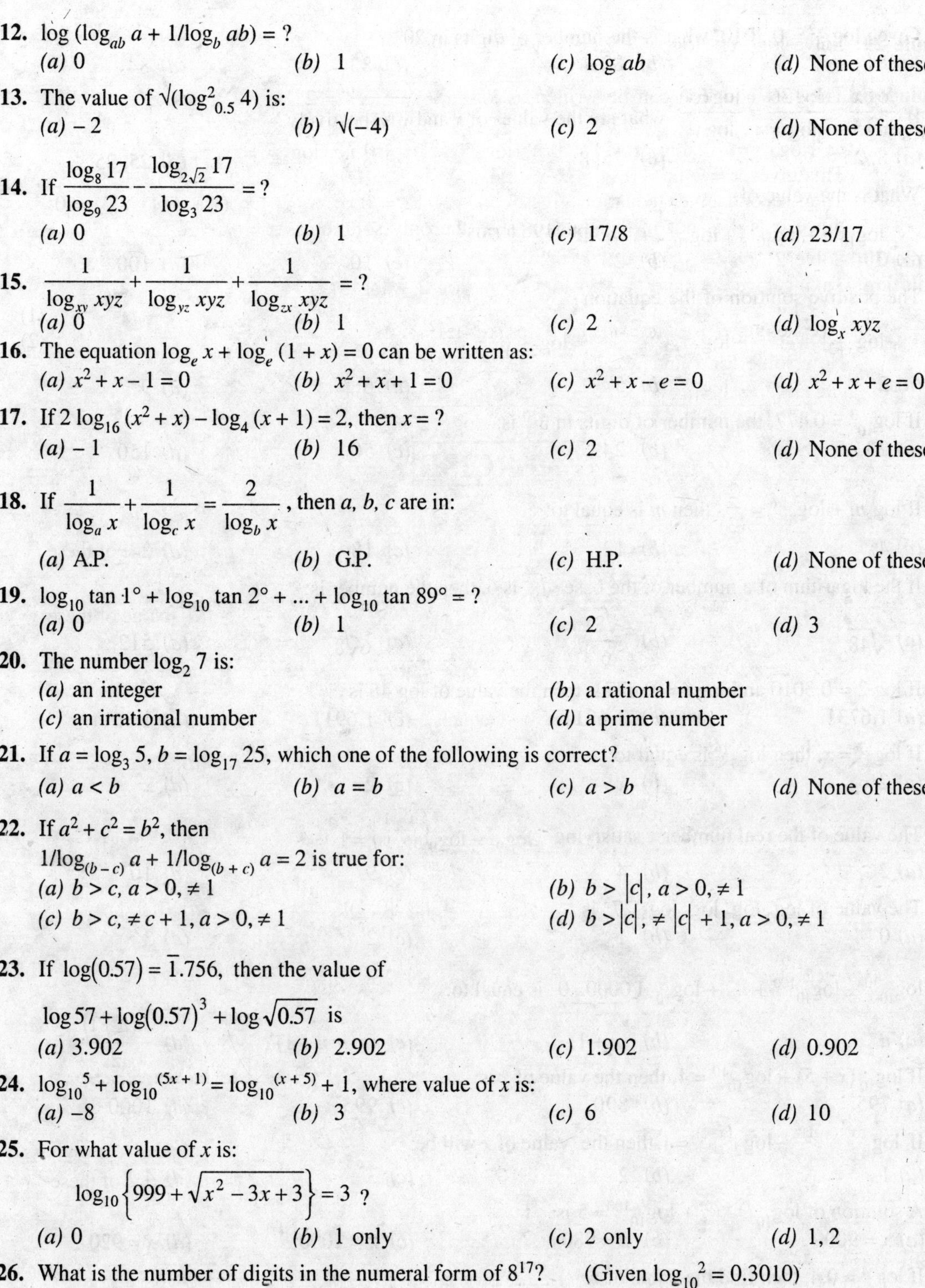

12. $\log(\log_{ab} a + 1/\log_b ab) = ?$

(a) 0 (b) 1 (c) $\log ab$ (d) None of these

13. The value of $\sqrt{(\log^2_{0.5} 4)}$ is:

(a) -2 (b) $\sqrt{(-4)}$ (c) 2 (d) None of these

14. If $\dfrac{\log_8 17}{\log_9 23} - \dfrac{\log_{2\sqrt{2}} 17}{\log_3 23} = ?$

(a) 0 (b) 1 (c) 17/8 (d) 23/17

15. $\dfrac{1}{\log_{xy} xyz} + \dfrac{1}{\log_{yz} xyz} + \dfrac{1}{\log_{zx} xyz} = ?$

(a) 0 (b) 1 (c) 2 (d) $\log_x xyz$

16. The equation $\log_e x + \log_e (1 + x) = 0$ can be written as:

(a) $x^2 + x - 1 = 0$ (b) $x^2 + x + 1 = 0$ (c) $x^2 + x - e = 0$ (d) $x^2 + x + e = 0$

17. If $2 \log_{16} (x^2 + x) - \log_4 (x + 1) = 2$, then $x = ?$

(a) -1 (b) 16 (c) 2 (d) None of these

18. If $\dfrac{1}{\log_a x} + \dfrac{1}{\log_c x} = \dfrac{2}{\log_b x}$, then a, b, c are in:

(a) A.P. (b) G.P. (c) H.P. (d) None of these

19. $\log_{10} \tan 1° + \log_{10} \tan 2° + ... + \log_{10} \tan 89° = ?$

(a) 0 (b) 1 (c) 2 (d) 3

20. The number $\log_2 7$ is:

(a) an integer (b) a rational number
(c) an irrational number (d) a prime number

21. If $a = \log_3 5$, $b = \log_{17} 25$, which one of the following is correct?

(a) $a < b$ (b) $a = b$ (c) $a > b$ (d) None of these

22. If $a^2 + c^2 = b^2$, then
$1/\log_{(b-c)} a + 1/\log_{(b+c)} a = 2$ is true for:

(a) $b > c, a > 0, \neq 1$ (b) $b > |c|, a > 0, \neq 1$
(c) $b > c, \neq c + 1, a > 0, \neq 1$ (d) $b > |c|, \neq |c| + 1, a > 0, \neq 1$

23. If $\log(0.57) = \bar{1}.756$, then the value of

$\log 57 + \log(0.57)^3 + \log\sqrt{0.57}$ is

(a) 3.902 (b) 2.902 (c) 1.902 (d) 0.902

24. $\log_{10}{}^5 + \log_{10}{}^{(5x+1)} = \log_{10}{}^{(x+5)} + 1$, where value of x is:

(a) -8 (b) 3 (c) 6 (d) 10

25. For what value of x is:

$$\log_{10}\left\{999 + \sqrt{x^2 - 3x + 3}\right\} = 3 \ ?$$

(a) 0 (b) 1 only (c) 2 only (d) 1, 2

26. What is the number of digits in the numeral form of 8^{17}? (Given $\log_{10}{}^2 = 0.3010$)

(a) 14 (b) 15 (c) 16 (d) 51

27. Given $\log_{10}{}^{2} = 0.3010$, what is the number of digits in 20^{64}?
(a) 81 (b) 82 (c) 83 (d) 84

28. If $\frac{\log x}{\log 5} = \frac{\log 36}{\log 6} = \frac{\log 64}{\log y}$; what are the values of x and y respectively?
(a) 8, 25 (b) 25, 8 (c) 8, 8 (d) 25, 25

29. What is the value of:
$\log_{10}{}^{1\frac{1}{2}} + \log_{10}{}^{1\frac{1}{3}} + \log_{10}{}^{1\frac{1}{4}} + \ldots..$ upto 198 terms?
(a) 0 (b) 2 (c) 10 (d) 100

30. The positive solution of the equation
$\log_{x+3}{}^{(x^2+6x+9)} + \log_{5x+2}{}^{(6x^2-6x)} = \log_{2x-1}{}^{(8x^3-12x^2+6x-1)}$ is
(a) 2 (b) 5 (c) 6 (d) 9

31. If $\log_{10}{}^{3} = 0.477$, the number of digits in 3^{50} is:
(a) 23 (b) 24 (c) 50 (d) 150

32. If $\log_8 m + \log_8{}^{1/6} = \frac{2}{3}$; then m is equal to:
(a) 4 (b) 12 (c) 18 (d) 24

33. If the logarithm of a number of the base $\sqrt{8}$ is 6, then the number is:
(a) $\sqrt{48}$ (b) $\frac{\sqrt{8}}{6}$ (c) $6\sqrt{8}$ (d) 512

34. If log 2 = 0.3010 and log 3 = 0.4771, then the value of log 48 is
(a) 1.6731 (b) 1.6811 (c) 1.6911 (d) 1.8611

35. If $\log_4{}^{7} = x$, then $\log_7{}^{16}$ is equal to:
(a) $2/x$ (b) x (c) $2x$ (d) x^2

36. The value of the real number x satisfying $\log_9{}^{x} - \log_9\left(\frac{x}{10}+\frac{1}{9}\right) = 1$ is:
(a) 2 (b) 4 (c) 9 (d) 10

37. The value of $\log_2 \log_2 \log_3 \log_3 27^3$ is
(a) 0 (b) 1 (c) 2 (d) 3

38. $\log_{10}{}^{10} + \log_{10}{}^{100} + \ldots. + \log_{10} 1\underbrace{0000\ldots0}_{n}$ is equal to:
(a) n (b) $(n+1)$ (c) (n^2+n+1) (d) $\frac{n(n+1)}{2}$

39. If $\log_{10}(x+5) + \log_{10}{}^{10} = 4$, then the value of x is:
(a) 795 (b) 890 (c) 995 (d) 1000

40. If $\log_4{}^{x^2(x-1)^2} - \log_2{}^{(x-1)} = 1$, then the value of x will be:
(a) 1 (b) 2 (c) 3 (d) 4

41. A solution of $\log_{10}{}^{(x+20)} + \log_{10}{}^{100} = 5$ is:
(a) $x = 900$ (b) $x = 980$ (c) $x = 1000$ (d) $x = 920$

42. If $\log_x{}^{4} = 0.4$, then find the value of x.
(a) 4 (b) 16 (c) 32 (d) 64

43. If $\log_x{}^y = 100$ and $\log_2 x = 10$, then find the value of y.

(a) 2^{100} (b) 2^{1000} (c) 2^{10000} (d) 2^{100000}

44. Find the value of $\dfrac{\log\sqrt{8}}{\log 8}$.

(a) $\dfrac{1}{2}$ (b) $\dfrac{1}{4}$ (c) $\dfrac{1}{2\sqrt{2}}$ (d) $\dfrac{1}{8}$

45. If $a^x = b^y$, then

(a) $\dfrac{\log a}{\log b} = \dfrac{x}{y}$ (b) $\dfrac{\log a}{\log b} = \dfrac{y}{x}$ (c) $\log\dfrac{a}{b} = \dfrac{x}{y}$ (d) None of these

46. $2\log_{10}5 + \log_{10}8 - \dfrac{1}{2}\log_{10}{}^4 = ?$

(a) 1 (b) 2 (c) 3 (d) 4

47. If $\log 2 = x$; $\log 3 = y$ and $\log 7 = z$, then find the value of $\log\left(4.\sqrt[3]{63}\right)$.

(a) $2x+\dfrac{2}{3}y+\dfrac{1}{3}z$ (b) $2x-\dfrac{2}{3}y+\dfrac{1}{3}z$ (c) $2x-\dfrac{2}{3}y-\dfrac{1}{3}z$ (d) $-2x+\dfrac{2}{3}y+\dfrac{1}{3}z$

48. If $\log a^{(ab)} = x$, then the value of $\log_b(ab)$ is:

(a) $\dfrac{x}{x-1}$ (b) $\dfrac{x}{x+1}$ (c) $\dfrac{x}{1-x}$ (d) $\dfrac{1}{x}$

49. If $\log_{12}{}^{27} = a$, then the value of $\log_6{}^{16}$ is:

(a) $\dfrac{3+a}{4(3-a)}$ (b) $\dfrac{3-a}{4(3+a)}$ (c) $\dfrac{4(3+a)}{(3-a)}$ (d) $\dfrac{4(3-a)}{(3+a)}$

50. If $\log_{10}{}^2 = 0.3010$, then find the value of $\log_2{}^{10}$.

(a) $\dfrac{301}{1000}$ (b) $\dfrac{1000}{301}$ (c) $\dfrac{301}{100}$ (d) $\dfrac{100}{301}$

51. If $\log_{10}{}^7 = a$, then find the value of $\log_{10}\left(\dfrac{1}{70}\right)$.

(a) $-(a+1)$ (b) $(a+1)$ (c) $(a-1)$ (d) $(1-a)$

52. If $\log 27 = 1.431$, then find the value of $\log 9$.

(a) 0.958 (b) 0.954
(c) 0.945 (d) 0.948

53. If $\log_{10}{}^2 = 0.3010$, then find the value of $\log_{10}{}^5$.

(a) 0.5990 (b) 0.6990
(c) 0.7090 (d) 0.7290

54. If $\log_2 = 0.3010$, then find the value of $\log_5{}^{512}$.

(a) 1.876 (b) 2.876
(c) 3.876 (d) 4.876

55. If $\log_{10}{}^2 = 0.3010$, then find the value of $\log_{10}{}^{80}$.

(a) 0.9030 (b) 1.9030 (c) 2.9030 (d) 3.9030

56. If $\log_{10}{}^2 = 0.3010$ and $\log_{10}{}^7 = 0.8451$, then find the value of $\log_{10}{}^{2.8}$.

(a) 0.4471 (b) 1.4471 (c) 2.4471 (d) 3.4471

SOLUTIONS

1. : Given expression $= 1.\log_{2^2} 3^2.\log_3 2$

$= \frac{2}{2}\log_2 3.1/(\log_2 3) = 1.$

2. : Given expression $= \log_3 27 = \log_3 3^3$

$= 3 \log_3 3 = 3.$

3. : $\log_{2\sqrt{2}} 512 = \log_{2^{3/2}} 2^9$

$= \{9/(3/2)\} \log_2 2 = 6.$

4. : $A = \log_2 \log_2 \log_4 4^4 + 2 \log_{2^{1/2}} 2$

$= \log_2 \log_2 4 + 2/(1/2) \log_2 2$

$= \log_2 \log_2 2^2 + 4 = \log_2 2 + 4 = 5.$

5. : Given expression

$= 5^{2\left(1/2+\log_{5^{-1}} 3^3+\log_{5^3} 3^4\right)}$

$= 5^{\left[1+2.\{3/(-1)\}\log_5 3+2(4/3)\log_5 3\right]}$

$= 5^{\left[\log_5 5+\log_5 3^{-6}+\log_5 3^{8/3}\right]}$

$= 5^{\log_5 5.3^{8/3}/3^6} = 5.3^{2/3}/3^4 = 5\sqrt[3]{9}/81$

6. : The function will be real if $\log_{0.5} x \geq 0$

i.e., if $0 < x \leq 1 \because$ base $= 0.5 < 1$

$\Rightarrow x \in (0, 1)$

7. : Let $x = 3^{40}$

$\therefore \log x = 40 \log_{10} 3$

$= 40 \times (0.477) = 19.08$

Hence the number of digits in x is 20.

8. : $a = c^z = (b^y)^z = b^{yz} = (a^x)^{yz}$

$= a^{xyz} \Rightarrow xyz = 1.$

9. : Given expression

$= 7(4 \log 2 - \log 3 - \log 5) + 5(2 \log 5 - \log 3 - 3 \log 2)$

$+ 3(4 \log 3 - 4 \log 2 - \log 5) = \log 2.$

10. : $\log_{16} x + \log_4 x + \log_2 x$

$= \log_{2^4} x + \log_{2^2} x + \log_2 x$

$= \frac{1}{4}\log_2 x + \frac{1}{2}\log_2 x + \log_2 x$

$= \frac{7}{4}\log_2 x = 14$

$\therefore \log_2 x = 8$

i.e., $x = 2^8 = 256.$

11. : Given expression

$= \log_N 2 + \log_N 3 + ... + \log_N m$

$= \log_N (2.3. ... m) = \log_N m!$

$= \log_{m!} m! = 1.$

12. : Given expression

$= \log(\log_{ab} a + \log_{ab} b)$

$= \log(\log_{ab} ab) = \log 1 = 0.$

13. : $\log_{0.5} 4 = \log_{2^{-1}} 2^2$

$= \{2/(-1)\}. \log_2 2 = -2$

$\therefore \sqrt{(\log^2_{0.5} 4)} = \sqrt{(-2)^2} = \sqrt{4} = 2.$

14. : Given expression

$$= \frac{\log_{2^3} 17}{\log_{3^2} 23} - \frac{\log_{2^{3/2}} 17}{\log_3 23}$$

$$= \frac{\frac{1}{3}\log_2 17}{\frac{1}{2}\log_3 23} - \frac{\frac{2}{3}\log_2 17}{\log_3 23} = 0.$$

15. : Given expression

$= \log_{xyz} xy + \log_{xyz} yz + \log_{xyz} zx$

$= \log_{xyz} (xy.yz.zx) = 2 \log_{xyz} (xyz)$

$= 2.$

16. : $\log_e x + \log_e (1 + x) = 0$

$\Rightarrow \log_e x(1 + x) = 0 \Rightarrow x(1 + x) = e^0 = 1$

$\Rightarrow x^2 + x - 1 = 0.$

17. : Given equation is equivalent to

$\log_4 [(x^2 + x)/(x + 1)] = 2$

i.e., $(x^2 + x)/(x + 1) = 16$

$$\Rightarrow \frac{x(x+1)}{x+1} = 16$$

$\therefore x = 16$

18. : The given expression

$= \log_x a + \log_x c = 2 \log_x b$

$\Rightarrow \log_x ac = \log_x b^2 \Rightarrow b^2 = ac$

Hence, a, b, c are in G.P.

19. : $\log \tan 89° = \log \cot 1°$

$= -\log \tan 1°$. etc.

$\therefore$ Given expression

$= \log \tan 1° + \log \tan 2° + ... + \log \tan 44° + \log \tan 45° - \log \tan 44° - ... - \log \tan 2° - \log \tan 1°$

$= \log \tan 45° = \log 1 = 0.$

20. : Suppose that $\log_2 7$ is rational number.

$\therefore$ Let $\log_2 7 = p/q$, where $p, q \in$ N.

$\Rightarrow 7 = 2^{p/q} \Rightarrow 7^q = 2^p$.

Obviously (1) is false, as the L.H.S. is odd while the R.H.S. is even and the two cannot be equal. Thus, $\log_2 7$ is not a rational number. Also $\log_2 7$ is not an integer and so it cannot be a prime number.

Hence, $\log_2 7$ is an irrational number.

21. : $b = 2\log_{17} 5 = 2/\log_5 17$
And $a = 1/\log_5 3 = 2/\log_5 9$
Since, $\log_5 17 > \log_5 9$ $\quad\therefore a > b.$

22. : $\log_a x$ is defined in real domain
if $x > 0,\ a > 0, \neq 1.$
$\therefore\ 1/\log_{(b-c)} a + 1/\log_{(b+c)} a$ is defined for $b - c > 0,\ b + c > 0,\ b - c \neq 1,\ b + c \neq 1$
$\therefore\ b > |c|$ and $b \neq |c| + 1.$
Also for $a = 1$, we get denominator $= 0$
So, $a > 0, \neq 1.$
$\therefore$ If $b > |c|, \neq |c| + 1$ and $a > 0, \neq 1$, then
$1/\log_{(b-c)}a + 1/\log_{(b+c)}a = \log_a (b - c) + \log_a (b + c)$

23. : Here, $\log 0.57 = \bar{1}.756$

Since, $\log 57 + \log (0.57)^3 + \log\sqrt{0.57}$

$= 1.756 + 3\log (0.57) + \dfrac{1}{2} \log (0.57)$

$= 1.756 + 3 \times \bar{1}.756 + \dfrac{1}{2} \times \bar{1}.756$

$= 1.756 + 3 (-1 + 0.756) + \dfrac{1}{2} (-1 + 0.756)$

$= 1.756 - 3 + 2.268 - 0.5 + 0.378$

$= 4.402 - 3.5 = 0.902$

24 : $\log_{10}{}^{5} + \log_{10}{}^{(5x+1)} = \log_{10}{}^{(x+5)} + 1$

$\Rightarrow \log_{10}{}^{5} + \log_{10}{}^{(5x+1)} = \log_{10}{}^{(x+5)} + \log_{10}{}^{10}$

$\Rightarrow \log_{10}{}^{5(5x+1)} = \log_{10}{}^{10(x+5)} + \log_{10}{}^{10}$

$\Rightarrow \log_{10}{}^{5(5x+1)} = \log_{10}{}^{10(x+5)} \quad \Rightarrow 5(5x + 1) = 10(x + 5)$

$\Rightarrow 5x + 1 = 2x + 10 \quad \Rightarrow 3x = 9 \quad \therefore x = 3$

25. : $\log_{10}\left\{999 + \sqrt{x^2 - 3x + 3}\right\} = 3 \quad \Rightarrow 999 + \sqrt{x^2 - 3x + 3} = 10^3$

$\Rightarrow \sqrt{x^2 - 3x + 3} = 1 \quad \Rightarrow x^2 - 3x + 3 - 1 = 0 \quad \Rightarrow x^2 - 3x + 2 = 0$

$\Rightarrow (x - 1)(x - 2) = 0$ Hence, $x = 1, 2$

26. : Let, $x = 8^{17}$

$\Rightarrow x = (2^3)^{17} \quad \Rightarrow x = 2^{51} \quad \Rightarrow \log x = 51 \log 2$

$\Rightarrow \log x = 51 \times 0.3010 \quad \therefore \log x = 15.3510$

Hence, the required number of digits $= 15 + 1 = 16$

27. : Let, $x = (20)^{64}$

$\Rightarrow x = (2 \times 10)^{64} \quad \Rightarrow \log x = 64 \log 2 + 64 \log 10$

$\Rightarrow \log x = 64 \times 0.3010 + 64 \times 1 = 19.2640 + 64 = 83.2640$

Hence, the required number of digits $= 83 + 1 = 84$

28. : $\dfrac{\log x}{\log 5}=\dfrac{\log 36}{\log 6}=\dfrac{\log 64}{\log y}$;

Since, $\dfrac{\log x}{\log 5}=\dfrac{\log 36}{\log 6}$ $\Rightarrow \dfrac{\log x}{\log 5}=\dfrac{\log 6^2}{\log 6}$

$\Rightarrow \dfrac{\log x}{\log 5}=\dfrac{2\log 6}{\log 6}$ $\Rightarrow \log x = 2\log 5$ $\therefore x = 5^2 = 25$

Again, $\dfrac{\log 64}{\log y}=\dfrac{\log 36}{\log 6}$ $\Rightarrow \dfrac{\log 2^6}{\log y}=\dfrac{\log 6^2}{\log 6}$ $\Rightarrow \dfrac{6\log 2}{\log y}=\dfrac{2\log 6}{\log 6}$

$\Rightarrow \dfrac{\log y}{6\log 2}=\dfrac{1}{2}$ $\Rightarrow \log y = 3\log 2$ $\Rightarrow y = 2^3 = 8$

29. : $\log_{10}{}^{1\frac{1}{2}}+\log_{10}{}^{1\frac{1}{3}}+\log_{10}{}^{1\frac{1}{4}}+\ldots$ upto 198 terms

$= \log_{10}{}^{\frac{3}{2}}+\log_{10}{}^{\frac{4}{3}}+\log_{10}{}^{\frac{5}{4}}+\ldots+\log_{10}{}^{\frac{199}{198}}+\log_{10}{}^{\frac{200}{199}}$

$= \log_{10}{}^{\left(\frac{3}{2}\times\frac{4}{3}\times\frac{5}{4}\times\ldots\times\frac{199}{198}\times\frac{200}{199}\right)}$

$= \log_{10}{}^{\frac{200}{2}} = \log_{10}{}^{100} = \log_{10}{}^{10^2} = 2\log_{10}{}^{10} = 2\times 1 = 2$

30. : $\log_{x+3}{}^{(x^2+6x+9)}+\log_{5x+2}{}^{(6x^2-6x)}=\log_{2x-1}{}^{(8x^3-12x^2+6x-1)}$

$\Rightarrow \log_{x+3}{}^{(x+3)^2}+\log_{(5x+2)}{}^{(6x^2-6x)}=\log_{2x-1}{}^{(2x-1)^3}$

$\Rightarrow 2\log_{x+3}{}^{(x+3)}+\log_{(5x+2)}{}^{(6x^2-6x)}=3\log_{2x-1}{}^{(2x-1)}$

$\Rightarrow \log_{(5x+2)}{}^{(6x^2-6x)}=3-2$ $\Rightarrow \log_{(5x+2)}{}^{(6x^2-6x)}=1$

$\Rightarrow 5x+2=6x^2-6x$ $\Rightarrow 6x^2-11x-2=0$ $\Rightarrow (6x+1)(x-2)=0$

Hence, $x = -\dfrac{1}{6}$ or 2

So, positive solution is $x = 2$

31. : Let $x = 3^{50}$

$\Rightarrow \log x = 50\log 3 = 50\times 0.477 = 23.850$

Hence, requried number of digits = 23 + 1 = 24

32. : $\log_8{}^m+\log_8{}^{1/6}=\dfrac{2}{3}$ $\Rightarrow \log_8{}^{\left(m\times\frac{1}{6}\right)}=\dfrac{2}{3}$

$\Rightarrow m\times\dfrac{1}{6}=8^{2/3}$ $\Rightarrow \dfrac{m}{6}=\left(2^3\right)^{2/3}$ $\Rightarrow \dfrac{m}{6}=4$ $\therefore m = 24$

33. : $\log_{\sqrt{8}}{}^x = 6$ $\Rightarrow x = \left(\sqrt{8}\right)^6 = \left(2^{3/2}\right)^6$

$\therefore x = 2^9 = 512$

34. : $\log 48 = \log(2^4\times 3) = 4\log 2 + \log 3 = 4\times 0.3010 + 0.4771 = 1.6811$

35. : $\log_4 7 = x$ $\Rightarrow \log_7^{4} = \dfrac{1}{x}$ $\Rightarrow 2\log_7^{4} = \dfrac{2}{x}$

$\Rightarrow \log_7^{4^2}$ $\Rightarrow \log_7^{16} = \dfrac{2}{x}$

36. : $\log_9 x - \log_9\left(\frac{x}{10}+\frac{1}{9}\right) = 1$ $\Rightarrow \log_9 x - \log_9\left(\frac{x}{10}+\frac{1}{9}\right) = \log_9^{9}$

$\Rightarrow \log_9^{x/\left(\frac{x}{10}+\frac{1}{9}\right)} = \log_9^{9}$ $\Rightarrow \log_9\left(\frac{90x}{9x+10}\right) = \log_9^{9}$

$\Rightarrow \dfrac{90x}{9x+10} = 9$ $\Rightarrow 90x = 81x + 90$ $\Rightarrow 9x = 90$ $\Rightarrow x = 10$

37. : $\log_2 \log_2 \log_3 \log_3^{27^3} = \log_2 \log_2 \log_3 \log_3\left(3^3\right)^3 = \log_2 \log_2 \log_3 9\log_3^{3}$

$= \log_2 \log_2 \log_3^{3^2} \times 1 = \log_2 \log_2^{2} \log_3^{3} = \log_2 \log_2^{2} \times 1$

$= \log_2 \times 1 = \log_2^{1} = 0$

38. : $\log_{10} 10 + \log_{10} 100 + \ldots\ldots + \log_{10} 1\underbrace{00000\ldots0}_{n}$

$= \log_{10}^{10} + \log_{10}^{10^2} + \ldots\ldots + \log_{10}^{10^n}$

$= \log_{10}^{10} + 2\log_{10}^{10} + \ldots\ldots + n\log_{10}^{10}$

$= 1 + 2 + \ldots\ldots + n = \dfrac{n(n+1)}{2}$

39. : $\log_{10}^{(x+5)} + \log_{10}^{10} = 4$ $\Rightarrow \log_{10}^{(x+5)} + 1 = 4$

$\Rightarrow \log_{10}^{(x+5)} = 3$ $\Rightarrow x + 5 = 10^3$ $\therefore x = 1000 - 5 = 995$

40. : $\log_4^{x^2(x-1)^2} - \log_2^{(x-1)} = 1$ $\Rightarrow \log_{2^2}^{[x(x-1)]^2} - \log_2^{(x-1)} = 1$

$\Rightarrow \dfrac{2}{2}\log_2^{x(x-1)} - \log_2^{(x-1)} = 1$ $\Rightarrow \log_2^{\frac{x(x-1)}{x-1}} = 1$

$\Rightarrow \log_2 x = 1$ $\therefore x = 2^1 = 2$

41. : $\log_{10}^{(x+20)} + \log_{10}^{100} = 5$ $\Rightarrow \log_{10}^{(x+20)} + \log_{10}^{10^2} = 5$

$\Rightarrow \log_{10}^{(x+20)} + 2\log_{10}^{10} = 5$ $\Rightarrow \log_{10}^{(x+20)} + 2 = 5$

$\Rightarrow \log_{10}^{(x+20)} = 3$ $\Rightarrow x + 20 = 10^3$ $\therefore x = 1000 - 20 = 980$

42. : $\log_x^{4} = 0.4$ $\Rightarrow x^{0.4} = 4$ $\therefore x = 4^{1/0.4} = (2^2)^{10/4} = 2^5 = 32$

43. : Here, $\log_2 x = 10$ $\therefore x = 2^{10}$

Now, $\log_x y = 100$ $\Rightarrow y = x^{100} = (2^{10})^{100} = 2^{1000}$

44. : $\dfrac{\log\sqrt{8}}{\log 8} = \dfrac{\log(8)^{1/2}}{\log 8} = \dfrac{\frac{1}{2}\log 8}{\log 8} = \dfrac{1}{2}$

45. : $a^x = b^y \Rightarrow \log_a x = \log_b y \Rightarrow x \log a = y \log b$

$\therefore \dfrac{\log a}{\log b} = \dfrac{y}{x}$

46. : $2\log_{10} 5 + \log_{10} 8 - \frac{1}{2}\log_{10} 4 = \log_{10} 5^2 + \log_{10} 8 - \log_{10}(4)^{1/2}$

$= \log_{10} 25 + \log_{10} 8 - \log_{10} 2 = \log_{10}\left(\dfrac{25\times 8}{2}\right) = \log_{10}^{100} = \log_{10} 10^2$

$= 2\log_{10}^{10} = 2 \times 1 = 2$

47. : $\log 4\sqrt[3]{63} = \log 4 + \frac{1}{3}\log 63 = \log 4 + \frac{1}{3}\log(3^2 \times 7)$

$= \log 2^2 + \frac{1}{3}(2\log 3 + \log 7) = 2\log 2 + \frac{2}{3}\log 3 + \frac{1}{3}\log 7$

$= 2x + \frac{2}{3}y + \frac{1}{3}z$

48. : Here, $\log_a^{(ab)} = x \Rightarrow \log_a^{a} + \log_a^{b} = x \Rightarrow 1 + \log_a^{b} = x$

$\Rightarrow \log_b^{a} = \dfrac{1}{x-1} \qquad \Rightarrow 1 + \log_b^{a} = 1 + \dfrac{1}{x-1}$

$\Rightarrow \log_b^{b} + \log_b^{a} = \dfrac{x}{x-1} \qquad \therefore \log_b^{(ab)} = \dfrac{x}{x-1}$

49. : $\log_{12}^{27} = a \Rightarrow \dfrac{\log 27}{\log 12} = a \Rightarrow \dfrac{\log 3^3}{\log(2^2 \times 3)} = a$

$\Rightarrow \dfrac{3\log 3}{2\log 2 + \log 3} = a \qquad \Rightarrow \dfrac{2\log 2 + \log 3}{3\log 3} = \dfrac{1}{a}$

$\Rightarrow \dfrac{2\log 2}{2\log 3} + \dfrac{\log 3}{3\log 3} = \dfrac{1}{a} \qquad \Rightarrow \dfrac{2\log 2}{3\log 3} = \dfrac{1}{a} - \dfrac{1}{3}$

$\Rightarrow \dfrac{2\log 2}{3\log 3} = \dfrac{3-a}{3a} \qquad \therefore \log 3 = \dfrac{2a}{(3-a)}\log 2$

Now, $\log_6^{16} = \dfrac{\log 16}{\log 6} = \dfrac{\log 2^4}{\log(2\times 3)} = \dfrac{4\log 2}{\log 2 + \log 3} = \dfrac{4\log 2}{\log 2 + \dfrac{2a}{3-a}\log 2} = \dfrac{4(3-a)}{3+a}$

50. : $\log_{10}^{2} = 0.3010 \qquad \therefore \log_2^{10} = \dfrac{1}{0.3010} = \dfrac{10000}{3010} = \dfrac{1000}{301}$

51. : $\log_{10}\left(\frac{1}{70}\right) = \log_{10}^{1} - \log_{10}^{70} = 0 - \log_{10}^{(10\times 7)}$

$= -\log_{10}^{10} - \log_{10}^{7} = -1 - a = -(a+1)$

52. : log 27 = 1.431 $\Rightarrow \log_3{}^3 = 1.431$ $\Rightarrow$ 3 log 3 = 1.431

$\Rightarrow \log 3 = \dfrac{1.431}{3}$ $\Rightarrow$ 2log3 = 2 × 0.477 $\Rightarrow \log_3{}^2 = 0.954$

Hence, log 9 = 0.954.

53. : $\log_{10}{}^2 = 0.3010$ (Given)

Since, $\log_{10}{}^5 = \log_{10}{}^{\left(\frac{10}{2}\right)} = \log_{10}{}^{10} - \log_{10}{}^2 = 1 - 0.3010 = 0.6990$

54. : $\log_5{}^{512} = \dfrac{\log 512}{\log 5} = \dfrac{\log 2^9}{\log\left(\dfrac{10}{2}\right)} = \dfrac{9\log 2}{\log 10 - \log 2}$

$= \dfrac{9 \times 0.3010}{1 - 0.3010} = \dfrac{2.7090}{0.6990} = \dfrac{2709}{699} \approx 3.876$

55. : $\log_{10}{}^{80} = \log_{10}{}^{(10 \times 2^3)} = \log_{10}{}^{10} + 3\log_{10}{}^2 = 1 + 3 \times 0.3010 = 1.9030$

56. : $\log_{10}{}^{2.8} = \log_{10}{}^{\left(\frac{7 \times 2^2}{10}\right)} = \log_{10}{}^7 + 2\log_{10}{}^2 - \log_{10}{}^{10}$

$= 0.8451 + 2 \times 0.3010 - 1 = 1.4471 - 1 = 0.4471$

29

AREA & PERIMETER

In this part of mensuration we often have to deal with the problem of finding the areas and perimeters of plane figures.

Triangle

1. Perimeter = 3 × side (Equilateral triangle)

2. Area = $\frac{1}{2} \times \text{base} \times \text{height}$, or

Area = $\sqrt{s(s-a)(s-b)(s-c)}$

where *a, b, c,* are the lengths of the sides of triangle and $s = \frac{a+b+c}{2}$

Right Angled Triangle : It is one whose one of the angles is right angle, *i.e.*, 90°.

1. $(\text{Hypotenuse})^2 = (\text{Perpendicular})^2 + (\text{Base})^2$

2. Area = $\frac{1}{2} \times \text{Base} \times \text{Perpendicular}$

Equilateral Triangle : All three sides are equal in length and all three angles are equal to 60°.

1. Area = $\frac{\sqrt{3}}{4} \times (\text{Side})^2$

2. Area = $\frac{(\text{Height})^2}{\sqrt{3}}$

3. Height = $\frac{\sqrt{3}}{2} \times \text{side}$

4. Perimeter = 3 × side

Isosceles Triangle : Two sides are equal in lengths.

1. Area = $\frac{b}{4}\sqrt{4a^2 - b^2}$

where a = lengths of equal sides b = length of unequal side

2. In an isosceles right triangle,

(*a*) Hypotenuse = $\sqrt{2} \times \text{congruent side (a)}$

(*b*) Area = $\frac{1}{2} \times a^2$

(*c*) Perimeter = $\sqrt{2} \times a\left(\sqrt{2}+1\right)$

Rectangle :

1. Area = length(l) × breadth(b)
2. Perimeter = $2(l + b)$
3. Diagonal = $\sqrt{l^2 + b^2}$

Square :

1. Area = $(\text{Side})^2$
2. Perimeter = 4 × side
3. Diagonal = side × $\sqrt{2}$

Parallelogram: In parallelogram opposite sides are parallel and equal. The two diagonals are not always equal but they bisect each other at the point of intersection.

Area = Base × Height.

Trapezium : It is a quadrilateral whose one pair of opposite sides is parallel. Other two opposite sides are oblique.

Area = $\frac{1}{2} \times \text{Height} \times (\text{Sum of parallel sides})$. Here, height is the distance between the two parallel sides.

Rhombus : It is parallelogram whose all sides are equal and diagonals are bisect each other at right angle.

1. Area = $\frac{1}{2} \times$ Product of diagonals
2. Side = $\sqrt{\left(\frac{d_1}{2}\right)^2 + \left(\frac{d_2}{2}\right)^2}$, where d_1 and d_2 are diagonals
3. Perimeter = 4 × side

Quadrilateral : Area = $\frac{1}{2} \times$ One diagonal × (Sum of perpendicular to it from the opposite vertices)

$$= \frac{1}{2} \times d \times (a + b)$$

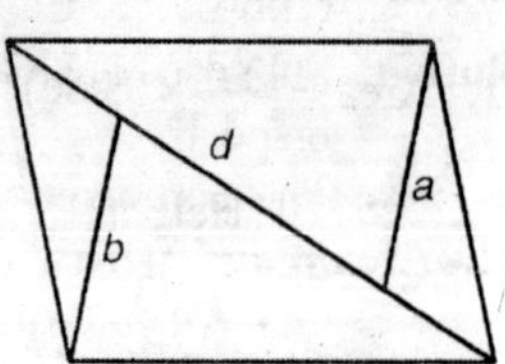

Circle :

1. Diameter = 2 × Radius
2. Area = $\pi r^2 = \frac{\pi}{4} d^2$; where d = diameter = $\sqrt{\frac{4A}{\pi}}$
3. Circumference = $2\pi r = \pi d$
4. Radius = $\frac{\text{Circumference}}{2\pi} = \frac{\sqrt{\text{Area}}}{\pi}$
5. Length of an Arc = $\frac{\theta}{360°} \times 2\pi r$
6. Area of sector = $\frac{\theta}{360°} \times \pi r^2 = \frac{1}{2} \times \text{Arc} \times r$

Polygon :

1. Interior angle + Exterior angle = 180°
2. Each interior angle = $\left(\frac{2n - 4}{n}\right) \times 90°$

   where n = number of sides

3. Sum of Exterior angles = 360°
4. Perimeter = Number of sides × Length of side.
5. For an equilateral triangle of side 'a' (a) radius of inscribed circle $=\frac{a}{2\sqrt{3}}$ and side of the triangle = $2\sqrt{3}r$, (b) radius of circumcircle = $\frac{a}{\sqrt{3}}$
6. Area of regular polygon $=\frac{1}{2}$(No. of sides) (Radius of the inscribed circle)
7. Area of regular hexagon = $\frac{3\sqrt{3}}{2}(\text{side})^2$ = 2.598 $(\text{side})^2$
8. Area of a regular octagon = $2(\sqrt{2}+1)(\text{side})^2$ = 4.828 $(\text{side})^2$
9. Area of quadrilateral, A = $\sqrt{s(s-a)(s-b)(s-c)(s-d)}$

   where, $s = \frac{a+b+c+d}{2}$

Example 1: Area of a rectangular field is 1600 sq. metre. If its length is four times its width, find the length of this rectangular field.

Solution: Suppose the length and the width of this field is $4x$ metres and x metres respectively.

∴ Area of the field $= 4x \times x = 4x^2$ sq. metre

Since, $4x^2 = 1600 \Rightarrow x^2 = 400$

$\Rightarrow x = \sqrt{400} \Rightarrow x = 20$

∴ Length of the rectangular field = 4 × 20 = 80 m.

Example 2: Perimeter of the rectangular floor of a room is 100 m. If its length and breadth are in the ratio 3 : 2, find the area of this rectangular floor.

Solution: Suppose the length and the breadth of this rectangular floor are $3x$ metre and $2x$ metre respectively.

The perimeter of the floor = $2 \times (l + b) = 2(3x + 2x) = 2 \times 5x = 10x$ metre

Since $10x = 100$

$\therefore x = \frac{100}{10} = 10$

∴Length of the floor = 3 × 10 = 30 m

And breadth of the floor = 2 × 10 = 20 m

∴Area of the floor = 30 × 20 = 600 sq. m.

Example 3: If the two diagonals of a rhombus are 72 cm and 30 cm respectively, find its perimeter.

Solution: Suppose the rhombus ABCD, diagonal AC =72 cm and diagonal BD = 30 cm

$\therefore OB = OD = \frac{BD}{2} = \frac{30}{2} = 15$ cm

and $OA = OC = \frac{AC}{2} = \frac{72}{2} = 36$ cm

$\therefore AB = BC = CD = DA = \sqrt{36^2 + 15^2}$

$= \sqrt{1296+225} = \sqrt{1521} = 39$

∴ Perimeter of the rhombus = 4 × 39 = 156 cm.

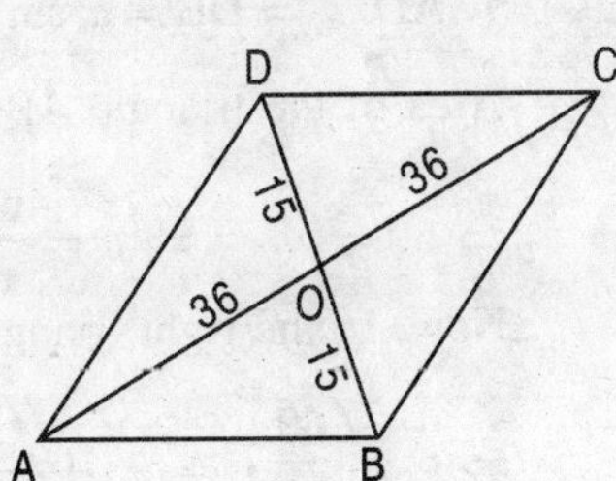

Example 4: Find the area of a triangle whose sides are 3 cm, 4 cm and 5 cm respectively.

Solution: Since the three sides of the triangle are 3 cm, 4 cm and 5 cm respectively and $5^2 = 3^2 + 4^2$

$\therefore$The triangle is a right angled triangle.

$\therefore$Area of the triangle $= \frac{1}{2} \times b \times p = \frac{1}{2} \times 3 \times 4 = 6$ sq. m.

Example 5: If the base of a triangle is made double and its height is halved, what will be the ratio of the area of the original triangle to that of the new triangle?

Solution: Suppose the base of the triangle = a and height = b

$\therefore$Area of the original triangle $= \frac{1}{2} \times a \times b = \frac{ab}{2}$

According to question :

Base of the new triangle = $2a$ and

height of the new triangle = $b/2$

$\therefore$ Area of the new triangle $= \frac{1}{2} \times 2a \times \frac{b}{2} = \frac{ab}{2}$

Hence, Ratio of their areas $= \frac{ab}{2} : \frac{ab}{2} = 1 : 1.$

Example 6: Of the two squares, the perimeter of one square is 12 cm and that of the other is 16 cm. Find the perimeter of a third square which is equal in area to the sum of the areas of these two given squares.

Solution: Side of the first square = 12/4 = 3 cm.

$\therefore$ Area of the first square = 3 × 3 = 9 sq cm.

Side of the second square $= \frac{16}{4} = 4$ cm.

Area of the second square = 4 × 4 = 16 sq. cm.

According to question :

Sum of Area of the two squares = 9 + 16 = 25 sq. cm.

$\therefore$ Side of the third square $= \sqrt{25} = 5$ cm.

Hence, Perimeter of the third square = 5 × 4 = 20 cm.

Example 7: The area of an isosceles triangle is 60 sq. cm. If one of the two equal sides is 13 cm, find its base.

Solution: Suppose in the isosceles triangle ABC,

AC = BC = 13 cm

DC = h cm

andBase, AB = $2a$ cm

$\therefore$ AD = DB = a cm

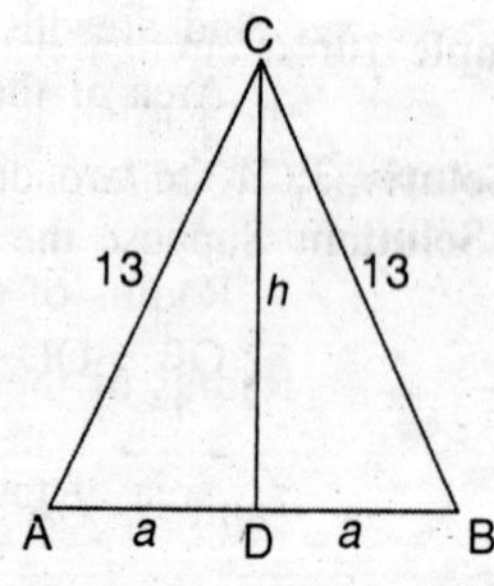

Area of the triangle ABC $= \frac{1}{2} \times 2a \times h$

$\Rightarrow 60 = ah \quad \Rightarrow h = \frac{60}{a}$

Now, In the right triangle ADC, $a^2 + h^2 = 13^2 = 169$ ... *(i)*

$\Rightarrow a^2 + \left(\frac{60}{a}\right)^2 = 169 \Rightarrow a^2 + \frac{3600}{a^2} = 169$

$$\Rightarrow \quad a^4 - 169a^2 + 3600 = 0$$
$$\Rightarrow \quad a^4 - 144a^2 - 25a^2 + 3600 = 0$$
$$\Rightarrow \quad a^2(a^2 - 144) - 25(a^2 - 144) = 0$$
$$\Rightarrow \quad (a^2 - 144)(a^2 - 25) = 0$$

Either, $a^2 - 144 = 0$

$\Rightarrow \quad a^2 = 144$

or, $a^2 = 25$

$\therefore \quad a = 12$

or, $a = 5$

$\therefore$ Base of $\Delta ABC = 2 \times 12 = 24$ cm or $2 \times 5 = 10$ cm.

Example 8: A rectangular field is 50 metre long and 40 metre wide. There is a path 5 metre wide outside the field along its sides. Find the cost of growing grass in this path at Rs. 10.50 per sq. metre.

Solution: Area of the field = 50 × 40 = 2000 sq. m.

And area of the field including the path = 60 × 50 = 3000 sq. m.

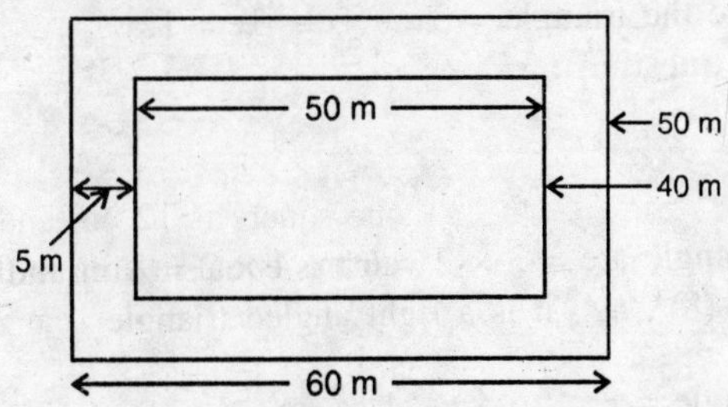

$\therefore$ Area of the path = 3000 – 2000 = 1000 sq. m.

$\therefore$ Cost of growing grass in the path = Rs. 1000 × 10.50 = Rs. 10500.

Example 9: The diagonal of a quadrilateral is 140 m and the offsets on it are 100 m and 30 m respectively. Find the area of this quadrilateral.

Sol: Area of the quadrilateral $= \frac{1}{2} \times \text{diagonal} \times \text{sum of the offsets}$

$$= \frac{1}{2} \times 140 \times (100 + 30)$$

$$= \frac{1}{2} \times 140 \times 130 = 9100 \text{ sq. m.}$$

Example 10: A circular path 3.5 m wide runs round outside a circular garden. If the circumference of the garden is 44 m, find the cost of levelling the path at 15 paise per sq. metre.

Solution: Circumference of the circular garden = $2\pi R = 44$ m

$\therefore$ Radius of the garden $= \frac{44}{2\pi} = \frac{44 \times 7}{2 \times 22} = 7$ m

Radius of the (garden + path) = 7 + 3.5 = 10.5 m

$\therefore$ Area of the (garden + path) $= \frac{22}{7} \times (10.5)^2 = 346.5$ sq. m.

Area of the garden $= \frac{22}{7} \times 7 \times 7 = 154$ sq. m.

$\therefore$ Area of the path = 346.5 – 154 = 192.5 sq. m.

Hence, Cost of levelling the path at 15 paise per sq. metre = 192.5 × 0.15 = Rs. 28.88.

Example 11: Find the side of a rhombus whose perimeter is equal to the circumference of the circle of radius 14 cm.

Solution: Suppose side of the rhombus = x cm

$\therefore$ Perimeter of the rhombus = $4x$ cm

According to question :

Perimeter of the rhombus = circumference of the circle

$\Rightarrow 4x = 2\pi \times 14$ ($\because$ radius of the circle = 14 cm) $\Rightarrow 4x = 2\times\frac{22}{7}\times 14$

Hence, $x = \frac{2\times 22\times 2}{4} = 22$ cm

$\therefore$ Side of the rhombus = 22 cm.

Example 12 : Three sides of a triangle are in the ratio 3 : 4 : 5. If its perimeter is 24 m, find area of this triangle.

Solution: Suppose sides of the triangle are $3x$ m, $4x$ m and $5x$ m respectively.

$\therefore$ Perimeter of the the triangle = $3x + 4x + 5x = 12x$

According to the question :

$12x = 24$

Hence, $x = \frac{24}{12} = 2$

$\therefore$ Sides of the triangle are = $3 \times 2 = 6$ m, $4 \times 2 = 8$ m and $5 \times 2 = 10$ m respectively

$\because (10)^2 = (6)^2 + (8)^2$, *i.e.,* it is a right angled triangle

$\therefore$ Area of the triangle = $\frac{1}{2}\times 6\times 8 = 24$ sq. m.

Example 13: The parallel sides of a trapezium are 60 cm and 99 cm and the other sides are 42 cm and 45 cm. Find the area.

Solution:

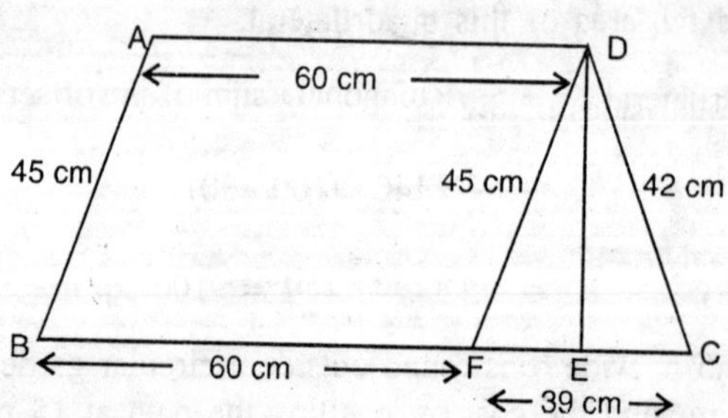

Here in the trapezium ABCD, the longer side BC = 99 cm and shorter side AD = 60 cm and CD = 42 cm and AB = 45 cm

$\because$ AD = BF = 60 cm

$\therefore$ FC = BC − BF = 99 − 60 = 39 cm

First of all we find the area of triangle DFC.

Here, $\frac{39+45+42}{2} = \frac{126}{2} = 63$

$\therefore$ Area of ΔDFC = $\sqrt{63\times 18\times 21\times 24} = 756$ sq. cm.

But area of ΔDFC = $\frac{1}{2}\times\text{base}\times\text{corresponding altitude (DE)}$

$\Rightarrow 756 = \frac{1}{2} \times 39 \times DE$

$\therefore DE = \frac{756 \times 2}{39} = \frac{504}{13}$ cm

Area of the trapezium ABCD $= \frac{1}{2} \times$ sum of parallel lines $\times$ distance between them (DE)

$= \frac{1}{2} \times (60 + 99) \times \frac{504}{13}$

$= \frac{1}{2} \times 159 \times \frac{504}{13} = 3082.15$ sq. cm.

Example 14: One side of a parallelogram is 45 cm and the corresponding altitude is 22 cm. Find its area.

Solution: Area of the parallelogram = 45 × 22 = 990 sq. m.

Example 15: A field is in the form of an isosceles triangle. If base of this triangle is 24 m and cost of growing grass in this triangular field at 25 paise per sq. metre is Rs. 15, find the length of any of the two equal sides.

Solution: Suppose the length of one of the equal sides = x m

And base of the triangular field = 24 m.

∵ Cost of growing grass at 25 paise per sq. m. = Rs. 15

$\therefore$ Area of the field $= \frac{15}{25} \times 100 = 60$ sq. m.

Now, area of the field $= \frac{a}{4}\sqrt{4x^2 - a^2}$

$\Rightarrow \frac{24}{4}\sqrt{4x^2 - 24^2} = 60$

$\Rightarrow 4x^2 - (24)^2 = \left(\frac{60 \times 4}{24}\right)^2$

$\Rightarrow 4x^2 - 576 = (10)^2 \Rightarrow 4x^2 = 576 + 100 = 676$

$\Rightarrow x^2 = 169 \Rightarrow x = 13$

$\therefore$ One of the equal sides of the isosceles triangle = 13 cm.

Example 16: Area of an equilateral triangle is $\sqrt{3}$ sq. cm. Find the length of its sides.

Solution: Area of equilateral triangle $= \frac{\sqrt{3}}{4} \times (\text{side})^2$

$\therefore \frac{\sqrt{3}}{4} \times (\text{side})^2 = \sqrt{3} \Rightarrow (\text{side})^2 = \frac{\sqrt{3} \times 4}{\sqrt{3}} = 4$

$\Rightarrow$ side $= \sqrt{4} = 2$

Hence, side of the triangle = 2 cm.

Example 17: A circular road runs round a circular garden. If the difference between the circumferences of the outer circle and the inner circle is 88 m, find the width of the road.

Solution: **According to question :**

$2\pi R - 2\pi r = 88 \Rightarrow 2\pi(R - r) = 88$

$\Rightarrow (R - r) = \frac{88}{2\pi} = \frac{88 \times 7}{2 \times 22} = 14$ m

$\therefore$ Width of the road = 14 m.

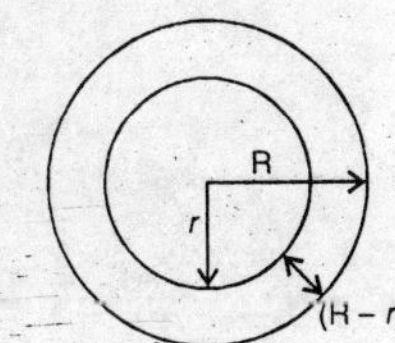

Example 18: Find the length of the longest rod that can be placed in a box 120 cm long, 40 cm wide and 30 cm high.

Solution: Length of the longest rod $= \sqrt{l^2 + b^2 + h^2}$

$= \sqrt{(120)^2 + (40)^2 + (30)^2}$

$= \sqrt{14400 + 1600 + 900} = \sqrt{16900} = 130$ cm.

Example 19: A park is in the form of a square of side 110 m. It has two mutually perpendicular paths in the central part of width 5 m. Find the cost of cementing the paths at Rs. 5 per sq. metre.

Solution: Suppose the two mutually perpendicular paths are PQ and RS

$\therefore$ Area of the rectangular path PQ $= l \times b = 110 \times 5 = 550$ sq. m.

Similarly, area of rectangular path RS $= 110 \times 5 = 550$ sq. m.

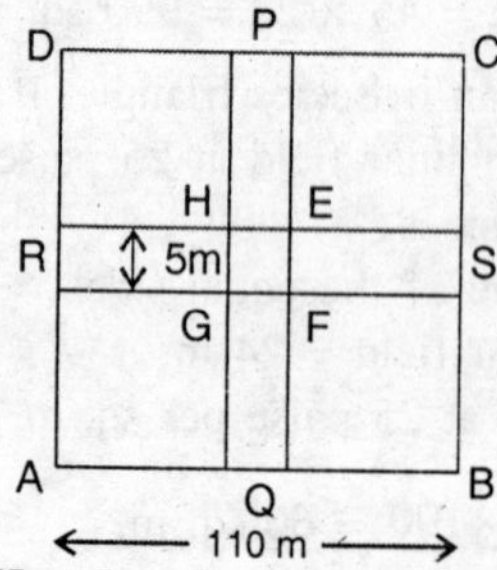

And area of square EFGH $= 5 \times 5 = 25$ sq. m.

$\therefore$ Area of the two paths $= 550 + 550 - 25 = 1075$ sq. m.

[$\because$ the central square EFGH is common in the two paths]

$\therefore$ Cost of cementing the two paths at Rs. 5 per square metre = Rs. 1075×5 = Rs. 5375.

Example 20: A rectangular tank is 25 m long, 12 m wide and 6 m high. Find the cost of plastering its walls and bottom at 75 paise per sq. metre.

Solution: Area of the four walls of the tank $= 2 \times$ height (length + breadth)

$= 2 \times 6 \times (25 + 12)$

$= 12 \times 37 = 444$ sq. m.

And area of the bottom of the tank = length × breadth $= 25 \times 12 = 300$ sq. m.

Total area $= 444 + 300 = 744$ sq. m.

$\therefore$ Cost of plastering $= 744 \times \frac{75}{100}$ = Rs. 558.

Example 21: Each side of a square measures 30 m. If the area of a triangle is equal to the area of this square, find the side of the triangle which is 36 m apart from the opposite vertex.

Solution: Area of the square $= 30 \times 30 = 900$ sq. m.

According to question :

Area of the triangle = Area of the square

$\therefore$ Area of the triangle = 900 sq. m.

$\because$ Area of the triangle $= \frac{1}{2} \times \text{base} \times \text{corresponding altitude}$

$\therefore 900 = \frac{1}{2} \times \text{base} \times 36$

$\therefore$ The said side of the triangle $= \frac{900 \times 2}{36} = 50$ m.

Example 22: A wire is looped in the form of a circle of radius 28 cm. It is re-bent into a square form. Find the length of the side of the square. (Use $\pi = \frac{22}{7}$).

Solution: Here, perimeter of square = circumferance of circle,

$\Rightarrow 4a = 2 \times \frac{22}{7} \times 28 \quad \therefore \quad a = \frac{2 \times 22 \times 4}{4} = 44$ cm

Hence, side of the square = 44 cm.

Example 23: The length of the minute-hand of a clock is 10 cm. What is the area swept by the minute hand in one minute? (Use, $\pi = 3.14$)

Solution: Angle formed by minute hand in 1 minute $= \frac{360}{60} = 6°$

Hence, required area $= \frac{6}{360} \times 3.14 \times (10)^2 = \frac{157}{30} = 5\frac{7}{30}$ cm^2

Example 24: What will be the area of a right angled triangle whose height is double that of base of 13 cm?

Solution: Area of right angled triangle $= \frac{1}{2} \times 13 \times 26 = 169$ cm^2

Example 25: What will be the area of a circle whose circumference is 132 cm?

Solution: Radius of the circle, $r = \frac{\text{circumference}}{2\pi} = \frac{132 \times 7}{2 \times 22} = 21$ cm

Hence, Area of the circle $= \frac{22}{7} \times 21 \times 21 = 1386$ cm^2

Example 26: If the area of a triangle is 1176 cm^2 and base : corresponding altitude is 3 : 4, then find the altitude of the triangle.

Solution: Let base and corresponding altitude of the triangle are $3x$ and $4x$ cm respectively; then

$\frac{1}{2} \times 3x \times 4x = 1176 \quad \Rightarrow \quad 6x^2 = 1176 \quad \Rightarrow \quad x^2 = 196 \quad \therefore \quad x = 14$

Hence, altitude of the triangle $= 4x = 4 \times 14 = 56$ cm

Example 27: The area of a circle is 154 cm^2. Find its radius.

Solution: Radius of a circie $= \sqrt{\frac{A}{\pi}} = \sqrt{\frac{154 \times 7}{22}} = 7$ cm

Example 28: Find the area of the ring between two concentric circles, whose circumferences are 88 cm and 132 cm.

Solution: Radius of inner circle, $r = \frac{88 \times 7}{2 \times 22} = 14$ cm

Radius of outer circle, $R = \frac{132 \times 7}{2 \times 22} = 21$ cm

Since, area of the ring $= \frac{22}{7}\left(21^2 - 14^2\right) = \frac{22}{7}(21 + 14)(21 - 14)$

$= \frac{22}{7} \times 35 \times 7 = 770$ cm^2

Example 29: The breadth of a rectangular field is 75% of its length. If the perimeter of the field is 1050 m. Find the area of the field.

Solution: Let length be x m then breadth will be $\frac{75}{100} \times x = \frac{3x}{4}$ m

Since, $2\left(x + \frac{3x}{4}\right) = 1050 \quad \Rightarrow \quad \frac{7x}{4} = 525 \quad \therefore \quad x = \frac{525 \times 4}{7} = 300$

Hence, length = x m = 300 m; breadth = $\frac{3x}{4} = \frac{3 \times 300}{4} = 225$ m

$\therefore$ Area of the rectangular field = 300 × 225 = 67500 m²

Example 30: Find the area of rhombus whose one side is 20 cm and a diagonal measures 24 cm.

Solution: Other diagonal = $2.\sqrt{(20)^2 - (12)^2} = 2\sqrt{400-144} = 2 \times 16 = 32$ cm

Hence, area of rhombus = $\frac{1}{2} \times 24 \times 32 = 384$ cm²

Example 31: Find the area of an equilateral triangle, each of whose side is 6 m.

Solution: Area of equilateral triangle = $\frac{\sqrt{3}}{4} \times a^2 = \frac{\sqrt{3}}{4}(6)^2 = 9 \times 1.732 = 15.588$ cm²

Example 32: Find the area of regular octagon with side 2 cm.

Solution: Area of regular octagon = $2\left(\sqrt{2}+1\right) \times (\text{side})^2 = 2\left(\sqrt{2}+1\right) \times 2^2 = 8\left(\sqrt{2}+1\right)$ cm²

Example 33: ABCMA is a quadrant of a circle of radius 14 cm with AC as diameter, a semicircle ANC is drawn. Find the area of the shaded portion.

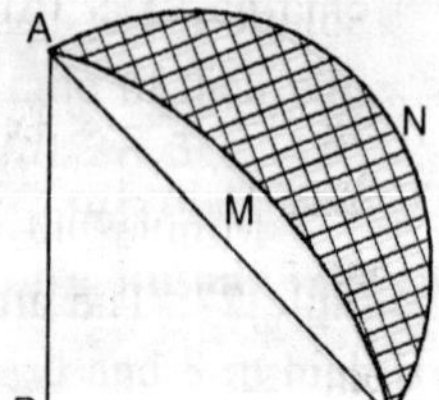

A
N
M
B
C

Solution: From the figure, AC = $\sqrt{AB^2 + BC^2} = \sqrt{14^2 + 14^2} = 14\sqrt{2}$ cm

Area of minor segment AMC = $\frac{1}{4} \times \frac{22}{7} \times (14)^2 - \frac{1}{2} \times 14 \times 14$

= 154 − 98 = 56 cm²

Area of shaded portion = $\frac{1}{2} \times \frac{22}{7} \times \left(7\sqrt{2}\right)^2 - 56 = \frac{1}{2} \times \frac{22}{7} \times 7 \times 7 \times 2 - 56$

= 154 − 56 = 98 cm²

Example 34: The area of a rectangle is 110 cm². If each of its sides is decreased by 4 cm, then the area is 42 cm². What is the width of the rectangle?

Sol: Here, lb = 110 cm² ...(i)

Again, $(l - 4)(b - 4) = 42 \quad \Rightarrow \quad lb - 4l - 4b + 16 = 42$

$\Rightarrow 4(l + b) = 110 + 16 - 42 \quad \Rightarrow \quad (l + b) = \frac{84}{4} = 21$

Now, $l - b = \sqrt{(l+b)^2 - 4lb} = \sqrt{(21)^2 - 4 \times 110} = \sqrt{1} = 1$

Since, $l + b = 11$ and $l - b = 1$; On solving we get, $l = 11$ cm and $b = 10$ cm

EXERCISE

1. A rectangle measures 50 cm × 25 cm. Its area is
(a) 1150 sq. cm. (b) 1250 sq. cm. (c) 1275 sq. cm. (d) 1280 sq. cm.

2. A field is in the form of a square whose perimeter is 580 m. Area of this field is
(a) 21025 sq. m. (b) 20225 sq. m. (c) 30025 sq. m. (d) 19975 sq. m.

3. Find the area of the square whose each side measures 20 cm.
(a) 300 sq. cm. (b) 380 sq. cm. (c) 360 sq. cm. (d) 400 sq. m.

4. Area of a circle is 154 sq. cm. Its circumference will be
(a) 44 cm (b) 48 cm (c) 54 cm (d) 68 cm

5. The base and the height of a triangle is 8 cm and 10 cm respectively. Its area will be
(a) 40 sq. cm. (b) 20 sq. cm. (c) 49 sq. cm. (d) 64 sq. cm.

6. If it is given that the parallel sides of a trapezium are 15 m and 25 m while the distance between them is 10 m. Its area will be:
(a) 150 sq. m. (b) 225 sq. m. (c) 200 sq. m. (d) 270 sq. m.

7. Perimeter of a rectangular field is 760 m and its length and breadth are in the ratio 11 : 8. Area of this rectangular field is
(a) 35200 sq. m. (b) 34700 sq. m. (c) 35600 sq. m. (d) 45200 sq. m.

8. If side of a square is reduced by 50%, its area will be reduced by
(a) 50% (b) 75% (c) 80% (d) 60%

9. If area of a square is equal to the area of a rectangle 6.4 m long and 2.5 m wide, then each side of this square measures
(a) 8 m (b) 5.4 m (c) 3.8 m (d) 4 m

10. If perimeter of a right angled triangle is six times its smallest side, then the three sides of this triangle are in the ratio of
(a) 13 : 5 : 12 (b) 13 : 12 : 5 (c) 12 : 5 : 13 (d) 13 : 5 : 10

11. The perimeter of a square is 24 m and that of another is 32 m. Find the perimeter of a third square, area of which is equal to sum of the areas of these two squares
(a) 40 m (b) 51 m (c) 37 m (d) 42 m

12. If each side of a square is doubled, its area will become
(a) double (b) four times (c) three times (d) eight times

13. The difference between the areas of two squares is 225 sq. metres and each side of the bigger square is 25 metres. The side of the smaller square is
(a) 18 m (b) 21 m (c) 20 m (d) 22 m

14. If the perimeter of an equilateral triangle is 72 cm, its area will be
(a) $144\sqrt{3}$ sq. cm (b) $142\sqrt{3}$ sq. cm (c) $154\sqrt{2}$ sq. cm. (d) $144\sqrt{2}$ sq. cm.

15. The radii of two circles are 5 cm and 12 cm respectively. Find the radius of a circle which is equal in area to these two circles.
(a) 15 cm (b) 13 cm (c) 10 cm (d) 8 cm

16. If the circumference of a circle is equal to the perimeter of a square, then their areas are in the ratio of
(a) 14 : 11 (b) 7 : 8 (c) 14 : 13 (d) 13 : 11

17. Three sides of a triangle are in the ratio of 17 : 15 : 8. If the perimeter of this triangle is 40 m, find its area

(*a*) 50 sq. m. (*b*) 49 sq. m. (*c*) 60 sq. m. (*d*) 69 sq. m.

18. If the length of a rectangle is increased by 20% and width is decreased by 15%, then its area

(*a*) decreases by 4% (*b*) increases by 2%
(*c*) decreases by 2% (*d*) increases by 3%

19. Find the perimeter of a rhombus whose diagonals measure 16 cm and 12 cm.

(*a*) 38 cm (*b*) 40 cm (*c*) 41 cm (*d*) 46 cm.

20. If the difference between the circumference and the radius of a circle is 37 cm, find its diameter.

(*a*) 11 cm (*b*) 12 cm (*c*) 16 cm (*d*) 14 cm

21. If the diagonal of a square is doubled to make another square, the area of the new square will

(*a*) become fourfold (*b*) become twofold
(*c*) become sixfold (*d*) become eightfold

22. The areas of two concentric circles, forming a ring, are 154 sq. cm and 616 sq. cm. respectively. The width of the ring is

(*a*) 6 cm (*b*) 7 cm (*c*) 9 cm (*d*) 11 cm

23. If the length of a rectangle is increased by 20%, then by how much per cent its breadth must be decreased so as to keep its area unaltered?

(*a*) 25% (*b*) $8\frac{1}{3}\%$ (*c*) $16\frac{2}{3}\%$ (*d*) 20%

24. Each side of a given square is 5 cm and assuming the two opposite sides of this square as diameters, two semicircles are drawn in the inside of the square. If these semicircles are cut out from the square, then the area of the remaining portion of the given square will be

(*a*) $(9 - 6.25\pi)$ sq. cm. (*b*) $(25 - 6.25\pi)$ sq. cm.
(*c*) $(25 - 4.25\pi)$ sq. cm. (*d*) $(36 - 6.25\pi)$ sq. cm.

25. If area of a traingle whose base is 6 cm is equal to the area of a square of side 6 cm, find the height of this triangle.

(*a*) 10 cm (*b*) 22 cm (*c*) 12 cm (*d*) 18 cm

26. If areas of two squares are in the ratio of 25 : 16, their perimeters will be in the ratio of

(*a*) 5 : 4 (*b*) 4 : 5 (*c*) 5 : 2 (*d*) 2 : 3

27. The length and breadth of a room are in the ratio 2 : 1. If the cost of cementing the floor at 75 paise per sq. metre comes to be Rs. 864 and the cost of polishing the walls at Rs. 3.25 per sq. metre comes to be Rs. 884, then the height of the room is

(*a*) $2\frac{8}{9}$ m (*b*) $1\frac{8}{9}$ m (*c*) $1\frac{2}{9}$ m (*d*) $1\frac{7}{9}$ m

28. A garden is 24 m long and 14 m wide. There is a path 1 m wide outside the garden along its sides. If the path is to be constructed with square marble tiles 20 cm × 20 cm, find the number of tiles required to cover the path.

(*a*) 1800 (*b*) 2200 (*c*) 2000 (*d*) 2150

29. Two adjacent sides of a parallelogram are 40 m and 30 m respectively. If one diagonal of the parallelogram measures 50 m, find its area.

(*a*) 1100 sq. m. (*b*) 1200 sq. m. (*c*) 1400 sq. m. (*d*) 1500 sq. m.

30. Four sides of a trapezium are 50 cm, 17 cm, 25 cm and 12 cm respectively. If the first of the four sides is parallel to the third, find the area of this trapezium.
(a) 280 sq. cm. *(b)* 810 sq. cm. *(c)* 270 sq. cm. *(d)* 225 sq. cm.

31. A rectangular sheet of paper is 8 cm × 6 cm. If a greatest possible circle is cut out from it, the area of the remaining paper will be :
(a) $(48 - 9\pi)$ sq. cm. *(b)* $(48 - 5\pi)$ sq. cm. *(c)* $(24 - 9\pi)$ sq. cm. *(d)* $(48 - 11\pi)$ sq. cm.

32. A circle and a square have same area. Therefore, the ratio of the side of the square and the radius of the circle is:
(a) $1 : \pi$ *(b)* $\pi : 1$ *(c)* $\sqrt{\pi} : 1$ *(d)* $1 : \sqrt{\pi}$

33. Base of a right angled triangle is 80 cm and its hypotenuse is 1 m. Find its area.
(a) 2400 cm² *(b)* 3600 cm² *(c)* 4000 cm² *(d)* 4800 cm²

34. The length of a rectangular plot is 88m. There are 3872 tiles in its floor. If the area of tile is 0.25 m², then find the breadth of the plot.
(a) 11 m *(b)* 12 m *(c)* 13 m *(d)* 14 m

35. A circular grass plot, whose diameter is 70m, contains a gravel walk 5m wide round it, 15m from the edge. The cost to turf the grass plot at Rs. 2 per m² is:
(a) Rs. 6000 *(b)* Rs. 6200 *(c)* Rs. 6400 *(d)* Rs. 6600

36. The area of the greatest circle, which can be inscribed in a square, whose perimeter is 120 cm, is:
(a) $\pi \times \left(\frac{7}{2}\right)^2$ cm² *(b)* $\pi \times \left(\frac{9}{2}\right)^2$ cm² *(c)* $\pi \times \left(\frac{15}{2}\right)^2$ cm² *(d)* $\pi \times (15)^2$ cm²

37. A lotus is seen 5 cm above the water level of a lake with the onset of the wind it sinks in the water 10 cm away from its place. How deep is the water in that place?
(a) 5 cm *(b)* 7.5 cm *(c)* 10 cm *(d)* $5\sqrt{5}$ cm

38. The lengths of the perpendiculrs drawn from any point in the interior of an equilateral triangle to the respective sides are p_1, p_2 and p_3. The length of each side of the triangle is:
(a) $\frac{1}{3}(p_1 + p_2 + p_3)$ *(b)* $\frac{1}{\sqrt{3}}(p_1 + p_2 + p_3)$
(c) $\frac{2}{\sqrt{3}}(p_1 + p_2 + p_3)$ *(d)* $\frac{4}{\sqrt{3}}(p_1 + p_2 + p_3)$

39. A brick, 5 cm thick (high) is placed against a wheel to act for a stop. The horizontal distance of the face of the brick stopping the wheel from the point, where the wheel touches the ground is 15 cm. Find the radius of the wheel.
(a) 20 cm *(b)* 25 cm *(c)* 30 cm *(d)* 35 cm

40. A chord AB of a circle of radius 10 cm makes a right angle at the centre of the circle. The areas of the major and minor segments are:
(a) 220 cm²; 30 cm² *(b)* 280 cm²; 30 cm²
(c) 285.5 cm²; 28.5 cm² *(d)* None of these

41. Two circles touch externally. The sum of their areas is 130 π cm² and the distance between their centres is 14 cm. Find the radii of the circles.
(a) 8 cm; 6 cm *(b)* 9 cm; 5 cm *(c)* 10 cm; 4 cm *(d)* 11 cm; 3 cm

42. The area of a circle inscribed in an equilateral triangle is 48 π cm^2. The perimeter of the triangle is:
(*a*) 24 cm (*b*) 36 cm (*c*) 48 cm (*d*) 72 cm

43. The length of the side of a square is 14 cm. Taking vertices of the squares as centres, four circles are drawn each with a radius of 7 cm. Find the area of the region of the square that remains outside the region of any of the circles.
(*a*) 30 cm^2 (*b*) 36 cm^2 (*c*) 42 cm^2 (*d*) 48 cm^2

44. The parallel sides of a field which is in the shape of trapezium are 20 m and 41 m and the remaining two sides are 10m and 17m. Find the cost of levelling the field at the rate of Rs. 30 per m^2.
(*a*) Rs. 7150 (*b*) Rs. 7220 (*c*) Rs. 7320 (*d*) Rs. 7350

45. The area of circle whose radius is 6 cm is trisected by two concentric circles. The radius of the smallest circle is:
(*a*) 2 cm (*b*) $2\sqrt{3}$ cm (*c*) $2\sqrt{6}$ cm (*d*) 3 cm

46. If the difference between the circumference and diameter of a circle is 30 cm, then the radius of the circle must be:
(*a*) 5 cm (*b*) 6 cm (*c*) 7 cm (*d*) 8 cm

47. If the length of a rectangle is increased by 20% and its breadth is decreased by 20%, then its area
(*a*) decreases by 4% (*b*) increases by 4%
(*c*) decreases by 1% (*d*) remains unchanged

48. If the diagonals of two squares are in the ratio of 2 : 5, their areas will be in the ratio of:
(*a*) $\sqrt{2}:\sqrt{5}$ (*b*) 2 : 5 (*c*) 4 : 5 (*d*) 4 : 25

49. The radius of a circular wheel is 1.75 m. The number of revolutions that it will make in travelling 11 km, is
(*a*) 10 (*b*) 100 (*c*) 1000 (*d*) 10,000

50. The difference between the length and breadth of a rectangle is 23 m. If its perimeter is 206m, then its area is:
(*a*) 1520 m^2 (*b*) 2420 m^2 (*c*) 2480 m^2 (*d*) 2520 m^2

51. If the radius of a circle is decreased by 50%, its area will decrease by:
(*a*) 25% (*b*) 50% (*c*) 75% (*d*) None of these

52. The diameter of a wheel of a cycle is 70 cm. It moves slowly along a road. How far will it go in 24 complete revolutions?
(*a*) 38.9 m (*b*) 52.8 m (*c*) 56.6 m (*d*) 60 m

53. The ratio of length and breadth of a rectangular plot is 71 : 61 respectively. The area of the plot is 17324 m^2. What is perimeter of the plot?
(*a*) 264 m (*b*) 284 m (*c*) 528 m (*d*) 614 m

54. The area of a circular plot is 3850 m^2. What is the circumference of the plot?
(*a*) 210 m (*b*) 220 m (*c*) 240 m (*d*) 260 m

55. X is a point on side CD of a square ABCD such that CX = 5 cm. If area of the triangle ADX is 42 cm^2. What is the length of the side of the square?
(*a*) 10 cm (*b*) 12 cm (*c*) 16 cm (*d*) 20 cm

56. A rectangular area having length 30 m, breadth 22 m is bounded by a series of trees. The distance between two trees is 1 m. How many number of trees could be planted?
(*a*) 52 (*b*) 104 (*c*) 156 (*d*) 208

57. A room having length 15m and breadth 12m. What will be the total cost if the floor is made at Rs. 125 per m^2?

(a) Rs. 20,050 *(b)* Rs. 20,500 *(c)* Rs. 22,050 *(d)* Rs. 22,500

58. A circular ground has area equal to 616 m^2. Inside the circle a small circle is there whose radius equal to half of the radius of circle. Find the remaining area of the circle.

(a) 154 m^2 *(b)* 156 m^2 *(c)* 460 m^2 *(d)* 462 m^2

59. What will be the area of the circle having circumference equal to 56 cm?

(a) 216 cm^2 *(b)* 249.45 cm^2 *(c)* 256.45 cm^2 *(d)* 260 cm^2

60. The sides of a rectangle are 8 cm and 6 cm. The corners of the rectangle lie on a circle. Find the area of circle without the rectangle.

(a) 30 cm^2 *(b)* 30.6 cm^2 *(c)* 32.4 cm^2 *(d)* 36 cm^2

61. The area of a circle is 1386 m^2. Find its circumference.

(a) 124 m *(b)* 132 m *(c)* 136 m *(d)* 140 m

62. What will be the cost of building a fence around a circular field with area equal to 18,634 m^2; if the cost of building the fence per metre is Rs. 365?

(a) Rs. 1,76,660 *(b)* Rs. 1,86,680 *(c)* Rs. 2,10,660 *(d)* Rs. 2,76,660

63. The area of a rectangle is 20 times its breadth. The perimeter of the rectangle is 76 cm. What is the length of the rectangle?

(a) 18 cm *(b)* 20 cm *(c)* 24 cm *(d)* 30 cm

64. If the length and breadth of a rectangular field are increased, the area increases by 50%. If the increase in length was 20%, by what percentage was the breadth increased?

(a) 20% *(b)* 25% *(c)* 30% *(d)* 40%

65. The area of a rectangular field is 2100 m^2. If the field is 60m long, what is its perimeter?

(a) 180 m *(b)* 190 m *(c)* 200 m *(d)* 220 m

66. If the length of a rectangular field is 48 m more than its breadth and the perimeter of the field is 800 m, what is the area of the field?

(a) 31,376 m^2 *(b)* 39424 m^2 *(c)* 40,424 m^2 *(d)* 42,424 m^2

67. The perimeter of a square and a rectangle is the same. If the rectangle is 12 cm by 10 cm, then by what percentage is the area of the square more than that of the rectangle?

(a) $\frac{5}{6}\%$ *(b)* $1\frac{1}{6}\%$ *(c)* $1\frac{5}{6}\%$ *(d)* None of these

68. What is the circumference of a circle whose area is 49π cm^2?

(a) 7π cm *(b)* 14π cm *(c)* 21π cm *(d)* 28π cm

69. What will be the cost of tiling the floor @ Rs. 38/- per m^2, if the hall is of a square shape and has perimeter of 400 m?

(a) Rs. 3,20,000 *(b)* Rs. 3,40,000 *(c)* Rs. 3,60,000 *(d)* 3,80,000

70. The area of a circle whose radius is 3.5 cm, is:

(a) 12.5 cm^2 *(b)* 22.5 cm^2 *(c)* 28.5 cm^2 *(d)* 38.5 cm^2

71. The radius of a wheel is 7 cm. How many revolutions it will make to cover a distance of 44 km?

(a) 1000 *(b)* 2000 *(c)* 5000 *(d)* 10000

72. The length of a rectangle is increased by 60%. By how many per cent its breadth will be reduced so that its area remains the same?

(a) 37.5% *(b)* 50% *(c)* 60% *(d)* 75%

73. The length of a room is 5.5 m and width is 3.75 m. What will be the cost of flooring by slab at the rate of Rs. 800 per m^2?
(a) Rs. 15500 *(b)* Rs. 16000 *(c)* Rs. 16500 *(d)* Rs. 17000

74. The area of a field in the shape of a trapezium measures 1440 m^2. The perpendicular distance between its parallel sides is 24m. If ratio of the parallel sides is 5 : 3, the length of the longer parallel sides is:
(a) 45 m *(b)* 60 m *(c)* 75 m *(d)* 120 m

75. The length of a rectangle is decreased by 10% and its breadth is increased by 10%. By what per cent is its area changed?
(a) 0% *(b)* 1% *(c)* 5% *(d)* 10%

76. The percentage increase in the area of a rectangle, if each of its sides is increased by 20%, is
(a) 40% *(b)* 44% *(c)* 48% *(d)* 50%

77. There is a rectangular tank of length 180 m and breadth 120 m in a circular field. If the area of the land portion of the field is 40,000 m^2, what is the radius of the field? (Take $\pi = 22/7$)
(a) 130 m *(b)* 135 m *(c)* 140 m *(d)* 145 m

78. Three coins of the same size (radius 1 cm) are placed on a table such that each of them touches the other two. The area enclosed by the coins is:
(a) $\left(\sqrt{3}-\pi/2\right)$ cm² *(b)* $\left(\pi/2-\sqrt{3}\right)$ cm² *(c)* $\left(2\sqrt{3}-\pi/2\right)$ cm² *(d)* $\left(3\sqrt{3}-\pi/2\right)$ cm²

79. The ratio of bases of two triangles is $x : y$ and their areas is $a : b$. Then ratio of their corresponding altitudes will be:
(a) $ax : by$ *(b)* $ay : bx$ *(c)* $\frac{a}{x}:\frac{b}{y}$ *(d)* $\frac{x}{a}:\frac{b}{y}$

80. The area of regular hexagon of side $2\sqrt{3}$ cm is:
(a) $12\sqrt{3}$ cm² *(b)* $18\sqrt{3}$ cm² *(c)* $27\sqrt{3}$ cm² *(d)* $36\sqrt{3}$ cm²

81. The length of a rectangle is increased by 30% and breadth is decreased by the same per cent, the effective change in area will be
(a) 6% decrease *(b)* 6% increase *(c)* 9% decrease *(d)* 9% increase

82. Find the area of cicular ring whose external and internal diameters are 20 cm and 6 cm respectively.
(a) 285 cm² *(b)* 286 cm² *(c)* 298 cm² *(d)* 1144 cm²

83. In the given diagram below, AB = CD = 9m, AC = BD = 5m. Length and breadth of the unshaded portion 3m and 1m. The area of the shaded portion is:

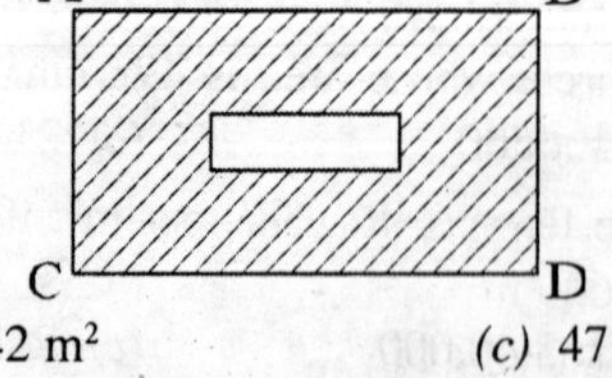

(a) 40 m² *(b)* 42 m² *(c)* 47 m² *(d)* 48 m²

84. The rectangle measures 140 m × 70 m. The circle at its centre has a diameter of 28 m. The area of the shaded portion is:

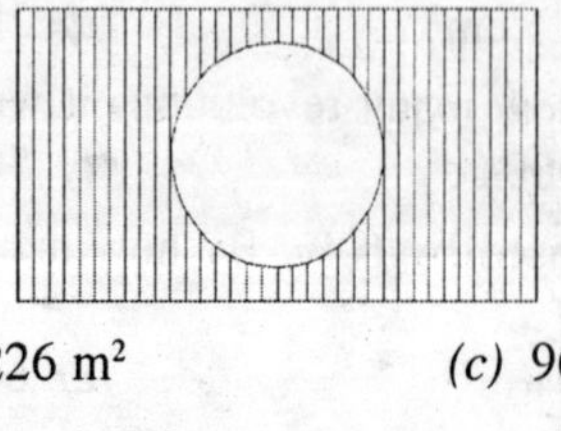

(a) 9184 m² *(b)* 9226 m² *(c)* 9624 m² *(d)* 9824 m²

85. A one metre long rope has been given the shape of a circle. The area of this circle is:
(a) 600 cm^2 (b) 795 .45 cm^2 (c) 810.45 cm^2 (d) 890.45 cm^2

86. The length and breadth of a varandah is 40 m and 15 m respectively. How many stone slabs of size 6 decimetre × 5 decimetre each are needed in flooring it:
(a) 1000 (b) 2000 (c) 3000 (d) 4000

87. A horse is tied to a peg hammered at one corner of a rectangular grass field of 40m by a rope 14m long. Over how much area of the field can the horse graze?
(a) 154 m^2 (b) 240 m^2 (c) 308 m^2 (d) 480 m^2

88. The sides of a triangle are in the ratio 3 : 5 : 7 and its perimeter is 30 cm. The length of the greatest side of the triangle is:
(a) 6 cm (b) 10 cm (c) 14 cm (d) 16 cm

89. The ratio of the length and the breadth of a rectangular plot is 7 : 6 respectively. The perimeter of the plot is 208 m. Find its area.
(a) 2538 m^2 (b) 2592 m^2 (c) 2688 m^2 (d) 2696 m^2

90. The circumference of a circular plot is 396 m. What is the area of the circular plot?
(a) 9,446 m^2 (b) 9,856 m^2 (c) 12,474 m^2 (d) 18,634 m^2

91. The length of the two diagonals of a rhombus are 10 cm and 8 cm. What is the area of the rhombus?
(a) 40 cm^2 (b) 80 cm^2 (c) 120 cm^2 (d) 160 cm^2

92. The circumference of a circle is 88 cm. Find its area.
(a) 544 cm^2 (b) 616 cm^2 (c) 724 cm^2 (d) 849 cm^2

93. The ratio between the length and breadth of a rectangle is 7:3. If the perimeter of the rectangle is 160 cm., what is its area?
(a) 1144 cm^2 (b) 1244 cm^2 (c) 1344 cm^2 (d) 1444 cm^2

94. If the sides of an equilateral triangle are increased by 20%, 30% and 50% respectively to form a new triangle, the increase in the perimeter of the equilateral triangle is:
(a) 25% (b) $33\frac{1}{3}\%$ (c) 50% (d) 100%

95. If each side of a rectangle is increased by 50%, its area will be increased by
(a) 50% (b) 100% (c) 125% (d) 150%

96. The floor of a corridor is 100 m long and 3 m wide. Cost of covering the floor with carpet 50 cm wide at the rate of Rs. 15 per m is
(a) Rs. 1900 (b) Rs. 4500 (c) Rs. 7500 (d) Rs. 9000

97. The area of a triangular field, the lengths of whose sides are 50m, 78m and 112m is:
(a) 1480 m^2 (b) 1600 m^2 (c) 1680 m^2 (d) 3360 m^2

98. The area of a circular jogging track is 3850 m^2. What is the circumference of the jogging track?
(a) 214 m (b) 220 m (c) 225 m (d) 235 m

99. The ratio of the length and the breadth of a rectangular plot is 6 : 5 respectively. If the breadth of the plot is 34 m less than the length, what is the perimeter of the rectangular plot?
(a) 448 m (b) 508 m (c) 748 m (d) 848 m

100. The length of a rectangular plot is thrice its breadth. What is the perimeter of that plot, if the area of the plot is 17328 m^2?
(a) 592 m (b) 604 m (c) 608 m (d) 616 m

101. The ratio of length and breadth of a rectangular plot is 8 : 5 repectively. if the breadth is 60 m less than the length, what is the perimeter of the rectangular plot?
(a) 260 m (b) 500 m (c) 520 m (d) 620 m

102. A rectangular garden is 100 m long, 80 m wide. It is surrounded on its outside by a uniformly broad path. If the area of the path is 1900 m^2, then what is its width?
(a) 2m (b) 3m (c) 4m (d) 5m

103. If a rectangular space 8 cm long and 6 cm wide is increased in its length and width by 25%, then what will be the percentage increase in the area of original rectangular space?
(a) 25% (b) 36% (c) 50% (d) 56¼%

104. The area of a rhombus is 96 cm^2. If one of the diagonals is 12 cm, then the other diagonal and the side of the rhombus are respectively:
(a) 8 cm and 10 cm (b) 10 cm and 16 cm (c) 16 cm and 10 cm (d) 16 cm and 8 cm

105. The three sides of a triangle are 3cm,. 4 cm and 5 cm respectively, then its area is:
(a) $\sqrt{32}$ cm^2 (b) 6 cm^2 (c) 9 cm^2 (d) 12 cm^2

106. If one side and one diagonal of a rhombus are 5 cm and 8 cm respectively, then its area is:
(a) 13 cm^2 (b) 20 cm^2 (c) 24 cm^2 (d) 40 cm^2

107. The perimeter of a rectangular field is 480 m and the ratio between the length and breadth is 5 : 3, the area is:
(a) 135 m^2 (b) 135 acres (c) 155 acres (d) 1550 m^2

108. A wire, in the form of a circle of radius 42 cm, is cut and bent in the form of square. The side of the square is:
(a) 29 cm (b) 33 cm (c) 44 cm (d) 66 cm

109. In a triangular field having sides 30 m, 72 m and 78 m, the length of the altitude to the side measuring 72 m is:
(a) 25 m (b) 28 m (c) 30 m (d) 35 m

110. If the perimeter of a right-angled isosceles triangle is $\left(4\sqrt{2}+4\right)$ cm, the length of the hypotenuse is:
(a) 4 cm (b) 6 cm (c) 8 cm (d) 10 cm

111. The length and breadth of a rectangle are inceased by 12% and 15% respectively. Its area will be increased by:
(a) 27% (b) $27\frac{1}{5}\%$ (c) 28% (d) $28\frac{4}{5}\%$

112. A piece of wire of 78 cm long is bent in the form of an isosceles triangle. If the ratio of one of the equal sides to the base is 5 : 3, then length of the base is:
(a) 16 cm (b) 17 cm (c) 18 cm (d) 19 cm

113. The area of a square is 2.25cm^2. What is its perimeter?
(a) 1.5 cm (b) 4.5 cm (c) 6 cm (d) 9 cm

114. The perimeter of a square is 48 m. The area of a rectangle is 4 m^2 less than the area of the given square. If the length of the rectangle is 14 m, find the breadth.
(a) 8 m (b) 10 m (c) 12 m (d) 14 m

115. Find the area of a parallelogram if two sides are 12 cm and 14 cm and the diagonal connecting the ends is 18 cm.
(a) 150 cm^2 (b) 160 cm^2 (c) 167.8 cm^2 (d) 170 cm^2

116. The diagonal of a farm in the shape of a quadrilateral is 180 m. The altitudes drawn from the other vertices on the diagonal are 57 m and 112 m. Find the area of the farm in hectares.
(*a*) 1.521 (*b*) 1.621 (*c*) 1.721 (*d*) 1.821

117. A sheet of paper is in the form of a rectangle ABCD in which AB = 40 cm and BC = 28 cm. A semi circular portion with BC as diameter is cut off. Find the area of remaining paper.
(*a*) 800 cm^2 (*b*) 812 cm^2 (*c*) 825 cm^2 (*d*) 850 cm^2

118. The circumference of two circles are in the ratio 2 : 3. Find the ratio of their areas.
(*a*) 2 : 3 (*b*) 4 : 3 (*c*) 4 : 9 (*d*) 2 : 9

119. A circular play ground is surrounded by a 21m road. The radius of the ground is 105 m. Find the area of the road.
(*a*) 15000 m^2 (*b*) 15246 m^2 (*c*) 15250 m^2 (*d*) 15260 m^2

120. A room measuring 7 m × 5.6 m is to be carpeted leaving 0.3 m space bare all around. Find the carepeted area.
(*a*) 25 m^2 (*b*) 30 m^2 (*c*) 32 m^2 (*d*) 35 m^2

121. If the area of a regular hexagon is $96\sqrt{3}$ m^2, find its side.
(*a*) 2 m (*b*) 4 m (*c*) 6 m (*d*) 8 m

122. The perimeter of a square whose area is equal to that of a circle with circumference $2\pi x$ is:
(*a*) $\sqrt{\pi}\, x$ (*b*) $4\sqrt{\pi}\, x$ (*c*) $4\sqrt{\pi x}$ (*d*) $2\pi x$

123. The cost of fencing a square garden is Rs. 400 at the rate of Re. 1 per metre. The area of the garden is:
(*a*) 10 m^2 (*b*) 100 m^2 (*c*) 1000 m^2 (*d*) 10000 m^2

124. A rectangular carpet has an area of 120 m^2 and a perimeter of 46 m. The length of its diagonal is:
(*a*) 15 m (*b*) 16 m (*c*) 17 m (*d*) 18 m

125. The parallel sides of a trapezium are p cm and q cm and the distance between them is d cm. Find the area of the trapezium.
(*a*) $\frac{p+q}{2d}$ cm^2 (*b*) $d(p+q)$ cm^2 (*c*) $\frac{1}{2}.d(p+q)$ cm^2 (*d*) dpq cm^2

126. The perimeter of a rectangle is 28 cm, one of its side is 8 cm. Find the area of the rectangle.
(*a*) 12 cm^2 (*b*) 24 cm^2 (*c*) 36 cm^2 (*d*) 48 cm^2

127. A sector of 120°, cut out from a circle, has an area of $9\frac{3}{7}$ cm^2. Find the radius of the circle.
(*a*) 3 cm (*b*) 6 cm (*c*) 9 cm (*d*) 10 cm

128. The length of a rectangular plot is 60% more than its breadth. If the difference between the length and the breadth of that rectangle is 24 cm, find the area of the rectangle.
(*a*) 2480 cm^2 (*b*) 2520 cm^2 (*c*) 2660 cm^2 (*d*) 2700 cm^2

129. The difference between the length and breadth of a rectangle is 23 cm. If the perimeter is 206 cm, then find its area.
(*a*) 2480 cm^2 (*b*) 2520 cm^2 (*c*) 2580 cm^2 (*d*) 2620 cm^2

130. A rectangular parking space is marked out painting three of its sides. If the length of the unpainted side is 9 m, and the sum of the lengths of the painted sides is 37m, then what is the area of the parking space?
(*a*) 126 m^2 (*b*) 130 m^2 (*c*) 136 m^2 (*d*) 140 m^2

131. The length of a rectangular plot is 20 m more than its breadth. If the cost of fencing the plot at the ratè of Rs. 26.50 per m is Rs. 5300, then find the length of the plot.
(*a*) 50 m (*b*) 60 m (*c*) 70 m (*d*) 80 m

132. The length of a rectangular hall is 5 m more than its breadth. The area of the hall is 750 m^2. What is the length of the hall?
(*a*) 25 m (*b*) 30 m (*c*) 35 m (*d*) 40 m

133. The ratio between length and the breadth of a rectangular park is 3 : 2. If a boy cycling along the boundary of the park at the speed of 12 km/hr completes one round in 8 minutes then what is the area of the park?
(*a*) 153600 m^2 (*b*) 154000 m^2 (*c*) 155000 m^2 (*d*) 163600 m^2

134. The area of a rectangle is 460 m^2. If the length is 15% more than the breadth, find the breadth of the rectangular field:
(*a*) 15 m (*b*) 20 m (*c*) 25 m (*d*) 30 m

135. The ratio between the perimeter and the breadth of a rectangle is 5 : 1. If the area of the rectangle is 216 m^2, what is the length of the rectangle?
(*a*) 12 m (*b*) 16 m (*c*) 18 m (*d*) 20 m

136. The sides of a rectangular field are in the ratio 3 : 4. If the area of the field is 7500 m^2, the cost of fencing the field at the rate of 25 paise per m is:
(*a*) Rs. 87.50 (*b*) Rs. 90 (*c*) Rs. 92.50 (*d*) Rs. 95

137. A rectangular field is to be fenced on three sides leaving a side of 20 m uncovered. If the area of the field is 680 m^2, how many metre of fencing will be required?
(*a*) 40 m (*b*) 44 m (*c*) 60 m (*d*) 88 m

138. A farmer wishes to start a 100 m^2 rectangular vegetable garden. Since he has 30 m barbed wire, he fences three sides of the garden letting his house compound wall as the fourth side fencing. What is the dimension of the garden?
(*a*) 40 m × 2.5 m (*b*) 2.5 m × 4 m (*c*) 20 m × 5 m (*d*) None of these

139. A rectangular paper, when folded into two congruent parts had a perimeter of 34 cm for each part folded along one set of sides and the same is 38cm when folded along the other set of sides. What is the area of the paper?
(*a*) 100 cm^2 (*b*) 120 cm^2 (*c*) 140 cm^2 (*d*) 160 cm^2

140. The diagonal of the floor of a rectangular closet is 7½m. The shorter side of the closet is 4½ m. Find the area of the closet.
(*a*) 13½ m^2 (*b*) 27 m^2 (*c*) 18½ m^2 (*d*) 37 m^2

141. Samir took 15 seconds to cross a rectangular field diagonally walking at the rate of 52 m/min. and Saurabh took the same to cross the same field along its sides walking at the rate of 68 m/min. What is the area of the field?
(*a*) 30 m^2 (*b*) 45 m^2 (*c*) 60 m^2 (*d*) 75 m^2

142. The length of a rectangle is three times of its breadth. If the length of the diagonal is $8\sqrt{10}$ cm, then find the perimeter of the rectangle.
(*a*) $24\sqrt{10}$ cm (*b*) $32\sqrt{10}$ cm (*c*) 60 cm (*d*) 64 cm

143. The diagonal of a rectangle is $\sqrt{41}$ cm and its area is 20 cm^2. What is the perimeter of the rectangle?
(*a*) 18 cm (*b*) 20 cm (*c*) 24 cm (*d*) 30 cm

144. If the length and breadth of a rectangular room are each increased by 1m, then the area of the floor is increased by 21 m^2. If the length is increased by 1m and breadth is decreased by 1m, then the area is decreased by $5m^2$. What is the perimeter of the floor?
(a) 40 m *(b)* 45 m *(c)* 50 m *(d)* 60 m

145. The length of a rectangle is halved, while its breadth is tripled. What is the percentage of increase in area?
(a) 25% *(b)* 50% *(c)* 75% *(d)* 100%

146. A typist uses a sheet measuring 20 cm by 30 cm lengthwise. If a margin of 2 cm is left on each side and a 3 cm margin on top and bottom. What is the per cent of the page used for typing?
(a) 60% *(b)* 64% *(c)* 70% *(d)* 74%

147. The length of a rectangle is decreased by *r*% and breadth is increased by $(r + 5)$%. If the area of the rectangle is unaltered then find the value of *r*.
(a) 20 *(b)* 25 *(c)* 30 *(d)* 40

148. What will be the cost of gardening 1m broad boundary around a rectangular plot having perimeter of 340 m at the rate of Rs. 10 per m^2?
(a) Rs. 1720 *(b)* Rs. 3400 *(c)* Rs. 3440 *(d)* Rs. 3540

149. The perimeter of five squares are 24 cm, 32 cm, 40 cm, 76 cm and 80 cm respectively. What is the perimeter of another square equal in area to the sum of the areas of these squares?
(a) 120 cm *(b)* 124 cm *(c)* 130 cm *(d)* 150 cm

150. 50 square stone slabs of equal size were needed to cover a floor area of 72 m^2. What is the length of each slab?
(a) 80 cm *(b)* 100 cm *(c)* 120 cm *(d)* 140 cm

151. What is the least number of square tiles required to pave the floor of a room 15m 17 cm long and 9m 2cm broad?
(a) 794 *(b)* 800 *(c)* 804 *(d)* 814

152. A boy walked diagonally across a square lot. What was the per cent saved approximately by not walking through the edges?
(a) 30 *(b)* 32 *(c)* 34 *(d)* 36

153. A park square in shape has a 3m wide road inside it running along its sides. The area occupied by the road is 1764 m^2. Find the perimeter along the outer edge of the road.
(a) 500 m *(b)* 525 m *(c)* 550 m *(d)* 600 m

154. The area of a square field is 69696 cm^2. What is its diagonal?
(a) $260\sqrt{2}$ cm *(b)* $262\sqrt{2}$ cm *(c)* $264\sqrt{2}$ cm *(d)* $266\sqrt{2}$ cm

155. If the length of the diagonal of a square is 20 cm, then find its perimeter.
(a) $20\sqrt{2}$ cm *(b)* 40 cm *(c)* $40\sqrt{2}$ cm *(d)* 80 cm

156. The ratio of the area of a square to that of the square drawn on its diagonal is
(a) 1 : 1 *(b)* 1 : 2 *(c)* 2 : 3 *(d)* 3 : 4

157. The diagonal of a square is $4\sqrt{2}$ cm. Find the diagonal of another square whose area is double that of the first square.
(a) 4 cm *(b)* $4\sqrt{2}$ cm *(c)* 8 cm *(d)* $8\sqrt{2}$ cm

158. If the ratio of areas of two squares is 225 : 256; then find the ratio of their perimeters.
(a) 15 : 16 *(b)* 16 : 15 *(c)* 225 : 256 *(d)* 256 : 225

159. An error of 2% in excess is made while measuring the side of a square. What is the percentge of error in the calculated area of the square?
(a) 4% (b) 4.04% (c) 8% (d) 8.04%

160. The length of one pair of opposite sides of a square is increased by 5 cm on each side; the ratio of the length and breadth of the newly formed rectangle becomes 3 : 2. Find the area of the original square.
(a) 81 cm^2 (b) 100 cm^2 (c) 121 cm^2 (d) 144 cm^2

161. The difference of the areas of two squares having different length of sides is 32 cm^2. Find the length of the side of greater square, if one is longer than other by 2 cm.
(a) 9 cm (b) 10 cm (c) 12 cm (d) 15 cm

162. A tank is 25 m long, 12 m wide and 6 m deep. The cost of plastering its walls and bottom at 75 paise per m^2 is
(a) Rs. 458 (b) Rs. 558 (c) Rs. 656 (d) Rs. 658

163. The areas of a square and a rectangle are equal. The length of the rectangle is greater than the length of the side of the square by 5 cm and breadth is less by 3 cm. What is the perimeter of the rectangle?
(a) 34 cm (b) 36 cm (c) 38 cm (d) 40 cm

164. The base of a triangle is 15 cm and height is 12 cm. What is the height of another triangle of double the area having the base 20 cm?
(a) 9 cm (b) 18 cm (c) 27 cm (d) 36 cm

165. The area of a triangle is 1176 cm^2 and base : corresponding altitude is 3 : 4, then what is the altitude of the triangle?
(a) 56 cm (b) 60 cm (c) 84 cm (d) 70 cm

166. The area of a right-angled triangle is 40 times its base. Find its height.
(a) 40 cm (b) 60 cm (c) 80 cm (d) 100 cm

167. The area of a triangle is 216 cm^2 and its sides are in the ratio 3 : 4 : 5. What is the perimeter of the triangle?
(a) 12 cm (b) 24 cm (c) 36 cm (d) 72 cm

168. The sides of of a triangle are in the ratio of $\frac{1}{2}:\frac{1}{3}:\frac{1}{4}$. If the perimeter is 52 cm, then find the length of the smallest side.
(a) 9 cm (b) 12 cm (c) 18 cm (d) 24 cm

169. The perimeter of a right-angled triangle is 60 cm. Its hypotenuse is 26 cm. What is the area of the triangle?
(a) 60 cm^2 (b) 100 cm^2 (c) 120 cm^2 (d) 240 cm^2

170. The sides of a triangle are 3 cm, 4 cm and 5 cm. What is the area of the triangle formed by joining the mid-points of the sides of this triangle?
(a) $\frac{3}{2}$ cm^2 (b) 3 cm^2 (c) $\frac{5}{2}$ cm^2 (d) 5 cm^2

171. The height of an equilateral triangle is 10 cm. Find its area.
(a) $\frac{100}{\sqrt{3}}$ cm^2 (b) $\frac{100}{3}$ cm^2 (c) 100 cm^2 (d) $\frac{200}{3}$ cm^2

172. The area of a square with side *a* is equal to the area of a triangle with base *a*, then find the altitude of the triangle.
(a) *a* (b) 2*a* (c) 4*a* (d) 6*a*

173. An equilateral triangle is described on the diagonal of a square. Find the ratio of the area of the triangle to that of the square.
(a) $4:\sqrt{3}$ (b) $2:\sqrt{3}$ (c) $\sqrt{3}:2$ (d) $\sqrt{3}:4$

174. If every side of equilateral triangle is doubled, the area of the new triangle is k times the area of the old one. Find the value of k.
(a) 2 (b) 3 (c) 4 (d) 5

175. A triangle and a parallelogram are constructed on the same base such that their areas are equal. If the altitude of the parallelogram is 100 m, then find the altitude of the triangle.
(a) 100 m (b) $100\sqrt{2}$ m (c) 200 m (d) $200\sqrt{2}$ m

176. One of the diagonals of a rhombus is double the other diagonal. Its area is 25 cm^2. Find the sum of diagonals.
(a) 9 cm (b) 10 cm (c) 12 cm (d) 15 cm

177. The area of a circle of radius 5 is numerically what per cent of its circumference?
(a) 150% (b) 200% (c) 250% (d) 300%

178. A circle and a rectangle have the same perimeter. The sides of the rectangle are 18 cm and 26 cm. Find the area of the circle.
(a) 512 cm^2 (b) 556 cm^2 (c) 600 cm^2 (d) 616 cm^2

179. If the circumference and the area of a circle are numerically equal, then find the diameter.
(a) 2 (b) 4 (c) 6 (d) 8

180. Between a square of perimeter 44 cm and a circle of circumference 44 cm, which figure has larger area and how much?
(a) Both have equal area (b) Circle, 33 cm^2 (c) Square, 33 cm^2 (d) Circle, 44 cm^2

181. The areas of two circular fields are in the ratio of 16 : 49. If the radius of the latter is 14m, then radius of the former is:
(a) 2 m (b) 4 m (c) 8 m (d) 12 m

182. The number of revolutions of a wheel of diameter 40 cm makes in travelling a distance of 176m, is:
(a) 140 (b) 150 (c) 160 (d) 200

183. If the ratio of areas of two circles is 4 : 9, then the ratio of circumferences will be:
(a) 4 : 9 (b) 9 : 4 (c) 2 : 3 (d) 3 : 4

184. The wheel of a motorcycle, 70 cm in diameter, makes 40 revolutions in every 10 seconds. Find the speed of the motorcycle in km/hr.
(a) 25.32 (b) 28.38 (c) 30.68 (d) 31.68

185. Find the diameter of a wheel that makes 113 revolutions to go 2 km 26 decametres.
(a) $2\frac{4}{11}$ m (b) $4\frac{4}{13}$ m (c) $6\frac{4}{11}$ m (d) $8\frac{4}{11}$ m

186. Wheels of diameters 7 cm and 14 cm start rolling simultaneously from X and Y, which are 1980 cm apart, towards each other in opposite directions. Both of them make the same number of revolutions per second. If both of them meet after 10 seconds, find the speed of smaller wheel.
(a) 88 cm/sec (b) 66 cm/sec (c) 55 cm/sec (d) 44 cm/sec

187. The front wheels of a wagon area 2π m in circumference and rear wheels are 3π m in circumference. When the front wheels have made 10 more revolutions than the rear wheels, how many metre has the wagon travelled?
(a) 20π m (b) 40π m (c) 60π m (d) 80π m

188. A circular park has a path of uniform width around it. The difference between outer and inner circumferences of the circular path is 132 m. Find its width.
(*a*) 21m (*b*) 22 m (*c*) 23 m (*d*) 24 m

189. What will be the area of semi-circle of 14 m diameter?
(*a*) 44 m^2 (*b*) 55 m^2 (*c*) 66 m^2 (*d*) 77 m^2

190. The ratio of the outer and inner perimeters of a circular path is 23 : 22. If the path is 5 metres wide, find the diameter of the inner circle.
(*a*) 44 m (*b*) 55 m (*c*) 110 m (*d*) 220 m

191. What will be the area of a semi-circle whose perimeter is 36 cm?
(*a*) 77 cm^2 (*b*) 154 cm^2 (*c*) 308 cm^2 (*d*) 330 cm^2

192. A semi-circular shaped window has diameter of 63 cm. Its perimeter is:
(*a*) 61 cm (*b*) 81 cm (*c*) 162 cm (*d*) 198 cm

193. The area of a circle is 220 cm^2. The area of a square inscribed in this circle will be:
(*a*) 50 cm^2 (*b*) 60 cm^2 (*c*) 70 cm^2 (*d*) 140 cm^2

194. The circumference of a circle is 100 cm. The side of a square inscribed in the circle is:
(*a*) $\frac{25\sqrt{2}}{\pi}$ cm (*b*) $\frac{50\sqrt{2}}{\pi}$ cm (*c*) $\frac{75\sqrt{2}}{\pi}$ cm (*d*) $\frac{100\sqrt{2}}{\pi}$ cm

195. The area of the incircle of an equilateral triangle of side 42 cm is
(*a*) 162 cm^2 (*b*) 231 cm^2 (*c*) 462 cm^2 (*d*) 562 cm^2

196. Four equal sized maximum circular plates are cut-off from a square paper sheet of area 784 cm^2. Find the circumference of each plate.
(*a*) 11 cm (*b*) 22 cm (*c*) 33 cm (*d*) 44 cm

197. An equilateral triangle, a square and a circle have equal perimeters. If T denotes the area of the triangle, S, the area of the square and C, the area of the circle then,
(*a*) $C < S < T$ (*b*) $T < S < C$ (*c*) $T < C < S$ (*d*) $S < T < C$

198. The area of the largest triangle that can be inscribed in a semi-circle of radius *r*, is:
(*a*) r^2 (*b*) $2r^2$ (*c*) $3r^2$ (*d*) $4r^2$

SOLUTIONS

1. Area of the rectangle $= l \times b = 50 \times 25 = 1250$ sq. cm

2. Here, $4 \times \text{side} = 580 \Rightarrow \text{side} = \frac{580}{4} = 145$ m

$\therefore$ Area $= (\text{side})^2 = (145)^2 = 21025$ sq. m.

3. Area of the square $= (\text{side})^2 = (20)^2 = 400$ sq. cm.

4. Area of the circle $= \pi r^2 \quad \Rightarrow \pi r^2 = 154 \quad \Rightarrow r^2 = \frac{154 \times 7}{22} \Rightarrow r = 7$ cm

$\therefore$ Circumference of the circle $= 2\pi r = 2 \times \frac{22}{7} \times 7 = 44$ cm.

5. Area of the triangle $= \frac{1}{2} \times 8 \times 10 = 40$ sq. cm.

6. Area of the trapezium $= \frac{1}{2} \times (15 + 25) \times 10 = 200$ sq. m.

7. Suppose length and breadth of the rectangular field are $11x$ m and $8x$ m.

$\therefore$ Perimeter of the field $= 2(11x + 8x) = 2 \times 19x = 38x$ m.

Now, $38x = 760 \Rightarrow x = \dfrac{760}{38} = 20$

$\therefore$ Length of the field $= 11 \times 20 = 220$ m

Breadth of the field $= 8 \times 20 = 160$ m

$\therefore$ Area of the field $= 220 \times 160 = 35200$ sq. m.

8. Area of the square $= x^2$ sq. m.

Side of the new square $= x - 50\%$ of $x = \dfrac{x}{2}$ m

$\therefore$ Area of the new square $= \left(\dfrac{x}{2}\right)^2 = \dfrac{x^2}{4}$ sq. m.

$\therefore$ Reduction in area of the square $= x^2 - \dfrac{x^2}{4} = \dfrac{3x^2}{4}$ sq. m.

$\therefore$ Percentage reduction $= \dfrac{3x^2/4}{x^2} \times 100 = 75\%$

9. Area of the rectangle $= 6.4 \times 2.5 = 16.00$ sq. m.

$\therefore$ Side of the square $= \sqrt{16} = \sqrt{4 \times 4} = 4$ m.

10. Suppose, the three sides of the triangle are a, b and c and a is the largest while c is the smallest side of the triangle.

Now, $(a + b + c) = c \times 6$

$\Rightarrow a + b = 5c$

Again, $a^2 - b^2 = c^2$

$\Rightarrow (a + b)(a - b) = c^2$

$\Rightarrow 5c(a - b) = c^2$

$\Rightarrow a - b = \dfrac{c}{5}$ $[\because a + b = 5c]$

Now, $a + b = 5c$, $a - b = \dfrac{c}{5}$

Since, $a = \dfrac{1}{2}\left(5c + \dfrac{c}{5}\right) = \dfrac{13c}{5}$ and $b = \dfrac{1}{2}\left(5c - \dfrac{c}{5}\right) = \dfrac{12c}{5}$

Hence, $a : b : c = \dfrac{13c}{5} : \dfrac{12c}{5} : c = 13 : 12 : 5$

11. Side of the 1st square $= \dfrac{24}{4} = 6$ m

And side of the 2nd square $= \dfrac{32}{4} = 8$ m

Now, area of the third square $= 6^2 + 8^2 = 36 + 64 = 100$ sq. m.

$\therefore$ Side of the third square $= \sqrt{100} = 10$ m

Hence, Perimeter of the third square $= 4 \times$ side $= 4 \times 10 = 40$ m.

12. Area of the square = x^2 sq. m
Now, area of the new square = $(2x)^2 = 4x^2$ sq. m
Hence, it is clear that if side of a square is doubled, its area becomes four times.

13. Area of smaller square, $x^2 = 25^2 - 225 = 625 - 225 = 400 \Rightarrow x = \sqrt{400} = 20$ m
$\therefore$ Side of the smaller square = 20 m.

14. Here, $3x = 72 \Rightarrow x = \frac{72}{3} = 24$ cm.

$\therefore$ Area of the equilateral triangle $= \frac{\sqrt{3}}{4} \times x^2 = \frac{\sqrt{3}}{4} \times (24)^2 = 144\sqrt{3}$ sq. cm.

15. Area of the new circle $= \pi.5^2 + \pi.12^2$
$= 25\pi + 144\pi = 169\pi$ sq. cm.
$= \pi(13)^2$ sq. cm
Hence, it is clear that the radius of the new circle will be 13 cm.

16. Here, $2\pi R = 4x \Rightarrow R = \frac{2x}{\pi}$

$\therefore$ Ratio between the areas of the circle and the square $= \pi R^2 : x^2$

$= \pi \times \left(\frac{2x}{p}\right)^2 : x^2 = \frac{4x^2}{\pi} : x^2 = 4 : \frac{22}{7} = 14 : 11$

17. Suppose sides of the triangle are $17x$ m, $15x$ m and $8x$ metres
$\therefore$ Perimeter $= 17x + 15x + 8x = 40x$
Now, $40x = 40$
$\Rightarrow x = 1$ m
Therefore, the sides are $17 \times 1 = 17$ m, $15 \times 1 = 15$ m and $8 \times 1 = 8$ m
$\because (17)^2 = (15)^2 + (8)^2$, *i.e.*, it is a right angled triangle

$\therefore$ Area of the right angled triangle $= \frac{1}{2} \times 8 \times 15 = 60$ sq. m.

18. Area of the rectangle = xy sq. metre

Area of the new rectangle $= \frac{120}{100} x \times \frac{85}{100} y = 1.020\, xy$ sq. metre

$\therefore$ Increase in the area $= 1.02\, xy - xy = .02\, xy$ sq. m.

$\therefore$ Percentage increase $= \frac{.02xy}{xy} \times 100 = 2\%$

19. Side of rhombus $= \sqrt{\left(\frac{16}{2}\right)^2 + \left(\frac{12}{2}\right)^2} = \sqrt{8^2 + 6^2} = \sqrt{100} = 10$ cm.

$\therefore$ Perimeter of the rhombus = 4 × side = 4 × 10 = 40 cm.

20. Here, $2\pi R - R = 37$

$\Rightarrow R\left(2 \times \frac{22}{7} - 1\right) = 37$

$\Rightarrow R(44 - 7) = 37 \times 7 \Rightarrow R \times 37 = 37 \times 7 \qquad \therefore R = 7$ cm

Hence, diameter of the circle = 2R = 2 × 7 = 14 cm.

21. Suppose side of the square = x cm

$\therefore$ Diagonal of the square = $\sqrt{2}\,x$ cm.

And area of the square = x^2 cm, *i.e.*, $\frac{(\text{Diagonal})^2}{2}$

Diagonal of the new square = $2 \times \sqrt{2}x = 2\sqrt{2}x$ cm.

$\therefore$ Area of the new square = $\frac{(\text{Diagonal of the new square})^2}{2}$

$$= \frac{(2\sqrt{2}x)^2}{2} = 4x^2 \text{ sq. cm.}$$

Thus area of the new square will become fourfold.

22. Here, $\pi R^2 = 616$ and $\pi r^2 = 154$

$\because$ $\pi R^2 = 616$

$\Rightarrow$ $R^2 = \frac{616 \times 7}{22} \Rightarrow R^2 = 196 \quad \therefore R = 14$ cm

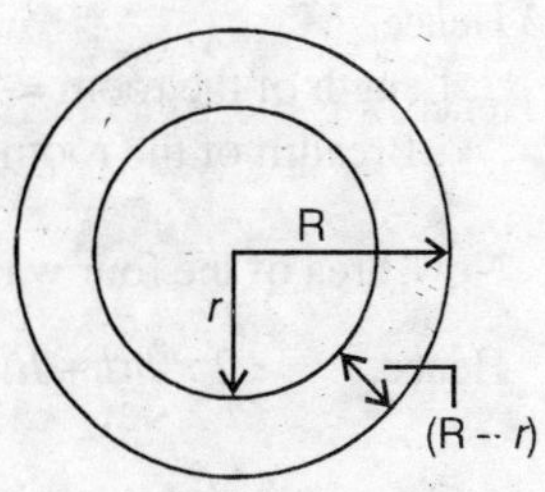

Now, and $\pi r^2 = 154 \Rightarrow r^2 = \frac{154 \times 7}{22} \quad \therefore r = 7$ cm

$\therefore$ Width of the ring $= 14 - 7 = 7$ cm.

23. Area of the rectangle = xy

On reducing the breadth by A% and increasing the length by 20%

Length of the new rectangle = $\frac{120x}{100}\, x = 1.2x$

Breadth of the new rectangle = y – A% of $y = y\left(1 - \frac{A}{100}\right)$

$\therefore$ Area of the new rectangle = $1.2x \times y\left(1 - \frac{A}{100}\right)$

Now, $xy = 1.2\,xy\left(1 - \frac{A}{100}\right) \Rightarrow 1 = 1.2\frac{(100 - A)}{100}$

$\Rightarrow$ $1.2\,A = 120 - 100$

$\therefore$ $A = \frac{20}{1.2} = 16\frac{2}{3}\%$

24. Area of the remaining portion of the square

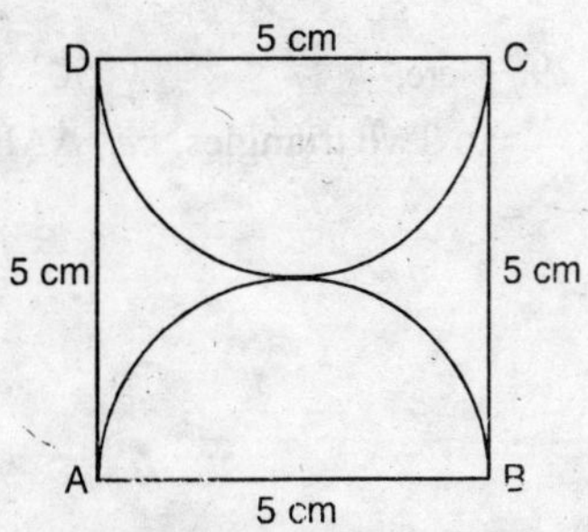

$$= 5^2 - 2 \times \frac{1}{2}\pi \times \left(\frac{5}{2}\right)^2 = 25 - \frac{25}{4}\pi$$

$$= (25 - 6.25\pi) \text{ sq. cm.}$$

25. Area of the square = 36 sq. cm

Now, $\frac{1}{2} \times \text{base} \times \text{height} = 36 \Rightarrow \frac{1}{2} \times 6 \times \text{height} = 36$

$\therefore$ Height of the triangle = $\frac{36 \times 2}{6} = 12$ cm.

26. Areas of the two circles are in the ratio 25 : 16

$\therefore$ $x^2 : y^2 = 25 : 16$

$\Rightarrow$ $x : y = 5 : 4$

Ratio of perimeters of the two squares = $4x : 4y = x : y = 5 : 4$.

27. Suppose the length and the breadth of the room are $2x$ metres and x metres respectively.

$\therefore$ Area of the floor $= 2x \times x = 2x^2$ sq. metres

Area of the floor $= \dfrac{864}{75/100} = \dfrac{864 \times 100}{75} = 1152$ sq. metre

Now, $2x^2 = 1152 \Rightarrow x^2 = \dfrac{1152}{2} = 576$

Hence, $x = 24$

$\therefore$ Length of the room $= 2 \times 24 = 48$ m

Breadth of the room = 24 m

Now, area of the four walls $= \dfrac{884}{3.25} = 272$ sq. metre

Hence, $2 \times h(l + b) = 272 \Rightarrow 2 \times h\,(48 + 24) = 272$

$\therefore$ $h = \dfrac{272}{2 \times 72} = 1\dfrac{8}{9}$ m

28. Area of the garden = 24 × 14 = 336 sq. m

Area of the (garden + path) = 26 × 16 = 416 sq. m

$\therefore$ Area of the path = 416 – 336 = 80 sq. m

Area of 1 tile = 20 × 20 = 400 sq. cm = .04 sq. m

$\therefore$ Number of tiles required to cover the path $= \dfrac{80}{.04} = 2000$.

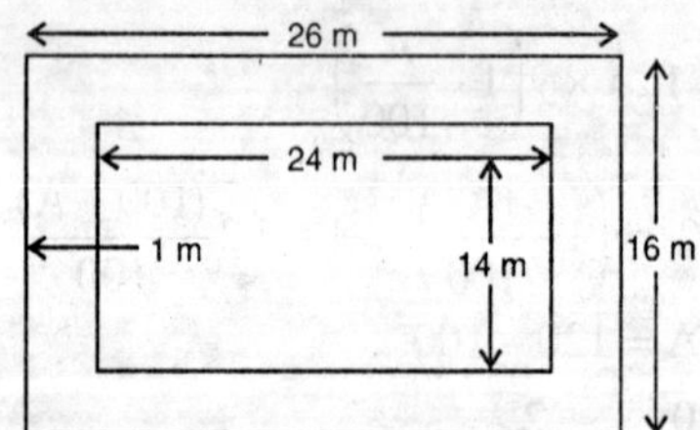

29. Here, $50^2 = 40^2 + 30^2$

$\therefore$ Two triangles, *i.e.*, ΔABC and ΔADC are right angled triangle.

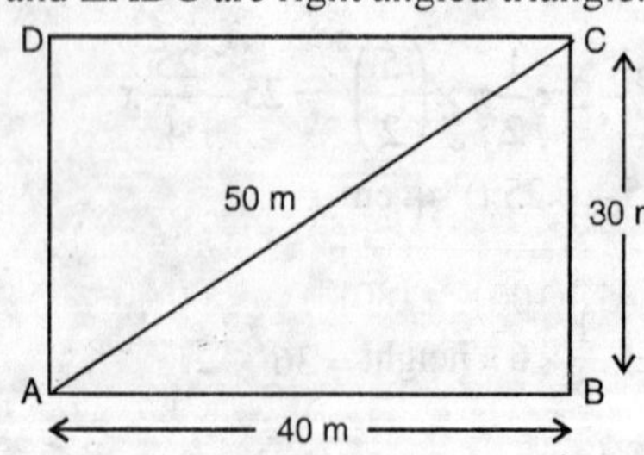

$\therefore$ Area of parallelogram ABCD = 2 × Area of Δ ABC $= 2 \times \dfrac{1}{2} \times 40 \times 30 = 1200$ sq.m.

30. First of all we will have to find the area of ΔBDF
Here, $a = 17, b = 25, c = 12$

$$\therefore \quad s = \frac{a+b+c}{2} = \frac{17+25+12}{2} = \frac{54}{2} = 27 \text{ m}$$

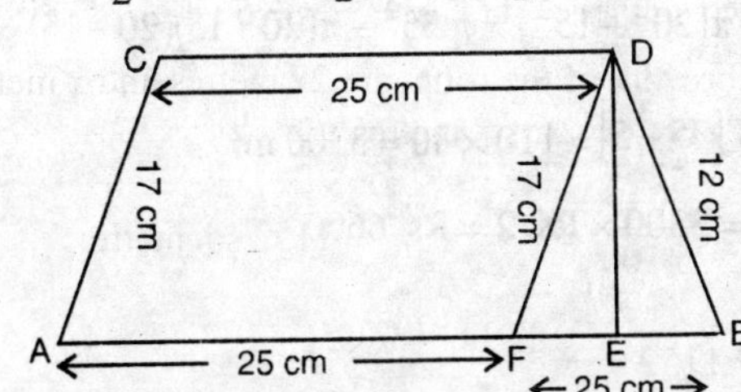

$$\therefore \quad \text{Area of } \Delta BDF = \sqrt{27(27-17)(27-25)(27-12)}$$
$$= \sqrt{27 \times 10 \times 2 \times 15}$$
$$= \sqrt{3 \times 3 \times 3 \times 2 \times 5 \times 2 \times 5 \times 3} = 3 \times 3 \times 5 \times 2$$
$$= 90 \text{ sq. m}$$

$$\because \quad \text{Area of } \Delta BDF = \frac{1}{2} \times \text{base} \times \text{height} \Rightarrow 90 = \frac{1}{2} \times 25 \times \text{height}$$

$\therefore$ Height of the triangle, *i.e.*, distance between the parallel sides of the trapezium

$$= \frac{90 \times 2}{25} = \frac{36}{5} \text{ m}$$

$$\therefore \text{ Area of the trapezium } = \frac{1}{2} \times (25+50) \times \frac{36}{5}$$

$$= \frac{1}{2} \times 75 \times \frac{36}{5} = 270 \text{ sq. cm.}$$

31. Area of the rectangular paper = $8 \times 6 = 48$ sq. cm.
$\because$ Diameter of the greatest possible circle will be 6 cm.
$\therefore$ Radius of the circle (R) = 6/2 = 3 cm
Now, Area of the circle = $\pi R^2 = \pi \times 3 \times 3 = 9\pi$ sq. cm
$\therefore$ Area of the remaining paper = $(48 - 9\pi)$ sq. cm.

32. Let the same area of the square and the circle be a; then side of the square = $\sqrt{a}$; radius of the cirlce = $\sqrt{\frac{a}{\pi}}$

Since, required ratio = $\sqrt{a} : \sqrt{\frac{a}{\pi}} = \sqrt{\pi} : 1$

33. Perpendicular of right triangle = $\sqrt{(100)^2 - (80)^2} = \sqrt{3600} = 60$ cm

Then, Area = $\frac{1}{2} \times 80 \times 60 = 2400 \text{ cm}^2$

34. Area of the rectangular plot = 3872×0.25 m² = 968 m²

Since, breadth of the plot $= \dfrac{968}{88} = 11$m

35. Area of grass plot $= \pi.35^2 - \pi\left(20^2 - 15^2\right) = \pi.35^2 - \pi(20+15)(20-15)$

$$= \frac{22}{7} \times 35\left[35 - 5\right] = 110 \times 30 = 3300 \text{ m}^2$$

The cost to turf the grass plot = 3300 × Rs. 2 = Rs. 6600

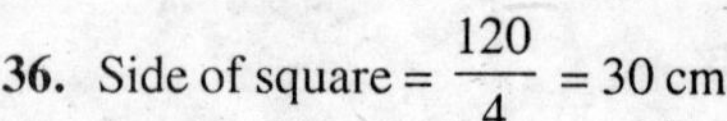

36. Side of square $= \dfrac{120}{4} = 30$ cm

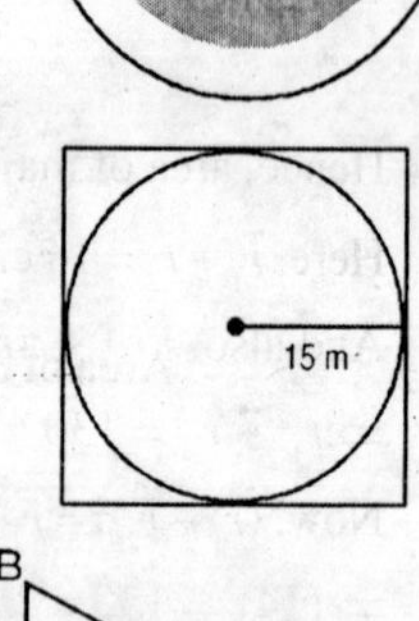

Hence, radius of the required circle $= \dfrac{30}{2} = 15$ cm

Since, area of the circle $= \pi \times (15)^2$ cm²

37. Here, AC is the water level, C is the point where lotus sinks.
Let, AD = x cm, then CD = $x + 5$ cm, now,

$(x+5)^2 - x^2 = 10^2 \Rightarrow 10x + 25 = 100 \quad \therefore x = \dfrac{75}{10} = 7.5$ cm

Hence, depth of the water = AD = 7.5 cm

38. Let side of the equilateral triangle be x.
From the figure,
Area of the equilateral triangle ABC
= Area of Δ BOD + Area of Δ AOC + Area of Δ AOB

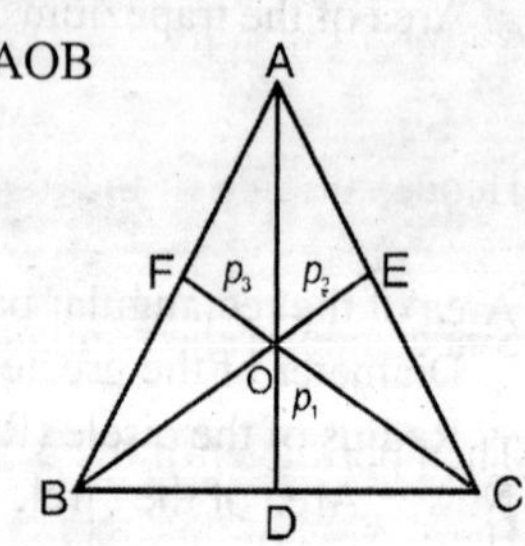

$$\Rightarrow \frac{\sqrt{3}}{4}x^2 = \frac{1}{2} \times x \times p_1 + \frac{1}{2} \times x \times p_2 + \frac{1}{2} \times x \times p_3$$

$$\Rightarrow \frac{\sqrt{3}}{2}x = p_1 + p_2 + p_3$$

$$\therefore x = \frac{2}{\sqrt{3}}(p_1 + p_2 + p_3)$$

39. Let ABCD is a brick in which AD = 5 cm and also AE = 15 cm.
If radius of the wheel = OD = OE = r cm
From the figure, OF = $r - 5$ cm, FD = 5 cm
Now, from the right Δ OFD,

$$\text{OD}^2 - \text{OF}^2 = \text{FD}^2$$
$$\Rightarrow r^2 - (r-5)^2 = 15^2$$
$$\Rightarrow 10r - 25 = 225$$
$$\Rightarrow 10r = 250$$
$$\Rightarrow r = \frac{250}{10} = 25 \text{ cm}$$

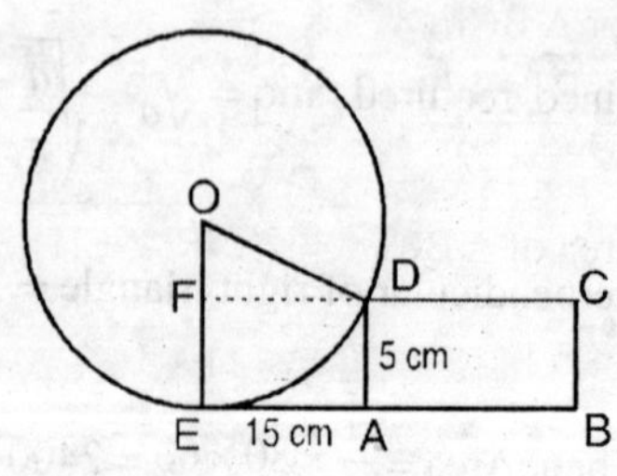

40. Area of circle = $\frac{22}{7} \times (10)^2 = \frac{2200}{7}$ cm² $\approx$ 314 cm²

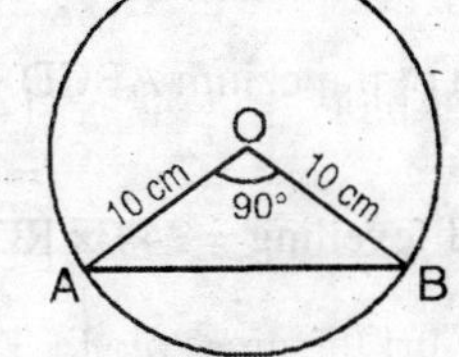

Area of minor segment = $\frac{90}{360} \times \frac{22}{7} \times 10^2 - \frac{1}{2} \times 10 \times 10$

$= \frac{550}{7} - 50$

$= \frac{200}{7} = 28.57 \approx 28.5$ cm²

Hence, area of major segment = 314 – 28.5 = 285.5 cm²

41. Here, $r_1 + r_2 = 14$ cm ...(i)

And also, $\pi r_1^2 + \pi r_2^2 = 130\,\pi$

$\Rightarrow r_1^2 + r_2^2 = 130$ ...(ii)

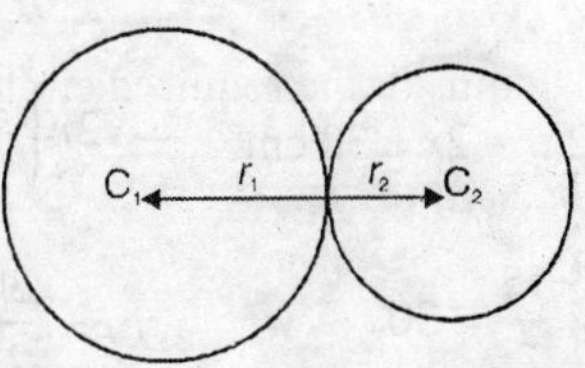

Now, $(r_1 + r_2)^2 = r_1^2 + r_2^2 + 2r_1r_2$

$\Rightarrow (14)^2 = 130 + 2r_1r_2 \quad \therefore r_1r_2 = 33$

Then, $r_1 - r_2 = \sqrt{(r_1 + r_2)^2 - 4r_1r_2} = \sqrt{(14)^2 - 4 \times 33} = \sqrt{64} = 8$

Hence, $r_1 = \frac{1}{2}(14 + 8) = 11$ cm

$r_2 = \frac{1}{2}(14 - 8) = 3$ cm

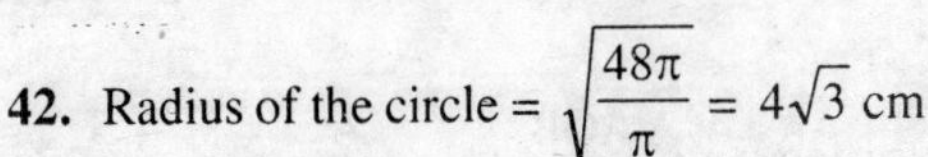

42. Radius of the circle = $\sqrt{\frac{48\pi}{\pi}} = 4\sqrt{3}$ cm

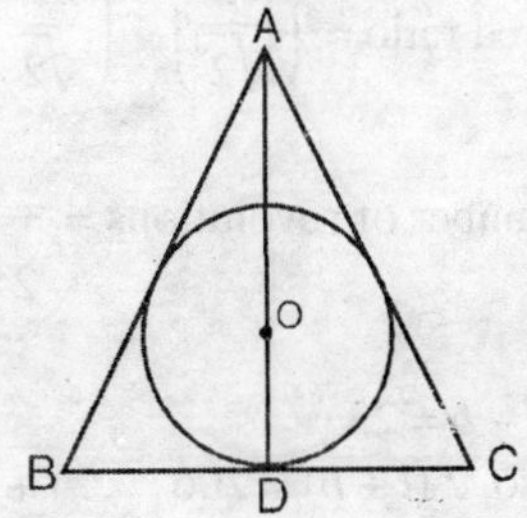

Hence, altitude of the triangle = $3 \times 4\sqrt{3} = 12\sqrt{3}$ cm

Since, side of the equilateral triangle = $\frac{2}{\sqrt{3}} \times 12\sqrt{3} = 24$ cm

Then perimeter of the triangle = 3 × 24 = 72 cm

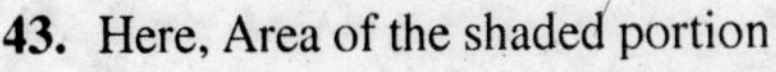

43. Here, Area of the shaded portion

$= (14)^2 - 4 \times \frac{1}{4} \times \frac{22}{7} \times 7^2$

$= 196 - 154 = 42$ cm²

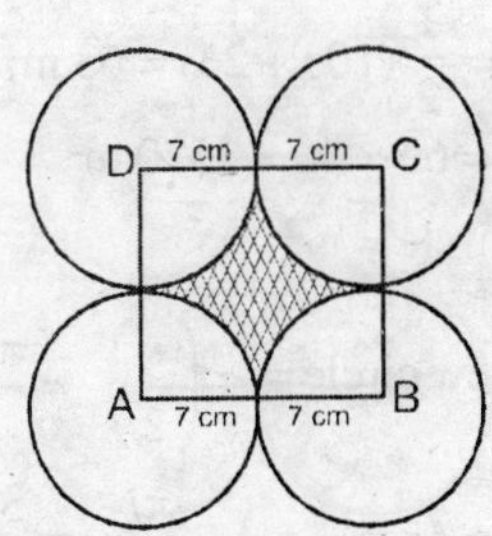

44. For Δ BCF

$s = \frac{21 + 17 + 10}{2} = 24$ m

Area of Δ BCF $= \sqrt{24(24 - 21)(24 - 17)(24 - 10)}$

$= \sqrt{24 \times 3 \times 7 \times 14}$

$= \sqrt{2 \times 2 \times 2 \times 3 \times 3 \times 7 \times 2 \times 7}$

$= 2 \times 2 \times 3 \times 7 = 84$ m²

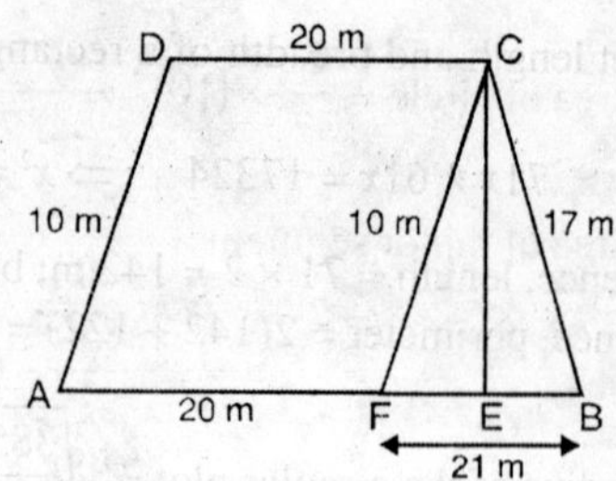

Now, $\frac{1}{2} \times 21 \times CE = 84 \quad \therefore CE = \frac{84 \times 2}{21} = 8$ m

Hence, Area of trapezium ABCD $= \frac{1}{2}(41+20) \times 8$

$= 61 \times 4 = 244$ m²

Total cost of levelling = 244 × Rs. 30 = Rs. 7320

45. Area of the smallest circle $= \frac{1}{3} \times \pi \times 6^2 = 12\pi$ cm²

Hence, radius of the smallest circle $= \sqrt{\frac{12\pi}{\pi}} = 2\sqrt{3}$ cm

46. Here, $2\pi r - 2r = 30$ cm $\Rightarrow 2r\left(\frac{22}{7} - 1\right) = 30$

$\Rightarrow 2r \times \frac{15}{7} = 30 \qquad \therefore r = \frac{30 \times 7}{2 \times 15} = 7$ cm

47. Required effect on area $= 20 + (-20) + \frac{20 \times -20}{100} = -4$

Hence, Area decreases by 4%

48. Required ratio $= \left(\frac{2x}{\sqrt{2}}\right)^2 : \left(\frac{5x}{\sqrt{2}}\right)^2 = 4 : 25$

49. The number of revolutions $= \frac{11 \times 1000}{2 \times \frac{22}{7} \times 1.75} = \frac{11 \times 1000 \times 7}{2 \times 22 \times 1.75} = 1000$

50. Here, $l - b = 23$ ...(i)

and also, $2(l + b) = 206 \quad \therefore l + b = 103$ ...(ii)

Hence, $l = \frac{1}{2}(103 + 23) = 63$ m; $b = \frac{1}{2}(103 - 23) = 40$ m

Since, A = 63 × 40 = 2520 m²

51. Area of circle $= \pi r^2$

Area of new circle $= \pi.\left(\frac{r}{2}\right)^2 = \frac{\pi r^2}{4}$

Change in Area $= \pi r^2 - \frac{\pi r^2}{4} = \frac{3}{4}\pi r^2$

Required percentage $= \frac{\frac{3}{4}\pi r^2}{\pi r^2} \times 100 = 75\%$

52. Distance, travelled in 24 revolutions $= 24 \times 2 \times \frac{22}{7} \times 35 = 5280$ cm $= 52.8$ cm

53. Let length and breadth of a rectangle be $71x$ and $61x$ m; then

$$71x \times 61x = 17324 \quad \Rightarrow x^2 = \frac{17324}{71 \times 61} = 4 \quad \therefore x = 2$$

Hence, length = 71 × 2 = 142 m; breadth = 61 × 2 = 122 m
Since, perimeter = 2(142 + 122) = 2 × 264 = 528 m

54. Radius of the circular plot = $\sqrt{\dfrac{3850 \times 7}{22}} = \sqrt{1225} = 35$ m

Circumference of the plot = $2 \times \dfrac{22}{7} \times 35 = 220$ m

55. Let side of the square = a cm; then

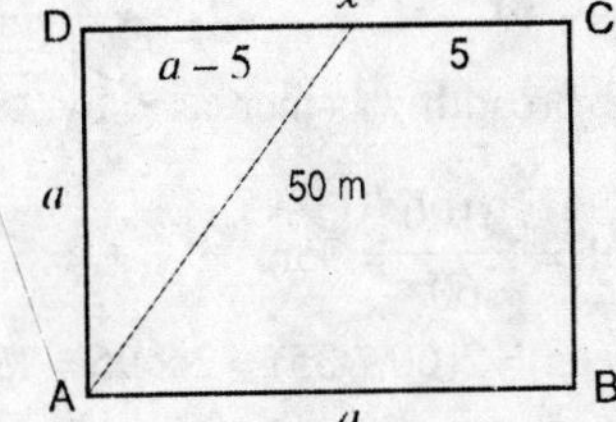

$\dfrac{1}{2} \times a \times (a - 5) = 42$
$\Rightarrow a^2 - 5a - 84 = 0$
$\Rightarrow a^2 - 12a + 7a - 84 = 0$
$\Rightarrow a(a - 12) + 7(a - 12) = 0$
$\Rightarrow (a - 12)(a + 7) = 0$
Hence, $a = 12$ cm

56. Required number of trees = $\dfrac{2(30+22)}{1} = \dfrac{104}{1} = 104$

57. Area of the floor = 15 × 12 = 180 m²
Hence, total cost of flooring = 180 × Rs. 125 = Rs. 22,500

58. Radius of the circular ground = $\sqrt{\dfrac{616 \times 7}{22}} = \sqrt{28 \times 7} = 14$ m

Area of the remaining portion = $616 - \dfrac{22}{7} \times 7^2$
$= 616 - 154 = 462$ m²

59. Radius of the circle = $\dfrac{56 \times 7}{2 \times 22} = 8.91$ cm

Area of the circle = $\dfrac{22}{7} \times 8.91 \times 8.91 = \dfrac{1746.58}{7} \approx 249.45$ cm²

60. Radius of the circle = $\dfrac{\sqrt{8^2 + 6^2}}{2} = \dfrac{10}{2} = 5$ cm

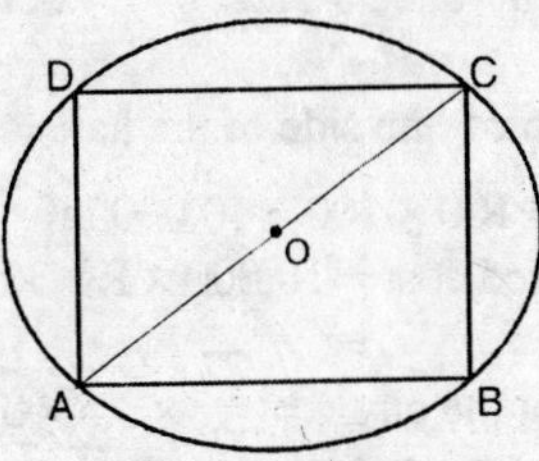

Required area = $\dfrac{22}{7} \times 5^2 - 8 \times 6$
$= 78.6 - 48 = 30.6$ cm²

61. Radius of the circle = $\sqrt{\dfrac{1386 \times 7}{22}} = \sqrt{63 \times 7} = 21$m

Circumference of the circle = $2 \times \dfrac{22}{7} \times 21 = 132$ m

62. Radius of the circular field = $\sqrt{\frac{18634 \times 7}{22}} = \sqrt{847 \times 7} = 77$ m

Circumference = $2 \times \frac{22}{7} \times 77 = 484\ m^2$

Required cost = 484 × Rs. 365 = Rs. 1,76,660

63. Let breadth of the rectangle be x cm

Since, Area = $l \times b = 20x$

$\therefore\ l = 20$ cm

64. Here, $20 + x + \frac{20 \times x}{100} = 50 \Rightarrow x + \frac{x}{5} = 30$

$\Rightarrow \frac{6x}{5} = 30 \qquad \therefore x = \frac{5 \times 30}{6} = 25$

Hence, breadth was increased by 25%

65. Breadth = $\frac{2100}{60} = 35$m

Perimeter = 2(60 + 35) = 2 × 95 = 190 m

66. Let breadth and length are x m and $(x + 48)$ m respectively, then

$2(x + x + 48) = 800 \quad \Rightarrow 2x + 48 = 400 \quad \Rightarrow 2x = 352 \quad \therefore x = 176$ m

Since, breadth = 176m and length = 176 + 48 = 224 m

Area = 224 × 176 = 39424 m^2

67. Perimeter of the rectangle = 2(12 + 10) = 44 cm

Hence, side of the square = $\frac{44}{4} = 11$ cm

Area of the square = $(11)^2 = 121\ cm^2$

Area of the rectangle = 12 × 10 = 120 cm^2

Required percentage = $\frac{121 - 120}{120} \times 100 = \frac{100}{120} = \frac{5}{6}\%$

68. Radius of the circle = $\sqrt{\frac{49\pi}{\pi}} = 7$ cm

circumference = $2\pi \times 7 = 14\pi$ cm

69. Length of one side of the hall = $\frac{400}{4} = 100$ m

Area = 100 × 100 = 10,000 m^2

Required cost = 10,000 × Rs. 38 = Rs. 3,80,000

70. Area of the circle = $\frac{22}{7} \times 3.5 \times 3.5 = 38.5\ cm^2$

71. Number of revolutions = $\frac{44 \times 1000 \times 100}{2 \times \frac{22}{7} \times 7} = 1,00,000$

72. Let breadth be reduced by $x\%$, then,

$$60 - x - \frac{60 \times x}{100} = 0 \Rightarrow x + \frac{3x}{5} = 60$$

$$\Rightarrow \frac{8x}{5} = 60 \qquad \therefore x = \frac{5 \times 60}{8} = 37.5\%$$

73. Area of the room = $5.5 \times 3.75 = 20.625$ m^2
Total cost of flooring = $20.625 \times$ Rs. 800 = Rs. 16500

74. Let the parallel sides of a trapezium be $5x$ and $3x$ m respectively,

Now, $\frac{1}{2}(5x + 3x) \times 24 = 1440 \Rightarrow 8x = \frac{1440}{12} \qquad \therefore x = \frac{120}{8} = 15$

Since, longest side = $5x = 5 \times 15 = 75$ m

75. Effective change in area $= -10 + 10 - \frac{10 \times 10}{100} = -1$

Hence, area is decreased by 1%.

76. Effective change in area $= 20 + 20 + \frac{20 \times 20}{100} = 44$

Hence, area is increased by 44%

77. Area of the circular field $= 40000 + 180 \times 120$
$= 40000 + 21600 = 61,600$ m^2

Hence, radius $= \sqrt{\frac{61600 \times 7}{22}} = \sqrt{2800 \times 7} = 140$ m

78. From the figure,
Area of shaded portion = Area of Δ ABC – Area of 3 equal sectors having central angle 60°.

$$= \frac{\sqrt{3}}{4} \times 2^2 - 3 \times \frac{60}{360} \times \pi \times 1^2$$

$$= \left(\sqrt{3} - \frac{\pi}{2}\right) \text{cm}^2$$

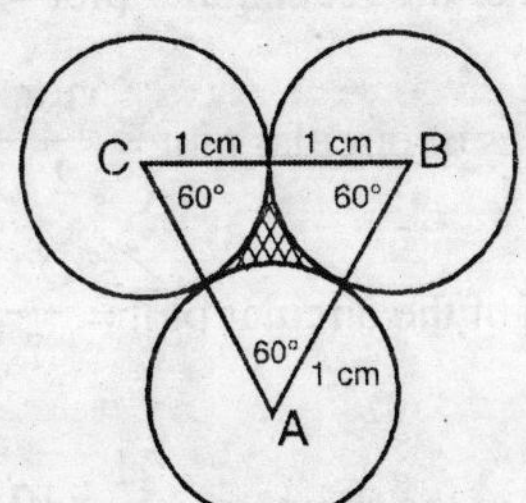

79. Required ratio $= \frac{2a}{x} : \frac{2b}{y} = ay : bx$

80. Area of regular hexagon $= \frac{3\sqrt{3}}{2} \times \left(2\sqrt{3}\right)^2 = 18\sqrt{3}$ cm^2

81. Effective change in area $= 30 - 30 - \frac{30 \times 30}{100} = -9$

Hence, area is decreased by 9%.

82. Area of circular ring $= \frac{22}{7}\left(10^2 - 3^2\right) = \frac{22}{7}(10+3)(10-3)$

$= 22 \times 13 = 286$ cm^2

83. The area of shaded portion $= 9 \times 5 - 3 \times 1 = 45 - 3 = 42 \text{ m}^2$

84. The area of shaded portion $= 140 \times 70 - \frac{22}{7} \times 14 \times 14$

$= 9800 - 616 = 9184 \text{ m}^2$

85. Radius of the circle $= \frac{100 \times 7}{2 \times 22} = \frac{175}{11}$ cm

Area of the circle $= \frac{22}{7} \times \frac{175}{11} \times \frac{175}{11} = \frac{8750}{11} = 795.45 \text{ cm}^2$

86. Required number of stone slabs $= \frac{40 \times 15}{\frac{6}{10} \times \frac{5}{10}} = \frac{40 \times 15 \times 100}{6 \times 5} = 2000$

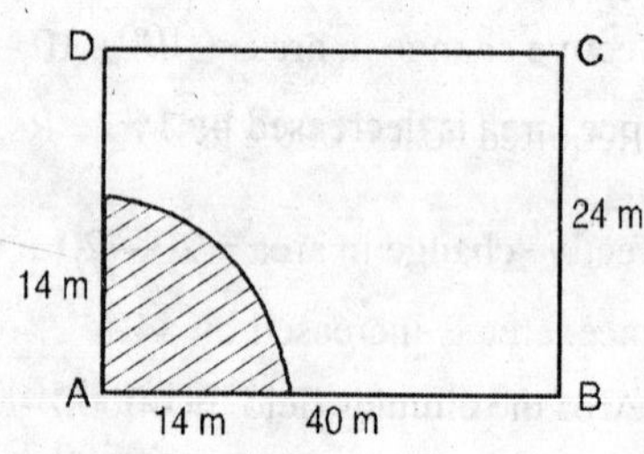

87. Required area (shaded portion) $= \frac{90}{360} \times \frac{22}{7} \times 14 \times 14$

$= 154 \text{ m}^2$

88. Let sides of the triangle are $3x$, $5x$ and $7x$ cm respectively,
Then, $3x + 5x + 7x = 30 \quad \Rightarrow 15x = 30 \quad \therefore x = 2$
Hence, length of the greatest side $= 7 \times 2 = 14$ cm

89. Let length and breadth be $7x$ and $6x$ m respectively; then,
$2(7x + 6x) = 208 \quad \Rightarrow 13x = 104 \quad \therefore x = 8$
Since, length $= 7 \times 8 = 56$ m; breadth $= 6 \times 8 = 48$m
Area of the rectangular plot $= 56 \times 48 = 2688 \text{ m}^2$

90. Radius of circular plot $= \frac{396 \times 7}{2 \times 22} = 63$ m

Area of the circular plot $= \frac{22}{7} \times 63 \times 63 = 12{,}474 \text{ m}^2$

91. Area of the rhombus $= \frac{1}{2} \times 10 \times 8 = 40 \text{ cm}^2$

92. Radius of the circle $= \frac{88 \times 7}{2 \times 22} = 14$ cm

Area of the circle $= \frac{22}{7} \times 14 \times 14 = 616 \text{ cm}^2$

93. Let length and breadth of a rectagle be $7x$ and $3x$ cm.
Then, $2(7x + 3x) = 160 \quad \Rightarrow 10x = 80 \quad \therefore x = 8$
Since, length $= 7 \times 8 = 56$ cm; breadth $= 3 \times 8 = 24$ cm
Hence, area of the rectangle $= 56 \times 24 = 1344 \text{ cm}^2$

94. Let side of the equilateral triangle be x m; then perimeter = $3x$ m

Again, three sides of the triangle are $1.20x$ cm, $1.30x$ cm and $1.50x$ cm respectively; then

Perimeter = $1.20x + 1.30x + 1.50x = 4x$ cm

Change in perimeter = $4x - 3x = x$ cm

Required percentage = $\frac{x}{3x} \times 100 = 33\frac{1}{3}\%$

95. Effective change in area = $50 + 50 + \frac{50 \times 50}{100} = 125$

Hence, area is increased by 125%.

96. Length of the carpet = $\frac{100 \times 3}{\frac{50}{100}} = 100 \times 3 \times 2 = 600$ m

Required cost = 600 × Rs. 15 = Rs. 9000

97. $s = \frac{50+78+112}{2} = \frac{240}{2} = 120$ m

Area of triangle $= \sqrt{120(120-50)(120-78)(120-112)}$

$= \sqrt{120 \times 70 \times 42 \times 8}$

$= \sqrt{2 \times 2 \times 2 \times 3 \times 5 \times 2 \times 5 \times 7 \times 2 \times 3 \times 7 \times 2 \times 2 \times 2}$

$= 2 \times 2 \times 2 \times 2 \times 3 \times 5 \times 7$

$= 1680 \text{ m}^2$

98. Radius of the circular jogging track = $\sqrt{\frac{3650 \times 7}{22}} = 35$ m

Hence, circumference = $2 \times \frac{22}{7} \times 35 = 220$ m

99. Let length and breadth be $6x$ and $5x$ m; then

$6x - 5x = 34 \quad \therefore x = 34$

Since, length = 6 × 34 = 204 m; breadth = 5 × 34 = 170 m

Hence, perimeter = 2(204 + 170) = 2 × 374 = 748 m

100. Let length and breadth be $3x$ and x m respectively, then

$3x \times x = 17328 \qquad \Rightarrow x^2 = \frac{17328}{3} \qquad \therefore x = \sqrt{5776} = 76$

Since, breadth = 76 m; length = 3 × 76 = 228 m

Hence, perimeter = 2 (228 + 76) = 2 × 304 = 608 m

101. Let length and breadth be $8x$ and $5x$ m; then,

$8x - 5x = 60 \qquad \Rightarrow 3x = 60 \qquad \therefore x = 20$

Since, length = 8 × 20 = 160 m; breadth = 5 × 20 = 100 m

Hence, perimeter = 2(160 + 100) = 2 × 260 = 520 m

102. Let width of the road be x m; then,

$(100 + 2x)(80 + 2x) - 100 \times 80 = 1900$

$\Rightarrow 4x^2 + 360x - 1900 = 0$

$\Rightarrow x^2 + 90x - 475 = 0$

$\Rightarrow x^2 + 95x - 5x - 475 = 0$

$\Rightarrow x(x + 95) - 5(x + 95) = 0$

Then, $x = 5$ m

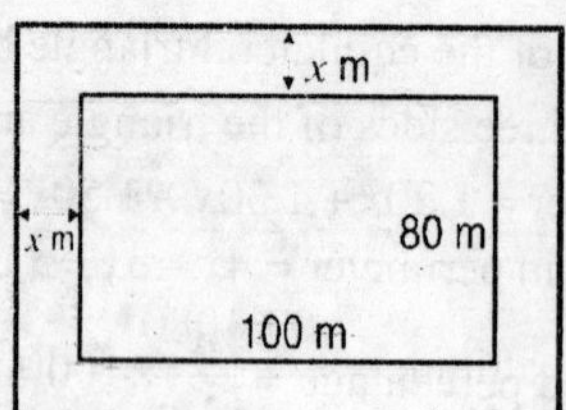

103. Area of the rectangular space $= 8 \times 6 = 48$ cm²

Now, new length $= 8 \times \frac{125}{100} = 10$ cm; New breadth $= 6 \times \frac{125}{100} = \frac{15}{2}$ cm

Since, new area $= 10 \times \frac{15}{2} = 75$ cm²

Change in area $= 75 - 48 = 27$ cm²

Required percentage $= \frac{27}{48} \times 100 = 56\frac{1}{4}\%$.

104. Other diagonal of the rhombus $= \frac{2 \times 96}{12} = 16$ cm

Side of the rhombus $= \sqrt{6^2 + 8^2} = \sqrt{100} = 10$ cm

105. Here, $3^2 + 4^2 = 5^2$; since triangle is right triangle.

Hence, its area $= \frac{1}{2} \times 3 \times 4 = 6$ cm²

106. Other diagonal $= 2 \times \sqrt{5^2 - 4^2} = 2 \times 3 = 6$ cm

Since, area of the rhombus $= \frac{1}{2} \times 8 \times 6 = 24$ cm²

107. Let length and breadth be $5x$ and $3x$ m respectively; then,

$2(5x + 3x) = 480 \quad \Rightarrow 8x = 240 \quad \therefore x = 30$

Since, length $= 5 \times 30 = 150$ m breadth $= 3 \times 30 = 90$ m

Hence, area $= 150 \times 90 = 13500$ m² $= 135$ acres.

108. Circumference of the circular wire $= 2 \times \frac{22}{7} \times 42 = 264$ cm

Since, side of the required square $= \frac{264}{4} = 66$ cm

109. $s = \frac{30 + 72 + 78}{2} = 90$ m

Area of the triangle $= \sqrt{90(90 - 30)(90 - 72)(90 - 78)}$

$= \sqrt{90 \times 60 \times 18 \times 12}$

$= \sqrt{2 \times 3 \times 3 \times 5 \times 2 \times 2 \times 3 \times 5 \times 2 \times 3 \times 3 \times 2 \times 2 \times 3}$

$= 2 \times 2 \times 2 \times 3 \times 3 \times 3 \times 5 = 1080 \text{ m}^2$

Required altitude $= \dfrac{2 \times 1080}{72} = 30$ m

110. Let equal sides of isosceles right triangle be x cm; then hypotenuse will be $\sqrt{2}\,x$ cm.

Since, $x + x + \sqrt{2}\,x = 4\sqrt{2} + 4 \quad \Rightarrow (2+\sqrt{2})x = 4(\sqrt{2}+1)$

$\therefore\ x = \dfrac{4(\sqrt{2}+1)}{\sqrt{2}(\sqrt{2}+1)} = 2\sqrt{2}$

Hence, length of hypotenuse $= 2\sqrt{2} \times \sqrt{2} = 4$ cm

111. Effective change in area $= 12 + 15 \dfrac{12 \times 15}{100} = 27 + \dfrac{9}{5} = 28\dfrac{4}{5}$

Hence, area is increased by $28\dfrac{4}{5}\%$

112. Let equal sides and base of the isosceles triangle be $5x$ and $3x$ m.

Then, $5x + 5x + 3x = 78 \quad \Rightarrow 13x = 78 \quad \therefore\ x = 6$

Hence, perimeter $= 3 \times 6 = 18$ cm.

113. Side of the square $= \sqrt{2.25} = 1.5$ cm

Hence, perimeter $= 4 \times 1.5 = 6$ cm

114. Side of the square $= \dfrac{48}{4} = 12$ m

Area of the square $= (12)^2 = 144 \text{ m}^2$

Since, area of required rectangle $= 144 - 4 = 140 \text{ m}^2$

Hence, breadth of the rectangle $= \dfrac{140}{14} = 10$ m

115. For Δ ABC, $\quad s = \dfrac{14+12+18}{2} = 22$ cm

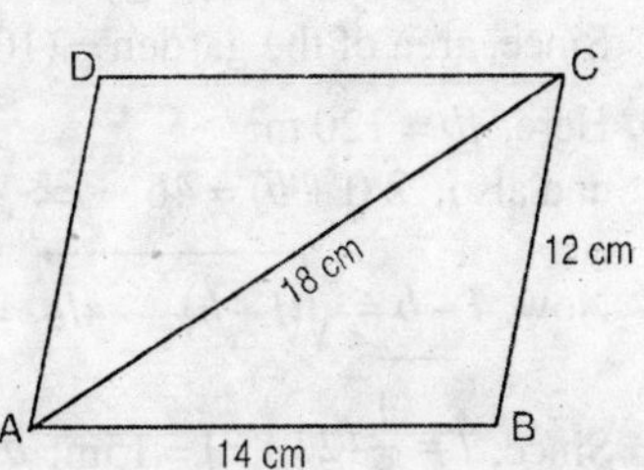

Area of Δ ABC $= \sqrt{22(22-14)(22-12)(22-18)}$

$= \sqrt{22 \times 8 \times 10 \times 4}$

$= \sqrt{7040} = 83.9 \text{ cm}^2$

Since, area of parallelogram ABCD $= 2 \times$ area of Δ ABC

$= 2 \times 83.9$

$= 167.8 \text{ cm}^2$

116. Area of the farm $= \frac{1}{2} \times 180 \times (57 + 112)$

$= 90 \times 169 = 15210 \text{ m}^2 = 1.521$ hectares

117. Area of remaining paper $= 40 \times 28 - \frac{1}{2} \times \frac{22}{7} \times 14 \times 14$

$= 1120 - 308$

$= 812 \text{ cm}^2$

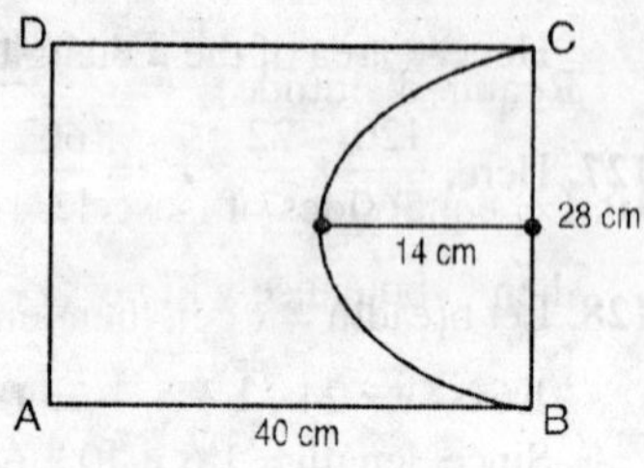

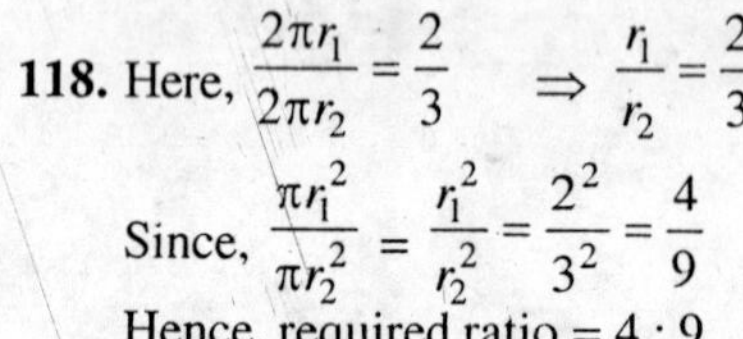

118. Here, $\frac{2\pi r_1}{2\pi r_2} = \frac{2}{3} \Rightarrow \frac{r_1}{r_2} = \frac{2}{3}$

Since, $\frac{\pi r_1^2}{\pi r_2^2} = \frac{r_1^2}{r_2^2} = \frac{2^2}{3^2} = \frac{4}{9}$

Hence, required ratio = 4 : 9

119. Area of the road (shaded portion)

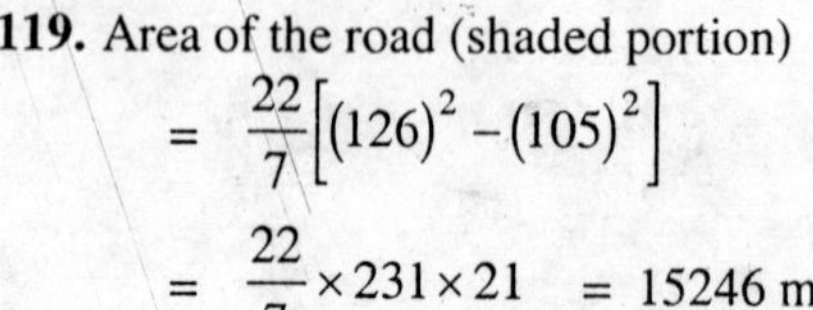

$= \frac{22}{7}\left[(126)^2 - (105)^2\right]$

$= \frac{22}{7} \times 231 \times 21 = 15246 \text{ m}^2$

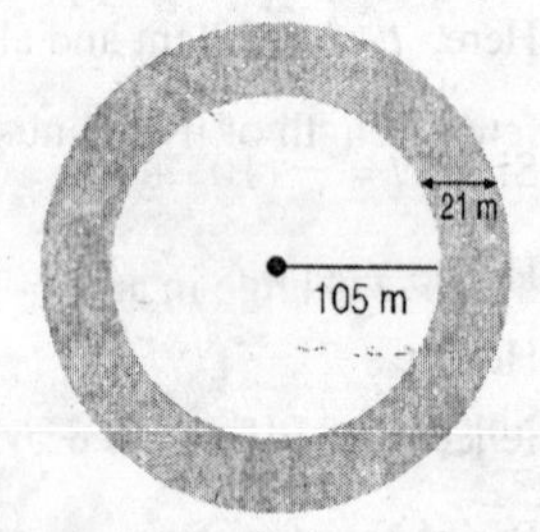

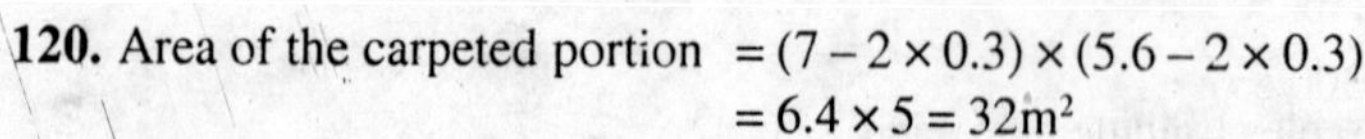

120. Area of the carpeted portion $= (7 - 2 \times 0.3) \times (5.6 - 2 \times 0.3)$

$= 6.4 \times 5 = 32\text{m}^2$

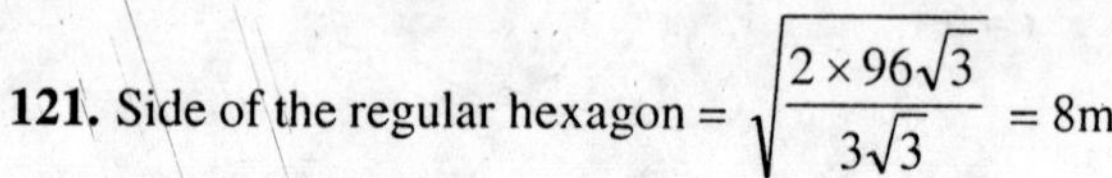

121. Side of the regular hexagon $= \sqrt{\frac{2 \times 96\sqrt{3}}{3\sqrt{3}}} = 8\text{m}$

122. Radius of the circle $= \frac{2\pi x}{2\pi} = x$

Hence, area of the circle $= \pi x^2$

Since, side of the given square $= \sqrt{\pi x^2} = \sqrt{\pi}x$

Hence, Perimeter of the square $= 4\sqrt{\pi}x$

123. Perimeter of the square garden$= \frac{400}{1} = 400$ m

Side of the garden $= \frac{400}{4} = 100$ m

Since, area of the garden $= (100)^2 = 10000 \text{ m}^2$

124. Here, $lb = 120 \text{ m}^2$

and also, $2(l + b) = 46 \Rightarrow l + b = 23$

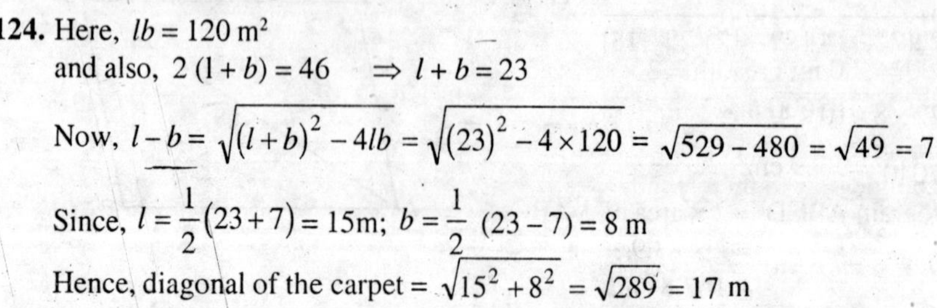

Now, $l - b = \sqrt{(l+b)^2 - 4lb} = \sqrt{(23)^2 - 4 \times 120} = \sqrt{529 - 480} = \sqrt{49} = 7$

Since, $l = \frac{1}{2}(23 + 7) = 15\text{m}$; $b = \frac{1}{2}(23 - 7) = 8$ m

Hence, diagonal of the carpet $= \sqrt{15^2 + 8^2} = \sqrt{289} = 17$ m

125. Area of the trapezium $= \frac{1}{2}d(p+q)$ cm²

126. Other side of the rectangle $= \frac{28}{2} - 8 = 6$m

Hence, area of the rectangle $= 8 \times 6 = 48$ cm²

127. Here, $\frac{120}{360} \times \frac{22}{7} \times r^2 = \frac{66}{7} \quad \Rightarrow r^2 = \frac{66 \times 3}{22} \quad \therefore r = 3$ cm

128. Let breadth $= x$ cm, then length $= \frac{160x}{100} = 1.6x$ cm; then

$1.6x - x = 24 \quad \Rightarrow 0.6x = 24 \quad \therefore x = 40$

Since, length $= 1.6 \times 40 = 64$ cm; breadth $= 40$ cm

Area $= 64 \times 40 = 2560$ cm²

129. Here, $l - b = 23$ cm and also $2(l + b) = 206 \quad \therefore l + b = 103$ cm

Since, $l = \frac{1}{2}(103 + 23) = 63$ cm, $\quad b = \frac{1}{2}(103 - 23) = 40$ cm

Hence, area $= 63 \times 40 = 2520$ cm²

130. Here, $9 + 2x = 37 \quad \Rightarrow 2x = 28 \quad \therefore x = 14$ m

Since, area of rectangular parking space $= 14 \times 9 = 126$ m²

131. Perimeter of rectangular plot $= \frac{5300}{26.50} = 200$ m

Let length and breadth be $(x + 20)$ and x m respectively; then

$2(x + 20 + x) = 200 \quad \Rightarrow 2x + 20 = 100 \quad \Rightarrow x = \frac{80}{2} = 40$ m

Hence, length $= 40 + 20 = 60$ m

132. Let length and breadth of the rectangular hall be $(x + 5)$ and x m respectively; then

$(x+5)x = 750 \quad \Rightarrow x^2 + 5x - 750 = 0 \quad \Rightarrow (x - 25)(x + 30) = 0$

Since, $x = 25$ m; then length $= 25 + 5 = 30$ m

133. Speed $= 12$ km/hr $= 12 \times \frac{5}{18} = \frac{10}{3}$ m/s

Since, perimeter of the rectangular park $= \frac{10}{3} \times 8 \times 60 = 1600$ m

Let length and breadth are $3x$ and $2x$ m respectively; then

$2(3x + 2x) = 1600 \quad \Rightarrow 5x = 800 \quad \therefore x = \frac{800}{5} = 160$

Since, length $= 3 \times 160 = 480$ m; breadth $= 2 \times 160 = 320$ m

Hence, area $= 480 \times 320 = 153600$ m²

134. Let breadth of the rectangle be x m then length $= \frac{115}{100}x = 1.15x$ m

Now, $1.15x \times x = 460 \quad \Rightarrow x^2 = \frac{460}{1.15} \quad \Rightarrow x^2 = 400 \quad \Rightarrow x = 20$ m

135. Let breadth and perimeter of a rectangle be x m and $5x$ m respectively.

Then, length $= \frac{5x}{2} - x = \frac{3x}{2}$

Since, $\frac{3x}{2} \times x = 216 \Rightarrow x^2 = \frac{216 \times 2}{3} \Rightarrow x^2 = 144 \quad \therefore x = 12$ m

Hence, length $= \frac{3}{2} \times 12 = 18$ m

136. Let sides of a rectangular field be $3x$ and $4x$ m respectively; then

$$3x \times 4x = 7500 \quad \Rightarrow x^2 = \frac{7500}{12} \quad \Rightarrow x^2 = 625 \quad \therefore x = 25$$

Since, sides are $3 \times 25 = 75$m and $4 \times 25 = 100$ m

Hence, perimeter $= 2\,(75 + 100) = 350$ m

$\therefore$ Cost of fencing $= 350 \times$ Re. $\frac{25}{100} =$ Rs. 87.50

137. Here, $20 \times x = 680 \quad \therefore x = \frac{680}{20} = 34$ m

Hence, length of fencing $= 2 \times 34 + 20 = 88$ m

138. Let one side of the garden be x m then another side $= \frac{30 - x}{2}$ m.

Now, $x \times \frac{(30 - x)}{2} = 100 \quad \Rightarrow 30x - x^2 = 200 \quad \Rightarrow x^2 - 30x + 200 = 0$

$\Rightarrow (x - 20)(x - 10) = 0$

Hence, $x = 20$ or 10; Taking $x = 20$ only because if we take $x = 10$ then plot will be square shape.

Since, another side $= \frac{30 - 20}{2} = 5$ m

Hence, dimension of the garden = 20 m × 5 m.

139. Let sides of the rectangular paper be x and y cm respectively;

then, $x + 2y = 34$ cm and $2x + y = 38$ cm

Solving these two equations we get $x = 14$ cm and $y = 10$ cm

Hence, area of the paper $= 14 \times 10 = 140$ cm^2

140. Here, $x^2 + \left(\frac{9}{2}\right)^2 = \left(\frac{15}{2}\right)^2 \quad \Rightarrow x^2 = \frac{225}{4} - \frac{81}{4} \quad \Rightarrow x^2 = \frac{144}{4} \quad \Rightarrow x = 6$m

Hence, area of the closet $= 6 \times \frac{9}{2} = 27$ m^2

141. Here, diagonal $= \sqrt{x^2 + y^2} = 52 \times \frac{15}{60} = 13$m $\quad \therefore x^2 + y^2 = 169$m^2

and also, $x + y = 68 \times \frac{15}{60} = 17$ m

Hence, area $= xy = \frac{(x+y)^2 - (x^2 + y^2)}{2} = \frac{(17)^2 - 169}{2} = \frac{289 - 169}{2} = 60$ m^2

142. Let length and breadth of a rectangle are $3x$ and x cm respectively;

Then, $(3x)^2 + x^2 = \left(8\sqrt{10}\right)^2 \Rightarrow 10x^2 = 640 \quad \therefore x^2 = 64 \quad \therefore x = 8$ cm

Since, length = 3 × 8 = 24 cm; breadth = 8 cm

Hence, perimeter = 2(24 + 8) = 2 × 32 = 64 cm

143. Here, $x^2 + y^2 = 41$ and also $xy = 20$; then

$(x + y)^2 = x^2 + y^2 + 2xy = 41 + 2 \times 20 = 81$

$\therefore x + y = 9$ cm

Hence, perimeter = $2(x + y) = 2 \times 9 = 18$ cm

144. Here, $(x + 1)(y + 1) = xy + 21 \Rightarrow xy + x + y + 1 = xy + 21$

$\therefore x + y = 20$ ...(i)

And also, $(x + 1)(y - 1) = xy - 5 \Rightarrow xy - x + y - 1 = xy - 5$

$\therefore -x + y = -4$ ...(ii)

Solving these two equations, we get x = 12m and y = 8m

Hence, Perimeter of the floor = $2(x + y) = 2(12 + 8) = 2 \times 20 = 40$ m

145. Here, area of the rectangle = $x \times y = xy$

Again, area of the new retangle = $\frac{x}{y} \times 3y = \frac{3xy}{2}$

Change in area = $\frac{3}{2}xy - xy = \frac{1}{2}xy$

Hence, required percentage = $\frac{1}{2} \, {}^{xy}\!/_{xy} \times 100 = 50\%$

146. Area of whole sheet = 30 × 20 = 600 cm^2

Area of sheet used = (30 – 2 × 3) × (20 – 2 × 2)

= 24 × 16 = 384 cm^2

Hence, required percentage = $\frac{384}{600} \times 100 = 64\%$

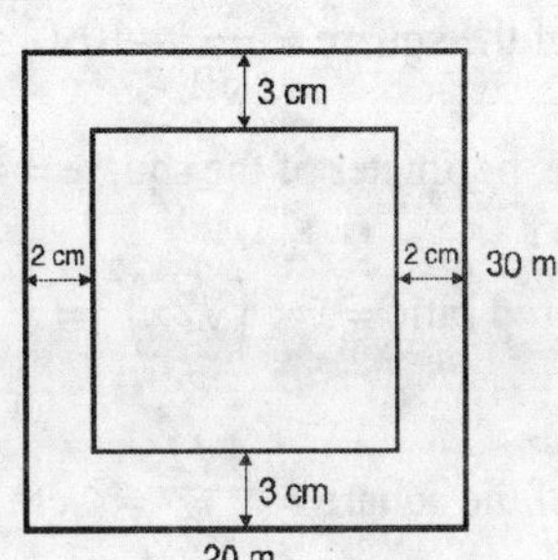

147. Here, $\frac{(100 - r)}{100} l \times \frac{(100 + r + 5)}{100} \times b = lb$

$\Rightarrow (100 - r)(105 + r) = 10000$

$\Rightarrow 10500 - 105r + 100r + r^2 = 10000$

$\Rightarrow r^2 + 5r - 500 \Rightarrow (r + 25)(r - 20) = 0$

Hence, $r = 20$

148. Here, $2(x + y) = 340$ m

Again, area of boundary $= [(x + 2)(y + 2)] - xy = xy + 2(x + y) + 4 - xy$

$= 2(x + y) + 4 = 340 + 4 = 344$ m

Hence, cost of gardening = 344 × Rs. 10 = Rs. 3440

149. Here sides of the given five squares are 6 cm, 8 cm, 10 cm, 19 cm and 20 cm respectively; then

Area of another new square = $6^2 + 8^2 + 10^2 + 19^2 + 20^2 = 961$ cm^2

Hence, side of the new square = $\sqrt{961}$ = 31 cm

$\therefore$ Perimeter of the new square = 4 × 31 = 124 cm

150. Area of one stone slabe = $\dfrac{72 \times 100 \times 100}{50} = 14400 \text{ cm}^2$

Hence, side of one stone slab = $\sqrt{14400} = 120$ cm

151. Length = 15m 17cm = 1517 cm; breadth = 9m 2cm = 902 cm
H.C.F. of 1517 and 902 = 41

Hence, required number of square tiles = $\dfrac{1517 \times 902}{41 \times 41} = 814$

152. Let side of the square lot = x m; then diagonal = $\sqrt{2}x = 1.41x$ m

Hence, required percentage = $\dfrac{2x - 1.41x}{2x} \times 100 = \dfrac{0.59}{2} \times 100 \approx 30\%$

153. Area of the road = $x^2 - (x-6)^2 = 1764 \quad \Rightarrow 12x - 36 = 1764$

$\Rightarrow 12x = 1800 \quad \therefore\ x = \dfrac{1800}{12} = 150$ m

Hence, required perimeter = 4 × 150 = 600 m

154. Side, of the square = $\sqrt{69696} = 264$ cm

Hence, diagonal of the square = $264\sqrt{2}$ cm

155. Side of the square = $\dfrac{20}{\sqrt{2}} = 10\sqrt{2}$ cm

Hence, perimeter of the square = $4 \times 10\sqrt{2} = 40\sqrt{2}$ cm

156. Required ratio = $x^2 : \left(\sqrt{2}x\right)^2 = x^2 : 2x^2 = 1 : 2$

157. Side of the square = $\dfrac{4\sqrt{2}}{\sqrt{2}} = 4$ cm
Area of the square = $(4)^2 = 16 \text{ cm}^2$
Since, area of the another square = $2 \times 16 = 32 \text{ cm}^2$
Hence, side of this square = $\sqrt{32} = 4\sqrt{2}$ cm

Then diagonal of this square = $4\sqrt{2} \times \sqrt{2} = 8$ cm

158. Ratio of their sides = $\sqrt{225} : \sqrt{256} = 15 : 16$

Since, ratio of their perimeters = 4 × 15 : 4 × 16 = 15 : 16

159. Actual area of the square = $x^2 \text{ cm}^2$
Measuring area of the square = $(1.02\,x)^2 = 1.0404\,x^2 \text{ cm}^2$
Their difference = $1.0404\,x^2 - x^2 = 0.0404\,x^2$

Hence, required percentage = $\dfrac{0.0404x^2}{x^2} \times 100 = 4.04\%$

160. $\frac{x+5}{x} = \frac{3}{2} \quad \Rightarrow 3x - 2x = 10 \quad \therefore\ x = 10$

Hence, area of the original square = $(10)^2 = 100\ \text{cm}^2$

161. Here, $(x+2)^2 - x^2 = 32 \quad \Rightarrow 4x + 4 = 32 \quad \Rightarrow x = \frac{28}{4} = 7\ \text{cm}$

Hence, length of the side of the greater square = 7 + 2 = 9 cm.

162. Area of 4 walls and bottom of the tank $= 2(25 + 12) \times 6 + 25 \times 12$
$= 744\ \text{m}^2$

The cost of plastering = $744 \times \text{Re.}\ \frac{75}{100}$ = Rs. 558

163. Here, $(x+5)(x-3) = x^2 \quad \Rightarrow 2x - 15 = 0 \quad \Rightarrow 2x = 15 \quad \therefore\ x = 7.5$ cm

Since, length = 7.5 + 5 = 12.5 cm; breadth = 7.5 – 3 = 4.5 cm

Hence, perimeter of the rectangle = $2(12.5 + 4.5) = 2 \times 17 = 34$ cm

164. Area of triangle = $\frac{1}{2} \times 15 \times 12 = 90\ \text{cm}^2$

Area of new triangle = $2 \times 90\ \text{cm}^2 = 180\ \text{cm}^2$

Since, height of new triangle = $\frac{2 \times 180}{20} = 18$ cm

165. Let base and altitude be $3x$ and $4x$ cm respectively; then

$\frac{1}{2} \times 3x \times 4x = 1176 \quad \Rightarrow 6x^2 = 1176 \quad \Rightarrow x^2 = 196 \quad \therefore\ x = 14$

Since, altitude = $4 \times 14 = 56$ cm

166. Let base and area of the right angled triangle are x cm and $40x$ cm² respectively; then

height = $\frac{2 \times 40x}{x} = 80$ cm

167. Let sides of the triangle are $3x$, $4x$ and $5x$ cm respectively; then

$s = \frac{3x + 4x + 5x}{2} = 6x$ cm

Now, $\sqrt{6x(6x-3x)(6x-4x)(6x-5x)} = 216 \quad \Rightarrow \sqrt{6x \times 3x \times 2x \times x} = 216$

$\Rightarrow 6x^2 = 216 \quad \Rightarrow x^2 = 36 \quad \Rightarrow x = 6$

Hence, sides are $3 \times 6 = 18$ cm, $4 \times 6 = 24$ cm and $5 \times 6 = 30$ cm

Since, perimeter = 18 + 24 + 30 = 72 cm

168. Ratio of the sides = $\frac{1}{2} : \frac{1}{3} : \frac{1}{4} = 6 : 4 : 3$

Hence, length of the smallest side = $\frac{3}{6+4+3} \times 52 = \frac{3}{13} \times 52 = 12$ cm

169. Let base of the right angled triangle = x cm; then

height = $60 - 26 - x = 34 - x$

Since, $x^2 + (34 - x)^2 = (26)^2$ $\Rightarrow x^2 + 1156 - 68x + x^2 = 676$

$\Rightarrow 2x^2 - 68x + 480 = 0$ $\Rightarrow x^2 - 34x + 240 = 0$ $\Rightarrow (x - 24)(x - 10) = 0$

Either, $x = 24$ or 10 then height = $34 - x = 10$ or , 24

Since, area of right angled triangle = $\frac{1}{2} \times 24 \times 10 = 120$ cm²

170. Here, $3^2 + 4^2 = 5^2$ Hence, triangle is right angled triangle.

Since, area of triangle = $\frac{1}{2} \times 3 \times 4 = 6$ cm²

Hence, area of required triangle = $\frac{1}{4} \times 6 = \frac{3}{2}$ cm²

171. Side of equilateral triangle = $\frac{2}{\sqrt{3}} \times 10 = \frac{20}{\sqrt{3}}$ cm

Hence, area of equilateral triangle = $\frac{\sqrt{3}}{4} \times \left(\frac{20}{\sqrt{3}}\right)^2 = \frac{\sqrt{3}}{4} \times \frac{400}{3} = \frac{100}{\sqrt{3}}$ cm²

172. Here, $\frac{1}{2} \times a \times h = a^2$ $\therefore h = 2a$

173. Let side of the square be x cm.

$$\text{Required ratio} = \frac{\frac{\sqrt{3}}{4} \times \left(\sqrt{2}x\right)^2}{x^2} = \frac{\frac{\sqrt{3}}{4} \times 2x^2}{x^2} = \frac{\sqrt{3}}{2} = \sqrt{3} : 2$$

174. Area of equilateral triangle = $\frac{\sqrt{3}}{4}a^2$

Area of new equilateral triangle = $\frac{\sqrt{3}}{4} \times (2a)^2 = 4.\frac{\sqrt{3}}{4}a^2$

Hence, $k = 4$

175. Here, $\frac{1}{2} \times b \times h = b \times 100$ Hence, $h = 200$ m

176. Let diagonals of the rhombus be d and $2d$ cm; then

$\frac{1}{2} \times d \times 2d = 25$ $\Rightarrow d^2 = 25$ $\therefore d = 5$ cm

Since, diagonals are 5 and 10 cm respectively,

Hence, sum of the diagonals = 5 + 10 = 15 cm

177. Area of circle = $\pi.5^2 = 25\pi$

Circumference of the circle = $2\pi \times 5 = 10\pi$

Required percentage = $\dfrac{25\pi}{10\pi} \times 100 = 250\%$

178. Perimeter of rectangle = $2(18 + 26) = 2 \times 44 = 88$ cm

Since, radius of the circle = $\dfrac{88 \times 7}{20 \times 22} = 14$ cm

Hence, area of the circle = $\dfrac{22}{7} \times 14 \times 14 = 616$ cm^2

179. Here, $\pi r^2 = 2\pi r \quad \therefore r = 2$

Hence, diameter = $2r = 2 \times 2 = 4$

180. Side of the square = $\dfrac{44}{4} = 11$ cm

Hence, area of the square = $(11)^2 = 121$ cm^2

Radius of the circle = $\dfrac{44 \times 7}{2 \times 22} = 7$ cm

Since, area of the circle = $\dfrac{22}{7} \times 7 \times 7 = 154$ cm^2

Hence, circle has larger area having $154 - 121 = 33$ cm^2 more

181. Here, $\dfrac{\pi r_1^2}{\pi r_2^2} = \dfrac{16}{49} \quad \therefore \dfrac{r_1}{r_2} = \dfrac{4}{7} \quad \therefore r_1 = \dfrac{4}{7} \times 14 = 8$ m

182. Required number of revolutions = $\dfrac{176 \times 100 \times 7}{2 \times 22 \times 20} = 140$

183. $\dfrac{A_1}{A_2} = \dfrac{\pi r_1^2}{\pi r_2^2} = \dfrac{r_1^2}{r_2^2} = \dfrac{4}{9} \quad \therefore \dfrac{r_1}{r_2} = \dfrac{2}{3}$

Hence, $\dfrac{2\pi r_1}{2\pi r_2} = \dfrac{2}{3}$

Since, required ratio = 2 : 3

184. Distance travelled in 10 seconds = $40 \times 2 \times \dfrac{22}{7} \times 35 = 8800$ cm = 0.088 km

Hence, distance travelled in 1 hour = $0.088 \times \dfrac{60}{10} \times 60 = 31.68$ km

Since, speed = 31.68 km/hr

185. Circumference of the wheel = $\dfrac{\text{2 km 26 decametres}}{113} = \dfrac{2260}{113} = 20$ m

Hence, diameter of the wheel = $\dfrac{20 \times 7}{22} = 6\dfrac{4}{11}$ m

186. Let the wheels make n revolutions per second, then

$\left(\frac{22}{7}\times 7+\frac{22}{7}\times 14\right)\times 10n = 1980 \quad \Rightarrow 66n = 198 \qquad \therefore n = 3$

Since, distance travelled by smaller wheel in 1 second = $\frac{22}{7}\times 7\times 3 = 66$ cm

Hence, speed of the smaller wheel = 66 cm/sec.

187. Let the front wheels and rear wheels made $(n + 10)$ and n revolutions respectively; then

$2\pi(n + 10) = 3\pi n \qquad \Rightarrow 2n + 20 = 3n \qquad \Rightarrow n = 20$

Since, wagon travelled = $3\pi \times 20 = 60\,\pi$ m

188. Here, $2\pi R - 2\pi r = 132$ m $\qquad \therefore R - r = \frac{132\times 7}{2\times 22} = 21$ m

Hence, width of the circular path = 21 m

189. Area of semi-circle = $\frac{1}{2}\times\frac{22}{7}\times 7\times 7 = 77\text{ m}^2$

190. Let inner and outer radius be r and (r + 5) m respectively;

Then, $\frac{2\pi(r+5)}{2\pi r} = \frac{23}{22} \qquad \Rightarrow 22r + 110 = 23r \qquad \therefore r = 110$ m

Since, diameter of the inner circle = $2r = 2 \times 110 = 220$ m

191. Here, $\frac{22}{7}\times r + 2r = 36 \quad \Rightarrow \frac{36r}{7} = 36 \qquad \therefore r = 7$ cm

Hence, area of semicircle = $\frac{1}{2}\times\frac{22}{7}\times 7\times 7 = 77\text{ cm}^2$

192. Perimeter of semi-circular shape = $\frac{22}{7}\times\frac{63}{2} + 63 = 99 + 63 = 162$ cm

193. Radius of circle = $\sqrt{\frac{220\times 7}{22}} = \sqrt{70}$ cm

Hence, diagonal of the square = $2\sqrt{70}$ cm

Since, side of the square = $\frac{2\sqrt{70}}{\sqrt{2}} = \sqrt{140}$ cm

$\therefore$ Area of the required square = $\left(\sqrt{140}\right)^2 = 140\text{ cm}^2$

194. Diameter of the circle = $\frac{100}{\pi}$ cm

So, diagonal of the inscribed square = $\frac{100}{\pi}$ cm

And, side of the inscribed square = $\frac{100}{\sqrt{2}\pi} = \frac{50\sqrt{2}}{\pi}$ cm

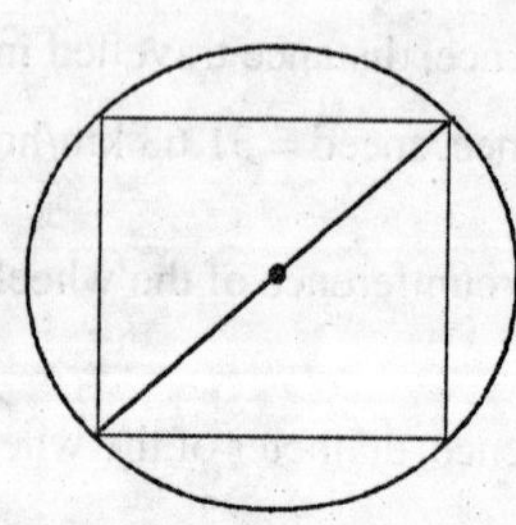

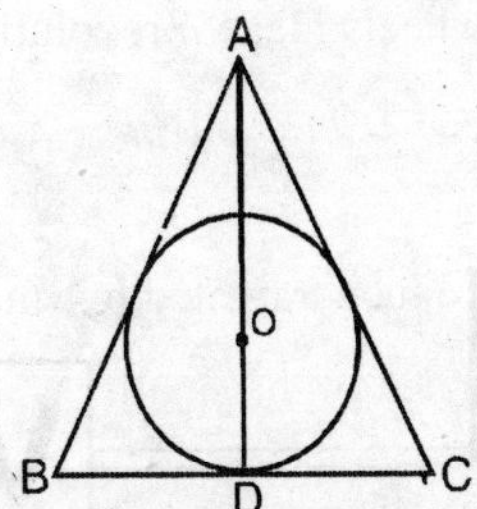

195. Height of equilateral triangle $= \dfrac{\sqrt{3}}{2} \times 42 = 21\sqrt{3}$ cm

Therefore, radius of incircle $= \dfrac{1}{3} \times 12\sqrt{3} = 7\sqrt{3}$ cm

Area of incircle $= \dfrac{22}{7} \times 7\sqrt{3} \times 7\sqrt{3} = 462\ \text{cm}^2$

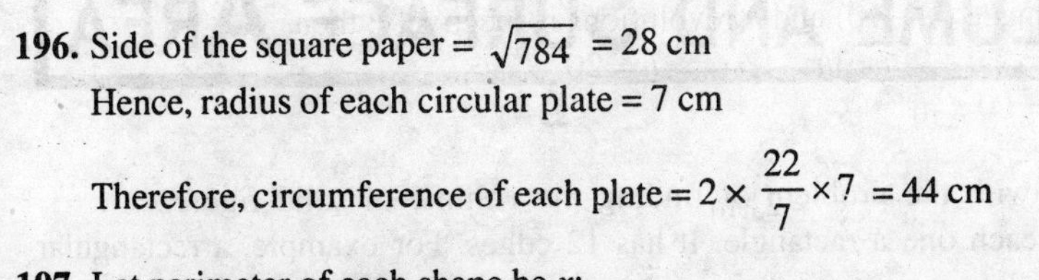

196. Side of the square paper $= \sqrt{784} = 28$ cm

Hence, radius of each circular plate = 7 cm

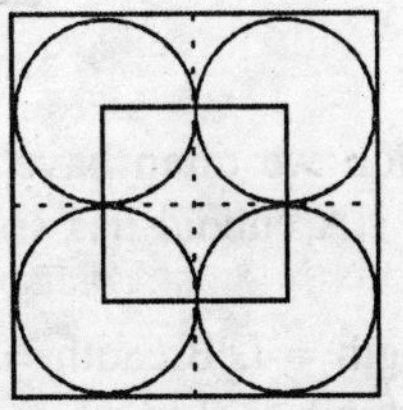

Therefore, circumference of each plate $= 2 \times \dfrac{22}{7} \times 7 = 44$ cm

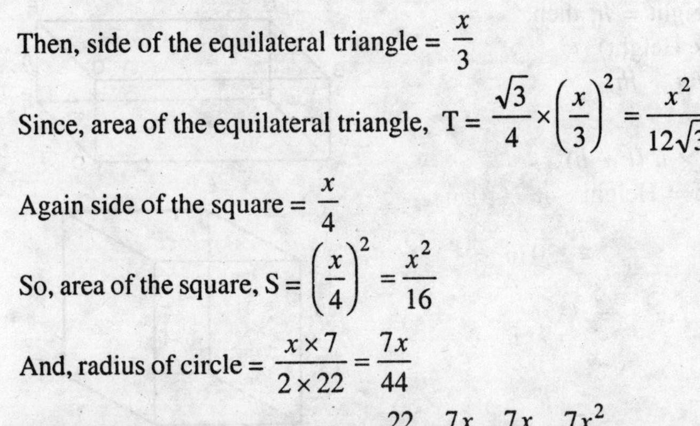

197. Let perimeter of each shape be x;

Then, side of the equilateral triangle $= \dfrac{x}{3}$

Since, area of the equilateral triangle, $T = \dfrac{\sqrt{3}}{4} \times \left(\dfrac{x}{3}\right)^2 = \dfrac{x^2}{12\sqrt{3}}$

Again side of the square $= \dfrac{x}{4}$

So, area of the square, $S = \left(\dfrac{x}{4}\right)^2 = \dfrac{x^2}{16}$

And, radius of circle $= \dfrac{x \times 7}{2 \times 22} = \dfrac{7x}{44}$

Therefore, area of the circle, $C = \dfrac{22}{7} \times \dfrac{7x}{44} \times \dfrac{7x}{44} = \dfrac{7x^2}{88}$

Hence, $C > S > T$.

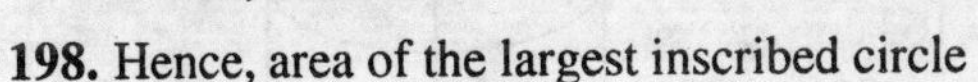

198. Hence, area of the largest inscribed circle

$= \dfrac{1}{2} \times 2r \times r$

$= r^2$

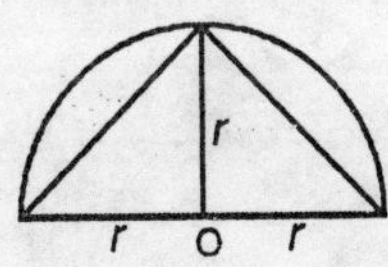

30

VOLUME AND SURFACE AREA

In mensuration we often have to deal with the problem of finding the volume of solid figure.

Cuboid : A cuboid has six faces, each one a ractangle. It has 12 edges. For example, a rectangular brick.

Let Length = l, Breadth = b and Height = h, then,

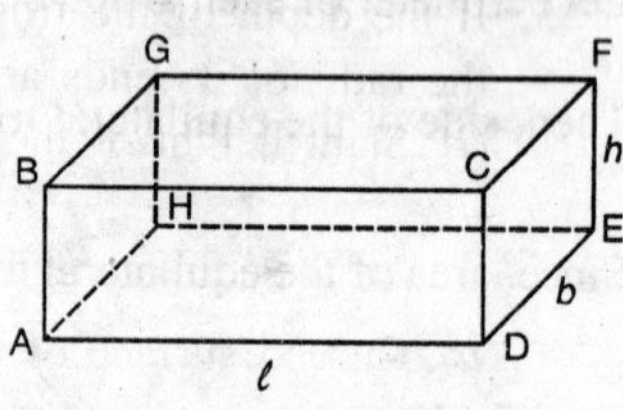

1. Volume = (Length × Breadth × Height)
2. Whole Surface Area = $2(lb + bh + lh)$
3. Diagonal = $\sqrt{l^2 + b^2 + h^2}$
4. Area of 4 walls of a room = $2 \times h\,(l + b)$

Cube : In a cube, Length = Breadth = Height

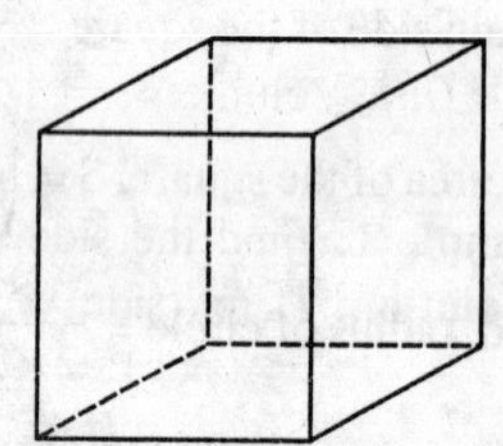

1. Volume = $(l)^3$
2. Length = $\sqrt[3]{\text{Volume}}$
3. Whole Surface Area = $6\,l^2$
4. Diagonal = $l \times \sqrt{3}$
5. Lateral Surface Area = $4\,l^2$

Cylinder :

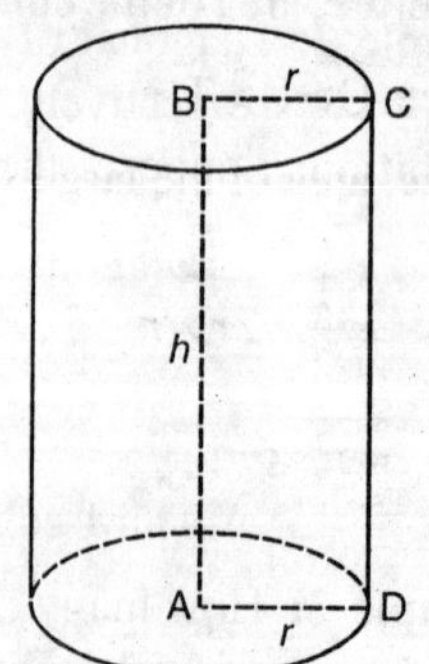

1. Volume = $\pi r^2 h$
2. Curved Surface Area = $2\pi rh$
3. Total Surface Area = $2\pi r(r + h)$
   where r = radius, h = height

Spherical Cell :

1. Volume = $\frac{4}{3}\pi\left(R^3 - r^3\right)$
2. Total Surface Area= $4\pi(R^2 - r^2)$
   where R = Outer radius
   r = Inner radius

Sphere :

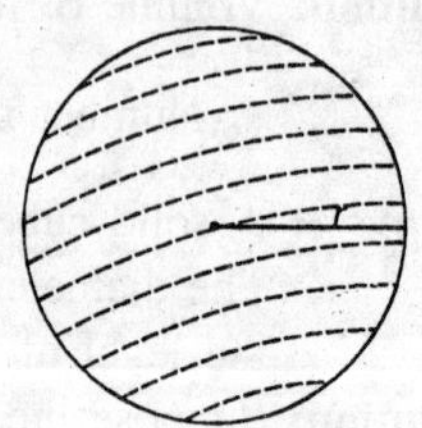

1. Volume = $\frac{4}{3}\pi r^3$
2. Surface Area = $4\pi r^2$

Semi-sphere :

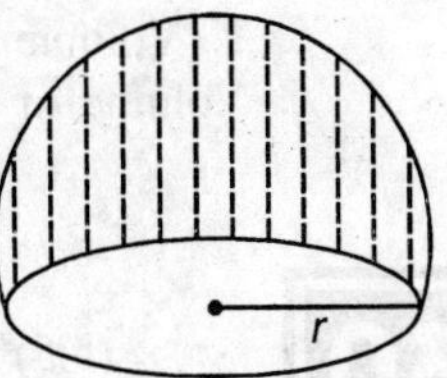

1. Volume = $\frac{2}{3}\pi r^3$
2. Curved surface area = $2\pi r^2$
3. Total surface area = $3\pi r^2$

Cone :

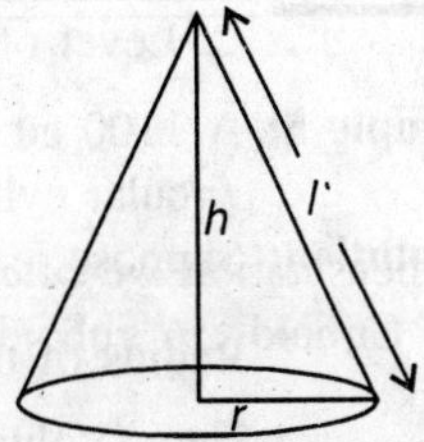

1. Slant height (l) = $\sqrt{r^2 + h^2}$
2. Volume = $\frac{1}{3}\pi r^2 h$
3. Curved surface area = πrl
4. Total surface area = $\pi r\ (l + r)$
5. If the depth of the frustum of a cone be k and the radii of its ends are r_1 and r_2, then

   (i) Slant height of the frustum of a cone

   $$= \sqrt{k^2 + (r_1 - r_2)^2}$$

   (ii) Curved surface of the frustum = $\pi(r_1 + r_2)\ l$.

   (iii) Volume = $\frac{\pi k}{3}\left(r_1^2 + r_1 r_2 + r_2^2\right)$

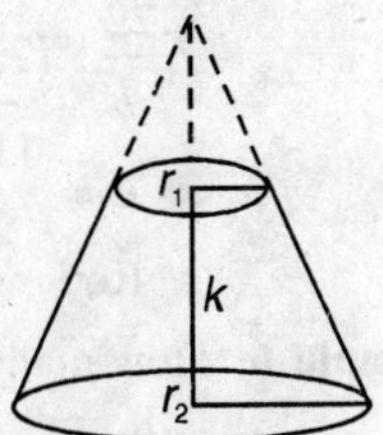

Example 1: Find the side and surface area of a cube whose volume is 729 cu cm.

Solution: Here, $(\text{side})^3 = 729$

$\Rightarrow (\text{side})^3 = (9)^3 \quad \Rightarrow \text{side} = 9$ cm

Since, surface area = $6 \times (9)^2 = 6 \times 81 = 486$ sq. cm.

Example 2: Diagonal of a rectangular solid figure is 17 cm long. If its two edges are 8 cm and 9 cm respectively, find its third edge.

Solution: Suppose, the length of the third edge = x cm

$$\text{Diagonal} = 17 = \sqrt{(8)^2 + (9)^2 + x^2} \Rightarrow (17)^2 = (8)^2 + (9)^2 + x^2$$

$$\Rightarrow \quad 289 = 64 + 81 + x^2 \Rightarrow 289 = 145 + x^2$$

$$\Rightarrow \quad x^2 = 289 - 145 = 144 \Rightarrow x = \sqrt{144} = 12$$

$\therefore$ Third edge is 12 cm long.

Example 3: How many cubical blocks can be packed in a carton of size 10 m × 6 m × 4 m, if the volume of each cubical block is 15 cu metre?

Solution: Volume of the carton = $l \times b \times h = 10 \times 6 \times 4 = 240$ cu m

$\therefore$ Number of cubical blocks that can be packed in the carton = $\frac{240}{15} = 16$

Example 4: A solid cube of side 5.5 cm is dropped into a cylindrical vessel partly filled with water. The diameter of the vessel is 11 cm. If the cube is wholly submerged, by how much will the level of the water rise?

Solution: Suppose the level of water in the cylindrical vessel is raised by h cm

Volume of the cubical solid = $(5.5)^3$ cu cm

∴ Volume of water displaced by the cubical solid = $(5.5)^3$ cu cm

Volume of water that is increased in the cylindrical vessel = $\pi r^2 h$

$$= \pi \times \left(\frac{11}{2}\right)^2 \times h = \pi \times (5.5)^2 \times h$$

$$\because \pi \times (5.5)^2 \times h = (5.5)^3 \Rightarrow h = \frac{(5.5)^3}{\pi (5.5)^2} = \frac{5.5}{\pi}$$

∴ Level of water raised in the cylinder = $h = \frac{5.5}{22/7} = \frac{5.5 \times 7}{22} = 1.75$ cm.

Example 5: A 1100 cu cm iron cube is to be melted and recast into a iron rod in the form of a right circular cylinder. If diameter of the rod is kept 4 cm, what will be the length of this rod?

Solution: Suppose length of the rod = h cm

Radius of the rod = $\frac{4}{2} = 2$ cm

Here, Volume of the rod = Volume of the iron cube

$$\therefore \frac{22}{7} \times (2)^2 \times h = 1100$$

$$\Rightarrow h = \frac{1100 \times 7}{22 \times 4} = 87.5 \text{ cm}$$

∴ Rod will be 87.5 cm long.

Example 6: How many spherical bullets of radius 2 cm can be made from a metallic sphere whose radius is 8 cm?

Solution: Here, Number of bullets = $\frac{\text{Volume of metallic sphere}}{\text{Volume of each bullet}} = \frac{\frac{4}{3}\pi (8)^3}{\frac{4}{3}\pi (2)^3} = (8)^2 = 64$

Example 7: Height of a right circular cone is double the base diameter. If volume of the cone is 36π cu cm, find the height of this cone.

Solution: Suppose the height and base radius of the cone are $4r$ cm and r cm respectively.

$$\because \text{Volume of the cone} = \frac{1}{3}\pi r^2 \times 4r = \frac{4}{3}\pi r^3 \text{ cu cm}$$

$$\therefore \frac{4}{3}\pi r^3 = 36\pi \Rightarrow r^3 = \frac{36\pi \times 3}{4\pi}$$

$$\Rightarrow r^3 = 27 \Rightarrow r = 3 \text{ cm}$$

∴Height of the cone = $4 \times r = 4 \times 3 = 12$ cm.

Example 8: If each edge of a cube is increased by 40%, then by how much per cent will the volume of the cube be increased?

Solution: Suppose each edge of the cube = a cm

∴Volume of the cube = a^3 cu cm

Each edge of the new cube = $1.4a$ cm

Volume of the new cube = $(1.4a)^3 = 2.744a^3$ cm

∴Increase in volume = $2.744a^3 - a^3 = 1.744a^3$ cu cm

∴ Percentage increase in volume = $\frac{1.744a^3}{a^3} \times 100 = 174.4\%$

Example 9: If external diameter of a 27 cm long hollow cylindrical pipe is 44 cm and thickness of the metal is 7 cm, find its total surface area.

Solution: External diameter of the pipe = 44 cm

∴ External radius (R) of the cylindrical pipe = 22 cm

Thickness of the metal = 7 cm

∴ Internal diameter of the pipe = 44 – (7 + 7) = 44 – 14 = 30 cm

Internal radius (r) of the pipe = 15 cm

Total surface area of the cylindrical pipe = Area of the outer curved surface + Area of the inner curved surface + Area of the two circular rings at the two ends.

$$= 2\pi Rh + 2\pi rh + 2(\pi R^2 - \pi r^2)$$

$$= 2\pi(Rh + rh + R^2 - r^2)$$

$$= 2\pi[22 \times 27 + 15 \times 27 + (22)^2 - (15)^2]$$

$$= 2\pi[27(22 + 15) + (22 + 15)(22 - 15)]$$

$$= 2\pi[37(27 + 7)]$$

$$= 2\pi[37 \times 34]$$

$$= 2 \times \frac{22}{7} \times 37 \times 34 = \frac{55352}{7}$$

$$= 7907\frac{3}{7} \text{ sq. cm.}$$

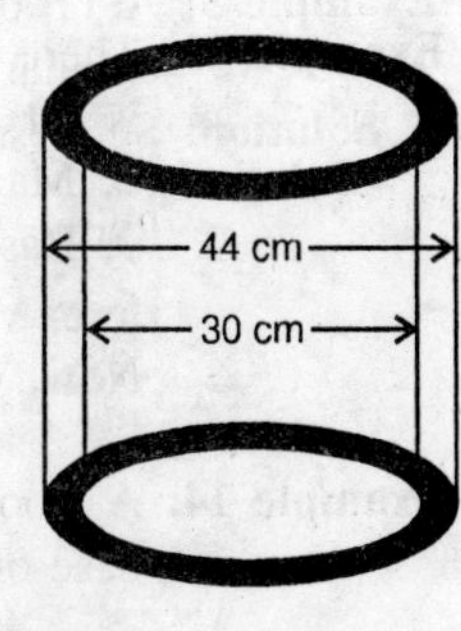

Example 10: A solid is composed of a right circular cone with hemispherical base. If whole volume of the solid is $\frac{32}{3}\pi$ cu cm and height of the cone is 4 cm, find the common radius of the hemisphere and that of the cone.

Solution: Suppose radius of the base = r cm

Here, Volume of the cone + Volume of the hemisphere = Whole volume of the solid

$$\frac{1}{3}\pi r^2 .4 + \frac{2}{3}\pi r^3 = \frac{32\pi}{3}$$

$$\therefore \frac{4}{3}\pi r^2 + \frac{2}{3}\pi r^3 = \frac{32\pi}{3}$$

$\Rightarrow \quad 2r^2 + r^3 = 16$

$\Rightarrow \quad r^2(2 + r) = 16$

$\Rightarrow \quad r^2(2 + r) = 2^2(2 + 2) \qquad [\because 16 = 2^2(2 + 2)]$

$\Rightarrow \quad r = 2$

∴ Common, radius of the cone and the hemisphere = 2 cm.

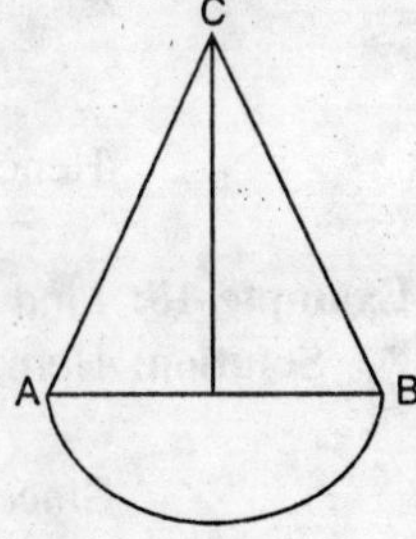

Example 11: A solid metallic cone having base radius 12 cm and height 24 cm is melted and beaten to form metallic shots of radius 2 cm. Find the number of metallic shots formed.

Solution: Number of shots $= \dfrac{\frac{1}{3}\pi(12)^2 \times 24}{\frac{4}{3}\pi(2)^3} = 108$

Example 12: How many bricks of size 6 cm × 5 cm × 4 cm will be required to construct a platform 15 m long, 8 m wide and 5 m high.

Solution: Volume of the platform = 15 × 8 × 5 = 600 cu m

Volume of one brick = $\frac{6}{100} \times \frac{5}{100} \times \frac{4}{100} = \frac{12}{100000}$ cu m

∴ Number of bricks required to construct the platform = $\frac{600}{\frac{12}{100000}} = 5000000 = 5 \times 10^6$.

Example 13: There is a cubical block of wood of side 8 cm. If a cylinder of the largest possible volume is carved out from it, find the volume of the remaining wood.

Solution: ∴ Maximum height of the cylinder (h) diameter = 8 cm

∴ Base radius (r) of the cylinder = 8/2 = 4 cm

Now, Volume of the remaining wood = $8^3 - \frac{22}{7} \times 4^2 \times 8 = 512 - \frac{2816}{7} = \frac{768}{7} = 109\frac{5}{7}$ cu cm.

Example 14: A wooden toy is in the form of a cone surmounted on a hemisphere. The diameter of the base of the cone is 6 cm and its height 4 cm. Find the cost of painting the toy at the rate of Rs. 7 per 100 cm². $\left(\text{Use, } \pi = \frac{22}{7}\right)$

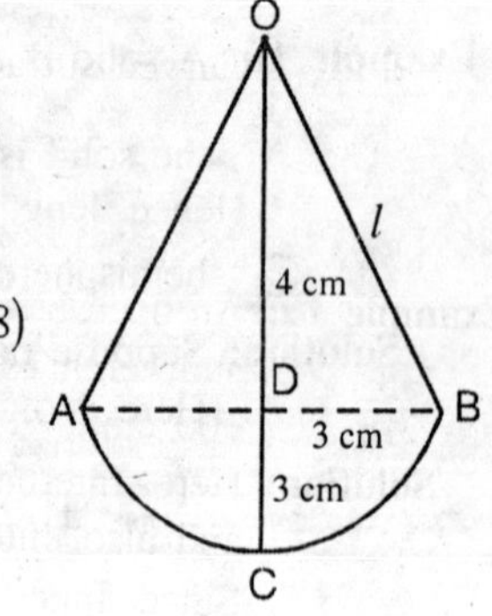

Solution: ∴ Slant height of the conical part, $l = \sqrt{4^3 + 3^2} = \sqrt{25} = 5$ cm

Curved surface area of the toy $= \pi \times 3 \times 5 + 2\pi.3^2$

$= \frac{22}{7}(15 + 18)$

$= \frac{726}{7}$ cm²

Hence, total cost of painting = $\frac{7}{100} \times \frac{726}{7}$ = Rs. 7.26

Example 15: Find the volume of a cone, whose height (h) is twice the radius (r) of its base.

Solution: Here, $h = 2r$

Since, volume of the cone = $\frac{1}{3}\pi r^2.2r = \frac{2}{3}\pi r^3$

Example 16: A sphere is melted to form a cylinder whose height is $4\frac{1}{2}$ times its radius. What is the ratio of radii of sphere to the cylinder?

Solution: Here, $\frac{4}{3}\pi r_1^3 = \pi r_2^2 \times \frac{9}{2} r_2 \Rightarrow \frac{r_1^3}{r_2^3} = \frac{9}{2} \times \frac{3}{4} \therefore \frac{r_1}{r_2} = \frac{3}{2}$

Hence, required ratio = 3 : 2.

Example 17: If the areas of the adjacent faces of a rectangular block are in the ratio of 2 : 3 : 4 and its volume is 9,000 cm³, then find the length of the shortest side.

Solution: Let length of the three sides are x, y and z cm respectively; then

$xy : yz : xz = 2 : 3 : 4$

Now, $\frac{xy}{yz} = \frac{2}{3}$ Hence, $x : z = 2 : 3$

Again, $\frac{xz}{yz} = \frac{4}{3}$ then, $x : y = 4 : 3$

Since, we get, $x : y : z = 4 : 3 : 6$

Now, $4a \times 3a \times 6a = 9000 \Rightarrow a^3 = \frac{9000}{72} = 125 \quad \therefore a = 5$

Hence, shortest side, $y = 3a = 3 \times 5 = 15$ cm

Example 18: Find the length of canvas 1.1 m wide required to build a conical tent of height 14m and the floor area of 346.5 m².

Solution: Here, $\pi r^2 = 346.5 \Rightarrow r^2 = \frac{346.5 \times 7}{22} = 110.25 \quad \therefore r = 10.5$ m

Now, slant height, $l = \sqrt{(14)^2 + (10.5)^2} = \sqrt{306.25} = 17.5$ m

Curved surface area of conical tent $= \frac{22}{7} \times 10.5 \times 17.5 = 577.5$ m³.

Hence, length of canvas required $= \frac{577.5}{1.1} = 525$ m

Example 19: An open box is made of wood 3 cm thick. Its external length is 1.46 m, breadth is 1.16 m and height is 83 cm. Find the cost of painting the inner surface of the box at 50 paise per 100 cm².

Solution: Here, Internal length = 146 − 2 × 3 = 140 cm; Internal breadth = 116 − 2 × 3 = 110 cm and also, internal height = 83 − 3 = 80 cm

Since, Inner surface area of the open box= 140 × 110 + 2 × (140 + 110) × 80

= 15400 + 40000

= 55400 cm²

Required cost of painting = Rs. $\frac{50}{100} \times \frac{1}{100} \times 55400 =$ Rs. 277

Example 20: An sphere and a cube have equal surface area. Find the ratio of their volumes?

Solution: Here, $4\pi r^2 = 6a^2 \Rightarrow \frac{r^2}{a^2} = \frac{6}{4\pi} = \frac{3}{2\pi} \quad \therefore \frac{r}{a} = \sqrt{\frac{3}{2\pi}}$

Now, $\frac{4/3\,\pi r^3}{a^3} = \frac{4\pi}{3} \times \left(\sqrt{\frac{3}{2\pi}}\right)^3 = \frac{4\pi}{3} \cdot \frac{3\sqrt{3}}{2\pi\sqrt{2\pi}} = \frac{\sqrt{6}}{\sqrt{\pi}}$

Hence, required ratio $= \sqrt{6} : \sqrt{\pi}$

Example 21 : A conical cavity is drilled in a circular cylinder of height 15 cm and base radius 8 cm. The height and the base radius of the cone are also same. Then find the whole surface of the remaining solid.

Solution: Slant height of the cone, $l = \sqrt{8^2 + 15^2} = \sqrt{289} = 17$ cm

Since, whole surface of the remaining solid $= 2\pi \times 8 \times 15 + \pi.8^2 + \pi.8.17$

$= 8\pi\ (30 + 8 + 17)$

$= 8\pi \times 55 = 440\pi$ cm²

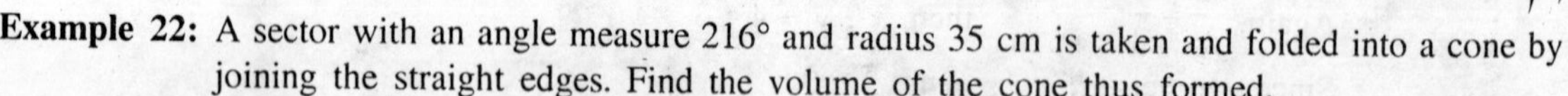

Example 22: A sector with an angle measure 216° and radius 35 cm is taken and folded into a cone by joining the straight edges. Find the volume of the cone thus formed.

Solution: Here, length of the arc of given sector $= \frac{216}{360} \times 2 \times \pi \times 35$

$= 42\pi$ cm

Now, $2\pi r = 42\pi \quad \therefore \quad r = 21$ cm

Thus vertical height of the cone, $h = \sqrt{(35)^2 - (21)^2} = \sqrt{784} = 28$ cm

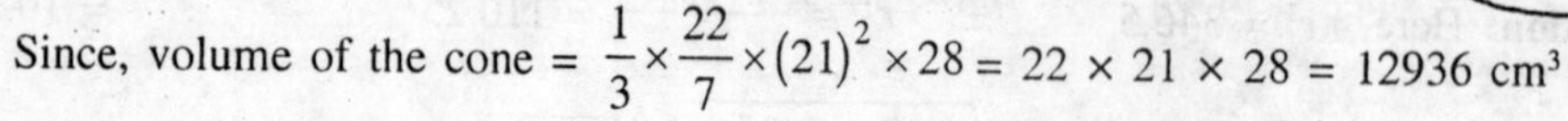

Since, volume of the cone $= \frac{1}{3} \times \frac{22}{7} \times (21)^2 \times 28 = 22 \times 21 \times 28 = 12936$ cm³

Example 23: If the heights of the two cones are in the ratio of 1 : 3 and their diameters are in the ratio of 3 : 5, find the ratio of their volumes.

Solution: Here, $\frac{V_1}{V_2} = \frac{\frac{1}{3}\pi(3)^2 \times 1}{\frac{1}{3}\pi(5)^2 \times 3} = \frac{3}{25}$

Since, required ratio = 3 : 25

Example 24: The diameter of a roller 120 cm long is 84 cm. If it takes 500 complete revolutions to level a playground, determine the cost of levelling at the rate of 30 paise per m².

Solution: Area of the playground $= 500 \times \frac{22}{7} \times 42 \times 120$

$= 15840000$ cm² $= 1584$ m²

Since, cost of lavelling = Rs. $\frac{30}{100} \times 1584$ = Rs. 475.20

Example 25: The diameter of a copper sphere is 6 cm. It is melted to form a wire of uniform cross-section. If the length of the wire is 36 cm then find the radius of the wire.

Solution: Here, $\pi r^2 \times 36 = \frac{4}{3}\pi \times 3^3 \quad \Rightarrow r^2 = \frac{4 \times 9}{36} \quad \therefore \ r = 1$ cm

Example 26: The trunk of a tree is a right cylinder 1.5 m in radius and 10 m high. Find the volume of the timber which remains when the trunk is trimmed just enough to reduce it to a rectangular parallelopiped on a square base.

Solution: Here length of diagonal of square base = 2 × 1.5 m

Since, area of the square base $= \frac{1}{2}(2 \times 1.5)^2 = 4.5$ m²

Hence, required volume of timber = 10 × 4.5 = 45 m³

Example 27: A semicircular sheet of a paper of diameter 28 cm is bent to cover the exterior surface of a conical ice cream cup. Find the depth of the ice cream cup.

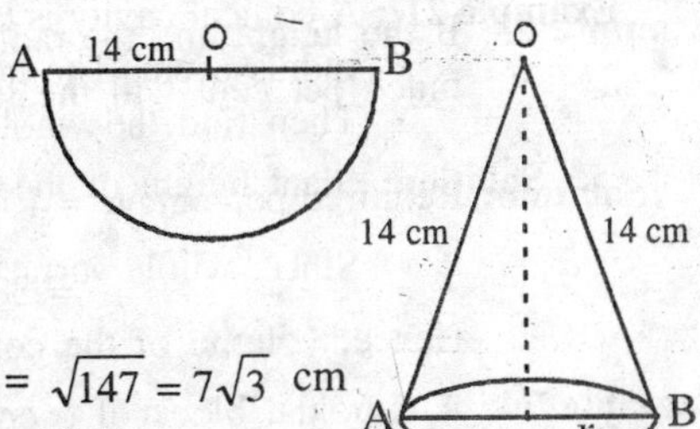

Sol: Here, $2\pi r = \pi.\frac{28}{2}$ $\therefore$ $r = 7$ cm

Hence, depth of the ice cream cup $= \sqrt{14^2 - 7^2} = \sqrt{147} = 7\sqrt{3}$ cm
$= 7 \times 1.732 = 12.12$ cm

Example 28: Find the volume of a cube whose diagonal measures $4\sqrt{3}$ cm.

Solution: Side of the cube $= \frac{4\sqrt{3}}{\sqrt{3}} = 4$ cm

Volume of the cube $= (4)^3 = 64$ cm^3

Example 29: Some solid metallic circular cones, each with radius of the base 3 cm and height 4 cm, are melted to form a solid sphere of radius 6 cm. Find the number of right circular cones.

Solution: Let number of right circular cones be n; then,

$$n \times \frac{1}{3}\pi \times 3^2 \times 4 = \frac{4}{3}\pi \times 6^3 \qquad \therefore \quad n = \frac{4 \times 6 \times 6 \times 6}{3 \times 3 \times 4} = 24$$

Example 30: If height of a right circular cone is increased by 200% and the radius of the base is reduced by 50%, then how much per cent will the volume of this cone be decrease?

Solution: Required percentage $= 200 - 50 - 50 + \frac{200 \times -50 + (-50) \times (-50) + (-50) \times 200}{100} + \frac{200 \times -50 \times -50}{(100)^2}$

$= 100 - 100 + 25 - 100 + 50 = -25\%$

Hence, volume of the cone decreased by 25%.

Example 31: If the ratio of volumes of two cones is 2 : 3 and ratio of radii of their bases is 1 : 2, then what will be the ratio of heights?

Solution: Here, $\frac{V_1}{V_2} = \frac{2}{3}$ and $\frac{r_1}{r_2} = \frac{1}{2}$; then

$$\frac{\frac{1}{3}\pi.(1)^2 \times h_1}{\frac{1}{3}\pi.(2)^2 \times h_2} = \frac{2}{3} \qquad \therefore \qquad \frac{h_1}{h_2} = \frac{2}{3} \times \frac{4}{1} = \frac{8}{3}$$

Hence, required ratio = 8 : 3

Example 32: Find the ratio of the surface area of the sphere and the curved surface area of the cylinder circumscribing the cylinder.

Solution: In this case, height of the cylinder, $h = 2r$ (diameter of the sphere)

Hence, required ratio $= \frac{4\pi r^2}{2\pi r.2r} = \frac{1}{1} = 1 : 1$

Example 33: If the height and the radius of the base of a cone are each increased by 100%, then how much per cent will the volume of the cone be increased?

Solution: Required percentage = $100 + 100 + 100 + \frac{100\times100+100\times100+100\times100}{100}+\frac{100\times100\times100}{100^2}$

$= 300 + 300 + 100 = 700\%$

Hence, volume of the cone increased by 700%

Example 34: A cuboidal block of 6 cm × 9 cm × 12 cm is cut up into exact number of equal cubes. What will be the least possible number of cubes?

Solution: Maximum possible length of the cube = H.C.F. of 6, 9, 12 = 3

Hence, required number of cubes = $\frac{6\times9\times12}{3\times3\times3}=24$

Example 35: If the volumes of two cubes are in the ratio of 27 : 1, What is the ratio of their edges?

Solution: $\frac{V_1}{V_2}=\frac{a_1^3}{a_2^3}=\frac{27}{1}\quad\therefore\quad\frac{a_1}{a_2}=\frac{3}{1}$

Hence, required ratio = 3 : 1

EXERCISE

1. A solid in the form of a cuboid is 4 cm × 3 cm × 2 cm. Its volume will be
(a) 20 cu cm (b) 22 cu cm (c) 28 cu cm (d) 24 cu cm

2. A reservoir is 3 m long, 2 m wide and 1 m deep. Its capacity in litres is
(a) 8000 litres (b) 10000 litres (c) 6500 litres (d) 6000 litres

3. Surface area of a cube is 1014 sq. cm. Its volume will be
(a) 2197 cu cm (b) 2297 cu cm (c) 2179 cu cm (d) 2117 cu cm

4. If the volumes of two cubical blocks are in the ratio of 8 : 1, what will be the ratio of their edges?
(a) 1 : 2 (b) 2 : 1 (c) 4 : 1 (d) 2 : 3

5. Two spheres have their surface areas in the ratio 9 : 16. Their volumes are in the ratio of
(a) 64 : 27 (b) 27 : 64 (c) 16 : 27 (d) 11 : 27

6. The length of the longest rod that can be placed in a room 12 m long, 9 m broad and 8 m high is
(a) 17 m (b) 18 m (c) 25 m (d) 16 m

7. The radius and the height of a right circular cone are in the ratio of 3 : 5. If its volume is 120π cu m, its slant height is
(a) $3\sqrt{34}$m (b) $2\sqrt{28}$m (c) $2\sqrt{44}$m (d) $2\sqrt{34}$m

8. Circumference of the base of a cylinder is 88 cm and height of the cylinder is 42 cm. Its volume is
(a) 25872 cu cm (b) 28572 cu cm (c) 25870 cu cm (d) 22584 cu cm

9. If two cubes each of 10 cm side are kept close to each other, then the cuboid so formed will have surface area equal to
(a) 1200 sq. cm (b) 5000 sq. cm (c) 1000 sq. cm (d) 1250 sq. cm

10. A rectangular piece of paper is 30 cm long and 20 cm wide. How many ways can be adopted if one wants to give this rectangular piece of paper a cylindrical form?
(a) Three (b) Two (c) One (d) Four

11. In the above question, the cylinders formed will have their volumes in the ratio of
(*a*) 2 : 3 (*b*) 3 : 1 (*c*) 3 : 2 (*d*) 1 : 3

12. If a solid sphere of 3 cm radius is melted and recast into a right circular cone whose base radius is same as that of the sphere, the height of the cone will be
(*a*) 8 cm (*b*) 12 cm (*c*) 6 cm (*d*) 5 cm

13. Diameter of a roller is 2.4 m and it is 1.68 m long. If it takes 1000 complete revolutions once over to level a field, the area of the field is
(*a*) 12672 sq. m (*b*) 12671 sq. m
(*c*) 12762 sq. m (*d*) 11768 sq. m

14. If each edge of a cube is increased by 10%, then by how much per cent will the surface area of this cube be increased?
(*a*) 21% (*b*) 18% (*c*) 15% (*d*) 20%

15. Height and base radius of a solid cylinder are 14 m and 4 m respectively. It is melted and recast into a solid cone of the same base radius as that of the cylinder, what will be the height of the cone?
(*a*) 21 m (*b*) 42 m (*c*) 48 m (*d*) 54 m

16. A room is in the form of a cube of side 10 m. How many bales of cotton can be kept in it if each bale covers 5 cu m space?
(*a*) 100 (*b*) 175 (*c*) 200 (*d*) 225

17. Three cubes having side 2 cm, 3 cm and 4 cm respectively are melted together to form a new cube. The side of the new cube will be
(*a*) 3.526 cm (*b*) 4.628 cm (*c*) 4.626 cm (*d*) 4.528 cm

18. If base diameter of a cylinder is increased by 50%, then by how much per cent its height must be decreased so as to keep its volume unaltered?
(*a*) 45.56% (*b*) 55.56% (*c*) 50.16% (*d*) 62.33%

19. The surface area of a cube is 600 sq. m. Its diagonal is
(*a*) $10\sqrt{3}$ cm (*b*) $5\sqrt{3}$ cm (*c*) $4\sqrt{2}$ cm (*d*) $10\sqrt{2}$ cm

20. The base diameter of a conical tomb is 28 m and its slant height is 50 m. Find the cost of white washing its curved surface at the rate of 80 paise per sq. m?
(*a*) Rs. 1860 (*b*) Rs. 1760 (*c*) Rs. 1950 (*d*) Rs. 1875

21. The volume of a cuboid is 1120 cu cm and its height is 5 cm while the length and the breadth of the cuboid are in the ratio 8 : 7. The length of this cylinder exceeds the breadth by
(*a*) 4 cm (*b*) 2 cm (*c*) 7 cm (*d*) 5 cm

22. If the base radius of a cylinder is decreased by 25% and height is increased by 10%, then the curved surface area
(*a*) Decreases by 17.5% (*b*) Increases by 16.5%
(*c*) Increases by 17.5% (*d*) Decreases by 11.5%

23. If the whole mass of a sphere can be tightly placed in a cube, then the volume of the cube and the volume of the sphere are in the ratio
(*a*) 7 : 12 (*b*) 22 : 21 (*c*) 21 : 11 (*d*) 20 : 7

24. If the radius of a sphere is decreased by 50%, then by how much per cent will the surface area of this sphere be decreased?
(*a*) 50% (*b*) 40% (*c*) 60% (*d*) 75%

25. A wall 8.0 m long, 3.6 m high and 0.8 m thick is to be constructed with bricks each 20 cm × 12 cm × 5.6 cm. If the mortar used increases the volume of each brick by $\frac{1}{7}$ of its original volume, find the number of bricks required to construct the wall.

(*a*) 15000 (*b*) 17000 (*c*) 14000 (*d*) 13000

26. The curved surface area of a cylinder is 528 sq. cm while its height is 8 cm. The volume of this cylinder will be

(*a*) 2882 cu cm (*b*) 2772 cu cm (*c*) 3772 cu cm (*d*) 2782 cu cm

27. Two cylindrical jars have their diameters in the ratio 3 : 1. If their heights are in the ratio 2 : 1, then the ratio of their volumes will be

(*a*) 18 : 1 (*b*) 14 : 3 (*c*) 3 : 5 (*d*) 1 : 18

28. A cone and a sphere have the same radius and the same volume. The ratio of the diameter of the sphere to the height of the cone is

(*a*) 1 : 3 (*b*) 3 : 2 (*c*) 1 : 2 (*d*) 2 : 3

29. The radius of the base and height of a right circular cone are in the ratio of 5 : 12. If its volume is 2512 cm^3, find its curved surface area and total surface area. (Use $\pi = 3.14$)

(*a*) 816.4 cm^2; 1130.4 cm^2 (*b*) 820.4 cm^2; 1125.4 cm^2
(*c*) 825.4 cm^2; 1130.4 cm^2 (*d*) None of these

30. The surface area of a cuboid is 22 cm^2 and sum of the lengths of all its edges is 24 cm. Find the length of a diagonal of the cuboid.

(*a*) 2.74 cm (*b*) 3 cm (*c*) 3.74 cm (*d*) 4 cm

31. The ratio of radii of two cylinders is 2 : 3 and the ratio of their heights is 5 : 3. Find the ratio of their volumes.

(*a*) 4 : 9 (*b*) 9 : 4 (*c*) 20 : 27 (*d*) 27 : 20

32. A cylindrical tank of diameter 35 cm is full of water. If 11 litres water is taken out from the tank, find the drop in the water level in the tank. $\left(\text{Use } \pi = \frac{22}{7}\right)$

(*a*) 9.425 cm (*b*) 10.428 cm (*c*) 11.428 cm (*d*) 12.428 cm

33. The diameters of the ends of a dustbin 24 cm high, which is in the shape of a frustum of a cone are 30 cm and 10 cm. Determine its capacity and surface area. $\left(\text{Use } \pi = \frac{22}{7}\right)$

(*a*) 8000 cm^3; 2000 cm^2 (*b*) 81100 cm^3; 2200 cm^2
(*c*) 81100 cm^3; 2400 cm^2 (*d*) 8171.43 cm^3; 2420 cm^2

34. A tank is of the shape of a cuboid whose length is 7.2 m and breadth is 2.5m. Water flows into it through a pipe whose cross-section is 5 cm × 3 cm at the rate of 10 m/s. Find the height to which water level will rise in the tank in 40 minutes.

(*a*) 1m (*b*) 2m (*c*) 3m (*d*) 4m

35. A well with 7m inside diameter is dug 22.5 m deep. Earth taken out of it is spread all around to a width of 10.5 m to form an embankment. Find the height of the embankment. $\left(\text{Use } \pi = \frac{22}{7}\right)$

(*a*) 1m (*b*) 1.5m (*c*) 2m (*d*) 2.5m

36. The difference between the outside and inside surfaces of a cylindrical metallic pipe 14 cm long is 44 cm^2. If the pipe is made of 99 cm^3 of metal, find the outer and inner radii of the pipe. $\left(\text{Use } \pi = \frac{22}{7}\right)$

(a) 1.5m; 1m (b) 2m; 1.5m (c) 2.5m; 2m (d) 3m; 2.5m

37. A sphere of maximum volume is cut out from a hemisphere of radius *r*. Find the ratio of the volume of the hemisphere to that of the sphere.

(a) 2 : 1 (b) 3 : 1 (c) 3 : 2 (d) 4 : 1

38. The volume of a cuboid is twice the volume of a cube. If the dimensions of the cuboid be 9 cm, 8 cm and 6 cm, then find the total surface area of the cube.

(a) 72 cm^2 (b) 108 cm^2 (c) 216 cm^2 (d) 432 cm^2

39. A solid is in the form of a right circular cylinder with hemispherical ends. The total length of the solid is 35 cm. The diameter of the cylinder is ¼th of its height. Find the volume and total surface area of the solid. $\left(\text{Use } \pi = \frac{22}{7}\right)$

(a) 1050.67 cm^3; 750 cm^2 (b) 1150.67 cm^3; 760 cm^2
(c) 1250.67 cm^3; 765 cm^2 (d) 1257.67 cm^3; 770 cm^2

40. The breadth of a cuboid is twice its height and half its length. If the volume of the cuboid is 512 m^3, then find the length of the cuboid.

(a) 8 m (b) 12 m (c) 16 m (d) 20 m

41. One cubic metre piece of copper is melted and recast into a square cross-section bar 36m long. An exact cube is cut off from this bar. If 1 cubic metre of copper costs Rs. 108, then the cost of the cube is

(a) 25 paise (b) 50 paise (c) 75 paise (d) one rupee

42. The volume of a rectangular block of stone is 10368 dm^2. Its dimensions are in the ratio of 3 : 2 : 1. If its entire surface is polished at 2 paise per dm^2, then find the total cost.

(a) Rs. 31.50 (b) Rs. 31.68 (c) Rs. 63.00 (d) RS. 63.36

43. Find the length of the longest rod that can be placed in a room 30m long, 24m broad and 18m high.

(a) $15\sqrt{2}$ m (b) 30 m (c) $30\sqrt{2}$ m (d) 60 m

44. If the volume of a cube is 512 cm^3, then find its total surface area.

(a) 192 cm^2 (b) 256 cm^2 (c) 329 cm^2 (d) 384 cm^2

45. If the volume of a cube is 216 cm^3, then find its total surface area.

(a) 212 cm^2 (b) 214 cm^2 (c) 216 cm^2 (d) 220 cm^2

46. Each side of a cube is 3 units. It is cut into cubes each of side 1 unit. Find the total surface area of all the smaller cubes thus obtained.

(a) 27 square units (b) 81 square units (c) 108 square units (d) 162 square units

47. If three equal cubes are placed adjacently in a row, then find the ratio of total surface area of the new cuboid to that sum of the surface areas of the three cubes.

(a) 1 : 3 (b) 2 : 3 (c) 5 : 9 (d) 7 : 9

48. If six cubes, each of 10 cm edge, are joined end to end, then find the surface area of the resulting solid.

(a) 2400 cm^2 (b) 2600 cm^2 (c) 3000 cm^2 (d) 3600 cm^2

49. If three cubes of copper, each with an edge of 6 cm, 8 cm and 10 cm respectively, are melted to form a single cube, then find the diagonal of the new cube.
(*a*) 18.8 cm (*b*) 20.8 cm (*c*) 22.8 cm (*d*) 24.8 cm

50. A rectangular tank is 80 m long and 25m broad. Water flows into it through a pipe whose cross-section is 25 cm^2, at the rate of 16 km/hr. How much will the level of water rise in the tank in 45 minutes?
(*a*) 3 cm (*b*) 3.375 cm (*c*) 4 cm (*d*) 5 cm

51. A field is 150 m long and 100 m wide. A plot (outside the field) 50 m long and 30 m wide is dug to a depth of 8 m and earth taken out from the plot is spread evenly in the field. By how much is the level of the field raised?
(*a*) 5 dm (*b*) 6 dm (*c*) 7 dm (*d*) 8 dm

52. The height of a right circular cylinder is 6 metres and three times the sum of the areas of its two end faces is twice the area of its curved surface, find the radius of its base.
(*a*) 4 m (*b*) 5 m (*c*) 6 m (*d*) 7 m

53. The circumference of the base of a right circular cylinder is 13.2 m and sum of its radius and height is 3m. Find the radius and total surface area of the cylinder.
(*a*) 1.5 m; 35.5 m^2 (*b*) 2m; 37.6m^2 (*c*) 2.1 m; 39.6m^2 (*d*) 2.5m; 40m^2

54. 96 equal circular plates, each half a centimetre thick are placed one above another to form a right circular cylinder of volume 7392 cm^3. Find the radius of each circular plate.
(*a*) 4 cm (*b*) 5 cm (*c*) 6 cm (*d*) 7 cm

55. A hollow cylinder whose internal diameter is 20 cm is closed at one end and is partly filled with water. By how much does the level of water in the cylinder rise when a cube, each of edge of which measures 11 cm is completely immersed in it?
(*a*) 4.235 cm (*b*) 5.532 cm (*c*) 6.325 cm (*d*) 7.253 cm

56. Find the number of coins 1.5 cm in diameter and 0.2 cm thick to be melted to form a right circular cylinder, whose height is 10 cm and diameter 4.5 cm.
(*a*) 400 (*b*) 425 (*c*) 450 (*d*) 500

57. A cylindrical cistern whose diameter is 14 cm is partly filled with water. If a conical block of iron whose radius of base is 3.5 cm and height 6 cm is wholly immersed in the water, by how much will the water level rise?
(*a*) 0.5 cm (*b*) 0.75 cm (*c*) 1 cm (*d*) 1.25 cm

58. The vertical height of a conical tent is $4\frac{2}{3}$ m and the diameter of its base is 6 m. It can be accommodate 11 persons. Find the average air space allowed per head.
(*a*) 2m^3 (*b*) 3m^3 (*c*) 4m^3 (*d*) 5m^3

59. Three solid metallic spheres of radii 6, 8 and 10 cm respectively are melted to form a single solid sphere. Find the radius of the sphere so formed.
(*a*) 8 cm (*b*) 10 cm (*c*) 12 cm (*d*) 14 cm

60. The vertical height of a conical tent is 42 dm and the diameter of its base is 5.4 m. Find the number of persons it can accommodate if each person is to be allowed 2916 dm^3.
(*a*) 10 (*b*) 11 (*c*) 12 (*d*) 13

61. How many metre of canvas will be required to make a conical tent whose slant height is $4\frac{2}{3}$ m and whose radius is 2.5 m. If width of the canvas be 1.25 m.
(*a*) $29\frac{1}{3}$ m (*b*) $32\frac{1}{3}$ m (*c*) $34\frac{1}{3}$ m (*d*) $36\frac{2}{3}$ m

62. Rain water which falls on a flat rectangular surface of length 6m and breadth 4m is transferred into a cylindrical vessesl of internal radius 20 cm. What will be the height of water in the cylindrical vessel if a rainfall of 1 cm has fallen?

(a) 191 cm *(b)* 193 cm *(c)* 195 cm *(d)* 197 cm

63. A conical vessel of radius 6 cm and height 8 cm is completely filled with water. A sphere is lowered into the water and its size is such that when it touches the sides it is just immersed. What fraction of water overflow?

(a) $\frac{1}{8}$ *(b)* $\frac{1}{4}$ *(c)* $\frac{3}{8}$ *(d)* $\frac{1}{2}$

64. A right circular cylinder and right cone have equal bases and equal heights. If their curved surface area in the ratio of 8 : 5, determine the ratio of the radius of the base to the height of either of them.

(a) 1 : 2 *(b)* 2 : 3 *(c)* 3 : 4 *(d)* 4 : 5

65. The volumes of two right circular cylinders are equal and the ratio between their heights is 1 : 3 respectively. What will be the ratio between their radii of bases?

(a) $1 : \sqrt{3}$ *(b)* $\sqrt{3} : 1$ *(c)* 1 : 3 *(d)* 3 : 1

66. If the height of the cone is doubled then its volume will be increased by

(a) 100% *(b)* 200% *(c)* 300% *(d)* 400%

67. The diameter of the iron ball used for the shot-put game is 14 cm. It is melted and then a solid cylinder of height $2\frac{1}{3}$ cm is made. What will be the diameter of the base of the cylinder?

(a) $\frac{14}{3}$ cm *(b)* $\frac{28}{3}$ cm *(c)* 14 cm *(d)* 28 cm

68. A cistern 6m long and 4m wide, contains water upto a depth of 1m 25cm. Find the total area of the wet surface.

(a) 49 m^2 *(b)* 50 m^2 *(c)* 53.5 m^2 *(d)* 55 m^2

69. The volume of a wall, 5 times as high as it is broad and 8 times as long as it is high, is 12.8 m^3. Find the breadth of the wall.

(a) 25 cm *(b)* 30 cm *(c)* 35 cm *(d)* 40 cm

70. A beam 9m long, 22.5 cm thick and 20 cm high is made up of iron which weighs 50 kg/m^3. Find the weight of the beam.

(a) 20.25 kg *(b)* 36 kg *(c)* 48 kg *(d)* 56 kg

71. The radius of a right circular cone is 3cm and its height is 4 cm. Find the curved surface of the cone.

(a) 12π cm^2 *(b)* 15π cm^2 *(c)* 18π cm^2 *(d)* 21π cm^2

72. An agricultural field is in the form of a rectangle of length 20m and width 14m. A pit 6m long, 3m wide and 2.5m deep is dug in a corner of a field and the earth taken out of the pit is spread uniformly over the remaining area of the field. The level of the field has been raised by:

(a) 15.16 cm *(b)* 16.17 cm *(c)* 17.18 cm *(d)* 18.19 cm

73. How many metres of cloth 5m wide will be required to make a conical tent, the radius of whose base is 7m and whose height is 24m? $\left(\text{Take } \pi = \frac{22}{7}\right)$

(a) 105m *(b)* 110m *(c)* 115m *(d)* 120m

74. The curved surface area of a cylindrical pillar is 264m^2 and its volume is 924m^3. What will be its height?

(a) 5m *(b)* 6m *(c)* 7m *(d)* 8m

75. Find the total surface area of a right circular cylinder whose diameter is 14 cm and height 18 cm.
(*a*) 1025 cm^2 (*b*) 1050 cm^2 (*c*) 1075 cm^2 (*d*) 1100 cm^2

76. If the radius of a right circular cylinder is decreased by 50% and its height is increased by 60%, its volume will be decreased by:
(*a*) 10% (*b*) 20% (*c*) 40% (*d*) 60%

77. The length, breadth and height of a cuboid are in the ratio 1 : 2 : 3. If they are increased by 100%, 200% and 200% respectively, then compared to the original volume the increase in the volume of the cuboid will be:
(*a*) 5 times (*b*) 12 times (*c*) 17 times (*d*) 18 times

78. If the radius of the sphere is doubled, its volume becomes:
(*a*) double (*b*) four times (*c*) six times (*d*) eight times

79. The areas of three adjacent faces of a cuboid are *x*, *y*, *z* square units respectively. If the volume of the cuboid are *V* cubic units, then find the correct relation between *V*, *x*, *y* and *z*.
(*a*) $V^2 = xyz$ (*b*) $V^2 = x^3y^3z^3$ (*c*) $V^3 = xyz$ (*d*) $V^3 = x^2y^2z^2$

80. A right circular cylinder is formed by rolling a rectangular paper 12 cm long and 3 cm wide along its length. Find the radius of the base of the cylinder.
(*a*) $\frac{3}{2\pi}$ cm (*b*) $\frac{6}{\pi}$ cm (*c*) $\frac{9}{2\pi}$ cm (*d*) 2π cm

81. A cone of height 7 cm and base-radius 1 cm is carved out from a cuboidal block of wood of size 10 cm × 5 cm × 2 cm. Find the wasted wood in this process. $\left(\text{Use } \pi = \frac{22}{7}\right)$
(*a*) $7\frac{1}{3}\%$ (*b*) $46\frac{1}{3}\%$ (*c*) $53\frac{2}{3}\%$ (*d*) $92\frac{2}{3}\%$

82. A rectangular tank of length 10 m, breadth 5m and depth 6m is full of water. How much water must be taken out of the tank to reduce the level of water in the tank by one metre?
(*a*) 30 m^3 (*b*) 50 m^3 (*c*) 60 m^3 (*d*) 100 m^3

83. Some oil is filled in a right circular cylindrical vessel. The radius of the base of the vessel is 6 cm. Some iron balls, each of diameter 3 cm, are completely dipped into the oil. If the level of oil in the vessel rises by 2 cm. Find the number of iron balls dipped in the oil.
(*a*) 4 (*b*) 8 (*c*) 16 (*d*) 32

84. If the area of the adjacent faces of a rectangular block are in the ratio of 2 : 3 : 4 and its volume is 9000 cm^3, then find the length of the shortest side.
(*a*) 10 cm (*b*) 15 cm (*c*) 20 cm (*d*) 30 cm

85. Find the volume of the wood required for making a closed box external measurements 14cm by 9.5 cm by 6 cm and wood is 7.5 mm thick.
(*a*) 215 cm^3 (*b*) 348 cm^3 (*c*) 352 cm^3 (*d*) 405 cm^3

86. A metal sheet 27 cm long, 8 cm broad and 1 cm thick is melted into a cube. The difference between the surface areas of two solids will be
(*a*) 216 cm^2 (*b*) 286 cm^2 (*c*) 300 cm^2 (*d*) 502 cm^2

87. The radii of the bases of two cylinders are in the ratio of 3 : 5 and their height in the ratio of 2 : 3. Find the ratio of their curved suface areas.
(*a*) 2 : 3 (*b*) 2 : 5 (*c*) 3 : 5 (*d*) 5 : 3

88. The radius of the base and height of a metallic solid cylinder are *r* cm and 6 cm rspectively. It is melted and recast into a solid cone of the same radius of base, find the height of the cone.
(*a*) 9 cm (*b*) 18 cm (*c*) 27 cm (*d*) 54 cm

89. If the radii of two spheres are in the ratio of 1 : 4, then find the ratio of their surface areas.
(*a*) 1 : 2 (*b*) 1 : 4 (*c*) 1 : 8 (*d*) 1 : 16

90. If the area of the base of a cone is 770 cm^2 and area of the curved surface is 814 cm^2. Then find its volume.
(*a*) $213\sqrt{5}$ cm^3 (*b*) $392\sqrt{5}$ cm^3 (*c*) $550\sqrt{5}$ cm^3 (*d*) $616\sqrt{5}$ cm^3

91. The radii of two spheres are in the ratio of 3 : 2. What will be ratio of their volumes?
(*a*) 3 : 2 (*b*) 9 : 4 (*c*) 8 : 27 (*d*) 27 : 8

92. A wall 3m × 2.7m × 0.2m of concrete weight 320 kg per cubic metre. What will be weight of the total wall?
(*a*) 51.84 kg (*b*) 518.4 kg (*c*) 5184.0 kg (*d*) 51840.0 kg

93. A solid sphere of radius 3 cm is melted and then cast into small spherical balls each of diameter 0.6 cm. Find the number of ball thus obtained.
(*a*) 10 (*b*) 100 (*c*) 1000 (*d*) 10000

94. Into a circular drum of radius 4.2 m and height 3.5m, how many full bags of wheat can be emptied if the space required for wheat in each bag is 2.1 cubic metre?
(*a*) 85 (*b*) 90 (*c*) 92 (*d*) 95

95. The volume of cuboid is twice that of a cube. If the dimensions of the cuboid are 9 cm, 8 cm and 6 cm, then find the total surface area of the cube.
(*a*) 72 cm^2 (*b*) 108 cm^2 (*c*) 216 cm^2 (*d*) 432 cm^2

96. A copper rod of 1 cm diameter and 8 cm length is drawn into a wire of uniform diameter and 18m length. Find the radius of the wire.
(*a*) $\frac{1}{10}$ cm (*b*) $\frac{1}{15}$ cm (*c*) $\frac{1}{20}$ cm (*d*) $\frac{1}{30}$ cm

97. A rectangular tank is 225m by 162m at the base. With what speed must water flow into it through an aperture 60 cm by 45 cm that the level may be raised 20 cm in 5 hours?
(*a*) 1800 m/hr (*b*) 3600 m/hr (*c*) 5400 m/hr (*d*) 7200 m/hr

98. A cube of edge 15 cm is immersed completely in a rectangular vessel containing water. If the dimensions of the base of vessel are 20 cm × 15 cm, find the rise in water level.
(*a*) 11.25 cm (*b*) 11.50 cm (*c*) 11.75 cm (*d*) 12 cm

99. How many iron rods, each of length 7m and diameter 2 cm can be made out of 0.88 cubic metre of iron?
(*a*) 40 (*b*) 400 (*c*) 4000 (*d*) 40000

100. How many spherical bullets can be made out of a lead cylinder 28 cm high and with base radius 6 cm, each bullet being 1.5 cm in diameter?
(*a*) 1790 (*b*) 1792 (*c*) 1794 (*d*) 1796

101. A hemispherical bowl of internal radius 9 cm contains a liquid. This liquid is to be filled into cylindrical shaped small bottles of diameter 3 cm and height 4 cm. How many bottles will be needed to empty thc bowl?
(*a*) 50 (*b*) 52 (*c*) 54 (*d*) 56

102. A boat having a length 3m and breadth 2m is floating on a lake. The boat sinks by 1 cm, when a man gets on it. Find the mass of the man.

(a) 50 kg *(b)* 60 kg *(c)* 65 kg *(d)* 70 kg

103. The height of a wall is six times of its width and the length of the wall is seven times of its height. If the volume of the wall is 16128 m^3, find its width.

(a) 3.5 m *(b)* 4 m *(c)* 4.5 m *(d)* 5 m

104. The edge of the cuboid are in the ratio of 1 : 2 : 3 and its surface area is 88cm^2. What will be the volume of the cuboid?

(a) 12 cm^3 *(b)* 24 cm^3 *(c)* 36 cm^3 *(d)* 48 cm^3

105. 50 men took a dip in a water tank 40 m long and 20 m broad on a religious day. If the average displacement of water by a man is 4 m^3, then rise in the water level in the tank will be:

(a) 15 cm *(b)* 20 cm *(c)* 25 cm *(d)* 30 cm

106. A rectangular water tank is 80m × 40m. Water flows into it through a pipe 40 cm^2 at the opening at a speed of 10 km/hr. By how much, the water level will rise in the tank in half an hour?

(a) $\frac{4}{7}$ cm *(b)* $\frac{5}{8}$ cm *(c)* $\frac{6}{11}$ cm *(d)* $\frac{8}{13}$ cm

107. A hall is 15m long and 12m broad. If the sum of the areas of the floor and ceiling is equal to the sum of areas of the four walls, then find the volume of the hall.

(a) 900 m^3 *(b)* 1000 m^3 *(c)* 1200 m^3 *(d)* 1500 m^3

108. A swimming pool 9m wide and 12m long is 1m deep on the shallow side and 4m deep on the deeper side. Find its volume.

(a) 270 m^3 *(b)* 300 m^3 *(c)* 360 m^3 *(d)* 420 m^3

109. A cistern of capacity 8000 litres measures externally 3.3m by 2.6m by 1.1m and its walls are 5 cm thick. Find the thickness of the bottom.

(a) 5 cm *(b)* 10 cm *(c)* 15 cm *(d)* 20 cm

110. A metallic sheet is of rectangular shape with dimensions 48m × 36m. From each of its corners, a square is cut off so as to make an open box. If the length of the square is 8m, find the volume of the box.

(a) 5120 m^3 *(b)* 5340 m^3 *(c)* 6120 m^3 *(d)* 6440 m^3

111. If the areas of the three adjacent faces of a cuboidal box are 120 cm^2, 72 cm^2 and 60 cm^2 respectively, then volume of the box is:

(a) 360 cm^3 *(b)* 480 cm^3 *(c)* 600 cm^3 *(d)* 720 cm^3

112. The cost of the paint is Rs. 36.50 per kg. If 1 kg of paint covers 16 square feet, then find the cost to paint outside of a cube having 8 feet each side.

(a) Rs. 678 *(b)* Rs. 768 *(c)* Rs. 876 *(d)* Rs. 968

113. An iron cube of side 10 cm is hammered into a rectangular sheet of thickness 0.5 cm. If the sides of the sheet are in the ratio of 1 : 5, then find its sides.

(a) 5 cm; 25 cm *(b)* 10 cm; 50 cm *(c)* 15 cm; 75 cm *(d)* 20 cm; 100 cm

114. Three cubes with sides in the ratio of 3 : 4 : 5 are melted to form a single cube whose diagonal is $12\sqrt{3}$ cm. Find the sides of the cube.

(a) 6 cm, 8 cm, 10 cm *(b)* 9 cm, 12 cm, 15 cm

(c) 12 cm, 16 cm, 20 cm *(d)* 15 cm, 20 cm, 25 cm

115. The capacity of a cylindrical tank is 246.4 litres. If the height is 4m, find the diameter of the base.
(a) 7 cm (b) 14 cm (c) 21 cm (d) 28 cm

116. A circular well with a diameter 2m, is dug to a depth of 14m, Find the volume of the earth dug out.
(a) 40 m^3 (b) 44 m^3 (c) 50 m^3 (d) 55 m^3

117. The radius of the cylinder is half of its height and area of the inner part is 616 cm^3. Find its volume.
(a) 1440 cc (b) 1538 cc (c) 1630 cc (d) 1740. cc

118. The curved surface area of a cylindrical pillar is 264 m^2 and its volume is 924m^3. The ratio of its diameter ot its height is
(a) 2 : 5 (b) 5 : 2 (c) 3 : 7 (d) 7 : 3

119. Find the height of a closed cylinder of given volume and minimum surface area.
(a) half of its diameter (b) equal to its diameter
(c) double of its diameter (d) None of these

120. Water flows through a cylindrical pipe of internal diameter 7cm at 2m/s. If the pipe is always half full, then find the volume of water discharged in 10 minutes.
(a) 1160 *l* (b) 2310 *l* (c) 3850 *l* (d) 4620 *l*

121. 66 cm^3 of silver is drawn into a wire of 1 mm in diameter. Find the length of the wire.
(a) 80m (b) 84m (c) 88m (d) 90m

122. A cylindrical tube open at both ends is made of metal. The internal diameter of the tube is 11.2 cm and its length is 21 cm. The metal everywhere is 0.4 cm thick. Find the volume of the metal used.
(a) 306.24 cm^3 (b) 310.24 cm^3 (c) 316 cm^3 (d) 324.24 cm^3

123. A hollow iron pipe is 21cm long and its external diameter is 8cm. If the thickness of the pipe is 1cm and iron weighs 8 gm/cm^3, then find the weight of the pipe.
(a) 3.696 kg (b) 36.96 kg (c) 39.6 kg (d) 40 kg

124. What is the total surface area of a right circular cone of height 14 cm and base radius 7 cm.
(a) 398.30 cm^2 (b) 462.30 cm^2 (c) 498.30 cm^2 (d) None of these

125. If a right circular cone of height 24 cm has a volume of 1232 cm^3, then find its curved surface area.
(a) 220 cm^2 (b) 330 cm^2 (c) 440 cm^2 (d) 550 cm^2

126. A solid cylindrical block of radius 12 cm and height 18 cm is mounted with a conical block of radius 12 cm and height 5 cm. What is the total lateral surface area of the solid thus formed?
(a) $2321\frac{5}{7}$ cm^2 (b) $2457\frac{5}{7}$ cm^2 (c) $2300\frac{4}{7}$ cm^2 (d) $1821\frac{5}{7}$ cm^2

127. If the volume of a sphere is divided by its surface area, the result is 27 cm. Find the radius of the sphere.
(a) 81 cm (b) 85 cm (c) 90 cm (d) 91 cm

128. If the radius of a sphere is increased by 2 cm, then its surface area increases by 352 cm^2. Find the radius of the original sphere.
(a) 3 cm (b) 6 cm (c) 9 cm (d) 12 cm

129. A hollow spherical metallic ball has an external diameter 6 cm and is $\frac{1}{2}$ cm thick. Find the volume of the metal used in the ball.
(a) $47\frac{2}{3}$ cm^3 (b) $51\frac{2}{3}$ cm^3 (c) $53\frac{2}{3}$ cm^3 (d) $61\frac{2}{3}$ cm^3

130. The surface area of a sphere is same as the curved surface area of a right circular cylinder, whose height and diameter are 12 cm each. Find the radius of the sphere.
(*a*) 2 cm (*b*) 4 cm (*c*) 6 cm (*d*) 9 cm

131. A hemisphere and a cone have equal bases. If their heights are equal, then find the ratio of their curved surfaces.
(*a*) $1:\sqrt{2}$ (*b*) $\sqrt{2}:1$ (*c*) 1 : 2 (*d*) 2 : 1

132. A metallic hemisphere is melted and recast the shape of a cone with same base radius (R) as that of the hemisphere. If H is the height of the cone, then
(*a*) $H = \frac{2}{3}R$ (*b*) H = 2R (*c*) H = 3R (*d*) $H = \sqrt{2}R$

133. A hollow sphere of internal and external diameters 4 cm and 8 cm respectively is melted into a cone of base diameter 8 cm. Find the height of the cone.
(*a*) 7 cm (*b*) 14 cm (*c*) 21 cm (*d*) 28 cm

134. A solid metallic spherical ball of diameter 6 cm is melted and recast into a cone with diameter of the base as 12 cm. Find the height of the cone.
(*a*) 3 cm (*b*) 4 cm (*c*) 5 cm (*d*) 6 cm

135. 12 spheres of the same size are made from melting a solid cylinder of 16 cm diameter and 2cm height. Find the diameter of each sphere.
(*a*) 2 cm (*b*) 4 cm (*c*) 6 cm (*d*) 8 cm

136. Find the volume of the greatest sphere that can be cut-off from a cylindrical log of wood of base radius 1 cm and height 5 cm.
(*a*) $\frac{2}{3}\pi\,cm^3$ (*b*) $\frac{4\pi}{3}cm^3$ (*c*) $\frac{8}{3}\pi\,cm^3$ (*d*) $\frac{10}{3}\pi\,cm^2$

SOLUTIONS

1. Volume of the cuboid = $l \times b \times h = 4 \times 3 \times 2 = 24$ cu. cm.

2. Volume of the reservoir = $l \times b \times h = 3 \times 2 \times 1 = 6$ cu. m
($\because$ 1 cu m = 1000 litre)
$\therefore$ Capacity of the reservoir = 6 × 1000 = 6000 litre.

3. Here, $6 \times (\text{side})^2 = 1014 \Rightarrow (\text{side})^2 = \frac{1014}{6} = 169$
$\therefore$ side $= \sqrt{169} = 13$ cm
Hence, Volume of the cube = $(\text{side})^3 = (13)^3 = 2197$ cu cm.

4. Here, $a_1^3 : a_2^3 = 8 : 1$
$\therefore \left(\frac{a_1}{a_2}\right)^3 = \left(\frac{2}{1}\right)^3 \Rightarrow a_1 : a_2 = 2 : 1$
Therefore, ratio of their edges = 2 : 1.

5. Here, $4\pi r_1^2 : 4\pi r_2^2 = 9 : 16 \Rightarrow r_1^2 : r_2^2 = 9 : 16$
$\Rightarrow \left(\frac{r_1}{r_2}\right)^2 = \left(\frac{3}{4}\right)^2 \Rightarrow r_1 : r_2 = 3 : 4 \Rightarrow \frac{r_1^3}{r_2^3} = \frac{27}{64} \Rightarrow r_1^3 : r_2^3 = 27 : 64.$

Therefore, ratio of their volumes = $\frac{4}{3}\pi r_1^3 : \frac{4}{3}\pi r_2^3 = r_1^3 : r_2^3 = 27 : 64$

6. The longest rod that can be placed in the cuboidal room = Length of the diagonal

$= \sqrt{l^2 + b^2 + h^2} = \sqrt{(12)^2 + (9)^2 + (8)^2} = \sqrt{144 + 81 + 64} = \sqrt{289} = 17$ m

7. Suppose the base radius and the height of the right circular cone are $3x$ m and $5x$ m respectively.

$\therefore$ Volume of the cone $= \frac{1}{3}\pi r^2 h = \frac{1}{3}\pi(3x)^2 \times 5x$ cu m

Now, $\frac{1}{3}\pi \times 9x^2 \times 5x = 120\pi \Rightarrow x^3 = \frac{120 \times 3}{9 \times 5}$

$\Rightarrow \quad x^3 = 8 \Rightarrow x^3 = (2)^3 \Rightarrow x = 2$ m

$\therefore$ The radius and the height of the cone will be $3 \times 2 = 6$ m and $5 \times 2 = 10$ m respectively.

$\therefore$ Slant height of the cone $= \sqrt{r^2 + h^2} = \sqrt{(6)^2 + (10)^2} = \sqrt{36 + 100} = \sqrt{136} = 2\sqrt{34}$m.

8. Here, $\quad 2\pi r = 88$

$\therefore \quad r = \frac{88}{2\pi} = \frac{88 \times 7}{2 \times 22} = 14$ cm

Since, volume of the cylinder $= \pi r^2 h = \frac{22}{7} \times (14)^2 \times 42 = 22 \times 2 \times 14 \times 42 = 25872$ cu cm.

9. Here, length of the cuboid = Edge of the first cube + Edge of the second cube

$= 10 + 10 = 20$ cm

$\therefore$ Surface area of the cuboid $= 2(20 \times 10 + 10 \times 10 + 10 \times 20)$

$= 2(200 + 100 + 200)$

$= 2 \times 500 = 1000$ sq. cm.

10. Obviously, two ways can be adopted if one wants to give the rectangular piece of paper a cylindrical form, *i.e.*, 1. *When the paper is bent towards its length.* In this case, the circumference of the base of the cylinder will be equal to the length of the rectangular piece of paper and the height of the cylinder will be equal to the breadth of the rectangular piece of paper.

2. *When the paper is bent towards its breadth.* In this case, the circumference of the base of the cylinder will be equal to the breadth of the rectangular piece of paper and the height of the cylinder will be equal to the length of the rectangular piece of paper.

11. In the first case :

$2\pi r = 30$

$r = \frac{15}{\pi}$ cm and $h = 20$ cm

$\Rightarrow \quad$ Volume $(V_1) = \pi r^2 h = \frac{15 \times 15 \times 20}{\pi} = \frac{4500}{\pi}$ cu cm

In the second case :

$2\pi r = 20 \Rightarrow r = \frac{10}{\pi}$ cm and $h = 30$ cm

$\therefore \quad$ Volume $(V_2) = \pi r^2 h = \frac{10 \times 10 \times 30}{\pi} = \frac{3000}{\pi}$ cu cm

Hence, ratio of the two volumes $= V_1 : V_2 = \frac{4500}{\pi} : \frac{3000}{\pi} = 3 : 2$

12. Volume of the cone = Volume of the sphere

$\therefore \quad \frac{1}{3}\pi(3)^2 \times h = \frac{4}{3}\pi \times 3^3 \Rightarrow h = 12$ cm

Hence, height of the cone = 12 cm.

13. Surface area of the roller = $2\pi rh = 2\times\frac{22}{7}\times 1.2\times 1.68 = 12.672$ sq. m

In one complete revolution, the roller covers 12.672 sq. m.

$\therefore$ It will cover in 1000 revolutions = 12.672 × 1000 = 12672 sq. m

Hence, area of the field = 12672 sq. m.

14. Percentage increase in the surface area of the cube = $\left(x+y+\frac{xy}{100}\right)\%$

$$= \left(10+10+\frac{10\times 10}{100}\right)\% = 21\%.$$

15. Here, volume of the cone = Volume of the cylinder

$\Rightarrow \quad \frac{1}{3}\pi r^2 \times \text{height} = \pi r^2 \times 14$

$\therefore \quad$ Height = 14 × 3 = 42 m

Thus, height of the cone = 42 m.

16. Volume of the cubical room = $(10)^3$ = 1000 cu m

Number of cotton bales which can be placed in the room

$$= \frac{\text{Volume of the room}}{\text{Volume of each cotton bale}} = \frac{1000}{5} = 200.$$

17. Volume of the new cube = $2^3 + 3^3 + 4^3 = 8 + 27 + 64 = 99$cu cm

$\therefore$ Side of the new cube = $\sqrt[3]{99} = 4.626$ cm.

18. Change in the volume of the cylinder

$$= \left(x+y+(-z)+\frac{xy+y(-z)+(-zx)}{100}+\frac{xy(-z)}{100^2}\right)\%$$

Since volume of the cylinder remains unchanged.

$\therefore \quad$ Change = 0%

Now, $\left(50+50+(-z)+\frac{50\times 50-50z-50z}{100}+\frac{50\times 50\times(-z)}{100^2}\right)=0$

$\therefore \quad 100 - z + 25 - z - .25z = 0$

$\Rightarrow 2.25z = 125 \Rightarrow z = \frac{125}{2.25} = 55.56$

$\therefore$ Height of the cylinder should be decreased by 55.56%.

19. Here, $\quad 6 \times (\text{side})^2 = 600$

$\Rightarrow \quad \text{side}^2 = 100 \Rightarrow \text{side} = \sqrt{100} = 10$ cm

$\therefore$ Diagonal of the cube = $\sqrt{3}\times\text{side} = \sqrt{3}\times 10 = 10\sqrt{3}$ cm.

20. Area of the curved surface of the cone $= \frac{22}{7} \times \frac{28}{2} \times 50 = 2200$ sq. m.

$\therefore$ Cost of white washing at 80 paise per sq. m $= 2200 \times \frac{80}{100} =$ Rs. 1760.

21. Suppose the length and the breadth of the cuboid are $8x$ cm and $7x$ cm

$\therefore$ Here, $8x \times 7x \times 5 = 1120 \Rightarrow x^2 = \frac{1120}{280} = 4 = (2)^2$

$\Rightarrow x = 2$

$\therefore$ Length of the cuboid $= 8 \times 2 = 16$ cm

Breadth of the cuboid $= 7 \times 2 = 14$ cm

Hence, it is clear that length of the cuboid exceeds the breadth by 2 cm.

22. Change in the curved surface of the cylinder $= \left(-25 + 10 + \frac{-25 \times 10}{100}\right)\%$

$= (-15 - 2.5)\% = -17.5\%$

$\therefore$ Curved surface of the cylinder will be decreased by 17.5%.

23. The sphere can be completely fitted in the cube. It means side of the cube is equal to the diameter of the sphere.

Volume of the sphere$= \frac{4}{3}\pi(r)^3$

And volume of the cube = $(\text{side})^3$

$\therefore$ Ratio of the volumes of the cube and the sphere $= (\text{side})^3 : \frac{4}{3}\pi r^3$

$\Rightarrow (2r)^3 : \frac{4}{3}\pi r^3 = 6 : \frac{22}{7} = 21:11$

24. Change in surface area of the sphere $= \left(-50 - 50 + \frac{-50 \times -50}{100}\right)\%$

$= (-100 + 25)\% = -75\%$

Hence, surface area of the sphere will be decreased by 75%.

25. Volume of the wall $= 8 \times 3.6 \times .8 = 23.04$ cu m $= 23040000$ cu cm

Volume of the brick $= 20 \times 12 \times 5.6 = 1344$ cu cm

Now, volume of a brick including the motar $= 1344 + \frac{1}{7}$ of 1344

$= 1344 + 192 = 1536$ cu cm

$\therefore$ Number of bricks required $= \frac{23040000}{1536} = 15000$

26. Here, $2\pi rh = 528$

$\therefore \quad r = \frac{528}{2\pi h} = \frac{528 \times 7}{2 \times 22 \times 8} = 10.5$ cm

Since, volume of the cylinder $= \frac{22}{7} \times (10.5)^2 \times 8 = 2772$ cu cm.

27. Required ratio $= \pi.3^2.2 : \pi.1^2.1 = 18 : 1$

28. Here, $4/3\pi r^3 = \frac{1}{3}\pi r^2 h \Rightarrow 4r = h \Rightarrow 2d = h \quad \therefore \frac{d}{h} = \frac{1}{2}$

Hence, required ratio = 1 : 2

29. Let radius and height of a right circular cone are $5x$ cm and $12x$ cm.

Then, $\frac{1}{3} \times 3.14 \times (5x)^2 \times 12x = 2512 \quad \Rightarrow x^3 = \frac{2512}{3.14 \times 25 \times 4} = 8$

$\therefore x = 2$

Since, radius = 5 × 2 = 10 cm; height = 12 × 2 = 24 cm

Now, slant height, $l = \sqrt{10^2 + 24^2} = \sqrt{676} = 26$ cm

Curved surface area = 3.14 × 10 × 26 = 816.4 cm^2

Total surface area = $3.14 \times 10 \times 26 + 3.14 \times (10)^2 = 816.4 + 314 = 1130.4$ cm^2

30. Here, $2(lb + bh + hl) = 22$ cm and

also, $4(l + b + h) = 24$ cm $\quad \Rightarrow (l + b + h) = 6$ cm

Now, $l^2 + b^2 + h^2 = (l + b + h)^2 - 2(lb + bh + hl) = (6)^2 - 22 = 14$

Since, diagonal, $d = \sqrt{l^2 + b^2 + h^2} = \sqrt{14} = 3.74$ cm

31. Here, $\frac{V_1}{V_2} = \frac{\pi \times 2^2 \times 5}{\pi \times 3^2 \times 3} = \frac{20}{27}$

Hence, required ratio = 20 : 27

32. Here, $\frac{22}{7} \times \left(\frac{35}{2}\right)^2 \times h = 11 \times 1000 \quad \therefore h = \frac{11 \times 1000 \times 2}{11 \times 5 \times 35} = \frac{80}{7} = 11.428$ cm

33. Slant height, $l = \sqrt{h^2 + (R - r)^2} = \sqrt{(24)^2 + (15 - 5)^2} = \sqrt{676} = 26$ cm

Now, Capacity of the dustbin $= \frac{\pi h}{3}\left(R^2 + r^2 + Rr\right) = \frac{22 \times 24}{7 \times 3}(15^2 + 5^2 + 15 \times 5)$

$$= \frac{22 \times 8}{7}(225 + 25 + 75) = \frac{22 \times 8}{7} \times 325$$

$$= \frac{57200}{7} = 8171.43 \text{ cm}^3$$

Surface area of the dustbin $= \pi\left[\left(R^2 + r^2\right) + l(R + r)\right] = \frac{22}{7}\left[(15)^2 + (5)^2 + 26(15 + 5)\right]$

$$= \frac{22}{7}[225 + 25 + 520] = \frac{22}{7} \times 770 = 2420 \text{ cm}^2$$

34. Here, length of water column in 40 min = 10 × 40 × 60 m

Since, $7.2 \times 2.5 \times h = \frac{5}{100} \times \frac{3}{100} \times 10 \times 40 \times 60 \quad \Rightarrow h = \frac{36 \times 100}{72 \times 25} = 2$m

35. Here, $\pi\left[(10.5+3.5)^2-(3.5)^2\right]h=\pi(3.5)^2\times 22.5$

$\Rightarrow (196-12.25)h = 12.25 \times 22.5 \qquad \therefore\ h=\dfrac{12.25\times 22.5}{183.75} = 1.5$ m

36. Here, $2\pi(R-r)h = 44 \qquad \Rightarrow 2\times\dfrac{22}{7}(R-r)\times 14 = 44 \quad \therefore\ (R-r)=\dfrac{1}{2}$

Again, $\pi(R^2-r^2)h = 99 \qquad \Rightarrow \dfrac{22}{7}(R+r)(R-r)\times 14 = 99$

$\Rightarrow \dfrac{22}{7}(R+r)\times\dfrac{1}{2}\times 14 = 99 \qquad \therefore\ (R+r)=\dfrac{99}{22}=\dfrac{9}{2}$

Since, $R=\dfrac{1}{2}\left(\dfrac{9}{2}+\dfrac{1}{2}\right)=\dfrac{5}{2}=2.5$ cm. $\quad r=\dfrac{1}{2}\left(\dfrac{9}{2}-\dfrac{1}{2}\right)=2$ cm

Hence, outer and inner radii of the pipe are 2.5 cm and 2 cm.

37. Required ratio $=\dfrac{\frac{2}{3}\pi r^3}{\frac{4}{3}\pi r^3}=\dfrac{8}{2}=\dfrac{4}{1}=4:1$

38. Here, volume of the cube $=\dfrac{9\times 8\times 6}{2}=216\text{ cm}^3$

Side of the cube $=(216)^{1/3}=6\text{ cm}^3$

Total sufrace area of the cube $=6\times 6^2=216\text{ cm}^2$

39. Here, $\dfrac{h}{4}=2r \qquad \therefore\ h=8r$

Since, $8r+r+r=35$

$\therefore\ r=\dfrac{35}{10}=3.5$ cm and also, $h=8\times 3.5=28$ cm

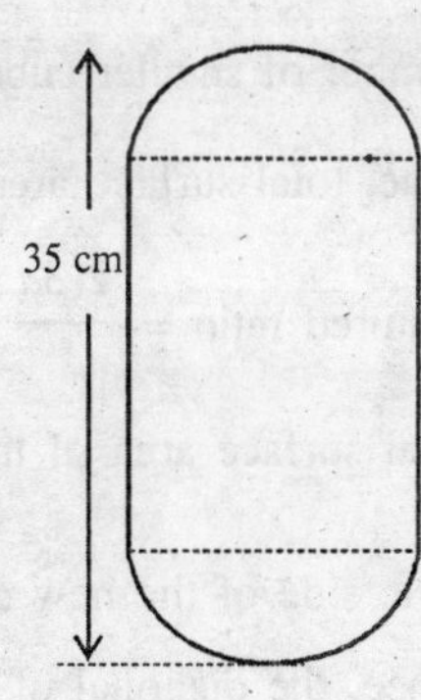

Volume of whole solid $=\pi r^2h+2\times\dfrac{2}{3}\pi r^3$

$=\dfrac{22}{7}\times(3.5)^2\left[28+\dfrac{4}{3}\times 3.5\right]$

$=38.5\times\dfrac{98}{3}$

$=\dfrac{3773}{3}=1257.67\text{ cm}^3$

Total surface area of the solid $=2\pi rh+2\times 2\pi r^2$

$=2\pi r(h+2r)$

$=2\times\dfrac{22}{7}\times 3.5\,(28+2\times 3.5)$

$=22\times 35=770\text{ cm}^2$

40. Let length, breadth and height of a cuboid are x, $x/2$ and $\frac{x}{4}$ cm respectively, then

$x \times \frac{x}{2} \times \frac{x}{4} = 512 \quad \Rightarrow x^3 = 8^3 \times 2^3 \quad \therefore x = 8 \times 2 = 16\text{m}$

41. Here, $a^2 \times 36 = 1 \quad \Rightarrow a^2 = \frac{1}{36} \quad \therefore a = \frac{1}{6}$ m

Volume of the required cube = $\left(\frac{1}{6}\right)^3 = \frac{1}{216}\text{m}^3$

Since, cost of the cube = Rs. $108 \times \frac{1}{216}$ = Re. $\frac{1}{2}$ = 50 paise

42. Let sides of the rectangular block are $3x$, $2x$ and x dm respectively; then,

$3x \times 2x \times x = 10368 \quad \Rightarrow x^3 = \frac{10368}{6} = (12)^3 \quad \therefore x = 12$

Since, three sides are 36, 24 and 12 dm respectively;
Hence, total surface area $= 2(36 \times 24 + 24 \times 12 + 12 \times 36)$
$= 2(864 + 288 + 432)$
$= 2 \times 1584 = 3168 \text{ dm}^2$

Hence, total cost of polishing = Re. $\frac{2}{100} \times 3168$ = Rs. 63.36

43. Length of the longest rod = $\sqrt{30^2 + 24^2 + 18^2} = \sqrt{1800} = 30\sqrt{2}$ m

44. Side of the cube = $(512)^{1/3} = 8$ cm
Total surface area = $6 \times 8^2 = 384 \text{ cm}^2$

45. Side of the cube = $(216)^{1/3} = 6$ cm
Total surface area = $6 \times 6^2 = 216 \text{ cm}^2$

46. Number of smaller cubes = $\frac{3^3}{1^3} = 27$

Since, total surface area of all the smaller cubes = $27 \times 6 \times 1^2 = 162$ square units

47. Required ratio = $\frac{2(3a \times a + a \times a + a \times 3a)}{3 \times 6a^2} = \frac{14a^2}{18a^2} = 7 : 9$

48. Total surface area of the resulting solid = $2\,(60 \times 10 + 10 \times 10 + 10 \times 60)$
$= 2 \times 1300 = 2600 \text{ cm}^2$

49. Here, side of the new cube = $(6^3 + 8^3 + 10^3)^{1/3} = (1728)^{1/3} = 12$ cm

Hence, the diagonal of the new cube = $12\sqrt{3} = 12 \times 1.73 = 20.8$ cm

50. 16 km/hr = $16 \times \frac{5}{8}$ = 10 m/s.

In 45 minutes length of water column = $10 \times 45 \times 60$

Hence, $80 \times 25 \times h = \frac{25}{100 \times 100} \times 10 \times 45 \times 60$

$\therefore h = \frac{45 \times 3}{2 \times 80 \times 25}\text{m} = \frac{27}{2 \times 80 \times 5} \times 100 \text{ cm} = \frac{27}{8}\text{cm} = 3.375 \text{ cm}.$

51. Here, $150 \times 100 \times h = 50 \times 30 \times 8$ $\quad \therefore\ h = \dfrac{50\times 30\times 8}{150\times 100} = \dfrac{8}{10}$ m = 8 dm

52. Here, $3 \times 2\ \pi r^2 = 2 \times 2\pi r \times 6$ $\quad \therefore\ r = \dfrac{12}{3} = 4$ m

53. Here, $2\pi r = 13.2$ m $\quad \therefore\ r = \dfrac{13.2\times 7}{2\times 22} = 2.1$ m.

Total surface area of the cylinder $= 2\pi r\ (h + r)$

$$= 2 \times \frac{22}{7} \times 2.1 \times 3 = 39.6\text{m}^2$$

54. Here, height of the cylinder $= 96 \times \dfrac{1}{2} = 48$ cm

Hence, $\pi r^2 \times 48 = 7392$ $\quad \Rightarrow r^2 = \dfrac{7392\times 7}{22\times 48} = 7 \times 7$ $\quad \therefore\ r = 7$ cm

55. Here, $\pi \times 10^2 \times h = 11^3$ $\quad \therefore\ h = \dfrac{1331\times 7}{22\times 100} = 4.235$ cm

56. Let number of coins be n; then

$$n \times \pi \times \left(\frac{1.5}{2}\right)^2 \times 0.2 = \pi\left(\frac{4.5}{2}\right)^2 \times 10$$

$$\Rightarrow n\times\frac{2.25}{4}\times 0.2 = \frac{20.25}{4}\times 10 \qquad \therefore\ n = \frac{20.25\times 10}{2.25\times 0.2} = 450$$

57. Here, $\pi.7^2.\ h = \dfrac{1}{3}\pi.(3.5)^2.6$ $\quad \therefore\ h = \dfrac{3.5\times 3.5\times 2}{7\times 7} = 0.5$ cm

58. Volume of the conical tent $= \dfrac{1}{3}\times\dfrac{22}{7}\times\left(3^2\right)\times\dfrac{14}{3} = 44\text{m}^3$

Hence, average air space allowed per head $= \dfrac{44}{11} = 4\text{m}^3$

59. Here, $\dfrac{4}{3}\pi R^3 = \dfrac{4}{3}\pi\left(6^3 + 8^3 + 10^3\right)$ $\quad \Rightarrow R^3 = 1728$ $\quad \therefore\ R = 12$-cm

60. Let n be the number of persons to be accomodated; then

$$n \times 2916 = \frac{1}{3}\times\frac{22}{7}\times(27)^2\times 42 \qquad \therefore\ n = \frac{22\times 27\times 27\times 2}{2916} = 111$$

61. Curved surface area of conical tent $= \dfrac{22}{7}\times 2.5\times\dfrac{14}{3} = \dfrac{110}{3}\text{m}^2$

Hence, length of the canvas $= \dfrac{110}{3\times 1.25} = 29\dfrac{1}{3}$ m

62. Here, $\pi.\left(\frac{20}{100}\right)^2 . h = 6 \times 4 \times \frac{1}{100}$ $\Rightarrow \frac{22}{7} \times \frac{1}{25} \times h = \frac{6}{25}$

$\therefore\ h = \frac{6 \times 7}{22}$ m $= \frac{2100}{11}$ cm $\approx$ 191 cm

63. Here, required fraction of water $= \frac{\frac{4}{3}\pi.(3^3)}{\frac{1}{3}\pi.(6^2)} = \frac{4 \times 27}{36 \times 8} = \frac{3}{8}$

64. Here, $\frac{2\pi rh}{\pi r\sqrt{r^2 + h^2}} = \frac{8}{5}$, $\Rightarrow \frac{h^2}{r^2 + h^2} = \frac{16}{25}$ $\Rightarrow 25h^2 = 16r^2 + 16h^2$

$\Rightarrow 16r^2 = 9h^2$ $\Rightarrow \frac{r^2}{h^2} = \frac{9}{16}$ $\therefore\ \frac{r}{h} = \frac{3}{4}$

Hence, required ratio = 3 : 4

65. Here, $\pi r_1^2.x = \pi r_2^2.3x$ $\Rightarrow \frac{r_1^2}{r_2^2} = \frac{3}{1}$ $\therefore\ \frac{r_1}{r_2} = \frac{\sqrt{3}}{1}$

Hence, required ratio = $\sqrt{3} : 1$

66. Volume of the original cone = $\frac{1}{3}\pi r^2 h$

Volume of the new cone = $\frac{1}{3}\pi r^2 .2h = 2 \times \frac{1}{3}\pi r^2 h$

Hence, volume increased by 100%.

67. Here, $\pi r^2.\frac{7}{3} = \frac{4}{3}\pi.7^3$ $\Rightarrow r^2 = \frac{4 \times 7 \times 7 \times 7}{7}$ $\therefore\ r = 14$ cm

Hence, diameter of the cylinder = $2r = 2 \times 14 = 28$ cm

68. Here, total surface area of the wet surface = $6 \times 4 + 2 \times 1.25 \times (6 + 4)$
$= 24 + 2.5 \times 10 = 49\text{m}^2$

69. Here, $5b = h$ $\therefore\ b = \frac{h}{5}$ and also $l = 8h$

Now, $8h \times \frac{h}{5} \times h = 12.8$ $\Rightarrow h^3 = \frac{12.8 \times 5}{8} = 8$ $\therefore\ h = 2$m

Hence, breadth of the wall = $\frac{h}{5} = \frac{2}{5}$ m $= \frac{2}{5} \times 100 = 40$ cm

70. Volume of the iron beam = $9 \times \frac{22.5}{100} \times \frac{20}{100} = 0.405\text{m}^3$

Hence, weight of the beam = 0.405×50kg = 20.25 kg

71. Curved surface area of the cone = $\pi.3.\sqrt{3^2 + 4^2} = 15\pi\ \text{cm}^2$.

72. Area of the agricultural field excluding pit = 20 × 14 – 6 × 3 = 262 m^2

Now, 262 × h = 6 × 3 × 2.5 $\quad \therefore h = \frac{6 \times 3 \times 2.5}{262} = \frac{22.5}{131}$ m $= \frac{2250}{131} = 17.18$ cm

73. Curved surface area of the conical tent $= \frac{22}{7} \times 7 \times \sqrt{24^2 + 7^2} = 22 \times 25 = 550$ m^2

Hence, length of the cloth required $= \frac{550}{5} = 110$ m

74. Here, $2\pi rh = 264$ m^2 and also $\pi r^2 h = 924$ m^3

Since, $\frac{\pi r^2 h}{2\pi rh} = \frac{924}{264} \quad \Rightarrow \frac{r}{2} = \frac{924}{264} \quad \Rightarrow r = \frac{924 \times 2}{264} = 7$ cm

Now, $2 \times \frac{22}{7} \times 7 \times h = 264 \quad \therefore h = \frac{264}{2 \times 22} = 6$m

75. Total surface area of the cylinder $= 2 \times \frac{22}{7} \times 7\ (18 + 7)$

$= 44 \times 25 = 1100$ cm^2

76. Change in volume $= 60 - 50 - 50 + \frac{60 \times -50 + (-50) \times (-50) + (-50 \times 60)}{100} + \frac{60 \times -50 \times -50}{100^2}$

$= -40 - 35 + 15 = -60$

Hence, volume will be decreased by 60%

77. Volume of the original cuboid = lbh

Volume of the new cuboid = $2l \times 3b \times 3h = 18\ lbh$

Hence, increase in volume = $18\ lbh - lbh = 17\ lbh$

So, volume of the cuboid will be increased by 17 times.

78. Volume of the original sphere $= \frac{4}{3}\pi r^3$

Volume of the new sphere $= \frac{4}{3}\pi.(2r)^3 = 8.\frac{4}{3}\pi r^3$

Hence, new volume becomes 8 times of the original volume.

79. Here, $xyz = lb\ .\ bh\ .\ hl = l^2b^2h^2 = V^2$

Hence, $V^2 = xyz$

80. Here, $2\pi r = 12 \quad \therefore r = \frac{12}{2\pi} = \frac{6}{\pi}$ cm

81. Volume of the cuboidal block of wood = 10 × 5 × 2 = 100 cm^3

Volume of the wasted wood $= 100 - \frac{1}{3} \times \frac{22}{7} \times 1^2 \times 7 = \frac{278}{3}$ cm^3

Since, percentage of wasted wood $= \frac{278}{3 \times 100} \times 100 = 92\frac{2}{3}\%$

82. Required volume of water = 10 × 5 × 1 = 50 m^3

83. Let n be the number of iron balls dipped in the oil; then

$$n \times \frac{4}{3}\pi \times \left(\frac{3}{2}\right)^3 = \pi \times 6^2 \times 2 \quad \Rightarrow \frac{9}{2} \times n = 36 \times 2 \quad \therefore\ n = \frac{36 \times 2 \times 2}{9} = 16$$

84. Here, $lb : bh : hl = 2 : 3 : 4$; then

$$\frac{lb}{bh} = \frac{2}{3} \quad \Rightarrow l : h = 2 : 3 \text{ and also, } \frac{lh}{bh} = \frac{4}{3} \quad \therefore\ l : b = 4 : 3$$

From these two, we get, $l : b : h = 4 : 3 : 6$

Let sides of rectangular block are $4x$, $3x$ and $6x$ cm respectively, then

$$4x \times 3x \times 6x = 9000 \quad \Rightarrow x^3 = \frac{9000}{4 \times 3 \times 6} = 125 \quad \therefore\ x = 5$$

Hence, shortest side $= 3x = 3 \times 5 = 15$ cm

85. Internal measurements:

$l = 14 - 2 \times 0.75 = 12.5$ cm; $\quad b = 9.5 - 2 \times 0.75 = 8$ cm

$h = 6 - 2 \times 0.75 = 4.5$ cm

Volume of the wood required $= 14 \times 9.5 \times 6 - 12.5 \times 8 \times 4.5$

$= 798 - 450 = 348\ \text{cm}^3$

86. Here, $a^3 = 27 \times 8 \times 1 \quad \therefore\ a = 3 \times 2 = 6$ cm

Total surface area of the cuboid $= 2\,(27 \times 8 + 8 \times 1 + 1 \times 27)$

$= 2 \times 251 = 502\ \text{cm}^2$

Total surface area of the cube $= 6 \times 6^2 = 216\ \text{cm}^2$

Hence, required difference $= 502 - 216 = 286\ \text{cm}^2$

87. Ratio of their curved surface areas $= \dfrac{2\pi \times 3 \times 2}{2\pi \times 5 \times 3} = \dfrac{2}{5} = 2 : 5$

88. Here, $\frac{1}{3}\pi r^2 \times h = \pi r^2 \times 6 \quad \therefore\ h = 18$ cm

89. Ratio of their surface areas $= \dfrac{4\pi.1^2}{4\pi.4^2} = \dfrac{1}{16} = 1 : 16$

90. Here, $\pi r^2 = 770 \quad \Rightarrow r^2 = \dfrac{770 \times 7}{22} \quad \therefore\ r = \sqrt{35 \times 7} = 7\sqrt{5}$ cm

and also $\pi r l = 814 \quad \Rightarrow \dfrac{22}{7} \times 7\sqrt{5} \times l = 814 \quad \therefore\ l = \dfrac{814}{22 \times \sqrt{5}} = \dfrac{37}{\sqrt{5}}$ cm

$$\text{Since, } h = \sqrt{\left(\frac{37}{\sqrt{5}}\right)^2 - \left(7\sqrt{5}\right)^2} = \sqrt{\frac{1369}{5} - 245} = \sqrt{\frac{144}{5}} = \frac{12}{\sqrt{5}} \text{ cm}$$

$$\text{Hence, volume of the cone} = \frac{1}{3} \times \frac{22}{7} \times \left(7\sqrt{5}\right)^2 \times \frac{12}{\sqrt{5}} = 616\sqrt{5}\ \text{cm}^3$$

91. Ratio of their volumes $= \dfrac{\frac{4}{3}\pi.(3^3)}{\frac{4}{3}\pi.(2^3)} = \dfrac{27}{8} = 27 : 8$

92. Weight of the total wall $= 3 \times 2.7 \times 0.2 \times 320 = 518.4$ kg

93. Let n be the number of balls; then

$$n \times \frac{4}{3}\pi.(0.3)^3 = \frac{4}{3}\pi.3^3 \qquad \therefore\ n = \frac{27}{0.027} = 1000$$

94. Required number of full bags $= \dfrac{\frac{22}{7}\times(4.2)^2\times 3.5}{2.1} = \dfrac{11\times 4.2\times 4.2}{2.1} = 92.4 \approx 92$

95. Volume of the cuboid $= 9 \times 8 \times 6 = 432$ cm^3

Hence, volume of required cube $= \dfrac{432}{2} = 216$ cm^3

Since, side of the cube $= (216)^{1/3} = 6$ cm

$\therefore$ Total surface area of the cube $= 6 \times 6^2 = 216$ cm^2

96. Here, $\pi r^2 \times 1800 = \pi.\left(\dfrac{1}{2}\right)^2 \times 8 \Rightarrow r^2 = \dfrac{2}{1800} \qquad \therefore\ r = \dfrac{1}{30}$ cm

97. Let x m/hr be the speed of the flow of water; then

Volume of water flowed in 5 hrs. $= 225 \times 162 \times \dfrac{20}{100}$ m^3

Hence, volume of water flowed in 1 hr $= \dfrac{45\times 162}{5} = 9 \times 162$ m^3

Since, $\dfrac{60}{100}\times\dfrac{45}{100}\times x = 9 \times 162 \qquad \therefore\ x = \dfrac{9\times 162\times 100\times 100}{60\times 45} = 5400$ m/hr.

98. Here, $20 \times 15 \times h = (15)^3 \qquad \therefore\ h = \dfrac{15\times 15}{20} = 11.25$ cm

99. Required number of iron rods $= \dfrac{0.88}{\frac{22}{7}\times\left(\frac{1}{100}\right)^2\times 7} = \dfrac{8800}{22} = 400$

100. Let n be the number of spherical bullets made; then

$$n \times \frac{4}{3}\pi \times \left(\frac{1.5}{2}\right)^3 = \pi \times 6^2 \times 28 \qquad \therefore\ n = \frac{36\times 28\times 8\times 3}{4\times 1.5\times 1.5\times 1.5} = 1792$$

101. Number of cylindrical bottles needed $= \dfrac{\frac{2}{3}\pi.9^3}{\pi.\left(\frac{3}{2}\right)^2\times 4} = 54$

102. Volume of water displaced $= 3 \times 2 \times \dfrac{1}{100} = \dfrac{6}{100}$ m^3

Mass of the man = Volume of water displaced × Density of water

$$= \frac{6}{100}\times 1000 = 60 \text{ kg}$$

103. Here, $h = 6b$ $\quad \therefore\ b = \frac{h}{b}$ and also, $l = 7h$; then

$7h \times \frac{h}{6} \times h = 16128 \quad \Rightarrow h^3 = \frac{16128 \times 6}{7}$

$\therefore\ h = (13824)^{1/3} = 24\text{m}$

Hence, width of the wall, $b = \frac{h}{6} = \frac{24}{6} = 4\text{m}$

104. Let sides of cuboid are x, $2x$ and $3x$ cm respectively; then

$2\,(x \times 2x + 2x \times 3x + 3x \times x) = 88 \quad \Rightarrow 22x^2 = 88 \quad \Rightarrow x^2 = 4 \quad \Rightarrow x = 2$

Since its, sides are 2cm, 4 cm and 6 cm respectively;

Hence, volume = $2 \times 4 \times 6 = 48\ \text{cm}^3$

105. Here $40 \times 20 \times h = 50 \times 4 \quad \therefore\ h = \frac{50 \times 4}{40 \times 20} = \frac{1}{4}\ \text{m} = \frac{1}{4} \times 100 = 25\ \text{cm}$

106. $10\text{km/hr} = 10 \times \frac{5}{18} = \frac{25}{9}\ \text{m/s}$

Length of water column in half an hour = $\frac{25}{9} \times 30 \times 60 = 25 \times 200\text{m}$

Since, $80 \times 40 \times h = \frac{40}{100 \times 100} \times 25 \times 200 \quad \therefore\ h = \frac{20}{80 \times 40}\ \text{m} = \frac{1}{80 \times 2} \times 100\ \text{cm} = \frac{5}{8}\ \text{cm}$

107. Here, $2h(l + b) = 2lb \quad \Rightarrow h(15 + 12) = 15 \times 12 \quad \therefore\ h = \frac{15 \times 12}{27} = \frac{20}{3}\ \text{m}$

Hence, volume of the hall = $15 \times 12 \times \frac{20}{3} = 1200\ \text{m}^3$

108. Volume of the swimming pool = $12 \times 9 \times \left(\frac{4+1}{2}\right) = 12 \times 9 \times \frac{5}{2} = 270\ \text{m}^3$

109. Let thickness of the bottom of the cistern be x cm; then internal measurements are $330 - 2 \times 5 = 320$ cm; $260 - 2 \times 5 = 250$ cm and $110 - x$ cm respectively.

Since, $320 \times 250 \times (110 - x) = 8000 \times 1000 \quad \Rightarrow 110 - x = \frac{8000 \times 1000}{320 \times 250}$

$\Rightarrow 110 - x = 100 \quad \therefore\ x = 110 - 100 = 10\ \text{cm}$

110. Here, $l = 48 - 16 = 32$ m; $b = 36 - 16 = 20$ m and $h = 8$m

Since, volume of the box = $32 \times 20 \times 8 = 5120\ \text{m}^3$

111. Here, $lb \times bh \times hl = 120 \times 72 \times 60 \quad \Rightarrow (lbh)^2 = 120 \times 72 \times 60$

$\Rightarrow lbh = \sqrt{120 \times 72 \times 60} \quad \therefore\ \text{V} = 720\ \text{cm}^3$

112. Quantity of paint needed = $\frac{6 \times 8^2}{16} = 24$ kg

Hence, cost of the paint = $24 \times$ Rs. 36.50 = Rs. 876

113. Let sides of the sheet are x and $5x$; then

$x \times 5x \times 0.5 = 10 \times 10 \times 10 \quad \Rightarrow x^2 = \dfrac{10\times10\times10}{5\times0.5} \quad \therefore\ x = 20$ cm

Hence, its sides are 20 cm and 5 × 20 = 100 cm respectively.

114. Let the sides of the three cubes are $3x$, $4x$ and $5x$ cm respectively,

$(3x)^3 + (4x)^3 + (5x)^3 = \left(\dfrac{12\sqrt{3}}{\sqrt{3}}\right)^3 \quad \Rightarrow 27x^3 + 64x^3 + 125x^3 = 12 \times 12 \times 12$

$\Rightarrow 216x^3 = 12 \times 12 \times 12 \quad \Rightarrow x^3 = \dfrac{12\times12\times12}{216} = 8 \quad \therefore\ x = 2$

Hence, its sides are 6 cm, 8 cm and 10 cm respectively.

115. Here, $\dfrac{22}{7}\times r^2\times400 = 246.4 \times 1000 \quad \Rightarrow r^2 = \dfrac{2464\times100\times7}{22\times400} = 28 \times 7 \quad \therefore\ r = 14$ cm

Hence, diameter of the base = $2r$ = 2 × 14 = 28 cm

116. Volume of the earth dug out = $\dfrac{22}{7} \times (1)^2 \times 14 = 44$ m^3

117. Here, $r = \dfrac{h}{2} \quad \therefore\ h = 2r$

Since, $\pi r^2 + 2\pi rh = 616 \quad \Rightarrow \pi r(r + 2h) = 616$

$\Rightarrow \pi r(r + 2 \times 2r) = 616 \quad \Rightarrow \pi \times 5r^2 = 616 \quad \therefore\ r^2 = \dfrac{616\times7}{22\times5} \quad \therefore\ r = \dfrac{14}{\sqrt{5}}$ cm

Then, $h = 2r = 2 \times \dfrac{14}{\sqrt{5}} = \dfrac{28}{\sqrt{5}}$ cm

Hence, Volume of the cylinder $= \dfrac{22}{7}\times\left(\dfrac{14}{\sqrt{5}}\right)^2\times\dfrac{28}{\sqrt{5}} = \dfrac{17248\sqrt{5}}{25}$

$= \dfrac{17248\times2.23}{25} = \dfrac{38463.04}{25} \approx 1538$ c.c.

118. Here, $2\pi rh = 264$ m^2 and also $\pi r^2h = 924$ m^3

Hence, $\dfrac{\pi r^2 h}{2\pi rh} = \dfrac{924}{264} \quad \therefore\ r = 2 \times \dfrac{924}{264} = 7$m

Now, $2 \times \dfrac{22}{7} \times 7 \times h = 264 \quad \therefore\ h = \dfrac{264}{2\times22} = 6$ m

Then, $\dfrac{d}{h} = \dfrac{2r}{h} = \dfrac{2\times7}{6} = \dfrac{7}{3}$

Hence, required ratio = 7 : 3

119. Here, $V = \pi r^2h \quad \therefore\ h = \dfrac{V}{\pi r^2}$

and also, $S = 2\pi rh + 2\pi r^2 = 2\pi r \times \dfrac{V}{\pi r^2} + 2\pi r^2$

$= \frac{2V}{r} + 2\pi r^2$

Since, $\frac{dS}{dr} = -\frac{2V}{r^2} + 4\pi r$ and also, $\frac{d^2S}{dr} = \left(\frac{4V}{r^3} + 4\pi\right) > 0$

Hence, S is minimum when $\frac{dS}{dr} = 0$

Then, $-\frac{2V}{r^2} + 4\pi r = 0 \quad \Rightarrow -\frac{2.\pi r^2 h}{r^2} + 4\pi r = 0$

$\therefore\ h = 2r = d$

Since, height is equal to its diameter.

120. Length of water column in 10 minutes = 2 × 10 × 60 × 100 cm

Since, volume of water discharged in 10 minutes $= \frac{22}{7} \times \frac{7}{2} \times \frac{7}{2} \times 2 \times 10 \times 60 \times 100$ c.c.

= 4620 × 1000 c.c.

= 4620 l

121. Here, $\pi.\left(\frac{1}{20}\right)^2 \times l = 66 \qquad \therefore\ l = \frac{66 \times 400 \times 7}{22} = 8400$ cm = 84 m

122. Volume of the metal used $= \frac{22}{7}\left[(5.6+0.4)^2 - (5.6)^2\right] \times 21$

= 66 × (6 + 5.6) × (6 – 5.6)

= 66 × 11.6 × 0.4 = 306.24 cm³

123. Volume of the iron used $= \frac{22}{7}[4^2 - (4-1)^2] \times 21$

= 66(16 – 9) = 66 × 7 = 462 cm³

Since, weight of the iron = 462 × 8 gm = 3696 gm = 3.696 kg

124. Slant height, $l = \sqrt{14^2 + 7^2} = \sqrt{245} = 15.65$ cm

Total surface area of the cone $= \pi r\ (l + r)$

$= \frac{22}{7} \times 7(15.65 + 7)$

= 22 × 22.65 = 498.30 cm²

125. Here, $\frac{1}{3}\pi r^2 \times 24 = 1232 \quad \Rightarrow r^2 = \frac{1232 \times 7}{22 \times 8} = 7 \times 7 \quad \therefore\ r = 7$ cm

Hence, curved surface area of the cone $= \frac{22}{7} \times 7 \times \sqrt{7^2 + 24^2} = 22 \times 25 = 550$ cm²

126. Slant height of cone, $l = \sqrt{12^2 + 5^2} = 13$ cm

Total lateral surface area of the solid

= Curved surface area of cone and cylinder + surface area of bottom

$= \pi rl + 2\pi rh + \pi r^2$

$= \pi r\,(l + 2h + r) = \frac{22}{7} \times 12\ \ (13 + 2 \times 18 + 12)$

$= \frac{22}{7} \times 12 \times 61 = \frac{16104}{7} = 2300\frac{4}{7}\ \text{cm}^2$

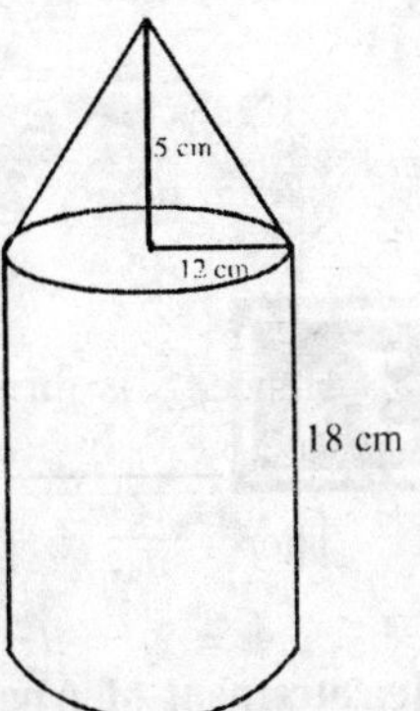

127. Here, $\frac{\frac{4}{3}\pi r^3}{4\pi r^2} = 27 \quad \Rightarrow \frac{r}{3} = 27 \quad \therefore\ r = 81$ cm

128. Here, $4\pi(r + 2)^2 = 4\pi r^2 + 352 \quad \Rightarrow 4\pi(r^2 + 4r + 4) = 4\pi r^2 + 352$

$\Rightarrow 4\pi r^2 + 16\pi r + 16\pi = 4\pi r^2 + 352 \quad \Rightarrow 16 \times \frac{22}{7}(r+1) = 352$

$\Rightarrow r + 1 = \frac{352 \times 7}{16 \times 22} = 7 \quad \Rightarrow r = 7 - 1 = 6$ cm

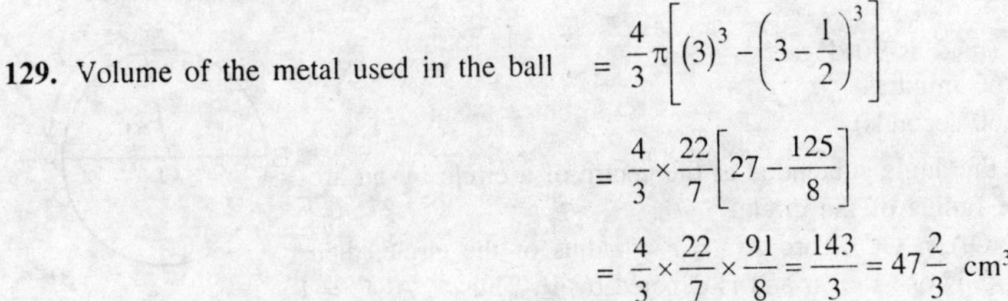

129. Volume of the metal used in the ball $= \frac{4}{3}\pi\left[(3)^3 - \left(3 - \frac{1}{2}\right)^3\right]$

$= \frac{4}{3} \times \frac{22}{7}\left[27 - \frac{125}{8}\right]$

$= \frac{4}{3} \times \frac{22}{7} \times \frac{91}{8} = \frac{143}{3} = 47\frac{2}{3}\ \text{cm}^3$

130. Here, $4\pi r^2 = 2\pi \times 6 \times 12 \quad \Rightarrow r^2 = \frac{2 \times 6 \times 12}{4} = 36 \quad \therefore\ r = 6$ cm

131. Here, $\frac{2\pi r^2}{\pi rl} = \frac{2\pi r^2}{\pi r\sqrt{r^2 + r^2}} = \frac{2r}{\sqrt{2}r} = \frac{\sqrt{2}}{1}$

Hence, ratio of their curved surface areas $= \sqrt{2} : 1$

132. Here, $\frac{2}{3}\pi R^3 = \frac{1}{3}\pi R^2 H \qquad \therefore\ H = 2R$

133. Here, $\frac{1}{3}\pi.4^2.h = \frac{4}{3}\pi\left(4^3 - 2^3\right) \quad \Rightarrow 16h = 4 \times 56 \qquad \therefore\ h = \frac{4 \times 56}{16} = 14$ cm

134. Here, $\frac{1}{3}\pi.6^2.h = \frac{4}{3}\pi.3^3 \quad \Rightarrow 36h = 4 \times 27 \qquad \therefore\ h = \frac{4 \times 27}{36} = 3$ cm

135. Here, $12 \times \frac{4}{3}\pi r^3 = \pi \times 8^2 \times 2 \Rightarrow r^3 = \frac{64 \times 2}{16} = 8 \qquad \therefore\ r = 2$ cm

Hence, diameter of each sphere $= 2r = 2 \times 2$ cm $= 4$ cm

136. In this case, base radius of the cylinder = radius of the sphere

Hence, volume of the required sphere $= \frac{4}{3}\pi.1^3 = \frac{4}{3}\pi\ \ \text{cm}^3$.

31

TRIGONOMETRICAL RATIOS

Measurement of Angles: In general, the angles are measured in degrees or in radians which are defined as follows:

(a) *Degrees*: A right angle is divided into 90 equal parts and each part is called a degree. Thus a right angle is equal to 90 degrees. One degree is denoted by 1°.
A degree is divided into sixty equal parts and each part is called a minute and is denoted by 1'.
A minute is divided into sixty equal parts and each part is called a second and is denoted by 1".
Thus, we have

1 right angle = 90° (read as 90 degrees)
1° = 60′ (read as 60 minutes)
1′ = 60″ (read as 60 seconds)

(b) *Radians*: A radian is the angle subtended at the centre of a circle by an arc equal in length to the radius of the circle.
In the adjacent figure OA = OC = arc AC = r = radius of the circle, then measurement of ∠ AOC is one radian and is denoted by 1^c. Thus ∠ AOC = 1^c.

A Constant Number π: The ratio of the circumference to the diameter of a circle is always equal to a constant and this constant is denoted by the Greek letter π. Thus π = circumference/diameter.

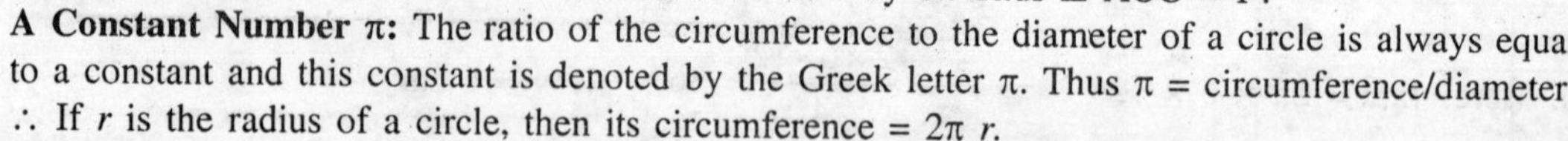

∴ If r is the radius of a circle, then its circumference = $2\pi r$.
The constant π is an irrational number and its approximate value is taken as 22/7.

Relation Between an Arc and an Angle: If s is the length of an arc of a circle of radius r, then the angle θ (in radians) subtended by this arc at the centre of the circle is given by $\theta = s/r$ or $s = r\theta$
i.e., arc = radius × angle in radians
Given in the figure,

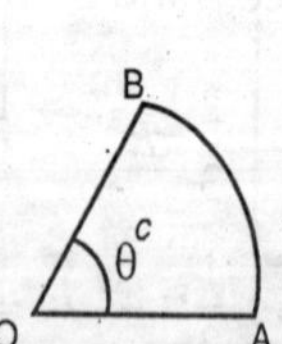

$$\angle AOB = \frac{\text{arc ACB}}{r} \text{ (in radians)} = \frac{\pi r}{r} = \pi \text{ radians.}$$

Thus we have, π radians = 180° = 2 right angles

$$\text{or 1 radian} = \frac{180}{\pi} \text{ degrees} = \frac{180}{22} \times 7 \text{ degrees} = 57^\circ\ 17'\ 44.8'' \text{ (Appr.)}$$

Sectorial Area: Let OAB be a sector having central angle θ^c and radius r. Then area of the sector OAB is given by $\frac{1}{2} r^2 \theta$.

Trigonometrical Ratios: In a right angled triangle ABC, if ∠ CAB = θ, then BC = side opposite to the angle θ = Perpendicular = p (say), AC = side opposite to the right angle = Hypotenuse = h (say) and AB = b (say).

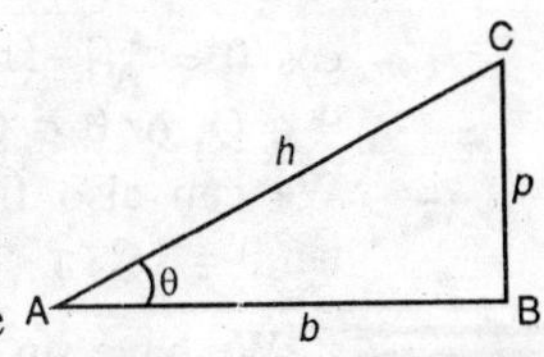

The six trigonometrical ratios are given as follows:
$\sin\theta = p/h$, $\cos\theta = b/h$, $\tan\theta = p/b$.
(Also $\tan\theta = \sin\theta/\cos\theta$, $\text{cosec}\,\theta = 1/\sin\theta$,
$\sec\theta = 1/\cos\theta$, $\cot\theta = 1/\tan\theta$,)

Basic Formulae Connecting Six Trigonometrical Ratios: The formulae connecting the six trigonometrical ratios are:

(i) $\sin^2\theta + \cos^2\theta = 1$ or $\cos^2\theta = 1 - \sin^2\theta$ or $\sin^2\theta = 1 - \cos^2\theta$.
(ii) $1 + \tan^2\theta = \sec^2\theta$ or $\sec^2\theta - \tan^2\theta = 1$
(iii) $1 + \cot^2\theta = \text{cosec}^2\,\theta$ or $\text{cosec}^2\,\theta - \cot^2\theta = 1$.

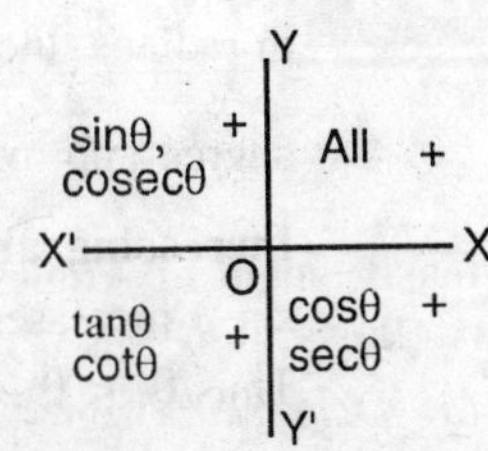

Sign of Trigonometrical Ratios:
1st quadrant $0 < \theta < 90°$, all trigonometrical ratios +ve,
2nd quadrant $90° < \theta < 180°$, only $\sin\theta$ and $\text{cosec}\,\theta$, +ve
3rd quadrant $180° < \theta < 270°$, only $\tan\theta$ and $\cot\theta$, +ve
4th quadrant $270° < \theta < 360°$, only $\cos\theta$ and $\sec\theta$, +ve.

Trigonometrical Ratios of Related Angles:

$\sin(-\theta) = -\sin\theta$	$\cos(-\theta) = \cos\theta$	$\tan(-\theta) = -\tan\theta$
$\sin(90° - \theta) = \cos\theta$	$\sin(180° + \theta) = -\sin\theta$	$\sin(270° + \theta) = -\cos\theta$
$\cos(90° - \theta) = \sin\theta$	$\cos(180° + \theta) = -\cos\theta$	$\cos(270° + \theta) = \sin\theta$
$\tan(90° - \theta) = \cot\theta$	$\tan(180° + \theta) = \tan\theta$	$\tan(270° + \theta) = -\cot\theta$
$\sin(90° + \theta) = \cos\theta$	$\sin(270° - \theta) = -\cos\theta$	$\sin(360° + \theta) = \sin\theta$
$\cos(90° + \theta) = -\sin\theta$	$\cos(270° - \theta) = -\sin\theta$	$\cos(360° + \theta) = \cos\theta$
$\tan(90° + \theta) = -\cot\theta$	$\tan(270° - \theta) = \cot\theta$	$\tan(360° + \theta) = \tan\theta$

Table giving sine, cosine and tangent of some angles less than 90°:

	0°	15°	18°	22.5°	30°	36°	45°	60°	67.5°	90°
sin	0	$\frac{\sqrt{6}-\sqrt{2}}{4}$	$\frac{\sqrt{5}-1}{4}$	$\frac{\sqrt{2-\sqrt{2}}}{2}$	$\frac{1}{2}$	$\frac{\sqrt{10-2\sqrt{5}}}{4}$	$\frac{1}{\sqrt{2}}$	$\frac{\sqrt{3}}{2}$	$\frac{\sqrt{\sqrt{2}+1}}{\sqrt{(2\sqrt{2})}}$	1
cos	1	$\frac{\sqrt{6}+\sqrt{2}}{4}$	$\frac{\sqrt{10+2\sqrt{5}}}{4}$	$\frac{\sqrt{\sqrt{2}+1}}{\sqrt{(2\sqrt{2})}}$	$\frac{\sqrt{3}}{2}$	$\frac{\sqrt{5}+1}{4}$	$\frac{1}{\sqrt{2}}$	$\frac{1}{2}$	$\frac{\sqrt{2-\sqrt{2}}}{2}$	0
tan	0	$2-\sqrt{3}$	$\frac{\sqrt{25-10\sqrt{5}}}{5}$	$\sqrt{2}-1$	$\frac{1}{\sqrt{3}}$	$\sqrt{5-2\sqrt{5}}$	1	$\sqrt{3}$	$\sqrt{2}+1$	not defined

Bounds of T-Ratios: Since $\sin^2\theta + \cos^2\theta = 1$, the absolute values of $\sin\theta$ and $\cos\theta$ can never be greater than 1. Thus $0 \le |\sin\theta| \le 1$, $0 \le |\cos\theta| \le 1$, *i.e.*, $-1 \le \sin\theta; \cos\theta \le 1$, or $0 \le \sin^2\theta; \cos^2\theta \le 1$.

Also $\quad \sec\theta; \text{cosec}\,\theta \ge 1$ or ≤ -1

i.e., $\quad \sec\theta$, $\text{cosec}\,\theta$ can never lie between -1 and 1.

It should be noted that $-\infty < \tan\theta; \cot\theta < \infty$.

To Determine the Values of Other Trigonometrical Ratios when one Trigonometrical Ratio is given: If one of the *t*-ratio is given, the values of other *t*-ratios can be found by using formulae. For example, $\sin\theta = 1/3$. Since sine is positive in Q_1 or Q_2, we have

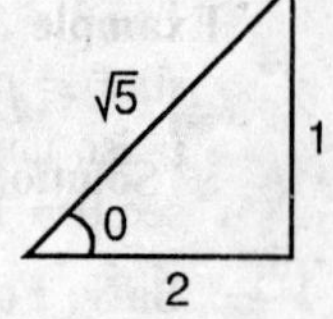

$\cos\theta = \sqrt{1-(1/9)}$ or $-\sqrt{1-(1/9)}$, *i.e.*, $2\sqrt{2}/3$ or $-2\sqrt{2}/3$ according to $\theta \in Q_1$ or $\theta \in Q_2$.

We can also find other ratios by forming right angled triangle, *e.g.*, Let $\tan\theta = 1/2$, $\pi < \theta < 3\pi/2$, then since θ in Q_3, sine and cosine both are negative,

$\therefore$ We have $\sin\theta = -1/\sqrt{5}$, $\cos\theta = -2/\sqrt{5}$.

Approximate Values of sin θ, cos θ and tan θ when θ is Small: Let θ be small and measured in radians, then $\sin\theta \approx \theta$, $\cos \approx 1$, $\tan\theta \approx \theta$. These are first degree approximations. The second degree approximations are given by $\sin\theta \simeq \theta$, $\cos\theta \simeq 1 - \frac{1}{2}\theta^2$, $\tan\theta = \theta$.

Increasing and Decreasing Behaviour of Trigonometrical Ratios: When $-\pi/2 \le \theta \le \pi/2$, $\sin\theta$ increases in Q_1 and Q_4 with angle while in Q_2, Q_3, $\sin\theta$ decreases from 1 to –1.

Thus $\theta_1 < \theta_2 \Rightarrow \sin\theta_1 < \sin\theta_2$ $(\theta_1, \theta_2 \in Q_1 \text{ or } Q_4)$

$\Rightarrow \sin\theta_1 > \sin\theta_2$ $(\theta_1, \theta_2 \in Q_2 \text{ or } Q_3)$

We can decide the behaviour of other ratios in a similar manner. If we denote ↑ for increasing and ↓ for decreasing, we have the following chart:

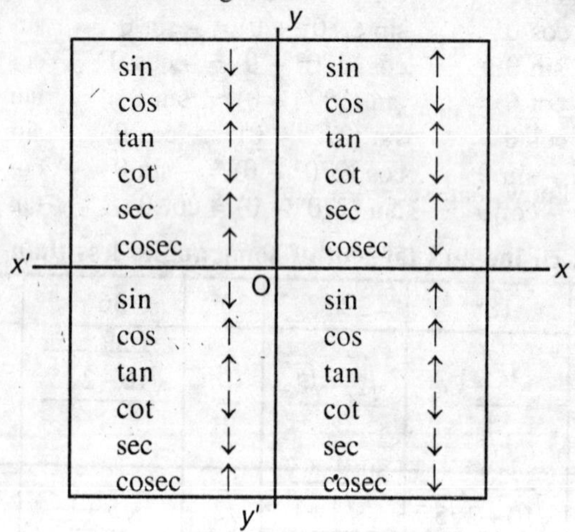

Example 1: *Prove that* $\dfrac{1}{\sec x - \tan x} - \dfrac{1}{\cos x} = \dfrac{1}{\cos x} - \dfrac{1}{\sec x + \tan x}$.

Solution: We have to prove that

$$\frac{1}{\sec x - \tan x} + \frac{1}{\sec x + \tan x} = \frac{2}{\cos x}$$

$$\text{L.H.S.} = \frac{2\sec x}{\sec^2 x - \tan^2 x} = 2\sec x = \frac{2}{\cos x} = \text{R.H.S.}$$

Example 2: Prove that (sec A + tan A – 1) (sec A – tan A + 1) – 2 tan A = 0.

Solution: L.H.S. = [sec A + (tan A – 1)] [sec A – (tan A – 1)] – 2 tan A

$= \sec^2 A - (\tan A - 1)^2 - 2\tan A$

$= \sec^2 A - \tan^2 A - 1 + 2\tan A - 2\tan A$.

$= 1 - 1 = 0 = \text{R.H.S.}$

Example 3: *If (sec A + tan A) (sec B + tan B) (sec C + tan C) = (sec A – tan A) (sec B – tan B) (sec C – tan C) prove that each of the side is equal to ± 1.*

Solution: Denoting the left hand and right hand sides by x and y, we have $x = y \Rightarrow x^2 = xy$.
or, $x^2 = (\sec^2 A - \tan^2 A)(\sec^2 B - \tan^2 B)(\sec^2 C - \tan^2 C) = 1 \therefore x = \pm 1 = y$

Example 4: *If (1 + sin A) (1 + sin B) (1 + sin C) = (1 – sin A) (1 – sin B) (1 – sin C), show that each side is equal to ± cos A cos B cos C.*

Solution: If $x = y$, then $x^2 = xy$.

$\therefore x^2 = (1 - \sin^2 A)(1 - \sin^2 B)(1 - \sin^2 C) = \cos^2 A \cos^2 B \cos^2 C$

$\therefore x = \pm \cos A \cos B \cos C = y$.

Example 5: Prove that $\sqrt{\left(\dfrac{1-\sin A}{1+\sin A}\right)} = \sec A - \tan A$

Solution: L.H.S. $= \sqrt{\left(\dfrac{(1-\sin A)^2}{1-\sin^2 A}\right)} = \dfrac{1-\sin A}{\cos A} = \dfrac{1}{\cos A} - \dfrac{\sin A}{\cos A} = \sec A - \tan A$

Example 6: *Prove that* $\dfrac{\tan A + \sec A - 1}{\tan A - \sec A + 1} = \dfrac{1+\sin A}{\cos A}$

Solution: We know that, $\sec^2 A - \tan^2 A = 1$; hence

$$\text{L.H.S.} = \frac{(\tan A + \sec A) - (\sec^2 A - \tan^2 A)}{\tan A - \sec A + 1} = \frac{(\tan A + \sec A)[1 - (\sec A - \tan A)]}{\tan A - \sec A + 1}$$

$$= \tan A + \sec A = \frac{1+\sin A}{\cos A}$$

Example 7: *Prove that* $\dfrac{\cot^2\theta(\sec\theta - 1)}{1+\sin\theta} = \sec^2\theta \cdot \dfrac{1-\sin\theta}{1+\sec\theta}$

Solution: L.H.S. $= \cot^2\theta \cdot \dfrac{\sec\theta - 1}{1+\sin\theta} \cdot \dfrac{\sec\theta+1}{\sec\theta+1} = \dfrac{\cot^2\theta(\sec^2\theta - 1)}{(\sec\theta+1)(1+\sin\theta)} = \dfrac{\cot^2\theta\tan^2\theta}{(\sec\theta+1)} \cdot \dfrac{1-\sin\theta}{1-\sin^2\theta}$

$$= \frac{1}{1+\sec\theta} \cdot \frac{1-\sin\theta}{\cos^2\theta} = \sec^2\theta \cdot \frac{1-\sin\theta}{1+\sec\theta}$$

Example 8: *Eliminate θ from the relations* $a \sec\theta = 1 - b\tan\theta$ *and* $a^2 \sec^2\theta = 5 + b^2\tan^2\theta$.

Solution: Squaring first relation $a^2 \sec^2\theta = (1 - b\tan\theta)^2 = 1 - 2b\tan\theta + b^2\tan^2\theta$.

Then second relation gives:

$1 - 2b\tan\theta + b^2\tan^2\theta = 5 + b^2\tan^2\theta$.

Which gives $\tan\theta = -2/b$.

Putting this value of $\tan\theta$ in the second given relation, we get

$a^2[1 + (4/b^2)] = 5 + b^2(4/b^2) = 9$

$\therefore a^2 b^2 + 4a^2 = 9b^2$.

Example 9: *Prove that* $\frac{\tan A}{1-\cot A}+\frac{\cot A}{1-\tan A}=\sec A \operatorname{cosec} A+1$

Solution: $\text{L.H.S.}=\frac{\sin^2 A}{\cos A(\sin A-\cos A)}-\frac{\cos^2 A}{\sin A(\sin A-\cos A)}=\frac{\sin^3 A-\cos^3 A}{\sin A\cos A(\sin A-\cos A)}$

$$=\frac{\sin^2 A+\cos^2 A+\sin A\cos A}{\sin A\cos A}=\frac{1+\sin A\cos A}{\sin A\cos A}=\frac{1}{\sin A\cos A}+1=\sec A \operatorname{cosec} A+1$$

Example 10: *Prove that* $(1+\cot A+\tan A)(\sin A-\cos A)=\frac{\sec A}{\operatorname{cosec}^2 A}-\frac{\operatorname{cosec} A}{\sec^2 A}$

Solution: $\text{L.H.S.}=(\sin A-\cos A)\left(1+\frac{\cos A}{\sin A}+\frac{\sin A}{\cos A}\right)$

$$=\frac{1}{\sin A\cos A}(\sin A-\cos A)(\sin^2 A+\cos^2 A+\sin A\cos A)=\frac{\sin^3 A-\cos^3 A}{\sin A\cos A}=\frac{\sin^2 A}{\cos A}-\frac{\cos^2 A}{\sin A}$$

$$=\frac{\sec A}{\operatorname{cosec}^2 A}-\frac{\operatorname{cosec} A}{\sec^2 A}$$

Example 11: *Prove that* $\frac{2\sin\theta\tan\theta(1-\tan\theta)+2\sin\theta\sec^2\theta}{(1+\tan\theta)^2}=\frac{2\sin\theta}{(1+\tan\theta)}$

Solution: $\text{L.H.S.}=\frac{2\sin\theta\left[\tan\theta-\tan^2\theta+\sec^2\theta\right]}{(1+\tan\theta)^2}=\frac{2\sin\theta(\tan\theta+1)}{(1+\tan\theta)^2}=\frac{2\sin\theta}{1+\tan\theta}$

Example 12: *Prove that* $(\tan\theta+\operatorname{cosec}\phi)^2-(\cot\phi-\sec\theta)^2=2\tan\theta\cot\phi(\operatorname{cosec}\theta+\sec\phi)$

Solution: $\text{L.H.S.}=(\tan^2\theta+\operatorname{cosec}^2\phi+2\tan\theta\operatorname{cosec}\phi)-(\cot^2\phi+\sec^2\theta-2\cot\phi\sec\theta)$

$$=(\operatorname{cosec}^2\phi-\cot^2\phi)-(\sec^2\theta-\tan^2\theta)+2\tan\theta\cot\phi\left(\frac{\operatorname{cosec}\phi}{\cot\phi}+\frac{\sec\theta}{\tan\theta}\right)$$

$$=1-1+2\tan\theta\cot\phi\,[1/\cos\phi+1/\sin\theta]=2\tan\theta\cot\phi(\sec\phi+\operatorname{cosec}\theta)$$

Example 13: *Prove that* $\left(\frac{1+\sin\theta-\cos\theta}{1+\sin\theta+\cos\theta}\right)^2=\frac{1-\cos\theta}{1+\cos\theta}$

Solution: $\text{L.H.S.}=\frac{(1+\sin\theta)^2+\cos^2\theta-2\cos\theta(1+\sin\theta)}{(1+\sin\theta)^2+\cos^2\theta+2\cos\theta(1+\sin\theta)}=\frac{1+\sin^2\theta+\cos^2\theta+2\sin\theta-2\cos\theta(1+\sin\theta)}{1+\sin^2\theta+\cos^2\theta+2\sin\theta+2\cos\theta(1+\sin\theta)}$

$$=\frac{2(1+\sin\theta)-2\cos\theta(1+\sin\theta)}{2(1+\sin\theta)+2\cos\theta(1+\sin\theta)}=\frac{1-\cos\theta}{1+\cos\theta}$$

Example 14: *Prove that* $(\operatorname{cosec}\theta-\sec\theta)(\cot\theta-\tan\theta)=(\operatorname{cosec}\theta+\sec\theta)(\sec\theta\operatorname{cosec}\theta-2)$.

Solution: $\text{L.H.S.}=\frac{\cos\theta-\sin\theta}{\sin\theta\cos\theta}\cdot\frac{\cos^2\theta-\sin^2\theta}{\sin\theta\cos\theta}$

$$=\frac{(\cos\theta-\sin\theta)^2}{\sin\theta\cos\theta}\cdot\frac{\cos\theta+\sin\theta}{\sin\theta\cos\theta}=\frac{1-2\sin\theta\cos\theta}{\sin\theta\cos\theta}\left[\frac{1}{\sin\theta}+\frac{1}{\cos\theta}\right]$$

$$=(\operatorname{cosec}\theta\sec\theta-2)(\operatorname{cosec}\theta+\sec\theta)=\text{R.H.S.}$$

Example 15: *If tan A + sin A = m and tan A – sin A = n, then show that* $m^2 - n^2 = 4\sqrt{mn}$.

Solution: $m^2 - n^2 = (m + n)(m - n) = 2 \tan A \,.\, 2 \sin A = 4 \tan A \sin A$,

$$4\sqrt{(mn)} = 4\sqrt{(\tan^2 A - \sin^2 A)} = 4 \sin A \sqrt{(\sec^2 A - 1)} = 4 \sin A \tan A.$$

$\therefore m^2 - n^2 = 4\sqrt{(mn)}$.

Example 16: *If cosec θ – sin θ = m, sec θ – cos θ = n, eliminate θ.*

Solution: cosec θ – sin θ = m and sec θ – cos θ = n.

or 1/sin θ – sin θ = m and 1/cos θ – cos θ = n

or $\dfrac{\cos^2\theta}{\sin\theta} = m$ and $\dfrac{\sin^2\theta}{\cos\theta} = n$

Multiplying, we get $\sin\theta\cos\theta = mn$ .....(1)

Again from $\cos^2\theta = m\sin\theta$, we get

$\cos^3\theta = m\sin\theta\cos\theta = m(mn) = m^2 n$ by (1) .....(2)

Also from $\sin^2\theta = n\cos\theta$, we get

$\sin^3\theta = n(\cos\theta\sin\theta) = n(mn) = mn^2$ by (1) .....(3)

But $\cos^2\theta + \sin^2\theta = 1$ or $(\cos^3\theta)^{2/3} + (\sin^3\theta)^{2/3} = 1$.

Put for $\cos^3\theta$ and $\sin^3\theta$ from (2) and (3),

$\therefore (m^2n)^{2/3} + (mn^2)^{2/3} = 1$

Example 17: *If* $\cos x + \sin x = \sqrt{2}\cos x$, *prove that* $\cos x - \sin x = \sqrt{2}\sin x$.

Solution: Squaring it, $1 + 2\sin x\cos x = 2(1 - \sin^2 x)$

$\Rightarrow 2\sin^2 x = 1 - 2\sin x\cos x = (\cos x - \sin x)^2 \therefore \sqrt{2}\sin x = \cos x - \sin x$.

Example 18: *If* $3\sin\theta + 5\cos\theta = 5$, *show that* $5\sin\theta - 3\cos\theta = \pm 3$.

Solution: Squaring $3\sin\theta + 5\cos\theta = 5$, we get

$9\sin^2\theta + 25\cos^2\theta + 30\sin\theta\cos\theta = 25$

$\Rightarrow 9(1 - \cos^2\theta) + 25(1 - \sin^2\theta) + 30\sin\theta\cos\theta = 25$

$\Rightarrow 9 - 9\cos^2\theta + 25 - 25\sin^2\theta + 30\sin\theta\cos\theta = 25$

$\Rightarrow 9 = 9\cos^2\theta + 25\sin^2\theta - 30\sin\theta\cos\theta = (5\sin\theta - 3\cos\theta)^2$

$\therefore 5\sin\theta - 3\cos\theta = \pm 3$.

Example 19: *If* $a\cos\theta + b\sin\theta = p$, $a\sin\theta - b\cos\theta = q$, *prove that* $a^2 + b^2 = p^2 + q^2$.

Solution: Square and add and put $\sin^2\theta + \cos^2\theta = 1$.

Example 20: *If* $a\cos\theta - b\sin\theta = c$, *show that* $a\sin\theta + b\cos\theta = \pm\sqrt{a^2 + b^2 + c^2}$

Solution: Square $a\cos\theta - b\sin\theta = c$.

$\Rightarrow a^2\cos^2\theta + b^2\sin^2\theta - 2ab\sin\theta\cos\theta = c^2$

$\Rightarrow a^2(1 - \sin^2\theta) + b^2(1 - \cos^2\theta) - 2ab\sin\theta\cos\theta = c^2 \therefore (a\sin\theta + b\cos\theta)^2 = a^2 + b^2 - c^2$

$\therefore a\sin\theta + b\cos\theta = \pm\sqrt{(a^2 + b^2 - c^2)}$

Example 21: *If* $\tan^2\theta = (1 - e^2)$, *prove that* $\sec\theta + \tan^3\theta \operatorname{cosec}\theta = (2 - e^2)^{3/2}$

Solution: $\tan^2\theta = 1 - e^2$ (given)

Now $\sec\theta + \tan^3\theta \operatorname{cosec}\theta$

$= \sec\theta(1 + \tan^3\theta \operatorname{cosec}\theta/\sec\theta) = \sec\theta(1 + \tan^3\theta\cot\theta)$

$= \sec\theta(1 + \tan^2\theta) = \sqrt{(1 + \tan^2\theta)\cdot(1 + \tan^2\theta)^2} = (1 + \tan^2\theta)^{3/2} = (1 + 1 - e^2)^{3/2} = (2 - e^2)^{3/2}$.

Example 22: *If* $\sin\theta = \dfrac{m^2 - n^2}{m^2 + n^2}$, *determine the values of* $\tan\theta$, $\sec\theta$ *and* $\operatorname{cosec}\theta$.

Sol. We know that $(m^2 + n^2)^2 - (m^2 - n^2)^2 = 4m^2 n^2$.

$$\therefore \tan\theta = \frac{m^2 - n^2}{2mn},\ \sec\theta = \frac{m^2 + n^2}{2mn},\ \operatorname{cosec}\theta = \frac{m^2 + n^2}{m^2 - n^2}$$

Example 23: *If* $\tan\theta = \dfrac{2x(x+1)}{2x+1}$, *determine* $\sin\theta$ *and* $\cos\theta$.

Solution: $\tan\theta = \dfrac{2x(x+1)}{2x+1}$

Make a triangle whose height is PM = $2x(x + 1)$ and base OM = $2x + 1$.

$\therefore$ Hypotenuse OP = $\sqrt{(\text{OM}^2 + \text{PM}^2)} = [4x^2 (x + 1)^2 + (2x + 1)^2]^{1/2}$,

$\Rightarrow$ OP = $[4x^4 + 8x^3 + 8x^2 + 4x + 1]^{1/2}$

$\Rightarrow$ OP = $[(2x^2)^2 + (2x)^2 + 1^2 + 2(2x)(2x^2) + 2(2x) \cdot 1 + 2.1\,(2x^2)]^{1/2}$

$= [(2x^2 + 2x + 1)^2]^{1/2} = 2x^2 + 2x + 1.$

$\sin\theta$ = PM/OP and $\cos\theta$ = OM/OP gives $\sin\theta = \dfrac{2x(x+1)}{2x^2 + 2x + 1}$, $\cos\theta = \dfrac{2x+1}{2x^2 + 2x + 1}$

Example 24: *Find the minimum values of* $\operatorname{cosec}^2\theta + \sin^2\theta$.

Solution: $\operatorname{cosec}^2\theta + \sin^2\theta = (\operatorname{cosec}\theta - \sin\theta)^2 + 2\operatorname{cosec}\theta\sin\theta = 2 + (\operatorname{cosec}\theta - \sin\theta)^2 \geq 2.$

$\therefore$ Minimum value of $\operatorname{cosec}^2\theta + \sin^2\theta$ is 2.

Example 25: *If* $\cos\theta = \dfrac{2x}{1+x^2}$, *find the values of* $\tan\theta$ *and* $\operatorname{cosec}\theta$.

Solution: $\tan\theta = \dfrac{1-x^2}{2x}$, $\operatorname{cosec}\theta = \dfrac{1+x^2}{1-x^2}$

$$\left[\because \sqrt{(1+x)^2 - 4x^2} = \sqrt{(1-x^2)^2} = (1-x^2)\right]$$

Example 26: *If* $\tan\theta = p/q$, *Show that* $\dfrac{p\sin\theta - q\cos\theta}{p\sin\theta - q\cos\theta} = \dfrac{p^2 - q^2}{p^2 + q^2}$

Solution: $\dfrac{p\sin\theta - q\cos\theta}{p\sin\theta - q\cos\theta} = \dfrac{p\tan\theta - q}{p\tan\theta + q}$, on dividing by $\cos\theta$

$$= \frac{p(p/q) - q}{p(p/q) + q} = \frac{p^2 - q^2}{p^2 + q^2} \qquad (\because \tan\theta = p/q)$$

Example 27: *Is the equation* $\sec^2\theta = \dfrac{4xy}{(x+y)^2}$ *possible for real values of x and y? If not, then find out a relation between x and y so that it may be possible.*

Solution: Since $\sec^2\theta \geq 1$, we have from the given relation,

$$\frac{4xy}{(x+y)^2} \geq 1 \text{ or } (x + y)^2 \leq 4xy \quad \Rightarrow (x + y)^2 - 4xy \leq 0 \quad \Rightarrow (x - y)^2 \leq 0.$$

Which implies that $x = y$. Thus the given equality can hold only when $x = y$.

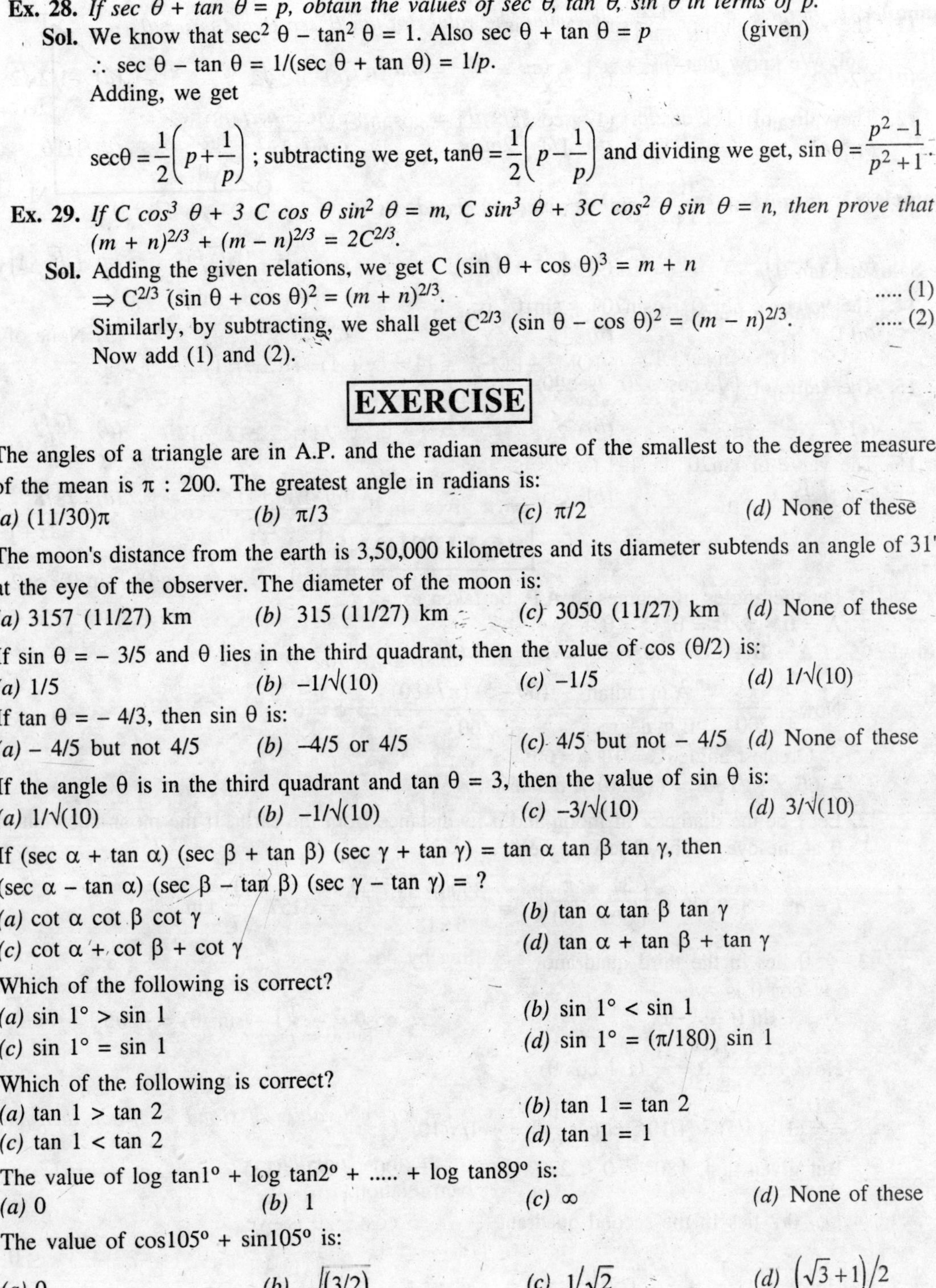

Ex. 28. *If* $\sec\theta + \tan\theta = p$, *obtain the values of* $\sec\theta$, $\tan\theta$, $\sin\theta$ *in terms of p.*

Sol. We know that $\sec^2\theta - \tan^2\theta = 1$. Also $\sec\theta + \tan\theta = p$ (given)

$\therefore\ \sec\theta - \tan\theta = 1/(\sec\theta + \tan\theta) = 1/p$.

Adding, we get

$\sec\theta = \dfrac{1}{2}\left(p + \dfrac{1}{p}\right)$; subtracting we get, $\tan\theta = \dfrac{1}{2}\left(p - \dfrac{1}{p}\right)$ and dividing we get, $\sin\theta = \dfrac{p^2-1}{p^2+1}$.

Ex. 29. *If* $C\cos^3\theta + 3C\cos\theta\sin^2\theta = m$, $C\sin^3\theta + 3C\cos^2\theta\sin\theta = n$, *then prove that* $(m+n)^{2/3} + (m-n)^{2/3} = 2C^{2/3}$.

Sol. Adding the given relations, we get $C(\sin\theta + \cos\theta)^3 = m + n$

$\Rightarrow C^{2/3}(\sin\theta + \cos\theta)^2 = (m+n)^{2/3}$. ..... (1)

Similarly, by subtracting, we shall get $C^{2/3}(\sin\theta - \cos\theta)^2 = (m-n)^{2/3}$. ..... (2)

Now add (1) and (2).

EXERCISE

1. The angles of a triangle are in A.P. and the radian measure of the smallest to the degree measure of the mean is $\pi : 200$. The greatest angle in radians is:

(a) $(11/30)\pi$ *(b)* $\pi/3$ *(c)* $\pi/2$ *(d)* None of these

2. The moon's distance from the earth is 3,50,000 kilometres and its diameter subtends an angle of 31' at the eye of the observer. The diameter of the moon is:

(a) 3157 (11/27) km *(b)* 315 (11/27) km *(c)* 3050 (11/27) km *(d)* None of these

3. If $\sin\theta = -3/5$ and θ lies in the third quadrant, then the value of $\cos(\theta/2)$ is:

(a) 1/5 *(b)* $-1/\sqrt{(10)}$ *(c)* $-1/5$ *(d)* $1/\sqrt{(10)}$

4. If $\tan\theta = -4/3$, then $\sin\theta$ is:

(a) $-4/5$ but not $4/5$ *(b)* $-4/5$ or $4/5$ *(c)* $4/5$ but not $-4/5$ *(d)* None of these

5. If the angle θ is in the third quadrant and $\tan\theta = 3$, then the value of $\sin\theta$ is:

(a) $1/\sqrt{(10)}$ *(b)* $-1/\sqrt{(10)}$ *(c)* $-3/\sqrt{(10)}$ *(d)* $3/\sqrt{(10)}$

6. If $(\sec\alpha + \tan\alpha)(\sec\beta + \tan\beta)(\sec\gamma + \tan\gamma) = \tan\alpha\tan\beta\tan\gamma$, then $(\sec\alpha - \tan\alpha)(\sec\beta - \tan\beta)(\sec\gamma - \tan\gamma) = ?$

(a) $\cot\alpha\cot\beta\cot\gamma$ *(b)* $\tan\alpha\tan\beta\tan\gamma$

(c) $\cot\alpha + \cot\beta + \cot\gamma$ *(d)* $\tan\alpha + \tan\beta + \tan\gamma$

7. Which of the following is correct?

(a) $\sin 1° > \sin 1$ *(b)* $\sin 1° < \sin 1$

(c) $\sin 1° = \sin 1$ *(d)* $\sin 1° = (\pi/180)\sin 1$

8. Which of the following is correct?

(a) $\tan 1 > \tan 2$ *(b)* $\tan 1 = \tan 2$

(c) $\tan 1 < \tan 2$ *(d)* $\tan 1 = 1$

9. The value of $\log\tan 1° + \log\tan 2° + ... + \log\tan 89°$ is:

(a) 0 *(b)* 1 *(c)* ∞ *(d)* None of these

10. The value of $\cos 105° + \sin 105°$ is:

(a) 0 *(b)* $\sqrt{(3/2)}$ *(c)* $1/\sqrt{2}$ *(d)* $\left(\sqrt{3}+1\right)/2$

11. The value of $\sin\left(67\frac{1}{2}°\right)\sin\left(22\frac{1}{2}°\right)$ is:

(a) $-2\sqrt{2}$ (b) $2\sqrt{2}$ (c) $1/2\sqrt{2}$ (d) $-1/2\sqrt{2}$

12. The value of $(1 + \cos\pi/8)(1 + \cos 3\pi/8)(1 + \cos 5\pi/8)(1 + \cos 7\pi/8)$ is:

(a) 1/2 (b) 1/4 (c) 1/8 (d) 1/16

13. The value of $\sin^2\frac{2\pi}{15} - \sin^2\frac{\pi}{30}$ is:

(a) $(\sqrt{5}-1)/4$ (b) $(\sqrt{5}-1)/8$ (c) $(\sqrt{5}+1)\sqrt{3}/2$ (d) $(\sqrt{5}-1)\sqrt{3}/2$

14. The value of $\sin 50° - \sin 70° + \sin 10°$ is:

(a) 0 (b) 1 (c) 2 (d) None of these

15. The value of $(\sqrt{3}\operatorname{cosec} 20° - \sec 20°)$ is:

(a) 2 (b) $2\sqrt{3}$ (c) 4 (d) $\sqrt{8}/2$

16. The value of $\tan 20° \tan 40° \tan 80°$ is:

(a) $1/\sqrt{3}$ (b) $\sqrt{3}$ (c) 1/8 (d) $\sqrt{8}/8$

SOLUTIONS

1. Let the angles in degrees in A.P. be taken as

$A = \theta - \phi, B = \theta, C = \theta + \phi$

$\therefore A + B + C = 180° = 3\theta \Rightarrow B = \theta = 60°$

Now $\frac{\pi}{200} = \frac{\text{A in radian}}{\text{B in degrees}} = \frac{(60-\phi)(\pi/180)}{60} \Rightarrow \phi = 6°$

$\therefore$ Greatest angle $C = \theta + \phi = 66°$

$= 66 \times (\pi/180) = (11/30)\,\pi$ radians.

2. Let l be the diameter of moon and a its distance from the earth. If the moon subtends an angle θ at the eye of the observer, then

$$l = a\theta = 350000 \times \left(\frac{31}{60}\times\frac{\pi}{180}\right) = \frac{3500\times 31}{6\times 18}\times\frac{22}{7} = 3157\ \frac{11}{27}\ \text{km.}$$

3. $\because$ θ lies in the third quadrant

$\because$ $\cos\theta$ is –ve

$\because$ $\sin\theta = -\ 3/5 \qquad \Rightarrow \cos\theta = -\sqrt{(1-\sin^2\theta)} = -\ 4/5$

Now, $\cos^2\frac{1}{2}\theta = \frac{1}{2}(1+\cos\theta)$

$= \frac{1}{2}(1 - 4/5) = 1/10 \Rightarrow \cos\frac{1}{2}\theta = \pm\ 1/\sqrt{(10)}$

But given that, $180° < \theta < 270° \Rightarrow 90° < \theta/2 < 135°$

i.e., $\theta/2$ lies in the second quadrant $\qquad \Rightarrow \cos\frac{1}{2}\theta$ is –ve

Hence $\cos\frac{1}{2}\theta = -\ 1/\sqrt{10}$.

4. $\tan\theta = -4/3$
$\Rightarrow \theta$ lies in 2nd or 4th quadrant.
$\therefore \sin\theta$ is positive or negative according as θ lie in 2nd or 4th quadrant respectively, *i.e.*, $\sin\theta$ may be positive or negative.
Now $\sin\theta = \tan\theta/\sqrt{(1 + \tan^2\theta)} = 4/5$
Hence $\sin\theta = -4/5$ or $4/5$.

5. $\because$ θ is in the third quadrant,
$\because \sin\theta < 0$.
Thus $\sin\theta = -\tan\theta/\sqrt{(1+\tan^2\theta)} = -3/\sqrt{(10)}$.

6. Multiplying both sides of the given expression by $(\sec\alpha - \tan\alpha).(\sec\beta - \tan\beta).(\sec\gamma - \tan\gamma)$, we get, $1.1.1 = (\sec\alpha - \tan\alpha).(\sec\beta - \tan\beta).(\sec\gamma - \tan\gamma).\tan\alpha\tan\beta\tan\gamma$
$\Rightarrow (\sec\alpha - \tan\alpha).(\sec\beta - \tan\beta).(\sec\gamma - \tan\gamma) = \cot\alpha.\cot\beta.\cot\gamma$.

7. 1 radian = $(180/\pi)$ Degrees = $57°$ (appr.)
$\therefore \sin 1° < \sin 57° \Rightarrow \sin 1° < \sin 1$.

8. 1 radian = $57°$ (appr.)
which lie in first quadrant. $\therefore \tan 1 > 0$,
and 2 radians = $114°$ (appr.), which lie in second quadrant $\therefore \tan 2 < 0$
Hence $\tan 1 > \tan 2$.

9. $\log\tan 1° + \log\tan 2° + \ldots + \log\tan 89°$

$$= \log[\tan 1°.\tan 2° \ldots \tan 45° \ldots \tan 88°.\tan 89°]$$

$$= \log[\tan 1°.\tan 2° \ldots \tan 45° \ldots \tan(90°-2°)\tan(90°-1°)]$$

$$= \log[\tan 1°.\cot 1°.\tan 2°.\cot 2° \ldots 1]$$

$$= \log 1 = 0$$

10. $\cos 105° + \sin 105°$
$= \cos(60° + 45°) + \sin(60° + 45°)$
$= \cos 60° \cos 45° - \sin 60° \sin 45° + \sin 60° \cos 45° + \cos 60° \sin 45°$

$$= \frac{1}{2}.\frac{1}{\sqrt{2}} - \frac{\sqrt{3}}{2}.\frac{1}{\sqrt{2}} + \frac{\sqrt{3}}{2}.\frac{1}{\sqrt{2}} + \frac{1}{2}.\frac{1}{\sqrt{2}}$$

$$= \frac{2}{2\sqrt{2}} = \frac{1}{\sqrt{2}}$$

11. $\sin\left(67\frac{1°}{2}\right)\sin\left(22\frac{1°}{2}\right)$

$$= \sin\left(45°+22\frac{1°}{2}\right)\sin\left(45°-22\frac{1°}{2}\right) \quad = \sin^2 45° - \sin^2 22\frac{1°}{2} = \left(\frac{1}{\sqrt{2}}\right)^2 - \frac{1-\cos 45°}{2}$$

$$= \frac{1}{2} - \frac{1}{2}\left(1 - \frac{1}{\sqrt{2}}\right) = \frac{1}{2}\left(1 - 1 + \frac{1}{\sqrt{2}}\right) = \frac{1}{2\sqrt{2}}$$

12. $\left(1+\cos\frac{\pi}{8}\right)\left(1+\cos\frac{3\pi}{8}\right)\left(1+\cos\frac{5\pi}{8}\right)\left(1+\cos\frac{7\pi}{8}\right)$

$= (1+\cos\pi/8)(1-\cos\pi/8)\ (1+\cos 3\pi/8)(1-\cos 3\pi/8)$

$= \sin^2 \pi/8.\ \sin^2 3\pi/8 = \frac{1}{4}\left(2\sin\frac{3\pi}{8}.\sin\pi/8\right)^2$

$= \frac{1}{4}\left[\cos\frac{\pi}{4}-\cos\frac{\pi}{2}\right]^2 = \frac{1}{4}\left(\frac{1}{\sqrt{2}}-0\right)^2$

$= \frac{1}{4}\times\frac{1}{2}=\frac{1}{8}$

13. $\sin^2\frac{2\pi}{5}-\sin^2\frac{\pi}{30}$

$= \sin\left(\frac{2\pi}{15}+\frac{\pi}{30}\right)\sin\left(\frac{2\pi}{15}-\frac{\pi}{30}\right)$

$= \sin\frac{\pi}{6}.\sin\frac{\pi}{10}=\frac{1}{2}\times\frac{\sqrt{5}-1}{4}$

$= \frac{1}{8}\ \left(\sqrt{5}-1\right)$

14. $\sin 50° - \sin 70° + \sin 10°$

$= 2\cos 60° \sin(-10)° + \sin 10°$

$= 2 \times \frac{1}{2} \times - \sin 10° + \sin 10°$

$= -\sin 10° + \sin 10° = 0$

15. $\sqrt{3}\ \text{cosec}\ 20° - \sec 20°$

$= \tan 60°\ \text{cosec} 20° - \sec 20° \quad = \frac{\sin 60°}{\cos 60°}.\frac{1}{\sin 20°}-\frac{1}{\cos 20°}$

$= \frac{\sin 60°\cos 20°-\cos 60°\sin 20°}{\cos 60°.\sin 20°\cos 20°} \quad = \frac{\sin(60°-20°)}{\frac{1}{2}.\frac{1}{2}(2\sin 20°\cos 20°)} = 4.\frac{\sin 40°}{\sin 40°} = 4$

16. $\tan 20° \times \tan 40° \times \tan 80°$

$= \tan 20° \times \tan(60° - 20°)\tan(60° + 20°)$

$= \tan(3 \times 20°) = \tan 60° = \sqrt{3}$

32 HEIGHT AND DISTANCE

Angle of Elevation and Depression: Let O and P be two points such that P is at higher level than O. Let PQ, OX be horizontal lines through P and O, respectively. If an observer (or eye) is at O and the object is at P, then ∠XOP is called the angle of elevation of P as seen from O. This angle is also called the angular height of P from O.

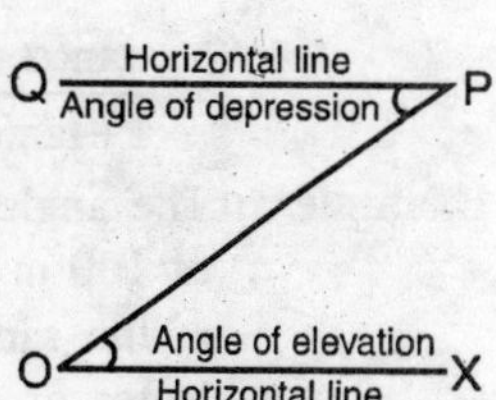

If an observer (or eye) is at P and the object is at O, then ∠QPO is called the angle of depression of O as seen from P.

Example 1: A kite is flying with the string inclined at 60° to the horizon. What is the height of the kite above the ground, when the string is 20 m long ?

Solution: Length of string = AP = 20 m.

Height of kite = OP = AP sin 60° = $20 \times \frac{\sqrt{3}}{2} = 10\sqrt{3}$ m.

Example 2: From the top of a light house 60 metres high with its base at the sea level, the angle of depression of a boat is 15°. What is the distance of the boat from the foot of the light house ?

Solution: Let P be the top of the light house at a height of 60m.

If A is the position of the boat, then

∠OAP = ∠LPA = 15°.

Now, tan 15° = OP/OA = 60/OA

∴ OA = 60 cot 15° = 60 cot (45° – 30°)

$$= 60 \frac{\cot 45° \cot 30° + 1}{\cot 30° - \cot 45°} = \left(\frac{\sqrt{3}+1}{\sqrt{3}-1}\right) 60 \text{ m}$$

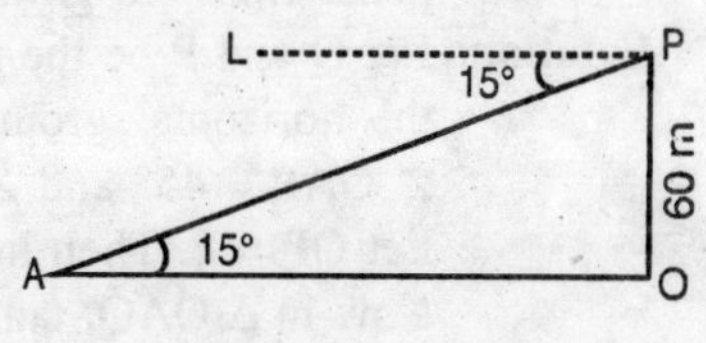

Example 3: From the top of a cliff 25 metres high, the angle of elevation of a tower is found to be equal to the angle of depression of the foot of the tower, then what is the height of the tower ?

Solution: AB is a cliff of height 25 m and OP the tower,

s.t. ∠ PBL = ∠ OBL = θ (say)

In Δ OAB, OA = AB cot θ = 25 cot θ = BL.

In Δ BPL,

PL = BL tan θ = 25 cot θ tan θ = 25 m

Height of the tower = OP = OL + PL = 50 m

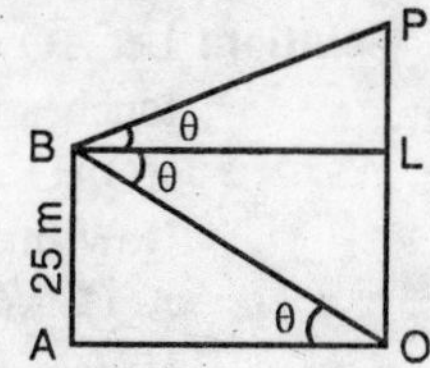

Example 4: AB is a vertical pole. The end A is on the level ground. C is the middle point of AB. P is a point on the ground. The portion BC subtends angle β at P. If AP = nAB, then what is the value of tan β ?

Solution: C is the middle point of the pole AB and P a point on the horizontal plane, s.t. $\angle$ BPC = β. Let $\angle$ APC = α

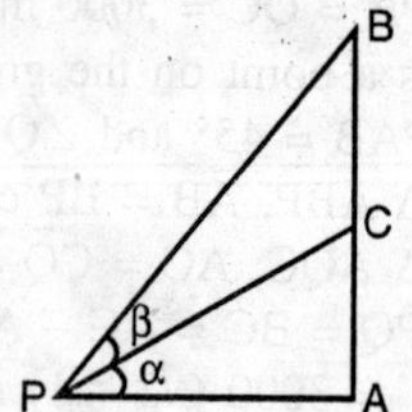

$\therefore$ tan α = AC/AP = AB/(2AP) = 1/(2n).

$\because$ AP = n AB (given)

In Δ APB, tan ($\alpha + \beta$) = AB/AP = 1/n

Now tan β = tan [($\alpha + \beta$) − α]

$$= \frac{\tan(\alpha+\beta)-\tan\alpha}{1+\tan(\alpha+\beta)\tan\alpha} = \frac{1/n-1/(2n)}{1+(1/n)(1/2n)} = \frac{n}{2n^2+1}.$$

Example 5: The angle of elevation of the top of an incomplete vertical pillar at a horizontal distance of 100 m. from its base is 45°. If the angle of elevation of the top of the complete pillar at the same point is to be 60°, then what is the height of the incomplete pillar is to be increased ?

Solution: Let OP be the incomplete and OQ the complete pillar. If A is a point on the horizontal plane, s.t. OA = 100 m

then $\angle$OAP = 45° and $\angle$OAQ = 60°

In Δ OAP, tan 45° = OP/OA

$\therefore$ OP = OA = 100 m

In Δ OAQ, tan 60° = OQ/OA

$\Rightarrow \sqrt{3} = (100 + x)/100$

$\Rightarrow x = 100\,(\sqrt{3} - 1)$m

Example 6: An aeroplane flying at a height of 300 metres above the ground passes vertically above another plane at an instant when the angles of elevation of the two planes from the same point on the ground are 60° and 45° respectively. Then what is the height of the lower plane from the ground (in metres)?

Solution: Let Q and P be the positions of the two aeroplanes at the instant when from a point A on the horizontal ground,

$\angle$ OAP = 45° and $\angle$OAQ = 60°, also given that OQ = 300 m.

Let OP = h. Then in Δ OAP, OA = OP = h.

Now in Δ OAQ, tan 60° = OQ/OA

$\Rightarrow \sqrt{3} = 300/h \quad \therefore \quad h = 100\sqrt{3}$ m

Example 7: A tree is broken by wind, its upper part touches the ground at a point 10 metres from the foot of the tree and makes an angle of 45° with the ground. What is the entire length of the tree ?

Solution: Let AQ (= PQ) be the broken part of the tree OP, whose upper part touches the ground at A such that

$\angle$QAO = 45°. $\therefore$ OA = 10 m. $\because$ OQ = 10 m.

Now in Δ OAQ,

AQ = $\sqrt{(OA^2 + OQ^2)} = 10\sqrt{2}$ m.

Hence, the entire length of the tree = OP = OQ + PQ = OQ + AQ
= 10 (1 + $\sqrt{2}$) m.

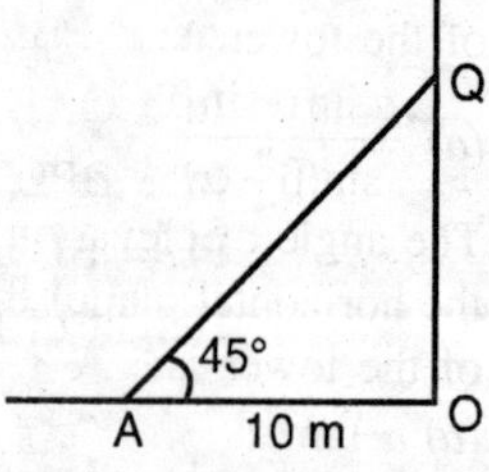

Example 8: The angle of elevation of an aeroplane flying at a height of 3000 m, from a point on the ground is 45°. After 15 seconds flight, the angle of elevation changes to 30°, what is the the speed of the plane ?

Solution: Let the P and Q be the two positions of the aeroplane flying at the height of 3000 m.

$\therefore$ PB = QC = 3000 m

A is a point on the ground s.t.

$\angle$ PAB = 45° and $\angle$QAC = 30°

In Δ ABP, AB = BP cot 45° = 3000 m

In Δ AQC, AC = CQ cot 30° = $3000\sqrt{3}$ m

$\therefore$ PQ = BC = AC – AB

= $3000(\sqrt{3}-1)$ m

Hence, the speed of the aeroplane

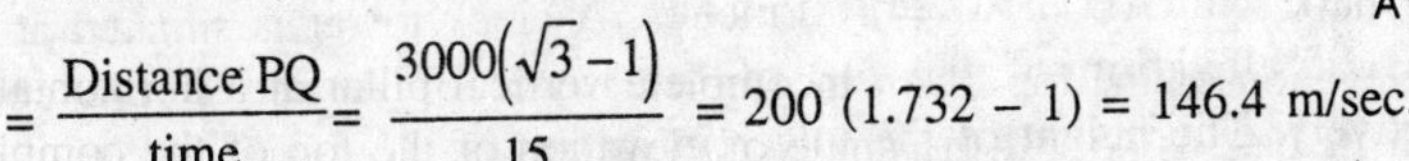

$$= \frac{\text{Distance PQ}}{\text{time}} = \frac{3000(\sqrt{3}-1)}{15} = 200\ (1.732 - 1) = 146.4 \text{ m/sec.}$$

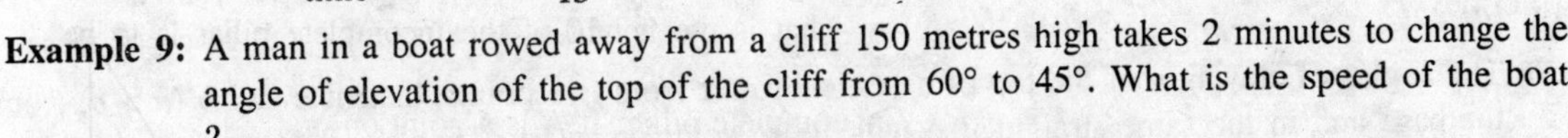

Example 9: A man in a boat rowed away from a cliff 150 metres high takes 2 minutes to change the angle of elevation of the top of the cliff from 60° to 45°. What is the speed of the boat ?

Solution: Let OP be the cliff of height 150 m and let A and B be two positions of the boat at an interval of 2 minutes s.t. $\angle$ OAP = 60° and $\angle$ OBP = 45°

In ΔOAP and ΔOBP,

OA = OP cot 60° = $150/\sqrt{3} = 50\sqrt{3}$ m and OB = OP cot 45° = 150 m

$\therefore$ AB = OB – OA = $50(3-\sqrt{3})$ metre

$\therefore$ Speed of the boat

$$= \frac{\text{Distance AB}}{\text{time}} = \frac{50(3-\sqrt{3})}{2} \text{ m/min.} = 25\ (3-\sqrt{3})\ \frac{60}{1000} \text{ km/hour} = \frac{9-3\sqrt{3}}{2} \text{ km/hour}$$

EXERCISE

1. A person standing on the bank of a river observes that the angle subtended by a tree on the opposite bank is 60°, when he retires 40 metres from the bank he finds the angle to be 30°. Then the breadth of the river is:

   (a) 40 m (b) 60 m (c) 20 m (d) 30 m

2. At a point on a level plane a tower subtends an angle θ and a flag-staff a ft. in length at the top of the tower subtends an angle ϕ. The height of the tower is:

   (a) $\dfrac{a\sin\theta\cos\phi}{\cos(\theta+\phi)}$ (b) $\dfrac{a\sin\theta\cos(\theta+\phi)}{\sin\phi}$ (c) $\dfrac{a\cos(\theta+\phi)}{\sin\theta\sin\phi}$ (d) None of these

3. The angle of elevation of the top of a tower standing on a horizontal plane from a point A is α. After walking a distance a towards the foot of the tower the angle of elevation is found to be β. The height of the tower is:

   (a) $\dfrac{a\sin\alpha\sin\beta}{\sin(\beta-\alpha)}$ (b) $\dfrac{a\sin\alpha\sin\beta}{\sin(\alpha-\beta)}$ (c) $\dfrac{a\sin(\beta-\alpha)}{\sin\alpha\sin\beta}$ (d) $\dfrac{a\sin(\alpha-\beta)}{\sin\alpha\sin\beta}$

4. The angle of elevation of the top of a TV tower from the three points A, B, C in a straight line (in the horizontal plane) through the foot of the tower are α, 2α, 3α respectively. If AB = a, the height of the tower is:

   (a) $a\tan\alpha$ (b) $a\sin\alpha$ (c) $a\sin 2\alpha$ (d) $a\sin 3\alpha$

5. The height of the centre of the round balloon of radius r, which subtend an angle α at the eye of an observer and the elevation of whose centre from the eye is β, is given by:

(a) $r \sin \alpha \sin \beta$ *(b)* $r \operatorname{cosec} \frac{1}{2} \alpha \sin \beta$ *(c)* $r \operatorname{cosec} \alpha \sin \beta$ *(d)* None of these

6. ABCD is a square plot. The angle of elevation of the top of a pole standing at D from A or C is 30° and that from B is θ, then $\tan \theta$ is equal to:

(a) $\sqrt{6}$ *(b)* $1/\sqrt{6}$ *(c)* $\sqrt{3}/\sqrt{2}$ *(d)* $\sqrt{2}/\sqrt{3}$

7. The angle of elevation of the top of two vertical towers as seen from the middle point of the line joining the foot of the towers are 60° and 30° respectively. The ratio of the heights of the towers is:

(a) 2 : 1 *(b)* $\sqrt{3}$: 1 *(c)* 3 : 2 *(d)* 3 : 1

8. ABC is a triangular park with AB = AC = 100 metres. A clock tower is situated at the mid-point of BC. The angles of elevation of the top of the tower of A and B are $\cot^{-1}$ (3.2) and $\operatorname{cosec}^{-1}$ (2.6) respectively. The height of the tower in metres is:

(a) 25/2 *(b)* 25 *(c)* 50 *(d)* None of these

9. The angles of elevation of the top of a vertical tower from two points, distant a and b ($a > b$) from the base and in the same straight line with it are complementary. Then the height of the tower is:

(a) $\sqrt{(ab)}$ *(b)* $\sqrt{(a^2 + b^2)}$ *(c)* $\sqrt{(a^2 - b^2)}$ *(d)* $\sqrt{a(a-b)}$

10. From the top of a h metre high cliff the angles of depression of the top and the bottom of a tower are observed to be 30° and 60° respectively. The height of the tower is:

(a) $h\sqrt{3}$ *(b)* $2h\sqrt{3}$ *(c)* $h/3$ *(d)* $2h/3$

11. A vertical pole is 75m high. Find the angle subtended by the pole a point 75 m away from its base.

(a) 30° *(b)* 45° *(c)* 60° *(d)* 90°

12. A person standing on the bank of river finds that the angle of elevation of the top of a tower on opposite side bank is 45°. Which of the following statement is correct?

(a) Breadth of the river is half of the height of the tower
(b) Breadth of the river and the height of the tower are equal
(c) Breadth of the river is twice the height of the tower
(d) None of these

13. The angles of depression of two ships from the top of a light house are 45° and 30° towards east. If the ships are 200 m apart, find the height of the light house.

(a) 100 m *(b)* 173 m *(c)* 200 m *(d)* 273 m

14. A man 2m high, walks at a uniform speed of 6m/min away from a lamp post, 5m high. Find the rate at which the length of his shadow increases.

(a) 4m/min *(b)* 8m/min *(c)* 9m/min *(d)* 14m/min

15. Two ships leave a port at the same instant. One sails at 30 km/hr in the direction N 32°E while the other sails at 20 km/hr in the direction S 58° E. After two hours the ships are distant from each other by:

(a) $15\sqrt{6}$ km *(b)* 36.5 km *(c)* $20\sqrt{13}$ km *(d)* 100 km

16. An observer measures angles of elevation of two towers of equal heights from a point between the towers. If the angles of elevation are 60° and 30° and distance of nearer tower is 100 m then the height of each tower and the distance between the towers, respectively are

(a) $\frac{100}{\sqrt{3}}$ m and 300m (b) $\frac{100}{\sqrt{3}}$ m and 400m

(c) $100\sqrt{3}$ m and 300m (d) $100\sqrt{3}$ m and 400 m

17. On the ground level the angle of elevation of the top of a tower is 30°. On moving 20 m nearer the tower, the angle of elevation found to be 60°. The height of the tower is:

(a) 10 m (b) $10\sqrt{3}$ m (c) 15 m (d) 20 m

18. A 6 ft.-tall man finds that the angle of elevation of the top of a 24 ft.-high pillar and the angle of depression its base are complementary angles. Then the distance between pillar and man is:

(a) $2\sqrt{3}$ ft (b) $4\sqrt{3}$ ft (c) $6\sqrt{3}$ ft (d) $8\sqrt{3}$ ft

19. A man on the top of a vertical towers observes a car moving at a uniform speed comming directly towards it. If it takes 12 minutes for the angle of depression to change from 30° to 45°, how soon after this will the car reach the tower?

(a) 14 min 20 sec. (b) 15 min 22 sec. (c) 16 min. (d) 16 min. 23 sec.

20. From a point P on a level ground, the angle of elevation of the top of a tower is 30°. If the tower is 100 m high, find the distance of point P from the foot of the tower.

(a) 100 m (b) 173 m (c) 200 m (d) 273 m

21. A man is observing from the top of a tower a boat speeding away from the tower. The boat makes an angle of depression of 45° with the man's eye when at a distance of 60 m from the tower. After 5 seconds, the angle of depression becomes 30°. Find the speed of the boat, assuming that it is running in still water.

(a) 30 km/hr. (b) 31.5 km/hr (c) 33 km/hr (d) 34 km/hr

SOLUTIONS

1. Let A be the position of a person on the bank of a river and OP the tree on the opposite bank and ∠OAP = 60°. When the person retires to the position B, s.t.

AB = 40 m then ∠ OBP = 30°

Let OA = x m and OP = h m

In Δ OAP, OP = OA tan 60° = $x\sqrt{3}$

and in Δ OBP, OP = OB tan 30° = $(x + 40)/\sqrt{3}$

∴ $(x + 40)/\sqrt{3} = x\sqrt{3} \Rightarrow x = 20$ m

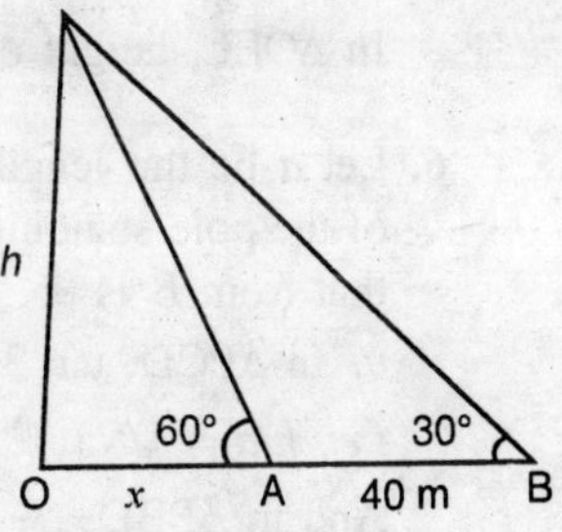

2. Let OP be the tower of height h (say) and PQ the flag-staff of height a, such that

$$\angle OAP = \theta \text{ and } \angle PAQ = \phi$$

In ΔOAP and ΔOAQ

$$OA = OP \cot\theta = h\cot\theta$$

and $$OA = OQ\cot(\theta+\phi) = (h+a)\cot(\theta+\phi)$$

∴ $$h\cot\theta = (h+a)\cot(\theta+\phi)$$

⇒ $$h = \frac{a\cot(\theta+\phi)}{\cot\theta - \cot(\theta+\phi)}$$

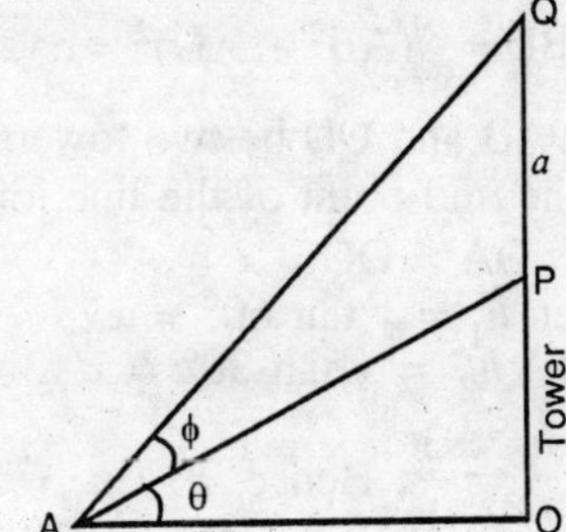

$$= \frac{a \sin \theta \cos (\theta + \phi)}{\sin \phi}.$$

3. Let OP be the tower of height h (say) and A and B be the two positions on the horizontal line through O, such that
$\angle$ OAP = α, $\angle$ OBP = β and OB = x
In ΔOBP, OB = $x = h \cot \beta$, and
in ΔOAP, OA = $a + x = h \cot \alpha$
$\therefore a = h (\cot \alpha - \cot \beta)$
$\Rightarrow h = a \sin \alpha \sin \beta / \sin (\beta - \alpha)$

4. OP is vertical tower. The elevations of the top of P from A, B, C are α, 2α, 3α respectively

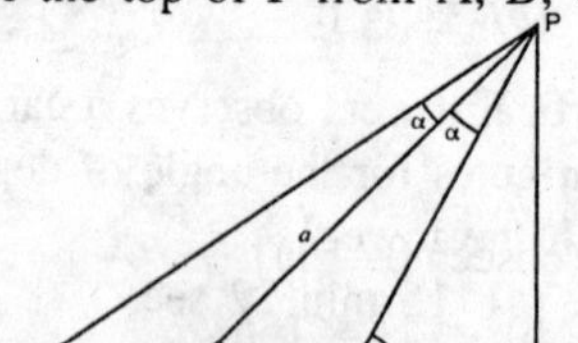

$\angle$OAP = $\angle$APB = α
$\therefore$ AB = PB = a
In ΔOBP,
OP = PB sin 2α
= $a \sin 2\alpha$

5. Let O be the centre of the balloon of radius r which subtend an angle α at the eye of an observer at E.
If EA and EB are the tangents to the balloon,

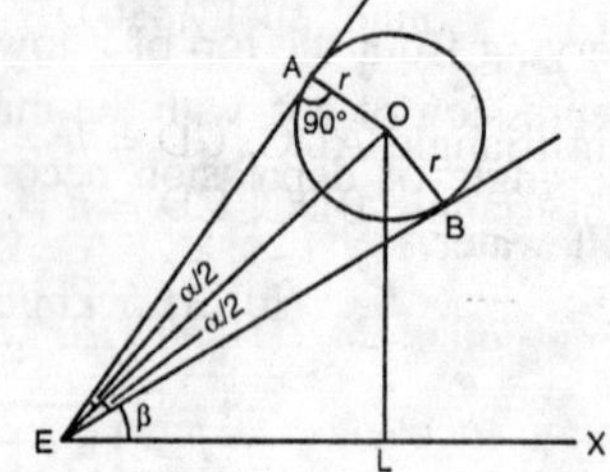

then $\angle$OEA = $\angle$OEB = $\frac{\alpha}{2}$

In ΔOAE, $\sin \frac{1}{2} \alpha$ = OA/OE

$\therefore$ OE = $r \operatorname{cosec} \frac{1}{2} \alpha$

In ΔOEL, height of the centre of the balloon = h = OE sin β = $r \operatorname{cosec} \frac{1}{2} \alpha \sin \beta$.

6. Let a be the length of a side of square plot ABCD and h, the height of the pole standing at D. Since elevations of P from A or C is 30° and that from B is θ,

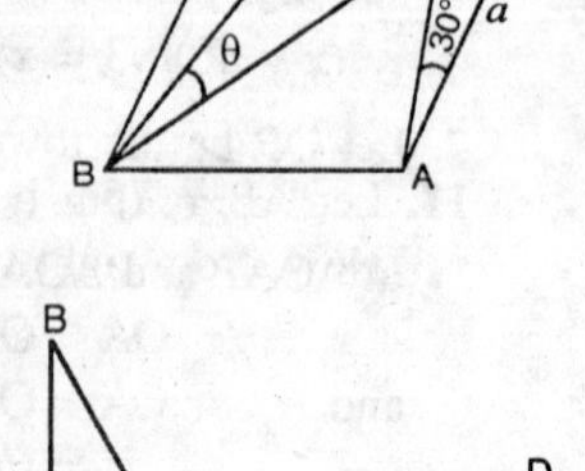

$\therefore$ In ΔPCD, tan 30° = h/a
i.e., $h/a = 1/\sqrt{3}$
And in ΔPBD,
$\tan \theta$ = PD/BD = $h/(a\sqrt{2}) = 1/\sqrt{6}$
$\therefore$ BD = $\sqrt{(AB^2 + AD)^2} = a\sqrt{2}$.

7. Let AB and CD be two towers of heights h_1 and h_2 respectively and O the mid-point of the line joining the foots A and C of the towers.
Let OA = OC = x
Then $h_1 = x \tan 60° = x\sqrt{3}$
and $h_2 = x \tan 30° = x/\sqrt{3}$

$\therefore \frac{h_1}{h_2} = \frac{3}{1}$, Hence, $h_1 : h_2 = 3 : 1$.

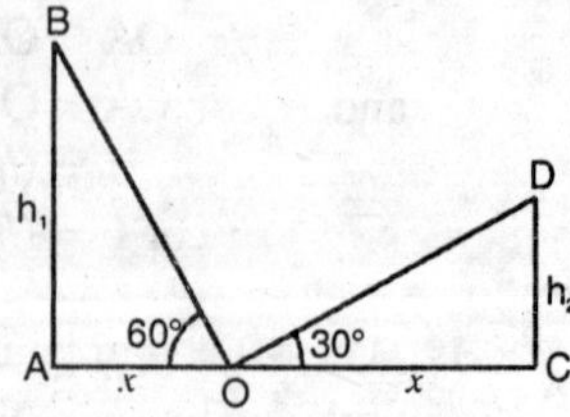

8. Given $\alpha = \cot^{-1}(3.2)$, $\beta = \text{cosec}^{-1}(2.6)$

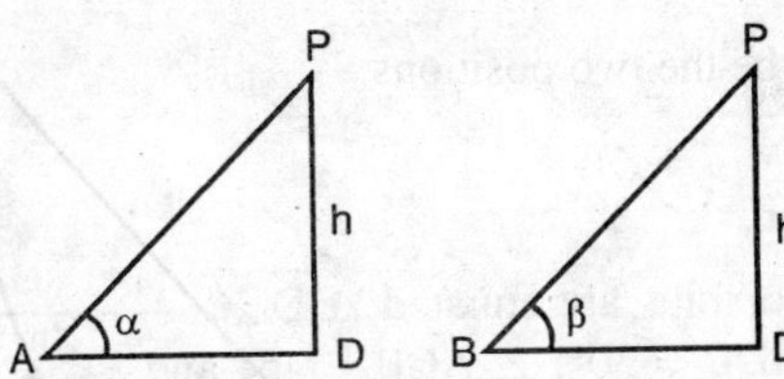

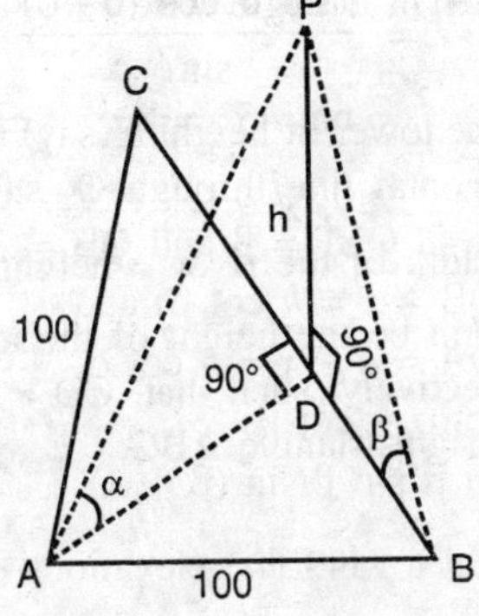

In ΔPAD, $AD = h \cot \alpha$,

In ΔPBD, $BD = h \cot \beta$

In ΔABD,

$AB^2 = AD^2 + BD^2$

$= h^2 (\cot^2 \alpha + \cot^2 \beta)$

$\Rightarrow 100^2 = h^2 \{\cot^2 \alpha + (\text{cosec}^2 \beta - 1)\}$

$\Rightarrow 100^2 = h^2 [(3.2)^2 + (2.6)^2 - 1] = 16h^2$

$\Rightarrow h = 25$ m.

9. Let $CD = h$ unit be the height of the tower and A and B be the two points on the ground, such that $DA = a$; $DB = b$; $\angle DAC = \alpha$ and $\angle DBC = 90° - \alpha$

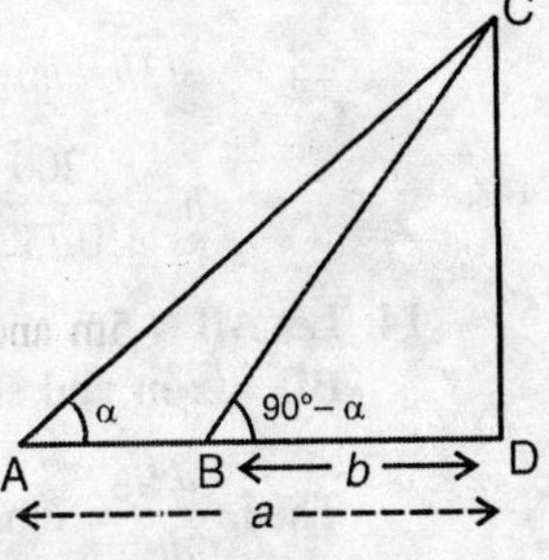

From right triangle ADC, $CD = h = a \tan\alpha$ ...(i)

From right triangle BDC, $CD = h = b \tan(90° - \alpha) = b \cot\alpha$ ...(ii)

Multiplying equations (i) and (ii), we get

$h^2 = a \tan\alpha \,.\, b\cot\alpha$ Hence, $h = \sqrt{ab}$

10. Let $AB = h$ m be the height of cliff and $CD = x$ m be the height of the tower and also $\angle ADB = 60°$ and $\angle ACE = 30°$.

Now, from the figure, $AE = (h - x)$m

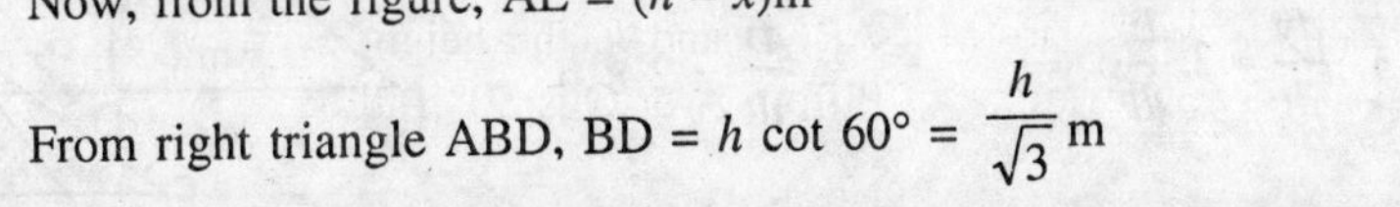

From right triangle ABD, $BD = h \cot 60° = \dfrac{h}{\sqrt{3}}$ m

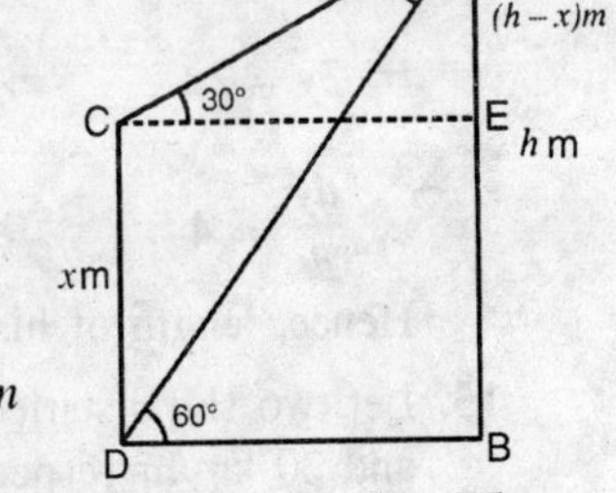

From right triangle CEA, $(h - x) = EC \tan 30° = BD \tan 30°$

$\Rightarrow h - x = \dfrac{h}{\sqrt{3}} \cdot \dfrac{1}{\sqrt{3}}$ $\quad \therefore x = h - \dfrac{h}{3} = \dfrac{2h}{3} m$

11. Let $AB = 75$m be the height of pole and C is a point on the ground such that $BC = 75$m

Now, from right triangle ABC,

$$\tan \alpha = \frac{AB}{BC} = \frac{75}{75}$$

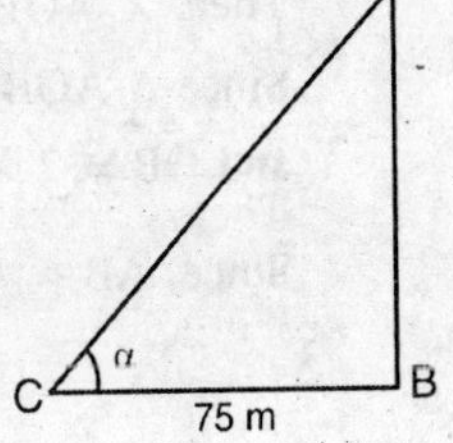

$\Rightarrow \quad \tan\alpha = 1$

$\therefore \quad \alpha = 45°$

12. Let $AB = h$ m be the height of the tower; $BC = x$ m be the breadth of the river and also $\angle ACB = 45°$

Now from right triangle ABC

$$\tan 45° = \frac{h}{x} \quad \Rightarrow 1 = \frac{h}{x}$$

$$\therefore x = h$$

Hence, breadth of the river = height of the tower

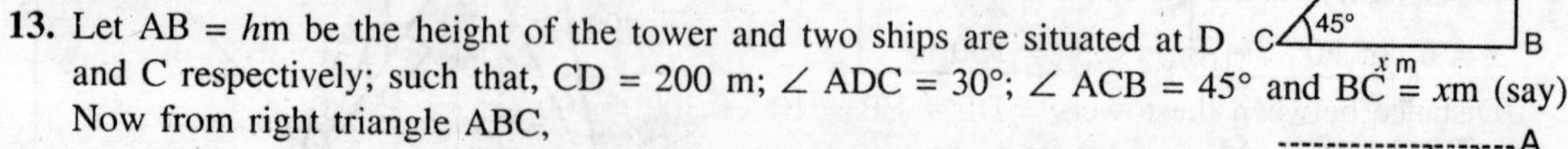

13. Let AB = hm be the height of the tower and two ships are situated at D and C respectively; such that, CD = 200 m; ∠ ADC = 30°; ∠ ACB = 45° and BC = xm (say)

Now from right triangle ABC,

$$\tan 45° = \frac{h}{x} \quad \Rightarrow 1 = \frac{h}{x}$$

$$\therefore \quad x = h$$

Again from right triangle ABD,

$$\text{tam } 30° = \frac{h}{200+x} \quad \Rightarrow \frac{1}{\sqrt{3}} = \frac{h}{200+h} \quad (\because x = h)$$

$$\Rightarrow \quad \sqrt{3}h - h = 200 \quad \Rightarrow h(1.732 - 1) = 200$$

$$\therefore \quad h = \frac{200}{0.732} = 273.2 \text{ m} \quad \simeq 273 \text{ m}$$

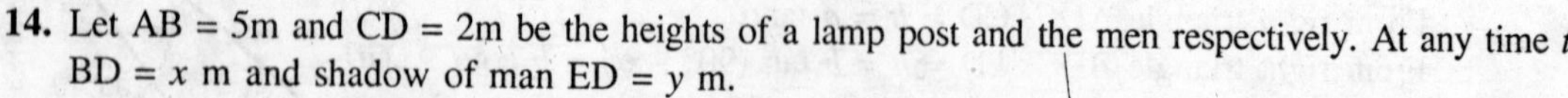

14. Let AB = 5m and CD = 2m be the heights of a lamp post and the men respectively. At any time t BD = x m and shadow of man ED = y m.

Then, $\frac{dx}{dt} = 6$m/min

Now, right triangles ABE and CDE are similar; then

$$\frac{AB}{CD} = \frac{BE}{DE} \quad \Rightarrow \frac{5}{2} = \frac{x+y}{y} \quad \Rightarrow 5y - 2y = 2x$$

$$\Rightarrow 3y = 2x \quad \Rightarrow 3.\frac{dy}{dt} = 2.\frac{dx}{dt} \quad \Rightarrow 3.\frac{dy}{dt} = 2 \times 6$$

$$\therefore \quad \frac{dy}{dt} = 4$$

Hence, length of his shadow increases at the rate of 4m/min.

15. Let two ships started from point O at the speed of 30 km/hr 0 and 20 km/hr respectively, after two hours they reach at points A and B.

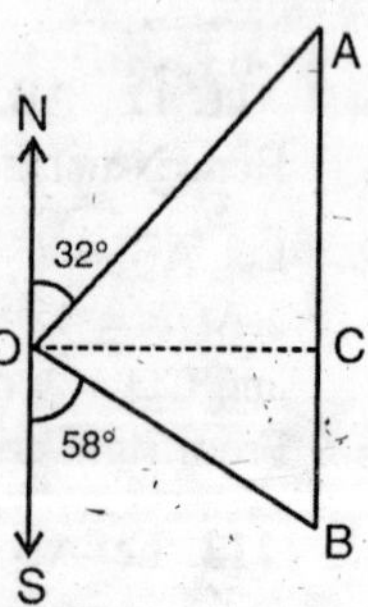

Now, ∠ NOA = 32° and ∠ SOB = 58°,

Then, ∠ AOB = 180° – (32° + 58°) = 90°

Since Δ AOB is a right triangle in which OA = 2 × 30 = 60 km and OB = 2 × 20 = 40 km

$$\text{Since, AB} = \sqrt{OA^2 + OB^2} = \sqrt{(60)^2 + (40)^2}$$

$$= \sqrt{5200} = 20\sqrt{13} \text{ km}$$

16. : Let AB = CD = h m be the heights of the towers. E is a point such that DE = 100m; $\angle CED = 60°$ and $\angle AEB = 30°$

Now, BE = x m (say)

From right triangle CDE,

$h = 100 \tan 60° = 100\sqrt{3}$ m

From right triangle ABE,

$x = h \cot 30° = 100\sqrt{3} \times \sqrt{3} = 300$ m

Distance between the towers = DE + EB = 100 + 300 = 400 m

Height of the tower = $100\sqrt{3}$ m

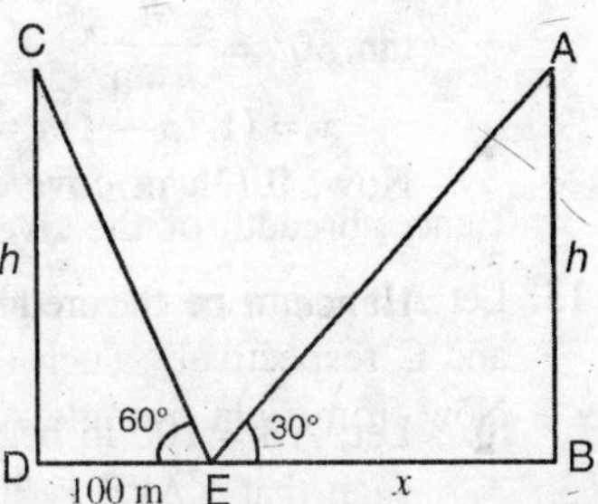

17. : Let AB = h m be the height of the tower; B and C are two points such that BC = 20 m; $\angle ADB = 30°$ and $\angle ACB = 60°$; BC = x m (say)

Now, from right triangle ABC,

$$x = h \cot 60° = \frac{h}{\sqrt{3}} \text{ m}$$

Again, from right triangle ABD,

$$h = (20 + x) \tan 30° = \left(20 + \frac{h}{\sqrt{3}}\right) \times \frac{1}{\sqrt{3}} \quad \left(\because\ x = \frac{h}{\sqrt{3}} \text{m}\right)$$

$$\Rightarrow h - \frac{h}{3} = \frac{20}{\sqrt{3}} \Rightarrow \frac{2h}{3} = \frac{20}{\sqrt{3}} \quad \therefore h = \frac{20 \times 3}{2\sqrt{3}} = 10\sqrt{3} \text{ m}$$

18. : Let AB = 24 ft and CD = 6 ft be the heights of the pillar and man respectively.

Here, $\angle ACE = \alpha$; $\angle CBD = 90° - \alpha$;

Now from right triangle CDB,

$$BD = 6 \cot (90° - \alpha) = 6 \tan\alpha \quad \therefore \tan \alpha = \frac{BD}{6} \quad ...(i)$$

From right triangle ACE,

$$\tan\alpha = \frac{18}{EC} = \frac{18}{BD} \quad ...(ii) \quad (\because EC = BD)$$

Now from *(i)* and *(ii)* we get,

$$\frac{BD}{6} = \frac{18}{BD} \quad \Rightarrow BD^2 = 18 \times 6 \quad \therefore BD = 6\sqrt{3} \text{ ft.}$$

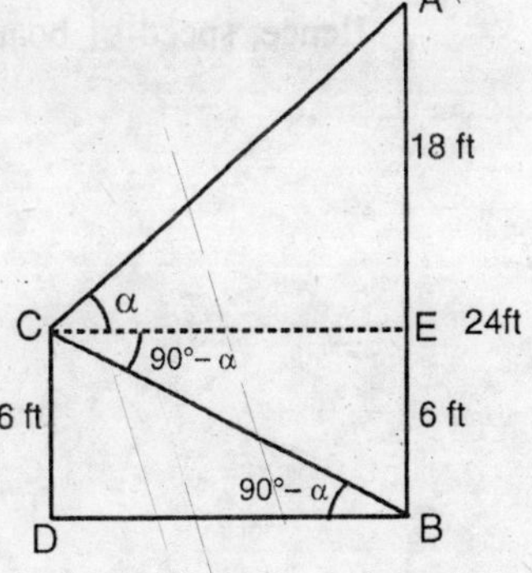

Hence, distance between pillar and man = $6\sqrt{3}$ ft

19. : Let AB = h m be the height of the tower; B and C are two points such that $\angle ACB = 30°$; $\angle ADB = 45°$

and CD = x m (say)

From right triangle ABD,

$$\tan 45° = \frac{h}{BD} \qquad \therefore BD = h \text{ m};$$

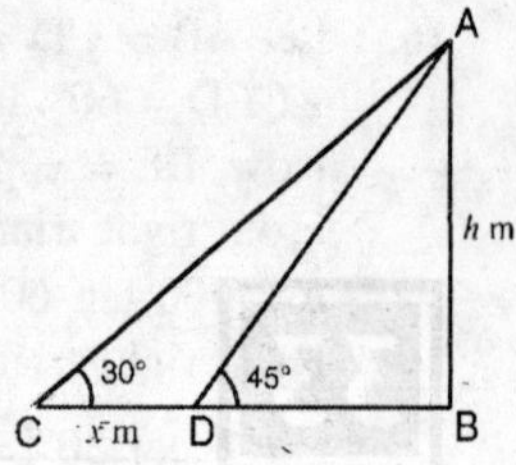

Again from right triangle ABC

$$\tan 30° = \frac{h}{h+x} \qquad \Rightarrow \quad h + x = \sqrt{3}\,h$$

$\therefore \quad x = (1.73 - 1)h = 0.73h$

Now, 0.73h m covered in 12 min

Hence, h m covered in $\frac{12}{0.73} = \frac{1200}{73}$ min $\simeq$ 16 min 23 sec.

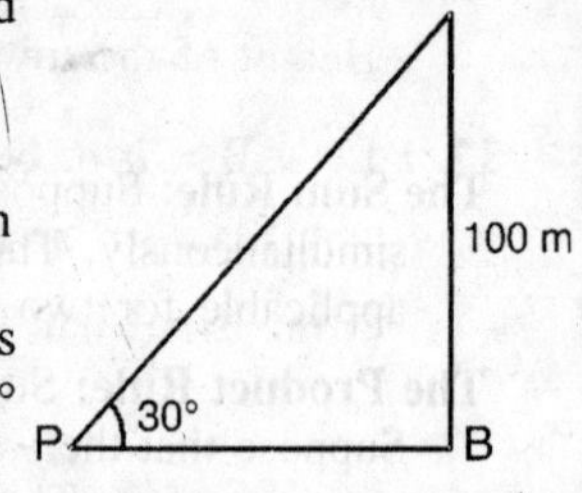

20. : Let, AB = 100 m be the height of a tower, P is a point on the ground such that ∠APB = 30°

From right triangle ABP,

$$BP = 100 \cot 30° = 100\sqrt{3} = 100 \times 1.73 = 173 \text{ m}$$

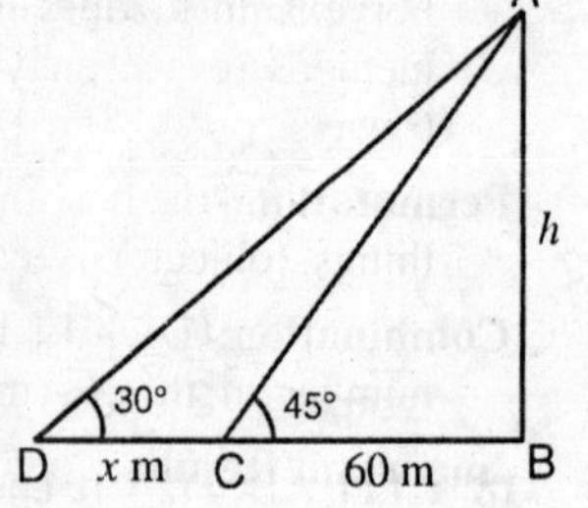

21. : Let AB = h m be the height of the tower; C and D are the two points on the ground such that BC = 60 m; ∠ ACB = 45° and ∠ ADB = 30°

Now from right triangle ABC,

$$\tan 45° = \frac{h}{60} \qquad \Rightarrow 1 = \frac{h}{60} \qquad \therefore h = 60 \text{ m;}$$

Again from right triangle ABD;

$$\tan 30° = \frac{h}{x+60} \qquad \Rightarrow \frac{1}{\sqrt{3}} = \frac{60}{x+60}$$

$$\Rightarrow x + 60 = 60\sqrt{3}$$

$\therefore \; x = 60\,(1.73 - 1) = 43.8\text{m}$

Hence, speed of boat = $\frac{43.8}{5}$ m/s = $\frac{43.8}{5} \times \frac{18}{5} \simeq 31.5$ km/hr.

33 Permutation & Combination

The Sum Rule: Suppose a work A can occur in m ways and B can occur in n ways and both cannot occur simultaneously. Then A or B (at least one of them) can occur in $(m + n)$ ways. This rule is also applicable for two or more exclusive events.

The Product Rule: Suppose there are two works A and B. Let A can occur in m ways and B in n ways. Suppose that the ways for A and B are not related in the sense that B occur in n ways regardless the outcome of A. Then both A and B occur in mn ways.

For example, let there are two questions A and B which can be solved by two methods and three methods respectively. Then A or B can be solved in 2 + 3 = 5 ways and both A and B in 2 × 3 = 6 ways.

Permutation: Each of the arrangements that can be made by taking some or all of a number of dissimilar things (objects) is called permutation.

Combination: Each of the different group or selection which can be made by taking some or all of a number of things (irrespective of order) is called a combination.

Important Results:

(i) Number of permutations of n distinct things taken r at a time, $0 \le r \le n$

$= n(n-1)(n-2)\ldots(n-r+1) = n!/(n-r)! = {}^nP_r$.

This is equivalent to filling r places by r objects taking from n distinct objects.

(ii) The number of permutations of n distinct objects taken all at a time $= n!$

(iii) The number of combinations of n objects taken r at a time, $0 \le r \le n$. $= {}^nC_r = \dfrac{n!}{(n-r)!.r!}$.

(iv) The number of permutations of n dissimilar things taken r at a time when each thing can be repeated any number of times $= n^r$.

(v) The number of combinations of n distinct objects taken r at a time when any object may be repeated any number of times

$=$ coefficient of x^r in $(1 + x + x^2 + \ldots + x^r)^n$

$=$ coefficient of x^r in $(1-x)^n = {}^{n+r-1}C_r$.

(vi) Number of combinations of n distinct things taken r at a time when p particular things always occur $= {}^{(n-p)}C_{(r-p)}$.

(vii) The number of permutations of n distinct things taken r at a time when p particular things always occur $= {}^{(n-p)}C_{(r-p)}.r!$.

(viii) Number of combinations of n distinct things taken r at a time when p particular things never occur $= {}^{(n-p)}C_r$.

(ix) Number of permutations (arrangements) of n distinct things taken r at a time when p particular things never occur = ${}^{(n-p)}C_r.r!$.

(x) Number of permutations of n things, taken all at a time when p_1 are alike of one kind, p_2 are alike of second kind, ..., p_r of them are alike of the r-th kind $p_1 + p_2 + ... + p_r \le n$, and remaining things are all different = $n!/\{p_1!p_2! ... p_r!\}$.

(xi) If $3n$ things are to be divided into three equal groups, then the number of ways = $\dfrac{(3n)!}{n!.n!.n!.3!}$.

(xii) If $3n$ things are to be divided equally between 3 persons (*i.e.*, division of $3n$ things into 3 equal groups with permutation of groups) then the number of ways = $\dfrac{(3n)!}{(n!)^3}$.

(xiii) Greatest value of ${}^nC_r$

${}^nC_r$ is greatest when $r = n/2$ if n is even

$r = (n - 1)/2$ or $(n + 1)/2$ if n is odd.

(xiv) ${}^nC_r = {}^nC_{n-r}$

(xv) ${}^nC_r + {}^nC_{r+1} = {}^{n+1}C_{r+1}$

(xvi) ${}^nC_r = {}^nC_s \Rightarrow r = s$ or $r + s = n$.

(xvii) The number of circular permutations of n different things taken all at a time = $(n - 1)!$

(xviii) The number of arrangements of n persons on a round table = $(n - 1)!$.

(xix) The number of arrangements of n flowers to make a garland = $\dfrac{1}{2}(n - 1)!$.

Example 1: Find the value of ${}^{47}C_4 + \sum_{r=1}^{5} {}^{(52-r)}C_3$.

Solution: The given expression on putting $r = 1, 2, 3, 4, 5$ is

${}^{47}C_4 + {}^{51}C_3 + {}^{50}C_3 + {}^{49}C_3 + {}^{48}C_3 + {}^{47}C_3$ = A, say. Combining 1st and last

${}^{47}C_3 + {}^{47}C_4 = {}^{48}C_4$

$\therefore A = {}^{48}C_4 + {}^{51}C_3 + {}^{50}C_3 + {}^{49}C_3 + {}^{48}C_3$.

Again combining 1st and last

$A = {}^{49}C_4 + {}^{51}C_3 + {}^{50}C_3 + {}^{49}C_3 = {}^{50}C_4 + {}^{51}C_3 + {}^{50}C_3 = {}^{51}C_4 + {}^{51}C_3 = {}^{52}C_4$.

Example 2: If ${}^{15}C_{3r} = {}^{15}C_{r+3}$; find r.

Solution: $\because$ ${}^{15}C_{3r} = {}^{15}C_{r+3}$, $\therefore$ $3r + r + 3 = 15$ $\therefore$ $r = 3$.

Example 3: If ${}^8C_r - {}^7C_3 = {}^7C_2$, find r.

Solution: ${}^8C_r - {}^7C_3 = {}^7C_2$

or, ${}^8C_r = {}^7C_2 + {}^7C_3 = {}^8C_3 = {}^8C_5$

$\therefore$ $r = 3$ or 5.

Example 4: If ${}^{15}C_r : {}^{15}C_{r-1} = 11 : 5$, find r.

Solution: $\dfrac{{}^{15}C_r}{{}^{15}C_{r-1}} = \dfrac{11}{5} \Rightarrow 5 \cdot \dfrac{15!}{r!(15-r)!} = 11 \cdot \dfrac{15!}{(r-1)!(15-r+1)(15-r)!}$

$\Rightarrow \dfrac{5}{r(r-1)!(15-r)!} = \dfrac{11}{(r-1)!(15-r+1)(15-r)!} \Rightarrow 5\,(15 - r + 1) = 11r$

$\Rightarrow 80 = 16r$, $\therefore$ $r = 5$.

Example 5: If ${}^{n}C_6 : {}^{n-3}C_3 = 33:4$, find n.

Solution: $\dfrac{{}^{n}C_6}{{}^{n-3}C_3} = 33/4 \Rightarrow \dfrac{n!}{6!(n-6)!} \cdot \dfrac{3!(n-6)!}{(n-3)!} = \dfrac{33}{4} \Rightarrow \dfrac{n(n-1)(n-2)}{6.5.4} = \dfrac{33}{4}$

$\Rightarrow n(n-1)(n-2) = 30 \times 33 = 11 \times 3 \times 3 \times 10 = 11 \times 10 \times 9 = 11(11-1)(11-2)$

Hence, clearly $n = 11$.

Example 6: If ${}^{10}P_r = 604800$ and ${}^{10}C_r = 120$, find r.

Solution: We know that ${}^{n}P_r = r!.\ {}^{n}C_r$

Put the values of ${}^{n}P_r$ and ${}^{n}C_r$

$\therefore 604800 = r!\ 120$

$r! = 5040 = 24 \times 210 = 4! \times 5 \times 42 = 5! \times 6 \times 7 = 6! \times 7 = 7!.\ \therefore r = 7.$

Example 7: If ${}^{2n+1}P_{n-1} : {}^{2n-1}P_n = 3 : 5$, find n.

Solution: $5 \cdot {}^{2n+1}P_{n-1} = 3.\ {}^{2n-1}P_n$ by given condition

$\therefore 5 \cdot \dfrac{(2n+1)!}{(n+2)!} = 3 \cdot \dfrac{(2n-1)!}{(n-1)!} \Rightarrow 5 \cdot \dfrac{(2n+1)2n \cdot (2n-1)!}{(n+2)(n+1)n \cdot (n-1)!} = 3 \cdot \dfrac{(2n-1)!}{(n-1)!}$

$\Rightarrow 10(2n+1) = 3(n+2)(n+1) \Rightarrow 20n + 10 = 3n^2 + 9n + 6$

$\Rightarrow 3n^2 - 11n - 4 = 0 \therefore (n-4)(3n+1) = 0 \Rightarrow n = 4.$

Example 8: If ${}^{n}P_r = {}^{n}P_{r+1}$ and ${}^{n}C_r = {}^{n}C_{r-1}$, find n and r.

Solution: ${}^{n}P_r = {}^{n}P_{r+1}$

$\therefore \dfrac{n!}{(n-r)!} = \dfrac{n!}{(n-r-1)!} \Rightarrow \dfrac{1}{(n-r)} = 1 \Rightarrow n - r = 1$ ...(1)

${}^{n}C_r = {}^{n}C_{r-1}$

$\therefore r + r - 1 = n \Rightarrow 2r - n = 1$ ...(2)

Solving (1) and (2), we get $r = 2$ and $n = 3$.

Example 9: Evaluate ${}^{15}C_8 + {}^{15}C_9 - {}^{15}C_6 - {}^{15}C_7$.

Solution: $({}^{15}C_8 + {}^{15}C_9) - ({}^{15}C_6 + {}^{15}C_7) = {}^{16}C_9 - {}^{16}C_7 = {}^{16}C_9 - {}^{16}C_{16-7} = {}^{16}C_9 - {}^{16}C_9 = 0,$

$[\because {}^{n}C_r = {}^{n}C_{n-r}]$

Example 10: Prove that ${}^{n}C_r + 2\ {}^{n}C_{r-1} + {}^{n}C_{r-2} = {}^{n+2}C_r$.

Solution: L.H.S. $= {}^{n}C_r + {}^{n}C_{r-1} + {}^{n}C_{r-1} + {}^{n}C_{r-2} = {}^{n+1}C_r + {}^{n+1}C_{r-1} = {}^{n+2}C_r$

Example 11: Prove that ${}^{n-1}C_3 + {}^{n-1}C_4 > {}^{n}C_3$ if $n > 7$.

Solution: ${}^{n-1}C_3 + {}^{n-1}C_4 > {}^{n}C_3 \Rightarrow {}^{n}C_4 > {}^{n}C_3$

$\Rightarrow \dfrac{n!}{(n-4)!\ 4!} > \dfrac{n!}{(n-3)!\ 3!} \Rightarrow \dfrac{1}{4.3!(n-4)!} > \dfrac{1}{3!(n-3)(n-4)!} \Rightarrow \dfrac{1}{4} > \dfrac{1}{n-3}$

$\Rightarrow n - 3 > 4 \qquad \Rightarrow n > 7$

Example 12: If ${}^{n}C_{r-1} = 36$, ${}^{n}C_r = 84$ and ${}^{n}C_{r+1} = 126$, find the values of n and r.

Solution: We have

$\dfrac{84}{36} = \dfrac{{}^{n}C_r}{{}^{n}C_{r-1}} = \dfrac{n-r+1}{r}$ ..(1) and $\dfrac{126}{84} = \dfrac{{}^{n}C_{r+1}}{{}^{n}C_r} = \dfrac{n-r}{r+1}$ ...(2)

From (1), $n - r = \frac{84}{36}r - 1 = \frac{7}{3}r - 1$ ...(3)

Substituting this value of $n - r$ in (2), we get

$$\frac{126}{84} = \frac{1}{r+1}\left(\frac{7}{3}r - 1\right) \Rightarrow \frac{3}{2} = \frac{7r-3}{3(r+1)} \Rightarrow 9(r + 1) = 14r - 6, \text{ giving } r = 3$$

$\therefore$ From (3), $n = \frac{10}{3}\ r - 1 = \frac{10}{3} \times 3 - 1 = 9$

Thus, $n = 9$, $r = 3$.

Example 13: In how many different words ending and beginning with a consonant can be made out of the letters of the word EQUATION?

Solution: 8 letters, *i.e.,* 3 consonants and 5 vowels.
The consonants are to occupy 1st and last place and it can be done in $^3P_2$ ways. We will now be left with 5 vowels and 1 consonant *i.e.* 6 letters which can be arranged in 6! ways. Hence, the number of words under condition is $^3P_2 \times 6! = 6 \times 720 = 4320$.

Example 14: In how many other ways can the letters of the word SIMPLETON be rearranged?

Solution: Nine letters. Total no. of words 9!. Hence no. of other words is $9! - 1$
We have excluded one arrangement, *i.e.,* Simpleton as we want other ways.

Example 15: How many different words can be formed with the letters of the word ORDINATE so that
(a) the vowels occupy odd places
(b) beginning with O
(c) beginning with O and ending with E.

Solution: 4 vowels and 4 consonants. Total 8 letters.
(a) No. of words $= 4! \times 4! = 24 \times 24 = 576$.
Because 4 vowels are to be adjusted in 4 odd places and the 4 consonants in the remaining 4 even places.
(b) 7! ways, O being fixed.
(c) 6! ways, O fixed in 1st and E fixed in last.

Example 16: How many different words can be formed out of the letters of the word MORADABAD taken four at a time?

Solution: In MORADABAD, we have 6 different types of letters 3As, 2Ds and rest four different.
We have to form words of 4 letters.
(i) All different, $^6P_4 = 6 \times 5 \times 4 \times 3 = 360$
(ii) Two different two alike $^2C_1 \times {^5C_2} \times \frac{4!}{2!} = 240$
(iii) 3 alike 1 different $^1C_1 \times {^5C_1} \times \frac{4!}{3!} = 20$
(iv) 2 alike of one type and 2 alike of other type $^2C_2 \times \frac{4!}{2!2!} = 6$
$\therefore$ Total number of words $= 360 + 240 + 20 + 6 = 626$

Example 17: Find the number of different permutations of the letters of the word BANANA.

Solution: BANANA
3A's, 2N's, B, *i.e.,* 6 letters, 3 alike of one type and 2 of another type. Number of words taken all at a time is $\frac{6!}{3!2!} = \frac{6 \times 5 \times 4}{2} = 60$

Example 18: How many different words can be formed out of the letters of the word ALLAHABAD ? In how many of them the vowels occupy the even positions?

Solution: ALLAHABAD.

4A's, 2L's, H, B, D, *i.e.*, 9 letters.

Number of words $\frac{9!}{4!2!} = \frac{9\times8\times7\times6\times5}{2} = 72 \times 105 = 7560.$

There are 4 vowels, and all are alike, *i.e.*, 4A's.

There are 4 even places, *i.e.*, 2nd, 4th, 6th, and 8th.

These 4 even positions can be filled by 4 vowels in $\frac{4!}{4!} = 1$ way.

Now we are left with 5 places in which 5 letters out of which 2L's are alike and rest different can be filled in $\frac{5!}{2!} = 5 \times 4 \times 3 = 60$ ways.

Hence, the total number of words is $60 \times 1 = 60$.

Example 19: How many different words can be formed with the letters of the word HARYANA? In how many of these H and N are together and how many of these begin with H and end with N ?

Solution: HARYANA 7 letters.

3A's, H, R, Y, N.

(i) The number of words = $\frac{7!}{3!} = 7 \times 6 \times 5 \times 4 = 840.$

(ii) Treating H and N together we have $7 - 2 + 1 = 6$ letters out of which three are alike, *i.e.*, A's and hence they can be arranged in $\frac{6!}{3!} = 120$ ways. But H and N can be arranged amongst themselves in $2! = 2$ ways.

Hence, the number of ways is $120 \times 2 = 240$.

(iii) Fixing up H in first and N in last; we have 5 letters out of these three are alike, *i.e.*, A's and hence the number of words is $\frac{5!}{3!} = 5 \times 4 = 20.$

Example 20: Prove that the number of words which can be formed out of the letters *a, b, c, d, e, f* taken 3 together, each word containing one vowel at least is 96.

Solution: Reqd. no of words = $({}^2C_1 \times {}^4C_2 + {}^2C_2 \times {}^4C_1)\, 3! = (12 + 4) \times 6 = 96.$

Example 21: A person wishes to make up as many different parties as he can out of 20 friends, each party consisting of the same number. How many should he invite at a time? In how many of these would the same man be found?

Solution: Since, $n = 20$ is even, ${}^{20}C_r$ is greatest when $r = \frac{20}{2} = 10$. Hence, the maximum number of parties = ${}^{20}C_{10}$. Thus, he should invite 10 friends at a time in order to form the maximum number of parties. Also, the same men will be found in ${}^{19}C_9$ parties.

Example 22: A box contains two white balls, three black balls and four red balls. In how many ways can three balls be drawn from the box if at least one black ball is to be included in the draw?

Solution: The required number of ways = ${}^3C_1 \times {}^6C_2 + {}^3C_2 \times {}^6C_1 + {}^3C_3 = 64$

Example 23: Five persons entered the lift cabin on the ground floor of an 8-floor house. Suppose that each of them independently and with equal probability can leave the cabin at any floor beginning with the first. Find out the probability of all five persons leaving at different floors.

Solution: Besides the ground floor, there are 7 floors. The total number of ways in which each of the five persons can leave the cabin at any of the 7 floors = 7^5. And the favourable number of ways, that is, the number of ways in which 5 persons leave at different floors is $^7P_5$.

∴ The required probability = $^7P_5/7^5$.

Example 24: How many different numbers of six digits each (without repetition of digits) can be formed from the digits 4, 5, 6, 7, 8, 9 ? How many of these are not divisible by 5?

Solution: Here, we have to use all six digits 4, 5, 6, 7, 8, 9.

∴ Number of six - digits numbers = 6! = 720.

Now 5! numbers are divisible by 5 as 5 is fixed in the last place. Hence, the number of numbers which are not divisible by 5 is 6! – 5! = 720 – 120 = 600.

Example 25: How many different numbers of 4 digits can be formed from the ten digits 0, 1, 2, ... 9, no digit being repeated in any number?

Solution: 0, 1, 2, ... 9. Ten digits.

Then required number of 4 - digit numbers = $^{10}P_4 - {}^9P_3$

Where $^9P_3$ corresponds to those numbers which will have zero in the first place

$$= \frac{10\times9\times8\times7\times6!}{6!} - \frac{9\times8\times7\times6!}{6!} = 9 \times 8 \times 7\ (10 - 1) = 81 \times 56 = 4536.$$

Example 26: Find the total number of 9 - digits numbers which have all different digits.

Solution: $^{10}P_9 - {}^9P_8 = \frac{10!}{1!} - \frac{9!}{1!} = 9!\,(10 - 1) = 9\,(9!) = 9 \times (9 \times 8 \times 7 \times 6!) = 81 \times 56 \times 720 =$ 3265920.

Example 27: How many numbers greater than 23000 can be formed from the digits 1, 2, 3, 4, 5?

Solution: The digits are 1, 2, 3, 4, 5. We have to form numbers greater than 23000. Required number will be

= Total – (those beginning with 1) – (those beginning with 21)

= 5! – 4! – 3! = 120 – 24 – 6 = 90.

Example 28: Prove that only 18 numbers with different digits greater than 1000 can be formed from the digits 1, 0, 2, 3.

Solution: The digits are 1, 0, 2, 3. We have to form numbers greater than 1000.

∴ Required number = 4! – 3! (3! for those having 0 in the 1st place) = 24 – 6 = 18.

Example 29: Prove that only 18 numbers can be formed by using all the digits 1, 2, 3, 4, 3, 2, 1 so that the odd digits always occupy the odd places.

Solution: There are 4 odd places and there are 4 odd numbers (2 are alike *i.e.* 1, 1; and 2 are alike, *i.e.*, 3, 3). These can be arranged in four places in $\frac{4!}{2!2!} = \frac{4\times3}{2} = 6$ ways.

There will be 3 even places namely 2nd, 4th and 6th in which 3 even numbers (2 are alike, *i.e.*, 2, 2). These can be arranged in $\frac{3!}{2!} = \frac{3\times2}{2} = 3$ ways.

Hence, the total number of the numbers thus formed is 6 × 3 = 18.

Example 30: How many numbers lying between 99 and 1000 can be formed from the digits 2, 3, 7, 0, 8, 6?

Solution: Digits are 2, 3, 7, 0, 8, 6, *i.e.,* six in all.

We have to form numbers between 99 and 1000. Clearly they will be of three digits and their number will be ${}^6P_3 = \frac{6!}{3!} = 6 \times 5 \times 4 = 120.$

Out of these we have to exclude those numbers by 3 digits which have zero in the first place.

Their number is ${}^5P_2 = \frac{5!}{3!} = 5 \times 4 = 20.$

$\therefore$ The required number = 120 – 20 = 100.

Example 31: How many numbers which are

(i) Even (ii) Less than 40,000, can be formed by taking all the digits 1, 2, 3, 4, 5?

Solution: 1, 2, 3, 4, 5 : 5 digits

(i) Even numbers which will have 2 in the last place = 4! = 24.

Similarly, those which will have 4 in the last place = 4! = 24.

$\therefore$ Total is 24 + 24 = 48.

(ii) Numbers less than 40,000 will have either 1 or 2 or 3 in the first place and hence as above total of such numbers will be 24 + 24 + 24 = 72.

Example 32: How many divisors are there of the numbers a = 38808 exclusive of the divisor 1 and a?

Solution: After factorising, we write the number a as $a = 2^3.3^2.7^2.\ 11$

the total number of divisors = (3 + 1) (2 + 1) (2 + 1) (1 + 1) = 72.

But this includes the divisions by 1 and a.

Hence, the required number of divisors = 72 – 2 = 70.

Example 33: How many natural numbers smaller than 10^4 are there, in the decimal notation of which all the digits are different?

Solution: The required natural numbers consist of 4 digits, 3 digits, 2 digits and one digit so that their number = 9.9.8.7 + 9.9.8 + 9.9 + 9 = 5274.

Example 34: Given five different green dyes, four different blue dyes and three different red dyes, how many combinations of dyes can be chosen taking at least one green and one blue dye?

Solution: At least one green dye can be selected out of five green dyes in $2^5 - 1$, *i.e.,* in 31 ways. Similarly, at least one blue dye can be selected out of 4 in $2^4 - 1$ *i.e.,* in 15 ways. And at least one red or no red dye can be selected in 2^3, *i.e.,* in 8 ways.

Hence, the required number of ways 31 × 15 × 8 = 3720.

Example 35: If some or all of n things be taken at a time, prove that the number of combinations is $2^n - 1$.

Solution: Each of the things can be taken or left out *i.e.* each gives two ways. So the combinations of n things will be 2 × 2 × 2 × ..... n factors = 2^n. But this includes the case when all have been left out. So the number of combinations is $2^n - 1$.

Example 36: In how many ways can 10 balls be divided between two boys, one receiving two and the other eight balls?

Solution: When A receives 2 and B gets 8, then $\frac{(10!)}{2!\cdot 8!} = 45,$

When A receives 8 and B gets 2, then also $\frac{(10!)}{2!\cdot 8!} = 45.$

$\therefore$ Total is 45 + 45 = 90.

Example 37: In how many ways can a pack of 52 cards be
(a) divided equally among four players in order?
(b) formed into 4 groups of 13 cards each?
(c) In 4 sets, three of them having 17 cards each and the fourth just 1 card?

Solution: *(a)* $\dfrac{52!}{(13!)^4}$ *(b)* $\dfrac{52!}{(13!)^4\,4!}$ *(c)* $\dfrac{52!}{(17!)^3\ 1!\ 3!}$

Example 38: Find the number of ways of dividing 15 things into groups of 8, 4 and 3 respectively.

Solution: $\dfrac{15!}{8!\ 4!\ 3!}$

Example 39: There are 3 copies each of 4 different books. In how many ways can they be arranged in a shelf?

Solution: $\dfrac{12!}{(3!)^4}$ [since there are 4 sets of 3 alike books.]

Example 40: In how many ways can three letters be posted in four letter boxes in a village? If all the three letters are not posted in the same letter box, find the corresponding number of ways of posting.

Solution: We can post the first letter in 4 ways and 2nd too in 4 ways, as well as the third. Therefore the total number of ways is $4 \times 4 \times 4 = 64$.
All the three letters can be posted in any of the four letter boxes in 4 ways.
Hence, the corresponding number when all are not posted in the same letter box is $64 - 4 = 60$.

Example 41: Three men have 4 coats, 5 waist coats and 6 caps. In how many ways can they wear them?

Solution: ${}^4P_3 \times {}^5P_3 \times {}^6P_3 = 172800$.

Example 42: There are 12 points in a plane of which 5 are collinear. Find (i) the number of straight lines obtained by joining these points in pairs (ii) the number of triangles that can be formed with vertices at these points.

Solution: *(i)* No. of lines = ${}^{12}C_2 - {}^5C_2 + 1 = 66 - 10 + 1 = 57$.
(ii) No. of $\Delta^s = {}^{12}C_3 - {}^5C_3 = 220 - 10 = 210$.

Example 43: Find the number of *(i) diagonals,* *(ii) triangles formed in a decagon.*

Solution: *(i)* ${}^{10}C_2 - 10 = 45 - 10 = 35$ *(ii)* ${}^{10}C_3 = \dfrac{10!}{3!\ 7!} = \dfrac{10 \times 9 \times 8}{6} = 120$.

Example 44: Show that the number of diagonals of a polygon of n sides is $n\ (n - 3)/2$.

Solution: The number of lines each joining 2 out of the n points is ${}^nC_2 = \dfrac{n!}{2!(n-2)!} = \dfrac{n(n-1)}{2}$.

Hence, the required no. of diagonals $= \dfrac{n(n-1)}{2} - n = \dfrac{n(n-3)}{2}$

Example 45: How many different signals can be given by using any number of flags from six flags of different colours?

Solution: By alteration in the arrangement of flags the signals will change. So we have to find permutations *i.e.* arrangements of flags. We are at liberty to use any number of flags at a time. Therefore, the required number of signals is
${}^6P_1 + {}^6P_2 + {}^6P_3 + {}^6P_4 + {}^6P_5 + {}^6P_6 = 6 + 30 + 120 + 360 + 720 + 720 = 1956.$

Example 46: A businessman hosts a dinner of 21 guests. He is having 2 round tables which can accomodate 15 and 6 persons each. In how many ways can he arrange the guests?

Solution: Out of 21, we can choose 15 for one table in $^{21}C_{15}$ ways and for each selection we are left with 6 guests for the second table having 6 seats. This can be chosen $^{6}C_{6}$ ways. Now 15 for table A can be arranged in (14)! ways and 6 for table B can be arranged in 5! ways. Hence, the total number is $^{21}C_{15} \times {}^{6}C_{6} \times 14! \times 5!$

Example 47: A round table conference is to be held between 20 delegates of 2 countries. In how many ways can they be seated if two particular delegates are *(i)* always to sit together *(ii)* or never to sit together?

Solution: *(i)* $(18)! \times 2! = 2\,(18)!$ *(ii)* $(19)! - 2\,(18)!$

Example 48: 20 persons were invited for a party. In how many ways can they and the host be seated at a circular table? In how many of these ways will two particular persons be seated on either side of the host?

Solution: 20 guest + 1 host = 21 persons. They can be seated in (20)! ways. Treat the host and two particular persons as one unit. So we have now 21–3 + 1 = 19 and the number of arrangements will be (18)!. But these two persons can be arranged on either side of the host in 2 ways. Hence, there will be 2 (18)! ways.

Example 49: A box contains two white balls, three black balls and 4 red balls. In how many ways can three balls be drawn from the box if at least one black ball is to be included in the draw?

Solution: Total no. of ways of selecting any three balls = $^{9}C_{3}$ and the no. of ways of selecting 3 non-black balls = $^{6}C_{3}$.

Hence, the number of ways of selecting at least one black ball

$$= {}^{9}C_{3} - {}^{6}C_{3} = \frac{9 \cdot 8 \cdot 7}{1 \cdot 2 \cdot 3} - \frac{6 \cdot 5 \cdot 4}{1 \cdot 2 \cdot 3} = 84 - 20 = 64.$$

Example 50: Find the number of ways of selecting 10 clerks from 27 male 17 female applicants if the selection is to consist of either all males or all females.

Solution: Males Females

$^{27}C_{10}$ + $^{17}C_{10}$.

Example 51: There are 16 vacancies for clerks in a certain office. 20 applications are received. In how many ways can the clerks be appointed? How many times may a particular candidate be selected?

Solution: $^{20}C_{16} = 4845$, $^{19}C_{15} = 3876$.

Example 52: To fill 12 vacancies there are 25 candidates of which 5 are from scheduled castes. If 3 of the vacancies are reserved for scheduled caste candidates while the rest are open to all, find the number of ways in which the selection can be made.

Solution: $5C_3 \times {}^{22}C_9 = 4974200$.

Example 53: A candidate is required to answer 6 out of 10 questions which are divided into two groups each containing 5 questions and he is not permitted to attempt more than 4 from each group. In how many ways can he make up his choice?

Solution: Group A5, Group B5, Questions to be attempted 6 but not more than 4 from any group

(4A, 2B), (3A, 3B), (2A, 4B)

$5C_4 \times {}^{5}C_2 + {}^{5}C_3 \times {}^{5}C_3 + {}^{5}C_2 \times {}^{5}C_4$

$= 50 + 100 + 50 = 200.$

Example 54: m men and n women are to be seated in a row so that no two women sit together. If $m > n$, then show that the number of ways in which they can be seated is $m!\,(m + 1)!/(m - n + 1)!$

Solution: m men can be arranged in $m!$ ways in a row and we have now $(m + 1)$ places in which n women can be arranged in ${}^{m+1}P_n = \dfrac{(m+1)!}{(m+1-n)!}$ ways.

Hence, required number of ways $= \dfrac{m!(m+1)!}{(m+1-n)!}$

EXERCISE

1. If ${}^9P_5 + 5.{}^9P_4 = {}^{10}P_r$, then r = ?
(a) 4 (b) 5 (c) 9 (d) 10

2. If ${}^nC_r + {}^nC_{r+1} = {}^{n+1}C_x$, then x = ?
(a) r (b) $r - 1$ (c) n (d) $r + 1$

3. The product of r consecutive positive integers, divided by $r!$, is:
(a) a proper fraction (b) equal to r (c) a positive integer (d) None of these

4. All the letters of the word EAMCET are arranged in possible ways. The number of such arrangement in which not two vowels are adjacent to each other is:
(a) 360 (b) 144 (c) 72 (d) 54

5. The number of arrangements which can be made by using all the letters of the word LAUGH, if the vowels are adjacent, is:
(a) 10 (b) 24 (c) 48 (d) 120

6. There are 10 persons named A, B, ...K. We have the capacity to accommodate only 5. In how many ways can we arrange them in a line if A is must and G and H must not be included in the team of 5?
(a) ${}^8P_5$ (b) ${}^7P_5$ (c) ${}^7C_3 . (4!)$ (d) ${}^7C_3 (5!)$

7. Let A be a set containing 10 distinct elements, then the total number of distinct functions from A to A is:
(a) 10! (b) 10^{10} (c) 2^{10} (d) $2^{10} - 1$

8. There are 10 lamps in a hall. Each one of them can be switched on independently. The number of ways in which the hall can be illuminated is:
(a) 10^2 (b) 1023 (c) 210 (d) 10!

9. How many 10 digits numbers can be written by using the digits 1 and 2?
(a) ${}^{10}C_1 + {}^9C_2$ (b) 2^{10} (c) ${}^{10}C_2$ (d) 10!

10. The number of 4 digit numbers, that can be formed by the digits 3, 4, 5, 6, 7, 8, 0, no digit is being repeated is:
(a) 720 (b) 840 (c) 280 (d) None of these

11. Five digit numbers are formed with 0, 1, 2, 3, 4. The number of numbers in which at least one digit is repeated is:
(a) 96 (b) 120 (c) 2500 (d) 2404

12. The number of positive integers greater than 6000 but not more than 7000, divisible by 5, using the digits 0, 1, 2, ... 9, any digits can be used any number of times, is:
(a) 200 (b) 112 (c) 119 (d) None of these

13. The expression 1.1! + 2.2! + ... + $n.n!$ is equal to:
(a) $(n+1)!$ *(b)* $(n+1)!+1$ *(c)* $(n+1)!-1$ *(d)* $(n+1)!-n!$

14. A five digit number divisible by 3 is to be formed using the numbers 0, 1, 2, 3, 4 and 5 without repetitions. The total number of ways this can be done is:
(a) 216 *(b)* 600 *(c)* 240 *(d)* 3125

15. Everybody in a room shakes hands with everybody else. The total number of hand shakes is 66. The total number of person in the room is:
(a) 11 *(b)* 12 *(c)* 8 *(d)* 14

16. A polygon has 44 diagonals, then the number of its side are:
(a) 11 *(b)* 7 *(c)* 8 *(d)* None of these

17. A cricket team of 11 players is to be selected from 13 players; 4 of which are bowlers and 2 wicket keepers. The number of ways to select the team, consisting one wicket keeper and at least 3 bowlers, is:
(a) 8 *(b)* 22 *(c)* 112 *(d)* None of these

18. A box contains two white, three red and four black balls. If at least one red ball is to be included in the draw, the number of ways of drawing 3 balls is given by (all balls are considered to be different):
(a) 45 *(b)* 64 *(c)* 63 *(d)* 46

19. The sides AB, BC, CA of a triangle ABC have 3, 5 and 6 interior points respectively on them. The number of triangles that can be constructed using these points as vertices is given by:
(a) 364 *(b)* 333 *(c)* 240 *(d)* None of these

20. Out of 18 points in a plane, no three are in the same straight line except five points which are collinear. The number of straight lines that can be formed joining them is:
(a) 143 *(b)* 144 *(c)* 153 *(d)* None of these

21. The number of triangles that are formed by choosing the vertices from a set of 12 points, seven of which lie on the same straight line, are:
(a) 105 *(b)* 115 *(c)* 175 *(d)* 185

22. The straight lines l_1, l_2, l_3 are parallel and lie in the same plane. A total number of m points are taken on l_1; n points on l_2, k points on l_3. The maximum number of triangles formed with vertices at these points are:
(a) ${}^{m+n+k}C_3$ *(b)* ${}^{m+n+k}C_3 - {}^{m}C_3 - {}^{n}C_3 - {}^{k}C_3$
(c) ${}^{m}C_3 + {}^{n}C_3 + {}^{k}C_3$ *(d)* None of these

23. The number of ways in which $4n$ students can be distributed equally among 4 sections is given by:
(a) $\dfrac{(4n)!}{n!}$ *(b)* $\dfrac{(4n)!}{4!n!}$ *(c)* $\dfrac{(4n)!}{(n!)^4}$ *(d)* $\dfrac{(4n)!}{4!(n!)^4}$

24. The number of ways in which 5 prizes be distributed among 4 boys, while each boy is capable of having any number of prizes is:
(a) 6^4 *(b)* 4^5 *(c)* $4!\,.\,2^4$ *(d)* $6\,.\,(4!)$

25. In an examination there are three multiple choice questions and each question has 4 choices. Number of ways in which a student can fail to get all answers correct, is:
(a) 11 *(b)* 12 *(c)* 27 *(d)* 63

26. The number of ways in which a team of eleven players can be selected from 22 players, always including 2 of them and excluding 4 of them, is:
(a) $^{16}C_{11}$ (b) $^{16}C_5$ (c) $^{16}C_9$ (d) $^{20}C_9$

27. The number of divisors of 9600 including 1 and 9600 are:
(a) 60 (b) 58 (c) 48 (d) 46

28. 7 men and 7 women are to sit round a table so that there is a man on either side of a woman. The number of seating arrangement is:
(a) $(7!)^2$ (b) $(6!)^2$ (c) $6! \times 7!$ (d) 7!

29. The number of 5-digit telephone numbers having at least one of their digits repeated is:
(a) 90000 (b) 10000 (c) 30240 (d) 69760

30. Set A contains n elements. A subset P of A is chosen. The set A is reconstructed by replacing the elements of P. A subset Q of A is again chosen. The number of ways of choosing P and Q so that $P \cap Q = \phi$ is:
(a) 2^n (b) 3^n (c) $2^n - 1$ (d) None of these

31. There are m points on a straight line AB and n points on another line AC, none of them being the point A. Triangles are formed from these points as vertices when (i) A is excluded (ii) A is included. Then the ratio of the number of triangles in the two cases is:
(a) $\dfrac{m+n-2}{m+n}$ (b) $\dfrac{m+n-2}{2}$ (c) $\dfrac{m+n-2}{m+n+2}$ (d) None of these

32. There are 60 greeting cards and 60 envelopes both marked 1 to 60. The number of ways in which the greeting cards can be put in the envelope so that exactly one of them is put in a wrong envelope is:
(a) (59)! (b) 3540 (c) (60)! – 1 (d) None of these

33. The number of times the digit 5 will be written when listing the integers from 1 to 1000 is:
(a) 271 (b) 272 (c) 300 (d) None of these

34. The number of triangles whose angular points are at the angular points of a given octagon, but none of whose sides are the sides of the octagon is:
(a) 56 (b) 24 (c) 16 (d) None of these

35. The number of ways in which we can choose a committee from four men and six women so that the committee includes at least two men and at least twice as many women as men is:
(a) 94 (b) 126 (c) 136 (d) None of these

36. Ten persons are to speak at a meeting. The number of ways in which it can be arranged if A wants to speak before B and B wants to speak before C, is:
(a) $\dfrac{10!}{3}$ (b) 7! (c) 10!/6 (d) $7! \times 3!$

SOLUTIONS

1. From the given relation,

$$\frac{9!}{4!}+5.\frac{9!}{5!}=\frac{(10)!}{(10-r)!} \Rightarrow \frac{2.9!}{4!}=\frac{10.9!}{(10-r)!}$$

$\Rightarrow (10-r)! = 5.4! = 5! \Rightarrow 10 - r = 5 \Rightarrow r = 5.$

2. $^{n+1}C_x = {}^nC_r + {}^nC_{r+1} = {}^{n+1}C_{r+1}$
$\Rightarrow x = r + 1.$

3. Consider r consecutive positive integers
$n + 1, ..., n + r - 1, n + r$

Then $\dfrac{(n+1)...(n+r)}{r!} = \dfrac{n!(n+1)...(n+r)}{n!r!}$

$= {}^{n+r}C_r$, which is a positive integer.

4. First we place 3 consonant in 3! ways and then at four places (2 between them and 2 on sides) 3 vowels in which one vowel is repeated can be placed in ${}^4P_3/2!$ ways.
Hence, required number = $3!.{}^4P_3/2! = 72$.

5. Considering two vowels together as a letter, there are 4 letters in all which can be arranged in 4! ways while 2 vowels can also be arranged in 2! ways.
∴ Total number of arrangements
= 4!.2! = 48.

6. Out of 10 persons, A is in and G and H are out of the team, so we have to select 4 more from 7 remaining. This can be done in ${}^7C_4$ ways. These 5 persons can be arranged in a line in 5! ways.
Hence, the number of possible arrangements is
${}^7C_4.5! = {}^7C_3.(5!)$.

7. Every element of the set A can be joined to ten elements of the set.
∴ Total number of mapping = 10^{10}.

8. Each bulb has two choices, either switched on or off.
∴ Required number = $2^{10} - 1 = 1023$
(Since in one way, when all switches are off, the hall will not be illuminated.)

9. Since each place of 10 digit number can be filled by 2 digits in two ways.
∴ Required number = 2^{10}

10. * * * *
Required number = 6 × 6 × 5 × 4 = 720.

11. If repetitions are allowed, the number of 5 digit numbers formed by 0, 1, 2, 3 and 4 is
* * * * *
4 × 5 × 5 × 5 × 5 = 2500
Number of numbers of 5 digits without repetition =
* * * * *
4 × 4 × 3 × 2 × 1 = 96
Hence, the number of numbers in which atleast one digit is repeated = 2500 – 96 = 2404

12. Any number, divisible by 5, should have 0 or 5 at unit place. Consider the numbers greater than or equal to 6000 and less than 7000. Such numbers can be counted as follows.
* * * *
(6) (0 or 5)
1 × 10 × 10 × 2 = 200.

13. $1.1! + 2.2! + 3.3! + ... + n.n!$
$= \{2.1! + 3.2! + 4.3! + ... + (n + 1)n!\} - \{1! + 2! + 3! + ... + n!\}$
$= (2! + 3! + ... + (n + 1)!) - (1! + 2! + ... + n!)$
$= (n + 1)! - 1$

14. The number is divisible by 3 if the sum of all its digits is divisible by 3.
Here sum of all six digits is 15. The sum of five digits will also be divisible by 3 if we leave either 0 or 3 from the six digits.
Leaving 3, total no. of numbers = 5! – 4!.
(Since the number having 0 as first place are of four digits like 01245).
And leaving 0, total no. of number = 5!.
Hence, the required number = (5! – 4!) + 5! = 216.

15. Let there be n persons in a room.
$\therefore$ Total no. of shakehands = ${}^nC_2 = 66$
$\Rightarrow \frac{1}{2}n(n-1) = 66 \Rightarrow n^2 - n - 132 = 0$
$\Rightarrow (n + 11)(n - 12) = 0$
$\therefore \; n = 12 \qquad (\because n \neq -11)$

16. If n is the number of sides, then the no. of diagonals = ${}^nC_2 - n = 44$
$\Rightarrow \frac{1}{2}n(n-1) - n = 44$
$\Rightarrow (n - 11)(n + 8) = 0$
$\therefore n = 11. \qquad (\because n \neq -8)$

17. There are two cases:
Case I. 3 bowlers : In this case, we have

W. Keeper		Bowlers		Others
1 from 2		3 from 4		7 from remaining 7
${}^2C_1$	×	${}^4C_3$	×	${}^7C_7 = 8$ ..... (1)

Case II. 4 bowlers : In this case, we have

W. Keeper		Bowlers		Others
1 from 2		4 from 4		6 from 7
${}^2C_1$	×	${}^4C_4$	×	${}^7C_6 = 14$ ..... (2)

Adding (1) and (2), we get the required number of selections = 8 + 14 = 22

18.

Red balls (3)	Others (6)	Ways
1	2	${}^3C_1 \times {}^6C_2 = 45$
2	1	${}^3C_2 \times {}^6C_1 = 18$
3	×	${}^3C_3 = 1$
		Total = 64

19. Selection of 3 points from given 14 pts can be made in ${}^{14}C_3 = 364$ ways.
But selection of 3 points from the points on one line cannot give any triangle. Such selections are ${}^3C_3 + {}^5C_3 + {}^6C_3 = 1 + 10 + 20 = 31$..... (2)
Hence total number of triangles that can be formed = 364 – 31 = 333.

20. The number of st. lines $= {}^{18}C_2 - ({}^5C_2 - 1) = 144$.

21. Total no. of Δ's = ${}^{12}C_3 - {}^7C_3 = 185$
(Since when all 3 points on a line are joined, then no Δ is formed.)

22. Total no. of points are $m + n + k$. The Δ's formed by these points = ${}^{m+n+k}C_3$.
Joining 3 points on the same point gives no triangle, such Δ's are ${}^mC_3 + {}^nC_3 + {}^kC_3$.
$\therefore$ Required number
$= {}^{m+n+k}C_3 - {}^mC_3 - {}^nC_3 - {}^kC_3$.

23. The number of ways = ${}^{4n}C_n . {}^{3n}C_n . {}^{2n}C_n . {}^{n}C_n$

$= \frac{(4n)!}{(3n)!n!} . \frac{(3n)!}{(2n)!n!} . \frac{(2n)!}{(n!)(n!)} .1 = (4n)!/(n!)^4.$

24. Since every prize can be given by any of the four boys, so number of ways

$= \dot{4} \times \dot{4} \times \dot{4} \times \dot{4} \times \dot{4} = 4^5.$

25. Each question can be answered in 4 ways and all questions can be answered correctly in only one way, so the required number of ways

$= 4^3 - 1 = 63.$

26. Leaving 4 from 22, we have to select 9 from the remaining

$22 - 4 - 2 = 16$ players

$\therefore$ No. of selection = ${}^{16}C_9$.

27. $\because$ $9600 = 2^7 \times 3 \times 5^2$

$\therefore$ No. of divisors

$= (7 + 1) \times (1 + 1) \times (2 + 1) = 48.$

28. First the seven women sit round the table in 6! ways and then seven men will sit in the spaces between every pair of two women in 7! ways.

$\therefore$ Required seating arrangements = $6! \times 7!$.

29. A telephone number can be started with zero. Therefore the number of numbers with atleast one digit repeated

$= 10^5 - {}^{10}P_5 = 10^5 - (10.9.8.7.6)$

$= 69760$

30. Let A = $\{a_1, a_2, \ldots , a_n\}$

For $a_1 \in$ A, we have the following choices:

(i) $a_i \in$ P; $a_i \in$ Q

(ii) $a_i \in$ P; $a_i \notin$ Q

(iii) $a_i \notin$ P; $a_i \in$ Q

(iv) $a_i \notin$ P; $a_i \notin$ Q

Out of these only *(ii)*, *(iii)* and *(iv)* imply $a_i \notin P \cap Q$. Hence, the number of ways in which none of $a_1, a_2, \ldots , a_n$ belong to $P \cap Q$ is 3^n.

31. Case I: When A is excluded.

Number of triangles = selection of (2 points from AB) (one point from AC) + selection of (one point from AB) (two points from AC)

$= {}^{m}C_2 \, {}^{n}C_1 + {}^{m}C_1 \, {}^{n}C_2 = \frac{1}{2}(m + n - 2)mn$ ..... (1)

Case II: When A is included.

The triangles with one vertex at A, one point from AB and one point from AC = mn are to be added in first case.

$\therefore$ Number of triangles

$= mn + \frac{1}{2} mn(m + n - 2)$

$= \frac{1}{2} mn\,(m + n)$ ..... (2)

$\therefore$ Required ratio = $(m + n - 2)/(m + n)$.

32. : Suppose card number p is placed in envelope number q, then card number q must be placed in a wrong envelope. Hence, at least two cards must be placed in wrong envelope if all of them are not kept in their corresponding envelopes.

33. : Since 5 does not occur in 1000, we have to count the number of times 5 occurs when we list the integers from 1 to 999. Any number between 1 and 999 is of the form xyz, $0 \le x, y, z \le 9$.
The number in which 5 occurs exactly once = $(^3C_1) \times 9 \times 9 = 243$.
The numbers in which 5 occurs exactly twice = $(^3C_2 \times 9) = 27$.
The numbers in which 5 occurs in all three digits = 1.
Hence, the number of times 5 occurs is
$1 \times 243 + 2 \times 27 + 3 \times 1 = 300$

34. : Consider the vertices of octagon as

$A_1, A_2, ..., A_8$

Triangles having only one side of the triangle as side of the octagon.
Consider this side as A_1A_2. Then third vertex may be any one from A_4, A_5, A_6, A_7 (adjacent vertices A_3 and A_8 are to be excluded). So number of triangles with one side A_1A_2 = 4.
∴ Number of triangles with one side as side of octagon = 8.4 = 32.
Now the number of triangles having 2 sides of octagon as their sides
= 8, $[A_1A_2A_3, A_2A_3A_4, ..., A_3A_1A_2]$
Also the number of all possible triangles
= $^8C_3 = 56$
Hence, required number = 56 − 32 − 8 = 16.

35. : We have the following pattern:

M	W	Ways
2	4	$^4C_2 . ^6C_4 = 90$
2	5	$^4C_2 . ^6C_5 = 36$
2	6	$^4C_2 . ^6C_6 = 6$
3	6	$^4C_3 . ^6C_6 = 4$

∴ Total number of ways = 136

36. : Number of arrangements of 10 persons is (10)!. In these arrangement A,B,C are also permuted 3! = 6 times, but ABC has a fixed order. Hence, the number of required arrangements is (10)!/6.

34 PROBABILITY

Random Experiment: If the result of an experiment is not certain and is any one of the several possible outcomes, the experiment is called a trial or a random experiment.

Sample Space: The set of all possible outcome of an experiment is called the sample space provided no two or more of these outcomes can occur simultaneously and exactly one of these outcomes must occur whenever the experiment is conducted.

Events: The outcomes of an experiment, *i.e.*, sample points of the sample space are usually known as simple events and any subset of the sample space 'S' is called an event.

Thus throwing of a dice is an experiment, S = {1, 2, 3, 4, 5, 6} is the sample space, {1}, ... {6} are simple events and {1, 2}, etc., are events. The empty set ϕ is also an event as $\phi \subset S$ and it is called an impossible event. The sample space S is also a subset of S and so it is also an event. S represents the sure event, *i.e.*, certainty.

Equally Likely Events: A set of events is said to be equally likely if taking into consideration all the relevant factors there is no reason to expect one of them in preference to others.

For example, when a fair coin is tossed, the occurrence of a tail or a head are equally likely.

Exhaustive Events: A set of events is said to be exhaustive if the performance of the experiment always results in the occurrence of atleast one of them.

For example, if we throw a dice, then the events $A_1 = \{1, 2\}$, $A_2 = \{2, 3, 3\}$ are not exhaustive as we can get 5 as outcome of the experiment which is not the member of any of the events A_1 and A_2. If we consider the events $E_1 = \{1, 2, 3\}$ and $E_2 = \{2, 4, 5, 6\}$, then the set E_1, E_2, is exhaustive.

Mutually Exclusive Events: A set of events is said to be mutually exclusive if they have no point in common, *i.e.*, happening of one of them eliminates the happening of any of the remaining events. Thus $E_1, E_2, E_3, \ldots$ are mutually exclusive iff $E_i \cap E_j = \phi$ for $i \neq E_1$ and E_2 are mutually exclusive.

Complement of An Events: The complement of an event A, denoted by $\overline{A}$, A' or A^c, is the set of all sample points of the space other than the sample points in A.

e.g., In the experiment of throwing a fair dice, S = {1, 2, 3, 4, 5, 6}. If A = {1, 3, 5, 6}, then $\overline{A} = \{2, 4\}$
Note that $A \cap \overline{A} = S$.

Classical Definition of Probability: If there are n exhaustive mutually exclusive and equally likely outcomes of an experiment and m of them are favourable to an event A, the probability of the happening of A is defined as the ratio m/n.
Thus, denoting the probability of the happening of an event A by p, we have $p = m/n$.

Clearly p is a positive number not greater than unity, so that $0 \leq p \leq 1$.

Since the number of cases in which the event A will not happen is $n - m$, the probability q that the event will not happen is given by $q = \frac{(n-m)}{n} = 1 - \frac{m}{n} = 1 - p. \therefore p + q = 1$

If probability of happening of an event A is 1, then A is certain event and if probability of happening of an event A is 0, then A is impossible event.

Odds in Favour and Odds against an Event: As a result of an experiment if a of the outcomes are favourable to an event E and b of the outcomes are against it, then we say that odds are a to b in favour of E or odds are b to a against E.

Thus, odds in favour of an event E = $\frac{\text{number of favourable cases}}{\text{number of unfavourable cases}}$.

Similarly, odds against an event E = $\frac{\text{number of unfavourable cases}}{\text{number of favourable cases}}$.

If odds in favour of an event are $a : b$ then the probability of the occurrence of that event is $\frac{a}{a+b}$ and the probability of the non-occurrence of that event is $\frac{b}{(a+b)}$.

Addition Theorem:

(a) If 'A' and 'B' are any two events in a sample space S, then $P(A \cup B) = P(A) + P(B) - P(A \cap B)$.

(b) If 'A' and 'B' are mutually exclusive then $P(A \cap B) = 0$ so that $P(A \cup B) = P(A) + P(B)$.

(c) If A is any event in S, then $P(A') = 1 - P(A)$.

Total Probability Theorem: The probability that one of several mutually exclusive events $A_1, A_2, ..., A_n$ will happen, is the sum of the probabilities of the separate events. In symbol,

$P(A_1 + A_2 + ... + A_n) = P(A_1) + P(A_2) + ... + P(A_n)$.

Conditional Probability: The probability of B under the assumption that A has occurred is called the conditional probability of B under the condition that the event A has taken place and is denoted by P(B/A). P(B/A) is read as "probability at the event B given A^B."

Conditional Probability Theorem: If A and B are any two events in the sample space S, the conditional probability of B relative to A is given by $P(B/A) = \frac{P(B \cap A)}{P(A)} = \frac{n(B \cap A)}{n(A)}, A \neq \phi$.

Some Important Remarks about Coins, Dice and Playing Cards:

(a) **Coins:** A coin has a head side and a tail side. If an experiment consist of more than a coin, coins are considered to be distinct if not otherwise stated.

(b) **Dice:** A die (cubical) has six faces marked 1, 2, 3, 4, 5, 6. We may have tetrahedral (having four faces 1, 2, 3, 4) or pentagonal (having five faces 1, 2, 3, 4, 5) die. As in the case of dice, if we have more than one die, all dice are considered to be distinct if not otherwise stated.

(c) **Playing Cards:** A pack of playing cards usually contain 52 cards.

There are 4 suits (spade, heart, diamond and club) each having 13 cards. There are two colours — red (heart and diamond) and black (spade and club) each having 26 cards.

In thirteen cards of each suit, there are 3 face cards namely king, queen and jack, so there are in all 12 face cards (4 kings, 4 queens and 4 jacks).

Also there are 16 honours cards, 4 of each suit namely ace, king, queen and jack.

Example 1: An urn contains 3 white and 5 black balls. One ball is drawn. What is the probability that it is black?

Solution: Total no. of ways $n = {}^{8}c_1 = 8$

and favourable no. of ways $m = {}^{5}c_1 = 5$. Hence, required probability $= \frac{m}{n} = \frac{5}{8}$.

Example 2: From a pack of 52 cards, four cards are drawn. Find the chance that they will be the four honours of the same suit.

Solution: Here, n = total no. of ways $m = {}^{52}C_4 = \frac{52 \times 51 \times 50 \times 49}{1 \times 2 \times 3 \times 4} = 13 \times 17 \times 25 \times 49 = 270725.$

There are four honours (ace, king, queen and jack) in each suit and so there are 4 sets of 4 honours each. To obtain the favourable number of ways, we have to select one suit of four honours from there fair sets.

$\therefore m = {}^{4}C_1 = 4 \qquad \therefore$ P = required probability $= \frac{m}{n} = \frac{4}{270725}$.

Example 3: In a certain city, two newspapers A and B published. It is known that 25% of the city population reads A and 20% reads B while 8% reads both A and B. It is also known that 30% of these who read A but not B look into advertisements and 40% of those who read B but not a look advertisement while 50% of those who read both A and B look into advertisements. What is the percentage of the population who reads an advertisements.

Solution: Let $p(A)$ and $p(B)$ denote the percentage of city population who read newspaper A and B, then from given data, we have

$$p(A) = 25\% = \frac{1}{4},\ p(B) = 20\% = \frac{1}{5},\ p\ (A \cap B) = 8\% = \frac{2}{25}$$

$\therefore$ percentage of those who read A but not B $= p\ (A \cap \overline{B}) = p(A) - p(A \cap B)$

$$= \frac{1}{4} - \frac{2}{25} = \frac{17}{100} = 17\%$$

Similarly, $p\ (\overline{A} \cap B) = p(B) - p\ (A \cap B) = \frac{1}{5} - \frac{2}{25} = \frac{3}{25} = 12\%$

If $p(C)$ denote the percentage of those who look into advertisement then from the given data we obtain

$$p(C) = 30\% \text{ of } p\ (A \cap \overline{B}) + 40\% \text{ of } p\ (\overline{A} \cap B) + 50\% \text{ of } p\ (A \cap B)$$

$$= \frac{3}{10} \times \frac{17}{100} + \frac{2}{5} \times \frac{3}{25} + \frac{1}{2} \times \frac{2}{25} = \frac{51 + 48 + 40}{1000} = \frac{139}{1000} = 13.9\%.$$

Example 4: In a hand at whist what is the chance that the 4 kings are held by a specified player?

Solution: We know that 13 cards are delivered to a hand at whist so that

$$n = \text{total no of ways} = {}^{52}C_{13} = \frac{52!}{13!\ 39!}$$

Since 4 kings are held by a specified player, 9 more cards are to be delivered to him from the remaining 48 cards so that

$$m = \text{favourable no. of ways} = {}^{48}C_9 = \frac{48!}{9!\ 39!}$$

Hence, p = required probability $= \frac{m}{n} = \frac{48!}{9!\ 39!} \times \frac{13!\,39!}{52!} = \frac{13.12.11.10}{52.51.50.49} = \frac{11}{4165}$.

Example 5: Five persons entered the lift cabin on the ground floor of an 8-floor house. Suppose that each of them independently and with equal probability can leave the cabin at any floor beginning with the first, find out the probability of all five persons leaving at different floors.

Solution: Besides the ground floor, there are seven floors. The total number of ways in which each of the five persons can leave cabin at any of the 7 floors: 7^5.
And the favourable number of ways, that is, the number of ways in which the 5 persons, leave at different floors ${}^7P_5$.
$\therefore$ The required probability = ${}^7P_5/7^5$.

Example 6: Two dice are thrown together first and secondly three dice are thrown together. Find the probability that the total in the first throw is 4 or more and at the same time the total in the second throw is 6 or more.

Solution: In the first throw a number less than 4 can came as (1, 1) (1, 2) (2, 1) that is in 3 ways and so 4 or more can come 36 – 3 = 33 ways. Since two dice can come up in 36 ways.

Hence, the probability of this case = $\frac{33}{36} = \frac{11}{12}$

In the II case, three dice are thrown. In this case the total of 3, 4 or 5 can come as (1, 1, 1) (2, 1, 1) (1, 2, 1) (1, 1, 2) (1, 1, 3) (3, 1, 1) (1, 3, 1) (1, 2, 2) (2, 1, 2) and (2, 2, 1) in 10 ways.
Hence, the number 6 or more can come in 216 –10 = 206 ways.

Hence the probability of this case = $\frac{206}{216} = \frac{103}{108}$

$\therefore$ The required probability = $\frac{11}{12} \times \frac{103}{108} = \frac{1133}{1296}$.

Example 7: A and B are two candidates seeking admission in J.N.U. The probability that A is selected is 0.5 and the probability that both A and B are selected is at most 0.3. It is possible that the probability of B getting selected is 0.9.

Solution: Let A denote the event that the candidate A is selected and B the event that B is selected.
It is given that P(A) = .5 ..... (1) and $P(A \cap B) \le .3$ ..... (2)
Now $p(A) + p(B) - p(A \cap B) = p(A \cup B) \le 1$
$\Rightarrow 0.5 + p(B) - p(A \cap B) \le 1$ by (1) $\Rightarrow p(B) \le 1 - 0.2$ by (2)
$\therefore$ $p(B) \le .8$. Hence, Probability of B cannot be 0.9.

Example 8: If on an average 1 vessel in every 10 is wrecked, find the chance that out of 5 vessels expected 4 at least will arrive safely.

Solution: Let the probability of a vessel wrecking be q and of safe arrival be p so that

$$q = \frac{1}{10} \text{ and } p = 1 - \frac{1}{10} = \frac{9}{10}$$

The probabilities of no vessel, one vessel, two vessels, arriving safely are the first, second, third terms, etc in the binomial expansion.
$(q + p)^5 = q^5 + {}^5C_1\, q^4p + {}^5C_2\, q^3 p^2 + {}^5C_3\, q^2 p^3 + {}^5C_4\, q\, p^4 + p^5$
$\therefore$ The probability of at least 4 vessels arriving safely is the sum of last two terms.

Hence, the required probability = ${}^5C_4\, qp^4 + p^5 = 5.\frac{1}{10}.\left(\frac{9}{10}\right)^4 + \left(\frac{9}{10}\right)^5 = \frac{45927}{5000}$.

Example 9: A lot of 100 bulbs from manufacturing process known to contain 10 defective and 90 non-defective bulbs. If a sample of 8 bulbs is selected at random what is the probability that?

Solution: q = probability of a bulb being defective = $\frac{10}{100} = \frac{1}{10}$ and p = probability of the bulb being non-defective = $\frac{9}{10}$. The probabilities of no defective, one defective, two defective bulbs etc. are the first, second, third terms etc. in the binomial expansion.

$(p + q)^8 = p^8 + {}^8C_1\, p^7\, q + {}^8C_2\, p^6\, q^2 + \ldots.. + q^8.$

Example 10: A five digit number is formed by the digits 1, 2, 3, 4, 5 without repetition. Find the probability that the number formed is divisible by 4.

Solution: n = total no. of five digit numbers = 5!. Now a number will be divisible by 4 if the last two digits are divisible by 4. Therefore the last two digits can be 12, 24, 32, 52 that can be filled in 4 ways.

Corresponding to each of these ways here are 3! = 6 ways of filling the remaining three places.

Hence, m = favourable no. of ways = 4 × 6 = 24.

$\therefore$ The required probability = $\frac{24}{120} = \frac{1}{5}$.

Example 11: Two dices are thrown simultaneously, what is the probability of obtaining a total score of seven?

Solution: There are 6 numbers (1, 2, 3, 4, 5, 6).

Thus, there are six possible ways as to the number of points on the first dice and to each of these ways, there correspond 6 possible numbers of point on the second dice. Hence, the total no. of ways $n = 6 \times 6 = 36$.

We now, find out how many ways are favourable to the total of 7 points. This may happen only in the following ways (1, 6) (6, 1) (2, 5) (5, 2) (3, 4) and (4, 3) that is, in 6 ways.

$\therefore m = 6$

$\therefore$ Hence, required probability $= \frac{m}{n} = \frac{6}{36} = \frac{1}{6}$.

Example 12: Six boys and six girls sit in a row randomly. Find the probability that

(i) The six girls sit together.

(ii) The boys and girls sit alternately.

Solution: *(i)* n = total no. of ways = 12!

and m = favourable no. of ways = 7! 6!

Since 7 objects (considering 6 boys as different objects and all the six girls together as one object) can be arranged in 7! ways, corresponding to each of these ways, the six girls can be arranged amongst themselves in 6! ways.

Hence, $p = \frac{m}{n} = \frac{7!6!}{12!} = \frac{1}{132}$

(ii) Here n = 12! and m = 2 × 6!; Hence, $p = \frac{m}{n} = \frac{2 \times 6!}{12!} = \frac{1}{924}$

Since the boys and girls can sit alternately, in 6! 6! ways if we begin with a boy and similarly, they can sit alternately in 6! 6! ways if we begin with a girl.

Example 13: In bridge game of playing cards, 4 players are distributed one card each by turn so that each player gets 13 cards. Find out the probability of a specified player getting a black ace and a king.

Solution: Here $n = 52C_{13}$ and $m = {}^2C_1 \times {}^4C_1 \times {}^{46}C_{11}$. Since one black ace out of 2 black aces can be chosen in $2C_1$ ways, one king out of 4 kings in $4C_1$ ways and the remaining 11 cards from the remaining 46 cards in ${}^{46}C_{11}$ ways.

$$\therefore \text{ The required probability } P = \frac{m}{n} = \frac{{}^2C_1 \times {}^4C_1 \times {}^{46}C_{11}}{{}^{52}C_{13}} = \frac{164502}{978775}.$$

Example 14: There are three events A, B, C one of which must and only one can happen the odds are 8 to 3 against A, 5 to 2 against B. Find the odds against C.

Solution: Since odds against A are as 8 : 3, the probability of A's occuring

$$p(A) = \frac{3}{8+3} = \frac{3}{11} \text{ and } p(B) = \frac{2}{5+2} = \frac{2}{7}$$

Since the events A, B, C are mutually exclusive and totally exhaustive, the sum of their probabilities must be unity that is

$$p(A) + p(B) + p(C) = 1$$

$$\Rightarrow \frac{3}{11} + \frac{2}{7} + p(C) = 1 \quad \therefore \quad p(C) = 1 - \frac{3}{11} - \frac{2}{7} = \frac{34}{77}$$

Hence, the odds against C are as (77 – 34) : 34 = 43 : 34.

Example 15: A coin is tossed twice. Events E and F are defined as follows: E = heads on first toss, F = heads on second toss. Find probability of $E \cup F$.

Solution: We denote the appearance of head by H and of tail by T. The sample space T consists of four points that is S = {(H, H), (H, T), (T, H) (T, T)}

Then E = {(H, H), (H, T)} and y = {(H, H) (T, H)}

So that $E \cup F$ = {(H, H), (H, T), (T, H)}

Hence, $n = n$ (S) = The number of points in S = 4 and $m = n(E \cup F) = 3$

$$\therefore \text{ Hence, } p(E \cup F) = \frac{n(E \cup F)}{n(s)} = \frac{3}{4}.$$

Example 16: A has 3 shares in a lottery containing 3 prizes and 9 blanks. B has two shares of lottery containing 2 prizes and 6 blanks. Compare their chances of success.

Solution: Since A has three shares in a lottery, his chance of success means that he gets at least one prize, that is he gets either one prize or 2 prizes or 3 prizes and his chance of failure means that he gets no prize. If p denotes his chance of success and q the chance of his failure then $p + q = 1$ or $p = 1 - q$

We now find q

$$n = \text{Total no. of ways} = {}^{12}C_3 = \frac{12 \times 11 \times 10}{1 \times 2 \times 3} = 220$$

Since out of 12 tickets in the lottery, he can draw any three tickets by virtue of his having three shares in the lottery and,

$$m = \text{favourable number of ways} = {}^9C_3 = \frac{9 \times 8 \times 7}{1 \times 2 \times 3} = 84$$

Since he will fail to draw a prize if all the tickets drawn by him are blanks.

$$\therefore \quad q = \frac{m}{n} = \frac{84}{220} = \frac{21}{55} \quad \therefore p = \text{A's chance of success} = 1 - \frac{21}{55} = \frac{34}{55}$$

Similarly, B's chance of success

$$p' = 1 - q' = 1 - \frac{^6C_2}{^8C_2} = 1 - \frac{6\times5}{8\times7} = 1 - \frac{15}{28} = \frac{13}{28}$$

$\therefore$ A's chance of success : B's chance of success $= p : p' = \frac{34}{55}:\frac{13}{28} = \frac{952}{1540}:\frac{715}{1540} = 952:715.$

Example 17: Two cards are drawn simultaneously from the same set. Find the probability that at least one of them will be the ace of hearts.

Solution: Let A = event that first card is an ace of hearts.

B = event that second card is an ace of hearts. Since here both the cards are drawn from the same set, they both cannot be the ace of hearts so that here events A and B are mutually exclusive.

$\therefore$ P (A $\cup$ B) = P(A) + P(B) and P(A) = P(B) = $\frac{1}{52}$

Hence, $P(A \cup B) = \frac{1}{52} + \frac{1}{52} = \frac{2}{52} = \frac{1}{26}$.

Example 18: What is the probability that in a group of N people, at least two of them will have the same birthday?

Solution: $n = 365^N$

$$m = 365.364 \ ..... \left(365 - \overline{N-1}\right) = \frac{365!}{(365-N)!}$$

The probability that no two birthdays coincide is $\frac{m}{n} = \frac{365!/(365-N)!}{365^N}$

$\therefore$ Hence, the required probability $= 1 - \frac{m}{n} = 1 - \frac{365!/(365-N)!}{365^N}$.

Example 19: Three groups of children contain 3 girls and one boy, 2 girls and 2 boys, one girl and 3 boys. One child is selected at random from each group. Show that the chance that the three selected consists of 1 girl and 2 boys is $\frac{13}{32}$.

Solution: Selection can be made in the following manner:

(i) Boy, boy, girl Probability $P_1 = \frac{1}{4}\cdot\frac{2}{4}\cdot\frac{1}{4} = \frac{1}{32}$

(ii) Boy, girl, boy Probability $P_2 = \frac{1}{4}\cdot\frac{2}{4}\cdot\frac{3}{4} = \frac{3}{32}$

(iii) Girl, boy, boy Probability $P_3 = \frac{3}{4}\cdot\frac{2}{4}\cdot\frac{3}{4} = \frac{9}{32}$

Since, these are mutually exclusive cases therefore, the required probability = $P_1 + P_2 + P_3 = \frac{13}{32}$.

Example 20: A speaks truth in 75% cases, and B in 80% of the cases. In what percentage of cases are they likely to contradict each other in stating the same fact?

Solution: If E_1 denotes the event that A speaks the truth, then $\overline{E}_1$ is the event that A does not speak the truth, similarly, we define the events E_2 and $\overline{E}_2$ for B.

Let E be the event that A and B contradict each other then according to the question we have,

$P(E_1) = \frac{75}{100} = \frac{3}{4}$, $P(\bar{E}_1) = 1 - \frac{3}{4} = \frac{1}{4}$, $P(E_2) = \frac{80}{100} = \frac{4}{5}$, $P(\bar{E}_2) = 1 - \frac{4}{5} = \frac{1}{5}$.

They will contradict each other if one speaks the truth and other does not.

Hence, $P(E) = P(E_1)\,P(\bar{E}_2) + P(\bar{E}_1)\,P(E_2)$

$$= \frac{3}{4}\times\frac{1}{5}+\frac{1}{4}\times\frac{4}{5} = \frac{7}{20} = 35\%$$

Example 21: What is the chance that a leap year selected at random will contain 53 sundays?

Solution: A leap year consists of 366 days and so it will have 52 complete weeks and two extra days. These two days can be

(i) Monday and Tuesday
(ii) Tuesday and Wednesday
(iii) Wednesday and Thursday
(iv) Thursday and Friday
(v) Friday and Saturday
(vi) Saturday and Sunday
(vii) Sunday and Monday

Of these 7 cases, the last two are favourable and hence the required probability = 2/7.

Example 22: The chance of an event happening is the square of the chance of a second event, but the odds against the first are the cubes of the odds against the second. Find the chance of each.

Solution: Let the chance of the second event be P. Then the chance of the first event is P^2.

$\therefore$ Odds against the first event are as $1 - P^2 : P^2$

and odds against the second event are $1 - P : P$.

Hence, according to the condition given in the question we have $\frac{1-P^2}{P^2} = \left(\frac{1-P}{P}\right)^3$

$$\Rightarrow \frac{(1-P)(1+P)}{P^2} = \frac{(1-P)^3}{P^3} \Rightarrow P(P+1) = (1-P)^2 \Rightarrow P^2 + P = P^2 - 2P + 1 \Rightarrow 3P = 1$$

$\therefore$ $P = 1/3$ and $P^2 = 1/9$

Hence, the Probability of the first event =1/9 and the second event = 1/9.

Example 23: A box contains 2 black, 4 white, and 3 red balls. One ball is drawn at random from the box, the kept side, from the remaining balls in the box, another ball is drawn at random and kept besides the first. This process is repeated till all the balls are drawn from the box. Find the probability that the balls drawn are in the sequence of 2 black, 4 white, and 3 red.

Solution: Let P_1, P_2, P_3 ..... P_9 denote the probabilities of drawing black, black, white, white, white, white, red, red and red respectively in this order without replacement then P = The required probability = P_1, P_2, P_3 ..... P_9.

$$P_1 = \frac{^2C_1}{^9C_1} = \frac{2}{9}$$

Since, one black ball can be drawn out of 2 in $^2C_1$ ways and total number of ways $^9C_1$.

$$P_2 = \frac{^1C_1}{^8C_1} = \frac{1}{8}$$

Since, one black ball remains after the I draw.

$$P_3 = \frac{^4C_1}{^7C_1} = \frac{4}{7}$$

Since, in the remaining 7 balls 4 are white.

Similarly, $P_4 = \frac{^3C_1}{^6C_1} = \frac{3}{6} = \frac{1}{2}$, $P_5 = \frac{^2C_1}{^5C_1} = \frac{2}{5}$; $P_6 = \frac{1}{4}$

Now, the remaining three balls are all red so that $P_7 = P_8 = P_9 = 1$.

Hence, $P = \frac{2}{9}\cdot\frac{1}{8}\cdot\frac{4}{7}\cdot\frac{1}{2}\cdot\frac{2}{5}\cdot\frac{1}{4} = \frac{1}{1260}$.

EXERCISE

1. Two dice are thrown simultaneously. The probability of obtaining a total score of 5 is
(a) 1/18 *(b)* 1/12 *(c)* 1/9 *(d)* None of these

2. Two dice are thrown simultaneously. The probability of obtaining total score of seven is
(a) 5/6 *(b)* 1/6 *(c)* 1/7 *(d)* 7/6

3. A card is drawn at random from a pack of 100 cards numbered 1 to 100. The probability of drawing a number, which is a square, is
(a) 1/5 *(b)* 2/5 *(c)* 1/10 *(d)* None of these

4. The probability of an event happening in one trial of an experiment is 0.6. Three independent trials are made. The probability that the event happens at least once is
(a) 0.432 *(b)* 0.064 *(c)* 0.936 *(d)* 0.568

5. One of the two exclusive events must occur the chance of one is 2/3 of the other, then odds in favour of the other are
(a) 1 : 3 *(b)* 3 : 1 *(c)* 2 : 3 *(d)* 3 : 2

6. Twelve coupons are numbered from 1 to 12. Six coupons are selected at random one at a time with replacement. The probability that the largest number appearing on a selected coupon is less than or equal to 8, is
(a) $(2/3)^6$ *(b)* $(7/12)^6$ *(c)* 1/33 *(d)* None of these

7. Seven chits are numbered 1 to 7. Four are drawn one by one with replacements. The probability that the least number on any selected chits is 5 is
(a) $1 - (2/7)^4$ *(b)* $4.(2/7)^4$ *(c)* $(3/7)^4$ *(d)* None of these

8. A bag contains 3 red, 4 white and 5 blue balls. All balls are different. Two balls are drawn at random. The probability that they are of different colours is
(a) 47/66 *(b)* 10/33 *(c)* 5/22 *(d)* None of these

9. The probabilities of three mutually exclusive events A, B and C are given by 2/3, 1/4 and 1/6 respectively. The statement
(a) is true *(b)* is false
(c) Nothing can be said *(d)* Could be either

10. A five digit number is formed by the digits 1, 2, 3, 4, 5, 6 and 8. The probability that the number has even digit at both ends is
(a) 2/7 *(b)* 3/7 *(c)* 4/7 *(d)* None of these

11. Three identical dice are rolled. The probability that the same number will appear on each of them is
(a) 1/6 *(b)* 1/18 *(c)* 1/36 *(d)* None of these

12. Three cards are drawn successively with replacement. The probability of selecting 2 aces and one king is
(a) $1/\{(13)^2 \times 17\}$ *(b)* $1/(13)^3$ *(c)* $3/(13)^3$ *(d)* None of these

13. If an integer p is chosen at random in the interval $0 \leq p \leq 5$, the probability that the roots of the equation $x^2 + px + p/4 + 1/2 = 0$ are real is
(*a*) 4/5 (*b*) 2/3 (*c*) 3/5 (*d*) None of these

14. There are 4 white and 4 black balls in a bag and 3 balls are drawn at random. If balls of same colour are identical, the probability that none of them is black, is
(*a*) 1/4 (*b*) 1/14 (*c*) 1/2 (*d*) None of these

15. Two events A and B have probabilities 0.25 and 0.50 respectively. The probability that both A and B occur simultaneously is 0.12. Then the probability that neither A nor B occurs is
(*a*) 0.13 (*b*) 0.38 (*c*) 0.63 (*d*) 0.37

16. The odds in favour of A solving a problem are 3 to 4 and the odds against B solving the same problem are 5 to 7. If they both try the problem, the probability that the problem is solved is
(*a*) 41/84 (*b*) 16/21 (*c*) 5/21 (*d*) 1/4

17. Cards are drawn from a pack of 52 cards one by one. The probability that exactly 10 cards will be drawn before the first ace is
(*a*) 241/1456 (*b*) 164/4165 (*c*) 451/884 (*d*) None of these

18. From eighty cards numbered 1 to 80, two cards are selected randomly. The probability that both the cards have the numbers divisible by 4 is given by
(*a*) 21/316 (*b*) 19/316 (*c*) 1/4 (*d*) None of these

19. A cubical dice is thrown 6 times. The probability that 2 and 4 will turn up exactly 3 times each is given by
(*a*) 5/11664 (*b*) 1/46656 (*c*) 1/5184 (*d*) None of these

20. The probability that an event A happens in one trial of an experiment is 0.7. Three independent trials of the experiment are performed. The probability that the event A happens atleast once is
(*a*) 0.657 (*b*) 0.973 (*c*) 0.189 (*d*) None of these

21. The probability of a problem being solved by two students are 1/2, 1/3. The probability of the problem being solved is
(*a*) 2/3 (*b*) 4/3 (*c*) 1/3 (*d*) 1

22. Let A and B be two events such that P(A) = 0.4, P(B) = 0.3 and P(A ∪ B) = 0.7. Then
(*a*) A and B are independent (*b*) A and B are exhaustive
(*c*) A and B are mutually exclusive (*d*) None of these

23. Probability of happening of at least one of the events is 0.6 and their simultaneous happening is 0.2. Then the value of P(A) + P(B) is
(*a*) 0.8 (*b*) 0.6 (*c*) 0.2 (*d*) 0.4

24. If the probabilities that A and B will die within a year are p and q respectively, then the probability that only one of them will be alive at the end of the year is
(*a*) $p + q$ (*b*) $p + q - 2pq$
(*c*) $p + q - pq$ (*d*) $p + q + pq$

25. A man is known to speak truth 3 out of 4 times. He throws a die and reports that it is a six, the probability that it is actually a six is
(*a*) 3/8 (*b*) 1/5 (*c*) 3/5 (*d*) None of these

26. An urn contains 8 blue and 4 green balls. Two balls are drawn at random. The probability that both balls are of the same colour (all balls are considered to be different) is
(*a*) 17/33 (*b*) 1/33 (*c*) 14/33 (*d*) 1/11

27. In order to get at least once a head with probability ≥ 0.9, the number of times a coin needs to be tossed is
(*a*) 3 (*b*) 4 (*c*) 5 (*d*) None of these

28. From a pack of cards, 2 are drawn at random one by one with replacement. The probability that first is heart and 2nd is king is
(*a*) 1/26 (*b*) 1/52 (*c*) 1/13 (*d*) None of these

29. A dice is thrown. Consider two events
A = {1, 2, 3, 4}, B = {4, 5, 6}. Then the events A and B are
(*a*) independent (*b*) dependent (*c*) mutually exclusive (*d*) exhaustive

30. Host, his wife and 8 guests are to be seated on a round dining table at random. The probability that the host and his wife sit together is
(*a*) 1/9 (*b*) 2/9 (*c*) 1/5 (*d*) 1/10

31. The letters of the word ALLAHABAD are arranged at random. The probability that in the word so formed, all similar letters are found together, is
(*a*) 16/21 (*b*) 16/17 (*c*) 5!/9! (*d*) None of these

32. Fifteen coupons are numbered 1, 2, ..., 15 respectively. Seven coupons are selected at random one at a time with replacement. The probability that the largest number appearing on a selected coupon is 9 is
(*a*) $(9/16)^6$ (*b*) $(8/15)^7$ (*c*) $(3/5)^5$ (*d*) None of these

33. If A and B are two events such that
$P(A \cup B) = 5/6$, $P(\overline{A}) = 1/4$, $P(B) = 1/3$, then A and B are
(*a*) mutually exclusive (*b*) dependent (*c*) independent (*d*) None of these

34. In a box containing 100 bulbs, 10 are defective. The probability that out of a sample of 5 bulbs none is defective is
(*a*) $1/10^5$ (*b*) $(9/10)^5$ (*c*) ${}^{90}C_5/{}^{100}C_5$ (*d*) None of these

35. A box contains 3 white and 2 red balls. If the first ball is being withdrawn, then the second ball withdrawn is red. The probability of the event is
(*a*) 8/25 (*b*) 2/5 (*c*) 3/5 (*d*) 21/25

36. Three rifle man take one shot each at the same target. The probability of the first rifle man hitting the target is 0.4, the probability of the second and third rifle man hitting the target are .5 and .8. Then the probability that exactly two of them hit the target is
(*a*) 0.92 (*b*) 0.44 (*c*) 0.94 (*d*) None of these

SOLUTIONS

1. Total ways = $6 \times 6 = 36$
Total 5 can be obtained in the following 4 ways : 1 + 4, 2 + 3, 3 + 2, 4 + 1
∴ Required probability = 4/36 = 1/9.

2. Total ways = $6 \times 6 = 36$
Total 7 can be obtained in the following 6 ways : 1 + 6, 2 + 5, 3 + 4, 4 + 3, 5 + 2, 6 + 1
∴ Required probability = 6/36 = 1/6.

3. Total number of ways = ${}^{100}C_1 = 100$
Favourable numbers are $1^2, 2^2, ..., 10^2$.
Therefore favourable ways = 10
∴ Probability = 10/100 = 1/10.

4. $P = 1 - (0.4)^3 = 0.936$.

5. Let $P(B) = x$, $P(A) = 2x/3$

$P(A) + P(B) = x + 2x/3 = 1 \Rightarrow 5x/3 = 1$

$\Rightarrow x = 3/5$

$P(A) = 2/5, P(B) = 3/5$

Odds in favours of B = $\frac{3/5}{1-3/5} = \frac{3}{2}$.

6. Probability of a coupon selected with any number from 1 to 8 = 8/12.

In six trails: P (number from 1 to 8) = $(8/12)^6$

$P = (2/3)^6$.

7. P (5 or 6 or 7) in one draw = 3/7

∴ Probabilty that in each of 4 draws, the chits bear 5 or 6 or 7 = $(3/7)^4$.

8. We have the following pattern:

I red, white $\quad P_I = 3 \times 4/{}^{12}C_2$

II red, blue $\quad P_{II} = 3 \times 5/{}^{12}C_2$

III blue, white $\quad P_{III} = 4 \times 5/{}^{12}C_2$

Since all these cases are exclusive, so the required probability = $(12 + 15 + 20)/{}^{12}C_2$

$= (47 \times 2)/(12 \times 11) = 47/66$.

9. Since the events A, B and C are mutually exclusive, we have

$P(A \cup B \cup C) = \frac{2}{3} + \frac{1}{4} + \frac{1}{6} = \frac{13}{12} > 1$, which is not possible.

Hence, the statement is false.

10. Total number of 5 digit numbers obtained by the digits 1, 2, 3, 4, 5, 6 and 8.

$= {}^7P_5 = 7.6.5.4.3 = 2520$

There are 4 even digits (2, 4, 6 and 8).

∴ 2 even digits can be selected in ${}^4C_2 = 6$ ways

∴ The two ends can be filled in $2 \times 6 = 12$ ways

Remaining 3 places from remaining 5 digits can be filled in ${}^5P_3 = 60$ ways.

Hence, the required probability $= \frac{12 \times 60}{2520} = \frac{2}{7}$.

11. Favourable cases = 6

Total cases = $6^3 = 216$

P(same number on three dice) = $\frac{6}{216} = \frac{1}{36}$.

12. $\quad P(\text{ace}) = \frac{4}{52} = \frac{1}{13} \quad P(\text{king}) = \frac{4}{52} = \frac{1}{13}$

P (2 aces and one king) $= {}^3C_2 \cdot \left(\frac{1}{13}\right)^2 \left(\frac{1}{13}\right) = \frac{3}{(13)^3}$.

13. Roots of the equation

$x^2 + px + p/4 + 1/2 = 0$ are real if $\Delta = p^2 - 4\,(p/4 + 1/2) \geq 0$

i.e., $(p-2)(p+1) \geq 0$ $\quad$ *i.e.*, $p \leq -1$ or $p \geq 2$

In $0 \leq p \leq 5$, possible values of p are 2, 3, 4, 5

Thus, probability = 4/6 = 2/3.

14. There are 4 identical white and 4 identical black balls and we have to select 3, which can be selected in the following pattern:

white	3	2	1	–
black	–	1	2	3

i.e., in all 4 ways.

It should be noted that the ways of selecting 3 white balls from 4 white balls is not equal to $^4C_3$ since the white balls are identical, it is equal to 1. Similar is the cases for 2, 1, etc.

Now the number of ways of selecting 3 white balls = 1.

Hence, required probability = 1/4.

15. $P(A \cup B) = P(A) + P(B) - P(A \cap B)$

$P(A \cup B) = 0.25 + 0.50 - 0.12 = 0.63$

$P(\overline{A \cup B}) = 1 - P(A \cup B) = 1 - 0.63 = 0.37.$

16. $P(A) = \dfrac{3}{7}, P(B) = \dfrac{7}{12}$

$P(\overline{A}) = \dfrac{4}{7}, P(\overline{B}) = \dfrac{5}{12}$

$\therefore P(A \cup B) = 1 - \dfrac{4}{7} \times \dfrac{5}{12} = \dfrac{16}{21}.$

17. P{(first 10 draws non-ace cards) (11th ace)}

$$= \frac{^{48}C_{10}}{^{52}C_{10}} \times \frac{4}{42} = \frac{164}{4165}.$$

18. Total ways = $^{80}C_2$

favourable ways = $^{20}C_2$

$$P = \frac{^{20}C_2}{^{80}C_2} = \frac{19}{316}.$$

19. $P(2) = \dfrac{1}{6}, P(4) = \dfrac{1}{6}$

Required probability, $P = {^6C_3}.\left(\dfrac{1}{6}\right)^3.\left(\dfrac{1}{6}\right)^3 = \dfrac{1}{6^6}.\dfrac{6!}{3!3!} = \dfrac{5}{11664}.$

20. $P(A) = 0.7 \therefore P(\overline{A}) = 0.3$

P(at least once) = 1 – P (no occurrence)

$= 1 - (0.3)^3 = 0.973.$

21. The probability that the problem is not being solved by any of the two students

= (1 – 1/2) (1 – 1/3) = 1/3

∴ Probability that the problem is solved = 1 – 1/3 = 2/3.

22. $P(A \cap B) = P(A) + P(B) - P(A \cup B) = 0.4 + 0.3 - 0.7 = 0$

$\therefore P(A \cap B) \neq P(A)\,P(B)$ so A and B are not independent.

{Since $P(A \cap B) \neq 1$, A and B are not exhaustive.}

$P(A \cap B) = 0$ gives A and B are mutually exclusive.

23. $P(A \cup B) = P(A) + P(B) - P(A \cap B)$
$\Rightarrow 0.6 = P(A) + P(B) - 0.2$
$\Rightarrow P(A) + P(B) = 0.8.$

24. P (only one of A and B will die in a year)
$= P(\overline{A}B) + P(A\overline{B})$
$= P(\overline{A})\, P(B) + P(A)\, P(\overline{B})$ [Since A and B are independent]
$= (1 - p)q + p(1 - q)$
$= p + q - 2pq.$

25. Let A denote the event that a six occurs and B the event that the man reports that it is a six. Then the probability that it is actually a six is given by

$$P(A/B) = \frac{P(A \cap B)}{P(B)}$$

Now $P(A \cap B) = \frac{1}{6}.\frac{3}{4} = \frac{3}{24} = \frac{1}{8}$ $P(B) = P(A \cap B) + P(\overline{A} \cap \overline{B}) = \frac{1}{6}.\frac{3}{4} + \frac{5}{6}.\frac{1}{4} = \frac{8}{24} = \frac{1}{3}$

Hence $P(A/B) = \frac{1/8}{1/3} = \frac{3}{8}$.

26. Required probability $= \frac{^8C_2 + ^4C_2}{^{12}C_2} = \frac{17}{33}$.

27. Probability of getting at least one head in n tosses $= 1 - (½)^n \geq 0.9$
$\Rightarrow$ $(½)^n \leq 0.1 \Rightarrow 2^n \geq 10$ $\Rightarrow n \geq 3$
Hence, least value of $n = 4$.

28. Probability of getting heart $= (13/52) = \frac{1}{4}$

Probability of getting king $= 4/52 = \frac{1}{13}$

∴ Probability that first is heart and 2nd is king is $1/4 \times 1/13 = 1/52$.

29. $P(A) = 4/6 = 2/3$, $P(B) = 3/6 = 1/2$
$P(AB) = 1/6$
$P(A).P(B) = 1/3$
As $P(AB) \neq P(A).P(B)$
∴ A and B are not independent. Occurrence of one do not effect the occurrence of other, $P(A \cap B) \neq$ null set
∴ Events are not mutually exclusive.
All the possible outcomes are existing, *i.e.*, $A \cup B$ is equal to sample space {1, 2, 3, 4, 5, 6}, therefore events A and B are exhaustive.

30. Favourable ways = 2!.8!.
Total ways of arrangement of 10 persons = (10 – 1)! = 9!

∴ $P = \frac{2!8!}{9!} = \frac{2}{9}$.

31. Total ways of arranging letters of words ALLAHABAD = $\frac{9!}{4!2!}$

Favourable ways = 4!.2!.5!

$\therefore \quad p = \frac{4!2!5!4!2!}{9!} = \frac{16}{21}$

32. Favourable ways = 9

Total ways = 15

∴ P (greatest number 9) in one chance =9/15 = 3/5

∴ P (greatest number 9 in all chances) =$(3/5)^7$.

33. $P(A \cup B) = P(A) + P(B) - P(A \cap B)$

∴ $P(A \cap B) = 1/3 + 3/4 - 5/6 = 3/12 = 1/4$

$P(A)\,P(B) = 1/3.3/4 = 1/4$

As $P(A)\,P(B) = P(A \cap B)$

∴ A and B are independent.

Also $P(A \cap B) \neq 0$

∴ A and B are not exclusive.

34. Favourable ways of selecting 5 non-defective bulbs = ${}^{90}C_5$.

Total no. of ways of selection = ${}^{100}C_5$

∴ P (non-defective bulbs) = $\frac{{}^{90}C_5}{{}^{100}C_5}$.

35. Probability $= \frac{2}{5}\cdot\frac{1}{4} + \frac{3}{5}\cdot\frac{2}{4} = \frac{2}{5}$.

36. Let A, B, C be the three rifle man. Given that $P(A) = 0.4, P(B) = 0.5$ and $P(C) = 0.8$.

P (exactly two success) $= P(AB\overline{C}) + P(A\overline{B}C) + P(\overline{A}BC)$

$= 0.4 \times 0.5 \times 0.2 + 0.4 \times 0.5 \times 0.8 + 0.6 \times 0.5 \times 0.8 = 0.44$

DATA INTERPRETATION: TABLES (Tabulation)

TABLES

Tables are often used in reports, magazines and newspaper to present as set of numerical data. It is one of the easiest and most accurate ways of presenting data. One of the main purposes of tables is to make complicated information easier to understand. Hence, the advantage of presenting data in a table is that one can see the information at a glance. We present below an example of tabular presentation of annual expenditure of 5 families for last 4 years.

Annual Expenditure of 5 families (in Rs. Thousands)

Years → Families ↓	2005	2006	2007	2008
A	35	50	55	60
B	40	60	65	75
C	45	50	70	80
D	30	40	45	50
E	50	55	60	70

Essentials of a Tables:

(i) **Title:** Heading of the table
(ii) **Stub:** The section of the table containing row headings in called Stub.
(iii) **Column Captions** : The heading of each column is designated as column caption.
(iv) **Body**
(v) **Footnotes**
(vi) **Source**

Example 1. Directions: *Study the folloiwng table and answer the questions given below:*

Categories of students according to their enrolment in various courses in a vocational college.

Courses	*Categories (Faculty)*			
	Arts		*Science*	
	Boys	*Girls*	*Boys*	*Girls*
1. Business Management	45	25	65	25
2. Typewriting	186	23	32	20
3. Stenography	120	25	58	12
4. Typewriting and Stenography	100	12	5	3

1. If 60% boys and 70% girls pass in their respective courses, then total pass percentage is:
   (a) 58% (b) 66% (c) 54% (d) 62%
2. The total number of students who have opted the course of Business Management and the course of Stenography exceeds the number of students studying in typewriting course by:
   (a) 44% (b) 66% (c) 33% (d) 55%
3. In which of the following courses, percentage of girls is the highest?
   (a) Stenography (b) Business Management
   (c) Typewriting (d) Typewriting and Stenography
4. In the art faculty number of students who have opted the course of stenography is how much per cent of the total student in the faculty?
   (a) 27% (b) 10% (c) 18% (d) 15%
5. Total number of boys studying in the college exceeds the total number of girls in the college by:
   (a) 321% (b) 280% (c) 308% (d) 250%

Solution 1. ∵ Total boys = 45 + 186 + 120 + 100 + 65 + 32 + 58 + 5 = 611

∴ Number of boys who pass in their respective courses = 60% of 611 = $611 \times \frac{60}{100} = 366.60$

Total number of girls = 25 + 23 + 25 + 12 + 25 + 20 + 12 + 3 = 145

Number of girls who pass in their respective courses = 70% of 145 = $\frac{145 \times 70}{100} = 101.50$

∴ Combined pass per cent = $\frac{(366.6+101.5)\times 100}{611+145} = \frac{46810}{756} = 61.92 \simeq 62\%$

Solution 2. ∵ Number of students in Business Management course = 160
Number of students in typewriting course = 261
Number of students in stenography corse = 215

∴ Required per cent = $\left(\frac{160+215-261}{261}\right)\times 100 \approx 44\%$

Solution 3. Percentage of girls in Business Management course = $\frac{(25+25)\times 100}{160} = 31.25$

Percentage of girls in typewriting course = $\frac{(23+20)\times 100}{261} = 16.47$

Percentage of girls in stenography course = $\frac{(25+12)\times 100}{215} = 12.56$

And percentage of girls in typewriting and stenography course = $\frac{(12+3)\times 100}{120} = 12.50$

Hence, it is clear from the above that percentage of girls in Business Management course is the highest.

Solution 4. Required percentage = $\frac{(25+120)\times 100}{536} \times 100 \simeq 27$

Solution 5. Total number of boys = 45 + 65 + 186 + 32 + 120 + 58 + 100 + 5 = 611
Total number of girls = 25 + 23 + 25 + 12 + 25 + 20 + 12 + 3 = 145

$\therefore$ Required percentage = $\left(\dfrac{611-145}{145}\right)\times 100 \simeq 321\%$

Example 2. Directions: *Figures of biscuit exports from a country during various years are given in the following table. Study the table carefully and answer the questions that follows:*

VOLUME OF EXPORT OF BISCUITS FROM A COUNTRY

Year	*Quantity (in lakh tins)*	*Price (in crores Rs.)*
2004	100	150
2005	75	150
2006	150	330
2007	160	400
2008	200	500

1. During which year per tin export price remained at lowest level?
(*a*) 2007 (*b*) 2006 (*c*) 2005 (*d*) 2004

2. During which years price per tin remained at the same level?
(*a*) 2006 and 2008 (*b*) 2006 and 2007 (*c*) 2007 and 2008 (*d*) 2006 and 2004

3. The export price of biscuit increased from 2004 to 2008 by how much per cent?
(*a*) 100 (*b*) $116\frac{2}{3}$ (*c*) $233\frac{1}{3}$ (*d*) 350

4. The difference between the number of biscuit tins exported in 2008 and that in 2007 is:
(*a*) 40 (*b*) 40,000 (*c*) 4,00,000 (*d*) 40,00,000

Solution 1. Export price per tin in 2004 = $\dfrac{\text{Rs. 150 crores}}{\text{Rs. 100 lakhs}}$ = Rs. 150

Export price per tin in 2005 = $\dfrac{\text{Rs. 150 crores}}{\text{Rs. 75 lakhs}}$ = Rs. 200

Export price per tin in 2006 = $\dfrac{\text{Rs. 330 crores}}{\text{Rs. 150 lakhs}}$ = Rs. 220

Export price per tin in 2007 = $\dfrac{\text{Rs. 400 crores}}{\text{Rs. 160 lakhs}}$ = Rs. 250

Export price per tin in 2008 = $\dfrac{\text{Rs. 500 crores}}{\text{Rs. 200 lakhs}}$ = Rs. 250

Hence, it is clear that per tin export price was at lowest level in 2004.

Solution 2. From the explanation given in the answer of Q.No. 1, it is clear that per tin export price was same in 2007 and 2008.

Solution 3. From the level of 2004 percentage increase in export price in 2008

$$= \left(\frac{500-150}{150}\right)\times 100 = 233\frac{1}{3}\%$$

Solution 4. Required difference = 200 – 160 = 40 lakh tins = 40,00,000 tins.

Example. 3. Directions: *Study the following table carefully and answer the questions given below:*

Number of Employees Working in Various departments of a Factory

Year	*Production Deptt.*	*Sale Deptt.*	*Procurement Deptt.*	*Administration & Accounts Deptt.*	*Research & Development Deptt.*
2003	150	25	50	45	75
2004	225	40	45	62	70
2005	450	65	30	90	73
2006	470	73	32	105	70
2007	500	80	35	132	74
2008	505	75	36	130	75

1. During which of the following years number of employees working in production deptt. of the factory was less than 50% of the total employees of the factory?
(a) 2003 *(b)* 2005 *(c)* 2006 *(d)* 2007

2. During which year the number of employees working in each department was more than those in the previous year and nearly equal to next year?
(a) 2007 *(b)* 2006 *(c)* 2005 *(d)* 2004

3. In which department of the factory number of employees remained nearly same during the years from 2003 to 2008?
(a) Production *(b)* Sale
(c) Research and Development *(d)* Administration and Accounts
(e) Procurement

4. In which department of the factory number of employees are maximum from 2003 to 2008?
(a) Production *(b)* Sale
(c) Research and Development *(d)* Administration and Accounts
(e) Sale and Procurement

5. During which year number of employees in the factory became nearly double the total number of employees working in the factory during 2003.
(a) 2008 *(b)* 2007 *(c)* 2006 *(d)* 2005

Solution 1. Number of total employees in 2003 = 150 + 25 + 50 + 45 + 70 = 442

∴ Percentage number of employees working in producton deptt. = $\frac{150\times 100}{345} = 43.48\%$

Number of total employees in 2004 = 225 + 40 + 45 + 62 + 70 = 442

∴ Percentage number of employees working in production deptt. = $\frac{225\times 100}{442} = 50.9\%$

Number of total employees in 2005 = 450 + 65 + 30 + 90 + 73 = 708

∴ Percentage number of employees working in proudction deptt. = $\frac{450 \times 100}{708}$ = 63.56%

Total number of employees in 2006 = 470 + 73 + 32 + 105 + 70 = 750

∴ Percentage number of employees working in production deptt. = $\frac{470 \times 100}{750}$ = 62.67%

Total number of employees in 2007 = 500 + 80 + 35 + 132 + 74 = 821

∴ Percentage number of employees working in production deptt. = $\frac{500 \times 100}{821}$ = 60.9%

Total number of employees in 2007 = 505 + 75 + 36 + 130 + 75 = 821

∴ Percentage number of employees working in production in deptt. = $\frac{505 \times 100}{821}$ = 61.51%

Hence, it is clear that percentage number of employees working in production deptt. was less than 50% in 2003.

Solution 2. It is clear from the table that it was the year 2007 when the number of employees working in each department was more than that in the previous year and nearly equal to next year.

Solution 3. According to the table in the research and development department number of employees remained nearly same during the year from 2003 to 2008.

Solution 4. Production.

Solution 5. Total number of employes in 2003 = 345
Total number of employees in 2005 = 708
Hence, it was the year 2005 when total number of employees in the factory became nearly double the total number of emplyees working in the factory during 2003.

Example. 4. *Study the table carefully to answer the questions that follow.*

Number of students studying in six different classes of six different schools.

Class → **School ↓**	**V**	**VI**	**VII**	**VIII**	**IX**	**X**
P	152	160	145	156	147	144
Q	148	166	150	155	157	143
R	161	152	140	145	143	165
S	159	142	149	140	142	168
T	147	144	158	163	154	150
U	150	160	162	160	161	140

1. What is the respective ratio of students studying in class IX of schools Q and R together to those studying in class VI of schools S and T together?
(*a*) 143 : 150 (*b*) 150 : 143 (*c*) 127 : 181 (*d*) 181 : 127

2. Number of students studying in class X from school P forms approximately what per cent of the total number of students studying in class X from all schools together?

(*a*) 9 (*b*) 12 (*c*) 16 (*d*) 24

3. Total number of students studying in school T from all classes together forms what per cent of total number of students studying in school S from all classes together?

(*a*) 100.26 (*b*) 101.78 (*c*) 102.64 (*d*) 103.52

4. The number of students studying in class VII from school U forms what per cent of the total number of students from all the classes together from that school?

(*a*) 15.93 (*b*) 16.14 (*c*) 17.36 (*d*) 18.28

5. Which class has the maximum number of students from all schools together?

(*a*) V (*b*) VI (*c*) VII (*d*) X

Solution 1. Number of students of class IX of schools Q and R = 157 + 143 = 300

Number of students of class VI of schools S and T = 142 + 144 = 286

Hence, required ratio = 300 : 286 = 150 : 143

Solution 2. Total number of students of class X from all schools

= 144 + 143 + 165 + 168 + 150 + 140 = 910

Required percentage = $\frac{144}{910} \times 100 = 15.82 \simeq 16\%$

Solution 3. Total number of students of school T from all classes

= 147 + 144 + 158 + 163 + 154 + 150 = 916

Total number of students of school S from all classes

= 159 + 142 + 149 + 140 + 142 + 168 = 900

Required percentage = $\frac{916}{900} \times 100 = 101.78\%$

Solution 4. Total number of students of school U from all the classes

= 150 + 160 + 162 + 160 + 161 + 140 = 933

Required percentage = $\frac{162}{933} \times 100 = 17.36\%$

Solution 5. Total number of students of class V from all the schools

= 152 + 148 + 161 + 159 + 147 + 150 = 917

Total number of students of class VI from all the schools

= 160 + 166 + 152 + 142 + 144 + 160 = 924

Total number of students of class VII from all the schools

= 145 + 150 + 140 + 149 + 158 + 162 = 904

Total number of students of class VIII from all the schools

= 156 + 155 + 145 + 140 + 163 + 160 = 919

Total number of students of class IX from all the schools

= 147 + 157 + 143 + 142 + 154 + 161 = 904

Total number of students of class X from all the schools

= 144 + 143 + 165 + 168 + 150 + 140 = 910

Hence, the class VI has maximum number of students.

EXERCISE

Directions (Qs. 1-5): *Study the table carefully to answer the questions that follow:*

PERCENTAGE OF MARKS OBTAINED BY SIX STUDENTS IN SIX DIFFERENT SUBJECTS

Subject → Student ↓	Science (Out of 150)	English (Out of 100)	Hindi (Out of 50)	Maths (Out of 150)	Social Studies (Out of 125)	Maithili (Out of 50)
Ravi	85	67	84	70	70	78
Riya	80	53	86	60	80	78
Amit	90	51	88	65	50	66
Kirti	65	78	90	85	70	68
Prasad	70	82	86	80	60	72
Tanya	60	84	80	65	50	76

1. What are the average marks obtained by all students together in Hindi?
   (a) 41.54 (b) 42.83 (c) 43.28 (d) 44.62
2. If to pass in the examination the minimum marks required in Maths are 95 and in Social studies are 85, how many students will pass?
   (a) One (b) Two (c) Three (d) Four
3. Which student has scored the highest marks in all subjects together?
   (a) Amit (b) Kirti (c) Prasad (d) Ravi
4. What are the total marks obtained by Tanya in all the subjects together?
   (a) 402 (b) 408 (c) 412 (d) 418
5. What is the Riya's overall percentage of marks in all subjects together?
   (a) 68.3 (b) 71.2 (c) 72.8 (d) 75.6

Directions (Qs. 6-9): *Study the table given below and answer the following questions:*

Loans Disbursed by Four Banks in Crores of Rupees in Different Years

Years → Banks ↓	2005	2006	2007	2008
A	18	23	45	30
B	27	33	18	41
C	29	29	22	17
D	13	19	28	32
Total	**87**	**104**	**113**	**120**

6. In which year the disbursement of loans by all the banks combined together was nearest to the average disbursement of loans over the years?
   (a) 2005 (b) 2006 (c) 2007 (d) 2008
7. In which year was the total disbursement of loans of banks A and B exactly equal to the total disbursement of loans of banks C and D?
   (a) 2005 (b) 2006 (c) 2008 (d) None of these

8. What was the percentage increase of disbursement of loans of all the banks together from 2007 to 2008?

(a) 6% (b) $6\frac{11}{113}\%$ (c) $6\frac{22}{113}\%$ (d) $7\frac{11}{113}\%$

9. In which bank was the loan disbursement more than 30% of the disbursement of all banks combined together in 2008?

(a) A (b) B
(c) C (d) D

Directions (Qs. 10-14): *Study the following table to answer the given questions.*

CENTRE AND POST-WISE NUMBER OF CANDIDATES

Centre ↓	Officer	Clerk	Field Officer	Supervisor	Specialist Officer
Bangluroo	2000	5000	50	2050	750
Delhi	15000	17000	160	11000	750
Mumbai	17000	19500	70	7000	900
Hyderabad	3500	20000	300	9000	1150
Kolkata	14900	17650	70	1300	1200
Lucknow	11360	15300	30	1500	650
Chennai	9000	11000	95	1650	500

10. Which centre has the highest number of candidates?

(a) Delhi (b) Hyderabad (c) Kolkata (d) Mumbai

11. What is the difference between total number of officers and clerks?

(a) 28680 (b) 29680 (c) 32690 (d) 34180

12. In Chennai, the number of clerks is approximately how much per cent more than that of officers?

(a) 2 (b) 18 (c) 20 (d) 22

13. Which centre has 300% more number of clerks as compared to Bangluroo?

(a) Chennai (b) Hyderabad (c) Mumbai (d) None of these

14. In Kolkata, number of specialist officers approximately what per cent of that of officers?

(a) 6.9 (b) 8 (c) 8.7 (d) 9

Directions (Qs. 15-19): *Study the table carefully to answer the questions that follow:*

Sale (in crores) of Numer of Units by Six Different Companies Over the Years

Year → Company ↓	2003	2004	2005	2006	2007	2008
A	110	118	143	126	152	195
B	91	93	85	99	69	35
C	103	153	100	128	96	56
D	112	166	78	83	135	198
E	72	169	154	98	140	192
F	64	56	120	70	176	54

15. Which company has sold the maximum number of units over the years?
(a) A *(b)* C *(c)* D *(d)* E

16. Which company has sold the minimum number of units over the years?
(a) A *(b)* B *(c)* D *(d)* F

17. What is the average number of units sold (in crores) in the year 2007?
(a) 121 *(b)* 127 *(c)* 128 *(d)* 130

18. What is the difference between number of units (in crores) sold by company D in the year 2003 and the year 2005?
(a) 32 *(b)* 34 *(c)* 36 *(d)* 38

19. Number of units sold by company B in the year 2005 is what per cent of the total number of units sold by all the companies together in the year?
(a) 12.5 *(b)* 12.76 *(c)* 15.5 *(d)* 20

Directions (Qs. 20-24): *Study the following table carefully and answer the questions given below:*

Number of people working in various departments from Various Organisations

	Organisations				
Department	**A**	**B**	**C**	**D**	**E**
H.R.	1050	1015	976	888	1004
Finance	1017	960	786	1025	963
Marketing	1382	1384	1275	1300	1290
Production	1542	1545	1550	1570	1580
Accounts	786	745	801	800	735
Legal	48	54	36	30	53

20. The total number of employees working in the Legal Department are approximately what per cent of the total number of employees working in H.R. Department of all the organisations together?
(a) 4 *(b)* 6 *(c)* 8 *(d)* 10

21. What is the respective ratio of the total number of employees working in organisation A to the total number of employees working in organisation E?
(a) 71 : 75 *(b)* 75 : 71 *(c)* 225 : 233 *(d)* 233 : 225

22. The number of people working in the Finance department from organisation B are approximately what per cent of the total number of employees working in organisation B?
(a) 12 *(b)* 15 *(c)* 17 *(d)* 20

23. What is the approximate difference between the average number of people working in Marketing and Production departments from all the organisations together?
(a) 231 *(b)* 300 *(c)* 330 *(d)* 578

24. What is the total number of employees from all the departments working in all the organisations together?
(a) 26960 *(b)* 28190 *(c)* 28910 *(d)* 29660

Directions (Qs. 25-29): *Study the following table carefully and answer the questions given below:*

Number of Males and Females staying in various societies		
Societies	**Males**	**Females**
A	250	350
B	400	150
C	300	275
D	280	300
E	180	250
F	325	300

Percentage of Children (Males and Females) in the societies			
Societies	**Children**	**Male**	**Female**
A	25%	40%	60%
B	40%	75%	25%
C	16%	25%	75%
D	25%	80%	20%
E	40%	50%	50%
F	24%	46%	54%

25. What is the respective ratio of the number of the adult females to the total number of female children staying in all the societies together?

(a) 82 : 243 *(b)* 243 : 82 *(c)* 71 : 112 *(d)* 112 : 71

26. What is the respective ratio of the total number of adult males in the societies A and B together to the total number of adult males in the societies E and F together?

(a) 14 ; 17 *(b)* 17 : 14 *(c)* 75 : 79 *(d)* 79 : 75

27. Wha is the difference between the number of male children in society B and the number of male children in society F?

(a) 14 *(b)* 26 *(c)* 84 *(d)* 96

28. What is the total number of female children staying in all the societies together?

(a) 314 *(b)* 343 *(c)* 410 *(d)* 433

29. What is the total number of members staying in all the societies together?

(a) 3000 *(b)* 3360 *(c)* 4100 *(d)* 4289

Directions (Qs. 30-34): *Study the folloiwng table carefully and answer the questions given below:*

Quantity of Rice produced by Various states over the years (Quantity in Tonnes)

States ↓	YEARS					
	2003	**2004**	**2005**	**2006**	**2007**	**2008**
A	1500	1480	1620	1700	1540	1650
B	1250	1190	1400	1450	1320	1380
C	1160	1190	1310	1300	1340	1360
D	1520	1500	1480	1590	1630	1580
E	1440	1350	1430	1280	1380	1400
F	1600	1620	1510	1610	1580	1590

30. In which state has the production of rice increased continuously over the years?

(a) B *(b)* C *(c)* D *(d)* None of these

31. Which state produced the lowest quantity of rice over the years?

(a) A *(b)* C *(c)* D *(d)* E

32. Rice produced by state C in the year 2006 is approximately what per cent of the rice produced by state A in the same year?
(a) 69 (b) 72 (c) 76 (d) 82

33. In which year was the production of rice the highest in all the states together?
(a) 2005 (b) 2006 (c) 2007 (d) 2008

34. What is the respective ratio of the average quantity of rice produced by state D to the average quantity of rice produced by State F over the years?
(a) 69 : 79 (b) 138 : 155 (c) 276 : 317 (d) 310 : 317

SOLUTIONS

1. The total percentage of marks obtained by all students in Hindi

$$= 84 + 86 + 88 + 90 + 86 + 80 = 514$$

Hence, total marks obtained by all students in Hindi $= \frac{50}{100} \times 514 = 257$

Since, their average $= \frac{257}{6} = 42.83\%$

2. Pass percentage in Maths $= 95 \times \frac{100}{150} = 63.3\%$

Pass percentage in Social studies $= 85 \times \frac{100}{125} = 68\%$

It is clear from the table that Ravi and Kirti will pass in the examination.

3. It is clear from the table that Kirti has scored the highest marks in all the subjects.

4. Total marks obtained by Tanya in all the subjects

$$= \frac{150}{100} \times 60 + 84 + \frac{50}{100} \times 80 + \frac{150}{100} \times 65 + \frac{125}{100} \times 50 + \frac{50}{100} \times 76$$

$$= 90 + 84 + 40 + 97.5 + 62.5 + 38 = 412$$

5. Riya's overall percentage of Marks in all subjects $= \frac{80+53+86+60+80+78}{6} = \frac{437}{6} \approx 72.8\%$

6. Average disbursement of loans over the years $= \frac{87+104+113+120}{4} = \frac{424}{4} = 106 \approx 104$

which is nearly equal to the disbursement of loans in year 2006.

7. In 2005,

Total disbursement of loans of banks A and B = 18 + 27 = 45

Total disbursement of loans of banks C and D = 19 + 13 = 32

In 2006,

Total disbursement of loans of banks A and B = 23 + 33 = 56

Total disbursement of loans of banks C and D = 29 + 19 = 48

In 2007,

Total disbursement of loans of banks A and B = 45 + 18 = 63

Total disbursement of loans of banks C and D = 22 + 28 = 50

In 2008,

Total disbursement of loans of banks A and B = 30 + 41 = 71

Total disbursement of loans of banks C and D = 17 + 32 = 49

Since, it is clear that total disbursement of loans of banks A and B is not equal to the total disbursement of loans of banks C and D in any year.

8. Required percentage = $\frac{120-113}{113}\times 100=\frac{700}{113}=6\frac{22}{113}\%$

9. In 2008, the percentage of loan disbursement of bank B to the disbursement of loans of all the banks = $\frac{41}{120}\times 100$ = 34.17% > 30%

10. Number of candidates :

Delhi → 15000 + 17000 + 160 + 11000 + 750 = 43910

Hyderabad → 3500 + 20000 + 300 + 9000 + 1150 = 33950

Kolkata → 14900 + 17650 + 70 + 1300 + 1200 = 35120

Mumbai → 17000 + 19500 + 70 + 7000 + 900 = 44470

Hence, Mumbai has the highest number of candidates.

11. Total number of officers = 2000 + 15000 + 17000 + 3500 + 14900 + 11360 + 9000 = 72760

Total number of clerks = 5000 + 17000 + 19500 + 20000 + 17650 + 15300 + 11000 = 105450

Their difference = 105450 – 72760 = 32690

12. Required percentage = $\frac{11000-9000}{9000}\times 100=\frac{2000}{90}\approx 22\%$

13. Number of clerks in Bangluroo = 5000

Number of clerks in Hyderabad = 20000

More number of clerks in Hyderabad as compared to Bangluroo = $\frac{20000-5000}{5000}\times 1000=300\%$

Hence, Hyderabad has 300% more number of clerks as compared to Bangluroo.

14. Required percentage = $\frac{1200}{14900}\times 100\approx 8\%$

15. The number of units sold by the company over the years:

A → 110 + 118 + 143 + 126 + 152 + 195 = 844

C → 103 + 153 + 100 + 128 + 96 + 56 = 636

D → 112 + 166 + 78 + 83 + 135 + 198 = 772

E → 72 + 169 + 154 + 98 + 140 + 192 = 825

Hence, company A has sold the maximum number of units over the years.

16. The number of units sold by the company over the years:

A → 110 + 118 + 143 + 126 + 152 + 195 = 844

B → 91 + 93 + 85 + 99 + 69 + 35 = 472

D → 112 + 166 + 78 + 83 + 135 + 198 = 772

F → 64 + 56 + 120 + 70 + 176 + 54 = 540

Hence, company B has sold the maximum number of units over the years.

17. In 2007, the average number of units sold (in crores) = $\frac{152+69+96+135+140+176}{6} = \frac{768}{6} = 128$

18. Required difference = 112 – 78 = 34 crores

19. In 2005, total number of units sold by all the companies = 143 + 85 + 100 + 78 + 154 + 120 = 680

Hence, required percentage = $\frac{85}{680} \times 100 = 12.5\%$

20. Total number of employees working in the legal department = 48 + 54 + 36 + 30 + 53 = 221
Total number of employees working in the H.R. department = 1050 + 1015 + 976 + 888 + 1004 = 4933

Required percentage = $\frac{221}{4933} \times 100 = 4.4 \approx 4\%$

21. Total number of employees working in Organisation A

= 1050 + 1017 + 1382 + 1542 + 786 + 48 = 5825

Total number of employees working in organisation E

= 1004 + 963 + 1290 + 1580 + 735 + 53 = 5625

Required ratio = 5825 : 5625 = 233 : 225

22. Total number of employees working in organisation B

= 1015 + 960 + 1384 + 1545 + 745 + 54 = 5703

Required percentage = $\frac{960}{5703} \times 100 = 16.83\% \approx 17\%$

23. Total number of employees working in Marketing department

= 1382 + 1384 + 1275 + 1300 + 1290 = 6631

Total number of employees working in Production department

= 1542 + 1545 + 1550 + 1570 + 1580 = 7787

Their difference = 7787 – 6631 = 1156

Hence, averagedifference = $\frac{1156}{5} = 231.2 \approx 231$

24. Number of employees working in different organisation are
A → 1050 + 1017 + 1382 + 1542 + 786 + 48 = 5825
B → 1015 + 960 + 1384 + 1545 + 745 + 54 = 5703
C → 976 + 786 + 1275 + 1550 + 801 + 36 = 5424
D → 888 + 1025 + 1300 + 1570 + 800 + 30 = 5613
E → 1004 + 963 + 1290 + 1580 + 735 + 53 = 5625
Hence, total numbr of employees = 5825 + 5703 + 5424 + 5613 + 5625
= 28190

25. In society A:

Number of children = $\frac{25}{100} \times (250+350) = \frac{1}{4} \times 600 = 150$

Number of male children = $\frac{40}{100} \times 150 = 60$

Number of female children = 150 – 60 = 90

In society B:

Number of children = $\frac{40}{100}\times(400+150)=\frac{2}{5}\times 550=220$

Number of male children = $\frac{75}{100}\times 220=165$

Number of female children = 220 -- 165 = 55

In society C:

Number of children = $\frac{16}{100}\times(300+275)=\frac{4}{25}\times 575=92$

Number of male children = $\frac{25}{100}\times 92=23$

Number of female children = 92 – 23 = 69

In society D:

Number of children = $\frac{25}{100}\times(280+300)=\frac{1}{4}\times 580=145$

Number of male children = $\frac{80}{100}\times 145=116$

Number of female children = 145 – 116 = 29

In society E:

Number of children = $\frac{40}{100}\times(180+250)=\frac{2}{5}\times 430=172$

Number of male children = $\frac{50}{100}\times 172=86$

Number of female children = 172 – 86 = 86

In society F :

Number of children = $\frac{24}{100}\times(325+300)=\frac{6}{25}\times 625=150$

Number of male children = $\frac{46}{100}\times 150=69$

Number of female children = 150 – 69 = 81

Hence, total number of female children = 90 + 55 + 69 + 29 + 86 + 81 = 410

Total number of adult females = (350 + 150 + 275 + 300 + 250 + 300) – 410
= 1625 – 410 = 1215

Hence, required ratio = 1215 : 410 = 283 : 82

26. Total number of adult males in the society A and B = (250 + 400) – (60 + 165)
(As shown in solution : 25)
= 650 – 225 = 425

Total number of adult males in the society E and F = (280 + 325) – (86 + 69)
(As shown in solution : 25)
= (180 + 325) – (86 + 69)
= 505 – 155 = 350

Hence, required ratio = 425 : 350 = 17 : 14

27. Male children in soeicty B = 165
Male children in society F = 69 (As shown in solution : 25)
Hence, their difference = 165 − 69 = 96

28. Total number of female children = 410 (As shown in solution : 25)

29. Number of all members

= (250 + 350) + (400 + 150) + (300 + 275) + (280 + 300) + (180 + 250) + (325 + 300) + 150 + 220 + 92 + 145 + 172 + 150

= 600 + 550 + 575 + 580 + 430 + 625 + 929

= 4289

30. It is clear from the table that none of the state has the production of rice increased continuously over the years.

31. Production of rice by different states over the years:

A → 1500 + 1480 + 1620 + 1700 + 1540 + 1650 = 9490 tonnes
B → 1250 + 1190 + 1400 + 1450 + 1320 + 1380 = 7990 tonnes
C → 1160 + 1190 + 1310 + 1300 + 1340 + 1360 = 7660 tonnes
D → 1520 + 1500 + 1480 + 1590 + 1630 + 1580 = 9300 tonnes
E → 1440 + 1350 + 1430 + 1280 + 1380 + 1400 = 8280 tonnes
F → 1600 + 1620 + 1510 + 1610 + 1580 + 1590 = 9510 tonnes

Hence, the state C produced the lowest quantity of rice.

32. : Required percentage = $\frac{1300}{1700} \times 100 = 76.47\% \approx 76\%$

33. : Production of rice in different years by all states together:

2003 → 1500 + 1250 + 1160 + 1520 + 1440 + 1600 = 8470 tonnes
2004 → 1480 + 1190 + 1190 + 1500 + 1350 + 1620 = 8330 tonnes
2005 → 1620 + 1400 + 1310 + 1480 + 1430 + 1510 = 8750 tonnes
2006 → 1700 + 1450 + 1300 + 1590 + 1280 + 1610 = 8930 tonnes
2007 → 1540 + 1320 + 1340 + 1630 + 1380 + 1580 = 8790 tonnes
2008 → 1650 + 1380 + 1360 + 1580 + 1400 + 1590 = 8960 tonnes

Hence, in year 2008 the production of rice was the highest.

34. : Average quantity of rice produced by state D = $\frac{9300}{6}$ = 1550 tonnes (As shown in soluton : 31)

Average quantity of rice produced by state F = $\frac{9510}{6}$ = 1585 tonnes (As shown in soluton : 31)

Hence, required ratio = 1550 : 1585 = 310 : 317

DATA INTERPRETATION: BAR GRAPHS

BAR GRAPHS

Given quantity of a bar graph can be compared by the height or length. A bar graph can have either vertical or horizontal bars. You can compare different quantities or the same quantity at the different times. The bars may be placed adjacent to each other or may be separated from each other by spaces depending upon the problem.

For Example:

Registration of New Vehicles in Delhi (in thousands)

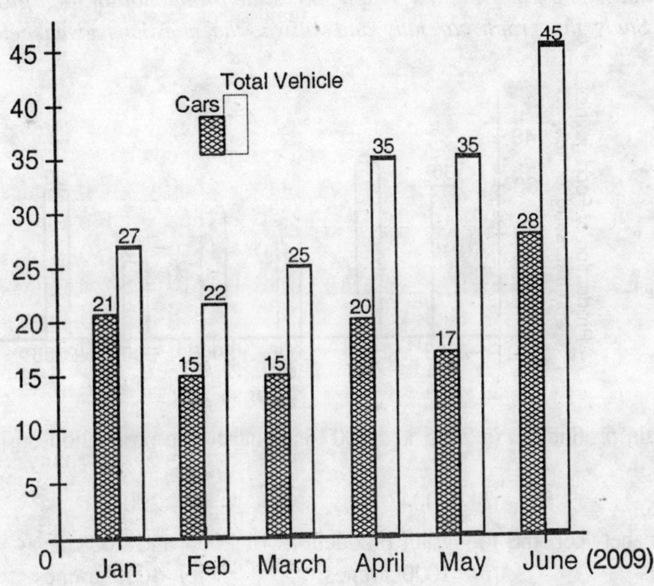

CUMULATIVE GRAPH

These are usually bar or line graphs where the height of the bar or line is divided up proportionally among various quantities presented in the graph. The representation of quantities may be done in terms of either percentage of the total or in absolute figures. These are also called sub-divided graphs. Thus, cumulative graph may be conveniently used for making comparisons.

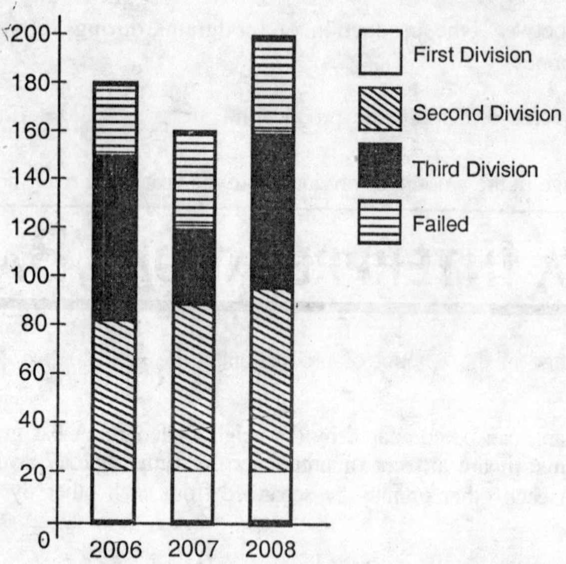

Example 1: Directions: *The following bar graph shows the production of food grains in India during certain year. Study the graph carefully and answer the questions given below:*

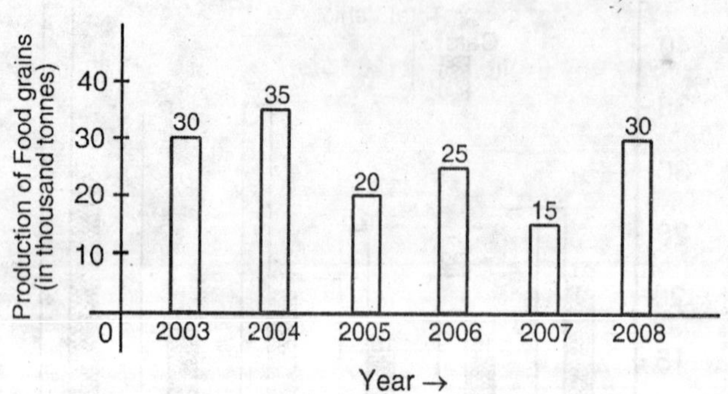

1. Total food grain production in 2005 and 2007 is equal to the production during which of the following years?
   (a) 2003 (b) 2004 (c) 2006 (d) 2008
2. The difference between the foodgrain productions of 2004 and 2008 is:
   (a) 500 tonnes (b) 1000 tonnes (c) 5000 tonnes (d) 10000 tonnes
3. Percentage increase in the production of foodgrains in the year 2008 over the year 2007 is:
   (a) 15% (b) 30% (c) 50% (d) 100%
4. Rate of change in quantity of production in which of the following two consecutive years is at the minimum level?
   (a) 2003 and 2004 (b) 2005 and 2006 (c) 2007 and 2008 (d) 2006 and 2007

Solution 1. Total production in 2005 and 2007 = 20 + 15 = 35 thousand tonnes. This total production is equal to the production in the year 2004.

Solution 2. Difference between the production of foodgrains during 2004 and 2008 = 35 – 30 = 5 thousand tonnes.

Solution 3. Percentage increase in foodgrain production = $\frac{30-15}{15} \times 100 = 100\%$

Solution 4. Rate of change in the amount of production in the year 2004 over the year 2003 = $\frac{35-30}{30} \times 100$

$= 16.67\%$

Rate of change in the amount of production in the year 2006 over the year 2005

$= \frac{(25-20)}{20} \times 100 = 25\%$

Rate of change in the amount of production in the year 2008 over the year 2007

$= \frac{(30-15)}{15} \times 100 = 100\%$

Rate of change in the amount of production in the year 2007 over the year 2006

$= \frac{(25-15)}{15} \times 100 = 66.67\%$

Hence, it is clear that the rate of change in the amount of production during the consecutive years 2007 and 2008 is at the highest level.

Example 2: Directions: *The bar graph as shown below gives information about the sale and profit details of a departmental store during the years from 2001–2008. Study the graph carefully and answer the questions asked here under.*

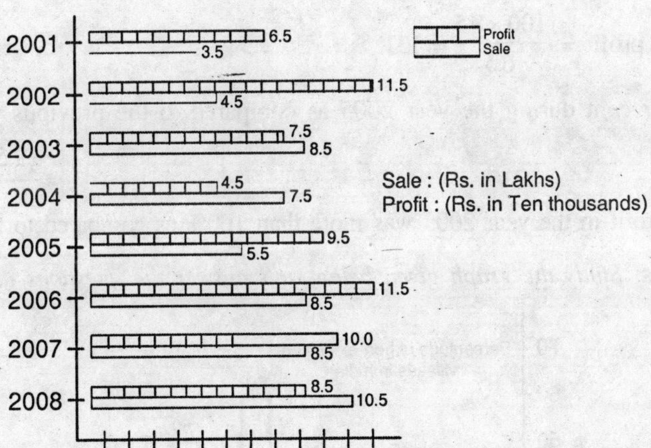

1. Mean of annual increase in sale from 2003 to 2008 (rupees in lakhs) is:
   (*a*) 0.1 (*b*) 0.2 (*c*) 0.3 (*d*) 0.4
2. Annual mean profit of the store (rupees in ten thousands) is approximately:
   (*a*) 8.5 (*b*) 8.6 (*c*) 8.7 (*d*) 9.0
3. During which of the following years percentage of profit earned by the store on the total sale was at the highest level?
   (*a*) 2001 (*b*) 2002 (*c*) 2003 (*d*) 2005

4. Assuming the profit earned during the year 2001 as base (100), the profit made by the store during the year 2008 was:
(*a*) 76 (*b*) 105 (*c*) 121 (*d*) 131

5. During which year between 2001 to 2006 profit made by the store as compared to the previous year was more than 100%?
(*a*) 2008 (*b*) 2007 (*c*) 2005 (*d*) 2003

Solution 1. Mean of annual increase in sale from 2003 to 2008 = $\frac{10.5-8.5}{5}=4$

Solution 2. Annual mean profit of the store (rupees in ten thousands)

$$=\frac{(6.5+11.5+7.5+4.5+9.5+11.5+10.0+8.5)}{8}=\frac{69.5}{8}=8.7 \text{ (approx.)}$$

Solution 3. Percentage of profit on the total sale in 2001 = $\frac{6.5\times10000\times100}{3.5\times100000}=18.57$

Percentage of profit on the total sale in 2002 = $\frac{11.5\times10000\times100}{4.5\times100000}=25.56$

Percentage of profit on the total sale in 2003 = $\frac{7.5\times10000\times100}{8.5\times100000}=8.82$

And percentage of profit on the total sale in 2005 = $\frac{9.5\times10000\times100}{5.5\times100000}=17.27$

∴ Percentage of profit on the total sale in 2002 was the highest level.

Solution 4. Required profit = $\frac{100\times8.5}{6.5}=131$

Solution 5. Profit per cent during the year 2005 as compared to the previous year

$$=\frac{(9.5-4.5)\times100}{4.5}=111.11\%$$

Hence, profit in the year 2005 was more than 100% as compared to the previous year.

Example 3: Directions: *Study the graph given below and answer the questions asked there under.*

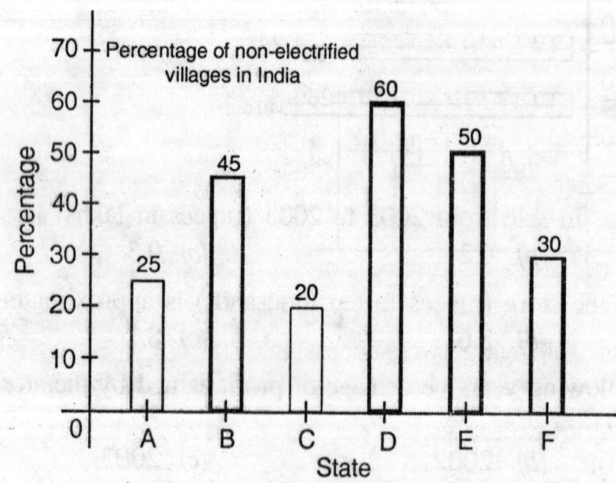

1. According to the table given below which state of India has the highest percentage of electritied villages?
(a) A (b) B (c) C (d) D (e) E
2. If central govt. decides to extend financial assistance for prompt electrification and begins with the state having the least electrified villages, then in the order of preference which of the following states will be fourth?
(a) C (b) B (c) A (d) E (e) F
3. How many states have at least 60% or more electrified villages?
(a) Five (b) Three (c) Four (d) Two (e) One
4. In which of the following states percentage of electrified villages is double the percentage of electrified villages in state (D)?
(a) C (b) F (c) A (d) B (e) E
5. What is the percentage of electrified villages in the state (A)?
(a) 65% (b) 25% (c) 35% (d) 75% (e) None of these

Solution 1. In the state (C) percentage of non-electrified villages is the least. It means the percentage of electrified villages for the state (C) is the highest.

Solution 2. The order of preference of the least electrified villages is given as: D, E, B, F, A, C.

Solution 3. In A, C and F states, percentage of non-electrified villages are 25, 20 and 30 per cent respectively. Hence, percentages of electrified villages for these three states are 75, 80 and 70 per cent respectively.

Solution 4. Percentage of electrified villages in state D = 100 – 60 = 40
Percentage of electrified villages in state C = 100 – 20 = 80
Hence, the percentage of electrified villages in the state C is double the percentage of electrified villages in state D.

Solution 5. Percentage of electrified villages in the state A = 100 – 25 = 75%

Example 4: Directions: *The following bar chart shows the amount accrued from additional taxation by the government during certain successive years. Study the chart carefully and answer the questions that follow:*

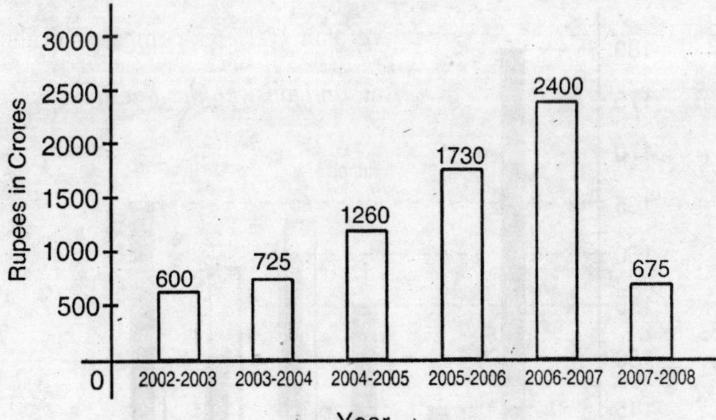

1. In between which of the following two successive financial years increase in taxation was at the highest level?
(a) 2002-2003 and 2003-04 (b) 2005-06 and 2006-07
(c) 2006-07 and 2007-08 (d) 2004-05 and 2005-06

2. Total increase in taxation was how much per cent between the years 2004-05 and 2005-06?
(a) 37.3% (b) 35.4% (c) 38.5% (d) 36.6%

3. Percentage decrease in taxation in between the years 2006-07 and 2007-08 was:
(a) 71.8% (b) 68.8% (c) 72.6% (d) 75%

4. Between the years 2005-06 and 2006-07 the taxation was increased by:
(a) Rs. 670 crores (b) Rs. 650 crores (c) Rs. 700 crores (d) Rs. 715 crores

5. What is the average amount of taxation during all these years?
(a) 1233.7 crores (b) Rs. 1433.5 crores (c) Rs. 1231.7 crores (d) Rs. 1400 crores

Solution 1. Between the financial years 2005-06 and 2006-07, maximum increase of Rs. 670 crores had been registered in taxation.

Solution 2. Percentage of total increase $= \frac{(1730-1260)}{1260} \times 100 = \frac{470 \times 100}{1260} = 37.3\%$

Solution 3. Percentage of total decrease in taxation between the years 2006-07 and 2007-08

$$= \frac{(2400-675)}{2400} \times 100 = \frac{1725 \times 100}{2400} = 71.8\%$$

Solution 4. Increase in taxation in between the financial years 2005-06 and 2006-07

$$= \text{Rs. } (2400 - 1730) = \text{Rs. } 670 \text{ crores}$$

Solution 5. Average of the total taxation during the years $= \frac{600+725+1260+1730+2400+625}{6}$

$$= \frac{7390}{6} = \text{Rs. } 1231.7 \text{ crores}$$

EXERCISE

Directions (Qs. 1-4): *The bar graph given here represents the number of persons killed in road accidents during rainy season in the year 2009. Study the graph carefully and answer the questions that follow:*

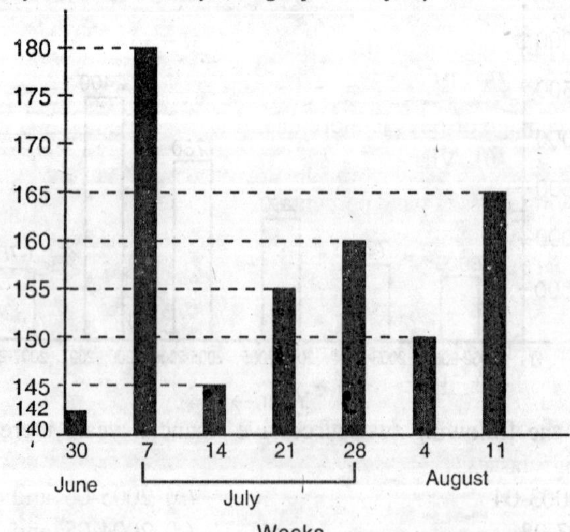

1. During which of the following successive weeks number of persons killed was the highest?
(a) 4 August – 11 August (b) 14 July – 21 July
(c) 30 June – 7 July (d) 21 July – 28 July

2. In how many weeks number of persons killed was more than 150?
(a) 3 (b) 2 (c) 4 (d) 1

3. In how many weeks number of persons killed was less than 150?
(a) 2 (b) 0 (c) 1 (d) 3

4. During which of the following successive weeks number of persons killed came down to a minimum level?
(a) 28 July – 4 August (b) 7 July – 14 July
(c) 30 June – 7 July (d) 21 July – 28 July

Directions (Qs. 5-9): *The bar graph given below shows annual result of different classes of a school. Study the graph carefully and attempt the questions that follow:*

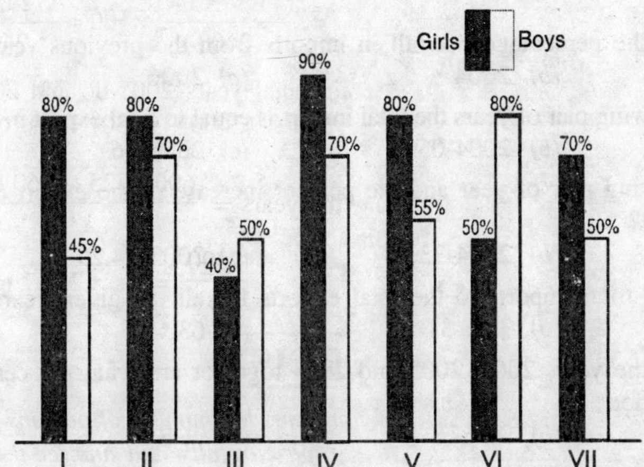

5. Result of which class shows maximum difference between pass percentage of the girls and the boys?
(a) I (b) IV (c) III (d) VI

6. In which class pass percentage of boys is more than the average pass percentage of girls of the school?
(a) VI (b) VII (c) III (d) V

7. In which of the following classes pass percentage of girls is less than the average pass percentage of the school?
(a) III-VI (b) V-VI
(c) VI-VII (d) III-IV

8. In which class number of failed girls is minimum?
(a) I (b) III (c) IV (d) VII

9. Average pass percentage of boys in classes II and III is equal to average pass percentage of girls in which of the following classes?
(a) II-VI (b) I-V
(c) VI-VII (d) V-VI

Directions (Qs. 10-14): *Study the following graph carefully to answer the questions given below it.*

Imports and Exports of spare parts by an automobile company over the given years

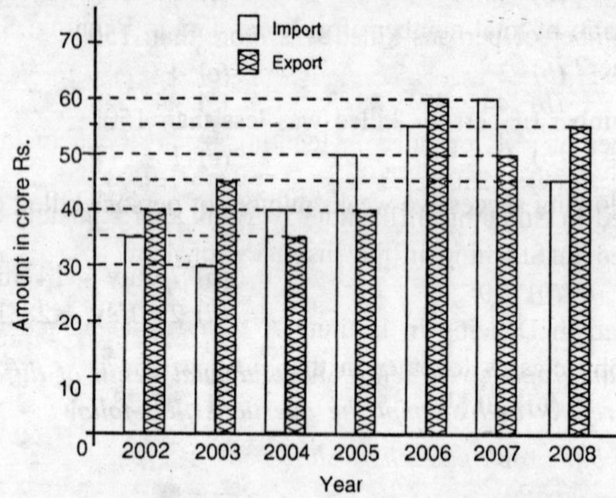

10. During which year the percentage rise/fall in imports from the previous year is the lowest?
(*a*) 2003 (*b*) 2004 (*c*) 2006 (*d*) 2007

11. In which of the following pair of years the total import is equal to total export in the same pair of years?
(*a*) 2002-03 (*b*) 2004-05 (*c*) 2005-06 (*d*) 2007-08

12. Which of the following pair of year and the percent increase in the export over the previous year is correctly matched?
(*a*) 2003-11.11 (*b*) 2004-33.33 (*c*) 2005-14.29 (*d*) 2008-20

13. What is the ratio of total imports to the total exports for all the given years together?
(*a*) 31 : 25 (*b*) 35 : 31 (*c*) 63 : 65 (*d*) 65 : 63

14. The total export in the years 2004, 2005 and 2008 together are what per cent of the total imports during the same period?
(*a*) 93.33 (*b*) 93.67 (*c*) 96.3% (*d*) 107.41

Directions (Qs. 15-19): *Study the graph carefully to answer the questions that follow:*

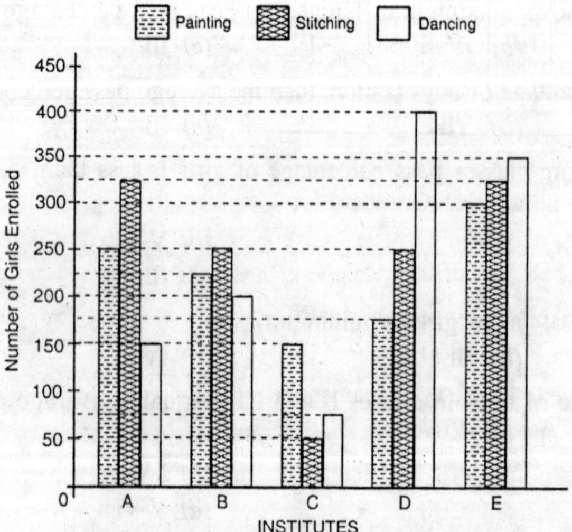

15. What is the respective ratio of total number of girls enrolled in Painting in the institutes A and C together to those enrolled in Stiching in the institutes D and E together?
(a) 5 : 4   *(b)* 5 : 7   *(c)* 9 : 8   *(d)* 16 : 23

16. What is the respective ratio of total number of girls enrolled in Painting, Stiching and Dancing from all the Institutes together?
(a) 43 : 47 : 48   *(b)* 44 : 47 : 48   *(c)* 44 : 48 : 47   *(d)* 47 : 48 : 44

17. What is the total number of girls enrolled in Painting from all the Institutes together?
(a) 1100   *(b)* 1150   *(c)* 1200   *(d)* 1275

18. Number of girls enrolled in Stitching in Institute B forms approximately what per cent of the total number of girls enrolled in Stitching in the Institutes together?
(a) 21   *(b)* 29   *(c)* 33   *(d)* 37

19. Number of girls enrolled in Dancing in Institute A forms what per cent of total number of girls enrolled in all the Hobby classes together in that Institute?
(a) 17.76   *(b)* 20.69   *(c)* 31.23   *(d)* 33.97

Directions (Qs. 20-23): *The bar graph given here shows the number of job-seekers of a state in various years at different stages of education.*

Job-seekers in Various Years

20. In which year was the number of Graduate job-seekers the same as that of Senior Secondary job-seekers?
(a) 2004   *(b)* 2005   *(c)* 2006   *(d)* 2007

21. The number of job-seekers having their qualification as Matriculation in the year 2005 was:
(a) 525   *(b)* 800   *(c)* 1050   *(d)* 1200

22. In comparison to the year 2003, how many job-seekers in all, were there in the year 2008?
(a) 1700   *(b)* 2075   *(c)* 2275   *(d)* 2375

23. In which year, was the number of Matriculate job-seekers maximum?
(a) 2003   *(b)* 2004   *(c)* 2006   *(d)* 2008

Directions (Qs. 24-28): *Study the following graph and answer the questions given below:*

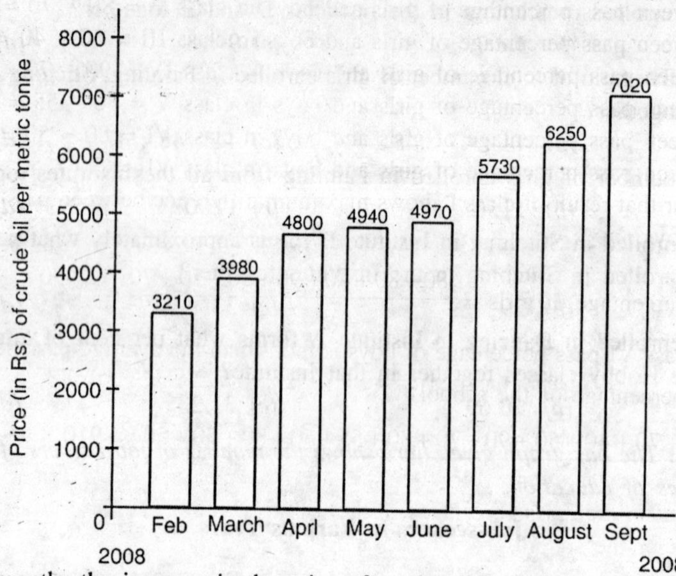

24. In how many months the increase in the price of crude oil was more than 10% with respect to the corresponding previous months?
(a) 2 (b) 3 (c) 4 (d) 5

25. What month/s experienced more than 10% but less than 20% increase in the crude oil price over the earlier month?
(a) March & July (b) April & July
(c) June & September (d) July & September

26. Which month had less than one per cent increase in crude oil price over the earlier month?
(a) April only (b) May only
(c) June only (d) April & August only

27. If in April the crude oil price would have been lesser than the given by Rs. 223 per metric tonne then how much would have been the percentage increase in price over the earlier month?
(a) 10 (b) 12 (c) 14 (d) 15

28. What is the approximate percentage increase in the price of crude oil from February to September?
(a) 80 (b) 100 (c) 130 (d) None of these

SOLUTIONS

1. According to the graph, the two successive weeks *vis.*, 30 June – 7 July shows highest increase of 180 – 142 = 38 in the number of persons killed.

2. According to the bar graph, number of person killed was more than 150 during the weeks beginning from 7 July, 21 July, 28 July and 11 August. Therefore number of such weeks = 4.

3. It is obvious from the bar graph that during the weeks beginning from 30 June, 14 July and 4 August, number of persons killed remained less than 150.

4. According to the bar graph, two successive weeks, *i.e.* 7 July – 14 July shows maximum decline in the number of persons killed in road accidents.

5. Difference between pass percentage of girls and boys in class I = 80 – 45 = 35%
Difference between pass percentage of girls and boys in class II = 80 – 70 = 10%
Difference between pass percentage of girls and boys in class III = 50 – 40 = 10%
Diffeence between pass percentage of girls and boys in class IV = 90 – 70 = 20%
Diffeence between pass percentage of girls and boys in class V = 80 – 55 = 25%
Diffeence between pass percentage of girls and boys in class VI = 80 – 50 = 30%
Diffeence between pass percentage of girls and boys in class VII = 70 – 50 = 20%
Hence, it is clear that result of class I shows maximum difference between pass percentage of the girls and the boys.

6. Average pass percentage of girls = $\frac{80+80+40+90+80+50+70}{7} = \frac{490}{7} = 70\%$.
Therefore, in class VI pass percentage of boys is more than the average pass percentage of girls.

7. Average pass percentage of the school

$$= \frac{80+45+80+70+40+50+90+70+80+55+50+80+70+50}{14} = \frac{910}{14} = 65\%$$

Therefore, it is clear that pass percentage of the girls in III and VI classes is less than the average pass percentage of the school.

8. In class IV pass percentage of girls is the highest. Thereore in this class only number of failed girls is the minimum.

9. Average pass percentage of the boys in classes II and III = $\frac{70+50}{2} = \frac{120}{2} = 60\%$

Average pass percentage of the girls in class VI and VII = $\frac{50+70}{2} = 60\%$

Therefore, average pass percentage of boys in classes II and III is equal to the average pass percentage of girls in classes VI and VII.

10. In 2003, change in imports = $\frac{35-30}{35} \times 100 = \frac{100}{7} = 13\frac{9}{7}\%$ fall

In 2004, change in imports = $\frac{40-30}{30} \times 100 = \frac{1}{3} \times 100 = 33\frac{1}{3}\%$ rise

In 2006, change in imports = $\frac{55-50}{50} \times 100 = 10\%$ rise

In 2007, change in imports = $\frac{60-55}{55} \times 100 = 9\frac{1}{11}\%$ rise

Hence, in 2007 the percentage rise/fall in imports from the previous year is the lowest.

11. In 2002-03, Total import = 35 + 30 = Rs. 65 crores
Total export = 40 + 55 = Rs. 95 crores

In 2004-05 , Total import = 40 + 50 = Rs. 90 crores
Total export = 35 + 40 = Rs. 75 crores

In 2005-06, Total import = 50 + 55 = Rs. 105 crores
Total export = 40 + 60 = Rs. 100 crores

In 2007-08, Total import = 60 + 45 = Rs. 105 crores
Total export = 50 + 55 = Rs. 105 crores
Hence, In 2007-08 pair of years the total import is equal to total export.

12. In 2003, percentage increase in export = $\frac{55-40}{40} \times 100 = 37.5\%$
In 2004, there is decrease in export over the previous year.

In 2005, percentage increase in export = $\frac{40-35}{35} \times 100 = 10\%$

In 2008, percentage increase in export = $\frac{55-50}{50} \times 100 = 10\%$

13. Total import = 35 + 30 + 40 + 50 + 55 + 60 + 45 = Rs. 315 crores
Total export = 40 + 55 + 35 + 40 + 60 + 50 + 55 = Rs. 335 crores
Since, their ratio = 315 : 335 = 63 : 65

14. In 2004, 2005 and 2008, total import = 40 + 50 + 45 = Rs. 135 crores
In 2004, 2005 and 2008, total export = 35 + 40 + 55 = Rs. 130 crores

Required percentage = $\frac{130}{135} \times 100 = 96.3\%$

15. Total number of girls enrolled in Painting in the Institutes A and C = 250 + 150 = 400
Total number of girls enrolled in Stitching in the Institutes D and E = 250 + 325 = 575
Required ratio = 400 : 575 = 16 : 23

16. Total number of girls enrolled in Painting = 250 + 225 + 150 + 175 + 300 = 1100
Total number of girls enrolled in Stitching = 325 + 250 + 50 + 250 + 325 = 1200
Tootal number of girls enrolled in Dancing = 150 + 200 + 75 + 400 + 350 = 1175
Hence, required ratio = 1100 : 1200 : 1175 = 44 : 48 : 47

17. Total number of girls enrolled in Painting = 250 + 225 + 150 + 175 + 300 = 1100

18. Number of girls enrolled in Stiching in Institute B = 250
Total number of girls enrolled in Stitching in all the Institutions
= 325 + 250 + 50 + 250 + 325 = 1200

Hence, required percentage = $\frac{250}{1200} \times 100 = 20.83 \approx 21\%$

19. Number of girls enrolled in Dancing in Institute A = 150
Total number of girls enrolled in all the Hobby classes in Institute A = 250 + 325 + 150 = 725

Hence, required percentage = $\frac{150}{725} \times 100 = 20.69$

20. In 2004, number of Graduate job-seekers = 375
In 2004, number of Senior Secondary job-seekers = 1000 – 375 = 635
In 2005, number of Graduate job-seekers = 525
In 2005, number of Senior Secondary job-seekers = 1050 – 525 = 525
Hence, In, 2005, number of Graduate job-seekers was the same as that of Senior Secondary job-seekers.

21. In the year 2005, the number of job-seekers having their qualification as Matriculation $= 1850 - 1050 = 800$

22. In 2004, total number of job seekers = 1625
In 2008, total number of job-seekers = 4000
Required difference = 4000 − 1625 = 2375

23. Number of Matriculate job-seekers :
In 2003 → 1400 − 650 = 750
In 2004 → 1625 − 1000 = 625
In 2006 → 2300 − 1250 = 1050
In 2008 → 4000 − 2200 = 1800
Hence, in 2008, number of Matriculate job-seekers was maximum.

24. Increase in the price of crude oil in the given months with respect to the corresponding previous months:

In March → $\frac{3980-3210}{3210}\times 100 \approx 24\% > 10\%$

In April → $\frac{4800\times 3980}{3980}\times 100 = 20.6\% > 10\%$

In May → $\frac{4940-4800}{4800}\times 100 \approx 3\% < 10\%$

In June → $\frac{4970-4940}{4970}\times 100 = 0.6\% < 10\%$

In July → $\frac{5730-4970}{4970}\times 100 \approx 15.3\% > 10\%$

In August → $\frac{6250-5730}{5730}\times 100 = 9.07\% < 10\%$

In September → $\frac{7020-6250}{6250}\times 100 = 12.32\% > 10\%$

Hence, in March, April, July and September *i.e.*, 4 months the increase in the price of crude oil was more than 10% with respect to the corresponding previous months.

25. It is shown in solution: 24 that in the months of July and September, increase in the crude oil price was more than 10% but less than 20% over the earlier month.

26. It is shown in solution: 24 that in the month of May only, increase in crude oil price has less than 1% *i.e.*, 0.6% over the earlier month.

27. In April, crude oil price = Rs. 4800 per metric tonne.
So, reduced crude oil price = 4800 − 223 = Rs. 4577

Hence, required percentage $= \frac{4577-3980}{3980}\times 100 = 15\%$

28. Required percentage $= \frac{7020-3210}{3210}\times 100 = \frac{381}{321}\times 100 = 118.69\%$

DATA INTERPRETATION: LINE GRAPHS

LINE GRAPHS

Line graphs are used to show how a quantity changes continuously. If the line goes up, the quantity is increasing; if the line goes down, the quantity is decreasing; if the line is horizontal, the quantity is not changing.

For Example:

Demand and Production of rubber (in thousand tons) in various years

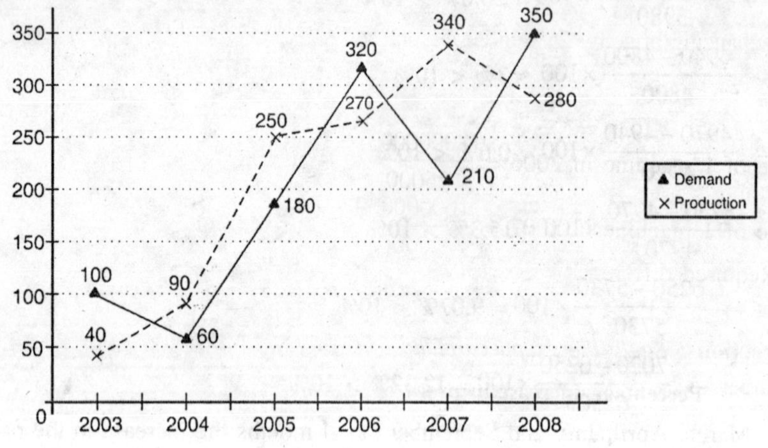

Example 1: Directions: *Study carefully the graph given below and answer the questions that follow:*

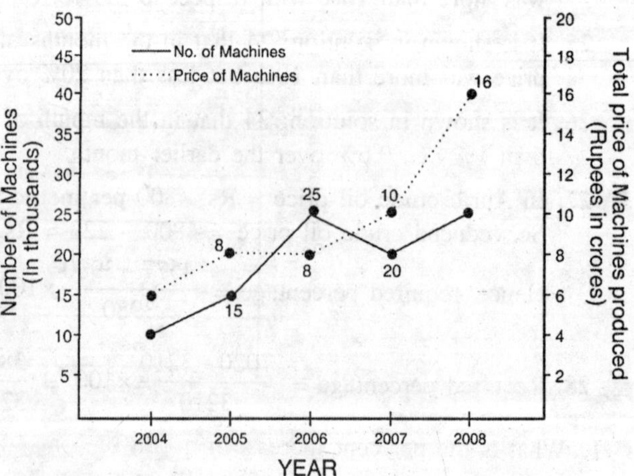

1. Price of a machine during 2005 was:

   (a) Rs. $5\frac{1}{3}$ thousand (b) Rs. 50 thousand

   (c) Rs. 5103 (d) Rs. 3 thousand

2. The percentage decrease in the production in 2007 over the previous year 2006 was:

   (a) 5% (b) 20%

   (c) 25% (d) 30%

3. The difference in revenue collection from the sale of machines during 2007 and 2008 was:
   (a) Rs. 10 lakhs (b) Rs. 1 crore (c) Rs. 4 crores (d) Rs. 6 crores
4. Had the company sold its machines in 2008 at 25% inhanced price of 2007, what would have been the total selling price of machines produced during the year?
   (a) Rs. 35 crores (b) Rs. 20 crores (c) Rs. 12.5 crores (d) Rs. 15.5 crores
5. Difference between the price of a machine in the year 2006 and that in the eyar 2007 was:
   (a) Rs. 1500 (b) Rs. 2500 (c) Rs. 1800 (d) Rs. 3200

Solution 1. No. of machines produced during the year 2005 = 15000
And price of the machines = Rs. 8,0000000

$\therefore$ Price of 1 machine in 2005 = Rs. $\frac{80000000}{15000}$ = Rs. $5\frac{1}{3}$ thousand

Solution 2. Percentage decrease in production of machines during 2007 over the previous year 2006

$$= \frac{(25-20)\times 100}{25} = 20\%$$

Solution 3. Difference in revenue collected from sale of machines during 2007 and 2008
= 16 – 10 = Rs. 6 crores.

Solution 4. On enhancing price by 25% in 2008, total price of the machines produced during the years 2008

$$= \frac{10\times 125}{100} = \text{Rs. } 12.5 \text{ crores}$$

Solution 5. Price of 1 machine in 2006 = $\frac{80000000}{25000}$ = Rs. 3200

Price of 1 machine in 2007 = $\frac{100000000}{20000}$ = Rs. 5000

$\therefore$ Required difference = Rs. (5000 – 3200) = Rs. 1800

Example 2: Directions: *Study the graph carefully to answer the questions that follow:*

Percentage Increase in profit of two companies over the years

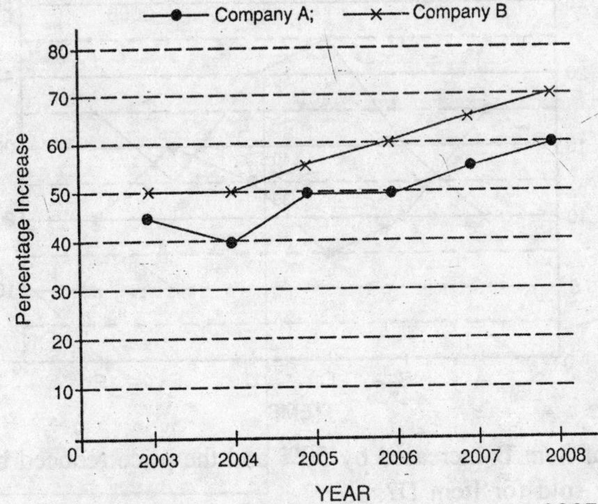

1. What is the per cent increase in profit of company A in the year 2007 from the previous year?
   (a) 5 (b) 10 (c) 45 (d) 60

2. What is the per cent increase in profit of company A in the year 2008 from the previous year?
(a) 7.64 *(b)* 9.09 *(c)* 8.12 *(d)* 10.11

3. What is the per cent increase in profit of company A in the year 2005 from the previous year?
(a) 10 *(b)* 15 *(c)* 20 *(d)* 25

4. If the profit of company B in the year 2003 was Rs. 6,79,995, what would its profit have been in the year 2002?
(a) Rs. 4,24,530 *(b)* Rs. 4,53,330 *(c)* Rs. 5,01,500 *(d)* Rs. 5,53,330

5. Based on the graph, which of the following statements is True?
(a) Company B has made the highest profit in the year 2008
(b) Company A has made the lowest profit in the year 2004
(c) Company B has made more amount of the profit than company A over the years
(d) There is no increase in the profit of company B in the year 2005 from the previous year.

Solution 1. Required percentage = $\frac{55-50}{50} \times 100 = 10\%$

Solution 2. Required percentage = $\frac{60-55}{55} \times 100 = 9.09\%$

Solution 3. Required percentage = $\frac{50-40}{40} \times 100 = 25\%$

Solution 4. Required profit = $\frac{100}{150} \times 6{,}79{,}995 =$ Rs. 4,53,330

Solution 5. It is clear from the graph that company B has made the highest profit in the year 2008, i.e., 70%

Example 3: Directions: *Study the following graph carefully to answer these questions:*

Quantity of Various items sold and price per kg

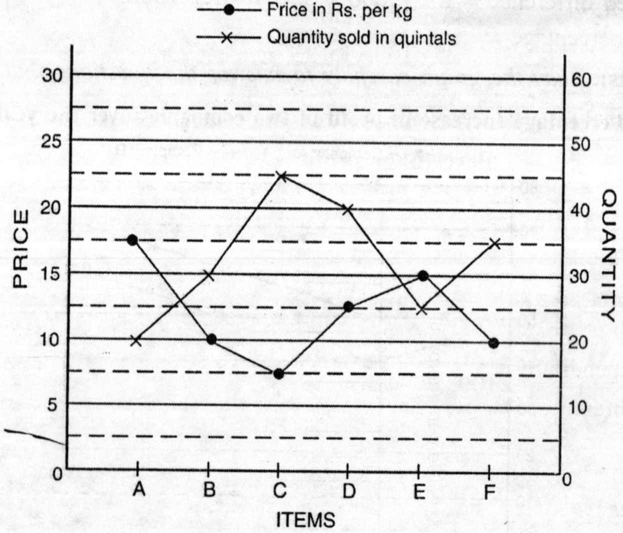

1. If the quantity sold of item D increased by 50% and the price reduced by 10%, what was the total value of the quantity sold for Item D?
(a) Rs. 675 *(b)* Rs. 6750 *(c)* Rs. 67500 *(d)* Rs. 67550

2. What is the ratio between the total values of quantity sold for items E and F respectively?
(*a*) 3 : 2 (*b*) 5 : 7 (*c*) 7 : 5 (*d*) 15 : 14

3. If the price as well as the quantity sold is increased by 20% for item A, what is the total value of quantity sold for item A?
(*a*) Rs. 42000 (*b*) Rs. 48500 (*c*) 49000 (*d*) 50400

4. What is the average price per kg. of items A, B and C?
(*a*) Rs. 7.50 (*b*) Rs. 9 (*c*) Rs. 9.50 (*d*) Rs. 11.67

5. Total value of quantity sold for item C is what per cent of the total value of the quantity sold for item E?
(*a*) 85 (*b*) 87.5 (*c*) 90 (*d*) 111

Solution 1. New quantity of item D = $\frac{150}{100} \times 40 = 60$ quintal

New price per kg of item D = $\frac{90}{100} \times 12.50 =$ Rs. 11.25

Since, total value = Rs (60 × 100 × 11.25) = Rs. 67500

Solution 2. Required ratio = (25 × 100 × 15) : (35 × 100 × 10) = 15 : 14

Solution 3. New price of item A per kg = $\frac{120}{100} \times 17.50 =$ Rs. 21

New quantity of item A = $\frac{120}{100} \times 20 = 24$ quintal

Since, total value = Rs. (24 × 100 × 21) = Rs. 50400

Solution 4. Average price per kg of items A, B and C = $\frac{17.50 + 10 + 7.50}{3}$ = Rs. 11.67

Solution 5. Required percentage = $\frac{45 \times 100 \times 750}{25 \times 100 \times 15} \times 100 = 90\%$

Example 4: Directions: *Study the following graph carefully and answer the questions that follow:*

Percentage profit earned by two companies over the given years

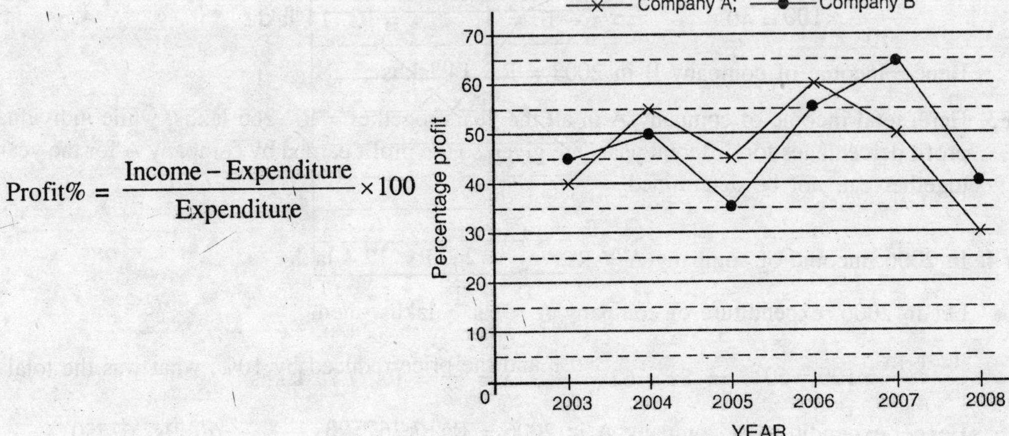

1. If the income of company A in 2005 was equal to its expenditue in 2007, what was the ratio between company's expenditure in the years 2005 and 2007 respectively?
   (a) 19 : 20 (b) 20 : 19 (c) 20 : 29 (d) 29 : 20
2. If the total expenditure of the two companies in 2008 was Rs. 18 lakhs and expenditure of companies A and B in that year in the ratio of 4 : 5 respectively, then what was the income of company B in that year (in lakh Rs.)?
   (a) 8 (b) 10 (c) 10.4 (d) 14
3. If the total income of company A in all the years together was equal to the total expenditure of company B in all the years together, which was Rs. 265 lakhs, then what was the total percentage profit earned by Company A for all the years together?
   (a) 37 (b) 45 (c) 52 (d) Cannot be determined
4. If the income of company B in 2006 was Rs. 18.6 lakhs and ratio of incomes of company A and B in 2006 was 2 : 3, what was the expenditure of company A in 2006 (in lakhs)?
   (a) 7.75 (b) 9.75 (c) 12 (d) 12.4
5. If the income of company A in 2006 was equal to the total expenditure of company B in 2007, then what was the ratio of expenditure of company A in 2006 to the income of company B in 2007?
   (a) 10 : 13 (b) 13 : 10 (c) 25 : 66 (d) 66 : 25

Solution 1. Let income of company A in 2005 = Expenditure of Company A in 2007 = Rs. x and also expenditure of company A in 2005 = Rs. x_1; then
For company A in 2005,

$$\frac{x - x_1}{x_1} \times 100 = 45 \quad \Rightarrow 29x_1 = 20x \quad \therefore \ x_1 = \frac{20x}{29}$$

Since, required ratio = $\frac{20x}{29} : x = 20 : 29$

Solution 2. In 2008, expenditure of company B = $\frac{5}{4+5} \times 18$ lakhs = Rs. 10 lakhs.
Let, income of company B in 2008 = Rs. x lakhs; then

$$\frac{x - 10}{10} \times 100 = 40 \quad \Rightarrow x - 10 = 4 \quad \therefore x = \text{Rs. } 14 \text{ lakhs}$$

Hence, income of company B in 2008 = Rs. 14 lakhs

Solution 3. Here, total income of company A in all the years together = Rs. 265 lakhs, while individual profit percentages for different years are given so the profit earned by company A for the years together can not be determined.

Solution 4. In 2006, income of company A = Rs. $\frac{18.6}{3} \times 2$ = Rs. 12.4 lakhs
Let in 2006, expenditure of company A = Rs. x lakhs, then

$$\frac{12.4 - x}{x} \times 100 = 60 \quad \Rightarrow 8x = 62 \quad \therefore x = \frac{62}{8} = \text{Rs. } 7.75 \text{ lakhs}$$

Hence, expenditure of company A in 2006 = Rs. 7.75 lakhs

Solution 5. Let income of company A in 2006 = Expenditure of company B in 2007 = Rs. x lakhs also Rs. x_1 lakhs, and Rs. x_2 lakhs be the expenditure of company A in 2006 and income of company B in 2007 respectively; then

For company A in 2006,

$$\frac{x - x_1}{x_1} \times 100 = 60 \quad \Rightarrow 8x_1 = 5x \quad \therefore\ x_1 = \text{Rs. } \frac{5x}{8} \text{ lakhs}$$

For company B in 2007,

$$\frac{x_2 - x}{x} \times 100 = 65 \quad \Rightarrow 20x_2 = 33x \quad \therefore\ x_2 = \text{Rs. } \frac{33x}{20} \text{ lakhs}$$

$$\text{Since, required ratio} = \frac{5x}{8} : \frac{33x}{20} = \frac{5x}{8} \times 40 : \frac{33x}{20} \times 40 = 25 : 66$$

EXERCISE

Directions (Qs. 1-5): *Study the following Graph carefully and answer the questions given below:*

Units of Raw Material Manufactured and Sold by a Company over the Years (Units in Crores)

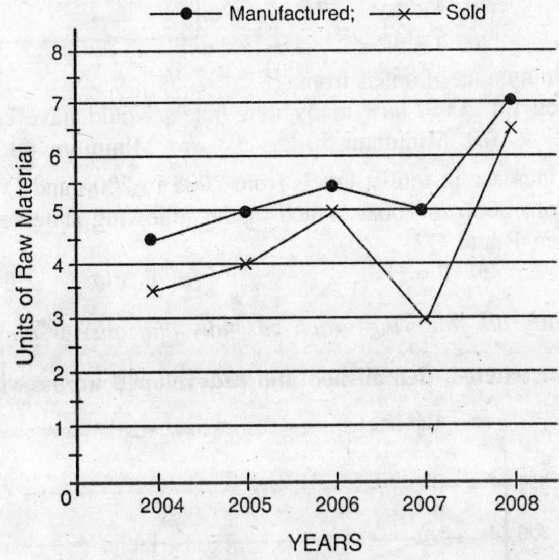

1. What is the average number of units sold over the years?

(*a*) 44 lakhs (*b*) 4.4 cores (*c*) 44 crores (*d*) None of these

2. What is the respective ratio of the number of units manufactured in the year 2004 to the number of units manufactured in the year 2008?

(*a*) 7 : 9 (*b*) 7 : 11 (*c*) 9 : 11 (*d*) 9 : 14

3. What is the difference between the number of units manufactured and the number of units sold over the years?

(*a*) 5 lakhs (*b*) 50 lakhs (*c*) 5 crores (*d*) 50 crores

4. What is respective ratio of the difference between the number of units manufactured and sold in the year 2006 to the difference between the number of units manufactured and sold in the year 2007?

(*a*) 1 : 2 (*b*) 1 : 4 (*c*) 2 : 3 (*d*) 3 : 5

5. What is the approximate per cent increase in the number of units sold in the year 2008 from the previous year?
(*a*) 60 (*b*) 70 (*c*) 95 (*d*) 117

Directions (Qs. 6-10): *Study the following graph carefully and answer the questions given below it:*

Number of Tourist Hotels in a State

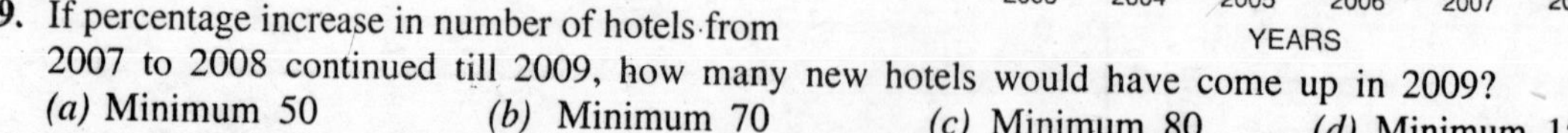

6. During which of the given years increase in number of hotels over the previous year was highest?
(*a*) 2004 (*b*) 2006
(*c*) 2005 (*d*) 2008

7. What is the approximate percentage increase in tourist hotels in 2008 over that in 2003?
(*a*) 75 (*b*) 100
(*c*) 125 (*d*) 150

8. If in 2005 new hotels constructed were fewer by 10, what would have been the ratio between the new hotels constructed in 2004 and that constructed in 2005?
(*a*) 1 : 4 (*b*) 4 : 1
(*c*) 4 : 5 (*d*) 5 : 4

9. If percentage increase in number of hotels from 2007 to 2008 continued till 2009, how many new hotels would have come up in 2009?
(*a*) Minimum 50 (*b*) Minimum 70 (*c*) Minimum 80 (*d*) Minimum 150

10. If P is the percentage increase in tourist hotels from 2005 to 2006 and Q is the percentage increase in the tourist hotels from 2006 to 2008. Which of the following statements is true with respect to the relationship between P and Q?
(*a*) P < Q (*b*) P = Q (*c*) P > Q (*d*) None of these

Directions (Qs. 11-15): *Study the following graph carefully and answer the questions given below.*

Number of Building constructed, demolished and redeveloped across various cities in a year

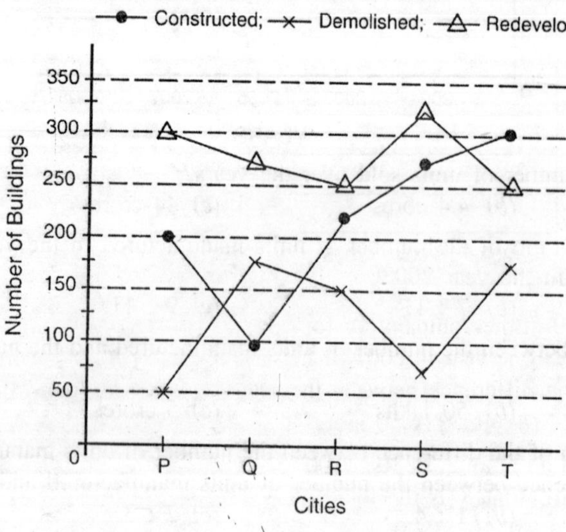

11. What is the difference between the total constructions (constructed, demolished and redeveloped) in city Q and city T?

(a) 125 (b) 175 (c) 180 (d) 200

12. The total number of buildings constructed across the cities is approximately what per cent of the total number of buildings redeveloped across the cities?

(a) 73 (b) 74 (c) 79 (d) 89

13. What is the respective ratio of the number of building demolished in city T to the number of buildings redeveloped in city P?

(a) 1 : 2 (b) 2 : 3 (c) 3 : 5 (d) 7 : 12

14. What is the average number of buildings demolished across the cities?

(a) 115 (b) 125 (c) 132 (d) 135

15. What is the approximate average number of constructions (constructed, demolished and redeveloped) in the city R?

(a) 198 (b) 208 (c) 216 (d) 222

Directions (Qs. 16-20): *These questions are based on the information given in the following graph.*

Rates of interest per cent per annum given by two companies 'A' and 'B' during the given years.

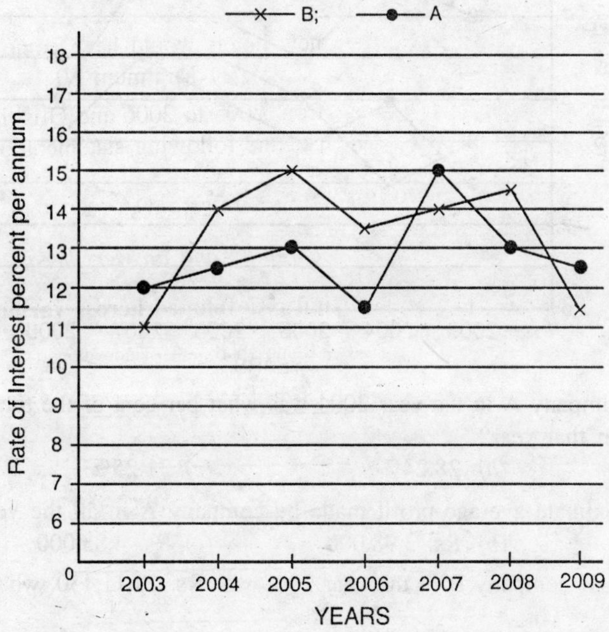

16. Samir invested Rs. 10,000 in the company 'A' for one year in 2006. He reinvested the total amount along with interest for next one year in 2007. If he had invested for both years in the Company 'B', what would have been the difference between the interests earned?

(a) Rs. 16.50 less (b) Rs. 116.50 more (c) Rs. 128.50 less (d) Rs. 128.50 more

17. In 2007 Saurabh invested an amount of Rs. 12000 in company 'A' and an amount of Rs. 15,000 in Company 'B' for one year. What was the total interest accrued?

(a) Rs. 3600 (b) Rs. 3800 (c) Rs. 3900 (d) Rs. 4100

18. Gopal invested an amount of Rs. 25,000 in company A in 2003 for one year. Thereafter in 2004 he invested the amount alongwith interest in Company 'B' for one year? What was the total amount of interest earned in the two years together?
(*a*) Rs. 6218.75 (*b*) Rs. 6800 (*c*) Rs. 6920 (*d*) Rs. 7200

19. An amount of Rs. 20,000 was invested in Company 'B' in 2008 and after one year the entire amount alongwith interest was will be reinvested in the Company A for one more year. What will be the total amount of interest accrued?
(*a*) Rs. 5199 (*b*) Rs. 5762.50 (*c*) Rs. 5533.75 (*d*) Rs. 54.25

20. Madhava invested Rs. 1500 in Company 'B' in 2005 for two years with a condition to get the compound interest at the same rate as 2005. What was the amount of interest earned?
(*a*) Rs. 4387.75 (*b*) Rs. 4578.50 (*c*) Rs. 4578.75 (*d*) Rs. 4837.50

Directions (Qs. 21-25): *Study the graph carefully to answer the questions that follow.*

Profit (in lakhs) made by three companies over the years
Profit = Income – Expenditure

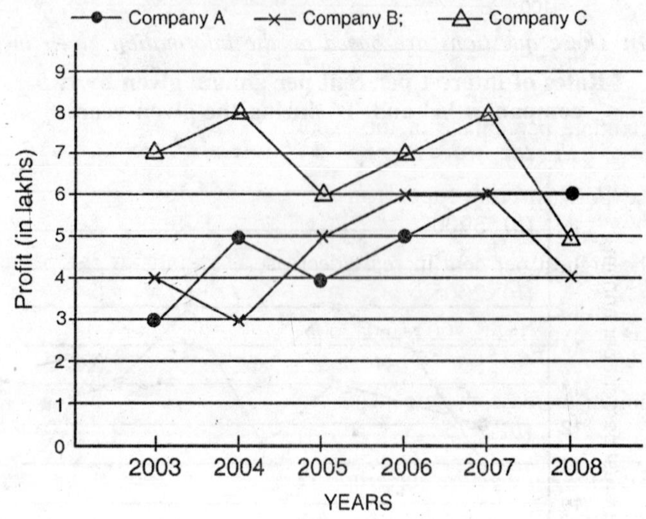

21. Profit made by Company A in the year 2004 was what per cent of the total profit made by all the three companies in that year?
(*a*) 21.43% (*b*) 28.24% (*c*) 31.25% (*d*) 36.25%

22. What is the approximate average profit made by company A in all the years together?
(*a*) Rs. 3,82,000 (*b*) Rs. 3,98,000 (*c*) Rs. 4,83,000 (*d*) Rs. 5,12,000

23. If the expenditure of company B in the year 2008 was Rs. 22,11,430, what was its income in that year?
(*a*) Rs. 26,11,430 (*b*) Rs. 27,11,430 (*c*) Rs. 28,14,680 (*d*) Rs. 32,09,670

24. If the income of company A in the year 2007 was Rs. 13,54,300, what was its expenditure in that year?
(*a*) Rs. 6,48,200 (*b*) Rs. 7,54,300 (*c*) Rs. 8,33,500 (*d*) Rs. 9,21,600

25. What is the per cent increase in profit of company C in the year 2004 from the previous year?
(*a*) 7 (*b*) 14 (*c*) 21 (*d*) 28

Directions (Qs. 26-30): *Study the folloiwng graph to answer the given questions.*

Export over the years (in crore Rs.)

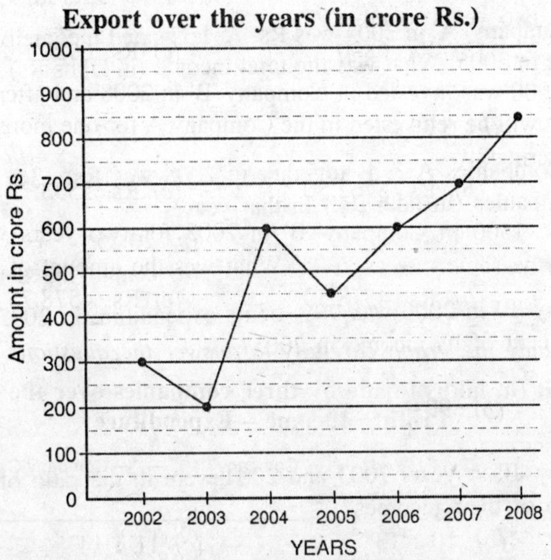

26. What is the approximate percentage of the export of 2004 from 2005?

(a) 120 *(b)* 135 *(c)* 145 *(d)* 150

27. What is the total export (in crore rupees) in the given years?

(a) 3700 *(b)* 3900 *(c)* 3950 *(d)* 4100

28. Which year has the highest per cent increase/decrease in exports as compared to the previous year?

(a) 2004 *(b)* 2005 *(c)* 2007 *(d)* Rs. 2008

29. What is difference in exports in 2004 and 2005?

(a) Rs. 15 crores *(b)* Rs. 100 crores *(c)* Rs. 150 crores *(d)* Rs. 1500 crores

30. What is the maximum increase in percentage from minimum export in the given years?

(a) 375 *(b)* 475 *(c)* 750 *(d)* 950

Directions (Qs. 31-35): *Study the following graph carefully and answer the questions given below it.*

Per cent profit earned by two Companies A and B over the years

—●— Company A; —×— Company B

Profit = Income − Expenditure

$$\text{Profit\%} = \frac{\text{Profit}}{\text{Expenditure}} \times 100$$

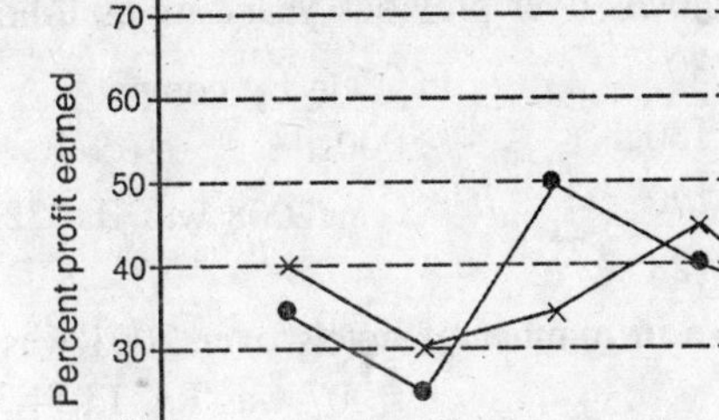

31. If the income of A in 2005 was Rs. 1,42,500, what was its expenditure in that year?
(a) Rs. 95000 *(b)* Rs. 95500 *(c)* Rs. 99,500 *(d)* Rs. 1,05,000

32. If the expenditure of company 'A' in 2004 was Rs. 75 lakhs and income of Company A in 2004 was equal to its expenditure in 2005. What was the total income (in lakhs Rs) of the company A in 2004 and 2005 together?
(a) 131.25 *(b)* 175 *(c)* 218.75 *(d)* 234.37

33. Total expenditure of Companies A & B together in 2008 was Rs. 13.5 lakhs. What was the total income of the two companies (in lakh Rs.) in that year?
(a) 19.75 *(b)* 20.25
(c) 19.575 *(d)* Cannot be determined

34. Expenditure of company 'B' in 2006 was 90% of its expenditure in 2005. Income of Company 'B' in 2006 was what per cent of its income in 2005?
(a) $96\frac{2}{3}$ *(b)* $99\frac{1}{3}$ *(c)* 121.5 *(d)* 130.5

35. Expenditure of company 'B' in years 2003 and 2004 were in the ratio of 5 : 7 respectively. What was the respective ratio of their incomes?
(a) 8 : 13 *(b)* 10 : 13 *(c)* 11 : 14 *(d)* 13 ; 14

SOLUTIONS

1. Average number of units sold $= \frac{3.5+4+5+3+6.5}{5} = \frac{22}{5} = 4.4$ crores

2. Required ratio = 4.5 : 7 = 45 : 70 = 9 : 14

3. Total number of units manufactured = 4.5 + 5 + 5.5 + 5 + 7 = 27 crores
Total number of units sold = 3.5 + 4 + 5 + 3 + 6.5 = 22 crores
Hence, their difference = 27 crores − 22 crores = 5 crores

4. Required ratio = (5.5 − 5) : (5 − 3) = 0.5 : 2 = 1 : 4

5. Required percentage of increase $= \frac{6.5-3}{3}\times 100 = \frac{3.5\times 100}{3} \approx 117\%$

6. Increase in number of hotels over previous years are as follows:
In 2004, 440 − 410 = 30
In 2005, 570 − 440 = 130
In 2006, 740 − 570 = 170
In 2008, 838 − 710 = 128
Hence, in 2006, increase in number of hotels over 2005 was highest.

7. Required percentage of increase $= \frac{838-410}{410}\times 100 = \frac{428}{410}\times 100$

$= 104.4\% \approx 100\%$

8. Required ratio = (440 − 410) : (570 − 10 − 440) = 30 : 120 = 1 : 4

9. Percentage increase in number of hotels from 2007 to 2008 = $\frac{838-710}{710}\times 100 = \frac{128}{710}\times 100 \approx 18\%$

Since, required number of new hotels in 2009 = $\frac{18}{100}\times 838 \approx 150$

10. Here, P = $\frac{740-570}{570}\times 100 = 29.8\%$

and also, Q = $\frac{838-740}{740}\times 100 = 13.2\%$

Hence, P > Q

11. Total constructions in City Q = 100 + 175 + 275 = 550
Total constructions in City T = 175 + 250 + 300 = 725
Their difference = 725 – 550 = 175

12. Total number of buildings constructed across the cities = 200 + 100 + 225 + 275 + 300 = 1100
Total number of buildings redeveloped across the cities = 300 + 275 + 250 + 325 + 250 = 1400

Required percentage = $\frac{1100}{1400}\times 100 = 78.57\% \approx 79\%$

13. Required ratio = 175 : 300 = 7 : 12

14. Average number of building demolished = $\frac{50+175+150+75+175}{5} = \frac{625}{5} = 125$

15. Average number of constructions in City R = $\frac{150+225+250}{3} = \frac{625}{3} = 208.33 \approx 208$

16. For Company A,

The amount received by Samir in 2008 $= 10000\left(1+\frac{11.5}{100}\right)\left(1+\frac{15}{100}\right)$

$= 10{,}000 \times \frac{223}{200}\times\frac{23}{20} =$ Rs. 12822.50

Hence, their interest = 12822.50 – 10000 = Rs. 2822.50
For Company B,
The amount received by Samir in 2008

$= 10{,}000\left(1+\frac{13.5}{100}\right)\left(1+\frac{14}{100}\right)$

$= 10{,}000 \times \frac{227}{200}\times\frac{57}{50} =$ Rs. 12939

Since, their interest = 12939 – 10000 = Rs. 2939
Hence, difference between the interests earned = 2939 – 2822.50 = Rs. 116.50
If Samir had invested the amount in company B for both years then he would get Rs. 116.50 more.

17. Total interests accrued by Saurabha = $\frac{12000\times 15\times 1}{100}+\frac{15000\times 14\times 1}{100}$ = 1800 + 2100 = Rs. 3900

18. Interest earned by Gopal from Company A in 2004 = $\frac{25000 \times 12 \times 1}{100}$ = Rs. 3000

Hence, their amount = 25000 + 3000 = Rs. 28000

Interest earned by Gopal from Company B in 2005 = $\frac{28000 \times 14 \times 1}{100}$ = Rs. 3920

Hence, total interests earned in the two years by him = 3000 + 3920 = Rs. 6920

19. Interest received in 2009 from Company B = $\frac{20000 \times 14.5 \times 1}{100}$ = Rs. 2900

Hence, their amount = 20000 + 2900 = Rs. 22900

Interest will be received in 2010 from Company A = $\frac{22900 \times 12.5 \times 1}{100}$ = Rs. 2862.50

Hence, total amount of interests for both years = 2900 + 2862.50 = Rs. 5762.50

20. Required amount of interest earned by Madhava in 2007 $= 15000\left[\left(1+\frac{15}{100}\right)^2 - 1\right]$

$$= 15000\left[\frac{529-400}{400}\right] = 15000 \times \frac{129}{400} = \frac{19350}{4}$$

= Rs. 4837.50

21. Required percentage = $\frac{5}{3+5+8} \times 100 = \frac{5}{16} \times 100 = 31.25\%$

22. Average profit made by company A in all the years = Rs. $\frac{(3+5+4+5+6+6) \text{ lakhs}}{6}$

$$= \text{Rs.}\frac{29 \text{ lakhs}}{6} \approx \text{Rs. } 4.83 \text{ lakh} = \text{Rs. } 4{,}83{,}000$$

23. Expenditure of Company B in 2008 = Rs. 22,11,430 and their profit = Rs. 4,00,000

Since, Income = 22,11,430 + 4,00,000 = Rs. 26,11,630

24. In 2007, income of Company A = Rs. 13,54,300 and their profit = Rs. 6,00,000

Since, their Expenditure = 13,54,300 – 6,00,000 = Rs. 7,54,300

25. Required percentage = $\frac{8-7}{7} \times 100 = 14.28\% \approx 14\%$

26. Required percentage = $\frac{600}{450} \times 100 = \frac{400}{3} = 133.33\% \approx 135\%$

27. Total export in given years = Rs. (300 + 200 + 600 + 450 + 600 + 800 + 950) crores

= Rs. 3900 crores

28. Required percentage for 2004 = $\frac{600-200}{200} \times 100 = 200\%$

Required percentage for 2005 = $\frac{600-450}{600} \times 100 = 25\%$

Required percentage for 2007 = $\frac{800-600}{600} \times 100 = 33\frac{1}{3}\%$

Required percentage for 2008 = $\frac{950-800}{800} \times 100 = 18.75$

Hence, required percentage is maximum for 2004.

29. Required difference = Rs. (600 – 450) crores = Rs. 150 crores

30. Required percentage = $\frac{950-200}{200} \times 100 = 375\%$

31. Let expenditure of Company A in 2005 = Rs. x; then

$x + \frac{50}{100} \times x = 1{,}42{,}500 \Rightarrow \frac{3x}{2} = 1{,}42{,}500 \quad \therefore x = \frac{2 \times 1{,}42{,}500}{3} = \text{Rs. } 95000$

32. In 2004, expenditure of Company 'A' = Rs. 75 lakh

Since, income of the company 'A' in 2004 = $75 + \frac{25}{100} \times 75$ = Rs. 93.75 lakhs

Now, expenditure of the company 'A' in 2005 = Rs. 93.75 lakhs

Since, their income = 93.75 + $\frac{50}{100} \times 93.75$ = Rs. 140.62 lakhs

Hence, total income for both the years = 93.75 + 140.62 = Rs. 234.37 lakhs

33. Here total expenditure of both companies are given while their individual expenditures are needed to determine their incomes. Since their total income of the two companies can not be determined by the given datas.

34. Let expenditure of company B in 2005 = Rs. x; then

I_1 (Income) = $x + \frac{35}{100} x = \text{Rs.} \frac{27x}{20}$

Since, expenditure of company B in 2006 = $\frac{90}{100} \times$ Rs. x = Rs. $\frac{9x}{10}$, then

I_2 (Income) = $\frac{9x}{10} + \frac{45}{100} \times \frac{9x}{10} = \frac{9x}{10} + \frac{81x}{200}$ = Rs. $\frac{261x}{200}$

Hence, required percentage = $\frac{261x/200}{27x/20} \times 100 = \frac{290}{3} = 96\frac{2}{3}\%$

35. Let expenditures of Company B in 2003 and 2004 are Rs. $5x$ and Rs. $7x$ respectively; then

their income in 2003, I_1 = $5x + \frac{40}{100} \times 5x$ = Rs. $7x$

Also their income in 2004, I_2 = $7x + \frac{30}{100} \times 7x$ = Rs. $\frac{91x}{10}$

Hence, the required ratio = $7x : \frac{91x}{10}$ = 10 : 13

38 DATA INTERPRETATION: PIE CHARTS

PIE CHARTS

These are used to show the share of various sectors in the total. They usually show the percentage share of each sector in the whole (taken as 100%). In such representation the total quantity in question is distributed over a total angle of 360°. The area of each sector is proportional to the relative frequency of the class represented by the sector.

$$\text{Sector angle} = \frac{\text{Class frequency}}{\text{Total frequency}} \times 360°$$

For Example: ***Distribution of Expenditure of a family***

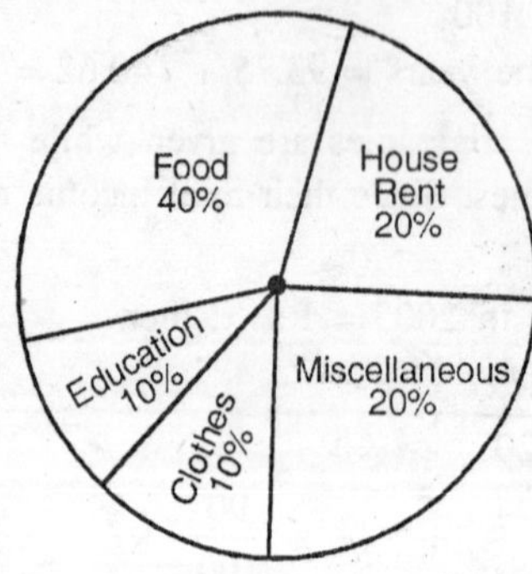

Example 1: Directions: *The pie-chart given below shows the household expenditure of a family on different items. Study the chart carefully and answer the questions that follows:*

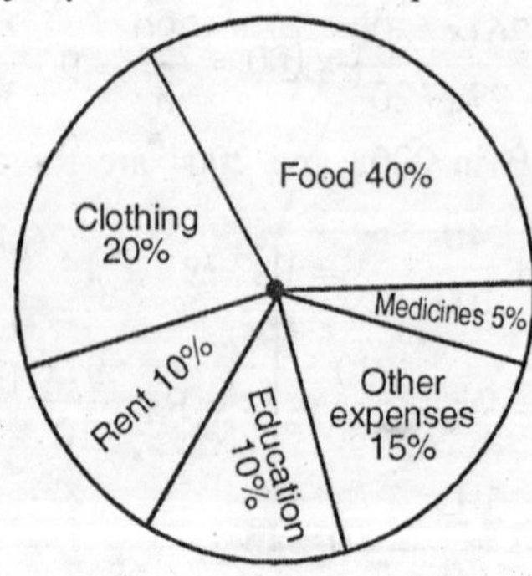

1. If the family's expenditure on education is Rs. 375 then the same amount is being expent by this family on which of the following items?
(a) Medicines *(b)* Other expenses *(c)* Rent *(d)* Clothing

2. If the family expends Rs. 750 per month on food, what is the annual expenditure of this family on education?
(a) Rs. 2150 *(b)* Rs. 1022.50 *(c)* Rs. 2250 *(d)* Rs. 1400

3. If total expenditure of this family is Rs. 4500, find the expenditure of the family on clothing?
(a) Rs. 800 *(b)* Rs. 900 *(c)* Rs. 840 *(d)* Rs. 950

4. What is the angle subtended on the centre by the segment representing other expenses?.
(a) 64° *(b)* 54° *(c)* 36° *(d)* 15°

5. What is the ratio of total expenses on rent and clothing to the total expenses on medicines and other expenses of this family?
(a) 2 : 3 *(b)* 3 : 4 *(c)* 3 : 5 *(d)* 3 : 2

Solution 1. Both segments representing education and rent respectively are each 10%. Hence, family's expenditure on these two items will be equal, *i.e.*, Rs. 375 will be expent on rent.

Solution 2. Here, 40% = Rs. 750

$\Rightarrow 10\% = \dfrac{750}{40} \times 10 = \text{Rs. } 187.50$

$\therefore$ Annual expenditure of the family on education = 187.50 × 12 = Rs. 2250

Solution 3. Expenditure on clothing = $\dfrac{20}{100} \times 4500 = \text{Rs. } 900$

Solution 4. Central angle for 15% = $\dfrac{15}{100} \times 360° = 54°$

Solution 5. Expenditure on rent and clothing = 10% + 20% = 30%
Expenditure on medicine and other expenses = 5% + 15% = 20%
$\therefore$ Ratio of the two = 30% : 20% = 3 : 2

Example 2: Directions: *The pie chart, drawn here, shows the spending of a country on various sports during a particular year. Study the graph carefully and answer the questions that follow:*

1. Graph shows that the most popular game of the country is:
(a) Football *(b)* Hockey *(c)* Cricket *(d)* Tennis

2. Out of the following the country spent the same amount on:
(a) Hockey and Cricket
(b) Hockey and Football
(c) Hockey and Golf
(d) Tennis and Golf

3. The ratio of the total amount spent on football to that spent on hockey is:
(a) 2 : 1 (b) 1 : 1 (c) 1 : 2 (d) 3 : 2

4. If the total amount spent on sports during the year was Rs. 1,20,00,000, how much was spent on basketball?
(a) Rs. 16,00,000 (b) Rs. 18,00,000 (c) Rs. 3,00,000 (d) Rs. 15,00,000

5. If the total amount spent on sports during the year was Rs. 30,00,000, the amount spent on cricket and hockey together was:
(a) Rs. 18,00,000
(b) Rs. 12,00,000
(c) Rs. 15,00,000
(d) Rs. 20,00,000

Solution 1. According to the graph, expenditure on cricket is the maximum. Therefore cricket is the most popular game.

Solution 2. According to the graph, equal amount has been spent on Hockey and Football.

Solution 3. Expenditure on the game of Football = 15% of total amount spent
Expenditure on the game of Hockey = 15% of total amount spent.
Therefore, the ratio of the expenditure on the two games = 1 : 1

Solution 4. 100% = Rs. 1,20,00,000
∴ Expenditure on the game of Basketball = 12½% of 1,20,00,000

$$= \frac{25 \times 1{,}20{,}00{,}000}{100} = \text{Rs. } 15{,}00{,}000$$

Solution 5. 100% = Rs. 30,00,000
∴ Expenditure on the games of Cricket and Hockey = 25% + 15% = 40%
∴ Total expenditure on the games of Cricket and Hockey = 20% of 30,00,000

$$= \frac{40 \times 30{,}00{,}000}{100} = \text{Rs. } 12{,}00{,}000.$$

Example 3: Directions: *Study the pie-charts carefully to answer the questions that follow.*

Percentage of Students in Six different Colleges
Total number of Students = 3500

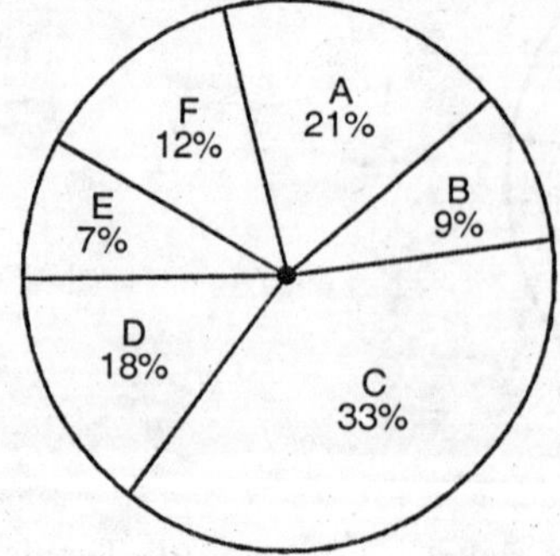

Percentage of Girls in each of the Colleges
Total number of Girls = 1800

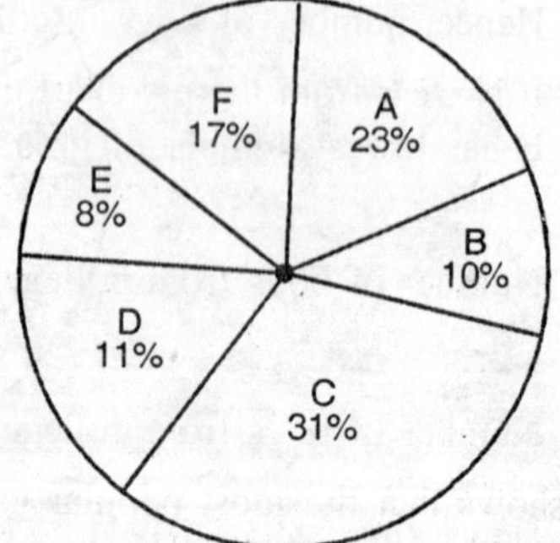

1. What is the number of girls in college D?
   (a) 176 (b) 188 (c) 192 (d) 198
2. The number of boys from College A form what per cent of total number of students from that college?
   (a) 22.83 (b) 38.41 (c) 43.67 (d) 56.29
3. Which college has the maximum number of boys?
   (a) A (b) B (c) C (d) D
4. Which college has lowest number of girls?
   (a) B (b) D (c) E (d) F
5. What is the total number of boys from Colleges E and F together?
   (a) 215 (b) 251 (c) 283 (d) 310

Solution 1. Number of girls in College D = $\frac{11}{100} \times 1800 = 198$

Solution 2. Number of students from College A = $\frac{21}{100} \times 3500 = 735$

Number of girls from College A = $\frac{23}{100} \times 1800 = 414$

Since, number of boys from college A = 725 – 414 = 321

Required percentage = $\frac{321}{735} \times 100 = \frac{2140}{49} = 43.67\%$

Solution 3. Number of boys in college A = $\frac{21}{100} \times 3500 - \frac{23}{100} \times 1800 = 735 - 414 = 321$

Number of boys in college B = $\frac{9}{100} \times 3500 - \frac{10}{100} \times 1800 = 315 - 180 = 135$

Number of boys in college C = $\frac{33}{100} \times 3500 - \frac{31}{100} \times 1800 = 1155 - 558 = 597$

Number of boys in college D = $\frac{18}{100} \times 3500 - \frac{11}{100} \times 1800 = 630 - 198 = 432$

Hence, number of boys in college C has maximum.

Solution 4. It is clear from the pie-chart that percentage of girls in college E is minimum, hence, college E has lowest number of girls.

Solution 5. Number of boys from college E = $\frac{7}{100} \times 3500 - \frac{8}{100} \times 1800 = 245 - 144 = 101$

Number of boys from college F = $\frac{12}{100} \times 3500 - \frac{17}{100} \times 1800 = 420 - 306 = 114$

Hence, their total = 101 + 114 = 215

Example 4: Directions: *Study the following pie-diagrams carefully to answer these questions.*

Number of students studying in different faculties in the years 2008 and 2009 from State X

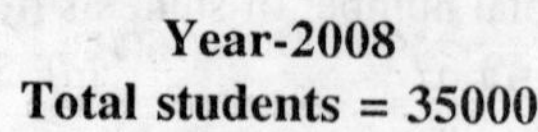

Year-2008
Total students = 35000

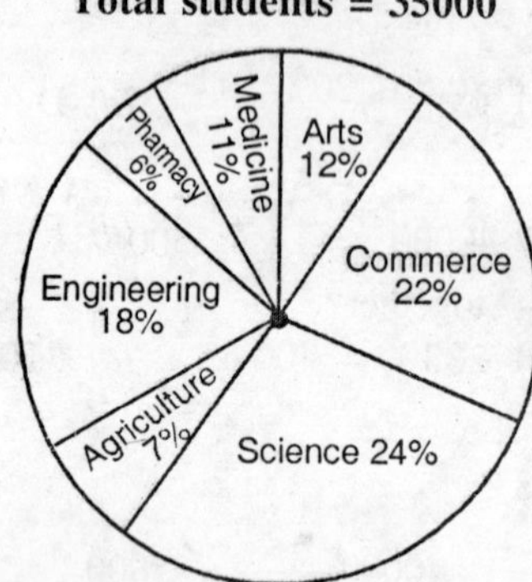

Year-2009
Total students = 40000

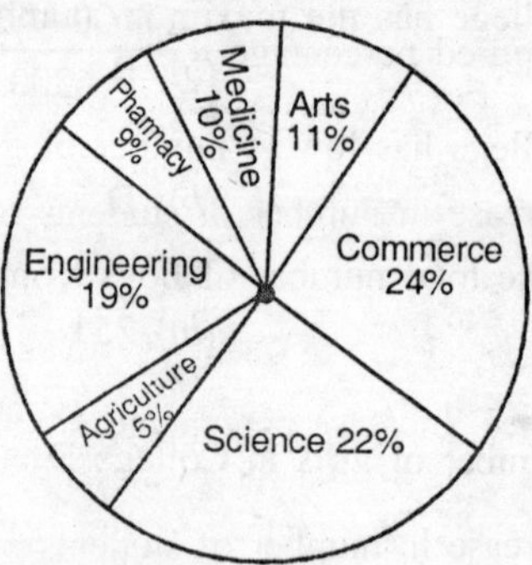

1. In which faculty there was decrease in the number of students from 2008 to 2009?
(a) Arts (b) Agriculture (c) Pharmacy (d) None of these
2. What was the approximate percentage increase in the number of students of Engineering from year 2008 to 2009?
(a) 15 (b) 17 (c) 20 (d) 25
3. In which of the following faculties the percentage increase in the number of students was minimum from 2008 to 2009?
(a) Science (b) Commerce (c) Arts (d) Medicine
4. What is the ratio between the number of students studying Pharmacy in the years 2008 and 2009 respectively?
(a) 4 : 3 (b) 5 : 7 (c) 7 : 12 (d) 8 : 13
5. In the year 2008, the number of students studying Arts and Commerce together is what per cent of the number of students studying these subjects together in 2009?
(a) 76 (b) 79 (c) 82 (d) 85

Solution 1. In 2008, number of students in Arts = $\frac{12}{100} \times 35000 = 4200$

In 2009, number of students in Arts = $\frac{11}{100} \times 40000 = 4400$

In 2008, number of students in Agriculture = $\frac{7}{100} \times 35000 = 2450$

In 2009, number of students in Agriculture = $\frac{5}{100} \times 40000 = 2000$

In 2008, number of students in Pharmacy = $\frac{6}{100} \times 35000 = 2100$

In 2009, number of students in Pharmacy = $\frac{9}{100} \times 40000 = 3600$

Hence, in Agriculture there was decrease in the number of students from 2008 to 2009.

Solution 2. In 2008, the number of students in Engineering = $\frac{18}{100} \times 35000 = 6300$

In 2009, the number of students in Engineering = $\frac{19}{100} \times 40000 = 7600$

Required percentage = $\frac{7600 - 6300}{6300} \times 100 = \frac{1300}{63} = 20.6 \approx 20\%$

Solution 3. Increase in number of students of Science = $\frac{22}{100} \times 40000 - \frac{24}{100} \times 35000$

$= 8800 - 8400 = 400$

Hence, Increase percentage = $\frac{400}{8400} \times 100 = 4\frac{16}{21}\%$

Increase in number of students of Commerce = $\frac{24}{100} \times 40000 - \frac{22}{100} \times 35000$

$= 9600 - 7700 = 1900$

Hence, their increase percentage = $\frac{1900}{7700} \times 100 = 24\frac{52}{77}\%$

Increase in number of students of Arts = $\frac{11}{100} \times 40000 - \frac{12}{100} \times 35000 = 4400 - 4200 = 200$

Hence, their increase percentage = $\frac{200}{4200} \times 100 = 4\frac{16}{21}\%$

Increase in number of students of Medicine = $\frac{10}{100} \times 40000 - \frac{11}{100} \times 35000 = 4000 - 3850 = 150$

Hence, their increase percentage = $\frac{150}{3850} \times 100 = 3\frac{69}{77}\%$

So, in Medicine the percentage increase in the number of students was minimum from 2008 to 2009.

Solution 4. In 2008, the number of students studying Pharmacy = $\frac{6}{100} \times 35000 = 2100$

In 2009, the number of students studying Pharmacy = $\frac{9}{100} \times 40000 = 3600$

Hence, their ratio = 2100 : 3600 = 7 : 12

Solution 5. In 2008, the number of students studying Arts and Commerce together

$= \frac{(12+22)}{100} \times 35000 = 34 \times 350 = 11900$

In 2009, the number of students studying Arts and Commerce together

$= \frac{(11+24)}{100} \times 40000 = 35 \times 400 = 14000$

Hence, required percentage = $\frac{11900}{14000} \times 100 = 85\%$

EXERCISE

Directions (Qs. 1-5): *Study the following Graph carefully and answer the questions given below:*

Percentage of students in various courses (A, B, C, D, E, F) and Percentage of girls out of these.
Total students = 1200 (800 girls + 400 boys)

Percentage in Various Courses

A 20%
B 15%
C 5%
D 35%
E 12%
F 13%

(Total girls = 800)
Percentage of Girls in Various courses

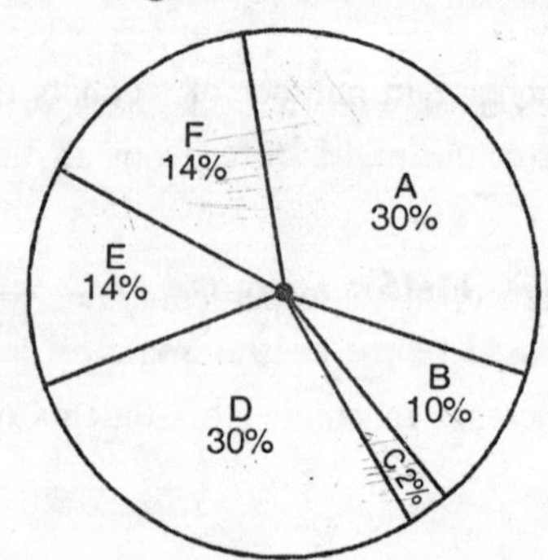

1. For which course is the number of boys the minimum?
   (a) A (b) C (c) E (d) F
2. For course D what is the respective ratio of boys and girls?
   (a) 3 : 4 (b) 3 : 5 (c) 4 : 5 (d) 5 : 6
3. For course E, the number of girls is how much per cent more than the boys for course E?
   (a) 80 (b) 150 (c) 250 (d) 350
4. How many girls are there in course C?
   (a) 16 (b) 40 (c) 44 (d) 160
5. For which pair of courses is the number of boys the same?
   (a) A and D (b) B and D (c) C and F (d) E and F

Directions (Qs. 6-10): *Study the following Pie-chart carefully and answer the questions given below:*

Percentage of People in a City working in Night shifts from various Industries
(Total number of people = 40250

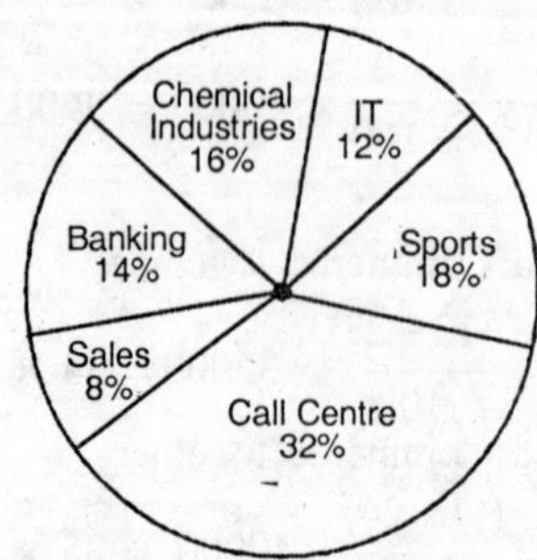

Percentage of Females from Various Industries working in Night shifts

Industries	*Females*
IT	*20%*
Sports	*20%*
Call Centre	*45%*
Sales	*60%*
Banking	*40%*
Chemical Industries	*15%*

6. What is the respective ratio of men to women working in night shifts from the Call centre Industry?
   (a) 9 : 11 (b) 11 : 9 (c) 8 : 13 (d) 13 : 8

7. What is the total number of men working in night shifts from all the industries together?
(a) 25788 (b) 26887 (c) 28297 (d) 28678

8. What is the difference between the total number of men and the total number of women working in night shifts from all the industries together?
(a) 13254 (b) 13363 (c) 13524 (d) 13542

9. What is the approximate average number of females working in night shifts from all the industries together?
(a) 2227 (b) 2823 (c) 3326 (d) 4107

10. The number of women from the sports industry are what per cent of the total number of people working in the night shifts from all the industries together?
(a) 3.2 (b) 3.6 (c) 4.4 (d) 5.6

Directions (Qs. 11-15): *Study the following pie-chart carefully and answer the following questions.*

Circle-graph given below shows the expenditure incurred in bringing out the steel production

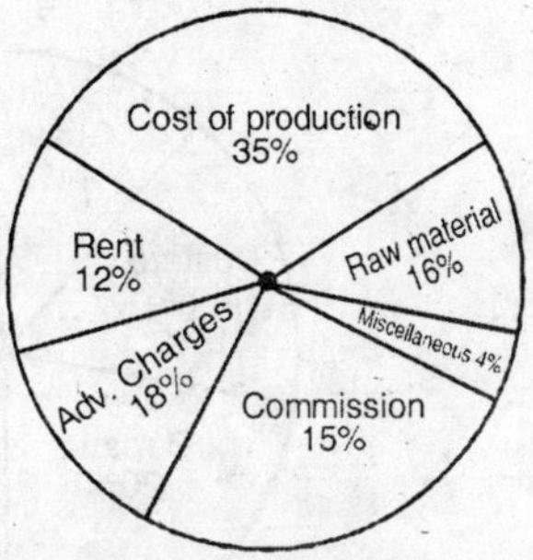

11. What should be the central angle of the sector for the cost of the raw material?
(a) 16° (b) 22.5°
(c) 54.8° (d) 57.6°

12. If the miscellaneous charges are Rs. 6000, the advertisement charges are:
(a) Rs. 10,000 (b) Rs. 12,000
(c) Rs. 25,000 (d) Rs. 27,000

13. Commission on the steel is less than the advertisement charges by
(a) 8% (b) $12\frac{2}{3}\%$
(c) $16\frac{2}{3}\%$ (d) 18%

14. If the cost of production is Rs. 17500, the commission is:
(a) Rs. 6500 (b) Rs. 7000 (c) Rs. 7500 (d) Rs. 8000

15. If 5500 kg are produced, miscellaneous expenditures amount to Rs. 1848 and manufacturer's profit is 25% then selling price per kg steel is:
(a) Rs. 6.50 (b) Rs. 8.50 (c) Rs. 10.50 (d) Rs. 12.50

Directions (Qs. 16-21): *Study the following pie-chart and answer the questions given below:*

Sales of car in U.K. according to their colour

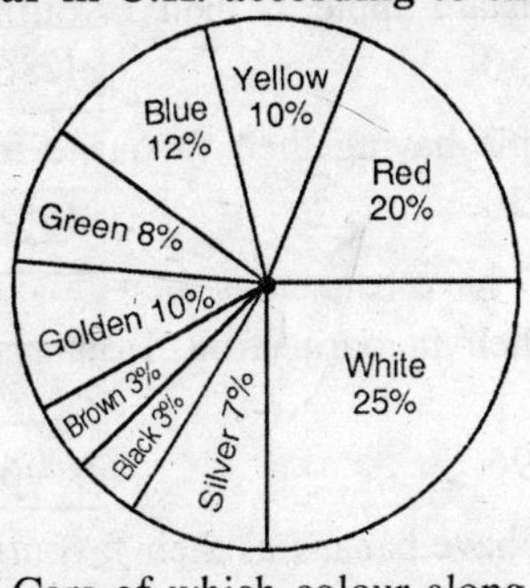

16. 3% increase in the production of Cars of which colour along with red cars will make them 35% of the total cars?
(a) Black (b) Blue (c) Silver (d) Yellow

17. Which car is 40% more popular than Black Cars?
(*a*) Blue (*b*) Brown (*c*) Red (*d*) Silver

18. Which colour is 68% less than white colour?
(*a*) Blue (*b*) Golden (*c*) Green (*d*) Yellow

19. The Cars of which colours together make them 50%?
(*a*) Blue, Black, Red (*b*) White, Black, Red
(*c*) White, Blue, Green (*d*) White, Silver, Blue

20. If the total production of cars during a certain period was 42000, how many more blue cars were sold in comparison to golden cars.
(*a*) 8400 (*b*) 12580 (*c*) 12850 (*d*) 13618

Directions (Qs. 21-25): *Study the following pie-graph carefully and answer the questions given below:*

A survey conducted on 5800 villagers staying in various villages and having various favourite fruits.

Favourite Fruits

Fruit	Percentage
Guava	14%
Apple	12%
Grapes	11%
Mango	28%
Banana	20%
Custard Apple	15%

People Staying in Various Villages

Village	Percentage
A	22%
B	21%
C	32%
D	25%

21. Mango is the favourite fruit of 50% of the people from village C. People having their favourite fruit as Mango from Village C form approximately what per cent of the people having their favourite fruit as mango from all the villages together?
(*a*) 48 (*b*) 53 (*c*) 57 (*d*) 61

22. How many people in all have custard apple as their favourite fruit?
(*a*) 812 (*b*) 850 (*c*) 864 (*d*) 870

23. What is the total number of people having their favourite fruit as apples and grapes together?
(*a*) 1286 (*b*) 1300 (*c*) 1334 (*d*) 1420

24. 20% of the people from village D have banana as their favourite fruit and 12% of the people from the same village have guava as their favourite fruit. How many people from the village like other fruits?
(*a*) 764 (*b*) 896 (*c*) 968 (*d*) 986

25. 50% of the people from village B have banana as their favourite fruit. How many people from other villages have the same favourite fruit?
(*a*) 551 (*b*) 609 (*c*) 1020 (*d*) 1160

Directions (Qs. 26-30): *Study the pie chart carefully to answer the questions that follow:*

Percentage of students enrolled in different Hobby classes in a school
Total number of students = 3600

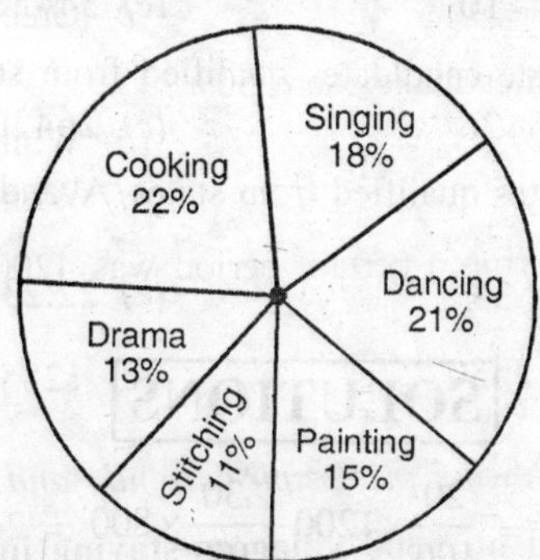

26. The number of students enrolled in Cooking classes is what per cent of those enrolled in Dancing classes?
(*a*) 101.45 (*b*) 104.76 (*c*) 110.28 (*d*) 113.84

27. How many students are enrolled in Painting Classes?
(*a*) 450 (*b*) 520 (*c*) 540 (*d*) 550

28. What is the ratio of number of students enrolled in Singing and Dancing Classes together to those enrolled in Drama Classes respectively?
(*a*) 3 : 1 (*b*) 3 : 5 (*c*) 4 : 7 (*d*) 7 : 5

29. What is the total number of students enrolled in Stiching and Drama Classes together?
(*a*) 648 (*b*) 684 (*c*) 846 (*d*) 864

30. Number of students enrolled in Painting Classes are approximately what per cent of those enrolled in Singing Classes?
(*a*) 72 (*b*) 78 (*c*) 83 (*d*) 92

Directions (Qs. 31-35): *Study the following graph and table carefully and answer the questions given below it:*

Distribution of Candidates appeared in a competitive examination from seven states
Total Candidates appeared = 3 lakh

G 7%
A 15%
B 18%
C 6%
D 23%
E 12%
F 19%

State-wise percentage and ratio of male and female qualified candidates

State	*% Qualified over appeared from a state*	*Ratio of qualified Candidates*
A	49	4 : 5
B	61	6 : 4
C	54	7 : 8
D	45	3 : 2
E	65	7 : 6
F	57	11 : 8
G	48	9 : 1

31. What is the number of male candidates qualified from state 'G'?
(*a*) 4536 (*b*) 4568 (*c*) 5454 (*d*) 5544

32. Which of the folloiwng pair of states have equal number of qualified male candidates?
(a) A and E (b) B and F (c) C and E (d) C and G

33. What is the total number of candidates qualified from states 'E' and D together?
(a) 45540 (b) 54410 (c) 54450 (d) 54540

34. What is the total number of female candidates qualified from states A and B together?
(a) 24526 (b) 25426 (c) 26426 (d) 26526

35. What is the percentage of candidates qualified from states 'A' and 'C' together of the total candidates appeared?
(a) 16.23 (b) 18.33 (c) 22.23 (d) 25.33

SOLUTIONS

1. Number of boys in course 'A' = $\frac{20}{100}\times 1200-\frac{30}{100}\times 800 = 240 - 240 = 0$

Number of boys in course 'C' = $\frac{5}{100}\times 1200-\frac{2}{100}\times 800 = 60 - 16 = 44$

Number of boys in course 'E' = $\frac{12}{100}\times 1200-\frac{14}{100}\times 800 = 144 - 112 = 32$

Number of boys in course 'F' = $\frac{13}{100}\times 1200-\frac{14}{100}\times 800 = 156 - 112 = 44$

Hence, in course 'A' number of boys is minimum *i.e.*, zero.

2. For course D,

Number of boys = $\frac{35}{100}\times 1200-\frac{30}{100}\times 800 = 420 - 240 = 180$

Number of girls = $\frac{30}{100}\times 800 = 240$

Since, required ratio = 180 : 240 = 3 : 4

3. For course E,

Number of boys = $\frac{12}{100}\times 1200-\frac{14}{100}\times 800 = 144 - 112 = 32$

Number of girls = $\frac{14}{100}\times 800 = 112$

Required percentage = $\frac{112-32}{32}\times 100 = \frac{80}{32}\times 100 = 250\%$

4. Number of girls in course 'C' = $\frac{2}{100}\times 800 = 16$

5. Number of boys in course A = $\frac{20}{100}\times 1200-\frac{30}{100}\times 800 = 240 - 240 = 0$

Number of boys in course B = $\frac{15}{100}\times1200-\frac{10}{100}\times800 = 180 - 80 = 100.$

Number of boys in course C = $\frac{5}{100}\times1200-\frac{2}{100}\times800 = 60 - 16 = 44$

Number of boys in course D = $\frac{35}{100}\times1200-\frac{30}{100}\times800 = 420 - 240 = 180$

Number of boys in course E = $\frac{12}{100}\times1200-\frac{14}{100}\times800 = 144 - 112 = 32$

Number of boys in course F = $\frac{13}{100}\times1200-\frac{14}{100}\times800 = 156 - 112 = 44$

Hence, number of boys in course 'C' and 'F' are same.

6. Number of people working in night shifts from Call Centre Industry = $\frac{32}{100}\times40250 = 12880$

Number of women working in night shifts from Call Centre Industry = $\frac{45}{100}\times12880 = 5796$

So, the number of men working from same Industry = 12880 − 5796 = 7084

Hence, Required ratio = 7084 : 5796 = 11 : 9

7. Number of men working in night shifts in different industries:

IT $\Rightarrow \frac{80}{100}\times\frac{12}{100}\times40250 = 3864$

Sports $\Rightarrow \frac{80}{100}\times\frac{18}{100}\times40250 = 5796$

Call Centre $\Rightarrow \frac{55}{100}\times\frac{32}{100}\times40250 = 7084$

Sales $\Rightarrow \frac{40}{100}\times\frac{8}{100}\times40250 = 1288$

Banking $\Rightarrow \frac{60}{100}\times\frac{14}{100}\times40250 = 3381$

Chemical Industries $\Rightarrow \frac{85}{100}\times\frac{16}{100}\times40250 = 5474$

Hence, total number of men working in night shifts in different industries

= 3864 + 5796 + 7084 + 1288 + 3381 + 5474 = 26887

8. Total number of men = 26887

Total number of women = 40250 − 26887 = 13363

Their difference = 26887 − 13363 = 13524

9. Required average number of females = $\frac{13363}{6} = 2227.16 \approx 2227$

10. Number of women from Sports Industry = $\frac{20}{100} \times \frac{18}{100} \times 40250 = 1449$

Required percentage = $\frac{1449}{40250} \times 100 = 3.6\%$

11. Required central angle = $\frac{16}{100} \times 360° = 57.6°$

12. Here, 4% = Rs. 6000

Since, 18% = $\frac{6000}{4} \times 18 =$ Rs. 27000

Hence, required advertisement charges = Rs. 27000

13. Required percentage = $\frac{18-15}{18} \times 100 = \frac{3}{18} \times 100 = 16\frac{2}{3}\%$

14. Here, 35% = Rs. 17500

Since, 15% = $\frac{17500}{35} \times 15 =$ Rs. 7500

Hence, required commission = Rs. 7500

15. Here, 4% = Rs. 1848

Since, 100% = $\frac{1848}{4} \times 100 =$ Rs. 46200

Hence, cost of 5500 kg = Rs. 46200

then cost of 1 kg = $\frac{46200}{5500} =$ Rs. 8.40

Hence, S.P. per kg = $\frac{125}{100} \times$ Rs. 8.40 = Rs. 10.50

16. If 3% increase in the production of Blue cars, then percentage of Blue cars = 12 + 3 = 15
Hence, percentage of (Blue + Red) cars = 15 + 20 = 35

17. 40% more popular than Black cars = $\frac{140}{100} \times 5 = 7\%$ popular i.e., Silver cars.

18. 68% less than white colour = $\frac{32}{100} \times 25 = 8\%$ *i.e.*, Green colour

19. The percentage of White, Black and Red Cars = 25 + 20 + 5 = 50%

20. Required difference = $\frac{(12-10)}{100} \times 420000 = \frac{2}{100} \times 420000 = 8400$

21. Percentage of people from village C, whose favourite fruit as Mango = 16%

Hence, required percentage = $\frac{16}{28} \times 100 = 57.14 \approx 57\%$

22. Number of people whose favourite fruit as custard apple $= \frac{15}{100} \times 5800 = 870$

23. Total number of people having their favourite fruit as apple and grapes together

$$= \frac{(12+11)}{100} \times 5800 = 23 \times 58 = 1334$$

24. Percentage of people from village D having their favourite fruit as Banana and Guava together $= 20 + 12 = 32\%$

Since, percentage of people from village D having their other favourite fruit $= 100 - 32 = 68\%$

Hence, required number of people $= \frac{68}{100} \times \frac{25}{100} \times 5800 = 986$

25. Required number of people $= \frac{20}{100} \times 5800 - \frac{1}{2} \times \frac{21}{100} \times 5800 = 1160 - 609 = 551$

26. Required percentage $= \frac{22}{21} \times 100 = 104.76$

27. Number of students enrolled in Painting classes $= \frac{15}{100} \times 3600 = 540$

28. Required ratio $= (18 + 21) : 13 = 39 : 13 = 3 : 1$

29. Required number of students $= \frac{(11+13)}{100} \times 3600 = 24 \times 36 = 864$

30. Required percentage $= \frac{15}{18} \times 100 = 83.33 \approx 83\%$

31. Number of candidates qualified from State G $= \frac{48}{100} \times \frac{7}{100} \times 3{,}00{,}000 = 10080$

Number of male candidates qualified from State G $= \frac{9}{9+11} \times 10080 = \frac{9}{20} \times 10080 = 4536$

32. Qualified Male Candidates from different states:

$A \to \frac{4}{9} \times \frac{49}{100} \times \frac{15}{100} \times 300000 = 9800$

$B \to \frac{6}{10} \times \frac{61}{100} \times \frac{18}{100} \times 300000 = 19764$

$C \to \frac{7}{15} \times \frac{54}{100} \times \frac{6}{100} \times 300000 = 4536$

$D \to \frac{3}{5} \times \frac{45}{100} \times \frac{23}{100} \times 300000 = 18630$

$E \to \times \frac{7}{13} \times \frac{65}{100} \times \frac{12}{100} \times 300000 = 12600$

$$F \to \frac{11}{19} \times \frac{57}{100} \times \frac{19}{100} \times 300000 = 18810$$

$$G \to \frac{9}{20} \times \frac{48}{100} \times \frac{7}{100} \times 300000 = 4536$$

Hence, State C and G have equal number of qualified male candidates.

33. Required number of candidates $= \frac{65}{100} \times \frac{12}{100} \times 300000 + \frac{45}{100} \times \frac{23}{100} \times 300000$

$= 23400 + 31050 = 54450$

34. Required number of female candidates $= \frac{5}{9} \times \frac{49}{100} \times \frac{15}{100} \times 300000 + \frac{4}{10} \times \frac{61}{100} \times \frac{18}{100} \times 300000$

$= 12250 + 13176 = 25426$

35. Number of Candidates qualified from States A and C together

$$= \frac{49}{100} \times \frac{15}{100} \times 300000 + \frac{61}{100} \times \frac{18}{100} \times 300000$$

$= 22050 + 32940 = 54990$

Required percentage $= \frac{54990}{300000} \times 100 = 18.33\%$